Fodor's

CALIFORNIA

D0032853

WELCOME TO CALIFORNIA

California's endless wonders, from Yosemite National Park to Disneyland, are both natural and man-made. Soul-satisfying wilderness often lies close to urbane civilization. With the iconic Big Sur coast, dramatic Mojave Desert, and majestic Sierra Nevada mountains, sunny California indulges those in search of great surfing, hiking, and golfing. Other pleasures await, too: superb food in San Francisco, studio tours in Los Angeles, winery visits and spas in Napa and Sonoma. Follow a beach picnic with a city stroll and live the California dream.

TOP REASONS TO GO

★ **Stunning Scenery:** Picture-perfect backdrops from the Golden Gate Bridge to redwoods.

★ **Beaches:** For surfing, swimming, or sunbathing, the state's beaches can't be beat.

★ **Cool Cities:** San Francisco, Los Angeles, San Diego, Palm Springs, and more.

★ **Feasts:** Cutting-edge restaurants, food trucks, fusion flavors, farmers' markets.

★ **Wine Country:** Top-notch whites and reds in Napa, Sonoma, and beyond.

★ **Road Trips:** The Pacific Coast Highway offers spectacular views and thrills aplenty.

Fodor's CALIFORNIA

Editorial: Douglas Stallings, *Editorial Director*; Salwa Jabado and Margaret Kelly, *Senior Editors*; Alexis Kelly, Jacinta O'Halloran, and Amanda Sadlowski, *Editors*; Teddy Minford, *Associate Editor*; Rachael Roth, *Content Manager*

Design: Tina Malaney, *Art Director*

Photography: Jennifer Arnow, *Senior Photo Editor*

Maps: Rebecca Baer, *Senior Map Editor*; Mark Stroud (Moon Street Cartography), David Lindroth, *Cartographers*

Production: Jennifer DePrima, *Editorial Production Manager*; Carrie Parker, *Senior Production Editor*; Elyse Rozelle, *Production Editor*; David Satz, *Director of Content Production*

Business & Operations: Chuck Hoover, *Chief Marketing Officer*; Joy Lai, *Vice President and General Manager*; Stephen Horowitz, *Head of Business Development and Partnerships*

Public Relations: Joe Ewaskiw, *Manager*

Writers: Michele Bigley, Cheryl Crabtree, Alene Dawson, Paul Feinstein, Marlise Kast-Myers, Amanda Kuehn Carroll, Denise M. Leto, Kai Oliver-Kurtain, Daniel Mangin, Kathy A. McDonald, Steve Pastorino, Joan Patterson, Andrea Powell, Rebecca Flint Marx, Archana Ram, Juliana Shallcross, Jerry James Stone, Jeff Terich, Ashley Tibbits, Claire Deeks van der Lee, and Clarissa Wei

Editors: Salwa Jabado (lead editor), Alexis Kelly (San Diego editor), Margaret Kelly (San Francisco and Napa and Sonoma editor), Rachael Roth (Los Angeles editor)

Production Editor: Jennifer DePrima

32nd Edition

ISBN 978-1-101-88008-1

ISSN 0192–9925

All details in this book are based on information supplied to us at press time. Always confirm information when it matters, especially if you're making a detour to visit a specific place. Fodor's expressly disclaims any liability, loss, or risk, personal or otherwise, that is incurred as a consequence of the use of any of the contents of this book.

PRINTED IN THE UNITED STATES OF AMERICA

10 9 8 7 6 5 4 3 2 1

CONTENTS

6 <

CONTENTS

CONTENTS

CONTENTS

MAPS

ABOUT THIS GUIDE

Fodor's Recommendations

Everything in this guide is worth doing—we don't cover what isn't—but exceptional sights, hotels, and restaurants are recognized with additional accolades. **Fodor's**Choice★ indicates our top recommendations. Care to nominate a new place? Visit Fodors.com/contact-us.

Trip Costs

We list prices wherever possible to help you budget well. Hotel and restaurant price categories from **$** to **$$$$** are noted alongside each recommendation. For hotels, we include the lowest cost of a standard double room in high season. For restaurants, we cite the average price of a main course at dinner or, if dinner isn't served, at lunch. For attractions, we always list adult admission fees; discounts are usually available for children, students, and senior citizens.

Hotels

Our local writers vet every hotel to recommend the best overnights in each price category, from budget to expensive. Unless otherwise specified, you can expect private bath, phone, and TV in your room. *For expanded hotel reviews and deals, visit Fodors.com.*

Top Picks	Hotels &
★ **Fodor's**Choice	**Restaurants**
	☷ Hotel
Listings	⤴ Number of
✉ Address	rooms
✉ Branch address	¶○| Meal plans
☏ Telephone	✗ Restaurant
🖷 Fax	⌖ Reservations
⊕ Website	𝄐 Dress code
✑ E-mail	▭ No credit cards
✏ Admission fee	$ Price
☉ Open/closed	
times	**Other**
Ⓜ Subway	⇨ See also
⊹ Directions or	☞ Take note
Map coordinates	🏌 Golf facilities

Restaurants

Unless we state otherwise, restaurants are open for lunch and dinner daily. We mention dress code only when there's a specific requirement and reservations only when they're essential or not accepted.

Credit Cards

The hotels and restaurants in this guide typically accept credit cards. If not, we'll say so.

EUGENE FODOR

Hungarian-born Eugene Fodor (1905–91) began his travel career as an interpreter on a French cruise ship. The experience inspired him to write *On the Continent* (1936), the first guidebook to receive annual updates and discuss a country's way of life as well as its sights. Fodor later joined the U.S. Army and worked for the OSS in World War II. After the war, he kept up his intelligence work while expanding his guidebook series. During the Cold War, many guides were written by fellow agents who understood the value of insider information. Today's guides continue Fodor's legacy by providing travelers with timely coverage, insider tips, and cultural context.

EXPERIENCE
CALIFORNIA

WHAT'S NEW IN CALIFORNIA

Foodie's Paradise

Great dining is a staple of the California lifestyle, and a new young generation of chefs is challenging old ideas about preparing and presenting great food. The food-truck frenzy continues to fuel movable feasts up and down the state. Esteemed chefs and urban foodies follow the trucks on Twitter as they move around cities 24/7 purveying delicious, cheap, fresh meals. You can find food-laden trucks at sports and entertainment venues, near parks and attractions, and on busy roads and boulevards—and the ensuing lines of hungry patrons.

Diners are also embracing the pop-up concept, where guest chefs offer innovative menus in unconventional settings for a limited time. These pop-up engagements are hosted anywhere from inside a warehouse to outside in a field. Often there is an air of secrecy and anticipation to them, with key details being revealed at the last moment. Visitors can look for local pop-ups listed on foodie websites such as Eater (⊕ *www.eater.com*).

California chefs continue to shop locally for produce and farmer-sourced meat, and many restaurants proudly display their vendors on the menu. Chefs and foodies alike engage in discourse on the ethics and politics of food and farming. Sustainably harvested seafood and "nose to tail" cooking, where as much of the animal as possible is used in an attempt to reduce food waste, are both hot topics these days.

Family Fun

California's theme parks work overtime to keep current and attract patrons of all ages. LEGOLAND California Resort keeps expanding with additional attractions such as the LEGOLAND Water Park and its 250-room LEGO-theme hotel.

Disneyland also continues to grow. Return visitors will notice changes around the park during the ongoing construction of the highly anticipated Star Wars Land, scheduled to open in 2019. In the meantime, visitors will enjoy the addition of new shows, parades and attractions, such as the transformation of the Tower of Terror into the Marvel Guardians of the Galaxy ride.

Both kids and adults will be fascinated by the creatures on display in "Tentacles: The Astounding Lives of Octopuses, Squid and Cuttlefishes," the newest exhibit at the Monterey Bay Aquarium.

The supersize and hands-on exhibits at San Francisco's Exploratorium continue to challenge and fascinate visitors of all ages. With trees as tall as they come, the Children's Redwood Forest in Humboldt Redwoods State Park is a great place for kids to romp through some awe-inspiring landscapes.

Wine Discoveries

California offers oenophiles ample opportunities for new discoveries beyond the traditional California Wine Country. Across the state, vineyards are going up in unlikely places.

In the hillsides of San Diego County, the Ramona Valley AVA is seeing an increasing number of visitors, and Escondido-based Orfila keeps snagging awards. North of Los Angeles, the boutique wineries in the hillsides of Malibu are garnering increased attention.

Venturing just beyond the traditional wine destinations of Napa and Sonoma counties will reward visitors with hidden gems. Areas such as the Petaluma Gap and the Sierra Foothills offer plenty of vineyards to explore. Visitors to Lake Tahoe can even take in some wine tasting at the Truckee River Winery, claiming to be the highest and coldest winery in the nation.

All Aboard

Riding the rails can be a satisfying experience, particularly in California where the distances between destinations sometimes run into the hundreds of miles. You can save money on gas and parking, avoid freeway traffic, and see some of the best the state has to offer. California just broke ground on a high-speed rail project linking San Francisco to Los Angeles. In 2030, when the $68-billion project is complete, the train will make the run between the two cities in less than three hours.

Until then, the best trip is on the luxuriously appointed *Coast Starlight*, a long-distance train with sleeping cars that runs between Seattle and Los Angeles, passing some of California's most beautiful coastline as it hugs the beach. For the best surfside viewing, get a seat or a room on the left side of the train and ride south to north.

Amtrak also has frequent Pacific Surfliner service between San Diego and Los Angeles, and San Diego and Santa Barbara. These are coach cars, but many of the trains have been upgraded and are comfortable and convenient, especially if you want to get off and on the train at several destinations—Anaheim near Disneyland, Downtown Los Angeles, coastal Ventura, Santa Barbara, and San Luis Obispo.

Homegrown Hospitality

Agritourism in California isn't new (remember, Knott's Berry Farm once *was* a berry farm), but it is on the rise, with farm tours and agricultural festivals sprouting up everywhere.

Wine Country is a particularly fertile area—spurred by the success of vineyards, the area's lavender growers and olive-oil producers have started welcoming visitors. Sonoma County Farm Trail maintains an excellent map and guide to visiting producers in the area.

In the Central Valley, America's number-one producer of stone fruit, you can travel themed tourist routes (like Fresno County's Blossom Trail) and tour herb gardens, fruit orchards, organic dairies, and pumpkin patches.

State of the Arts

California's beauty-obsessed citizens aren't the only ones opting for a fresh look these days: its esteemed art museums are also having a bit of work done.

The Los Angeles County Museum of Art (LACMA) keeps expanding its Wilshire Boulevard campus following the 2010 opening of the Renzo Piano–designed Resnick Pavilion. It is now gearing up for a major expansion under the direction of architect Peter Zumthor, estimated to be complete in 2023.

The San Francisco Museum of Modern Art (SFMOMA) reopened in 2016 after a major expansion project vastly increased the museum's exhibition and support space.

WHAT'S WHERE

The following numbers refer to chapters.

3 San Diego. San Diego's Gaslamp Quarter and early California-themed Old Town have a human scale—but big-ticket animal attractions like the San Diego Zoo pull in visitors.

4 Orange County. A diverse destination with premium resorts and restaurants, strollable waterfront communities, and kid-friendly attractions.

5 Los Angeles. Go for the glitz of the entertainment industry, but stay for the rich cultural attributes and communities.

6 The Central Coast. Three of the state's top stops— swanky Santa Barbara, Hearst Castle, and Big Sur—sit along the scenic 200-mile route. A quick boat trip away lies scenic Channel Islands National Park.

13 The Inland Empire. The San Bernardino Mountains provide seasonal escapes, and the Temecula Valley will challenge your ideas of "California Wine Country."

14 Palm Springs. Golf on some of the West's most challenging courses, lounge at fabulous resorts, check out mid-century-modern architectural gems, and trek through primitive desert parks.

15 Joshua Tree National Park. Proximity to major urban areas—as well as world-class rock climbing and nighttime celestial displays—help make this one of the most visited national parks.

16 Mojave Desert. Material pleasures are in short supply here, but Mother Nature's stark beauty more than compensates.

17 Death Valley National Park. America's second-largest national park is vast, beautiful, and often the hottest place in the nation.

18 Eastern Sierra. In the Mammoth Lakes region, sawtooth mountains and deep powdery snowdrifts create the state's premier conditions for skiing and snowboarding.

19 Yosemite National Park. The views immortalized by photographer Ansel Adams—towering granite monoliths, verdant glacial valleys, and lofty waterfalls—are still camera-ready.

20 Sequoia and Kings Canyon National Parks. The sight of ancient redwoods towering above jagged mountains is breathtaking.

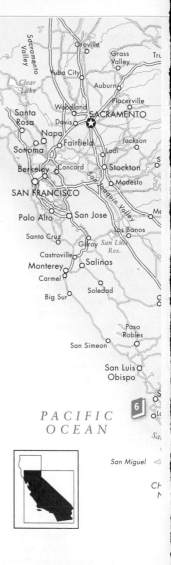

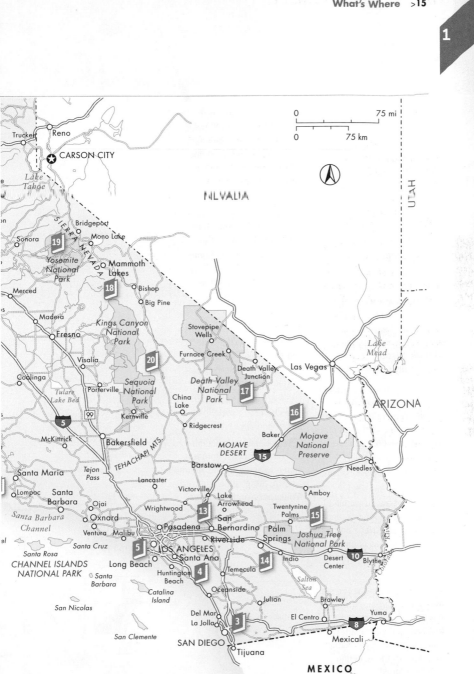

Truckee
Reno
CARSON CITY
Lake Tahoe
NEVADA

0   75 mi
0   75 km

UTAH

Sonora
Bridgeport
Mono Lake
19
Yosemite National Park
Mammoth Lakes
18
Merced
Bishop
Big Pine
Madera
Kings Canyon National Park
Fresno
Stovepipe Wells
Lake Mead
Visalia
Furnace Creek
20
Coalinga
Sequoia National Park
Death Valley Junction
Las Vegas
Tulare Lake Bed
Porterville
Death Valley National Park
17
ARIZONA
McKittrick
Kernville
China Lake
5
99
Ridgecrest
Baker
16
Bakersfield
TEHACHAPI MTS.
Mojave National Preserve
Santa Maria
Tejon Pass
Lancaster
Barstow
MOJAVE DESERT
15
Needles
Lompoc
Santa Barbara
Victorville
Lake Arrowhead
Amboy
Santa Barbara Channel
Ojai
Wrightwood
13
Twentynine Palms
15
Oxnard
San Bernardino
Joshua Tree National Park
Ventura Malibu
Pasadena
Palm Springs
Santa Cruz
5
LOS ANGELES
Riverside
Indio
Desert Center
10
Blythe
Santa Rosa
Santa Ana
14
CHANNEL ISLANDS NATIONAL PARK
Long Beach
Huntington Beach
4
Temecula
Salton Sea
Santa Barbara
Catalina Island
Oceanside
Julian
Brawley
San Nicolas
Del Mar
La Jolla
3
El Centro
Yuma
San Clemente
SAN DIEGO
8
Tijuana
Mexicali
MEXICO

WHAT'S WHERE

The following numbers refer to chapters.

7 Monterey Bay Area. Postcard-perfect Monterey, Victorian-flavored Pacific Grove, and exclusive Carmel all share this stretch of California coast. To the north, Santa Cruz boasts a boardwalk, a UC campus, ethnic clothing shops, and plenty of surfers.

8 San Francisco. To see why so many have left their hearts here, you need to visit the city's iconic neighborhoods— posh Pacific Heights, the Hispanic Mission, and gay-friendly Castro.

9 The Bay Area. The area that rings San Francisco is nothing like the city—but it is home to some of the nation's great universities, fabulous bay views, Silicon Valley, and Alice Waters's Chez Panisse.

10 Napa and Sonoma. By virtue of award-winning vintages, luxe lodgings, and epicurean eats, Napa and Sonoma counties retain their title as *the* California Wine Country.

11 The North Coast. The star attractions here are natural ones, from the secluded beaches and wave-battered bluffs of Point Reyes National Seashore to the towering redwood forests.

12 Redwood National Park. More than 200 miles of trails, ranging from easy to strenuous, allow visitors to see these spectacular trees in their primitive environments.

21 Sacramento and the Gold Country. The 1849 gold rush that built San Francisco and Sacramento began here, and the former mining camps strung along 185 miles of Highway 49 replay their past to the hilt.

22 Lake Tahoe. With miles of crystalline water reflecting the peaks of the High Sierra, Lake Tahoe is the perfect setting for activities like hiking and golfing in summer and skiing and snowmobiling in winter.

23 The Far North. California's far northeast corner is home to snowcapped Mount Shasta, the pristine Trinity Wilderness, and abundant backwoods character.

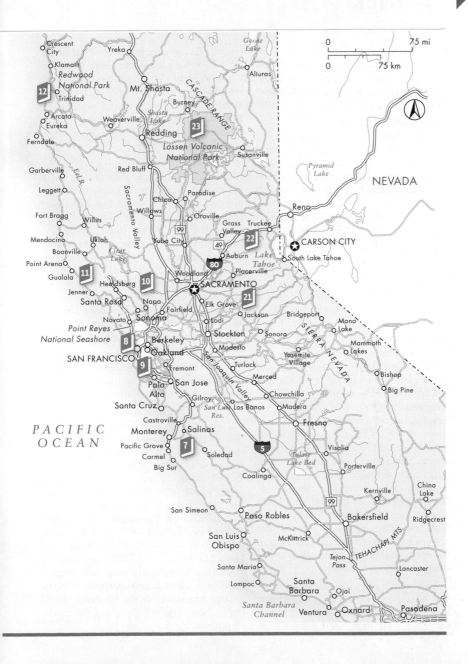

PLANNER

When to Go

Because they offer activities indoors and out, the top California cities rate as all-seasons destinations. Ditto for Southern California's coastal playgrounds.

Death Valley and Joshua Tree National Park are best in spring when desert blooms offset their austerity and temperatures are still manageable. Early spring—when the gray whale migration overlaps with the end of the elephant seal breeding season and the start of the bird migration—is the optimal time to visit Point Reyes National Seashore. Yosemite is ideal in late spring because roads closed in winter are reopened, and the park's waterfalls—swollen with melting snow—run fast. Autumn is "crush time" in all the wine destinations. Ski resorts typically open around Thanksgiving (they sometimes remain in operation into June).

Car Travel

Driving may be a way of life in California, but it isn't cheap (gas prices here are usually among the highest in the nation). It's also not for the fainthearted; you've surely heard horror stories about L.A.'s freeways, but even the state's scenic highways and byways have their own hassles. For instance, on the dramatic coastal road between San Simeon and Carmel, twists, turns, and divinely distracting vistas frequently slow traffic; in rainy season, mudslides can close the road altogether. ⚠ Never cross the double line to pass a slower car ahead of you. If you see that cars are backing up behind you, stop at the first available pullout to allow faster drivers to pass.

On California's notorious freeways, other rules apply. Nervous Nellies must resist the urge to stay in the two slow-moving lanes on the far right, used primarily by trucks. To drive at least the speed limit, get yourself in a middle lane. If you're ready to bend the rules a bit, the second lane (lanes are numbered from 1 starting at the center) moves about 5 mph faster. But avoid the far-left lane (the one next to the carpool lane), where speeds range from 75 mph to 90 mph.

Air Travel

Air travelers beginning or ending their vacation in San Francisco have two main airports to choose from: San Francisco International (SFO) or Oakland International (OAK). The former lands you closer to the city core (ground transportation will take about 20 minutes), but the latter is less heavily trafficked and less prone to fog delays. BART, the Bay Area's affordable rapid-transit system, serves both airports. So your decision will probably rest on which one has the best fares and connections for your route.

If your final destination is Monterey or Carmel, San Jose International Airport (SJC), about 40 miles south of San Francisco, is another alternative.

Around Los Angeles, there are several airport options to choose from. LAX, the world's sixth-busiest airport, gets most of the attention—and not usually for good reasons. John Wayne Airport (SNA), about 25 miles south in Orange County, is a solid substitute—especially if you're planning to visit Disneyland or Orange County. You might also consider Bob Hope Airport (BUR) in Burbank (close to Hollywood and its studios) or Long Beach Airport (LGB), convenient if you're catching a cruise ship. San Diego's Lindbergh International Airport (SAN) is located minutes from the Gaslamp Quarter, Balboa Park and Zoo, and the cruise ship terminal.

CALIFORNIA'S TOP EXPERIENCES

Hit the Road

Kings Canyon Highway, Redwood Highway, Tioga Pass, 17-Mile Drive, the Lake Tahoe loop: California has some splendid and challenging roads. You'll drive through a tunnel formed by towering redwood trees on the Redwood Highway. If you venture over the Sierras by way of Tioga Pass (through Yosemite in summer only), you'll see emerald green meadows, gray granite monoliths, and pristine blue lakes—and very few people.

Ride a Wave

Surfing—which has influenced everything from fashion to moviemaking to music—is a quintessential California activity. You can find great surf breaks in many places along the coast, but one of the best places to try it is Huntington Beach. Lessons are widely available. If you're not ready to hang 10, you can hang out at "Surf City's" International Surfing Museum or stroll the Surfing Walk of Fame.

Pan for Gold

Though California's gold rush ended more than a hundred years ago, you can still feel the forty-nine fever on the western face of the Sierra Nevada in Columbia, a well-preserved town populated by costumed interpreters, where you can pan for gold or tour a mine. Or visit Bodie, an eerie ghost town in the eastern Sierra that remains in a state of "arrested decay."

Think Globally, Eat Locally

Over the years California cuisine has evolved from a mere trend into a respected gastronomic tradition: one that pairs local, often organic or sustainable, ingredients with techniques inspired by European, Asian, and, increasingly, Indian and Middle Eastern cookery.

See Eccentric Architecture

California has always drawn creative and, well, eccentric people. And all that quirkiness has left its mark in the form of oddball architecture that makes for some fun sightseeing. Begin by touring Hearst Castle—the beautifully bizarre estate William Randolph Hearst built above San Simeon. In Death Valley, the late Marta Becket's Amargosa Opera House offers a variation on the theme. And Lake Tahoe's Vikingsholm (a re-created Viking castle) is equally odd.

Get Behind the Scenes

In L.A. it's almost obligatory to do some Hollywood-style stargazing. Cue the action with a behind-the-scenes tour of one of the dream factories. (Warner Bros. Studios' five-hour deluxe version, which includes lunch in the commissary, is just the ticket for cinephiles.) Other must-sees include the Dolby Theatre, home to the Academy Awards; Grauman's Chinese Theatre, where celebs press feet and hands into cement for posterity's sake; Hollywood Boulevard's star-paved Walk of Fame; and the still-iconic Hollywood sign.

People-Watch

Opportunities for world-class people-watching abound in California. Just saunter the rainbow-flagged streets of San Francisco's Castro neighborhood or the century-old boardwalk in time-warped, resiliently boho Santa Cruz. Better yet, hang around L.A.'s Venice Boardwalk, where chain-saw jugglers, surfers, fortune-tellers, and well-oiled bodybuilders take beachfront exhibitionism to a new high (or low, depending on your point of view). The result is pure eye candy.

CALIFORNIA TODAY

The People

California is as much a state of mind as a state in the union—a kind of perpetual promised land that has represented many things to many people. In the 18th century, Spanish missionaries came seeking converts and gold. In the 19th, miners rushed here to search for gold. And, in the years since, a long line of Dust Bowl farmers, land speculators, Haight-Ashbury hippies, migrant workers, dot-commers, real estate speculators, and would-be actors have come chasing their own dreams.

The result is a population that leans toward idealism—without necessarily being as liberal as you might think. (Remember, this is Ronald Reagan's old stomping ground.) And despite the stereotype of the blue-eyed, blond surfer, California's population is not homogeneous either. Ten million people who live here (more than 27% of Californians) are foreign born. Almost half hail from Latin American countries; another third emigrated from Asia, following the waves of Chinese workers who arrived in the 1860s to build the railroads and subsequent waves of refugees from the Vietnam War.

The Politics

What's blue and red and green all over? California: a predominantly Democratic state with an aggressive "go green" agenda and policies that make California the greenest state in the nation, supporting more green construction, wind farms, and solar panels.

The Economy

Leading all other states in terms of the income generated by agriculture, tourism, entertainment, and industrial activity, California has the country's most diverse state economy. Moreover, with a gross state product of more than $2 trillion, California would be one of the top 10 economies *in the world* if it were an independent nation.

Despite its wealth ($61,818 median household income) and productivity, California took a large hit in the 2007 recession, but the Golden State's economic history is filled with boom and bust cycles—beginning with the mid-19th-century gold rush that started it all. Optimists already have their eyes on the next potential boom: high-tech and bioresearch, "green companies" focused on alternative energy, renewables, electric cars, and the like.

The Culture

Cultural organizations flourish in California. San Francisco—a city with less than 900,000 residents—has well-regarded ballet, opera, and theater companies, and is home to one of the continent's most noteworthy orchestras. Museums like San Francisco Museum of Modern Art (SFMOMA) and the de Young also represent the city's ongoing commitment to the arts.

Art and culture thrive in San Diego. Balboa Park alone holds 17 museums, opulent gardens, and three performance venues, in addition to the San Diego Zoo. The Old Globe Theater and La Jolla Playhouse routinely originate plays that capture coveted Tony Awards in New York.

But California's *real* forte is pop culture, and L.A. and its environs are the chief arbiters. Movie, TV, and video production have been centered here since the early 20th century. Capitol Records set up shop in L.A. in the 1940s, and this area has been instrumental in the music industry ever since. And while these industries continue to influence national trends, today they are only part of the pop culture equation. Websites are also a growing part of that creativity—Facebook, YouTube, and Google are California companies.

The Parks and Preserves

Cloud-spearing redwood groves, snow-tipped mountains, canyon-slashed deserts, primordial lava beds, and a seemingly endless coast: California's natural diversity is staggering—and efforts to protect it started early. Yosemite, the first national park, was established here in 1890, and the National Park Service now oversees 32 sites in California (more than in any other state). When you factor in 280 state parks—which encompass underwater preserves, historic sites, wildlife reserves, dune systems, and other sensitive habitats—the number of acres involved is almost as impressive as the topography itself.

Due to encroaching development and pollution, keeping these natural treasures in pristine condition is an ongoing challenge. For instance, Sequoia and Kings Canyon (which is plagued by pesticides and other agricultural pollutants blown in from the San Joaquin Valley) has been named America's "smoggiest park" by the National Parks Conservation Association, and the Environmental Protection Agency has designated it as an "ozone nonattainment area with levels of ozone pollution that threaten human health."

There is no question that Californians love their 280 state parks. Nearly every park has its grass-roots supporters, who volunteer to raise money, volunteer as rangers, and work other jobs to keep the parks open.

The Cuisine

California gave us McDonald's, Denny's, Carl's Jr., Taco Bell, and, of course, In-N-Out Burger. Fortunately for those of us with fast-clogging arteries, the state also kick-started the health-food movement. Back in the 1970s, California-based chefs put American cuisine on the culinary map by focusing on freshly prepared seasonal ingredients.

Today, this focus has spawned the "locavore" or sustainable food movement—followers try to consume only food produced within a 100-mile radius of where they live, since processing and refining food and transporting goods over long distances is bad for both the body and the environment. This isn't much of a restriction in California, where a huge variety of crops grow year-round. Some 350 cities and towns have certified farmers' markets—and their stalls are bursting with a variety of goods. California has been America's top agricultural producer for the last 50 years, growing more fruits and vegetables than any other state. Dairies and ranches also thrive here, and fishing fleets harvest fish and shellfish from the rich waters offshore.

SOUTHERN CALIFORNIA TOP ATTRACTIONS

Balboa Park

(A) What's not to like about San Diego's Balboa Park? A huge space in the heart of downtown where you can spend a whole day, the park is filled with open green lawns, great play areas for kids, colorful gardens, historic fountains, and beautiful Spanish-style buildings that are more than 100 years old. Fifteen museums display collections ranging from natural history to fine art and photography, from sports to classic cars to science.

Big Sur Coastline

(B) A drive along Highway 1 through the winding Big Sur Coastline is hard to beat. With towering forests on one side and rocky seaside cliffs on the other, drivers must take care not to become distracted by the spectacular ocean views. While the vistas are stunning from the road, travelers will be rewarded by short detours to visit elephant seals, relax on secluded beaches or hike through the redwoods.

This 90-mile stretch of road between San Simeon and Carmel is arguably one of the most stunning in the state.

Death Valley

(C) For well-prepared travelers, a trip to Death Valley is more awe-inspiring than ominous. Within the largest national park in the contiguous United States you'll find the brilliantly colored rock formations of Artist's Palette, the peaks of the Panamint Mountains, and the desolate salt flats of Badwater, 282 feet below sea level.

Disneyland Resort

(D) A trip to Disneyland is indeed a dream come true for many. Built in 1955, Disneyland is the original Disney amusement park. Today, the Anaheim resort has grown to include Disneyland, Disney's California Adventure, Downtown Disney, and three Disney hotels. Its proximity to Los Angeles and San Diego makes it easy to incorporate a visit into almost any Southern California itinerary.

Hollywood

(E) When people think of Los Angeles, it is Hollywood that most often comes to mind. Visitors can't help but be star-struck while wandering the Hollywood Walk of Fame, standing at the epicenter of Hollywood and Vine, or gazing up at the famous Hollywood sign. A visit to one of the studios that makes the magic happen, such as Paramount Pictures, Universal Studios Hollywood, or Warner Bros. Studios, is a must.

Mission Santa Barbara

Santa Barbara is the most beautiful of the 21 remaining settlements along California's Mission Trail. Originally built in 1786, the Mission is home to an excellent collection of Native American and Spanish and Mexican colonial art. Santa Barbara has many more attractions to warrant a visit, including its walkable downtown, and an excellent wine region.

Palm Springs and Beyond

In this improbably situated bastion of Bentleys and bling, worldly pleasures rule. Glorious golf courses, tony shops and restaurants, decadent spa resorts—they're all here. Fans of mid-century modernist architecture will love the many gems on display in Palm Springs. Solitude seekers can still slip away to nearby Joshua Tree National Park or Anza-Borrego Desert State Park.

San Diego Zoo

(F) The world-renowned San Diego Zoo is a must-see for adults and kids alike. Set in 100 acres within Balboa Park, the zoo is admired for its conservation efforts. Famous for its giant panda research, the zoo's resident pandas are the stars of the show.

NORTHERN CALIFORNIA TOP ATTRACTIONS

The Golden Gate Bridge

(A) Catching that first glimpse of the iconic Golden Gate Bridge is bound to take your breath away. Completed in 1937, the art deco suspension bridge has become the internationally recognized symbol of San Francisco. While often swathed in an otherworldly fog, on a clear day the city and bay views from the bridge are spectacular.

Lake Tahoe

(B) Deep, clear, and intensely blue, this forest-rimmed body of water straddling the California–Nevada border is one of the continent's prettiest alpine lakes. That environmental controls can keep it that way is something of a miracle, given Tahoe's popularity. Throngs of outdoor adventurers flock to the California side to ski, hike, bike, and boat. On the Nevada side, where casinos are king, gambling often wins out over fresh-air activities— but natural wonders are never far away.

Monterey Bay Aquarium

This aquarium is one of the nation's most spectacular and most respected. A multistory kelp forest, the million-plus-gallon tank in the Open Seas exhibit, and a dramatically lit jellyfish experience are just some of the highlights. The aquarium also impresses behind the scenes with its extensive marine research programs and conservation efforts.

Napa Valley

(C) Despite impressive wines being produced throughout the state, the Napa Valley remains California's original and most famous destination for wine. Although the vineyard-blanketed hills are undeniably scenic, the wine itself remains the big draw here. From household names to producers with a cult following, budding oenophiles can educate their palettes on scores of tours and tasting sessions.

Point Reyes National Seashore

(D) Aside from the namesake seashore, this Marin County preserve encompasses ecosystems that range from woodlands and marshlands to heathlike grasslands. The range of wildlife here is equally diverse—depending on when you visit, expect to see gray whales, rare Tule elk, and almost 500 species of birds. December through March you can also see male elephant seals compete for mates.

Redwood National and State Park

A United Nations World Heritage Site, this park along California's north coast is one of the most serene spots on earth. It holds groves of towering ancient redwood trees, including the world's tallest tree at nearly 380 feet. Drive along the Redwood Highway to experience the majesty of the trees.

San Francisco's Cable Cars

(E) Pricey and touristy for sure, but a chance to ride on one of San Francisco's classic cable cars should not be passed up. Clutching a handrail while riding downhill on one of the exterior running boards can be exhilarating or downright frightening, depending on whom you ask. Sitting inside offers a tamer ride, yet you can watch the gripman at work, listen to the clanging of the bell, and take in the sights as you roll by.

Yosemite National Park

(F) Nature looms large here, both literally and figuratively. In addition to hulking Half Dome, the park is home to El Capitan (the world's largest exposed granite monolith, rising 3,593 feet above the glacier-carved valley floor) and Yosemite Falls (North America's tallest cascade). In Yosemite's signature stand of giant sequoias—the Mariposa Grove—even the trees are Bunyanesque.

IF YOU LIKE

One-of-a-Kind Accommodations

Hoteliers statewide have done their utmost to create accommodations that match the glories of the region's landscape, in the process creating lodgings that boast character as well as comfort. Some are unconventional, while others are genuine old-school gems.

Hotel Del Coronado, Coronado. A turreted beauty and veritable Victorian extravaganza, this spot inspired L. Frank Baum's description of Oz. Iconic architecture aside, Hotel Del Coronado is also famous as the filming locale for *Some Like It Hot,* and has hosted most of the U.S. presidents in the last century. Today it caters more to tour groups than Tinseltown stars, but fans remain loyal.

Mission Inn, Riverside. This sprawling Spanish colonial revival estate has welcomed a who's who of politicos. Ronald and Nancy Reagan spent their wedding night here, Richard and Pat Nixon were married in its chapel, and eight U.S. heads of state have patronized its Presidential Lounge.

Movie Colony Hotel, Palm Springs. Hollywood's 1930s heyday comes alive at this glamorous boutique hotel designed by Albert Frey, who created mid-century minimalism in Palm Springs. It now attracts a lively clientele and has a cool vibe.

Fairmont San Francisco, San Francisco. It got off to a shaky start (the 1906 earthquake delayed its opening by exactly a year), but this Nob Hill hotel has hosted groundbreaking events like the drafting of the United Nations Charter and Tony Bennett's debut of "I Left My Heart in San Francisco."

Off-the-Beaten-Path Adventures

Mother Nature has truly outdone herself in California. But at the state's most popular sites, it can be hard to approach her handiwork with a sense of awe when you're encircled by souvenir hawkers and camera-wielding tourists. Step off the beaten path, though, and all you'll be able to hear will be the echo of your own voice saying "wow."

Hiking. Steam is the theme at Lassen Volcanic National Park: especially along the 3-mile Bumpass Hell Trail, which has hot springs, steam vents, and mud pots. If you're looking for a cooler hiking experience (temperature-wise), it's hard to top the rugged beauty of Point Reyes National Seashore.

Climbing. Joshua Tree National Park is California's epicenter for rock climbing; within the park there are hundreds of formations and thousands of routes to choose from. No experience? No problem. J-Tree Outfitters offers crash courses for beginners.

Kayaking. Paddling around the lichen-covered sea caves of Channel Islands National Park or the surreal tufa towers of Mono Lake, you'll feel as if you're on another planet. But kayaking in San Francisco or La Jolla proves you can still find peace close to the big city.

Ballooning. Hot-air ballooning—whether over Wine Country, Temecula, Palm Desert, Mammoth Lakes, or Shasta Valley—lets you sightsee from a totally new perspective.

Amusement Parks

You're on vacation, so why not enjoy some carefree pleasures? For concentrated doses of old-fashioned fun, indulge in creaky waterfront amusements—like Musée Mécanique on San Francisco's Fisherman's Wharf and the antique carousel at Santa Monica Pier. Or opt for a full day at an over-the-top theme park.

Disneyland, Anaheim. Walt Disney set the gold standard for theme parks, and his original "magic kingdom" (the only one built during his lifetime) remains at the top of its class due to innovative rides, animatronics, and a liberal sprinkling of pixie dust.

LEGOLAND California, Carlsbad. Dedicated to the plastic bricks that have been a playtime staple for more than 60 years, this park has more than 60 LEGO-inspired attractions (including the popular Driving School, Fun Town Fire Academy, plus get-all-wet Splash Battle and Pirate Reef) and some 15,000 LEGO models ranging from teeny working taxis to a 9-foot-tall dinosaur.

San Diego Zoo Safari Park, Escondido. Get up close and personal with lions and tigers at this huge park where animals appear to be roaming free. You can feed a giraffe, talk to the gorillas, and track herds of elk as they cross the plain. Cheetahs bound, hippos huff, and zebras zip.

Santa Cruz Beach Boardwalk, Santa Cruz. Now well over 100 years old, the state's oldest amusement park is a sentimental favorite. Expect vintage rides (most notably a 1911 carousel and wooden roller coaster) alongside contemporary attractions, as well as corn dogs, cotton candy, and loads of kitsch.

Spas

Ancient Romans coined the word "spa" as an acronym for *solus per aqua* (or "health by water"). There's plenty of the wet stuff in the Golden State, yet California spas—like California kitchens—are known for making the most of any indigenous ingredient. The resulting treatments are at once distinctive, decadent, and most important, relaxing.

The Golden Door, Escondido. Relax and renew at this destination spa tucked into a secluded canyon north of San Diego. Serenity and simplicity rule here, where every moment reflects its Zen-like ambience.

Glen Ivy Hot Springs Spa, Corona. The outdoor bath at this historic day spa couples red clay from Temescal Canyon with naturally heated, mineral-rich water from its own thermal springs.

Post Ranch Inn & Spa, Big Sur. Like its organic architecture, this luxe retreat's spa treatments are designed to capture the tone of Big Sur—case in point, the Crystal and Gemstone Therapy. It combines Native American tradition (a ceremonial burning of sage) with an aromatherapy massage that employs jade collected from nearby beaches and essences of local wildflowers.

Spa Terra, Napa. While other Wine Country spas often overlook vineyards, the one at the Meritage Resort occupies an estate cave 40 feet below them. Appropriately, the facility specializes in vinotherapy treatments incorporating—you guessed it—the fruit of the vine.

CALIFORNIA MADE EASY

I'm not particularly active. Will I still enjoy visiting a national park? Absolutely. The most popular parks really do have something for everyone. Take Yosemite. When the ultrafit embark on 12-hour trail treks, mere mortals can hike Cook's Meadow—an easy 1-mile loop that's also wheelchair accessible. If even that seems too daunting, you can hop on a free shuttle or drive yourself to sites like Glacier Point or the Mariposa Grove of Giant Sequoias. Further north in Redwood National Park, the 8-mile Coastal Drive offers breathtaking views of the giant trees as well as the Pacific Ocean from the comfort of your vehicle. If you do want to stretch your legs, the trail through the otherworldly Fern Canyon is less than a mile long.

What's the single best place to take the kids? Well, that depends on your children's ages and interests, but for its sheer smorgasbord of activities, San Diego is hard to beat. Between the endless summer weather and sites such as the San Diego Zoo and LEGOLAND (about 30 minutes away), California's southernmost city draws families in droves. Once you've covered the mega-attractions, enjoy an easy-to-swallow history lesson in Old Town or the Maritime Museum. Want to explore different ecosystems? La Jolla Cove has kid-friendly tidal pools and cliff caves, while Anza-Borrego Desert State Park is a doable two-hour drive east.

If you're traveling in Northern California, San Francisco is also chockablock with kid-friendly attractions. A cable-car ride is a no-brainer—but if you have a Thomas the Tank Engine fan in tow, be sure to also take a spin on the historic F-line trolleys. Other classic kid-friendly SF sights include the Exploratorium, the San Francisco Zoo, Alcatraz, the Ferry Building, and the California Academy of Sciences. Take the kids for dim sum in Chinatown. Or head to Musée Mécanique to see what kids played (way) before Nintendo's Wii came out.

That said, there are kid-friendly attractions all over the state—your kids are going to have to try really hard to be bored.

I am planning on visiting several top attractions on my trip. How can I beat the crowds? If you are visiting a theme park during a peak time, consider a timed pass such as Disneyland's FASTPASS tickets (free on participating rides) or LEGOLAND's Reserve N' Ride (from $25 per person). Be sure to start your day early and have a plan for what you want to see prior to arriving. Popular state and national parks can definitely be crowded during the summer, however, for every crowded trail and visitor center, there are many under-the-radar hikes and pockets of solitude to be found. Ask a park ranger to point you in the right direction. And don't forget about rush hour—time your travel through major urban areas to avoid commuter traffic.

California sounds expensive. How can I save on sightseeing? CityPass (☎ *888/330–5008* ⊕ *www.citypass.com*) includes admission and some upgrades for main attractions in San Francisco, Hollywood, and Southern California (Disneyland, Universal Studios, San Diego Zoo/Safari Park, and LEGOLAND). Also, many museums set aside free-admission days. Prefer the great outdoors? An $80 America the Beautiful annual pass (☎ *888/275–8747* ⊕ *www. nps.gov*) admits you to every site under the National Park Service umbrella.

CALIFORNIA'S BEST ROAD TRIPS

GREAT ITINERARIES

No trip to California would be complete without a drive through the state's spectacular scenery. However, adding a road trip to your itinerary is not just a romantic idea: it's often a practical one, too. A road trip is a great way to link together more than one urban area (San Francisco to Los Angeles with a drive down the coast, for example) or to venture into some more remote areas of this massive state. Whether you have just a few days or longer to spare, these itineraries will help you hit the road.

THE BEST OF THE NORTHERN COAST, 5 DAYS

Hit the highlights of Northern California in one itinerary: scenic coastal drives, quaint windswept towns, wine tasting, culinary delights, and majestic redwood forests. This route can be done as part of a longer trip north towards the Oregon border, or as part of a loop back down to San Francisco.

Day 1: Marin County and Point Reyes National Seashore

(Without stops, Point Reyes National Seashore is about 1½ hrs by car from San Francisco on Hwy 1. Point Reyes Lighthouse is 45 mins by car from the visitor center.)

As you head out of San Francisco on the Golden Gate Bridge, be sure to pull over at the **scenic lookout** on the north side and take in the spectacular views looking back at the city skyline. If you haven't yet checked out the picturesque harbor community of **Sausalito** just north of the bridge, now is your chance. It will be hard not to linger, but there is much to see today. Bidding San Francisco farewell, you will quickly find yourself in the natural beauty of Marin County. Exit the 101 onto Highway 1

at the chic suburb **Mill Valley,** and head towards **Muir Woods National Monument.** Walking among the coastal redwoods, it is hard to imagine San Francisco lies just a few miles away. However, the proximity to the city means that Muir Woods is often crowded, and parking can be difficult if you don't arrive early.

From Muir Woods, continue on Highway 1 past the laid-back beach towns of **Stinson Beach** and **Bolinas** before continuing on to **Point Reyes National Seashore.** Spend the remainder of the day at the park tide pooling, kayaking, hiking one of the many trails, or exploring the **Point Reyes Lighthouse.** In the winter, be on the lookout for migrating gray whales.

The tiny town of **Point Reyes Station** offers a selection of shops and dining options, including **Tomales Bay Foods,** a provisions stop favored by foodies. Spend a quiet evening in town and overnight at one of the small inns nearby.

Day 2: Healdsburg

(Point Reyes Station to Healdsburg, via Jenner, is 2 hrs by car.)

Continue north on Highway 1 past **Bodega Bay,** made famous by the Alfred Hitchcock movie *The Birds.* At Jenner, known for its resident harbor seals, turn on Route 116 and follow the Russian River inland, taking time to stop at a winery or two along the way.

Ditch the car in **Healdsburg** and enjoy strolling through the appealing town square with its excellent selection of tasting rooms and boutiques. The town is home to many acclaimed restaurants and luxurious hotels and is an excellent place to stop for the night. The town's compact layout and quality offerings make Healdsburg a favorite among wine-country destinations.

Days 3 and 4: Anderson Valley and Mendocino

(Mendocino is 2 hrs by car from Healdsburg. Budget plenty of time for stops in Anderson Valley to ensure the end of this scenic drive is done in the daylight.)

Driving north on the 101 from Healdsburg, pick up Highway 128 at Cloverdale and head into the **Anderson Valley.** This wine region is famous for its excellent Pinot Noir and Gewürztraminer, and the laid-back atmosphere of its tasting rooms can be a refreshing alternative to those in Napa Valley. **Navarro Vineyards, Roederer Estate,** and **Husch Vineyards** are all recommended. The small towns of **Boonville** and **Philo** have several high-quality dining options, and the latter is home to the **Philo Apple Farm's** beloved farm stand.

Continuing on to the coast, Highway 128 follows the Navarro River through several miles of dense and breathtaking redwood forest ending at the ocean. From here you meet up again with Highway 1 as it winds its way along a spectacularly scenic portion of the coast.

With their excellent dining and lodging options, the towns of **Mendocino** and **Little River,** just to the south, are great choices for your overnight stay. Spend the next day and a half exploring the area. Opportunities for stunning coastal walks abound, including **MacKerricher** and **Van Damme State Parks.** Hike through the unique Pygmy Forest in Van Damme and visit the **Glass Beach** in Fort Bragg. Be sure to save some time to explore the town of Mendocino itself with its quaint New England–style architecture and selection of art galleries and boutiques.

Day 5: Humboldt Redwoods State Park and the Avenue of the Giants

(Mendocino to Eureka via the Avenue of the Giants is 3 hrs by car.)

Driving north on Highway 1, the road eventually curves inland and meets up with U.S. 101 near Leggett. Head north on the 101 to Garberville, a good place to take a break before heading on to the redwoods.

For all the hype, a drive through **The Avenue of the Giants** will still take your breath away. Pick up a copy of the self-guided tour as you enter the 32-mile stretch of road running alongside some of the tallest trees on the planet. The drive weaves through portions of the larger **Humboldt Redwoods State Park.** Take time to get out of the car and take a short hike through Founders Grove or Rockefeller Forest.

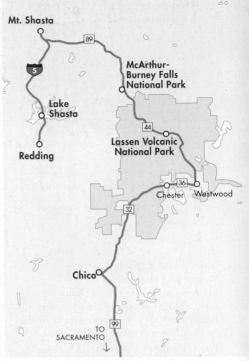

Continue on to **Ferndale,** a picturesque town of colorful Victorian buildings that is now largely a tourist destination. You can overnight here, or carry on to the regional city of **Eureka** for a wider variety of dining and accommodation.

From here, you can continue your way up the coast through the **Redwood National Forest** and on to the Oregon border. Alternatively, you can head south on the 101 and either return to **San Francisco,** or easily combine this itinerary with a trip to **Napa Valley** and the rest of **Sonoma.**

ROADS LESS TRAVELED: DISCOVERING THE NORTHERN INTERIOR, 5 DAYS

Mountain peaks, alpine lakes, a lush waterfall, and a striking volcanic landscape are all included on this tour of California's far north. The drive packs a big scenic punch in a short amount of time, and without the crowds found elsewhere in California's national parks. The remote roads and high elevations make parts of this route subject to snow closures well into the spring. Check current road conditions before setting out.

Day 1: Sacramento to Chico
(1½ hrs by car.)

Start your trip with a tour of the highlights of California's capital city, **Sacramento.** Wander the cobblestone streets and historic storefronts of Old Sacramento to get a sense of the city during its gold-rush days. Enjoy a horse-drawn-carriage ride through the historic neighborhood or take a cruise along the riverfront. Train enthusiasts of all ages will enjoy the walk-through exhibits at the nearby **California State Railroad**

Museum. Finally, don't leave town without taking a guided tour of the magnificent **Capitol** building.

When you have finished your tour of Sacramento, drive north on Highway 99 to **Chico.** Overnighting in Chico gets you a jump-start on the next day's drive, with the added bonus of spending time in this surprisingly bustling agricultural-meets-university town. Stop at the legendary **Sierra Nevada Brewing Company** for a free tour, or enjoy a meal at the brewpub.

Days 2 and 3: Lassen Volcanic National Park
(1½–2 hrs by car from Chico.)

Get an early start on your day, as spectacular scenery awaits you. From Chico, follow Highway 32 towards Chester and branch north at Highway 36 to reach the southern entrance of **Lassen Volcanic National Park.** Spend the next two days exploring the area's geothermal activity and dramatic landscape. Highlights

2

include a hike alongside the bubbling mud pots and hot springs of **Bumpass Hell trail,** views of **Lassen Peak** from Manzanita Lake, or an ascent of the peak itself. The 185-mile **Lassen Scenic Byway** circles the volcanic park and neighboring Lassen National Forest. If you plan ahead, you might score a reservation at **Drakesbad Guest Ranch** or at one of the campgrounds within the park. Otherwise, you will need to bunk in Chester or another neighboring town. Note: in winter, the park is closed to vehicles. Check current road conditions before setting out. If the park is closed, the itinerary can easily be modified to skip it and continue straight to McArthur-Burney Falls from Chico via Highway 299.

Day 4: McArthur-Burney Falls National Park and Mt. Shasta
(McArthur-Burney Falls is about 45 mins by car from Manzanita Lake; the start of the Everitt Memorial Hwy. is approximately 1 hr and 10 mins from the falls.)
Follow Highway 89 north out of Lassen to **McArthur-Burney Falls Memorial State Park.** Arrive early on busy holidays and weekends, as the park entrance will close when filled to capacity. Inside the park, the 129-foot-high falls are a sight to behold as water cascades over the moss-covered rocks. The falls are located near the park visitor center, with a vista point and hiking trail leading down to the bottom.

When you've had your fill of the falls, continue north on Highway 89 to **Mt. Shasta.** Drive up the mountain on the paved Everitt Memorial Highway for incredible views. Time permitting, choose from one of the many day hikes along the route. Alternatively, in winter you can hit the slopes at the nearby **Mt. Shasta Board & Ski Park.** The charming

town of Mount Shasta makes a great place to overnight. Train enthusiasts might prefer to venture 10 miles south to **Dunsmuir** and overnight at the **Railroad Park Resort,** a collection of antique cabooses transformed into a motel.

Day 5: Lake Shasta and Redding
(The exit for Lake Shasta Caverns is approximately 50 mins by car from the town of Mount Shasta. It's another ½ hr by car to reach Redding.)
Drive south on Interstate 5 to Lakehead and take Exit 695 to the **Lake Shasta Caverns.** The two-hour tour of the glittering caverns also includes a boat ride. Tours are offered throughout the day, more frequently in summer.

Back aboveground, anglers and boating enthusiasts should head to one of the marinas dotting the lakeshore to charter the craft of their choice. Houseboats are particularly popular on Lake Shasta, but many rentals come with a two-night minimum. For those more interested in engineering than angling, the hour-long tour of the **Shasta Dam** takes you inside the second-largest concrete dam in the United States. If you are not staying overnight on the lake, drive south and conclude your tour in the nearby city of **Redding** for the best selection of dining and accommodation. Note: this itinerary is designed for those wanting to loop back around to Sacramento and the Bay Area, or to continue on toward either Lake Tahoe or the North Coast. If you plan on driving north into Oregon, visit Shasta Lake prior to Mt. Shasta (take Highway 299 west from Burney) and then continue on Interstate 5 north across the state line.

THE ULTIMATE WINE TRIP: NAPA AND SONOMA, 4 DAYS

On this four-day extravaganza, you'll taste well-known and under-the-radar wines, bed down in plush hotels, and dine at restaurants operated by celebrity chefs. Appointments are required for some of the tastings.

Day 1: Sonoma County
(1½–2 hrs by car from San Francisco, depending on traffic.)

Begin your tour in Geyserville, about 78 miles north of San Francisco on U.S. 101. Visit **Locals Tasting Room,** which pours the wines of special small wineries. Have lunch at nearby **Diavola** or **Catelli's,** then head south on U.S. 101 and Old Redwood Highway to **Healdsburg's J Vineyards and Winery,** known for sparkling wines, Pinot Grigio, and Pinot Noir. After a tasting, backtrack on Old Redwood to Healdsburg. **Hôtel Les Mars** and **h2hotel** are two well-located spots to spend the night. Have dinner at **Chalkboard, Bravas Bar de Tapas,** or **Campo Fina,** all close by.

Day 2: Sonoma Wineries
(1 hr by car from Healdsburg to Glen Ellen.)

Interesting wineries dot the countryside surrounding Healdsburg, among them **Dry Creek Vineyard, Jordan Vineyard & Winery,** and **Unti Vineyards.** Dry Creek produces Zinfandel, Jordan makes Cabernet Sauvignon and Chardonnay, and Unti specializes in Zinfandel, Sangiovese, and obscure Italian and Rhône varietals. In the afternoon, head south on U.S. 101 and east on scenic Highway 12 to **Glen Ellen.** Visit **Jack London State Historic Park,** the memorabilia-filled home of the famous writer. Dine at **Aventine Glen Ellen** or **Glen Ellen Star** and stay at the **Olea Hotel.**

Day 3: Napa Valley
(Glen Ellen to St. Helena is about 30 mins by car without traffic. St. Helena to Yountville is about 15 mins by car, without stops.)

On Day 3, head east from Glen Ellen on Trinity Road, which twists and turns over the Mayacamas Mountains, eventually becoming the Oakville Grade. Unless you're driving, bask in the stupendous **Napa Valley** views. At Highway 29, drive north to **St. Helena.** Focus on history and architecture at **Charles Krug Winery** or let the art and wines at **Hall St. Helena** transport you. Take lunch downtown at **Cindy's Backstreet Kitchen.** Check out St. Helena's shopping, then head south on Highway 29 to Yountville for more shopping. With its mix of gift stores and galleries, **V Marketplace** is a good place to start.

Stay overnight at **Bardessono** or the **North Block Hotel,** both within walking distance of Yountville's famous restaurants. A meal at **The French Laundry** is many visitors' holy grail, but dining at **Bouchon, Bistro Jeanty, Redd,** or Chiarello's **Bottega** will also leave you feeling well served.

2

Day 4: Oakville to Carneros

(Just over 1 hr by car from Napa to San Francisco, without traffic.)

After breakfast, head north on Highway 29 to **Oakville,** where sipping wine at **Silver Oak Cellars, Nickel & Nickel,** or **B Cellars** will make clear why collectors covet Oakville Cabernet Sauvignons. Nickel & Nickel is on Highway 29; Silver Oak and B Cellars are east of it on Oakville Cross Road. Have a picnic at **Oakville Grocery,** in business on Highway 29 since 1881. Afterward, head south to Highway 121 and turn west to reach the Carneros District. Tour the **di Rosa** arts center (appointment required), then repair across the street to **Domaine Carneros,** which makes French-style sparkling wines. There's hardly a more elegant way to bid a Wine Country adieu than on the Domaine château's vineyard-view terrace before heading back to San Francisco. Give yourself plenty of time to get to your departure airport; traffic is generally heavy as you close in on the Bay Area.

Modifiying the Route from San Francisco

The above itinerary is useful if traveling to wine country from points further north. If you prefer to make a loop beginning and ending in San Francisco, the itinerary can be easily modified as follows: Day 1: Head north from San Francisco to the town of Sonoma (1 to 1½ hours by car, depending on traffic) and spend some time exploring the restaurants, shops, and tasting rooms lining the downtown plaza. Several excellent wineries operate nearby, including **Walt Wines** and **Patz & Hall.** From Sonoma, head north to Glen Ellen (20 minutes by car) and pick up the Glen Ellen itinerary described above. Day 2: Continue north to Healdsburg, following

the above itinerary in reverse. Overnight in Healdsburg as described. Day 3: Head south on Highway 101 to River Road and then east on Mark Springs Road toward Calistoga (45 minutes by car), a town made famous by its hot springs and mud baths. If time permits, overnight at one of Calistoga's luxury retreats, such as the **Calistoga Ranch,** or enjoy a day of pampering at **Spa Solage.** Otherwise, head south to St. Helena (15 minutes by car) and complete the remainder of the road trip as outlined above.

SIERRA RICHES: YOSEMITE, GOLD COUNTRY, AND TAHOE, 10 DAYS

This tour will show you why Tony Bennett left his heart in San Francisco. It also includes some of the most beautiful places in a very scenic state, plus gold-rush-era history, and a chance to hike a trail or two.

Day 1: San Francisco

Straight from the airport, drop your bags at the lighthearted **Hotel Monaco** near **Union Square** and request a goldfish for your room. A Union Square stroll packs a wallop of people-watching, window-shopping, and architecture viewing. **Chinatown,** chock-full of dim sum shops, storefront temples, and open-air markets, promises authentic bites for lunch. Catch a Powell Street **cable car** to the end of the line and get off to see the bay views and the antique arcade games at **Musée Mécanique,** the hidden gem of otherwise mindless **Fisherman's Wharf.** No need to go any farther than cosmopolitan North Beach for cocktail hour, dinner, and live music.

Day 2: Golden Gate Park
(15 mins by car or taxi, 45 mins by public transport from Union Square.)

In **Golden Gate Park,** linger amid the flora of the **Conservatory of Flowers** and the **San Francisco Botanical Garden at Strybing Arboretum,** soak up some art at the **de Young Museum,** and find serene refreshment at the **San Francisco Japanese Tea Garden.** The Pacific surf pounds the cliffs below the **Legion of Honor** art museum, which has an exquisite view of the **Golden Gate Bridge**—when the fog stays away. Sunset cocktails at the circa-1909 **Cliff House** include a prospect over Seal Rock (actually occupied by sea lions). Eat dinner elsewhere: Pacific Heights, the Mission, and SoMa teem with excellent restaurants.

Day 3: Into the High Sierra
(4–5 hrs by car from San Francisco.)

First thing in the morning, pick up your rental car and head for the hills. Arriving in **Yosemite National Park, Bridalveil Fall** and **El Capitan,** the 350-story granite monolith, greet you on your way to **Yosemite Village.** Ditch the car and pick up information and refreshment before hopping on the year-round shuttle to explore. Justly famous sights cram Yosemite Valley: massive **Half Dome** and **Sentinel Dome,** thundering **Yosemite Falls,** and wispy **Ribbon Fall** and **Nevada Fall.** Invigorating short hikes off the shuttle route lead to numerous vantage points. Celebrate your arrival in one of the world's most sublime spots with dinner in the dramatic **Majestic Hotel Dining Room** (formerly the Ahwahnee) and stay the night there (reserve well in advance).

Day 4: Yosemite National Park
(Yosemite shuttles run every 10–30 mins.)

Ardent hikers consider **John Muir Trail to Half Dome** a must-do, tackling the rigorous 12-hour round-trip to the top of Half Dome in search of life-changing vistas. Mere mortals hike downhill from Glacier Point on Four-Mile Trail or **Panorama Trail,** the latter an all-day trek past waterfalls. Less demanding still is a drive to Wawona for a stroll in the **Mariposa Grove of Big Trees** and lunch at the 19th-century **Big Trees Lodge Dining Room** (formerly the Wawona). In bad weather, take shelter in the **Ansel Adams Gallery** and **Yosemite Museum;** in fair conditions, drive up to **Glacier Point** for a breathtaking sunset view.

Day 5: Gold Country South
(2½–3 hrs by car from Yosemite.)

Highway 49 traces the mother lode that yielded many fortunes in gold in the 1850s and 1860s. Step into a living gold-rush town at **Columbia State Historic Park,** where you can ride a stagecoach and pan for riches. **Sutter Creek's** well-preserved downtown bursts with shopping opportunities, but the vintage goods displayed at **Monteverde Store Museum** are not for sale. A different sort of vintage powers the present-day bonanza of **Shenandoah Valley,** heart of the Sierra Foothills Wine Country. Taste your way through Rhône-style blended Zinfandels and Syrahs at boutique wineries such as **Shenandoah Vineyards** and **Sobon Estate.** Amador City's 1879 **Imperial Hotel** places you firmly in the past for the night.

Day 6: Gold Country North
(2 hrs by car from Amador City to Nevada City.)

In **Placerville,** a mineshaft invites investigation at **Hangtown's Gold Bug Mine,** while **Marshall Gold Discovery State Historic Park** encompasses most of **Coloma** and preserves the spot where James Marshall's 1849 find set off the California gold rush. Old Town **Auburn,** with its museums and courthouse, makes a good lunch stop, but

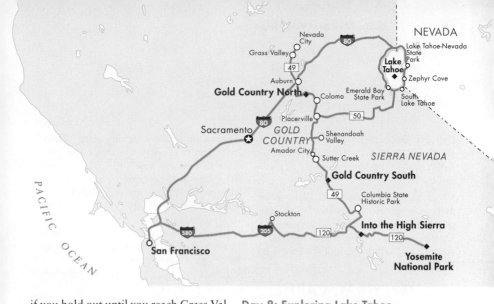

if you hold out until you reach Grass Valley you can try authentic miners' pasties. A tour of **Empire Mine State Historic Park** takes you into a mine, and a few miles away horse-drawn carriages ply the narrow, shop-lined streets of downtown **Nevada City**. Both Nevada City and **Grass Valley** hold a collection of bed-and-breakfast inns that date back to gold-rush days. For more contemporary accommodations backtrack to Auburn or Placerville.

Day 7: Lake Tahoe
(1 hr by car from Nevada City, 2 hrs from Placerville.)

Jewel-like **Lake Tahoe** is a straight shot east of Placerville on Highway 50; stop for picnic provisions in commercial **South Lake Tahoe**. A stroll past the three magnificent estates in **Pope-Baldwin Recreation Area** hints at the sumptuous lakefront summers once enjoyed by the elite. High above a glittering cove, **Emerald Bay State Park** offers one of the best lake views as well as a steep hike down to (and back up from) **Vikingsholm**, a replica 9th-century Scandinavian castle. Another fine, old mansion—plus a nature preserve and many hiking trails—lies in **Sugar Pine Point State Park**. Tahoe City offers more history and ample dining and lodging choices.

Day 8: Exploring Lake Tahoe
(Sightseeing cruise lasts 2 hrs.)

The picture-perfect beaches and bays of **Lake Tahoe–Nevada State Park** line the Nevada shoreline, a great place to bask in the sun or go mountain biking. For a different perspective of the lake, get out on the azure water aboard the sternwheeler MS *Dixie II* from **Zephyr Cove.** In South Lake Tahoe, another view unfurls as the **Heavenly Gondola** travels 2½ miles up a mountain. Keep your adrenaline pumping into the evening with some action at the massive casinos clustered in Stateline, Nevada.

Day 9: Return to San Francisco
(About 4 hrs by car from Tahoe City.)

After a long morning of driving, return your rental car in San Francisco and soak up some more urban excitement. Good options include a late lunch at the **Ferry Building,** followed by a visit to the **San Francisco Museum of Modern Art,** or lunch in **Japantown** followed by shopping in **Pacific Heights.** There is excellent people-watching in the **Castro** and the **Haight.** Say good-bye to Northern California at one of the plush lounges or trendy bars in the downtown hotels.

Day 10: Departure
(SFO is 30 mins from downtown both by BART public transport and by car, without traffic.)

Check the weather and your flight information before you start out for the airport: fog sometimes causes delays at SFO. On a clear day, your flight path might give you one last fabulous glimpse of the City by the Bay.

MONTEREY BAY, CARMEL, AND BIG SUR, 4 DAYS

In a nutshell, this drive is all about the jaw-dropping scenery of the Pacific Coast. Visitors pressed for time often make the drive from Monterey through Big Sur in one day. However, those who linger will be rewarded with more time to venture off the road and to enjoy the solitude of Big Sur once the day-trippers have gone. ⚠ Heavy rainfall in early 2017 caused a series of mudslides and the destabilization of the Pfeiffer Canyon Bridge along Highway 1 in Big Sur, and at press time several sections of the highway remain closed with no alternate routes through Big Sur. Before planning a drive in the area, check the latest reconstruction updates on the Caltrans website at www.dot.ca.gov.

Day 1: Monterey
Monterey, with its federally protected national marine sanctuary and its world-renowned aquarium, is the perfect spot to kick off your tour of the coast. Start the day with a visit to the enthralling **Monterey Bay Aquarium.** Exhibits such as the dramatic three-story kelp forest near the entrance give you a true sense of the local marine environment. For an even closer encounter, take to the water yourself on

a kayak or whale-watching tour. While undoubtedly touristy, the shops and galleries of **Cannery Row** still make for an interesting diversion and it's fun to watch the colony of sea lions at **Fisherman's Wharf.** There are plenty of excellent dining and lodging choices within walking distance of downtown, so enjoy a seafood dinner and an evening stroll before hitting the road the next morning.

Day 2: 17-Mile Drive and Carmel-By-The-Sea
(The 17-Mile Drive's Pacific Grove entrance gate is 15 mins by car from Monterey.)

If your visit falls between October and March, begin your drive with a quick detour to visit the migrating monarch butterflies at the **Monarch Grove Sanctuary** in the charming Victorian town of **Pacific Grove.**

Enter the **17-Mile Drive** through the tollgate ($10 per car) off Sunset Drive in Pacific Grove. This scenic road winds its way along the coast through a hushed and refined landscape of stunning homes and the renowned golf links at **Pebble Beach.** Perhaps the most famous (and photographed) resident is the **Lone Cypress,** which has come to symbolize the solitude and natural beauty of the coast. Even though the drive is only 17 miles, plan on taking your time. If you stop for lunch or souvenir shopping, inquire about a refund on the entry toll.

Upon exiting the drive, continue south to the charming town of **Carmel-by-the-Sea.** Spend the afternoon browsing the town's boutiques and galleries before walking to **Carmel Beach** for sunset and dinner at one of the many fine restaurants here. Similarly, there is no shortage of stylish, but pricey, lodging. Venture outside of the village for less expensive accommodation.

Day 3: Big Sur
(30 mins by car.)

The coastal drive through **Big Sur** is justifiably one of the most famous stretches of road in the world. The winding curves, endless views, and scenic waypoints are the stuff of road-trip legend. Keep your camera handy, fill up the tank, and prepare to be wowed. Traffic can easily back up along the route and drivers should take caution navigating the road's twists and turns. While you will only drive about 30 miles today, allow several hours for hikes and stops.

Heading into Big Sur you will first come upon the extremely photogenic **Bixby Creek Bridge.** Pull over in the turnout on the north side of the bridge to get that perfect shot. About 10 miles down the road look for a small cluster of services known as Big Sur Village just before the entrance to **Pfeiffer Big Sur State Park,** the perfect place to stop for a hike.

One mile south of the park, watch carefully for the sharp turnout and unmarked road leading to **Pfeiffer Beach.** Following the unpaved road 2 miles toward the sea you may question whether you are lost, but your perseverance will be rewarded when you reach the secluded beach with its signature rocky arch just offshore. Don't miss it!

There are several lodging options around this portion of Big Sur, ranging from rustic to luxurious. If room rates at the legendary **Post Ranch Inn** are not in your budget, consider splurging on the nine-course tasting menu at its spectacular cliff-side **Sierra Mar** restaurant instead. Alternatively, the terrace at **Nepenthe** offers decent food and gorgeous views at a lower price point. Be sure to check the time for sunset when making your dinner reservation.

Day 4: Big Sur to Cambria
(About 2 hrs by car. Allow ample time for hiking and 2 hrs to tour Hearst Castle.)

Start the morning off with a hike in **Julia Pfeiffer Burns State Park,** popular for its waterfall tumbling dramatically into the sea. Back on the road, several scenic overlooks will beckon as you head through the southern stretch of Big Sur. Treasure hunters should consider a stop at **Jade Cove.**

As you enter **San Simeon,** don't miss the **Piedras Blancas Elephant Seal Rookery.** Depending on your timing, you might catch a late afternoon tour at **Hearst Castle.** If not, you can make a reservation for a tour early the following morning. End the day with a walk at **Moonstone Beach** in the town of **Cambria,** 10 miles south of the castle, and overnight in one of the reasonably priced lodgings here.

From here, you can continue your travels south through the central coast to **Santa Barbara**. Or head inland to visit the **Paso Robles** wine region before returning to Monterey via Highway 101.

THE INLAND ROUTE: SAN FRANCISCO TO LOS ANGELES VIA THE SIERRAS, 5 DAYS

This itinerary provides an alternate to the more frequented coastal route between San Francisco and Los Angeles and takes in the splendid scenery of the Sierras. This trip just touches the surface of all that Yosemite, Kings Canyon, and Sequoia national parks have to offer. Avid naturalists might want to extend their time in the parks. Either way, plan on spending a few days on either end of the road trip to explore California's two most popular cities.

Day 1: San Francisco to Yosemite
(Yosemite is about 4 hrs from San Francisco by car, depending on traffic.)

Hit the road early for the day's long drive to **Yosemite National Park**. As you approach from Route 120, be sure to top up the tank as there are only a few gas stations within the park. Drive straight to the **Valley Visitor Center** to get an overview of the park. Stretch your legs on the easy loop trail to **Lower Yosemite Falls**. If daylight permits and you are looking for something a bit more strenuous, tackle the **Mist Trail** leading to **Bridalveil and Vernal Falls**. Reserve lodging early at the central valley lodges or campgrounds. Even if you aren't staying there, treat yourself to dinner at the renowned **Majestic Hotel Dining Room** (formerly the Ahwahnee).

Day 2: Exploring Yosemite
Spend today tackling some of the sights in the northern and central areas of the park. Options include the 8½ mile **Panorama Trail** from **Glacier Point** back down to the valley or a drive along the impossibly scenic Tioga Road to **Tuolumne Meadows**. Alternatively, consider a horseback or photography tour. Hikers looking to tackle the strenuous ascent of **Half Dome** should plan on spending an additional day in the park. While some do attempt to complete the trail in one very long day, many consider camping overnight in Little Yosemite Valley to be preferable. If attempting Half Dome, don't forget to secure your wilderness permit in advance. Spend a second night in Yosemite Valley.

Day 3: Yosemite to Kings Canyon
(The Wawona area of the park is about 1 hr by car from Yosemite Valley. From Wawona, Grants Grove Village in Kings Canyon is about 3 hrs by car.)

Make your way south to the **Wawona** section of Yosemite and don't miss the **Mariposa Grove of Big Trees** to see the famous Grizzly Giant before leaving the park. From here, drive south out of Yosemite and link up with Route 180 heading into **Kings Canyon National Park**. Again, remember to get gas along the route. Once inside Kings Canyon, continue along Route 180 for the 30-mile stretch known as the **Kings Canyon Scenic Byway** as it winds between Grant Grove Village and Zumwalt Meadow. There are several vista points or opportunities to stretch your legs en route. Towards the end, enjoy an easy 1½-mile hike along the **Zumwalt Meadows Trail**. Drive back (allow about an hour without stops) and overnight in the Grant Grove area of the park.

San Francisco · 580 · 120 · Yosemite · Mariposa Grove of Big Trees · 41 · NEVADA · Fresno · 180 · 180 · Zumwalt Meadows · Kings Canyon National Park · 198 · Wuksachi Lodge · Sequoia National Park · 65 · Bakersfield · 99 · PACIFIC OCEAN · Santa Barbara Channel · 5 · Los Angeles

Days 4 and 5: Kings Canyon to Sequoia

(Allow ample time to drive Generals Hwy. as parts are steep and winding, and there are many stops to make on the way. Los Angeles is about 3½–4 hrs by car from the Foothills Visitor Center. Bakersfield is about 2 hrs from Foothills by car.)

Spend the next two days exploring **Generals Highway**, the 43-mile scenic route connecting Kings Canyon and Sequoia national parks. Warm up with a hike into Redwood Canyon Grove, one of the largest sequoia groves in the world. You can choose between a shorter hike to an overlook point or longer 6- and 10-mile trails that lead deep into the grove. From there, continue the drive into **Sequoia National Park** and spend the rest of the day and the majority of the next exploring its highlights with an overnight at the **Wuksachi Lodge.**

Don't miss the 2-mile **Congress Trail**, an excellent opportunity to walk among the big trees, and the nearby **General Sherman Tree,** a massive specimen. If you want to tour the marble interior of **Crystal Cave,** be sure to reserve tour tickets in advance online or purchase them at the **Lodgepole visitor center.** Challenge your calves on the 350 stone steps of

Moro Rock and reward your efforts with views over the Middle Fork Canyon. Don't leave the park without making the requisite photo stop at **Tunnel Log,** which, as its name suggests, is a drive-through tunnel carved out of the trunk of a fallen tree. It might take some discipline to pull away from the spectacular scenery, but a 3½-hour drive to Los Angeles awaits. With any luck, an evening arrival will mean you miss much of the city's notorious traffic. However, if you linger a bit longer than expected or simply don't feel up to the drive, Bakersfield is a closer alternative to stop for the night. Note: for the particularly intrepid traveler, this itinerary can be modified to take in **Yosemite and Death Valley national parks** via the **Tioga Pass** and **Mono Lake.** However, travelers should be aware that Tioga Pass is only open in the summer and early fall. By the time the pass opens (usually late May or June), temperatures in Death Valley are already searing hot and the extreme conditions should not be taken lightly. Always travel with an ample supply of drinking water and food, take precautions against the burning sun, limit physical activity, and time outings for early or late in the day.

SANTA BARBARA WINE COUNTRY, 3 DAYS

It has been well over a decade since the popular movie *Sideways* brought the Santa Barbara wine country to the world's attention, and interest in this wine-growing area continues to grow. On this trip you will explore one of the most beautiful cities in the West, enjoy time along the gorgeous coast, and then head inland for a delightful wine-tasting adventure. This itinerary makes a perfect add-on to a trip to Los Angeles, or for those driving the coastal route between Los Angeles and San Francisco.

Day 1: Santa Barbara

(2 hrs by car from LAX to Santa Barbara without traffic.)

Santa Barbara is a gem, combining elegance with a laid-back coastal vibe. It provides a tranquil escape from the congestion of Los Angeles, and a dose of sophistication to the largely rural central coast.

Start your day at the beautiful **Old Mission Santa Barbara**, known as the "Queen" of the 21 missions that comprise the California Mission Trail. Plan to spend some time here; if your visit doesn't coincide with one of the 60-minute docent-led tours, self-guided tours are also available. From here, head to the waterfront and spend some time enjoying the wide stretch of sand at **East Beach** and a seafood lunch at one of the restaurants on **Stearns Wharf.**

Next stop is a tour of the **Santa Barbara County Courthouse** and the beautiful red-tile-roofed buildings of the surrounding downtown. Don't miss the murals in the ceremonial chambers or the incredible views from the top of the courthouse tower.

Back on the ground, enjoy superb shopping along **State Street** and consider kicking off your wine tour early with some tastings along the **Urban Wine Trail,** a collection of tasting rooms spread over a few blocks between downtown and the beach. Enjoy the lively dining and nightlife scene downtown, or head towards tony **Montecito** for an elegant dinner or overnight stay at the ultra-exclusive (and expensive) **San Ysidro Ranch.**

Day 2: Santa Rita Hills, Lompoc, and Los Olivos

(Without stops, this route takes about 2 hrs by car. Plan to linger and to detour down side roads to reach the wineries.)

Take the scenic drive along the coast on Highway 101 before heading inland towards Buellton. Exit onto Santa Rosa Road to begin your loop through the Santa Rita Hills. This area's cooler climate produces top-notch Chardonnay and Pinot Noir. Vineyards line the loop as you head out on Santa Rosa Road and return on Highway 246 towards Buellton. **Lafond Winery and Vineyards, Alma Rosa Winery,** and **Ken Brown Wines** are just a few of the wineries found along this route. Don't miss a stop at the so-called **Lompoc Wine Ghetto,** located midway around the route. Don't let the industrial-park setting deter you—several tasting rooms are clustered together, including well-regarded producers such as **Stolpman** and **Longoria,** making it a convenient and worthwhile stop.

Back on Highway 101, head north about 6 miles before exiting towards **Los Olivos.** Here you can park the car and spend the rest of the day exploring on foot. Tasting rooms, galleries, boutiques, and restaurants have made this former stagecoach town quite wine-country chic. **Carhartt**

PACIFIC
OCEAN

Vineyard and **Daniel Gehrs** are just two of the producers with tasting rooms in town. Los Olivos is a good base to overnight in, or stay just outside town at the lovely **Ballard Inn.** Or, dine at the chic locavore **Root 246** restaurant and stay at the **Hotel Corque** in nearby **Solvang.**

Day 3: Solvang, Foxen Canyon, and the Santa Ynez Valley

(The drive from Santa Ynez to Santa Barbara is about 45 mins by car via Hwy. 154.)

Start the next morning with pastries at the Danish town of **Solvang,** 10 minutes south of Los Olivos. The collection of windmills and distinct half-timber architecture of this village is charming, even if it is touristy. Spend some time exploring the town before hitting the road.

The towns of Los Olivos, Santa Ynez, and Solvang are located just a few minutes apart, with wineries spread between them in an area known as the Santa Ynez Valley. Heading north from Los Olivos, the Foxen Canyon wine trail extends all the way to Santa Maria and is home to excellent producers such as **Zaca Mesa** and the aptly named **Foxen Vineyards.** Expect some backtracking along your route today as you wind between the towns and venture into

Foxen Canyon. The tour at **Firestone Vineyard** is worthwhile, but very popular. The tasting rooms throughout the Santa Ynez region can get crowded, but there are plenty to choose from—if you see a tour bus parked outside one winery, just keep driving to the next one. Don't blink or you might miss the tiny town of **Santa Ynez;** it is worth a wander or a stop for lunch.

When you've had your fill of the wine region, take scenic Highway 154 over the San Marcos Pass and back to Santa Barbara. Wind down the day with a stroll along the beach, and perhaps one last glass of wine at sunset.

ROUTE 66 AND THE MOJAVE DESERT, 4 DAYS

Route 66 was the original road trip and California the ultimate destination. The Mother Road travels west from the Arizona border, skirting the Mojave Desert before passing through Los Angeles and ending at the Pacific Ocean. What makes this journey so compelling is actually what it lacks. Desolate stretches of road through windswept towns are reminders of the tough conditions faced by dust-bowl pioneers, while faded neon signs and

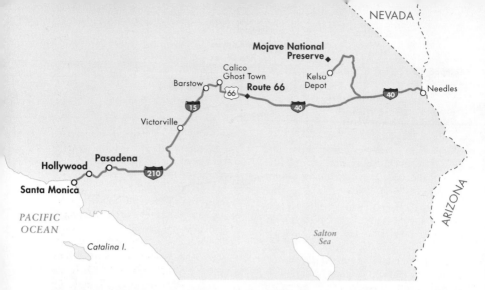

abandoned motels offer nostalgic glimpses of Route 66's heyday. Nearby, the solitary beauty of the Mojave National Preserve beckons with its volcanic rock formations, Joshua trees, and seemingly endless sand dunes.

Day 1: Santa Monica

By reversing the typical Route 66 journey and traveling from west to east you can hit the road upon arrival at LAX, or spend a few days exploring Los Angeles first. Starting your journey off in **Santa Monica** may feel a bit like eating your dessert first. For road-trippers on Route 66, reaching the Pacific Ocean after a long dusty drive through the desert was certainly a treat. The official end of Route 66 is marked with a plaque in **Palisades Park,** on a bluff overlooking **Santa Monica State Beach.** Soak in the quintessential SoCal beach scene on the wide expanse of sand below before heading to the famous **Santa Monica Pier.** From here, you can rent a bike and cruise south to **Venice Beach** for the ultimate people-watching experience.

In the evening, stroll the pedestrian-only **Third Street Promenade** and neighboring **Santa Monica Place** mall for a good selection of shopping, dining, and entertainment. Relax in luxury at the legendary **Shutters on the Beach.** Or, in keeping with

the true Route 66 spirit, opt for the more modest motor-lodge vibe of the **Sea Shore Motel.**

Day 2: Hollywood and Pasadena
(1½ hrs by car from Santa Monica to Pasadena and another 1½–2 hrs by car to Victorville.)

Heading inland through **Beverly Hills** and **Hollywood,** the remnants of Route 66 are easily overshadowed by the surrounding glitz and glamour. A stop at the **Hollywood Museum** or the **Hollywood Walk of Fame** will help transport you back in time to Tinseltown's golden age.

The route continues through **Pasadena,** with its stately homes and spacious gardens. Fans of Craftsman architecture won't want to miss a tour of the **Gamble House,** while a stroll around **Old Town Pasadena** is a great way to stretch your legs and grab a bite to eat.

Depending on your interests and how much sightseeing you've done, you might choose to stay in Pasadena for the night to enjoy a wider choice of dining and lodging options. Or, head to **Victorville** to maximize time on Route 66 tomorrow.

2

Day 3: Route 66

(Barstow to Needles is 2 hrs by car along I–40. However, add several more hrs to trace Route 66. Plan on spending 1–2 hrs at the Calico Ghost Town.)

Today is all about the drive. Hit the road early if you didn't spend the night in Victorville. First stop is the **California Route 66 Museum** in **Victorville**, where you'll learn all about the history of the Mother Road. Be sure to pick up a copy of their self-guided tour book and consult one of the many Route 66–related websites, such as ⊕ *www.historic66.com*, to help you navigate the old road as it crosses back and forth alongside Interstate 40 between Barstow and Needles. Abandoned service stations, shuttered motels, and faded signs dot the desert landscape in various states of alluring decay. Grab a meal at the famous **Baghdad Café** in Barstow . For a non–Route 66–related diversion spend a few hours exploring **Calico Ghost Town,** a restored old mining town just north of Barstow. In the evening, catch a flick at the **Skyline Drive-In Theatre.**

Accommodations in this area are mostly of the chain-motel variety. Victorville, Barstow, and Needles are your best bets for lodging.

Day 4: Mojave National Preserve

(There are several access points to the park along I–15 and I–40. Kelso Dunes Visitor Center is about 1½ hrs by car from either Barstow or Needles. Stick to the major roads in the park, which are either paved or gravel—others require four-wheel drive.)

In the morning, head north from Route 66 into the beautiful and remote landscape of the **Mojave National Preserve**. Reaching the top of the stunning golden **Kelso Dunes** requires some athleticism, but your efforts

will be rewarded with incredible scenery and the eerie sounds of "singing" sand. If you spent the night in Needles, explore the volcanic gas formations of **Hole-in-the-Wall** first. Farther north in the park, the Cima Road will bring you to the Teutonia Peak Trailhead and the largest concentration of Joshua trees in the world. Visitor centers at **Kelso Depot** and **Hole-in-the-Wall** provide information on additional sights, hiking trails, and campgrounds in the park.

There are several options for the next leg of your journey. You can drive back to Los Angeles in about three hours or drive onward to **Las Vegas** even faster. If you have more time, you can continue north and spend a few days in **Death Valley National Park,** or head south towards **Joshua Tree** and **Palm Springs** before making your way back to **Los Angeles.**

PALM SPRINGS AND THE DESERT, 5 DAYS

The Palm Springs area is paradise for many. Most go for more than a good tan or to play golf on championship courses. Expect fabulous and funky spas, a dog-friendly atmosphere, and sparkling stars at night.

Day 1: Palm Springs

(Just over 2 hrs by car from LAX, without traffic.)

Somehow in harmony with the harsh environment, midcentury-modern homes and businesses with clean, low-slung lines define the **Palm Springs** style. Although the desert cities comprise a trendy destination with beautiful hotels, fabulous multicultural food, abundant nightlife, and plenty of culture, a quiet atmosphere prevails. Fans of Palm Springs' legendary architecture and style won't want to miss the

home tours, lectures, and other events at the annual Modernism Week held each February, or the smaller fall preview event in October. If your visit doesn't coincide with these events, swing by the Palm Springs Visitor's Center for information on self-guided architecture tours. The city seems far away when you hike in hushed **Tahquitz** or **Indian Canyon**; cliffs and palm trees shelter rock art, irrigation works, and other remnants of Agua Caliente culture. If your boots aren't made for walking, you can always practice your golf game or indulge in some sublime or funky spa treatments at an area resort instead. Embrace the Palm Springs vibe and park yourself at the retro **Orbit In Hotel** or the legendary **Parker Palm Springs**. Alternatively, base yourself at the desert oasis, **La Quinta Resort**, about 40 minutes outside downtown Palm Springs.

Day 2: Explore Palm Springs
(The Aerial Tram is 15 mins by car from central Palm Springs. Plan at least a half day for the excursion.)

If riding a tram up an 8,516-foot mountain for a stroll or even a snowball fight above the desert sounds like fun to you, then show up at the **Palm Springs Aerial Tramway** before the first morning tram leaves (later, the line can get discouragingly long). Just

don't forget to dress in layers and wear decent footwear as it can be significantly colder when you reach the top. Afterward stroll through the **Palm Springs Art Museum** where you can see a shimmering display of contemporary studio glass, an array of enormous Native American baskets, and significant works of 20th-century sculpture by Henry Moore and others. After all that walking you may be ready for an early dinner. Nearly every restaurant in Palm Springs offers a happy hour, when you can sip a cocktail and nosh on a light entrée, usually for half price. Using your hotel as a base, take a few day trips to discover the natural beauty of the desert.

Day 3: Joshua Tree National Park
(1 hr by car from Palm Springs.)

Due to its proximity to Los Angeles and the highway between Las Vegas and coastal cities, **Joshua Tree** is one of the most popular and accessible of the national parks. You can see most of it in a day, entering the park at the town of Joshua Tree, exploring sites along **Park Boulevard**, and exiting at **Twentynine Palms**. With its signature trees, piles of rocks, glorious spring wildflowers, starlit skies, and colorful pioneer history, the experience is a bit more like the Wild West than Sahara sand dunes. Whether planning to take a day hike or a scenic drive, be sure to load up on plenty of drinking water prior to entering the park.

Day 4: Anza-Borrego Desert State Park and the Salton Sea

(About 2 hrs by car from Palm Springs.)

The **Salton Sea,** about 60 miles south of Palm Springs via Interstate 10 and Highway 86S, is one of the largest inland seas on earth. A new sea, formed by the flooding of the Colorado River in 1905, it attracts thousands of migrating birds and bird-watchers every fall. **Anza-Borrego Desert State Park** is the largest state park in California, with 600,000 acres of mostly untouched wilderness; it offers one of the best spring-wildflower displays in California and also displays a large collection of life-size bronze sculptures of animals that roamed this space millions of years ago. **Borrego Springs,** a tiny hamlet, lies in the center of it all. The desert is home to an archaeological site, where scientists continue to uncover remnants of prehistoric animals ranging from mastodons to horses. If you have four-wheel drive, a detour down the sandy track to **Font's Point** rewards the intrepid with spectacular views of the Borrego badlands. However, do not take the challenging road conditions lightly—inquire with park rangers before setting out.

Day 5: Return to L.A.

(LAX is just over 2 hrs by car from Palm Springs without traffic, but the drive often takes significantly more time. Allow plenty of extra time if catching a flight.)

If you intend to depart from LAX, plan for a full day of driving from the desert to the airport. Be prepared for heavy traffic at any time of day or night. If possible, opt to fly out of Palm Springs International or LA/Ontario International Airport instead.

SOUTHERN CALIFORNIA WITH KIDS, 7 DAYS

SoCal offers many opportunities to entertain the kids beyond the Magic Kingdom. LEGOLAND is a blast for kids 12 and under, and families can't beat the San Diego Zoo and San Diego's historic Old Town.

Days 1–2: Disneyland

(45 mins by car from LAX to Disneyland.)

Get out of Los Angeles International Airport as fast as you can. Pick up your rental car and head south on the Interstate 405 freeway, which can be congested day or night, toward Orange County and **Disneyland.** Skirt the lines at the box office with advance-purchased tickets in hand and storm the gates of the Magic Kingdom. You can cram the highlights into a single day, but if you get a two-day ticket and stay the night you can see the parade and visit **Downtown Disney** before heading south. The **Grand Californian Hotel** is a top choice for lodging within the Disney Resort. If tackling Disneyland after a long flight is too much, head south from LAX to the surfer's haven at **Huntington Beach,** where you can relax at the beach and spend the night in one of several beachfront hotels before heading inland to Anaheim the next morning.

Day 3: LEGOLAND

(1 to 1½ hrs by car from Huntington Beach or Anaheim, depending on traffic.)

Get an early start for your next roller-coaster ride at **LEGOLAND,** about an hour's drive south of Huntington Beach via the Pacific Coast Highway. Check into the **LEGOLAND Hotel** or the **Sheraton Carlsbad Resort & Spa**; both offer direct access to the park. LEGOLAND has a water park and aquarium in addition to

the LEGO-based rides, shows, and roller coasters. The little ones can live out their fairy-tale fantasies and bigger ones can spend all day on waterslides, shooting water pistols, driving boats, or water fighting with pirates.

Day 4: La Jolla and San Diego
(La Jolla is just over an hour's drive from Carlsbad along scenic S21, or 40 mins on the I–5 freeway; Downtown San Diego is a 20-min drive from La Jolla.)

Take a leisurely drive south to San Diego by using the "old road," the original Pacific Coast Highway that hugs the shore all the way. It's a slow drive through Leucadia, Encinitas, Solana Beach, and Del Mar, all of which are popular surfing beaches. When you get to **La Jolla**, swing around the cove to see one of the area's most beautiful beaches. Look, but don't go in the water at the Children's Pool, as it's likely to be filled with barking seals. The **Birch Aquarium at Scripps** here offers a look at how scientists study the oceans.

Hop onto Interstate 5 and head for Downtown **San Diego**. Go straight for the city's nautical heart by exploring the restored ships of the **Maritime Museum** at the waterfront in Downtown. Victorian buildings—and plenty of other tourists—surround you on a stroll through

the **Gaslamp Quarter.** Plant yourself at a Downtown hotel and graze your way through the neighborhood's many restaurants.

Day 5: San Diego Zoo
(10 mins by car from Downtown San Diego.)

Malayan tapirs in a faux-Asian rain forest, polar bears in an imitation Arctic, and pandas frolicking in the trees—the **San Diego Zoo** maintains a vast and varied collection of creatures in a world-renowned facility comprised of meticulously designed habitats. Come early, wear comfy shoes, and stay as long as you like.

Day 6: SeaWorld and Old Town
(From Downtown San Diego, both SeaWorld and Old Town are 10 mins by car.)

Two commercial and touristy sights are on the agenda today. **SeaWorld**, with its walk-through shark tanks, can be a lot of fun if you surrender to the experience. Also touristy, but with genuine historical significance, **Old Town** drips with Mexican and early Californian heritage. Soak it up in the plaza at **Old Town San Diego State Historic Park,** then browse the stalls and shops at **Fiesta de Reyes** and along San Diego Avenue. Unwind after a long day with dinner and margaritas at one of Old Town's many Mexican restaurants.

2

Day 7: Departure from San Diego or Los Angeles

(San Diego Airport is 10 mins by car from Downtown. Depending on traffic, allow 2½–4 hrs to drive from Downtown San Diego to LAX.)

Pack up your Mouseketeer gear and give yourself ample time to reach the airport. San Diego International Airport lies within a 10-minute drive from Old Town. Although you'll be driving on freeways the entire way to LAX, traffic is always heavy and you should allot at least a half day to get there.

THE SOUTHERN PACIFIC COAST HIGHWAY: SAND, SURF, AND SUN, 3 DAYS

This tour along the southern section of the Pacific Coast Highway (PCH) is a beach vacation on wheels, taking in the highlights of the Southern California coast and its world-famous surfer-chic vibe. If at any point the drive feels like something out of a movie, that's because it likely is—this is the California of Hollywood legend. The itinerary is easily combined with the Big Sur and Northern Coast itineraries to do a full run of the legendary coastal route. Roll the top down on the convertible and let the adventure begin.

Day 1: Santa Barbara to Santa Monica

(About 2 hrs by car via the 101 and Hwy. 1. Allow plenty of time for beach stops and be aware of rush-hour traffic as you approach Santa Monica.)

Don't leave **Santa Barbara** without exploring the highlights of this Mediterranean-inspired city. Take a stroll along State Street, through the red-tile-roofed buildings of downtown to the gorgeous **Santa Barbara County Courthouse** and take in the views from its tower. Before leaving town, make a stop at the **Mission Santa Barbara**, widely considered one of the finest of all the California missions.

Heading south out of town the 101 runs along the coast past the low-key beach communities of Carpinteria and Mussel Shoals. Approaching **Ventura** on a clear day, the Channel Islands are visible in the distance. Stretch your legs on the **Ventura Oceanfront** with a walk on San Buenaventura State Beach, or around the picturesque Ventura Harbor. There are several spots to grab lunch at the harbor too, including an outpost of Santa Barbara's famous **Brophy Bros.** seafood restaurant.

Leaving Ventura, trade the 101 for Highway 1 and continue south through miles of protected, largely unpopulated coastline. Hike the trails at **Point Mugu State Park**, scout for offshore whales at **Point Dume State Beach**, or ride a wave at **Zuma Beach**. The PCH follows the curve of Santa Monica Bay from Point Mugu through Malibu and on to Santa Monica.

Chances are you'll experience déjà vu driving this stretch of road: mountains on one side, ocean on the other, opulent homes perched on hillsides; you've seen this piece of coast countless times on TV and film. As you approach Malibu proper, affectionately known as "the 'bu", be sure to walk out on the **Malibu Pier** for a great photo op, then check out **Surfrider Beach,** with three famous points where perfect waves ignited a worldwide surfing rage in the 1960s.

If you plan to visit the **Getty Villa Malibu,** with its impressive antiquities collection and jaw-dropping setting overlooking the Pacific, you will need to obtain free timed-entry tickets online prior to your arrival. Otherwise, continue the drive to Santa Monica where you can overnight near the **Santa Monica Pier** and grab dinner along the **Third Street Promenade** or at Santa Monica Place.

Day 2: Santa Monica to Newport Beach
(About 2 hrs by car without traffic, but plan for traffic.)

Start the day with a morning walk along **Santa Monica State Beach** and, if you didn't visit it the night before, the **Santa Monica Pier.** Rent some beach cruisers and pedal your way south along the bike path to **Venice Beach** (about 3 miles each way) to take in the action along the boardwalk. Once you tire of the skateboarders, body builders, and street performers, head inland a few blocks to Abbott Kinney Boulevard for lunch at **Gjelina** and a browse in the local boutiques.

Pedal back to Santa Monica and trade two wheels for four to continue the drive toward Newport Beach. If time permits, you can follow Highway 1 through Marina del Ray and the trio of beach towns well-known among beach-volleyball enthusiasts: Manhattan, Hermosa, and Redondo Beach. From here Highway 1 skirts through Long Beach and continues into Orange County. If time is short, this section of the PCH can be skipped in favor of the 405 freeway. However, as is always advisable near L.A., check current traffic reports before choosing your route.

The affluent coastal cities of Orange County, or the O.C., are familiar to many thanks to several popular television shows. However, the dazzling yachts and multimillion dollar mansions of Newport Beach still may take you by surprise after the more laid-back brand of luxe found elsewhere on the coast.

Choose from among the many excellent restaurants and overnight at **The Island Hotel**.

Day 3: Newport Beach to Dana Point
(1 hr by car.)

The next morning, pick out your dream yacht or estate, and then head to Balboa Island in the middle of Newport Harbor. This far quainter (but equally expensive) community is a popular getaway for locals and tourists alike. Browse the boutiques along Marine Avenue before hopping in a Duffy (electric boat) for a tour around the harbor. Back on land, don't leave without enjoying a Balboa Bar—the ice-cream treat is essentially mandatory for all Balboa Island visitors. Leaving Newport Beach on the PCH, your next stop is Crystal Cove State Park just past Corona Del Mar. If the tide is low, this is a great spot for tide pooling. Otherwise, don't miss the collection of historic beach cottages dating as far back as 1935.

Back on the road, **Laguna Beach** is the final stop of this journey. In an area not often noted for its cultural offerings, Laguna Beach is the exception. Browse the art galleries and enjoy a meal in the charming downtown before taking in one last walk along the Pacific. The PCH terminates 10 miles south of Laguna Beach near Dana Point, a town famous for its harbor and whale-watching excursions. From here, you can continue towards San Diego, or return north to Anaheim or Los Angeles via Interstate 5.

HOORAY FOR HOLLYWOOD, 4 DAYS

If you are a movie fan, there's no better place to see it all than L.A. Always keep your eyes out for a familiar face: you never know when you might spot a celebrity.

Day 1: Los Angeles

As soon as you land at LAX, make like a local and hit the freeway. Even if L.A.'s top-notch art, history, and science museums don't tempt you, the hodgepodge of art deco, Beaux Arts, and futuristic architecture begs at least a drive-by. Heading east from Santa Monica, Wilshire Boulevard cuts through a historical and cultural cross section of the city. Two stellar sights on its Miracle Mile are the encyclopedic **Los Angeles County Museum of Art** and the fossil-filled **La Brea Tar Pits.** Come evening, the open-air **Farmers' Market** and its many eateries hum. Hotels in Beverly Hills or West Hollywood beckon, just a few minutes away.

Day 2: Hollywood and the Movie Studios

(Avoid driving to the studios during rush hour. Studio tours vary in length—plan at least a half day for the excursion.)

Every L.A. tourist should devote at least one day to the movies and take at least one studio tour in the San Fernando Valley. For fun, choose the special-effects theme park at **Universal Studios Hollywood**; for the nitty-gritty, choose **Warner Bros. Studios.** Nostalgic musts in Hollywood include the **Walk of Fame** along **Hollywood Boulevard** and the celebrity footprints cast in concrete outside **Grauman's Chinese Theatre** (now known as the TCL Chinese Theater). When evening arrives, the Hollywood scene boasts a bevy of trendy restaurants and nightclubs.

Days 3 and 4: Beverly Hills and Santa Monica

(15–20 mins by car between destinations, but considerably longer in traffic.)

Even without that extensive art collection, the **Getty Center**'s pavilion architecture, hilltop gardens, and frame-worthy L.A. views make it a dazzling destination. Descend to the sea via Santa Monica Boulevard for lunch along **Third Street Promenade,** followed by a ride on the historic carousel on the pier. The buff and the bizarre meet at **Venice Beach Oceanfront Walk** (strap on some Rollerblades if you want to join them!). **Rodeo Drive** in Beverly Hills specializes in exhibitionism with a heftier price tag, but voyeurs are still welcome.

Splurge on breakfast or brunch at a posh café in the **Farmers' Market,** then stroll through aisles and aisles of gorgeous produce and specialty food before you take a last look at the Pacific Ocean through the camera obscura at **Palisades Park** in Santa Monica.

SAN DIEGO

WELCOME TO SAN DIEGO

TOP REASONS TO GO

★ **Beautiful beaches:** San Diego's shore shimmers with crystalline Pacific waters rolling up to some of the prettiest stretches of sand on the West Coast.

★ **Good eats:** Taking full advantage of the region's bountiful vegetables, fruits, herbs, and seafood, San Diego's chefs dazzle and delight diners with inventive California-colorful cuisine.

★ **History lessons:** The well-preserved and reconstructed historic sites in California's first European settlement help you imagine what the area was like when explorers first arrived.

★ **Stellar shopping:** The Gaslamp Quarter, Seaport Village, Coronado, Old Town, La Jolla … no matter where you go in San Diego, you'll find great places to do a little browsing.

★ **Urban oasis:** Balboa Park's 1,200 acres contain world-class museums and the San Diego Zoo, but also well-groomed lawns and gardens and wild, undeveloped canyons.

1 Downtown. San Diego's Downtown area is delightfully urban and accessible, filled with walkable A-list attractions like the Gaslamp Quarter and the waterfront.

2 Balboa Park. San Diego's cultural heart is where you'll find most of the city's museums and its world-famous zoo.

3 Old Town and Uptown. California's first permanent European settlement is now preserved as a state historic park in Old Town. Uptown is composed of several smaller neighborhoods that showcase a unique blend of historical charm and modern urban community.

4 Mission Bay and Beaches. Home to 27 miles of shoreline, this 4,600 acre aquatic park is San Diego's monument to sports and fitness. SeaWorld lies south of the bay.

5 La Jolla. This luxe, blufftop enclave fittingly means "the jewel" in Spanish. Come here for fantastic upscale shopping and unspoiled stretches of the coast.

6 Point Loma and Coronado. Home to the Hotel Del, Coronado's island-like isthmus is a favorite celebrity haunt. Visit the site of the first European landfall on Point Loma.

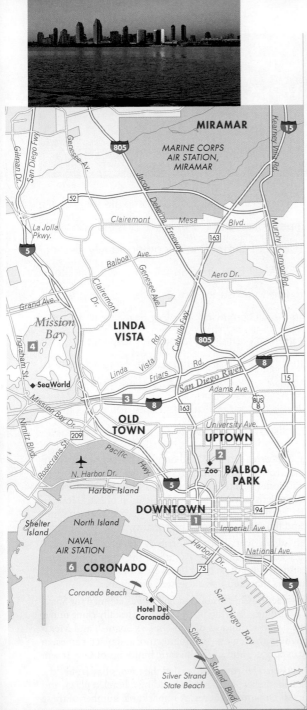

GETTING ORIENTED

Exploring San Diego may be an endless adventure, but there are limitations, especially if you don't have a car. San Diego is more a chain of separate communities than a cohesive city, and many of the major attractions are miles apart. Walking is good for getting an up close look at neighborhoods like the Gaslamp Quarter, but true Southern Californians use the freeways that criss-cross the county. Interstate 5 runs a direct north–south route through the coastal communities from Orange County in the north to the Mexican border. Interstates 805 and 15 do much the same inland. Interstate 8 is the main east–west route. Routes 163, 52, and 94 serve as connectors.

Updated by
Claire Deeks
Van Der Lee,
Marlise Kast,
Kai Oliver-
Kurtin, Archana
Ram, Juliana
Shallcross,
and Jeff Terich

San Diego is a vacationer's paradise, complete with idyllic year-round temperatures and 70 miles of pristine coastline. Recognized as one of the nation's leading family destinations, with LEGOLAND and the San Diego Zoo, San Diego is equally attractive to those in search of art, history, world-class shopping, and culinary exploration. San Diego's beaches are legendary, offering family-friendly sands, killer surf breaks, and spectacular scenery. San Diego's cultural sophistication often surprises visitors, as the city is better known for its laid-back vibe. Tourists come for some fun in the sun, only to discover a city with much greater depth.

San Diego is a big California city—second only to Los Angeles in population—with a small-town feel. San Diego's many neighborhoods offer diverse adventures: from the tony boutiques in La Jolla to the yoga and surf shops of Encinitas; from the subtle sophistication of Little Italy to the flashy nightlife of the Downtown Gaslamp Quarter, each community adds flavor and flair to San Diego's personality.

San Diego County also covers a lot of territory, roughly 400 square miles of land and sea. To the north and south of the city are its famed beaches. Inland, a succession of chaparral-covered mesas is punctuated with deep-cut canyons that step up to forested mountains.

Known as the birthplace of California, San Diego was claimed for Spain by explorer Juan Rodríguez Cabrillo in 1542 and eventually came under Mexican rule. You'll find reminders of San Diego's Spanish and Mexican heritage throughout the region—in architecture and place-names, in distinctive Mexican cuisine, and in the historic buildings of Old Town.

In 1867 developer Alonzo Horton, who called the town's bay front "the prettiest place for a city I ever saw," began building a hotel, a plaza, and prefab homes on 960 Downtown acres. A remarkable number of these buildings are preserved in San Diego's historic Gaslamp Quarter today. The city's fate was sealed in the 1920s when the U.S. Navy, impressed by the city's excellent harbor and temperate climate, decided to build a destroyer base on San Diego Bay. Today, the military operates many bases and installations throughout the county (which, added together, form the largest military base in the world) and continues to be a major contributor to the local economy.

PLANNING

WHEN TO GO

San Diego's weather is so ideal that most locals shrug off the high cost of living and relatively lower wages as a "sunshine tax." Along the coast, average temperatures range from the mid-60s to the high 70s, with clear skies and low humidity. Annual rainfall is minimal, less than 10 inches per year.

The peak season for sun seekers is July through October. In July and August, the mercury spikes and everyone spills outside. From mid-December to mid-March, whale-watchers can glimpse migrating gray whales frolicking in the Pacific. In spring and early summer, a marine layer hugs the coastline for much or all of the day (locals call it "June Gloom"), which can be dreary and disappointing for those who were expecting to bask in Southern California sunshine.

GETTING HERE AND AROUND

AIR TRAVEL

The major airport is San Diego International Airport (SAN), called Lindbergh Field locally. Major airlines depart and arrive at Terminal 1 and Terminal 2. A red shuttle bus provides free transportation between terminals.

Airport San Diego International Airport. ⊠ *3225 N. Harbor Dr., off I–5* ☎ *619/400–2400* ⊕ *www.san.org.*

Airport Transfers SuperShuttle. ⊠ *123 Caminio de la Riena* ☎ *800/974–8885* ⊕ *www.supershuttle.com.* **San Diego Transit.** ☎ *619/233–3004* ⊕ *transit.511sd.com.*

BUS AND TROLLEY TRAVEL

Under the umbrella of the Metropolitan Transit System, there are two major transit agencies in the area: San Diego Transit and North County Transit District (NCTD). The bright-red trolleys of the San Diego Trolley light-rail system operate on three lines that serve Downtown San Diego, Mission Valley, Old Town, South Bay, the U.S. border, and East County. The trolley system connects with San Diego Transit bus routes—connections are posted at each trolley station.

San Diego Transit bus fares range from $2.25 to $5; North County Transit District bus fares are $4. You must have exact change in coins and/or bills. Pay upon boarding. Transfers are not included; the $5 day pass is the best option for most bus travel and can be purchased on board.

San Diego Trolley tickets cost $2.50 and are good for two hours, but for one-way travel only. For a round-trip journey or longer, day passes are available for $5.

Bus and Trolley Information North County Transit District. ☎ 760/966–6500 ⊕ www.gonctd.com. **San Diego Transit.** ☎ 619/233–3004 ⊕ transit.511sd.com. **Transit Store.** ✉ 102 Broadway ☎ 619/234–1060 ⊕ www.sdmts.com.

CAR TRAVEL

A car is necessary for getting around greater San Diego on the sprawling freeway system and for visiting the North County beaches, mountains, and desert. Driving around San Diego County is pretty simple: most major attractions are within a few miles of the Pacific Ocean. Interstate 5, which stretches north–south from Oregon to the Mexican border, bisects San Diego. Interstate 8 provides access from Yuma, Arizona, and points east. Drivers coming from the Los Angeles area, Nevada, and the mountain regions beyond can reach San Diego on I–15. During rush hours there are jams on I–5 and on I–15 between I–805 and Escondido.

There are a few border inspection stations along major highways in San Diego County, the largest just north of Oceanside on I–5 near San Clemente. Travel with your driver's license, and passport if you're an international traveler.

TAXI TRAVEL

Fares vary among companies. If you're heading to the airport from a hotel, ask about the flat rate, which varies according to destination; otherwise you'll be charged by the mile (which works out to $20 or so from any Downtown location). Taxi stands are at shopping centers and hotels; otherwise you must call and reserve a cab. For on-demand private transportation, Uber is readily available throughout San Diego County with competitive rates up to 40% less than that of a taxi. The companies listed *below* don't serve all areas of San Diego County. If you're going somewhere other than Downtown, ask if the company serves that area.

Taxi Companies Orange Cab. ☎ 619/223–5555 ⊕ www.orangecabsandiego.net. **Silver Cabs.** ☎ 619/280–5555 ⊕ www.sandiegosilvercab.com. **Yellow Cab.** ☎ 619/444–4444 ⊕ www.driveu.com.

TRAIN TRAVEL

Amtrak serves Downtown San Diego's Santa Fe Depot with daily trains to and from Los Angeles, Santa Barbara, and San Luis Obispo. Amtrak trains stop in San Diego North County at Solana Beach and Oceanside. Coaster commuter trains, which run between Oceanside and San Diego Monday through Saturday, stop at the same stations as Amtrak as well as others. The frequency is about every half hour during the weekday rush hour, with four trains on Saturday. One-way fares are $4 to $5.50, depending on the distance traveled. The Sprinter runs between Oceanside and Escondido, with many stops along the way.

Metrolink operates high-speed rail service ($17) between the Oceanside Transit Center and Union Station in Los Angeles.

Information Coaster. ☎ 760/966–6500 ⊕ www.gonctd.com/coaster. **Metrolink.** ☎ 800/371–5465 ⊕ www.metrolinktrains.com.

TOURS

BIKE TOURS

Biking is popular in San Diego. You can find trails along the beach, in Mission Bay, and throughout the mountains.

Where You Want to Be Tours (*Secret San Diego*). Taking in spectacular views of the beach, bay, and skyline, these bike rides cover everything from historic neighborhoods to historic Highway 101. The walking tours, urban scavenger hunts, and Rent-a-Local custom tours are popular options as well. ✉ *611 K St., #B224* ☎ *619/917–6037* ⊕ *www.wheretours.com* ✍ *From $45.*

BOAT TOURS

Visitors to San Diego can get a great overview of the city from the water. Tour companies offer a range of harbor cruises, from one-hour jaunts to dinner and dancing cruises. In season, whale-watching voyages are another popular option.

Flagship Cruises and Events. One- and two-hour tours of the San Diego harbor loop north or south from the Broadway Pier throughout the day. Other offerings include dinner and dance cruises, brunch cruises, and winter whale-watching tours December–mid-April. ✉ *990 N. Harbor Dr., Embarcadero* ☎ *619/234–4111* ⊕ *www.flagshipsd.com* ✍ *From $23.*

H&M Landing. From mid-December to March, this outfitter offers three-hour tours to spot migrating gray whales just off the San Diego coast. From June to October—during slow fishing seasons only—six-hour cruises search for the gigantic blue whales that visit the California coast in summer. Winter gray whale cruises are offered December–March; summer blue whale tours are available Thursday, Saturday, and Sunday. ✉ *2803 Emerson St.* ☎ *619/222–1144* ⊕ *www.whalewatchingathm-landing.com* ✍ *From $45.*

Hornblower Cruises & Events. One- and two-hour cruises around San Diego harbor depart from the Embarcadero several times a day and alternate between the northern and southern portion of the bay. If you're hoping to spot some sea lions, take the North Bay route. Dinner and brunch cruises are also offered, as well as whale-watching tours in winter. ✉ *970 N. Harbor Dr.* ☎ *619/234–8687, 800/668–4322* ⊕ *www.hornblower.com* ✍ *From $25.*

San Diego SEAL Tours. This amphibious tour drives along the Embarcadero before splashing into the San Diego Harbor for a cruise. The 90-minute tours depart from Seaport Village year-round, and from outside the Maritime Museum seasonally. Call for daily departure times and locations. ✉ *500 Kettner Blvd., Embarcadero* ☎ *619/298–8687* ⊕ *www.sealtours.com* ✍ *$42.*

Seaforth Boat Rentals. For those seeking a private tour on the water, this company can provide a skipper along with your boat rental. Options include harbor cruises, whale-watching, and sunset sails. Seaforth has four locations and a diverse fleet of sail and motorboats to choose from. ✉ *1641 Quivira Rd., Mission Bay* ☎ *888/834–2628* ⊕ *www.seaforth-boatrental.com* ✍ *From $225.*

BUS AND TROLLEY TOURS

For those looking to cover a lot of ground in a limited time, narrated trolley tours include everything from Balboa Park to Coronado. To venture farther afield, consider a coach tour to the desert, Los Angeles, or even Baja, Mexico.

DayTripper Tours. Single- and multiday trips throughout Southern California, the Southwest, and Baja depart from San Diego year-round. Popular day trips include the Getty Museum, and theater performances in Los Angeles. Call or check the website for pickup locations. ☎ *619/299–5777, 800/679–8747* ⊕ *www.daytripper.com* ✄ *From $75.*

Five Star Tours. Private and group sightseeing bus tour options around San Diego and beyond include everything from the San Diego Zoo to Brewery tours and trips to Baja, Mexico. ✉ *1050 Kettner Blvd.* ☎ *619/232–5040* ⊕ *www.fivestartours.com* ✄ *From $48.*

Old Town Trolley Tours. Combining points of interest with local history, trivia, and fun anecdotes, this hop-on, hop-off trolley tour provides an entertaining overview of the city and offers easy access to all the highlights. The tour is narrated, and you can get on and off as you please. Stops include Old Town, Seaport Village, the Gaslamp Quarter, Coronado, Little Italy, and Balboa Park. The trolley leaves every 30 minutes, operates daily, and takes two hours to make a full loop. ✉ *San Diego* ☎ *619/298–8687* ⊕ *www.trolleytours.com/san-diego* ✄ *From $40.*

San Diego Scenic Tours. Half- and full-day bus tours of San Diego and Tijuana depart daily, and some include a harbor cruise. Tours depart from several hotels around town. ✉ *San Diego* ☎ *858/273–8687* ⊕ *www.sandiegoscenictours.com* ✄ *From $38.*

WALKING TOURS

Several fine walking tours are available on weekdays or weekends; upcoming walks are usually listed in the *San Diego Reader.*

Balboa Park Offshoot Tours. On Saturday at 10 am, free, hour-long walks start from the Balboa Park Visitor Center. The tour's focus rotates weekly, covering topics such as the park's history, palm trees, and desert vegetation. Reservations are not required, but no tours are scheduled between Thanksgiving and the New Year. ✉ *Balboa Park Visitor Center, 1549 El Prado, Balboa Park* ☎ *619/239–0512* ⊕ *www.balboapark.org* ✄ *Free.*

Coronado Walking Tours. Departing from the Glorietta Bay Inn at 11 am Tuesday, Thursday, and Saturday, this 90-minute stroll through Coronado's historic district takes in the island's mansions, old Tent City, the Hotel del Coronado, and the castles and cottages that line the beautiful beach. Reservations are recommended. ✉ *1630 Glorietta Blvd.* ☎ *619/435–5993* ⊕ *coronadowalkingtour.com* ✄ *$12* ☞ *Cash only.*

Gaslamp Quarter Historical Foundation. Two-hour walking tours of the Downtown historic district depart from the William Heath Davis House at 11 am on Saturday. ✉ *410 Island Ave.* ☎ *619/233–4692* ⊕ *www.gaslampquarter.org* ✄ *$20.*

Urban Safaris. Led by longtime San Diego resident Patty Fares, these two-hour Saturday walks through diverse neighborhoods like Hillcrest, Ocean Beach, and Point Loma are popular with tourists and locals alike. The tours, which always depart from a neighborhood coffeehouse, focus on art, history, and ethnic eateries, among other topics. Reservations are required, and private walks can be arranged during the week. ☎ 619/944–9255 ⊕ *www.walkingtoursofsandiego. com* ✉ *$10.*

VISITOR INFORMATION

For general information and brochures before you go, contact the San Diego Tourism Authority, which publishes the helpful *San Diego Visitors Planning Guide.* When you arrive, stop by one of the local visitor centers for general information.

Citywide Contacts San Diego Tourism Authority. ✉ *750 B St., Suite 1500* ☎ *619/232–3101* ⊕ *www.sandiego.org.* **San Diego Visitor Information Center.** ✉ *996 N. Harbor Dr., Downtown* ☎ *619/236–1242* ⊕ *www.sandiego.org.*

EXPLORING SAN DIEGO

DOWNTOWN

Nearly written off in the 1970s, today Downtown San Diego is a testament to conservation and urban renewal. Once derelict Victorian storefronts now house the hottest restaurants, and the *Star of India*, the world's oldest active sailing ship, almost lost to scrap, floats regally along the Embarcadero. Like many modern U.S. cities, Downtown San Diego's story is as much about its rebirth as its history. Although many consider Downtown to be the 16½-block Gaslamp Quarter, it's actually comprised of eight neighborhoods, including East Village, Little Italy, and Embarcadero.

GASLAMP QUARTER

Considered the liveliest of the Downtown neighborhoods, the Gaslamp Quarter's 4th and 5th avenues are peppered with trendy nightclubs, swanky lounge bars, chic restaurants, and boisterous sports pubs. The Gaslamp has the largest collection of commercial Victorian-style buildings in the country. Despite this, when the move for Downtown redevelopment gained momentum in the 1970s, there was talk of bulldozing them and starting from scratch. In response, concerned history buffs, developers, architects, and artists formed the Gaslamp Quarter Council to clean up and preserve the quarter. The majority of the quarter's landmark buildings are on 4th and 5th avenues, between Island Avenue and Broadway.

WORTH NOTING

Gaslamp Museum at the Davis-Horton House. The oldest wooden house in San Diego houses the Gaslamp Quarter Historical Foundation, the district's curator. Before developer Alonzo Horton came to town, Davis, a prominent San Franciscan, had made an unsuccessful attempt to develop the waterfront area. In 1850 he had this prefab saltbox-style house, built in Maine, shipped around Cape Horn and assembled in San Diego (it originally stood at State and Market streets). Ninety-minute walking tours ($20) of the historic district leave from the house on Thursday at 1 pm (summer only) and Saturday at 11 am (year-round). If you can't time your visit with the tour, a self-guided tour map ($2) is available. ⊠ *410 Island Ave., at 4th Ave., Gaslamp Quarter* ☎ *619/233–4692* ⊕ *www.gaslampfoundation.org* ⌖ *$5 self-guided, $10 with audio tour* ⊘ *Closed Mon.*

EMBARCADERO

The Embarcadero cuts a scenic swath along the harbor front and connects today's Downtown San Diego to its maritime routes. The bustle of Embarcadero comes less these days from the activities of fishing folk than from the throngs of tourists, but this waterfront walkway, stretching from the Convention Center to the Maritime Museum, remains the nautical soul of the city. There are several seafood restaurants here, as well as sea vessels of every variety—cruise ships, ferries, tour boats, and navy destroyers.

A huge revitalization project is under way along the northern Embarcadero. The overhaul seeks to transform the area with large mixed-use development projects, inviting parks, walkways, and public art installations. The redevelopment will eventually head south along the waterfront, with plans under way for a major overhaul of the entire Central Embarcadero and Seaport Village.

TOP ATTRACTIONS

FAMILY
Fodor'sChoice
★

Maritime Museum. From sailing ships to submarines, the Maritime Museum is a must for anyone with an interest in nautical history. This collection of restored and replica ships affords a fascinating glimpse of San Diego during its heyday as a commercial seaport. The jewel of the collection, the *Star of India*, was built in 1863 and made 21 trips around the world in the late 1800s. Saved from the scrap yard and painstakingly restored, the windjammer is the oldest active iron sailing ship in the world. The newly constructed *San Salvador* is a detailed historic replica of the original ship first sailed into San Diego Bay by explorer Juan Rodriguez Cabrillo back in 1542. And, the popular *HMS Surprise* is a replica of an 18th-century British Royal Navy frigate. The museum's headquarters are on the *Berkeley*, an 1898 steam-driven ferryboat, which served the Southern Pacific Railroad in San Francisco until 1958.

Numerous cruises of San Diego Bay are offered, including a daily 45-minute narrated tour aboard a 1914 pilot boat and 3-hour weekend sails aboard the topsail schooner the *Californian*, the state's official tall ship, and 75-minute tours aboard a historic swift boat, which highlights the city's military connection. Partnering with the museum, the renowned yacht *America* also offers sails on the bay, and whale-watching excursions are available in winter. ⊠ *1492 N. Harbor Dr., Embarcadero* ☎ *619/234–9153* ⊕ *www.sdmaritime.org* ⌖ *$16, $5 more for Pilot Boat Bay Cruise.*

Fodor'sChoice
★

Museum of Contemporary Art San Diego (MCASD). At the Downtown branch of the city's contemporary art museum, explore the works of international and regional artists in a modern, urban space. The Jacobs Building—formerly the baggage building at the historic Santa Fe

Depot—features large gallery spaces, high ceilings, and natural lighting, giving artists the flexibility to create large-scale installations. MCASD's collection includes many Pop Art, minimalist, and conceptual works from the 1950s to the present. The museum showcases both established and emerging artists in temporary exhibitions, and has permanent, site-specific commissions by Jenny Holzer and Richard Serra. ✉ *1100 and 1001 Kettner Blvd., Downtown* ☎ *858/454–3541* ⊕ *www.mcasd.org* 💰 *$10; free 3rd Thurs. of the month 5–7* ⊘ *Closed Wed.*

FAMILY
Fodor'sChoice
★
The New Children's Museum (NCM). The NCM blends contemporary art with unstructured play to create an environment that appeals to children as well as adults. The 50,000-square-foot structure was constructed from recycled building materials, operates on solar energy, and is convection-cooled by an elevator shaft. It also features a nutritious and eco-conscious café. Interactive exhibits include designated areas for toddlers and teens, as well as plenty of activities for the entire family. Several art workshops are offered each day, as well as hands-on studios where visitors are encouraged to create their own art. The studio projects change frequently and the entire museum changes exhibits every 18 to 24 months, so there is always something new to explore. The adjoining 1-acre park and playground is across from the convention center trolley stop. ✉ *200 W. Island Ave., Embarcadero* ☎ *619/233–8792* ⊕ *www.thinkplaycreate. org* 💰 *$13; 2nd Sun. each month $3* ⊘ *Closed Tues.*

FAMILY
Seaport Village. You'll find some of the best views of the harbor at Seaport Village, three bustling shopping plazas designed to reflect the New England clapboard, and Spanish Mission architectural styles of early California. On a prime stretch of waterfront the dining, shopping, and entertainment complex connects the harbor with hotel towers and the convention center. Specialty shops offer everything from a kite store and swing emporium to a shop devoted to hot sauces. You can dine at snack bars and restaurants, many with harbor views.

Live music can be heard daily from noon to 4 at the main food court. Additional free concerts take place every Sunday from 1 to 4 at the East Plaza Gazebo. The **Seaport Village Carousel** (rides $3) has 54 animals, hand-carved and hand-painted by Charles Looff in 1895. Across the street, the **Headquarters at Seaport Village** converted the historic police headquarters into several trendsetting shops and restaurants. ✉ *849 W. Harbor Dr., Downtown* ☎ *619/235–4014 office and events hotline* ⊕ *www.seaportvillage.com.*

FAMILY
Fodor'sChoice
★
USS Midway Museum. After 47 years of worldwide service, the retired USS *Midway* began a new tour of duty on the south side of the Navy pier in 2004. Launched in 1945, the 1,001-foot-long ship was the largest in the world for the first 10 years of its existence. The most visible landmark on the north Embarcadero, it now serves as a floating interactive museum—an appropriate addition to the town that is home to one-third of the Pacific fleet and the birthplace of naval aviation. A free audio tour guides you through the massive ship while offering insight from former sailors. As you clamber through passageways and up and down ladder wells, you'll get a feel for how the *Midway*'s 4,500 crew members lived and worked on this "city at sea."

Though the entire tour is impressive, you'll really be wowed when you step out onto the 4-acre flight deck—not only the best place to get an idea of the ship's scale, but also one of the most interesting vantage points for bay and city skyline views. An F-14 Tomcat jet fighter is just one of many vintage aircraft on display. Free guided tours of the bridge and primary flight control, known as "the Island," depart every 10 minutes from the flight deck. Many of the docents stationed throughout the ship served in the Navy, some even on the *Midway*, and they are eager to answer questions or share stories. The museum also offers multiple flight simulators for an additional fee, climb-aboard cockpits, and interactive exhibits focusing on naval aviation. There is a gift shop and a café with pleasant outdoor seating. This is a wildly popular stop, with most visits lasting several hours. ⚠ **Despite efforts to provide accessibility throughout the ship, some areas can only be reached via fairly steep steps; a video tour of these areas is available on the hangar deck.** ⊠ *910 N. Harbor Dr., Embarcadero* ☎ *619/544–9600* ⊕ *www.midway.org* ⊠ *$20.*

EAST VILLAGE

The most ambitious of the Downtown projects is East Village, not far from the Gaslamp Quarter, and encompassing 130 blocks between the railroad tracks up to J Street, and from 6th Avenue east to around 10th Street. Sparking the rebirth of this former warehouse district was the 2004 construction of the San Diego Padres' baseball stadium, PETCO Park. The Urban Art Trail has added pizzazz to drab city thoroughfares by transforming such things as trash cans and traffic controller boxes into works of art. As the city's largest Downtown neighborhood, East Village is continually broadening its boundaries with its urban design of redbrick cafés, spacious galleries, rooftop bars, sleek hotels, and warehouse restaurants.

LITTLE ITALY

Home to many in San Diego's design community, Little Italy exudes a sense of urban cool while remaining authentic to its roots and marked by old-country charms: church bells ring on the half hour, and Italians gather daily to play bocce in Amici Park. The main thoroughfare, India Street, is filled with lively cafés, chic shops, and many of the city's trendiest restaurants. Little Italy is one of San Diego's most walkable neighborhoods, and a great spot to wander. Art lovers can browse gallery showrooms, while shoppers adore the Fir Street cottages. The neighborhood bustles each Saturday during the wildly popular Mercato farmers' market.

BALBOA PARK AND SAN DIEGO ZOO

Overlooking Downtown and the Pacific Ocean, 1,200-acre Balboa Park is the cultural heart of San Diego. Ranked as one of the world's best parks by the Project for Public Spaces, it's also where you can find most of the city's museums, art galleries, the Tony Award–winning Old Globe Theatre, and the world-famous San Diego Zoo. Often referred to as the "Smithsonian of the West" for its concentration of museums, Balboa Park is also a series of botanical gardens, performance spaces, and outdoor playrooms endeared to the hearts of residents and visitors alike.

In addition, the captivating architecture of Balboa's buildings, fountains, and courtyards gives the park an enchanted feel. Historic buildings dating from San Diego's 1915 Panama–California International Exposition are strung along the park's main east–west thoroughfare, El Prado. The parkland across the Cabrillo Bridge, at the west end of El Prado, is set aside for picnics and athletics. East of Plaza de Panama, El Prado becomes a pedestrian mall and ends at a footbridge that crosses over Park Boulevard, to rose and desert gardens.

Bankers Hill is a small neighborhood west of Balboa Park, with gorgeous views ranging from Balboa Park's greenery in the east to the San Diego Bay in the west. It's become one of San Diego's hottest restaurant destinations.

TOP ATTRACTIONS

Bea Evenson Fountain. A favorite of barefoot children, this fountain shoots cool jets of water upwards of 50 feet. Built in 1972 between the Fleet Center and Natural History Museum, the fountain offers plenty of room to sit and watch the crowds go by. ⊠ *Balboa Park ✛ East end of El Prado* ⊕ *www.balboapark.org.*

Fodor'sChoice ★ **Botanical Building.** The graceful redwood-lath structure, built for the 1915 Panama–California International Exposition, now houses more than 2,000 types of tropical and subtropical plants plus changing seasonal flower displays. Ceiling-high tree ferns shade fragile orchids and feathery bamboo. There are benches beside miniature waterfalls for resting in the shade. The rectangular pond outside, filled with lotuses and water lilies that bloom in spring and fall, is popular with photographers. ⊠ *1549 El Prado, Balboa Park* ☎ *619/239–0512* ⊕ *www. balboapark.org* ⌨ *Free* ☿ *Closed Thurs.*

Cabrillo Bridge. The official gateway into Balboa Park soars 120 feet above a canyon floor. Pedestrian-friendly, the 1,500-foot bridge provides inspiring views of the California Tower and El Prado beyond. ■TIP➔ **This is a great spot for photo-capturing a classic image of the park.** ⊠ *Balboa Park ✛ On El Prado, at 6th Ave. park entrance* ⊕ *www. balboapark.org.*

FAMILY
Fodor'sChoice ★ **Carousel.** Suspended an arm's length away on this antique merry-go-round is the brass ring that could earn you an extra free ride (it's one of the few carousels in the world that continue this bonus tradition). Hand-carved in 1910, the carousel features colorful murals, big-band music, and bobbing animals including zebras, giraffes, and dragons; real horsehair was used for the tails. ⊠ *1889 Zoo Pl., behind zoo parking lot, Balboa Park* ☎ *619/239–0512* ⊕ *www.balboapark.org* ⌨ *$2.75* ☿ *Closed weekdays Labor Day–mid-June.*

Fodor'sChoice ★ **Inez Grant Parker Memorial Rose Garden and Desert Garden.** These neighboring gardens sit just across the Park Boulevard pedestrian bridge and offer gorgeous views over Florida Canyon. The formal rose garden contains 2,500 roses representing nearly 200 varieties; peak bloom is usually in April and May. The adjacent Desert Garden provides a striking contrast, with 2.5 acres of succulents and desert plants seeming to blend into the landscape of the canyon below. ⊠ *2525 Park Blvd., Balboa Park* ⊕ *www.balboapark.org.*

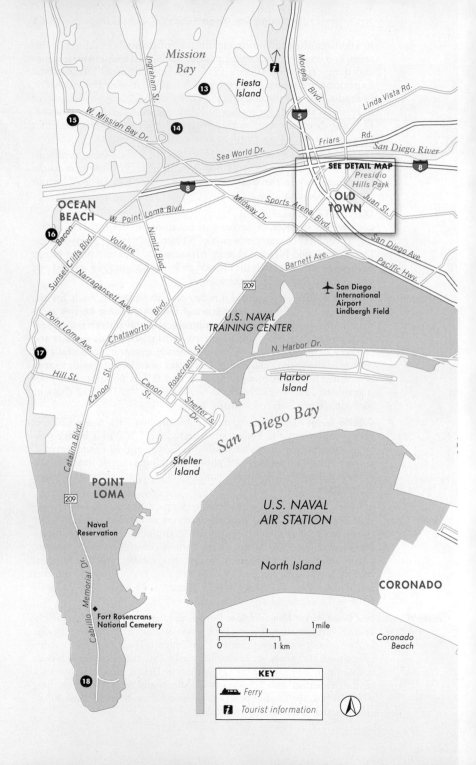

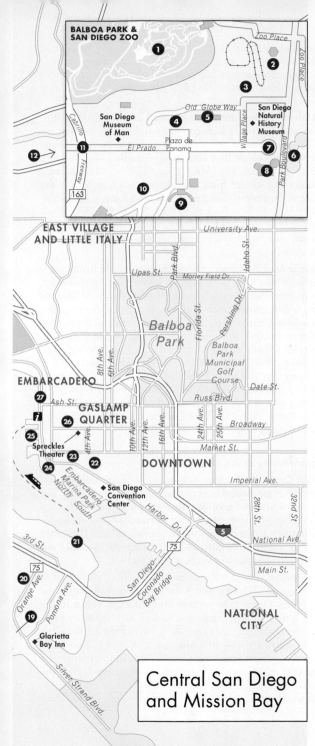

Palm Canyon. Enjoy an instant escape from the buildings and concrete of urban life in this Balboa Park oasis. Lush and tropical, with hundreds of palm trees, the 2-acre canyon has a shaded path perfect for those who love walking through nature. ✉ *1549 El Prado, south of House of Charm, Balboa Park.*

FAMILY **Reuben H. Fleet Science Center.** Interactive exhibits here are artfully educational and for all ages: older kids can get hands-on with inventive projects in the Tinkering Studio, while the five-and-under set can be easily entertained with interactive play stations like the Ball Wall and Fire Truck in the center's Kid City. The IMAX Dome Theater, which screens exhilarating nature and science films, was the world's first, as was the Fleet's "NanoSeam" (seamless) dome ceiling that doubles as a planetarium. ✉ *1875 El Prado, Balboa Park* ☎ *619/238–1233* ⊕ *www.rhfleet. org* ☒ *The Fleet experience includes gallery exhibits and 1 IMAX film $19.95; additional cost for special exhibits or add-on 2nd IMAX film or planetarium show.*

Fodor'sChoice **San Diego Museum of Art.** Known for its Spanish baroque and Renaissance
★ paintings, including works by El Greco, Goya, Rubens, and van Ruisdael, San Diego's most comprehensive art museum also has strong holdings of South Asian art, Indian miniatures, and contemporary California paintings. The museum's exhibits tend to have broad appeal, and if traveling shows from other cities come to town, you can expect to see them here. Free docent tours are offered throughout the day. An outdoor Sculpture Court and Garden exhibits both traditional and modern pieces. Enjoy the view over a craft beer and some locally sourced food in the adjacent Panama 66 courtyard restaurant. ■TIP➜ **The museum hosts "Art After Hours" most Friday nights, with discounted admission 5–8 pm.** ✉ *1450 El Prado, Balboa Park* ☎ *619/232–7931* ⊕ *www.sdmart.org* ☒ *$15; $5 Fri. 5–8 pm; sculpture garden free* ⊙ *Closed Wed.*

Fodor'sChoice **San Diego Zoo.**
★ *See the highlighted listing in this chapter.*

Fodor'sChoice **Spanish Village Art Center.** More than 200 local artists, including glass-
★ blowers, enamel workers, woodcarvers, sculptors, painters, jewelers, and photographers work and give demonstrations of their craft on a rotating basis in these red tile–roof studio-galleries that were set up for the 1935–36 exposition in the style of an old Spanish village. The center is a great source for memorable gifts. ✉ *1770 Village Pl., Balboa Park* ☎ *619/233–9050* ⊕ *www.spanishvillageart.com* ☒ *Free.*

Fodor'sChoice **Spreckels Organ Pavilion.** The 2,400-bench-seat pavilion, dedicated in
★ 1915 by sugar magnates John D. and Adolph B. Spreckels, holds the 4,518-pipe Spreckels Organ, the largest outdoor pipe organ in the world. You can hear this impressive instrument at one of the year-round, free, 2 pm Sunday concerts, regularly performed by the city's civic organist and guest artists—a highlight of a visit to Balboa Park. On Monday evenings from late June to mid-August, internationally renowned organists play evening concerts. At Christmastime the park's Christmas tree and life-size Nativity display turn the pavilion into a seasonal wonderland. ✉ *2211 Pan American Rd., Balboa Park* ☎ *619/702–8138* ⊕ *spreckelsorgan.org.*

Continued on page 74

Polar bear, San Diego Zoo

LIONS AND TIGERS AND PANDAS:
The World-Famous San Diego Zoo

From cuddly pandas and diving polar bears to 6-ton elephants and swinging great apes, San Diego's most famous attraction has it all. Nearly 4,000 animals representing 800 species roam the 100-acre zoo in expertly crafted habitats that replicate the animals' natural environments. While the pandas get top billing, there are plenty of other cool creatures to see here, from teeny-tiny mantella frogs to two-story-tall giraffes. But it's not all just fun and games. Known for its exemplary conservation programs, the zoo educates visitors on how to go green and explains its efforts to protect endangered species.

SAN DIEGO ZOO TOP ATTRACTIONS

Underwater viewing area at the Hippo Trail

❶ Children's Zoo (Discovery Outpost). Goats and sheep beg to be petted, and there is a viewer-friendly nursery where you may see baby animals bottle-feed and sleep peacefully in large cribs.

❷ Monkey Trails and Forest Tales (Lost Forest). Follow an elevated trail at treetop level and trek through the forest floor observing African mandrill monkeys, Asia's clouded leopard, the rare pygmy hippopotamus, and Visayan warty pigs.

❸ Orangutan and Siamang Exhibit (Lost Forest). Orangutans and siamangs climb and swing in this lush, tropical environment lined with 110-foot-long and 12-foot-high viewing windows.

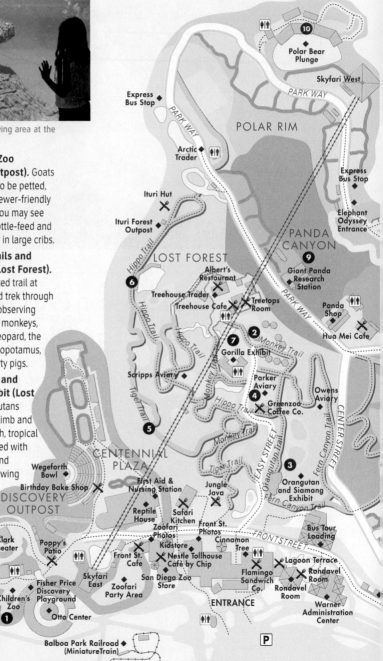

4 Scripps, Parker, and Owens Aviaries (Lost Forest). Wandering paths climb through the enclosed aviaries where brightly colored tropical birds swoop between branches inches from your face.

5 Tiger Trail (Lost Forest). The mist-shrouded trails of this simulated rainforest wind down a canyon. Tigers, Malayan tapirs, and Argus pheasants wander among the exotic trees and plants.

6 Hippo Trail (Lost Forest). Glimpse huge but surprisingly graceful hippos frolicking in the water through an underwater viewing window and buffalo cavorting with monkeys on dry land.

7 Gorilla Exhibit (Lost Forest). The gorillas live in one of the zoo's bioclimatic zone exhibits modeled on their native habitat with waterfalls, climbing areas, and an open meadow. The sounds of the tropical rain forest emerge from a 144-speaker sound system that plays CDs recorded in Africa.

8 Sun Bear Forest (Asian Passage). Playful beasts claw apart the trees and shrubs that serve as a natural playground for climbing, jumping, and general merrymaking.

9 Giant Panda Research Station (Panda Canyon). An elevated pathway provides visitors with great access

Lories at Owen's Aviary

to the zoo's most famous residents in their side-by-side viewing areas. The adjacent discovery center features lots of information about these endangered animals and the zoo's efforts to protect them.

10 Polar Bear Plunge (Polar Rim). Watch polar bears take a chilly dive from the underwater viewing room. There are also Siberian reindeer, white foxes, and other Arctic creatures here. Kids can learn about the Arctic and climate change through interactive exhibits.

11 Elephant Odyssey. Get a glimpse of the animals that roamed Southern California 12,000 years ago and meet their living counterparts. The 7.5-acre, multispecies habitat features elephants, California condors, jaguars, and more.

12 Koala Exhibit (Outback). The San Diego Zoo houses the largest number of koalas outside Australia. Walk through the exhibit for photo ops of these marsupials from Down-Under curled up on their perches or dining on eucalyptus branches.

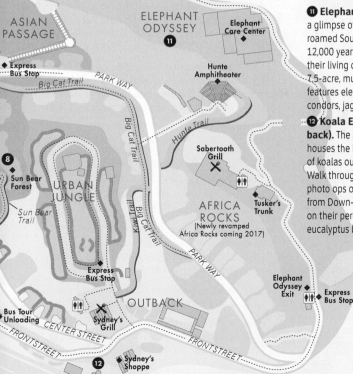

ASIAN PASSAGE

ELEPHANT ODYSSEY
11

Elephant Care Center

◆ Express Bus Stop

Big Cat Trail

PARK WAY

Hunte Amphitheater

Big Cat Trail

Hunte Trail

Sabertooth Grill

8 ◆
Sun Bear Forest

Sun Bear Trail

URBAN JUNGLE

Big Cat Trail

AFRICA ROCKS
(Newly revamped Africa Rocks coming 2017)

Tusker's Trunk

Express Bus Stop

PARK WAY

OUTBACK

Elephant Odyssey Exit ◆

◆ Express Bus Stop

Bus Tour Unloading

CENTER STREET

Sydney's Grill

FRONTSTREET

FRONTSTREET

12 ◆ Sydney's Shoppe
◆ Koala Exhibit

PLANNING YOUR DAY AT THE ZOO

Left: Main entrance of the San Diego Zoo. Right: Sunbear

PLANNING YOUR TIME

Plan to devote at least a half-day to exploring the zoo, but with so much to see it is easy to stay a full day or more.

If you're on a tight schedule, opt for the guided **35 minute bus tour** that lets you zip through three-quarters of the exhibits. However, lines to board the busses can be long, and you won't get as close to the animals.

Another option is to take the **Skyfari Aerial Tram** to the far end of the park, choose a route, and meander back to the entrance. The Skyfari trip gives a good overview of the zoo's layout and a spectacular view.

The **Elephant Odyssey,** while accessible from two sides of the park, is best entered from just below the Polar Rim. The extremely popular **Panda exhibit** can develop long lines, so get there early.

The zoo offers several entertaining **live shows** daily. Check the website or the back of the map handed out at the zoo entrance for the day's offerings and showtimes.

BEFORE YOU GO

■ To avoid ticket lines, purchase and print tickets online using the zoo's Web site.

■ To avoid excessive backtracking or a potential meltdown, plan your route along the zoo map before setting out. Try not to get too frustrated if you lose your way, as there are exciting exhibits around every turn and many paths intersect at several points.

■ The zoo offers a variety of program extras, including behind-the-scenes tours, backstage pass animal encounters, and sleepover events. Call in advance for pricing and reservations.

AT THE ZOO

■ Don't forget to explore at least some of the exhibits on foot—a favorite is the lush Tiger Trail.

■ If you visit on the weekend, find out when the Giraffe Experience is taking place. You can purchase leaf–eater biscuits to hand feed the giraffes!

■ Splurge a little at the gift shop: your purchases help support zoo programs.

■ The zoo rents strollers, wheelchairs, and lockers; it also has a first-aid office, a lost and found, and an ATM.

Fern Canyon, San Diego Zoo

GETTING HERE AND AROUND

The zoo is easy to get to, whether by bus or car.

Bus Travel: Take Bus No. 7 and exit at Park Boulevard and Zoo Place.

Car Travel: From Downtown, take Route 163 north through Balboa Park. Exit at Zoo/Museums (Richmond Street) and follow signs.

Several options help you get around the massive park: express buses loop through the zoo and the Skyfari Aerial Tram will take you from one end to the other. The zoo's topography is fairly hilly, but moving sidewalks lead up the slopes between some exhibits.

QUICK BITES

There is a wide variety of food available for purchase at the zoo from food carts to ethnic restaurants such as the Pan-Asian **Hua Mei Cafe**.

One of the best restaurants is **Albert's**, near the Gorilla exhibit, which features grilled fish, homemade pizza, and fresh pasta along with a full bar.

SERVICE INFORMATION

✉ 2920 Zoo Dr., Balboa Park

☎ 619/234-3153

🌐 www.sandiegozoo.org

Gorilla

SAN DIEGO ZOO SAFARI PARK

About 45 minutes north of the zoo in Escondido, the 1,800-acre San Diego Zoo Safari Park is an extensive wildlife sanctuary where animals roam free—and guests can get close in escorted caravans and on backcountry trails. This park and the zoo operate under the auspices of the San Diego Zoo's nonprofit organization; joint tickets are available.

OLD TOWN AND UPTOWN

San Diego's Spanish and Mexican roots are most evident in Old Town and the surrounding hillside of Presidio Park. Visitors can experience settlement life in San Diego from Spanish and Mexican rule to the early days of U.S. statehood. Nearby Uptown is composed of several smaller neighborhoods near Downtown and around Balboa Park: the vibrant neighborhoods of Hillcrest, Mission Hills, North Park, and South Park showcase their unique blend of historical charm and modern urban community.

OLD TOWN

As the first European settlement in Southern California, Old Town began to develop in the 1820s. But its true beginnings took place on a nearby hillside in 1769 with the establishment of a Spanish military outpost and the first of California's missions, San Diego de Alcalá. In 1774 the hilltop was declared a *presidio reál*, a fortress built by the Spanish Empire, and the mission was relocated along the San Diego River. Over time, settlers moved down from the presidio to establish Old Town. A central plaza was laid out, surrounded by adobe and, later, wooden structures. San Diego became an incorporated U.S. city in 1850, with Old Town as its center. In the 1860s, however, the advent of Alonzo Horton's New Town to the southeast caused Old Town to wither. Efforts to preserve the area began early in the 20th century, and Old Town became a state historic park in 1968.

Today Old Town is a lively celebration of history and culture. The Old Town San Diego State Historic Park re-creates life during the early settlement, while San Diego Avenue buzzes with art galleries, gift shops, festive restaurants, and open-air stands selling inexpensive Mexican handicrafts.

TOP ATTRACTIONS

FAMILY

Fodor's Choice

★

Fiesta de Reyes. North of San Diego's Old Town Plaza lies the area's unofficial center, built to represent a colonial Mexican plaza. The collection of more than a dozen shops and restaurants around a central courtyard in blossom with magenta bougainvillea, scarlet hibiscus, and other flowers in season reflects what early California might have looked like from 1821 to 1872. Shops are even stocked with items reminiscent of that era. Mariachi bands and folklorico dance groups frequently perform on the plaza stage—check the website for times and upcoming special events. ■TIP→ Casa de Reyes is a great stop for a margarita and some chips and guacamole. ⊠ *4016 Wallace St., Old Town* ☎ *619/297–3100* ⊕ *www.fiestadereyes.com.*

FAMILY

Fodor's Choice

★

Old Town San Diego State Historic Park. The six square blocks on the site of San Diego's original pueblo are the heart of Old Town. Most of the 20 historic buildings preserved or re-created by the park cluster around **Old Town Plaza,** bounded by Wallace Street on the west, Calhoun Street on the north, Mason Street on the east, and San Diego Avenue on the south. The plaza is a pleasant place to rest, plan your tour of the park, and watch passers-by. San Diego Avenue is closed to vehicle traffic here.

Some of Old Town's buildings were destroyed in a fire in 1872, but after the site became a state historic park in 1968, reconstruction and restoration of the remaining structures began. Five of the original adobes are still intact.

Facing Old Town Plaza, the **Robinson-Rose House** was the original commercial center of Old San Diego, housing railroad offices, law offices, and the first newspaper press. The largest and most elaborate of the original adobe homes, the **Casa de Estudillo** was occupied by members of the Estudillo family until 1887 and later gained popularity for its billing as "Ramona's Marriage Place" based on a popular novel of the time. Albert Seeley, a stagecoach entrepreneur, opened the **Cosmopolitan Hotel** in 1869 as a way station for travelers on the daylong trip south from Los Angeles. Next door to the Cosmopolitan Hotel, the **Seeley Stable** served as San Diego's stagecoach stop in 1867 and was the transportation hub of Old Town until 1887, when trains became the favored mode of travel.

Several reconstructed buildings serve as restaurants or as shops purveying wares reminiscent of those that might have been available in the original Old Town. **Racine & Laramie**, a painstakingly reproduced version of San Diego's first cigar store in 1868, is especially interesting.

Pamphlets available at the Robinson-Rose House give details about all the historic houses on the plaza and in its vicinity. Tours of the historic park are offered daily at 11:30, 1, and 2; purchase tickets at the Robinson-Rose House. A free history program is also offered daily in the Seely Stable Theater. ■ TIP→ **The covered wagon located near the intersection of Mason and Calhoun streets provides a great photo op.** ⊠ *Visitor center (Robinson-Rose House), 4002 Wallace St., Old Town* ☎ *619/220–5422* ⊕ *www.parks.ca.gov* ⊒ *Free; walking tour $10.*

Thomas Whaley House Museum. A New York entrepreneur, Thomas Whaley came to California during the gold rush. He wanted to provide his East Coast wife with all the comforts of home, so in 1857 he had Southern California's first two-story brick structure built, making it the oldest double-story brick building on the West Coast. The house, which served as the county courthouse and government seat during the 1870s, stands in strong contrast to the Spanish-style adobe residences that surround the nearby historic plaza and marks an early stage of San Diego's "Americanization." A garden out back includes many varieties of prehybrid roses from before 1867. The place is perhaps most famed, however, for the ghosts that are said to inhabit it. You can tour on your own during the day, but must visit by guided tour starting at 5 pm. The evening tours are geared toward the supernatural aspects of the house. They are offered every half hour, with the last tour departing at 9:30 pm, and last about 45 minutes. ⊠ *2476 San Diego Ave., Old Town* ☎ *619/297–7511* ⊕ *www.whaleyhouse.org* ⊒ *$8 before 5 pm; $13 after 5 pm* ☉ *Closed Sept.–May, Wed.*

HILLCREST

The large retro Hillcrest sign over the intersection of University and 5th avenues makes an excellent landmark at the epicenter of this vibrant section of Uptown. Strolling along University Avenue between 4th and 6th avenues from Washington Street to Robinson Avenue will reveal a mixture of retail shops and restaurants. A few blocks east, another interesting stretch of stores and restaurants runs along University Avenue to Normal Street. Long established as the center of San Diego's gay community, the neighborhood bustles both day and night with a mixed crowd of shoppers, diners, and partygoers. If you are visiting Hillcrest on Sunday between 9 and 2 be sure to explore the Hillcrest Farmers Market.

MISSION VALLEY

Although Mission Valley's charms may not be immediately apparent, it offers many conveniences to visitors and residents alike. One of the area's main attractions is the Fashion Valley mall, with its mix of high-end and mid-range retail stores and dining options, and movie theater. The Mission Basilica San Diego de Alcalá provides a tranquil refuge from the surrounding suburban sprawl.

TOP ATTRACTIONS

Fodor's Choice **Mission Basilica San Diego de Alcalá.** It's hard to imagine how remote
★ California's earliest mission must have once been; these days, however, it's accessible by major freeways (I–15 and I–8) and via the San Diego Trolley. The first of a chain of 21 missions stretching northward along the coast, Mission San Diego de Alcalá was established by Father

Junípero Serra on Presidio Hill in 1769 and moved to this location in 1774. In 1775, it proved vulnerable to enemy attack, and Padre Luis Jayme, a young friar from Spain, was clubbed to death by the Kumeyaay Indians he had been trying to convert. He was the first of more than a dozen Christians martyred in California. The present church, reconstructed in 1931 following the outline of the 1813 church, is the fifth built on the site. It measures 150 feet long but only 35 feet wide because, without easy means of joining beams, the mission buildings were only as wide as the trees that served as their ceiling supports were tall. Father Jayme is buried in the sanctuary; a small museum named for him documents mission history and exhibits tools and artifacts from the early days; there is also a gift shop. From the peaceful, palm-bedecked gardens out back you can gaze at the 46-foot-high *campanario* (bell tower), the mission's most distinctive feature, with five bells. Mass is celebrated on the weekends. ✉ *10818 San Diego Mission Rd., Mission Valley* ✥ *From I–8 east, exit and turn left on Mission Gorge Rd., then left on Twain Rd.; mission is on right* ☎ *619/281–8449* ⊕ *www.missionsandiego.com* ✆ *$5.*

NORTH PARK

Named for its location north of Balboa Park, this evolving neighborhood is home to an exciting array of restaurants, bars, and shops. High-end condominiums and local merchants are often cleverly disguised behind historic signage from barbershops, bowling alleys, and theater marquees. The stretch of Ray Street near University Avenue is home to several small galleries. With a steady stream of new openings in the neighborhood, North Park is one of San Diego's top dining and nightlife destinations. Beer enthusiasts won't want to miss the breweries and tasting rooms along the 30th St. Beer Corridor for a chance to sample San Diego's famous ales.

MISSION BAY AND THE BEACHES

Mission Bay and the surrounding beaches are the aquatic playground of San Diego. The choice of activities available is astonishing, and the perfect weather makes you want to get out there and play. If you're craving downtime after all the activity, there are plenty of peaceful spots to relax and simply soak up the sunshine.

Mission Bay welcomes visitors with its protected waters and countless opportunities for fun. The 4,600-acre **Mission Bay Park** is the place for water sports like sailing, stand-up paddleboarding, and waterskiing. With 19 miles of beaches and grassy areas, it's also a great place for a picnic. And if you have kids, don't miss **SeaWorld,** one of San Diego's most popular attractions.

Mission Beach is a famous and lively fun zone for families and young people; if it isn't party time at the moment, it will be five minutes from now. The pathways in this area are lined with vacation homes, many for rent by the week or month.

North of Mission Beach is the college-packed party town of Pacific Beach, or "PB" as locals call it. The laid-back vibe of this surfer's mecca draws in free-spirited locals who roam the streets on skateboards and beach cruisers. The energy level peaks during happy hour, when PB's cluster of nightclubs, bars, and 150 restaurants open their doors to those ready to party.

TOP ATTRACTIONS

FAMILY

Fodor'sChoice

★

Belmont Park. The once-abandoned amusement park between the bay and Mission Beach Boardwalk is now a shopping, dining, and recreation complex. Twinkling lights outline the **Giant Dipper,** an antique wooden roller coaster on which screaming thrill-seekers ride more than 2,600 feet of track and 13 hills (riders must be at least 4 feet, 2 inches tall). Created in 1925 and listed on the National Register of Historic Places, this is one of the few old-time roller coasters left in the United States.

Other Belmont Park attractions include miniature golf, laser tag, a video arcade, bumper cars, a tilt-a-whirl, and an antique carousel. The zip line thrills as it soars over the crowds below, while the rock wall challenges both junior climbers and their elders. Belmont Park also has the most consistent wave in the county at the **Wave House,** where the FlowRider provides surfers and bodyboarders a near-perfect simulated wave on which to practice their skills. ✉ *3146 Mission Blvd., Mission Bay* ☎ *858/488–1549 for rides* ⊕ *www.belmontpark.com* ✉ *Unlimited ride day package $30 for 48 inches and taller, $20 for under 48 inches, some attractions not included in price; individual ride tickets and other ride/attraction combo packages are also available.*

Fodor'sChoice

★

Mission Bay Park. San Diego's monument to sports and fitness, this 4,600-acre aquatic park has 27 miles of shoreline including 19 miles of sandy beaches. Playgrounds and picnic areas abound on the beaches and low, grassy hills. On weekday evenings, joggers, bikers, and skaters take over. In the daytime, swimmers, water-skiers, paddleboarders, anglers, and boaters—some in single-person kayaks, others in crowded power-boats—vie for space in the water. ✉ *2688 E. Mission Bay Dr., Mission Bay* ✛ *Off I–5 at Exit 22 E. Mission Bay Dr.* ☎ *858/581–7602 park ranger's office* ⊕ *www.sandiego.gov/park-and-recreation* ✉ *Free.*

FAMILY

SeaWorld San Diego. Spread over 189 tropically landscaped bayfront acres, SeaWorld is one of the world's largest marine-life amusement parks. The majority of its exhibits are walk-through marine environments like **Shark Encounter,** where guests walk through a 57-foot acrylic tube and come face-to-face with a variety of sharks that call the 280,000-gallon habitat home. **Turtle Reef** offers an incredible up-close encounter with the green sea turtle, while the moving sidewalk at **Penguin Encounter** whisks you through a colony of nearly 300 penguins. The park also wows with its adventure rides like **Journey to Atlantis,** with a heart-stopping 60-foot plunge, and **Manta,** a thrilling double-launch coaster. Younger children will enjoy the rides, climbing structures and splash pads at the **Sesame Street Bay of Play.**

SeaWorld is most famous for its large-arena entertainments, but this is an area in transition. A new orca experience debuted in the summer of 2017 that features a nature-inspired backdrop and demonstrates orca behaviors in the wild. This change is part of SeaWorld's efforts to refocus it's orca program toward education and conservation. Other live-entertainment shows feature dolphins, sea otters, and

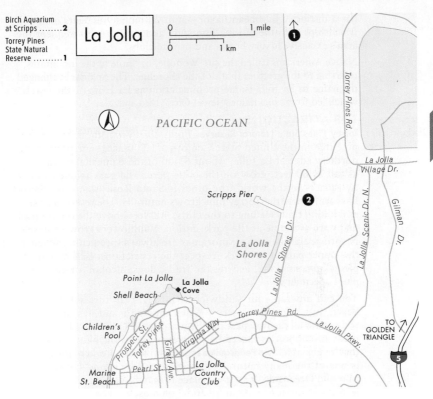

La Jolla

PACIFIC OCEAN

3

even household pets. Several upgraded animal encounters are available including the Dolphin Interaction Program, which gives guests the chance to interact with SeaWorld's bottlenose dolphins in the water. The hour-long program (20 minutes in the water), during which visitors can feed, touch, and give behavior signals, costs $215. ✉ *500 SeaWorld Dr., near west end of I–8, Mission Bay* ☎ *800/257–4268* ⊕ *www.seaworldparks.com* ✑ *$90 ages 3 and older; advanced purchase discounts available online; parking $17.*

LA JOLLA

La Jollans have long considered their village to be the Monte Carlo of California, and with good cause. Its coastline curves into natural coves backed by verdant hillsides covered with homes worth millions. La Jolla is both a natural and cultural treasure trove. The upscale shops, galleries, and restaurants of La Jolla Village satisfy the glitterati, while secluded trails, scenic overlooks, and abundant marine life provide balance and refuge.

Although La Jolla is a neighborhood of the city of San Diego, it has its own postal zone and a coveted sense of class; the ultrarich from around the globe own second homes here—the seaside zone between the neighborhood's bustling Downtown and the cliffs above the Pacific has a distinctly European flavor—and old-money residents maintain friendships with the visiting film stars and royalty who frequent the area's exclusive luxury hotels and private clubs.

Native Americans called the site Woholle, or "hole in the mountains," referring to the grottoes that dot the shoreline. The Spaniards changed the name to La Jolla (same pronunciation as La Hoya), "the jewel," which led to the nickname "Jewel City."

TOP ATTRACTIONS

Fodor's Choice ★ **Torrey Pines State Natural Reserve.** *Pinus torreyana,* the rarest native pine tree in the United States, enjoys a 1,700-acre sanctuary at the northern edge of La Jolla. About 6,000 of these unusual trees, some as tall as 60 feet, grow on the cliffs here. The park is one of only two places in the world (the other is Santa Rosa Island, off Santa Barbara) where the Torrey pine grows naturally. The reserve has several hiking trails leading to the cliffs, 300 feet above the ocean; trail maps are available at the park station. Wildflowers grow profusely in spring, and the ocean panoramas are always spectacular. When in this upper part of the park, respect the restrictions. Not permitted: picnicking, smoking, leaving the trails, dogs, alcohol, or collecting plant specimens.

You can unwrap your sandwiches, however, at Torrey Pines State Beach, just below the reserve. When the tide is out, it's possible to walk south all the way past the lifeguard towers to Black's Beach over rocky promontories carved by the waves (avoid the bluffs, however; they're unstable). **Los Peñasquitos Lagoon** at the north end of the reserve is one of the many natural estuaries that flow inland between Del Mar and Oceanside. It's a good place to watch shorebirds. Volunteers lead guided nature walks at 10 and 2 on most weekends. ✉ *12600 N. Torrey Pines Rd., La Jolla* ✛ *N. Torrey Pines Rd. exit off I–5 onto Carmel Valley Rd. going west, then turn left (south) on Coast Hwy. 101* ☎ *858/755–2063* ⊕ *www.torreypine.org* 🚗 *Parking $10–$20, varies by day of week and by season.*

WORTH NOTING

FAMILY **Birch Aquarium at Scripps.** Affiliated with the world-renowned Scripps Institution of Oceanography, this excellent aquarium sits at the end of a signposted drive leading off North Torrey Pines Road and has sweeping views of La Jolla coast below. More than 60 tanks are filled with colorful saltwater fish, and a 70,000-gallon tank simulates a La Jolla kelp forest. A special exhibit on sea horses features several examples of the species, plus mesmerizing sea dragons and a sea horse nursery. Besides the fish themselves, attractions include interactive educational exhibits based on the institution's ocean-related research and a variety of environmental issues. ✉ *2300 Expedition Way, La Jolla* ☎ *858/534–3474* ⊕ *www.aquarium.ucsd.edu* 🚗 *$18.50.*

POINT LOMA AND CORONADO WITH HARBOR AND SHELTER ISLANDS, AND OCEAN BEACH

Although Coronado is actually an isthmus, easily reached from the mainland if you head north from Imperial Beach, it has always seemed like an island and is often referred to as such. To the west, Point Loma protects the San Diego Bay from the Pacific's tides and waves. Both Coronado and Point Loma have stately homes, sandy beaches, private marinas, and prominent military installations. Nestled between the two, Harbor and Shelter islands owe their existence to dredging in the bay.

POINT LOMA

The hilly peninsula of Point Loma curves west and south into the Pacific and provides protection for San Diego Bay. Its high elevations and sandy cliffs provide incredible views, and make Point Loma a visible local landmark. Its maritime roots are evident, from its longtime ties to the U.S. Navy to its bustling sport fishing and sailing marinas. The funky community of Ocean Beach coexists alongside the stately homes of Sunset Cliffs and the honored graves at Fort Rosecrans National Cemetery.

TOP ATTRACTIONS

FAMILY
Fodor's Choice
★

Cabrillo National Monument. This 160-acre preserve marks the site of the first European visit to San Diego, made by 16th-century explorer Juan Rodríguez Cabrillo when he landed at this spot on September 15, 1542. Today the site, with its rugged cliffs and shores and outstanding overlooks, is one of the most frequently visited of all the national monuments.

The **visitor center** presents films and lectures about Cabrillo's voyage, the sea-level tide pools, and migrating gray whales. **Interpretive stations** have been installed along the walkways that edge the cliffs. The moderately steep **Bayside Trail**, 2½ miles round-trip, winds through coastal sage scrub, curving under the cliff-top lookouts and taking you ever closer to the bay-front scenery. You cannot reach the beach from this trail; you must stick to the path to protect the cliffs from erosion and yourself from thorny plants and snakes—including rattlers. The climb back is long but gradual, leading up to the **Old Point Loma Lighthouse.** The restored lighthouse dates to 1855 and is open to visitors. An exhibit in the Assistant Keepers Quarters next door tells the story of the Old Lighthouse and the daily lives of its keepers.

The western and southern cliffs of Cabrillo National Monument are prime whale-watching territory. A sheltered **viewing station** has wayside exhibits describing the great gray whales' yearly migration from Baja California to Alaska. High-powered telescopes help you focus on the whales' waterspouts. Whales are visible on clear days from late December through early March, with the highest concentration in January and February. More-accessible sea creatures (starfish, crabs, anemones) can be seen in the **tide pools** at the foot of the monument's western cliffs. Tide pooling is best when the tide is at its lowest, so call ahead or check tide charts online before your visit. Exercise caution on the slippery rocks. Drive north from the visitor center to Cabrillo Road, which winds down to the Coast Guard station and the shore. ⊠ *1800 Cabrillo Memorial Dr., Point Loma* ☎ *619/557–5450* ⊕ *www.nps.gov/cabr* ⊞ *$10 per car, $5 per person on foot/bicycle, entry good for 7 days.*

A surfer prepares to head out before sunset at La Jolla's Torrey Pines State Beach and Reserve.

Sunset Cliffs. As the name suggests, the 60-foot-high bluffs on the western side of Point Loma south of Ocean Beach are a perfect place to watch the sun set over the sea. To view the tide pools along the shore, use the staircase off Sunset Cliffs Boulevard at the foot of Ladera Street.

The dramatic coastline here seems to have been carved out of ancient rock. The impact of the waves is very clear: each year more sections of the cliffs are posted with caution signs. Don't ignore these warnings—it's easy to slip in the crumbling sandstone, and the surf can be extremely rough. The small coves and beaches that dot the coastline are popular with surfers drawn to the pounding waves. The homes along the boulevard—pink stucco mansions beside shingled Cape Cod–style cottages—are fine examples of Southern California luxury. ⊠ *Sunset Cliffs Blvd., Point Loma.*

OCEAN BEACH

At the northern end of Point Loma lies the chilled-out, hippyesque town of Ocean Beach, commonly referred to as "OB." The main thoroughfare of this funky neighborhood is dotted with dive bars, coffeehouses, surf shops, and 1960s diners. OB is a magnet for everyone from surfers to musicians and artists. Fans of OB applaud its resistance to "selling out" to upscale development, whereas detractors lament its somewhat scruffy edges.

Ocean Beach Pier. This T-shape pier is a popular fishing spot and home to the Ocean Beach Pier Café and a small tackle shop. Constructed in 1966, it is the longest concrete pier on the West Coast and a perfect place to take in views of the harbor, ocean, and Point Loma Peninsula. Surfers flock to the waves that break just below. ⊠ *1950 Abbott St., Ocean Beach.*

SHELTER ISLAND

In 1950 San Diego's port director decided to raise the shoal that lay off the eastern shore of Point Loma above sea level with the sand and mud dredged up during the course of deepening a ship channel in the 1930s and '40s. The resulting peninsula, **Shelter Island**, became home to several marinas and resorts, many with Polynesian details that still exist today, giving them a retro flair. This reclaimed peninsula now supports towering palms and resorts, restaurants, and side-by-side marinas. A long sidewalk runs past boat brokerages to the hotels and marinas that line the inner shore, facing Point Loma. On the bay side, fishermen launch their boats and families relax at picnic tables along the grass, where there are fire rings and permanent barbeque grills.

HARBOR ISLAND

Following the successful creation of Shelter Island, in 1961 the U.S. Navy used the residue from digging berths deep enough to accommodate aircraft carriers to build **Harbor Island**. Restaurants and high-rise hotels dot the inner shore of this 1½-mile-long man-made peninsula adjacent to the airport. The bay's shore is lined with pathways, gardens, and scenic picnic spots. The east-end point has killer views of the Downtown skyline.

CORONADO

As if freeze-framed in the 1950s, Coronado's quaint appeal is captured in its old-fashioned storefronts, well-manicured gardens, and charming **Ferry Landing Marketplace**. The streets of Coronado are wide, quiet, and friendly, and many of today's residents live in grand Victorian homes handed down for generations. Naval Air Station North Island was established in 1911 on Coronado's north end, across from Point Loma, and was the site of Charles Lindbergh's departure on the transcontinental flight that preceded his famous solo flight across the Atlantic. Coronado's long relationship with the U.S. Navy and its desirable real estate have made it an enclave for military personnel; it's said to have more retired admirals per capita than anywhere else in the United States.

Coronado is accessible via the arching blue 2.2-mile-long San Diego–Coronado Bay Bridge, which offers breathtaking views of the harbor and downtown. Alternatively, pedestrians and bikes can reach Coronado via the popular ferry service. Bus 904 meets the ferry and travels as far as Silver Strand State Beach. Bus 901 runs daily between the Gaslamp Quarter and Coronado.

TOP ATTRACTIONS

FAMILY **Coronado Ferry Landing.** This collection of shops at Ferry Landing is on a smaller scale than the Embarcadero's Seaport Village, but you do get a great view of the Downtown San Diego skyline. The little bayside shops and restaurants resemble the gingerbread domes of the Hotel Del Coronado. **Bikes and Beyond** (*619/435–7180, www.bikes-and-beyond.com*) rents bikes and surreys, perfect for riding through town and along Coronado's scenic bike path. ⊠ *1201 1st St., at B Ave., Coronado ⊕ www.coronadoferrylandingshops.com.*

Fodor's Choice **Hotel Del Coronado.** The Del's distinctive red-tile roofs and Victorian
★ gingerbread architecture have served as a set for many movies, political meetings, and extravagant social happenings. It's speculated that the

Duke of Windsor may have first met the Duchess of Windsor Wallis Simpson here. Eleven presidents have been guests of the Del, and the film *Some Like It Hot*—starring Marilyn Monroe, Jack Lemmon, and Tony Curtis—used the hotel as a backdrop.

The Hotel Del, as locals call it, was the brainchild of financiers Elisha Spurr Babcock Jr. and H. L. Story, who saw the potential of Coronado's virgin beaches and its view of San Diego's emerging harbor. It opened in 1888 and has been a National Historic Landmark since 1977. The History Gallery displays photos from the Del's early days, and books elaborating on its history are sold, along with logo apparel and gifts, in the hotel's 15-plus shops.

Although the pool area is reserved for hotel guests, several surrounding dining patios make great places to sit back and imagine the scene during the 1920s, when the hotel rocked with good times. Behind the pool area, an attractive shopping arcade features a classic candy shop as well as several fine clothing and accessories stores. A lavish Sunday brunch is served in the Crown Room. During the holidays, the hotel hosts Skating by the Sea, an outdoor beachfront ice-skating rink open to the public. ■TIP➔ Whether or not you're staying at the Del, enjoy a drink at the Sun Deck Bar and Grill in order to gaze out over the ocean—it makes for a great escape.

Tours of the Del are $20 per person and take place on Monday, Wednesday, and Friday at 10:30, and weekends at 2; reservations are required. ✉ *1500 Orange Ave., at Glorietta Blvd., Coronado* ☎ *619/435–6611, 619/434–7242 tour reservations (through the Coronado Historical Association)* ⊕ *www.hoteldel.com.*

Fodor's Choice **Orange Avenue.** Comprising Coronado's business district and its village-
★ like heart, this avenue is surely one of the most charming spots in Southern California. Slow-paced and very "local" (the city fights against chain stores), it's a blast from the past, although entirely up to date in other respects. The military presence—Coronado is home to the U.S. Navy Sea, Air and Land (SEAL) forces—is reflected in shops selling military gear and places like **McP's Irish Pub,** at No. 1107. A family-friendly stop for a good, all-American meal, it's the unofficial SEALs headquarters. Many clothing boutiques, home-furnishings stores, and upscale restaurants cater to visitors with deep pockets, but you can buy plumbing supplies, too, or get a genuine military haircut at **Crown Barber Shop,** at No. 947. If you need a break, stop for a latte at the sidewalk café of **Bay Books,** San Diego's largest independent bookstore, at No. 1029. ✉ *Orange Ave., near 9th St., Coronado.*

BEACHES

San Diego's beaches have a different vibe from their northern counterparts in neighboring Orange County and glitzy Los Angeles farther up the coast. San Diego is more laid-back and less of a scene. Cyclists on cruiser bikes whiz by as surfers saunter toward the waves and sunbathers bronze under the sun, be it July or November.

Even at summer's hottest peak, San Diego's beaches are cool and breezy. Ocean waves are large, and the water will be colder than what you experience at tropical beaches—temperatures range from 55°F to 65°F from October through June, and 65°F to 73°F from July through September.

Finding a parking spot near the ocean can be hard in summer. Del Mar has a pay lot and metered street parking around the 15th Street Beach. La Jolla Shores has free street parking up to two hours. Mission Beach, and other large beaches have unmetered parking lots, but space can be limited. Your best bet is to arrive early.

Pay attention to signs listing illegal activities; undercover police often patrol the beaches. Smoking and alcoholic beverages are completely banned on city beaches. Drinking in beach parking lots, on boardwalks, and in landscaped areas is also illegal. Glass containers are not permitted on beaches, cliffs, and walkways, or in park areas and adjacent parking lots. Littering is not tolerated, and skateboarding is prohibited at some beaches. Fires are allowed only in fire rings or elevated barbecue grills. Although it may be tempting to take a sea creature from a tide pool as a souvenir, it may upset the delicate ecological balance, and it's illegal, too.

Year-round, lifeguards are stationed at nine permanent stations from Sunset Cliffs to Black's Beach. All other beaches are covered by roving patrols in the winter, and seasonal towers in the summer. When swimming in the ocean be aware of rip currents, which are common in California shores. For a surf and weather report, call San Diego's Lifeguard Services at *619/221–8824.* Visit ⊕ *www.surfline.com.* for live webcams on surf conditions and water temperature forecasts.

CORONADO

FAMILY **Silver Strand State Beach.** This quiet beach on a narrow sand-spit allows visitors a unique opportunity to experience both the Pacific Ocean and the San Diego Bay. The 2½ miles of ocean side is great for surfing and other water sports while the bay side, accessible via foot tunnel under Highway 75, has calmer, warmer water and great views of the San Diego skyline. Lifeguards and rangers are on duty year-round, and there are places for biking, volleyball, and fishing. Picnic tables, grills, and fire pits are available in summer, and the Silver Strand Beach Cafe is open Memorial Day through Labor Day. The beach is close to Loews Coronado Bay Resort and the Coronado Cays, an exclusive community popular with yacht owners. You can reserve RV sites ($65 beach; $50 inland) online (*www.reserveamerica.com*). Three day-use parking lots provide room for 800 cars. **Amenities:** food and drink, lifeguards, parking (fee), showers, toilets. **Best for:** walking, swimming, surfing. ✉ *5000 Hwy. 75, Coronado* ✛ *4½ miles south of city of Coronado* ☎ *619/435–5184* ⊕ *www.parks.ca.gov/silverstrand* ⊒ *Parking $10, motorhome $30.*

FAMILY
Fodor's Choice
★
Coronado Beach. This wide beach is one of San Diego's most picturesque thanks to its soft white sand and sparkly blue water. The historic Hotel Del Coronado serves as a backdrop, and it's perfect for sunbathing, people-watching, and Frisbee tossing. The beach has limited surf, but

it's great for bodyboarding and swimming. Exercisers might include Navy SEAL teams or other military units that conduct training runs on beaches in and around Coronado. There are picnic tables, grills, and popular fire rings, but don't bring lacquered wood or pallets. Only natural wood is allowed for burning. There's also a dog beach on the north end. There's free parking along Ocean Boulevard, though it's often hard to snag a space. **Amenities:** food and drink, lifeguards, showers, toilets. **Best for:** walking, swimming. ⊠ *Ocean Blvd., between S. O St. and Orange Ave., Coronado* ✛ *From the San Diego–Coronado bridge, turn left on Orange Ave. and follow signs.*

MISSION BAY AND LA JOLLA

Sunset Cliffs. As the name would suggest this natural park near Point Loma Nazerene University is one of the best places in San Diego to watch the sunset thanks to its cliff-top location and expansive ocean views. Some limited beach access is accessible via an extremely steep stairway at the foot of Ladera Street. Beware of the treacherous cliff trails and pay attention to warning signs. The cliffs are very unstable and several fatalities have occurred over the last few years. If you're going to make your way to the narrow beach below, it's best to go at low tide when the southern end, near Cabrillo Point, reveals tide pools teeming with small sea creatures. Farther north the waves lure surfers, and Osprey Point offers good fishing off the rocks. Keep your eyes peeled for migrating California gray whales during the winter months. Check WaveCast (*www.wavecast.com/tides*) for tide schedules. **Amenities:** parking (no fee). **Best for:** solitude, sunset, surfing. ⊠ *Sunset Cliffs Blvd., between Ladera St. and Adair St., Point Loma* ⊕ *www.sunsetcliffs.info.*

MISSION BAY

FAMILY **Mission Beach.** With a roller coaster, artificial wave park, and hot dog stands, this 2-mile-long beach has a carnival vibe and is the closest thing you'll find to Coney Island on the West Coast. It's lively year-round but draws a huge crowd on hot summer days. A wide boardwalk paralleling the beach is popular with walkers, joggers, skateboarders, and bicyclists. To escape the crowds, head to South Mission Beach. It attracts surfers, swimmers, and scantily clad volleyball players, who often play competitive pickup games on the courts near the north jetty. The water near the Belmont Park roller coaster can be a bit rough but makes for good bodyboarding and bodysurfing. For free parking, you can try for a spot on the street, but your best bets are the two big lots at Belmont Park. **Amenities:** lifeguards, parking (no fee), showers, toilets. **Best for:** swimming, surfing, walking. ⊠ *3000 Mission Blvd., Mission Bay* ✛ *Parking near roller coaster at West Mission Bay Dr.* ⊕ *www. sandiego.gov/lifeguards/beaches/mb.shtml.*

Pacific Beach/North Pacific Beach. This beach, known for attracting a young college-age crowd and surfers, runs from the northern end of Mission Beach to Crystal Pier. The scene here is lively on weekends, with nearby restaurants, beach bars, and nightclubs providing a party atmosphere. In P.B. (as the locals call it) Sundays are known as "Sunday Funday," and pub crawls can last all day. So although drinking is no longer allowed on the beach, it's still likely you'll see people who have had one too many. The mood changes just north of the pier at North Pacific Beach, which attracts families and surfers. Although not quite pillowy, the sand at both beaches is nice and soft, which makes for great sunbathing and sand-castle building. ■TIP➜ **Kelp and flies can be a problem on this stretch, so choose your spot wisely.** Parking at Pacific Beach can also be a challenge. A few coveted free angle parking spaces are available along the boardwalk, but you'll most likely have to look for spots in the surrounding neighborhood. If you're staying at nearby Pacific Terrace Hotel, you can simply walk to the beach. **Amenities:** food and drink, lifeguards, parking (no fee), showers, toilets. **Best for:** partiers, swimming, surfing. ✉ *4500 Ocean Blvd., Pacific Beach* ⊕ *www.sandiego.gov/lifeguards/beaches/pb.shtml.*

Tourmaline Surfing Park. Offering slow waves and frequent winds, this is one of the most popular beaches for surfers. For windsurfing and kiteboarding, it's only sailable with northwest winds. The 175-space parking lot at the foot of Tourmaline Street normally fills to capacity by midday. Just like Pacific Beach, Tourmaline has soft, tawny-colored sand, but when the tide is in the beach becomes quite narrow, making finding a good sunbathing spot a bit of a challenge. **Amenities:** seasonal lifeguards, parking (no fee), showers, toilets. **Best for:** windsurfing, surfing. ✉ *600 Tourmaline St., Pacific Beach.*

LA JOLLA

Fodor'sChoice
★
Windansea Beach. With its rocky shoreline and strong shore break, Windansea stands out among San Diego beaches for its dramatic natural beauty. It's one of the best surf spots in San Diego County. Professional surfers love the unusual A-frame waves the reef break here creates. Although the large sandstone rocks that dot the beach might sound like a hindrance, they actually serve as protective barriers from the wind, making this one of the best beaches in San Diego for sunbathing. The beach's palm-covered surf shack is a protected historical landmark, and a seat here at sunset may just be one of the most romantic spots on the West Coast. The name Windansea comes from a hotel that burned down in the late 1940s. You can usually find nearby street parking. **Amenities:** seasonal lifeguards, toilets. **Best for:** sunset, surfing, solitude. ✉ *Neptune Pl. at Nautilus St., La Jolla* ⊕ *www.sandiego.gov/lifeguards/ beaches/windan.shtml.*

FAMILY
Fodor'sChoice
★
La Jolla Cove. This shimmering blue-green inlet surrounded by cliffs is what first attracted everyone to La Jolla, from Native Americans to the glitterati. "The Cove," as locals refer to it, beyond where Girard Avenue dead-ends into Coast Boulevard, is marked by towering palms that line a promenade where people strolling in designer clothes are as common as Frisbee throwers. Ellen Browning Scripps Park sits atop cliffs formed by the incessant pounding of the waves and offers a great spot for picnics with a view. The Cove has beautiful white sand that is a bit course near the water's edge, but the beach is still a great place for sunbathing and lounging. At low tide, the pools and cliff caves are a destination for explorers. With visibility at 30-plus feet, this is the best place in San Diego for snorkeling, where bright-orange Garibaldi fish and other marine life populate the waters of the **San Diego–La Jolla Underwater**

Park Ecological Reserve. From above water, it's not uncommon to spot sea lions and birds basking on the rocks, or dolphin fins just offshore. The cove is also a favorite of rough-water swimmers, while the area just north is best for kayakers wanting to explore the Seven La Jolla Sea Caves. **Amenities:** lifeguards, showers, toilets. **Best for:** snorkeling, swimming, walking. ⊠ *1100 Coast Blvd., east of Ellen Browning Scripps Park, La Jolla ⊕ www.sandiego.gov/lifeguards/beaches/cove.shtml.*

FAMILY **La Jolla Shores.** This is one of San Diego's most popular beaches due to its wide sandy shore, gentle waves, and incredible views of La Jolla Peninsula. There's also a large grassy park, and adjacent to La Jolla Shores lies the **San Diego La Jolla Underwater Park Ecological Reserve,** 6,000 acres of protected ocean bottom and tide lands. The white powdery sand at La Jolla Sands is some of San Diego's best, and several surf and scuba schools teach here. Kayaks can also be rented nearby. A concrete boardwalk parallels the beach, and a boat launch for small vessels lies 300 yards south of the lifeguard station at Avenida de Playa. Arrive early to get a parking spot in the lot near Kellogg Park at the foot of Calle Frescota. Street parking is limited to one or two hours. **Amenities:** lifeguards, parking (no fee), showers, toilets. **Best for:** surfing, swimming, walking. ⊠ *8200 Camino del Oro, in front of Kellogg Park, La Jolla ✛ 2 miles north of downtown La Jolla ⊕ www.sandiego. gov/lifeguards/beaches/shores.shtml.*

Fodor'sChoice **Torrey Pines State Beach and Reserve.** With sandstone cliffs and hiking
★ trails adjacent to the beach rather than urban development, Torrey Pines State Beach feels far away from the SoCal sprawl. The beach and reserve encompass 1,600 acres of sandstone cliffs and deep ravines, and a network of meandering trails lead to the wide, pristine beach below. Along the way enjoy the rare Torrey pine trees, found only here and on Santa Rosa Island, offshore. Guides conduct free tours of the nature preserve on weekends. Torrey Pines tends to get crowded in summer, but you'll find more isolated spots heading south under the cliffs leading to Black's Beach. Smooth rocks often wash up on stretches of the beach making it a challenge, at times, to go barefoot. If you can find a patch that is clear of debris, you'll encounter the nice soft, golden sand San Diego is known for. There is a paid parking lot at the entrance to the park but also look for free angle parking along N. Torrey Pines Road. **Amenities:** lifeguards, parking (fee), showers, toilets. **Best for:** swimming, surfing, walking. ⊠ *12600 N. Torrey Pines Rd.* ☎ *858/755–2063 ⊕ www.torreypine.org* ▨ *Parking $15 per vehicle.*

NORTH COUNTY BEACHES

DEL MAR

FAMILY **Del Mar Beach.** This famously clean 2-mile-long beach is the perfect place for long barefoot walks and sunbathing due to its extremely fine, soft sand and lack of seaweed and other debris. Del Mar Beach is also a great place for families. It has year-round lifeguards and areas clearly marked for swimming and surfing. Depending on the swell, you may see surfers at the 15th Street surf break, right below two coastal parks, Powerhouse and Seagrove; volleyball players love the courts at the beach's far North end. The section of beach south of 15th is lined with cliffs and tends to be less crowded than Main Beach, which extends from 15th north to 29th. Leashed dogs are permitted on most sections of the beach, except Main Beach, where they are prohibited from June 15 through the Tuesday after Labor Day. For the rest of the year, dogs may run under voice control at North Beach, just north of the River Mouth, also known locally as Dog Beach. Food, shopping, and hotels including L'Auberge Del Mar, are near Del Mar Beach. Parking costs from $1.50 to $3 per hour at meters and pay lots on Coast Boulevard and along Camino Del Mar. **Amenities:** food and drink, lifeguards, parking (fee), showers, toilets. **Best for:** swimming, walking. ⊠ *Main Beach, 1700 Coast Blvd., North Beach 3200–3300 Camino Del Mar, Del Mar* ☎ *858/755–1556* ⊕ *www.delmar.ca.us/203/Beaches-Parks.*

ENCINITAS

Swami's. The palms and the golden lotus-flower domes of the nearby Self-Realization Fellowship temple and ashram earned this picturesque beach, also a top surfing spot, its name. Extreme low tides expose tide pools that harbor anemones, starfish, and other sea life. The only access is by a long stairway leading down from the cliff-top Swami's Seaside Park, where there's free parking. A shower is at the base of the steps. On big winter swells, the bluffs are lined with gawkers watching the area's best surfers take on—and be taken down by—some of the county's best big waves. The beach has flat, packed sand and can accumulate seaweed and some flies, so if laying out is your main objective you might want to head north to Moonlight Beach. Offshore, divers do their thing at North County's underwater park, Encinitas Marine Life Refuge. The small park next to the Swami's parking lot offers shade trees, picnic tables, barbecues, and clean bathrooms. Across the street is the cheerful Swami's Cafe, where surfers refuel postsurf. **Amenities:** lifeguards, parking (no fee), showers, toilets. **Best for:** snorkeling, surfing, swimming. ⊠ *1298 S. Coast Hwy. 101 (Rte. S21), Encinitas* ✛ *1 mile north of Cardiff.*

WHERE TO EAT

San Diego is an up-and-coming culinary destination, thanks to its stunning Pacific Ocean setting, proximity to Mexico, diverse population, and the area's extraordinary farming community. Increasingly the city's veteran top chefs are being joined by a new generation of talented chefs and restaurateurs who are adding stylish restaurants with innovative food and drink programs to the dining scene at a record pace. Yes, visitors still are drawn to the San Diego Zoo and miles of beaches, but now they come for memorable dining experiences as well.

The city's culinary scene got a significant boost when San Diego emerged as one of the world's top craft beer destinations, with artisan breweries and gastropubs now in almost every neighborhood. These neighborhoods are also ethnically diverse with modest eateries offering affordable authentic international cuisines that add spice to the dining mix.

The trendy Gaslamp Quarter delights visitors looking for a broad range of innovative and international dining and nightlife, while bustling

Little Italy offers a mix of affordable Italian fare and posh new eateries. Modern restaurants and cafés thrive in East Village, amid the luxury condos near PETCO Park. The Uptown neighborhoods centered on Hillcrest—an urbane district with San Francisco flavor—are a mix of bars and independent restaurants, many of which specialize in ethnic cuisine. North Park, in particular, has a happening restaurant and craft beer scene, with just about every kind of cuisine you can think of, and laid-back prices to boot. And scenic La Jolla offers some of the best fine dining in the city with dramatic water views as an added bonus.

Use the coordinate (✣ A1) at the end of each listing to locate a site on the corresponding map.

PRICES

Meals in San Diego popular dining spots can be pricey, especially in areas like La Jolla, the Gaslamp Quarter, and Coronado. Many other restaurants are very affordable or offer extra value with fixed-price menus, early-dining specials and early and late happy hours.

WHAT IT COSTS

	$	$$	$$$	$$$$
Restaurants	under $18	$18–$27	$28–$35	over $35

Prices in the reviews are the average cost of a main course at dinner or, if dinner is not served, at lunch.

DOWNTOWN

GASLAMP QUARTER

$$$ AMERICAN

🍴 **Searsucker.** Since opened by celebrity chef Brian Malarkey a few years ago, this high-energy flagship restaurant has become the Gaslamp's best for food and energetic atmosphere. Foodies from near and far savor Malarkey's upscale down-home fare like small plates of biscuits with spicy honey, duck fat fries, and shrimp and grits. **Known for:** detailed, home-inspired decor; crispy duck fat fries; late-night menu on Fridays and Saturdays from 11 pm–1 am. [$] *Average main: $30* ✉ *611 5th Ave., Gaslamp Quarter* ☎ *619/233–7327* 🌐 *www.searsucker.com* ✣ *H2.*

$$ JAPANESE

🍴 **Taka.** Pristine fish imported from around the world and presented creatively attracts crowds nightly to this intimate Gaslamp restaurant. Take a seat at the bar and watch one of the sushi chefs preparing appetizers, perhaps the monkfish liver with ponzu or spicy tuna tartar. **Known for:** uni sushi topped with wasabi; omakase tasting menu; upscale sake offerings. [$] *Average main: $18* ✉ *555 5th Ave., Gaslamp Quarter* ☎ *619/338–0555* 🌐 *www.takasushi.com* 🕒 *No lunch* ✣ *H2.*

EAST VILLAGE

$$ MODERN MEXICAN FAMILY

🍴 **The Blind Burro.** East Village families, baseball fans heading to or from PETCO Park and happy-hour bound singles flock to this airy restaurant with Baja-inspired food and drink. Traditional margaritas get a fresh kick from fruit juices or jalapeno peppers; other libations include sangrias and Mexican beers, all perfect pairings for house-made guacamole, ceviche, or salsas with chips. **Known for:** house margarita with fruit infusions; surf-and-turf Baja-style tacos; gluten-free menu. [$] *Average main: $18* ✉ *639 J St., East Village* ☎ *619/795–7880* 🌐 *www.theblindburro.com* ✣ *H3.*

LITTLE ITALY

$$$ MODERN AMERICAN 🍴 **Juniper and Ivy.** Celebrity chef Richard Blais's addition to San Diego's restaurant scene fills an open-beamed space with seating for 250 and an open stainless-steel dream kitchen where diners can watch the chef and team in action. Blais sources local farm fresh ingredients for his "left coast cookery" with a molecular gastronomy twist. **Known for:** a California-Baja-inspired Carne Crudo Asada topped with quail eggs; an off-menu "In & Haute" burger; very shareable Yodel chocolate dessert. [$] *Average main: $35* ✉ *2228 Kettner Blvd., Little Italy* ☎ *619/269–9036* 🌐 *www.juniperandivy.com* 🕓 *Closed for lunch* ✣ *E5.*

$$ MODERN AMERICAN Fodor's Choice ★ 🍴 **Prepkitchen Little Italy.** Urbanites craving a hip casual setting and gourmet menu pack architectural salvage-styled Prepkitchen Little Italy, tucked upstairs above a busy corner in this thriving neighborhood. With first-date cocktails, after-work brews or birthday champagne, diners relish familiar choices like meatball sandwiches, chops, and pork belly with kimchi brussels. **Known for:** weekend brunch featuring popular chilaquiles dish; bacon-wrapped dates. [$] *Average main: $23* ✉ *1660 India St., Little Italy* ☎ *619/398–8383* 🌐 *www.prepkitchenlittleitaly.com* ✣ *E5.*

BALBOA PARK AND BANKERS HILL

BALBOA PARK

$ AMERICAN 🍴 **Panama 66.** Adding a dose of hip to Balboa Park, this gastropub, located adjacent to the San Diego Museum of Art, offers a stylish pit-stop pre-theater or between museum-hopping. Decor is contemporary, with café-style seating, sculptures in the garden, and a view of the California Tower. **Known for:** rotating cocktails pegged to museum exhibits; live music most nights. [$] *Average main: $11* ✉ *1450 El Prado, Balboa Park* ☎ *619/696–1966* 🌐 *www.panama66.com* 🕓 *No dinner Mon. and Tues.* ✣ *E5.*

BANKERS HILL

$$ MODERN AMERICAN Fodor's Choice ★ 🍴 **Bankers Hill Bar and Restaurant.** The living wall of succulents, hip warehouse interior, and wine bottle chandeliers suit this vibrant restaurant where good times and great eats meet. An after-work crowd joins residents of this quiet stretch of Bankers Hill for happy hour cocktails, craft beers, and well-curated wines served from the zinc bar. **Known for:** popular burger with truffle fries; soft-shell crab lettuce wraps with a vodka-infused batter; living plant wall on the sun-drenched patio. [$] *Average main: $21* ✉ *2202 4th Ave., Bankers Hill* ☎ *619/231–0222* 🌐 *www.bankershillsd.com* 🕓 *No lunch* ✣ *E5.*

$$ ITALIAN Fodor's Choice ★ 🍴 **Cucina Urbana.** Twentysomethings mingle with boomers in this convivial Bankers Hill dining room and bar, one of the most popular restaurants in town. Country-farmhouse decor that mixes rolling pins with modern art looks and feels festive. **Known for:** vasi appetizer platters; seasonal polenta with ragu; ricotta-stuffed zucchini blossoms. [$] *Average main: $20* ✉ *505 Laurel St., Bankers Hill* ☎ *619/239–2222* 🌐 *www.cucinaurbana.com* 🕓 *No lunch Sat.–Mon.* ✣ *E5.*

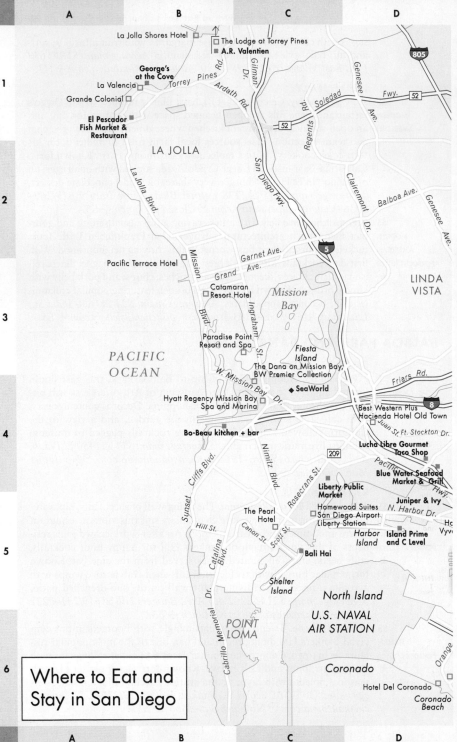

Where to Eat and Stay in San Diego

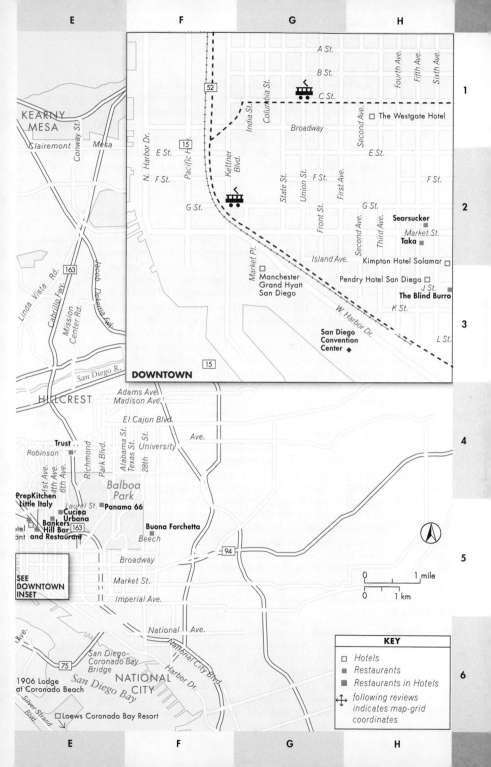

OLD TOWN AND UPTOWN

OLD TOWN

$ **✗ Blue Water Seafood Market & Grill.** Blame a television segment by Guy
SEAFOOD Fieri on "Diners, Drive-ins and Dives" for the long lines of fans from
FAMILY around the globe. But it's the fresh seafood cooked to order that keeps
them coming back to this no-frills fish market and restaurant. **Known
for:** beer-battered cod tacos; classic cioppino plate with mussels and
clams, scallops, shrimp, and red snapper. $ *Average main: $15 ✉ 3667
India St., Mission Hills ☎ 619/497–0914 ⊕ www.bluewaterseafood-
sandiego.com ✛ D4.*

HILLCREST AND MISSION HILLS

$ **✗ Lucha Libre Gourmet Taco Shop.** Named for a form of Mexican wres-
MEXICAN tling, this taco shop with its hot-pink walls and shiny booths was
famous mostly for its lack of parking until it appeared on the Travel
Channel's "Man v. Food." Then long lines of burrito-crazed fans began
forming outside the walk-up window for lunch. **Known for:** Tap Me
Out taco with fried cheese; Champion nachos with french fries; lively
and festive interior seating. $ *Average main: $7 ✉ 1810 W. Washington
St., Mission Hills ☎ 619/296–8226 ⊕ www.tacosmackdown.com ✛ D4.*

$$ **✗ Trust.** Old-school wood-fire techniques meet modern architecture in
MODERN this busy bistro where comic book–style art covers the concrete walls
AMERICAN and the bottle-lined bar beckons locals and visitors alike. Dishes feature
Fodor'sChoice popular items like the braised oxtail raviolini with horseradish and
★ whipped ricotta, and wood-grilled cauliflower dressed in a curry vin-
aigrette. **Known for:** five-hour braised oxtail raviolini; roomy outdoor
patio. $ *Average main: $20 ✉ 3752 Park Blvd., Hillcrest ☎ 619/795–
6901 ⊕ www.trustrestaurantsd.com ✛ E4.*

SOUTH PARK

$ **✗ Buona Forchetta.** A golden-domed pizza oven, named Sofia after the
ITALIAN owner's daughter, delivers authentic Neapolitan-style pizza to fans who
FAMILY often line up for patio tables at this dog- and kid-friendly Italian res-
Fodor'sChoice taurant in South Park. Slices of classic margherita or truffle-flavored
★ mozzarella and mushroom pizzas make a meal or can be shared, but
don't miss the equally delicious appetizers like the tender calamari or
succulent artichokes, heaping salads, or fresh pastas, including a hearty
lasagna, delicate ravioli, or gnocchi with pesto. **Known for:** house red
wine; bubbly Neapolitan-style pizzas; bustling patio. $ *Average main:
$14 ✉ 3001 Beech St., South Park ☎ 619/381–4844 ⊕ www.buonafor-
chettasd.com ⊙ No lunch Mon. and Tues. ✛ F5.*

LA JOLLA

$$$$ **✗ A.R. Valentien.** Champions of in-season, fresh-today produce and sea-
AMERICAN food, executive chef Jeff Jackson and chef de cuisine Kelli Crosson have
Fodor'sChoice made this cozy room in the luxurious, Craftsman-style Lodge at Torrey
★ Pines one of San Diego's top fine dining destinations. Their food combina-
tions are simultaneously simple and delightfully inventive—duck breast
with celery root risotto; ahi tuna with grapefruit and crispy quinoa; or
swordfish with chorizo and charred scallion salsa verde. **Known for:**

red-wine braised short rib; creamy chicken liver pâté; patio that overlooks the resort pool and the famed 18th green at Torrey Pines South Course. $ *Average main: $38* ✉ *The Lodge at Torrey Pines, 11480 N. Torrey Pines Rd., La Jolla* ☎ *858/777–6635* ⊕ *www.arvalentien.com* ✚ *B1.*

$ ✕ **El Pescador Fish Market & Restaurant.** This bustling fish market and
SEAFOOD café in the heart of La Jolla Village has been popular with locals for its superfresh fish for more than 30 years. Order the char-grilled, locally caught halibut, swordfish, or yellowtail on a toasted torta roll to enjoy in-house or to-go for an oceanfront picnic at nearby La Jolla Cove. **Known for:** superfresh fish; bustling on-site fish market. $ *Average main: $15* ✉ *634 Pearl St., La Jolla* ☎ *858/456–2526* ⊕ *www.elpescadorfishmarket.com* ✚ *B1.*

$$$$ ✕ **George's at the Cove.** La Jolla's ocean-view destination restaurant
AMERICAN includes three dining areas: California Modern on the bottom floor,
Fodor'sChoice the Level2 bar in the middle, and Ocean Terrace on the roof. The
★ sleek main dining room presents elegant preparations of seafood, beef, and venison, which star-chef Trey Foshee enlivens with amazing local produce. **Known for:** beef tartare with 67-degree egg; excellent ocean views; attention to detail for special occasion dinners. $ *Average main: $37* ✉ *1250 Prospect St., La Jolla* ☎ *858/454–4244* ⊕ *www.georgesatthecove.com* ✚ *B1.*

POINT LOMA, SHELTER ISLAND, AND HARBOR ISLAND

POINT LOMA

$$ ✕ **Bo-Beau kitchen + bar.** Ocean Beach is a slightly eccentric beach town,
BISTRO not a place diners would expect to find this warm, romantic bistro that evokes a French farmhouse. The satisfying French-inspired menu of soups, woodstone-oven flatbreads, mussels, and other bistro classics is served in cozy dining rooms and a rustic outdoor patio. **Known for:** popular crispy Brussels sprouts with pancetta; Tuesday date night special. $ *Average main: $22* ✉ *4996 W. Point Loma Blvd., Ocean Beach* ☎ *619/224–2884* ⊕ *www.cohnrestaurants.com/bobeaukitchenbar* ☾ *No lunch* ✚ *B4.*

$ ✕ **Liberty Public Market.** The city's former Naval Training Center is now
INTERNATIONAL home to nearly 30 vendors so even the pickiest of diners will be pleased.
FAMILY Options include tacos and quesadillas at Cecilia's Taqueria; fried rice,
Fodor'sChoice pad Thai, and curries at Mama Made Thai; gumbo, fried chicken, jam-
★ balaya, and other Southern specialties at Cane Patch Kitchen; smoothies and cold-pressed juices at Fully Loaded; and croissants, eclairs, and macarons at Le Parfait Paris. **Known for:** colossal burgers with creative fillings at Stuffed!; lively kid- and dog-friendly patio. $ *Average main: $10* ✉ *2820 Historic Decatur Rd., Liberty Station* ☎ *619/487–9346* ⊕ *www.libertypublicmarket.com* ✚ *C4.*

SHELTER ISLAND

$$ ✕ **Bali Hai.** For more than 50 years, generations of San Diegans and visi-
HAWAIIAN tors have enjoyed this Polynesian-theme icon with its stunning bay and city skyline views. Much of the kitsch has been replaced by contemporary decor, but you'll still spot tikis here and there. **Known for:** potent Bali Hai mai tais; Sunday brunch buffet with a DIY sundae bar. $ *Average main:*

$25 ✉ *2230 Shelter Island Dr., Shelter Island* ☎ *619/222–1181* 🌐 *www.balihairestaurant.com* 🕑 *No lunch Sun.* ⊕ *C5.*

HARBOR ISLAND

$$$$ MODERN AMERICAN

🍴 **Island Prime and C Level.** Two restaurants in one share this enviable spot on the shore of Harbor Island: the splurge-worthy Island Prime steak house and the relaxed C Level with a choice terrace. Both venues tempt with unrivaled views of downtown San Diego's skyline. **Known for:** sunset views; popover bread served with jalapeño jelly butter. [$] *Average main: $39* ✉ *880 Harbor Island Dr., Harbor Island* ☎ *619/298–6802* 🌐 *www.cohnrestaurants.com/islandprime* 🕑 *No lunch at Island Prime* ⊕ *D5.*

WHERE TO STAY

Sharing the city's postcard-perfect sunny skies are neighborhoods and coastal communities that offer great diversity; San Diego is no longer the sleepy beach town it once was. In action-packed Downtown, luxury hotels cater to solo business travelers and young couples with trendy restaurants and cabana-encircled pools. Budget-friendly options can be found in smaller neighborhoods just outside the Gaslamp Quarter such as Little Italy and Uptown.

You'll need a car if you stay outside Downtown, but the beach communities are rich with lodging options. Across the bridge, Coronado's hotels and resorts offer access to a stretch of glistening white sand that's often recognized as one of the best beaches in the country. La Jolla offers many romantic, upscale ocean-view hotels and some of the area's best restaurants and specialty shopping. But it's easy to find a water view in any price range: surfers make themselves at home at the casual inns and budget stays of Pacific Beach and Mission Bay. If you're planning to fish, check out hotels located near the marinas in Shelter Island, Point Loma, or Coronado.

For families, Uptown, Mission Valley, and Old Town are close to SeaWorld and the San Diego Zoo, offering good-value accommodations with extras like sleeper sofas and video games. Mission Valley is ideal for business travelers; there are plenty of well-known chain hotels with conference space, modern business centers, and kitchenettes for extended stays.

When you make reservations, book well in advance and ask about specials. Several properties in the Hotel Circle area of Mission Valley offer reduced rates and even free tickets to the San Diego Zoo and other attractions. You can save on hotels and attractions by visiting the San Diego Tourism Authority website (🌐 *www.sandiego.org*) for special seasonal offers.

Use the coordinate (⊕ A1) at the end of each listing to locate a site on the corresponding map.

PRICES

Note that even in the most expensive areas, you can find affordable rooms. High season is summer, and rates are lowest in fall. If an ocean view is important, request it when booking, but it will cost you.

Hotel reviews have been shortened. For full information, visit Fodors.com.

	WHAT IT COSTS			
	$	$$	$$$	$$$$
Hotels	under $150	$150–$225	$226–$300	over $300

Hotel prices are the cost of a standard double room in high season, excluding 10.5% tax.

3

DOWNTOWN

GASLAMP QUARTER

$$$ HOTEL FAMILY Fodor's Choice ★ **Kimpton Hotel Solamar.** Best known for Upper East Bar, its pool-side rooftop bar, and stylish lobby decor, Solamar's recently refreshed guest rooms reflect this urban escape's mixture of luxury and fun, with prints galore and subtle nods to San Diego's happy beach culture. **Pros:** great restaurant; attentive service; upscale rooms. **Cons:** busy valet parking; daily facility fee. [$] *Rooms from: $279* ✉ *435 6th Ave., Gaslamp Quarter* ☎ *619/819–9500, 877/230–0300* 🌐 *www.hotelsolamar.com* 🛏 *235 rooms* 🍴 *No meals* ✣ *H2.*

$$$$ HOTEL Fodor's Choice ★ **Pendry San Diego.** Opened in early 2017, the Pendry San Diego is the Gaslamp's newest stunner. **Pros:** well-situated in Gaslamp Quarter; excellent dining options; complimentary coffee in the mornings. **Cons:** pricey room rates; meals are expensive. [$] *Rooms from: $480* ✉ *550 J St., Gaslamp Quarter* ☎ *619/738–7000* 🌐 *www.pendryhotels.com* 🛏 *317 rooms* 🍴 *No meals* ✣ *H3.*

$$$ HOTEL **The Westgate Hotel.** A modern high-rise near Horton Plaza hides San Diego's most opulent old world–style hotel, featuring a lobby outfitted with bronze sculptures and Baccarat chandeliers. **Pros:** affordable luxury; serene rooftop pool deck. **Cons:** dated guest rooms; mandatory facility fee. [$] *Rooms from: $299* ✉ *1055 2nd Ave., Gaslamp Quarter* ☎ *619/238–1818, 800/522–1564* 🌐 *www.westgatehotel.com* 🛏 *223 rooms* 🍴 *No meals* ✣ *H1.*

LITTLE ITALY

$ B&B/INN **Hotel Vyvant.** You'll find more amenities at other Downtown hotels but it's hard to beat this property's value and charm. **Pros:** good location; historic property; welcoming staff. **Cons:** some shared baths; no parking. [$] *Rooms from: $139* ✉ *505 W. Grape St., Little Italy* ☎ *619/230–1600, 800/518–9930* 🌐 *www.hotelvyvant.com* 🛏 *23 rooms* 🍴 *Breakfast* ✣ *E5.*

EMBARCADERO

$$$ HOTEL FAMILY **Manchester Grand Hyatt San Diego.** Primarily a draw for business travelers, this hotel between Seaport Village and the convention center also works well for leisure and family travelers. **Pros:** great views; conference facilities; good location; spacious rooms. **Cons:** lots of convention-goers; some trolley noise. [$] *Rooms from: $259* ✉ *1 Market Pl., Embarcadero* ☎ *619/232–1234, 800/233–1234* 🌐 *www.manchester.grand.hyatt.com* 🛏 *1628 rooms* 🍴 *No meals* ✣ *G3.*

OLD TOWN, MISSION VALLEY

OLD TOWN

$$ HOTEL FAMILY **Best Western Plus Hacienda Hotel Old Town.** Perched on a hill in the heart of Old Town, this hotel is known for its expansive courtyards, outdoor fountains, and maze of stairs that connect eight buildings of guest rooms. **Pros:** airport shuttle; well-maintained outdoor areas. **Cons:** some rooms need renovating; complicated layout. *Rooms from: $210 4041 Harney St., Old Town 619/298–4707 www.haciendahotel-oldtown.com 198 rooms No meals D4.*

MISSION BAY AND BEACHES

MISSION BAY

$$ RESORT FAMILY **The Dana on Mission Bay, BW Premier Collection.** A part of Best Western's BW Premier Collection, this waterfront resort, just down the road from SeaWorld, has an ideal location for active leisure travelers. **Pros:** water views; many outdoor activities. **Cons:** expensive resort fee. *Rooms from: $209 1710 W. Mission Bay Dr., Mission Bay 619/222–6440, 800/445–3339 www.thedana.com 271 rooms No meals C4.*

$$$ RESORT FAMILY **Hyatt Regency Mission Bay Spa and Marina.** This modern property has many desirable amenities, including balconies with excellent views of the garden, bay, ocean, or swimming pool courtyard. **Pros:** proximity to water sports; 120-foot waterslides in pools, plus kiddie slide. **Cons:** daily resort fee; not centrally located. *Rooms from: $299 1441 Quivira Rd., Mission Bay 619/224–1234, 800/233–1234 www.missionbay.regency.hyatt.com 429 rooms No meals C4.*

$$$ RESORT FAMILY **Paradise Point Resort and Spa.** Minutes from SeaWorld but hidden in a quiet part of Mission Bay, the beautiful landscape of this 44-acre resort offers plenty of space for families to play and relax. **Pros:** water views; five pools; good service. **Cons:** not centrally located; motel-thin walls; parking and resort fees. *Rooms from: $289 1404 Vacation Rd., Mission Bay 858/274–4630, 800/344–2626 www.paradisepoint.com 462 rooms No meals C3.*

PACIFIC BEACH

$$$$ RESORT **Pacific Terrace Hotel.** Travelers love this terrific beachfront hotel and the ocean views from most rooms; it's a perfect place for watching sunsets over the Pacific. **Pros:** beach views; large rooms; friendly service. **Cons:** busy and sometimes noisy area; expensive in peak season. *Rooms from: $549 610 Diamond St., Pacific Beach 858/581–3500, 800/344–3370 www.pacificterrace.com 73 rooms No meals B3.*

LA JOLLA

$$$$ HOTEL Fodor's Choice ★ **Grande Colonial.** This white wedding cake–style hotel in the heart of La Jolla village has ocean views and charming European details that include chandeliers, mahogany railings, and French doors. **Pros:** great location; superb restaurant. **Cons:** somewhat busy street; no fitness center; valet parking only. *Rooms from: $369 910 Prospect St., La Jolla 888/828–5498 www.thegrandecolonial.com 93 rooms No meals B1.*

$$$$ HOTEL FAMILY **La Jolla Shores Hotel.** One of San Diego's few hotels actually on the beach, this property is part of La Jolla Beach and Tennis Club. **Pros:** on beach; great views. **Cons:** not centrally located; pool can be noisy; three-night minimum in summer. [$] *Rooms from: $319 ✉ 8110 Camino del Oro, La Jolla ☎ 858/923–8058, 877/346–6714 🌐 www.ljshoreshotel.com ⇨ 128 rooms 🍴 No meals ✣ B1.*

$$$$ HOTEL **La Valencia.** This pink Spanish-Mediterranean confection drew Hollywood film stars in the 1930s and '40s with its setting and views of La Jolla Cove; now it draws the Kardashians. **Pros:** upscale rooms; views; near beach. **Cons:** standard rooms are tiny; lots of traffic outside. [$] *Rooms from: $449 ✉ 1132 Prospect St., La Jolla ☎ 858/454–0771 🌐 www.lavalencia.com ⇨ 114 rooms 🍴 No meals ✣ B1.*

$$$$ RESORT Fodor's Choice ★ **The Lodge at Torrey Pines.** This beautiful Craftsman-style lodge sits on a bluff between La Jolla and Del Mar and commands a coastal view. **Pros:** spacious upscale rooms; good service; adjacent the famed Torrey Pines Golf Course. **Cons:** not centrally located; expensive. [$] *Rooms from: $379 ✉ 11480 N. Torrey Pines Rd., La Jolla ☎ 858/453–4420, 888/826–0224 🌐 www.lodgetorreypines.com ⛳ Two 18-hole championship golf courses ⇨ 170 rooms 🍴 No meals ✣ B1.*

POINT LOMA AND CORONADO WITH HARBOR AND SHELTER ISLANDS

POINT LOMA

$$$$ HOTEL FAMILY Fodor's Choice ★ **Homewood Suites San Diego Airport Liberty Station.** Families and business travelers will benefit from the space and amenities at this all-suites hotel. **Pros:** complimentary grocery shopping service; close to paths for joggers and bikers. **Cons:** no pets allowed; far from nightlife. [$] *Rooms from: $349 ✉ 2576 Laning Rd., Point Loma ☎ 619/222–0500 🌐 www.homewoodsuites.com ⇨ 150 suites 🍴 Breakfast ✣ C5.*

$$$ HOTEL Fodor's Choice ★ **The Pearl Hotel.** This previously vintage motel received a makeover, turning it into a retro-chic hangout decorated with kitschy lamps and original, in-room art by local children. **Pros:** near marina; hip bar/restaurant on-site (dinner only, except for seasonal specials). **Cons:** not centrally located; one bed in rooms. [$] *Rooms from: $233 ✉ 1410 Rosecrans St., Point Loma ☎ 619/226–6100 🌐 www.thepearlsd.com ⇨ 23 rooms 🍴 No meals ✣ C5.*

CORONADO

$$$$ RESORT FAMILY Fodor's Choice ★ **Hotel Del Coronado.** As much of a draw today as it was when it opened in 1888, the Victorian-style "Hotel Del" is always alive with activity, as guests—including U.S. presidents and celebrities—and tourists marvel at the fanciful architecture and ocean views. **Pros:** 17 on-site shops; on the beach; well-rounded spa. **Cons:** some rooms are small; expensive dining; hectic public areas. [$] *Rooms from: $425 ✉ 1500 Orange Ave., Coronado ☎ 800/468–3533, 619/435–6611 🌐 www.hoteldel.com ⇨ 757 rooms 🍴 No meals ✣ D6.*

$$$$ RESORT FAMILY **Loews Coronado Bay Resort.** You can park your boat at the 80-slip marina of this romantic retreat set on a secluded 15-acre peninsula on the Silver Strand. **Pros:** great restaurants; lots of activities; all rooms have furnished balconies with water views. **Cons:** far from anything;

confusing layout. $ *Rooms from: $349* ✉ *4000 Coronado Bay Rd., Coronado* ☎ *619/424–4000, 800/815–6397* ⊕ *www.loewshotels.com/ CoronadoBay* ➣ *439 rooms* ⏀ *No meals* ✛ *E6.*

$$$$ ☷ **1906 Lodge at Coronado Beach.** Smaller but no less luxurious than
B&B/INN   the sprawling beach resorts of Coronado, this lodge—whose name
Fodor's Choice   alludes to the main building's former life as a boardinghouse built in
★   1906—welcomes couples for romantic retreats two blocks from the
ocean. **Pros:** most suites feature Jacuzzi tubs, fireplaces, and porches;
historic property; free underground parking. **Cons:** too quiet for families; no pool. $ *Rooms from: $329* ✉ *1060 Adella Ave., Coronado*
☎ *619/437–1900, 866/435–1906* ⊕ *www.1906lodge.com* ➣ *17 rooms*
⏀ *Breakfast* ✛ *D6.*

NIGHTLIFE

A couple of decades ago, San Diego scraped by on its superb daytime offerings. Those sleepy-after-dark days are over; San Diego now sizzles when the sun goes down. Of particular interest to beer lovers, the city has become internationally acclaimed for dozens of breweries, beer pubs, and festivals.

The Gaslamp Quarter is still one of the most popular areas to go for a night on the town. Named for actual gaslights that once provided illumination along its once-seedy streets (it housed a number of gambling halls and brothels), the neighborhood bears only a trace of its debauched roots. Between the Gaslamp and nearby East Village, Downtown San Diego mostly comprises chic nightclubs, tourist-heavy pubs, and a handful of live music venues. Even most of the hotels Downtown have a street-level or rooftop bar—so plan on making it a late night if that's where you intend to bunk. On weekends, parking can be tricky; most lots run about $20, and though there is metered parking (free after 6 pm and all day Sunday), motorists don't give up those coveted spots so easily. Some restaurants and clubs offer valet, though that can get pricey.

Hillcrest is a popular area for LGBT nightlife and culture, whereas just a little bit east of Hillcrest, ever-expanding North Park features a diverse range of bars and lounges that cater to a twenty- and thirtysomething crowd, bolstering its reputation as the city's hipster capital. Nearby Normal Heights is a slightly less pretentious alternative, though whichever of these neighborhoods strikes your fancy, a cab from Downtown will run about the same price: $15.

Nightlife along the beaches is more of a mixed bag. Where the scene in Pacific Beach might feel like every week is Spring Break, La Jolla veers toward being more cost-prohibitive. And although Point Loma is often seen as a sleeper neighborhood in terms of nightlife, it's coming into its own with some select destinations.

If your drink involves caffeine and not alcohol, there's no shortage of coffeehouses in San Diego, and some of the better ones in Hillcrest and North Park stay open past midnight. Many of them also serve beer and wine, if the caffeine buzz isn't enough.

DOWNTOWN

GASLAMP QUARTER

BARS

Fluxx. Arguably the hottest club in the Gaslamp, this Vegas-style, multitheme space is packed to the gills on weekends with pretty people dancing to house and electro music and dropping major cash at the bar. ■TIP→ Get here early for a lower cover and to avoid the epic lines that snake around the block. ✉ *500 4th Ave., Gaslamp Quarter* ☎ *619/232–8100* ⊕ *www.fluxxsd.com.*

FodorsChoice **Rooftop600 @Andaz.** At this rooftop bar and lounge atop the Andaz
★ hotel, a fashionable crowd sips cocktails poolside while gazing at gorgeous views of the city. Thursday through Saturday, the scene heats up with a DJ spinning dance music, while velvet ropes and VIP bottle service please the A-listers (like Prince Harry) in the crowd. ✉ *600 F St., Gaslamp Quarter* ☎ *619/814–2060* ⊕ *sandiego.andaz.hyatt.com.*

MUSIC CLUBS

House of Blues. The local branch of the renowned music chain is decorated floor to ceiling with colorful folk art and features three different areas to hear music. There's something going on here just about every night of the week, and the gospel brunch on select Sundays is one of the most praiseworthy events in town. Can we get a hallelujah? ✉ *1055 5th Ave., Gaslamp Quarter* ☎ *619/299–2583* ⊕ *www.houseofblues.com.*

EAST VILLAGE

BARS

Cat Eye Club. Separated from the hectic hustle of East Village by just a short and dimly lit foyer, Cat Eye Club might as well be in an entirely different world. More specifically, it's a trip back to the 1960s, with mid-century modern furnishings, a Wurlitzer jukebox and Rat Pack flicks on regular rotation. Their menu of tiki cocktails ranges from simple sips to punch bowls, or for those who prefer their drinks flashier, the Cradle of Life, garnished with a flaming lime wedge. ✉ *370 7th Ave., East Village* ⊕ *cateyeclubsd.com.*

LITTLE ITALY

BARS

FodorsChoice **The Waterfront Bar & Grill.** It isn't really *on* the waterfront, but San Diego's
★ oldest bar was once the hangout of Italian fishermen. Most of the collars are now white, and patrons enjoy an excellent selection of beers, along with chili, burgers, fish-and-chips, and other great-tasting grub, including fish tacos. Get here early, as there's almost always a crowd. ✉ *2044 Kettner Blvd., Little Italy* ☎ *619/232–9656* ⊕ *www.waterfrontbarandgrill.com.*

OLD TOWN AND UPTOWN

HILLCREST

GAY NIGHTLIFE

FodorsChoice **Baja Betty's.** Although it draws plenty of gay customers, the festive and
★ friendly atmosphere is popular with just about everyone in the Hillcrest area (and their pets are welcome, too). The bar staff stocks more than

100 brands of tequila and mixes plenty of fancy cocktails. ⊠ *1421 University Ave., Hillcrest* ☎ *619/269–8510* ⊕ *www.bajabettyssd.com.*

Urban Mo's Bar and Grill. Cowboys gather for line dancing and two-stepping on the wooden dance floor—but be forewarned, yee-hawers, it can get pretty wild on Western nights. There are also Latin, hip-hop, and drag revues but the real allure is in the creative drinks ("Gone Fishing"—served in a fishbowl, for example) and the breezy patio where love (or something like it) is usually in the air. ⊠ *308 University Ave., Hillcrest* ☎ *619/491–0400* ⊕ *www.urbanmos.com.*

MISSION HILLS

BARS

Fodor'sChoice **Starlite.** Bar-goers are dazzled by Starlite's award-winning interior ★ design, which includes rock walls, luxe leather booths, and a massive mirror-mounted chandelier. A hexagonal wood-plank entryway leads to a sunken white bar, where sexy tattooed guys and girls mix creative cocktails, such as the signature Starlite Mule, served in a copper mug. An iPod plays eclectic playlists ranging from old-timey jazz and blues to obscure vintage rock (and DJs are on hand on certain evenings). During warmer months, procuring a spot on the outside wood-decked patio is an art form. ⊠ *3175 India St., Mission Hills* ☎ *619/358–9766* ⊕ *www.starlitesandiego.com.*

NORTH PARK

BARS

Fodor'sChoice **Seven Grand.** This whiskey lounge is a swanky addition to an already ★ thriving North Park nightlife scene and a welcome alternative to the neighboring dives and dance clubs. Live jazz, a tranquil atmosphere, and a bourbon-loving craft cocktail list keep locals flocking. ⊠ *3054 University Ave., North Park* ☎ *619/269–8820* ⊕ *213hospitality.com.*

BREWPUBS

Tiger! Tiger! A communal vibe prevails at this wood, metal, and brick gastropub, where patrons sit at picnic tables to schmooze and sip from one of the dozens of carefully selected craft and microbrews on tap. ⊠ *3025 El Cajon Blvd., North Park* ☎ *619/487–0401* ⊕ *www.tiger-tigertavern.com.*

MISSION BAY AND THE BEACHES

PACIFIC BEACH

BARS

JRDN. This contemporary lounge (pronounced "Jordan") occupies the ground floor of Pacific Beach's chicest boutique hotel, Tower23, and offers a more sophisticated vibe in what is a very party-happy neighborhood. Sleek walls of windows and an expansive patio overlook the boardwalk. ⊠ *723 Felspar St., Pacific Beach* ☎ *858/270–2323* ⊕ *www.t23hotel.com.*

CLOSE UP

San Diego On Tap

The secret is out: San Diego is the nation's best beer town. In addition to more than 60 local breweries, San Diego has a stretch of beer-nerd heaven nicknamed the Belgian Corridor (30th Street in North/South Park). You can find all styles of beer in San Diego, from the meek to the mighty, but many local brewers contend that the specialty is the big, bold Double IPA (also called an Imperial IPA). It's an India Pale Ale with attitude—and lots of hops. Nearly every local brewery has its own version.

Bars with the best microbrew selection: Blind Lady Ale House, Hamilton's Tavern, Live Wire, O'Brien's, Toronado.

Best fests: Want one location and a seemingly endless supply of beer? Try the San Diego Festival of Beers (September ⊕ *www.sdbeerfest.org*), San Diego Beer Week (November ⊕ *www.sdbw.org*), and the Strong Ale Fest (December). Find more listings at ⊕ *www.sandiegobrewersguild.org*.

Best way to sample it all: Sign up for Brewery Tours of San Diego (⊕ *www.brewerytoursofsandiego.com*) to sample the best craft beers without a second thought about directions or designated drivers.

SAN DIEGO'S BEST BREWERIES
You can also head to the source, where beer is brewed. These are outside the city center, but worth the trek for beer aficionados.

Alpine Brewing Co. Well worth the mountain drive, this family-owned operation may be itty-bitty, but it's also a big champ: brewmaster Pat McIlhenney, a former fire captain, has won national and international kudos for his hopped-up creations and took the title of the fifth-best brewery in the nation from *Beer Advocate.* Tasters are only a buck each, or fill a growler, which holds a half gallon, for future imbibing. If they're on tap, don't pass up Duet, Pure Hoppiness, or Exponential Hoppiness. Alpine recently opened a pub a few doors down where you can taste flights of their various beers. ⊠ *2363 Alpine Blvd., Alpine* ☎ *619/445–2337* ⊕ *www. alpinebeerco.com.*

Ballast Point Brewing Co. Until recently, you had to head to the Miramar/Scripps Ranch area for a tasting at Ballast Point, but now there's a local taproom in Little Italy (2215 India Street). There are also plenty of opportunities to sample the beers at local pubs—the Sculpin IPA is outstanding, and for more adventurous drinkers, the much hotter Habanero sculpin is brewed with Habanero peppers. ⊠ *10051 Old Grove Rd., Scripps Ranch* ☎ *858/695– 2739* ⊕ *www.ballastpoint.com.*

Stone Brewing World Gardens and Bistro. The Big Daddy of San Diego craft brewing was founded by a couple of basement beer tinkerers in 1996; the company now exports its aggressively hoppy beers—instantly identifiable by their leering gargoyle labels—across the nation. Stone's monumental HQ is out of the way, but worth a visit for its tours ($3 includes a souvenir glass), vast on-tap selection (not just Stone beers), and hard-to-beat bistro eats. ⊠ *1999 Citracado Pkwy., Escondido* ☎ *760/294–7899* ⊕ *www.stonebrewing.com.*

3

PERFORMING ARTS

DANCE

California Ballet Company. The company performs high-quality contemporary and classical works September–May at the **Civic Theatre.** The *Nutcracker* is staged annually around the holiday season. ⊠ *San Diego Civic Theatre, 1100 3rd Ave., Downtown* ☎ *619/560–5676* ⊕ *www. californiaballet.org.*

MUSIC

Fodor'sChoice ★ **Copley Symphony Hall.** The great acoustics here are surpassed only by the incredible Spanish baroque interior. Not just the home of the San Diego Symphony Orchestra, the renovated 2,200-seat 1920s-era theater has also hosted major stars like Elvis Costello, Leonard Cohen, and Sting. ⊠ *750 B St., Downtown* ☎ *619/235–0804* ⊕ *www.sandiegosymphony.org.*

San Diego Symphony Orchestra. The orchestra's events include classical concerts and summer and winter pops, nearly all of them at Copley Symphony Hall. The outdoor Summer Pops series is held on the Embarcadero, on North Harbor Drive beyond the convention center. ⊠ *Box office, 750 B St., Downtown* ☎ *619/235–0804* ⊕ *www.sandiegosymphony.org.*

THEATER

Fodor'sChoice ★ **La Jolla Playhouse.** Under the artistic direction of Christopher Ashley, the playhouse presents exciting and innovative plays and musicals on three stages. Many Broadway shows—among them *Memphis, Tommy,* and *Jersey Boys*—have previewed here before their East Coast premieres. Its Without Walls program also ensures that the productions aren't limited to the playhouse, having put on site-specific shows in places like outdoor art spaces, cars, and even the ocean. ⊠ *University of California at San Diego, 2910 La Jolla Village Dr., La Jolla* ☎ *858/550–1010* ⊕ *www.lajollaplayhouse.org.*

Fodor'sChoice ★ **The Old Globe.** This complex, comprising the Sheryl and Harvey White Theatre, the Lowell Davies Festival Theatre, and the Old Globe Theatre, offers some of the finest theatrical productions in Southern California. Theater classics such as *The Full Monty* and *Dirty Rotten Scoundrels,* both of which went on to Broadway, premiered on these famed stages. The Old Globe presents the family-friendly *How the Grinch Stole Christmas* around the holidays, as well as a renowned summer Shakespeare Festival with three to four plays in repertory. ⊠ *1363 Old Globe Way, Balboa Park* ☎ *619/234–5623* ⊕ *www.oldglobe.org.*

SPORTS AND THE OUTDOORS

BASEBALL

Fodor's Choice ★ Long a favorite spectator sport in San Diego, where games are rarely rained out, baseball gained even more popularity in 2004 with the opening of PETCO Park, a stunning 42,000-seat facility in the heart of Downtown.

Fodor's Choice ★ **San Diego Padres.** From April into October, the Padres slug it out for bragging rights in the National League West. Home games are played at PETCO Park. Tickets are usually available on game day, but rival matchups against the Los Angeles Dodgers and the San Francisco Giants often sell out quickly. For an inexpensive day at the ballpark, go for "The Park at the Park" tickets ($10 and up, depending on demand; available for purchase at the park only) and have a picnic on the grass while watching the game on one of several giant-screen TVs. You also get access to the full concourse. Head to the fifth floor to find a Stone Brewing outdoor beer garden with sweeping views of Downtown and the San Diego Bay. ⊠ *100 Park Blvd., East Village* ☎ *619/795–5000, 877/374–2784* ⊕ *sandiego.padres.mlb.com* ⊠ *From $10.*

BIKING

San Diego offers bountiful opportunities for bikers, from casual boardwalk cruises to strenuous rides into the hills. The mild climate makes biking in San Diego a year-round delight. Bike culture is respected here, and visitors are often impressed with the miles of designated bike lanes running alongside city streets and coastal roads throughout the county.

Cheap Rentals. One block from the boardwalk, this place has good daily and weekly prices for surfboards, paddleboards, kayaks, snorkel gear, skateboards, ice chests, umbrellas, chairs, and bike rentals, including beach cruisers, tandems, hybrids, and two-wheeled baby carriers. Kids bikes are also available. Demand is high during the busy season (May through September), so call to reserve equipment ahead of time. ⊠ *3689 Mission Blvd., Mission Beach* ☎ *858/488–9070, 800/941–7761* ⊕ *www.cheap-rentals.com* ⊠ *From $12.*

Holland's Bicycles. This is a great bike rental source on Coronado Island, so you can ride the Silver Strand Bike Path on an electric bike, beach cruiser, road bike, or tandem. ⊠ *977 Orange Ave., Coronado* ☎ *619/435–3153* ⊕ *www.hollandsbicycles.com* ⊠ *From $25.*

Route S21 (*Coast Highway 101*). On many summer days, Route S21, aka Old Highway 101, from La Jolla to Oceanside looks like a freeway for cyclists. About 24 miles long, it's easily the most popular and scenic bike route around, never straying far from the beach. Although the terrain is fairly easy, the long, steep Torrey Pines grade is famous for weeding out the weak. Another Darwinian challenge is dodging slow-moving pedestrians and cars pulling over to park in towns like Encinitas and Del Mar. ⊠ *La Jolla.*

DIVING

Ocean Enterprises Scuba Diving. Stop in for everything you need to plan a diving adventure, including equipment, advice, and instruction. ⊠ *7710 Balboa Ave., Suite 101, Clairemont* ☎ *858/565–6054* ⊕ *www.ocean-enterprises.com.*

Scuba San Diego. This center is well regarded for its top-notch instruction and certification programs, as well as for guided dive tours. Trips include dives to kelp reefs in La Jolla Cove, and night diving at La Jolla Canyon. They also have snorkeling tours to La Jolla's Sea Caves, plus evening kayaking tours under the firework-lit sky on Mission Bay (in summer only). ⊠ *San Diego Hilton Hotel, 1775 E. Mission Bay Dr., Mission Bay* ☎ *619/260–1880* ⊕ *www.scubasandiego.com* 🎫 *From $70.*

FISHING

Fisherman's Landing. You can book space on a fleet of luxury vessels from 57 feet to 124 feet long and embark on multiday trips in search of yellowfin tuna, yellowtail, and other deep-water fish. Half-day fishing and whale-watching trips are also available. ⊠ *2838 Garrison St., Point Loma* ☎ *619/221–8500* ⊕ *www.fishermanslanding.com* 🎫 *From $45.*

H&M Landing. Join one of the West's oldest sportfishing companies for year-round fishing trips plus whale-watching excursions from December through March. ⊠ *2803 Emerson St., Point Loma* ☎ *619/222–1144* ⊕ *www.hmlanding.com* 🎫 *From $24.*

GOLF

Balboa Park Golf Course. San Diego's oldest public course is 5 minutes from Downtown in the heart of Balboa Park and offers impressive views of the city and the bay. The course includes a 9-hole executive course and a challenging 18-hole course that weaves among the park's canyons with some tricky drop-offs. Finish off your round with biscuits and gravy and a mimosa at Tobey's 19th Hole Cafe, a greasy spoon that's also Balboa Park's best-kept secret. ⊠ *2600 Golf Course Dr., Balboa Park* ☎ *619/235–1184* ⊕ *www.sandiego.gov* 🎫 *$40 weekdays, $50 weekends* 🏌 *27 holes, 6339 yards, par 72.*

Fodor'sChoice **Coronado Municipal Golf Course.** Spectacular views of Downtown San
★ Diego and the Coronado Bridge as well as affordable prices make this public course one of the busiest in the world. Bordered by the bay, the trick is to keep your ball out of the water. Wind can add some difficulty, but otherwise this is a leisurely course and a good one to walk. It's difficult to get on unless you reserve a tee time 3 to 14 days in advance. The course's Bayside Grill restaurant is well-known for its Thursday and Sunday night prime rib dinner. Reservations are recommended. ⊠ *2000 Visalia Row, Coronado* ☎ *619/522–6590* ⊕ *www. golfcoronado.com* 🎫 *$37 weekdays, $42 weekends* 🏌 *18 holes, 6590 yards, par 72.*

Omni La Costa Resort and Spa. One of the premier golf resorts in Southern California, La Costa over the years has hosted many of the best professional golfers in the world as well as prominent politicians and Hollywood celebrities. The Dick Wilson–designed Champions course has Bermuda fairways and bunkers. The more spacious Legends Course received a complete makeover in 2013 including a redesign of all 18 greens, as well as new bunkers and turfgrass plantings. After a day on the links you can wind down with a massage, steam bath, and dinner at the resort. ⊠ *2100 Costa del Mar Rd., Carlsbad* ☎ *760/438–9111* ⊕ *www. omnihotels.com* 🖃 *$210 Mon.–Thurs., $230 Fri.–Sun.* ⅄ *Champions: 18 holes, 6747 yards, par 72. Legends: 18 holes, 6587 yards, par 72.*

Fodor'sChoice **Park Hyatt Aviara Golf Club.** This golf course consistently ranks as one
★ of the best in California and is the only course in San Diego designed by Arnold Palmer. The course features gently rolling hills dotted with native wildflowers and views of the protected adjacent Batiquitos Lagoon and the Pacific Ocean. There are plenty of bunkers and water features for those looking for a challenge, and the golf carts, included in the cost, come fitted with GPS systems that tell you the distance to the pin. The two-story Spanish colonial clubhouse has full-size lockers, lounge areas, a bar, and a steak house. ⊠ *7447 Batiquitos Dr., Carlsbad* ☎ *760/603–6900* ⊕ *www.golfaviara.com* 🖃 *$235 Mon.– Thurs., $255 Fri.–Sun.* ⅄ *18 holes, 7007 yards, par 72.*

Fodor'sChoice **Torrey Pines Golf Course.** Due to its clifftop location overlooking the
★ Pacific and its classic championship holes, Torrey Pines is one of the best public golf courses in the United States. The course was the site of the 2008 U.S. Open and has been the home of the Farmers Insurance Open since 1968. The par-72 South Course, redesigned by Rees Jones in 2001, receives rave reviews from touring pros; it is longer, more challenging, and more expensive than the North Course. Tee times may be booked from 8 to 90 days in advance (858/522–1662) and are subject to an advance booking fee ($45). ⊠ *11480 N. Torrey Pines Rd., La Jolla* ☎ *858/452–3226, 800/985–4653* ⊕ *www.torreypinesgolfcourse. com* 🖃 *South: $192 weekdays, $240 weekends. North: $105 weekdays, $131 weekends; $40 for golf cart* ⅄ *South: 18 holes, 7227 yards, par 72. North: 18 holes, 6874 yards, par 72.*

HIKING AND NATURE TRAILS

Fodor'sChoice **Bayside Trail at Cabrillo National Monument.** Driving here is a treat in itself,
★ as a vast view of the Pacific unfolds before you. The view is equally enjoyable on Bayside Trail (2 miles round-trip), which is home to the same coastal sagebrush that Juan Rodriguez Cabrillo saw when he first discovered the California coast in the 16th century. After the hike, you can explore nearby tide pools, the monument statue, and the Old Point Loma Lighthouse. Don't worry if you don't see everything on your first visit; your entrance receipt ($10 per car) is good for 7 days. ⊠ *1800 Cabrillo Memorial Dr., Point Loma* ✛ *From I–5, take Rosecrans exit and turn right on Canon St. then left on Catalina Blvd. (also known as Cabrillo Memorial Dr.); follow until end* ☎ *619/557–5450* ⊕ *www. nps.gov/cabr* 🖃 *Parking $10.*

Torrey Pines State Reserve. Hikers and runners will appreciate this park's many winning features: switch-back trails that descend to the sea, an unparalleled view of the Pacific, and a chance to see the Torrey pine tree, one of the rarest pine breeds in the United States. The reserve hosts guided nature walks as well. All food is prohibited at the reserve, so save the picnic until you reach the beach below. Parking is $12–$15, depending on day and season. ⊠ *12600 N. Torrey Pines Rd., La Jolla* ✢ *Exit I–5 at Carmel Valley Rd. and head west toward Coast Hwy. 101 until you reach N. Torrey Pines Rd.; turn left.* ☎ *858/755–2063* ⊕ *www.torreypines.org* ⊠ *Parking $12–$15.*

KAYAKING, SAILING, AND BOATING

Hike Bike Kayak Adventures. This shop offers several kayak tours, from easy excursions in Mission Bay that are well suited to families and beginners to more advanced jaunts. Tours include kayaking the caves off La Jolla coast, whale-watching (from a safe distance) December through March, moonlight and sunset trips, and a cruise into the bay to see SeaWorld's impressive fireworks shows over the water in the summer. Tours last two to three hours and require a minimum of four people. ⊠ *2222 Ave. de la Playa, La Jolla* ☎ *858/551–9510* ⊕ *www. hikebikekayak.com* ⊠ *From $65.*

SURFING

If you're a beginner, consider paddling in the waves off Mission Beach, Pacific Beach, Tourmaline Surfing Park, La Jolla Shores, Del Mar, or Oceanside. More experienced surfers usually head for Sunset Cliffs, La Jolla reef breaks, Black's Beach, or Swami's in Encinitas. All necessary equipment is included in the cost of all surfing schools. Beach-area Y's offer surf lessons and surf camp in the summer months and during spring break.

Cheap Rentals. Many local surf shops rent both surf and bodyboards. Cheap Rentals is right off the boardwalk, just steps from the waves. It rents wet suits, bodyboards, and skimboards in addition to soft surfboards and long and short fiberglass rides. It also has good hourly to weekly pricing on paddleboards and accessories. ⊠ *3689 Mission Blvd., Mission Beach* ☎ *858/488–9070, 800/941–7761* ⊕ *www.cheap-rentals.com* ⊠ *From $5/hour.*

SHOPPING

San Diego's retail landscape has changed radically in recent years with the opening of several new shopping centers—some in historic buildings—that are focused more on locally owned boutiques than national retailers. Where once the Gaslamp was the place to go for urban apparel and unique home decor, many independently owned boutiques have decided to set up shop in the charming neighborhoods east of Balboa Park known as North Park and South Park. Although Downtown is still thriving, any shopping trip to San Diego should include venturing out to the city's diverse and vibrant neighborhoods. Not far from Downtown, Little Italy is the place to find contemporary art, modern furniture, and home accessories.

Old Town is a must for pottery, ceramics, jewelry, and handcrafted baskets. Uptown is known for its mélange of funky bookstores, offbeat gift shops, and nostalgic collectibles and vintage stores. The beach towns offer the best swimwear and sandals. La Jolla's chic boutiques offer a more intimate shopping experience, along with some of the classiest clothes, jewelry, and shoes in the county. The new La Plaza La Jolla is an open-air shopping center with boutiques and galleries in a Spanish-style building overlooking the cove. Point Loma's Liberty Station shopping area in the former Naval Training Center has art galleries, restaurants, and home stores. Trendsetters will have no trouble finding must-have handbags and designer apparel at the world-class Fashion Valley mall in Mission Valley, a haven for luxury brands such as Hermès, Gucci, and Jimmy Choo.

Enjoy near-perfect weather year-round as you explore shops along the scenic waterfront. The Headquarters at Seaport is a new open-air shopping and dining center in the city's former Police Headquarters building. Here there are some big names, but mostly locally owned boutiques selling everything from gourmet cheese to coastal-inspired home accessories. Just next door, Seaport Village is still the place to go for trinkets and souvenirs. If you don't discover what you're looking for in the boutiques, head to Westfield Horton Plaza, the Downtown mall with more than 120 stores. The sprawling mall completed a major restoration project in 2016 to include a new public plaza, amphitheater, and fountains.

Most malls have free parking in a lot or garage, and parking is not usually a problem. Some of the shops in the Gaslamp Quarter offer validated parking or valet parking.

OLD TOWN AND UPTOWN

OLD TOWN
MARKET
Fodor'sChoice **Bazaar del Mundo Shops.** With a Mexican villa theme, the Bazaar hosts
★ riotously colorful gift shops such as **Ariana,** for ethnic and artsy women's fashions; **Artes de Mexico,** which sells handmade Latin American crafts and Guatemalan weavings; and **The Gallery,** which carries handmade jewelry, Native American crafts, collectible glass, and original silk-screen prints. The **Laurel Burch Gallerita** carries the complete collection of its namesake artist's signature jewelry, accessories, and totes. ✉ *4133 Taylor St., at Juan St., Old Town* ☎ *619/296–3161* ⊕ *www. bazaardelmundo.com.*

MISSION VALLEY
MALL
Fodor'sChoice **Fashion Valley.** More than 18 million shoppers visit Fashion Valley
★ each year. That's more than the combined attendance of SeaWorld San Diego, LEGOLAND California, the San Diego Padres, the San

Diego Chargers, and the San Diego Zoo. San Diego's best and most upscale mall has a contemporary Mission theme, lush landscaping, and more than 200 shops and restaurants. Acclaimed retailers like Nordstrom, Neiman Marcus, Bloomingdale's, and Tiffany & Co. are here, along with boutiques from fashion darlings like Michael Kors, Jimmy Choo, Tory Burch, and James Perse. H&M is a favorite of fashionistas in search of edgy and affordable styles. Free wireless Internet service is available throughout the mall. Select "Simon WiFi" from any Wi-Fi–enabled device to log onto the network. ■TIP➔ If you're visiting from out of state, are a member of the military, or have a AAA membership, you can pick up a complimentary Style Pass at Simon Guest Services (located on the lower level beneath AMC Theaters near Banana Republic), which can get you savings at more than 70 of Fashion Valley's stores and restaurants. ⊠ *7007 Friars Rd., Mission Valley* 🕾 *619/688–9113* ⊕ *www.simon.com/mall/fashion-valley.*

NORTH PARK

CLOTHING AND ACCESSORIES

Fodor's Choice ★ **Aloha Sunday Supply Co.** This carefully curated boutique with high ceilings and blonde-wood accents carries no Billabong or Quiksilver, but make no mistake, this is a surf shop. The store sells only handcrafted pieces like Matuse wet suits, Thorogood leather boots, and the store's own brand of tailored men's clothing designed by co-owner and former pro surfer Kahana Kalama. ⊠ *3039 University Ave., North Park* 🕾 *619/269–9838* ⊕ *www.alohasunday.com.*

CORONADO

SHOPPING CENTER

Fodor's Choice ★ **Hotel Del Coronado.** At the gift shops within the peninsula's main historic attraction, you can purchase sportswear, designer handbags, jewelry, and antiques. **Babcock & Story Emporium** carries an amazing selection of home decor items, garden accessories, and classy gifts. **Blue Octopus** is a children's store featuring creative toys, gifts, and apparel. **Spreckels Sweets & Treats** offers old-time candies, freshly made fudge, and decadent truffles. **Kate's** has designer fashions and accessories, while **Brady's for Men,** with its shirts and sport coats, caters to well-dressed men. **Crown Jewels Coronado** features fine jewelry, some inspired by the sea. ⊠ *1500 Orange Ave., Coronado* 🕾 *619/435–6611* ⊕ *www.hoteldel.com/coronado-shopping.*

SIDE TRIPS TO NORTH COUNTY

A whole world of scenic grandeur, fascinating history, and scientific wonder lies just beyond San Diego's city limits. If you travel north along the coast, you'll encounter the great beaches for which the region is famous, along with some sophisticated towns holding fine restaurants, great galleries, and museums.

DEL MAR

23 miles north of Downtown San Diego on I–5, 9 miles north of La Jolla on Rte. S21.

Del Mar is best known for its quaint old section west of Interstate 5 marked with a glamorous racetrack, half-timber buildings, chic shops, tony restaurants, celebrity visitors, and wide beaches.

EXPLORING

FAMILY **Del Mar Fairgrounds.** The Spanish Mission–style fairground is the home of the **Del Mar Thoroughbred Club** (*www.dmtc.com*). Crooner Bing Crosby and his Hollywood buddies—Pat O'Brien, Gary Cooper, and Oliver Hardy, among others—organized the club in the 1930s, and the racing here (usually July through September, Wednesday through Monday, posttime 2 pm) remains a fashionable affair. Del Mar Fairgrounds hosts more than 100 different events each year, including the San Diego County Fair, the Del Mar National Horse Show in April and May, and the fall Scream Zone that's popular with local families. ⊠ *2260 Jimmy Durante Blvd.* ☎ *858/755–1161* ⊕ *www.delmarfairgrounds.com.*

WHERE TO EAT

$$$$ ✕ **Addison.** Indulge in the finer things in life at this AAA 5-Diamond
FRENCH restaurant by acclaimed chef William Bradley who serves up haute
Fodor's Choice French flavors in his 4- and 10-course prix-fixe dinners. Beyond the
★ swanky bar and wine cave is a sophisticated Tuscan-style dining room with intricately carved dark-woods, marble pillars, and arched windows draped in red velvet. **Known for:** decadent tasting menus; the ultimate fine-dining experience; impeccable service. Ⓢ *Average main: $110* ⊠ *5200 Grand Del Mar Way* ☎ *858/314–1900* ⊕ *www.addisondelmar.com* ☾ *Closed Sun. and Mon. No lunch.*

$$$ ✕ **Market Restaurant + Bar.** Carl Schroeder, one of California's hottest
AMERICAN young chefs, draws well-heeled foodies to his creative and locally
Fodor's Choice sourced California fare, much of it with an Asian influence from his
★ time in Japan. The menu changes regularly depending upon what's fresh, but might include carrot-ginger soup or crispy duck confit with candied kumquats. **Known for:** succulent short ribs; award-winning chef; seasonal menu. Ⓢ *Average main: $30* ⊠ *3702 Via de la Valle* ☎ *858/523–0007* ⊕ *www.marketdelmar.com* ☾ *No lunch.*

WHERE TO STAY

$$$$ ▦ **Fairmont Grand Del Mar.** Mind-blowing indulgence in serene surround-
RESORT ings, from drop-dead gorgeous guest accommodations to myriad out-
FAMILY door adventures, sets the opulent Mediterranean-style Fairmont Grand
Fodor's Choice Del Mar apart from any other luxury hotel in San Diego. **Pros:** ulti-
★ mate luxury; secluded, on-site golf course; enormous rooms; has most acclaimed fine-dining restaurant in San Diego. **Cons:** floor plan may be confusing; hotel is not on the beach. Ⓢ *Rooms from: $415* ⊠ *5200 Grand Del Mar Ct., San Diego* ☎ *858/314–2000, 855/314–2030* ⊕ *www.fairmont.com/san-diego* ⚐ *Greens fees $250; 18 holes, 7160 yards, par 72* ⟿ *249 rooms* ⦿ *No meals.*

CARLSBAD

6 miles north of Encinitas on Rte. S21, 36 miles north of Downtown San Diego on I–5.

Once-sleepy Carlsbad has long been popular with beachgoers and sun seekers. On a clear day in this village, you can take in sweeping ocean views that stretch from La Jolla to Oceanside by walking the 2-mile-long sea walk running between the Encina power plant and Pine Street. En route, you'll find several stairways leading to the beach and quite a few benches. Inland are LEGOLAND California and other attractions in its vicinity.

EXPLORING

FAMILY
Fodor'sChoice
★

Flower Fields at Carlsbad Ranch. The largest bulb production farm in Southern California has hillsides abloom here each spring, when thousands of Giant Tecolote ranunculus produce a stunning 50-acre display of color against the backdrop of the blue Pacific Ocean. Other knockouts include the rose gardens—with examples of every All-American Rose Selection award-winner since 1940—and a historical display of Paul Ecke poinsettias. Open to the public during this time, the farm offers family activities that include wagon rides, panning for gold, and a kids' playground. ⊠ *5704 Paseo del Norte, east of I–5* ☎ *760/431–0352* ⊕ *www.theflowerfields.com* ⊠ *$14* ⊘ *Closed mid-May–Feb.*

FAMILY
Fodor'sChoice
★

LEGOLAND California Resort. The centerpiece of a development that includes resort hotels, a designer discount shopping mall, an aquarium, and a water park, LEGOLAND has rides and diversions geared to kids ages 2 to 12. Fans of *Star Wars*, and building Legos in general, should head straight to *Star Wars* **Miniland,** where you can follow the exploits of Yoda, Princess Leia, Obi-Wan, Anakin, R2, Luke, and the denizens of the *Star Wars* films. There's also **Miniland U.S.A.,** which features a miniature, animated, interactive collection of U.S. icons that were constructed out of 34 million LEGO bricks! **LEGO Heartlake City,** features LEGO Friends and Elves, and you can test your ninja skills in **LEGO NINJAGO WORLD.**

If you're looking for rides, **NINJAGO The Ride** uses hand gesture technology to throw fireballs, shock waves, ice, and lightning to defeat villains in this interactive 4-D experience. Journey through ancient Egyptian ruins in a desert roadster, scoring points as you hit targets with a laser blaster at **Lost Kingdom Adventure.** Or, jump on the **Dragon Coaster,** an indoor/outdoor steel roller coaster that goes through a castle. Don't let the name frighten you—the motif is more humorous than scary. Kids ages 6 to 13 can stop by the **Driving School** to drive speed-controlled cars (not on rails) on a miniature road; driver's licenses are awarded after the course. Junior Driving School is the pint-size version for kids 3 to 5.

Bring bathing suits—there are lockers at the entrance and at Pirate Shores—if you plan to go to **Soak-N-Sail,** which has 60 interactive features, including a pirate shipwreck–theme area. You'll also need your swimsuit for **LEGOLAND Water Park,** where an additional $30 gives you access to slides, rides, rafts, and the CHIMA Water Park, as well as Surfer's Bay with competitive water raceways and a "spray ground" with water jets.

A LEGOLAND model worker puts the finishing touches on the San Francisco portion of Miniland U.S.A.

Be sure to try Granny's Apple Fries, Castle Burgers, and Pizza Mania for pizzas and salads. The Market near the entrance has excellent coffee, fresh fruit, and yogurt. The LEGOLAND Hotel is worth a visit even if you're not staying overnight. There are activities and a LEGO pit in the lobby that will entertain kids while parents recover with a cocktail. ■ **TIP→ The best value is one of the Hopper Tickets that give you one admission to LEGOLAND plus Sea Life Aquarium and/or the LEGOLAND Water Park for $119. These can be used on the same day or on different days. Purchase tickets online for discounted pricing. Go midweek to avoid the crowds.** ✉ *1 Legoland Dr.* ✣ *Exit I–5 at Cannon Rd. and follow signs east ¼ mile* ☎ *760/918–5346* 🌐 *www.legoland.com/california* 🎟 *LEGOLAND $95 adults, $89 children; parking $15; water park additional $30; hopper ticket $119* ⏲ *Closed Tues. and Wed. Sept.–Feb.*

WHERE TO EAT

$$ BARBECUE Fodor's Choice ★

🍴 **Campfire.** Paying tribute to community around the campfire, it's all about connecting here, both with the cool crowd and with the distinctive cocktail and dinner menus. Throughout the restaurant, subtle hints of the camping theme—canvas-backed booths, servers in flannels, leather menus branded with the Campfire log—are visible, but it's the food that will leave you setting up camp, as chefs work their magic behind glass walls grilling, roasting, and smoking almost every dish including the shrimp with pumpkin chili butter. **Known for:** smoky cocktails; wood-fired American fare. [$] *Average main: $23* ✉ *2725 State St.* ☎ *760/637–5121* 🌐 *www.thisiscampfire.com* ⏲ *No lunch Mon.*

WHERE TO STAY

$$$$ RESORT FAMILY **Omni La Costa Resort & Spa.** This chic Spanish colonial oasis on 400 tree-shaded acres has ample guest rooms, two golf courses, and is known for being family-friendly, with plenty of kids' activities (including a kids' club, a game room, eight swimming pools, three waterslides, and a water play zone). **Pros:** adult-only pool; excellent kids' facilities; spa under the stars. **Cons:** very spread out, making long walks necessary; lots of kids; $30 daily resort fee. [$] *Rooms from: $349* ✉ *2100 Costa del Mar Rd.* ☎ *760/438–9111, 800/439–9111* 🌐 *www.lacosta.com* 🛏 *748 rooms* 🍴 *No meals.*

$$$$ RESORT FAMILY Fodor's Choice ★ **Park Hyatt Aviara Resort.** This former Four Seasons hilltop retreat is one of the most luxurious hotels in San Diego, boasting an Arnold Palmer–designed golf course, a tennis club, two pools, six restaurants, and views overlooking Batiquitos Lagoon and the Pacific among it's 250 acres. **Pros:** unbeatable location; best golf course in San Diego; surrounding nature trails. **Cons:** $25 resort fee and $35 parking; expensive; breakfast not included. [$] *Rooms from: $309* ✉ *7100 Aviara Resort Dr.* ☎ *800/233–1234, 760/448–1234* 🌐 *www.parkhyattaviara.com* 🕒 *Greens fees $255; 18 holes, 7007 yards, par 72* 🛏 *327 rooms* 🍴 *No meals.*

ESCONDIDO

8 miles north of Rancho Bernardo on I–15, 31 miles northeast of Downtown San Diego on I–15.

Escondido and the lovely rolling hills around it were originally a land grant bestowed by the governor of Mexico on Juan Bautista Alvarado in 1843. For a century and a half, these hills supported citrus and avocado trees, plus large vineyards. The rural character of the area began to change when the San Diego Zoo established its Safari Park in the San Pasqual Valley east of town in the 1970s. Despite its urbanization, Escondido still supports several pristine open-space preserves that attract nature lovers, hikers, and mountain bikers. And, the area's abundant farms are slowly luring award-winning chefs who are taking the lead on opening farm-to-fork establishments.

EXPLORING

FAMILY Fodor's Choice ★ **San Diego Zoo Safari Park.** A branch of the San Diego Zoo, 35 miles to the north, the 1,800-acre preserve in the San Pasqual Valley is designed to protect endangered species from around the world. Exhibit areas have been carved out of the dry, dusty canyons and mesas to represent the animals' natural habitats in various parts of Africa and Asia.

The best way to see these preserves is to take the 25-minute, 2½-mile Africa tram safari, included with admission. More than 3,500 animals of more than 400 species roam or fly above the expansive grounds. Predators are separated from prey by deep moats, but only the elephants, tigers, lions, and cheetahs are kept in enclosures. Good viewpoints are at the Elephant Viewing Patio, African Plains Outlook, and Kilmia Point. The park's newest project is the **Tull Family Tiger Trail,** a Sumatran tiger habitat opened in 2014, where you can get face-to-face (with a glass between) with the gorgeous cats. The 5-acre exhibit

features a waterfall and swimming hole, and addresses poaching and other environmental threats to the species. ■TIP➜ In summer, when the park stays open late, the trip is especially enjoyable in the early evening, when the heat has subsided and the animals are active and feeding. When the tram travels through the park after dark, sodium-vapor lamps illuminate the active animals. Photographers with zoom lenses can get spectacular shots of zebras, gazelles, and rhinos.

For a more focused view of the park, you can take one of several other safaris that are well worth the additional charge. You can choose from several behind-the-scenes safaris, fly above it all via the zip-line safari, or get up close to giraffes and rhinos on a Caravan safari.

The park is as much a botanical garden as a zoo, serving as a "rescue center" for rare and endangered plants. Unique gardens include cacti and succulents from Baja California, a bonsai collection, a fuchsia display, native plants, and protea.

The gift shops are well worth a visit for their limited-edition items. There are lots of restaurants, snack bars, and some picnic areas. Rental lockers, strollers, and wheelchairs are available. You can also arrange to stay overnight in the park in summer on a Roar and Snore Sleepover ($140 and up, plus admission).

⊠ *15500 San Pasqual Valley Rd.* ⊹ *Take I–15 north to Via Rancho Pkwy. and follow signs for 6 miles* ☎ *760/747–8702* ⊕ *www.sdzsafaripark.org* ▧ *$52 one-day pass including Africa tram ride; multipark and multiday passes are available; special safaris are extra starting at $50 per person; parking $12.*

ORANGE COUNTY AND CATALINA ISLAND

with Disneyland and Knott's Berry Farm

WELCOME TO ORANGE COUNTY AND CATALINA ISLAND

TOP REASONS TO GO

★ **Disney Magic:** Walking down Main Street, U.S.A., with Cinderella's Castle straight ahead, you really will feel that you're in one of the happiest places on Earth.

★ **Beautiful Beaches:** Surf, swim, paddleboard, or just relax on one of the state's most breathtaking stretches of coastline. Keep in mind, the water may be colder than you expect.

★ **Island Getaways:** Just a short high-speed catamaran ride away, Catalina Island feels 1,000 miles from the mainland. Wander around charming Avalon, or explore the unspoiled beauty of the island's wild interior.

★ **The Fine Life:** Some of the state's wealthiest communities are in coastal Orange County, so spend at least part of your stay here experiencing how the other half lives.

★ **Family Fun:** Spend some quality time with the kids riding roller coasters, eating ice cream, fishing off ocean piers, and bodysurfing.

1 Disneyland Resort. Southern California's top family destination has expanded from the humble park of Walt Disney's vision to a megaresort with more attractions spilling over into Disney's California Adventure. But kids (and many adults) still consider it the happiest place on Earth.

2 Knott's Berry Farm. Amusement park lovers should check out this Buena Park attraction, with thrill rides, the *Peanuts* gang, and lots of fried chicken and boysenberry pie.

3 Coastal Orange County. OC's beach communities may not be quite as glamorous as seen on TV, but coastal spots like Huntington Beach, Newport Harbor, and Laguna Beach are perfect for chilling out in a beachfront hotel.

GETTING ORIENTED

Like Los Angeles, Orange County stretches over a large area, lacks a singular focal point, and has limited public transportation. You'll need a car and a sensible game plan to make the most of your visit. Anaheim, home of Disneyland, has every style of hotel imaginable, from family-friendly motels to luxurious high-rises. The coastal cities are more expensive but have cooler weather in summer, and marvelous beaches that you can enjoy throughout the year.

4 Catalina Island. This unspoiled island paradise—with its pocket-size town, Avalon, and large nature preserve—is just off the Orange County coast.

Updated
by Kathy A.
McDonald

With its tropical flowers and palm trees, the stretch of coast between Seal Beach and San Clemente is often called the California Riviera. Exclusive Newport Beach, artsy Laguna, and the surf town of Huntington Beach are the stars, but lesser-known gems on the glistening coast—such as Corona del Mar—are also worth visiting. Offshore, meanwhile, lies gorgeous Catalina Island, a terrific spot for diving, snorkeling, and hiking.

Few of the citrus groves that gave Orange County its name remain. This region south and east of Los Angeles is now ruled by tourism and high-tech business rather than agriculture. Despite a building boom that began in the 1990s, the area is still a place to find wilderness trails, canyons, greenbelts, and natural environs. Just offshore is a deep-water wilderness that's possible to explore via daily whale-watching excursions.

PLANNING

GETTING HERE AND AROUND
AIR TRAVEL
Orange County's main facility is John Wayne Airport Orange County (SNA), which is served by eight major domestic airlines and a commuter line. Long Beach Airport (LGB) is served by three airlines, including its major player, JetBlue. It's roughly 20 to 30 minutes by car from Anaheim.

Super Shuttle and Prime Time Airport Shuttle provide transportation from John Wayne and LAX to the Disneyland area of Anaheim. Round-trip fares average about $25 per person from John Wayne and $16 to $42 from LAX.

BUS TRAVEL

The Orange County Transportation Authority will take you virtually anywhere in the county, but it will take time; OCTA buses go from Knott's Berry Farm and Disneyland to Huntington Beach and Newport Beach. Bus 1 travels along the coast; buses 701 and 721 provide express service to Los Angeles.

Bus Contacts Orange County Transportation Authority. ☎ 714/636–7433 ⊕ www.octa.net.

CAR TRAVEL

The San Diego Freeway (Interstate 405), the coastal route, and the Santa Ana Freeway (Interstate 5), the inland route, run north–south through Orange County. South of Laguna, Interstate 405 merges into Interstate 5 (called the San Diego Freeway south from this point). A toll road, Highway 73, runs 15 miles from Newport Beach to San Juan Capistrano; it costs $6.65–$7.35 (lower rates are for weekends and off-peak hours) and is usually less jammed than the regular freeways. Keep in mind, however, there are no toll booths on OC toll roads; payment is required via a FastTrak transponder (available at AAA, Costco, and Albertson's). Some car-rental companies (like Avis) provide them for a daily service fee; Hertz does not. You can always pay the toll fee online (⊕ thetollroads.com). Do your best to avoid all Orange County freeways during rush hours (6–9 am and 3:30–6:30 pm). Highway 55 leads to Newport Beach. The Pacific Coast Highway (Highway 1) allows easy access to beach communities, and is the most scenic route, but expect it to be crowded, especially on summer weekends and holidays.

FERRY TRAVEL

There are two ferries that service Catalina Island; Catalina Express runs from Long Beach (about 90 minutes) and from Newport Beach (about 75 minutes). Reservations are strongly advised for summers and weekends. During the winter months, ferry crossings are not as frequent as in the summer high season.

TRAIN TRAVEL

Amtrak makes daily stops in Orange County at all major towns. Metrolink is a weekday commuter train that runs to and from Los Angeles and Orange County.

Train Contacts Amtrak. ☎ 800/872–7245 ⊕ www.amtrak.com. **Metrolink.** ☎ 800/371–5465 ⊕ www.metrolinktrains.com.

RESTAURANTS

Much like those of L.A., restaurants in Orange County are generally casual, and you'll rarely see suits and ties. Nevertheless, at top resort hotel dining rooms, many guests choose to dress up.

Of course, there's also a swath of casual places along the beachfronts— seafood takeout, taquerias, burger joints—that won't mind if you wear flip-flops. Reservations are recommended for the nicest restaurants.

Many places don't serve past 11 pm, and locals tend to eat early. Remember that according to California law, smoking is prohibited in all enclosed areas. *Restaurant reviews have been shortened. For full information, visit Fodors.com.*

HOTELS

Along the coast there are remarkable luxury resorts; if you can't afford a stay, pop in for the view at Laguna Beach's Montage or the always-welcoming Ritz-Carlton at Dana Point. For a taste of the OC glam life, have lunch overlooking the yachts of Newport Bay at the Balboa Bay Resort.

As a rule, lodging prices tend to rise the closer the hotels are to the beach. If you're looking for value, consider a hotel that is inland along the Interstate 405 freeway corridor.

In most cases, you can take advantage of some of the facilities of the high-end resorts, such as restaurants and spas, even if you aren't an overnight guest. *Hotel reviews have been shortened. For full information, visit Fodors.com.*

WHAT IT COSTS			
$	$$	$$$	$$$$
RESTAURANTS under $16	$16–$22	$23–$30	over $30
HOTELS under $120	$120–$175	$176–$250	over $250

Restaurant prices are the average cost of a main course at dinner or, if dinner is not served, at lunch, excluding sales tax. Hotel prices are the lowest cost of a standard double room in high season, excluding service charges and tax.

VISITOR INFORMATION

The Anaheim/Orange County Visitor and Convention Bureau on the main floor of the Anaheim Convention Center is an excellent resource for both leisure and business travelers.

The Orange County Tourism Council's website is also a useful source of information.

Information Visit Anaheim. ⊠ *Anaheim Convention Center, 800 W. Katella Ave., Anaheim* ☎ *714/765–8888* ⊕ *www.visitanaheim.org.* **Orange County Visitors Association.** ⊕ *www.visittheoc.com.*

DISNEYLAND RESORT

26 miles southeast of Los Angeles, via I-5.

The snowcapped Matterhorn, the centerpiece of the Magic Kingdom, punctuates the skyline of Anaheim. Since 1955, when Walt Disney chose this once-quiet farming community for the site of his first amusement park, Disneyland has attracted more than 616 million visitors and tens of thousands of workers, and Anaheim has been their host.

To understand the symbiotic relationship between Disneyland and Anaheim, you need only look at the $4.2 billion spent in a combined effort to revitalize Anaheim's tourist center and run-down areas, and to expand and renovate the Disney properties into what is known now as Disneyland Resort.

The resort is a sprawling complex that includes Disney's two amusement parks, three hotels, and Downtown Disney, a shopping, dining, and entertainment promenade. Anaheim's tourist center includes Angel Stadium of Anaheim, home of baseball's 2002 World Series Champions Los Angeles Angels of Anaheim; the Honda Center (formerly the Arrowhead Pond), which hosts concerts and the Anaheim Ducks hockey team; and the enormous Anaheim Convention Center.

GETTING HERE

Disney is about a 30-mile drive from either LAX or Downtown. From LAX, follow Sepulveda Boulevard south to the Interstate 105 freeway and drive east 16 miles to the Interstate 605 north exit. Exit at the Santa Ana Freeway (Interstate 5) and continue south for 12 miles to the Disneyland Drive exit. Follow signs to the resort. From Downtown, follow Interstate 5 south 28 miles and exit at Disneyland Drive. **Disneyland Resort Express** (☎ *800/828–6699* ⊕ *graylineanaheim.com*) offers daily nonstop bus service between LAX, John Wayne Airport, and Anaheim. Reservations are not required. The cost is $30 one-way from LAX, and $20 from John Wayne Airport.

SAVING TIME AND MONEY

If you plan to visit for more than a day, you can save money by buying two- three-, four-, and five-day Park Hopper tickets that grant same-day "hopping" privileges between Disneyland and Disney's California Adventure. You get a discount on the multiple-day passes if you buy online through the Disneyland website.

A one-day Park Hopper pass costs $155–$169 for anyone 10 or older, and $149–$163 for kids ages 3–9 depending on what day you go. Admission to either park (but not both) is $97–$124 or $89–$119 for kids ages 3–9; kids 2 and under are free.

In addition to tickets, parking is $18–$35 (unless your hotel has a shuttle or is within walking distance), and meals in the parks and at Downtown Disney range from $10 to $50 per person.

DISNEY'S TOP ATTRACTIONS

Indiana Jones: You're at the wheel for this thrilling ride through a cursed temple. Watch out for boulders!

Matterhorn Bobsleds: This ride is modeled after the Matterhorn mountain in Switzerland; beware the Abominable Snowman.

Pirates of the Caribbean: Watch buccaneers wreak havoc as you float along in a rowboat.

Space Mountain: This scary and thrilling roller coaster is mostly in the dark.

Star Tours 3D: Fly through a 3-D galaxy with your favorite Star Wars characters.

4

DISNEYLAND

FAMILY **Disneyland.** One of the biggest misconceptions people have about Dis-
Fodor's Choice neyland is that it's the same as Florida's mammoth Walt Disney World,
★ or one of the Disney parks overseas. But Disneyland, which opened in 1955 and is the only one of the parks to have been overseen by Walt

himself, has a genuine historic feel and occupies a unique place in the Disney legend. Expertly run, perfectly maintained, with polite and helpful staff ("cast members" in the Disney lexicon), the park has plenty that you won't find anywhere else—such as the Indiana Jones Adventure ride and Storybook Land, with its miniature replicas of animated Disney scenes from classics such as *Pinocchio* and *Alice in Wonderland*. Characters appear for autographs and photos throughout the day; times and places are posted at the entrances. Live shows, parades, strolling musicians, fireworks on weekends, and endless snack choices add to the carnival atmosphere. You can also meet some of the animated icons at one of the character meals served at the three Disney hotels (open to the public). Belongings can be stored in lockers just off Main Street; stroller rentals at the entrance gate are a convenient option for families with small tykes. ⊠ *1313 S. Disneyland Dr., between Ball Rd. and Katella Ave., Anaheim* ☎ *714/781–4636 guest information* ⊕ *www.disneyland. com* ⊡ *$95–$119; parking $18.*

PARK NEIGHBORHOODS
Neighborhoods for Disneyland are arranged in geographic order.

MAIN STREET, U.S.A.
Walt's hometown of Marceline, Missouri, was the inspiration behind this romanticized image of small-town America, circa 1900. The sidewalks are lined with a penny arcade, an endless supply of sugar confections, shops that sell everything from tradable pins to Disney-theme clothing, and a photo shop that offers souvenirs created via Disney's PhotoPass (on-site photographers capture memorable moments digitally—you can access in person or online). Main Street opens a half hour before the rest of the park, so it's a good place to explore if you're getting an early start to beat the crowds (it's also open an hour after the other attractions close, so you may want to save your shopping for the end of the day). **Main Street Cinema** offers a cool respite from the crowds, and six classic Disney animated shorts, including *Steamboat Willie*. There's rarely a wait to enter. Grab a cappuccino and fresh-made pastry at the Jolly Holiday bakery to jump-start your visit. Board the **Disneyland Railroad** here to save on walking; it tours all the lands plus offers unique views of Splash Mountain and the Grand Canyon and Primeval World dioramas.

NEW ORLEANS SQUARE
This mini–French Quarter, with narrow streets, hidden courtyards, and live street performances, is home to two iconic attractions and the Cajun-inspired Blue Bayou restaurant. **Pirates of the Caribbean** now features Jack Sparrow and the cursed Captain Barbossa, in a nod to the blockbuster movies of the same name, plus enhanced special effects and battle scenes (complete with cannonball explosions). Nearby, the **Haunted Mansion** continues to spook guests with its stretching room and "doombuggy" rides (plus there's now an expanded storyline for the beating-heart bride). Its *Nightmare Before Christmas* holiday overlay is an annual tradition. This is a good area to get a casual bite to eat; the clam chowder in sourdough bread bowls, sold at the French Market Restaurant and Royal Street Veranda, is a popular choice. Food carts offer everything from just-popped popcorn to churros, and even fresh fruit.

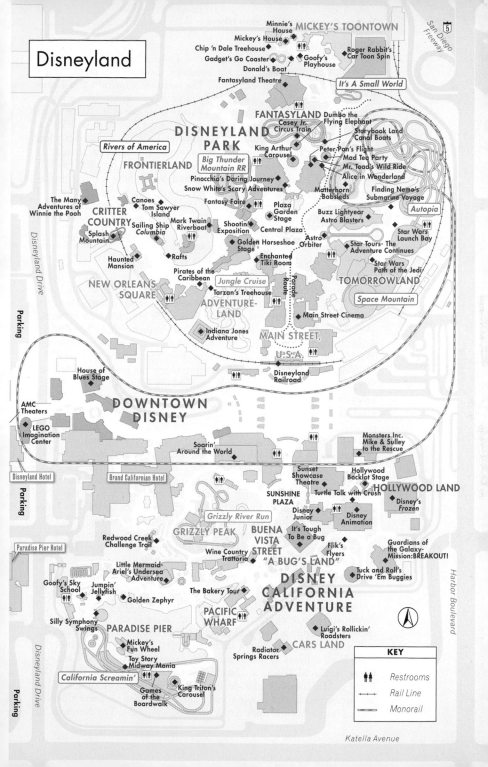

FRONTIERLAND

Between Adventureland and Fantasyland, Frontierland transports you to the Wild, Wild West with its rustic buildings, shooting gallery, mountain range, and foot-stompin' dance hall. The marquee attraction, **Big Thunder Mountain Railroad,** is a relatively tame roller-coaster ride (no steep descents) that takes the form of a runaway mine car as it rumbles past desert canyons and an old mining town. Tour the Rivers of America on the **Mark Twain Riverboat,** in the company of a grizzled old river pilot, or circumnavigate the globe on the **Sailing Ship Columbia,** though its operating hours are usually limited to weekends. From here you can raft over to Pirate's Lair on **Tom Sawyer Island,** which now features pirate-theme caves, treasure hunts, and music, along with plenty of caves and hills to climb and explore. If you don't mind tight seating, have a snack at the Golden Horseshoe Restaurant while enjoying the always-entertaining comedy and bluegrass show of Billy Hill and the Hillybillies. Children won't want to miss **Big Thunder Ranch,** a small petting zoo featuring pigs, goats, and cows, beyond Big Thunder Mountain.

CRITTER COUNTRY

Down-home country is the theme in this shady corner of the park, where Winnie the Pooh and Davy Crockett make their homes. Here you can find **Splash Mountain,** a classic flume ride accompanied by music and appearances by Brer Rabbit and other characters from *Song of the South*. Don't forget to check out your photo (the camera snaps close-ups of each car just before it plunges into the water) on the way out. The patio of the popular Hungry Bear Restaurant has great views of Tom Sawyer's Island and Davy Crockett's Explorer Canoes.

ADVENTURELAND

Modeled after the lands of Africa, Polynesia, and Arabia, this tiny tropical paradise is worth braving the crowds that flock here for the ambience and better-than-average food. Sing along with the animatronic birds and tiki gods in the **Enchanted Tiki Room,** sail the rivers of the world with joke-cracking skippers on **Jungle Cruise,** and climb the *Disneyodendron semperflorens* (aka always-blooming Disney tree) to **Tarzan's Treehouse,** where you can walk through scenes, some interactive, from the 1999 animated film. Cap off the visit with a wild Jeep ride at **Indiana Jones Adventure,** where the special effects and decipherable hieroglyphics distract you while you're waiting in line. The skewers (some vegetarian options available) at Bengal Barbecue and pineapple whip at Tiki Juice Bar are some of the best options for quick bites in the park.

FANTASYLAND

Sleeping Beauty Castle marks the entrance to Fantasyland, a visual wonderland of princesses, spinning teacups, flying elephants, and other classic storybook characters. Rides and shops (such as the princess-theme Once Upon a Time and Gepetto's Toys and Gifts) take precedence over restaurants in this area of the park, but outdoor carts sell everything from churros to turkey legs. Tots love the **King Arthur Carousel, Casey Jr. Circus Train,** and **Storybook Land Canal Boats.** This is also home to **Mr. Toad's Wild Ride, Peter Pan's Flight,** and **Pinocchio's Daring Journey**—classic, movie-theater-dark rides that immerse riders in Disney fairy tales and appeal to adults and kids alike. The Abominable

BEST TIPS FOR DISNEYLAND

■TIP➜ As of 2017, all visitors must pass through metal detectors, and bags are searched before entering the Disneyland Resort. Allot 10–15 extra minutes for passing through the security line.

Buy entry tickets in advance. Many nearby hotels sell park admission tickets; you can also buy them through the Disney website. If you book a package deal, such as those offered through AAA, tickets are included, too.

The lines at the ticket booths can take more than an hour on busy days, so you'll definitely save time by buying in advance, especially if you're committed to going on a certain day regardless of the weather.

Come midweek. Weekends, especially in summer, are a mob scene. Holidays are crowded, too. A rainy winter weekday is often the least crowded time to visit.

Plan your times to hit the most popular rides. Fodorites recommend getting to the park as early as possible and staying as late as possible. If you're at the park when the gates open, make a beeline for the top rides before the crowds reach a critical mass. Another good time is the late evening, when the hordes thin out, and, if planned right, during a parade or other show. Save the quieter attractions for midafternoon.

Use FASTPASS. These passes allow you to reserve your place in line at some of the most crowded attractions (only one at a time). Distribution machines are posted near the entrances of each attraction. Feed in your park admission ticket, and you'll receive a pass with a printed time frame (generally up to 1–1½ hours later) during which you can return to wait in a much shorter line.

Plan your meals to avoid peak mealtime crowds. Start the day with a big breakfast, so you won't be too hungry at noon, when restaurants and vendors get swarmed. Wait to have lunch until after 1 pm.

If you want to eat at the **Blue Bayou** in New Orleans Square, you can make a reservation up to six months in advance online. Another (cheaper) option is to bring your own food. There are areas just outside the park gates with picnic tables set up for this. It's always a good idea to bring water.

Check the daily events schedule online or at the park entrance. During parades, fireworks, and other special events, sections of the parks clog with crowds. This can work for you or against you. An event could make it difficult to get around a park—but if you plan ahead, you can take advantage of the distraction to hit popular rides.

Send the teens next door. Disneyland's newer sister park, California Adventure, features more intense rides suitable for older kids (Park Hopper passes include admission to both parks).

4

Snowman pops up on the **Matterhorn Bobsleds,** a roller coaster that twists and turns up and around on a made-to-scale model of the real Swiss mountain. Anchoring the east end of Fantasyland is **It's a Small World,** a smorgasbord of dancing animatronic dolls, cuckoo clock–covered walls, and variations of the song everyone knows, or soon *will* know, by heart. Beloved Disney characters like Ariel from *Under the Sea* are also part of the mix. Fantasy Faire is a fairy tale–style village that collects all the Disney princesses together. Each has her own reception nook in the Royal Hall. Condensed retellings of *Tangled* and *Beauty and the Beast* take place at the Royal Theatre.

MICKEY'S TOONTOWN

Geared toward small fries, this lopsided cartoonlike downtown, complete with cars and trolleys that invite exploring, is where Mickey, Donald, Goofy, and other classic Disney characters hang their hats. One of the most popular attractions is **Roger Rabbit's Car Toon Spin,** a twisting, turning cab ride through the Toontown of *Who Framed Roger Rabbit?* You can also walk through **Mickey's House** to meet and be photographed with the famous mouse, take a low-key ride on **Gadget's Go Coaster,** or bounce around the fenced-in playground in front of **Goofy's House.**

TOMORROWLAND

This popular section of the park continues to tinker with its future, adding and enhancing rides regularly. *Star Wars*–themed attractions can't be missed, like the immersive, 3-D **Star Tours – The Adventures Continue,** where you can join the Rebellion in a galaxy far, far away. **Finding Nemo's Submarine Voyage** updates the old Submarine Voyage ride with the exploits of Nemo, Dory, Marlin, and other characters from the Disney-Pixar film. Try to visit this popular ride early in the day if you can, and be prepared for a wait. The interactive **Buzz Lightyear Astro Blasters** lets you zap your neighbors with laser beams and compete for the highest score. Hurtle through the cosmos on **Space Mountain** or check out mainstays like the futuristic **Astro Orbiter** rockets, **Star Wars Launch Bay,** which showcases costumes, models, and props from the franchise, and **Star Wars, Path of the Jedi,** which catches viewers up on all the movies with a quick 12-minute film. Disneyland Monorail and Disneyland Railroad both have stations here. There's also a video arcade and dancing water fountain that makes a perfect playground for kids on hot summer days. The Jedi Training Academy spotlights future Luke Skywalkers in the crowd.

Besides the eight lands, the daily live-action shows and parades are always crowd-pleasers. Among these is **Fantasmic!** a musical, fireworks, and laser show in which Mickey and friends wage a spellbinding battle against Disneyland's darker characters. ■ **TIP➜ Arrive early to secure a good view; if there are two shows scheduled for the day, the second one tends to be less crowded. A fireworks display illuminates the sky weekends and most summer evenings.** Brochures with maps, available at the entrance, list show and parade times.

Sleeping Beauty Castle was actually built before the movie *Sleeping Beauty* came out, because it took so long to produce animated feature films.

DISNEY CALIFORNIA ADVENTURE

FAMILY

Fodor's Choice

★

Disney California Adventure. The sprawling Disney California Adventure, adjacent to Disneyland (their entrances face each other), pays tribute to the Golden State with eight theme areas that re-create vintage architectural styles and embrace several hit Pixar films via engaging attractions. Visitors enter through the art deco–style Buena Vista Street, past shops and a helpful information booth that advises wait times on attractions. The 12-acre Cars Land features Radiator Springs Racers, a speedy trip in six-passenger speedsters through scenes featured in the blockbuster hit. (FASTPASS tickets for the ride run out early most days.) Other popular attractions include World of Color, a nighttime water-effects show, and Toy Story Mania!, an interactive adventure ride hosted by Woody and Buzz Lightyear. At night the park takes on neon hues as glowing signs light up Route 66 in Cars Land and Mickey's Fun Wheel, a giant Ferris wheel on the Paradise Pier. Unlike at Disneyland, cocktails, beer, and wine are available; craft beers and premium wines from California are poured. Live nightly entertainment also features a 1930s jazz troupe that arrives in a vintage jalopy. ✉ *1313 S. Disneyland Dr., between Ball Rd. and Katella Ave., Anaheim* ☎ *714/781–4636* ⊕ *www.disneyland.com* ▧ *$95–$119; parking $18.*

PARK NEIGHBORHOODS

Neighborhoods for Disney California Adventure are arranged in geographic order.

BUENA VISTA STREET

California Adventure's grand entryway re-creates the lost 1920s of Los Angeles that Walt Disney encountered when he moved to the Golden State. There's a **Red Car trolley** (modeled after Los Angeles's bygone streetcar line); hop on for the brief ride to Hollywood Land. Buena Vista Street is also home to a Starbucks outlet—within the Fiddler, Fifer & Practical Café—and the upscale Carthay Circle Restaurant and Lounge, which serves modern craft cocktails and beer.

GRIZZLY PEAK

This woodsy land celebrates the great outdoors. Test your skills on the **Redwood Creek Challenge Trail,** a challenging trek across net ladders and suspension bridges. **Grizzly River Run** mimics the river rapids of the Sierra Nevadas; be prepared to get soaked.

Soarin' Around the world is a spectacular simulated hang-gliding ride over internationally known landmarks like Switzerland's Matterhorn and India's Taj Mahal.

HOLLYWOOD LAND

With a main street modeled after Hollywood Boulevard, a fake sky backdrop, and real soundstages, this area celebrates California's film industry. **Disney Animation** gives you an insider's look at how animators create characters. **Turtle Talk with Crush** lets kids have an unscripted chat with a computer-animated Crush, the sea turtle from *Finding Nemo.* The Hyperion Theater hosts **Frozen,** a 45-minute live performance from a Broadway-sized cast with terrific visual effects. ■TIP➔ Plan on getting in line about half an hour in advance; the show is worth the wait. On the film-inspired ride, **Monsters, Inc. Mike & Sulley to the Rescue,** visitors climb into taxis and travel the streets of Monstropolis on a mission to safely return Boo to her bedroom. **Guardians of the Galaxy – Mission: BREAKOUT!** which opened in summer 2017, replaced the now-closed Twilight Zone Tower of Terror.

A BUG'S LAND

Inspired by the 1998 film *A Bug's Life,* this section skews its attractions to an insect's point of view. Kids can spin around in giant takeout Chinese food boxes on **Flik's Flyers,** and hit the bug-shaped bumper cars on **Tuck and Roll's Drive 'Em Buggies.** The short show *It's Tough to Be a Bug!* gives a 3-D look at insect life.

CARS LAND

Amble down Route 66, the main thoroughfare of Cars Land, a pitch-perfect re-creation of the vintage highway. Quick eats are found at the Cozy Cone Motel (in a teepee-shape motor court), while Flo's V8 café serves hearty comfort food. Start your day at Radiator Springs Racers, the park's most popular attraction, where waits can be two hours or longer. Strap into a nifty sports car and meet the characters of Pixar's *Cars*; the ride ends in a speedy auto race through the red rocks and desert of Radiator Springs.

PACIFIC WHARF

The Wine Country Trattoria is a great place for Italian specialties paired with California wine; relax outside on the restaurant's terrace for a casual bite. Mexican cuisine and potent margaritas are available at the Cocina Cucamonga Mexican Grill and Rita's Baja Blenders.

PARADISE PIER

This section re-creates the glory days of California's seaside piers. If you're looking for thrills, the **California Screamin'** roller coaster takes its riders from 0 to 55 mph in about four seconds and proceeds through scream tunnels, steeply angled drops, and a 360-degree loop. **Goofy's Sky School** is a rollicking roller-coaster ride that goes up three stories and covers more than 1,200 feet of track. **Mickey's Fun Wheel,** a giant Ferris wheel, provides a good view of the grounds, though some cars spin and sway for more kicks. There are also carnival games, an aquatic-themed carousel, and Ariel's Grotto, where future princesses can dine with the mermaid and her friends (reservations are a must). Get a close-up look at Ariel's world on **Little Mermaid—Ariel's Undersea Adventure.** The best views of the nighttime music, water, and light show, **World of Color,** are from the paths along Paradise Bay. FASTPASS tickets are available. Or for a guaranteed spot, book dinner at the Wine Country Trattoria that includes a ticket to a viewing area to catch all the show's stunning visuals.

4

OTHER ATTRACTIONS

FAMILY **Downtown Disney District.** The Downtown Disney District is a 20-acre promenade of dining, shopping, and entertainment that connects the resort's hotels and theme parks. At **Ralph Brennan's Jazz Kitchen** you can dig into New Orleans–style food and music. Sports fans gravitate to **ESPN Zone,** which serves American food from the grill, and lets visitors play video games or watch worldwide sports events telecast through 120 HDTVs. An **AMC** multiplex movie theater with stadium-style seating plays the latest blockbusters and, naturally, a couple of kid flicks. Shops sell everything from Disney goods to antique jewelry—don't miss **Disney Vault 28,** a hip boutique that sells designer-made Disney wear and couture clothing and accessories. At the mega-sized **Lego Store** there are hands-on demonstrations and space to play with the latest Lego creations. Anna & Elsa's Store speedily makes over kids into their favorite character from the hit film *Frozen.* Parking is a deal: the first two hours are free, or four hours with validation. All visitors must pass through a security checkpoint and metal detectors before entering. ✉ *1580 Disneyland Dr., Anaheim* ☎ *714/300–7800* 🌐 *disneyland.disney.go.com/downtown-disney* 🎟 *Free.*

WHERE TO EAT

$$$ MEDITERRANEAN 🍴 **Catal Restaurant & Uva Bar.** Famed chef Joachim Splichal and his staff take a relaxed approach at this bi-level Mediterranean spot where 40 wines by the glass, craft beers, and craft cocktails pair well with his Spanish-influenced dishes. Upstairs, Catal's menu has tapas, a variety of flavorful paellas (lobster is worth the splurge), and charcuterie. **Known for:** people-watching; gourmet burgers; paella. [$] *Average main: $30* ✉ *Downtown Disney District, 1580 S. Disneyland Dr., Suite 103, Anaheim* ☎ *714/774–4442* 🌐 *www.patinagroup.com.*

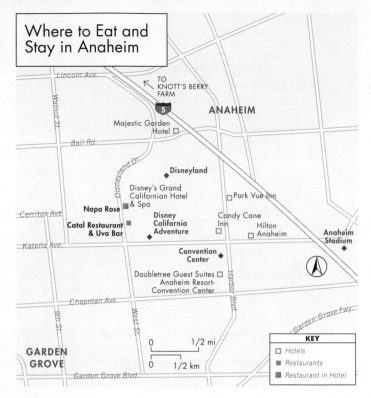

Where to Eat and Stay in Anaheim

$$$$
AMERICAN

✕**Napa Rose.** Done up in a handsome Craftsman style, Napa Rose's rich seasonal cuisine is matched with an extensive wine list, with 1,000 labels and 80 available by the glass. For a look into the open kitchen, sit at the counter and watch the chefs as they whip up such signature dishes as grilled diver scallops and chanterelles, and roasted lamp chops topped with pomegranate. **Known for:** excellent wine list; kid-friendly options; grilled diver scallops. Ⓢ *Average main: $45* ⊠ *Disney's Grand Californian Hotel, 1600 S. Disneyland Dr., Anaheim* ☎ *714/300–7170, 714/781–3463 reservations* ⊕ *disneyland.disney. go.com/grand-californian-hotel/napa-rose.*

WHERE TO STAY

$$
HOTEL
FAMILY

⌂ **Candy Cane Inn.** One of the Disneyland area's first hotels, the Candy Cane is one of Anaheim's most relaxing properties, with spacious and understated rooms and an inviting palm-fringed pool. **Pros:** proximity to everything Disney; friendly service; well-lighted property. **Cons:** rooms and lobby are on the small side; all rooms face parking lot. Ⓢ *Rooms from: $158* ⊠ *1747 S. Harbor Blvd., Anaheim* ☎ *714/774–5284, 800/345–7057* ⊕ *www.candycaneinn.net* ⤳ *171 rooms* ⦿*Breakfast.*

$$$$
RESORT
FAMILY
Fodor'sChoice
★

Disney's Grand Californian Hotel & Spa. The most opulent of Disneyland's three hotels, the Craftsman-style Grand Californian offers views of Disney California Adventure and Downtown Disney. **Pros:** gorgeous lobby; family friendly; direct access to California Adventure. **Cons:** the self-parking lot is across the street; standard rooms are on the small side. $ *Rooms from: $461* ✉ *1600 S. Disneyland Dr., Anaheim* ☎ *714/635–2300* ⊕ *disneyland.disney.go.com/grand-californian-hotel* ⤳ *998 rooms* ◯|*No meals.*

$$
HOTEL

Doubletree Guest Suites Anaheim Resort-Convention Center. This busy hotel near the Anaheim Convention Center and a 20-minute walk from Disneyland caters to business travelers and vacationers alike. **Pros:** huge suites; walking distance to a variety of restaurants. **Cons:** a bit far from Disneyland; pool area is small. $ *Rooms from: $129* ✉ *2085 S. Harbor Blvd., Anaheim* ☎ *714/750–3000, 800/215–7316* ⊕ *doubletreeanaheim.com* ⤳ *252 rooms* ◯|*No meals.*

$$
HOTEL
FAMILY

Hilton Anaheim. Next to the Anaheim Convention Center, this busy Hilton is one of the largest hotels in Southern California, with a restaurant and food court, cocktail lounges, a full-service gym, and its own Starbucks. **Pros:** efficient service; great children's programs; some rooms have views of the park fireworks. **Cons:** huge size can be daunting; fee to use health club. $ *Rooms from: $159* ✉ *777 Convention Way, Anaheim* ☎ *714/750–4321, 800/445–8667* ⊕ *www.anaheim.hilton.com* ⤳ *1,572 rooms* ◯|*No meals.*

$$
HOTEL
FAMILY

Park Vue Inn. Watch the frequent fireworks from the rooftop sundeck at this bougainvillea-covered Spanish-style inn, one of the closest lodgings to Disneyland's main gate. **Pros:** easy walk to Disneyland, Downtown Disney, and Disney California Adventure; free parking until midnight on checkout day; some rooms have bunk beds. **Cons:** all rooms face the parking lot; rooms near the breakfast room can be noisy. $ *Rooms from: $159* ✉ *1570 S. Harbor Blvd., Anaheim* ☎ *714/772–3691, 800/334–7021* ⊕ *www.parkvueinn.com* ⤳ *86 rooms* ◯|*Breakfast.*

$$
HOTEL
FAMILY

Majestic Garden Hotel. If you're hoping to escape from the commercial atmosphere of the hotels near Disneyland and California Adventure, consider this sprawling replica of a Tudor castle. **Pros:** large, attractive lobby; game room; spacious rooms with comfortable beds. **Cons:** confusing layout; hotel sits close to a busy freeway; small bathrooms. $ *Rooms from: $144* ✉ *900 S. Disneyland Dr., Anaheim* ☎ *714/778–1700, 844/326–7122* ⊕ *www.majesticgardenhotel.com* ⤳ *489 rooms* ◯|*No meals.*

SPORTS AND THE OUTDOORS

Anaheim Ducks. The National Hockey League's Anaheim Ducks, winners of the 2007 Stanley Cup, play at Honda Center. ✉ *Honda Center, 2695 E. Katella Ave., Anaheim* ☎ *877/945–3946* ⊕ *nhl.com/ducks.*

Los Angeles Angels of Anaheim. Professional baseball's Los Angeles Angels of Anaheim play at Angel Stadium. An "Outfield Extravaganza" celebrates great plays on the field, with fireworks and a geyser exploding over a model evoking the California coast. ✉ *Angel Stadium, 2000 E. Gene Autry Way, Anaheim* ☎ *714/426–4357* ⊕ *www.angels.com* Ⓜ *Metrolink Angels Express.*

KNOTT'S BERRY FARM

25 miles south of Los Angeles, via I-5, in Buena Park.

FAMILY **Knott's Berry Farm.** The land where the boysenberry was invented (by crossing raspberry, blackberry, and loganberry bushes) is now occupied by Knott's Berry Farm. In 1934 Cordelia Knott began serving chicken dinners on her wedding china to supplement her family's income. The dinners and her boysenberry pies proved more profitable than husband Walter's farm, so the two moved first into the restaurant business and then into the entertainment business. The park is now a 160-acre complex with 40 rides, dozens of restaurants and shops, arcade games, live shows, a brick-by-brick replica of Philadelphia's Independence Hall, and loads of Americana. Although it has plenty to keep small children occupied, the park is best known for its awesome rides. The Boardwalk area is home to several coasters, including the stomach-churning Rip Tide that turns thrill-seekers upside down and around several times, plus water features to cool things off on hot days, and a lighted promenade. And, yes, you can still get that boysenberry pie (and jam, juice— you name it). ⊠ *8039 Beach Blvd., Buena Park* ✥ *Between La Palma Ave. and Crescent St., 2 blocks south of Hwy. 91* ☎ *714/220–5200* ⊕ *www.knotts.com* ⊡ *$75.*

PARK NEIGHBORHOODS

Neighborhoods for Knott's Berry Farm are arranged in geographic order.

CAMP SNOOPY

It can be gridlocked on weekends, but small fries love this miniature High Sierra wonderland where the *Peanuts* gang hangs out. Tykes can push and pump their own mini–mining cars on **Huff and Puff,** zip around a pint-size racetrack on **Charlie Brown Speedway,** and hop aboard **Woodstock's Airmail,** a kids' version of the park's Supreme Scream ride. Most of the rides here are geared toward kids only, leaving parents to cheer them on from the sidelines. **Sierra Sidewinder,** a roller coaster near the entrance of Camp Snoopy, is aimed at older children, with spinning saucer–type vehicles that go a maximum speed of 37 mph.

FIESTA VILLAGE

Over in **Fiesta Village** are two more musts for adrenaline junkies: **Montezooma's Revenge,** a roller coaster that goes from 0 to 55 mph in less than five seconds, and **Jaguar!,** which simulates the motions of a cat stalking its prey, twisting, spiraling, and speeding up and slowing down as it takes you on its stomach-dropping course. There's also **Hat Dance,** a version of the spinning teacups but with sombreros, and a 100-year-old **Dentzel carousel,** complete with an antique organ and menagerie of hand-carved animals. In a nod to history, there are restored scale models of the California Missions at Fiesta Village's southern entrance.

THE BOARDWALK

Not-for-the-squeamish thrill rides and skill-based games dominate the scene at the **boardwalk.** New roller coasters—Coast Rider, Surfside Glider, and Pacific Scrambler—were added in 2013 and surround a pond that keeps things cooler on hot days. Go head over heels on the **Boomerang** roller coaster, then do it again—backward. The boardwalk is also home to a string of test-your-skill games that are fun to watch whether you're playing or not, and Johnny Rockets, the park's newest restaurant.

GHOST TOWN

Clusters of authentic old buildings relocated from their original mining-town sites mark this section of the park. You can stroll down the street, stop and chat with a blacksmith, pan for gold (for a fee), crack open a geode, check out the chalkboard of a circa-1875 schoolhouse, and ride an original Butterfield stagecoach. Looming over it all is **GhostRider,** Orange County's first wooden roller coaster. Traveling up to 56 mph and reaching 118 feet at its highest point, the park's biggest attraction is riddled with sudden dips and curves, subjecting riders to forces up to three times that of gravity. On the Western-theme **Silver Bullet,** riders are sent to a height of 146 feet and then back down 109 feet. Riders spiral, corkscrew, fly into a cobra roll, and experience overbanked curves. The **Calico Mine** ride descends into a replica of a working gold mine. The **Timber Mountain Log Ride** is a visitor favorite—the flume ride underwent a complete renovation in 2013. Also found here is the park's newest thrill ride, the **Pony Express,** a roller coaster that lets riders saddle up on packs of "horses" tethered to platforms that take off on a series of hairpin turns and travel up to 38 mph. Don't miss the **Western Trails Museum,** a dusty old gem full of Old West memorabilia and rural Americana, plus menus from the original chicken restaurant, and an impressive antique button collection. **Calico Railroad** departs regularly from Ghost Town station for a round-trip tour of the park (bandit holdups notwithstanding).

This section is also home to **Big Foot Rapids,** a splash-fest of white-water river rafting over towering cliffs, cascading waterfalls, and wild rapids. Don't miss the visually stunning show at **Mystery Lodge,** which tells the story of Native Americans in the Pacific Northwest with lights, music, and beautiful images.

KNOTT'S SOAK CITY WATERPARK

Knott's Soak City Waterpark is directly across from the main park on 13 acres next to Independence Hall. It has a dozen major water rides; **Pacific Spin** is an oversize waterslide that drops riders 75 feet into a catch pool. There's also a children's pool; a 750,000-gallon wave pool; and a funhouse. Soak City's season runs mid-May to mid-September. It's open daily after Memorial Day, weekends only after Labor Day, and then closes for the season.

WHERE TO EAT AND STAY

$$ AMERICAN FAMILY

🍴 **Mrs. Knott's Chicken Dinner Restaurant.** Cordelia Knott's fried chicken and boysenberry pies drew crowds so big that Knott's Berry Farm was built to keep the hungry customers occupied while they waited. The restaurant's current incarnation (outside the park's entrance) still serves crispy fried chicken, along with fluffy handmade biscuits, mashed potatoes, and Mrs. Knott's signature chilled cherry-rhubarb compote. **Known for:** fried chicken; family friendly; outdoor dining. [$] *Average main: $22* ✉ *Knott's Berry Farm Marketplace, 8039 Beach Blvd., Buena Park* ☎ *714/220–5055* 🌐 *www.knotts.com/california-marketplace/mrs-knott-s-chicken-dinner-restaurant.*

A mural at Huntington Beach

$ RESORT FAMILY 🏨 **Knott's Berry Farm Hotel.** This convenient high-rise hotel is run by the park and sits right on park grounds surrounded by graceful palm trees. **Pros:** easy access to Knott's Berry Farm; plenty of family activities; basketball court. **Cons:** lobby and hallways can be noisy; public areas show significant wear and tear. [$] *Rooms from: $99* ✉ *7675 Crescent Ave., Buena Park* ☎ *714/995–1111, 866/752–2444* 🌐 *www.knottshotel.com* 🛏 *320 rooms* 🍴 *No meals.*

THE COAST

Running along the Orange County coastline is scenic Pacific Coast Highway (Highway 1, known locally as the PCH). Older beachfront settlements, with their modest bungalow-style homes, are joined by posh gated communities. The pricey land between Newport Beach and Laguna Beach is where ex-Laker Kobe Bryant, novelist Dean Koontz, those infamous Real Housewives of Bravo, and a slew of finance moguls live.

Though the coastline is rapidly being filled in, there are still a few stretches of beautiful, protected open land. And at many places along the way you can catch an idealized glimpse of the Southern California lifestyle: surfers hitting the beach, boards under their arms.

LONG BEACH

About 25 miles southeast of Los Angeles, via I-110 south.

Long Beach is L.A.'s gateway to the Pacific with ferries to Catalina Island and fishing charters. Long Beach also welcomes cruise ships, offers whale-watching excursions, and is home to the now retired grande dame of trans-Atlantic crossings, *The Queen Mary*.

EXPLORING

FAMILY **Aquarium of the Pacific.** Sea lions, nurse sharks, and penguins, oh my!—this aquarium focuses on creatures of the Pacific Ocean. The main exhibits include large tanks of sharks, sting rays, and ethereal sea dragons, which the aquarium has successfully bred in captivity. The Great Hall features the multimedia attraction *Penguins*, a panoramic film that captures the world of this endangered species. Be sure to say hello to Betty, a rescue at the engaging sea otter exhibit. For a non-aquatic experience, head to Lorikeet Forest, a walk-in aviary full of the friendliest parrots from Australia. Buy a cup of nectar and smile as you become a human bird perch. If you're a true animal lover, book an up-close-and-personal Animal Encounters Tour ($109) to learn about and assist in the care and feeding of the animals; or find out how the aquarium functions with the extensive Behind the Scenes Tour ($42.95 for adults, including admission). Certified divers can book a supervised dive in the aquarium's Tropical Reef Habitat ($299). Twice daily whale-watching trips on the *Harbor Breeze* depart from the dock adjacent to the aquarium; summer sightings of blue whales are an unforgettable thrill. ⊠ *100 Aquarium Way, Long Beach* ☎ *562/590–3100* ⊕ *www.aquariumofpacific.org* ⊠ *$29.95.*

WHERE TO STAY

$$ · HOTEL · FAMILY **Queen Mary Hotel.** Experience the golden age of transatlantic travel without the seasickness: a 1936–art deco style reigns on *The Queen Mary,* from the ship's mahogany paneling to its nickel-plated doors to the majestic Grand Salon. **Pros:** a walkable historic Promenade deck; views from Long Beach out to the Pacific; art deco details. **Cons:** spotty service; vintage soundproofing makes for a challenging night's sleep; mandatory Wi-Fi fee. $ *Rooms from: $149* ⊠ *1126 Queens Hwy., Long Beach* ☎ *562/435–3511, 877/342–0742* ⊕ *www.queenmary.com* ⊐ *346 staterooms* ⊠ *No meals.*

$$ · B&B/INN **The Varden.** Constructed in 1929 to house Bixby Knolls Sr.'s mistress, Dolly Varden, this small, historic, European-style hotel, on the metro line in downtown Long Beach, now caters to worldly budget travelers. Compact rooms are mostly white and blend modern touches like flat-screen TVs and geometric silver fixtures with period details like exposed beams, Dakota Jackson periwinkle chairs, and round penny-tile baths. **Pros:** great value for downtown location; discount passes to Gold's Gym across the street; complimentary Continental breakfast. **Cons:** no resort services; small rooms. $ *Rooms from: $159* ⊠ *335 Pacific Ave., Long Beach* ☎ *562/432–8950* ⊕ *www.thevardenhotel.com* ⊐ *35 rooms.*

NEWPORT BEACH

6 miles south of Huntington Beach via the Pacific Coast Highway.

Newport Beach has evolved from a simple seaside village to an icon of chic coastal living. Its ritzy reputation comes from mega-yachts bobbing in the harbor, boutiques that rival those in Beverly Hills, and spectacular homes overlooking the ocean.

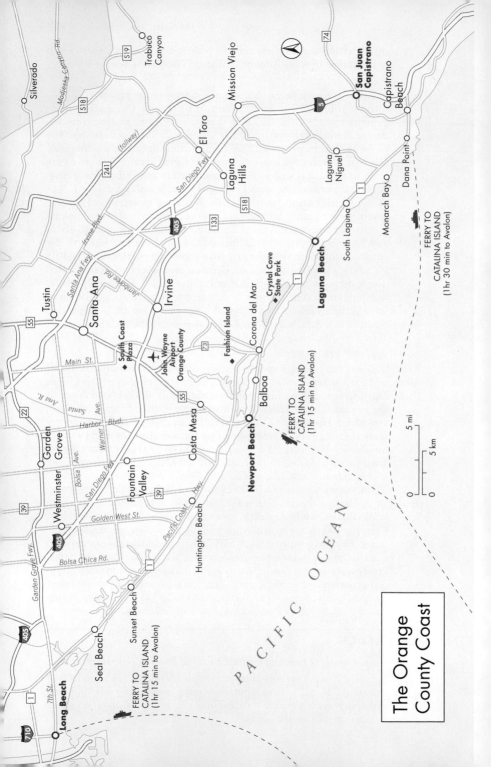

The Orange County Coast

The city boasts some of the cleanest beaches in Southern California; inland Newport Beach's concentration of high-rise office buildings, shopping centers, and luxury hotels drive the economy. But on the city's Balboa Peninsula, you can still catch a glimpse of a more humble, down-to-earth town scattered with taco spots, tackle shops, and sailor bars.

ESSENTIALS

Visitor Information Visit Newport Beach. ⌧ *Atrium Court at Fashion Island, 401 Newport Center Dr.* ☎ *855/563–9767* ⊕ *www.visitnewportbeach.com.*

EXPLORING

Balboa Island. This sliver of terra firma in Newport Harbor boasts quaint streets tightly packed with impossibly charming multimillion-dollar cottages. The island's main drag, Marine Avenue, is lined with equally picturesque cafés and shops.

NEED A BREAK

Sugar 'N Spice. Stop by ice cream parlor Sugar 'N Spice for a Balboa Bar—a slab of vanilla ice cream dipped first in chocolate and then in a topping of your choice such as hard candy or Oreo crumbs. Other parlors serve the concoction, but Sugar 'N Spice claims to have invented it back in 1945.

⌧ *310 Marine Ave., Balboa Island* ☎ *949/673–8907.*

FAMILY **Balboa Peninsula.** Newport's best beaches are on Balboa Peninsula, where many jetties pave the way to ideal swimming areas. The most intense spot for bodysurfing in Orange County, and arguably on the West Coast, known as the **Wedge,** is at the south end of the peninsula. It was created by accident in the 1930s when the Federal Works Progress Administration built a jetty to protect Newport Harbor. ■TIP➔ Rip currents mean it's strictly for the pros—but it sure is fun to watch an experienced local ride it. ⊕ *www.visitnewportbeach.com/vacations/balboa-peninsula.*

FAMILY **Discovery Cube's Ocean Quest.** This family-friendly destination has exhibits on the history of the harbor, ocean explorers, and scientific aspects of the Pacific Ocean. There's a fleet of ship models: some date to 1798, and one is made entirely of gold and silver. Other fun features include a touch tank holding local sea creatures and a lab for kids that encourages innovation. ⌧ *600 E. Bay Ave.* ☎ *949/675–8915* ⊕ *www.oceanquestoc.org* ⌧ *$3* ⊗ *Closed Mon.–Thurs.*

Newport Harbor. Sheltering nearly 16,000 small boats, Newport Harbor may seduce even those who don't own a yacht. Spend an afternoon exploring the charming avenues and surrounding alleys; take California's longest running auto ferry across to Balboa Island. The fare is $2 for car and driver for the scenic crossing. Several grassy areas on the primarily residential Lido Isle have views of the water. ⌧ *Pacific Coast Hwy.* ⊕ *www.balboaislandferry.com.*

FAMILY **Newport Pier.** Jutting out into the ocean near 20th Street, Newport Pier is a popular fishing spot. Street parking is difficult, so grab the first space you find and be prepared to walk. Early on Wednesday–Sunday mornings you're likely to encounter dory fishermen hawking their predawn catches, as they've done for generations. On weekends the area is alive with kids of all ages on in-line skates, skateboards, and bikes dodging pedestrians and whizzing past fast-food joints and classic dive bars. ⌧ *72 McFadden Pl.*

4

Riding the waves at Newport Beach

WHERE TO EAT

$$$$
BRASSERIE
✕ **Basilic.** This intimate French-Swiss bistro adds a touch of old-world elegance to the island with its white linen and flower-topped tables. Chef Bernard Althaus grows the herbs used in his classic French dishes. **Known for:** French classics; fine wine; old-school ambience. $ *Average main: $32 ⊠ 217 Marine Ave., Balboa Island ☎ 949/673–0570 ⊕ www. basilicrestaurant.com ⊘ Closed Sun. No lunch Mon.*

$
SEAFOOD
FAMILY
✕ **Bear Flag Fish Co.** Expect long lines in summer at this indoor/outdoor dining spot serving up the freshest local fish (swordfish, sea bass, halibut, and tuna) and a wide range of creative seafood dishes (the Hawaiian-style *poke* salad with ahi tuna is a local favorite). Order at the counter, which doubles as a seafood market, and sit inside the airy dining room or outside on a grand patio. **Known for:** freshest seafood; fish tacos; craft beers. $ *Average main: $12 ⊠ Newport Peninsula, 3421 Via Lido ☎ 949/673–3474 ⊕ www.bearflagfishco.com.*

$$$$
SEAFOOD
✕ **The Cannery.** This 1920s cannery building still teems with fish, but now they go into dishes on the eclectic Pacific Rim menu rather than being packed into crates. Settle in at the sushi bar, in the dining room, or on the patio before choosing between sashimi, seafood platters, or the upscale surf-and-turf with filet mignon and grilled Maine lobsters. **Known for:** waterfront views; seafood specialties; craft cocktails. $ *Average main: $35 ⊠ 3010 Lafayette Rd. ☎ 949/566–0060 ⊕ www.cannerynewport.com.*

$$$
SEAFOOD
✕ **Gulfstream.** This on-trend restaurant has an open kitchen, comfortable booths, and outdoor seating. The patio is a fantastic place to hang out. **Known for:** oysters on the half shell; local hangout; outdoor patio. $ *Average main: $30 ⊠ 850 Avocado Ave. ☎ 949/718–0188 ⊕ www. hillstone.com.*

$$$ AMERICAN 🍴 **3-Thirty-3.** This stylish eatery attracts a convivial crowd—both young and old—for midday, sunset, and late-night dining. A long list of small, shareable plates heightens the camaraderie. **Known for:** happy hour; brunch burritos; generous portions. [$] *Average main: $26* ✉ *333 Bayside Dr.* ☎ *949/673–8464* 🌐 *www.3thirty3nb.com.*

WHERE TO STAY

$$$$ RESORT FAMILY 🏨 **Balboa Bay Resort.** Sharing the same frontage as the private Balboa Bay Club that long ago hosted Humphrey Bogart, Lauren Bacall, and the Reagans, this waterfront resort has one of the best bay views around. **Pros:** exquisite bay-front views; comfortable beds; a raked beach for guests. **Cons:** not much within walking distance; $25 nightly hospitality fee. [$] *Rooms from: $309* ✉ *1221 W. Coast Hwy.* ☎ *949/645–5000* 🌐 *www.balboabayresort.com* 🛏 *159 rooms* 🍽 *No meals.*

$$$$ HOTEL 🏨 **The Island Hotel.** Across a palm tree-lined boulevard from stylish Fashion Island, this 20-story tower caters to business types during the week and luxury seekers on weekends. **Pros:** lively lounge scene; first-class spa; great location. **Cons:** steep valet parking prices; some rooms have views of mall parking. [$] *Rooms from: $259* ✉ *690 Newport Center Dr.* ☎ *949/759–0808, 877/591–9145* 🌐 *www.islandhotel.com* 🛏 *378 rooms* 🍽 *No meals.*

$$$ RESORT 🏨 **Newport Beach Marriott Hotel and Spa.** Here you'll be smack in the moneyed part of town: across from Fashion Island, next to a country club, and with a view toward Newport Harbor. **Pros:** four concierge floors offer enhanced amenities; fantastic spa; complimentary bike rentals. **Cons:** sprawling floor plan; small bathrooms; car is essential for exploring beyond Fashion Island. [$] *Rooms from: $229* ✉ *900 Newport Center Dr.* ☎ *949/640–4000* 🌐 *www.marriott.com* 🛏 *532 rooms.*

SPORTS AND THE OUTDOORS

BOAT RENTALS

FAMILY **Balboa Boat Rentals.** You can tour Lido and Balboa isles with kayaks ($18 an hour), stand-up paddleboards ($25 an hour), small motorboats ($75 an hour), and electric boats ($80 to $95 an hour) at Balboa Boat Rentals. ✉ *510 E. Edgewater Ave.* ☎ *949/673–7200* 🌐 *www.boats4rent.com.*

BOAT TOURS

FAMILY **Catalina Flyer.** At Balboa Pavilion, the Catalina Flyer operates a 90-minute daily round-trip passage to Catalina Island for $70. Reservations are required; check the schedule in January and February, as crossings may be canceled due to annual maintenance. ✉ *400 Main St.* ☎ *949/673–5245* 🌐 *www.catalinainfo.com.*

Hornblower Cruises & Events. This operator books three-hour weekend dinner cruises with dancing for $87. The two-hour Sunday brunch cruise starts at $68. Cruises traverse the mostly placid and scenic waters of Newport Harbor. ✉ *2431 W. Coast Hwy.* ☎ *888/467–6256* 🌐 *www.hornblower.com.*

FISHING

FAMILY **Davey's Locker.** In addition to a complete tackle shop, Davey's Locker offers half-day sportfishing trips starting at $41.50. Whale-watching excursions begin at $26 for weekdays. ✉ *Balboa Pavilion, 400 Main St.* ☎ *949/673–1434* 🌐 *www.daveyslocker.com.*

SHOPPING

Fodor'sChoice **Fashion Island.** Shake the sand out of your shoes to head inland to the
★ ritzy Fashion Island outdoor mall, a cluster of arcades and courtyards
complete with koi pond, fountains, and a family-friendly trolley—plus
some awesome ocean views. It has the luxe department stores Neiman
Marcus and Bloomingdale's, plus expensive spots like Jonathan Adler,
Kate Spade, and Michael Stars. ⊠ *401 Newport Center Dr., between
Jamboree and MacArthur Blvds., off PCH* ☎ *949/721–2000, 855/658–
8527* ⊕ *www.shopfashionisland.com.*

LAGUNA BEACH

*10 miles south of Newport Beach on PCH, 60 miles south of Los
Angeles on I-5 south to Hwy. 133, which turns into Laguna Canyon Rd.*

Fodor'sChoice Driving in along Laguna Canyon Road from the I-405 freeway gives you
★ the chance to cruise through a gorgeous coastal canyon, large stretches of
which remain undeveloped, before arriving at a glistening wedge of ocean.

Laguna's welcome mat is legendary. On the corner of Forest and Park
avenues is a gate proclaiming, "This gate hangs well and hinders none,
refresh and rest, then travel on." A gay community has long been established here; art galleries dot the village streets, and there's usually someone daubing up in Heisler Park. Along the Pacific Coast Highway you'll
find dozens of clothing boutiques, jewelry stores, and cafés.

ESSENTIALS

Visitor Information Visit Laguna Beach Visitors Center. ⊠ *381 Forest Ave.*
☎ *949/497–9229, 800/877–1115* ⊕ *www.visitlagunabeach.com.*

EXPLORING

Laguna Art Museum. This museum displays American art, with an emphasis on California artists from all periods. Special exhibits change quar-
terly. ⊠ *307 Cliff Dr.* ☎ *949/494–8971* ⊕ *www.lagunaartmuseum.org*
⊠ *$7* ⊗ *Closed Wed.*

Festival of Arts and Pageant of the Masters. An outdoor amphitheater near
the mouth of the canyon hosts the annual Pageant of the Masters, Laguna's most impressive event. Local participants arrange tableaux vivants,
in which live models and carefully orchestrated backgrounds merge in
striking mimicry of classical and contemporary paintings. The pageant
is part of the **Festival of Arts,** held in July and August; tickets are in high
demand, so plan ahead. ⊠ *650 Laguna Canyon Rd.* ☎ *949/497–6582,
800/487–3378* ⊕ *www.foapom.com.*

BEACHES

FAMILY **1,000 Steps Beach.** Off South Coast Highway at 9th Street, 1,000 Steps
Beach is a hard-to-find spot tucked away in a neighborhood with great
waves and hard-packed, white sand. There aren't really 1,000 steps
down (but when you hike back up, it'll certainly feel like it). Sea caves
and tide pools enhance this already beautiful natural spot. **Amenities:**
parking. **Best for:** sunset; surfing; swimming. ⊠ *S. Coast Hwy., at 9th St.*

FAMILY **Main Beach Park.** A stocky 1920s lifeguard tower marks Main Beach
Fodor'sChoice Park, where a wooden boardwalk separates the sand from a strip of
★ lawn. Walk along this soft-sand beach, or grab a bench and watch

people bodysurfing, playing volleyball, or scrambling around two half-basketball courts. The beach also has children's play equipment. Most of Laguna's hotels are within a short (but hilly) walk. **Amenities:** lifeguards; showers; toilets. **Best for:** sunset; swimming; walking. ✉ *Broadway at S. Coast Hwy.* 🌐 *www.visitlagunabeach.com.*

FAMILY **Wood's Cove.** Off South Coast Highway, Wood's Cove is especially quiet during the week. Big rock formations hide lurking crabs. This is a prime scuba-diving spot, and at high tide much of the beach is underwater. Climbing the steps to leave, you can see a Tudor-style mansion that was once home to Bette Davis. Street parking is limited. **Amenities:** none. **Best for:** snorkeling; scuba diving; sunset. ✉ *Diamond St. and Ocean Way* 🌐 *www.visitlagunabeach.com.*

4

WHERE TO EAT

$$$ INTERNATIONAL 🍴 **Sapphire Laguna.** This Laguna Beach establishment set in a historic Craftsman is part gourmet pantry (a must-stop for your every picnic need) and part global dining adventure. Iranian-born chef Azmin Ghahreman takes you on a journey through Europe and Asia with dishes ranging from a summer vegetable gazpacho to banana-curried black cod. **Known for:** cheese selection; weekend brunch; pet-friendly patio. [$] *Average main: $27* ✉ *The Old Pottery Place, 1200 S. Coast Hwy.* ☎ *949/715–9888* 🌐 *www.sapphirelaguna.com.*

$ VEGETARIAN FAMILY 🍴 **The Stand.** If an eatery can be called old-school, artsy Laguna, this is it. Only organic vegan ingredients are used to prepare the salads, burritos with brown rice and hummus, pita sandwiches, and smoothies. [$] *Average main: $10* ✉ *238 Thalia St.* ☎ *949/494–8101* 🌐 *www.thestandnaturalfoods.com.*

$$$$ MODERN AMERICAN Fodor's Choice ★ 🍴 **Studio.** In a nod to Laguna's art history, Studio has house-made specialties that entice the eye as well as the palate. The restaurant occupies its own Craftsman-style bungalow, atop a 50-foot bluff overlooking the Pacific. **Known for:** attentive service; chef's tasting menu; great for special occasions. [$] *Average main: $55* ✉ *Montage Laguna Beach, 30801 S. Coast Hwy.* ☎ *949/715–6420* 🌐 *www.studiolagunabeach.com* ⏲ *Closed Mon. No lunch.*

$ MEXICAN 🍴 **Taco Loco.** This may look like a fast-food taco stand, and the hemp brownies on the menu may make you think the kitchen's *really* laid-back, but the quality of the food here equals that in many higher-price restaurants. Some Mexican standards get a Louisiana twist, like Cajun-spiced seafood tacos. **Known for:** vegetarian tacos; sidewalk seating; surfer clientele. [$] *Average main: $9* ✉ *640 S. Coast Hwy.* ☎ *949/497–1635* 🌐 *www.tacoloco.net.*

$ VEGETARIAN FAMILY 🍴 **Zinc Café & Market.** Families flock to this small Laguna Beach institution for reasonably priced breakfast and lunch options. Try the signature quiches or poached egg dishes in the morning, or swing by later in the day for healthy salads, house-made soups, quesadillas, or pizzettes. **Known for:** gourmet goodies; avocado toast; busy outdoor patio. [$] *Average main: $15* ✉ *350 Ocean Ave.* ☎ *949/494–6302* 🌐 *www.zinccafe.com* ⏲ *No dinner Nov.–Apr.*

WHERE TO STAY

$$$$ HOTEL FAMILY **Inn at Laguna Beach.** On a bluff overlooking the ocean, this inn is steps from the surf. **Pros:** large rooms; oceanfront location; sustainable design. **Cons:** ocean-view rooms are pricey; rooms on highway can be noisy. [$] *Rooms from: $379* ✉ *211 N. Coast Hwy.* ☎ *949/497–9722, 800/544–4479* 🌐 *www.innatlagunabeach.com* *70 rooms.*

$$$ HOTEL **La Casa del Camino.** The look is Old California at the 1929-built La Casa del Camino, with dark woods, arched doors, and wrought iron in the lobby. **Pros:** breathtaking views from rooftop lounge; personable service; close to beach. **Cons:** some rooms face the highway; frequent events can make hotel noisy; some rooms are very small. [$] *Rooms from: $229* ✉ *1289 S. Coast Hwy.* ☎ *949/497–2446, 855/634–5736* 🌐 *www.lacasadelcamino.com* *36 rooms* 🍴 *No meals.*

$$$$ RESORT FAMILY Fodor's Choice ★ **Montage Laguna Beach.** Laguna's connection to the Californian plein-air artists is mined for inspiration at this head-turning, lavish hotel. **Pros:** top-notch, enthusiastic service; idyllic coastal location; numerous sporty pursuits available offshore. **Cons:** multi-night stays required on weekends and holidays; $40 valet parking; $38 daily resort fee. [$] *Rooms from: $695* ✉ *30801 S. Coast Hwy.* ☎ *949/715–6000, 866/271–6953* 🌐 *www.montagehotels.com/lagunabeach* *248 rooms* 🍴 *No meals.*

$$$$ RESORT **Surf & Sand Resort.** One mile south of downtown, on an exquisite stretch of beach with thundering waves and gorgeous rocks, this is a getaway for those who want a boutique hotel experience without all the formalities. **Pros:** easy beach access; intimate property; slightly removed from Main Street crowds. **Cons:** pricey valet parking; surf can be quite loud. [$] *Rooms from: $575* ✉ *1555 S. Coast Hwy.* ☎ *949/497–4477, 877/741–5908* 🌐 *www.surfandsandresort.com* *167 rooms* 🍴 *No meals.*

NIGHTLIFE AND PERFORMING ARTS

Laguna Playhouse. Dating back to the 1920s, the Laguna Playhouse mounts a variety of productions, from classics to youth-oriented plays. ✉ *606 Laguna Canyon Rd.* ☎ *949/497–2787* 🌐 *www.lagunaplayhouse.com.*

Sandpiper Lounge. A hole-in-the-wall joint with live music, the Sandpiper Lounge attracts an eclectic crowd. ✉ *1183 S. Coast Hwy.* ☎ *949/494–4694.*

White House. This hip club on the main strip has nightly entertainment and dancing, which begins at 9:30 nightly. From early morning on, it's also a landmark Laguna Beach restaurant serving pasta, burgers, and brunch favorites. ✉ *340 S. Coast Hwy.* ☎ *949/494–8088* 🌐 *www.whitehouserestaurant.com.*

SHOPPING

Coast Highway, Forest and Ocean avenues, and Glenneyre Street are full of art galleries, fine jewelry stores, and clothing boutiques.

Adam Neeley Fine Art Jewelry. Be prepared to be dazzled at Adam Neeley Fine Art Jewelry, where artisan proprietor Adam Neeley creates one-of-a-kind modern pieces. ✉ *352 N. Coast Hwy.* ☎ *949/715–0953* 🌐 *www.adamneeley.com* ⏱ *Closed Sun. and Mon.*

Art for the Soul. A riot of color, Art for the Soul has hand-painted furniture, crafts, and unusual gifts. ⊠ *272 Forest Ave.* ☎ *949/497–8700* ⊕ *www.art4thesoul.com.*

Fetneh Blake. Hit Fetneh Blake for pricey, Euro-chic clothes. The emerging designers found here lure Angelenos to make the trek south. ⊠ *427 N. Coast Hwy.* ☎ *949/494–3787* ⊕ *www.fetnehblake.com.*

La Rue du Chocolat. This shop dispenses chocolate-covered strawberries and handcrafted chocolates in seasonal flavors. ⊠ *Peppertree La., 448 S. Coast Hwy., Suite B* ☎ *949/494–2372* ⊕ *www.larueduchocolat.com.*

SAN JUAN CAPISTRANO

4

5 miles north of Dana Point via Hwy. 74, 60 miles north of San Diego via I-5.

San Juan Capistrano is best known for its historic mission, where the swallows traditionally return each year, migrating from their winter haven in Argentina (though these days they are more likely to choose other local sites for nesting). St. Joseph's Day, March 19, launches a week of fowl festivities. Charming antiques stores, which range from pricey to cheap, line Camino Capistrano.

GETTING HERE AND AROUND

If you arrive by train, which is far more romantic and restful than battling freeway traffic, you'll be dropped off across from the mission at the San Juan Capistrano depot. With its appealing brick café and preserved Santa Fe cars, the depot retains much of the magic of early American railroads. If driving, park near Ortega and Camino Capistrano, the city's main streets.

EXPLORING

FAMILY

Fodor'sChoice

★

Mission San Juan Capistrano. Founded in 1776 by Father Junípero Serra, Mission San Juan Capistrano was one of two Roman Catholic outposts between Los Angeles and San Diego. The Great Stone Church, begun in 1797, is the largest structure created by the Spanish in California. Many of the mission's adobe buildings have been preserved to illustrate mission life, with exhibits of an olive millstone, tallow ovens, tanning vats, metalworking furnaces, and the padres' living quarters. The gardens, with their fountains, are a lovely spot in which to wander. The bougainvillea-covered Serra Chapel is believed to be the oldest church still standing in California, and is the only building remaining in which Fr. Serra actually led Mass. Mass takes place weekdays at 7 am in the chapel. Enter via a small gift shop in the gatehouse. ⊠ *Camino Capistrano and Ortega Hwy.* ☎ *949/234–1300* ⊕ *www.missionsjc.com* 🎟 *$9.*

FAMILY

San Juan Capistrano Library. Near Mission San Juan Capistrano is the San Juan Capistrano Library, a postmodern structure built in 1983. Architect Michael Graves combined classical and Mission styles to striking effect. Its courtyard has secluded places for reading. ⊠ *31495 El Camino Real* ☎ *949/493–1752* ⊕ *ocpl.org/libloc/sjc* ⊘ *Closed Fri.*

WHERE TO EAT

$$$

AMERICAN

FAMILY

✕ Cedar Creek Inn. Just across the street from Mission San Juan Capistrano, this restaurant has a patio that's perfect for a late lunch or a romantic dinner. The menu is fairly straightforward, dishes are tasty,

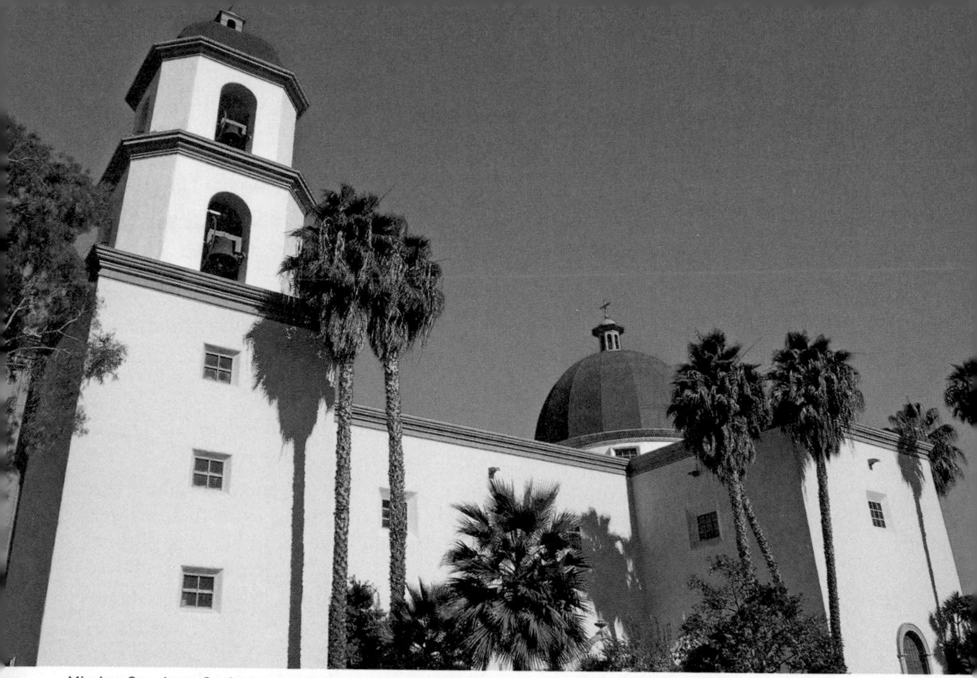
Mission San Juan Capistrano

and portions are substantial—try the Monte Cristo or a burger at lunch, or splurge on the prime rib for dinner. **Known for:** brunch; rich desserts; comfortable seating. [$] *Average main: $30* ✉ *26860 Ortega Hwy.* ☎ *949/240–2229* 🌐 *www.cedarcreekinn.com.*

$$$$ FRENCH 🍴 **L'Hirondelle.** Locals have romanced at cozy tables for decades at this delightful restaurant. Such classic dishes as beef bourguignonne and a New York strip in a black peppercorn and brandy sauce are the hallmark of this French and Belgian restaurant, whose name means "the little swallow." The extensive wine list is matched by an impressive selection of Belgian beers. **Known for:** Sunday brunch; traditional French cuisine; composed salads. [$] *Average main: $32* ✉ *31631 Camino Capistrano* ☎ *949/661–0425* 🌐 *www.lhirondellesjc.com* ⏲ *Closed Mon.*

$$ AMERICAN 🍴 **The Ramos House Cafe.** It may be worth hopping the Amtrak to San Juan Capistrano just for the chance to have breakfast or lunch at one of Orange County's most beloved restaurants located in an historic board-and-batten home dating back to 1881. This café sits practically on the railroad tracks across from the depot—nab a table on the patio and dig into a hearty breakfast, such as the smoked bacon scramble. **Known for:** Southern specialties; weekend brunch; historic setting. [$] *Average main: $20* ✉ *31752 Los Rios St.* ☎ *949/443–1342* 🌐 *www.ramoshouse.com* ⏲ *Closed Mon. No dinner.*

NIGHTLIFE

Coach House. A roomy, casual club with long tables and a dark-wood bar, Coach House draws crowds of varying ages for dinner and entertainment ranging from hip new bands to legacy blues bands to famed musicians from yesteryear like surf guitarist Dick Dale to rockers like Hot Tuna. ✉ *33157 Camino Capistrano* ☎ *949/496–8930* 🌐 *www.thecoachhouse.com.*

Swallow's Inn. Across the way from Mission San Juan Capistrano you'll spot a line of Harleys in front of the Swallow's Inn. Despite a somewhat tough look, it attracts all kinds—bikers, surfers, modern-day cowboys, grandparents—for a drink, a casual bite, karaoke nights, and some rowdy live country music. ✉ *31786 Camino Capistrano* ☎ *949/493–3188* ⊕ *www.swallowsinn.com.*

CATALINA ISLAND

Fodor'sChoice ★

Just 22 miles out from the L.A. coastline, across from Newport Beach and Long Beach, Catalina has virtually unspoiled mountains, canyons, coves, and beaches; best of all, it gives you a glimpse of what undeveloped Southern California once looked like.

Water sports are a big draw, as divers and snorkelers come for the exceptionally clear water surrounding the island. Kayakers are attracted to the calm cove waters and thrill seekers have made the eco-themed zip line so popular that there are nighttime tours via flashlight in summer. The main town, Avalon, is a charming, old-fashioned beach community, where yachts and pleasure boats bob in the crescent bay. Wander beyond the main drag and find brightly painted little bungalows fronting the sidewalks; golf carts are the preferred mode of transport.

In 1919 William Wrigley Jr., the chewing-gum magnate, purchased a controlling interest in the company developing Catalina Island, whose most famous landmark, the Casino, was built in 1929 under his orders. Because he owned the Chicago Cubs baseball team, Wrigley made Catalina the team's spring training site, an arrangement that lasted until 1951.

In 1975 the Catalina Island Conservancy, a nonprofit foundation, acquired about 88% of the island to help preserve the area's natural flora and fauna, including the bald eagle and the Catalina Island fox. These days the conservancy is restoring the rugged interior country with plantings of native grasses and trees. Along the coast you might spot oddities like electric perch, saltwater goldfish, and flying fish.

GETTING HERE AND AROUND
BUS TRAVEL
Catalina Safari Shuttle Bus has regular bus service (in season) between Avalon, Two Harbors, and several campgrounds. The trip between Avalon and Two Harbors takes two hours and costs $54 one-way.

Bus Contacts Catalina Safari Shuttle Bus. ☎ *310/510–4205, 877/778-8322.*

FERRY TRAVEL
Two companies offer ferry service to Catalina Island. The boats have both indoor and outdoor seating and snack bars. Excessive baggage is not allowed, and there are extra fees for bicycles and surfboards. The waters around Santa Catalina can get rough, so if you're prone to seasickness, come prepared. Winter, holiday, and weekend schedules vary, so reservations are recommended.

Catalina Express makes an hour-long run from Long Beach or San Pedro to Avalon and a 90-minute run from Dana Point to Avalon with some stops at Two Harbors. Round-trip fares begin at $73.50, with

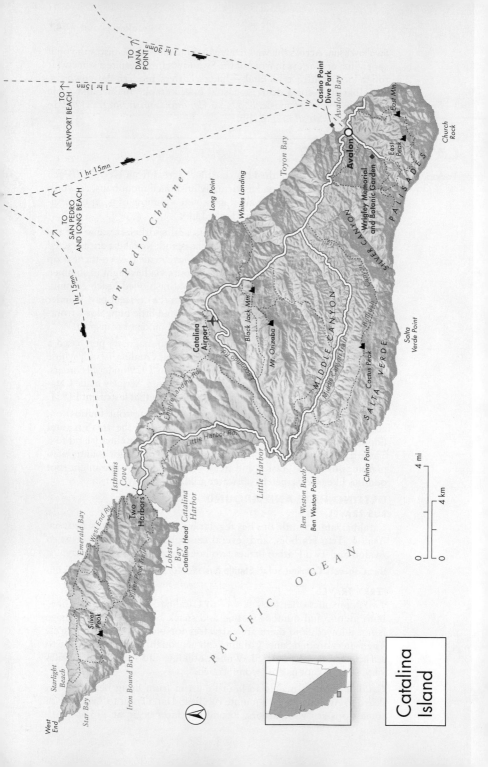

Catalina Island

TO DANA POINT 1 hr 30mn

TO NEWPORT BEACH 1 hr 15mn

TO SAN PEDRO AND LONG BEACH 1 hr 15mn

1 hr 15mn

Casino Point Dive Park
Avalon Bay
Avalon
Wrigley Memorial and Botanic Garden
East Mtn
East Peak
Church Rock
PALISADES
SILVER CANYON
Toyon Bay
Long Point
Whites Landing
San Pedro Channel
Bullrush
MIDDLE CANYON
Chuckua Canyon Trail
Salta Verde Point
SALTA VERDE
Catalina Airport
Black Jack Mtn
Mt. Orizaba
Cactus Peak
China Point
Escondido Rd.
Middle Canyon Rd.
Empire Landing Rd.
Little Harbor Rd.
Little Harbor
Ben Weston Beach
Ben Weston Point
Two Harbors
Isthmus Cove
West End Rd.
Emerald Bay
Lobster Bay
Catalina Head
Catalina Harbor
Silver Peak Trail
Silver Peak
Starlight Beach
West End
Star Bay
Iron Bound Bay

PACIFIC OCEAN

4 mi
4 km
0
0

discounts for seniors and kids. On busy days a $15 upgrade to the Commodore Lounge, when available, is worth it. Service from Newport Beach to Avalon is available through the Catalina Flyer. Boats leave from Balboa Pavilion at 9 am (in season), take 75 minutes to reach the island, and cost $70 round-trip. Return boats leave Catalina at 4:30 pm. Reservations are required for the Catalina Flyer and recommended for all weekend and summer trips. ■ TIP→ Keep an eye out for dolphins, which sometimes swim alongside the ferries.

Ferry Contacts Catalina Express. ☎ *800/481–3470, 562/485–3300* ⊕ *www.catalinaexpress.com.* **Catalina Flyer.** ☎ *949/673–5245* ⊕ *www.catalinainfo.com.*

GOLF CARTS
Golf carts constitute the island's main form of transportation for sightseeing in the area, however some parts of town are off limits, as is the island's interior. You can rent them along Avalon's Crescent Avenue and Pebbly Beach Road for about $40 per hour with a $40 deposit, payable via cash or traveler's check only.

Golf Cart Rentals Island Rentals. ⊠ *125 Pebbly Beach Rd., Avalon* ☎ *310/510–1456* ⊕ *www.catalinagolfcartrentals.com.*

HELICOPTER TRAVEL
Island Express helicopters depart hourly from San Pedro, Santa Ana, and Long Beach next to the retired *Queen Mary* (8 am–dusk). The trip from Long Beach takes about 15 minutes and costs $125 one-way, $250 round-trip (plus tax). Winter rates are lower. Reservations a week in advance are recommended.

Helicopter Contacts Island Express. ☎ *800/228–2566* ⊕ *www.islandexpress.com.*

TIMING
Although Catalina can be seen in one very hectic day, several inviting hotels make it worth extending your stay for one or more nights. A short itinerary might include breakfast on the pier, a tour of the interior, a snorkeling excursion at Casino Point, or a beach day at the Descanso Beach Club and a romantic waterfront dinner in Avalon.

After late October, rooms are much easier to find on short notice, rates drop dramatically, and many hotels offer packages that include transportation from the mainland and/or sightseeing tours. January to March you have a good chance of spotting migrating gray whales on the ferry crossing.

TOURS
FAMILY **Catalina Adventure Tours.** Catalina Adventure Tours, which has booths at the boat landing and on the pier, arranges tours inland as well as on the water via glass-bottom boat and other crafts. ☎ *877/510–2888* ⊕ *www.catalinaadventuretours.com.*

Catalina Island Conservancy. The Catalina Island Conservancy organizes custom ecotours and hikes of the interior. Naturalist guides drive open Jeeps through some gorgeously untrammeled parts of the island. Tours start at $70 per person for a two-hour trip (two-person minimum); you can also book half- and full-day tours. The tours run year-round. ⊠ *125 Claressa Ave., Avalon* ☎ *310/510–2595* ⊕ *www.catalinaconservancy.org.*

FAMILY   **Santa Catalina Island Company.** Santa Catalina Island Company runs 15 land and sea tours, including the Flying Fish boat trip (summer evenings only); a comprehensive inland motor tour; a tour of Skyline Drive; several Casino tours; a scenic tour of Avalon; a glass-bottom boat tour; an undersea tour on a semisubmersible vessel; an eco-themed zip-line tour that traverses a scenic canyon; a speedy Ocean Runner expedition that searches for all manner of sea creatures. Reservations are highly recommended for the inland tours. Tours cost $13 to $129. There are ticket booths on the Green Pleasure Pier, at the Casino, in the plaza, and at the boat landing. ✉ *Avalon* ☎ *877/778–8322* ⊕ *www.visitcatalinaisland.com.*

VISITOR INFORMATION

Visitor Contacts Catalina Island Chamber of Commerce & Visitors Bureau.
✉ *1 Green Pleasure Pier, Avalon* ☎ *310/510–1520* ⊕ *www.catalinachamber.com.*

AVALON

A 1- to 2-hour ferry ride from Long Beach, Newport Beach, or San Pedro; a 15-minute helicopter ride from Long Beach or San Pedro, slightly longer from Santa Ana.

Avalon, Catalina's only real town, extends from the shore of its natural harbor to the surrounding hillsides. Its resident population is about 3,800, but it swells with tourists on summer weekends. Most of the city's activity, however, is centered on the pedestrian mall on Crescent Avenue, and most sights are easily reached on foot. Private cars are restricted, and rental cars aren't allowed, but taxis, trams, and shuttles can take you anywhere you need to go. Bicycles, electric bikes, and golf carts can be rented from shops along Crescent Avenue.

EXPLORING

Fodor's Choice
★
  Casino. This circular white structure is one of the finest examples of art deco architecture anywhere. Its Spanish-inspired floors and murals gleam with brilliant blue and green Catalina tiles. In this case, *casino,* the Italian word for "gathering place," has nothing to do with gambling. First-run movies are screened nightly at the Avalon Theatre, noteworthy for its classic 1929 theater pipe organ and art deco wall murals.

The Santa Catalina Island Company leads two tours of the Casino—the 30-minute basic tour ($13) and the 90-minute behind-the-scenes tour ($27), which leads visitors through the green room and into the Wrigleys' private lounge. ✉ *1 Casino Way* ☎ *310/510–0179 theater* ⊕ *www. visitcatalinaisland.com.*

Casino Point Dive Park. In front of the Casino are the crystal-clear waters of the Casino Point Dive Park, a protected marine preserve where moray eels, bat rays, spiny lobsters, harbor seals, and other sea creatures cruise around kelp forests and along the sandy bottom. It's a terrific site for scuba diving, with some shallow areas suitable for snorkeling. Equipment can be rented on and near the pier. The shallow waters of Lover's Cove, east of the boat landing, are also good for snorkeling. ✉ *Avalon.*

Wrigley Memorial and Botanic Garden. Two miles south of the bay is Wrigley Memorial and Botanic Garden, home to plants native to Southern California. Several grow only on Catalina Island—Catalina ironwood, wild tomato, and rare Catalina mahogany. The Wrigley family commissioned the garden as well as the monument, which has a grand staircase and a Spanish-style mausoleum inlaid with colorful Catalina tile. Wrigley Jr. was once buried here but his remains were moved to Pasadena during the Second World War. ✉ *Avalon Canyon Rd.* ☎ *310/510–2897* 🌐 *www.catalinaconservancy.org* 🎫 *$7.*

WHERE TO EAT

$$$ SEAFOOD FAMILY ✕ **Bluewater Grill.** Overlooking the ferry landing and the entire harbor, the open-to-the-salt-air Bluewater Grill offers freshly caught fish, savory chowders, and all manner of shellfish. If they're on the menu, don't miss the swordfish steak or the sand dabs. **Known for:** fresh local fish; happy hour; harbor views. $ *Average main: $25* ✉ *306 Crescent Ave.* ☎ *310/510–3474* 🌐 *www.bluewatergrill.com.*

$ AMERICAN ✕ **Eric's on the Pier.** This little snack bar has been an Avalon family–run institution since the 1920s. It's a good place to people-watch while drinking a draft beer and munching on a breakfast burrito, hot dog, or signature buffalo burger. **Known for:** comfort foods; quick eats; beachside location. $ *Average main: $12* ✉ *Green Pier No. 2* ☎ *310/510–0894* ⏲ *Closed Mon. No dinner.*

$$$ SEAFOOD ✕ **The Lobster Trap.** Seafood rules at the Lobster Trap—the restaurant's owner has his own boat and fishes for the catch of the day and, in season, spiny lobster. Ceviche is a great starter, always fresh and brightly flavored. **Known for:** locally caught seafood; convivial atmosphere; locals' hangout. $ *Average main: $24* ✉ *128 Catalina St.* ☎ *310/510–8585* 🌐 *catalinalobstertrap.com.*

WHERE TO STAY

$$$ HOTEL **Aurora Hotel & Spa.** In a town dominated by historic properties, the Aurora is refreshingly contemporary, with a hip attitude and sleek furnishings. **Pros:** trendy design; quiet location off main drag; close to restaurants. **Cons:** standard rooms are small, even by Catalina standards; no elevator. $ *Rooms from: $249* ✉ *137 Marilla Ave.* ☎ *310/510–0454* 🌐 *www.auroracatalina.com* *18 rooms* 🍴 *Breakfast.*

$$ HOTEL FAMILY **Hermosa Hotel.** This historic 1896 hotel offers small rooms, some well-worn character, and a friendly vibe. **Pros:** quiet enforced after 10 pm; kitchenettes available; reasonably priced; nearby grocery store. **Cons:** no frills; combo rooms share a bath; some rooms lack heating and/or a/c; no elevator. $ *Rooms from: $175* ✉ *131 Metropole St.* ☎ *310/510–1010, 800/668–5963* 🌐 *www.hermosahotel.com* *50 rooms.*

$$$ HOTEL FAMILY **Hotel Villa Portofino.** Steps from the Green Pleasure Pier, this European-style hotel creates an intimate feel with brick courtyards and walkways and suites named after Italian cities. **Pros:** romantic; close to beach; incredible sundeck. **Cons:** ground-floor rooms can be noisy; some rooms are on small side; no elevator. $ *Rooms from: $179* ✉ *111 Crescent Ave.* ☎ *310/510–0555, 888/510–0555* 🌐 *www.hotelvillaportofino.com* *35 rooms* 🍴 *Breakfast.*

$$$$ HOTEL FAMILY **Hotel Vista del Mar.** On the bay-facing Crescent Avenue, this third-floor property is steps from the beach, where complimentary towels, chairs, and umbrellas await guests. **Pros:** comfortable beds; central location; modern decor. **Cons:** no restaurant or spa facilities; few

rooms with ocean views; no elevator. $ *Rooms from: $295* ✉ *417 Crescent Ave.* ☎ *310/510–1452, 800/601–3836* ⊕ *www.hotel-vistadel-mar.com* ⇆ *14 rooms* ⏐◯⏐ *Breakfast.*

$$$$
B&B/INN
⊡ **Mt. Ada.** If you stay in the mansion where Wrigley Jr. once lived, you can enjoy all the comforts of a millionaire's home—at a millionaire's prices. **Pros:** timeless charm; shuttle from heliport and dock; incredible views. **Cons:** smallish rooms and bathrooms; expensive. $ *Rooms from: $480* ✉ *398 Wrigley Rd.* ☎ *310/510–2030, 877/778–8322* ⊕ *www.visitcatalinaisland.com* ☯ *Closed mid-Jan.–early Feb.* ⇆ *6 rooms* ⏐◯⏐ *Some meals.*

$$$$
HOTEL
FAMILY
⊡ **Pavilion Hotel.** This mid-century-modern-style hotel is Avalon's most citified spot, though just a few steps from the sand. **Pros:** centrally located, steps from the beach and harbor; friendly staff; plush bedding. **Cons:** no pool. $ *Rooms from: $265* ✉ *513 Crescent Ave.* ☎ *310/510–1788, 877/778–8322* ⊕ *www.visitcatalinaisland.com* ⇆ *71 rooms* ⏐◯⏐ *Breakfast.*

SPORTS AND THE OUTDOORS

BICYCLING

FAMILY
Brown's Bikes. Look for rentals on Crescent Avenue and Pebbly Beach Road, where Brown's Bikes is located. Beach cruisers and mountain bikes start at $20 per day. Electric bikes are also on offer. ✉ *107 Pebbly Beach Rd.* ☎ *310/510–0986* ⊕ *www.catalinabiking.com.*

DIVING AND SNORKELING

The Casino Point Underwater Park, with its handful of wrecks, is best suited for diving. Lover's Cove is better for snorkeling (but you'll share the area with glass-bottom boats). Both are protected marine preserves.

Catalina Divers Supply. Head to Catalina Divers Supply to rent equipment, sign up for guided scuba and snorkel tours, and attend certification classes. It also has an outpost at the Dive Park at Casino Point. ✉ *7 Green Pleasure Pier* ☎ *310/510–0330* ⊕ *www.catalinadiverssupply.com.*

HIKING

Catalina Island Conservancy. Permits from the Catalina Island Conservancy are required for hiking into Santa Catalina Island's interior. If you plan to backpack overnight, you'll need a camping reservation. The interior is dry and desert-like; bring plenty of water, sunblock, and all necessary supplies. The permits are free and can be picked up at the main house of the conservancy or at the airport. You don't need a permit for shorter hikes, such as the one from Avalon to the Botanical Garden. The conservancy has maps of the island's east-end hikes, such as Hermit's Gulch Trail. It's possible to hike between Avalon and Two Harbors, starting at the Hogsback Gate, above Avalon, but the 28-mile journey has an elevation gain of 3,000 feet and is not for the weak. ■TIP→ For a pleasant 4-mile hike out of Avalon, take Avalon Canyon Road to the Wrigley Botanical Garden and follow the trail to Lone Pine. At the top there's an amazing view of the Palisades cliffs and, beyond them, the sea. ✉ *125 Claressa Ave.* ☎ *310/510–2595* ⊕ *www. catalinaconservancy.org.*

LOS ANGELES

WELCOME TO LOS ANGELES

TOP REASONS TO GO

★ **Stargazing:** Both through the telescope atop Griffith Park and among the residents of Beverly Hills.

★ **Eating:** From food trucks to fine dining, an unparalleled meal awaits your palate.

★ **Beaches and Boardwalks:** The dream of '80s Venice is alive in California.

★ **Shopping:** Peruse eclectic boutiques or window-shop on Rodeo Drive.

★ **Architecture:** Art deco wonders to Frank Gehry masterpieces abound.

★ **Scenic Drives:** You haven't seen the sunset until you've seen it from a winding L.A. road.

1 Downtown. Downtown L.A. shows off spectacular modern architecture with the swooping Walt Disney Concert Hall, the brand new art museum, The Broad, and the stark Cathedral of Our Lady of the Angels. The Music Center and the Museum of Contemporary Art anchor a world-class arts scene, while Olvera Street, Chinatown, and Little Tokyo reflect the city's history and diversity.

2 Hollywood and the Studios. Glitzy and tarnished, good and bad—Hollywood is just like the entertainment business itself. The Walk of Fame, TCL Chinese Theatre, Paramount Pictures, and the Hollywood Bowl keep its glamorous past alive. Universal Studios Hollywood, Warner Bros., and NBC Television Studios are in the San Fernando Valley.

3 Beverly Hills and the Westside. Go for the glamour, the restaurants, and the scene. Rodeo Drive is particularly good for a look at excess. But don't forget the Westside's cultural attractions—especially the dazzling Getty Center. West Hollywood is an area for urban indulgences—shopping, restaurants, nightlife—rather than sightseeing. Its main arteries are the Sunset Strip

and Melrose Avenue, lined with shops that range from punk to postmodern.

4 Santa Monica and the Beaches. These desirable beach communities move from ultrarich, ultracasual Malibu to bohemian/transitioning Venice, with liberal, Mediterranean-style Santa Monica in between.

5 Pasadena. Its own separate city, Pasadena is a quiet area with outstanding Arts and Crafts homes, good dining, and a pair of exceptional museums: Huntington Library and Norton Simon Museum.

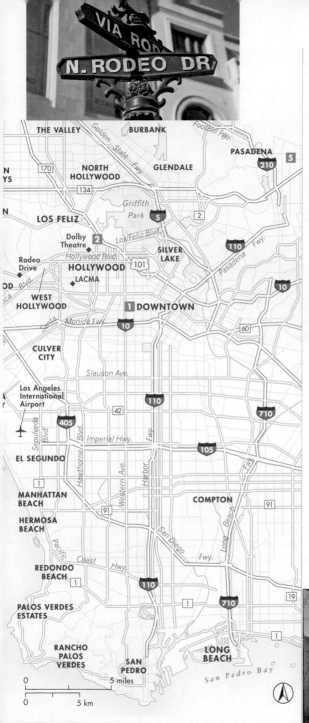

GETTING ORIENTED

Looking at a map of sprawling Los Angeles, first-time visitors are sometimes overwhelmed. Where to begin? What to see first? And what about all those freeways? Start by setting your priorities—movie and television buffs should first head to Hollywood, Universal Studios, and a taping of a television show. Beach and nature lovers might start out in Santa Monica, Venice, or Malibu, or spend an afternoon in Griffith Park, one of the country's largest city parks. Culture vultures should make a beeline for top museums: the twin Gettys (the center in Brentwood and the villa near Malibu), the Los Angeles County Museum of Art (LACMA), or Downtown's MOCA. Urban explorers might begin with Downtown L.A.

5

SOUTH-OF-THE-BORDER FLAVOR

From Cal-Mex burritos to Mexico City–style tacos, Southern California is a top stateside destination for experiencing Mexico's myriad culinary styles.

Many Americans are surprised to learn that the Mexican menu goes far beyond Tex-Mex (or Cal-Mex) favorites like burritos, chimichangas, enchiladas, fajitas, and nachos—many of which were created or popularized stateside. Indeed, Mexico has rich, regional food styles, like the complex *mole* sauces of Puebla and Oaxaca and the fresh *ceviches* of Veracruz, as well as the trademark snack of Mexico City: tacos.

In Southern California tacos are an obsession, with numerous blogs and websites dedicated to the quest for the perfect taco. They're everywhere—in ramshackle taco stands, roving trucks, and strip-mall taquerias. Whether you're looking for a cheap snack or a lunch on-the-go, SoCal's taco selection can't be beat. But be forewarned: there may not be an English menu. Here we've noted unfamiliar taco terms, along with other potentially new-to-you items from the Mexican menu.

THIRST QUENCHERS

Spanish for "fresh water," *agua fresca* is a nonalcoholic Mexican drink made from fruit, rice, or seeds that are blended with sugar and water. Fruit flavors like lemon, lime, and watermelon are common. Other varieties include *agua de Jamaica*, flavored with red hibiscus petals; *agua de horchata*, a cinnamon-scented rice milk; and *agua de tamarindo*, a bittersweet variety flavored with tamarind. For something with more of a kick, try a *Michelada*, a beer with a mixture of lime juice, chili sauce, and other savory ingredients. It's typically served in a salt-rimmed glass with ice.

5

DECODING THE MENU

Ceviche—Citrus-marinated raw seafood appetizer from the Gulf shores of Veracruz. Often eaten with tortilla chips.

Chile relleno—Roasted poblano pepper that is stuffed with ingredients like ground meat or cheese, then dipped in egg batter, fried, and served in tomato sauce.

Clayuda—An Oaxacan dish similar to pizza. Large corn tortillas are baked until hard, then topped with ingredients like refried beans, cheese, and salsa.

Fish taco—A specialty in Southern California, the fish taco is a soft corn tortilla stuffed with grilled or fried white fish (mahimahi, tilapia, or wahoo), pico de gallo, *crema*, and shredded cabbage.

Gordita—"Little fat one" in Spanish, this dish is like a taco, but the cornmeal shell is thicker, similar to pita bread.

Mole—A complex, sweet sauce with Aztec roots made from more than 20 ingredients, including chilies, cinnamon, cumin, anise, black pepper, sesame seeds, and Mexican chocolate. There are many types of mole using various chilies and ingredient combinations, but the most common is *mole poblano* from the Puebla region.

Quesadilla—A snack made from a fresh tortilla that is folded over and stuffed with simple fillings like cheese, then toasted on a griddle. Elevated versions of the quesadilla may be stuffed with

sautéed *flor de calabaza* (squash blossoms) or *huitlacoche* (corn mushrooms).

Salsa—A class of cooked or raw sauces made from chilies, tomatoes, and other ingredients. Popular salsas include *pico de gallo*, a fresh sauce made from chopped tomatoes, onions, chilies, cilantro, and lime; *salsa verde*, made with tomatillos instead of tomatoes; and *salsa roja*, a cooked sauce made with chilies, tomatoes, onion, garlic, and cilantro.

Sopes—A small, fried corn cake topped with ingredients like refried beans, shredded chicken, and salsa.

Taco—In Southern California, as in Mexico, tacos are made from soft, palm-sized corn tortillas folded over and filled with meat, chopped onion, cilantro, and salsa. Common taco fillings include *al pastor* (spiced pork), *barbacoa* (braised beef), *carnitas* (roasted pork), *cecina* (chili-coated pork), *carne asada* (roasted, chopped beef), *chorizo* (spicy sausage), *lengua* (beef tongue), *sesos* (cow brain), and *tasajo* (spiced, grilled beef).

Tamales—Sweet or savory corn cakes that are steamed, and may be filled with cheese, roasted chilies, shredded meat, or other fillings.

Torta—A Mexican sandwich served on a crusty sandwich roll. Fillings often include meat, refried beans, and cheese.

Updated
by Michele
Bigley, Alene
Dawson, Paul
Feinstein,
Ashley Tibbits,
and Clarissa
Wei

Los Angeles is a polarizing place, but those who hate it just haven't found their niche—there's truly a corner of the city for everyone. Drive for miles between towering palm trees, bodega-lined streets, and Downtown's skyscrapers, and you'll still never discover all of L.A.'s hidden gems.

Yes, you'll encounter traffic-clogged freeways, but there are also walkable pockets like Venice's Abbot Kinney. You'll drive past Beverly Hills mansions and spy palaces perched atop hills, but you'll also see the roots of midcentury modern architecture in Silver Lake. You'll soak up the sun in Santa Monica and then find yourself barhopping in the city's revitalized Downtown while enjoying scrumptious fish tacos along the way.

You might think that you'll have to spend most of your visit in a car, but that's not the case. In fact, exploring by foot is the only way to really get to know the various fringe neighborhoods and mini-cities that make up the vast L.A. area. But no single locale—whether it's Malibu, Downtown, Beverly Hills, or Burbank—fully embodies Los Angeles. It's in the mix that you'll discover the city's character.

PLANNING

WHEN TO GO
Almost any time of the year is the right time to go to Los Angeles; the climate is mild and pleasant year-round. Winter brings crisp, sunny, unusually smogless days from about November to May (expect brief rains from December to April). Los Angeles summers, which are virtually rainless, can lead to air-quality alerts. Prices skyrocket and reservations are a must when tourism peaks from July through early October.

GETTING HERE AND AROUND
AIR TRAVEL
It's generally easier to navigate the secondary airports than to get through sprawling LAX, the city's major gateway. Bob Hope Airport in Burbank is closest to Downtown, and domestic flights to it can be cheaper than those to LAX—it's definitely worth checking out. From

Long Beach Airport it's equally convenient to go north to central Los Angeles or south to Orange County. Flights to Orange County's John Wayne Airport are often more expensive than those to the other secondary airports. Parking at the smaller airports is cheaper than at LAX.

At LAX, SuperShuttle allows walk-on shuttle passengers without prior reservations. FlyAway buses travel between LAX and Van Nuys, Westwood, La Brea, and Union Station in Downtown.

Airports Hollywood Burbank Airport (*BUR*). ✉ *2627 N. Hollywood Way, near I-5 and U.S. 101, Burbank* ☎ *818/840–8840* ⊕ www.bobhopeairport.com. **John Wayne Airport** (*SNA*). ✉ *18601 Airport Way, Santa Ana* ☎ *949/252–5200* ⊕ www.ocair.com. **L.A./Ontario International Airport** (*ONT*). ✉ *E. Airport Dr., off I-10, Ontario* ☎ *909/937–2700* ⊕ www.flyontario.com. **Long Beach Airport** (*LGB*). ✉ *4100 Donald Douglas Dr., Long Beach* ☎ *562/570–2600* ⊕ www.lgb. org. **Los Angeles International Airport** (*LAX*). ✉ *1 World Way, off Hwy. 1* ☎ *855/463–5252* ⊕ www.lawa.org.

Shuttles FlyAway. ☎ *866/435–9529* ⊕ www.lawa.org/flyaway. **SuperShuttle.** ☎ *323/775–6600, 800/258–3826* ⊕ www.supershuttle.com.

BUS TRAVEL

Inadequate public transportation has plagued L.A. for decades. That said, many local trips can be made, with time and patience, by buses run by the Los Angeles County Metropolitan Transit Authority. In certain cases—visiting the Getty Center, for instance, or Universal Studios—buses may be your best option. There's a special Dodger Stadium Express that shuttles passengers between Union Station and the ballpark for home games. It's free if you have a ticket in hand, and saves you parking-related stress.

Metro Buses cost $1.75, plus 50¢ for each transfer to another bus or to the subway. A one-day pass costs $7, and a weekly pass is $25 for unlimited travel on all buses and trains. Passes are valid from Sunday through Saturday. For the fastest service, look for the red-and-white Metro Rapid buses; these stop less frequently and are able to extend green lights. There are 25 Metro Rapid routes, including along Wilshire and Vermont boulevards.

Other bus services make it possible to explore the entire metropolitan area. DASH minibuses cover six different circular routes in Hollywood, Mid-Wilshire, and Downtown. You pay 50¢ every time you get on. The Santa Monica Municipal Bus Line, also known as the Big Blue Bus, is a pleasant and inexpensive way to move around the Westside. Trips cost $1, and transfers are free. An express bus to and from Downtown L.A., run by Culver CityBus, costs $1.

Bus Information Culver CityBus. ☎ *310/253–6510* ⊕ www.culvercity.org. **DASH.** ☎ *310/808–2273* ⊕ www.ladottransit.com. **Los Angeles County Metropolitan Transit Authority.** ☎ *323/466–3876* ⊕ www.metro.net. **Santa Monica Municipal Bus Line.** ☎ *310/451–5444* ⊕ www.bigbluebus.com.

CAR TRAVEL

If you're used to driving in a congested urban area, you shouldn't have too much trouble navigating the streets of Los Angeles. If not, L.A. can be unnerving. Nevertheless, the city evolved with drivers in mind. Streets are wide and parking garages abound, so it's more car-friendly than many older big cities.

Remember that most freeways are known by a name and a number; for example, the San Diego Freeway is Interstate 405 (or just The 405), the Hollywood Freeway is U.S. 101, the Ventura Freeway is a different stretch of U.S. 101, the Santa Monica Freeway is Interstate 10, and the Harbor Freeway is Interstate 110. It helps, too, to know which direction you're traveling; say, west toward Santa Monica or east toward Downtown Los Angeles. Distance in miles doesn't mean much, depending on the time of day you're traveling: the short 10-mile drive between the San Fernando Valley and Downtown Los Angeles might take an hour to travel during rush hour but only 20 minutes at other times.

There are plenty of identical or similarly named streets in L.A. (Beverly Boulevard and Beverly Drive, for example), so be as specific as you can when asking directions. Expect sudden changes in addresses as streets pass through neighborhoods, then incorporated cities, then back into neighborhoods. This can be most bewildering on Robertson Boulevard, an otherwise useful north–south artery that, by crossing through L.A., West Hollywood, and Beverly Hills, dips in and out of several such numbering shifts in a matter of miles.

Information Caltrans Current Highway Conditions. ☎ *800/427–7623 for road conditions* ⊕ *www.dot.ca.gov.*

Emergency Services Metro Freeway Service Patrol. ☎ *511 for breakdowns* ⊕ *www.go511.com.*

METRO RAIL TRAVEL

Metro Rail covers only a small part of L.A.'s vast expanse, but it's convenient, frequent, and inexpensive. Most popular with visitors is the underground Red Line, which runs from Downtown's Union Station through Mid-Wilshire, Hollywood, and Universal City on its way to North Hollywood, stopping at the most popular tourist destinations along the way.

The light-rail Green Line stretches from Redondo Beach to Norwalk, while the partially underground Blue Line travels from Downtown to the South Bay. The monorail-like Gold Line extends from Union Station to Pasadena and Sierra Madre. The Orange Line, a 14-mile bus corridor, connects the North Hollywood subway station with the western San Fernando Valley.

Most recently unveiled was the Expo Line, which connects Downtown to Culver City and ends in Santa Monica, two blocks from the Pacific Ocean.

There's daily service from about 4:30 am to 12:30 am, with departures every 5 to 15 minutes. On weekends trains run until 2 am. Buy tickets from station vending machines; fares are $1.75, or $7 for an all-day pass.

Metro Rail Information Los Angeles County Metropolitan Transit Authority. ☎ *323/466–3876* ⊕ *www.metro.net.*

TAXI AND LIMOUSINE TRAVEL

Instead of trying to hail a taxi on the street, phone one of the many taxi companies. The metered rate is $2.70 per mile, plus a $2.85 per-fare charge. Taxi rides from LAX have an additional $4 surcharge. Be aware that distances are greater than they might appear on the map, so fares add up quickly.

On the other end of the price spectrum, limousines come equipped with everything from full bars to nightclub-style sound-and-light systems. Most charge by the hour, with a three-hour minimum.

Limo Companies Apex Limo. ☎ *818/637–2277, 877/427–1777 for 24-hr pickup* ⊕ *www.apexlimola.com.* **Dav El Chauffeured Transportation Network.** ☎ *800/922–0343* ⊕ *www.davel.com.* **First Class Limousine Service.** ☎ *800/400–9771* ⊕ *www.first-classlimo.com.* **Wilshire Limousine Services.** ☎ *888/813–8420* ⊕ *www.wilshirelimousine.com.*

Taxi Companies Beverly Hills Cab Co. ☎ *800/273–6611* ⊕ *www.beverlyhillscabco.com.* **LA Checker Cab.** ☎ *800/300–5007* ⊕ *www.ineedtaxi.com.* **United Independent Taxi.** ☎ *800/822–8294, 323/207–8294 text to order taxi* ⊕ *www.unitedtaxi.com.* **Yellow Cab Los Angeles.** ☎ *424/222–2222* ⊕ *www.layellowcab.com.* **Independent Cab Co.** ☎ *800/521–8294* ⊕ *www.taxi4u.com.*

TRAIN TRAVEL

Downtown's Union Station is one of the great American railroad terminals. The interior includes comfortable seating, a restaurant, and several snack bars. As the city's rail hub, it's the place to catch an Amtrak or Metrolink commuter train. Among Amtrak's Southern California routes are 22 daily trips to San Diego and five to Santa Barbara. Amtrak's luxury *Coast Starlight* travels along the spectacular coastline from Seattle to Los Angeles in just a day and a half (though it's often a little late). The *Sunset Limited* arrives from New Orleans, and the *Southwest Chief* comes from Chicago.

Information Amtrak. ☎ *800/872–7245* ⊕ *www.amtrak.com.* **Metrolink.** ☎ *800/371–5465* ⊕ *www.metrolinktrains.com.* **Union Station.** ✉ *800 N. Alameda St.* ☎ *213/683–6979* ⊕ *www.unionstationla.com.*

VISITOR INFORMATION

Discover Los Angeles publishes an annually updated general information packet with suggestions for entertainment, lodging, and dining, as well as a list of special events. There are two visitor information centers, both accessible to Metro stops: the Hollywood & Highland entertainment complex and Union Station.

Contacts Beverly Hills Conference and Visitors Bureau. ☎ *310/248–1015, 800/345–2210* ⊕ *www.lovebeverlyhills.com.* **Discover Los Angeles.** ☎ *213/624–7300, 800/228–2452* ⊕ *www.discoverlosangeles.com.* **Hollywood Chamber of Commerce.** ☎ *323/469–8311* ⊕ *www.hollywoodchamber.net.* **Long Beach Area Convention and Visitors Bureau.** ☎ *562/436–3645* ⊕ *www.visitlongbeach.com.* **Pasadena Convention & Visitor Bureau.** ☎ *800/307–7977* ⊕ *www.visitpasadena.com.* **Santa Monica Travel & Tourism.** ☎ *310/393–7593, 800/544–5319* ⊕ *www.santamonica.com.* **Visit California.** ☎ *916/444–4429, 800/862–2543* ⊕ *www.visitcalifornia.com.* **Visit West Hollywood.** ☎ *310/289–2525, 800/368–6020* ⊕ *www.visitwesthollywood.com.*

EXPLORING LOS ANGELES

Starstruck. Excessive. Smoggy. Superficial…. There's a modicum of truth to each of the adjectives regularly applied to L.A., but the locals dismiss their prevalence as envy from those who aren't as blessed with year-round sunshine.

Pop culture does permeate life here, its massive economy employing millions of Southern Californians, but the city where dreams are made accommodates those from all avenues of life.

DOWNTOWN

Updated by Clarissa Wei

If there's one thing Angelenos love, it's a makeover, and city planners have put the wheels in motion for a dramatic revitalization. Downtown is both glamorous and gritty and is an example of Los Angeles's complexity as a whole. There's a dizzying variety of experiences not to be missed here if you're curious about the artistic, historic, ethnic, or sports-loving sides of L.A.

Downtown Los Angeles isn't just one neighborhood: it's a cluster of pedestrian-friendly enclaves where you can sample an eclectic mix of flavors, wander through world-class museums, and enjoy great live performances or sports events.

TOP ATTRACTIONS

Fodor's Choice ★ **The Broad Museum.** The talk of the Los Angeles art world when it opened in 2015, this museum in an intriguing, honeycomb-looking building created by philanthropists Eli and Edythe Broad (rhymes with "road") to showcase their stunning private collection of contemporary art, amassed over five decades and still growing. With upward of 2,000 pieces by more than 200 artists, the collection has in-depth representations of the work of such prominent names as Jean Michel Basquiat, Jeff Koons, Ed Ruscha, Cindy Sherman, Cy Twombly, Kara Walker, and Christopher Wool. The "veil and vault" design of the main building integrates gallery space and storage space (visitors can glimpse the latter through a window in the stairwell): the veil refers to the fiberglass, concrete, and steel exterior; the vault is the concrete base. Temporary exhibits and works from the permanent collection are arranged in the small first-floor rooms and in the more expansive third floor of the museum, so you can explore everything in a few hours. Next door to The Broad is a small plaza with olive trees and seating, as well as the museum restaurant, Otium. Admission to the museum is free, but book timed tickets in advance to guarantee entry. ⊠ *221 S. Grand Ave., Downtown* ☎ *213/232–6200* ⊕ *www.thebroad.org* ⊠ *Free* ☉ *Closed Mon.*

FAMILY **California Science Center.** You're bound to see excited kids running up to the dozens of interactive exhibits here that illustrate the prevalence of science in everyday life. Clustered in different "worlds," the center keeps young guests busy for hours. They can design their own buildings and learn how to make them earthquake-proof; watch Tess, the dramatic 50-foot animatronic star of the exhibit "Body Works," demonstrate how the body's organs work together; and ride a bike across a trapeze wire three stories high in the air. One of the exhibits in the Air

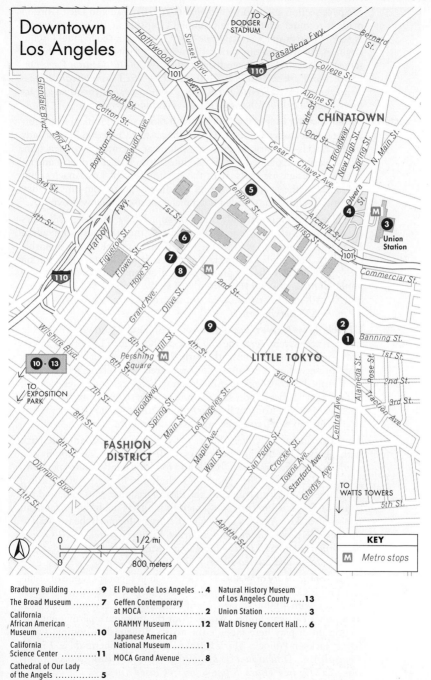

Downtown Los Angeles

5

& Space section shows how astronauts Pete Conrad and Dick Gordon made it to outer space in the Gemini 11 capsule in 1966; also here is NASA's massive space shuttle *Endeavor*, located in the Samuel Oschin Pavilion, for which a timed ticket is needed to visit. The IMAX theater screens science-related large-format films. ⊠ *700 Exposition Park Dr., Exposition Park* ☎ *213/744–7400, 323/724–3623* ⊕ *www.californiasciencecenter.org* ✉ *Free to permanent exhibitions; fees for some attractions, special exhibitions, and IMAX screenings vary.*

Fodor's Choice
★
Cathedral of Our Lady of the Angels. A half block from Frank Gehry's curvaceous Walt Disney Concert Hall sits the austere Cathedral of Our Lady of the Angels—a spiritual draw as well as an architectural attraction. Controversy surrounded Spanish architect José Rafael Moneo's unconventional design for the seat of the Archdiocese of Los Angeles. But judging from the swarms of visitors and the standing-room-only holiday masses, the church has carved out a niche for itself in Downtown L.A.

The plaza in front is glaringly bright on sunny days, though a children's play garden with bronze animals mitigates the starkness somewhat. Head underground to wander the mausoleum's mazelike white-marble corridors. Free guided tours start at the entrance fountain at 1 pm on weekdays. ■ TIP→ There's plenty of underground visitors parking; the vehicle entrance is on Hill Street. ⊠ *555 W. Temple St., Downtown* ☎ *213/680–5200* ⊕ *www.olacathedral.org* ✉ *Free, parking $4 every 15 mins, $19 maximum.*

El Pueblo de Los Angeles. The oldest section of the city, known as El Pueblo de Los Angeles, represents the rich Mexican heritage of L.A. It had a close shave with disintegration in the early 20th century, but key buildings were preserved, and eventually **Olvera Street,** the district's heart, was transformed into a Mexican-American marketplace. Today vendors still sell puppets, leather goods, sandals, and woolen shawls from stalls lining the narrow street. You can find everything from salt and pepper shakers shaped like donkeys, to gorgeous glassware and pottery.

At the beginning of Olvera Street is the Plaza, a Mexican-style park with plenty of benches and walkways shaded by a huge Moreton Bay fig tree. On weekends, mariachi bands and folkloric dance groups perform. Nearby places worth investigating include the historic Avila Adobe, the Chinese American Museum, the Plaza Firehouse Museum, and the America Tropical Interpretive Center. Exhibits at the Italian American Museum of Los Angeles chronicle the area's formerly heavy Italian presence. ⊠ *Avila Adobe/Olvera Street Visitors Center, E-10 Olvera St., Downtown* ☎ *213/628–1274* ⊕ *www.elpueblo.lacity.org* ✉ *Free for Olvera St. and guided tours, fees at some museums.*

Geffen Contemporary at MOCA. The Geffen Contemporary is one of architect Frank Gehry's boldest creations. The largest of the three MOCA branches, with 40,000 square feet of exhibition space, it was once used as a police car warehouse. Works from the museum's permanent collection on display here include the artists Willem de Kooning, Franz Kline, Jackson Pollock, Mark Rothko, and Cindy Sherman. ⊠ *152 N. Central Ave., Downtown* ☎ *213/626–6222* ⊕ *www.moca.org/exhibitions* ✉ *$12; free Thurs. 5 pm–8 pm* ⊗ *Closed Tues.*

Frank Gehry's Walt Disney Concert Hall became an instant L.A. icon.

GRAMMY Museum. The interactive GRAMMY Museum brings the music industry's history to life. Throughout 30,000 square feet of space, the museum shows rare footage of GRAMMY performances, plus rotating exhibits on award-winning musicians. ✉ *800 W. Olympic Blvd., Downtown* ☎ *213/765–6800* ⊕ *www.grammymuseum.org* ✉ *$12.95.*

MOCA Grand Avenue. The main branch of the Museum of Contemporary Art, designed by Arata Isozaki, contains underground galleries and presents elegant exhibitions. A huge Nancy Rubins sculpture fashioned from used airplane parts graces the museum's front plaza. ■ **TIP→ Take advantage of the free audio tour.** ✉ *250 S. Grand Ave., Downtown* ☎ *213/626–6222* ⊕ *www.moca.org* ✉ *$12; free Thurs. 5 pm–8 pm* ☉ *Closed Tues.*

Fodor'sChoice
★

Walt Disney Concert Hall. One of the architectural wonders of Los Angeles, the 2,265-seat hall is a sculptural monument of gleaming, curved steel designed by Frank Gehry. It's part of a complex that includes a public park, gardens, shops, and two outdoor amphitheaters, one of them atop the concert hall. The acoustically superlative venue is the home of the city's premier orchestra, the Los Angeles Philharmonic, whose music director, Gustavo Dudamel, is an international celebrity in his own right. The orchestra's season runs from late September to early June, before they head to the Hollywood Bowl for the summer. The highly praised Los Angeles Master Chorale also performs here. Look for big-name acts such as Pink Martini during the off-season, and special holiday events like the Deck the Hall Holiday Sing-Along. ■ **TIP→ Free 60-minute guided tours are offered on most days, and there are self-guided audio tours.** ✉ *111 S. Grand Ave., Downtown* ☎ *323/850–2000* ⊕ *www.laphil.org* ✉ *Tours free.*

WORTH NOTING

Bradbury Building. Stunning wrought-iron railings, ornate plaster moldings, pink marble staircases, a birdcage elevator, and a skylighted atrium that rises almost 50 feet—it's easy to see why the Bradbury Building leaves visitors awestruck. Designed in 1893 by a novice architect who drew his inspiration from a science-fiction story and a conversation with his dead brother via Ouija board, the office building was originally the site of turn-of-the-20th-century sweatshops, but now it houses a variety of businesses. Scenes from *Blade Runner* and *Chinatown* were filmed here, which means there's often a barrage of tourists snapping photos. Visits are limited to the lobby and the first-floor landing. ⊠ *304 S. Broadway, at 3rd St., Downtown* ☎ *213/626–1893.*

California African American Museum. With more than 3,500 historical artifacts, this museum showcases contemporary art of the African diaspora. Artists represented here include Betye Saar, Charles Haywood, and June Edmonds. The museum has a research library with more than 20,000 books available for public use. ■TIP➜ If possible, visit on a Sunday, when there's almost always a diverse lineup of speakers and performances. ⊠ *600 State Dr., Exposition Park* ☎ *213/744–7432* ⊕ *www. caamuseum.org* ⧉ *Free* ⊘ *Closed Mon.*

Japanese American National Museum. What was it like to grow up on a sugar plantation in Hawaii? How difficult was life for Japanese Americans interned in concentration camps during World War II? These questions are addressed by changing exhibitions at this museum in Little Tokyo that also include fun tributes to anime and Hello Kitty. Volunteer docents are on hand to share their own stories and experiences. The museum occupies its original site in a renovated 1925 Buddhist temple and an 85,000-square-foot adjacent pavilion. ⊠ *100 N. Central Ave., off E. 1st St., Downtown* ☎ *213/625–0414* ⊕ *www.janm.org* ⧉ *$10* ⊘ *Closed Mon.*

FAMILY **Natural History Museum of Los Angeles County.** The hot ticket at this beaux arts–style museum completed in 1913 is the Dinosaur Hall, whose more than 300 fossils include adult, juvenile, and baby skeletons of the fearsome Tyrannosaurus rex. The Discovery Center lets kids and curious grown-ups touch real animal pelts, and the Insect Zoo gets everyone up close and personal with the white-eyed assassin bug and other creepy crawlers. A massive hall displays dioramas of animals in their natural habitats. Also look for pre-Columbian artifacts and crafts from the South Pacific. Outdoors, the 3½-acre Nature Gardens shelter native plant and insect species and contain an expansive edible garden. ⊠ *900 Exposition Blvd., off I–110, near Vermont Ave., Exposition Park* ☎ *213/763–3466* ⊕ *www.nhm.org* ⧉ *$12.*

Union Station. Even if you don't plan on traveling by train anywhere, head here to soak up the ambience of a great rail station. Envisioned by John and Donald Parkinson, the architects who also designed the grand City Hall, the 1939 masterpiece combines Spanish Colonial Revival and art deco elements that have retained their classic warmth and quality. The waiting hall's commanding scale and enormous chandeliers have provided the backdrop for countless scenes in films, TV shows, and music videos. ⊠ *800 N. Alameda St., Downtown* ⊕ *www.unionstationla.com.*

HOLLYWOOD AND THE STUDIOS

Updated by
Clarissa Wei

The Tinseltown mythology of Los Angeles was born in Hollywood. Daytime attractions can be found on foot around the home of the Academy Awards at the Dolby Theatre, part of the Hollywood & Highland entertainment complex. The adjacent TCL Chinese Theatre delivers silver screen magic with its cinematic facade and ornate interiors from a bygone era. Walk the renowned Hollywood Walk of Stars to find your favorite celebrities' hand- and footprints. In summer, visit the crown jewel of Hollywood, the Hollywood Bowl, which hosts the Los Angeles Philharmonic.

To the north is Studio City, a thriving commercial strip at the base of the Hollywood Hills that's home to many smaller film companies and lunching studio execs; Universal City, where you'll find Universal Studios Hollywood; and bustling Burbank, home of several of the major studios. In Los Feliz, to the east, Griffith Park connects L.A.'s largest greenbelt with the trendy Vermont Avenue area. Beyond that you'll find Silver Lake and Echo Park.

TOP ATTRACTIONS

Dolby Theatre. The interior design of the theater that hosts the Academy Awards was inspired by European opera houses, but underneath all the trimmings the space has one of the finest technical systems in the world. A tour of the Dolby, which debuted in 2001 as the Kodak Theatre, is a worthwhile expense for movie buffs who just can't get enough insider information. Tour guides share plenty of behind-the-scenes tidbits about Oscar ceremonies as they escort you through the theater. You'll get to step into the VIP lounge where celebrities mingle on the big night and get a bird's-eye view from the balcony seating. ■TIP➔ If you have the Go Los Angeles Card, the tour is included. ⊠ *6801 Hollywood Blvd., Hollywood* ☏ *323/308–6300* ⊕ *www.dolbytheatre.com* ⊠ *Tour $22.*

Fodor's Choice
★

Griffith Observatory. High on a hillside overlooking the city, Griffith Observatory is one of the area's most celebrated landmarks. Its interior is just as impressive as its exterior, thanks to a massive expansion and cosmic makeover completed a decade ago. Highlights of the building include the Foucault's pendulum hanging in the main lobby, the planet exhibitions on the lower level, and the playful wall display of galaxy-themed jewelry along the twisty indoor ramp.

In true L.A. style, the Leonard Nimoy Event Horizon Theater presents guest speakers and shows on space-related topics and discoveries. The Samuel Oschin Planetarium features an impressive dome, digital projection system, theatrical lighting, and a stellar sound system. Shows are $7.

Grab a meal at the Café at the End of the Universe, which serves up dishes created by celebrity chef Wolfgang Puck. ■TIP➔ For a fantastic view, come at sunset to watch the sky turn fiery shades of red with the city's skyline silhouetted. ⊠ *2800 E. Observatory Ave., Los Feliz* ☏ *213/473–0800* ⊕ *www.griffithobservatory.org* ⊙ *Closed Mon.* ☞ *Observatory grounds and parking are open daily.*

5

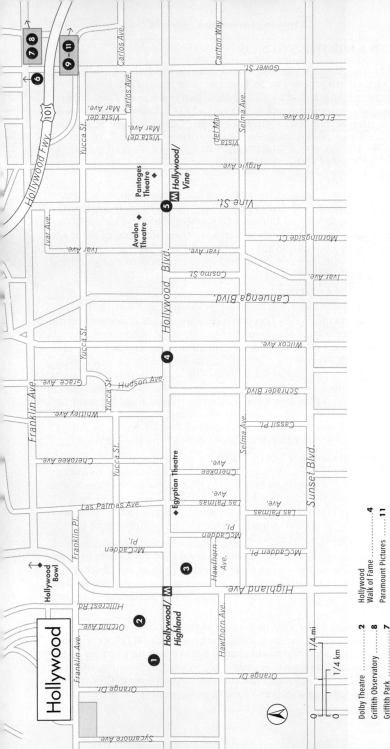

Hollywood

Hollywood Bowl

Hollywood Fwy • 101

Hollywood/Highland

Hollywood/Vine

Pantages Theatre

Avalon Theatre

Egyptian Theatre

Hollywood Blvd.

Cahuenga Blvd.

Sunset Blvd.

Franklin Ave.

Yucca St.

Carlos Ave.

Carlton Way

Gower St.

Selma Ave.

El Centro Ave.

Vista del Mar Ave.

Argyle Ave.

Vine St.

Morningside Ct.

Ivar Ave.

Cosmo St.

Wilcox Ave.

Schrader Blvd

Cassil Pl.

Cherokee Ave.

Las Palmas Ave.

McCadden Pl.

Hawthorn Ave.

Highland Ave.

Orange Dr.

Sycamore Ave.

Grace Ave.

Whitley Ave.

Hudson Ave.

Cahuenga Blvd.

Ivar Ave.

Ivar Ave.

Hillcrest Rd.

Orchid Ave.

Franklin Pl.

Cherokee Ave.

1/4 mi
1/4 km

Griffith Park. The country's largest municipal park, the 4,210-acre Griffith Park is a must for nature lovers, the perfect spot for respite from the hustle and bustle of the surrounding urban areas. Plants and animals native to Southern California can be found within the park's borders, including deer, coyotes, and even a reclusive mountain lion. Bronson Canyon (where the Batcave from the 1960s *Batman* TV series is located) and Crystal Springs are favorite picnic spots.

The park is named after Colonel Griffith J. Griffith, a mining tycoon who donated 3,000 acres to the city in 1896. As you might expect, the park has been used as a film and television location for at least a century. Here you'll find the Griffith Observatory, the Los Angeles Zoo, the Greek Theater, two golf courses, hiking and bridle trails, a swimming pool, a merry-go-round, and an outdoor train museum. ⊠ *4730 Crystal Springs Dr., Los Feliz* ☎ *323/913–4688* ⊕ *www.laparks.org/dos/parks/ griffithpk* ⊠ *Free; attractions inside park have separate admission fees.*

Fodor'sChoice **Hollywood Museum.** Lovers of Tinseltown's glamorous past may find
★ themselves humming "Hooray for Hollywood" as they tour this gem of cinema history inside the Max Factor Building. For years, Factor's famous makeup was manufactured on the top floors, and on the ground floor was a salon. After an extensive renovation, this art deco landmark that Factor purchased in 1928 now holds this museum with more than 10,000 bits of film memorabilia.

Exhibits include sections dedicated to Marilyn Monroe, Michael Jackson, and Bob Hope, and to costumes and props from such films as *Moulin Rouge, The Silence of the Lambs,* and *Planet of the Apes.* There's also an impressive gallery of photos showing movie stars frolicking at the Brown Derby, Ciro's, the Trocadero, the Mocambo, and other fabled venues.

Hallway walls are covered with the autograph collection of ultimate fan Joe Ackerman; aspiring filmmakers may want to check out the early film equipment. The museum's showpiece is the Max Factor exhibit, where separate dressing rooms are dedicated to Factor's "color harmony," which created distinct looks for "brownettes" (Factor's term), redheads, and, of course, bombshell blondes. You can practically smell the peroxide of Marilyn Monroe getting her trademark platinum look here. Also worth a peek are makeup cases owned by Lucille Ball, Lana Turner, Ginger Rogers, Bette Davis, Rita Hayworth, and others who made Max Factor makeup popular. ⊠ *1660 N. Highland Ave., at Hollywood Blvd., Hollywood* ☎ *323/464–7776* ⊕ *www.thehollywoodmuseum.com* ⊠ *$15* ⊗ *Closed Mon. and Tues.*

Hollywood Walk of Fame. Along Hollywood Boulevard (and part of Vine Street) runs a trail of affirmations for entertainment-industry overachievers. On this mile-long stretch of sidewalk, inspired by the concrete handprints in front of TLC Chinese Theatre, names are embossed in brass, each at the center of a pink star embedded in dark-gray terrazzo. They're not all screen deities; many stars commemorate people who worked in a technical field, such as sound or lighting. The first eight stars were unveiled in 1960 at the northwest corner of Highland Avenue and Hollywood Boulevard: Olive Borden, Ronald

Colman, Louise Fazenda, Preston Foster, Burt Lancaster, Edward Sedgwick, Ernest Torrence, and Joanne Woodward (some of these names have stood the test of time better than others). Since then, more than 2,000 others have been immortalized, though that honor doesn't come cheap—upon selection by a special committee, the personality in question (or more likely his or her movie studio or record company) pays about $30,000 for the privilege. To aid you in spotting celebrities you're looking for, stars are identified by one of five icons: a motion-picture camera, a radio microphone, a television set, a record, or a theatrical mask. ⊠ *Hollywood Blvd. and Vine St., Hollywood* ☎ *323/469–8311* ⊕ *www.walkoffame.com.*

Fodor'sChoice ★ **Paramount Pictures.** With a history dating to the early 1920s, the Paramount lot was home to some of Hollywood's most luminous stars, including Mary Pickford, Rudolph Valentino, Mae West, Marlene Dietrich, and Bing Crosby. Director Cecil B. DeMille's base of operations for decades, Paramount offers probably the most authentic studio tour, giving you a real sense of the film industry's history. This is the only major studio from film's golden age left in Hollywood—all the others are in Burbank, Universal City, or Culver City.

Memorable movies and TV shows with scenes shot here include *Sunset Boulevard, Forrest Gump,* and *Titanic.* Many of the *Star Trek* movies and TV series were shot entirely or in part here, and several seasons of *I Love Lucy* were shot on the portion of the lot Paramount acquired in 1967 from Lucille Ball. You can take a 2-hour studio tour or a 4½-hour VIP tour, led by guides who walk and trolley you around the back lots. As well as gleaning some gossipy history, you'll spot the sets of TV and film shoots in progress. Reserve ahead for tours, which are for those ages 10 and up. ■TIP➔ You can be part of the audience for live TV tapings (tickets are free), but you must book ahead. ⊠ *5555 Melrose Ave., Hollywood* ☎ *323/956–1777* ⊕ *www.paramountstudiotour.com* ⊠ *$55 regular tour, $178 VIP tour.*

TCL Chinese Theatre. The stylized Chinese pagodas and temples of the former Grauman's Chinese Theatre have become a shrine both to stardom and the combination of glamour and flamboyance that inspire the phrase "only in Hollywood." Although you have to buy a movie ticket to appreciate the interior trappings, the courtyard is open to the public. The main theater itself is worth visiting, if only to see a film in the same setting as hundreds of celebrities who have attended big premieres here.

And then, of course, outside in front are the oh-so-famous cement hand- and footprints. This tradition is said to have begun at the theater's opening in 1927, with the premiere of Cecil B. DeMille's *King of Kings,* when actress Norma Talmadge just happened to step in wet cement. Now more than 160 celebrities have contributed imprints for posterity, including some oddball specimens, such as casts of Whoopi Goldberg's dreadlocks. ⊠ *6925 Hollywood Blvd., Hollywood* ☎ *323/461–3331* ⊕ *www.tclchinesetheatres.com* ⊠ *Tour $15.*

FAMILY **Universal Studios Hollywood.** A theme park with classic attractions like roller coasters and thrill rides, Universal Studios also provides a tour of some beloved television and movie sets. A favorite attraction is the tram tour, during which you can experience the parting of the Red Sea; duck from dinosaurs in Jurassic Park; visit Dr. Seuss's Whoville; see the airplane wreckage of *War of the Worlds*; and get chills looking at the house from *Psycho*. ■ TIP→ The tram ride is usually the best place to begin your visit, because the lines become longer as the day goes on.

Most attractions are designed to give you a thrill in one form or another, including the spine-tingling Transformers: The Ride 3-D, or the bone-rattling roller coaster, Revenge of the Mummy. The Simpsons Ride takes you on a hair-raising animated journey through the clan's hometown of Springfield. Don't forget to indulge in magical moments at The Wizarding World of Harry Potter and try some Butterbeer in Hogsmeade. Geared more toward adults, CityWalk is a separate venue run by Universal Studios, where you'll find shops, restaurants, nightclubs, and movie theaters. ⊠ *100 Universal City Pl., Universal City* ☎ *818/622–3801* ⊕ *www.universalstudioshollywood.com* ☑ *$99.*

Warner Bros. Studios. If you're looking for an authentic behind-the-scenes look at how films and TV shows are made, head to this major studio center, one of the world's busiest. After a short film on the studio's movies and TV shows, hop aboard a tram for a ride through the sets and soundstages of such favorites as *Casablanca* and *Rebel Without a Cause*. You'll see the bungalows where Marlon Brando, Bette Davis, and other icons relaxed between shots, and the current production offices for Clint Eastwood and George Clooney. You might even spot a celeb or see a shoot in action—tours change from day to day depending on the productions taking place on the lot.

Tours are given at least every hour, more frequently from May to September, and last 2 hours and 25 minutes. Reservations are required, and advance notice is needed for people with mobility issues. Children under eight are not admitted. A five-hour deluxe tour costing $295 includes lunch, and lets you spend more time exploring the sets. ⊠ *3400 W. Riverside Dr., Burbank* ☎ *877/492–8687* ⊕ *www.wbstudiotour.com* ☑ *$62, $295 for deluxe tour.*

WORTH NOTING

Hollywood and Vine. The mere mention of this intersection inspires images of a street corner bustling with movie stars, hopefuls, and moguls arriving on foot or in a Duesenberg or a Rolls-Royce. In the old days this was the hub of the radio and movie industry: film stars like Gable and Garbo hustled in and out of their agents' office buildings (some now converted to luxury condos) at these fabled cross streets. Even the Red Line Metro station here keeps up the Hollywood theme, with a *Wizard of Oz*–style yellow brick road, vintage movie projectors, and old film reels on permanent display. Sights visible from this intersection include the Capitol Records Building, the Avalon Hollywood nightclub, Pantages Theater, and the W Hollywood Hotel. ⊠ *Hollywood Ave. and Vine St., Hollywood.*

Hollywood Sign. With letters 50 feet tall, Hollywood's trademark sign can be spotted from miles away. The icon, which originally read "Hollywoodland," was erected in the Hollywood Hills in 1923 to advertise a segregated housing development and was outfitted with

4,000 light bulbs. In 1949 the "land" portion of the sign was taken down. By 1973 the sign had earned landmark status, but since the letters were made of wood, its longevity came into question. A make-over project was launched and the letters were auctioned off (rocker Alice Cooper bought an "O" and singing cowboy Gene Autry sponsored an "L") to make way for a new sign made of sheet metal. Inevitably, the sign has drawn pranksters who have altered it over the years, albeit temporarily, to spell out "Hollyweed" (in the 1970s, to push for more lenient marijuana laws), "Go Navy" (before a Rose Bowl game), and "Perotwood" (during businessman Ross Perot's 1992 presidential bid). A fence and surveillance equipment have since been installed to deter intruders, but another vandal managed to pull the "Hollyweed" prank once again in 2017 after Californians voted to make recreational use of marijuana legal statewide. ■TIP➔ Use caution if driving up to the sign on residential streets; many cars speed around the blind corners. ✉ *Griffith Park, Mt. Lee Dr., Hollywood* ⊕ *www.hollywoodsign.org.*

BEVERLY HILLS AND THE WESTSIDE

Updated by
Clarissa Wei

The rumors are true: Beverly Hills delivers on a dramatic, cinematic scale of wealth and excess. A known celebrity haunt, come here to daydream, or to live like the rich and famous for a day. In West Hollywood you'll find nightclubs, world-famous eateries, and gallery openings.

The three-block stretch of Wilshire Boulevard known as Museum Row, east of Fairfax Avenue, features intriguing museums and a prehistoric tar pit. Wilshire Boulevard itself is something of a cultural monument—it begins its grand 16-mile sweep to the sea in Downtown L.A.

West of La Cienega Boulevard, you'll find chic, attractive neighborhoods with coveted postal codes—Bel Air, Brentwood, Westwood, West Los Angeles, and Pacific Palisades. The Westside is rich in culture—and not just entertainment-industry culture: it's home to the monumental Getty Center and the engrossing Museum of Tolerance.

TOP ATTRACTIONS

FAMILY
Fodor's Choice
★

The Getty Center. With its curving walls and isolated hilltop perch, the Getty Center resembles a pristine fortified city of its own. You may have been lured here by the beautiful views of Los Angeles—on a clear day stretching all the way to the Pacific Ocean—but the amazing architecture, uncommon gardens, and fascinating art collections will be more than enough to capture and hold your attention. When the sun is out, the complex's rough-cut travertine marble skin seems to soak up the light.

Getting to the center involves a bit of anticipatory lead-up. At the base of the hill, a pavilion disguises the underground parking structure. From there you either walk or take a smooth, computer-driven tram up the steep slope, checking out the Bel Air estates across the humming 405 freeway. The five pavilions that house the museum surround a central courtyard and are bridged by walkways. From the courtyard, plazas, and walkways, you can survey the city from the San Gabriel Mountains to the ocean.

The *Urban Light* assemblage sculpture outisde of LACMA consists of 202 restored street lamps from the 1920s and 1930s.

In a ravine separating the museum and the Getty Research Institute, conceptual artist Robert Irwin created the playful Central Garden in stark contrast to Meier's mathematical architectural geometry. The garden's design is what Hollywood feuds are made of: Meier couldn't control Irwin's vision, and the two men sniped at each other during construction, with Irwin stirring the pot with every loose twist his garden path took. The result is a refreshing garden walk whose focal point is an azalea maze (some insist the Mickey Mouse shape is on purpose) in a reflecting pool.

Inside the pavilions are the galleries for the permanent collections of European paintings, drawings, sculpture, illuminated manuscripts, and decorative arts, as well as photographs gathered internationally. The Getty's collection of French furniture and decorative arts, especially from the early years of Louis XIV (1643–1715) to the end of the reign of Louis XVI (1774–92), is renowned for its quality and condition; you can see a pair of completely reconstructed salons. In the paintings galleries, a computerized system of louvered skylights allows natural light to filter in, creating a closer approximation of the conditions in which the artists painted. Notable among the paintings are Rembrandt's *The Abduction of Europa*, Van Gogh's *Irises*, Monet's *Wheatstack, Snow Effects*, and *Morning*, and James Ensor's *Christ's Entry into Brussels*.

If you want to start with a quick overview, pick up the brochure in the entrance hall that guides you to collection highlights. There's also an instructive audio tour (free, but you have to leave your ID) with commentaries by art historians and other experts. Art information rooms with multimedia computer stations contain more details about the collections. The Getty also presents lectures, films, concerts, and special programs for kids, families, and all-around culture lovers. The complex includes an upscale restaurant and downstairs cafeteria with panoramic window views. There are also outdoor coffee carts. ■TIP→ On-site parking is subject to availability and can fill up by midday on holidays and in the summer, so try to come early in the day or after lunch. A tram takes you from the street-level entrance to the top of the hill. Public buses (Metro Rapid Line 734) also serve the center and link to the Expo Rail extension. ✉ *1200 Getty Center Dr., Brentwood* ☎ *310/440–7300* ⊕ *www.getty.edu* ✆ *Free; parking $15* ⊘ *Closed Mon.*

FAMILY   **La Brea Tar Pits Museum.** Show your kids where Ice Age fossils come from by taking them to the stickiest park in town. The area formed when deposits of oil rose to the earth's surface, collected in shallow pools, and coagulated into asphalt. In the early 20th century geologists discovered that all that goo contained the largest collection of Pleistocene (Ice Age) fossils ever found at one location: more than 600 species of birds, mammals, plants, reptiles, and insects. Roughly 100 tons of fossil bones have been removed in excavations during the last 100 years, making this one of the world's most famous fossil sites. You can see most of the pits through chain-link fences, and the new Excavator Tour gets you as close as possible to the action.

Pit 91 and Project 23 are ongoing excavation projects; tours are offered, and you can volunteer to help with the excavations in the summer. Several pits are scattered around Hancock Park and the surrounding neighborhood; construction in the area has often had to accommodate them, and in nearby streets and along sidewalks, little bits of tar occasionally ooze up. The museum displays fossils from the tar pits and has a glass-walled laboratory that allows visitors to view paleontologists and volunteers as they work on specimens. ✉ *5801 Wilshire Blvd., West Hollywood* ☎ *323/857–6300* ⊕ *www.tarpits.org* ✆ *$12; parking $12.*

Fodor's Choice   **Los Angeles County Museum of Art (LACMA).** Without a doubt, this is the
★   focal point of the museum district that runs along Wilshire Boulevard. Chris Burden's *Urban Light* sculpture, composed of 202 restored cast-iron antique street lamps, elegantly marks the location. Inside you'll find one of the country's most comprehensive art collections, with more than 120,000 objects dating from ancient times to the present. The museum, which opened in 1965, now includes numerous buildings that cover more than 20 acres.

The permanent collection's strengths include works by prominent Southern California artists; Latin American artists such as Diego Rivera and Frida Kahlo; Islamic and European art; paintings by Henri Matisse, Rene Magritte, Paul Klee, and Wassily Kandinsky; art representing the ancient civilizations of Egypt, the Near East, Greece, and Rome; and costumes and textiles dating back to the 16th century.

The Broad Contemporary Art Museum, designed by Renzo Piano, opened in 2008 and impresses with three vast floors. BCAM presents contemporary art from LACMA's collection in addition to temporary exhibitions that explore the interplay between the present and the past.

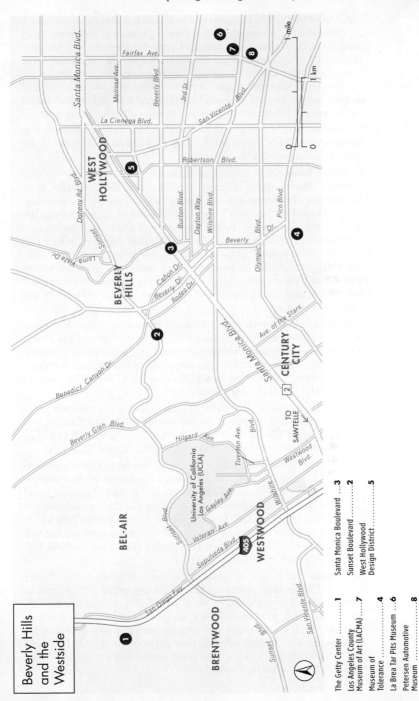

Beverly Hills and the Westside

The Getty Center **1**
Los Angeles County
Museum of Art (LACMA) **7**
Museum of
Tolerance **4**
La Brea Tar Pits Museum ...**6**
Petersen Automotive
Museum **8**

Santa Monica Boulevard ...**3**
Sunset Boulevard **2**
West Hollywood
Design District **5**

LACMA's other spaces include the Ahmanson Building, a showcase for Art of the Pacific, European, Middle Eastern, South and Southeast Asian collections; the Robert Gore Rifkind Center for German Expressionist Studies; the Art of the Americas Building; the Pavilion for Japanese Art, featuring scrolls, screens, drawings, paintings, textiles, and decorative arts from Japan; the Bing Center, a research library, resource center, and theater; and the Boone Children's Gallery, located in the Hammer Building, where story time and art lessons are among the activities offered. ■TIP→ Temporary exhibits sometimes require tickets purchased in advance. ⊠ *5905 Wilshire Blvd., West Hollywood* ☎ *323/857–6000* ⊕ *www.lacma.org* ⊴ *$15.*

FAMILY **Museum of Tolerance.** This museum unflinchingly confronts bigotry and racism. One of the most affecting sections covers the Holocaust, with film footage of deportations and concentration camps. Upon entering, you are issued a "passport" bearing the name of a child whose life was dramatically changed by the Nazis; as you go through the exhibit, you learn the fate of that child. An exhibit called "Anne: The Life and Legacy of Anne Frank," brings her story to life through immersive environments, multimedia presentations, and interesting artifacts. Simon Wiesenthal's Vienna office is set exactly as the famous "Nazi hunter" had it while performing his research that brought more than 1,000 war criminals to justice.

Interactive exhibits include the Millennium Machine, which engages visitors in finding solutions to human rights abuses around the world; Globalhate.com, which examines hate on the Internet by exposing problematic sites via touch-screen computer terminals; and the Point of View Diner, a re-creation of a 1950s diner that "serves" a menu of controversial topics on video jukeboxes. ■TIP→ Plan to spend at least three hours touring the museum; making a reservation is especially recommended for Friday, Sunday, and holiday visits. ⊠ *9786 W. Pico Blvd., south of Beverly Hills* ☎ *310/772–2505 for reservations* ⊕ *www.museumoftolerance.com* ⊴ *$15.50.*

Santa Monica Boulevard. From La Cienega Boulevard in the east to Doheny Drive in the west, Santa Monica Boulevard is the commercial core of West Hollywood's gay community, with restaurants and cafés, bars and clubs, bookstores and galleries, and other establishments catering largely to the LGBTQ scene. Twice a year—during June's L.A. Pride and on Halloween—the boulevard becomes an open-air festival. ⊠ *Santa Monica Blvd., between La Cienega Blvd. and Doheny Dr., West Hollywood* ⊕ *weho.org.*

Sunset Boulevard. One of the most fabled avenues in the world, Sunset Boulevard began humbly enough in the 18th century as a route from El Pueblo de Los Angeles to the Pacific Ocean. Today, as it passes through West Hollywood, it becomes the sexy and seductive Sunset Strip, where rock and roll had its heyday and cocktail bars charge a premium for the views. It slips quietly into the tony environs of Beverly Hills and Bel Air, twisting and winding past gated estates and undulating vistas. ⊠ *Sunset Blvd., West Hollywood.*

WORTH NOTING

FAMILY **Petersen Automotive Museum.** L.A. is a mecca for car lovers, which explains the popularity of this museum with a collection of more than 300 automobiles and other motorized vehicles. But you don't have to be a gearhead to appreciate the Petersen; there's plenty of fascinating history here for all to enjoy. Learn how Los Angeles grew up around its freeways, how cars evolve from the design phase to the production line, and how automobiles have influenced film and television. To see how the vehicles, many of them quite rare, are preserved and maintained, take the 90-minute tour of the basement-level Vault (young kids aren't permitted in the Vault, but they'll find plenty to keep them occupied throughout the museum). ⊠ *6060 Wilshire Blvd., Mid-Wilshire* ☎ *323/930–2277* ⊕ *www.petersen.org* ⊠ *$15.*

West Hollywood Design District. More than 200 businesses—art galleries, antiques shops, fashion outlets (including Rag & Bone and Christian Louboutin), and interior design stores—are found in the design district. There are also about 40 restaurants, including the famous paparazzi magnet, The Ivy. All are clustered within walking distance of each other—rare for L.A. ⊠ *Melrose Ave. and Robertson and Beverly Blvds., West Hollywood* ☎ *310/289–2534* ⊕ *wehodesigndistrict.com.*

5

SANTA MONICA AND THE BEACHES

Updated by Clarissa Wei

Hugging the Santa Monica Bay in an arch, the desirable communities of Malibu, Santa Monica, and Venice move from ultrarich and ultracasual Malibu to bohemian, borderline-seedy Venice. What they have in common is cleaner air, mild temperatures, heavy traffic, and an emphasis on beach culture.

Fodor's Choice ★ **Getty Villa Malibu.** Feeding off the cultures of ancient Rome, Greece, and Etruria, the villa exhibits astounding antiquities, though on a first visit even they take a backseat to their environment. This megamansion sits on some of the most valuable coastal property in the world. Modeled after an Italian country home, the Villa dei Papiri in Herculaneum, the Getty Villa includes beautifully manicured gardens, reflecting pools, and statuary. The structures blend thoughtfully into the rolling terrain and significantly improve the public spaces, such as the new outdoor amphitheater, gift store, café, and entry arcade. Talks and educational programs are offered at an indoor theater. ■**TIP→ An advance timed entry ticket is required for admission. Tickets are free and may be ordered from the museum's website or by phone.** ⊠ *17985 Pacific Coast Hwy., Pacific Palisades* ☎ *310/440–7300* ⊕ *www.getty.edu* ⊠ *Free, tickets required; parking $15* ☉ *Closed Tues.*

FAMILY **Santa Monica Pier.** Souvenir shops, carnival games, arcades, eateries, an outdoor trapeze school, a small amusement park, and an aquarium all contribute to the festive atmosphere of this truncated pier at the foot of Colorado Boulevard below Palisades Park. The pier's trademark 46-horse Looff Carousel, built in 1922, has appeared in several films, including *The Sting*. The Soda Jerks ice cream fountain (named for the motion the attendant makes when pulling the machine's arm) inside

the carousel building is a pier staple. Free concerts are held on the pier in the summer. ⊠ *Colorado Ave. and the ocean, Santa Monica* ☎ *310/458–8901* ⊕ *www.santamonicapier.org.*

Third Street Promenade. Stretch your legs along this pedestrians-only three-block stretch of 3rd Street, close to the Pacific, lined with jacaranda trees, ivy-topiary dinosaur fountains, strings of lights, and branches of nearly every major U.S. retail chain. Outdoor cafés, street vendors, movie theaters, and a rich nightlife make this a main gathering spot for locals, visitors, street musicians, and performance artists. Plan a night just to take it all in or take an afternoon for a long people-watching stroll. There's plenty of parking in city structures on the streets flanking the promenade. **Santa Monica Place,** at the south end of the promenade, is a sleek outdoor mall and foodie haven. Its three stories are home to Bloomingdale's, Louis Vuitton, Coach, and other upscale retailers. Don't miss the ocean views from the rooftop food court. ⊠ *Third St., between Colorado and Wilshire Blvds., Santa Monica* ⊕ *www.downtownsm.com.*

Venice Beach Boardwalk. The surf and sand of Venice are fine, but the main attraction here is the boardwalk scene, which is a cosmos all its own. Go on weekend afternoons for the best people-watching experience. You can also swim, fish, surf, and skateboard, or play racquetball, handball, shuffleboard, and basketball (the boardwalk is the site of hotly contested pickup games). You can rent a bike or in-line skates and hit The Strand bike path, then pull up a seat at a sidewalk café and watch the action unfold. ⊠ *1800 Ocean Front Walk, west of Pacific Ave., Venice* ☎ *310/392–4687* ⊕ *www.venicebeach.com.*

BEACHES

Malibu Lagoon State Beach. Bird-watchers, take note: in this 5-acre marshy area near Malibu Beach Inn you can spot egrets, blue herons, avocets, and gulls. (You need to stay on the boardwalks so as not to disturb their habitats.) The path leads out to a rocky stretch of Surfrider Beach, and makes for a pleasant stroll. The sand is soft, clean, and white, and you're also likely to spot a variety of marine life. Look for the signs to help identify these sometimes exotic-looking creatures. The lagoon is particularly enjoyable in the early morning and at sunset—and even more so now, thanks to a restoration effort that improved the lagoon's scent. The parking lot has limited hours, but street-side parking is usually available at off-peak times. Close by are shops and a theater. **Amenities:** lifeguards; parking (fee); showers; toilets. **Best for:** sunset; walking. ⊠ *23200 Pacific Coast Hwy., Malibu* ☎ *310/457–8143* ⊕ *www.parks. ca.gov* ⌑ *$12 parking.*

Fodor's Choice ★ **Robert H. Meyer Memorial State Beach.** Part of Malibu's most beautiful coastal area, this beach is made up of three minibeaches—El Pescador, La Piedra, and El Matador—each with the same spectacular view. Scramble down the steps to the rocky coves via steep, steep stairways; all food and water needs to be toted in, as there are no services. Portable toilets at the trailhead are the only restrooms. "El Mat" has a series of caves, Piedra some nifty rock formations, and Pescador a secluded feel, but they're all picturesque and fairly private. ⚠ **Keep track of the incoming tide so you won't get trapped between those otherwise scenic boulders. Amenities:** parking (fee); toilets. **Best for:** snorkeling; solitude; sunset; surfing; walking; windsurfing. ⊠ *32350, 32700, and 32900 Pacific Coast Hwy., Malibu* ☎ *818/880–0363* ⊕ *www.parks.ca.gov.*

Santa Monica State Beach. The first beach you'll hit after the Santa Monica Freeway (I–10) runs into the Pacific Coast Highway, wide and sandy Santa Monica is *the* place for sunning and socializing. Be prepared for a mob scene on summer weekends, when parking becomes an expensive ordeal. Swimming is fine (with the usual post-storm pollution caveat); for surfing, go elsewhere. For a memorable view, climb up the stairway over the PCH to Palisades Park, at the top of the bluffs. Free summer-evening concerts are held on the pier on Thursday nights. **Amenities:** food and drink; lifeguards; parking; showers; toilets; water sports. **Best for:** partiers; sunset; surfing; swimming; walking. ⊠ *1642 Promenade, PCH at California Incline, Santa Monica* ☎ *310/458–8573* ⊕ *www. smgov.net/portals/beach* ⌑ *$10 parking.*

PASADENA AREA

Updated by
Clarissa Wei

Although seemingly absorbed into the general Los Angeles sprawl, Pasadena is a separate and distinct city. Noted for its Tournament of Roses, seen around the world each New Year's Day, the city brims with noteworthy spots, from its gorgeous Craftsman homes to its exceptional museums, particularly the Norton Simon and the Huntington Library, Art Collections, and Botanical Gardens. Where else can you see a Chaucer manuscript and rare cacti in one place?

TOP ATTRACTIONS

Gamble House. Built by Charles and Henry Greene in 1908, this American Arts and Crafts bungalow illustrates the incredible craftsmanship that went into early L.A. architecture. The term *bungalow* can be misleading, since the Gamble House is a huge three-story home. To wealthy Easterners such as the Gambles (as in Procter & Gamble), this type of vacation home seemed informal compared with their mansions back home. Admirers swoon over the teak staircase and cabinetry, the Greene and Greene–designed furniture, and an Emil Lange glass door. The dark exterior has broad eaves, with sleeping porches on the second floor. An hour-long, docent-led tour of the Gamble's interior will draw your eye to the exquisite details. For those who want to see more of the Greene and Greene homes, there are guided walks around the historic Arroyo Terrace neighborhood. Advance tickets are highly recommended. ⊠ *4 Westmoreland Pl., Pasadena* ☎ *626/793–3334* ⊕ *www.gamblehouse.org* ⊠ *$15.*

Fodor's Choice
★

Huntington Library, Art Collections, and Botanical Gardens. If you have time for just one stop in the Pasadena area, be sure to see this sprawling estate built for railroad tycoon Henry E. Huntington in the early 1900s. Henry and his wife, Arabella (who was also his aunt by marriage), voraciously collected rare books and manuscripts, botanical specimens, and 18th-century British art. The institution they established became one of the most extraordinary cultural complexes in the world.

The library contains more than 700,000 books and 4 million manuscripts, including one of the world's biggest history of science collections.

Don't resist being lured outside into the Botanical Gardens, which extend out from the main building. The 10-acre Desert Garden has one of the world's largest groups of mature cacti and other succulents (visit on a cool morning or late afternoon). The Shakespeare Garden, meanwhile, blooms with plants mentioned in Shakespeare's works. The Japanese Garden features an authentic ceremonial teahouse built in Kyoto in the 1960s. A waterfall flows from the teahouse to the ponds below. In the Rose Garden Tea Room, afternoon tea is served (reserve in advance). The Chinese Garden, which is among the largest outside of China, sinews around waveless pools.

The Bing Children's Garden lets tiny tots explore the ancient elements of water, fire, air, and earth. A 1¼-hour guided tour of the Botanical Gardens is led by docents at posted times, and a free brochure with a map and property highlights is available in the entrance pavilion. ⊠ *1151 Oxford Rd., San Marino* ☎ *626/405–2100* ⊕ *www.huntington. org* ⊠ *$20 weekdays, $23 weekends* ⊙ *Closed Tues.*

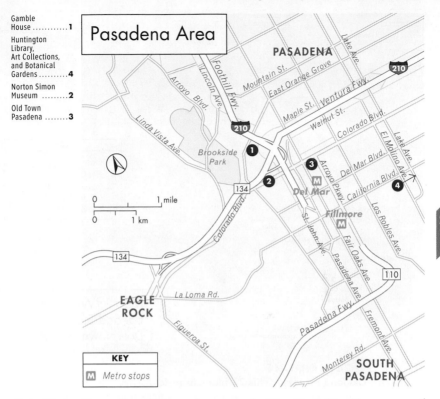

Fodor's Choice **Norton Simon Museum.** As seen in the New Year's Day Tournament of
★ Roses Parade, this low-profile brown building is one of the finest midsize museums anywhere, with a collection that spans more than 2,000
years of Western and Asian art. It all began in the 1950s when Norton
Simon (Hunt-Wesson Foods, McCalls Corporation, and Canada Dry)
started collecting works by Degas, Renoir, Gauguin, and Cézanne. His
collection grew to include old masters, impressionists, and modern
works from Europe, as well as Indian and Southeast Asian art.

Today the Norton Simon Museum is richest in works by Rembrandt,
Picasso, and, most of all, Degas—this is one of the only two U.S. institutions (the other is New York's Metropolitan Museum of Art) to hold
nearly all of the artist's model bronzes.

Head down to the bottom floor to see temporary exhibits and phenomenal Southeast Asian and Indian sculptures and artifacts, where
pieces like a Ban Chiang black ware vessel date back to well before
1000 BC. Don't miss a living artwork outdoors: the garden, conceived
by noted Southern California landscape designer Nancy Goslee Power.
The tranquil pond was inspired by Monet's gardens at Giverny. ⊠ *411
W. Colorado Blvd., Pasadena* ☎ *626/449–6840* ⊕ *www.nortonsimon.
org* 💲 *$12, free 1st Fri. of month 5–8 pm* ☽ *Closed Tues.*

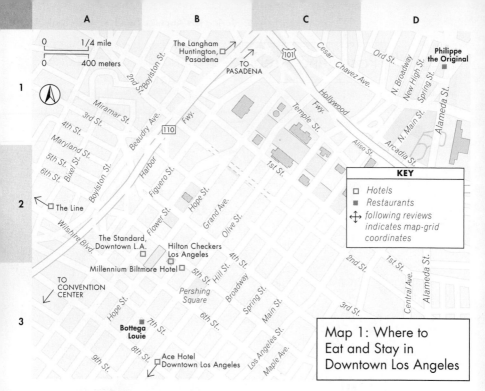

Map 1: Where to Eat and Stay in Downtown Los Angeles

KEY

□ Hotels
■ Restaurants
⊕ following reviews indicates map-grid coordinates

WORTH NOTING

Old Town Pasadena. This 22-block historic district contains a vibrant mix of restored 19th-century brick buildings interspersed with contemporary architecture. Chain stores have muscled in, but there are still some homegrown shops, plenty of tempting cafés and restaurants, and a bustling beer scene. In recent years, a vibrant Asian food scene has popped up in the vicinity as well. In the evening and on weekends, the streets are packed with people. Old Town's main action takes place on Colorado Boulevard between Pasadena Avenue and Arroyo Parkway. ⊠ *Pasadena.*

WHERE TO EAT

Updated by
Paul Feinstein

Los Angeles may be known for its beach living and celebrity-infused backdrop, but it was once a farm town. The hillsides were covered in citrus orchards and dairy farms, and agriculture was a major industry. Today, even as L.A. is urbanized, the city's culinary landscape has re-embraced a local, sustainable, and seasonal philosophy at many levels—from fine dining to street snacks.

Use the coordinate (⊕ 1:A1) at the end of each listing to locate a site on the corresponding map.

WHAT IT COSTS			
$	**$$**	**$$$**	**$$$$**
Restaurants	under $18	$18–$24	$25–$35	over $35

Prices are the average cost of a main course at dinner or, if dinner is not served, at lunch, excluding 9.75% tax.

DOWNTOWN

$$$
ITALIAN
✕**Bottega Louie.** A Downtown dining staple, this lively Italian restaurant and gourmet market features open spaces, stark white walls, and majestic floor-to-ceiling windows. If the wait is too long at this no-reservations eatery, you can sip on prosecco and nibble on pastries at the bar. **Known for:** mouthwatering crab beignets; one-of-a-kind portobello fries. $ *Average main: $25* ⊠ *700 S. Grand Ave., Downtown* ☎ *213/802–1470* ⊕ *www.bottegalouie.com* ✛ *1:A3.*

$
AMERICAN
FAMILY
Fodor'sChoice
★
✕**Philippe the Original.** First opened in 1908, Philippe's is one of L.A.'s oldest restaurants and claims to be the originator of the French dip sandwich. While the debate continues around the city, one thing is certain: the dips made with beef, pork, ham, lamb, or turkey on a freshly baked roll stand the test of time. **Known for:** $0.50 coffee; communal tables; post–Dodgers game eats. $ *Average main: $8* ⊠ *1001 N. Alameda St., Downtown* ☎ *213/628–3781* ⊕ *www.philippes.com* ✛ *1:D1.*

HOLLYWOOD AND THE STUDIOS

BURBANK

$
CUBAN
FAMILY
✕**Porto's Bakery.** Waiting in line at Porto's is as much a part of the experience as is indulging in a roasted pork sandwich or a chocolate-dipped croissant. This Cuban bakery and café has been an L.A. staple for more than 50 years, often bustling during lunch. **Known for:** counter service; potato balls; roasted pork sandwiches. $ *Average main: $10* ⊠ *3614 W. Magnolia Blvd., Burbank* ☎ *818/846–9100* ⊕ *www.portosbakery. com* ✛ *2:E1.*

HOLLYWOOD

$
AMERICAN
FAMILY
✕**Pink's Hot Dogs.** Since 1939, Angelenos and tourists alike have been lining up at this roadside hot dog joint. Open until 3 am on weekends, the chili dogs are the main draw, but don't shy away from themed and celebrity-inspired specials like the Emeril Legasse Bam Dog, the Lord of the Rings Dog, or the Giada De Laurentiis Dog. **Known for:** long lines; outside seating. $ *Average main: $6* ⊠ *709 N. La Brea Ave., Hollywood* ☎ *323/931–4223* ⊕ *www.pinkshollywood.com* ✛ *2:D2.*

$$
ITALIAN
✕**Pizzeria Mozza.** Mario Batali and Nancy Silverton own this upscale pizza and antipasti eatery. The pies—thin-crusted delights with golden, blistered edges—are more Campania than California, and are served piping hot daily. **Known for:** affordable Italian-only wines; walk-ins welcome at bar. $ *Average main: $19* ⊠ *641 N. Highland Ave., Hollywood* ☎ *323/297–0101* ⊕ *www.pizzeriamozza.com* ✛ *2:D2.*

5

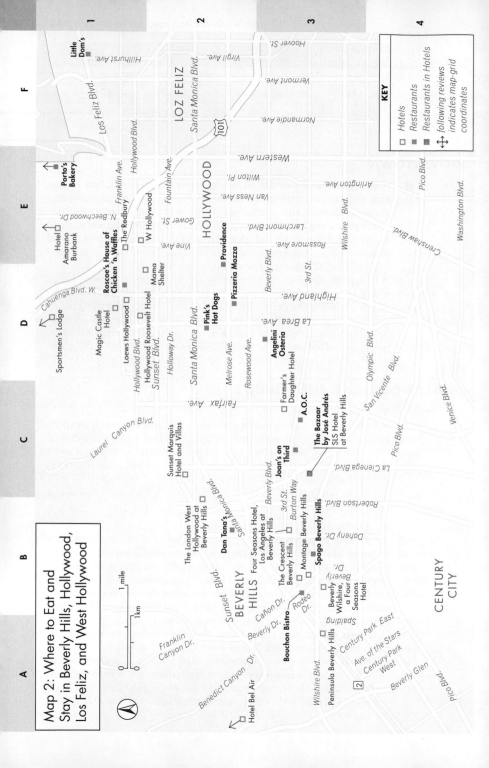

Map 2: Where to Eat and Stay in Beverly Hills, Hollywood, Los Feliz, and West Hollywood

KEY
□ Hotels
■ Restaurants
■ Restaurants in Hotels
↔ following reviews indicates map-grid coordinates

BEVERLY HILLS
HOLLYWOOD
LOZ FELIZ
CENTURY CITY

Little Dom's
Porto's Bakery
Sportsmen's Lodge
Hotel Amarano Burbank
Magic Castle Hotel
Roscoe's House of Chicken 'n Waffles
The Redbury
W Hollywood
Loews Hollywood
Hollywood Roosevelt Hotel
Mama Shelter
Providence
Pink's Hot Dogs
Pizzeria Mozza
Angelini Osteria
Farmer's Daughter Hotel
A.O.C.
The Bazaar by José Andrés
SLS Hotel at Beverly Hills
Joan's on Third
Sunset Marquis Hotel and Villas
The London West Hollywood at Beverly Hills
Dan Tana's
Four Seasons Hotel, Los Angeles at Beverly Hills
The Crescent Beverly Hills
Montage Beverly Hills
Spago Beverly Hills
Beverly Wilshire, a Four Seasons Hotel
Bouchon Bistro
Peninsula Beverly Hills
Hotel Bel Air

Los Feliz Blvd.
Hillhurst Ave.
Hollywood Blvd.
Virgil Ave.
Hoover St.
Vermont Ave.
Normandie Ave.
Santa Monica Blvd.
Western Ave.
Wilton Pl.
Van Ness Ave.
Arlington Ave.
Pico Blvd.
Washington Blvd.
Crenshaw Blvd.
Wilshire Blvd.
Larchmont Blvd.
Rossmore Ave.
3rd St.
Beverly Blvd.
Highland Ave.
La Brea Ave.
Rosewood Ave.
Melrose Ave.
Fairfax Ave.
Olympic Blvd.
San Vicente Blvd.
La Cienega Blvd.
Robertson Blvd.
Pico Blvd.
Venice Blvd.
Doheny Dr.
Burton Way
3rd St.
Beverly Blvd.
Santa Monica Blvd.
Beverly Dr.
Cañon Dr.
Rodeo Dr.
Spalding Dr.
Century Park East
Ave. of the Stars
Century Park West
Beverly Glen
Pico Blvd.
Wilshire Blvd.
Franklin Canyon Dr.
Benedict Canyon Dr.
Laurel Canyon Blvd.
Sunset Blvd.
Holloway Dr.
Gower St.
Vine Ave.
Fountain Ave.
Franklin Ave.
N. Beechwood Dr.
Cahuenga Blvd. W.
101

1 mile
1 km

$$$$ ✕ **Providence.** Widely considered one of the best seafood restaurants in the
SEAFOOD country, chef-owner Michael Cimarusti and co-owner Donato Poto ele-
Fodor'sChoice vate sustainably driven fine dining to an art form. The elegant space is the
★ perfect spot to sample exquisite seafood with the chef's signature application of French technique, traditional American themes, and Asian accents.
Known for: pastries by chef Jessie Liu; Friday lunch special. $ *Average
main: $120* ✉ *5955 Melrose Ave., Hollywood* ☎ *323/460–4170* ⊕ *www.
providencela.com* ☉ *No lunch Mon.–Thurs. and weekends* ✛ *2:E2.*

$ ✕ **Roscoe's House of Chicken 'n Waffles.** Roscoe's is *the* place for down-
SOUTHERN home Southern cooking in Southern California. Just ask the patrons
FAMILY who drive from all over L.A. for bargain-priced fried chicken and
waffles. The name of this casual eatery honors a late-night combo
popularized in Harlem jazz clubs. Known for: busy; late-night eats;
lemonade. $ *Average main: $15* ✉ *1514 N. Gower St., Hollywood*
☎ *323/466–7453* ⊕ *www.roscoeschickenandwaffles.com* ✛ *2:E1.*

LOS FELIZ
$$ ✕ **Little Dom's.** With a vintage bar and dapper barkeep who mixes up
ITALIAN seasonally inspired retro cocktails, an attached Italian deli where you
can pick up a pork-cheek sub, and an $18 Monday-night supper, it's not
surprising that Little Dom's is a neighborhood gem. Cozy and inviting,
with big leather booths you can sink into for the night, the restaurant
puts a modern spin on classic Italian dishes such as wild-boar meatballs,
almond-milk ricotta agnolotti, and grilled steak slathered in Parmesan.
Known for: spaghetti and meatballs; outdoor seating; brunch. $ *Av-
erage main: $20* ✉ *2128 Hillhurst Ave., Los Feliz* ☎ *323/661–0055*
⊕ *www.littledoms.com* ✛ *2:F1.*

BEVERLY HILLS AND THE WESTSIDE

BEVERLY HILLS
$$$$ ✕ **The Bazaar by José Andrés.** Celebrity Spanish chef José Andrés has con-
SPANISH quered L.A. with this colorful and opulent Beverly Hills spot, which fea-
tures a bar stocked with liquid nitrogen and a super-flashy patisserie. Pore
over a menu of items like Spanish tapas (with a twist), and "liquid" olives
(created through a technique called spherification). Known for: molecular
gastronomy; foie gras cotton candy. $ *Average main: $65* ✉ *SLS Hotel
at Beverly Hills, 465 S. La Cienega Blvd., Beverly Hills* ☎ *310/246–5555*
⊕ *slshotels.com/beverlyhills/bazaar* ☉ *No lunch* ✛ *2:C3.*

$$$ ✕ **Bouchon Bistro.** Chef Thomas Keller of Napa Valley's The French
FRENCH Laundry fame is at the head of this majestic bistro in Beverly Hills. Start
FAMILY with the classic onion soup that arrives with a bubbling lid of cheese,
Fodor'sChoice or the salmon rillettes, which are big enough to share. Known for: tasty
★ steak frites; sumptuous croque madame; sweet profiteroles for dessert.
$ *Average main: $35* ✉ *235 N. Canon Dr., Beverly Hills* ☎ *310/271–
9910* ⊕ *www.thomaskeller.com/bouchonbeverlyhills* ✛ *2:B3.*

$$$ ✕ **Spago Beverly Hills.** Wolfgang Puck's flagship restaurant is a modern
MODERN L.A. classic. Spago centers on a buzzing redbrick outdoor courtyard
AMERICAN shaded by 100-year-old olive trees, and a daily-changing menu offers
Fodor'sChoice dishes like Cantonese-style striped bass, traditional Austrian specialties,
★ or pizza with white truffles. Known for: great people-watching; magical

5

CLOSE UP

Local Chains Worth Stopping For

It's said that the drive-in burger joint was invented in L.A., probably to meet the demands of an ever-mobile car culture. Burger aficionados line up at all hours outside **In-N-Out Burger** (🌐 *www.in-n-out.com, multiple locations*), still a family-owned operation whose terrific made-to-order burgers are revered by Angelenos. Visitors may recognize the chain as the infamous spot where Paris Hilton got nabbed for drunk driving, but locals are more concerned with getting their burger fix off the "secret" menu, with variations like "Animal Style" (mustard-grilled patty with grilled onions and extra spread), a "4 x 4" (four burger patties and four cheese slices, for big eaters) or the bun-less "Protein Style" that comes wrapped in a bib of lettuce. Go online for a list of every "secret" menu item.

Tommy's is best known for their delightfully sloppy chili burger. Visit their no-frills original location (✉ *2575 Beverly Blvd., Los Angeles* ☎ *213/389-9060*)—a culinary landmark. For rotisserie chicken that will make you forget the Colonel altogether, head to **Zankou Chicken** (✉ *5065 Sunset Blvd., Hollywood* ☎ *323/665-7845* 🌐 *www.zankouchicken.com*), a small chain noted for its golden crispy-skinned birds, potent garlic sauce, and Armenian specialties. One-of-a-kind-sausage lovers will appreciate **Wurstküche** (✉ *800 E. 3rd St., Downtown* ☎ *213/687-4444* 🌐 *www.jerrysfamousdeli.com*), where the menu includes items like rattlesnake and rabbit or pheasant with Herbs de Provence. With a lively bar scene, the occasional celebrity sighting, and a spot directly across from the beach, **BOA Steakhouse** (✉ *101 Santa Monica Blvd., Santa Monica* ☎ *310/899-4466* 🌐 *www.hillstone.com*) is a popular hangout, while **Lemonade** (✉ *9001 Beverly Blvd., West Hollywood* ☎ *310/247-2500* 🌐 *www.senorfish.net*) is known for its healthy seasonally driven menu, pulled straight from L.A.'s farmers' markets.

mango soufflé. [$] *Average main: $32* ✉ *176 N. Cañon Dr., Beverly Hills* ☎ *310/385-0880* 🌐 *www.wolfgangpuck.com* 🕒 *No lunch Sun.* ✥ *2:B3.*

WEST HOLLYWOOD

$$$$ ITALIAN Fodor's Choice ★ 🍴 **Angelini Osteria.** Despite its modest, rather congested dining room, this is one of L.A.'s most celebrated Italian restaurants. The key is chef-owner Gino Angelini's consistently impressive dishes, like whole branzino, tender veal kidneys, or rich oxtail stew, as well as lasagna oozing with besciamella. **Known for:** large Italian wine selection; bold flavors. [$] *Average main: $40* ✉ *7313 Beverly Blvd., West Hollywood* ☎ *323/297-0070* 🌐 *www.angeliniosteria.com* 🕒 *Closed Mon. No lunch weekends* ✥ *2:D3.*

$$$$ MEDITERRANEAN 🍴 **A.O.C.** An acronym for Appellation d'Origine Contrôlée, the regulatory system that ensures the quality of local wines and cheeses in France, A.O.C. upholds this standard of excellence from shared plates to perfect wine pairings. Try the Spanish fried chicken, diver scallops with rapini pesto, or arroz negro with squid. **Known for:** amazing bacon-wrapped dates; quaint outdoor seating; fireplaces indoors. [$] *Average main: $36*

✉ *8700 W. 3rd St., West Hollywood* ☎ *310/859–9859* 🌐 *www.aocwine-bar.com* 🕑 *No lunch weekends* ⊕ *2:C3.*

$$$ ITALIAN 🍴 **Dan Tana's.** If you're looking for an Italian vibe straight out of *Goodfellas*, your search ends here. Checkered tablecloths cover the tightly packed tables as Hollywood players dine on the city's best chicken and veal Parm, and down Scotches by the finger. **Known for:** elbow-room-only bar; lively atmosphere; long lines. [$] *Average main: $35* ✉ *9071 California Rte. 2, West Hollywood* ☎ *310/275–9444* 🌐 *www.dantanasrestaurant.com* ⊕ *2:B2.*

$ CAFÉ FAMILY 🍴 **Joan's on Third.** Part restaurant, part bakery, part market, Joan's on Third has a little bit of everything. This roadside French-style café caters to families, the occasional local celebrity, and lovers of all things wholesome. **Known for:** crispy baguettes; fresh pastries; long lines. [$] *Average main: $16* ✉ *8350 W. 3rd St., West Hollywood* ☎ *323/655–2285* 🌐 *www.joansonthird.com* ⊕ *2:C3.*

WEST LOS ANGELES

$ AMERICAN Fodor'sChoice ★ 🍴 **The Apple Pan.** A favorite since 1947, this unassuming joint with a horseshoe-shaped counter—no tables here—turns out one heck of a good burger. Try the cheeseburger with Tillamook cheddar, or the hickory burger with barbecue sauce. **Known for:** indulgent apple pie; perfect fries; Sanka coffee. [$] *Average main: $8* ✉ *10801 W. Pico Blvd., West L.A.* ☎ *310/475–3585* 💳 *No credit cards* 🕑 *Closed Mon.* ⊕ *3:D2.*

SANTA MONICA AND VENICE

SANTA MONICA

$ DELI 🍴 **Bay Cities Italian Deli.** Part deli, part market, Bay Cities has been home to incredible Italian subs since 1925. This renowned counter service spot is always crowded (best to order ahead), but monster subs run the gamut from the mighty meatball, to their signature "Godmother" made with prosciutto, ham, capicola, mortadella, Genoa salami, and provolone. **Known for:** market with rare imports; excellent service. [$] *Average main: $10* ✉ *1517 Lincoln Blvd., Santa Monica* ☎ *310/395–8279* 🌐 *www.baycitiesitaliandeli.com* 🕑 *Closed Mon.* ⊕ *3:B2.*

$ AMERICAN 🍴 **Father's Office.** Distinguished by its vintage neon sign, this pub is famous for handcrafted beers and a brilliant signature burger. Topped with Gruyère and Maytag blue cheeses, arugula, caramelized onions, and applewood-smoked bacon compote, the "Office Burger" is a guilty pleasure worth waiting in line for, which is usually required. **Known for:** addictive sweet-potato fries; strict no-substitutions policy. [$] *Average main: $15* ✉ *1018 Montana Ave., Santa Monica* ☎ *310/736–2224* 🌐 *www.fathersoffice.com* 🕑 *No lunch weekdays* ⊕ *3:B2.*

$$$$ FRENCH Fodor'sChoice ★ 🍴 **Mélisse.** Chef-owner Josiah Citrin enhances his modern French cooking with seasonal California produce. The tasting menu might feature a white-corn ravioli in brown butter-truffle froth, lobster Bolognese, or elegant table-side presentations of Dover sole and stuffed rotisserie chicken. **Known for:** domestic and European cheese cart; contemporary/elegant decor. [$] *Average main: $135* ✉ *1104 Wilshire Blvd., Santa Monica* ☎ *310/395–0881* 🌐 *www.melisse.com* 🕑 *Closed Sun. and Mon. No lunch* ⊕ *3:B2.*

5

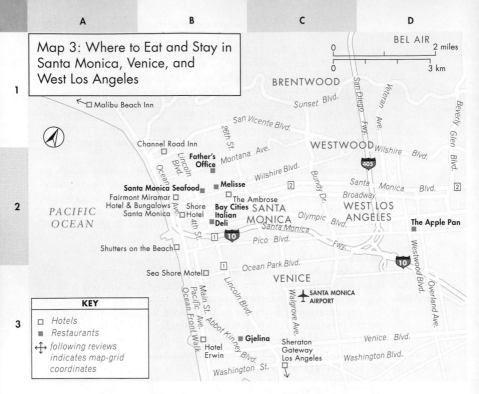

Map 3: Where to Eat and Stay in Santa Monica, Venice, and West Los Angeles

KEY

□ Hotels
■ Restaurants
✛ following reviews indicates map-grid coordinates

$$ ✕ **Santa Monica Seafood.** A Southern California favorite, this Italian sea-
SEAFOOD food haven has been serving up fresh fish since 1939. Come for lunch
FAMILY or dinner, but make sure to take time to stroll around the market, read
up on the history, and enjoy free tastings of the specials. **Known for:**
deliciously seasoned rainbow trout; oyster bar; kids' meals. $ *Aver-
age main: $20* ⊠ *1000 Wilshire Blvd., Santa Monica* ☎ *310/393–5244*
⊕ *www.santamonicaseafood.com* ✛ *3:B2.*

VENICE

$$ ✕ **Gjelina.** Gjelina comes alive the minute you walk through the rustic
AMERICAN wooden door and into a softly lit dining room with long communal
tables. The menu is seasonal, with outstanding small plates, charcuterie, pastas, and pizza. **Known for:** lively crowd on the patio; late-night
menu; wild nettle pizza. $ *Average main: $20* ⊠ *1429 Abbot Kinney
Blvd., Venice* ☎ *310/450–1429* ⊕ *www.gjelina.com* ✛ *3:B3.*

WHERE TO STAY

Updated by
Michele Bigley

When looking for a hotel, don't write off the pricier establishments
immediately. Price categories are determined by "rack rates"—the list
price of a hotel room, which is usually discounted. Specials abound,
particularly Downtown on the weekends. Many hotels have packages
that include breakfast, theater tickets, spa services, or exotic rental cars.
Pricing is very competitive, so always check the hotel website in advance
for current special offers.

Use the coordinate (✛ 1:B2) at the end of each listing to locate a site on the corresponding map. Hotel reviews have been shortened. For full information, visit Fodors.com.

WHAT IT COSTS				
	$	**$$**	**$$$**	**$$$$**
Hotels	under $200	$200–$300	$301–$400	over $400

Hotel prices are the lowest cost of a standard double room in high season, excluding taxes (as high as 14%, depending on the region).

DOWNTOWN

$$
HOTEL **Ace Hotel Downtown Los Angeles.** The L.A. edition of this bohemian-chic hipster haven is at once a hotel, theater, bar, and poolside lounge, housed in the gorgeous Spanish Gothic–style United Artists building in the heart of Downtown. **Pros:** lively rooftop lounge/pool area, aptly named Upstairs; gorgeous building and views; heart of Downtown. **Cons:** expensive parking rates compared to nightly rates ($36); some kinks in the service; compact rooms. $ *Rooms from: $239* ⊠ *929 S. Broadway, Downtown* ☎ *213/623–3233* ⊕ *www.acehotel.com/losangeles* ⇆ *183 rooms* ❐⊙❐ *No meals* ✛ *1:B3.*

$$
HOTEL **Hilton Checkers Los Angeles.** Opened as the Mayflower Hotel in 1927, Checkers combines its original character and period detail with contemporary luxuries such as pillow-top mattresses and high-speed Internet, and offers views of the L.A. Library and the Downtown skyline from its rooftop deck. **Pros:** historic charm; 24-hour room service; business-friendly. **Cons:** no on-street parking and valet is over $38.50; some rooms are compact. $ *Rooms from: $229* ⊠ *535 S. Grand Ave., Downtown* ☎ *213/624–0000, 800/445–8667* ⊕ *www.hilton.com* ⇆ *193 rooms* ❐⊙❐ *No meals* ✛ *1:B2.*

$$$
HOTEL **The Line.** This boutique hotel pays homage to its Koreatown address (about 20 minutes from Downtown) with a dynamic dining concept by superstar chef Roy Choi, and a hidden karaoke speakeasy. **Pros:** on-site bikes to explore the area; cheery staff; houses the Houston Brothers' '80s-themed bar. **Cons:** expensive parking; lobby club crowds public spaces; far from parts of the city you may want to explore. $ *Rooms from: $349* ⊠ *3515 Wilshire Blvd.* ☎ *213/381–7411* ⊕ *www.thelinehotel.com* ⇆ *384 rooms* ❐⊙❐ *No meals* ✛ *1:A2.*

$$$
HOTEL **Millennium Biltmore Hotel.** As the local headquarters of John F. Kennedy's 1960 presidential campaign and the location of some of the earliest Academy Awards ceremonies, this Downtown treasure, with its gilded 1923 beaux-arts design, exudes ambience and history. **Pros:** 24-hour business center; tiled indoor pool and steam room; multimillion-dollar refurbishment in 2017. **Cons:** pricey valet parking ($45); standard rooms are compact. $ *Rooms from: $349* ⊠ *506 S. Grand Ave., Downtown* ☎ *213/624–1011, 866/866–8086* ⊕ *www.millenniumhotels.com* ⇆ *683 rooms* ❐⊙❐ *No meals* ✛ *1:B3.*

5

$$ ⌂ **The Standard, Downtown L.A.** Built in 1955 as the headquarters of
HOTEL Standard Oil, the building was completely revamped in 2002 under the sharp eye of owner André Balazs, to become a sleek, cutting-edge hotel with spacious guest rooms. **Pros:** Rudy's barbershop on-site; 24/7 coffee shop; lively rooftop lounge. **Cons:** disruptive party scene on weekends and holidays; street noise; pricey valet parking ($44). $ *Rooms from: $279* ⊠ *550 S. Flower St., Downtown* ☎ *213/892–8080* ⊕ *www.standardhotels.com* ⌁ *207 rooms* ⎺⎔⎹ *No meals* ✛ *1:B2.*

HOLLYWOOD AND THE STUDIOS

BURBANK

$$ ⌂ **Hotel Amarano Burbank.** Close to Burbank's TV and movie studios,
HOTEL the smartly designed Amarano feels like a Beverly Hills boutique hotel, complete with 24-hour room service, a homey on-site restaurant and lounge, and spiffy rooms. **Pros:** fireplace, cocktails, and tapas in lobby; penthouse with private gym; saltwater pool. **Cons:** street noise. $ *Rooms from: $269* ⊠ *322 N. Pass Ave., Burbank* ☎ *818/842–8887, 888/956–1900* ⊕ *www.hotelamarano.com* ⌁ *98 rooms, 34 suites* ⎺⎔⎹ *No meals* ✛ *2:E1.*

HOLLYWOOD

$$$$ ⌂ **Hollywood Roosevelt Hotel.** Poolside cabana rooms are adorned with
HOTEL cow-skin rugs and marble bathrooms, while rooms in the main build-
Fodor'sChoice ing accentuate the property's history at this party-centric hotel in the
★ heart of Hollywood. **Pros:** Spare Room bowling alley on-site; pool is a popular weekend hangout; great burgers at the on-site 25 Degrees restaurant. **Cons:** reports of noise and staff attitude; stiff parking fees ($42). $ *Rooms from: $419* ⊠ *7000 Hollywood Blvd., Hollywood* ☎ *323/466–7000, 800/950–7667* ⊕ *www.hollywoodroosevelt.com* ⌁ *353 rooms* ⎺⎔⎹ *No meals* ✛ *2:D2.*

$$$ ⌂ **Loews Hollywood.** Part of the massive Hollywood and Highland shop-
HOTEL ping, dining, and entertainment complex, the 20-story Loews is at the
FAMILY center of Hollywood's action but manages to deliver a quiet night's sleep. **Pros:** large rooms with contemporary furniture; free Wi-Fi; Red Line Metro station adjacent. **Cons:** corporate feeling; very touristy; pricey parking ($50). $ *Rooms from: $349* ⊠ *1755 N. Highland Ave., Hollywood* ☎ *323/856–1200, 800/769–4774* ⊕ *www.loewshotels.com/en/hollywood-hotel* ⌁ *628 rooms* ⎺⎔⎹ *No meals* ✛ *2:D1.*

$ ⌂ **Magic Castle Hotel.** Guests at the hotel can secure advanced dinner
HOTEL reservations and attend magic shows at the Magic Castle, a private club
FAMILY in a 1908 mansion next door for magicians and their admirers. **Pros:**
Fodor'sChoice heated pool; near Hollywood and Highland; lush patio. **Cons:** strict
★ dress code; no elevator; highly trafficked street. $ *Rooms from: $199* ⊠ *7025 Franklin Ave., Hollywood* ☎ *323/851–0800, 800/741–4915* ⊕ *magiccastlehotel.com* ⌁ *43 rooms* ⎺⎔⎹ *Breakfast* ✛ *2:D1.*

$ ⌂ **Mama Shelter.** Even locals are just catching on to Hollywood's sexiest
HOTEL new property, complete with a rooftop bar populated with beautiful
Fodor'sChoice people lounging on loveseats, simple affordable rooms with quirky
★ amenities like Bert and Ernie masks, and a down-home lobby restaurant that serves a mean Korean-style burrito. **Pros:** delicious food and

cocktails on the property; affordable rooms don't skimp on style; foosball in lobby. **Cons:** spare and small rooms; creaky elevators. $ *Rooms from: $159* ✉ *6500 Selma Ave., Hollywood* ☎ *323/785–6666* ⊕ *www. mamashelter.com/en/los-angeles* ⤳ *70 rooms* |○| *No meals* ✥ *2:D1.*

$$$
HOTEL
Fodor's Choice
★

🎞 **The Redbury.** In the heart of Hollywood's nightlife, near the intersection of Hollywood and Vine, the Redbury is designed to appeal to guests' inner bohemian with paisley-patterned wallpaper, vibrant Persian rugs, and vintage rock posters. **Pros:** on-site kitchenettes and washer-dryer; excellent dining options; spacious suites. **Cons:** no pool or on-site gym; noisy on lower floors; some guests may find the Hollywood scene too chaotic. $ *Rooms from: $329* ✉ *1717 Vine St., Hollywood* ☎ *323/962–1717, 977/962–1717* ⊕ *www.theredbury.com* ⤳ *57 suites* |○| *No meals* ✥ *2:E1.*

$$$$
HOTEL

🎞 **W Hollywood.** This centrally located, ultramodern-it location is outfitted for the wired traveler, and features a rooftop pool deck and popular on-site bars, like the Station Hollywood and the mod Living Room lobby bar. **Pros:** metro stop outside the front door; comes with in-room party necessities, from ice to cocktail glasses; comfy beds with petal-soft duvets. **Cons:** small pool; pricey dining and valet parking; in noisy part of Hollywood. $ *Rooms from: $659* ✉ *6250 Hollywood Blvd., Hollywood* ☎ *323/798–1300, 888/625–4955* ⊕ *www.whotels.com/hollywood* ⤳ *305 rooms* |○| *No meals* ✥ *2:E1.*

STUDIO CITY

$$
HOTEL
FAMILY

🎞 **Sportsmen's Lodge.** This sprawling five-story hotel, a San Fernando Valley landmark just a short jaunt over the Hollywood Hills, has an updated contemporary look highlighted by the Olympic-size pool and summer patio with an outdoor bar. **Pros:** close to Ventura Boulevard restaurants; free shuttle to Universal Hollywood; quiet garden-view rooms worth asking for. **Cons:** pricey daily self-parking fee ($18); a distance from the city. $ *Rooms from: $249* ✉ *12825 Ventura Blvd., Studio City* ☎ *818/769–4700, 800/821–8511* ⊕ *www.sportsmenslodge. com* ⤳ *190 rooms* |○| *No meals* ✥ *2:D1.*

BEVERLY HILLS AND THE WESTSIDE

BEL AIR

$$$$
HOTEL
Fodor's Choice
★

🎞 **Hotel Bel-Air.** This Spanish Mission–style icon has been a discreet hillside retreat for celebrities and society types since 1946, and was given a face-lift by star designers Alexandra Champalimaud and David Rockwell. **Pros:** Bang & Olfusen TVs; fireplace and private patio in many rooms; alfresco dining at Wolfgang Puck restaurant. **Cons:** attracts society crowd; hefty price tag; a car is essential. $ *Rooms from: $525* ✉ *701 Stone Canyon Rd., Bel Air* ☎ *310/472–1211, 800/648–4097* ⊕ *www.hotelbelair.com* ⤳ *91 rooms* |○| *No meals* ✥ *2:A2.*

BEVERLY HILLS

$$$$
HOTEL

🎞 **Beverly Wilshire, a Four Seasons Hotel.** Built in 1928, this Rodeo Drive–adjacent hotel is part Italian Renaissance (with elegant details like crystal chandeliers) and part contemporary. **Pros:** complimentary car service; Wolfgang Puck restaurant on-site; first-rate spa. **Cons:** small lobby; valet parking backs up at peak times; expensive dining options.

$ *Rooms from: $845* ✉ *9500 Wilshire Blvd., Beverly Hills* ☎ *310/275–5200, 800/427–4354* ⊕ *www.fourseasons.com/beverlywilshire* ⤳ *395 rooms* ¶⊙¶ *No meals* ✛ *2:B3.*

$ **The Crescent Beverly Hills.** Built in 1926 as a dorm for silent-film actors,
HOTEL the Crescent is now a sleek boutique hotel with a great location—within
Fodor's Choice the Beverly Hills shopping triangle—and with an even better price.
★ **Pros:** indoor/outdoor fireplace; lively on-site restaurant Crescent Bar and Terrace; economic room available for $148. **Cons:** gym an additional fee; no elevator. $ *Rooms from: $149* ✉ *403 N. Crescent Dr., Beverly Hills* ☎ *310/247–0505* ⊕ *www.crescentbh.com* ⤳ *35 rooms* ¶⊙¶ *No meals* ✛ *2:B3.*

$$$$ **Four Seasons Hotel, Los Angeles at Beverly Hills.** High hedges and patio
HOTEL gardens make this hotel a secluded retreat that even the hum of traffic can't permeate—one reason it's a favorite of Hollywood's elite, whom you might spot at the pool and espresso bar. **Pros:** tropical terrace with pool; high-end Italian eatery Culina on-site; great massages and nail salon. **Cons:** Hollywood scene in bar and restaurant means rarefied prices. $ *Rooms from: $625* ✉ *300 S. Doheny Dr., Beverly Hills* ☎ *310/273–2222, 800/332–3442* ⊕ *www.fourseasons.com/losangeles* ⤳ *285 rooms* ¶⊙¶ *No meals* ✛ *2:B3.*

$$$$ **Montage Beverly Hills.** The nine-story, Mediterranean-style palazzo
HOTEL is dedicated to welcoming those who relish luxury, providing classic
FAMILY style and exemplary service. **Pros:** secret whiskey bar tucked upstairs;
Fodor's Choice Gornick & Drucker Barber Shop on-site; obliging, highly trained
★ staff; families love the kids' club Paintbox. **Cons:** the hefty tab for all this finery. $ *Rooms from: $695* ✉ *225 N. Cañon Dr., Beverly Hills* ☎ *310/860–7800, 888/860–0788* ⊕ *www.montagebeverlyhills.com/ beverlyhills* ⤳ *201 rooms* ¶⊙¶ *No meals* ✛ *2:B3.*

$$$$ **Peninsula Beverly Hills.** This French Rivera–style palace overflowing
HOTEL with antiques and art is a favorite of boldface names, but visitors consis-
Fodor's Choice tently describe a stay here as near perfect. **Pros:** Belvedere restaurant on-
★ site is a lunchtime favorite; sunny pool area with cabanas; complimentary Rolls-Royce takes you to nearby Beverly Hills. **Cons:** very expensive; room decor might feel too ornate for some. $ *Rooms from: $595* ✉ *9882 S. Santa Monica Blvd., Beverly Hills* ☎ *310/551–2888, 800/462–7899* ⊕ *beverlyhills.peninsula.com* ⤳ *195 rooms* ¶⊙¶ *No meals* ✛ *2:A3.*

$$$$ **SLS Hotel at Beverly Hills.** From the sleek, Philippe Starck–designed lobby
HOTEL and lounge with fireplaces, hidden nooks, and a communal table, to pool-side cabanas with DVD players, this hotel offers a cushy, dreamlike stay. **Pros:** on-property cuisine masterminded by Jose Andres; fully stocked bar in each room; dreamy Ciel spa. **Cons:** standard rooms are compact; pricey dining and parking; design might seem cold to some. $ *Rooms from: $639* ✉ *465 S. La Cienega Blvd., Beverly Hills* ☎ *310/247–0400* ⊕ *www.slshotels.com* ⤳ *297 rooms* ¶⊙¶ *No meals* ✛ *2:C3.*

WEST HOLLYWOOD

$$ **Farmer's Daughter Hotel.** A favorite of *The Price Is Right* and *Danc-*
HOTEL *ing with the Stars* hopefuls (both TV shows tape at the CBS studios
Fodor's Choice nearby), this hotel has a tongue-in-cheek country style with a hopping
★ Sunday brunch, and a little pool accented by giant rubber duckies. **Pros:** bikes for rent; daily yoga; book lending library. **Cons:** shaded pool; no

bathtubs; staff can be stiff. [$] *Rooms from: $260* ✉ *115 S. Fairfax Ave., West Hollywood* ☎ *323/937–3930, 800/334–1658* 🌐 *www.farmersdaughterhotel.com* 🛏 *65 rooms* 🍴 *No meals* ✥ *2:C3.*

$$$ HOTEL 🏨 **The London West Hollywood at Beverly Hills.** Just off the Sunset Strip, cosmopolitan and chic in design, especially after the $27-million renovation in 2015, the London West Hollywood is known for its large suites, rooftop pool with citywide views, and luxury touches throughout. **Pros:** state-of-the-art fitness center; Chef Anthony Keen oversees dining program; 110-seat screening room. **Cons:** too refined for kids to be comfortable; lower floors have mundane views. [$] *Rooms from: $395* ✉ *1020 N. San Vicente Blvd., West Hollywood* ☎ *310/854–1111, 866/282–4560* 🌐 *www.thelondonwesthollywood.com* 🛏 *225 suites* 🍴 *No meals* ✥ *2:B2.*

$$$ HOTEL Fodor's Choice ★ 🏨 **Sunset Marquis Hotel & Villas.** If you're in town to cut your new hit single, you'll appreciate this near-the-Strip hidden retreat in the heart of WeHo, with two on-site recording studios. **Pros:** favorite among rock stars; 53 villas with lavish extras; exclusive Bar 1200; free passes to Equinox nearby. **Cons:** rooms can feel dark; small balconies. [$] *Rooms from: $365* ✉ *1200 N. Alta Loma Rd., West Hollywood* ☎ *310/657–1333, 800/858–9758* 🌐 *www.sunsetmarquis.com* 🛏 *154 rooms* 🍴 *No meals* ✥ *2:C2.*

5

SANTA MONICA AND THE BEACHES

LOS ANGELES INTERNATIONAL AIRPORT

$ HOTEL 🏨 **Sheraton Gateway Los Angeles.** LAX's swanky hotel just had some serious work done to its already sleek look, yet the appeal is in more than just the style; in-transit visitors love the 24-hour room service, fitness center, and airport shuttle. **Pros:** significantly lower weekend rates; free LAX shuttle; on-site restaurant, Costero California Bar and Bistro, slings craft beer. **Cons:** convenient to airport but not much else. [$] *Rooms from: $149* ✉ *6101 W. Century Blvd., Los Angeles International Airport* ☎ *310/642–1111, 800/325–3535* 🌐 *www.sheratonlosangeles.com* 🛏 *802 rooms* 🍴 *No meals* ✥ *3:C3.*

MALIBU

$$$$ B&B/INN 🏨 **Malibu Beach Inn.** Set right on exclusive Carbon Beach, Malibu's hideaway for the super-rich remains the room to nab along the coast, with an ultrachic new look thanks to designer Waldo Fernandez, and an upscale restaurant and wine bar overlooking the Pacific. **Pros:** see the ocean from your private balcony; wine list curated by sommelier Laurie Sutton. **Cons:** billionaire's travel budget required; noise of PCH; no pool, gym, or hot tub. [$] *Rooms from: $575* ✉ *22878 Pacific Coast Hwy., Malibu* ☎ *310/456–6444* 🌐 *www.malibubeachinn.com* 🛏 *47 rooms* 🍴 *No meals* ✥ *3:A1.*

SANTA MONICA

$$$ HOTEL 🏨 **The Ambrose.** An air of tranquillity pervades the beach-chic four-story Ambrose, which blends right into its mostly residential Santa Monica neighborhood. **Pros:** "green" practices: nontoxic cleaners, recycling bins; partial ocean view. **Cons:** quiet, residential area of Santa Monica; parking fee ($27). [$] *Rooms from: $345* ✉ *1255 20th St., Santa Monica* ☎ *310/315–1555, 877/262–7673* 🌐 *www.ambrosehotel.com* 🛏 *77 rooms* 🍴 *Breakfast* ✥ *3:B2.*

$$
B&B/INN
Fodor's Choice
★

🏨 **Channel Road Inn.** A quaint surprise in Southern California, the Channel Road Inn is every bit the country retreat bed-and-breakfast lovers adore, with four-poster beds, fluffy duvets, and a cozy living room with a fireplace. **Pros:** free wine and hors d'oeuvres every evening; home-cooked breakfast included; meditative rose garden on-site. **Cons:** no pool; need a car to get around. $ *Rooms from: $225 ⊠ 219 W. Channel Rd., Santa Monica* ☎ *310/459–1920* ⊕ *www.channelroadinn.com* ⇆ *15 rooms* ⭘ *Breakfast* ✛ *3:B2.*

$$$$
HOTEL

🏨 **Fairmont Miramar Hotel & Bungalows Santa Monica.** A mammoth Moreton Bay fig tree dwarfs the main entrance of the 5-acre beach-adjacent Santa Monica wellness retreat, and lends its name to the inviting on-site Mediterranean-inspired restaurant, FIG, which focuses on local ingredients. **Pros:** guests can play games on the heated patio; swanky open-air cocktail spot The Bungalow on-site; stay in retrofitted '20s and '40s bungalows. **Cons:** all this luxury comes at a big price. $ *Rooms from: $439 ⊠ 101 Wilshire Blvd., Santa Monica* ☎ *310/576–7777, 866/540–4470* ⊕ *www.fairmont.com/santamonica* ⇆ *334 rooms* ⭘ *No meals* ✛ *3:B2.*

$
HOTEL

🏨 **Sea Shore Motel.** On Santa Monica's busy Main Street, the Sea Shore is a throwback to Route 66 and to '60s-style, family-run roadside motels, and is surrounded by an ultra-trendy neighborhood. **Pros:** close to beach and restaurants; free Wi-Fi and parking; popular rooftop deck and on-site restaurant, Amelia's. **Cons:** street noise; motel-style decor and beds. $ *Rooms from: $155 ⊠ 2637 Main St., Santa Monica* ☎ *310/392–2787* ⊕ *www.seashoremotel.com* ⇆ *24 rooms* ⭘ *No meals* ✛ *3:B3.*

$$$$
HOTEL
Fodor's Choice
★

🏨 **Shore Hotel.** With views of the Santa Monica Pier, this hotel with a friendly staff offers eco-minded travelers stylish rooms with a modern design, just steps from the sand and sea. **Pros:** near beach and Third Street Promenade; rainfall showerheads; solar-heated pool and hot tub. **Cons:** expensive rooms and parking fees; fronting busy Ocean Avenue. $ *Rooms from: $539 ⊠ 1515 Ocean Ave., Santa Monica* ☎ *310/458–1515* ⊕ *shorehotel.com* ⇆ *164 rooms* ⭘ *No meals* ✛ *3:B2.*

$$$$
HOTEL
FAMILY
Fodor's Choice
★

🏨 **Shutters on the Beach.** Set right on the sand, this inn has become synonymous with staycations, and while the hotel's service gets mixed reviews from some readers, the beachfront location and show-house decor make this one of SoCal's most popular luxury hotels. **Pros:** built-in cabinets filled with art books and curios; rooms designed by Michael Smith; rooms come with whirlpool tub. **Cons:** service could improve; very expensive. $ *Rooms from: $800 ⊠ 1 Pico Blvd., Santa Monica* ☎ *310/458–0030, 800/334–9000* ⊕ *www.shuttersonthebeach.com* ⇆ *198 rooms* ⭘ *No meals* ✛ *3:B2.*

VENICE

$$$
HOTEL

🏨 **Hotel Erwin.** A boutique hotel a block off the Venice Beach Boardwalk, the Erwin has spacious, airy rooms and a local-favorite rooftop bar and lounge (appropriately named High). **Pros:** dining emphasizes fresh ingredients; playful design in guest rooms. **Cons:** some rooms face a noisy alley; no pool. $ *Rooms from: $319 ⊠ 1697 Pacific Ave., Venice* ☎ *310/452–1111, 800/786–7789* ⊕ *www.hotelerwin.com* ⇆ *119 rooms* ⭘ *No meals* ✛ *3:B3.*

PASADENA

$$$$ 🔲 **The Langham Huntington, Pasadena.** Fronted by the historic Horseshoe
HOTEL   Garden, this 1907 grande dame spans 23 acres and includes an Italianate-
FAMILY   style main building, Spanish Revival cottages, a lanai, an azalea-filled Japa-
Fodor's Choice   nese garden, and several dining options. **Pros:** great for a romantic escape;
★   delicious Cal-French restaurant Royce; top-notch Chuan Spa. **Cons:** in a
suburban neighborhood far from local shopping and dining. $ *Rooms
from: $429* ✉ *1401 S. Oak Knoll Ave., Pasadena* ☎ *626/568–3900*
⊕ *www.pasadena.langhamhotels.com* ↝ *380 rooms* ⦿ *No meals* ✢ *1:B1.*

NIGHTLIFE AND PERFORMING ARTS

Local publications *Los Angeles* magazine (⊕ *www.lamag.com*) and *LA
Weekly* (⊕ *www.laweekly.com*), or sites like TimeOut (⊕ *www.timeout.
com/los-angeles*), are great places to discover what's happening in the city.

NIGHTLIFE

Updated
by Meg
Butler, Audrey
Farnsworth,
Rachael Levitt,
Rachael Roth,
Jesse Tabit,
and Jeremy
Tarr

The focus of L.A. nightlife once centered on the Sunset Strip, with its
multitude of bars and rock clubs; now most corners of the city have their
own distinct after-hours culture. Whether you plan to test your limits at
historic establishments Downtown or take advantage of a cheap happy
hour at a Hollywood dive, this city's nightlife has something for you.

Utilize a ride-share app to avoid pricey parking. Most neighborhoods
near party-heavy areas like West Hollywood require residential parking
permits, so if you do drive, you're often better off with a garage or valet
parking. Either option costs from $5 to $20.

HOLLYWOOD

BARS

FAMILY   **Musso & Frank Grill.** The prim and proper vibe of this old-school steak
Fodor's Choice   house won't appeal to those looking for a raucous night out; instead, its
★   appeal lies in its history and sturdy drinks. Established in 1919, its dark
wood decor, red tuxedo–clad waiters, and highly skilled bartenders can
easily shuttle you back to its Hollywood heyday when Marilyn Monroe,
F. Scott Fitzgerald, and Greta Garbo once hung around and sipped martinis. ✉ *6667 Hollywood Blvd., Hollywood* ☎ *323/467–7788* ⊕ *www.
mussoandfrank.com.*

Three Clubs. Part martini lounge, part biker bar, this spot right on the
corner of Santa Monica and Vine has plush leather booths and cozy bar
seats. The focus is on fresh and local ingredients for all the cocktails,
and they offer a daily happy hour. There's a small cover charge to watch
bands, comedy, or burlesque shows on the stage in the back room.
✉ *1123 Vine St., Hollywood* ☎ *323/462–6441* ⊕ *www.threeclubs.com.*

Yamashiro Hollywood. Modeled after a mansion in Kyoto, this Japanese
place with a hillside perch has spectacular koi ponds and gardens, as
well as sweeping views of Hollywood's twinkling lights. Additional lures
here include the tasty, if pricey, food and delicious drinks. ■**TIP➜ The
mandatory valet parking costs $10.** ✉ *1999 N. Sycamore Ave., Hol-
lywood* ☎ *323/466–5125* ⊕ *www.yamashirohollywood.com.*

5

CLUBS

Boardner's. This neighborhood lounge has been around for decades, and its dim lighting and leather booths give it a well-worn feel. The adjoining open-air Club 52, with an ornate tiled fountain in the center, has its own cover charge and entrance, and often hosts burlesque shows or live bands. The long-running Saturday Goth night, Bar Sinister, remains popular here after 19 years. ⊠ *1652 N. Cherokee Ave., Hollywood* ☎ *323/462–9621* ⊕ *www.boardners.com.*

COMEDY

Fodor's Choice ★ **Upright Citizens Brigade.** The L.A. offshoot of New York's famous troupe continues its tradition of sketch comedy and improv with weekly shows like "Facebook" (where the audience's online profiles are mined for material), and "Doug Loves Movies," where comedian Doug Benson invites three surprise guests (Zach Galifianakis and Sarah Silverman have both made appearances) to play a movie-themed game show with loose rules. Arrive early as space is limited. A second theater on Sunset Boulevard opened in 2014. ⊠ *5919 Franklin Ave., Hollywood* ☎ *323/908–8702* ⊕ *www.ucbtheatre.com.*

LIVE MUSIC

Avalon. This multitasking art deco venue offers both live music and club nights. The killer sound system, cavernous space, and multiple bars make it a perfect venue for both. The club is best known for its DJs, who often spin well past the 2 am cutoff for drinks. The crowd can be a mixed bag, depending on the night, but if you're looking to dance, you likely won't be disappointed. Upstairs is **Bardot,** which hosts a free Monday night showcase of up-and-coming artists called School Night! that's always a good time. Remember to RSVP online in advance; they'll be checking names at the door. ⊠ *1735 Vine St., Hollywood* ☎ *323/462–8900* ⊕ *www.avalonhollywood.com.*

Fodor's Choice ★ **El Floridita.** Although the exterior might not look like much, El Floridita is a popular live salsa music spot on Monday, Friday, and Saturday, with dancers ranging from enthusiasts to those just trying to keep up. There's a $15 cover to listen to the band, although admission is free with dinner. Reservations are recommended to guarantee a table. ⊠ *1253 N. Vine St., Hollywood* ☎ *323/871–8612* ⊕ *www.elfloridita.com.*

Largo at the Coronet. The welcoming vibe of this venue attracts big-name performers who treat its stage as their home away from home in Los Angeles. Standouts include musician and music producer Jon Brion, who often appears here with special drop-in guests (Fiona Apple and Andrew Bird have both been on the bill). Comedians Sarah Silverman and Patton Oswalt each host a monthly comedy show. Bring cash for drinks in the Little Room before the show. ⊠ *366 N. La Cienega Blvd., Hollywood* ☎ *310/855–0350* ⊕ *www.largo-la.com.*

WEST HOLLYWOOD

BARS

Rainbow Bar & Grill. Its location next door to a long-running music venue, the Roxy, helped cement this bar and restaurant's status as a legendary watering hole for musicians (as well as their entourages and groupies). The Who, Guns N' Roses, Poison, Kiss, and many others have all passed through the doors. Expect a $5–$10 cover, but you'll get the money back in drink tickets or a food discount. ✉ *9015 W. Sunset Blvd., West Hollywood* ☎ *310/278–4232* ⊕ *www.rainbowbarandgrill.com.*

The Standard. Weekend pool parties in the summer are downright notorious at the Standard Hollywood. Party on the pool deck with DJs, or hear acoustic sets in the Cactus Lodge on Wednesday evenings. Check the calendar for special events like film screenings. ✉ *The Standard Hollywood, 8300 Sunset Blvd., West Hollywood* ☎ *323/650–9090* ⊕ *www.standardhotels.com.*

CLUBS

Rage. The various events at this gay bar and dance club draw different crowds—show queens for Broadway musical sing-alongs, drag queens (and more show queens) for the Dreamgirls Revue, half-nude chiseledbodied men for Fetch Tuesdays and Thursday Night College Night. There's lots of eye candy, even more so on weekends. ✉ *8911 Santa Monica Blvd., West Hollywood* ☎ *310/652–7055* ⊕ *www.ragenightclub.com.*

COMEDY

Comedy Store. Three stages give seasoned and unseasoned comedians a place to perform and try out new material, with performers such as Louis C.K. and Sarah Silverman dropping by just for fun. The front bar along Sunset Boulevard is a popular hangout after or between shows, oftentimes with that night's comedians mingling with fans. ✉ *8433 Sunset Blvd., West Hollywood* ☎ *323/650–6268* ⊕ *www.thecomedystore.com.*

Laugh Factory. Top stand-up comics appear at this Sunset Boulevard mainstay, often working out the kinks in new material in advance of national tours. Stars such as Kevin Hart and Tim Allen sometimes drop by unannounced, and Kevin Nealon puts on a monthly show. Midnight Madness on the weekends is extremely popular, with comics performing more daring sets. ✉ *8001 W. Sunset Blvd., West Hollywood* ☎ *323/656–1336* ⊕ *www.laughfactory.com* 🎫 *$20.*

LIVE MUSIC

The Troubadour. The intimate vibe of the Troubadour helps make this club a favorite with music fans. Around since 1957, this venue has a storied past. These days, the eclectic lineup is still attracting the crowds, with the focus mostly on rock, indie, and folk music. Those looking for drinks can imbibe to their heart's content at the adjacent bar. ✉ *9081 Santa Monica Blvd., West Hollywood* ⊕ *www.troubadour.com.*

Viper Room. This rock club on the edge of the Sunset Strip has been around for more than 20 years and is famously known as the site of much controversial Hollywood history. Today the venue books rising alt-rock acts, and covers typically range from $5 to $10. ✉ *8852 W. Sunset Blvd., West Hollywood* ☎ *310/358–1881* ⊕ *www.viperroom.com.*

Whisky A Go Go. The hard-core metal and rock scene is alive and well at the legendary Whisky A Go Go (the full name includes the prefix "World Famous"), where Janis Joplin, Led Zeppelin, Alice Cooper, Van Halen, the Doors (they were the house band for a short stint), and Frank Zappa have all played. On the Strip for more than five decades, they book both underground acts, and huge names in rock. ✉ *8901 Sunset Blvd., West Hollywood* ☎ *310/652–4202* ⊕ *www.whiskyagogo.com.*

ECHO PARK AND SILVER LAKE

BARS

Cha Cha Lounge. This place's decor—part tiki hut, part tacky party palace—shouldn't work, but it does. An import from Seattle, its cheap drinks, foosball tables, and jovial atmosphere make it a natural party scene. ⊠ *2375 Glendale Blvd., Silver Lake* ☎ *323/660–7595* ⊕ *www. chachalounge.com.*

Fodor's Choice ★ **Tiki-Ti.** The cozy feel of this Polynesian-theme bar is due in part to its small size—12 seats at the bar, plus a few tables along one side. Open since 1961, it serves strong drinks (92 to be exact), one of which will have the entire place yelling your order. Don't be surprised to find a line outside. ⊠ *4427 Sunset Blvd., Silver Lake* ☎ *323/669–9381* ⊕ *www. tiki-ti.com.*

LIVE MUSIC

Fodor's Choice ★ **The Echo.** A neighborhood staple, this beloved spot showcases up-and-coming indie bands that are soon to be big names, with soul or reggae dance nights and DJ mash-up sessions rounding out the calendar. ⊠ *1822 Sunset Blvd., Echo Park* ☎ *213/413–8200* ⊕ *www.theecho.com.*

Echoplex. It may surprise you that while this spot is in the basement of the Echo, you have to cross the street and walk under the bridge to access it. A larger space than its sister theater, the Echoplex books bigger national tours and events. Comedians like Marc Maron, and a slew of big names in indie rock have graced the stage. ⊠ *1154 Glendale Blvd., Echo Park* ☎ *213/413–8200* ⊕ *www.attheecho.com.*

Fodor's Choice ★ **The Satellite.** This venue hosts a variety of bands, mostly indie rock acts, as well as a popular DJ night, Dance Yourself Clean (with a great range of highly danceable jams), which is held every Saturday. Monday nights are free, and feature exciting up-and-coming acts. Cover charges on other days range from $8 to $15. ⊠ *1717 Silver Lake Blvd., Silver Lake* ☎ *323/661–4380* ⊕ *www.thesatellitela.com.*

Silverlake Lounge. Discover new indie, rock, and classical acts at this divey venue. Cheap beer and well drinks abound, with happy hour specials daily. Order delivery from one of the restaurants nearby and eat it at the bar. ⊠ *2906 Sunset Blvd., Silver Lake* ☎ *323/663–9636* ⊕ *www.thesilverlakelounge.com.*

PERFORMING ARTS

Updated by
Alene Dawson

CONCERT HALLS

Fodor's Choice ★ **Dorothy Chandler Pavilion.** Though half a century old, this theater maintains the glamour of its early years, richly decorated with crystal chandeliers and classical theatrical drapes. Part of the Los Angeles Music Center, a large portion of programming is made up of dance and ballet performances, like Shen Yun Performing Arts, a large production showcasing classical Chinese dance and music. Ticket-holders can attend free talks that take place an hour before opera performances. ■ TIP➔ Reservations for the talks aren't required, but it's wise to arrive early as space is limited. ⊠ *135 N. Grand Ave., Downtown* ☎ *213/972–7211* ⊕ *www.musiccenter.org.*

Greek Theatre. With a robust lineup from May through November, acts such as Beck, John Legend, and Chicago have all graced the stage at this scenic outdoor venue. The 5,900-capacity amphitheater is at the base of Griffith Park, and you may want to make a day of it by hiking or stargazing beforehand. There is usually slow, preshow traffic on concert nights, but it'll give you a chance to take in the beautiful park foliage and homes in the Hollywood Hills. Paid lots are available for parking, but wear comfortable shoes and expect to walk, as some lots are fairly far from the theater. Or, park and enjoy cocktails in the trendy and chic Los Feliz neighborhood below before a show, then walk up to the venue. ⊠ *2700 N. Vermont Ave., Los Feliz* ☎ *323/665–5857* ⊕ *www.greektheatrela.com.*

Fodor's Choice
★
Hollywood Bowl. For those seeking a quintessential Los Angeles experience, a concert on a summer night at the Bowl, the city's iconic outdoor venue, is unsurpassed. The Bowl has presented world-class performers since it opened in 1920. The L.A. Philharmonic plays here from June to September; its performances and other events draw large crowds. Parking is limited near the venue, but there are additional remote parking locations serviced by shuttles. You can bring food and drink to any event, which Angelenos often do, though you can only bring alcohol when the LA Phil, as the orchestra is known, is performing. (Bars sell alcohol at all events, and there are dining options.) It's wise to bring a jacket even if daytime temperatures have been warm—the Bowl can get quite chilly at night. ■TIP➔ Visitors can sometimes watch the LA Phil practice for free, usually on a weekday; call ahead for times. ⊠ *2301 Highland Ave., Hollywood* ☎ *323/850–2000* ⊕ *www.hollywoodbowl.com.*

Microsoft Theatre. Formerly known as the Nokia Theatre L.A., the Microsoft Theatre is host to a variety of concerts and big-name awards shows—the Emmys, American Music Awards, BET Awards, and the ESPYs. This theater and the surrounding L.A. Live complex are a draw for those looking for a fun night out. The building's emphasis on acoustics and versatile seating arrangements means that all the seats are good, whether you're at an intimate Neil Young concert or the People's Choice Awards. Outside, the L.A. Live complex hosts restaurants and attractions, including the Grammy Museum, to keep patrons entertained before and after shows (though it's open whether or not there's a performance). ⊠ *777 Chick Hearn Ct., Downtown* ☎ *213/763–6030* ⊕ *www.nokiatheatrelalive.com.*

Shrine Auditorium. Since opening in 1926, the auditorium has hosted nearly every major awards show at one point or another. Today, the venue and adjacent Expo Hall hosts performers like Radiohead, and festivals, including Tenacious D's comedy/music extravaganza, Festival Supreme, in October. The Shrine's Moorish Revival–style architecture is a spectacle all its own. ⊠ *665 W. Jefferson Blvd., Downtown* ☎ *213/748–5116* ⊕ *www.shrineauditorium.com.*

FILM

Watching movies here isn't merely an efficient way to kill time, but it's an *event*. With theaters this close to the movie studios, it's not unusual for major directors or actors to participate in a post-film discussion. Whether it's a first-run film or a revival, the show will likely be worth the trip out.

The American Cinémathèque at the Aero and Egyptian Theatres. American Cinémathèque screens classic and independent films at two theaters, the Aero and the Egyptian. Expect everything from Hitchcock thrillers, to anime by Hayao Miyazaki, plus occasional Q&A sessions with directors and actors following film screenings. The Egyptian Theatre in Hollywood has the distinction of hosting the first-ever movie premiere when it opened back in 1922. Its ornate courtyard and columns have been restored to preserve the building's history. The Aero Theatre in Santa Monica opened in 1940. ✉ *6712 Hollywood Blvd., Hollywood* ☎ *323/466–3456* ⊕ *www.americancinematheque.com.*

Fodor's Choice ★ **ArcLight.** This big multiplex includes the historic Cinerama Dome, that impossible-to-miss golf ball–looking structure on Sunset Boulevard, which was built in 1963. Like many L.A. theaters, the ArcLight has assigned seating (you will be asked to select seats when purchasing tickets). The complex is a one-stop shop with a parking garage, shopping area, restaurant, and in-house bar. The events calendar is worth paying attention to, as directors and actors often drop by to chat with audiences. Amy Adams and Samuel L. Jackson, for example, have both made time for post-screening Q&As. Movies here can be pricey (ranging from around $18–$25), but the theater shows just about every new release. ■TIP➜ Evening shows on the weekend feature "21+" shows, during which moviegoers can bring alcoholic beverages into the screening rooms. ✉ *6360 Sunset Blvd., Hollywood* ☎ *323/464–4226* ⊕ *www.arclightcinemas.com.*

Cinefamily at The Silent Movie Theatre. Although the name may imply that only silent movies are shown here, this theater also has a packed schedule of film screenings, from rare to indie to foreign. Regular events include Doug Benson's Movie Interruption, Haunted Hangovers (early matinees paired with coffee or mimosas on weekends leading up to Halloween), and The Silent Treatment—pre–sound era films that run on the second Saturday of every month (though it's best to check the calendar for changes). Also expect special guests, live music, dance parties, and potlucks. ✉ *611 N. Fairfax Ave., Fairfax District* ☎ *323/655–2510* ⊕ *www.cinefamily.org.*

THEATER

Center Theatre Group. Celebrating their 50th anniversary, Center Theatre Group is comprised of three venues: The Ahmanson and the Taper (both at the Music Center campus Downtown), and the Kirk Douglas Theatre in Culver City. They show an array of productions, from the world premiere of newcomer Nigerian playwright Ngozi Anyanwu's *Good Grief*, to touring productions of Broadway hits like *Jersey Boys*. ✉ *135 N. Grand Ave., Downtown* ☎ *213/972–7211* ⊕ *www.center-theatregroup.org.*

Ahmanson Theatre. The largest of L.A.'s Center Group's three theaters, Ahmanson Theatre presents larger-scale classic revivals, dramas, musicals, and comedies like *Into the Woods,* that are either going to, or coming from Broadway and the West End. The ambience is a theater-lover's delight. ⊠ *135 N. Grand Ave., Downtown* ☎ *213/628–2772* ⊕ *www. centertheatregroup.org.*

Mark Taper Forum. Both dramas and comedies dominate the stage at the Mark Taper Forum, next door to the Ahmanson Theatre in Downtown. Plenty of shows that premiered here have gone on to Broadway and off-Broadway theaters (a number of Pulitzer Prize–winning plays have also been developed here). ⊠ *135 N. Grand Ave., Downtown* ☎ *213/628–2772* ⊕ *www.centertheatregroup.org.*

Kirk Douglas Theatre. This theater, located in a walkable Culver City neighborhood (close to cocktail bars and trendy restaurants), stages modern works and world premieres. The smallest venue of the group at 317 seats, the theater also hosts intimate workshops and readings. ⊠ *9820 W. Washington Blvd., Culver City* ☎ *213/628–2772* ⊕ *www. centertheatregroup.org.*

Geffen Playhouse. Well-known actors are often on the bill at the Geffen, and plays by established playwrights, such as Neil LaBute and Lynn Nottage, happen regularly. With two stages hosting world premieres and critically acclaimed works, there's always something compelling to watch. ■TIP➜ Free events are frequently put on for ticket holders, including Wine Down Sundays, which feature music and wine sampling before evening shows. ⊠ *10886 Le Conte Ave., Westwood* ☎ *310/208–5454* ⊕ *www.geffenplayhouse.com.*

Ricardo Montalbán Theatre. Plays, musicals, and concerts all happen at this midsize theater, mostly focusing on Latin culture. When the weather warms up, they host the Rooftop Cinema Club, where you can watch a flick on the roof (they give out blankets on cold nights), indulge at the snack bar, and take in views of Hollywood. ⊠ *1615 N. Vine St., Hollywood* ☎ *323/871–2420* ⊕ *www.themontalban.com.*

Pantages Theatre. For the grand-scale theatrics of a Broadway show, such as *Hamilton* and *The Book of Mormon,* the 2,703-seat Pantages Theatre (the last theater built by Greek-American vaudeville producer Alexander Pantages) lights up Hollywood Boulevard on show nights, when lines of excited patrons extend down the block. ⊠ *6233 Hollywood Blvd., Hollywood* ☎ *800/982–2787* ⊕ *www.hollywoodpantages.com.*

SPORTS AND THE OUTDOORS

BASEBALL

Los Angeles Angels of Anaheim. The Angels often contend for the top slot in the Western Division of pro baseball's American League. ⊠ *Angel Stadium of Anaheim, 2000 E. Gene Autry Way, Anaheim* ☎ *714/940–2000* ⊕ *www.angelsbaseball.com.*

Los Angeles Dodgers. The Dodgers take on their National League rivals at one of major league baseball's most comfortable ballparks, Dodger Stadium. ⊠ *Dodger Stadium, 1000 Elysian Park Ave., exit off I–110, Pasadena Fwy.* ☎ *323/224–1507* ⊕ *www.dodgers.com.*

BASKETBALL

L.A.'s pro basketball teams play at the Staples Center.

Los Angeles Clippers. L.A.'s "other" pro basketball team, the Clippers, was formerly an easy ticket, but these days the club routinely sells out its home games. ⊠ *Staples Center, 1111 S. Figueroa St.* ☎ *213/742–7100* ⊕ *www.nba.com/clippers.*

Los Angeles Lakers. The team of pro-basketball champions Magic and Kareem, and Shaq and Kobe has slipped in recent years, but games are still intense, especially if the Lakers are playing a rival team. ⊠ *Staples Center, 1111 S. Figueroa St., Downtown* ☎ *310/426–6000* ⊕ *www. nba.com/lakers.*

Los Angeles Sparks. The women's pro basketball team has made it to the WNBA playoffs more than a dozen times in the past two decades. ⊠ *Staples Center, 1111 S. Figueroa St.* ☎ *310/426–6031* ⊕ *www.wnba. com/sparks.*

SHOPPING

DOWNTOWN

Updated by
Ashley Tibbits

Los Angeles's close association to the rich and famous has long made it a major shopping destination, but in recent years the city has grown beyond just a locale for luxe clothing and accessories—although high-end goods will always be a cornerstone of L.A.'s retail scene. With a wealth of stellar vintage spots, purveyors of affordable on-the-pulse products, and an ever-growing number of shops selling local artisanal goods, there is truly something for every type of spender here.

SHOPPING STREETS AND DISTRICTS

Fashion District. With the influx of emerging designers in this pocket of Downtown, it's become much more than just a wholesale market. Besides containing the plant paradise that is the Flower District as well as the Fabric District, the neighborhood now boasts a bevy of boutiques and cool coffee shops, thanks in part to the opening of the stylish Ace Hotel. ⊠ *Roughly between I–10 and 7th St., and S. San Pedro and S. Main Sts., Downtown* ⊕ *www.fashiondistrict.org.*

Santee Alley. Situated in the Fashion District, Santee Alley is known for back-alley deals on knockoffs of designer sunglasses, jewelry, handbags, shoes, and clothing. Be prepared to haggle, and don't lose sight of your wallet. Weekend crowds can be overwhelming, but there's plenty of street food to keep your energy up. ⊠ *Santee St. and Maple Ave. from Olympic Blvd. to 11th St., Downtown* ⊕ *www.thesanteealley.com.*

The Santa Monica Pier is packed with fun diversions and hosts free concerts in summer.

Jewelry District. Filled with bargain hunters, these crowded sidewalks resemble a slice of Manhattan. While you can save big on everything from wedding bands to sparkling belt buckles, the neighborhood also offers several more upscale vendors for those in search of super-special pieces. ⊠ *Between Olive St. and Broadway from 5th to 8th St., Downtown.*

Fodor's Choice
★ **Olvera Street.** Historic buildings line this redbrick walkway overhung with grape vines. At dozens of clapboard stalls you can browse south-of-the-border goods—leather sandals, woven blankets, and devotional candles, as well as cheap toys and souvenirs—and sample outstanding tacos. With the musicians and cafés providing the soundtrack, the area is constantly lively. ⊠ *Between Cesar Chavez Ave. and Arcadia St., Downtown ⊕ www.olvera-street.com.*

HOLLYWOOD AND THE STUDIOS

Here you can find everything from records to lingerie to movie memorabilia.

BOOKS AND MUSIC

Fodor's Choice
★ **Amoeba Records.** Touted as the "World's Largest Independent Record Store," Amoeba is a playground for music-lovers, with a knowledgeable staff and a focus on local artists. Catch free in-store appearances and signings by artists and bands that play sold-out shows at venues down the road. There's a rich stock of new and used CDs and DVDs, LPs, and 45s, an impressive cache of collectibles, and walls filled with concert posters. ⊠ *6400 W. Sunset Blvd., at Cahuenga Blvd., Hollywood* ☎ *323/245–6400 ⊕ www.amoeba.com.*

CLOTHING

Lost & Found. Specializing in emerging local and indie designers, this impeccably curated retailer keeps posh housewares such as lambswool throws, Brazilian soapstone cookware, and hand-thrown ceramics regularly in stock. But while you're here, don't sleep on the men's French shirting, modern bohemian clothing by Los Angeles' own Raquel Allegra, and luxurious baby blankets; there's something chic for everyone in the family. ✉ *6320 Yucca St., Hollywood* ☎ *323/856–5872* ⊕ *www.lostandfoundshop.com.*

MALLS AND SHOPPING CENTERS

Hollywood & Highland. Full of designer shops (BCBGMaxAzria, Louis Vuitton) and chain stores (Victoria's Secret, Fossil, and Sephora), this entertainment complex is a huge tourist magnet. The design pays tribute to the city's film legacy, with a grand staircase leading up to a pair of three-story-tall stucco elephants, a nod to the 1916 movie *Intolerance*. Pause at the entrance arch, called Babylon Court, which frames a picture-perfect view of the Hollywood sign. On the second level, next to the Dolby Theatre, is a visitor information center with maps, brochures, and a multilingual staff. The streets nearby provide the setting for Sunday's Hollywood Farmers Market, where you're likely to spot a celebrity or two picking up fresh produce or stopping to pick up breakfast from the food vendors. ✉ *Hollywood Blvd. and Highland Ave., Hollywood* ☎ *323/817–0220* ⊕ *www.hollywoodandhighland.com.*

BEVERLY HILLS AND THE WESTSIDE

BEVERLY HILLS

The shops of Beverly Hills, particularly Rodeo Drive, are a big draw for window-shopping, and leave visitors awestruck by L.A.'s excess. In this highly walkable neighborhood you'll find big-name luxury jewelers and department stores such as Cartier and Barneys New York.

BOOKS

Taschen. Philippe Starck designed the Taschen space to evoke a cool 1920s Parisian salon—a perfect showcase for the publisher's design-forward coffee table books about architecture, travel, culture, and photography. A suspended glass cube gallery in back hosts art exhibits and features limited-edition books. ✉ *354 N. Beverly Dr., Beverly Hills* ☎ *310/274–4300* ⊕ *www.taschen.com.*

CLOTHING

Tory Burch. Preppy, stylish, and colorful clothes appropriate for a road trip to Palm Springs or a flight to Palm Beach fill this flagship boutique. ✉ *142 S. Robertson Blvd., Beverly Hills* ☎ *310/248–2612* ⊕ *www.toryburch.com.*

DEPARTMENT STORES

Barneys New York. This is truly an impressive one-stop shop for high fashion. Deal hunters will appreciate the co-op section, which introduces indie designers before they make it big. Shop for beauty products, shoes, and accessories on the first floor, then wind your way up the staircase for couture. Keep your eyes peeled for fabulous and/or famous folks spearing salads at Fred's on the top floor. ✉ *9570 Wilshire Blvd., Beverly Hills* ☎ *310/276–4400* ⊕ *www.barneys.com.*

MALLS AND SHOPPING CENTERS

Beverly Center. In addition to luxury retailers like Bloomingdale's, Henri Bendel, and Dolce & Gabbana (which are always ideal for window-shopping if you don't have the means to splurge), this eight-level shopping center also offers plenty of outposts for more affordable brands including Aldo, H&M, and Uniqlo. ✉ *8500 Beverly Blvd., West Hollywood* ☎ *310/854–0071* ⊕ *www.beverlycenter.com.*

WEST HOLLYWOOD

This is prime shopping real estate, with everything from bridal couture design shops to furnishing stores sharing sidewalk space along posh streets like Melrose Place and Robertson Boulevard. It's also worth strolling West 3rd Street, which is lined with independent but affordable boutiques and several of the city's hottest restaurants and cafés.

CLOTHING

Fodor's Choice ★ **American Rag Cie.** Half the store features new clothing from established and emerging labels, while the other side is stocked with well-preserved vintage clothing organized by color and style. You'll also find plenty of shoes and accessories being picked over by the hippest of Angelenos. ✉ *150 S. La Brea Ave., West Hollywood* ☎ *323/935–3154* ⊕ *www.amrag.com.*

Fodor's Choice ★ **Fred Segal.** The ivy-covered building and security guards in the parking lot might tip you off that this is *the* place to be. Visit during the lunch hour to stargaze at the super-trendy café. This L.A. landmark is subdivided into smaller boutiques purveying everything from couture clothing to skateboard wear. The entertainment industry's fashion fiends are addicted to these exclusive creations, many from cult designers just beginning to excite the masses. ✉ *8100 Melrose Ave., West Hollywood* ☎ *323/651–4129* ⊕ *www.fredsegal.com.*

Fodor's Choice ★ **Maxfield.** This modern concrete structure is one of L.A.'s most desirable destinations for ultimate high fashion. The space is stocked with sleek offerings from Chanel, Saint Laurent, Balmain, and Rick Owen, plus occasional pop-ups by fashion's labels-of-the-moment. For serious shoppers (or gawkers) only. ✉ *8825 Melrose Ave., at Robertson Blvd., West Hollywood* ☎ *310/274–8800* ⊕ *www.maxfieldla.com.*

MALLS AND SHOPPING CENTERS

The Grove. Come to this popular (and polarizing) outdoor mall for familiar names like Anthropologie, Nike, and Nordstrom; stay for the central fountain with "dancing" water and light shows, people-watching from the trolley, and, during the holiday season, artificial snowfall and a winter wonderland. Feel-good pop blasting over the loudspeakers aims to boost your mood while you spend. The adjacent Farmers' Market offers tons of great dining options. ✉ *189 The Grove Dr., West Hollywood* ☎ *323/900–8080* ⊕ *www.thegrovela.com.*

SANTA MONICA AND THE BEACHES

The breezy beachside communities of Santa Monica and Venice are ideal for leisurely shopping. Scads of tourists (and some locals) gravitate toward Santa Monica Place and Third Street Promenade, a popular pedestrians-only shopping area that is within walking distance of the beach and historic Santa Monica Pier. ■TIP→ Parking in Santa Monica is next to impossible on Wednesday, when some streets are blocked off for the farmers' market, but there are several parking structures with free parking for an hour or two.

MALLS AND SHOPPING CENTERS

Malibu Lumber Yard. Emblematic Malibu lifestyle stores in this shopping complex include James Perse, Maxfield, and a too-chic J. Crew outpost. The playground and alfresco dining area make this an ideal weekend destination for families. ⊠ *3939 Cross Creek Rd., Malibu* ⊕ *www.themalibulumberyard.com.*

PASADENA

In Pasadena the stretch of Colorado Boulevard between Pasadena Avenue and Arroyo Parkway, known as Old Town, is a popular pedestrian shopping destination, with retailers such as Crate & Barrel and H&M, and Tiffany's, which sits a block away from Forever 21.

BOOKS

Vroman's Bookstore. Southern California's oldest and largest independent bookseller is justly famous for its great service. A newsstand, café, and stationery store add to the appeal. A regular rotation of events including trivia night, kids' story time, author meet-and-greets, crafting sessions, discussions, and more get the community actively involved. ⊠ *695 E. Colorado Blvd., Pasadena* ☎ *626/449–5320* ⊕ *www.vromansbookstore.com.*

THE CENTRAL COAST

from Ventura to Big Sur with
Channel Island National Park

WELCOME TO THE CENTRAL COAST

TOP REASONS TO GO

★ **Incredible nature:** The wild and wonderful Central Coast is home to Channel Islands National Park, two national marine sanctuaries, state parks and beaches, and the rugged Los Padres National Forest.

★ **Edible bounty:** Land and sea provide enough fresh regional foods to satisfy the most sophisticated foodies—grapes, strawberries, seafood, olive oil, and much more. Get your fill at countless farmers' markets, wineries, and restaurants.

★ **Outdoor activities:** Kick back and revel in the California lifestyle. Surf, golf, kayak, hike, play tennis—or just hang out and enjoy the gorgeous scenery.

★ **Small-town charm, big-city culture:** With all the amazing cultural opportunities—museums, theater, music, and festivals—you might start thinking you're in L.A. or San Francisco.

★ **Wine tasting:** Central Coast wines earn high critical praise. Sample them in urban tasting rooms, dusty crossroads towns, and at high- and low-tech rural wineries.

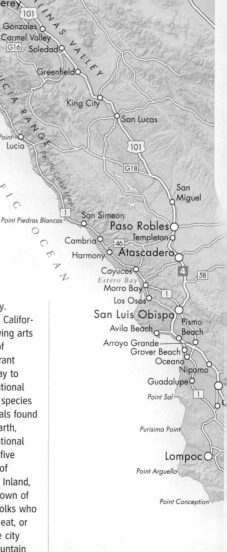

1 Ventura County.
Ventura is a classic California city with a thriving arts community, miles of beaches, and a vibrant harbor—the gateway to Channel Islands National Park. Home to 145 species of plants and animals found nowhere else on Earth, Channel Islands National Park encompasses five islands and a mile of surrounding ocean. Inland, the tiny and artsy town of Ojai plays host to folks who want to golf, shop, eat, or meditate, to escape city life in an idyllic mountain setting.

2 Santa Barbara. Down-home surfers rub elbows with Hollywood celebrities in sunny, well-scrubbed Santa Barbara, 95 miles north of Los Angeles. Its Spanish-Mexican heritage is reflected in the architectural style of its mission, court-house, and many homes and public buildings.

3 Northern Santa Barbara County. Wineries, ranches, and small villages dominate the quintessentially Californian landscape here. The quaint Danish town of Solvang is worth a stop for its half-timber buildings, galleries, and bakeries.

4 San Luis Obispo County. Friendly college town San Luis Obispo serves as the hub of a burgeoning wine region that stretches nearly 100 miles from Pismo Beach north to Paso Robles; the 230-plus wineries here have earned reputations for high-quality vintages that rival those of Northern California.

5 Big Sur Coastline. Rugged cliffs meet the Pacific for more than 60 miles—one of the most scenic and dramatic drives in the world.

GETTING ORIENTED

The Central Coast region begins about 60 miles north of Los Angeles, near the seaside city of Ventura. North along the sinuous coastline from here lie the cities of Santa Barbara and San Luis Obispo, and beyond them the smaller towns of Morro Bay, Cambria, and Big Sur. The nearly 300-mile drive through this region, especially the section of Highway 1 from San Simeon to Big Sur, is one of the most scenic in the state.

6

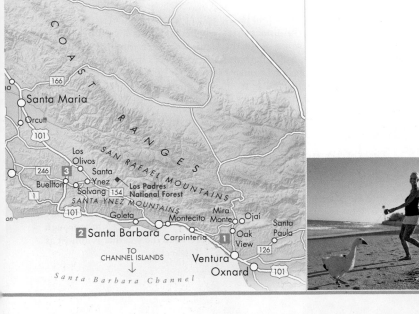

0 _____ 20 miles
0 _____ 30 kilometers

Updated
by Cheryl
Crabtree

Balmy weather, glorious beaches, crystal clear air, and serene landscapes have lured people to the Central Coast since prehistoric times. Today it's also known for its farm-fresh bounty, from grapes vintners crafted into world-class wines, to strawberries and other produce incorporated by chefs into distinctive cuisine. The scenic variety along the Pacific coast is equally impressive—you'll see everything from dramatic cliffs and grass-tufted bluffs to wildlife estuaries and miles of dunes. It's an ideal place to relax, slow down, and appreciate the abundant natural beauty.

Offshore, a pristine national park and a vast marine sanctuary protect the wild, wonderful underwater resources of this incredible corner of the planet. But not all of the Central Coast's top attractions are natural: Ventura, Santa Barbara, and San Luis Obispo are filled with sparkling examples of Spanish-Mediterranean architecture, bustling shopping districts, and first-rate restaurants showcasing regional foods and wines.

PLANNING

WHEN TO GO

The Central Coast climate is mild year-round. If you like to swim in warmer (if still nippy) ocean waters, July and August are the best months to visit. Be aware that this is also high season. Fog often rolls in along the coastal areas in early summer; you'll need a jacket, especially after sunset, close to the shore. It usually rains from December through March. From April to early June and early fall the weather is almost as fine as in high season, and the pace is less hectic.

GETTING HERE AND AROUND
AIR TRAVEL
Alaska Air, American, and United fly to Santa Barbara Airport (SBA), 9 miles from downtown. The same airlines provide service to San Luis Obispo County Regional Airport (SBP), 3 miles from downtown San Luis Obispo.

Santa Barbara Airbus shuttles travelers between Santa Barbara and Los Angeles for $55 one-way and $100 round-trip. The Santa Barbara Metropolitan Transit District Bus 11 ($1.75) runs every 30 minutes from the airport to the downtown transit center. A taxi between the airport and the hotel districts costs between $22 and $40.

Airport Contacts San Luis Obispo County Regional Airport. ⊠ *901 Airport Dr., off Hwy. 227, San Luis Obispo* ☎ *805/781–5205* ⊕ *sloairport.com.* **Santa Barbara Airport.** ⊠ *500 Fowler Rd., off U.S. 101 Exit 104B, Santa Barbara* ☎ *805/683–4011* ⊕ *flysba.com.* **Santa Barbara Airbus.** ☎ *805/964–7759, 800/423–1618* ⊕ *www.sbairbus.com.* **Santa Barbara Metropolitan Transit District.** ☎ *805/963–3366* ⊕ *sbmtd.gov.*

BUS TRAVEL
Greyhound provides service from Los Angeles and San Francisco to San Luis Obispo, Ventura, and Santa Barbara. Local transit companies serve these three cities and several smaller towns. Buses can be useful for visiting some urban sights, particularly in Santa Barbara; they're less so for rural ones.

Bus Contacts Greyhound. ☎ *800/231–2222* ⊕ *www.greyhound.com.*

CAR TRAVEL
Driving is the easiest way to experience the Central Coast. U.S. 101 and Highway 1, which run north–south, are the main routes to and through the Central Coast from Los Angeles and San Francisco. Highly scenic Highway 1 hugs the coast, and U.S. 101 runs inland. Between Ventura County and northern Santa Barbara County, the two highways are the same road. Highway 1 again separates from U.S. 101 north of Gaviota, then rejoins the highway at Pismo Beach. Along any stretch where these two highways are separate, U.S. 101 is the quicker route.

The most dramatic section of the Central Coast is the 70 miles between San Simeon and Big Sur. The road is narrow and twisting, with a single lane in each direction. In fog or rain the drive can be downright nerve-racking; in wet seasons mudslides can close portions of the road.

Other routes into the Central Coast include Highway 46 and Highway 33, which head, respectively, west and south from Interstate 5 near Bakersfield.

Road Conditions Caltrans. ☎ *800/427–7623, 888/836–0866 Hwy. 1 visitor hotline (Cambria north to Carmel)* ⊕ *www.dot.ca.gov.*

TRAIN TRAVEL
The Amtrak *Coast Starlight,* which runs between Los Angeles and Seattle via Oakland, stops in Paso Robles, San Luis Obispo, Santa Barbara, and Oxnard. Amtrak runs several *Pacific Surfliner* trains and buses daily between San Luis Obispo, Santa Barbara, Los Angeles, and

San Diego. Metrolink Regional Rail Service trains connect Ventura and Oxnard with Los Angeles and points between.

Train Contacts Amtrak. ☎ *800/872–7245* ⊕ *www.amtrak.com, www. amtrakcalifornia.com, www.pacificsurfliner.com.* **Metrolink.** ☎ *800/371–5465* ⊕ *metrolinktrains.com.*

RESTAURANTS

The cuisine in Ventura and Santa Barbara is every bit as eclectic as it is in California's bigger cities; fresh seafood is a standout. A foodie renaissance has overtaken the entire region from Ventura to Paso Robles, spawning dozens of restaurants touting locavore cuisine made with fresh organic produce and meats. Dining attire on the Central Coast is generally casual, though slightly dressy casual wear is the custom at pricier restaurants. *Restaurant reviews have been shortened. For full information, visit Fodors.com.*

HOTELS

Expect to pay top dollar for rooms along the shore, especially in summer. Moderately priced hotels and motels do exist—most just a short drive inland from their higher-price counterparts. Make your reservations as early as possible, and take advantage of midweek specials to get the best rates. It's common for lodgings to require two-day minimum stays on holidays and some weekends, especially in summer, and to double rates during festivals and other events. *Hotel reviews have been shortened. For full information, visit Fodors.com.*

WHAT IT COSTS			
$	**$$**	**$$$**	**$$$$**
Restaurants	under $16	$16–$22	$23–$30	over $30
Hotels	under $120	$120–$175	$176–$250	over $250

Restaurant prices are the average cost of a main course at dinner or, if dinner is not served, at lunch, excluding sales tax of 8%–8.25% (depending on location). Hotel prices are the lowest cost of a standard double room in high season, excluding service charges and 9%–12% occupancy tax.

TOURS

Many tour companies will pick you up at your hotel or central locations; ask about this when booking.

Central Coast Food Tours. Food and wine destinations are the focus of this outfit's walking tours of shops, restaurants, wineries, and other spots in San Luis Obispo, Paso Robles, and elsewhere. Some tours combine wine tasting with an ocean sail or a zip-line adventure. ☎ *800/656–0713* ⊕ *centralcoastfoodtours.com* ✉ *From $69.*

Cloud Climbers Jeep and Wine Tours. This outfit conducts trips in open-air, six-passenger jeeps to the Santa Barbara/Santa Ynez mountains and Wine Country. Tour options include wine tasting, mountain, sunset, and a discovery adventure for families. The company also offers a four-hour All Around Ojai Tour and arranges horseback riding and trap-shooting tours. ☎ *805/646–3200* ⊕ *ccjeeps.com* ✉ *From $89.*

Grapeline Wine Tours. Wine and vineyard picnic tours in Paso Robles and the Santa Ynez Valley are Grapeline's specialty. ☎ *888/894–6379* ⊕ *gogrape.com* ✉ *From $119.*

Santa Barbara Wine Country Cycling Tours. The company leads half- and full-day tours of the Santa Ynez wine region, conducts hiking and cycling tours, and rents out bicycles. ☎ *888/557–8687, 805/686–9490* ⊕ *winecountrycycling.com* ✉ *From $100.*

Stagecoach Wine Tours. Locally owned and operated, Stagecoach runs daily wine-tasting excursions through the Santa Ynez Valley in vans, minicoaches, and SUVs. ✉ *Solvang* ☎ *805/686–8347* ⊕ *winetourssantaynez.com* ✉ *From $171.*

Sustainable Vine Wine Tours. This green-minded company specializes in eco-friendly Santa Ynez Valley wine tours in luxury vans and Tesla SUVs. Trips include tastings at limited-production wineries committed to sustainable practices. An organic picnic lunch is served. ☎ *805/698–3911* ⊕ *sustainablevine.com* ✉ *$150.*

VISITOR INFORMATION

Contacts Central Coast Tourism Council. ⊕ *centralcoast-tourism.com.*

6

VENTURA COUNTY

Ventura County was first settled by the Chumash Indians. Spanish missionaries were the first Europeans to arrive, followed by Americans and other Europeans, who established towns, transportation networks, and highly productive farms. Since the 1920s, agriculture has been steadily replaced as the area's main industry—first by the oil business and more recently by tourism.

Accessible via boat or plane from Ventura and Santa Barbara, Channel Islands National Park is a series of five protected islands just 11 miles offshore where hiking, kayaking, and wildlife viewing abound.

VENTURA

60 miles north of Los Angeles.

Like Los Angeles, the city of Ventura enjoys gorgeous weather and sun-kissed beaches—but without the smog and congestion. The miles of beautiful beaches attract athletes—body-surfers and boogie boarders, runners and bikers—and those who'd rather doze beneath an umbrella all day. Ventura Harbor is home to myriad fishing boats, restaurants, and water-activity centers where you can rent boats and take harbor cruises. Foodies can get their fix all over Ventura—dozens of upscale cafés and wine and tapas bars have opened in recent years. Arts and antiques buffs have long trekked downtown to browse the galleries and shops here. One of the greatest perks of Ventura is its walkability. If you drive here, park your car in one of the free 24-hour parking lots sprinkled around the city and hoof it on foot, or board a free trolley that cruises from downtown along the waterfront (Thursday–Sunday 11 am –11 pm).

GETTING HERE AND AROUND

Amtrak and Metrolink trains serve the area from Los Angeles. Greyhound buses stop in Ventura; Gold Coast Transit serves the city and the rest of Ventura County.

U.S. 101 is the north–south main route into town, but for a scenic drive, take Highway 1 north from Santa Monica. The highway merges with U.S. 101 just south of Ventura. ■TIP➔ Traveling north to Ventura from Los Angeles on weekdays, it's best to depart before 6 am, between 10 and 2, or after 7 pm, or you'll get caught in the extended rush-hour traffic. Coming south from Santa Barbara, depart before 1 or after 6 pm. On weekends, traffic is generally fine except southbound on U.S. 101 between Santa Barbara and Ventura on Sunday late afternoon and early evening.

ESSENTIALS

Bus Contact Gold Coast Transit. ☎ 805/487-4222 ⊕ www.goldcoasttransit.org.

Visitor Information Ventura Visitors and Convention Bureau. ✉ Downtown Visitor Center, 101 S. California St. ☎ 805/648-2075, 800/483-6214 ⊕ visitventuraca.com.

EXPLORING

Mission San Buenaventura. The ninth of the 21 California missions, Mission San Buenaventura was established in 1782 and the current church was rebuilt and rededicated in 1809. A self-guided tour takes you through a small museum, a quiet courtyard, and a chapel with 250-year-old paintings. ✉ 211 E. Main St., at Figueroa St. ☎ 805/643-4318 ⊕ www.sanbuenaventuramission.org ☜ $4.

Museum of Ventura County. Exhibits in a contemporary complex of galleries and a sunny courtyard plaza tell the story of Ventura County from prehistoric times to the present. A highlight is the gallery that contains Ojai artist George Stuart's historical figures, dressed in exceptionally detailed, custom-made clothing reflecting their particular eras. In the courtyard, eight panels made with 45,000 pieces of cut glass form a history time line. ✉ 100 E. Main St., at S. Ventura Ave. ☎ 805/653-0323 ⊕ www.venturamuseum.org ☜ $5, free 1st Sun. of month.

Fodor'sChoice ★ **Ventura Oceanfront.** Four miles of gorgeous coastline stretch from the county fairgrounds at the northern border of the city of San Buenaventura, through San Buenaventura State Beach, down to Ventura Harbor in the south. The main attraction here is the San Buenaventura City Pier, a landmark built in 1872 and restored in 1993. Surfers rip the waves just north of the pier, and sunbathers relax on white-sand beaches on either side. The mile-long promenade and the Omer Rains Bike Trail north of the pier attract scores of joggers, surrey cyclers, and bikers throughout the year. ✉ California St., at ocean's edge.

WHERE TO EAT

$$$ ✕ **Brophy Bros.** The Ventura outpost of the wildly popular Santa Bar-
SEAFOOD bara restaurant provides the same fresh seafood-oriented meals in a spacious second-story setting overlooking the harbor. Feast on everything from fish-and-chips and crab cakes to chowder and delectable

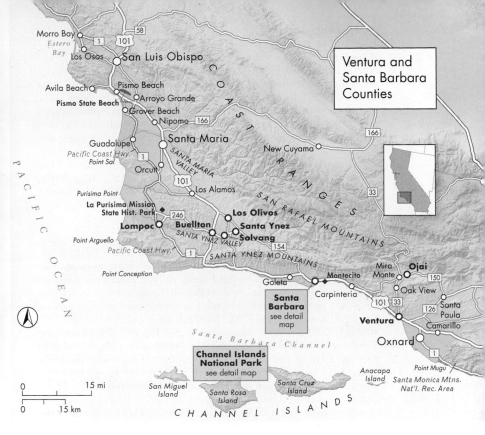

fish—often straight from the boats moored below. **Known for:** lively atmosphere; harbor views; killer clam bar. $ *Average main: $25* ✉ *1559 Spinnaker Dr., in Ventura Harbor Village* ☎ *805/639–0865* ⊕ *brophybros.com.*

$$$ ✕ **Café Zack.** A local favorite for anniversaries and other celebrations,
AMERICAN Zack's serves classic European dishes in an intimate, two-room 1930s
Fodor'sChoice cottage adorned with local art. Entrées of note include seafood spe-
★ cials (depending on the local catch), slow-roasted boar shank and filet mignon, the latter typically crusted in peppercorns or topped with porcini mushrooms. **Known for:** personal service; house-made desserts; excellent California wines. $ *Average main: $30* ✉ *1095 E. Thompson Blvd., at S. Ann St.* ☎ *805/643–9445* ⊕ *cafezack.com* ⊗ *Closed Sun. No lunch Sat.*

$$ ✕ **Lure Fish House.** Fresh, sustainably caught seafood charbroiled over
SEAFOOD a mesquite grill, a well-stocked oyster bar, specialty cocktails, and a wine list heavy on local vintages lure diners into this slick, nautical-themed space downtown. The menu centers on the mostly local catch and organic vegetables, and includes tacos, sandwiches, and salads. **Known for:** shrimp-and-chips; cioppino; citrus crab-cake salad. $ *Average main: $22* ✉ *60 S. California St.* ☎ *805/567–4400* ⊕ *lurefish-house.com.*

$$$
CARIBBEAN
✕ **Rumfish y Vino.** The sibling of a popular namesake restaurant in Placencia, Belize, Rumfish y Vino serves up zesty Caribbean fare with a California wine country twist in a courtyard venue just off Main Street near the mission. Dine in the beach-chic dining room or in the heated patio with a roaring fireplace, where live music plays several nights a week, The seafood-heavy menu changes depending on the local catch, but you might start with Peruvian ceviche conch fritters with rumfish sauce or zesty local yellowtail carpaccio, then dig into Caribbean seafood stew or a hangar steak with crispy avocado. **Known for:** delectable fish tacos and flatbreads; happy hour and creative cocktails; chile-braised beef lasagne. $ *Average main: $26* ⊠ *434 N. Palm St.* ☎ *805/667–9288* ⊕ *www.rumfishyvinoventura.com.*

WHERE TO STAY

$$$
RESORT
🏨 **Four Points by Sheraton Ventura Harbor Resort.** An on-site restaurant, spacious rooms, and a slew of amenities make this 17-acre property—which includes sister hotel Holiday Inn Express—a popular and practical choice for Channel Islands visitors. **Pros:** close to island transportation; quiet location; short drive to historic downtown. **Cons:** not in the heart of downtown; noisy seagulls sometimes congregate nearby. $ *Rooms from: $179* ⊠ *1050 Schooner Dr.* ☎ *805/658–1212, 800/368–7764* ⊕ *fourpoints.com/ventura* ⟿ *106 rooms* ⫶⦶ *No meals.*

$$$
HOTEL
🏨 **Holiday Inn Express Ventura Harbor.** A favorite among Channel Islands visitors, this quiet, comfortable, lodge-inspired property sits right at the Ventura Harbor entrance. **Pros:** quiet at night; easy access to harbor restaurants and activities; five-minute drive to downtown. **Cons:** busy area on weekends; complaints of erratic service. $ *Rooms from: $179* ⊠ *1080 Navigator Dr.* ☎ *805/856–9533, 888/233–9450* ⊕ *holidayinnexpress.com/venturaca* ⟿ *69 rooms* ⫶⦶ *Breakfast.*

$$$
HOTEL
🏨 **Ventura Beach Marriott.** Spacious, contemporary rooms, a peaceful location just steps from San Buenaventura State Beach, and easy access to downtown arts and culture make the Marriott a popular choice. **Pros:** walk to beach and biking/jogging trails; a block from historic pier; great value for location. **Cons:** close to highway; near busy intersection. $ *Rooms from: $195* ⊠ *2055 E. Harbor Blvd.* ☎ *805/643–6000, 888/236–2427* ⊕ *marriottventurabeach.com* ⟿ *285 rooms* ⫶⦶ *No meals.*

SPORTS AND THE OUTDOORS

The most popular outdoor activities in Ventura are beach-going and whale-watching. California gray whales migrate offshore through the Santa Barbara Channel from late December through March; giant blue and humpback whales feed here from mid-June through September. The channel teems with marine life year-round, so tours, which depart from Ventura Harbor, include more than just whale sightings.

Island Packers Cruises. A cruise through the Santa Barbara Channel with Island Packers will give you the chance to spot dolphins, seals, and sometimes even whales. ⊠ *Ventura Harbor, 1691 Spinnaker Dr.* ☎ *805/642–1393* ⊕ *islandpackers.com.*

CHANNEL ISLANDS NATIONAL PARK

11 miles southwest of Ventura Harbor via boat.

On crystal clear days the craggy peaks of the Channel Islands are easy to see from the mainland, jutting from the Pacific in such sharp detail it seems you could reach out and touch them. The islands are not too far away—a high-speed boat will whisk you to the closest ones in less than an hour—yet very few people ever visit them. Those who do venture out to the islands will experience one of the most splendid land-and-sea wilderness areas on the planet. Camping is your only lodging choice on the islands, but it's a fantastic way to experience the natural beauty and isolation of the park. Campsites are primitive, with no water (except on Santa Rosa and Santa Cruz) or electricity. Campsites are $15 per night; you must arrange your transportation before you reserve your site (☎ *(800) 444–6777*) or online (⊕ *www.recreation.gov*) up to five months in advance.

Channel Islands National Park includes five of the eight Channel Islands and the one nautical mile of ocean that surrounds them. Six nautical miles of surrounding channel waters are designated a National Marine Sanctuary, and are teeming with life, including giant kelp forests, 345 fish species, dolphins, whales, seals, sea lions, and seabirds. To maintain the integrity of their habitats, pets are not allowed in the park.

GETTING HERE AND AROUND

Most visitors access the Channel Islands via an Island Packers boat from Ventura Harbor. To reach the harbor by car, exit U.S. 101 in Ventura at Seaward Boulevard or Victoria Avenue and follow the signs to Ventura Harbor/Spinnaker Drive. An Island Packers boat heads to Anacapa Island from Oxnard's Channel Islands Harbor, which you can reach from Ventura Harbor by following Harbor Boulevard south about 6 miles and continuing south on Victoria Avenue. Private vehicles are not permitted on the islands.

BOAT TOURS

Island Packers. Sailing on high-speed catamarans from Ventura or a mono-hull vessel from Oxnard, Island Packers goes to Santa Cruz Island daily most of the year, weather permitting. The boats also go to Anacapa several days a week, and to the outer islands from April through November. They also cruise along Anacapa's north shore on three-hour wildlife tours (no disembarking) several times a week. ⊠ *3550 Harbor Blvd., Oxnard* ☎ *805/642–1393* ⊕ *islandpackers.com.*

EXPLORING

TOP ATTRACTIONS

Channel Islands National Park Visitor Center. The park's Robert J. Lagomarsino Visitor Center has a museum, a bookstore, and a three-story observation tower with telescopes. The museum's exhibits and a 24-minute film, *Treasure in the Sea*, provide an engaging overview of the islands. In the marine life exhibit, sea stars cling to rocks, and a brilliant orange Garibaldi darts around. Also on display are full-size reproductions of a male northern elephant seal and the pygmy mammoth skeleton unearthed on Santa Rosa Island in 1994.

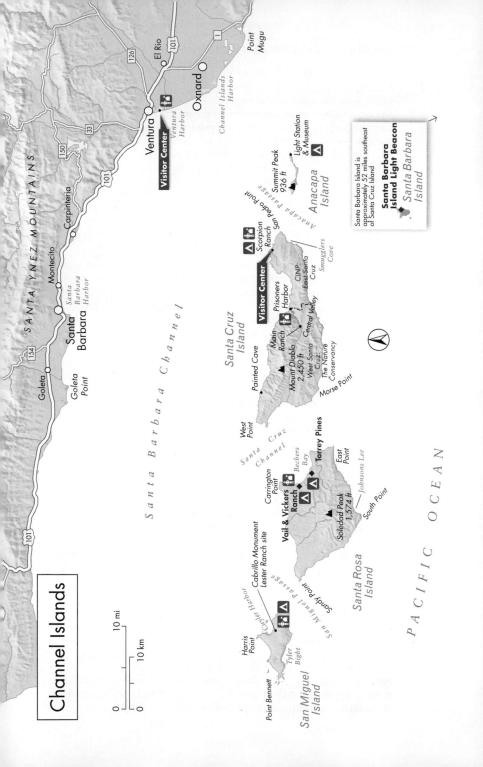

Channel Islands

Santa Ynez Mountains

El Rio
Oxnard
Point Mugu
Channel Islands Harbor
Ventura
Visitor Center
Ventura Harbor

Montecito
Carpinteria
Santa Barbara
Santa Barbara Harbor

Goleta
Goleta Point

Santa Barbara Channel

Santa Barbara is approximately 52 miles southeast of Santa Cruz Island

Santa Barbara Island Light Beacon

Santa Barbara Island

Anacapa Passage
Light Station & Museum
Summit Peak 936 ft
Anacapa Island

San Pedro Point
Scorpion Ranch
Smugglers Cove
Visitor Center
Prisoners Harbor
CINP: East Santa Cruz
Central Valley
Main Ranch
Mount Diablo 2,450 ft
West Santa Cruz: The Nature Conservancy
Morse Point

Santa Cruz Island
Painted Cave

West Point
Santa Cruz Channel

Bechers Bay
Carrington Point
Torrey Pines
East Point
Johnsons Lee
Vail & Vickers Ranch
Soledad Peak 1,574 ft
South Point

Santa Rosa Island

Cabrillo Monument
Lester Ranch site
Cuyler Harbor
Harris Point
Tyler Bight
Point Bennett
Sandy Point
San Miguel Passage

San Miguel Island

PACIFIC OCEAN

10 mi
10 km

On weekends and holidays at 11 am and 3 pm, rangers lead various free public programs describing park resources, and from Wednesday through Saturday in summer the center screens live ranger broadcasts of hikes and dives on Anacapa Island. Webcam images of bald eagles and other land and sea creatures are shown at the center and on the park's website. ⊠ *1901 Spinnaker Dr., Ventura* ☎ *805/658–5730* ⊕ *www.nps.gov/chis.*

Fodor's Choice
★
Santa Cruz Island. Five miles west of Anacapa, 96-square-mile Santa Cruz Island is the largest of the Channel Islands. The National Park Service manages the easternmost 24% of the island; the rest is owned by the Nature Conservancy, which requires a permit to land. When your boat drops you off on a portion of the 70 miles of craggy coastline, you see two rugged mountain ranges with peaks soaring to 2,500 feet and deep canyons traversed by streams. This landscape is the habitat of a remarkable variety of flora and fauna—more than 600 types of plants, 140 kinds of land birds, 11 mammal species, five varieties of reptiles, and three amphibian species live here. Bird-watchers may want to look for the endemic island scrub jay, which is found nowhere else in the world.

One of the largest and deepest sea caves in the world, **Painted Cave** lies along the northwest coast of Santa Cruz. Named for the colorful lichen and algae that cover its walls, Painted Cave is nearly ¼ mile long and 100 feet wide. In spring a waterfall cascades over the entrance. Kayakers may encounter seals or sea lions cruising alongside their boats inside the cave. The Channel Islands hold some of the richest archaeological resources in North America; all artifacts are protected within the park. Remnants of a dozen Chumash villages can be seen on the island. The largest of these villages, at the eastern end, occupied the area now called **Scorpion Ranch.** The Chumash mined extensive chert deposits on the island for tools to produce shell-bead money, which they traded with people on the mainland. You can learn about Chumash history and view artifacts, tools, and exhibits on native plant and wildlife at the interpretive visitor center near the landing dock. Visitors can also explore remnants of the early-1900s ranching era in the restored historic adobe and outbuildings. ⊠ *Channel Islands National Park.*

WORTH NOTING

Anacapa Island. Most people think of Anacapa as an island, but it's actually comprised of three narrow islets. Although the tips of these volcanic formations nearly touch, the islets are inaccessible from one another except by boat. All three have towering cliffs, isolated sea caves, and natural bridges; Arch Rock, on East Anacapa, is one of the best-known symbols of Channel Islands National Park.

Wildlife viewing is the main activity on East Anacapa, particularly in summer when seagull chicks are newly hatched and sea lions and seals lounge on the beaches. Exhibits at East Anacapa's compact **museum** include the original lead-crystal Fresnel lens from the 1932 lighthouse.

On West Anacapa, depending on the season and the number of desirable species lurking about here, boats travel to **Frenchy's Cove.** On a voyage here you might see anemones, limpets, barnacles, mussel beds, and colorful marine algae in the pristine tide pools. The rest of West Anacapa is closed to protect nesting brown pelicans. ⊠ *Channel Islands National Park.*

San Miguel Island. The westernmost of the Channel Islands, San Miguel Island is frequently battered by storms sweeping across the North Pacific. The 15-square-mile island's wild windswept landscape is lush with vegetation. Point Bennett, at the western tip, offers one of the world's most spectacular wildlife displays when more than 100,000 pinnipeds hit its beach. Explorer Juan Rodríguez Cabrillo was the first European to visit this island; he claimed it for Spain in 1542. Legend holds that Cabrillo died on one of the Channel Islands—no one knows where he's buried, but there's a memorial to him on a bluff above Cuyler Harbor. ⊠ *Channel Islands National Park.*

Santa Barbara Island. At about 1 square mile, Santa Barbara Island is the smallest of the Channel Islands and nearly 35 miles south of the others. Triangular in shape, Santa Barbara's steep cliffs—which offer a perfect nesting spot for the Scripps's murrelet, a rare seabird—are topped by twin peaks. In spring you can enjoy a brilliant display of yellow coreopsis. Learn about the wildlife on and around the islands at the island's small museum. ⊠ *Channel Islands National Park.*

Santa Rosa Island. Between Santa Cruz and San Miguel, Santa Rosa is the second largest of the Channel Islands. The terrain along the coast varies from broad, sandy beaches to sheer cliffs—a central mountain range, rising to 1,589 feet, breaks the island's relatively low profile. Santa Rosa is home to about 500 species of plants, including the rare Torrey pine, and three unusual mammals, the island fox, the spotted skunk, and the deer mouse. They hardly compare, though, to their predecessors: a nearly complete skeleton of a 6-foot-tall pygmy mammoth was unearthed in 1994.

From 1901 to 1998, cattle were raised at the island's **Vail & Vickers Ranch.** The route from Santa Rosa's landing dock to the campground passes by the historic ranch buildings, barns, equipment, and the wooden pier where cattle were brought onto the island. ⊠ *Channel Islands National Park.*

SPORTS AND THE OUTDOORS

Channel Islands Adventure Company (owned and operated by Santa Barbara Adventure Company) *(see Santa Barbara Sports and the Outdoors)* arranges paddling, kayaking, and other Channel Islands excursions out of Ventura, and various concessionaires at Ventura Harbor Village (☏ *805/477–0470* ⊕ *www.venturaharborvillage.com*) arrange diving, kayaking, and other rentals and tours. Island Packers conducts whale-watching cruises.

DIVING

Some of the best snorkeling and diving in the world can be found in the cool waters surrounding the Channel Islands. In the relatively warm water around Anacapa and eastern Santa Cruz, photographers can get great shots of rarely seen giant black bass swimming among the kelp forests. Here you also find a reef covered with red brittle starfish. If you're an experienced diver, you might swim among five species of seals and sea lions, or try your hand at spearing rockfish or halibut near San Miguel and Santa Rosa. The best time to scuba dive is in summer and fall, when the water is often clear up to a 100-foot depth.

KAYAKING

The most remote parts of the Channel Islands are accessible only by a sea kayak. Some of the best kayaking in the park can be found on Anacapa, Santa Barbara, and the eastern tip of Santa Cruz. It's too far to kayak from the mainland out to the islands, but outfitters have tours that take you to the islands. Tours are offered year-round, but high seas may cause trip cancellations between December and March. ⚠ Channel waters can be unpredictable and challenging. Guided trips are highly recommended.

WHALE-WATCHING

About a third of the world's cetacean species (27 to be exact) can be seen in the Santa Barbara Channel. In July and August, humpback and blue whales feed off the north shore of Santa Rosa. From late December through March, up to 10,000 gray whales pass through the Santa Barbara Channel on their way from Alaska to Mexico and back again; if you go on a whale-watching trip during this time frame you're likely to spot one or more of them. Other types of whales, but fewer in number, swim the channel from June through August.

OJAI

15 miles north of Ventura.

The Ojai Valley, which director Frank Capra used as a backdrop for his 1936 film *Lost Horizon,* sizzles in the summer when temperatures routinely reach 90°F. The acres of orange and avocado groves here evoke postcard images of long-ago agricultural Southern California. Many artists and celebrities have sought refuge from life in the fast lane in lush Ojai.

GETTING HERE AND AROUND

From northern Ventura, Highway 33 veers east from U.S. 101 and climbs inland to Ojai. From Santa Barbara, exit U.S. 101 at Highway 150 in Carpinteria, then travel east 20 miles on a twisting, two-lane road that is not recommended at night or during poor weather. You can also access Ojai by heading west from Interstate 5 on Highway 126. Exit at Santa Paula and follow Highway 150 north for 16 miles to Ojai. Gold Coast Transit provides service to Ojai from Ventura.

Ojai can be easily explored on foot; you can also hop on the Ojai Trolley ($1, or $2 day pass), which until about 5 pm follows two routes around Ojai and neighboring Miramonte on weekdays and one route on weekends. Tell the driver you're visiting and you'll get an informal guided tour.

ESSENTIALS

Bus Contacts Gold Coast Transit. ☎ 805/487–4222 ⊕ goldcoasttransit.org. **Ojai Trolley.** ☎ 805/646–5581 ⊕ ojaitrolley.com.

Visitor Information Ojai Visitors Bureau. ✉ 109 N. Blanche St., Suite 103, at W. Matilija St. ☎ 888/652–4669 ⊕ ojaivisitors.com.

EXPLORING

Meditation Mount. Enter through a Peace Portal hewn from reclaimed 1,200-year-old Douglas Fir to walk through the International Garden of Peace and sit in a beautiful meditation room at this nonprofit meditation center, open to the public from 8 am to sunset. ✉ *10340 Reeves Rd.* ✥ *5 miles east of downtown Ojai* ☎ *805/646–5508* 🌐 *meditationmount.org* 🕓 *Closed Mon. and Tues.*

Ojai Art Center. California's oldest nonprofit, multipurpose arts center exhibits visual art from various disciplines and presents theater, dance, and other performances. ✉ *113 S. Montgomery St., near E. Ojai Ave.* ☎ *805/646–0117* 🌐 *www.ojaiartcenter.org.*

Ojai Avenue. The work of local artists is displayed in the Spanish-style shopping arcade along the avenue downtown. On Sunday between 9 and 1, organic and specialty growers sell their produce at the outdoor market behind the arcade.

Ojai Valley Museum. The museum collects, preserves, and presents exhibits about the art, history, and culture of Ojai and Ojai Valley. Walking tours of Ojai depart from here. ✉ *130 W. Ojai Ave.* ☎ *805/640–1390* 🌐 *ojaivalleymuseum.org* 🎟 *Museum $5, walking tour $7 ($15 family)* 🕓 *Closed Mon.*

Ojai Valley Trail. The 18-mile trail is open to pedestrians, joggers, equestrians, bikers, and others on nonmotorized vehicles. You can access it anywhere along its route. ✉ *Parallel to Hwy. 33 from Soule Park in Ojai to ocean in Ventura* ☎ *888/652–4669* 🌐 *ojaivisitors.com.*

WHERE TO EAT

$$$ MEDITERRANEAN
🍴 **Azu.** Slick furnishings, piped-in jazz, craft cocktails, and local beers and wines draw diners to this artsy Mediterranean bistro known for tapas made from organic ingredients. You can also order soups, salads, and bistro fare such as steak frites and paella. **Known for:** many vegan and gluten-free options; amazing homemade gelato; more than 30 wines by the glass. [$] *Average main: $25* ✉ *457 E. Ojai Ave.* ☎ *805/640–7987* 🌐 *azuojai.com.*

$ ITALIAN
🍴 **Boccali's.** Edging a ranch, citrus groves, and a seasonal garden that provides produce for menu items, the modest but cheery Boccali's attracts many loyal fans. When it's warm, you can dine alfresco in the oak-shaded patio and lawn area and sometimes listen to live music. **Known for:** family-run operation; handrolled pizzas and home-style pastas; seasonal strawberry shortcake. [$] *Average main: $15* ✉ *3277 Ojai Ave., about 2 miles east of downtown* ☎ *805/646–6116* 🌐 *boccalis.com* 🕓 *No lunch Mon. and Tues.*

$ AMERICAN
🍴 **Farmer and the Cook.** An organic farmer and his chef-wife run this funky café/bakery/market in Meiners Oaks, just a few miles west of downtown Ojai. Fill up at the soup and salad bar, order a wood-fired pizza, bento box, sandwich, or a daily special, then grab a table indoors or out on the patio, Vegans have ample choices from the Mexican-inspired menu. **Known for:** many veggie and gluten-free options; grab-and-go meals; weekend breakfasts. [$] *Average main: $12* ✉ *339 W. El Roblar* ☎ *805/640–9608* 🌐 *www.farmerandcook.com.*

$$$ ITALIAN Fodor's Choice ★ 🍴 **Nocciola.** Authentic northern Italian dishes with a California twist, a cozy fireplace dining room in a century-old Craftsman-style house, and a covered patio amid the oaks draw locals and visitors alike to this popular eatery, owned by an Italian chef and his American wife (the family lives upstairs). The menu changes seasonally, but regular stars include seared sea scallops with Parmesan fondue and truffle shavings, homemade pastas made with organic egg yolks, and *pappardelle* with slow-roasted wild boar. **Known for:** great wild fish and game; Moment Pink signature cocktail; five-course tasting menu. [$] *Average main: $29* ✉ *314 El Paseo Rd.* ☎ *805/640–1648* 🌐 *nocciolaojai.com* ⏲ *Closed Mon.*

$$$$ EUROPEAN 🍴 **Suzanne's Cuisine.** Peppered filet mignon, linguine with steamed clams, and pan-roasted salmon with a roasted mango sauce are among the offerings at this European-style restaurant. Seafood, roasted meats, and poultry, as well as vegetarian dishes dominate the dinner menu, and salads and soups star at lunchtime. **Known for:** professional service; cozy dining room with fireplace; all desserts made on the premises. [$] *Average main: $32* ✉ *502 W. Ojai Ave.* ☎ *805/640–1961* 🌐 *suzannescuisine.com* ⏲ *Closed Tues.*

6

WHERE TO STAY

$$ B&B/INN 🏨 **The Iguana Inns of Ojai.** Artists own and operate these two bohemian-chic inns: The Blue Iguana, a cozy Southwestern-style hotel about 2 miles west of downtown, and the Emerald Iguana, which has art nouveau rooms, suites, and cottages in a secluded residential setting near downtown Ojai. **Pros:** colorful art everywhere; secluded. **Cons:** 2 miles from downtown; on a highway; small. [$] *Rooms from: $139* ✉ *11794 N. Ventura Ave.* ☎ *805/646–5277* 🌐 *iguanainnsofojai.com* 🛏 *12 rooms, 8 cottages* 🍽 *Breakfast.*

$$$$ RESORT 🏨 **Oaks at Ojai.** Rejuvenation is the name of the game at this destination spa where you can work out all day or just lounge by the pool. **Pros:** all-inclusive fitness package available; hikes and fitness classes; healthful meals. **Cons:** some rooms are basic; on main road through town. [$] *Rooms from: $265* ✉ *122 E. Ojai Ave.* ☎ *805/646–5573, 800/753–6257* 🌐 *oaksspa.com* 🛏 *46 rooms* 🍽 *All meals* ☞ *2-night minimum stay.*

$$ HOTEL 🏨 **Ojai Rancho Inn.** A collection of one-story buildings and cottages tucked between Ojai Avenue and the bike trail, this ranch-style motel attracts hipsters and those who appreciate a rustic getaway with modern comforts and a laid-back vintage vibe. **Pros:** free loaner cruiser bikes; small on-site bar; nice pool area with lounge chairs. **Cons:** not fancy or luxurious; rooms could use soundproofing; some road noise in rooms close to the road. [$] *Rooms from: $150* ✉ *615 W. Ojai Ave.* ☎ *805/646–1434* 🌐 *ojairanchoinn.com* 🛏 *17 rooms* 🍽 *No meals.*

$$$$ RESORT Fodor's Choice ★ 🏨 **Ojai Valley Inn & Spa.** This outdoorsy, golf-oriented resort and spa is set on beautifully landscaped grounds, with hillside views in nearly all directions. **Pros:** Spanish-colonial architecture; exceptional outdoor activities; seven on-site restaurants serving regional cuisine. **Cons:** expensive; areas near restaurants can be noisy. [$] *Rooms from: $349* ✉ *905 Country Club Rd.* ☎ *805/646–1111, 855/697–8780* 🌐 *ojairesort.com* 🛏 *303 rooms* 🍽 *No meals.*

$$$ B&B/INN 🏨 **Su Nido Inn.** A short walk from downtown Ojai sights and restaurants, this posh Mission Revival–style inn sits in a quiet neighborhood a few blocks from Libbey Park. **Pros:** walking distance from downtown; homey feel. **Cons:** no pool; can get hot during summer. [$] *Rooms from: $199* ✉ *301 N. Montgomery St.* ☎ *805/646–7080, 866/646–7080* 🌐 *www.sunidoinn.com* 🛏 *12 rooms* 🍴 *No meals* ☞ *2-night minimum stay on weekends.*

SANTA BARBARA

27 miles northwest of Ventura and 29 miles west of Ojai.

Santa Barbara has long been an oasis for Los Angelenos seeking respite from big-city life. The attractions begin at the ocean and end in the foothills of the Santa Ynez Mountains. A few miles up the coast east and west—but still very much a part of Santa Barbara—are the exclusive residential districts of Montecito and Hope Ranch. Santa Barbara is on a jog in the coastline, so the ocean is actually to the south, instead of the west. "Up" the coast toward San Francisco is west, "down" toward Los Angeles is east, and the mountains are north.

GETTING HERE AND AROUND

U.S. 101 is the main route into Santa Barbara. If you're staying in town, a car is handy but not essential; the beaches and downtown are easily explored by bicycle or on foot. Visit the Santa Barbara Car Free website for bike-route and walking-tour maps, suggestions for car-free vacations, and transportation discounts.

Santa Barbara Metropolitan Transit District's Line 22 bus serves major tourist sights. Several bus lines connect with the very convenient electric shuttles that cruise the downtown and waterfront every 10 to 15 minutes (50¢ each way).

Santa Barbara Trolley Co. operates a motorized San Francisco–style cable car that loops past major hotels, shopping areas, and attractions from 10 am to 4 pm. Get off whenever you like, and pick up another trolley (they come every hour) when you're ready to move on. The fare is $22 for the day.

TOURS

Land and Sea Tours. This outfit conducts 90-minute narrated tours in an amphibious 49-passenger vehicle nicknamed the Land Shark. The adventure begins with a drive through the city, followed by a plunge into the harbor for a cruise along the coast. ✉ *10 E. Cabrillo Blvd., at Stearns Wharf* ☎ *805/683–7600* 🌐 *out2seesb.com* 🎟 *From $30.*

Segway Tours of Santa Barbara. After a brief training session, a guide leads you around town on electric-powered personal balancing transporters. Tour options include the waterfront (1¼ hours), Butterfly Beach and Montecito (2 hours), historic downtown Santa Barbara (2½ hours), and through town to the mission (3 hours). ✉ *16 Helena Ave., at Cabrillo Blvd.* ☎ *805/963–7672* 🌐 *segwayofsb.com* 🎟 *$75–$115.*

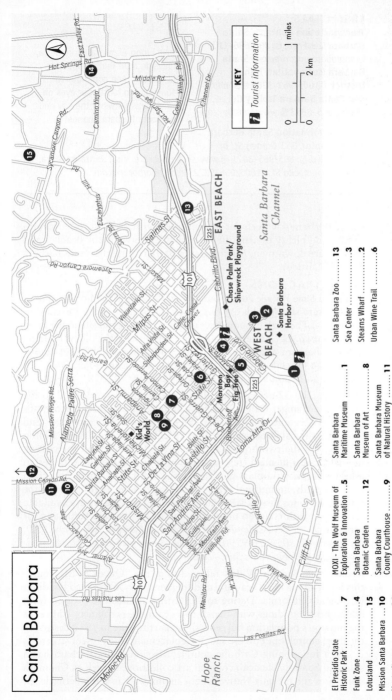

Santa Barbara

KEY

ℹ️ Tourist information

1 miles

2 km

EAST BEACH

WEST BEACH

Santa Barbara Channel

Chase Palm Park/
Shipwreck Playground

Santa Barbara
Harbor

6

ESSENTIALS

Transportation Contacts Santa Barbara Car Free. ☎ *805/696–1100* ⊕ *santabarbaracarfree.org.* **Santa Barbara Metropolitan Transit District.** ☎ *805/963–3366* ⊕ *sbmtd. gov.* **Santa Barbara Trolley Co.** ☎ *805/965–0353* ⊕ *www.sbtrolley.com.*

Visitor Information Santa Barbara Visitor Center. ✉ *1 Garden St., at Cabrillo Blvd.* ☎ *805/965–3021* ⊕ *www.sbchamber.org.* **Visit Santa Barbara.** ✉ *500 E. Montecito St.* ☎ *805/966–9222* ⊕ *santabarbaraca.com.*

BEST VIEWS

Drive along Alameda Padre Serra, a hillside road that begins near the mission and continues to Montecito, to feast your eyes on spectacular views of the city and the Santa Barbara Channel.

EXPLORING

Santa Barbara's waterfront is beautiful, with palm-studded promenades and plenty of sand. In the few miles between the beaches and the hills are downtown, Mission Santa Barbara, and the Santa Barbara Botanic Garden.

TOP ATTRACTIONS

El Presidio State Historic Park. Founded in 1782, El Presidio was one of four military strongholds established by the Spanish along the coast of California. The park encompasses much of the original site in the heart of downtown. El Cuartel, the adobe guardhouse, is the oldest building in Santa Barbara and the second oldest in California. ■TIP→ Admission is free for children 16 and under. ✉ *123 E. Canon Perdido St., at Anacapa St.* ☎ *805/965–0093* ⊕ *www.sbthp.org* ⊡ *$5.*

FAMILY
Fodor'sChoice
★
Lotusland. The 37-acre estate called Lotusland once belonged to the Polish opera singer Ganna Walska, who purchased it in the late 1940s and lived here until her death in 1984. Many of the exotic trees and other subtropical flora were planted in 1882 by horticulturist R. Kinton Stevens. On the two-hour guided tour—the only option for visiting unless you're a member (reserve well ahead in summer)—you'll see an outdoor theater, a topiary garden, a lotus pond, and a huge collection of rare cycads, an unusual plant genus that has been around since the time of the dinosaurs. ■TIP→ Child-friendly family tours are available for groups with children under the age of 10; contact Lotusland for scheduling. ✉ *695 Ashley Rd., off Sycamore Canyon Rd. (Hwy. 192), Montecito* ☎ *805/969–9990* ⊕ *lotusland.org* ⊡ *$48* ☉ *Closed mid-Nov.–mid-Feb. No tours Sun.–Tues.*

Fodor'sChoice
★
Mission Santa Barbara. Widely referred to as the "Queen of Missions," this is one of the most beautiful and frequently photographed buildings in coastal California. Dating to 1786, the architecture evolved from adobe-brick buildings with thatch roofs to more permanent edifices as the mission's population burgeoned. An earthquake in 1812 destroyed the third church built on the site. Its replacement, the present structure, is still a functioning Catholic church. Mission Santa Barbara has a splendid Spanish/Mexican colonial art collection, as well as Chumash sculptures and the only Native American–made altar and tabernacle left

CALIFORNIA'S MISSIONS

California history changed forever in the 18th century when Spanish explorers founded a series of missions along the Pacific coast. Believing they were following God's will, they wanted to spread the gospel and convert as many natives as possible. The process produced a collision between the Hispanic and California Indian cultures, resulting in one of the most striking legacies of Old California: the Spanish mission churches. Rising like mirages in the middle of desert plains and rolling hills, these historic sites transport you back to the days of the Spanish colonial period.

FATHER OF THE MISSIONS

Father Junípero Serra is an icon of the Spanish colonial period. At the behest of the Spanish government, the diminutive padre—then well into his fifties, and despite a chronic leg infection—started out on foot from Baja California to search for suitable mission sites, with a goal of reaching Monterey. In 1769 he helped establish Alta California's first mission in San Diego and continued his travels until his death in 1784, by which time he had founded eight more missions.

EL CAMINO REAL

The system ended about a decade after the Mexican government took control of Alta California in the early 1820s and began to secularize the missions. In 1848, the Americans assumed control of the territory, and California became part of the United States. Today, all 21 of these missions stand as extraordinary monuments to their colorful past. Many are found on or near the "King's Road"—El Camino Real—which linked these mission outposts. At the height of the mission system the trail was approximately 600 miles long, eventually extending from San Diego to Sonoma. Today the road is commemorated on portions of routes 101 and 82 in the form of roadside bell markers erected by CalTrans every 1 to 2 miles between San Diego and San Francisco.

MISSION ARCHITECTURE

Mission architecture reflects a gorgeous blend of European and New World influences. While naves followed the simple forms of Franciscan Gothic, cloisters (with beautiful arcades) adopted aspects of the Romanesque style, and ornamental touches of the Spanish Renaissance—including red-tiled roofs and wrought-iron grilles—added even more elegance. In the 20th century, the Mission Revival Style had a huge impact on architecture and design in California, as seen in examples ranging from San Diego's Union Station to Stanford University's main quadrangle. For information on California's missions, see ⊕ *californiamissionsfoundation.org*.

in the California missions. Docents lead 60-minute tours ($13 adult) Thursday and Friday at 11 am, and Saturday at 10:30 am. ✉ *2201 Laguna St., at E. Los Olivos St.* ☎ *805/682–4149 gift shop, 805/682–4713 tours* ⊕ *www.santabarbaramission.org* 🎫 *$9 self-guided tour.*

FAMILY
Fodor's Choice
★

MOXI–The Wolf Museum of Exploration and Innovation. It took more than two decades of unrelenting community advocacy to plan and build this exceptional science hub, which opened in early 2017 in a gorgeous three-story Spanish-Mediterranean building next to the train station and a block from Stearns Wharf and the beach. MOXI ignites learning through interactive activities in science and creativity for curious minds of all ages, from pre-K to gray. The 70-plus interactive exhibits—devoted to science, technology, engineering, arts, and mathematics (STEAM)—are integrated so visitors can explore seven themed areas (called tracks) in concert with one another and discover connections between them, for example, the relationship between music and electricity. In the Speed and Motion track you can build a model car and

challenge two others to a race on a Tesla track—then use the collected data to reconfigure your car for improved performance. In the Fantastic Forces space, build a contraption to send on a test flight in a wind column. Other sections include Light and Color, The Tech Track, Innovation Lab, Sound Track, and interactive media spaces. Up on the rooftop "sky, which has some of the best panoramic views in downtown, you can listen to an orchestra of wind and solar-powered instruments and peer down through glass floor-windows to view the happy faces of explorers on the floors below. ⊠ *125 State St.* ☎ *805/770–5000* ⊕ *moxi.org* ⊠ *$14.*

Santa Barbara Botanic Garden. Five miles of scenic trails meander through the garden's 78 acres of native plants. The Mission Dam, built in 1806, stands just beyond the redwood grove and above the restored aqueduct that once carried water to Mission Santa Barbara. More than a thousand plant species thrive in various themed sections, including mountains, deserts, meadows, redwoods, and Channel Islands. ■**TIP→ A conservation center dedicated to rare and endangered plant species opened in 2016 and presents rotating exhibitions.** ⊠ *1212 Mission Canyon Rd., north of Foothill Rd. (Hwy. 192)* ☎ *805/682–4726* ⊕ *www.sbbg.org* ⊠ *$12.*

Fodor's Choice ★ **Santa Barbara County Courthouse.** Hand-painted tiles and a spiral staircase infuse the courthouse, a national historic landmark, with the grandeur of a Moorish palace. This magnificent building was completed in 1929. An elevator rises to an arched observation area in the tower that provides a panoramic view of the city. Before or after you take in the view, you can (if it's open) visit an engaging gallery devoted to the workings of the tower's original, still operational Seth Thomas clock. The murals in the ceremonial chambers on the courthouse's second floor were painted by an artist who did backdrops for some of Cecil B. DeMille's films. ■**TIP→ Join a free guided tour weekdays at 10:30, daily at 2** ⊠ *1100 Anacapa St., at E. Anapamu St.* ☎ *805/962–6464* ⊕ *sbcourthouse.org.*

QUICK BITES

Jeannine's. Take a break from shopping at Jeannine's, revered locally for its wholesome sandwiches, salads, and baked goods, made from scratch with organic and natural ingredients. Pick up a turkey cranberry or chicken pesto sandwich to go, and picnic in the courthouse gardens a block away. Known for: fantastic pastries; hearty, healthful breakfasts; turkey roasted or smoked in house. ⊠ *La Arcada, 15 E. Figueroa St., at State St.* ☎ *805/966–1717* ⊕ *jeannines.com/restaurants.*

Santa Barbara Museum of Art. The highlights of this museum's permanent collection include ancient sculpture, Asian art, impressionist paintings, contemporary art, photography, and American works in several mediums. ⊠ *1130 State St., at E. Anapamu St.* ☎ *805/963–4364* ⊕ *sbma.net* ⌨ *$10, free Thurs. 5–8* ⊙ *Closed Mon.*

FAMILY **Santa Barbara Museum of Natural History.** The gigantic blue whale skeleton greets you at the entrance to this complex whose major draws include its planetarium, space lab, and gem and mineral display. Startlingly alive-looking stuffed specimens, complete with nests and eggs, roost in the bird hall, and a room of dioramas illustrates Chumash Indian history and culture. Outdoors, nature trails wind through the serene oak-studded grounds. A Nature Pass, available at the museum and the associated Sea Center, is good for discounted admission to both facilities. ⊠ *2559 Puesta del Sol Rd., off Mission Canyon Rd.* ☎ *805/682–4711* ⊕ *sbnature.org* ⌨ *$12; free 3rd Sun. of month Sept.–Apr.*

FAMILY **Santa Barbara Zoo.** This compact zoo's gorgeous grounds shelter elephants, gorillas, exotic birds, and big cats. For small children, there's a scenic railroad and barnyard petting zoo. Three high-tech dinosaurs and an eight-foot-tall grizzly bear puppet perform in live stage shows (free with admission), daily in summer and on weekends the rest of the year. Kids especially love feeding the giraffes from a view deck overlooking the beach. ■TIP➔ The palm-studded lawns on a hilltop overlooking the beach are perfect spots for family picnics. ⊠ *500 Niños Dr., off El Cabrillo Blvd.* ☎ *805/962–5339 main line* ⊕ *santabarbarazoo.org* ⌨ *Zoo $17, parking $7.*

FAMILY **Sea Center.** A branch of the Santa Barbara Museum of Natural History, the center specializes in Santa Barbara Channel marine life and conservation. Though small compared to aquariums in Monterey and Long Beach, this is a fascinating, hands-on marine science laboratory that lets you participate in experiments, projects, and exhibits, including touch pools. The two-story glass walls here open to stunning ocean, mountain, and city views. ■TIP➔ Purchase a Nature Pass, available here, for discounted admission to the center and the natural history museum. ⊠ *211 Stearns Wharf* ☎ *805/962–2526* ⊕ *sbnature.org* ⌨ *$8.50.*

Stearns Wharf. Built in 1872, Stearns Wharf is Santa Barbara's most visited landmark. Expansive views of the mountains, cityscape, and harbor unfold from every vantage point on the three-block-long pier. Although it's a nice walk from the Cabrillo Boulevard parking areas, you can also park on the pier and then wander through the shops or stop for a meal at one of the wharf's restaurants. ⊠ *Cabrillo Blvd. and State St.* ⊕ *stearnswharf.org.*

6

Be sure to visit Santa Barbara's beautiful—and usually uncrowded—beaches.

WORTH NOTING

Funk Zone. A formerly run-down industrial neighborhood near the waterfront and train station, the Funk Zone has evolved into a hip hangout filled with wine-tasting rooms, arts-and-crafts studios, murals, breweries, restaurants, and small shops. It's fun to poke around the three-square-block district. ■**TIP**➔ **Street parking is limited, so leave your car in a nearby city lot and cruise up and down the alleys on foot.** ✉ *Between State and Garden Sts. and Cabrillo Blvd. and U.S. 101* ⊕ *funkzone.net.*

Montecito. Since the late 1800s the tree-studded hills and valleys of this town have attracted the rich and famous: Hollywood icons, business tycoons, tech moguls, and old-money families who installed themselves years ago. Shady roads wind through the community, which consists mostly of gated estates. Swank boutiques line **Coast Village Road,** where well-heeled residents such as Oprah Winfrey sometimes browse for truffle oil, picture frames, and designer jeans. Residents also hang out in the Upper Village, a chic shopping area with restaurants and cafés at the intersection of San Ysidro and East Valley roads.

FAMILY **Santa Barbara Maritime Museum.** California's seafaring history is the focus here. High-tech, hands-on exhibits, such as a virtual sportfishing activity that lets participants haul in a "big one" and a local surfing history retrospective, make this a fun stop for families. The museum's shining star is a rare, 17-foot-tall Fresnel lens from the historic Point Conception Lighthouse. Ride the elevator to the fourth-floor observation area for great harbor views. ✉ *113 Harbor Way, off Shoreline Dr.* ☎ *805/962–8404* ⊕ *sbmm.org* ✉ *$8* ⊗ *Closed Wed.*

Urban Wine Trail. Nearly two dozen winery tasting rooms form the Urban Wine Trail; most are within walking distance of the waterfront and the lower State Street shopping and restaurant district. **Santa Barbara Winery,** at 202 Anacapa Street, and **Au Bon Climat,** at 813 Anacapa Street, are good places to start your oenological trek. ✉ *Santa Barbara* 🌐 *urbanwinetrailsb.com.*

BEACHES

FAMILY **Arroyo Burro Beach.** The beach's usually gentle surf makes it ideal for families with young children. It's a local favorite because you can walk for miles in both directions when tides are low. Leashed dogs are allowed on the main stretch of beach and westward; they are allowed to romp off-leash east of the slough at the beach entrance. The parking lots fill early on weekends and throughout the summer, but the park is relatively quiet at other times. Walk along the beach just a few hundreds yards away from the main steps at the entrance to escape crowds on warm-weather days. Surfers, swimmers, stand-up paddlers, and boogie boarders regularly ply the waves, and photographers come often to catch the vivid sunsets. **Amenities:** food and drink; lifeguard in summer; parking, showers, toilets. **Best for:** sunset; surfing; swimming; walking. ✉ *Cliff Dr. and Las Positas Rd.* 🌐 *countyofsb.org/parks.*

FAMILY Fodor's Choice ★ **East Beach.** The wide swath of sand at the east end of Cabrillo Boulevard is a great spot for people-watching. East Beach has sand volleyball courts, summertime lifeguard and sports competitions, and arts-and-crafts shows on Sundays and holidays. You can use showers, a weight room, and lockers (bring your own towel) and rent umbrellas and boogie boards at the Cabrillo Bathhouse. Next door, there's an elaborate jungle-gym play area for kids. Hotels line the boulevard across from the beach. **Amenities:** food and drink; lifeguards in summer; parking (fee); showers; toilets; water sports. **Best for:** walking; swimming; surfing. ✉ *1118 Cabrillo Blvd., at Ninos Dr.* ☎ *805/897–2680.*

WHERE TO EAT

$$$ JAPANESE 🍴 **Arigato Sushi.** You might have to wait for a table at this two-story restaurant and sushi bar—locals line up early for the wildly creative combination rolls and other delectables (first come, first served). Fans of authentic Japanese food sometimes disagree about the quality of the seafood, but all dishes are fresh and artfully presented. **Known for:** innovative creations; lively atmosphere; patio and second-floor balcony seating. [$] *Average main: $30* ✉ *1225 State St., near W. Victoria St.* ☎ *805/965–6074* 🌐 *www.arigatosb.com* 🕒 *No lunch.*

$$ MODERN AMERICAN 🍴 **Barbareño.** Determined to push the boundaries of farm-to-table, three college friends who worked at the same Los Angeles eatery banded together in 2014 to launch Barbareño. The three churn their own butter, bake their own breads, make condiments from scratch, and forage mushrooms, eucalyptus leaves, and other ingredients from the wild. **Known for:** youthful, sophisticated vibe; chef's sampler plate; monthly seasonal menu. [$] *Average main: $22* ✉ *205 W. Canon Perdido St., at De La Vina St.* ☎ *805/963–9591* 🌐 *barbareno.com* 🕒 *No lunch weekdays.*

$$$ SEAFOOD **🍴 Brophy Bros.** The outdoor tables at this casual harborside restaurant have perfect views of the marina and mountains. Staffers serve enormous, exceptionally fresh fish dishes and provide guests with a pager so you can stroll along the waterfront until the beep lets you know your table is ready. **Known for:** seafood salad and chowder; stellar clam bar; long wait times. [$] *Average main: $25* ✉ *119 Harbor Way, off Shoreline Dr.* ☎ *805/966–4418* 🌐 *brophybros.com.*

$ MEXICAN **🍴 La Super-Rica.** This food stand on the east side of town serves some of the spiciest and most authentic Mexican dishes between Los Angeles and San Francisco. Fans (the late chef Julia Child was one) fill up on the soft tacos served with yummy spicy or mild sauces and legendary beans. **Known for:** house-made tortillas; daily specials such as chilaquiles; vegetarian and gluten-free dishes. [$] *Average main: $12* ✉ *622 N. Milpas St., at Alphonse St.* ☎ *805/963–4940* 💳 *No credit cards* 🕒 *Closed Tues. and Wed.*

$$$ MODERN AMERICAN Fodor's Choice ★ **🍴 The Lark.** Shared dining—small plates and larger—and a seasonal menu showcasing local ingredients are the focus at this urban-chic restaurant named for an overnight all-Pullman train that chugged into the nearby railroad station for six decades. Sit at the 24-seat communal table set atop vintage radiators, or at tables and booths crafted from antique Spanish church pews and other repurposed or recycled materials. **Known for:** social environment; wines curated by a master sommelier; handcrafted locavore cocktails. [$] *Average main: $28* ✉ *131 Anacapa St., at E. Yanonali St.* ☎ *805/284–0370* 🌐 *www.thelarksb.com* 🕒 *No lunch.*

$$$ SPANISH **🍴 Loquita.** In a cozy space in a prime corner at the gateway to the Funk Zone near Stearns Wharf, Loquita honors Santa Barbara's Spanish heritage by serving up authentic Spanish dishes, wines, and cocktails made with fresh, sustainably sourced local ingredients. The menu covers all bases, from tapas, to wood-fired seafood, and grilled meats, to Spanish wines, vermouth, gin and tonics, and sangria. **Known for:** multiple types of paella; counter and takeaway items; great gin and tonic. [$] *Average main: $28* ✉ *202 State St.* 🌐 *www.loquitasb.com.*

$$$$ ITALIAN **🍴 Olio e Limone.** Sophisticated Italian cuisine with an emphasis on Sicily is served at this restaurant near the Arlington. The juicy veal chop is popular, but surprises abound here; be sure to try unusual dishes such as ribbon pasta with quail and sausage in a mushroom ragout, or the duck ravioli. **Known for:** grilled veal and lamb chops; cozy white-tablecloth dining room; adjacent raw bar and casual pizzeria. [$] *Average main: $31* ✉ *17 W. Victoria St., at State St.* ☎ *805/899–2699* 🌐 *www.olioelimone.com* 🕒 *No lunch Sun.*

TAKE THE KIDS

Two fun playgrounds provide welcome interludes for the young set. Children love tooling around **Kids' World** (✉ *Garden and Micheltorena Sts.*), a public playground with a castle-shaped maze of climbing structures, slides, and tunnels. At **Shipwreck Playground** (✉ *Chase Palm Park, E. Cabrillo Blvd., east of Garden St.*), parents take as much pleasure in the waterfront views as the kids do in the nautical-themed diversions and the antique carousel.

$$$ SOUTHERN 🍴 **Palace Grill.** Mardi Gras energy, team-style service, lively music, and great Cajun, creole, and Caribbean food have made the Palace a Santa Barbara icon. Be prepared to wait for a table on Friday and Saturday nights (when reservations are taken for a 5:30 seating only), though the live entertainment and free appetizers, sent out front when the line is long, will whet your appetite for the feast to come. **Known for:** blackened fish and meats; Louisiana bread pudding soufflé; Cajun martini served in a mason jar. [$] *Average main: $30* ✉ *8 E. Cota St., at State St.* ☎ *805/963–5000* 🌐 *palacegrill.com.*

$$$$ AMERICAN Fodor's Choice ★ 🍴 **Somerset.** A romantic courtyard shaded by century-old olive trees, an elegant interior that reflects European Grand Café style (marble walls, candles on zinc-topped tables), and cuisine that aims to please the most discerning of foodies quickly launched Somerset to the pinnacle of swank Santa Barbara dining when it opened in early 2017. Just a few steps away from The Granada and Arlington theaters in the arts and culture district, Somerset is an ideal upscale choice for pre- or postperformance dining. **Known for:** California cuisine with Mediterranean/European influences; full bar with craft cocktails; prime arts district location. [$] *Average main: $34* ✉ *7 E. Anapamu St.* ☎ *805/845–7112* 🌐 *somersetsb.com.*

$$$$ AMERICAN Fodor's Choice ★ 🍴 **The Stonehouse.** The elegant Stonehouse—consistently lauded as one of the nation's top restaurants—is inside a century-old granite former farmhouse at the San Ysidro Ranch resort. The menu changes constantly, but might include pan-seared abalone or classic steak Diane flambéed table-side. **Known for:** ingredients from on-site garden; heated oceanview deck with fireplace; elegant dining room. [$] *Average main: $49* ✉ *900 San Ysidro La., off San Ysidro Rd., Montecito* ☎ *805/565–1700* 🌐 *www.sanysidroranch.com.*

$$$ ITALIAN Fodor's Choice ★ 🍴 **Toma.** Seasonal, locally sourced ingredients and softly lit muted-yellow walls evoke the flavors and charms of Tuscany and the Mediterranean at this rustic-romantic restaurant across from the harbor and West Beach. Ahi sashimi tucked in a crisp sesame cone is a popular appetizer, after which you can proceed to a house-made pasta dish or rock shrimp gnocchi. **Known for:** house-made pastas and gnocchi; wines from Italy and California's Central Coast; romantic waterfront setting. [$] *Average main: $29* ✉ *324 W. Cabrillo Blvd., near Castillo St.* ☎ *805/962–0777* 🌐 *www.tomarestaurant.com* 🕒 *No lunch.*

$$$$ AMERICAN 🍴 **Wine Cask.** The Wine Cask serves bistro-style meals in a comfortable and classy dining room with a huge fireplace and wood-beam ceiling decorated with gold leaf. The more casual bar-café, Intermezzo, across the courtyard, serves pizzas, salads, small plates, wines, and cocktails and is open late. **Known for:** extensive wine list and pairing suggestions; historic courtyard patio; late hours. [$] *Average main: $31* ✉ *El Paseo, 813 Anacapa St., at E. De La Guerra St.* ☎ *805/966–9463* 🌐 *winecask.com* 🕒 *Closed Sun. and Mon.*

WHERE TO STAY

$$$$ RESORT Fodor's Choice ★ 🏨 **Bacara Resort & Spa.** A luxury resort with four restaurants and a 42,000-square-foot spa and fitness center with 36 treatment rooms, the Bacara provides a gorgeous setting for relaxing retreats. **Pros:** serene natural setting; three zero-edge pools; three golf courses nearby. **Cons:**

pricey; not close to downtown; sand on beach not pristine enough for some. [$] *Rooms from: $450* ✉ *8301 Hollister Ave., Goleta* ☎ *844/610–9688* 🌐 *bacararesort.com* 🛏 *358 rooms* 🍴 *No meals.*

$$$$ HOTEL Fodor's Choice ★ 🏨 **Belmond El Encanto.** Following nearly seven years and more than $100 million of extensive renovations, this Santa Barbara icon lives on to thrill a new generation of guests with its relaxed-luxe bungalow rooms, lush gardens, and personalized service. **Pros:** revitalized historic landmark; stellar spa facility; has hosted luminaries including Franklin D. Roosevelt. **Cons:** long walk to downtown; pricey; guests staying for more than a few days may find the restaurant menus limited. [$] *Rooms from: $404* ✉ *800 Alvarado Pl.* ☎ *805/845–5800, 800/393–5315* 🌐 *www.belmond.com/elencanto* 🛏 *92 rooms* 🍴 *No meals.*

$$$$ HOTEL 🏨 **Canary Hotel.** The only full-service hotel in the heart of downtown, this Kimpton property blends a casual, beach-getaway feel with urban sophistication. **Pros:** upscale local cuisine at Finch & Fork; rooms come with candles, yoga mats, and binoculars (for touring); adjacent fitness center. **Cons:** across from transit center; a mile from the beach. [$] *Rooms from: $415* ✉ *31 W. Carrillo St.* ☎ *805/884–0300, 866/999–5401* 🌐 *www.canarysantabarbara.com* 🛏 *97 rooms* 🍴 *No meals.*

$$$$ RESORT 🏨 **The Fess Parker, A DoubleTree by Hilton Resort.** A full-scale resort with seven buildings spread over 24 landscaped acres across from East Beach, the hotel was founded by the late TV actor Fess Parker, best known for playing Davy Crockett and Daniel Boone. **Pros:** numerous amenities; right across from the beach; free shuttle to train station and airport. **Cons:** train noise filters into some rooms; too spread out for some. [$] *Rooms from: $269* ✉ *633 East Cabrillo Blvd.* ☎ *800/879–2929, 805/564–4333* 🌐 *www.fessparkersantabarbarahotel.com* 🛏 *360 rooms* 🍴 *No meals.*

$$$$ RESORT Fodor's Choice ★ 🏨 **Four Seasons Resort The Biltmore Santa Barbara.** Surrounded by lush, perfectly manicured gardens and across from the beach, Santa Barbara's grande dame has long been a favorite for quiet, California-style luxury. **Pros:** spa with 11 treatment rooms; access to members-only clubs and restaurant on site; steps from the beach. **Cons:** back rooms are close to train tracks; expensive. [$] *Rooms from: $795* ✉ *1260 Channel Dr.* ☎ *805/969–2261, 805/332–3442 for reservations only* 🌐 *www.fourseasons.com/santabarbara* 🛏 *207 rooms* 🍴 *No meals.*

$$$$ HOTEL 🏨 **The Goodland.** A vintage Woody car, a silver Airstream trailer, and a digital photo booth are among the elements that bring 1960s California surf culture to life at this Kimpton hotel in Goleta. **Pros:** cool and casual vibe; short walk to shops and services; a short drive to the beach. **Cons:** not close to downtown Santa Barbara; some rooms on the small side. [$] *Rooms from: $284* ✉ *5650 Calle Real, Goleta* ☎ *877/480–1465, 805/964–6241* 🌐 *www.thegoodland.com* 🛏 *158 rooms* 🍴 *No meals.*

$$$$ HOTEL Fodor's Choice ★ 🏨 **Hotel Californian.** A sprawling collection of Spanish-Moorish buildings that opened in summer 2017 at the site of the historic 1925 Hotel Californian, this sophisticated hotel with a hip youthful vibe occupies nearly three full blocks on State Street just steps from Stearns Wharf, MOXI, the Funk Zone, beaches, and the harbor. **Pros:** steps from the waterfront, Funk Zone, and beaches; resort-style amenities; on-site parking. **Cons:** pricey; must walk or ride the shuttle to downtown attractions; train whistle noise in rooms close to station. [$] *Rooms from: $550* ✉ *36 State St.* ☎ *805/882–0100* 🌐 *www.thehotelcalifornian.com* 🛏 *121 rooms.*

$$$
HOTEL

Hotel Indigo. The closest hotel to the train station and across the street from the Funk Zone, artsy Hotel Indigo is a fine choice for travelers who appreciate contemporary art and want easy access to dining, nightlife, and the beach. **Pros:** multilingual staff; a block from Stearns Wharf; great value for location. **Cons:** showers only (no bathtubs); train whistles early morning; rooms on small side. $ *Rooms from: $189* ⊠ *121 State St.* ☎ *805/966–6586* ⊕ *www.indigosantabarbara. com* ⇒ *41 rooms* ⊚ *No meals.*

$$$$
HOTEL

Hyatt Santa Barbara. A complex of four buildings on three landscaped acres, the Hyatt provides an appealing lodging option in a prime location right across from East Beach. **Pros:** steps from the beach; many room types and rates; walk to the zoo and waterfront shuttle. **Cons:** motel feel; busy area in summer. $ *Rooms from: $289* ⊠ *1111 E. Cabrillo Blvd.* ☎ *805/882–1234, 800/643–1994* ⊕ *santabarbara.centric.hyatt.com* ⇒ *174 rooms* ⊚ *No meals.*

$$
HOTEL

Motel 6 Santa Barbara Beach. A half block from East Beach amid fancier hotels sits this basic but comfortable motel—the first Motel 6 in existence, and the first in the chain to transform into a contemporary Euro-style abode. **Pros:** very close to zoo and beach; friendly staff; clean. **Cons:** no frills; motel-style rooms; no breakfast. $ *Rooms from: $146* ⊠ *443 Corona Del Mar Dr.* ☎ *805/564–1392, 800/466–8356* ⊕ *motel6. com* ⇒ *51 rooms* ⊚ *No meals.*

$$$$
RESORT
Fodor's Choice
★

San Ysidro Ranch. At this romantic hideaway on a historic property in the Montecito foothills—where John and Jackie Kennedy spent their honeymoon and Oprah sends her out-of-town visitors—guest cottages are scattered among groves of orange trees and flower beds. **Pros:** rooms come with private outdoor spas; 17 miles of hiking trails nearby; Plow & Angel Bistro and Stonehouse restaurants on site are Santa Barbara institutions. **Cons:** very expensive; too remote for some. $ *Rooms from: $845* ⊠ *900 San Ysidro La., Montecito* ☎ *805/565–1700, 800/368–6788* ⊕ *www.sanysidroranch.com* ⇒ *41 rooms and cottages* ⊚ *No meals* ⟳ *2-day minimum stay on weekends, 3 days on holiday weekends.*

$$$$
HOTEL
Fodor's Choice
★

Santa Barbara Inn. After a two-year closure to undergo a massive remodel and expansion, this full-service family-owned hotel reopened in summer 2016 in sparkling Spanish-Mediterranean style in a prime waterfront corner across from East Beach. **Pros:** more than half the rooms have ocean views; suites come with whirlpool tubs; delicious on-site restaurant Convivo. **Cons:** on a busy boulevard; limited street parking. $ *Rooms from: $280* ⊠ *901 E. Cabrillo Blvd.* ✛ *At Milpas St.* ☎ *805/966–3636* ⊕ *www.santabarbarainn.com* ⇒ *70 rooms* ⊚ *Breakfast.*

$$$$
B&B/INN
Fodor's Choice
★

Simpson House Inn. If you're a fan of traditional bed-and-breakfast inns, this property, with its beautifully appointed Victorian main house and acre of lush gardens, is for you. **Pros:** elegant; impeccable landscaping; within walking distance of downtown. **Cons:** some rooms in main building are small; two-night minimum stay on weekends May–October. $ *Rooms from: $325* ⊠ *121 E. Arrellaga St.* ☎ *805/963–7067, 800/676–1280* ⊕ *www.simpsonhouseinn.com* ⇒ *15 rooms* ⊚ *Breakfast.*

$$$$
B&B/INN

Spanish Garden Inn. A half block from the Presidio in the heart of downtown, this Spanish-Mediterranean retreat celebrates Santa Barbara style, from the tile floors, wrought-iron balconies, and exotic plants to

6

the original art by local plein-air artists. **Pros:** walking distance from downtown; classic Spanish-Mediterranean style; free parking. **Cons:** no restaurant. $ *Rooms from: $399* ✉ *915 Garden St.* ☎ *805/564–4700* ⊕ *www.spanishgardeninn.com* ⤳ *24 rooms* ❍❙ *Breakfast.*

$$$$
B&B/INN

The Upham. Built in 1871, this downtown Victorian in the arts and culture district has been restored as a full-service hotel. **Pros:** 1-acre garden; easy walk to theaters; excellent on-site restaurant. **Cons:** some rooms are small; not near beach or waterfront. $ *Rooms from: $285* ✉ *1404 De la Vina St.* ☎ *805/962–0058, 800/727–0876* ⊕ *www. uphamhotel.com* ⤳ *50 rooms* ❍❙ *Breakfast* ⤳ *2-night minimum stay on weekends.*

$$$
HOTEL

The Wayfarer. One of the nicest international hostels you'll ever come across, the hip and stylish Wayfarer opened in 2014 in a prime Funk Zone location, three blocks from Stearns Wharf and the beach, and across the street from the train station. **Pros:** outdoor heated pool; breakfast included; free parking. **Cons:** some rooms on the small side; freeway and train noise bothers some guests; pricey during high season. $ *Rooms from: $239* ✉ *12 E. Montecito St.* ☎ *805/845–1000* ⊕ *wayfarersb.com* ⤳ *31 rooms* ❍❙ *Breakfast.*

NIGHTLIFE AND PERFORMING ARTS

The bar, club, and live music scene centers on lower State Street, between the 300 and 800 blocks. The arts district, with theaters, restaurants, and cafés, starts around the 900 block of State and continues north to the 1300 block. To see what's scheduled around town, pick up the free weekly *Santa Barbara Independent* newspaper or visit its website, ⊕ *www.independent.com.*

NIGHTLIFE

Dargan's. Lively Dargan's pub has pool tables, great draft beers and Irish whiskies, and serves a full menu of traditional Irish dishes. ✉ *18 E. Ortega St., at Anacapa St.* ☎ *805/568–0702* ⊕ *darganssb.com.*

The Good Lion. The cocktail menu at this intimate neighborhood bar near The Granada Theatre changes weekly, depending on the fresh organic bounty available at the markets. All juices are organic and squeezed fresh daily, and all syrups are made in house with organic produce and sweeteners. ✉ *1212 State St.* ☎ *805/845–8754* ⊕ *www. goodlioncocktails.com.*

James Joyce. A good place to have a few beers and while away an evening; the James Joyce hosts rock, blues, jazz, and other performers six nights a week. ✉ *513 State St., at W. Haley St.* ☎ *805/962–2688* ⊕ *sbjamesjoyce.com.*

Joe's Cafe. Steins of beer and stiff cocktails accompany hearty bar food at Joe's. It's a fun, if occasionally rowdy, collegiate scene. ✉ *536 State St., at E. Cota St.* ☎ *805/966–4638* ⊕ *joescafesb.com.*

Les Marchands. Brian McClintic, one of four real-life candidates trying to achieve master sommelier status in the 2013 film *Somm* (he succeeded), co-owns and operates this combination wine bar, store, and eatery in the Funk Zone. ✉ *131 Anacapa St., at Yananoli St.* ☎ *805/284–0380* ⊕ *www.lesmarchandswine.com.*

Lucky's. A slick sports bar attached to an upscale steak house owned by the maker of Lucky Brand dungarees, this place attracts hip patrons hoping to see and be seen. ✉ *1279 Coast Village Rd., near Olive Mill Rd., Montecito* ☎ *805/565–7540* ⊕ *luckys-steakhouse.com.*

Milk & Honey. Artfully prepared tapas, mango mojitos, and exotic cocktails lure trendy crowds to swank M&H, despite high prices and a reputation for inattentive service. ✉ *30 W. Anapamu St., at State St.* ☎ *805/275–4232* ⊕ *www.milknhoneytapas.com.*

SOhO. A lively restaurant, bar, and music venue, SOhO books all kinds of musical acts, from jazz to blues to rock. ✉ *1221 State St., at W. Victoria St.* ☎ *805/962–7776* ⊕ *www.sohosb.com.*

PERFORMING ARTS

Arlington Theatre. This Moorish-style auditorium presents touring performers and films throughout the year. ✉ *1317 State St., at Arlington Ave.* ☎ *805/963–4408* ⊕ *thearlingtontheatre.com.*

Center Stage Theatre. This venue hosts plays, music, dance, and readings. ✉ *Paseo Nuevo Center, Chapala and De la Guerra Sts., 2nd fl.* ☎ *805/963–0408* ⊕ *www.centerstagetheater.org.*

Ensemble Theatre Company (ETC). The company stages classic and contemporary comedies, musicals, and dramas. ✉ *33 W. Victoria St., at Chapala St.* ☎ *805/965–5400* ⊕ *www.etcsb.org.*

The Granada Theatre. A restored, modernized landmark that dates from 1924, the Granada hosts Broadway touring shows and dance, music, and other cultural events. ✉ *1214 State St., at E. Anapamu St.* ☎ *805/899–2222* ⊕ *granadasb.org.*

Lobero Theatre. A state landmark, the Lobero hosts community theater groups and touring professionals. ✉ *33 E. Canon Perdido St., at Anacapa St.* ☎ *805/963–0761* ⊕ *www.lobero.com.*

Santa Barbara Bowl. Built in 1936 and recently renovated to meet the highest standards of visiting musicians, the 4,500-seat Bowl attracts world-class entertainers (past acts include Radiohead, The Who, John Legend, and Natalie Merchant), from April through October. ✉ *1122 N. Milpas St. ✛ At Anapamu St.* ☎ *805/962–7411* ⊕ *www.sbbowl.com.*

Fodor'sChoice
★ **Old Spanish Days Fiesta.** The city celebrates its Spanish, Mexican, and Chumash heritage in early August with events that include music, dancing, an all-equestrian parade, a carnival, and a rodeo. ✉ *Santa Barbara* ⊕ *oldspanishdays-fiesta.org.*

Fodor'sChoice
★ **Santa Barbara International Film Festival.** The 12-day festival in late January and early February attracts film enthusiasts and major stars to downtown venues for screenings, panels, and tributes. ✉ *Santa Barbara* ⊕ *www.sbiff.org.*

Summer Solstice Celebration. More than 100,000 revelers celebrate the arts at this mid-June event whose highlight is a huge parade of costumed participants who dance, drum, and ride people-powered floats up State Street. ✉ *Santa Barbara* ☎ *805/965–3396* ⊕ *www.solsticeparade.com.*

SPORTS AND THE OUTDOORS

BIKING

Cabrillo Bike Lane. The level, two-lane, 3-mile Cabrillo Bike Lane passes the Santa Barbara Zoo, the Andree Clark Bird Refuge, beaches, and the harbor. Stop for a meal at one of the restaurants along the way, or for a picnic along the palm-lined path looking out on the Pacific.

Wheel Fun Rentals. You can rent bikes, quadricycles, and skates here. ⊠ *23 E. Cabrillo Blvd.* ☎ *805/966–2282* ⊕ *wheelfunrentalssb.com.*

BOATS AND CHARTERS

Fodor's Choice **Condor Express.** From SEA Landing, the *Condor Express,* a 75-foot ★ high-speed catamaran, whisks up to 149 passengers toward the Channel Islands on whale-watching excursions and sunset and dinner cruises. ⊠ *301 W. Cabrillo Blvd.* ☎ *805/882–0088, 888/779–4253* ⊕ *condorexpress.com.*

Paddle Sports Center. A full-service paddle-sports center in the harbor, this outfit rents kayaks, stand-up paddleboards, surfboards, boogie boards, and water-sports gear. ⊠ *117 B Harbor Way, off Shoreline Dr.* ☎ *805/617–3425 rentals* ⊕ *www.paddlesportsca.com.*

Santa Barbara Sailing Center. The center offers sailing instruction, rents and charters sailboats, kayaks, and stand-up paddleboards, and organizes dinner and sunset champagne cruises, island excursions, and whale-watching trips. ⊠ *Santa Barbara Harbor launching ramp* ☎ *805/962–2826* ⊕ *sbsail.com.*

Truth Aquatics. Truth runs kayaking, paddleboarding, hiking, snorkeling, and scuba excursions to the National Marine Sanctuary and Channel Islands National Park. ⊠ *Departures from SEA Landing, Santa Barbara Harbor* ☎ *805/962–1127* ⊕ *truthaquatics.com* ▤ *From $120.*

SHOPPING

CLOTHING

DIANI. This upscale, European-style women's boutique dresses clients in designer clothing from around the world. Sibling shoe and home-and-garden shops are nearby. ⊠ *1324 State St., at Arlington Ave.* ☎ *805/966–3114, 805/966–7175 shoe shop* ⊕ *dianiboutique.com.*

Surf N Wear's Beach House. This shop carries surf clothing, gear, and collectibles; it's also the home of Santa Barbara Surf Shop and the exclusive local dealer of Surfboards by Yater. ⊠ *10 State St., at Cabrillo Blvd.* ☎ *805/963–1281* ⊕ *www.surfnwear.com.*

Wendy Foster. This store sells casual-chic women's fashions. ⊠ *833 State St., at W. Canon Perdido St.* ☎ *805/966–2276* ⊕ *wendyfoster.com.*

FOOD AND WINE

Santa Barbara Public Market. A dozen food and beverage vendors occupy this spacious arts district galleria. Stock up on olive oils, vinegars, and other gourmet goodies; sip on handcrafted wines and beers while watching sports events; and nosh on noodle bowls, sushi and baked goods. ⊠ *38 W. Victoria St., at Chapala St.* ☎ *805/770–7702* ⊕ *sb-publicmarket.com.*

SHOPPING AREAS

Fodor's Choice ★ **El Paseo.** Wine-tasting rooms, shops, art galleries, and studios share the courtyard and gardens of this historic arcade. ⊠ *Canon Perdido St., between State and Anacapa Sts.*

Fodor's Choice ★ **State Street.** Between Cabrillo Boulevard and Sola Street, State Street is a shopper's paradise. Chic malls, quirky storefronts, antiques emporia, elegant boutiques, and funky thrift shops abound. You can shop on foot or ride a battery-powered trolley (50¢) that runs between the waterfront and the 1300 block. Nordstrom and Macy's anchor **Paseo Nuevo,** an open-air mall in the 700 block. Shops, restaurants, galleries, and fountains line the tiled walkways of **La Arcada,** a small complex of landscaped courtyards in the 1100 block designed by architect Myron Hunt in 1926.

EARTH DAY

In 1969, 200,000 gallons of crude oil spilled into the Santa Barbara Channel, causing an immediate outcry from residents. The day after the spill, Get Oil Out (GOO) was established; the group helped lead the successful fight for legislation to limit and regulate offshore drilling in California. The Santa Barbara spill also spawned Earth Day, which is still celebrated across the nation today.

6

NORTHERN SANTA BARBARA COUNTY

The Santa Ynez Mountains divide Santa Barbara County geographically; U.S. 101 passes through a mountain tunnel leading inland. Northern Santa Barbara County used to be known for sprawling ranches and strawberry and broccoli fields. Today its 200-plus wineries and 22,000 acres of vineyards dominate the landscape from the Santa Ynez Valley in the south to Santa Maria in the north. Though more than 50 grape varietals are grown in the county, more than half the vineyards are planted to Chardonnay, Pinot Noir, and Syrah.

GETTING HERE AND AROUND

Two-lane Highway 154 over San Marcos Pass is the shortest and most scenic route from Santa Barbara into the Santa Ynez Valley. You can also drive along U.S. 101 north 43 miles to Buellton, then 7 miles east through Solvang to Santa Ynez. Santa Ynez Valley Transit shuttle buses serve Santa Ynez, Los Olivos, Ballard, Solvang, and Buellton. COLT Wine Country Express buses connect Lompoc, Buellton, and Solvang on weekdays except holidays.

ESSENTIALS

Bus Contacts COLT Wine Country Express. ☎ *805/736-7666* ⊕ *www.cityoflompoc.com/transit.* **Santa Ynez Valley Transit.** ☎ *805/688-5452* ⊕ *www.syvt.com.*

Visitor Information Santa Barbara Vintners. ☎ *805/688-0881* ⊕ *www.sbcountywines.com.* **Visit Santa Barbara.** ⊕ *www.santabarbaraca.com.* **Visit the Santa Ynez Valley.** ⊕ *www.visitsyv.com.*

SANTA YNEZ

31 miles north of Goleta.

Founded in 1882, the tiny town of Santa Ynez still has many of its original frontier buildings. You can walk through the three-block downtown area in a few minutes, shop for antiques, and hang around the old-time saloon. At some of the Santa Ynez Valley's best restaurants, you just might bump into one of the celebrities who own nearby ranches.

GETTING HERE AND AROUND

Take Highway 154 over San Marcos Pass or U.S. 101 north 43 miles to Buellton, then 7 miles east.

EXPLORING

Gainey Vineyard. The 1,800-acre Gainey Ranch, straddling the banks of the Santa Ynez River, includes about 100 acres of organic vineyards: Sauvignon Blanc, Merlot, Cabernet Sauvignon, and Cabernet Franc. The winery also makes wines from Chardonnay, Pinot Noir, and Syrah grapes from the Santa Rita Hills. You can taste the latest releases—the estate Pinot Noir is especially good—in a Spanish-style hacienda overlooking the ranch. Barrel tasting is also available through the week (except in winter). ✉ *3950 E. Hwy. 246* ☎ *805/688–0558* 🌐 *www.gaineyvineyard.com* 🎟 *Tasting $15–$45.*

WHERE TO EAT AND STAY

$$$ ITALIAN 🍴 **Santa Ynez Kitchen.** The owners of Toscana, a popular eatery in L.A.'s Brentwood neighborhood, run this rustic-chic restaurant with an Italy-meets-California Wine Country vibe. Chef and co-owner Luca Crestanelli, a native of Verona, Italy, typically offers about 10 seasonal daily specials. **Known for:** wood-fired pizzas and oak-grilled entrées; creative craft cocktails; gelatos and "not-so-classic" tiramisu. [$] *Average main: $25* ✉ *1110 Faraday St., at Sagunto St.* ☎ *805/691–9794* 🌐 *www.sykitchen.com* ⏲ *No lunch Mon.–Thurs.*

$$$ ITALIAN 🍴 **Trattoria Grappolo.** Authentic Italian fare, an open kitchen, and festive, family-style seating make this trattoria equally popular with celebrities from Hollywood and ranchers from the Santa Ynez Valley. The noise level tends to rise in the evening, so this isn't the best spot for a romantic getaway. **Known for:** thin-crust wood-fired pizzas; risottos and homemade pastas; carpaccio. [$] *Average main: $25* ✉ *3687–C Sagunto St.* ☎ *805/688–6899* 🌐 *trattoriagrappolo.com* ⏲ *No lunch Mon.*

$$$$ B&B/INN 🏨 **ForFriends Inn.** Four close friends—Jim and Debbie Campbell and Dave and Katie Pollock—own and operate this luxury bed-and-breakfast, designed as a social place where friends gather to enjoy good wine, food, and music in a casual backyard setting. **Pros:** three-course breakfast, evening wine and appetizers included; friendly innkeepers; "Friendship Pass" provides perks and savings at restaurants and wineries. **Cons:** not suitable for children; no pets allowed. [$] *Rooms from: $295* ✉ *1121 Edison St.* ☎ *805/693–0303* 🌐 *www.forfriendsinn.com* 🛏 *5 rooms, 2 cottages* 🍽 *Breakfast.*

$$$$ B&B/INN 🏨 **Santa Ynez Inn.** This posh two-story Victorian inn in downtown Santa Ynez was built from scratch in 2002, and the owners have furnished all the rooms with authentic historical pieces. **Pros:** near

restaurants; unusual antiques; spacious rooms. **Cons:** high price for location; building not historic. $ *Rooms from: $339* ✉ *3627 Sagunto St.* ☎ *805/688–5588, 800/643–5774* ⊕ *www.santaynezinn.com* ⇄ *20 rooms* ❖ *Breakfast.*

SPORTS AND THE OUTDOORS

Santa Barbara Soaring. The outfit's scenic glider rides last from 10 to 50 minutes. Tour options include the Santa Ynez Valley, coastal mountains and the Channel Islands, and celebrity homes. ✉ *Santa Ynez Airport, 900 Airport Rd.* ☎ *805/688–2517* ⊕ *www.sbsoaring.com* ✉ *$185–$475.*

LOS OLIVOS

4 miles north of Santa Ynez.

This pretty village was once on Spanish-built El Camino Real (Royal Road) and later a stop on major stagecoach and rail routes. Tasting rooms, art galleries, antiques stores, and country markets line Grand Avenue and intersecting streets for several blocks.

GETTING HERE AND AROUND

From U.S. 101 north or south, exit at Highway 154 and drive east about 8 miles. From Santa Barbara, travel 30 miles northwest on Highway 154.

EXPLORING

Blair Fox Cellars. Blair Fox, a Santa Barbara native, crafts small-lot Rhône-style wines made from organic grapes. The bar in his rustic Los Olivos tasting room, where you can sample exceptional vineyard-designated Syrahs and other wines, was hewn from Australian white oak reclaimed from an old Tasmanian schoolhouse. ✉ *2902–B San Marcos Ave.* ☎ *805/691–1678* ⊕ *www.blairfoxcellars.com* ✉ *Tasting $15* ⊗ *Closed Tues. and Wed.*

Coquelicot Estate Vineyard. Named for the vivid red poppy flowers that blanket the French countryside and appear on all its labels, this limited-production winery focuses on handcrafted Bordeaux wines made from grapes at its certified organic 58-acre Santa Ynez Valley vineyard. Don't miss samples of the flagship wines: Sixer (a Syrah and Viogner blend), Mon Amour (a Bordeaux blend), and the estate Sauvignon Blanc and Rosé. ✉ *2884 Grand Ave.* ☎ *805/688–1500* ⊕ *www.coquelicotwines. com* ✉ *Tastings $15–$20.*

Firestone Vineyard. Heirs to the Firestone tire fortune developed (but no longer own) this winery known for Chardonnay, Gewürztraminer, Cabernet Sauvignon, and Syrah—and for the fantastic valley views from its tasting room and picnic area. The tour here is highly informative. ✉ *5017 Zaca Station Rd., off U.S. 101* ☎ *805/688–3940* ⊕ *www.firestonewine.com* ✉ *Tastings $10–$15.*

WHERE TO EAT AND STAY

$$$

AMERICAN

✕ **Los Olivos Wine Merchant Cafe.** Part wine store and part social hub, this café focuses on wine-friendly fish, pasta, and meat dishes, plus salads, pizzas, and burgers. Don't miss the homemade muffuletta and olive tapenade spreads, or the French toast soufflé for breakfast (weekends only). **Known for:** nearly everything made in-house; ingredients from own organic café farm; wines from own estate winery. $ *Average main: $23* ✉ *2879 Grand Ave.* ☎ *805/688–7265* ⊕ *www.winemerchantcafe. com* ⊙ *No breakfast weekdays.*

$$$ ✕ **Sides Hardware & Shoes: A Brothers Restaurant.** Inside a historic store-
AMERICAN front they renovated, brothers Matt and Jeff Nichols serve comfort food prepared with panache. The Kobe-style burgers, especially the one with bacon and white cheddar, make a great lunch, and the dinner favorites include za'atar chicken, Scottish salmon, and lamb sirloin with goat cheese gnocchi. **Known for:** in-house cured and smoked bacon; juicy burgers; jalapeño margaritas. $ *Average main: $30* ✉ *2375 Alamo Pintado Ave.* ☎ *805/688–4820* ⊕ *brothersrestaurant.com.*

$$$$ ⚄ **The Ballard Inn.** Set among orchards and vineyards in the tiny town of
B&B/INN Ballard, 2 miles south of Los Olivos, this inn makes an elegant wine-
Fodor's Choice country escape. **Pros:** exceptional food; attentive staff; secluded. **Cons:**
★ some baths could use updating. $ *Rooms from: $315* ✉ *2436 Baseline Ave., Ballard* ☎ *805/688–7770, 800/638–2466* ⊕ *ballardinn.com* ⇌ *15 rooms* ⏏ *Breakfast.*

$$$$ ⚄ **Fess Parker's Wine Country Inn and Spa.** This luxury inn includes an
B&B/INN elegant, tree-shaded French country–style main building and an equally attractive annex across the street with a pool and day spa. **Pros:** con-venient wine-touring base; walking distance from restaurants and gal-leries; rate includes full breakfast at The Bear and Star on site. **Cons:** pricey; not pet-friendly. $ *Rooms from: $395* ✉ *2860 Grand Ave.* ☎ *805/688–7788, 800/446–2455* ⊕ *www.fessparkerinn.com* ⇌ *19 rooms* ⏏ *Breakfast.*

SOLVANG

5 miles south of Los Olivos.

You'll know you've reached the town of Solvang when the architecture suddenly changes to half-timber buildings and windmills. Danish edu-cators settled the town in 1911—the flatlands and rolling green hills reminded them of home. Solvang has attracted tourists for decades, but it's lately become more sophisticated, with smorgasbords giving way to galleries, upscale restaurants, and wine-tasting rooms by day and wine bars by night. The visitor center on Copenhagen Drive has walking-tour maps (also available online). The Sweet Treats tour covers the town's Danish bakeries, confectionary stores, and ice-cream parlors. The Olsen's and Solvang bakeries and Ingeborg's Danish Chocolates are worth investigating.

GETTING HERE AND AROUND

Highway 246 West (Mission Drive) traverses Solvang, connecting with U.S. 101 to the west and Highway 154 to the east. Alamo Pintado Road connects Solvang with Ballard and Los Olivos to the north. Park your car in one of the free public lots and stroll the town. Or take the bus: Santa Ynez Valley Transit shuttles run between Solvang and nearby towns.

ESSENTIALS

Visitor Information Solvang Conference & Visitors Bureau. ✉ *1639 Copen-hagen Dr., at 2nd St.* ☎ *805/688–6144* ⊕ *www.solvangusa.com.*

EXPLORING

Mission Santa Inés. The mission holds an impressive collection of paintings, statuary, vestments, and Chumash and Spanish artifacts in a serene bluff-top setting. You can tour the museum, sanctuary, and gardens. ⊠ *1760 Mission Dr., at Alisal Rd.* ☎ *805/688–4815* ⊕ *missionsantaines. org* ⊡ *$5.*

Rideau Vineyard. This winery celebrates its locale's rich history—the King of Spain himself once owned this land, and the tasting room occupies a former guest ranch inn—but fully embraces the area's wine-making present. Wines made from the Rhône varietals Mourvèdre, Roussanne, Syrah, and Viognier are the specialty here. ⊠ *1562 Alamo Pintado Rd., 2 miles north of Hwy. 246* ☎ *805/688–0717* ⊕ *rideauvineyard.com* ⊡ *Tastings $12–$16.*

Sevtap. Winemaker Art Sevtap, an Istanbul native, is often on hand to pour samples of his limited-production wines—mostly from Bordeaux varietals—in this artsy wine bar that's decked out with Tibetan prayer flags and chalkboard walls and has a stage where guests can pick up a guitar and strum away. ⊠ *1622 Copenhagen Dr., at 2nd St.* ☎ *805/693–9200* ⊕ *www.sevtapwinery.com* ⊡ *Tasting $15.*

WHERE TO EAT

$$$$
AMERICAN
Fodor's Choice
★

✕ **First & Oak.** Create your own custom tasting menu by choosing among five different groups of eclectic California-French dishes paired with local wines at this elegant farm-to-table restaurant inside the Mirabelle Inn. The seasonal menu changes constantly, but regulars include smoked sweet-and-spicy duck wings, truffle-roasted cauliflower, local spot prawns, short rib bourguignonne, and pears poached in red wine from the sommelier-owner's organic Coceliquot Estate Vineyard, **Known for:** intimate fine-dining setting; sommelier-owner selected wine list; complex dishes and presentation. Ⓢ *Average main: $34* ⊠ *409 1st St.* ⊹ *at Oak St.* ☎ *805/688–1703* ⊕ *www.firstandoak.com.*

$$$$
AMERICAN
Fodor's Choice
★

✕ **Root 246.** This chic restaurant's chefs tap local purveyors and shop for organic ingredients at farmers' markets before deciding on the day's menu. Depending on the season, you might feast on Dungeness crab, a savory cassoulet, Santa Maria–style tri-tip grilled over an oak fire, or seaweed-crusted steelhead trout in a smoky red wine broth. **Known for:** gorgeous contemporary Native American-influenced design; 1,800-bottle wine selection; popular happy hour with craft cocktails. Ⓢ *Average main: $33* ⊠ *Hotel Corque, 420 Alisal Rd., at Molle Way* ☎ *805/686–8681* ⊕ *www.root-246.com* ☾ *Closed Mon. No lunch. No breakfast weekdays.*

$$$
AMERICAN

✕ **Succulent Café.** Locals flock to this cozy café for its comfort cuisine and regional wines and craft beers. Order at the counter, and staffers will deliver your meal to the interior dining areas or the sunny outdoor patio. **Known for:** artisanal charcuterie plates; pet-friendly patio; homemade biscuits and gravy, house-roasted turkey. Ⓢ *Average main: $26* ⊠ *1555 Mission Dr., at 4th Pl.* ☎ *805/691–9444* ⊕ *succulentcafe. com* ☾ *Closed Tues.*

6

WHERE TO STAY

$$$$ RESORT Fodor's Choice ★ 🏨 **Alisal Guest Ranch and Resort.** Since 1946 this 10,000-acre ranch has been popular with celebrities and plain folk alike. **Pros:** Old West atmosphere; many activities; ultraprivate. **Cons:** isolated; not close to downtown. [$] *Rooms from: $600* ✉ *1054 Alisal Rd.* ☎ *805/688–6411, 800/425–4725* 🌐 *alisal.com* 🛏 *73 rooms* 🍴 *Some meals.*

$$$ HOTEL Fodor's Choice ★ 🏨 **Hotel Corque.** Owned by the Santa Ynez Band of Chumash Indians, the stunning three-story "Corque" provides a full slate of upscale amenities. **Pros:** friendly, professional staff; short walk to shops, tasting rooms and restaurants; free Wi-Fi. **Cons:** no kitchenettes or laundry facilities; pricey. [$] *Rooms from: $239* ✉ *400 Alisal Rd.* ☎ *805/688–8000, 800/624–5572* 🌐 *hotelcorque.com* 🛏 *132 rooms* 🍴 *No meals.*

$$$ B&B/INN Fodor's Choice ★ 🏨 **Mirabelle Inn.** French, Danish, and American flags at the entrance and crystal chandeliers, soaring ceilings, and skylights in the lobby set the tone from the get-go in this elegant four-story inn a few blocks from the main tourist hub. **Pros:** excellent farm-to-table restaurant (dinner only); full cook-to-order breakfast included; away from noisy crowds. **Cons:** some rooms on the small side; not in the heart of town. [$] *Rooms from: $250* ✉ *409 1st St.* ✣ *at Oak St.* ☎ *805/688–1703, 800/786–7925* 🛏 *12 rooms* 🍴 *Breakfast.*

PERFORMING ARTS

Solvang Festival Theater. Pacific Conservatory of the Performing Arts presents crowd-pleasing musicals like *Lend Me a Tenor* and *Beauty and the Beast*, as well as Shakespeare's *Twelfth Night*, and contemporary plays at this 700-seat outdoor amphitheater. ✉ *420 2nd St., at Molle Way* ☎ *805/922–8313* 🌐 *pcpa.org* ☞ *Performances June–Oct.*

BUELLTON

3 miles west of Solvang.

A crossroads town at the intersection of U.S. 101 and Highway 246, Buellton has evolved from a sleepy gas and coffee stop into an enclave of wine-tasting rooms, beer gardens, and restaurants. It's also a gateway to Lompoc and the Santa Rita Hills Wine Trail to the west, and to Solvang, Santa Ynez, and Los Olivos to the east.

GETTING HERE AND AROUND

Driving is the easiest way to get to Buellton. From Santa Barbara, follow U.S. 101 north to the Highway 246 exit. Santa Ynez Valley Transit serves Buellton with shuttle buses from Solvang and nearby towns.

ESSENTIALS

Visitor Information **Buellton Visitors Bureau.** ✉ *597 Ave. of the Flags, No. 101* ☎ *805/688–7829, 800/324–3800* 🌐 *visitbuellton.com.* **Santa Rita Hills Wine Trail.** 🌐 *santaritahillswinetrail.com.*

EXPLORING

Alma Rosa Winery. Winemaker Richard Sanford helped put Santa Barbara County on the international wine map with a 1989 Pinot Noir. For Alma Rosa, started in 2005, he crafts wines from grapes grown on 100-plus acres of certified organic vineyards in the Santa Rita Hills.

The Pinot Noirs and Chardonnays are exceptional. Vineyard tours and tastings are available by appointment, ✉ *181 C Industrial Way, off Hwy. 246, west of U.S. 101* ☎ *805/688–9090* 🌐 *almarosawinery.com* 🎫 *Tastings $15* 🕒 *Sun.–Thurs., daily 11–4:30; Fri. and Sat., daily 11–6:30.*

Industrial Way. A half-mile west of U.S. 101, head south from Highway 246 on Industrial Way to explore a hip and happening collection of food and drink destinations. Top stops include **Industrial Eats** (a craft butcher shop and restaurant), **Figueroa Mountain Brewing Co.**, the **Alma Rosa Winery** tasting room, **Terravant, Tesora Sweets,** and the **Ascendant Spirits Distillery.** ✉ *Industrial Way, off Hwy. 246.*

Lafond Winery and Vineyards. A rich, concentrated Pinot Noir is the main attention-getter at this winery that also produces noteworthy Chardonnays and Syrahs. Bottles with Lafond's SRH (Santa Rita Hills) label are an especially good value. The winery also has a tasting room at 111 East Yanonali Street in Santa Barbara's Funk Zone. ✉ *6855 Santa Rosa Rd., west off U.S. 101 Exit 139* ☎ *805/688–7921* 🌐 *lafondwinery.com* 🎫 *Tasting $12 (includes logo glass).*

WHERE TO EAT

$$$$ AMERICAN

🍴 **The Hitching Post II.** You'll find everything from grilled artichokes to quail at this casual eatery, but most people come for the smoky Santa Maria–style barbecue. Be sure to try a glass of owner-chef-winemaker Frank Ostini's signature Highliner Pinot Noir, a star in the film *Sideways*. **Known for:** entrées grilled over local red oak; chef-owner makes his own wines. [$] *Average main: $32* ✉ *406 E. Hwy. 246, off U.S. 101* ☎ *805/688–0676* 🌐 *www.hitchingpost2.com* 🕒 *No lunch.*

LOMPOC

20 miles west of Solvang.

Known as the flower-seed capital of the world, Lompoc is blanketed with vast fields of brightly colored flowers that bloom from May through August. Also home to a starkly beautiful mission, Lompoc has emerged as a major Pinot Noir and Chardonnay grape-growing region. Overlapping the Santa Rita Hills Wine Trail in parts, the Lompoc Wine Trail includes wineries in the Wine Ghetto, a downtown industrial park, and along Highway 246 and (to the south) Santa Rosa Road, which form a loop between Lompoc and Buellton.

GETTING HERE AND AROUND

Driving is the easiest way to get to Lompoc. From Santa Barbara, follow U.S. 101 north to Highway 1 exit off Gaviota Pass, or Highway 246 west at Buellton.

ESSENTIALS

Visitor Information Lompoc Valley Chamber of Commerce & Visitors Bureau. ✉ *111 S. I St., at Hwy. 246* ☎ *805/736–4567, 800/240–0999* 🌐 *lompoc.com.*

EXPLORING

FAMILY **La Purísima Mission State Historic Park.**
The state's most fully restored mission, founded in 1787, stands in a stark and still remote location that powerfully evokes the lives and isolation of California's Spanish settlers. Docents lead tours every afternoon, and vivid displays illustrate the secular and religious activities that formed mission life. ⊠ *2295 Purísima Rd., off Hwy. 246* ☎ *805/733–3713* ⊕ *www.lapurisimamission.org* 🎟 *$6 per vehicle.*

> **VOLCANOES?**
>
> Those eye-catching sawed-off peaks along the drive from Pismo Beach to Morro Bay are called the Nine Sisters—a series of ancient volcanic plugs. Morro Rock, the northernmost sibling and a state historic monument, is the most famous and photographed of the clan.

Lompoc Wine Ghetto. Laid-back tasting rooms can be found in a downtown industrial park. Taste of Sta. Rita Hills and Flying Goat are two rooms worth checking out here. ⊠ *200 N. 9th St.* ⊕ *lompoctrail.com* 🎟 *Tasting fees vary, some free* ⊙ *Many tasting rooms closed Mon.–Wed.*

SAN LUIS OBISPO COUNTY

San Luis Obispo County's pristine landscapes and abundant wildlife areas, especially those around Morro Bay, have long attracted nature lovers. In the south, Pismo Beach and other coastal towns have great sand and surf; inland, a booming wine region stretches from the Edna, Arroyo Grande, and Avila valleys and Nipomo in the south, to Paso Robles in the north. A good way to explore the county is to follow the Highway 1 Discovery Route, a 101-mile road trip that takes you off the beaten track through 10 small towns and cities, from Ragged Point, San Simeon, Cambria, and Cayucos in the north to Los Osos/Baywood Park, Avila Beach, Edna Valley, Arroyo Grande, and Oceano/Nipomo in the south (⊕ *www.highway1discoveryroute.com*).

GETTING HERE AND AROUND

San Luis Obispo Regional Transit Authority operates buses in San Luis Obispo and serves Paso Robles as well as Pismo Beach and other coastal towns.

ESSENTIALS

Transportation Contact San Luis Obispo Regional Transit Authority.
☎ *805/541–2228* ⊕ *www.slorta.org.*

Visitor Information California Highway 1 Discovery Route. ⊕ *highway-1discoveryroute.com.* **SLO Wine Country.** ☎ *805/541–5868* ⊕ *www.slowine.com.* **Visit SLO CAL.** ⊠ *1334 Marsh St., San Luis Obispo* ☎ *805/541–8000* ⊕ *slocal.com.*

PISMO BEACH

40 miles north of Lompoc.

About 20 miles of sandy shoreline—nicknamed the Bakersfield Riviera for the throngs of vacationers who come here from the Central Valley—begins at the town of Pismo Beach. The southern end of town runs along sand dunes, some of which are open to cars and off-road vehicles. Sheltered by the dunes, a grove of eucalyptus trees attracts thousands of migrating monarch butterflies from November through February. A long, broad beach fronts the center of town, where a municipal pier extends into the sea at the foot of shop-lined Pomeroy Street. To the north, hotels and homes perch atop chalky oceanfront cliffs. Fewer than 10,000 people live in this quintessential surfer haven, but Pismo Beach has a slew of hotels and restaurants with great views of the Pacific Ocean.

GETTING HERE AND AROUND

Pismo Beach straddles both sides of U.S. 101. If you're coming from the south and have time for a scenic drive, exit U.S. 101 in Santa Maria and take Highway 166 west for 8 miles to Guadalupe and follow Highway 1 north 16 miles to Pismo Beach. South County Area Transit (SCAT; ⊕ *www.slorta.org*) buses run throughout San Luis Obispo and connect the city with nearby towns. On summer weekends, the free Avila Trolley extends service to Pismo Beach.

ESSENTIALS

Visitor Information California Welcome Center. ⊠ *333 Five Cities Dr.* ☏ *805/773-7924.* **Pismo Beach Visitors Information Center.** ⊠ *Dolliver St./ Hwy. 1, at Hinds Ave.* ☏ *800/443-7778, 805/773-4382* ⊕ *classiccalifornia.com.*

BEACHES

Fodor's Choice ★ **Oceano Dunes State Vehicular Recreation Area.** Part of the spectacular Guadalupe-Nipomo Dunes, this 3,600-acre coastal playground is one of the few places in California where you can drive or ride off-highway vehicles on the beach and sand dunes. Hike, ride horses, kiteboard, join a Hummer tour, or rent an ATV or a dune buggy and cruise up the white-sand peaks for spectacular views. At **Oso Flaco Lake Nature Area**—3 miles west of Highway 1 on Oso Flaco Road—a 1½-mile boardwalk over the lake leads to a platform with views up and down the coast. Leashed dogs are allowed in much of the park except Oso Flaco and Pismo Dunes Natural Reserve. **Amenities:** food and drink; lifeguards (seasonal); parking (fee); showers; toilets; water sports. **Best for:** sunset; surfing; swimming; walking. ⊠ *West end of Pier Ave., off Hwy. 1, Oceano* ☏ *805/473-7220* ⊕ *www.parks.ca.gov* ⊲ *$5 per vehicle.*

Pismo State Beach. Hike, surf, ride horses, swim, fish in a lagoon or off the pier, and dig for Pismo clams at this busy state beach. One of the day-use parking areas is off Highway 1 near the **Monarch Butterfly Grove,** where from November through February monarch butterflies nest in eucalyptus and Monterey pines. The other parking area is about 1½ miles south at Pier Avenue. **Amenities:** food and drink; lifeguards (seasonal); parking (fee); showers; toilets; water sports. **Best for:** sunset; surfing; swimming; walking. ⊠ *555 Pier Ave., off Hwy. 1, 3 miles south of downtown Pismo Beach, Oceano* ☏ *805/489-1869* ⊕ *www.parks. ca.gov* ⊲ *Day use $5 per vehicle if parking at the beach.*

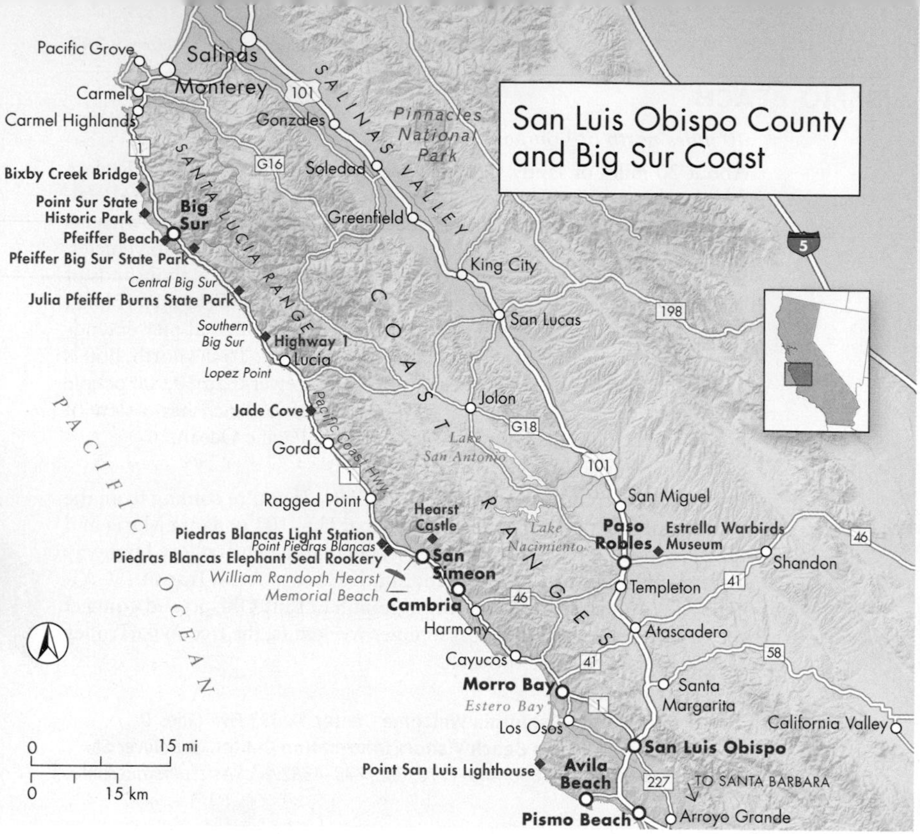
San Luis Obispo County and Big Sur Coast
Pacific Grove
Salinas
Monterey
Carmel
Carmel Highlands
Gonzales
Pinnacles National Park
Salinas Valley
Soledad
Greenfield
King City
San Lucas
Santa Lucia Range
Coast Ranges
Bixby Creek Bridge
Point Sur State Historic Park
Big Sur
Pfeiffer Beach
Pfeiffer Big Sur State Park
Central Big Sur
Julia Pfeiffer Burns State Park
Southern Big Sur
Highway 1
Lucia
Lopez Point
Jade Cove
Pacific Coast Hwy.
Gorda
Jolon
Lake San Antonio
Ragged Point
Hearst Castle
Lake Nacimiento
San Miguel
Paso Robles
Estrella Warbirds Museum
Shandon
Piedras Blancas Light Station
Point Piedras Blancas
Piedras Blancas Elephant Seal Rookery
San Simeon
William Randoph Hearst Memorial Beach
Cambria
Templeton
Harmony
Atascadero
Cayucos
Morro Bay
Estero Bay
Santa Margarita
Los Osos
California Valley
San Luis Obispo
Point San Luis Lighthouse
Avila Beach
TO SANTA BARBARA
Pismo Beach
Arroyo Grande
Pacific Ocean
101
1
5
198
G16
G18
46
41
58
227
0
15 mi
15 km

WHERE TO EAT

$$$ SEAFOOD 🍴 **Cracked Crab.** This traditional New England–style crab shack imports fresh seafood daily from Australia, Alaska, and the East Coast. Fish is line-caught, much of the produce is organic, and everything is made from scratch. **Known for:** shellfish meals in a bucket, dumped on the table; casual setting; menu changes daily. [$] *Average main: $30* ✉ *751 Price St., near Main St.* ☎ *805/773–2722* 🌐 *www.crackedcrab.com.*

$ AMERICAN FAMILY 🍴 **Doc Burnstein's Ice Cream Lab.** The delectable ice creams are churned on site at this beloved old-fashioned parlor east of Pismo Beach. Top-selling flavors include the Elvis Special (banana and peanut butter) and Motor Oil, a blend of dark chocolate and Kahlua with a fudge swirl. [$] *Average main: $7* ✉ *114 W. Branch St., at Nevada St., east off U.S. 101, Arroyo Grande* ☎ *805/474–4068* 🌐 *docburnsteins.com.*

$$ MODERN AMERICAN Fodor's Choice ★ 🍴 **Ember.** A barn-style restaurant with high ceilings and an open kitchen, Ember enjoys a red-hot reputation for Italian-inflected dishes prepared in an authentic Tuscan fireplace or a wood-burning oven. Chef-owner Brian Collins, a native of Arroyo Grande, the town bordering Pismo Beach, honed his culinary skills at Berkeley's legendary Chez Panisse Restaurant. **Known for:** seasonal menu changes monthly; wood-fired flatbread pizzas; long lines during prime time (no reservations). [$] *Average main: $22* ✉ *1200 E. Grand Ave., at Brisco Rd., Arroyo Grande* ☎ *805/474–7700* 🌐 *www.emberwoodfire.com* 🕒 *Closed Mon. and Tues. No lunch.*

$ SEAFOOD 🍴 **Splash Café.** Folks stand in line down the block for clam chowder served in a sourdough bread bowl at this wildly popular seafood stand. You can also order beach food such as fresh steamed clams, burgers, and fried calamari at the counter (no table service). **Known for:** famous clam chowder; sourdough bread bowls baked in house; cheery hole-in-the-wall. [$] *Average main: $9* ✉ *197 Pomeroy St., at Cypress St.* ☎ *805/773–4653* 🌐 *splashcafe.com.*

$$$ FUSION 🍴 **Ventana Grill.** Perched on a bluff at the northern edge of Pismo Beach, Ventana Grill offers ocean views from nearly every table, unusual seafood-centered Latin American-California fusion dishes, and more than 50 tequilas plus craft cocktails at the bar. Reservations are essential—this place is almost always packed, especially during the weekday happy hour. **Known for:** happy hour with sunset views; salsas and sauces made from scratch; more than 50 tequila selections. [$] *Average main: $25* ✉ *2575 Price St.* ☎ *805/773–0000.*

WHERE TO STAY

$$$ RESORT 🏨 **The Cliffs Resort.** Lawns and palm trees surround this full-service resort that perches dramatically on an oceanfront cliff. **Pros:** beach access via short downhill path; oceanfront restaurant and lounge; bluff-top walking trail. **Cons:** not close to downtown; rooms near service areas and elevator can be noisy. [$] *Rooms from: $195* ✉ *2757 Shell Beach Rd.* ☎ *805/773–5000, 800/826–7827* 🌐 *www.cliffsresort.com* 🛏 *160 rooms* 🍽 *No meals.*

$$$$ RESORT 🏨 **Dolphin Bay Resort & Spa.** On grass-covered bluffs overlooking Shell Beach, this luxury resort looks and feels like an exclusive community of villas; choose among sprawling one- or two-bedroom suites, each with a gourmet kitchen, laundry room with washer and dryer, and contemporary furnishings. **Pros:** lavish apartment units; killer views; walking distance from the beach. **Cons:** hefty price tag; vibe too upper-crust for some. [$] *Rooms from: $419* ✉ *2727 Shell Beach Rd.* ☎ *805/773–4300, 800/516–0112 reservations, 805/773–8900 restaurant* 🌐 *www.thedolphinbay.com* 🛏 *60 suites* 🍽 *No meals.*

$$$ HOTEL 🏨 **Hilton Garden Inn.** A slew of on-site amenities, easy access to the freeway and state beaches, and reasonable rates for the location make this chain hotel a good choice at the southern edge of Pismo Beach. **Pros:** newly renovated rooms with adjustable beds; on-site restaurant, bar and lounge; free parking and Wi-Fi. **Cons:** chain hotel; some rooms overlook freeway; not pet-friendly. [$] *Rooms from: $179* ✉ *601 James Way* ☎ *805/773–6020* 🌐 *www.sanluisobispopismobeach.hgi.com* 🛏 *120 rooms* 🍽 *Breakfast.*

$$$$ HOTEL 🏨 **Pismo Lighthouse Suites.** Each of the well-appointed two-room, two-bath suites at this oceanfront resort has a private balcony or patio. **Pros:** sport court features life-size chess game; nautical-style furnishings; nice pool area. **Cons:** not easy to walk to main attractions; some units are next to busy road. [$] *Rooms from: $259* ✉ *2411 Price St.* ☎ *805/773–2411, 800/245–2411* 🌐 *www.pismolighthousesuites.com* 🛏 *70 suites* 🍽 *Breakfast.*

$$$ HOTEL 🏨 **SeaVenture Beachfront Hotel & Restaurant.** The bright, homey rooms at this hotel all have fireplaces and featherbeds; most have balconies with private hot tubs, and some have beautiful ocean views. **Pros:** on

6

the beach; excellent food; romantic rooms. **Cons:** touristy area; some rooms and facilities dated; dark hallways. $ *Rooms from: $235* ⊠ *100 Ocean View Ave.* ☎ *805/773–4994* ⊕ *www.seaventure.com* ⇨ *50 rooms* |◯| *No meals.*

$ ☲ **Shell Beach Inn.** Just 2½ blocks from the beach, this basic but cozy
HOTEL   motor court is a great bargain for the area. **Pros:** walking distance from the beach; free parking; friendly and dependable service. **Cons:** sits on a busy road; small rooms; tiny pool. $ *Rooms from: $100* ⊠ *653 Shell Beach Rd.* ☎ *805/773–4373, 800/549–4727* ⊕ *shellbeachinn.com* ⇨ *10 rooms* |◯| *No meals.*

AVILA BEACH

4 miles north of Pismo Beach.

Because the village of Avila Beach and the sandy, cove-front shoreline for which it's named face south into the Pacific Ocean, they get more sun and less fog than any other stretch of coast in the area. With its fortuitous climate and protected waters, Avila's public beach draws sunbathers and families; summer weekends are very busy. Downtown Avila Beach has a lively seaside promenade and some shops and hotels, but for real local color, head to the far end of the cove and watch the commercial fishers offload their catch on the old Port San Luis wharf. On Friday from mid-April through mid-September, a fish and farmers' market livens up the beach area with music, fresh local produce and seafood, and children's activities.

GETTING HERE AND AROUND

Exit U.S. 101 at Avila Beach Drive and head 3 miles west to reach the beach. The free Avila Trolley operates weekends year-round, plus Friday afternoon and evening from April to September. The minibuses connect Avila Beach and Port San Luis to Shell Beach, with multiple stops along the way. Service extends to Pismo Beach in summer.

ESSENTIALS

Visitor Information Avila Beach Tourism Alliance. ⊕ *visitavilabeach.com.*

EXPLORING

FAMILY   **Avila Valley Barn.** An old-fashioned, family-friendly country store jam-packed with local fruits and vegetables, prepared foods, and gifts, Avila Valley Barn also gives visitors a chance to experience rural American traditions. You can pet farm animals and savor homemade ice cream and pies daily, and on weekends ride a hay wagon out to the fields to pick your own produce. ⊠ *560 Avila Beach Dr., San Luis Obispo* ☎ *805/595–2816* ⊕ *www.avilavalleybarn.com.*

Central Coast Aquarium. You'll learn all about local marine plants and animals from the hands-on exhibits at this science center next to the main beach. ⊠ *50 San Juan St., at 1st St., off Avila Beach Dr.* ☎ *805/595–7280* ⊕ *www.centralcoastaquarium.com* ⌷ *$8* ⊙ *Closed Tues.–Fri. Sept.–May.*

FAMILY   **Point San Luis Lighthouse.** Docents lead hikes along scenic Pecho Coast Trail (3½ miles round-trip) to see the historic 1890 lighthouse and its rare Fresnel lens. ■**TIP→** If you'd prefer a lift out to the lighthouse,

join a trolley tour. Hikes and tours require reservations. ✉ *Point San Luis, 1¾ miles west of Harford Pier, Port San Luis* ☎ *805/540–5771, 805/528–8758 hikes reservations* 🌐 *www.pointsanluislighthouse.org* 🎟 *Trolley tours $20; hikes free ($5 to enter lighthouse).*

BEACHES

FAMILY **Avila State Beach.** At the edge of a sunny cove next to downtown shops and restaurants, Avila's ½-mile stretch of white sand is especially family-friendly, with a playground, barbecue and picnic tables, volleyball and basketball courts, and lifeguards on watch in summer and on many holiday weekends. The free beachfront parking fills up fast, but there's a nearby pay lot ($6 for the day, $2 after 4 pm). Dogs aren't allowed on the beach from 10 to 5. **Amenities:** food and drink; lifeguards (seasonal); parking; showers; toilets; water sports. **Best for:** sunset; surfing; swimming; walking. ✉ *Avila Beach Dr., at 1st St.* 🌐 *www.visitavilabeach.com* 🎟 *Free.*

WHERE TO EAT AND STAY

$ SEAFOOD 🍴 **Mersea's.** Walk down the pier to this casual crabshack where you can order at the counter, grab a drink at the bar, and find a seat on the deck or in the casual indoor dining area to gaze at spectacular Avila Bay views while you dine. The menu includes chowder bowls, burgers, sandwiches, seafood, and salads, plus bowls of fish, shrimp, or chicken served over rice pilaf and veggies. **Known for:** clam chowder in sourdough bread bowls; fish tacos; fresh local ingredients. [$] *Average main: $13* ✉ *3985 Port San Luis Pier* ✥ *At Port San Luis* ☎ *805/548–2290* 🌐 *www.merseas.com.*

$$$ SEAFOOD 🍴 **Ocean Grill.** Across from the promenade, beach, and pier, Ocean Grill serves up fresh seafood to diners who typically arrive before sunset to enjoy the views. Boats anchored in the bay provide much of the seafood, which pairs well with the mostly regional wines on the list. **Known for:** fantastic ocean views; wood-fired pizzas; gluten-free and vegetarian options. [$] *Average main: $29* ✉ *268 Front St.* ☎ *805/595–4050* 🌐 *www.oceangrillavila.com* ⏲ *No lunch Mon.–Thurs.*

$$$$ HOTEL 🏨 **Avila La Fonda.** Modeled after a village in early California's Mexican period, Avila La Fonda surrounds guests with rich jewel tones, fountains, and upscale comfort; its facade replicates eight different casitas, including several famous historic homes in Mexico. **Pros:** one-of-a-kind theme and artwork; flexible room combinations; a block from the beach. **Cons:** pricey; most rooms don't have an ocean view. [$] *Rooms from: $329* ✉ *101 San Miguel St.* ☎ *805/595–1700* 🌐 *www.avilalafondahotel.com* 🛏 *29 rooms* 🍽 *No meals.*

$$$$ HOTEL 🏨 **Avila Lighthouse Suites.** Families, honeymooners, and business travelers all find respite at this two-story, all-suites luxury hotel. **Pros:** directly across from beach; easy walk to restaurants and shops; on-site activities like golf course and life-size checkerboard. **Cons:** noise from passersby can be heard in room; some ocean-view rooms have limited vistas. [$] *Rooms from: $359* ✉ *550 Front St.* ☎ *805/627–1900, 800/372–8452* 🌐 *www.avilalighthousesuites.com* 🛏 *54 suites* 🍽 *Breakfast.*

$$$ HOTEL 🏨 **Avila Village Inn.** This intimate hotel embraces Craftsman style in its wood-and-stone architecture and in custom furnishings such as faux-Tiffany lampshades. **Pros:** in a residential community; access to great

fitness center with pool; gorgeous lobby. **Cons:** some rooms are small and dark; several miles from the beach. [$] *Rooms from: $200* ✉ *6655 Bay Laurel Dr.* ☎ *800/454–0840, 805/627–1810* 🌐 *www.avilavillage-inn.com* 🛏 *30 rooms* 🍴 *Breakfast.*

$$ RESORT 🏨 **Sycamore Mineral Springs Resort.** This wellness resort's hot mineral springs bubble up into private outdoor tubs on an oak-and-sycamore-forest hillside. **Pros:** great place to rejuvenate; nice hiking nearby; incredible spa services. **Cons:** rooms vary in quality; 2½ miles from the beach. [$] *Rooms from: $169* ✉ *1215 Avila Beach Dr., San Luis Obispo* ☎ *805/595–7302* 🌐 *www.sycamoresprings.com* 🛏 *72 rooms* 🍴 *No meals.*

SAN LUIS OBISPO

8 miles north of Avila Beach.

About halfway between San Francisco and Los Angeles, San Luis Obispo spreads out below gentle hills and rocky extinct volcanoes. Its main appeal lies in its architecturally diverse, pedestrian-friendly downtown, which bustles with shoppers, restaurant goers, and students from California Polytechnic State University, known as Cal Poly. On Thursday evening from 6 to 9 the city's famed farmers' market fills Higuera Street with local produce, entertainment, and food stalls.

GETTING HERE AND AROUND

U.S. 101/Highway 1 traverses the city for several miles. From the north, Highway 1 merges with U.S. 101 when it reaches the city limits. The wineries of the Edna Valley and Arroyo Grande Valley wine regions lie south of town off Highway 227, the parallel (to the east) Orcutt Road, and connecting roads.

SLO City Transit buses operate daily; Regional Transit Authority (SLORTA) buses connect with north county towns. The Downtown Trolley provides evening service to the city's hub every Thursday, on Friday from June to early September, and Saturday from April through October.

ESSENTIALS

Visitor Information San Luis Obispo Chamber of Commerce. ✉ *895 Monterey St.* ☎ *805/781–2777* 🌐 *www.visitslo.com.* **San Luis Obispo City Visitor Information.** ☎ *877/756–8698* 🌐 *www.sanluisobispovacations.com.*

EXPLORING

TOP ATTRACTIONS

Mission San Luis Obispo de Tolosa. Sun-dappled Mission Plaza fronts the fifth mission established in 1772 by Franciscan friars. A small museum exhibits artifacts of the Chumash Indians and early Spanish settlers. ✉ *751 Palm St., at Chorro St.* ☎ *805/543–6850* 🌐 *www.missionsan-luisobispo.org* 🎟 *$3.*

Fodor's Choice ★ **Talley Vineyards.** Acres of Chardonnay and Pinot Noir, plus smaller parcels of Sauvignon Blanc, Syrah, and other varietals blanket Talley's mountain-ringed dell in the Arroyo Grande Valley. The estate tour ($40), worth a splurge, includes wine and cheese, a visit to an

1860s adobe, and barrel-room tastings of upcoming releases. ⊠ *3031 Lopez Dr., off Orcutt Rd., Arroyo Grande ☎ 805/489–0446 ⊕ www.talleyvineyards.com ☞ Tastings $12–$18; tours $20–$40.*

WORTH NOTING

Biddle Ranch Vineyard. Glass doors and walls in a converted dairy barn fill the Biddle Ranch Vineyard tasting room with light and sweeping valley, mountain, and vineyard

views. The small-production winery focuses on estate Chardonnay (the adjacent 17-acre vineyard is planted exclusively to the grape), plus Pinot Noir and sparkling wines. The winery also crafts Sangiovese and Cabernet and Syrah blends. ⊠ *2050 Biddle Ranch Rd.* ✛ *At Hwy. 227 ☎ 805/543–2399 ⊕ www.biddleranch.com ☞ Tasting $15 ⊗ Closed Tues. and Wed.*

Claiborne & Churchill. An eco-friendly winery built from straw bales, C&C makes small lots of aromatic Alsatian-style wines such as dry Riesling and Gewürztraminer, plus Pinot Noir blends, Syrah and Chardonnay. ⊠ *2649 Carpenter Canyon Rd., at Price Canyon Rd. ☎ 805/544–4066 ⊕ www.claibornechurchill.com ☞ Tasting $15.*

Edna Valley Vineyard. For sweeping valley views and crisp Sauvignon Blancs and Chardonnays, head to the modern tasting bar here. ■**TIP**➜ **The reserve tasting ($20) is the best option.** ⊠ *2585 Biddle Ranch Rd., off Edna Rd. ☎ 805/544–5855 ⊕ www.ednavalleyvineyard.com ☞ Tastings $15–$20.*

Madonna Inn Trail Rides. Experts and novices enjoy the Madonna Inn concession's one-hour rides on dirt trails fringed by sagebrush, cacti, and lava rock. After a brief lesson in rein control, a congenial guide leads participants partway up 1,292-foot-high Cerro San Luis, one of the flattop volcanic peaks that stretch from San Luis Obispo to Morro Bay. In addition to viewing plant life, the city, and rocky terrain that recalls the Old West, riders often spot hawks and woodpeckers, and occasionally a roadrunner or two. ⊠ *Madonna Inn, 100 Madonna Rd., off U.S. 101 ☎ 805/305–5470 ⊕ www.madonnainn.com ☞ $65 1 hr ride, $80 ride plus wine and cheese tasting.*

Niven Family Wine Estates. A refurbished 1909 schoolhouse serves as tasting room for six Niven Family wineries: Baileyana, Cadre, Tangent, Trenza, True Myth, and Zocker. The winemaker for all these labels is Christian Roguenant, whose Cadre Pinot Noirs are worth checking out. ⊠ *5828 Orcutt Rd., at Righetti Rd. ☎ 805/269–8200 ⊕ www.nivenfamilywines.com ☞ Tasting $15.*

Old Edna. This peaceful, 2-acre site once *was* the town of Edna. Nowadays you can peek at the vintage 1897 and 1908 farmhouse cottages, taste Sextant wines, pick up sandwiches at the gourmet deli, and stroll along Old Edna Lane. ⊠ *1655 Old Price Canyon Rd., at Hwy. 227 ☎ 805/710–3701 Old Edna Townsite, 805/542–0133 tasting room and deli ⊕ oldedna.com.*

6

FAMILY **San Luis Obispo Children's Museum.** Activities at this facility geared to kids under age eight include an "imagination-powered" elevator that transports visitors to a series of underground caverns. Elsewhere, simulated lava and steam sputter from an active volcano. Kids can pick rubber fruit at a farmers' market and race in a fire engine to fight a fire. ✉ *1010 Nipomo St., at Monterey St.* ☎ *805/544–5437* 🌐 *www.slocm.org* 🎫 *$8* 🕓 *Closed nonholiday Mon. Sept.–Apr.*

Wolff Vineyards. Syrah, Petite Sirah, and Riesling join the expected Pinot Noir and Chardonnay as the stars at this family-run winery 6 miles south of downtown. The pourers are friendly, and you'll often meet one of the owners or their children in the tasting room. With its hillside views, the outdoor patio is a great place to enjoy an afternoon picnic. ✉ *6238 Orcutt Rd., near Biddle Ranch Rd.* ☎ *805/781–0448* 🌐 *www.wolffvineyards.com* 🎫 *Tasting $10.*

WHERE TO EAT

$$ ECLECTIC 🍴 **Big Sky Café.** Family-friendly Big Sky turns local and organically grown ingredients into global dishes, starting with breakfast. Just pick your continent: Brazilian churrasco chicken breast, Thai catfish, North African vegetable stew, Maryland crab cakes. **Known for:** artsy, creative vibe; ample choices for vegetarians; locavore pioneer. [$] *Average main: $19* ✉ *1121 Broad St., at Higuera St.* ☎ *805/545–5401* 🌐 *bigskycafe.com.*

$$ ITALIAN 🍴 **Buona Tavola.** Northern Italian dishes are this casual spot's specialty. You might find homemade pumpkin-stuffed tortellini in a creamy mascarpone sauce on the menu, or porcini-mushroom risotto with river shrimp. **Known for:** daily fresh fish and salad specials; impressive wine list; gluten-free menus. [$] *Average main: $22* ✉ *1037 Monterey St., near Osos St.* ☎ *805/545–8000* 🌐 *btslo.com* 🕓 *No lunch weekends.*

$$ NORTHERN ITALIAN 🍴 **Café Roma.** At this Railroad Square restaurant you can dine on authentic northern Italian cuisine in the warmly lit dining room or out on the covered patio. Menu favorites include ricotta-filled squash blossoms, and beef tenderloin glistening with porcini butter and a Pinot Noir reduction. **Known for:** classic Italian dining room and bar; well-selected international wine list with more than 200 choices; attentive service. [$] *Average main: $22* ✉ *1020 Railroad Ave., at Osos St.* ☎ *805/541–6800* 🌐 *www.caferomaslo.com* 🕓 *No lunch weekends.*

$$$ MODERN AMERICAN 🍴 **Foremost Wine Company.** A hip combination restaurant, wine bar, lounge, and wine shop in the Creamery building, a former dairy, Foremost focuses on community-linked food and wine and sustainable practices. The bar, dining areas, and wine store occupy a huge interior space with copper-topped tables and other furnishings made with repurposed materials. **Known for:** seasonal menu with many dishes to share; plentiful vegan and vegetarian options; delicious burrata and charcuterie. [$] *Average main: $29* ✉ *570 Higuera St., near Nipomo St.* ☎ *805/439–3410* 🌐 *www.foremostwineco.com* 🕓 *Closed Mon.*

$$$ INTERNATIONAL 🍴 **Luna Red.** A spacious, contemporary space with a festive outdoor patio, this restaurant near Mission Plaza serves creative tapas and cocktails. The small plates include lamb sausage flatbread, avocado-tuna ceviche, and *piquillo* peppers stuffed with goat cheese. **Known for:** excellent traditional Valencian paellas; craft cocktails; lively

music scene. $ *Average main: $25* ⊠ *1023 Chorro St., at Monterey St.* ☎ *805/540–5243* ⊕ *www.lunaredslo.com.*

$$
ECLECTIC

✕ **Novo Restaurant & Lounge.** In the colorful dining room or on the large creek-side deck, this animated downtown eatery will take you on a culinary world tour. The salads, small plates, and entrées come from nearly every continent. **Known for:** value-laden happy hour from 3 to 6; savory curry and noodle dishes; local farmers' market ingredients. $ *Average main: $22* ⊠ *726 Higuera St., at Broad St.* ☎ *805/543–3986* ⊕ *www.novorestaurant.com.*

$$
MODERN
AMERICAN

✕ **Sidecar.** Sidecar serves farm-fresh meals and small plates along with inventive cocktails and 16 beers on tap, most of them local. Burger patties made from grass-fed beef and free-range chicken are served on a brioche bun with inventive sauces such as bacon-maple ketchup. **Known for:** comfort food and artisanal cocktails made with local ingredients; many vegetarian and vegan options; daily happy hour and Sunday brunch. $ *Average main: $22* ⊠ *1127 Broad St., at Marsh St.* ☎ *805/540–5340* ⊕ *sidecarslo.com.*

$$$
FUSION
Fodor'sChoice
★

✕ **Thomas Hill Organic Kitchen.** This hip eatery—the chic sibling of a much-lauded restaurant in Paso Robles—opened on the second story of a downtown building near the mission in early 2017. Organic locavore dishes take center stage here, spiced up with international flavors and paired with an extensive list of local wines. **Known for:** signature wood-fired pizzas; global cuisine; excellent craft cocktails and spirits. $ *Average main: $27* ⊠ *858 Monterey St., Santa Barbara* ☎ *805/457–1616* ⊕ *www.thomashillorganics.com.*

WHERE TO STAY

$$$
HOTEL

⊡ **Apple Farm.** Decorated to the hilt with floral bedspreads and watercolors by local artists, this Wine Country–theme hotel is highly popular. **Pros:** flowers everywhere; convenient to Cal Poly and U.S. 101; creekside setting. **Cons:** hordes of tourists during the day; some rooms too floral for some people's tastes. $ *Rooms from: $219* ⊠ *2015 Monterey St.* ☎ *800/255–2040, 805/544-2040* ⊕ *www.applefarm.com* ⤳ *104 rooms* ⦿*No meals.*

$$$
B&B/INN

⊡ **Garden Street Inn.** From this restored 1887 Italianate Queen Anne downtown, you can walk to many restaurants and attractions; uniquely decorated rooms, each with private bath, are filled with antiques, and some rooms have stained-glass windows, fireplaces, and decks. **Pros:** lavish homemade breakfast; convenient location; complementary wine-and-cheese reception. **Cons:** city noise filters into some rooms; not great for families. $ *Rooms from: $199* ⊠ *1212 Garden St.* ☎ *805/545–9802, 800/488–2045* ⊕ *www.gardenstreetinn.com* ⤳ *13 rooms* ⦿*Breakfast.*

$$$
HOTEL

⊡ **Granada Hotel & Bistro.** Built in 1922 and sparkling again after renovations completed in 2012, the Granada is one of the few full-service hotels in the heart of downtown. **Pros:** vintage style retreat; easy walk to downtown; popular farm-to-table hangout Granada Bistro on site. **Cons:** some rooms are tiny; sometimes noisy near restaurant kitchen. $ *Rooms from: $249* ⊠ *1126 Morro St.* ☎ *805/544–9100* ⊕ *www.granadahotelandbistro.com* ⤳ *17 rooms* ⦿*No meals.*

6

$$$ HOTEL 🏨 **Madonna Inn.** From its rococo bathrooms to its pink-on-pink froufrou steak house, the Madonna Inn is fabulous or tacky, depending on your taste. **Pros:** fun, one-of-a-kind experience; on-site horseback riding for all levels; each room has its own distinct identity, for example, Safari Room. **Cons:** rooms vary widely; must appreciate kitsch. [$] *Rooms from: $209* ✉ *100 Madonna Rd.* ☎ *805/543–3000, 800/543–9666* 🌐 *www.madonnainn.com* 🛏 *110 rooms* 🍴 *No meals.*

$ HOTEL 🏨 **Peach Tree Inn.** Extra touches such as rose gardens, a porch with rockers, and flower-filled vases turn this modest, family-run motel into a relaxing creek-side haven. **Pros:** bargain rates; cozy rooms; picnic area. **Cons:** near a busy intersection; basic amenities. [$] *Rooms from: $99* ✉ *2001 Monterey St.* ☎ *805/543–3170, 800/227–6396* 🌐 *www.peachtreeinn.com* 🛏 *37 rooms* 🍴 *Breakfast.*

$$$ B&B/INN 🏨 **Petit Soleil.** A cobblestone courtyard, country-French custom furnishings, and Gallic music piped through the halls evoke a Provençal mood at this cheery inn. **Pros:** includes wine and appetizers at cocktail hour; includes scrumptious breakfasts; cozy rooms with luxury touches. **Cons:** sits on a busy avenue; cramped parking. [$] *Rooms from: $179* ✉ *1473 Monterey St.* ☎ *805/549–0321, 800/676–1588* 🌐 *www.psslo.com* 🛏 *16 rooms* 🍴 *Breakfast.*

$$$$ HOTEL 🏨 **SLO Brew Lofts.** If you want to be in the heart of the downtown nightlife action, you can't get much closer than this contemporary collection of apartment-stye rooms on the second floor of the historic brick SLO Brew building. **Pros:** in the heart of downtown; upscale amenities; residential vibe. **Cons:** live music plays on the first floor Thursday–Monday; no on-site desk staff after business hours; parking is in a city lot several blocks away. [$] *Rooms from: $350* ✉ *738 Higuera St,* ☎ *805/543–1843* 🌐 *www.slobrew.com/the-lofts* 🛏 *5 suites* 🍴 *No meals.*

NIGHTLIFE AND PERFORMING ARTS

SLO's club scene is centered on Higuera Street, off Monterey Street.

Koberl at Blue. A trendy crowd hangs out at this upscale restaurant's slick bar to sip on exotic martinis and the many local and imported beers and wines. ✉ *998 Monterey St., at Osos St.* ☎ *805/783–1135* 🌐 *www.epkoberl.com.*

The Libertine Brewing Company. Come to Libertine to savor 76 craft beers and wines on tap, housemade brews of kombucha and cold brew coffee, and pub food infused with the brewery's own wild ales. ✉ *1234 Broad St.* ☎ *805/548–2337* 🌐 *www.libertinebrewing.com/san-luis-obispo.*

Linnaea's. A mellow java joint, Linnaea's hosts poetry readings, as well as blues, jazz, and folk music performances. ✉ *1110 Garden St., at Higuera St.* ☎ *805/541–5888* 🌐 *linnaeas.com* ☞ *No events Mon.*

MoTav. Chicago-style MoTav draws crowds with good pub food and live entertainment in a turn-of-the-20th-century setting, complete with antique U.S. flags and a wall-mounted moose head. ✉ *725 Higuera St., at Broad St.* ☎ *805/541–8733* 🌐 *motherstavern.com.*

Performing Arts Center, San Luis Obispo. A truly great performance space, the center hosts live theater, dance, and music. ✉ *Cal Poly, 1 Grand Ave., off U.S. 101* ☎ *805/756–4849* 🌐 *www.calpolyarts.org.*

San Luis Obispo Repertory Theatre. SLO County's only nonprofit, fully professional theater group presents dramas, musicals, readings, and other performances year-round. ⊠ *888 Morro St.* ☎ *805/786–2440 box office* ⊕ *www.slolittletheatre.org.*

SLO Brew. Handcrafted microbrews and live music most nights make for a winning combination at this downtown watering hole and restaurant in a restored historic brick building. In 2017 SLO Brew opened The Rock, a satellite brewing and tasting facility near the airport with a beer garden, restaurant, and regular live music performances. ⊠ *736 Higuera St.* ☎ *805/543–1843* ⊕ *www.slobrewingco.com.*

MORRO BAY

14 miles north of San Luis Obispo.

Commercial fishermen slog around Morro Bay in galoshes, and beat-up fishing boats bob in the bay's protected waters. Nature-oriented activities take center stage here: kayaking, hiking, biking, fishing, and wildlife-watching around the bay and national marine estuary and along the state beach.

GETTING HERE AND AROUND

From U.S. 101 south or north, exit at Highway 1 in San Luis Obispo and head west. Scenic Highway 1 passes through the eastern edge of town. From Atascadero, two-lane Highway 41 West treks over the mountains to Morro Bay. San Luis Obispo RTA Route 12 buses travel year-round between Morro Bay, San Luis Obispo, Cayucos, Cambria, San Simeon, and Hearst Castle. The Morro Bay Shuttle picks up riders throughout the town from Friday through Monday in summer ($1.25 one-way, $3 day pass).

ESSENTIALS

Visitor Information Morro Bay Visitors Center. ⊠ *695 Harbor St., at Napa Ave.* ☎ *805/225–1570* ⊕ *www.morrobay.org.*

EXPLORING

Embarcadero. The center of Morro Bay action on land is the Embarcadero, where vacationers pour in and out of souvenir shops and seafood restaurants and stroll or bike along the scenic half-mile Harborwalk to Morro Rock. From here, you can get out on the bay in a kayak or tour boat. ⊠ *On waterfront from Beach St. to Tidelands Park.*

FAMILY **Morro Bay State Park Museum of Natural History.** The museum's entertaining interactive exhibits explain the natural environment and how to preserve it—in the bay and estuary and on the rest of the planet. ■TIP➔ **Kids age 16 and under are admitted free.** ⊠ *20 State Park Rd., south of downtown* ☎ *805/772–2694* ⊕ *centralcoastparks.org* ⊠ *$3.*

Morro Rock. At the mouth of Morro Bay stands 576-foot-high Morro Rock, one of nine small volcanic peaks, or morros, in the area. A short walk leads to a breakwater, with the harbor on one side and crashing ocean waves on the other. You may not climb the rock, where endangered falcons and other birds nest. Sea lions and otters often play in the water below the rock. ⊠ *Northern end of Embarcadero.*

6

WHERE TO EAT

$$ SEAFOOD 🍴 **Dorn's Original Breakers Cafe.** This restaurant overlooking the harbor has satisfied local appetites since 1942. In addition to straight-ahead dishes such as cod or shrimp fish-and-chips or calamari tubes sautéed in butter and wine, Dorn's serves breakfast. **Known for:** sweeping views of Morro Rock and the bay; fresh local seafood; friendly, efficient service. [$] *Average main: $22* ✉ *801 Market Ave., at Morro Bay Blvd.* ☎ *805/772–4415* 🌐 *www.dornscafe.com.*

$ SOUTHWESTERN 🍴 **Taco Temple.** This family-run diner serves some of the freshest food around. The seafood-heavy menu includes salmon burritos, superb fish tacos with mango salsa, and other dishes hailing from somewhere between California and Mexico. **Known for:** fresh seafood and salsa bar; hefty portions; daily specials. [$] *Average main: $15* ✉ *2680 Main St., at Elena St., just north of Hwy. 1/Hwy. 41 junction* ☎ *805/772–4965.*

$$ SEAFOOD Fodor's Choice ★ 🍴 **Tognazzini's Dockside.** Captain Mark Tognazzini catches seasonal seafood and delivers the bounty to his family's collection of down-home, no frills enterprises in the harbor: a fish market with patio dining and up-close views of Morro Rock (Dockside Too), the original Dockside restaurant, and a combination smokehouse, oyster bar, and pub (Dockside 3). Local musicians play live music nearly every day at the outdoor patio at Dockside Too, and Dockside 3 serves more than 50 brews on tap and in the bottle. **Known for:** fresh-as-it-gets local seafood; live music nearly every day year-round; front-row seats to Morro Rock views. [$] *Average main: $18* ✉ *1245 Embarcadero* ☎ *805/772–8100 restaurant, 805/772–8120 fish market and patio dining, 805/772–8130 smokehouse, oyster bar, and pub.*

$$$$ SEAFOOD 🍴 **Windows on the Water.** Diners at this second-floor restaurant view the sunset through giant picture windows. Meanwhile, fresh fish and other dishes based on local ingredients emerge from the wood-fired oven in the open kitchen, and oysters on the half shell beckon from the raw bar. **Known for:** sustainably farmed seafood; 20-plus wines by the glass; menu changes nightly. [$] *Average main: $33* ✉ *699 Embarcadero, at Pacific St.* ☎ *805/772–0677* 🌐 *www.windowsmb.com* ⏲ *No lunch.*

WHERE TO STAY

$$$$ B&B/INN Fodor's Choice ★ 🏨 **Anderson Inn.** Friendly, personalized service and an oceanfront setting keep loyal patrons returning to this Embarcadero inn, which was built from scratch in 2008, and features well-appointed rooms with state-of-the-art tiled bathrooms and cozy comforters atop queen beds. **Pros:** walk to restaurants and sights; spacious rooms; oceanfront rooms have fireplaces and private balconies. **Cons:** not low-budget; waterfront area can get crowded. [$] *Rooms from: $269* ✉ *897 Embarcadero* ☎ *805/772–3434, 866/950–3434 toll-free reservations* 🌐 *andersoninnmorrobay.com* 🛏 *8 rooms* 🍽 *No meals.*

$$$$ B&B/INN 🏨 **Cass House.** In tiny Cayucos, 4 miles north of Morro Bay, a shipping pioneer's 1867 home is now a luxurious bed-and-breakfast surrounded by rose and other gardens. **Pros:** historic property; some ocean views; delicious lobster roll at The Grill. **Cons:** away from nightlife and attractions; not good for families. [$] *Rooms from: $265* ✉ *222 N. Ocean Ave., Cayucos* ☎ *805/995–3669* 🌐 *casshouseinn.com* 🛏 *5 rooms* 🍽 *Breakfast.*

$$$ HOTEL **456 Embarcadero.** The rooms at this waterfront hotel are cheery and welcoming, and many have fireplaces. **Pros:** across from waterfront. **Cons:** tiny lobby; no pool. [$] *Rooms from: $189* ✉ *456 Embarcadero* ☎ *805/772–2700, 800/292–7625* 🌐 *www.embarcaderoinn.com* 🛏 *33 rooms* 🍴 *Breakfast.*

$$$ RESORT **The Inn at Morro Bay.** Surrounded by eucalyptus trees, this inn abuts a heron rookery and Morro Bay State Park. **Pros:** great for wildlife lovers; stellar views from restaurant and some rooms; nearby golf course, wellness center on-site. **Cons:** some rooms on the small side; birds and seals can wake you early. [$] *Rooms from: $229* ✉ *60 State Park Rd.* ☎ *805/772–5651* 🌐 *innatmorrobay.com* 🛏 *98 rooms* 🍴 *No meals.*

$$ HOTEL **Pleasant Inn.** A friendly staff, bright flower boxes, and comfy, clean rooms are the hallmarks of this basic but cheery lodge less than two blocks from the waterfront. **Pros:** great value for the location; friendly staff; cozy and clean. **Cons:** small rooms; few amenities. [$] *Rooms from: $169* ✉ *235 Harbor St.* ☎ *805/772–8521, 888/772–8521* 🌐 *www.pleasantinnmotel.com* 🛏 *11 rooms* 🍴 *No meals.*

SPORTS AND THE OUTDOORS

Kayak Horizons. This outfit rents kayaks and paddleboards and gives lessons and guided tours. ✉ *551 Embarcadero, near Marina St.* ☎ *805/772–6444* 🌐 *kayakhorizons.com.*

The Paddleboard Co. Come to this waterfront shop to rent stand-up paddleboards and to take paddleboard lessons and yoga and fitness classes (for all ages and skill levels), and stock up on outdoor wear and paddling gear. You can sign up for classes online as well. ✉ *575 Embarcadero* ☎ *805/225–5555* 🌐 *www.thepaddleboardcompany.com* 🎟 *board rentals $25 per hr, $10 additional ½ hr, lessons from $85.*

Sub-Sea Tours & Kayaks. You can view sea life aboard this outfit's glass-bottom boat, watch whales from its catamaran, or rent a kayak, canoe, or stand-up paddleboard. ✉ *699 Embarcadero* ☎ *805/772–9463* 🌐 *subseatours.com.*

Virg's Landing. Virg's conducts deep-sea-fishing and whale-watching trips. ✉ *1169 Market Ave.* ☎ *805/772–1222* 🌐 *virgslanding.com.*

PASO ROBLES

30 miles north of San Luis Obispo, 25 miles northwest of Morro Bay.

In the 1860s, tourists began flocking to this ranching outpost to "take the cure" in a bathhouse fed by underground mineral hot springs. An Old West town emerged, and grand Victorian homes went up, followed in the 20th century by Craftsman bungalows. These days, the wooded hills of Paso Robles west of U.S. 101 and the flatter, more open land to the freeway's east hold more than 250 wineries, many with tasting rooms. Hot summer days, cool nights, and varied soils and microclimates allow growers to cultivate an impressive array of Bordeaux, Rhône, and other grape types. Cabernet Sauvignon grows well in the Paso Robles AVA—32,000 of its 600,000-plus acres are planted to grapes—as do Petit Verdot, Grenache, Syrah, Viognier, and Zinfandel. In recognition of the diverse growing conditions, the AVA was divided into 11 subappellations in 2014. Pick up a wine-touring map at lodgings, wineries, and attractions around town. The fee at most tasting rooms is between $10 and $25; many lodgings pass out discount coupons.

Upmarket restaurants, bars, antiques stores, and little shops fill the streets around oak-shaded City Park, where special events of all kinds— custom car shows, an olive festival, Friday-night summer concerts— take place on many weekends. Despite its increasing sophistication, Paso (as the locals call it) retains a small-town vibe. The city celebrates its cowboy roots in late July and early August with the two-week California Mid-State Fair, complete with livestock auctions, carnival rides, and corn dogs.

GETTING HERE AND AROUND

U.S. 101 runs north–south through Paso Robles. Highway 46 West links Paso Robles to Highway 1 and Cambria on the coast. Highway 46 East connects Paso Robles with Interstate 5 and the San Joaquin Valley. Public transit is not convenient for wine touring and sightseeing.

Visitor Information Paso Robles CAB Collective. ☎ *805/543–2288* ⊕ *pasoroblescab.com.* **Paso Robles Wine Country Alliance.** ☎ *805/239–8463* ⊕ *pasowine.com.* **Paso Robles Visitor Center.** ✉ *1225 Park St., near 12th St.* ☎ *805/238–0506* ⊕ *travelpaso.com.* **Rhone Rangers/Paso Robles.** ⊕ *rhonerangers.org/pasorobles.*

EXPLORING

TOP ATTRACTIONS

Fodor's Choice ★ **Calcareous Vineyard.** Elegant wines, a stylish tasting room, and knockout hilltop views make for a winning experience at this winery along winding Peachy Canyon Road. Cabernet Sauvignon, Syrah, and Zinfandel grapes thrive in the summer heat and limestone soils of the two vineyards near the tasting room; and a third vineyard on cooler York Mountain produces Pinot Noir, Chardonnay, and a Cabernet with a completely different character from the Peachy Canyon edition. ■ TIP→ The picnic area's expansive eastward views invite lingering. ✉ *3430 Peachy Canyon Rd.* ☎ *805/239–0289* ⊕ *calcareous.com* ☞ *Tasting $10; tour and tasting (reservations required) $15–$35.*

FAMILY **Estrella Warbirds Museum.** An entertaining homage to fighter planes, flyboys, and flygirls, this museum maintains indoor exhibits about wartime aviation and displays retired aircraft outdoors and in repair shops. Bonus attraction: a huge building with spruced-up autos, drag racers, and "funny cars." ✉ *4251 Dry Creek Rd., off Airport Rd., north off Hwy. 46E* ☎ *805/238–9317* ⊕ *ewarbirds.org* ☞ *$10* ☉ *Closed Mon.–Wed. except legal holidays.*

Firestone Walker Brewing Company. At this working craft brewery you can sample medal-winners such as the Double Barrel Ale and learn about the beer-making process on 30-minute guided tours of the brew house and cellar. ✉ *1400 Ramada Dr., east side of U.S. 101; exit at Hwy. 46 W/Cambria, but head east* ☎ *805/225–5911* ⊕ *www.firestonebeer.com* ☞ *Tastings $1.50–$3 per sample, tour free.*

Halter Ranch Vineyard. A good place to learn about contemporary Paso Robles wine making, this ultramodern operation produces high-quality wines from estate-grown Bordeaux and Rhône grapes grown in sustainably farmed vineyards. The gravity-flow winery, which you can view on tours, is a marvel of efficiency. Ancestor, the flagship wine, a potent Bordeaux-style blend of Cabernet Sauvignon, Petit Verdot, and Malbec, is named for the ranch's huge centuries-old coast oak tree. ⊠ *8910 Adelaida Rd., at Vineyard Dr.* ☎ *888/367–9977* ⊕ *www.halterranch. com* 🖅 *Tasting $10.*

Fodor's Choice **HammerSky Vineyards.** Owner Doug Hauck bucks a few trends by focusing on Merlot and Zinfandel, two varietals of variable popularity in
★ recent years. Hauck makes excellent small lots of each, along with a Merlot-heavy Bordeaux-style blend; on the lighter side are Sauvignon Blanc and a Rosé of Zinfandel. Set amid rolling hills of vineyards punctuated by a huge oak, HammerSky's bright-white contemporary structure houses both the tasting and barrel-aging rooms; an outdoor patio has views of the estate vines. ⊠ *7725 Vineyard Dr., at Jensen Rd.* ☎ *805/239–0930* ⊕ *www.hammersky.com* 🖅 *Tasting $10* ☾ *Closed Wed.*

Fodor's Choice **Jada Vineyard & Winery.** Winemaker David Galzignato, formerly of
★ the Napa Valley's Charles Krug Winery, crafts Jada's nuanced, highly structured wines. Two worth checking out are Jack of Hearts, starring Petit Verdot, and Passing By, a Cabernet-heavy blend. Galzignato also shines with Tannat and with Rhône-style wines, particularly Grenache. At tastings, the wines are paired with gourmet cheeses. ⊠ *5620 Vineyard Dr., north of Hwy. 46 W* ☎ *805/226–4200* ⊕ *jadavineyard.com* 🖅 *Tastings $15.*

JUSTIN Vineyards & Winery. This suave winery built its reputation on Isosceles, a hearty Bordeaux blend, usually of Cabernet Sauvignon, Cabernet Franc, and Merlot. JUSTIN's Cabernet Sauvignon is also well regarded, as is the Right Angle blend of Cab and three other varietals. Tastings here take place in an expansive room whose equally expansive windows provide views of the hillside vineyards. ⊠ *11680 Chimney Rock Rd., 15 miles west of U.S. 101's Hwy 46 E exit; take 24th St. west and follow road (name changes along the way) to Chimney Rock Rd.* ☎ *805/238–6932* ⊕ *justinwine.com* 🖅 *Tasting $20, tour and tasting $25* ☞ *Tours 10 and 2:30 (reservations recommended).*

Fodor's Choice **Pasolivo.** While touring the idyllic west side of Paso Robles, take a break
★ from wine tasting by stopping at Pasolivo. Find out how the artisans here make their Tuscan-style olive oils on a high-tech Italian press, and test the acclaimed results. ⊠ *8530 Vineyard Dr., west off U.S. 101 (Exit 224) or Hwy. 46 W (Exit 228)* ☎ *805/227–0186* ⊕ *www.pasolivo.com* 🖅 *Free.*

Tablas Creek Vineyard. Tucked in the western hills of Paso Robles, Tablas Creek is known for its blends of organically grown, hand-harvested Rhône varietals. Roussanne and Viognier are the standout whites; the Mourvèdre-heavy blend called Panoplie (it also includes Grenache and Syrah) has received high praise in recent years. ■ TIP→ There's a fine picnic area here. ⊠ *9339 Adelaida Rd., west of Vineyard Dr.* ☎ *805/237–1231* ⊕ *www.tablascreek.com* 🖅 *Tasting $15 (reserve $40 by appointment), tour free.*

WORTH NOTING

Eberle Winery. Even if you don't drink wine, stop here for a tour of the huge wine caves beneath the vineyards (departs every half hour all day). Eberle produces wines from Bordeaux, Rhône, and Italian varietals and makes intriguing blends including Grenache Blanc–Viognier and Cabernet Sauvignon–Syrah. ⊠ *3810 Hwy. 46 E, 3½ miles east of U.S. 101* ☎ *805/238–9607* ⊕ *www.eberlewinery.com* ⊠ *Basic tasting and tour free, weekend reserve tasting $25, private tour and tasting $35 by appointment.*

Paso Robles Pioneer Museum. The delightful museum's one-room schoolhouse and its displays of ranching paraphernalia, horse-drawn vehicles, hot-springs artifacts, and photos evoke Paso's rural heritage. ⊠ *2010 Riverside Ave., at 21st St.* ☎ *805/239–4556* ⊕ *www.pasoroblespioneermuseum.org* ⊠ *Free.*

FAMILY **Pomar Junction Vineyard & Winery.** A vintage railroad boxcar and a caboose provide a visual change of pace at Pomar Junction. Its flagship wine, Train Wreck, is a daring but usually winning blend of Cabernet Sauvignon, Zinfandel, Mourvèdre, Syrah, and Petite Sirah. With sparkling wine, a Grenache Blanc, Pinot Noir, a smooth Merlot, and several white and red blends, there's something for pretty much everyone here. ■TIP➔ Picnic areas shaded by elms, oaks, and other trees—not to mention old farm equipment and those train cars—make this a popular stop for wine tasters with kids. ⊠ *5036 S. El Pomar Rd., at El Pomar Dr.* ☎ *805/238–9940* ⊕ *pomarjunction.com* ⊠ *Tastings $10–$15.*

River Oaks Hot Springs & Spa. The lakeside spa, on 240 hilly acres near the intersection of U.S. 101 and Highway 46 East, is a great place to relax after wine tasting or festival-going. Soak in a private indoor or outdoor hot tub fed by natural mineral springs, or indulge in a massage or facial. ⊠ *800 Clubhouse Dr., off River Oaks Dr., just north of River Oaks Golf Course* ☎ *805/238–4600* ⊕ *riveroakshotsprings.com* ⊠ *$12–$15 per hr.*

Robert Hall Winery. The late Robert Hall's winery made its reputation on a well-made, reasonably priced Cabernet Sauvignon from Paso Robles AVA grapes, but at the high-ceilinged tasting room you can sample less widely distributed wines. These include a reserve Cabernet, a Merlot, a Malbec, a Bordeaux-style Meritage blend, and a Port made from Portuguese grapes. Whites of note include Roussanne, Sauvignon Blanc, and Viognier. ■TIP➔ Ask for a 30-minute tour if you'd like to see the production facilities. ⊠ *3443 Mill Rd., at Hwy. 46E, 3 miles east of U.S. 101* ☎ *805/239–1616* ⊕ *roberthallwinery.com* ⊠ *Tastings $10; tour free.*

SIP CERTIFICATION

Many wineries in Paso Robles take pride in being SIP (Sustainability in Practice) Certified, for which they undergo a rigorous third-party audit of their entire operations. Water and energy conservation practices are reviewed, along with pest management and other aspects of farming. Also considered are the wages, benefits, and working conditions of the employees, and the steps taken to mitigate the impact of grape growing and wine production on area habitats.

SummerWood Winery. Rhône varietals do well in the Paso Robles AVA, where many wineries, including this one, produce "GSM" (Grenache, Syrah, Mourvèdre) red blends, along with whites such as Viognier, Marsanne, and Grenache Blanc. Winemaker Mauricio Marchant displays a subtle touch with Rhône whites and reds, as well as Sentio, a Petit Verdot–heavy Bordeaux red blend. Tastings here are relaxed and informal, and there's a patio from which you can enjoy the vineyard views. ✉ *2175 Arbor Rd., off Hwy. 46W* ☎ *805/227–1365* 🌐 *summerwoodwine.com* 🎫 *Tasting $15.*

Villa San-Juliette Vineyard & Winery. Nigel Lithgoe (co-creator of *So You Think You Can Dance* is one of his many titles), and Ken Warwick (executive producer of *American Idol,* among other programs) established this winery northeast of Paso Robles. With a cast that includes Petit Verdot, a fine Grenache, and a perky Albariño (a Spanish white varietal), their stylish operation is no flash in the pan. From 11 to 4 you can order snacks, panini, pizzas, soup and salad, and cheese and charcuterie plates to enjoy with your wine in the tasting room or on the view-filled outdoor terrace. ✉ *6385 Cross Canyons Rd., at Ranchita Canyon Rd., San Miguel* ☎ *805/467–0014* 🌐 *www.villasanjuliette.com* 🎫 *Tasting $10* 🕒 *Closed Tues. and Wed. except by appointment.*

6

Wild Horse Winery & Vineyards. High-profile Wild Horse, these days part of the Constellation Brands lineup, is known for its Central Coast Pinot Noir and other widely distributed wines. The draws at its winery, though, are smaller-production, vineyard-designated Pinot Noirs, several made from grapes grown in Santa Barbara County's Santa Maria Valley and Sta. Rita Hills AVAs. ✉ *1437 Wild Horse Winery Ct., off Templeton Rd., Templeton* ☎ *805/788–6300* 🌐 *www.wildhorsewinery.com* 🎫 *Tasting $10–$15, tour $15.*

WHERE TO EAT

$$$$ FRENCH

🍴 **Bistro Laurent.** Owner-chef Laurent Grangien's handsome, welcoming French bistro occupies an 1890s brick building across from City Park. He focuses on traditional dishes such as duck confit, rack of lamb, and onion soup, but always prepares a few au courant daily specials as well. **Known for:** classic French dishes made with local ingredients; good selection of local and international wines; four- or five-course tasting menus. [$] *Average main: $32* ✉ *1202 Pine St., at 12th St.* ☎ *805/226–8191* 🌐 *www.bistrolaurent.com* 🕒 *Closed Sun. and Mon.*

$$$ MODERN ITALIAN Fodor's Choice ★

🍴 **Il Cortile.** One of two Paso establishments owned by chef Santos MacDonal and his wife, Carole, this Italian restaurant entices diners with complex flavors and a contemporary space with art deco overtones. Consistent crowd-pleasers often on the menu include beef carpaccio with white truffle cream sauce and shaved black truffles, pappardelle with wild boar ragu, and pork osso buco, perhaps served with Parmesan herb risotto. **Known for:** house-made pastas; excellent wine pairings; ingredients from chef's garden. [$] *Average main: $30* ✉ *608 12th St., near Spring St.* ☎ *805/226–0300* 🌐 *www.ilcortileristorante.com* 🕒 *Closed Tues. No lunch.*

$$$ SOUTH AMERICAN

🍴 **La Cosecha.** At barlike, tin-ceilinged La Cosecha (Spanish for "the harvest"), Honduran-born chef Santos MacDonal faithfully re-creates dishes from Spain and South America. Noteworthy starters include *pastelitos catracho,* Honduran-style empanadas in a light tomato sauce served with *queso fresco* (fresh cheese) and micro cilantro. **Known for:** fusion of Latin spices and fresh local fare; daily paella special; artisanal cocktails. $ *Average main: $29* ✉ *835 12th St., near Pine St.* ☎ *805/237–0019* ⊕ *www.lacosechabr.com* ☾ *Closed Mon.*

$$$$
AMERICAN

✗ **McPhee's Grill.** Just south of Paso Robles in tiny Templeton, this casual chophouse in an 1860s wood-frame storefront serves sophisticated, contemporary versions of traditional Western fare such as oak-grilled filet mignon and fresh seafood tostadas. The house-label wines, made especially for the restaurant, are quite good. **Known for:** meats grilled over red oak; local seasonal menu; excellent wine selections. $ *Average main: $32* ✉ *416 S. Main St., at 5th St., Templeton* ☎ *805/434–3204* ⊕ *mcpheesgrill.com* ☾ *No lunch Sun.*

$$$
FRENCH

✗ **Panolivo Family Bistro.** Affordable French fare draws patrons to this café north of the town square. For breakfast, try a fresh pastry or quiche, or build your own omelet. **Known for:** vegan and gluten-free menus; three-course prix-fixe dinner option; all-day breakfast (until 4). $ *Average main: $26* ✉ *1344 Park St., at 14th St.* ☎ *805/239–3366* ⊕ *www.panolivo.com.*

$$$$
MODERN
AMERICAN
Fodor's Choice
★

✗ **Thomas Hill Organics.** The Central Coast's abundance of organic and sustainably sourced bounty—veggies, seafood, meats, and breads—are creatively woven into innovative dishes at this brick-walled downtown favorite. The wine list celebrates local wines; with many by the half-glass, you can sample a good cross-section. **Known for:** organic sustainable menu; local-centric wine list; regional locavore pioneer. $ *Average main: $31* ✉ *1313 Park St., at 13th St.* ☎ *805/226–5888* ⊕ *thomashillorganics.com.*

$$$
SOUTHWESTERN

✗ **Villa Creek.** Within a spacious brick-and-wood building at the northeast corner of the main square, chef Tim Veatch Fundaro conjures rustic wine country cuisine with sustainably sourced ingredients from small Californian farms and ranches. The seasonal menu changes often, and might include Sicilian fried cauliflower with caper mayo and Calabrian chilies, and Liberty Farms duck with crispy potatoes, house-fermented sauerkraut, and caraway onions. **Known for:** popular bar with small plates; potent margaritas; lively vibe. $ *Average main: $26* ✉ *1144 Pine St., at 12th St.* ☎ *805/238–3000* ⊕ *www.villacreek.com* ☾ *No lunch.*

WHERE TO STAY

$
HOTEL
FAMILY

⊞ **Adelaide Inn.** Family-owned and -managed, this clean oasis with meticulous landscaping offers spacious rooms and everything you need: coffeemaker, iron, hair dryer, and peace and quiet. **Pros:** good bargain; attractive pool area; ideal for families. **Cons:** not a romantic retreat; near a busy intersection. $ *Rooms from: $104* ✉ *1215 Ysabel Ave.* ☎ *805/238–2770, 800/549–7276* ⊕ *adelaideinn.com* ↝ *108 rooms* ⦿◯ *Breakfast.*

$$$$
RESORT
Fodor's Choice
★

⊞ **Allegretto.** This swank, 20-acre Tuscan-style resort amid estate vineyards is also a private museum where owner Doug Ayres displays hundreds of artworks and artifacts collected on his world travels: ancient Indian river stones and statues; a massive cross section from a giant Sequoia; Russian and California impressionist paintings; mandalas, and more (nonguests are welcome to walk around). **Pros:** yoga in medieval alley; full-service restaurant Cello and spa; bocce ball, fire pit, and other diversions. **Cons:** not close to downtown square; pricey; some rooms close to courtyard music. ⓢ *Rooms from: $349* ⊠ *2700 Buena Vista Dr.* ☎ *805/369–2500* ⊕ *www.allegrettoresort.com* ⮑ *171 rooms.*

$$$$
HOTEL
Fodor'sChoice
★

⌂ **Hotel Cheval.** Equestrian themes surface throughout this intimate European-style boutique hotel a half-block from the main square and near some of Paso's best restaurants. **Pros:** most rooms have fireplaces; sip wine and champagne at the on-site Pony Club and zinc bar; extremely personalized service. **Cons:** views aren't great; no pool or hot tub. ⓢ *Rooms from: $330* ⊠ *1021 Pine St.* ☎ *805/226–9995, 866/522–6999* ⊕ *www.hotelcheval.com* ⮑ *16 rooms* ⍟*Breakfast.*

$$$$
B&B/INN

⌂ **JUST Inn.** Fine wines, a destination restaurant, and a vineyard's-edge setting make a stay at Justin winery's on-site inn an exercise in sophisticated seclusion. **Pros:** secluded; vineyard views; destination restaurant. **Cons:** half-hour drive to town; location may be too secluded for some. ⓢ *Rooms from: $400* ⊠ *11680 Chimney Rock Rd.* ☎ *805/238–6932, 800/726–0049* ⊕ *www.justinwine.com* ⮑ *4 suites* ⍟*Breakfast.*

$$$
HOTEL

⌂ **La Bellasera Hotel & Suites.** A full-service hotel just off Highway 101 at the Highway 46 exit, La Bellasera caters to those looking for high-tech amenities and easy access to major Central Coast roadways. **Pros:** oversize rooms; Romanesque architectural features; close to freeways. **Cons:** far from downtown; at a major intersection. ⓢ *Rooms from: $199* ⊠ *206 Alexa Ct.* ☎ *805/238–2834, 866/782–9669* ⊕ *labellasera. com* ⮑ *35 rooms, 25 suites* ⍟*No meals.*

$$$
HOTEL

⌂ **La Quinta Inn & Suites.** A good value for Paso Robles, this three-story chain property attracts heavy repeat business with its upbeat staff and slew of perks. **Pros:** apartment-style suites in separate building; free happy hour with local wines and appetizers; good for leisure or business travelers. **Cons:** conventional decor; not downtown. ⓢ *Rooms from: $189* ⊠ *2615 Buena Vista Dr.* ☎ *805/239–3004, 800/753–3757* ⊕ *www.laquintapasorobles.com* ⮑ *101 rooms* ⍟*Breakfast.*

$$
HOTEL

⌂ **Paso Robles Inn.** On the site of an old spa hotel of the same name, the inn is built around a lush, shaded garden with a pool (the water is still the reason to stay here), and each of the 18 deluxe rooms has a spring-fed hot tub in its bathroom or on its balcony. **Pros:** private spring-fed hot tubs; special touches like unique photography in each room; across from town square. **Cons:** fronts a busy street; rooms vary in size and amenities. ⓢ *Rooms from: $149* ⊠ *1103 Spring St.* ☎ *805/238–2660, 800/676–1713* ⊕ *www.pasoroblesinn.com* ⮑ *92 rooms, 6 suites* ⍟*No meals.*

$$$$
B&B/INN
Fodor'sChoice
★

⌂ **SummerWood Inn.** Easygoing hospitality, vineyard-view rooms, and elaborate breakfasts make this inn a mile west of U.S. 101 worth seeking out. **Pros:** convenient wine-touring base; elaborate breakfasts; complimentary tastings at associated winery. **Cons:** some noise from nearby highway during the day. ⓢ *Rooms from: $275* ⊠ *2130 Arbor Rd., 1 mile west of U.S. 101, at Hwy. 46W* ☎ *805/227–1111* ⊕ *www.sum-merwoodwine.com/inn* ⮑ *9 rooms* ⍟*Breakfast.*

PERFORMING ARTS

Vina Robles Amphitheatre. At this 3,300-seat, Mission-style venue with good food, wine, and sight lines, you can enjoy acclaimed musicians in concert. ⊠ *Vina Robles winery, 3800 Mill Rd., off Hwy. 46* ☎ *805/286–3680* ⊕ *www.vinaroblesamphitheatre.com* ⌕ *Performances Apr.–Nov.*

6

CAMBRIA

28 miles west of Paso Robles, 20 miles north of Morro Bay.

Cambria, set on piney hills above the sea, was settled by Welsh miners in the 1890s. In the 1970s the isolated setting attracted artists and other independent types; the town now caters to tourists, but it still bears the imprint of its bohemian past. Both of Cambria's downtowns, the original East Village and the newer West Village, are packed with art and crafts galleries, antiques shops, cafés, restaurants, and bed-and-breakfasts.

Two diverting detours lie between Morro Bay and Cambria. In the laid-back beach town of **Cayucos,** 4 miles north of Morro Bay, you can stroll the long pier, feast on chowder (at Duckie's), and sample the namesake delicacies of the Brown Butter Cookie Co. Over in **Harmony,** a quaint former dairy town 7 miles south of Cambria (population 18), you can take in the glassworks, pottery, and other artsy enterprises.

GETTING HERE AND AROUND

Highway 1 leads to Cambria from the north and south. Highway 246 West curves from U.S. 101 through the mountains to Cambria. San Luis Obispo RTA Route 12 buses stop in Cambria (and Hearst Castle).

ESSENTIALS

Visitor Information Cambria Chamber of Commerce. ⊠ *767 Main St.* ☎ *805/927–3624* ⊕ *www.cambriachamber.org.*

EXPLORING

Covells California Clydesdales. Come to the vast 2,000-acre Covell Ranch to see one of the world's largest private stands of endangered Monterey pines and witness herds of gentle Clydesdales roaming the range. Much of the ranch is in a conservation easement that will never be developed. The two-hour guided tours include a 3-mile ride that takes you through an historic picnic grove amid the pines to the barn. The ranch also offers trail rides and Saturday night barbecue dinners at the barn, where you can take a hayride on a custom-built "people mover" wagon. ⊠ *5694 Bridge St.* ☎ *805/927–3398* ⊕ *www.covellscaliforni-aclydesdales.com* ⊠ *Tours $100 per person, Sat. night barbecues $100 per person* ☉ *Tours, trail rides, and barbecues by appointment only.*

Fiscalini Ranch Preserve. Walk down a mile-long coastal bluff trail to spot migrating whales, otters, and shore birds at this 450-acre public space. Miles of additional scenic trails crisscross the protected habitats of rare and endangered species of flora and fauna, including a Monterey pine forest, western pond turtles, monarch butterflies, and burrowing owls. Dogs are permitted on-leash everywhere and off-leash on all trails except the bluff. ⊠ *Hwy. 1, between Cambria Rd. and Main St. to the north, and Burton Dr. and Warren Rd. to the south; access either end of bluff trail off Windsor Blvd.* ☎ *805/927–2856* ⊕ *www.ffrpcambria.org.*

Leffingwell Landing. A state picnic ground, the landing is a good place for examining tidal pools and watching otters as they frolic in the surf. ⊠ *North end of Moonstone Beach Dr.* ☎ *805/927–2070.*

Moonstone Beach Drive. The drive runs along a bluff above the ocean, paralleled by a 3-mile boardwalk that winds along the beach. On this photogenic walk you might glimpse sea lions and sea otters, and perhaps a gray whale during winter and spring. Year-round, birds fly about, and tiny creatures scurry amid the tidepools. ✉ *Off Hwy. 1.*

Nit Wit Ridge. Arthur Beal (aka Captain Nit Wit, Der Tinkerpaw) spent 51 years building a home above Cambria's West Village out of collected junk: beer cans, rocks, abalone shells, car parts, TV antennas—you name it. The site, sometimes signed as Nitt Witt Ridge, is a state landmark. ■ **TIP→ You can drive by and peek in—from the 700 block of Main Street, head southeast on Cornwall Street and east on Hillcrest Drive. Or, schedule a guided tour.** ✉ *881 Hillcrest Dr.* ☎ *805/927–2690* 🎟 *$10.*

WHERE TO EAT

$$ MODERN AMERICAN

🍴 **Centrally Grown at Off the Grid.** A collection of sustainably conscious spaces fashioned from repurposed materials, Centrally Grown encompasses a coffee shop, market, wine tasting, exotic gardens, and a second-floor restaurant with fantastic views of San Simeon Bay and the Big Sur Coast. The restaurant, decorated in a "planet-friendly chic" style that includes a driftwood archway, serves classic California cuisine with global influences. **Known for:** all day dining; great place to stop before or after driving the Big Sur Coast; exotic gardens with meandering paths. [$] *Average main: $22* ✉ *7432 Exotic Garden Dr., off Hwy. 1* ☎ *800/927–3563* 🌐 *www.centrallygrown.com.*

$$$ AMERICAN FAMILY

🍴 **Linn's Restaurant.** Homemade olallieberry pies, soups, potpies, and other farmhouse comfort foods share the menu at this spacious East Village restaurant with fancier farm-to-table dishes such as organic, free-range chicken topped with raspberry-orange-cranberry sauce. Also on-site are a bakery, a café serving more casual fare (take-out available), and a gift shop that sells gourmet foods. **Known for:** ollallieberry pie; numerous gluten-free and vegan options; family owned and operated for decades. [$] *Average main: $23* ✉ *2277 Main St., at Wall St.* ☎ *805/927–0371* 🌐 *www.linnsfruitbin.com.*

$$ ECLECTIC

🍴 **Robin's.** A multiethnic, vegetarian-friendly dining experience awaits you at this cozy East Village cottage. Dinner choices include wild prawn enchiladas, grilled Skuna Bay salmon, Japanese scallops, and short ribs. **Known for:** savory curries; top-notch salmon bisque; secluded (heated) garden patio. [$] *Average main: $22* ✉ *4095 Burton Dr., at Center St.* ☎ *805/927–5007* 🌐 *robinsrestaurant.com.*

$$$ SEAFOOD Fodor's Choice ★

🍴 **Sea Chest Oyster Bar and Restaurant.** Cambria's best place for seafood fills up soon after it opens at 5:30 (no reservations taken). Those in the know grab seats at the oyster bar and take in spectacular sunsets while watching the chefs broil fresh halibut, steam garlicky clams, and fry crispy calamari steaks. **Known for:** New England chowder house vibe; savory cioppino; waiting areas in wine bar, game room, and patio with fire pit. [$] *Average main: $30* ✉ *6216 Moonstone Beach Dr., near Weymouth St.* ☎ *805/927–4514* 🌐 *www.seachestrestaurant.com* 💳 *No credit cards* ⏲ *Closed Tues. mid-Sept.–May. No lunch.*

WHERE TO STAY

$$ HOTEL **Bluebird Inn.** This sweet motel in Cambria's East Village sits amid beautiful gardens along Santa Rosa Creek. **Pros:** excellent value; well-kept gardens; friendly staff. **Cons:** few frills; basic rooms; not on beach. [$] *Rooms from: $125* ✉ *1880 Main St.* ☎ *805/927–4634, 800/552–5434* 🌐 *bluebirdmotel.com* *37 rooms* 🍴 *Breakfast.*

$$ RESORT **Cambria Pines Lodge.** This 25-acre retreat up the hill from the East Village is a good choice for families; accommodations range from basic fireplace cabins to motel-style standard rooms to large fireplace suites and deluxe suites with spa tubs. **Pros:** short walk from downtown; live music nightly in the lounge; verdant gardens. **Cons:** service and housekeeping not always top-quality; some units need updating. [$] *Rooms from: $149* ✉ *2905 Burton Dr.* ☎ *805/927–4200, 800/966–6490* 🌐 *www.cambriapineslodge.com* *152 rooms* 🍴 *Breakfast.*

$$$ B&B/INN **J. Patrick House.** Monterey pines and flower gardens surround this Irish-themed inn, which sits on a hilltop above Cambria's East Village. **Pros:** fantastic breakfasts; friendly innkeepers; quiet neighborhood. **Cons:** few rooms; fills up quickly. [$] *Rooms from: $195* ✉ *2990 Burton Dr.* ☎ *805/927–3812, 800/341–5258* 🌐 *jpatrickhouse.com* *7 rooms* 🍴 *Breakfast.*

$$$ HOTEL **Moonstone Landing.** This up-to-date motel's amenities, reasonable rates, and accommodating staff make it a Moonstone Beach winner. **Pros:** sleek furnishings; across from the beach; cheery lounge. **Cons:** narrow property; some rooms overlook a parking lot. [$] *Rooms from: $189* ✉ *6240 Moonstone Beach Dr.* ☎ *805/927–0012, 800/830–4540* 🌐 *www.moonstonelanding.com* *29 rooms* 🍴 *Breakfast.*

SAN SIMEON

9 miles north of Cambria, 65 miles south of Big Sur.

Whalers founded San Simeon in the 1850s, but had virtually abandoned it by 1865, when Senator George Hearst began purchasing most of the surrounding ranch land. Hearst turned San Simeon into a bustling port, and his son, William Randolph Hearst, further developed the area while erecting Hearst Castle (one of the many remarkable stops you'll encounter when driving along Highway 1). Today San Simeon is basically a strip of unremarkable gift shops and so-so motels that straddle Highway 1 about 4 miles south of the castle's entrance, but **Old San Simeon,** right across from the entrance, is worth a peek. Julia Morgan, William Randolph Hearst's architect, designed some of the village's Mission Revival–style buildings.

GETTING HERE AND AROUND

Highway 1 is the only way to reach San Simeon. Connect with the highway off U.S. 101 directly or via rural routes such as Highway 41 West (Atascadero to Morro Bay) and Highway 46 West (Paso Robles to Cambria).

San Simeon Chamber of Commerce Visitor Center. ✉ *250 San Simeon Ave.* ☎ *805/927–3500* 🌐 *www.sansimeonchamber.org.*

EXPLORING
TOP ATTRACTIONS

Fodor's Choice **Hearst Castle.** Officially known as "Hearst San Simeon State Historical
★ Monument," Hearst Castle sits in solitary splendor atop La Cuesta
Encantada (the Enchanted Hill). Its buildings and gardens spread over
127 acres that were the heart of newspaper magnate William Randolph
Hearst's 250,000-acre ranch. Hearst commissioned renowned California architect Julia Morgan to design the estate, but he was very much
involved with the final product, a blend of Italian, Spanish, and Moorish
styles. The 115-room main structure and three huge "cottages" are connected by terraces and staircases and surrounded by pools, gardens, and
statuary. In its heyday the castle, whose buildings hold about 22,000
works of fine and decorative art, was a playground for Hearst and his
guests—Hollywood celebrities, political leaders, scientists, and other
well-known figures. Construction began in 1919 and was never officially completed. Work was halted in 1947 when Hearst had to leave
San Simeon because of failing health. The Hearst Corporation donated
the property to the State of California in 1958, and it is now part of
the state park system.

Access to the castle is through the visitor center at the foot of the hill,
where you can view educational exhibits and a 40-minute film about
Hearst's life and the castle's construction. Buses from the center zigzag
up to the hilltop estate, where guides conduct four daytime tours, each
with a different focus: Grand Rooms, Upstairs Suites, Designing the
Dream, and Cottages and Kitchen. These tours take about three hours
and include a movie screening, and time at the end to explore the castle's
exterior and gardens. In spring and fall, docents in period costume
portray Hearst's guests and staff for the Evening Tour, which begins
around sunset. Reservations are recommended for all tours, which
include a ½-mile walk and between 150 and 400 stairs. ⊠ *San Simeon
State Park, 750 Hearst Castle Rd.* ☎ *800/444–4445, 518/218–5078
international reservations* ⊕ *www.hearstcastle.org* ✉ *Daytime tours
$25–$30, evening tours $36.*

FAMILY **Piedras Blancas Elephant Seal Rookery.** A large colony of elephant seals (at
last count 22,000) gathers every year at Piedras Blancas Elephant Seal
Rookery, on the beaches near Piedras Blancas Lighthouse. The huge
males with their pendulous, trunklike noses typically start appearing
on shore in late November, and the females begin to arrive in December
to give birth—most babies are born in the last two weeks of January.
The newborn pups spend about four weeks nursing before their mothers head out to sea, leaving them on their own; the "weaners" leave
the rookery when they are about 3½ months old. The seals return in
the spring and summer months to molt or rest, but not en masse as in
winter. You can watch them from a boardwalk along the bluffs just a
few feet above the beach; do not attempt to approach these as they are
wild animals. The nonprofit Friends of the Elephant Seal runs a small
visitor center and gift shop (*250 San Simeon Avenue*) in San Simeon.
⊠ *Off Hwy. 1, 4½ miles north of Hearst Castle, just south of Piedras
Blancas Lighthouse* ☎ *805/924–1628* ⊕ *www.elephantseal.org.*

6

DID YOU KNOW?

Newspaper magnate William Randolph Hearst's dream estate, Hearst Castle, is a blend of Italian, Spanish, and Moorish architectural styles. Fans of *Citizen Kane* won't want to pass up a visit to this opulent "castle" where Hollywood celebrities and other notable figures of the era played.

Piedras Blancas Light Station. If you think traversing craggy, twisting Highway 1 is tough, imagine trying to navigate a boat up the rocky coastline (*piedras blancas* means "white rocks" in Spanish) near San Simeon before lighthouses were built. Captains must have cheered wildly when the beam began to shine here in 1875. Try to time a visit to include a morning tour (reservations not required). Tours are at 9:45 am on Tuesday, Thursday, and Saturday year-round (except for on major holidays). ■ **TIP→ Do not meet at the gate to the lighthouse—you'll miss the tour. Meet your guide instead at the former Piedras Blancas Motel, a mile and a half north of the light station.** ✉ *San Simeon* ☎ *805/927–7361,* 🌐 *www.piedrasblancas.org* 🎟 *$10* ☞ *No pets allowed.*

WORTH NOTING

Hearst Ranch Winery. Old whaling equipment and Hearst Ranch and Hearst Castle memorabilia decorate this winery's casual Old San Simeon outpost. The tasting room occupies part of Sebastian's, a former whaling store built in 1852 and moved by oxen to its present location in 1878. The flagship wines include a Bordeaux-style red blend with Petite Sirah added to round out the flavor, and Rhône-style white and red blends. Malbec and Tempranillo are two other strong suits. ■ **TIP→ Templeton chef Ian McPhee serves burgers and other lunch items at the adjacent deli, whose outdoor patio is a delight in good weather.** ✉ *442 SLO San Simeon Rd., off Hwy. 1* ☎ *805/927–4100* 🌐 *www.hearstranchwinery.com* 🎟 *Tasting $10–$15.*

6

BEACHES

William Randolph Hearst Memorial Beach. This wide, sandy beach edges a protected cove on both sides of San Simeon Pier. Fish from the pier or from a charter boat, picnic and barbecue on the bluffs, or boogie board or bodysurf the relatively gentle waves. In summer you can rent a kayak and paddle out into the bay for close encounters with marine life and sea caves. The NOAA Coastal Discovery Center, next to the parking lot, has interactive exhibits and hosts educational activities and events. **Amenities:** food and drink; parking; toilets; water sports. **Best for:** sunset; swimming; walking. ✉ *750 Hearst Castle Rd., off Hwy. 1, west of Hearst Castle entrance* ☎ *805/927–2020, 805/927–6575 Coastal Discovery Center* 🌐 *www.slostateparks.com* 🎟 *Free.*

WHERE TO STAY

$$$ HOTEL 🏨 **Cavalier Oceanfront Resort.** Reasonable rates, an oceanfront location, evening bonfires, and well-equipped rooms—some with wood-burning fireplaces and private patios—make this motel a great choice. **Pros:** on the bluffs; fantastic views; close to Hearst Castle. **Cons:** room amenities and sizes vary; pools are small and sometimes crowded. [$] *Rooms from: $229* ✉ *9415 Hearst Dr.* ☎ *805/927–4688, 800/826–8168* 🌐 *www.cavalierresort.com* 🛏 *90 rooms* 🍴 *No meals.*

$$ HOTEL 🏨 **The Morgan San Simeon.** On Highway 1's ocean side, the Morgan offers motel-style rooming options in two buildings designed to reflect the life and style of Hearst Castle architect, Julia Morgan. **Pros:** fascinating artwork; easy access to Hearst Castle; some ocean views. **Cons:** not right on beach; no fitness room or laundry facilities. [$] *Rooms from: $149* ✉ *9135 Hearst Dr.* ☎ *805/927–3878, 800/451–9900* 🌐 *www.hotel-morgan.com* 🛏 *55 rooms* 🍴 *Breakfast.*

BIG SUR COASTLINE

Long a retreat of artists and writers, Big Sur is a place of ancient forests and rugged shoreline, stretching 90 miles from San Simeon to Carmel. Residents have protected it from overdevelopment, and much of the region lies within several state parks and the more than 165,000-acre Ventana Wilderness, itself part of the Los Padres National Forest.

ESSENTIALS

Visitor Information Big Sur Chamber of Commerce. ☎ *831/667–2100* ⊕ *bigsurcalifornia.org.*

SOUTHERN BIG SUR

Hwy. 1 from San Simeon to Julia Pfeiffer Burns State Park.

This especially rugged stretch of oceanfront is a rocky world of mountains, cliffs, and beaches.

GETTING HERE AND AROUND

Highway 1 is the only major access route from north or south. From the south, access Highway 1 from U.S. 101 in San Luis Obispo. From the north, take rural route Highway 46 West (Paso Robles to Cambria) or Highway 41 West (Atascadero to Morro Bay). Nacimiento-Fergusson Road snakes through mountains and forest from U.S. 101 at Jolon about 25 miles to Highway 1 at Kirk Creek, about 4 miles south of Lucia; this curving, at times precipitous road is a motorcyclist favorite, not recommended for the faint of heart or during inclement weather.

EXPLORING

Fodor's Choice
★

Highway 1. One of California's most spectacular drives, Highway 1 snakes up the coast north of San Simeon. Numerous pullouts along the way offer tremendous views and photo ops. On some of the beaches huge elephant seals lounge nonchalantly, seemingly oblivious to the attention of rubberneckers. Heavy rain sometimes causes mudslides that block the highway north and south of Big Sur. ⚠ Sections of Highway 1 are sometimes closed for general maintenance or to repair damage from natural incidents such as mudslides. It's wise to visit bigsurcalifornia.org and click on the Highway 1 Conditions and Information link for the latest news before you travel. ⊕ *www.dot.ca.gov.*

Jade Cove. In Los Padres National Forest just north of the town of Gorda is Jade Cove, a well-known jade-hunting spot. Rock hunting is allowed on the beach, but you may not remove anything from the walls of the cliffs. ✉ *Hwy. 1, 34 miles north of San Simeon.*

Julia Pfeiffer Burns State Park. The park provides fine hiking, from an easy ½-mile stroll with marvelous coastal views to a strenuous 6-mile trek through redwoods. The big draw here, an 80-foot waterfall that drops into the ocean, gets crowded in summer; still, it's an astounding place to contemplate nature. Migrating whales, harbor seals, and sea lions can sometimes be spotted just offshore. ✉ *Hwy. 1, 15 miles north of Lucia* ☎ *831/667–2315* ⊕ *www.parks.ca.gov* 🎟 *$10.*

WHERE TO STAY

$$$ ⬚ **Ragged Point Inn.** At this cliff-top resort—the only inn and restaurant
HOTEL for miles around—glass walls in most rooms open to awesome ocean
views. **Pros:** on the cliffs; good burgers and locally made ice cream;
idyllic views. **Cons:** busy road stop during the day; often booked for
weekend weddings. $ *Rooms from: $199* ⌧ *19019 Hwy. 1, 20 miles
north of San Simeon, Ragged Point* ☎ *805/927–4502, 805/927–5708
restaurant* ⊕ *www.raggedpointinn.com* ⤳ *39 rooms* ❖❘ *No meals.*

$$$$ ⬚ **Treebones Resort.** Perched on a hilltop surrounded by national forest
RESORT and stunning, unobstructed ocean views, this yurt resort provides a
stellar back-to-nature experience along with creature comforts. **Pros:**
luxury yurts with cozy beds; lodge with fireplace and games; local food
at Wild Coast Restaurant and decked sushi bar. **Cons:** steep paths; no
private bathrooms; not good for families with young children. $ *Rooms
from: $320* ⌧ *71895 Hwy. 1, Willow Creek Rd., 32 miles north of
San Simeon, 1 mile north of Gorda* ☎ *805/927–2390, 877/424–4787*
⊕ *www.treebonesresort.com* ⤳ *16 yurts, 5 campsites, 1 human nest w/
campsite* ❖❘ *Breakfast* ⤳ *2-night minimum.*

CENTRAL BIG SUR

Hwy. 1, from Partington Cove to Bixby Bridge.

The countercultural spirit of Big Sur—which instead of a conventional
town is a loose string of coast-hugging properties along Highway 1—is
alive and well today. Its few residents include the very wealthy, the
enthusiastically outdoorsy, and the thoroughly evolved: since the 1960s
the Esalen Institute, a center for alternative education and East–West
philosophical study, has attracted seekers of higher consciousness and
devotees of the property's hot springs. Today posh and rustic resorts
hidden among the redwoods cater to visitors drawn from near and far
by the extraordinary scenery and serene isolation.

GETTING HERE AND AROUND

From the north, follow Highway 1 south from Carmel. From the south,
continue the drive north from Julia Pfeiffer Burns State Park on High-
way 1. Monterey-Salinas Transit operates the Line 22 Big Sur bus from
Monterey and Carmel to Central Big Sur (the last stop is Nepenthe), daily
from late May to early September and weekends only the rest of the year.

Bus Contact Monterey-Salinas Transit. ☎ *888/678–2871* ⊕ *www.mst.org.*

EXPLORING

Bixby Creek Bridge. The graceful arc of Bixby Creek Bridge is a photogra-
pher's dream. Built in 1932, the bridge spans a deep canyon, more than
100 feet wide at the bottom. From the north-side parking area you can
admire the view or walk the 550-foot structure. ⌧ *Hwy. 1, 6 miles north
of Point Sur State Historic Park, 13 miles south of Carmel, Big Sur.*

Pfeiffer Big Sur State Park. Among the many hiking trails at Pfeiffer Big
Sur, a short route through a redwood-filled valley leads to a waterfall.
You can double back or continue on the more difficult trail along the
valley wall for views over miles of treetops to the sea. ⌧ *47225 Hwy.
1, Big Sur* ☎ *831/667–2315* ⊕ *www.parks.ca.gov* ⤳ *$10 per vehicle.*

6

DID YOU KNOW?

McWay cove at Julia Pfeiffer Burns State Park is one of the most famous spots on the Big Sur Coast.

Point Sur State Historic Park. An 1889 lighthouse at this state park still stands watch from atop a large volcanic rock. Four lighthouse keepers lived here with their families until 1974, when the light station became automated. Their homes and working spaces are open to the public only on 2½- to 3-hour ranger-led tours. Considerable walking, including up two stairways, is involved. Strollers are not allowed. ⊠ *Hwy. 1, 7 miles north of Pfeiffer Big Sur State Park, Big Sur* 🕾 *831/625–4419* ⊕ *www.pointsur.org* 🎟 *$12* 🕾 *Call or visit website for current tour schedule.*

BEACHES
Pfeiffer Beach. Through a hole in one of the gigantic boulders at secluded Pfeiffer Beach, you can watch the waves break first on the seaside and then on the beach side. Keep a sharp eye out for the unsigned, non-gated road to the beach: it branches west of Highway 1 between the post office and Pfeiffer Big Sur State Park. The 2-mile, one-lane road descends sharply. **Amenities:** parking (fee); toilets. **Best for:** solitude; sunset. ⊠ *Off Hwy. 1, 1 mile south of Pfeiffer Big Sur State Park, Big Sur* 🎟 *$10 per vehicle.*

WHERE TO EAT

$$$
AMERICAN
Fodor's Choice
★

✕ **Deetjen's Big Sur Inn.** The candle-lighted, creaky-floor restaurant in the main house at the historic inn of the same name is a Big Sur institution. It serves spicy seafood paella, grass-fed filet mignon, and rack of lamb for dinner and flavorful eggs Benedict for breakfast. **Known for:** rustic, romantic setting; ingredients from sustainable purveyors; stellar weekend brunch. 💲 *Average main: $30* ⊠ *Hwy. 1, 3½ miles south of Pfeiffer Big Sur State Park, Big Sur* 🕾 *831/667–2378* ⊕ *www.deetjens. com* ⊗ *No lunch.*

$$$$
AMERICAN
Fodor's Choice
★

✕ **Nepenthe.** It may be that no other restaurant between San Francisco and Los Angeles has a better coastal view than Nepenthe, named for an opiate mentioned in Greek literature that would induce a state of "no sorrow." For the real show, settle on the terraced deck in the late afternoon, order a glass from the extensive wine list, and watch the sun slip into the Pacific Ocean. The food and drink are overpriced but good; there are burgers, sandwiches, and salads for lunch, and fresh fish and hormone-free steaks for dinner. **Known for:** ambrosia burger, fresh fish, hormone-free steaks; multiple view decks; brunch and lunch at casual outdoor Café Kevah. 💲 *Average main: $32* ⊠ *48510 Hwy. 1, 2½ miles south of Big Sur Station, Big Sur* 🕾 *831/667–2345* ⊕ *nepenthebigsur.com.*

$$$$
AMERICAN
Fodor's Choice
★

✕ **The Restaurant at Ventana.** The Ventana Inn's restaurant sits high on a ridge, and magnificent terraces offer stunning ocean views and a full-service outdoor bar. Regional and international wines on a comprehensive list pair well with the California-inspired dishes, many of whose ingredients are sourced from local purveyors, and the bar serves seasonal specialty cocktails and California craft beers. **Known for:** stunning views; local ingredients; excellent wine list. 💲 *Average main: $40* ⊠ *48123 Hwy. 1, 1½ miles south of Pfeiffer Big Sur State Park, Big Sur* 🕾 *831/667–4242* ⊕ *www.ventanainn.com.*

$$$$ · AMERICAN · **Fodor's**Choice · ★ · ✕ **Sierra Mar.** At cliff's edge 1,200 feet above the Pacific at the ultrachic Post Ranch Inn, Sierra Mar serves cutting-edge American cuisine made from mostly organic, seasonal ingredients, some from the on-site chef's garden. The four-course prix-fixe option always shines, and the nine-course Taste of Big Sur menu centers on ingredients grown or foraged on the property or sourced locally. **Known for:** stunning panoramic ocean views; one of the nation's most extensive wine lists; iconic Big Sur farm-to-table experience. $ *Average main: $125* ✉ *Hwy. 1, 1½ miles south of Pfeiffer Big Sur State Park, Big Sur* ☎ *831/667–2800* ⊕ *www. postranchinn.com/dining.*

WHERE TO STAY

$$$$ · HOTEL · ⛺ **Big Sur Lodge.** The lodge's modern, motel-style cottages with Mission-style furnishings and vaulted ceilings sit in a meadow surrounded by redwood trees and flowering shrubbery. **Pros:** secluded setting near trail-heads; good camping alternative; rates include state parks pass. **Cons:** basic rooms; walk to main lodge. $ *Rooms from: $309* ✉ *Pfeiffer Big Sur State Park, 47225 Hwy. 1, Big Sur* ☎ *831/667–3100, 800/424–4787* ⊕ *www.bigsurlodge.com* ⤳ *62 rooms* ⦿❘ *No meals.*

$$$ · B&B/INN · ⛺ **Big Sur River Inn.** During summer at this rustic property you can sip drinks beside—or in—the Big Sur River fronted by the inn's wooded grounds; if you're here on a Sunday afternoon between May and September you can enjoy live music on the restaurant's deck. **Pros:** riverside setting; next to a restaurant and small market; outdoor pool; recently renovated baths. **Cons:** standard rooms across the road; no phone in rooms. $ *Rooms from: $250* ✉ *Hwy. 1, 2 miles north of Pfeiffer Big Sur State Park, Big Sur* ☎ *831/667–2700, 831/667–2743, 800/548–3610* ⊕ *www.bigsurriverinn.com* ⤳ *22 rooms* ⦿❘ *No meals.*

$$ · B&B/INN · ⛺ **Deetjen's Big Sur Inn.** This historic 1930s Norwegian-style property is endearingly rustic, with its village of cabins nestled in the redwoods; many of the very individual rooms have their own fireplaces. **Pros:** tons of character; wooded grounds. **Cons:** thin walls; some rooms don't have private baths; no TVs or Wi-Fi, limited cell service. $ *Rooms from: $170* ✉ *Hwy. 1, 3½ miles south of Pfeiffer Big Sur State Park, Big Sur* ☎ *831/667–2377* ⊕ *www.deetjens.com* ⤳ *20 rooms, 15 with bath* ⦿❘ *No meals* ⤳ *2-night minimum stay on weekends.*

$$$$ · HOTEL · ⛺ **Glen Oaks Big Sur.** At this rustic-modern cluster of adobe-and-redwood buildings, you can choose between motel-style rooms, cabins, and cottages in the woods. **Pros:** in the heart of town; natural river-rock radiant-heated tiles; gas fireplaces in each room. **Cons:** near busy road and parking lot; no TVs. $ *Rooms from: $300* ✉ *Hwy. 1, 1 mile north of Pfeiffer Big Sur State Park, Big Sur* ☎ *831/667–2105* ⊕ *www.glenoaksbigsur.com* ⤳ *16 rooms, 2 cottages, 7 cabins* ⦿❘ *No meals.*

$$$$ · RESORT · **Fodor's**Choice · ★ · ⛺ **Post Ranch Inn.** This luxurious retreat is perfect for getaways; the redwood guesthouses, all of which have views of the sea or the mountains, blend almost invisibly into a wooded cliff 1,200 feet above the ocean. **Pros:** units come with fireplaces and private decks; on-site activities like yoga and stargazing; gorgeous property with hiking trails and spectacular views. **Cons:** expensive; austere design; not a good choice if you're afraid of heights. $ *Rooms from: $925* ✉ *Hwy.*

6

1, 1½ miles south of Pfeiffer Big Sur State Park, Big Sur ☎ *831/667–2200, 800/527–2200* 🌐 *www.postranchinn.com* 🛏 *39 rooms, 2 houses* 🍴 *Breakfast.*

$$$$ HOTEL Fodor's Choice ★ **Ventana.** Hundreds of celebrities, from Oprah Winfrey to Sir Anthony Hopkins, have escaped to Ventana, a romantic resort on 243 tranquil acres 1,200 feet above the Pacific. **Pros:** secluded; nature trails everywhere; rates include daily guided hike, yoga, wine and cheese hour. **Cons:** expensive; some rooms lack an ocean view; not family-friendly. [$] *Rooms from: $650* ✉ *Hwy. 1, almost 1 mile south of Pfeiffer Big Sur State Park, Big Sur* ☎ *831/667–2331, 800/628–6500* 🌐 *www.ventanainn.com* 🛏 *59 rooms* 🍴 *Breakfast.*

MONTEREY BAY AREA

from Carmel to Santa Cruz

WELCOME TO MONTEREY BAY AREA

TOP REASONS TO GO

★ **Marine life:** Monterey Bay is the location of the world's third-largest marine sanctuary, home to whales, otters, and other underwater creatures.

★ **Getaway central:** For more than a century, urbanites have come to the Monterey Bay area to unwind, relax, and have fun. It's a great place to browse unique shops and galleries, ride a giant roller coaster, or play a round of golf on a world-class course.

★ **Nature preserves:** More than the sea is protected here: the region boasts nearly 30 state parks, beaches, and preserves—fantastic places for walking, jogging, hiking, and biking.

★ **Wine and dine:** The area's rich agricultural bounty translates into abundant fresh produce, great wines, and fabulous dining. It's no wonder more than 300 culinary events take place here every year.

★ **Small-town vibes:** Even the cities here are friendly, walkable places where you'll feel like a local.

0 ____ 5 mi

0 ____ 5 km

Santa Cruz

17

9

1

4

1 Carmel and Pacific Grove. Exclusive Carmel-by-the-Sea and Carmel Valley Village burst with historic charm, fine dining, and unusual boutiques that cater to celebrity residents and well-heeled visitors. Nearby 17-Mile Drive—quite possibly the prettiest stretch of road you'll ever travel—runs between Carmel-by-the-Sea and Victorian-studded Pacific Grove, home to thousands of migrating monarch butterflies between October and February.

2 Monterey. A former Spanish military outpost, Monterey's well-preserved historic district is a hands-on history lesson. Cannery Row, the center of Monterey's once-thriving sardine industry, has been reborn as a tourist attraction with shops, restaurants, hotels, and the Monterey Bay Aquarium.

3 Around Monterey Bay. Much of California's lettuce, berries, artichokes, and brussels sprouts is grown in Salinas and other towns. Salinas is also home to the National Steinbeck Center, and Moss Landing encompasses pristine wildlife wetlands. Aptos, Capitola, and Soquel are former lumber towns that became popular seaside resorts more than a century ago. Today they're filled with antiques shops, restaurants, and wine-tasting rooms; you'll also find some of the bay's best beaches along the shore here.

4 Santa Cruz. Santa Cruz shows its colors along an old-time beach boardwalk and municipal wharf. A University of California campus imbues the town with arts and culture and a liberal mind-set.

GETTING ORIENTED

North of Big Sur the coastline softens into lower bluffs, windswept dunes, pristine estuaries, and long, sandy beaches, bordering one of the world's most amazing marine environments—Monterey Bay. On the Monterey Peninsula, at the southern end of the bay, are Carmel-by-the-Sea, Pacific Grove, and Monterey; Santa Cruz sits at the northern tip of the crescent. In between, Highway 1 cruises along the coastline, passing windswept beaches piled high with sand dunes. Along the route are wetlands and artichoke and strawberry fields.

7

Updated
by Cheryl
Crabtree

Natural beauty is at the heart of the Monterey Bay area's enormous appeal—it's everywhere, from the redwood-studded hillsides to the pristine shoreline with miles of walking paths and bluff-top vistas. Nature even takes center stage indoors at the world-famous Monterey Bay Aquarium, but history also draws visitors, most notably to Monterey's well-preserved waterfront district. Quaint, walkable towns and villages such as Carmel-by-the-Sea and Carmel Valley Village lure with smart restaurants and galleries, while sunny Aptos, Capitola, Soquel, and Santa Cruz, with miles of sand and surf, attract surfers and beach lovers.

Monterey Bay life centers on the ocean. The bay itself is protected by the Monterey Bay National Marine Sanctuary, the nation's largest undersea canyon—bigger and deeper than the Grand Canyon. On-the-water activities abound, from whale-watching and kayaking to sailing and surfing. Bay cruises from Monterey and Moss Landing almost always encounter other enchanting sea creatures, among them sea otters, sea lions, and porpoises.

Land-based activities include hiking, zip-lining in the redwood canopy, and wine tasting along urban and rural trails. Golf has been an integral part of the Monterey Peninsula's social and recreational scene since the Del Monte Golf Course opened in 1897. Pebble Beach's championship courses host prestigious tournaments, and though the greens fees at these courses can run up to $500, elsewhere on the peninsula you'll find less expensive options. And, of course, whatever activity you pursue, natural splendor appears at every turn.

PLANNING

WHEN TO GO

Summer is peak season; mild weather brings in big crowds. In this coastal region a cool breeze generally blows and fog often rolls in from offshore; you will frequently need a sweater or windbreaker. Off-season, from November through April, fewer people visit and the mood is mellower. Rainfall is heaviest in January and February. Fall and spring days are often clearer than those in summer.

GETTING HERE AND AROUND

AIR TRAVEL

Monterey Regional Airport, 3 miles east of downtown Monterey off Highway 68, is served by Alaska, Allegiant, American, and United. Taxi service costs from $20 to $22 to downtown, and from $28 to $37 to Carmel. Monterey Airbus service between the region and the San Jose and San Francisco airports starts at $40; the Early Bird Airport Shuttle costs from $85 to $195 ($205 from Oakland).

Airport Contacts Monterey Regional Airport (*MRY*). ✉ *200 Fred Kane Dr., at Olmsted Rd., off Hwy. 68, Monterey* ☎ *831/648-7000* ⊕ *www.montereyairport.com.*

Ground Transportation Central Coast Cab Company. ☎ *831/626-3333* ⊕ *www.centralcoastcab.com.* **Early Bird Airport Shuttle.** ☎ *831/462-3933* ⊕ *www.earlybirdairportshuttle.com.* **Monterey Airbus.** ☎ *831/373-7777* ⊕ *www.montereyairbus.com.* **Yellow Cab.** ☎ *831/333-1234.*

BUS TRAVEL

Greyhound serves Santa Cruz and Salinas from San Francisco and San Jose. The trips take about 3 and 4½ hours, respectively. Monterey-Salinas Transit (MST) provides frequent service in Monterey County (from $1.75 to $3.50; day pass $10), and Santa Cruz METRO ($2; day pass from $6 to $10) buses operate throughout Santa Cruz County. You can switch between the lines in Watsonville.

Bus Contacts Greyhound. ☎ *800/231-2222* ⊕ *www.greyhound.com.* **Monterey-Salinas Transit.** ☎ *888/678-2871* ⊕ *mst.org.* **Santa Cruz METRO.** ☎ *831/425-8600* ⊕ *scmtd.com.*

CAR TRAVEL

Highway 1 runs south–north along the coast, linking the towns of Carmel-by-the-Sea, Monterey, and Santa Cruz; some sections have only two lanes. The freeway, U.S. 101, lies to the east, roughly parallel to Highway 1. The two roads are connected by Highway 68 from Pacific Grove to Salinas; Highway 156 from Castroville to Prunedale; Highway 152 from Watsonville to Gilroy; and Highway 17 from Santa Cruz to San Jose. ■TIP→ Traffic near Santa Cruz can crawl to a standstill during commuter hours. In the morning, avoid traveling between 7 and 9; in the afternoon avoid traveling between 4 and 7.

The drive south from San Francisco to Monterey can be made comfortably in three hours or less. The most scenic way is to follow Highway 1 down the coast. A generally faster route is Interstate 280 south to Highway 85 to Highway 17 to Highway 1. The drive from the Los

Angeles area takes five or six hours. Take U.S. 101 to Salinas and head west on Highway 68. You can also follow Highway 1 up the coast.

TRAIN TRAVEL

Amtrak's *Coast Starlight* runs between Los Angeles, Oakland, and Seattle. You can also take the *Pacific Surfliner* to San Luis Obispo and connect to Amtrak buses to Salinas or San Jose. From the train station in Salinas you can connect with buses serving Carmel and Monterey, and from the train station in San Jose with buses to Santa Cruz.

Train Contacts Amtrak. ☎ *800/872-7245* ⊕ *pacificsurfliner.com.*

RESTAURANTS

The Monterey Bay area is a culinary paradise. The surrounding waters are full of fish, wild game roams the foothills, and the inland valleys are some of the most fertile in the country—local chefs draw on this bounty for their fresh, truly Californian cuisine. Except at beachside stands and inexpensive eateries, where anything goes, casual but neat dress is the norm. *Restaurant reviews have been shortened. For full information, visit Fodors.com.*

HOTELS

Accommodations in the Monterey area range from no-frills motels to luxurious hotels. Pacific Grove, amply endowed with ornate Victorian houses, is the region's bed-and-breakfast capital; Carmel also has charming inns. Lavish resorts cluster in exclusive Pebble Beach and pastoral Carmel Valley.

High season runs from May through October. Rates in winter, especially at the larger hotels, may drop by 50% or more, and smaller inns often offer midweek specials. Whatever the month, some properties require a two-night stay on weekends. *Hotel reviews have been shortened. For full information, visit Fodors.com.* ■TIP➜ Many of the fancier accommodations aren't suitable for children; if you're traveling with kids, ask before you book.

WHAT IT COSTS			
	$	$$	$$$	$$$$
Restaurants	under $16	$16–$22	$23–$30	over $30
Hotels	under $120	$120–$175	$176–$250	over $250

Restaurant prices are the average cost of a main course at dinner or, if dinner is not served, at lunch, excluding sales tax of 8¼%–9½% (depending on location). Hotel prices are the lowest cost of a standard double room in high season, excluding service charges and 10%–10½% tax.

TOUR OPTIONS

Ag Venture Tours & Consulting. Crowd-pleasing half- and full-day wine tasting, sightseeing, and agricultural tours are Ag Venture's specialty. Tastings are at Monterey and Santa Cruz Mountains wineries; sightseeing opportunities include the Monterey Peninsula, Big Sur, and Santa Cruz; and the agricultural forays take in the Salinas and Pajaro valleys. Customized itineraries can be arranged. ☎ *831/761–8463* ⊕ *agventure-tours.com* ✉ *From $85 (day) and $363 (overnight).*

California Parlor Car Tours. This outfit operates motor-coach tours from San Francisco that include one or two days in Monterey and Carmel. The company's three-day San Francisco–Los Angeles tours include stops in Monterey and Carmel. ☎ *415/474–7500, 800/227–4250* ⊕ *www. californiaparlorcar.com* ✉ *From $80 (day) and $267 (overnight).*

Monterey Guided Wine Tours. The company's guides lead customized wine tours in Monterey, and Carmel Valley, along with the Santa Lucia Highlands, the Santa Cruz Mountains, and the Paso Robles area. Tours, which typically last from four to six hours, take place in a town car, a stretch limo, or a party bus. ☎ *831/920–2792* ⊕ *montereyguidedwinetours.com* ✉ *From $85.*

VISITOR INFORMATION

Contacts Monterey County Convention & Visitors Bureau. ☎ *888/221–1010* ⊕ *www.seemonterey.com.* **Monterey Wine Country.** ☎ *831/375–9400* ⊕ *www. montereywines.org.* **Santa Cruz County Conference & Visitors Council.** ✉ *303 Water St., No. 100, Santa Cruz* ☎ *831/425–1234, 800/833–3494* ⊕ *santacruz. org.* **Santa Cruz Mountains Winegrowers Association.** ✉ *725 Front St., No. 112, Santa Cruz* ☎ *831/685–8463* ⊕ *www.scmwa.com.*

CARMEL AND PACIFIC GROVE

As Highway 1 swings inland about 30 miles north of Big Sur, historic Carmel-by-the Sea anchors the southern entry to the Monterey Peninsula—a gorgeous promontory at the southern tip of Monterey Bay. Just north of Carmel along the coast, the legendary 17-Mile Drive wends its way through private Pebble Beach and the town of Pacific Grove. Highway 1 skirts the peninsula to the east with more direct access to Pebble Beach and Pacific Grove.

CARMEL-BY-THE-SEA

26 miles north of Big Sur.

Even when its population quadruples with tourists on weekends and in summer, Carmel-by-the-Sea, commonly referred to as Carmel, retains its identity as a quaint village. Self-consciously charming, the town is populated by many celebrities, major and minor, and has its share of quirky ordinances. For instance, women wearing high heels do not have the right to pursue legal action if they trip and fall on the cobblestone streets, and drivers who hit a tree and leave the scene are charged with hit-and-run.

Buildings have no street numbers—street names are written on discreet white posts—and consequently no mail delivery. One way to commune with the locals: head to the post office. Artists started this community, and their legacy is evident in the numerous galleries.

GETTING HERE AND AROUND

From north or south follow Highway 1 to Carmel. Head west at Ocean Avenue to reach the main village hub.

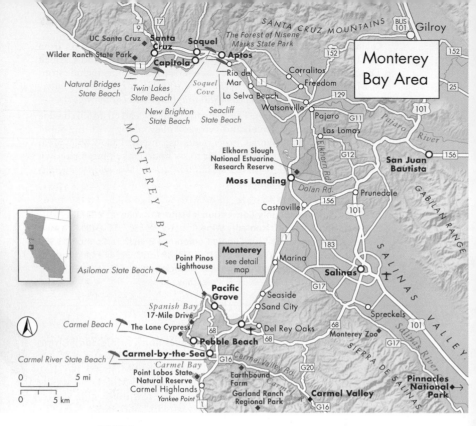

TOURS

Carmel Walks. For insight into Carmel's history and culture, join one of these guided two-hour ambles through hidden courtyards, gardens, and pathways. Tours depart from the Pine Inn courtyard, on Lincoln Street. Call to reserve a spot. ✉ *Lincoln St. at 6th Ave., Carmel* ☎ *888/284–8405 reservations, 831/373–2813 group reservations* ⊕ *carmelwalks. com* ✉ *From $30.*

ESSENTIALS

Visitor Information Carmel Chamber of Commerce. ✉ *Visitor Center, in Carmel Plaza, Ocean Ave. between Junipero and Mission Sts., Carmel* ☎ *831/624–2522, 800/550–4333* ⊕ *carmelchamber.org.*

EXPLORING

TOP ATTRACTIONS

Carmel Mission. Long before it became a shopping and browsing destination, Carmel was an important religious center during the establishment of Spanish California. That heritage is preserved in the Mission San Carlos Borroméo del Rio Carmelo, more commonly known as the Carmel Mission. Founded in 1771, it served as headquarters for the mission system in California under Father Junípero Serra. Adjoining the stone church is a tranquil garden planted with California poppies. Museum rooms at the mission include an early kitchen, Serra's spartan sleeping quarters and burial shrine, and the first college library in California. ✉ *3080 Rio Rd., at Lasuen Dr., Carmel* ☎ *831/624–1271* ⊕ *carmelmission.org* 🗨 *$6.50.*

Fodor'sChoice **Ocean Avenue.** Downtown Carmel's chief lure is shopping, especially
★ along its main street, Ocean Avenue, between Junipero Avenue and Camino Real. The architecture here is a mishmash of ersatz Tudor, Mediterranean, and other styles. ✉ *Carmel.*

Fodor'sChoice **Point Lobos State Natural Reserve.** A 350-acre headland harboring a
★ wealth of marine life, the reserve lies a few miles south of Carmel. The best way to explore here is to walk along one of the many trails. The Cypress Grove Trail leads through a forest of Monterey cypress (one of only two natural groves remaining) that clings to the rocks above an emerald-green cove. Sea Lion Point Trail is a good place to view sea lions. From those and other trails, you might also spot otters, harbor seals, and (in winter and spring) migrating whales. An additional 750 acres of the reserve is an undersea marine park open to qualified scuba divers. No pets are allowed. ■**TIP➔ Arrive early (or in late afternoon) to avoid crowds; the parking lots fill up.** ✉ *Hwy. 1, Carmel* ☎ *831/624–4909, 831/624–8413 water sports reservations* ⊕ *www.pointlobos.org* 🗨 *$10 per vehicle.*

WORTH NOTING

Carmel Wine Walk By-the-Sea. If you purchase a Wine Walk Passport, you can park the car and sample local wines at any 10 of 14 tasting rooms, all within a few blocks of each other in downtown Carmel. Individual passports can be used by two or more people at the same tasting room, and they entitle holders to free corkage at some local restaurants. ✉ *Carmel Chamber of Commerce Visitor Center, San Carlos St., between 5th and 6th Aves., Carmel* ☎ *831/624–2522, 800/550–4333* ⊕ *www.carmelchamber.org/store/wine-walk-by-the-sea* 🗨 *$100.*

Dawson Cole Fine Art. Amazing images of dancers, athletes, and other humans in motion come to life in this gallery that is devoted to the artworks of Monterey Bay resident Richard MacDonald, one of the most famed figurative sculptors of our time. ✉ *Lincoln St., at 6th Ave., Carmel* ☎ *800/972–5528* ⊕ *dawsoncolefineart.com* 🗨 *Free.*

Tor House. Scattered throughout the pines of Carmel-by-the-Sea are houses and cottages originally built for the writers, artists, and photographers who discovered the area decades ago. Among the most impressive dwellings is Tor House, a stone cottage built in 1919 by poet Robinson Jeffers on a craggy knoll overlooking the sea. Portraits, books, and unusual art objects fill the low-ceilinged rooms. The highlight of the small estate is Hawk Tower, a detached edifice set with stones from the Carmel coastline—as well as one from the Great Wall of China. The docents who lead tours (six people maximum) are well informed about the poet's work and life. Reservations are required. Call the reservation line or click on the reservation link on the website. ✉ *26304 Ocean View Ave., Carmel* ☎ *844/285–0244, 831/624–1840 direct docent office line, Fri. and Sat. only* ⊕ *www.torhouse.org* 🗨 *$12* ☞ *No children under 12.*

7

BEACHES

Carmel Beach. Carmel-by-the-Sea's greatest attraction is its rugged coastline, with pine and cypress forests and countless inlets. Carmel Beach, an easy walk from downtown shops, has sparkling white sands and magnificent sunsets. **■TIP→ Dogs are allowed to romp off-leash here.** **Amenities:** parking (no fee); toilets. **Best for:** sunset; surfing; walking. ✉ *End of Ocean Ave., Carmel.*

Carmel River State Beach. This sugar-white beach, stretching 106 acres along Carmel Bay, is adjacent to a bird sanctuary, where you might spot pelicans, kingfishers, hawks, and sandpipers. Dogs are allowed on leash. **Amenities:** parking (no fee); toilets. **Best for:** sunrise; sunset; walking. ✉ *Off Scenic Rd., south of Carmel Beach, Carmel* ☎ *831/649–2836* 🌐 *www.parks.ca.gov* 🎟 *Free.*

WHERE TO EAT

$$$$ EUROPEAN

🍴 **Anton and Michel.** Carefully prepared European cuisine is the draw at this airy restaurant. The rack of lamb is carved at the table, the grilled halloumi cheese and tomatoes are meticulously stacked and served with basil and Kalamata olive tapenade, and the desserts are set aflame before your eyes. **Known for:** romantic courtyard with fountain; elegant interior with fireplace lounge; flambé desserts. [$] *Average main: $32* ✉ *Mission St. and 7th Ave., Carmel* ☎ *831/624–2406* 🌐 *antonandmichel.com.*

$$$$ AMERICAN Fodor's Choice ★

🍴 **Aubergine.** To eat and sleep at luxe L'Auberge Carmel is an experience in itself, but even those staying elsewhere can splurge at the inn's intimate restaurant. Chef Justin Cogley's eight-course prix-fixe tasting menu (your only option at dinner, $150 per person) is a gastronomical experience unrivaled in the region. **Known for:** exceptional chef's choice tasting menu; expert wine pairings; intimate 12-table dining room. [$] *Average main: $150* ✉ *Monte Verde at 7th Ave., Carmel* ☎ *831/624–8578* 🌐 *auberginecarmel.com* 🕒 *No lunch.*

$$$ MODERN AMERICAN Fodor's Choice ★

🍴 **Basil.** Eco-friendly Basil was Monterey County's first restaurant to achieve a green dining certification, recognition of chef-owner Soerke Peters's commitment to using organic, sustainably cultivated ingredients in his cuisine. Peters grows many of his own herbs, which find their way into creative dishes such as black squid linguine with sea urchin sauce, creamy duck liver–pear pâté, and smoked venison and other housemade charcuterie. **Known for:** organic ingredients; creative cocktails; year-round patio dining. [$] *Average main: $25* ✉ *Paseo Square, San Carlos St., between Ocean Ave. and 7th Ave., Carmel* ☎ *831/636–8226* 🌐 *basilcarmel.com.*

$$$$ MEDITERRANEAN

🍴 **Casanova.** This restaurant inspires European-style celebration and romance: accordions hang from the walls, and tiny party lights flicker along the low ceilings. Dishes from southern France and northern Italy—osso buco, Wagyu beef tartare—predominate. **Known for:** housemade pastas and gnocchi; private dining at antique Van Gogh's table; romantic candlelight dining room. [$] *Average main: $32* ✉ *5th Ave., between San Carlos and Mission Sts., Carmel* ☎ *831/625–0501* 🌐 *www.casanovarestaurant.com.*

$ AMERICAN

🍴 **The Cottage Restaurant.** This family-friendly spot serves sandwiches, pizzas, and homemade soups at lunch, but the best meal is breakfast (good thing it's served all day). The menu offers six variations on eggs

Point Lobos State Natural Reserve offers stunning vistas of sea and sky.

Benedict, and all kinds of sweet and savory crepes. **Known for:** artichoke soup; eggs Benedict and crepes; daily specials. [$] *Average main: $15* ✉ *Lincoln St. between Ocean and 7th Aves., Carmel* ☎ *831/625–6260* 🌐 *cottagerestaurant.com* 🕒 *No dinner.*

$$$$ AMERICAN 🍴 **Grasing's Coastal Cuisine.** Chef Kurt Grasing draws from fresh Carmel Coast and Central Valley ingredients to whip up contemporary adaptations of European-provincial and American cooking. Longtime menu favorites include artichoke lasagna in a roasted tomato sauce, duck with fresh cherries in a red wine sauce, a savory paella, and grilled steaks and chops. **Known for:** artichoke heart lasagne; grilled steaks; sophisticated setting. [$] *Average main: $39* ✉ *6th Ave. and Mission St., Carmel* ☎ *831/612–0082* 🌐 *grasings.com.*

$$ TAPAS 🍴 **Mundaka.** The traditional Spanish-style tapas, made with fresh local ingredients, and the full bar attract legions of locals to this downtown spot. Longtime favorites include the chorizo slider with truffle fries, the authentic Valencian paella, and a charcuterie platter made in-house. **Known for:** Spanish-style tapas; live music; Valencian paella. [$] *Average main: $22* ✉ *San Carlos St., between Ocean and 7th Aves., Carmel* ☎ *831/624–7400* 🌐 *www.mundakacarmel.com.*

$$$ ITALIAN 🍴 **Vesuvio.** Chef and restaurateur Rich Pèpe heats up the night with this lively trattoria downstairs and swinging rooftop terrace, the Starlight Lounge 65°. Pèpe's elegant take on traditional Italian cuisine yields dishes such as wild-boar Bolognese pappardelle, lobster ravioli, and velvety limoncello mousse cake. **Known for:** traditional cuisine of Campania, Italy; popular gathering spot; live music on rooftop terrace in summer. [$] *Average main: $28* ✉ *6th and Junipero Aves., Carmel* ☎ *831/625–1766* 🌐 *vesuviocarmel.com* 🕒 *No lunch.*

WHERE TO STAY

$$$$ B&B/INN **Cypress Inn.** This luxurious inn has a fresh Mediterranean ambience with Moroccan touches. **Pros:** luxury without snobbery; popular lounge and restaurant; British-style afternoon tea on weekends. **Cons:** not for the pet-phobic. [$] *Rooms from: $279* ✉ *Lincoln St. and 7th Ave., Carmel* ☎ *831/624–3871, 800/443–7443* 🌐 *cypress-inn.com* 🛏 *44 rooms* 🍴 *Breakfast.*

$$$$ HOTEL **The Hideaway.** On a quiet street with a residential vibe, The Hideway is a peaceful haven for those seeking stylish comfort in the heart of town. **Pros:** easy walk to shops, restaurants, galleries; recently refurbished; short walk to Carmel Beach; pet-friendly amenities. **Cons:** street parking only; no pool or hot tub. [$] *Rooms from: $295* ✉ *Junipero St. at 8th Ave., Carmel* ☎ *831/625–5222* 🌐 *hideawaycarmel.com* 🛏 *24 rooms* 🍴 *Breakfast.*

$$$$ HOTEL **Hyatt Carmel Highlands.** High on a hill overlooking the Pacific, this place has superb views; accommodations include king rooms with fireplaces, suites with personal Jacuzzis, and full town houses with many perks. **Pros:** killer views; romantic getaway; great food. **Cons:** thin walls; must drive to Carmel. [$] *Rooms from: $399* ✉ *120 Highlands Dr., Carmel* ☎ *831/620–1234, 800/233–1234* 🌐 *carmelhighlands.hyatt.com* 🛏 *48 rooms.*

$$$$ B&B/INN Fodor's Choice ★ **L'Auberge Carmel.** Stepping through the doors of this elegant inn is like being transported to a little European village. **Pros:** in town but off the main drag; four blocks from the beach; full-service luxury. **Cons:** touristy area; not a good choice for families. [$] *Rooms from: $465* ✉ *Monte Verde at 7th Ave., Carmel* ☎ *831/624–8578* 🌐 *www.laubergecarmel.com* 🛏 *20 rooms* 🍴 *Breakfast.*

$$$$ HOTEL **La Playa Carmel.** A historic complex of lush gardens and Mediterranean-style buildings, La Playa has light and airy interiors done in Carmel Bay beach-cottage style. **Pros:** residential neighborhood; manicured gardens; two blocks from the beach. **Cons:** four stories (no elevator); busy lobby; some rooms are on the small side. [$] *Rooms from: $458* ✉ *Camino Real at 8th Ave., Carmel* ☎ *831/293–6100, 800/582–8900* 🌐 *laplayahotel.com* 🛏 *75 rooms* 🍴 *Breakfast.*

$$ HOTEL **Mission Ranch.** Movie star Clint Eastwood owns this sprawling property whose accommodations include rooms in a converted barn, and several cottages, some with fireplaces. **Pros:** farm setting; pastoral views; great for tennis buffs. **Cons:** busy parking lot; must drive to the heart of town. [$] *Rooms from: $175* ✉ *26270 Dolores St., Carmel* ☎ *831/624–6436, 800/538–8221, 831/625–9040 restaurant* 🌐 *www.missionranchcarmel.com* 🛏 *31 rooms* 🍴 *Breakfast.*

$$$$ B&B/INN **Tickle Pink Inn.** Atop a towering cliff, this inn has views of the Big Sur coastline, which you can contemplate from your private balcony. **Pros:** close to great hiking; intimate; dramatic views. **Cons:** close to a big hotel; lots of traffic during the day. [$] *Rooms from: $309* ✉ *155 Highland Dr., Carmel* ☎ *831/624–1244, 800/635–4774* 🌐 *ticklepink.com* 🛏 *33 rooms, 1 cottage* 🍴 *Breakfast.*

$$$ B&B/INN **Tradewinds Carmel.** This converted motel with sleek decor inspired by the South Seas encircles a courtyard with waterfalls, a meditation garden, and a fire pit. **Pros:** serene; within walking distance of restaurants;

friendly service. **Cons:** no pool; long walk to the beach. [$] *Rooms from: $250* ✉ *Mission St. at 3rd Ave., Carmel* ☎ *831/624–2776* 🌐 *tradewinds-carmel.com* 🛏 *28 rooms* 🍴 *Breakfast.*

NIGHTLIFE

BARS AND PUBS

Barmel. Al Capone and other Prohibition-era legends once sidled up to this hip nightspot's carved wooden bar. Rock to DJ music and sit indoors, or head out to the pet-friendly patio. Some menu items pay homage to California's early days, and you can order Spanish tapas and wines from the adjacent Mundaka restaurant, which is under the same ownership. ✉ *San Carlos St., between Ocean and 7th Aves., Carmel* ☎ *831/626–2095* 🌐 *www.mundakacarmel.com.*

Mulligan Public House. A sports bar with seven TV screens, 12 beers on tap, and extensive menu packed with hearty American pub food, Mulligan usually stays open until midnight. ✉ *5 Dolores St., at Ocean* ☎ *831/250–5910* 🌐 *mulliganspublichouse.com.*

SHOPPING

ART GALLERIES

Carmel Art Association. Carmel's oldest gallery, established in 1927, exhibits original paintings and sculptures by local artists. ✉ *Dolores St., between 5th and 6th Aves., Carmel* ☎ *831/624–6176* 🌐 *carmelart.org.*

Galerie Plein Aire. The gallery showcases the oil paintings of a group of local artists. ✉ *Dolores St., between Ocean and 6th Aves., Carmel* ☎ *831/277–6165* 🌐 *galeriepleinaire.com* 🕒 *Closed Tues.*

Gallery Sur. Fine art photography of the Big Sur Coast and the Monterey Peninsula, including scenic shots and golf images, is the focus here. ✉ *6th Ave., between Dolores and Lincoln Sts., Carmel* ☎ *831/626–2615* 🌐 *gallerysur.com.*

Fodor's Choice ★ **Weston Gallery.** Run by the family of the late Edward Weston, this is hands down the best photography gallery around, with contemporary color photography and classic black-and-whites. ✉ *6th Ave., between Dolores and Lincoln Sts., Carmel* ☎ *831/624–4453* 🌐 *westongallery.com* 🕒 *Closed Mon.*

MALLS

Carmel Plaza. Tiffany & Co. and J. Crew are among the name brands doing business at this mall on Carmel's east side, but what makes it worth a stop are homegrown enterprises such as Blue Lemon, for artsy, handcrafted clothing and jewelry; Madrigal for women's fashion; and J. Lawrence Khaki's for debonair menswear. Flying Fish Grill and several other restaurants are here, along with the Wrath Wines tasting room (Chardonnay and Pinot Noir). The Carmel Chamber of Commerce Visitor Center (open daily) is on the second floor. ✉ *Ocean Ave. and Mission St., Carmel* ☎ *831/624–1385* 🌐 *carmelplaza.com.*

SPECIALTY SHOPS

Bittner. The shop carries collectible and vintage pens from around the world. ✉ *Ocean Ave., between Mission and San Carlos Sts., Carmel* ☎ *831/626–8828* 🌐 *bittner.com.*

elizabethW. Named after the designer and owner's pioneering great-grandmother, elizabethW handcrafts fragrances, essential oils, candles, silk eye pillows, and other soul-soothing goods for bath, body, and home. ⊠ *Ocean Ave., between Monte Verde and Lincoln, Carmel* ☎ *831/626–3892* ⊕ *elizabethw.com.*

Foxy Couture. Shop for one-of-a-kind treasures at this curated collection of gently used luxury couture and vintage clothes and accessories—think Chanel, Hermes, and Gucci—without paying a hefty price tag. ⊠ *San Carlos St., in Vanervort Court, between Ocean and 7th Aves., Carmel* ☎ *831/625–9995* ⊕ *foxycouturecarmel.com.*

Jan de Luz. This shop monograms and embroiders fine linens (including bathrobes) while you wait. ⊠ *Dolores St., between Ocean and 7th Aves., Carmel* ☎ *831/622–7621* ⊕ *www.jandeluz.com.*

CARMEL VALLEY

10 miles east of Carmel.

Carmel Valley Road, which heads inland from Highway 1 south of Carmel, is the main thoroughfare through this valley, a secluded enclave of horse ranchers and other well-heeled residents who prefer the area's sunny climate to coastal fog and wind. Once thick with dairy farms, the valley has evolved into an esteemed wine appellation. Carmel Valley Village has crafts shops, art galleries, and the tasting rooms of numerous local wineries.

GETTING HERE AND AROUND

From U.S. 101 north or south, exit at Highway 68 and head west toward the coast. Scenic, two-lane Laureles Grade winds west over the mountains to Carmel Valley Road north of the village.

TOURS

Carmel Valley Grapevine Express. An incredible bargain, the express—aka MST's Bus 24—travels between downtown Monterey and Carmel Valley Village, with stops near wineries, restaurants, and shopping centers. ☎ *888/678–2871* ⊕ *mst.org* 🚍 *$10 all-day pass.*

EXPLORING
TOP ATTRACTIONS

Bernardus Tasting Room. At the tasting room of Bernardus, known for its Bordeaux-style red blend, called Marinus, and Chardonnays, you can sample current releases and library and reserve wines. ⊠ *5 W. Carmel Valley Rd., at El Caminito Rd.* ☎ *831/298–8021, 800/223–2533* ⊕ *bernardus.com* 🚍 *Tastings $12–$20.*

Cowgirl Winery. Cowgirl chic prevails in the main tasting building here, and it's just plain rustic at the outdoor tables, set amid chickens, a tractor, and a flatbed truck. The wines include Chardonnay, Cabernet Sauvignon, Rosé, and some blends. You can order a wood-fired pizza from sister business Corkscrew Café, and play boccie ball, horseshoes, or corn hole until your food arrives. ⊠ *25 Pilot Rd., off W. Carmel Valley Rd.* ☎ *831/298–7030* ⊕ *cowgirlwinery.com* 🚍 *Tasting $15.*

Fodor'sChoice ★ **Folktale Winery & Vineyards.** The expansive winery on a 15-acre estate (formerly Chateau Julienne) offers daily tastings, live music on weekends (plus Friday in summer and fall), and special events and programs such as Saturday yoga in the vineyard. Best-known wines include the estate Pinot Noir, Sparkling Rosé, and Le Mistral Joseph's Blend. Celebrity chef Todd Fisher cooks up small plates with wine pairing suggestions at the on-site restaurant. Tours of the winery and organically farmed vineyards are available by appointment. ✉ *8940 Carmel Valley Rd.* ✥ *At Schetter Rd.* ☎ *831/293–7500* 🌐 *folktalewinery.com* 🎫 *Tastings $20–$25.*

Holman Ranch Vineyards Tasting Room. Estate-grown Pinot Gris and Pinot Noir are among the standout wines made by Holman Ranch, which operates a tasting room in Carmel Valley village. If the Heather's Hill Pinot is being poured, be sure to try it. The ranch itself occupies rolling hills once part of the Carmel mission's land grant. You can book winery and vineyard tours by appointment, and the ranch welcomes overnight guests at its 10-room hacienda. ✉ *19 E. Carmel Valley Rd., Suite C* ☎ *831/659–2640* 🌐 *holmanranch.com* 🎫 *Tastings $8–$12.*

WORTH NOTING

FAMILY **Earthbound Farm.** Pick up fresh vegetables, ready-to-eat meals, gourmet groceries, flowers, and gifts at Earthbound Farm, the world's largest grower of organic produce. You can also take a romp in the kids' garden, cut your own herbs, and stroll through the chamomile aromatherapy labyrinth. Special events, on Saturday from April through December, include bug walks and garlic-braiding workshops. ✉ *7250 Carmel Valley Rd., Carmel* ☎ *831/625–6219* 🌐 *www.ebfarm.com* 🎫 *Free.*

Garland Ranch Regional Park. Hiking trails stretch across much of this park's 4,500 acres of meadows, forested hillsides, and creeks. ✉ *Carmel Valley Rd., 9 miles east of Carmel-by-the-Sea* ☎ *831/659–4488* 🌐 *www.mprpd.org.*

WHERE TO EAT

$$$ EUROPEAN 🍴 **Café Rustica.** European country cooking is the focus at this lively roadhouse. Specialties include roasted meats, seafood, pastas, and thin-crust pizzas from the wood-fired oven. **Known for:** Tuscan-flavored dishes from Alsace; open kitchen with wood-fired oven; outdoor patio seating. [$] *Average main: $24* ✉ *10 Delfino Pl., at Pilot Rd., off Carmel Valley Rd.* ☎ *831/659–4444* 🌐 *caferusticavillage.com* 🕒 *Closed Mon.*

$$ MODERN AMERICAN 🍴 **Corkscrew Café.** Farm-fresh food is the specialty of this casual, Old Monterey–style bistro. Herbs and seasonal produce come from the Corkscrew's own organic gardens; the catch of the day comes from local waters; and the meats are hormone-free. **Known for:** woodfired pizzas; fish tacos; antique corkscrew collection. [$] *Average main: $22* ✉ *55 W. Carmel Valley Rd., at Pilot Rd.* ☎ *831/659–8888* 🌐 *corkscrewcafe.com.*

WHERE TO STAY

$$$$ RESORT Fodor's Choice ★ 🏨 **Bernardus Lodge & Spa.** The spacious guest rooms at this luxury spa resort, have vaulted ceilings, French oak floors, featherbeds, fireplaces, patios, and bathrooms with heated-tile floors and soaking tubs for two. **Pros:** exceptional personal service; outstanding food and wine. **Cons:** pricey; some guests can seem snooty. [$] *Rooms from: $475* ✉ *415 W. Carmel Valley Rd.* ☎ *831/658–3400* 🌐 *bernarduslodge.com* 🛏 *73 rooms and villas.*

7

$$$$ RESORT Fodor's Choice ★ **Carmel Valley Ranch.** The activity options at this luxury ranch are so varied that the resort provides a program director to guide you through them. **Pros:** stunning natural setting; tons of activities; state-of-the-art amenities. **Cons:** must drive several miles to shops and nightlife; pricey. [$] *Rooms from: $400* ✉ *1 Old Ranch Rd., Carmel* ☎ *831/625–9500, 855/687–7262 toll free reservations* 🌐 *carmelvalleyranch.com* 🛏 *181 suites* 🍴 *No meals.*

$$$ HOTEL FAMILY **Quail Lodge & Golf Club.** A sprawling collection of ranch-style buildings on 850 acres of meadows, fairways, and lakes, Quail Lodge offers luxury rooms and outdoor activities at surprisingly affordable rates. **Pros:** on the golf course; on-site restaurant. **Cons:** extra fees for athletic passes and some services; 5 miles from the beach and Carmel Valley Village. [$] *Rooms from: $195* ✉ *8205 Valley Greens Dr., Carmel* ☎ *866/675–1101 reservations, 831/624–2888* 🌐 *www.quaillodge.com* 🛏 *93 rooms* 🍴 *No meals.*

$$$$ RESORT Fodor's Choice ★ **Stonepine Estate Resort.** Set on 330 pastoral acres, the former estate of the Crocker banking family has been converted to a luxurious inn. **Pros:** supremely exclusive. **Cons:** difficult to get a reservation; far from the coast. [$] *Rooms from: $300* ✉ *150 E. Carmel Valley Rd.* ☎ *831/659–2245* 🌐 *www.stonepineestate.com* 🛏 *12 rooms, 3 cottages.*

SPORTS AND THE OUTDOORS

GOLF

Quail Lodge & Golf Club. Robert Muir Graves designed this championship semiprivate 18-hole course next to Quail Lodge that provides challenging play for golfers of all skill levels. The scenic course, which incorporates five lakes and edges the Carmel River, was completely renovated in 2015 by golf architect Todd Eckenrode to add extra challenge to the golf experience, white sand bunkers, and other enhancements. For the most part flat, the walkable course is well maintained, with stunning views, lush fairways, and ultrasmooth greens. ✉ *8000 Valley Greens Dr., Carmel* ☎ *831/620–8808 golf shop, 831/620–8866 club concierge* 🌐 *www.quaillodge.com* 🎟 *$185* ⛳ *18 holes, 6500 yards, par 71.*

SPAS

Fodor's Choice ★ **Refuge.** At this co-ed, European-style center on 2 serene acres you can recharge without breaking the bank. Heat up in the eucalyptus steam room or cedar sauna, plunge into cold pools, and relax indoors in zero-gravity chairs or outdoors in Adirondack chairs around fire pits. Repeat the cycle a few times, then lounge around the thermal waterfall pools. Talk is not allowed, and bathing suits are required. ✉ *27300 Rancho San Carlos Rd., south off Carmel Valley Rd., Carmel* ☎ *831/620–7360* 🌐 *refuge.com* 🎟 *$44* ☞ *$46 admission; $125 50-min massage (includes Refuge admission), $12 robe rental, hot tubs (outdoor), sauna, steam room. Services: Aromatherapy, hydrotherapy, massage.*

PEBBLE BEACH

Off North San Antonio Ave. in Carmel-by-the-Sea or off Sunset Dr. in Pacific Grove.

Fodor'sChoice
★
In 1919 the Pacific Improvement Company acquired 18,000 acres of prime land on the Monterey Peninsula, including the entire Pebble Beach coastal region and much of Pacific Grove. Pebble Beach Golf Links and The Lodge at Pebble Beach opened the same year, and the private enclave evolved into a world-class golf destination with three posh lodges, five golf courses, hiking and riding trails, and some of the West Coast's ritziest homes. Pebble Beach has hosted major international golf tournaments and will host the U.S. Open in 2019. The annual Pebble Beach Food & Wine, a four-day event in late April with 100 celebrity chefs, is one of the West Coast's premier culinary festivals.

GETTING HERE AND AROUND

If you drive south from Monterey on Highway 1, exit at 17-Mile Drive/Sunset Drive in Pacific Grove to find the northern entrance gate. Coming from Carmel, exit at Ocean Avenue and follow the road almost to the beach; turn right on North San Antonio Avenue to the Carmel Gate. You can also enter through the Highway 1 Gate off Highway 68. Monterey–Salinas Transit buses provide regular service in and around Pebble Beach.

EXPLORING

Fodor'sChoice
★
The Lone Cypress. The most-photographed tree along 17-Mile Drive is the weather-sculpted Lone Cypress, which grows out of a precipitous outcropping above the waves about 1½ miles up the road from Pebble Beach Golf Links. You can't walk out to the tree, but you can stop for a view of it at a small parking area off the road.

Fodor'sChoice
★
17-Mile Drive. Primordial nature resides in quiet harmony with palatial, mostly Spanish Mission–style estates along 17-Mile Drive, which winds through an 8,400-acre microcosm of the Pebble Beach coastal landscape. Dotting the drive are rare Monterey cypresses, trees so gnarled and twisted that Robert Louis Stevenson described them as "ghosts fleeing before the wind." The most famous of these is the **Lone Cypress.** Other highlights include **Bird Rock** and **Seal Rock,** home to harbor seals, sea lions, cormorants, and pelicans and other sea creatures and birds, and the **Crocker Marble Palace,** inspired by a Byzantine castle and easily identifiable by its dozens of marble arches.

Enter 17-Mile Drive at the Highway 1 Gate, at Highway 68; the Carmel Gate, off North San Antonio Avenue; the Pacific Grove Gate, off Sunset Drive; S.F.B. Morse Gate, Morse Drive off Highway 68; and Country Club Gate, at Congress Avenue and Forest Lodge Road. ■ **TIP→ If you spend $30 or more on dining or shopping in Pebble Beach and show a receipt upon exiting, you'll receive a refund off the drive's $10 per car fee.** ⊠ *Hwy. 1 Gate, 17-Mile Dr., west of Hwy. 1 and Hwy. 68 intersection* ⌨ *$10 per car, free for bicyclists.*

7

WHERE TO STAY

$$$$
RESORT
Fodor'sChoice
★

Casa Palmero. This exclusive boutique hotel evokes a stately Mediterranean villa. **Pros:** ultimate in pampering; sumptuous decor; more private than sister resorts; right on the golf course. **Cons:** pricey; may be *too* posh for some. *$ Rooms from: $975 ⊠1518 Cypress Dr. ☎831/622–6650, 866/508–9268 reservations ⊕ www.pebblebeach. com ⤸ 24 rooms ❚❍❙ Breakfast.*

$$$$
RESORT

The Inn at Spanish Bay. This resort sprawls across a breathtaking stretch of shoreline, and has lush, 600-square-foot rooms. **Pros:** attentive service; many amenities; spectacular views. **Cons:** huge hotel; 4 miles from other Pebble Beach Resorts facilities. *$ Rooms from: $720 ⊠2700 17-Mile Dr. ☎831/647–7500, 866/508–9268 ⊕ www.pebble-beach.com ⤸ 269 rooms.*

$$$$
RESORT

The Lodge at Pebble Beach. Most rooms have wood-burning fireplaces and many have wonderful ocean views at this circa-1919 resort, which expanded to include Fairway One, an additional 38-room complex, in August 2017. **Pros:** world-class golf; borders the ocean and fairways; fabulous facilities. **Cons:** some rooms are on the small side; very pricey. *$ Rooms from: $840 ⊠1700 17-Mile Dr. ☎831/624–3811, 866/508–9268 ⊕ www.pebblebeach.com ⤸ 199 rooms ❚❍❙ No meals.*

SPORTS AND THE OUTDOORS
GOLF

Links at Spanish Bay. This course, which hugs a choice stretch of shoreline, was designed by Robert Trent Jones Jr., Tom Watson, and Sandy Tatum in the rugged manner of traditional Scottish links, with sand dunes and coastal marshes interspersed among the greens. A bagpiper signals the course's closing each day. ■**TIP→** Nonguests of the Pebble Beach Resorts can reserve tee times up to two months in advance. ⊠ *17-Mile Dr., north end ☎866/508–9268 ⊕ www.pebblebeach.com ⛳$280 ⅊ 18 holes, 6821 yards, par 72.*

Fodor'sChoice
★

Pebble Beach Golf Links. Each February, show-business celebrities and golf pros team up at this course, the main site of the glamorous AT&T Pebble Beach National Pro-Am tournament. On most days the rest of the year, tee times are available to guests of the Pebble Beach Resorts who book a minimum two-night stay. Nonguests can reserve a tee time only one day in advance on a space-available basis; resort guests can reserve up to 18 months in advance. ⊠ *17-Mile Dr., near The Lodge at Pebble Beach ☎866/508–9268 ⊕ www.pebblebeach.com ⛳$525 ⅊ 18 holes, 6828 yards, par 72.*

Peter Hay. The only 9-hole, par-3 course on the Monterey Peninsula open to the public, Peter Hay attracts golfers of all skill levels. It's an ideal place for warm ups, practicing short games, and for those who don't have time to play 18 holes. ⊠ *17-Mile Dr. and Portola Rd. ☎866/508–9268 ⊕ www.pebblebeach.com ⛳$30 ⅊ 9 holes, 725 yards, par 27.*

Poppy Hills. An 18-hole course designed in 1986 by Robert Trent Jones Jr., Poppy Hills reopened in 2014 after a yearlong renovation that Jones supervised. Each hole has been restored to its natural elevation along the forest floor, and all 18 greens have been rebuilt with bent grass. Individuals may reserve up to a month in advance. Chef Johnny De Vivo grows and

DID YOU KNOW?

The Lone Cypress has stood on this rock for more than 250 years. The tree is the official symbol of the Pebble Beach Company.

sources organic ingredients that inspire the menus at the course's restaurant. ■ TIP→ **Poppy Hills, owned by a golfing nonprofit, represents good value for this area.** ✉ *3200 Lopez Rd., at 17-Mile Dr.* ☎ *831/250–1819* ⊕ *poppyhillsgolf.com* ✉ *$225* ⚐ *18 holes, 7002 yards, par 73.5.*

Spyglass Hill. With three holes rated among the toughest on the PGA tour, Spyglass Hill, designed by Robert Trent Jones Sr. and Jr., challenges golfers with its varied terrain but rewards them with glorious views. The first five holes border the Pacific, and the other 13 reach deep into the Del Monte Forest. Reservations are essential and may be made up to one month in advance (18 months for resort guests). ✉ *Stevenson Dr. and Spyglass Hill Rd.* ☎ *866/508–9268* ⊕ *www.pebblebeach.com* ✉ *$395* ⚐ *18 holes, 6960 yards, par 72.*

PACIFIC GROVE

3 miles north of Carmel-by-the-Sea.

This picturesque town, which began as a summer retreat for church groups more than a century ago, recalls its prim and proper Victorian heritage in its host of tiny board-and-batten cottages and stately mansions. However, long before the church groups flocked here the area received thousands of annual pilgrims—in the form of bright orange-and-black monarch butterflies. They still come, migrating south from Canada and the Pacific Northwest to take residence in pine and eucalyptus groves from October through March. In Butterfly Town USA, as Pacific Grove is known, the sight of a mass of butterflies hanging from the branches like a long, fluttering veil is unforgettable.

A prime way to enjoy Pacific Grove is to walk or bicycle the 3 miles of city-owned shoreline along Ocean View Boulevard, a cliff-top area landscaped with native plants and dotted with benches meant for sitting and gazing at the sea. You can spot many types of birds here, including the web-footed cormorants that crowd the massive rocks rising out of the surf. Two Victorians of note along Ocean View are the Queen Anne–style Green Gables, at No. 301—erected in 1888, it's now an inn—and the 1909 Pryor House, at No. 429, a massive, shingled, private residence with a leaded- and beveled-glass doorway.

GETTING HERE AND AROUND
Reach Pacific Grove via Highway 68 off Highway 1, just south of Monterey. From Cannery Row in Monterey, head north until the road merges with Ocean Boulevard and follow it along the coast. MST buses travel within Pacific Grove and surrounding towns.

EXPLORING
FAMILY **Lovers Point Park.** The coastal views are gorgeous from this waterfront park whose sheltered beach has a children's pool and a picnic area. The main lawn has a volleyball court and a snack bar. ✉ *Ocean View Blvd. northwest of Forest Ave.* ☎ *831/648–5730.*

FAMILY **Monarch Grove Sanctuary.** The sanctuary is a reliable spot for viewing monarch butterflies between November and February. ■ TIP→ **The best time to visit is between noon and 3 pm.** ✉ *250 Ridge Rd., off Lighthouse Ave.* ⊕ *www.pgmuseum.org/monarch-viewing.*

Pacific Grove Museum of Natural History. The museum, a good source for the latest information about monarch butterflies, has permanent exhibitions about the butterflies, birds of Monterey County, biodiversity, and plants. There's a native plant garden, and a display documents life in Pacific Grove's 19th-century Chinese fishing village. ✉ *165 Forest Ave., at Central Ave.* ☎ *831/648–5716* 🌐 *pgmuseum.org* 🎟 *$9, free last Sat. of month* 🕒 *Closed Mon.*

FAMILY **Point Pinos Lighthouse.** At this 1855 structure, the West Coast's oldest continuously operating lighthouse, you can learn about the lighting and foghorn operations and wander through a small museum containing U.S. Coast Guard memorabilia. ✉ *Asilomar Ave., between Lighthouse Ave. and Del Monte Blvd.* ☎ *831/648–3176* 🌐 *pointpinoslighthouse.org* 🎟 *$2* 🕒 *Closed Tues. and Wed.*

BEACHES

Asilomar State Beach. A beautiful coastal area, Asilomar State Beach stretches between Point Pinos and the Del Monte Forest. The 100 acres of dunes, tidal pools, and pocket-size beaches form one of the region's richest areas for marine life—including surfers, who migrate here most winter mornings. Leashed dogs are allowed on the beach. **Amenities:** none. **Best for:** sunrise; sunset; surfing; walking. ✉ *Sunset Dr. and Asilomar Ave.* ☎ *831/646–6440* 🌐 *www.parks.ca.gov.*

WHERE TO EAT

$$ | MODERN AMERICAN

🍴 **Beach House.** Patrons of this blufftop perch sip classic cocktails, sample California fare, and watch the otters frolic on Lovers Point Beach below. Standout dishes include the crispy shrimp appetizer—tossed in a creamy, spicy sauce—entrées such as bacon-wrapped meat loaf, and crab-stuffed sole topped with citrus beurre blanc. **Known for:** sweeping blufftop views; sunset discounts; heated outdoor patio. [$] *Average main: $22* ✉ *620 Ocean View Blvd.* ☎ *831/375–2345* 🌐 *beachhousepg.com* 🕒 *No lunch.*

$$$$ | MEDITERRANEAN | Fodor's Choice ★

🍴 **Fandango.** The menu here is mostly Mediterranean and southern French, with such dishes as osso buco and paella. The decor follows suit: stone walls and country furniture lend the restaurant the earthy feel of a European farmhouse. **Known for:** wood-fire-grilled rack of lamb, seafood, and beef; convivial residential vibe; traditional European flavors. [$] *Average main: $32* ✉ *223 17th St., south of Lighthouse Ave.* ☎ *831/372–3456* 🌐 *fandangorestaurant.com.*

$$$ | ITALIAN

🍴 **Joe Rombi's La Mia Cucina.** Pasta, fish, steaks, and veal dishes are the specialties at this modern trattoria, the best in town for Italian food. The look is spare and clean, with colorful antique wine posters decorating the white walls. **Known for:** house-made gnocchi, ravioli, and sausage; festive dining room. [$] *Average main: $25* ✉ *208 17th St., at Lighthouse Ave.* ☎ *831/373–2416* 🌐 *lamiacucinaristorante.com* 🕒 *Closed Mon. and Tues. No lunch.*

$$$ | MODERN AMERICAN | Fodor's Choice ★

🍴 **Passionfish.** South American artwork and artifacts decorate Passionfish, and Latin and Asian flavors infuse the dishes. The chef shops at local farmers' markets several times a week to find the best produce, fish, and meat available, then pairs it with creative sauces like a caper, raisin, and walnut relish. **Known for:** sustainably sourced seafood and organic ingredients; reasonably priced wine list that supports small producers; slow-cooked meats. $ *Average main: $24* ✉ *701 Lighthouse Ave., at Congress Ave.* ☎ *831/655–3311* ⊕ *passionfish. net* ⊘ *No lunch.*

$$
AMERICAN

✕ **Red House Café.** When it's nice out, sun pours through the big windows of this cozy restaurant and across tables on the porch; when fog rolls in, the fireplace is lit. The American menu changes with the seasons but grilled lamb chops atop mashed potatoes are often on offer for dinner, and a grilled calamari steak might be served for lunch, either in a salad or as part of a sandwich. **Known for:** cozy homelike dining areas; comfort food; stellar breakfast and brunch. $ *Average main: $21* ✉ *662 Lighthouse Ave., at 19th St.* ☎ *831/643–1060* ⊕ *redhousecafe. com* ⊘ *No dinner Mon.*

$$
AMERICAN
FAMILY

✕ **Taste Café and Bistro.** Grilled marinated rabbit, roasted half chicken, filet mignon, and other meats are the focus at Taste, which serves hearty European-inspired food in a casual, open-kitchen setting. **Known for:** grilled meats; house-made desserts; kids' menu. $ *Average main: $22* ✉ *1199 Forest Ave., at Prescott La.* ☎ *831/655–0324* ⊕ *tastecafebistro. com* ⊘ *Closed Sun. and Mon.*

WHERE TO STAY

$$
B&B/INN
Fodor's Choice
★

🏨 **Green Gables Inn.** Stained-glass windows and ornate interior details compete with spectacular ocean views at this Queen Anne–style mansion. **Pros:** exceptional views; impeccable attention to historic detail. **Cons:** some rooms are small; thin walls. $ *Rooms from: $169* ✉ *301 Ocean View Blvd.* ☎ *831/375–2095* ⊕ *www.greengablesinnpg.com* ⇨ *11 rooms, 8 with bath* ⊙| *Breakfast.*

$$$
B&B/INN

🏨 **Martine Inn.** The glassed-in parlor and many guest rooms at this 1899 Mediterranean-style villa have stunning ocean views. **Pros:** romantic; exquisite antiques; fancy breakfast; ocean views. **Cons:** not child-friendly; sits on a busy thoroughfare. $ *Rooms from: $219* ✉ *255 Ocean View Blvd.* ☎ *831/373–3388, 800/852–5588* ⊕ *martineinn.com* ⇨ *25 rooms* ⊙| *Breakfast.*

MONTEREY

2 miles southeast of Pacific Grove, 2 miles north of Carmel.

Monterey is a scenic city filled with early California history: adobe buildings from the 1700s, Colton Hall, where California's first constitution was drafted in 1849, and Cannery Row, made famous by author John Steinbeck. Thousands of visitors come each year to mingle with otters and other sea creatures at the world-famous Monterey Bay Aquarium and in the protected waters of the national marine sanctuary that hugs the shoreline.

GETTING HERE AND AROUND

From San Jose or San Francisco, take U.S. 101 south to Highway 156 West at Prunedale. Head west about 8 miles to Highway 1 and follow it about 15 miles south. From San Luis Obispo, take U.S. 101 north to Salinas and drive west on Highway 68 about 20 miles.

Many MST bus lines connect at the Monterey Transit Center, at Pearl Street and Munras Avenue. In summer (daily from 10 until at least 7) and on weekends and holidays the rest of the year, the free MST Monterey Trolley travels from downtown Monterey along Cannery Row to the Aquarium and back.

TOURS

Monterey Movie Tours. Board a customized motorcoach and relax while a film-savvy local takes you on a scenic tour of the Monterey Peninsula enhanced by film clips from the more than 200 movies shot in the area. The three-hour adventure travels a 32-mile loop through Monterey, Pacific Grove, and Carmel. ⊠ *Departs from Monterey Conference Center, 1 Portola Plaza* ☎ *831/372–6278, 800/343–6437* ⊕ *montereymovietours.com* ✉ *$55.*

Old Monterey Walking Tour. Learn all about Monterey's storied past by joining a guided walking tour through the historic district. Tours begin at the Pacific House Museum in Custom House Plaza, across from Fisherman's Wharf and are offered Thursday through Sunday at 10:30, 12:30, and 2. ⊠ *Monterey* ⊕ *www.parks.ca.gov/?page_id=951.*

The Original Monterey Walking Tours. Learn more about Monterey's storied past, primarily the Mexican period until California statehood, on a guided tour through downtown Monterey. You can also join a guided walking tour of Cannery Row in the afternoon. Tours last 1½ to 2 hours and are offered Thursday–Sunday at 10 am and 2. Reservations are essential. ⊠ *Monterey* ☎ *831/521–4884* ⊕ *www.walkmonterey.com* ✉ *From $25.*

ESSENTIALS

Visitor Information Monterey County Convention & Visitors Bureau. ☎ *888/221–1010* ⊕ *seemonterey.com.*

EXPLORING

TOP ATTRACTIONS

Cannery Row. When John Steinbeck published the novel *Cannery Row* in 1945, he immortalized a place of rough-edged working people. The waterfront street, edging a mile of gorgeous coastline, once was crowded with sardine canneries processing, at their peak, nearly 200,000 tons of the smelly silver fish a year. During the mid-1940s, however, the sardines disappeared from the bay, causing the canneries to close. Through the years the old tin-roof canneries have been converted into restaurants, art galleries, and malls with shops selling T-shirts, fudge, and plastic sea otters. Recent tourist development along the row has been more tasteful, however, and includes stylish inns and hotels, wine tasting rooms, and upscale specialty shops. ⊠ *Cannery Row, between Reeside and David Aves.* ⊕ *canneryrow.com.*

Colton Hall. A convention of delegates met here in 1849 to draft the first state constitution. The stone building, which has served as a school, a courthouse, and the county seat, is a city-run museum furnished as it was during the constitutional convention. The extensive grounds outside the hall surround the Old Monterey Jail. ⊠ *570 Pacific St., between Madison and Jefferson Sts.* ☎ *831/646–5640* ⊕ *www.monterey.org/museums* ✉ *Free.*

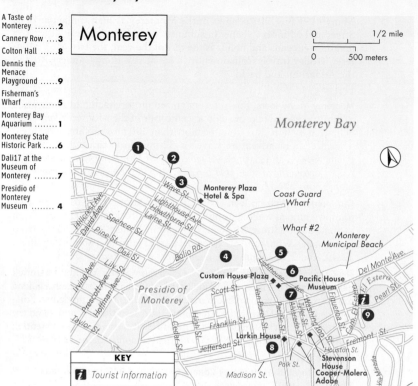

Dali17 at the Museum of Monterey. Whether you're a fan of surrealist art or not, come to Dali17 to gain rare insight into the life and work of famed Spanish artist Salvador Dali, who lived in Monterey in the 1940s. The permanent exhibition houses nearly 600 artworks in various media, including 300 Dali originals. The museum's name reflects Dali's ties to nearby 17 Mile Drive, where he lived, worked, and hosted parties that included Andy Warhol, Walt Disney, Bob Hope, and other celebrities, ⊠ *5 Custom House Plaza* ☎ *831/372–2608* ⊕ *dali17.com* ⊒ *$20.*

FAMILY **Fisherman's Wharf.** The mournful barking of sea lions provides a steady soundtrack all along Monterey's waterfront, but the best way to actually view the whiskered marine mammals is to walk along one of the two piers across from Custom House Plaza. Lined with souvenir shops, the wharf is undeniably touristy, but it's lively and entertaining. At Wharf No. 2, a working municipal pier, you can see the day's catch being unloaded from fishing boats on one side and fishermen casting their lines into the water on the other. The pier has a couple of low-key restaurants, from whose seats lucky customers might spot otters and harbor seals. ⊠ *At end of Calle Principal* ⊕ *www.montereywharf.com.*

FAMILY **Monterey Bay Aquarium.** Sea creatures surround you the minute you hand
Fodor's Choice over your ticket at this extraordinary facility: right at the entrance
★ dozens of them swim in a three-story-tall, sunlit kelp-forest tank. All

the exhibits here provide a sense of what it's like to be in the water with the animals—sardines swim around your head in a circular tank, and jellyfish drift in and out of view in dramatically lighted spaces that suggest the ocean depths. A petting pool puts you literally in touch with bat rays, and the million-gallon Open Seas tank illustrates the variety of creatures, from sharks to placid-looking turtles, that live in the eastern Pacific. At the Splash Zone, which has 45 interactive bilingual exhibits, kids can commune with African black-footed penguins, potbellied seahorses, and other creatures. The only drawback to the aquarium experience is that it must be shared with the throngs that congregate daily, but most visitors think it's worth it. The *¡Viva Baja! Life on the Edge* exhibit explores the delicate balance of life where the sea meets the sand in Baja, Mexico. Another must-see is *Tentacles: The Astounding Lives of Octopuses, Squid, and Cuttlefishes*, a huge and fascinating display of marine mollusks. ✉ *886 Cannery Row, at David Ave.* ☎ *831/648–4800 info, 866/963–9645 for advance tickets* ⊕ *montereybayaquarium.org* ✆ *$50.*

> ### JOHN STEINBECK'S CANNERY ROW
>
> "Cannery Row in Monterey in California is a poem, a stink, a grating noise, a quality of light, a tone, a habit, a nostalgia, a dream. Cannery Row is the gathered and scattered, tin and iron and rust and splintered wood, chipped pavement and weedy lots and junk heaps, sardine canneries of corrugated iron, honky tonks, restaurants and whore houses, and little crowded groceries, and laboratories and flophouses." —
> John Steinbeck, *Cannery Row*

Fodor's Choice
★ **Monterey State Historic Park.** You can glimpse Monterey's early history in several well-preserved adobe buildings downtown. Some of the structures have gardens that are themselves worthy sights, and they're visitable even if the buildings—among them **Casa Soberanes,** the **Larkin House,** and the **Stevenson House**—are closed.

A good place to start is the **Pacific House Museum.** Once a hotel and saloon, this facility, also a visitor center, commemorates life in pioneer-era California with gold-rush relics and photographs of old Monterey. On the upper floor are Native American artifacts, including gorgeous baskets and pottery. In the same plaza is the **Custom House.** Built by the Mexican government in 1827, it's California's oldest standing public building.

■TIP→ If buildings are closed when you visit you can access a cell phone tour 24/7 at 831/998–9458. ✉ *Pacific House Museum visitor center, 10 Custom House Plaza* ☎ *831/649–7118* ⊕ *www.parks.ca.gov/ mshp* ✆ *Free–$5.*

WORTH NOTING

A Taste of Monterey. Without driving the back roads, you can taste the wines of nearly 100 area vintners (craft beers, too) while taking in fantastic bay views. Bottles are available for purchase, and food is served from noon until closing. ✉ *700 Cannery Row, Suite KK* ☎ *831/646– 5446* ⊕ *atasteofmonterey.com* ✆ *Tastings $10–$20.*

Trained "seals" that perform in circuses are actually California sea lions—intelligent, social animals that live (and sleep) close together in groups.

FAMILY **Dennis the Menace Playground.** The late cartoonist Hank Ketcham designed this play area. Its equipment is on a grand scale and made for Dennis-like daredevils: kid favorites include the roller slide, rock-climbing area, and clanking suspension bridge. You can rent a rowboat or a paddleboat for cruising around U-shaped Lake El Estero, populated with an assortment of ducks, mud hens, and geese. ✉ *El Estero Park, Pearl St. and Camino El Estero* ☎ *831/646–3866* 🌐 *www.monterey.org/parks* 🕒 *Closed Tues., Sept.–May.*

Presidio of Monterey Museum. This spot has been significant for centuries. Its first incarnation was as a Native American village for the Rumsien tribe. The Spanish explorer Sebastián Vizcaíno landed here in 1602, and Father Junípero Serra arrived in 1770. Notable battles fought here include the 1818 skirmish in which the corsair Hipólito Bruchard conquered the Spanish garrison that stood on this site and claimed part of California for Argentina. The indoor museum tells the stories; plaques mark the outdoor sites. ✉ *Presidio of Monterey, Corporal Ewing Rd., off Lighthouse Ave.* ☎ *831/646–3456* 🌐 *www.monterey.org/museums* 🎟 *Free* 🕒 *Closed Tues. and Wed.*

WHERE TO EAT

$$ SEAFOOD 🍴 **Monterey's Fish House.** Casual yet stylish and always packed, this seafood restaurant is removed from the hubbub of the wharf. If the dining room is full, you can wait at the bar and savor plump oysters on the half shell. **Known for:** seafood, steaks, house-made pasta; festive atmosphere. [$] *Average main: $22* ✉ *2114 Del Monte Ave., at Dela Vina Ave.* ☎ *831/373–4647* 🌐 *montereyfishhouse.com* 🕒 *No lunch weekends.*

FORMER CAPITAL OF CALIFORNIA

In 1602 Spanish explorer Sebastián Vizcaíno stepped ashore on a remote California peninsula. He named it after the viceroy of New Spain—Count de Monte Rey. Soon the Spanish built a military outpost, and the site was the capital of California until the state came under American rule.

$$$ AMERICAN Fodor's Choice ★ 🍴 **Montrio Bistro.** This quirky converted firehouse, with its rawhide walls and iron indoor trellises, has a wonderfully sophisticated menu. Organic produce and meats and sustainably sourced seafood are used in imaginative dishes that reflect the area's agriculture—crispy artichoke hearts with Mediterranean baba ganoush, for instance, and scallop crudo with avocado-jalapeño panna cotta. **Known for:** green-certified restaurant; historic firehouse setting; inventive cocktails. [$] *Average main: $30* ✉ *414 Calle Principal, at W. Franklin St.* ☎ *831/648–8880* 🌐 *montrio.com* 🕒 *No lunch.*

$$$ SEAFOOD 🍴 **Old Fisherman's Grotto.** Otters and seals frolic in the water just below this nautical-theme Fisherman's Wharf restaurant famous for its creamy clam chowder. Seafood paella, sand dabs, filet mignon, teriyaki chicken, and several pastas are among the many entrée options. **Known for:** Monterey-style clam chowder and calamari; Monterey Bay views. [$] *Average main: $29* ✉ *39 Fisherman's Wharf* ☎ *831/375–4604* 🌐 *oldfishermansgrotto.com.*

$ AMERICAN 🍴 **Old Monterey Café.** Breakfast here gets constant local raves. The café's fame rests on familiar favorites: a dozen kinds of omelets, and pancakes from blueberry to cinnamon-raisin-pecan. [$] *Average main: $15* ✉ *489 Alvarado St., at Munras Ave.* ☎ *831/646–1021* 🕒 *No dinner.*

$$$$ MODERN AMERICAN Fodor's Choice ★ 🍴 **Restaurant 1833.** Inside the two-story Stokes Adobe, built in 1833, this popular restaurant and bar showcases the region's colorful history and local bounty. Each of the seven dining rooms honors an era and characters from the adobe's past, which includes an early stint as an apothecary. **Known for:** tree-shaded courtyard with fire pits; craft cocktails; extensive wine list. [$] *Average main: $32* ✉ *500 Hartnell St., at Polk St.* ☎ *831/643–1833* 🌐 *www.restaurant1833.com* 🕒 *No lunch. Closed Mon.*

$$$ AMERICAN 🍴 **Tarpy's Roadhouse.** Fun, dressed-up American favorites—a little something for everyone—are served in this renovated early-1900s stone farmhouse several miles east of town. The kitchen cranks out everything from Cajun-spiced prawns to meat loaf with marsala–mushroom gravy to grilled ribs and steaks. **Known for:** American comfort food with a California twist; rustic dining: indoor fireplace or garden courtyard. [$] *Average main: $28* ✉ *2999 Monterey–Salinas Hwy., Hwy. 68* ☎ *831/647–1444* 🌐 *tarpys.com.*

WHERE TO STAY

$$$ HOTEL FAMILY 🏨 **InterContinental The Clement Monterey.** Spectacular bay views, upscale amenities, assiduous service, and a superb location next to the aquarium propelled this luxury hotel to immediate stardom. **Pros:** a block from the aquarium; fantastic waterfront views from some rooms; great for families. **Cons:** a tad formal; pricey. [$] *Rooms from: $229* ✉ *750 Cannery Row* ☎ *831/375–4500, 866/781–2406 toll free* 🌐 *www.icthe-clementmonterey.com* 🛏 *208 rooms* 🍽 *No meals.*

CLOSE UP

The Monterey Bay National Marine Sanctuary

Although Monterey's coastal landscapes are stunning, their beauty is more than equaled by the wonders that lie offshore. The Monterey Bay National Marine Sanctuary—which stretches 276 miles, from north of San Francisco almost down to Santa Barbara—teems with abundant life, and has topography as diverse as that aboveground.

The preserve's 5,322 square miles include vast submarine canyons, which reach down 10,663 feet at their deepest point. They also encompass dense forests of giant kelp—a kind of seaweed that can grow more than a hundred feet from its roots on the ocean floor. These kelp forests are especially robust off Monterey.

The sanctuary was established in 1992 to protect the habitat of the many species that thrive in the bay. Some animals can be seen quite easily from land. In summer and winter you might glimpse the offshore spray of gray whales as they migrate between their summer feeding grounds in Alaska and their breeding grounds in Baja. Clouds of marine birds—including white-faced ibis, three types of albatross, and more than 15 types of gull—skim the waves, or roost in the rock islands along 17-Mile Drive. Sea otters dart and gambol in the calmer waters of the bay; and of course, you can watch the sea lions—and hear their round-the-clock barking—on the wharves in Santa Cruz and Monterey.

The sanctuary supports many other creatures, however, that remain unseen by most on-land visitors. Some of these are enormous, such as the giant blue whales that arrive to feed on plankton in summer; others, like the more than 22 species of red algae in these waters, are microscopic. So whether you choose to visit the Monterey Bay Aquarium, take a whale-watch trip, or look out to sea with your binoculars, remember you're seeing just a small part of a vibrant underwater kingdom.

$$ HOTEL FAMILY
🏨 **Monterey Bay Lodge.** Its superior amenities and location bordering El Estero Park give this cheerful facility the edge over other area motels. **Pros:** within walking distance of the beach and a playground; quiet at night; good family choice. **Cons:** near a busy boulevard. [$] *Rooms from: $150* ✉ *55 Camino Aguajito* ☎ *831/372–8057, 800/558–1900* 🌐 *montereybaylodge.com* 🛏 *46 rooms* 🍴 *No meals.*

$$$$ HOTEL
🏨 **Monterey Plaza Hotel & Spa.** Guests at this waterfront Cannery Row hotel can see frolicking sea otters from its wide outdoor patio and many room balconies. **Pros:** on the ocean; many amenities; attentive service. **Cons:** touristy area; heavy traffic. [$] *Rooms from: $269* ✉ *400 Cannery Row* ☎ *831/920–6710, 855/421–0264* 🌐 *www.montereyplazahotel.com* 🛏 *290 rooms.*

$$$$ B&B/INN Fodor's Choice ★
🏨 **Old Monterey Inn.** This three-story manor house was the home of Monterey's first mayor, and today it remains a private enclave within walking distance of downtown, set off by lush gardens shaded by huge old trees and bordered by a creek. **Pros:** gorgeous gardens; refined luxury; serene. **Cons:** must drive to attractions and sights; fills quickly. [$] *Rooms from: $289* ✉ *500 Martin St.* ☎ *831/652–8999, 800/350–2344* 🌐 *www.oldmontereyinn.com* 🛏 *9 rooms, 1 cottage* 🍴 *Breakfast.*

$$$ HOTEL **Spindrift Inn.** This boutique hotel on Cannery Row has beach access and a rooftop garden that overlooks the water. **Pros:** close to aquarium; steps from the beach; friendly staff. **Cons:** throngs of visitors outside; can be noisy; not good for families. [$] *Rooms from: $209* ✉ *652 Cannery Row* ☎ *831/646–8900, 800/841–1879* 🌐 *spindriftinn.com* 🛏 *45 rooms* 🍴 *Breakfast.*

NIGHTLIFE AND PERFORMING ARTS

NIGHTLIFE

BARS

Peter B's Brewpub. House-made beers, 15 HDTVs, a decent pub menu, and a pet-friendly patio ensure lively crowds at this craft brewery in back of the Portola Plaza Hotel. ✉ *2 Portola Plaza* ☎ *831/649–2699* 🌐 *www.peterbsbrewpub.com.*

Turn 12 Bar & Grill. The motorcycles and vintage photographs at this downtown watering hole pay homage to nearby 11-turn Laguna Seca Raceway. The large-screen TVs, heated outdoor patio, happy-hour specials, and live entertainment keep the place jumpin' into the wee hours. ✉ *400 Tyler St., at E. Franklin St.* ☎ *831/372–8876* 🌐 *turn12barandgrill.com.*

MUSIC FESTIVALS

Monterey Jazz Festival. The world's oldest jazz festival attracts top-name performers to the Monterey Fairgrounds on the third full weekend of September. ☎ *888/248–6499 ticket office, 831/373–3366* 🌐 *montereyjazzfestival.org.*

7

PERFORMING ARTS

THEATER

Bruce Ariss Wharf Theater (*The New Wharf Theatre*). American musicals past and present are the focus here, with dramas and comedies also in the mix. ✉ *One Fisherman's Wharf* ☎ *831/649–2332.*

SPORTS AND THE OUTDOORS

Monterey Bay waters never warm to the temperatures of their Southern California counterparts—the warmest they get is the low 60s. That's one reason why the marine life here is so diverse, which in turn brings out the fishers, kayakers, and whale-watchers. During the rainy winter, the waves grow larger, and surfers flock to the water. On land pretty much year-round, bikers find opportunities to ride, and walkers have plenty of waterfront to stroll.

BIKING

Adventures by the Sea. You can rent surreys plus tandem, standard, and electric bicycles from this outfit that also conducts bike and kayak tours, and rents kayaks and stand-up paddleboards. There are multiple locations along Cannery Row and Custom House Plaza as well as branches at Lovers Point in Pacific Grove and 17-Mile Drive in Pebble Beach. ✉ *299 Cannery Row* ☎ *831/372–1807, 800/979–3370 reservations* 🌐 *adventuresbythesea.com.*

Bay Bikes. For bicycle and surrey rentals, visit Bay Bikes at here or at 486 Washington Street. ■TIP→ You can rent a bike on Cannery Row and drop it off at the company's Carmel location at 3600 The Barnyard. ⊠ *585 Cannery Row* ☎ *831/655–2453* ⊕ *www.baybikes.com.*

FISHING

Randy's Fishing and Whale Watching Trips. In business since 1949, Randy's takes beginning and experienced fishers out to sea. ⊠ *66 Fisherman's Wharf* ☎ *831/372–7440, 800/251–7440* ⊕ *randysfishingtrips.com.*

KAYAKING

Fodor's Choice **Monterey Bay Kayaks.** For many visitors the best way to see the bay is
★ by kayak. This company rents equipment and conducts classes and natural-history tours. ⊠ *693 Del Monte Ave.* ☎ *831/373–5357* ⊕ *www. montereybaykayaks.com.*

WALKING

Monterey Bay Coastal Recreation Trail. From Custom House Plaza, you can walk along the coast in either direction on this 29-mile-long trail and take in spectacular views of the sea. The trail runs from north of Monterey in Castroville south to Pacific Grove, with sections continuing around Pebble Beach. Much of the path follows an old Southern Pacific Railroad route. ☎ *888/221–1010* ⊕ *seemonterey.com/things-to-do/ parks/coastal-trail/.*

WHALE-WATCHING

Thousands of gray whales pass close by the Monterey Coast on their annual migration between the Bering Sea and Baja California, and a whale-watching cruise is the best way to see these magnificent mammals close up. The migration south takes place from December through March; January is prime viewing time. The whales migrate north from March through June. Blue whales and humpbacks also pass the coast; they're most easily spotted in late summer and early fall.

Fast Raft Ocean Safaris. Naturalists lead whale-watching and sightseeing tours of Monterey Bay aboard the 33-foot *Ranger,* a six-passenger, rigid-hull inflatable boat. The speedy craft slips into coves inaccessible to larger vessels; its quiet engines enable intimate marine experiences without disturbing wildlife. Children ages eight and older are welcome to participate. ⊠ *32 Cannery Row, Suite F2* ☎ *408/659–3900* ⊕ *www. fastraft.com* ⌨ *$150.*

Monterey Bay Whale Watch. The marine biologists here lead three- to five-hour whale-watching tours. ⊠ *84 Fisherman's Wharf* ☎ *831/375–4658* ⊕ *montereybaywhalewatch.com.*

Princess Monterey Whale Watching. Tours are offered daily on a 100-passenger high-speed cruiser and a large 100-foot boat. ⊠ *96 Fisherman's Wharf* ☎ *831/372–2203, 831/205–2370 reservations* ⊕ *monterey-whalewatching.com.*

SHOPPING

Alvarado and nearby downtown streets are good places to start a Monterey shopping spree, especially if you're interested in antiques and collectibles.

Cannery Row Antique Mall. Bargain hunters can sometimes find little treasures at the mall, which houses more than 100 local vendors under one roof. ✉ *471 Wave St.* ☎ *831/655–0264* ⊕ *canneryrowantiquemall.com.*

Old Monterey Book Co. Antiquarian books and prints are this shop's specialties. ✉ *136 Bonifacio Pl., off Alvarado St.* ☎ *831/372–3111* ⊙ *Closed Sun. and Mon.*

AROUND MONTEREY BAY

North and east of Monterey is what many call Steinbeck country—the rich agricultural setting for many of famed author John Steinbeck's novels—and it's home to California's newest national park, Pinnacles. North of Monterey, Highway 1 follows the curve of the bay between Monterey and Santa Cruz: passing through a protected national marine estuary at Moss Landing, where otters and seals play alongside humans in kayaks; up to some of the bay's best beaches, including Seacliff and New Brighton state beach parks; to classic California seaside villages Aptos, Soquel, and Capitola; to Santa Cruz, home of surf legends, an historic boardwalk, and UC Santa Cruz. Salinas and Moss Landing are in Monterey County; the other cities and towns covered here are in Santa Cruz County.

GETTING HERE AND AROUND

All the towns in this area are on or just off Highway 1. MST buses serve Monterey County destinations, connecting in Watsonville with Santa Cruz METRO buses, which operate throughout Santa Cruz County.

7

SALINAS

17 miles east of Monterey on Hwy. 68.

Salinas, a hardworking city surrounded by vineyards and fruit and vegetable fields, honors the memory and literary legacy of John Steinbeck, its most famous native, with the National Steinbeck Center. The facility is in Old Town Salinas, where renovated turn-of-the-20th-century stone buildings house shops and restaurants.

ESSENTIALS

Train Information Salinas Amtrak Station. ✉ *11 Station Pl., at W. Market St.* ☎ *800/872–7245* ⊕ *www.amtrak.com.*

Visitor Information California Welcome Center. ✉ *1213 N. Davis Rd., west of U.S. 101, exit 330* ☎ *831/757–8687* ⊕ *visitcalifornia.com/attraction/ california-welcome-center-salinas.*

EXPLORING

FAMILY **Monterey Zoo.** Exotic animals, many of them retired from film, television, and live production work or rescued from less than ideal environments, find sanctuary here. The zoo offers daily tours, but for an in-depth experience, stay in a safari bungalow on-site at Vision Quest Safari B&B, where breakfast is delivered in a basket by an elephant. The inn's room rate includes a complimentary zoo tour. ✉ *400 River Rd., off Hwy. 68* ☎ *831/455–1901, 800/228–7382* ⊕ *www.montereyzoo.com* 🎟 *Tours $12; posttour elephant feeding $5.*

National Steinbeck Center. The center's exhibits document the life of Pulitzer- and Nobel-prize winner John Steinbeck and the history of the nearby communities that inspired novels such as *East of Eden*. Highlights include reproductions of the green pickup-camper from *Travels with Charley* and the bunk room from *Of Mice and Men*. **Steinbeck House,** the author's Victorian birthplace, at 132 Central Avenue, is two blocks from the center. Now a decent restaurant (only open for lunch) and gift shop with docent-led tours, it displays memorabilia. ⊠ *1 Main St., at Central Ave.* ☎ *831/775–4721* ⊕ *steinbeck.org* ⊒ *$13.*

PINNACLES NATIONAL PARK

38 miles southeast of Salinas.

Pinnacles may be the nation's newest national park, but Teddy Roosevelt recognized the uniqueness of this ancient volcano—its jagged spires and monoliths thrusting upward from chaparral-covered mountains—when he made it a national monument in 1908. Though only about two hours from the bustling Bay Area, the outside world seems to recede even before you reach the park's gates.

GETTING HERE AND AROUND

One of the first things you need to decide when visiting Pinnacles is which entrance—east or west—you'll use, because there's no road connecting the two rugged peaks separating them. Entering from Highway 25 on the east is straightforward. The gate is only a mile or so from the turnoff. From the west, once you head east out of Soledad on Highway 146, the road quickly becomes narrow and hilly, with many blind curves. Drive slowly and cautiously along the 10 miles or so before you reach the west entrance.

ESSENTIALS

Pinnacles Visitor Center. At the park's main visitor center, located at the eastern entrance, you can purchase admission passes, get maps, browse books, and buy gifts. The adjacent campground store sells snacks and drinks. ⊠ *Hwy. 146, 2 miles west of Hwy. 25, Paicines* ☎ *831/389–4485* ⊕ *www.nps.gov/pinn.*

West Pinnacles Visitor Contact Station. This station is just past the park's western entrance, about 10 miles east of Soledad. Here you can get maps and information, watch a 13-minute film about Pinnacles, and view some displays. Food and drink aren't available here. ⊠ *Hwy. 146, off U.S. 101, Soledad* ☎ *831/389–4427* ⊕ *www.nps.gov/pinn.*

EXPLORING

FAMILY　**Pinnacles National Park.** The many attractions at Pinnacles include talus caves, 30 miles of hiking trails, and hundreds of rock-climbing routes. A mosaic of diverse habitats supports an amazing variety of wildlife species: 185 birds, 49 mammals, 70 butterflies, and nearly 400 bees. The park is also home to some of the world's remaining few hundred condors in captivity and release areas. Fourteen of California's 25 bat species live in caves and other habitats in the park. President Theodore Roosevelt declared this remarkable 26,000-acre geologic and wildlife preserve a national monument in 1908. President Barack Obama officially designated it a national park in 2013.

The pinnacles are believed to have been created when two major tectonic plates collided and pushed a smaller plate down beneath the earth's crust, spawning volcanoes in what's now called the Gabilan Mountains, southeast of Salinas and Monterey. After the eruptions ceased, the San Andreas Fault split the volcanic field in two, carrying part of it northward to what is now Pinnacles National Park. Millions of years of erosion left a rugged landscape of rocky spires and crags, or pinnacles. Boulders fell into canyons and valleys, creating talus caves and a paradise for modern-day rock climbers. Spring is the most popular time to visit, when colorful wildflowers blanket the meadows; the light and scenery can be striking in fall and winter; the summer heat is often brutal. The park has two entrances—east and west—but they are not connected. The Pinnacles Visitor Center, Bear Gulch Nature Center, Park Headquarters, the Pinnacles Campground, and the Bear Gulch Cave and Reservoir are on the east side. The Chaparral Parking Area is on the west side, where you can feast on fantastic views of the Pinnacles High Peaks from the parking area. Dogs are not allowed on hiking trails. ■TIP➔ **The east entrance is 32 miles southeast of Hollister via Highway 25. The west entrance is about 12 miles east of Soledad via Highway 146.** ✉ *5000 Hwy. 146, Paicines* ☎ *831/389–4486, 831/389–4427 Westside* ⊕ *www.nps.gov/pinn* ◐ *$10 per vehicle, $5 per visitor if biking or walking.*

SPORTS AND THE OUTDOORS

HIKING

Hiking is the most popular activity at Pinnacles, with more than 30 miles of trails for every interest and level of fitness. Because there isn't a road through the park, hiking is also the only way to experience its interior, including the High Peaks, the talus caves, and the reservoir.

Balconies Cliffs-Cave Loop. Grab your flashlight before heading out from the Chaparral Trailhead parking lot for this 2.4-mile loop that takes you through the Balconies Caves. This trail is especially beautiful in spring, when wildflowers carpet the canyon floor. About 0.6 mile from the start of the trail, turn left to begin ascending the Balconies Cliffs Trail, where you'll be rewarded with close-up views of Machete Ridge and other steep, vertical formations; you may run across rock climbers testing their skills. *Easy.* ✉ *West side of park* ✛ *Trailhead: from West Pinnacles Visitor Contact Station, drive about 2 miles to Chaparral Trailhead parking lot. Trail picks up on west side of lot.*

FAMILY **Moses Spring-Rim Trail Loop.** Perhaps the most popular hike at Pinnacles, this relatively short (2.2 miles) trail is fun for kids and adults. It leads to the Bear Gulch cave system, and if your timing is right, you'll pass by several seasonal waterfalls inside the caves. If it has been raining, check with a ranger, as the caves could be flooded. The upper side of the cave is usually closed in spring and early summer to protect the Townsend's big-ear bats and their pups. *Easy.* ✉ *East side of park* ✛ *Trailhead: just past Bear Gulch Nature Center, on south side of overflow parking lot.*

SAN JUAN BAUTISTA

20 miles northeast of Salinas.

Much of the small town that grew up around Mission San Juan Bautista, still a working church, has been protected from development since 1933, when a state park was established here. Small antiques shops and restaurants occupy the Old West and art deco buildings that line 3rd Street.

GETTING HERE AND AROUND

From Highway 1 north or south, exit east onto Highway 156. MST buses do not serve San Juan Bautista.

EXPLORING

San Juan Bautista State Historic Park. With the low-slung, colonnaded **Mission San Juan Bautista** as its drawing card, this park 20 miles northeast of Salinas is about as close to early-19th-century California as you can get. Historic buildings ring the wide green plaza, among them an adobe home furnished with Spanish-colonial antiques, a hotel frozen in the 1860s, a blacksmith shop, a pioneer cabin, and a jailhouse. The mission's cemetery contains the unmarked graves of more than 4,300 Native American converts. ■TIP→ On the first Saturday of the month, costumed volunteers engage in quilting bees, tortilla making, and other frontier activities; and sarsaparilla and other nonalcoholic drinks are served in the saloon. ⊠ *19 Franklin St., off Hwy. 156, east of U.S. 101* ☎ *831/623–4881* ⊕ *www.parks.ca.gov* ⊠ *$3 park, $4 mission.*

MOSS LANDING

17 miles north of Monterey, 12 miles north of Salinas.

Moss Landing is not much more than a couple of blocks of cafés and restaurants, art galleries, and studios, plus a busy fishing port, but therein lies its charm. It's a fine place to overnight or stop for a meal and get a dose of nature.

GETTING HERE AND AROUND

From Highway 1 north or south, exit at Moss Landing Road on the ocean side. MST buses serve Moss Landing.

TOURS

Elkhorn Slough Safari Nature Boat Tours. This outfit's naturalists lead two-hour tours of Elkhorn Sough aboard a 27-foot pontoon boat. Reservations are required. ⊠ *Moss Landing Harbor* ☎ *831/633–5555* ⊕ *elkhornslough.com* ⊠ *$38.*

ESSENTIALS

Visitor Information Moss Landing Chamber of Commerce. ☎ *831/633–4501* ⊕ *mosslandingchamber.com.*

EXPLORING

Elkhorn Slough National Estuarine Research Reserve. The reserve's 1,400 acres of tidal flats and salt marshes form a complex environment that supports some 300 species of birds. A walk along the meandering waterways and wetlands can reveal hawks, white-tailed kites, owls, herons, and egrets. Also living or visiting here are sea otters, sharks, rays, and many other animals. ■ **TIP→ On weekends, guided walks from the visitor center begin at 10 and 1. On the first Saturday of the month, an early-bird tour departs at 8:30.** ✉ *1700 Elkhorn Rd., Watsonville* ☎ *831/728–2822* 🌐 *elkhornslough.org* 🎫 *$4 day use fee (credit card only)* ⏲ *Closed Mon.–Tues.*

WHERE TO EAT AND STAY

$$$ SOUTH AMERICAN 🍴 **Haute Enchilada.** Part of a complex that includes art galleries and an events venue, the Haute adds bohemian character to the seafaring village of Moss Landing. The inventive Latin American–inspired dishes include shrimp and black corn enchiladas topped with a citrus cilantro cream sauce, and roasted *pasilla* chilies stuffed with mashed plantains and caramelized onions. **Known for:** extensive cocktail and wine list; many vegan and gluten-free options; artsy atmosphere. [$] *Average main: $24* ✉ *7902 Moss Landing Rd.* ☎ *831/633–5843* 🌐 *hauteenchilada.com.*

$$ SEAFOOD 🍴 **Phil's Fish Market & Eatery.** Exquisitely fresh, simply prepared seafood (try the cioppino) is on the menu at this warehouselike restaurant on the harbor; all kinds of glistening fish are for sale at the market in the front. **Known for:** cioppino; clam chowder; myriad artichoke dishes. [$] *Average main: $21* ✉ *7600 Sandholdt Rd.* ☎ *831/633–2152* 🌐 *philsfishmarket.com.*

$$ B&B/INN 🏨 **Captain's Inn.** Commune with nature and pamper yourself with upscale creature comforts at this green-certified complex in the heart of town. **Pros:** walk to restaurants and shops; tranquil natural setting; free Wi-Fi and parking. **Cons:** rooms in historic building don't have water views; far from urban amenities; not appropriate for young children. [$] *Rooms from: $170* ✉ *8122 Moss Landing Rd.* ☎ *831/633–5550* 🌐 *www.captainsinn.com* 🛏 *10 rooms* 🍽 *Breakfast.*

SPORTS AND THE OUTDOORS

KAYAKING

Monterey Bay Kayaks. Rent a kayak to paddle out into Elkhorn Slough for up-close wildlife encounters. ✉ *2390 Hwy. 1, at North Harbor* ☎ *831/373–5357* 🌐 *montereybaykayaks.com.*

APTOS

17 miles north of Moss Landing.

Backed by a redwood forest and facing the sea, downtown Aptos—known as Aptos Village—is a place of wooden walkways and false-fronted shops. Antiques dealers cluster along Trout Gulch Road, off Soquel Drive east of Highway 1.

GETTING HERE AND AROUND

Use Highway 1 to reach Aptos from Santa Cruz or Monterey. Exit at State Park Drive to reach the main shopping hub and Aptos Village. You can also exit at Freedom Boulevard or Rio del Mar. Soquel Drive is the main artery through town.

ESSENTIALS

Visitor Information Aptos Chamber of Commerce. ✉ *7605-A Old Dominion Ct.* ☎ *831/688–1467* 🌐 *aptoschamber.com.*

7

BEACHES

FAMILY Fodor's Choice ★ **Seacliff State Beach.** Sandstone bluffs tower above popular Seacliff State Beach. The 1.5 mile walk north to adjacent New Brighton State Beach in Capitola is one of the nicest on the bay. Leashed dogs are allowed on the beach. **Amenities:** food and drink; lifeguards; parking (fee); showers; toilets. **Best for:** sunset; swimming; walking. ✉ *201 State Park Dr., off Hwy. 1* ☎ *831/685–6500* 🌐 *www.parks.ca.gov* 🎟 *$10 per vehicle.*

WHERE TO EAT AND STAY

$$$ MEDITERRANEAN 🍴 **Bittersweet Bistro.** A large old tavern with cathedral ceilings houses this popular bistro, where chef-owner Thomas Vinolus draws culinary inspiration from the Mediterranean. The menu changes seasonally, but regular highlights include paella, seafood puttanesca, and pepper-crusted rib-eye steak with Cabernet demi-glace. **Known for:** value-laden happy hour; seafood specials; house-made desserts. [$] *Average main: $28* ✉ *787 Rio Del Mar Blvd., off Hwy. 1* ☎ *831/662–9799* 🌐 *www.bittersweetbistro.com* 🕒 *Closed Mon.*

$$$ HOTEL FAMILY 🏨 **Best Western Seacliff Inn.** Families and business travelers like this 6-acre property near Seacliff State Beach that's more resort than hotel. **Pros:** walking distance to the beach; family-friendly; hot breakfast buffet. **Cons:** close to freeway; occasional nighttime bar noise. [$] *Rooms from: $180* ✉ *7500 Old Dominion Ct.* ☎ *831/688–7300, 800/780–7234* 🌐 *seacliffinn.com* 🛏 *149 rooms* 🍽 *Breakfast.*

$$$ HOTEL 🏨 **Rio Sands Hotel.** A property-wide makeover completed in 2015 has made this casual two-building complex near the beach an even more exceptional value. **Pros:** two-minute walk to Rio Del Mar Beach (Seacliff State Beach is also nearby); free parking and Wi-Fi; close to a deli and restaurants. **Cons:** some rooms and suites are small; neighborhood becomes congested in summer. [$] *Rooms from: $179* ✉ *116 Aptos Beach Dr.* ☎ *831/688–3207, 800/826–2077* 🌐 *riosands.com* 🛏 *50 rooms* 🍽 *Breakfast.*

$$$$ RESORT FAMILY 🏨 **Seascape Beach Resort.** It's easy to unwind at this full-fledged resort on a bluff overlooking Monterey Bay. The spacious suites sleep from two to eight people. **Pros:** time share–style apartments; access to miles of beachfront; superb views. **Cons:** far from city life; most bathrooms are small. [$] *Rooms from: $300* ✉ *1 Seascape Resort Dr.* ☎ *831/688–6800, 800/929–7727* 🌐 *seascaperesort.com* 🛏 *285 suites* 🍽 *No meals.*

CAPITOLA AND SOQUEL

4 miles northwest of Aptos.

On the National Register of Historic places as California's first seaside resort town, the village of Capitola has been in a holiday mood since the late 1800s. Casual eateries, surf shops, and ice cream parlors pack its walkable downtown. Inland, across Highway 1, antiques shops line Soquel Drive in the town of Soquel. Wineries dot the Santa Cruz Mountains beyond.

GETTING HERE AND AROUND

From Santa Cruz or Monterey, follow Highway 1 to the Capitola/Soquel (Bay Avenue) exit about 7 miles south of Santa Cruz and head west to reach Capitola and east to access Soquel Village. On summer weekends, park for free in the lot behind the Crossroads Center, a block west of the freeway, and hop aboard the free Capitola Shuttle to the village.

CALIFORNIA'S OLDEST RESORT TOWN

As far as anyone knows for certain, Capitola is the oldest seaside resort town on the Pacific Coast. In 1856 a pioneer acquired Soquel Landing, the picturesque lagoon and beach where Soquel Creek empties into the bay, and built a wharf. Another man opened a campground along the shore, and his daughter named it Capitola after a heroine in a novel series. After the train came to town in the 1870s, thousands of vacationers began arriving to bask in the sun on the glorious beach.

ESSENTIALS

Visitor Information Capitola-Soquel Chamber of Commerce. ✉ *716-G Capitola Ave., Capitola* ☎ *831/475-6522* 🌐 *capitolachamber.com.*

BEACHES

FAMILY Fodor's Choice ★ **New Brighton State Beach.** Once the site of a Chinese fishing village, New Brighton is now a popular surfing and camping spot. Its Pacific Migrations Visitor Center traces the history of the Chinese and other peoples who settled around Monterey Bay. It also documents the migratory patterns of the area's wildlife, such as monarch butterflies and gray whales. Leashed dogs are allowed in the park. New Brighton connects with Seacliff Beach, and at low tide you can walk or run along this scenic stretch of sand for nearly 16 miles south (though you might have to wade through a few creeks). ■ **TIP→ The 1½-mile stroll from New Brighton to Seacliff's concrete ship is a local favorite.** **Amenities:** parking (fee); showers; toilets. **Best for:** sunset; swimming; walking. ✉ *1500 State Park Dr., off Hwy. 1, Capitola* ☎ *831/464–6329* 🌐 *www.parks.ca.gov* 🎫 *$10 per vehicle.*

7

WHERE TO EAT

$ SEAFOOD FAMILY 🍴 **Carpo's.** Locals love this casual counter where seafood predominates, but you can also order burgers, salads, and steaks. Baskets of battered snapper are among the favorites, along with calamari, prawns, seafood kebabs, fish and chips, and homemade olallieberry pie. **Known for:** large portions of healthy comfort food; lots of options under $10; soup and salad bar. [$] *Average main: $13* ✉ *2400 Porter St., at Hwy. 1, Soquel* ☎ *831/476–6260* 🌐 *carposrestaurant.com.*

$$ CAFÉ FAMILY 🍴 **Gayle's Bakery & Rosticceria.** Whether you're in the mood for an orange-olallieberry muffin, a wild rice and chicken salad, or tri-tip on garlic toast, this bakery-deli's varied menu is likely to satisfy. Munch on your lemon meringue tartlet or chocolate brownie on the shady patio, or dig into the daily blue-plate dinner—teriyaki grilled skirt steak with edamame-shiitake sticky rice, perhaps, or roast turkey breast with Chardonnay gravy—amid the whirl of activity inside. **Known for:** prepared meals to go; on-site bakery and rosticceria; deli and espresso bar. [$] *Average main: $16* ✉ *504 Bay Ave., at Capitola Ave., Capitola* ☎ *831/462–1200* 🌐 *gaylesbakery.com.*

$$$ AMERICAN 🍴 **Michael's on Main.** Creative variations on classic comfort food and live music five nights a week draw lively crowds to this upscale but casual creekside eatery. Cordon Bleu-trained chef Peter Henry's menu changes seasonally, but might include skirt steak with pickled strawberry chimichurri

or chargrilled prawns with a Thai chili glaze. **Known for:** locally sourced, usually within 50 miles; excellent wine list; romantic patio overlooking Soquel Creek. $ *Average main: $28* ⊠ *2591 Main St., at Porter St., Soquel* 🕾 *831/479–9777* ⊕ *michaelsonmain.net* ⊘ *Closed Mon.*

$$$$ ✕ **Shadowbrook.** To get to this romantic spot overlooking Soquel Creek,
EUROPEAN   you can take a cable car or walk the stairs down a steep, fern-lined bank beside a running waterfall. Dining room options include the rooftop Redwood Room, the wood-paneled Wine Cellar, the creekside, glass-enclosed Greenhouse, the Fireplace Room, and the airy Garden Room. **Known for:** romantic creekside setting; prime rib and grilled seafood; local special-occasion favorite for nearly 70 years. $ *Average main: $32* ⊠ *1750 Wharf Rd., at Lincoln Ave., Capitola* 🕾 *831/475–1511* ⊕ *www. shadowbrook-capitola.com* ⊘ *No lunch.*

WHERE TO STAY

$$$$ ⬚ **Inn at Depot Hill.** This inventively designed bed-and-breakfast in a
B&B/INN   former rail depot views itself as a link to the era of luxury train travel. **Pros:** short walk to beach and village; historic charm; excellent service. **Cons:** fills quickly; hot-tub conversation audible in some rooms. $ *Rooms from: $299* ⊠ *250 Monterey Ave., Capitola* 🕾 *831/462–3376, 800/572–2632* ⊕ *www.innatdepothill.com* ⇆ *12 rooms* ⦿*Breakfast.*

SANTA CRUZ

5 miles west of Capitola, 48 miles north of Monterey.

The big city on this stretch of the California coast, Santa Cruz (pop. 63,364) is less manicured than Carmel or Monterey. Long known for its surfing and its amusement-filled beach boardwalk, the town is a mix of grand Victorian-era homes and rinky-dink motels. The opening of the University of California campus in the 1960s swung the town sharply to the left politically, and the counterculture more or less lives on here. At the same time, the revitalized downtown and an insane real-estate market reflect the city's proximity to Silicon Valley and to a growing wine country in the surrounding mountains. Amble around the downtown Santa Cruz Farmer's Market (Wednesday afternoons year-round) to experience the local culture, which derives much of its character from close connections to food and farming. The market covers a city block and includes not just the expected organic produce, but also live music and booths with local crafts and prepared food.

GETTING HERE AND AROUND

From the San Francisco Bay Area, take Highway 17 south over the mountains to Santa Cruz, where it merges with Highway 1. Use Highway 1 to get around the area. The Santa Cruz Transit Center is at 920 Pacific Avenue, at Front Street, a short walk from the Wharf and Boardwalk, with connections to public transit throughout the Monterey Bay and San Francisco Bay areas. You can purchase day passes for Santa Cruz METRO buses (*Bus Travel, in Planner*) here.

ESSENTIALS

Visitor Information Visit Santa Cruz County. ⊠ *303 Water St., No. 100* 🕾 *831/425–1234, 800/833–3494* ⊕ *visitsantacruz.org.*

EXPLORING

TOP ATTRACTIONS

Pacific Avenue. When you've had your fill of the city's beaches and waters, take a stroll in downtown Santa Cruz, especially on Pacific Avenue between Laurel and Water streets. Vintage boutiques and mountain-sports stores, sushi bars, and Mexican restaurants, day spas, and nightclubs keep the main drag and the surrounding streets hopping from midmorning until late evening.

FAMILY

Fodor'sChoice

★

Santa Cruz Beach Boardwalk. Santa Cruz has been a seaside resort since the mid-19th century. Along one end of the broad, south-facing beach, the Boardwalk has entertained holidaymakers for more than a century. Its Looff carousel and classic wooden Giant Dipper roller coaster, both dating from the early 1900s, are surrounded by high-tech thrill rides and easygoing kiddie rides with ocean views. Video and arcade games, a minigolf course, and a laser-tag arena pack one gigantic building, which is open daily even if the rides aren't running. You have to pay to play, but you can wander the entire boardwalk for free while sampling carnival fare such as corn dogs and garlic fries. ⊠ *Along Beach St.* ☎ *831/423–5590 info line* ⊕ *beachboardwalk.com* ✉ *$37 day pass for unlimited rides, or pay per ride* ⊙ *Some rides closed Sept.–May.*

FAMILY

Santa Cruz Municipal Wharf. Jutting half a mile into the ocean near one end of the boardwalk, the century-old Municipal Wharf is lined with seafood restaurants, a wine bar, souvenir shops, and outfitters offering bay cruises, fishing trips, and boat rentals. A salty soundtrack drifts up from under the wharf, where barking sea lions lounge in heaps on the crossbeams. Docents from the Seymour Marine Discovery Center lead free 30-minute tours on spring and summer weekends at 1 and 3; meet at the stage on the west side of the wharf between Olitas Cantina and Marini's Candies. ⊠ *Beach St. and Pacific Ave.* ☎ *831/459–3800 tour information.*

Santa Cruz Surfing Museum. This museum inside the Mark Abbott Memorial Lighthouse chronicles local surfing history. Photographs show old-time surfers, and a display of boards includes rarities such as a heavy redwood plank predating the fiberglass era and the remains of a modern board chomped by a great white shark. Surfer docents reminisce about the good old days. ⊠ *Lighthouse Point Park, 701 W. Cliff Dr. near Pelton Ave.* ☎ *831/420–6289* ⊕ *santacruzsurfingmuseum.org* ✉ *$2 suggested donation* ⊙ *Closed Tues. and Wed.*

Fodor'sChoice

★

West Cliff Drive. The road that winds along an oceanfront bluff from the municipal wharf to Natural Bridges State Beach makes for a spectacular drive, but it's even more fun to walk or bike the paved path that parallels the road. Surfers bob and swoosh in Monterey Bay at several points near the foot of the bluff, especially at a break known as **Steamer Lane.** Named for a surfer who died here in 1965, the nearby Mark Abbott Memorial Lighthouse stands at Point Santa Cruz, the cliff's major promontory. From here you can watch pinnipeds hang out, sunbathe, and frolic on Seal Rock. ⊠ *Santa Cruz.*

7

WORTH NOTING

FAMILY **Monterey Bay National Marine Sanctuary Exploration Center.** The interactive and multimedia exhibits at this fascinating interpretive center reveal and explain the treasures of the nation's largest marine sanctuary. The two-story building, across from the main beach and municipal wharf, has films and exhibits about migratory species, watersheds, underwater canyons, kelp forests, and intertidal zones. The second-floor deck has stellar ocean views and an interactive station that provides real-time weather, surf, and buoy reports. ⊠ *35 Pacific Ave., near Beach St.* ☎ *831/421–9993* ⊕ *montereybay.noaa.gov/vc/sec* ✍ *Free* ⊘ *Closed Mon. and Tues.*

Mystery Spot. Hokey tourist trap or genuine scientific enigma? Since 1940, curious throngs baffled by the Mystery Spot have made it one of the most visited attractions in Santa Cruz. The laws of gravity and physics don't appear to apply in this tiny patch of redwood forest, where balls roll uphill and people stand on a slant. ■TIP→ On weekends and holidays, it's wise to purchase tickets online in advance. ⊠ *465 Mystery Spot Rd., off Branciforte Dr. (north off Hwy. 1)* ☎ *831/423–8897* ⊕ *mysteryspot.com* ✍ *$8, parking $5.*

OFF THE BEATEN PATH

Surf City Vintners. A dozen tasting rooms of limited-production wineries occupy renovated warehouse spaces west of the beach. MJA, Sones Cellars, and Equinox are good places to start. Also here are the Santa Cruz Mountain Brewing Company and El Salchicheroa, popular for its homemade sausages, jams, and pickled and candied vegetables. ⊠ *Swift Street Courtyard, 334 Ingalls St., at Swift St., off Hwy. 1 (Mission St.)* ⊕ *surfcityvintners.com.*

UC Santa Cruz. The 2,000-acre University of California Santa Cruz campus nestles in the forested hills above town. Its sylvan setting, ocean vistas, and redwood architecture make the university worth a visit, as does its **arboretum** ($5, open daily from 9 to 5), whose walking path leads through areas dedicated to the plants of California, Australia, New Zealand, and South Africa. ■TIP→ Free shuttles help students and visitors get around campus, and you can join a guided tour (online reservation required). ⊠ *Main entrance at Bay and High Sts. (turn left on High for arboretum)* ☎ *831/459–0111* ⊕ *www.ucsc.edu/visit.*

Wilder Ranch State Park. In this park's Cultural Preserve you can visit the homes, barns, workshops, and bunk house of a 19th-century dairy farm. Nature has reclaimed most of the ranch land, and native plants and wildlife have returned to the 7,000 acres of forest, grassland, canyons, estuaries, and beaches. Hike, bike, or ride horseback on miles of ocean-view trails. Dogs aren't allowed at Wilder Ranch. ⊠ *Hwy. 1, 1 mile north of Santa Cruz* ☎ *831/426–0505 Interpretive Center, 831/423–9703 trail information* ⊕ *www.parks.ca.gov* ✍ *$10 per car* ⊘ *Interpretive center closed Mon.–Wed.*

BEACHES

FAMILY **Natural Bridges State Beach.** At the end of West Cliff Drive lies this stretch of soft sand edged with tide pools and sea-sculpted rock bridges. **■ TIP→ From September to early January a colony of monarch butterflies roosts in the eucalyptus grove.** **Amenities:** lifeguards; parking (fee); toilets. **Best for:** sunrise; sunset; surfing; swimming. ✉ *2531 W. Cliff Dr.* ☎ *831/423–4609* 🌐 *www.parks.ca.gov* 🎫 *Beach free, parking $10.*

FAMILY **Twin Lakes State Beach.** Stretching a half-mile along the coast on both sides of the small-craft jetties, Twin Lakes is one of Monterey Bay's sunniest beaches. It encompasses Seabright State Beach (with access in a residential neighborhood on the upcoast side) and Black's Beach on the downcoast side. Families often come here to sunbathe, picnic, and hike the nature trail around adjacent Schwann Lake. Parking is tricky on weekends from April through September—you need to pay for an $8 day use permit at a kiosk and the lot fills quickly—but you can park all day in the harbor pay lot and walk here. Leashed dogs are allowed. **Amenities:** food and drink; lifeguards (seasonal); parking; showers; toilets; water sports (seasonal). **Best for:** sunset; surfing; swimming; walking. ✉ *7th Ave., at East Cliff Dr.* ☎ *831/427–4868* 🌐 *www.parks.ca.gov.*

WHERE TO EAT

$$ MODERN AMERICAN 🍴 **Assembly.** Seasonal, sustainably farmed local ingredients inspire this downtown eatery's rustic California cuisine. An adjacent pop-up space temporarily hosts rising chefs who create dishes with ingredients sourced from local purveyors before moving on. **Known for:** rustic locavore fare and seasonal menus; live music Thursday. [$] *Average main: $19* ✉ *1108 Pacific Ave., at Cathcart St.* ☎ *831/824–6100* 🌐 *assembly.restaurant* 🕒 *Closed Mon. and Tues. during off-season; call to verify hrs.*

$$ SEAFOOD FAMILY 🍴 **Crow's Nest.** A classic California beachside restaurant, the Crow's Nest sits right on the water in Santa Cruz Harbor. Vintage surfboards and local surf photography line the walls in the main dining room, and nearly every table overlooks sand and surf. **Known for:** house-smoked salmon and calamari apps; crab-cake eggs Benedict and olallieberry pancakes; ocean views. [$] *Average main: $21* ✉ *2218 E. Cliff Dr., west of 7th Ave.* ☎ *831/476–4560* 🌐 *crowsnest-santacruz.com.*

$$ MEDITERRANEAN Fodor's Choice ★ 🍴 **Laili Restaurant.** Exotic Mediterranean flavors with an Afghan twist take center stage at this artsy, stylish space with soaring ceilings. Evenings are especially lively, when locals come to relax over wine and soft jazz at the blue-concrete bar, the heated patio with twinkly lights, or at a communal table near the open kitchen. **Known for:** house-made pastas and numerous vegetarian and vegan options; fresh naan, chutneys and dips with every meal. [$] *Average main: $20* ✉ *101–B Cooper St., near Pacific Ave.* ☎ *831/423–4545* 🌐 *lailirestaurant.com* 🕒 *Closed Mon.*

$$$ ITALIAN 🍴 **La Posta.** Authentic Italian fare made with fresh local produce lures diners into cozy, modern-rustic La Posta. Nearly everything is made in-house, from the pizzas and breads baked in the brick oven to the pasta and the vanilla-bean gelato. **Known for:** seasonal wild-nettle lasagne; braised lamb shank. [$] *Average main: $24* ✉ *538 Seabright Ave., at Logan St.* ☎ *831/457–2782* 🌐 *lapostarestaurant.com* 🕒 *Closed Mon. No lunch.*

$$$ EUROPEAN 🍴 **Oswald.** Sophisticated yet unpretentious European-inspired California cooking is the order of the day at this intimate and stylish bistro. The menu changes seasonally, but might include such items as seafood risotto or crispy duck breast in a pomegranate reduction sauce. **Known for:** classic American burger; craft cocktails. [$] *Average main: $30* ✉ *121 Soquel Ave., at Front St.* ☎ *831/423–7427* 🌐 *oswaldrestaurant.com* 🕒 *Closed Mon. No lunch Sun.–Tues.*

$$$ MEDITERRANEAN Fodor's Choice ★ 🍴 **Soif.** Wine reigns at this sleek bistro and wineshop that takes its name from the French word for thirst. The selections come from near and far, and you can order many of them by the taste or glass. **Known for:** Mediterranean-style dishes; well-stocked wine shop. [$] *Average main: $25* ✉ *105 Walnut Ave., at Pacific Ave.* ☎ *831/423–2020* 🌐 *soifwine.com* 🕒 *No lunch.*

WHERE TO STAY

$$$ B&B/INN 🏨 **Babbling Brook Inn.** Though it's in the middle of Santa Cruz, this bed-and-breakfast has lush gardens, a running stream, and tall trees that make you feel like you're in a secluded wood. **Pros:** close to UCSC; within walking distance of downtown shops; woodsy feel. **Cons:** near a high school; some rooms close to a busy street. [$] *Rooms from: $249* ✉ *1025 Laurel St.* ☎ *831/427–2437, 800/866–1131* 🌐 *babblingbrookinn.com* 🛏 *13 rooms* 🍽 *Breakfast.*

$$ HOTEL 🏨 **Carousel Beach Inn.** This basic but comfy motel, decorated in bold, retro seaside style and across the street from the Boardwalk is ideal for travelers who want easy access to the sand and the amusement park rides without spending a fortune. **Pros:** steps from Santa Cruz Main Beach; affordable lodging rates and ride packages; free parking and Wi-Fi. **Cons:** no pool or spa; no exercise room; not pet-friendly. [$] *Rooms from: $159* ✉ *110 Riverside Ave.* ☎ *831/425–7090* 🌐 *santacruzmotels.com/carousel.html* 🛏 *34 rooms* 🍽 *Breakfast.*

$$$$ RESORT 🏨 **Chaminade Resort & Spa.** Secluded on 300 hilltop acres of redwood and eucalyptus forest with hiking trails, this Mission-style complex commands expansive views of Monterey Bay. Guest rooms were completely remodeled in 2016 and are furnished in an eclectic, bohemian style that pays homage to the artsy local community and the city's industrial past, while incorporating vintage game elements throughout. **Pros:** far from city life; spectacular property; ideal spot for romance and rejuvenation. **Cons:** must drive to attractions and sights; near a major hospital. [$] *Rooms from: $269* ✉ *1 Chaminade La.* ☎ *800/283–6569 reservations, 831/475–5600* 🌐 *www.chaminade.com* 🛏 *156 rooms* 🍽 *No meals.*

$$$ HOTEL 🏨 **Fairfield Inn & Suites by Marriott Santa Cruz.** Built from scratch in 2016, this four-story hotel sits at the far northwestern end of Santa Cruz just off Highway 1 and is a good choice for families and business travelers who want to be close to the beach or UC Santa Cruz, but not in the thick of the boardwalk action. **Pros:** convenient location near UC Santa Cruz and Highway 1; great sunset views from some rooms; biking trails near property. **Cons:** no on-site restaurant; open parking lot (not locked). [$] *Rooms from: $179* ✉ *2956 Mission St.* ✣ *At Western Dr.* ☎ *831/420–0777* 🌐 *marriott.com/sjccr* 🛏 *82 rooms* 🍽 *Breakfast.*

$$$$ HOTEL **Hotel Paradox.** About a mile from the ocean and two blocks from Pacific Avenue, this stylish, forest-theme complex (part of the Marriott Autograph Collection) is among the few full-service hotels in town. **Pros:** close to downtown and main beach; alternative to beach-oriented lodgings; contemporary feel. **Cons:** pool area can get crowded on warm-weather days; some rooms on the small side. [$] *Rooms from: $279* ✉ *611 Ocean St.* ☎ *831/425-7100, 855/425-7200* 🌐 *hotelparadox.com* *172 rooms* 🍴 *No meals.*

$$$ B&B/INN **Pacific Blue Inn.** Green themes predominate in this three-story, eco-friendly bed-and-breakfast, on a sliver of prime downtown property. **Pros:** free parking; free bicycles; downtown location. **Cons:** tiny property; not suitable for children. [$] *Rooms from: $189* ✉ *636 Pacific Ave.* ☎ *831/600-8880* 🌐 *pacificblueinn.com* *9 rooms* 🍴 *No meals.*

$$$$ HOTEL Fodor's Choice ★ **Santa Cruz Dream Inn.** A short stroll from the boardwalk and wharf, this full-service luxury hotel is the only lodging in Santa Cruz directly on the beach. **Pros:** directly on the beach; easy parking; walk to boardwalk and downtown. **Cons:** expensive; area gets congested on summer weekends. [$] *Rooms from: $369* ✉ *175 W. Cliff Dr.* ☎ *831/426-4330* 🌐 *dreaminnsantacruz.com* *165 rooms* 🍴 *No meals.*

$$$ B&B/INN Fodor's Choice ★ **West Cliff Inn.** With views of the boardwalk and Monterey Bay, the West Cliff perches on the bluffs across from Cowell Beach. **Pros:** killer views; walking distance of the beach; close to downtown. **Cons:** boardwalk noise; street traffic. [$] *Rooms from: $249* ✉ *174 West Cliff Dr.* ☎ *800/979-0910 toll free, 831/457-2200* 🌐 *www.westcliffinn.com* *9 rooms, 1 cottage* 🍴 *Breakfast.*

7

NIGHTLIFE AND PERFORMING ARTS

NIGHTLIFE

Catalyst. This huge, grimy, and fun club books rock, indie rock, punk, death-metal, reggae, and other acts. ✉ *1011 Pacific Ave.* ☎ *877/987-6487 tickets* 🌐 *catalystclub.com.*

Kuumbwa Jazz Center. The center draws top performers such as the Lee Ritenour and Dave Grusin, Chris Potter, and the Dave Holland Trio; the café serves meals an hour before most shows. ✉ *320-2 Cedar St.* ☎ *831/427-2227* 🌐 *kuumbwajazz.org.*

Moe's Alley. Blues, salsa, reggae, funk: delightfully casual Moe's presents it all (and more). ✉ *1535 Commercial Way* ☎ *831/479-1854* 🌐 *moesalley.com* ⏲ *Closed Mon.*

PERFORMING ARTS

Tannery Arts Center. The former Salz Tannery now contains nearly 30 studios and live-work spaces for artists whose disciplines range from ceramics and glass to film and digital media; most have public hours of business. The social center is the **Artbar & Cafe,** which in the late afternoons and evenings hosts poets, all types of performers, and live music. Performances also take place at the on-site Colligan Theater. The center also hosts assorted arts events on weekends and occasionally on weekdays. ✉ *1060 River St., at intersection of Hwys. 1 and 9* 🌐 *tanneryartscenter.org/.*

SPORTS AND THE OUTDOORS

ADVENTURE TOURS

Mount Hermon Adventures. Zip-line through the redwoods at this adventure center in the Santa Cruz Mountains. On some summer weekends there's an aerial adventure course with obstacles and challenges in the redwoods. ■ TIP→ To join a tour (reservations essential), you must be at least 10 years old and weigh between 75 and 250 pounds. ⊠ *17 Conference Dr., 9 miles north of downtown Santa Cruz near Felton, Mount Hermon* ☎ *831/430–4357* ⊕ *mounthermonadventures.com* ☜ *From $65.*

BICYCLING

Another Bike Shop. Mountain bikers should head here for tips on the best area trails and to browse cutting-edge gear made and tested locally. ⊠ *2361 Mission St., at King St.* ☎ *831/427–2232* ⊕ *www.anotherbikeshop.com.*

BOATS AND CHARTERS

Chardonnay II Sailing Charters. The 70-foot *Chardonnay II* departs year-round from Santa Cruz yacht harbor on whale-watching, sunset, and other cruises around Monterey Bay. Most regularly scheduled excursions cost $64; food and drink are served on many of them. Reservations are essential. ⊠ *Santa Cruz West Harbor, 790 Mariner Park Way* ☎ *831/423–1213* ⊕ *chardonnay.com.*

Stagnaro Sport Fishing, Charters & Whale Watching Cruises. Stagnaro operates salmon, albacore, and rock-cod fishing expeditions; the fees include bait. The company (aka Santa Cruz Whale Watching) also runs whale-watching, dolphin, and sea-life cruises year-round. ⊠ *1718 Brommer St., near Santa Cruz Harbor* ☎ *831/427–0230 whale watching, 888/237–7084 tickets, 831/427–2334 fishing* ⊕ *stagnaros.com* ☜ *From $50.*

GOLF

Pasatiempo Golf Club. Designed by famed golf architect Dr. Alister MacKenzie in 1929, this semiprivate course, set amid undulating hills just above the city, is among the nation's top championship courses. Golfers rave about the spectacular views and challenging terrain. According to the club, MacKenzie, who designed Pebble Beach's exclusive Cypress Point course and Augusta National in Georgia, the home of the Masters Golf Tournament, declared this his favorite layout. ⊠ *20 Clubhouse Rd.* ☎ *831/459–9155* ⊕ *www.pasatiempo.com* ☜ *From $260* ⚑ *18 holes, 6125 yards, par 72.*

KAYAKING

Kayak Connection. From March through May, participants in this outfit's tours mingle with gray whales and their calves on their northward journey to Alaska. Throughout the year, the company rents kayaks and paddleboards and conducts tours of Natural Bridges State Beach, Capitola, and Elkhorn Slough. ⊠ *Santa Cruz Harbor, 413 Lake Ave., No. 3* ☎ *831/479–1121* ⊕ *kayakconnection.com* ☜ *From $60 for scheduled tours.*

O'Neill: A Santa Cruz Icon

O'Neill wet suits and beachwear weren't exactly born in Santa Cruz, but as far as most of the world is concerned, the O'Neill brand is synonymous with Santa Cruz and surfing legend.

The O'Neill wet-suit story began in 1952, when Jack O'Neill and his brother Robert opened their first Surf Shop in a garage across from San Francisco's Ocean Beach. While shaping balsa surfboards and selling accessories, the O'Neills experimented with solutions to a common surfer problem: frigid waters. Tired of being forced back to shore, blue-lipped and shivering, after just 20 or 30 minutes riding the waves, they played with various materials and eventually designed a neoprene vest.

In 1959 Jack moved his Surf Shop 90 miles south to Cowell's Beach in Santa Cruz. It quickly became a popular surf hangout, and O'Neill's new wet suits began to sell like hotcakes. In the early 1960s, the company opened a warehouse for manufacturing on a larger scale. Santa Cruz soon became a major surf city, attracting wave riders to prime breaks at Steamer Lane, Pleasure Point, and the Hook. In 1965 O'Neill pioneered the first wet-suit boots, and in 1971 Jack's son invented the surf leash. By 1980, O'Neill stood at the top of the world wet-suit market. On June 2, 2017, Jack O'Neill passed away at the age of 94, in his longtime Pleasure Point residence overlooking the surf.

Venture Quest Kayaking. Explore hidden coves and kelp forests on guided two-hour kayak tours that depart from Santa Cruz Wharf. The tours include a kayaking lesson. Venture Quest also rents kayaks (and wet suits and gear), and arranges tours at other Monterey Bay destinations, including Elkhorn Slough. ⊠ *2 Santa Cruz Wharf* ☎ *831/427–2267 kayak hotline, 831/425–8445 rental office* ⊕ *kayaksantacruz.com* ▱ *From $35 for rentals, $60 for tours.*

SURFING

EQUIPMENT AND LESSONS

Club-Ed Surf School and Camps. Find out what all the fun is about at Club-Ed. Your first private or group lesson ($90 and up) includes all equipment. ⊠ *Cowell's Beach, at Santa Cruz Dream Inn* ☎ *831/464–0177* ⊕ *club-ed.com.*

Cowell's Beach Surf Shop. This shop sells gear, clothing, and swimwear; rents surfboards, stand-up paddle boards, and wet suits; and offers lessons. ⊠ *30 Front St.* ☎ *831/427–2355* ⊕ *cowellssurfshop.com.*

Richard Schmidt Surf School. Since 1978 Richard Schmidt has shared the stoke of surfing and the importance of ocean awareness and conservation with legions of students of all ages. Today the outfit offers surfing and standup paddleboard lessons (equipment provided) and marine adventure tours in Santa Cruz and elsewhere on the bay. Locations depend on where the waves are breaking or the wind's a'blowing, but typically convene at Cowell's Beach or Pleasure Point. ⊠ *Santa Cruz* ☎ *831/423–0928* ⊕ *www.richardschmidt.com* ▱ *From $90.*

SHOPPING

Bookshop Santa Cruz. In 2016 the town's best and most beloved independent bookstore celebrated its 50th anniversary of selling new, used, and remaindered titles. The children's section is especially comprehensive, and the shop's special events calendar is packed with readings, social mixers, book signings, and discussions. ✉ *1520 Pacific Ave.* ☎ *831/423–0900* ⊕ *bookshopsantacruz.com.*

O'Neill Surf Shop. Local surfers get their wetties (wet suits) and other gear at this O'Neill store or the one in Capitola, at 1115 41st Avenue. There's also a satellite shop on the Santa Cruz Boardwalk. ✉ *110 Cooper St.* ☎ *831/469–4377* ⊕ *www.oneill.com.*

FAMILY **Santa Cruz Downtown Farmers' Market.** Santa Cruz is famous for its long tradition of organic growing and sustainable living, and its downtown market (one of five countywide) especially reflects the incredible diversity and quality of local agriculture and synergistic daily life of community-minded residents. The busy market, which always has live music, happens every Wednesday from 1:30 to 5:30 (6:30 in summer), rain or shine. The stalls cover much of an entire city block near Pacific Avenue and include fresh produce plus everything from oysters, beer, bread, and charcuterie, to arts and crafts and hot prepared foods made from ingredients sourced from on-site vendors. ✉ *Cedar Street at Lincoln Street* ☎ *831/454–0566* ⊕ *www.santacruzfarmersmarket.org.*

The True Olive Connection. Taste your way through boutique extra-virgin olive oils and balsamic vinegars from around the world at this family-run shop. You can also pick up gourmet food products and olive-oil-based gift items. There's another location in Aptos. ✉ *106 Lincoln St., at. Pacific Ave.* ☎ *831/458–6457* ⊕ *trueoliveconnection.com.*

SAN FRANCISCO

WELCOME TO SAN FRANCISCO

TOP REASONS TO GO

★ **The bay:** It's hard not to gasp as you catch sight of sunlight dancing on the water when you crest a hill, or watch the Golden Gate Bridge vanish and reemerge in the summer fog.

★ **The food:** San Franciscans are serious about what they eat, and with good reason. Home to some of the nation's best chefs, top restaurants, and finest local produce, it's hard not to eat well here.

★ **The shopping:** Shopaholics visiting the city will not be disappointed— San Francisco is packed with browsing destinations, everything from quirky boutiques to massive malls.

★ **The good life:** A laid-back atmosphere, beautiful surroundings, and oodles of cultural, culinary, and aesthetic pleasures … if you spend too much time here, you might not leave.

★ **The great outdoors:** From Golden Gate Park to sidewalk cafés in North Beach, San Franciscans relish their outdoor spaces.

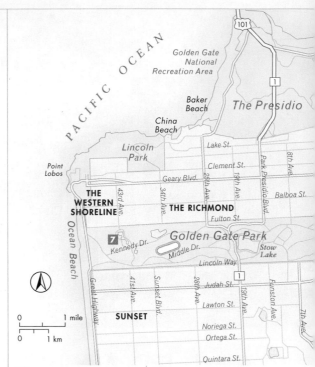

1 **Union Square and Chinatown.** Union Square has hotels, public transportation, and shopping; walking through Chinatown is like visiting a bustling street in Beijing.

2 **SoMa and Civic Center.** SoMa is anchored by SFMOMA and Yerba Buena Gardens; the city's performing arts venues are in Civic Center.

3 **Nob Hill and Russian Hill.** Nob Hill is old-money San Francisco; Russian Hill's steep streets have excellent eateries and shopping.

4 **North Beach.** The city's small Italian neighborhood makes even locals feel as if they're on holiday.

5 **On the Waterfront.** Wandering the shops and attractions of Fisherman's Wharf, Pier 39, and Ghirardelli Square, the only locals you'll meet will be the ones with visitors in tow.

6 **The Marina and the Presidio.** The Marina has trendy boutiques, restaurants, and cafés; the wooded Presidio offers great views of the Golden Gate Bridge.

5 **WATERFRONT**
Fisherman's Wharf ◆ Pier 39
◆
Marina Green
4
Ghirardelli Square ◆ Bay St. **NORTH BEACH**
6 **MARINA**
◆ Coit Tower
RUSSIAN HILL TELEGRAPH HILL
Lombard St. 101
Broadway **3** (tunnel)
NOB HILL **CHINATOWN**
PACIFIC HEIGHTS Washington St.
Sacramento St. California St. **FINANCIAL DISTRICT**
Pine St. **10**
Bush St. **1**
UNION SQUARE
Post St. **SF MOMA**
Geary Blvd. Geary St.
Turk St. Yerba Buena ◆ Gardens
JAPANTOWN **80**
San Francisco Bay
CIVIC CENTER **2** **SOMA**
Hayes St.
WESTERN ADDITION
Fell St. Duboce
HAIGHT Haight St.
Buena Vista Park **280**
Central Basin
CASTRO
8 **9** 17th St. Mariposa St.
MISSION
NOE VALLEY 20th St.
Twin Peaks ▲
24th St.
25th St.
Cesar Chavez St. *Islais Cr. Channel*

101

San Francisco–Oakland Bay Bridge

The Embarcadero

Columbus Ave.

8

---

7 **Golden Gate Park and the Western Shoreline.** San Francisco's 1,000-acre backyard has sports fields, windmills, museums, and gardens; the windswept Western Shoreline stretches for miles.

8 **The Haight, the Castro, and Noe Valley.** After you've seen the blockbuster sights, come to these neighborhoods to see where the city's heart beats.

9 **The Mission.** When the sun sets, people descend on the Mission for destination restaurants, excellent bargain-price ethnic eateries, and the hippest bar scene around.

10 **Pacific Heights and Japantown.** Pacific Heights has some of the city's most opulent real estate; Japantown is packed with authentic Japanese shops and restaurants.

GETTING ORIENTED

San Francisco is a compact city; just 46.7 square miles. Essentially a tightly packed cluster of extremely diverse neighborhoods, the city dearly rewards walking. The areas that most visitors cover are easy (and safe) to reach on foot, but many have steep— make that *steep*—hills.

Updated by Amanda Kuehn Carroll, Rebecca Flint Marx, Denise Leto, Danny Mangin, Andrea Powell, and Jerry James Stone

On a 46½-square-mile strip of land between San Francisco Bay and the Pacific Ocean, San Francisco has charms great and small. Residents cherish their city for the same reasons visitors do: the proximity to the bay, rows of Victorian homes clinging precariously to the hillsides, the sun setting behind the Golden Gate Bridge, the world-class cuisine. Locals and visitors alike spend hours exploring downtown, Chinatown, North Beach, the northern and western waterfronts, and Golden Gate Park, along with colorful neighborhoods like the Haight, the Mission murals, and the Castro.

The city's attraction, though, goes much deeper than its alluring physical space, from the diversity of its neighborhoods to its free-spirited tolerance. Take all these things together and you'll understand why many San Franciscans—despite the dizzying cost of living and the chilly summers—can't imagine calling any place else home.

You won't want to miss the City by the Bay's highlights, whether it's a cable car ride over Nob Hill; a walk down the Filbert Street Steps; gazing at the thundering Pacific from the cliffs of Lincoln Park; cheering the San Francisco Giants to *beat L.A.* in lively AT&T Park; or eating freshly shucked oysters at the Ferry Building. San Francisco is a beautiful metropolis packed with diverse wonders that inspire at every turn.

PLANNING

WHEN TO GO
You can visit San Francisco comfortably any time of year. Possibly the best time is September and October, when the city's summerlike weather brings outdoor concerts and festivals. The climate here always feels Mediterranean and moderate - with a foggy, sometimes chilly bite. The temperature rarely drops below 40°F, and anything warmer than 80°F

is considered a heat wave. Be prepared for rain in winter, especially December and January. Winds off the ocean can add to the chill factor. That old joke about summer in San Francisco feeling like winter is true at heart, but once you move inland, it gets warmer. (And some locals swear that the thermostat has inched up in recent years.)

GETTING HERE AND AROUND

AIR TRAVEL

The major gateway to San Francisco is San Francisco International Airport (SFO), 15 miles south of the city. It's off U.S. 101 near Millbrae and San Bruno. Oakland International Airport (OAK) is across the bay, not much farther away from downtown San Francisco (via I-80 east and I-880 south), but rush-hour traffic on the Bay Bridge may lengthen travel times considerably. San Jose International Airport (SJC) is about 40 miles south of San Francisco; travel time depends largely on traffic flow, but plan on an hour and a half with moderate traffic.

Airports San Francisco International Airport (SFO). ⊠ McDonnell and Link Rds., San Francisco ☏ 800/435-9736, 650/821-8211 ⊕ www.flysfo.com. **Oakland International Airport** (OAK). ⊠ 1 Airport Dr., Oakland ⊹ 2 miles west of I-880 ☏ 510/563-3300 ⊕ www.flyoakland.com.

Airport Transfers American Airporter. ☏ 415/202-0733 ⊕ www.americanair-porter.com. **Caltrain.** ☏ 800/660-4287 ⊕ www.caltrain.com. **East Bay Shuttle.** ☏ 925/800-4500 ⊕ www.eastbayshuttle.net. **GO Lorrie's Airport Shuttle.** ☏ 415/334-9000 ⊕ www.gosfovan.com. **Marin Airporter.** ☏ 415/461-4222 ⊕ www.marinairporter.com. **Marin Door to Door.** ☏ 415/457-2717 ⊕ www.marindoortodoor.com. **SamTrans.** ☏ 800/660-4287 ⊕ www.samtrans.com. **SuperShuttle.** ☏ 800/258-3826 ⊕ www.supershuttle.com.

BART TRAVEL

BART (Bay Area Rapid Transit) trains, which run until midnight, travel under the bay via tunnel to connect San Francisco with Oakland, Berkeley, and other cities and towns beyond. Within San Francisco, stations are limited to downtown, the Mission, and a couple of outlying neighborhoods.

Trains travel frequently from early morning until evening on weekdays. After 8 pm weekdays and on weekends there's often a 20-minute wait between trains on the same line. Trains also travel south from San Francisco as far as Millbrae. BART trains connect downtown San Francisco to San Francisco International Airport; the ride costs $8.95.

Intracity San Francisco fares are $1.95; intercity fares are $3.20 to $11.45. BART bases its ticket prices on miles traveled and doesn't offer price breaks by zone. The easy-to-read maps posted in BART stations list fares based on destination, radiating out from your starting point of the current station.

During morning and evening rush hour, trains within the city are crowded—even standing room can be hard to come by. Cars at the far front and back of the train are less likely to be filled to capacity. Smoking, eating, and drinking are prohibited on trains and in stations.

Contacts Bay Area Rapid Transit (BART). ☏ 415/989-2278 ⊕ www.bart.gov.

BOAT TRAVEL

Several ferry lines run out of San Francisco. Blue & Gold Fleet operates a number of routes, including service to Sausalito ($11.50 one-way) and Tiburon ($11.50 one-way). Tickets are sold at Pier 39; boats depart from Pier 41 nearby. Alcatraz Cruises, owned by Hornblower Cruises and Events, operates the ferries to Alcatraz Island ($35.50 including audio tour and National Park Service ranger-led programs) from Pier 33, about a half-mile east of Fisherman's Wharf. Boats leave 14 times a day (more in summer), and the journey itself takes 30 minutes. Allow at least 2½ hours for a round-trip jaunt. Golden Gate Ferry runs daily to and from Sausalito and Larkspur ($11.75 and $11 one-way), leaving from Pier 1, behind the San Francisco Ferry Building. The Alameda/Oakland Ferry operates daily between Alameda's Main Street Terminal, Oakland's Jack London Square, and San Francisco's Pier 41 and the Ferry Building ($6.60 one-way); some ferries go only to Pier 41 or the Ferry Building, so ask when you board. Purchase tickets on board.

Information Alameda/Oakland Ferry. ☎ 877/643-3779 ⊕ *sanfranciscobay-ferry.com*. **Alcatraz Cruises.** ☎ 415/981-7625 ⊕ *www.alcatrazcruises.com*. **Blue & Gold Fleet.** ☎ 415/705-8200 ⊕ *www.blueandgoldfleet.com*. **Ferry Building Marketplace.** ✉ *1 Ferry Bldg., at foot of Market St. on Embarcadero, San Francisco* ☎ 415/983-8030 ⊕ *www.ferrybuildingmarketplace.com*. **Golden Gate Ferry.** ☎ 415/923-2000 ⊕ *www.goldengateferry.org*.

CABLE-CAR TRAVEL

Don't miss the sensation of moving up and down some of San Francisco's steepest hills in a clattering cable car. Jump aboard as it pauses at a designated stop, and wedge yourself into any available space. Then just hold on.

The fare (for one direction) is $7. You can buy tickets on board (exact change isn't required but operators can only make change up to $20) or at the kiosks at the cable-car turnarounds at Hyde and Beach Streets and at Powell and Market Streets.

The heavily traveled Powell–Mason and Powell–Hyde lines begin at Powell and Market Streets near Union Square and terminate at Fisherman's Wharf; lines for these routes can be long, especially in summer. The California Street line runs east and west from Market and California Streets to Van Ness Avenue; there's often no wait to board this route.

CAR TRAVEL

Driving in San Francisco can be a challenge because of the one-way streets, snarly traffic, and steep hills. The first two elements can be frustrating enough, but those hills are tough for unfamiliar drivers. ■TIP➔ Remember to curb your wheels when parking on hills—turn wheels away from the curb when facing uphill, toward the curb when facing downhill. You can get a ticket if you don't do this.

MUNI TRAVEL

The San Francisco Municipal Railway, or Muni, operates light-rail vehicles, the historic F-line streetcars along Fisherman's Wharf and Market Street, buses, and the world-famous cable cars. Light rail travels along Market Street to the Mission District and Noe Valley (J line), the Ingleside District (K line), and the Sunset District (L, M, and N lines) while also passing through the West Portal, Glen Park, and Castro neighborhoods. The N line continues around the Embarcadero to the Caltrain station at 4th and King Streets; the T-line light rail runs from the Castro, down Market Street, around the Embarcadero, and south past Mission Bay and Hunters Point to Sunnydale Avenue and Bayshore Boulevard. Muni provides 24-hour service on select lines to all areas of the city.

On buses and streetcars the fare is $2.50. Exact change is required, and dollar bills are accepted in the fare boxes. For all Muni vehicles other than cable cars, 90-minute transfers are issued free upon request at the time the fare is paid. These are valid for unlimited transfers in any direction until they expire (time is indicated on the ticket). Cable cars cost $7 and include no transfers *(see Cable-Car Travel)*.

One-day ($21), three-day ($32), and seven-day ($42) Passports valid on the entire Muni system can be purchased at several outlets, including the cable-car ticket booth at Powell and Market Streets and the visitor information center downstairs in Hallidie Plaza. A monthly ticket is available for $80, and can be used on all Muni lines (including cable cars) and on BART within city limits. The San Francisco CityPass ($86), a discount ticket booklet to several major city attractions, also covers all Muni travel for seven consecutive days.

The San Francisco Municipal Transit and Street Map ($5) is a useful guide to the extensive transportation system. You can buy the map at most bookstores and at the San Francisco Visitor Information Center, on the lower level of Hallidie Plaza at Powell and Market Streets.

BUS OPERATORS — Outside the city, AC Transit serves the East Bay, and Golden Gate Transit serves Marin County and a few cities in southern Sonoma County.

Bus and Muni Information **San Francisco Municipal Transportation Agency** *(Muni).* ☎ *311, 415/701–3000* ⊕ *www.sfmta.com.*

TAXI TRAVEL

Taxi service is notoriously bad in San Francisco, and finding a cab can be frustratingly difficult. Popular nightspots such as the Mission, SoMa, North Beach, and the Castro are the easiest places to hail a cab off the street; hotel taxi stands are also an option. If you're going to the airport, make a reservation or book a shuttle instead. Taxis in San Francisco charge $3.50 for the first 0.5 mile (one of the highest base rates in the United States), 55¢ for each additional 0.2 mile, and 55¢ per minute in stalled traffic; a $4 surcharge is added for trips from the airport. There's no charge for additional passengers; there's no surcharge for luggage. For trips further than 15 miles outside city limits, multiply the metered rate by 1.5; tolls and tip are extra.

That said, San Francisco's poor taxi service was a direct factor in the creation of ride-sharing services such as Uber and Lyft, which are easy to use and prominent throughout the city and its surrounding areas. San Franciscans generally regard taxis as a thing of the past and use ride-sharing on a day-to-day basis. If you're willing to share a car with strangers, a trip within the city can run as low as $4; rates go up for private rides and during peak demand times. These services are especially economical when going to or from the airport, where a shared ride will run you about $25—half the cost of a cab.

8

Taxi Companies Flywheel Taxi. ☎ *415/970–1303* ⊕ *flywheeltaxi.com.* **Luxor Cab.** ☎ *415/282–4141* ⊕ *www.luxorcab.com.* **National Veterans Cab.** ☎ *415/321–8294* ⊕ *sfnationalcab.sftaxischool.com/index.html.* **Yellow Cab.** ☎ *415/333–3333* ⊕ *yellowcabsf.com.*

Complaints San Francisco Police Department Taxi Complaints. ☎ *415/701–4400.*

TRAIN TRAVEL

Amtrak trains travel to the Bay Area from some cities in California and the United States. The *Coast Starlight* travels north from Los Angeles to Seattle, passing the Bay Area along the way, but contrary to its name, the train runs inland through the Central Valley for much of its route through Northern California; the most scenic stretch is in Southern California, between San Luis Obispo and Los Angeles. Amtrak also has several routes between San Jose, Oakland, and Sacramento. The *California Zephyr* travels from Chicago to the Bay Area, and has spectacular alpine vistas as it crosses the Sierra Nevada range. San Francisco doesn't have an Amtrak train station but does have an Amtrak bus stop at the Ferry Building, from which shuttle buses transport passengers to trains in Emeryville, just over the Bay Bridge. Shuttle buses also connect the Emeryville train station with BART and other points in downtown San Francisco. You can buy a California Rail Pass, which gives you 7 days of travel in a 21-day period for $159.

Caltrain connects San Francisco to Palo Alto, San Jose, Santa Clara, and many smaller cities en route. In San Francisco, trains leave from the main depot, at 4th and Townsend Streets, and a rail-side stop at 22nd and Pennsylvania Streets. One-way fares are $3.75 to $13.75, depending on the number of zones through which you travel; tickets are valid for four hours after purchase time. A ticket is $7.75 from San Francisco to Palo Alto, at least $9.75 to San Jose. You can also buy a day pass ($7.50–$27.50) for unlimited travel in a 24-hour period. It's worth waiting for an express train for trips that last from 1 to 1¾ hours. On weekdays, trains depart three or four times per hour during the morning and evening, only once or twice per hour during daytime non-commute hours and late night. Weekend trains run once per hour, though there are two bullet trains per day, one in late morning and one in early evening. The system shuts down after midnight. There are no onboard ticket sales. You must buy tickets before boarding the train or risk paying up to $250 for fare evasion.

Information Amtrak. ☎ *800/872–7245* ⊕ *www.amtrak.com.* **Caltrain.** ☎ *800/660–4287* ⊕ *www.caltrain.com.* **San Francisco Caltrain station.** ✉ *700 4th St., near Townsend St., San Francisco* ☎ *800/660–4287.*

VISITOR INFORMATION

The San Francisco Convention and Visitors Bureau can mail you brochures, maps, and events listings. Once in town, you can stop by the bureau's info center near Union Square.

Contacts San Francisco Visitor Information Center. ✉ *Hallidie Plaza, lower level, 900 Market St., at Powell St., Union Sq.* ☎ *415/391–2000* ⊕ *www.sftravel.com.*

EXPLORING SAN FRANCISCO

UNION SQUARE AND CHINATOWN

The Union Square area bristles with big-city bravado, while just a stone's throw away is a place that feels like a city unto itself, Chinatown. The two areas share a strong commercial streak, although manifested very differently. In Union Square—a plaza but also the neighborhood around it—the crowds zigzag among international brands, trailing glossy shopping bags. A few blocks north, people dash between small neighborhood stores, their arms draped with plastic totes filled with groceries or souvenirs.

UNION SQUARE

TOP ATTRACTIONS

Union Square. Ground zero for big-name shopping in the city and within walking distance of many hotels, Union Square is home base for many visitors. The Westin St. Francis Hotel and Macy's line two of the square's sides, and Saks, Neiman-Marcus, and Tiffany & Co. edge the other two. Four globular lamp sculptures by the artist R. M. Fischer preside over the landscaped, 2½-acre park, which has a café with outdoor seating, an open-air stage, and a visitor-information booth—along with a familiar kaleidoscope of characters: office workers sunning and brown-bagging, street musicians, shoppers taking a rest, kids chasing pigeons, and a fair number of homeless people. The constant clang of cable cars traveling up and down Powell Street helps maintain a festive mood.

The heart of San Francisco's downtown since 1850, the square takes its name from the violent pro-Union demonstrations staged here before the Civil War. At center stage, Robert Ingersoll Aitken's *Victory Monument* commemorates Commodore George Dewey's victory over the Spanish fleet at Manila in 1898. The 97-foot Corinthian column, topped by a bronze figure symbolizing naval conquest, was dedicated by Theodore Roosevelt in 1903 and withstood the 1906 earthquake. After the earthquake and fire of 1906, the square was dubbed "Little St. Francis" because of the temporary shelter erected for residents of the St. Francis Hotel. Actor John Barrymore (grandfather of actress Drew Barrymore and a notorious carouser) was among the guests pressed into volunteering to stack bricks in the square. His uncle, thespian John Drew, remarked, "It took an act of God to get John out of bed and the United States Army to get him to work." ⊠ *Bordered by Powell, Stockton, Post, and Geary Sts., Union Sq.*

WORTH NOTING

Maiden Lane. Known as Morton Street in the raffish Barbary Coast era, this former red-light district reported at least one murder a week during the late 19th century. Things cooled down after the 1906 fire destroyed the brothels, and these days Maiden Lane is a chic, boutique-lined pedestrian mall (favored by brides-to-be) stretching two blocks, between Stockton and Kearny Streets. Wrought-iron gates close the street to traffic most days between 11 and 5, when the lane becomes a patchwork of umbrella-shaded tables. At **140 Maiden Lane** is the only

The epicenter of high-end shopping, Union Square is lined with department stores.

Frank Lloyd Wright building in San Francisco, fronted by a large brick archway. The graceful, curving ramp and skylights of the interior are said to have been his model for the Guggenheim Museum in New York. ⊠ *Between Stockton and Kearny Sts., Union Sq.*

San Francisco Visitor Information Center. Head downstairs from the cable-car terminus to the visitor center, where multilingual staffers answer questions and provide maps and pamphlets. Muni Passports are sold here, and you can pick up discount coupons—the savings can be significant, especially for families. If you're planning to hit the big-ticket stops like the California Academy of Sciences and the Exploratorium and ride the cable cars, consider purchasing a CityPass (*www.citypass.com/san-francisco*) here. ■**TIP➜** The CityPass ($94, $69 ages 5–11), good for nine days, including seven days of transit, will save you 50%. The pass is also available at the attractions it covers, though if you choose the pass that includes Alcatraz—an excellent deal—you'll have to buy it directly from Alcatraz Cruises. ⊠ *Hallidie Plaza, lower level, 900 Market St., at Market and Powell Sts., Union Sq.* ☎ *415/391–2000,* ⊕ *www.sftravel.com* ☉ *Closed Sun. Nov.–Apr.*

Westin St. Francis Hotel. Built in 1904 and barely established as the most sumptuous hotel in town before it was ravaged by fire following the 1906 earthquake, this grande-dame hotel designed by Walter Danforth Bliss and William Baker Faville reopened in 1907 with the addition of a luxurious Italian Renaissance–style residence designed to attract loyal clients from among the world's rich and powerful. The hotel's checkered past includes the ill-fated 1921 bash in the suite of the silent-film superstar Fatty Arbuckle, at which a woman became ill and later died.

Arbuckle endured three sensational trials for rape and murder before being acquitted, by which time his career was kaput. In 1975, Sara Jane Moore, standing among a crowd outside the hotel, attempted to shoot then-President Gerald Ford. Of course the grand lobby contains no plaques commemorating these events. ■**TIP➔ Some visitors make the St. Francis a stop whenever they're in town, soaking up the lobby ambience or enjoying a cocktail in Clock Bar or a meal at the Oak Room Restaurant.** ⊠ *335 Powell St., at Geary St., Union Sq.* ☎ *415/397–7000* ⊕ *westinstfrancis.com.*

CHINATOWN

TOP ATTRACTIONS

Chinatown Gate. This is the official entrance to Chinatown. Stone lions flank the base of the pagoda-topped gate; the lions, dragons, and fish up top symbolize wealth, prosperity, and other good things. The four Chinese characters immediately beneath the pagoda represent the philosophy of Sun Yat-sen (1866–1925), the leader who unified China in the early 20th century. Sun Yat-sen, who lived in exile in San Francisco for a few years, promoted the notion of friendship and peace among all nations based on equality, justice, and goodwill. The vertical characters under the left pagoda read "peace" and "trust," the ones under the right pagoda "respect" and "love." The whole shebang telegraphs the internationally understood message of "photo op." Immediately beyond the gate, dive into souvenir shopping on Grant Avenue, Chinatown's tourist strip. ⊠ *Grant Ave. at Bush St., Chinatown.*

Fodor's Choice
★

Tin How Temple. Duck into the inconspicuous doorway, climb three flights of stairs, and be assaulted by the aroma of incense in this tiny, altar-filled room. In 1852, Day Ju, one of the first three Chinese to arrive in San Francisco, dedicated this temple to the Queen of the Heavens and the Goddess of the Seven Seas, and the temple looks largely the same today as it did more than a century ago. In the entryway, elderly ladies can often be seen preparing "money" to be burned as offerings to various Buddhist gods or as funds for ancestors to use in the afterlife. Hundreds of red-and-gold lanterns cover the ceiling; the larger the lamp, the larger its donor's contribution to the temple. Gifts of oranges, dim sum, and money left by the faithful, who kneel mumbling prayers, rest on altars to different gods. Tin How presides over the middle back of the temple, flanked by one red and one green lesser god. Take a good look around, since taking photographs is not allowed. ⊠ *125 Waverly Pl., between Clay and Washington Sts., Chinatown* ☐ *Free, donations accepted.*

WORTH NOTING

Chinese Historical Society of America Museum and Learning Center. The displays at this small, light-filled gallery document the Chinese-American experience—from 19th-century agriculture to 21st-century food and fashion trends—and include a thought-provoking collection of racist games and toys. The facility also has temporary exhibits of works by contemporary Chinese-American artists. ⊠ *965 Clay St., between Stockton and Powell Sts., Chinatown* ☎ *415/391–1188* ⊕ *www.chsa. org* ☐ *$15, free 1st Sun. of month* ☾ *Closed Mon.*

8

FAMILY **Golden Gate Fortune Cookie Factory.**
Follow your nose down Ross Alley to this tiny but fragrant cookie factory. Two workers sit at circular motorized griddles and wait for dollops of batter to drop onto a tiny metal plate, which rotates into an oven. A few moments later out comes a cookie that's pliable and ready for folding. It's easy to peek in for a moment, and hard to leave without a few free samples. A bagful of cookies—with mildly racy "adult" fortunes or more benign ones—costs under $5. ⊠ *56 Ross Alley, off Washington or Jackson St. west of Grant Ave., Chinatown* ☎ *415/781–3956* ⌕ *Free.*

> ## CABLE CAR TERMINUS
>
> Two of the three cable-car lines begin and end their runs at Powell and Market streets, a couple blocks south of Union Square. These two lines are the most scenic, and both pass near Fisherman's Wharf, so they're usually clogged with first-time sightseers. The wait to board a cable car at this intersection is longer than at any other stop in the system. If you'd rather avoid the mob, board the less-touristy California line at the bottom of Market Street, at Drumm Street.

Portsmouth Square. Chinatown's living room buzzes with activity. The square, with its pagoda-shape structures, is a favorite spot for morning tai chi; by noon dozens of men huddle around Chinese chess tables, engaged in competition. Kids scamper about the square's two grungy playgrounds (warning: the bathrooms are sketchy). Back in the late 19th century this land was near the waterfront. The square is named for the USS *Portsmouth*, the ship helmed by Captain John Montgomery, who in 1846 raised the American flag here and claimed the then-Mexican land for the United States. A couple of years later, Sam Brannan kicked off the gold rush at the square when he waved his loot and proclaimed, "Gold from the American River!" Robert Louis Stevenson, the author of *Treasure Island,* often dropped by, chatting up the sailors who hung out here. Some of the information he gleaned about life at sea found its way into his fiction. A bronze galleon sculpture, a tribute to Stevenson, anchors the square's northwest corner. A plaque marks the site of California's first public school, built in 1847. ⊠ *Bordered by Walter Lum Pl. and Kearny, Washington, and Clay Sts., Chinatown.*

SOMA, CIVIC CENTER, AND HAYES VALLEY

To a newcomer, SoMa (short for "south of Market") and the Civic Center may look like cheek-by-jowl neighbors—they're divided by Market Street. To locals, though, these areas are separate entities, especially since Market Street itself is considered such a strong demarcation line. Both neighborhoods have a core of cultural sights but more than their share of sketchy blocks. North of the Civic Center lies the western section of the frisky Tenderloin neighborhood, while to the east is hip Hayes Valley.

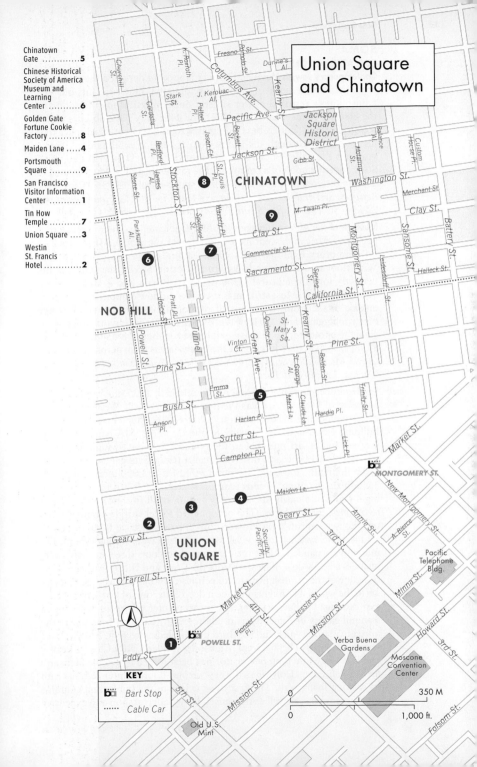

Union Square and Chinatown

CHINATOWN

Jackson Square Historic District

NOB HILL

UNION SQUARE

Yerba Buena Gardens

Moscone Convention Center

Pacific Telephone Bldg.

Old U.S. Mint

MONTGOMERY ST.

POWELL ST.

KEY

b Bart Stop

...... Cable Car

0   350 M

0   1,000 ft.

SOMA
TOP ATTRACTIONS

Contemporary Jewish Museum. Daniel Liebeskind designed the postmodern CJM, whose impossible-to-ignore diagonal blue cube juts out of a painstakingly restored power substation. A physical manifestation of the Hebrew phrase *l'chaim* (to life), the cube may have obscure philosophical origins, but Liebeskind created a unique, light-filled space that merits a stroll through the lobby even if current exhibits don't entice you into the galleries. ■TIP➔ San Francisco's best Jewish deli, Wise Sons, recently opened a counter in the museum, giving you a chance to sample the company's wildly popular smoked trout. ⊠ *736 Mission St., between 3rd and 4th Sts., SoMa* ☎ *415/655–7800* ⊕ *www.thecjm.org* ⊞ *$14; $5 Thurs. after 5 pm, free 1st Tues. of month* ☉ *Closed Wed.*

Museum of the African Diaspora (MoAD). Dedicated to the influence that people of African descent have had all over the world, MoAD focuses on temporary exhibits in its three galleries over two upper floors. With floor-to-ceiling windows onto Mission Street, the museum fits perfectly into the cultural scene of Yerba Buena and is well worth a 30-minute foray. Most striking is its front-window exhibit: a three-story mosaic, made from thousands of photographs, that forms the image of a young girl's face. ■TIP➔ Walk up the stairs inside the museum to view the photographs up close—Malcolm X is there, Muhammad Ali, too, along with everyday folks—but the best view is from across the street. ⊠ *685 Mission St., SoMa* ☎ *415/358–7200* ⊕ *www.moadsf.org* ⊞ *$10* ☉ *Closed Mon. and Tues.*

Fodor'sChoice
★ **San Francisco Museum of Modern Art.** Founded in 1935, the San Francisco Museum of Modern Art was the first museum on the West Coast dedicated to modern and contemporary art. In 2016, after a major three-year building expansion designed by Snøhetta, SFMOMA emerged as the largest modern art museum in the country and the revitalized anchor of the Yerba Buena arts district. Nearly tripling its gallery space over seven floors, the museum displays 1,900 of its 33,000-work collection, including a daunting 20-plus temporary exhibits. It can be overwhelming—you could easily spend a day taking it all in, but allow at least two hours; three is better. The original 3rd Street entrance remains, but use the new entrance on Howard Street to experience Richard Serra's gigantic *Sequence*, a gorgeous 15-foot-tall metal walk-through spiral. The museum's expanded collection, showcased on floors three through seven, includes a heavy dose of new art from the Doris and Donald Fisher Collection, one of the greatest private collections of modern and contemporary art in the world. Highlights include a deep collection of German abstract expressionist Gerhard Richter, American painter Ellsworth Kelly, and a tranquil gallery of Agnes Martin. Photography has long been one of the museum's strong suits, and the third floor is dedicated to it. Also look for seminal works by Diego Rivera, Alexander Calder, Chuck Close, Matisse, and Picasso. More than one visitor has been fooled by Duane Hanson's lifelike *Policeman*. Don't miss the new second-floor sculpture terrace with its striking living wall. The first floor is free to the public and contains four large works, as well as the museum's wonderful shop and expensive

Continued on page 343

CHINATOWN

Chinatown's streets flood the senses. Incense and cigarette smoke mingle with the scents of briny fish and sweet vanilla. Rooflines flare outward, pagoda-style. Loud Cantonese bargaining and honking car horns rise above the sharp clack of mah-jongg tiles and the eternally humming cables beneath the street.

Most Chinatown visitors march down Grant Avenue, buy a few trinkets, and call it a day. Do yourself a favor and dig deeper. This is one of the largest Chinese communities outside Asia, and there is far more to it than buying a back-scratcher near Chinatown Gate. To get a real feel for the neighborhood, wander off the main drag. Step into a temple or an herb shop and wander down a flag-draped alley. And don't be shy: residents welcome guests warmly, though rarely in English.

Whatever you do, don't leave without eating something. Noodle houses, bakeries, tea houses, and dim sum shops seem to occupy every other storefront. There's a feast for your eyes as well: in the market windows on Stockton and Grant, you'll see hanging whole roast ducks, fish, and shellfish swimming in tanks, and strips of shiny, pink-glazed Chinese-style barbecued pork.

CHINATOWN'S HISTORY

Sam Brannan's 1848 cry of "Gold!" didn't take long to reach across the world to China. Struggling with famine, drought, and political upheaval at home, thousands of Chinese jumped at the chance to try their luck in California. Most came from the Pearl River Delta region, in the Guangdong province, and spoke Cantonese dialects. From the start, Chinese businesses circled around Portsmouth Square, which was conveniently central. Bachelor rooming houses sprang up, since the vast majority of new arrivals were men. By 1853, the area was called Chinatown.

The Street of Gamblers (Ross Alley), 1898 (top). The first Chinese telephone operator in Chinatown (bottom).

COLD WELCOME

The Chinese faced discrimination from the get-go. Harrassment became outright hostility as first the gold rush, then the work on the Transcontinental Railroad petered out. Special taxes were imposed to shoulder aside competing "coolie labor." Laws forbidding the Chinese from moving outside Chinatown kept the residents packed in like sardines, with nowhere to go but up and down—thus the many basement establishments in the neighborhood. State and federal laws passed in the 1870s deterred Chinese women from immigrating, deeming them prostitutes. In the late 1870s, looting and arson attacks on Chinatown businesses soared.

The coup de grace, though, was the Chinese Exclusion Act, passed by the U.S.

Chinatown's Grant Avenue.

Women and children flooded into the neighborhood after the Great Quake.

Congress in 1882, which slammed the doors to America for "Asiatics." This was the country's first significant restriction on immigration. The law also prevented the existing Chinese residents, including American-born children, from becoming naturalized citizens. With a society of mostly men (forbidden, of course, from marrying white women), San Francisco hoped that Chinatown would simply die out.

OUT OF THE ASHES

When the devastating 1906 earthquake and fire hit, city fathers thought they'd seize the opportunity to kick the Chinese out of Chinatown and get their hands on that desirable piece of downtown real estate. Then Chinatown businessman Look Tin Eli had a brainstorm of Disneyesque proportions.

He proposed that Chinatown be rebuilt, but in a tourist-friendly, stylized, "Oriental" way. Anglo-American architects would design new buildings with pagoda roofs and dragon-covered columns. Chinatown would attract more tourists—the curious had been visiting on the sly for decades—and add more tax money to the city's coffers. Ka-ching: the sales pitch worked.

PAPER SONS

For the Chinese, the 1906 earthquake turned the virtual "no entry" sign into a flashing neon "welcome!" All the city's immigration records went up in smoke, and the Chinese quickly began to apply for passports as U.S. citizens, claiming their old ones were lost in the fire. Not only did thousands of Chinese become legal overnight, but so did their sons in China, or "sons," if they weren't really related. Whole families in Chinatown had passports in names that weren't their own; these "paper sons" were not only a windfall but also an uncomfortable neighborhood conspiracy. The city caught on eventually and set up an immigration center on Angel Island in 1910. Immigrants spent weeks or months being inspected and interrogated while their papers were checked. Roughly 250,000 people made it through. With this influx, including women and children, Chinatown finally became a more complete community.

A GREAT WALK THROUGH CHINATOWN

■ Start at the Chinatown Gate and walk ahead on Grant Avenue, entering the souvenir gauntlet. (You'll also pass Old St. Mary's Cathedral.)

■ Make a right on Clay Street and walk to Portsmouth Square. Sometimes it feels like the whole neighborhood's here, playing chess and exercising.

■ Head up Washington Street to the Old Chinese Telephone Exchange building, now the EastWest Bank. Across Grant, look left for Waverly Place. Here Free Republic of China (Taiwanese) flags flap over some of the neighborhood's most striking buildings, including Tin How Temple.

■ At the Sacramento Street end of Waverly Place stands the First Chinese Baptist Church of 1908. Just across the way, the Clarion Music Center is full of unusual instruments, as well as exquisite lion-dance sets.

■ Head back to Washington Street and check out the many herb shops.

■ Follow the scent of vanilla down Ross Alley (entrance across from Superior Trading Company) to the Golden Gate Fortune Cookie Factory. Then head across the alley to Sam Bo Trading Co., where religious

items are stacked in the narrow space. Tell the owners your troubles and they'll prepare a package of joss papers, joss sticks, and candles, and tell you how and when to offer them up.

■ Turn left on Jackson Street; ahead is the real Chinatown's main artery, Stockton Street, where most residents do their

grocery shopping. Vegetarians will want to avoid Luen Fat Market (No. 1135), with tanks of live frogs, turtles, and lobster as well as chickens and ducks. Look toward the back of stores for Buddhist altars with offerings of oranges and grapefruit. From here you can loop one block east back to Grant.

restaurant. If you don't have hours, save the steep entrance fee and take a spin through here. Ticketing, information, and one gallery are on the second floor; save time and reserve timed tickets online. Take advantage of the variety of well-done audio tours, which focus on specific exhibits or subjects and use positioning technology to locate you in the museum and talk about what you're seeing. Daily guided tours—a quick 25 minutes or 45 minutes—are an excellent way to get a foothold in this expansive space. And if you start to fade, grab a cup of Sightglass coffee at the café on the third floor; another café/restaurant is located by the fifth-floor sculpture garden. The monochromatic bathrooms—a different color on each floor—are surprising and fun. ⊠ *151 3rd St., SoMa* ☏ *415/357–4000* ⊕ *www.sfmoma.org* ☞ *$25.*

> **LOOK UP!**
>
> When wandering around Chinatown, don't forget to look up! Above the chintziest souvenir shop might loom an ornate balcony or a curly pagoda roof. The best examples are on the 900 block of Grant Avenue (at Washington Street) and at Waverly Place.

FAMILY

Fodor's Choice

★

Yerba Buena Gardens. There's not much south of Market Street that encourages lingering outdoors—or indeed walking at all—with this notable exception. These two blocks encompass the Center for the Arts, the Metreon, and Moscone Convention Center, but the gardens themselves are the everyday draw. Office workers escape to the green swath of the East Garden, the focal point of which is the memorial to Martin Luther King Jr. Powerful streams of water surge over large, jagged stone columns, mirroring the enduring force of King's words that are carved on the stone walls and on glass blocks behind the waterfall. Moscone North is behind the memorial, and an overhead walkway leads to Moscone South and its rooftop attractions. ■TIP→ **The gardens are liveliest during the week and especially during the Yerba Buena Gardens Festival, from May through October (www.ybgfestival.org), with free performances of everything from Latin music to Balinese dance.**

Atop the Moscone Convention Center perch a few lures for kids. The historic Looff carousel (*$4 for two rides*) twirls daily 10–5. South of the carousel is the Children's Creativity Museum (*415/820–3320 creativity. org*), a high-tech, interactive arts-and-technology center (*$12*) geared to children ages 3–12. Just outside, kids adore the excellent slides, including a 25-foot tube slide, at the play circle. Also part of the rooftop complex are gardens, an ice-skating rink, and a bowling alley. ⊠ *Bordered by 3rd, 4th, Mission, and Folsom Sts., SoMa* ⊕ *yerbabuenagardens.com* ☞ *Free.*

WORTH NOTING

Yerba Buena Center for the Arts. You never know what's going to be on display at this facility in Yerba Buena Gardens, but whether it's an exhibit of Mexican street art (graffiti to laypeople), innovative modern dance, or a baffling video installation, it's likely to be memorable. The productions here, which lean toward the cutting edge, tend to draw a young, energetic crowd. ■TIP→ **Present any public library card or public transit ticket to receive a 10% discount.** ⊠ *701 Mission St., SoMa* ☏ *415/978–2787* ⊕ *www.ybca.org* ☞ *Galleries $10, free 1st Tues. of month* ☽ *Closed Mon.*

CIVIC CENTER

Asian Art Museum. You don't have to be a connoisseur of Asian art to appreciate a visit to this museum whose monumental exterior conceals a light, open, and welcoming space. The fraction of the Asian's collection on display (about 2,500 pieces out of 15,000-plus total) is laid out thematically and by region, making it easy to follow historical developments.

Begin on the third floor, where highlights of Buddhist art in Southeast Asia and early China include a large, jewel-encrusted, exquisitely painted 19th-century Burmese Buddha, and clothed rod puppets from Java. On the second floor you can find later Chinese works, as well as pieces from Korea and Japan. The joy here is all in the details: on a whimsical Korean jar, look for a cobalt tiger jauntily smoking a pipe, or admire the delicacy of the Japanese tea implements. The ground floor is devoted to temporary exhibits and the museum's wonderful gift shop. During spring and summer, visit the museum the first Thursday evening of the month for extended programs and sip drinks while a DJ spins tunes. ✉ *200 Larkin St., between McAllister and Fulton Sts., Civic Center* 🖥 *415/581–3500* ⊕ *www.asianart.org* 🗺 *$20 weekdays, $25 weekends, free 1st Sun. of month; $10 Thurs. 5–9* ⊗ *Closed Mon.*

City Hall. This imposing 1915 structure with its massive gold-leaf dome—higher than the U.S. Capitol's—is about as close to a palace as you're going to get in San Francisco. The classic granite-and-marble behemoth was modeled after St. Peter's Basilica in Rome. Architect Arthur Brown Jr., who also designed Coit Tower and the War Memorial Opera House, designed an interior with grand columns and a sweeping central staircase. San Franciscans were thrilled, and probably a bit surprised, when his firm built City Hall in just a few years. The 1899 structure it replaced had taken 27 years to erect, as corrupt builders and politicians lined their pockets with funds earmarked for it. That building collapsed in about 27 seconds during the 1906 earthquake, revealing trash and newspapers mixed into the construction materials.

City Hall was spruced up and seismically retrofitted in the late 1990s, but the sense of history remains palpable. Some noteworthy events that have taken place here include the marriage of Marilyn Monroe and Joe DiMaggio (1954); the hosing—down the central staircase—of civil-rights and freedom-of-speech protesters (1960); the murders of Mayor George Moscone and openly gay supervisor Harvey Milk (1978); the torching of the lobby by angry members of the gay community in response to the light sentence given to the former supervisor who killed both men (1979); and the registrations of scores of gay couples in celebration of the passage of San Francisco's Domestic Partners Act (1991). In 2004, Mayor Gavin Newsom took a stand against then-current state law by issuing marriage licenses to same-sex partners.

On display in the South Light Court are city artifacts including maps, documents, and photographs. That enormous, 700-pound iron head once crowned the *Goddess of Progress* statue, which topped the old City Hall building until it crumbled during the 1906 earthquake.

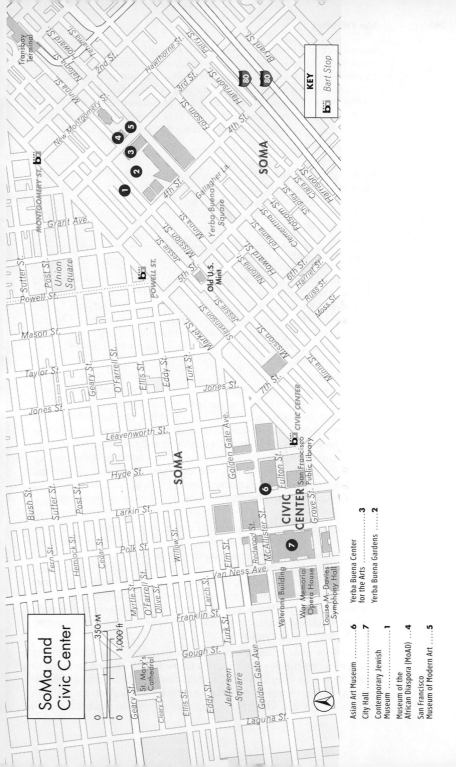

SoMa and Civic Center

0 ─────── 350 M
0 ─────── 1,000 ft

KEY

🅱 Bart Stop

Across Polk Street from City Hall is **Civic Center Plaza,** with lawns, walkways, seasonal flower beds, a playground, and an underground parking garage. This sprawling space is generally clean but somewhat grim. Many homeless people hang out here, so the plaza can feel dodgy. ⊠ *Bordered by Van Ness Ave. and Polk, Grove, and McAllister Sts., Civic Center* ☎ *415/554–6023 recorded tour info, 415/554–6139 tour reservations* ⊕ *sfgov.org/cityhall/city-hall-tours* ⊡ *Free* ⊙ *Closed weekends.*

HAYES VALLEY

SFJAZZ Center. Devoted entirely to jazz, the center hosts performances by jazz greats such as McCoy Tyner, Joshua Redman, Regina Carter, and Chick Corea. Walk by and the street-level glass walls will make you feel as if you're inside; head indoors and the acoustics will knock your socks off. ⊠ *201 Franklin St., at Fell St., Hayes Valley* ☎ *866/920–5299* ⊕ *www.sfjazz.org.*

NOB HILL AND RUSSIAN HILL

In place of the quirky charm and cultural diversity that mark other San Francisco neighborhoods, Nob Hill exudes history and good breeding. Topped with some of the city's most elegant hotels, Gothic Grace Cathedral, and private blue-blood clubs, it's the pinnacle of privilege. One hill over, across Pacific Avenue, is another old-family bastion, Russian Hill. It may not be quite as wealthy as Nob Hill, but it's no slouch—and it's got jaw-dropping views.

NOB HILL

FAMILY **Cable Car Museum.** One of the city's best free offerings, this museum is an absolute must for kids. You can even ride a cable car here—all three lines stop between Russian Hill and Nob Hill. The facility, which is inside the city's last cable-car barn, takes the top off the system to let you see how it all works. Eternally humming and squealing, the massive powerhouse cable wheels steal the show. You can also climb aboard a vintage car and take the grip, let the kids ring a cable-car bell (briefly), and check out vintage gear dating from 1873. ⊠ *1201 Mason St., at Washington St., Nob Hill* ☎ *415/474–1887* ⊕ *www.cablecarmuseum. org* ⊡ *Free.*

Grace Cathedral. Not many churches can boast an altarpiece by Keith Haring and not one but two labyrinths. The seat of the Episcopal Church in San Francisco, this soaring Gothic-style structure, erected on the site of the 19th-century railroad baron Charles Crocker's mansion, took 53 years to build, wrapping up in 1964. The gilded bronze doors at the east entrance were taken from casts of Lorenzo Ghiberti's incredible Gates of Paradise, which are on the Baptistery in Florence, Italy. A black-and-bronze stone sculpture of St. Francis by Beniamino Bufano greets you as you enter.

The 35-foot-wide limestone labyrinth is a replica of the 13th-century stone maze on the floor of Chartres Cathedral. All are encouraged to walk the ¼-mile-long labyrinth, a ritual based on the tradition of meditative walking. There's also a terrazzo outdoor labyrinth on the church's north side. The AIDS Interfaith Chapel, to the right as you enter Grace,

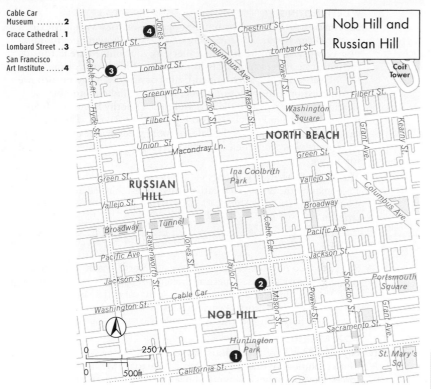

contains a metal triptych by the late artist Keith Haring and panels from the AIDS Memorial Quilt. ■TIP→ **Especially dramatic times to view the cathedral are during Thursday-night evensong (5:15 pm) and during special holiday programs.** ✉ *1100 California St., at Taylor St., Nob Hill* ☎ *415/749–6300* ⊕ *www.gracecathedral.org* ☞ *Free; tours $25.*

RUSSIAN HILL
TOP ATTRACTIONS

Lombard Street. The block-long "Crookedest Street in the World" makes eight switchbacks down the east face of Russian Hill between Hyde and Leavenworth Streets. Residents bemoan the traffic jam outside their front doors, but the throngs continue. Join the line of cars waiting to drive down the steep hill, or avoid the whole mess and walk down the steps on either side of Lombard. You take in super views of North Beach and Coit Tower whether you walk or drive—though if you're the one behind the wheel, you'd better keep your eye on the road lest you become yet another of the many folks who ram the garden barriers. ■TIP→ **Can't stand the traffic? Thrill seekers of a different stripe may want to head two blocks south of Lombard to Filbert Street. At a gradient of 31.5%, the hair-raising descent between Hyde and Leavenworth Streets is the city's steepest. Go slowly!** ✉ *Lombard St. between Hyde and Leavenworth Sts., Russian Hill.*

WORTH NOTING

San Francisco Art Institute. The number-one reason for a visit is Mexican master Diego Rivera's *The Making of a Fresco Showing the Building of a City* (1931), in the student gallery to your immediate left inside the entrance. Rivera himself is in the fresco—his broad behind is to the viewer—and he's surrounded by his assistants. They in turn are surrounded by a construction scene, laborers, and city notables such as sculptor Robert Stackpole and architect Timothy Pfleuger. *Making* is one of three San Francisco murals painted by Rivera. The number-two reason to come here is the café, or more precisely the eye-popping, panoramic view from the café, which serves surprisingly decent food for a song.

The **Walter & McBean Galleries** *(415/749–4563; Tues. 11–7, Wed.–Sat. 11–6)* exhibit the often provocative works of established artists. ⊠ *800 Chestnut St., Russian Hill* ☎ *415/771–7020* ⊕ *www.sfai.edu* ✉ *Galleries free.*

NORTH BEACH

San Francisco novelist Herbert Gold calls North Beach "the longest-running, most glorious, American bohemian operetta outside Greenwich Village." Indeed, to anyone who's spent some time in its eccentric old bars and cafés, North Beach evokes everything from the Barbary Coast days to the no-less-rowdy Beatnik era.

TOP ATTRACTIONS

Fodor's Choice ★ **City Lights Bookstore.** Take a look at the exterior of the store: the replica of a revolutionary mural destroyed in Chiapas, Mexico, by military forces; the art banners hanging above the windows; and the sign that says "Turn your sell [sic] phone off. Be here now." This place isn't just doling out best sellers. Designated a city landmark, the hangout of Beat-era writers—Allen Ginsberg and store founder Lawrence Ferlinghetti among them—and independent publishers remains a vital part of San Francisco's literary scene. Browse the three levels of poetry, philosophy, politics, fiction, history, and local zines, to the tune of creaking wood floors. ■TIP➜ Be sure to check the calendar of literary events.

Back in the day, the basement was a kind of literary living room, where writers like Ginsberg and Jack Kerouac would read and even receive mail. Ferlinghetti cemented City Lights' place in history by publishing Ginsberg's *Howl and Other Poems* in 1956. The small volume was ignored in the mainstream … until Ferlinghetti and the bookstore manager were arrested for obscenity and corruption of youth. In the landmark First Amendment trial that followed, the judge exonerated both men, declaring that a work that has "redeeming social significance" can't be obscene. *Howl* went on to become a classic.

Stroll Kerouac Alley, branching off Columbus Avenue next to City Lights, to read the quotes from Ferlinghetti, Maya Angelou, Confucius, John Steinbeck, and the street's namesake embedded in the pavement. ⊠ *261 Columbus Ave., North Beach* ☎ *415/362–8193* ⊕ *www. citylights.com.*

Continued on page 353

SAN FRANCISCO'S CABLE CARS

The moment it dawns on you that you severely underestimated the steepness of the San Francisco hills will likely be the same moment you look down and realize those tracks aren't just for show—or just for tourists.

Sure, locals rarely use the cable cars for commuting these days. (That's partially due to the $7 fare—hear that, Muni?) So you'll likely be packed in with plenty of fellow sightseers. You may even be approaching cable-car fatigue after seeing its image on so many souvenirs. But if you fear the magic is gone, simply climb on board, and those jaded thoughts will dissolve. Grab the pole and gawk at the view as the car clanks down an insanely steep grade toward the bay. Listen to the humming cable, the clang of the bell, and the occasional quip from the gripman. It's an experience you shouldn't pass up, whether on your first trip or your fiftieth.

HOW CABLE CARS WORK

The mechanics are pretty simple: cable cars grab a moving subterranean cable with a "grip" to go. To stop, they release the grip and apply one or more types of brakes. Four cables, totaling 9 miles, power the city's three lines. If the gripman doesn't adjust the grip just right when going up a steep hill, the cable will start to slip and the car will have to back down the hill and try again. This is an extremely rare occurrence—imagine the ribbing the gripman gets back at the cable car barn!

Gripman: Stands in front and operates the grip, brakes, and bell. Favorite joke, especially at the peak of a steep hill: "This is my first day on the job folks…"

Conductor: Moves around the car, deals with tickets, alerts the grip about what's coming up, and operates the rear wheel brakes.

❶ **Cable:** Steel wrapped around flexible sisal core; 2 inches thick; runs at a constant 9½ mph.

❷ **Bells:** Used for crew communication; alerts other drivers and pedestrians.

❸ **Grip:** Vice-like lever extends through the center slot in the track to grab or release the cable.

❹ **Grip Lever:** Left-hand lever; operates grip.

❺ **Car:** Entire car weighs 8 tons.

❻ **Wheel Brake:** Steel brake pads on each wheel.

❼ **Wheel Brake Lever:** Foot pedal; operates wheel brakes.

❽ **Rear Wheel Brake Lever:** Applied for extra traction on hills.

❾ **Track Brake:** 2-foot-long sections of Monterey pine push down against the track to help stop the car.

❿ **Track Brake Lever:** Middle lever; operates track brakes.

⓫ **Emergency Brake:** 18-inch steel wedge, jams into street slot to bring car to an immediate stop.

⓬ **Emergency Brake Lever:** Right-hand lever, red; operates emergency brake.

ROUTES

Powell–Hyde line: Most scenic, with classic Bay views. Begins at Powell and Market streets, then crosses Nob Hill and Russian Hill before a white-knuckle descent down Hyde Street, ending near the Hyde Street Pier.

Powell–Mason line: Also begins at Powell and Market streets, but winds through North Beach to Bay and Taylor streets, a few blocks from Fisherman's Wharf.

California line: Runs from the foot of Market Street, at Drumm Street, up Nob Hill and back. Great views (and aromas and sounds) of Chinatown on the way up. Sit in back to catch glimpses of the Bay. ■TIP→ Take the California line if it's just the cable-car experience you're after—the lines are shorter, and the grips and conductors say it's friendlier and has a slower pace.

Cars run at least every 15 minutes, from around 6 AM to about 1 AM.

RULES OF THE RIDE

Tickets. There are ticket booths at all three turnarounds, or you can pay the conductor after you board (they can make change). Try not to grumble about the price—they're embarrassed enough as it is.

■TIP→ If you're planning to use public transit a few times, or if you'd like to ride back and forth on the cable car without worrying about the price, consider a one-day Muni passport. You can get passports online, at the Powell Street turnaround, the TIX booth on Union Square, or the Fisherman's Wharf cable-car ticket booth at Beach and Hyde streets.

All Aboard. You can board on either side of the cable car. It's legal to stand on the running boards and hang on to the pole, but keep your ears open for the grip-man's warnings. ■TIP→ Grab a seat on the outside bench for the best views.

Most people wait (and wait) in line at one of the cable car turnarounds, but you can also hop on along the route. Board wherever you see a white sign showing a figure climbing aboard a brown cable car; wave to the approaching driver, and wait until the car stops.

Riding on the running boards can be part of the thrill.

8

CABLE CAR HISTORY

HALLIDIE FREES THE HORSES

In the 1850s and '60s, San Francisco's streetcars were drawn by horses. Legend has it that the horrible sight of a car dragging a team of horses downhill to their deaths roused Andrew Smith Hallidie to action. The English immigrant had invented the "Hallidie Ropeway," essentially a cable car for mined ore, and he was convinced that his invention could also move people. In 1873, Hallidie and his intrepid crew prepared to test the first cable car high on Russian Hill. The anxious engineer peered down into the foggy darkness, failed to see the bottom of the hill, and promptly turned the controls over to Hallidie. Needless to say, the thing worked . . . but rides were free for the first two days because people were afraid to get on.

SEE IT FOR YOURSELF

The **Cable Car Museum** is one of the city's best free offerings and an absolute must for kids. (You can even ride a cable car there, since all three lines stop between Russian Hill and Nob Hill.) The museum, which is inside the city's last cable-car barn, takes the top off the system to let you see how it all works.

Eternally humming and squealing, the massive powerhouse cable wheels steal the show. You can also climb aboard a vintage car and take the grip, let the kids ring a cable-car bell (briefly, please!), and check out vintage gear dating from 1873.

■ **TIP➔** The gift shop sells cable car paraphernalia, including an authentic gripman's bell for $600 (it'll sound like Powell Street in your house every day). For significantly less, you can pick up a key chain made from a piece of worn-out cable.

CHAMPION OF THE CABLE CAR BELL

Each September the city's best and brightest come together to crown a bell-ringing champion at Union Square. The crowd cheers gripmen and conductors as they stomp, shake, and riff with the rope. But it's not a popularity contest; the ringers are judged by former bell-ringing champions who take each ping and gong very seriously.

Coit Tower. Whether or not you agree that it resembles a fire-hose nozzle, this 210-foot tower is among San Francisco's most distinctive skyline sights. Although the monument wasn't intended as a tribute to firemen, it's often considered as such because of the donor's special attachment to the local fire company. As the story goes, a young gold rush–era girl, Lillie Hitchcock Coit (known as Miss Lil), was a fervent admirer of her local fire company—so much so that she once deserted a wedding party and chased down the street after her favorite engine, Knickerbocker No. 5, while clad in her bridesmaid finery. She became the Knickerbocker Company's mascot and always signed her name "Lillie Coit 5." When Lillie died in 1929 she left the city $125,000 to "expend in an appropriate manner … to the beauty of San Francisco."

You can ride the elevator to the top of the tower—the only thing you have to pay for here—to enjoy the view of the Bay Bridge and the Golden Gate Bridge; due north is Alcatraz Island. Most visitors saunter right past the 19 fabulous Depression-era murals inside the tower that depict California's economic and political life, but take the time to appreciate the first New Deal art project supported by taxpayer money. The federal government commissioned the paintings from 25 local artists, and ended up funding a controversy. The radical Mexican painter Diego Rivera inspired the murals' socialist-realist style, with its biting cultural commentary, particularly about the exploitation of workers. At the time the murals were painted, clashes between management and labor along the waterfront and elsewhere in San Francisco were widespread. ✉ *Telegraph Hill Blvd. at Greenwich St. or Lombard St., North Beach* ☎ *415/362–0808* ⊕ *sfrecpark.org* ✎ *Free; elevator to top $8.*

Grant Avenue. Originally called Calle de la Fundación, Grant Avenue is the oldest street in the city, but it's got plenty of young blood. Here dusty bars such as the Saloon and perennial favorites like the Savoy Tivoli mix with hotshot boutiques, odd curio shops like the antique jumble that is Aria, atmospheric cafés such as the boho haven Caffè Trieste, and authentic Italian delis. While the street runs from Union Square through Chinatown, North Beach, and beyond, the fun stuff in this neighborhood is crowded into the four blocks between Columbus Avenue and Filbert Street. ✉ *North Beach.*

Fodor's Choice ★ **Telegraph Hill.** Residents here have some of the city's best views, as well as the most difficult ascents to their aeries. The hill rises from the east end of Lombard Street to a height of 284 feet and is capped by Coit Tower. Imagine lugging your groceries up that! If you brave the slope, though, you can be rewarded with a "secret treasure" San Francisco moment. Filbert Street starts up the hill, then becomes the **Filbert Steps** when the going gets too steep. You can cut between the Filbert Steps and another flight, the **Greenwich Steps**, on up to the hilltop. As you climb, you can pass some of the city's oldest houses and be surrounded by beautiful, flowering private gardens. In some places the trees grow over the stairs so it feels like you're walking through a green tunnel; elsewhere, you'll have wide-open views of the bay. The cypress trees that grow on the hill are a favorite roost of local avian celebrities, the wild parrots of Telegraph Hill; you'll hear the cries of the cherry-headed conures if they're

8

Parrots of Telegraph Hill

While on Telegraph Hill, you might be startled by a chorus of piercing squawks and a rushing sound of wings. No, you're not about to have a Hitchcock bird-attack moment. These small, vivid green parrots with cherry red heads number in the hundreds; they're descendants of former pets that escaped or were released by their owners. (The birds dislike cages, and they bite if bothered—must've been some disillusioned owners along the way.)

The parrots like to roost high in the aging cypress trees on the hill, chattering and fluttering, sometimes taking wing en masse. They're not popular with some residents, but they did find a champion in local bohemian Mark Bittner, a former street musician. Bittner began chronicling their habits, publishing a book and battling the homeowners who wanted to cut down the cypresses. A documentary, *The Wild Parrots of Telegraph Hill*, made the issue a cause célèbre. In 2007 City Hall, which recognizes a golden goose when it sees one, stepped in and brokered a solution to keep the celebrity birds in town. The city would cover the homeowners' insurance worries and plant new trees for the next generation of wild parrots.

nearby. And the telegraphic name? It comes from the hill's status as the first Morse code signal station back in 1853. ⊠ *Bordered by Lombard, Filbert, Kearny, and Sansome Sts., North Beach.*

Washington Square. Once the daytime social heart of Little Italy, this grassy patch has changed character numerous times over the years. The Beats hung out here in the 1950s, hippies camped out in the 1960s and early '70s, and nowadays you're more likely to see elderly Asians doing tai chi than Italian folks reminiscing about the old country. You might also see homeless people hanging out on the benches and young locals sunbathing or running their dogs. Lillie Hitchcock Coit, in yet another show of affection for San Francisco's firefighters, donated the statue of two firemen with a child they rescued. ⊠ *Bordered by Columbus Ave. and Stockton, Filbert, and Union Sts., North Beach.*

WORTH NOTING

Beat Museum. "Museum" might be a stretch for this tiny storefront that's half bookstore, half memorabilia collection. You can see the 1949 Hudson from the movie version of *On the Road* and the shirt Neal Cassady wore while driving Ken Kesey's Merry Prankster bus, "Further." There are also manuscripts, letters, and early editions by Jack Kerouac, Allen Ginsberg, and Lawrence Ferlinghetti; but the true treasure here is the passionate and well-informed staff, which often includes the museum's founder, Jerry Cimino: your short visit may turn into an hours-long trip through the Beat era. ■TIP➔ The excellent Saturday walking tour goes beyond the museum to take in favorite Beat watering holes and hangouts in North Beach. ⊠ *540 Broadway, North Beach* ☎ 415/399–9626 ⊕ *www.thebeatmuseum.org* ⊒ *$8; walking tours $25.*

ON THE WATERFRONT

San Francisco's waterfront neighborhoods have fabulous views and utterly different personalities. Kitschy, overpriced Fisherman's Wharf struggles to maintain the last shreds of its existence as a working wharf, while Pier 39 is a full-fledged consumer circus. The Ferry Building draws well-heeled locals with its culinary pleasures, firmly connecting the Embarcadero and downtown. Between the Ferry Building and Pier 39 a former maritime no-man's-land is filling in with the recently relocated Exploratorium, a new $90-million cruise-ship terminal, Alcatraz Landing, fashionable waterfront restaurants, and restored, pedestrian-friendly piers.

TOP ATTRACTIONS

FAMILY **Alcatraz.** Thousands of visitors come every day to walk in the footsteps of Alcatraz's notorious criminals. The stories of life and death on "the Rock" may sometimes be exaggerated, but it's almost impossible to resist the chance to wander the cell block that tamed the country's toughest gangsters and saw daring escape attempts of tremendous desperation. Fewer than 2,000 inmates ever did time on the Rock, and though they weren't the worst criminals, they were definitely the worst prisoners, including Al "Scarface" Capone, Robert "The Birdman" Stroud, and George "Machine Gun" Kelly.

Some tips for escaping to Alcatraz: 1) Buy your ticket in advance. Visit the website for Alcatraz Cruises (*www.alcatrazcruises.com*) to scout out available departure times for the ferry. Prepay by credit card and keep a receipt record; the ticket price covers the boat ride and the audio tour. Pick up your ticket at the "will call" window at Pier 33 up to an hour before sailing. 2) Dress smart. Bring a jacket to ward off the chill from the boat ride and wear comfortable shoes. 3) Go for the evening tour. You'll get even more out of your Alcatraz experience at night. The evening tour has programs not offered during the day, the bridge-to-bridge view of the city twinkles at night, and your "prison experience" will be amplified as darkness falls. 4) Be mindful of scheduled and limited-capacity talks. Some programs are given only once a day (the schedule is posted in the cell house) and have limited seating, so keep an eye out for a cell-house staffer handing out passes shortly before the start time.

The boat ride to the island is brief (15 minutes), but affords beautiful views of the city, Marin County, and the East Bay. The audio tour, highly recommended, includes observations by guards and prisoners about life in one of America's most notorious penal colonies. Plan your schedule to allow at least three hours for the visit and boat rides combined. Not inspired by the prison? Wander around the lovely native plant gardens and (if the tide is cooperating) the tide pools on the north side of the island. ⊠ *Pier 33, Embarcadero* ☎ *415/981–7625* ⊕ *www.nps.gov/alca* ⊠ *$35.50, including audio tour; $42.50 evening tour, including audio.*

FAMILY
Fodor's Choice
★

Exploratorium. Walking into this fascinating "museum of science, art, and human perception" is like visiting a mad-scientist's laboratory. Most of the exhibits are supersize, and you can play with everything. Signature experiential exhibits include the Tinkering Studio and a glass Bay Observatory building, where the exhibits inside help visitors better understand what they see outside.

8

Get an *Alice in Wonderland* feeling in the distortion room, where you seem to shrink and grow as you walk across the slanted, checkered floor. In the shadow room, a powerful flash freezes an image of your shadow on the wall; jumping is a favorite pose. "Pushover" demonstrates cow-tipping, but for people: stand on one foot and try to keep your balance while a friend swings a striped panel in front of you (trust us, you're going to fall).

More than 650 other exhibits focus on sea and insect life, computers, electricity, patterns and light, language, the weather, and more. "Explainers"—usually high-school students on their days off—demonstrate cool scientific tools and procedures, like DNA-sample collection and cow-eye dissection. One surefire hit is the pitch-black, touchy-feely Tactile Dome ($8–$15 extra; reservations required). In this geodesic dome strewn with textured objects, you crawl through a course of ladders, slides, and tunnels, relying solely on your sense of touch. Lovey-dovey couples sometimes linger in the "grope dome," but be forewarned: the staff will turn on the lights if necessary. ■TIP➔ Patrons must be at least seven years old to enter the Tactile Dome, and the space is not for the claustrophobic. ✉ *Piers 15–17, Embarcadero* ☎ *415/561–0360 general information, 415/561–0362 Tactile Dome reservations* ⊕ *www.exploratorium.edu* ▨ *$30.*

F-line. The city's system of vintage electric trolleys, the F-line, gives the cable cars a run for their money as a beloved mode of transportation. The beautifully restored streetcars—some dating from the 19th century—run from the Castro District down Market Street to the Embarcadero, then north to Fisherman's Wharf. Each car is unique, restored to the colors of its city of origin, from New Orleans and Philadelphia to Moscow and Milan. ■TIP➔ Purchase tickets on board; exact change is required. ✉ *San Francisco* ⊕ *www.streetcar.org* ▨ *$2.50.*

Fodor's Choice
★

Ferry Building. The jewel of the Embarcadero, erected in 1896, is topped by a 230-foot clock tower modeled after the campanile of the cathedral in Seville, Spain. On the morning of April 18, 1906, the tower's four clock faces, powered by the swinging of a 14-foot pendulum, stopped at 5:17—the moment the great earthquake struck—and stayed still for 12 months.

Today San Franciscans flock to the street-level marketplace, stocking up on supplies from local favorites such as Acme Bread, Scharffen Berger Chocolate, Cowgirl Creamery, Blue Bottle Coffee, and Humphry Slocombe ice cream. Slanted Door, the city's beloved high-end Vietnamese restaurant, is here, along with highly regarded Bouli Bar. The seafood bar at Hog Island Oyster Company has fantastic bay view panoramas. On the plaza side, the outdoor tables at Gott's Roadside offer great people-watching with their famous burgers. On Saturday morning the plazas outside the building buzz with an upscale farmers' market where you can buy exotic sandwiches and other munchables. Extending south from the piers north of the building all the way to the Bay Bridge, the waterfront promenade out front is a favorite among joggers and picnickers, with a front-row view of sailboats plying the bay. True to its name, the Ferry Building still serves actual ferries: from its eastern flank

Thousands of visitors take ferries to Alcatraz each day to walk in the footsteps of the notorious criminals who were held on "The Rock."

they sail to Sausalito, Larkspur, Tiburon, and the East Bay. ⊠ *Embarcadero at foot of Market St., Embarcadero* ☎ *415/983–8030* ⊕ *www. ferrybuildingmarketplace.com.*

QUICK BITES

Buena Vista Café. At the end of the Hyde Street cable-car line, the Buena Vista packs 'em in for its famous Irish coffee—which, according to owners, was the first served stateside (in 1952). The place oozes nostalgia, drawing devoted locals as well as out-of-towners relaxing after a day of sightseeing. It's narrow and can get crowded, but this spot provides a fine alternative to the overpriced tourist joints nearby. ⊠ *2765 Hyde St., at Beach St., Fisherman's Wharf* ☎ *415/474–5044* ⊕ *www.thebuenavista.com.*

FAMILY
Fodor'sChoice
★

Hyde Street Pier. Cotton candy and souvenirs are all well and good, but if you want to get to the heart of the Wharf—boats—there's no better place to do it than at this pier, one of the Wharf area's best bargains. Depending on the time of day, you might see boatbuilders at work or children pretending to man an early-1900s ship.

Don't pass up the centerpiece collection of historic vessels, part of the **San Francisco Maritime National Historic Park,** almost all of which can be boarded. The *Balclutha,* an 1886 full-rigged three-masted sailing vessel that's more than 250 feet long, sailed around Cape Horn 17 times. Kids especially love the *Eureka,* a side-wheel passenger and car ferry, for her onboard collection of vintage cars. The *Hercules* is a steam-powered tugboat, and the *C.A. Thayer* is a beautifully restored three-masted schooner.

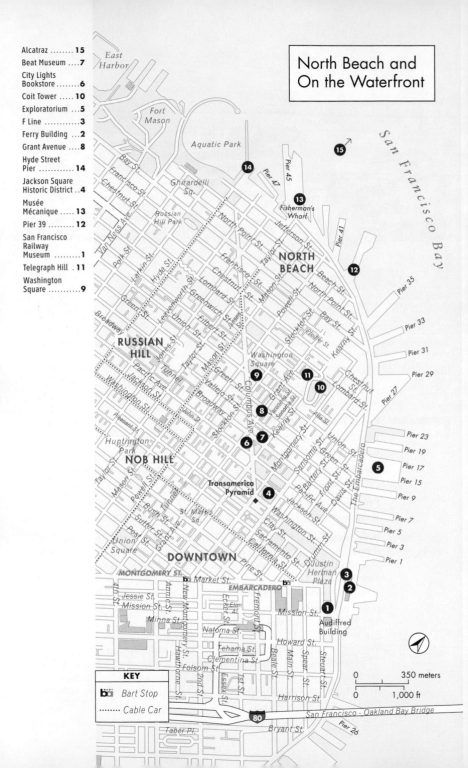

North Beach and On the Waterfront

East Harbor

San Francisco Bay

Fort Mason

Aquatic Park

Bay St.

Francisco St.

Chestnut St.

Ghirardelli Sq.

Russian Hill Park

14

Pier 47

Pier 45

15

13

Fisherman's Wharf

Jefferson St.

Pier 41

North Point St.

NORTH BEACH

Francisco St.

Chestnut St.

Lombard St.

Filbert St.

Greenwich St.

Union St.

Green St.

Van Ness Ave.

Polk St.

Larkin St.

Hyde St.

Leavenworth St.

Jones St.

Taylor St.

Mason St.

Powell St.

Stockton St.

Beach St.

North Point St.

Bay St.

Pier 35

Pier 33

Pier 31

Pier 29

12

Broadway

RUSSIAN HILL

Tunnel

Vallejo St.

Broadway

Washington Square

9

11

10

Grant Ave.

Columbus Ave.

Chestnut St.

Lombard St.

Pier 27

8

7

6

Kearny St.

Montgomery St.

Sansome St.

Battery St.

Front St.

Davis St.

Union St.

Green St.

Alta St.

Pacific Ave.

Pier 23

Pier 19

Pier 17

Pier 15

5

Pacific Ave.

4

Transamerica Pyramid

Jackson St.

Washington St.

Clay St.

Sacramento St.

California St.

Pier 9

Pier 7

Pier 5

Pier 3

Pier 1

NOB HILL

Huntington Park

Pleasant St.

Washington St.

Jackson St.

Pacific Ave.

Taylor St.

Mason St.

Powell St.

Bush Tunnel

St. Mary's Sq.

Pine St.

DOWNTOWN

Union Square

Sutter St.

Grant Ave.

Post St.

The Embarcadero

Justin Herman Plaza

3

2

1

MONTGOMERY ST.

Market St.

EMBARCADERO

New Montgomery St.

Mission St.

Fremont St.

Mission St.

Audiffred Building

Jessie St.

Mission St.

Minna St.

Annie St.

Elim Al.

Ecker St.

Natoma St.

Minna St.

Howard St.

Tehama St.

Clementina St.

Folsom St.

Hawthorne St.

2nd St.

Essex St.

1st St.

Beale St.

Main St.

Spear St.

Steuart St.

Harrison St.

80

San Francisco – Oakland Bay Bridge

Taber Pl.

Bryant St.

Pier 26

KEY

🅱 **Bart Stop**

.... Cable Car

0   350 meters

0   1,000 ft

Across the street from the pier and a museum in itself is the maritime park's **Visitor Center** (*499 Jefferson St., 415/447–5000; June–Aug., daily 9:30–5:30; Sept.–May, daily 9:30–5*), whose fun, large-scale exhibits make it an engaging stop. See a huge First Order Fresnel lighthouse lens and a shipwrecked boat. Then stroll through time in the exhibit "The Waterfront," where you can touch the timber from a gold rush–era ship recovered from below the Financial District; peek into 19th-century storefronts, and see the sails of an Italian fishing vessel. ✉ *Hyde and Jefferson Sts., Fisherman's Wharf* ☎ *415/561–7100* ⊕ *www.nps. gov/safr* ⚓ *Ships $10 (ticket good for 7 days).*

Jackson Square Historic District. This was the heart of the Barbary Coast of the Gay '90s—the 1890s, that is. Although most of the red-light district was destroyed in the fire that followed the 1906 earthquake, the remaining old redbrick buildings, many of them now occupied by advertising agencies, law offices, and antiques firms, retain hints of the romance and rowdiness of San Francisco's early days.

With its gentrified gold rush–era buildings, the 700 block of **Montgomery Street** just barely evokes the Barbary Coast days, but this was a colorful block in the 19th century and on into the 20th. Writers Mark Twain and Bret Harte were among the contributors to the spunky *Golden Era* newspaper, which occupied No. 732 (now part of the building at No. 744). From 1959 to 1996, the late ambulance-chaser extraordinaire, lawyer Melvin Belli, had his headquarters at Nos. 722 and 728–730. There was never a dull moment in Belli's world; he represented clients from the actress Mae West to Gloria Sykes (who in 1964 claimed that a cable-car accident turned her into a nymphomaniac) to the disgraced televangelists Jim and Tammy Faye Bakker. Whenever he won a case, he fired a cannon and raised the Jolly Roger. Belli was also known for receiving a letter from the never-caught Zodiac killer.

Restored 19th-century brick buildings line Hotaling Place, which connects Washington and Jackson Streets. The lane is named for the **A.P. Hotaling Company whiskey distillery** (*451 Jackson St., at Hotaling Pl.*), the largest liquor repository on the West Coast in its day. The exceptional City Guides (*415/557–4266, www.sfcityguides.org*) Gold Rush City walking tour covers this area and brings its history to life. ✉ *Bordered by Columbus Ave., Broadway, and Washington and Sansome Sts., San Francisco.*

FAMILY
Fodor's Choice
★

Musée Mécanique. Once a staple at Playland-at-the-Beach, San Francisco's early 20th-century amusement park, the antique mechanical contrivances at this time-warped arcade—including peep shows and nickelodeons—make it one of the most worthwhile attractions at the Wharf. Some favorites are the giant and rather creepy "Laffing Sal," an arm-wrestling machine, the world's only steam-powered motorcycle, and mechanical fortune-telling figures that speak from their curtained boxes. Note the depictions of race that betray the prejudices of the time: stoned Chinese figures in the "Opium-Den" and clown-faced African Americans eating watermelon in the "Mechanical Farm." ■ **TIP→ Admission is free, but you'll need quarters to bring the machines to life.** ✉ *Pier 45, Shed A, Fisherman's Wharf* ☎ *415/346–2000* ⊕ *museemecaniquesf.com* ⚓ *Free.*

FAMILY   **Pier 39.** The city's most popular waterfront attraction draws millions of visitors each year, who come to browse through its shops and concessions hawking every conceivable form of souvenir. The pier can be quite crowded, and the numerous street performers may leave you feeling more harassed than entertained. Arriving early in the morning ensures you a front-row view of the sea lions that bask here, but if you're here to shop—and make no mistake about it, Pier 39 wants your money—be aware that most stores don't open until 9:30 or 10 (later in winter).

Brilliant colors enliven the double-decker **San Francisco Carousel** (*$5 per ride*), decorated with images of such city landmarks as the Golden Gate Bridge and Lombard Street.

Follow the sound of barking to the northwest side of the pier to view the **sea lions** that flop about the floating docks. During the summer, orange-clad naturalists answer questions and offer fascinating facts about the playful pinnipeds—for example, that most of the animals here are males.

At the **Aquarium of the Bay** (*415/623–5300 or 888/732–3483, www. aquariumofthebay.org; $19.95, hrs vary but at least 10–6 daily*) moving walkways transport you through a space surrounded on three sides by water filled with indigenous San Francisco Bay marine life, from fish and plankton to sharks. Many find the aquarium overpriced; if you can, take advantage of the family rate (*$70 for 2 adults and 2 kids under 12*). ⊠ *Beach St. at Embarcadero, Fisherman's Wharf* ⊕ *www.pier39.com.*

WORTH NOTING

FAMILY   **San Francisco Railway Museum.** A labor of love brought to you by the same vintage-transit enthusiasts responsible for the F-line's revival, this one-room museum and store celebrates the city's streetcars and cable cars with photographs, models, and artifacts. The permanent exhibit includes the replicated end of a streetcar with a working cab—complete with controls and a bell—for kids to explore; the cool, antique Wiley birdcage traffic signal; and models and display cases to view. Right on the F-line track, just across from the Ferry Building, this is a great quick stop. ⊠ *77 Steuart St., Embarcadero* ☎ *415/974–1948* ⊕ *www. streetcar.org* ▣ *Free.*

THE MARINA, COW HOLLOW, AND THE PRESIDIO

Yachts bob at their moorings, satisfied-looking folks jog along the Marina Green, and multimillion-dollar homes overlook the bay in the picturesque, if somewhat sterile, Marina neighborhood. Does it all seem a bit too perfect? Well, it got this way after the hard knock of Loma Prieta—the current pretty face was put on after hundreds of homes collapsed in the 1989 earthquake. Just west of this waterfront area is a more natural beauty: the Presidio. Once a military base, this beautiful, sprawling park is mostly green space, with hills, woods, and the marshlands of Crissy Field. Between old-money Pacific Heights and the well-heeled, postcollegiate Marina lies comfortably upscale Cow Hollow.

THE MARINA

Fodor's Choice ★ **Palace of Fine Arts.** At first glance this stunning, rosy rococo palace seems to be from another world, and indeed, it's the sole survivor of the many tinted-plaster structures (a temporary classical city of sorts) built for the 1915 Panama-Pacific International Exposition, the world's fair that celebrated San Francisco's recovery from the 1906 earthquake and fire. The expo buildings originally extended about a mile along the shore. Bernard Maybeck designed this faux-Roman classic beauty, which was reconstructed in concrete and reopened in 1967. A victim of the elements, the Palace required a piece-by-piece renovation that was completed in 2008.

The pseudo-Latin language adorning the Palace's exterior urns continues to stump scholars. The massive columns (each topped with four "weeping maidens"), great rotunda, and swan-filled lagoon have been used in countless fashion layouts, films, and wedding photo shoots. After admiring the lagoon, look across the street to the house at 3460 Baker St. If the maidens out front look familiar, they should—they're original casts of the "garland ladies" you can see in the Palace's colonnade. ⊠ *3301 Lyon St., at Beach St., Marina* 🕾 ⊠ *Free.*

COW HOLLOW

Octagon House. This eight-sided home sits across the street from its original site on Gough Street; it's one of two remaining octagonal houses in the city (the other is on Russian Hill), and the only one open to the public. White quoins accent each of the eight corners of the pretty blue-gray exterior, and a colonial-style garden completes the picture. The house is full of antique American furniture, decorative arts (paintings, silver, rugs), and documents from the 18th and 19th centuries, including the contents of a time capsule left by the original owners in 1861 that was discovered during a 1950s renovation. A deck of Revolutionary-era hand-painted playing cards takes an anti-monarchist position: in place of kings, queens, and jacks, the American upstarts substituted American statesmen, Roman goddesses, and Indian chiefs. ⊠ *2645 Gough St., near Union St., Cow Hollow* 🕾 *415/441–7512* ⊕ *nscda-ca.org/octagon-house/* ⊠ *Free, donations encouraged.*

THE PRESIDIO

TOP ATTRACTIONS

Fodor's Choice ★ **Golden Gate Bridge.** With its simple but powerful Art Deco design, the 1.7-mile suspension span that connects San Francisco and Marin County was built to withstand winds of more than 100 mph. It's also not a bad place to be in an earthquake: designed to sway almost 28 feet, the Golden Gate Bridge (unlike the Bay Bridge) was undamaged by the 1989 Loma Prieta quake. If you're walking on the bridge when it's windy, stand still and you can feel it swaying a bit.

Crossing the Golden Gate Bridge under your own power is exhilarating—a little scary, and definitely chilly. From the bridge's eastern-side walkway, the only side pedestrians are allowed on, you can take in the San Francisco skyline and the bay islands; look west for the wild hills of the Marin Headlands, the curving coast south to Lands End, and the Pacific Ocean. On sunny days, sailboats dot the water, and brave windsurfers test the often-treacherous tides beneath the bridge. A vista point on the Marin County side provides a spectacular city panorama.

8

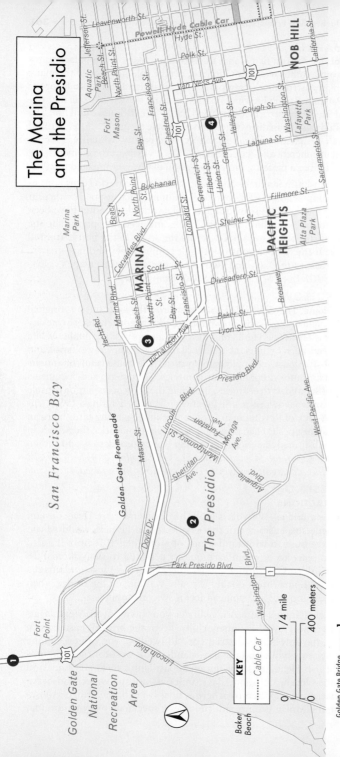

The Marina and the Presidio

San Francisco Bay

Golden Gate National Recreation Area

Fort Point

Baker Beach

The Presidio

Golden Gate Promenade

Lincoln Blvd.

Doyle Dr.

Mason St.

Lincoln Blvd.

Montgomery St.

Funston Ave.

Moraga Ave.

Sheridan Ave.

Arguello Blvd.

West Pacific Ave.

Park Presido Blvd.

Washington Blvd.

Presidio Blvd.

Yacht Rd.

Richardson Ave.

MARINA

Marina Park

Marina Blvd.

Cervantes Blvd.

Beach St.

North Point St.

Bay St.

Francisco St.

Scott St.

Bay St.

Lyon St.

Baker St.

Divisadero St.

Steiner St.

Fillmore St.

Broadway

PACIFIC HEIGHTS

Alta Plaza Park

Lombard St.

Greenwich St.

Filbert St.

Union St.

Green St.

Vallejo St.

Laguna St.

Lafayette Park

Sacramento St.

Washington St.

Gough St.

Van Ness Ave.

Chestnut St.

Buchanan St.

North Point St.

Fort Mason

Aquatic Park

Beach St.

North Point St.

Leavenworth St.

Jefferson St.

Hyde St.

Polk St.

Francisco St.

NOB HILL

California St.

Powell-Hyde Cable Car

KEY

······· Cable Car

0 — 1/4 mile
0 — 400 meters

A structural engineer, dreamer, and poet named Joseph Strauss worked tirelessly for 20 years to make the bridge a reality, first promoting the idea of it and then overseeing design and construction. Though the final structure bore little resemblance to his original plan, Strauss guarded his legacy jealously, refusing to recognize the seminal contributions of engineer Charles A. Ellis. In 2007, the Golden Gate Bridge district finally recognized Ellis's role, though Strauss, who died less than a year after opening day in 1937, would doubtless be pleased with the inscription on his statue, which stands sentry in the southern parking lot: "The Man Who Built the Bridge."

You won't see it on a T-shirt, but the bridge is perhaps the world's most publicized suicide platform, with an average of one jumper about every 10 days. Signs on the bridge refer the disconsolate to special telephones, and officers patrol the walkway and watch by security camera to spot potential jumpers. A suicide barrier, an unobtrusive net not unlike the one that saved 19 workers during the bridge's construction, is expected to be completed in 2020.

While at the bridge, you can grab a healthy snack at the art deco–style Bridge Café. The Bridge Pavilion sells attractive, high-quality souvenirs and has a small display of historical artifacts. At the outdoor exhibits, you can see the bridge rise before your eyes on hologram panels, learn about the features that make it art deco, and read about the personalities behind its design and construction. City Guides offers free walking tours of the bridge every Thursday and Sunday at 11 am. ✉ *Lincoln Blvd. near Doyle Dr. and Fort Point, Presidio* ☎ *415/921–5858* ⊕ *www. goldengatebridge.org* ✎ *Free.*

Fodor's Choice **Presidio.** When San Franciscans want to spend a day in the woods, they
★ come here. The Presidio has 1,400 acres of hills and majestic woods, two small beaches, and stunning views of the bay, the Golden Gate Bridge, and Marin County. Famed environmental artist Andy Goldsworthy's work greets visitors at the Arguello Gate entrance. The 100-plus-foot *Spire,* made of 37 cypress logs reclaimed from the Presidio, looks like a rough, natural version of a church spire. ■TIP➔ The Presidio's best lookout points lie along Washington Boulevard, which meanders through the park.

Part of the **Golden Gate National Recreation Area,** the Presidio was a military post for more than 200 years. Don Juan Bautista de Anza and a band of Spanish settlers first claimed the area in 1776. It became a Mexican garrison in 1822, when Mexico gained its independence from Spain; U.S. troops forcibly occupied the Presidio in 1846. The U.S. Sixth Army was stationed here until 1994.

The Presidio is now a thriving community of residential and nonresidential tenants, who help to fund its operations by rehabilitating and leasing its more than 700 buildings. Bay Area filmmaker George Lucas's 23-acre **Letterman Digital Arts Center,** a digital studio "campus," along the eastern edge of the land, is exquisitely landscaped and largely open to the public. If you have kids in tow or are a *Star Wars* fan yourself, sidle over to the **Yoda Fountain** (Letterman Drive at Dewitt Road), between two of the arts-center buildings, then take your picture with the life-size Darth Vader statue in the lobby, open to the public on weekdays.

8

The Presidio Trust, created to manage the Presidio and guide its transformation from military post to national park, has now turned its focus to rolling out the welcome mat to the public. The Presidio's visitor-serving tenants, such as the Asian-theme SenSpa, the House of Air Trampoline Park, Planet Granite climbing gym, the Walt Disney museum, and a fabulous lodge at the Main Post, have helped with this goal. The rental of old military houses and apartments helps too, with top rents pushing $20,000 a month.

Especially popular is **Crissy Field**, a stretch of restored marshland along the sand of the bay. Kids on bikes, folks walking dogs, and joggers share the paved path along the shore, often winding up at the Warming Hut, a combination café and fun gift store at the end of the path, for a hot chocolate in the shadow of the Golden Gate Bridge. Midway along the Golden Gate Promenade that winds along the shore is the Gulf of the Farallones National Marine Sanctuary Visitor Center, where kids can get a close-up view of small sea creatures and learn about the rich eco-system offshore. Just across from the Palace of Fine Arts, Crissy Field Center offers great children's programs and has cool science displays. West of the Golden Gate Bridge is sandy **Baker Beach**, beloved for its spectacular views and laid-back vibe (read: you'll see naked people here). This is one of those places that inspires local pride.

The Presidio also has a golf course, picnic sites, and the only camp-ground in the city; the views from the many overlooks are sublime. For background and to help plan your time here, stop at the high-tech **Visitor Center** *(210 Lincoln Blvd., 415/561–4323).* ⊠ *Between Marina and Lincoln Park, Presidio* ⊕ *www.presidio.gov.*

GOLDEN GATE PARK AND THE WESTERN SHORELINE

More than 1,000 acres, stretching from the Haight all the way to the windy Pacific coast, Golden Gate Park is a vast patchwork of woods, trails, lakes, lush gardens, sports facilities, museums—even a herd of buffalo. There's more natural beauty beyond the park's borders, along San Francisco's wild Western Shoreline.

GOLDEN GATE PARK
TOP ATTRACTIONS

FAMILY
Fodor'sChoice
★

California Academy of Sciences. With its native plant–covered living roof, retractable ceiling, three-story rain forest, gigantic planetarium, living coral reef, and frolicking penguins, the California Academy of Sciences is one of the city's most spectacular treasures. Dramatically designed by Renzo Piano, it's an eco-friendly, energy-efficient adventure in biodiversity and green architecture. The roof's large mounds and hills mirror the local topography, and Piano's audacious design completes the dramatic transformation of the park's Music Concourse. Moving away from a restrictive role as a museum that catalogued natural history, the acad-emy these days is all about sustainability and the future. The locally beloved dioramas in African Hall have survived the transition, however.

By the time you arrive, hopefully you've decided which shows and pro-grams to attend, looked at the academy's floor plan, and designed a plan to cover it all in the time you have. And if not, here's the quick version:

Armed with only helmets, safety harnesses, and painting equipment, a full-time crew of 38 painters keeps the Golden Gate Bridge clad in International Orange.

Head left from the entrance to the wooden walkway over otherworldly rays in the Philippine Coral Reef, then continue to the Swamp to see Claude, the famous albino alligator. Swing through African Hall and gander at the penguins, take the elevator up to the living roof, then return to the main floor and get in line to explore the Rainforests of the World, ducking free-flying butterflies and watching for other live surprises. You'll end up below ground in the Amazonian Flooded Rainforest, where you can explore the academy's other aquarium exhibits. Phew.

■ **TIP→** Considering the hefty price of admission here, start out early and take advantage of in-and-out privileges to take a break. ⊠ *55 Music Concourse Dr., Golden Gate Park* ☎ *415/379–8000* ⊕ *www.calacademy.org* ⧪ *$34.95, save $3 if you bike, walk, or take public transit here; free 1 Sun. per quarter.*

Conservatory of Flowers. Whatever you do, be sure to at least drive by the Conservatory of Flowers—it's too darn pretty to miss. The gorgeous, white-framed 1878 glass structure is topped with a 14-ton glass dome. Stepping inside the giant greenhouse is like taking a quick trip to the rain forest, with its earthy smell and humid warmth. The undeniable highlight is the Aquatic Plants section, where lily pads float and carnivorous plants dine on bugs to the sounds of rushing water. On the east side of the conservatory (to the right as you face the building), cypress, pine, and redwood trees surround the Dahlia Garden, which blooms in summer and fall. Adding to the allure are temporary exhibits such as a past one devoted to prehistoric plants; an annual model-train display punctuated with mini buildings, found objects, and dwarf plants; and a butterfly garden that returns periodically. To the

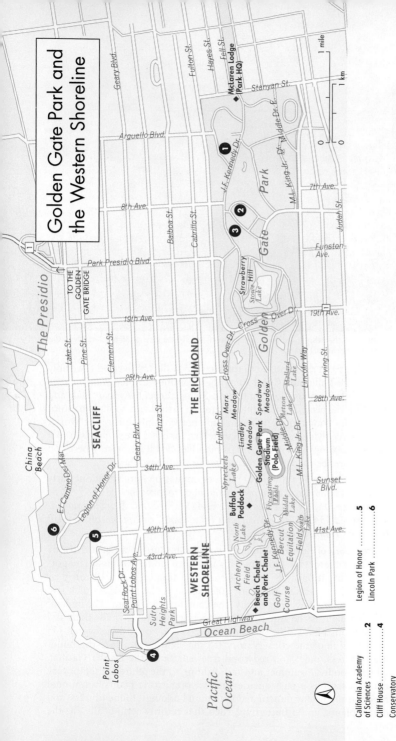

Golden Gate Park and
the Western Shoreline

west is the **Rhododendron Dell,** which contains 850 varieties, more than any other garden in the country. It's a favorite local Mother's Day picnic spot. ✉ *John F. Kennedy Dr. at Conservatory Dr., Golden Gate Park* ☎ *415/666–7001* ⊕ *www.conservatoryofflowers.org* ⌨ *$8, free 1st Tues. of month* ☞ *No strollers allowed inside.*

de Young Museum. It seems that everyone in town has a strong opinion about the de Young Museum: some adore its striking copper facade, while others just hope that the green patina of age will mellow the effect. Most maligned is the 144-foot tower, but the view from its ninth-story observation room, ringed by floor-to-ceiling windows and free to the public, is worth a trip here by itself. The building almost overshadows the de Young's respected collection of American, African, and Oceanic art. The museum also plays host to major international exhibits, such as 100 works from Paris's Musée National Picasso and a collection of the work of Jean Paul Gaultier from the Montreal Museum of Fine Arts; there's often an extra admission charge for these. The annual Bouquets to Art is a fanciful tribute to the museum's collection by notable Bay Area floral designers. On many Friday evenings, the museum hosts fun, free, family-centered events, with live music, art projects for children, and a wine and beer bar (the café stays open late, too). ✉ *50 Hagiwara Tea Garden Dr., Golden Gate Park* ☎ *415/750–3600* ⊕ *deyoung.famsf. org* ⌨ *$15, good for same-day admittance to the Legion of Honor; free 1st Tues. of month.*

THE WESTERN SHORELINE
TOP ATTRACTIONS

Cliff House. A meal at the Cliff House isn't just about the food—the spectacular ocean view is what brings folks here—but the cuisine won't leave you wanting. The vistas, which include offshore Seal Rock (the barking marine mammals who reside there are actually sea lions), can be 30 miles or more on a clear day—or less than a mile on foggy days. ■TIP➜ Come for drinks just before sunset; then head back into town for dinner.

Three buildings have occupied this site since 1863. The current building dates from 1909; a 2004 renovation has left a strikingly attractive restaurant and a squat concrete viewing platform out back. The complex, owned by the National Park Service, includes a gift shop.

Sitting on the observation deck is the **Giant Camera,** a camera obscura with its lens pointing skyward housed in a cute yellow-painted wooden shack. Built in the 1940s and threatened many times with demolition, it's now on the National Register of Historic Places. Step into the dark, tiny room inside (for a $3 fee); a fascinating 360-degree image of the surrounding area—which rotates as the "lens" on the roof rotates—is projected on a large, circular table. ■TIP➜ In winter and spring you may also glimpse migrating gray whales from the observation deck.

To the north of the Cliff House lie the ruins of the once grand glass-roof **Sutro Baths,** which you can explore on your own (they look a bit like water-storage receptacles). Adolph Sutro, eccentric onetime San Francisco mayor and Cliff House owner, built the bath complex, including a train out to the site, in 1896, so that everyday folks could

8

enjoy the benefits of swimming. Six enormous baths (some freshwater and some seawater), more than 500 dressing rooms, and several restaurants covered 3 acres north of the Cliff House and accommodated 25,000 bathers. Likened to Roman baths in a European glass palace, the baths were for decades the favorite destination of San Franciscans in search of entertainment. The complex fell into disuse after World War II, was closed in 1952, and burned down (under questionable circumstances) during demolition in 1966. ⌂ *1090 Point Lobos Ave., Richmond* ☎ *415/386–3330* ⊕ *www.cliffhouse.com* ☲ *Free.*

Legion of Honor. The old adage of real estate—location, location, location—is at full force here. You can't beat the site of this museum of European art atop cliffs overlooking the ocean, the Golden Gate Bridge, and the Marin Headlands. A pyramidal glass skylight in the entrance court illuminates the lower-level galleries, which exhibit prints and drawings, English and European porcelain, and ancient Assyrian, Greek, Roman, and Egyptian art. The 20-plus galleries on the upper level display the permanent collection of European art (paintings, sculpture, decorative arts, and tapestries) from the 14th century to the present day.

The noteworthy Auguste Rodin collection includes two galleries devoted to the master and a third with works by Rodin and other 19th-century sculptors. An original cast of Rodin's *The Thinker* welcomes you as you walk through the courtyard. As fine as the museum is, the setting and view outshine the collection and also make a trip here worthwhile. ⌂ *34th Ave. at Clement St., Richmond* ☎ *415/750–3600* ⊕ *legionofhonor.famsf.org* ☲ *$15, free 1st Tues. of month.*

Fodor's Choice
★

Lincoln Park. Although many of the city's green spaces are gentle and welcoming, Lincoln Park is a wild, 275-acre park in the Outer Richmond with windswept cliffs and panoramic views. The Coastal Trail, the park's most dramatic one, leads out to **Lands End**; pick it up west of the Legion of Honor (at the end of El Camino del Mar) or from the parking lot at Point Lobos and El Camino del Mar. Time your hike to hit Mile Rock at low tide, and you might catch a glimpse of two wrecked ships peeking up from their watery graves. ⚠ Be careful if you hike here; landslides are frequent, and people have fallen into the sea by standing too close to the edge of a crumbling bluff top.

On the tamer side, large Monterey cypresses line the fairways at Lincoln Park's 18-hole golf course, near the Legion of Honor. At one time this land was the Golden Gate Cemetery, where the dead were segregated by nationality; most were indigent and interred without ceremony in the potter's field. In 1900 the Board of Supervisors voted to ban burials within city limits, and all but two city cemeteries (at Mission Dolores and the Presidio) were moved to Colma, a small town just south of San Francisco. When digging has to be done in the park, bones occasionally surface again. ⌂ *Entrance at 34th Ave. at Clement St., Richmond.*

A colorful mosaic mural in the Castro

THE HAIGHT, THE CASTRO, AND NOE VALLEY

These distinct neighborhoods wear their personalities large and proud, and all are perfect for just strolling around. Like a slide show of San Franciscan history, you can move from the Haight's residue of 1960s counterculture to the Castro's connection to 1970s and '80s gay life to 1990s gentrification in Noe Valley. Although historic events thrust the Haight and the Castro onto the international stage, both are anything but stagnant—they're still dynamic areas well worth exploring.

THE HAIGHT

Haight-Ashbury Intersection. On October 6, 1967, hippies took over the intersection of Haight and Ashbury Streets to proclaim the "Death of Hip." If they thought hip was dead then, they'd find absolute confirmation of it today, what with the only tie-dye in sight on the famed corner being Ben & Jerry's storefront. ⊠ *Haight*.

THE CASTRO

Fodor'sChoice
★
Castro Theatre. Here's a classic way to join in the Castro community: grab some popcorn and catch a flick at this 1,500-seat art-deco theater; opened in 1922, it's the grandest of San Francisco's few remaining movie palaces. The neon marquee, which stands at the top of the Castro strip, is the neighborhood's great landmark. The Castro was the fitting host of 2008's red-carpet preview of Gus Van Sant's film *Milk*, starring Sean Penn as openly gay San Francisco supervisor Harvey Milk. The theater's elaborate Spanish baroque interior is fairly well preserved. Before many shows the theater's pipe organ rises from the orchestra pit and an organist plays pop and movie tunes, usually ending with the

Jeanette McDonald standard "San Francisco" (go ahead, sing along). The crowd can be enthusiastic and vocal, talking back to the screen as loudly as it talks to them. Classics such as *Who's Afraid of Virginia Woolf?* take on a whole new life, with the assembled beating the actors to the punch and fashioning even snappier comebacks for Elizabeth Taylor. Head here to catch sing-along classics like *Mary Poppins*, a Fellini film retrospective, or the latest take on same-sex love. ⊠ *429 Castro St., Castro* ☎ *415/621–6120* ⊕ *www.castrotheatre.com.*

Harvey Milk Plaza. An 18-foot-long rainbow flag, the symbol of gay pride, flies above this plaza named for the man who electrified the city in 1977 by being elected to its Board of Supervisors as an openly gay candidate. In the early 1970s Milk had opened a camera store on the block of Castro Street between 18th and 19th Streets. The store became the center for his campaign to open San Francisco's social and political life to gays and lesbians.

The liberal Milk hadn't served a full year of his term before he and Mayor George Moscone, also a liberal, were shot in November 1978 at City Hall. The murderer was a conservative ex-supervisor named Dan White, who had recently resigned his post and then became enraged when Moscone wouldn't reinstate him. Milk and White had often been at odds on the board, and White thought Milk had been part of a cabal to keep him from returning to his post. Milk's assassination shocked the gay community, which became infuriated when the infamous "Twinkie defense"—that junk food had led to diminished mental capacity—resulted in a manslaughter verdict for White. During the so-called White Night Riot of May 21, 1979, gays and their allies stormed City Hall, torching its lobby and several police cars.

Milk, who had feared assassination, left behind a tape recording in which he urged the community to continue the work he had begun. His legacy is the high visibility of gay people throughout city government; a bust of him was unveiled at City Hall on his birthday in 2008, and the 2008 film *Milk* gives insight into his life. A plaque at the base of the flagpole lists the names of past and present openly gay and lesbian state and local officials. ⊠ *Southwest corner of Castro and Market Sts., Castro.*

NOE VALLEY

Golden fire hydrant. When all the other fire hydrants went dry during the fire that followed the 1906 earthquake, this one kept pumping. Noe Valley and the Mission District were thus spared the devastation wrought elsewhere in the city, which explains the large number of pre-quake homes here. Every year on April 18 (the anniversary of the quake), folks gather here to share stories about the earthquake, and the famous hydrant gets a fresh coat of gold paint. ⊠ *Church and 20th Sts., southeastern corner, across from Dolores Park, Noe Valley.*

CASTRO AND NOE WALK

The Castro and Noe Valley are both neighborhoods that beg to be walked—or ambled through, really, without time pressure or an absolute destination. Hit the Castro first, beginning at **Harvey Milk Plaza** under the gigantic rainbow flag. If you're going on to Noe Valley, first head east down **Market Street** for the cafés, bistros, and shops, then go back to **Castro Street** and head south, past the glorious Art-Deco **Castro Theatre**, checking out boutiques and cafés along the way (Cliff's Variety, at 479 Castro Street, is a must). To tour Noe Valley, go east down 18th Street to Church (at Dolores Park), and then either strap on your hiking boots and head south over the hill or hop the J–Church to 24th Street, the center of this rambling neighborhood.

MISSION DISTRICT

The Mission has a number of distinct personalities: it's the Latino neighborhood, where working-class folks raise their families and where gangs occasionally clash; it's the hipster hood, where tattooed and pierced twenty- and thirtysomethings hold court in the coolest cafés and bars in town; it's a culinary epicenter, with the strongest concentration of destination restaurants and affordable ethnic cuisine; it's the face of gentrification, where high-tech money prices out longtime commercial and residential renters; and it's the artists' quarter, where murals adorn literally blocks of walls long after the artists have moved to cheaper digs. It's also the city's equivalent of the Sunshine State—this neighborhood's always the last to succumb to fog.

TOP ATTRACTIONS

Balmy Alley murals. Mission District artists have transformed the walls of their neighborhood with paintings, and Balmy Alley is one of the best-executed examples. Many murals adorn the one-block alley, with newer ones continually filling in the blank spaces. In 1971, artists began teaming with local children to create a space to promote peace in Central America, community spirit, and (later) AIDS awareness; since then dozens of artists have added their vibrant works. ⚠ Be alert here: the 25th Street end of the alley adjoins a somewhat dangerous area. ✉ *24th St. between and parallel to Harrison and Treat Sts., alley runs south to 25th St., Mission District.*

Fodor'sChoice
★

Dolores Park. A two-square-block microcosm of life in the Mission, Dolores Park is one of San Francisco's liveliest green spaces: dog lovers and their pampered pups congregate, kids play at the extravagant, recently reconstructed playground, and hipsters hold court, drinking beer on sunny days. During the summer, the park hosts movie nights; performances by Shakespeare in the Park, the San Francisco Mime Troupe, and the San Francisco Symphony; and any number of pop-up events and impromptu parties. Spend a warm day here—maybe sitting at the top of the park with a view of the city and the Bay Bridge—surrounded by locals and that laid-back San Francisco energy, and you may well find yourself plotting your move to the city. ✉ *Between 18th and 20th Sts. and Dolores and Church Sts., Mission District.*

Mission Dolores. Two churches stand side by side here, including the small adobe **Mission San Francisco de Asís,** which, along with the Presidio's Officers' Club, is the oldest standing structure in San Francisco. Completed in 1791, it's the sixth of the 21 California missions founded by Franciscan friars in the 18th and early 19th centuries. Its ceiling depicts original Ohlone Indian basket designs, executed in vegetable dyes. The tiny chapel includes frescoes and a hand-painted wooden altar.

8

The Haight, the Castro, Noe Valley, and the Mission District

Hampshire St.
York St.
Bryant St.
Florida St.
Alabama St.
Harrison St.
Mariposa St.
16th St.
17th St.
Folsom St.
Shotwell St.
South Van Ness Ave.
Capp St.
18th St.
19th St.
Mission St.
Valencia St.
Guerrero St.
Dolores St.

20th St.

Museum of Craft and Design ◆

7 **8**

POTRERO

16th St Mission 🅱

MISSION

U.S. Mint

Landers St.
Reservoir St.
Germania St.
Herman St.
Duboce Ave.
Belcher St.
Church St.
Steiner St.
Walter St.
Market St.
Potomac St.
Carmelita St.
Noe St.
14th St.
15th St.
Castro St.
Lloyd St.
Waller St.
Alpine Ter.
Buena Vista Ter.
Buena Vista Ave. East
Roosevelt Way
Corona Heights Playground
Buena Vista Park

16th St.
17th St.
Ford St.
Hancock St.

4

6 Mission Dolores Park

5

21st St.

Noe St.
22nd St.

NOE VALLEY

2
3

CASTRO

Castro St.
Collingwood St.
Diamond St.
Eureka St.
Douglass St.

17th St.
18th St.
19th St.
Caselli St.

Market St.

HAIGHT ASHBURY
1
Ashbury St.
Frederick St.
Delmar St.
Clayton St.
Belvedere St.
Cole St.
Shrader St.
Sunset Tunnel Pk.
Stanyan St.
Haight St.
Waller St.

0 ——— 350 M
0 ——— 1,000 ft

Balmy Alley murals **7**
Castro Theatre **2**
Dolores Park **6**
Galería de la Raza **8**
Golden fire hydrant.........**5**
Haight-Ashbury
intersection **1**
Harvey Milk Plaza **3**
Mission Dolores **4**

There's a hidden treasure here, too. In 2004 an archaeologist and an artist crawling along the ceiling's rafters opened a trapdoor behind the altar and rediscovered the mission's original mural, painted with natural dyes by Native Americans in 1791. The centuries have taken their toll, so the team photographed the 20-by-22-foot mural and began digitally restoring the photographic version. Among the images is a dagger-pierced Sacred Heart of Jesus.

The small museum here covers the mission's founding and history, and the pretty little cemetery—which appears in Alfred Hitchcock's film *Vertigo*—contains the graves of mid-19th-century European immigrants. The remains of an estimated 5,000 Native Americans lie in unmarked graves. Services are held in both the old mission and next door in the handsome multidome basilica. ⊠ *Dolores and 16th Sts., Mission District* ☎ *415/621–8203* ⊕ *www.missiondolores.org* ⊠ *Suggested donation $7.*

OFF THE BEATEN PATH

Museum of Craft and Design. Right at home in this once-industrial neighborhood now bursting with creative energy, this small, four-room space—definitely a quick view—mounts temporary art and design exhibitions. The focus might be sculpture, metalwork, furniture, or jewelry—or industrial design, architecture, or other topics. The MakeArt Lab gives kids the opportunity to create their own exhibit-inspired work, and the beautifully curated shop sells tempting textiles, housewares, jewelry, and other well-crafted items. ⊠ *2569 3rd St., near 22nd St., Dogpatch* ☎ *415/773–0303* ⊕ *sfmcd.org* ⊠ *$8, free 1st Tues. of month.*

WORTH NOTING

Galería de la Raza. San Francisco's premier showcase for contemporary Latino art, the gallery exhibits the works of mostly local artists. Events include readings and spoken word by local poets and writers, screenings of Latin American and Spanish films, and theater works by local minority theater troupes. The gallery may close between exhibits, so call ahead. Just across the street, murals and mosaics festoon the 24th Street/York Street Minipark, a tiny urban playground. A mosaic-covered Quetzalcoatl serpent plunges into the ground and rises, creating hills for little ones to clamber over, and mural-covered walls surround the space. ⊠ *2857 24th St., at Bryant St., Mission District* ☎ *415/826–8009* ⊕ *www.galeriadelaraza.org.*

8

PACIFIC HEIGHTS AND JAPANTOWN

Pacific Heights and Japantown are something of an odd couple: privileged, old-school San Francisco and the workaday commercial center of Japanese American life in the city, stacked virtually on top of each other. The sprawling, extravagant mansions of Pacific Heights gradually give way to the more modest Victorians and unassuming housing tracts of Japantown. The most interesting spots in Japantown huddle in the Japan Center, the neighborhood's two-block centerpiece, and along Post Street. You can find plenty of authentic Japanese treats in the shops and restaurants.

PACIFIC HEIGHTS

TOP ATTRACTIONS

Haas-Lilienthal House. A small display of photographs on the bottom floor of this elaborate, gray 1886 Queen Anne house makes clear that despite its lofty stature and striking, round third-story tower, the house was modest compared with some of the giants that fell victim to the 1906 earthquake and fire. The Foundation for San Francisco's Architectural Heritage operates the home, whose carefully kept rooms provide a glimpse into late-19th-century life through period furniture, authentic details (antique dishes in the kitchen built-in), and photos of the family that occupied the house until 1972. ■TIP➜ You can admire hundreds of gorgeous San Francisco Victorians from the outside, but this is the only one that's open to the public, and it's worth a visit. Volunteers conduct one-hour house tours three days a week, and informative two-hour walking tours of Pacific Heights on Sunday afternoon (call or check website for schedule). ✉ *2007 Franklin St., between Washington and Jackson Sts., Pacific Heights* ☎ *415/441–3004* ⊕ *www.sfheritage.org* ▨ *Tours $8.*

Spreckels Mansion. Shrouded behind tall juniper hedges at the corner of winding, redbrick Octavia Street, overlooking Lafayette Park, the estate was built for sugar heir Adolph Spreckels and his wife, Alma. Mrs. Spreckels was so pleased with her house that she commissioned George Applegarth to design another building in a similar vein: the Legion of Honor. One of the city's great iconoclasts, Alma Spreckels was the model for the bronze figure atop the Victory Monument in Union Square. These days an iconoclast of another sort owns the mansion: romance novelist Danielle Steel, whose dustup with local columnists over the size of those hedges entertained aficionados of local gossip in 2014. ✉ *2080 Washington St., at Octavia St., Pacific Heights.*

JAPANTOWN

Japan Center. Cool and curious trinkets, noodle houses and sushi joints, a destination bookstore, and a peek at Japanese culture high and low await at this 5-acre complex designed in 1968 by noted American architect Minoru Yamasaki. The Japan Center includes the shop- and restaurant-filled Kintetsu and Kinokuniya buildings; the excellent Kabuki Springs & Spa; the Hotel Kabuki; and the Sundance Kabuki, Robert Redford's fancy, reserved-seating cinema/restaurant complex.

The Kinokuniya Bookstore, in the Kinokuniya Building, has an extensive selection of Japanese-language books, *manga* (graphic novels), books on design, English-language translations, and books on Japanese topics. Just outside, follow the Japanese teenagers to Pika Pika, where you and your friends can step into a photo booth and then use special effects and stickers to decorate your creation. On the bridge connecting the center's two buildings, check out Shige Antiques for *yukata* (lightweight cotton kimonos) for kids and lovely silk kimonos, and Asakichi and its tiny incense shop for tinkling wind chimes and display-worthy teakettles. Continue into the Kintetsu Building for a selection of Japanese restaurants.

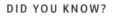

DID YOU KNOW?

These pastel Victorian homes in Pacific Heights are closer to the original hues sported back in the 1900s. It wasn't until the 1960s that the bold, electric colors now seen around San Francisco gained popularity. Before that, the most typical house paint color was a standard gray.

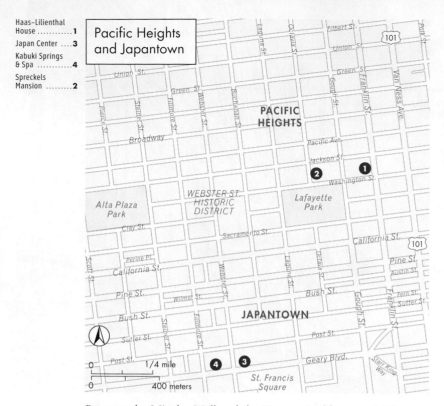

Between the Miyako Mall and the Kintetsu Building are the five-tier, 100-foot-tall **Peace Pagoda** and the Peace Plaza, where seasonal festivals are held. The pagoda, which draws on the 1,200-year-old tradition of miniature round pagodas dedicated to eternal peace, was designed in the late 1960s by Yoshiro Taniguchi to convey the "friendship and goodwill" of the Japanese people to the people of the United States. The plaza itself is a shadeless, unwelcoming space with little seating. Continue into the Miyako Mall to Ichiban Kan, a Japanese dollar store where you can pick up fun Japanese kitchenware, tote bags decorated with hedgehogs, and erasers shaped like food. ⊠ *Bordered by Geary Blvd. and Fillmore, Post, and Laguna Sts., Japantown.*

Fodor's Choice **Kabuki Springs & Spa.** This serene spa is one Japantown destination that
★ draws locals from all over town, from hipster to grandma, Japanese-American or not. Balinese urns decorate the communal bath area of this house of tranquility.

The extensive service menu includes facials, salt scrubs, and mud and seaweed wraps, in addition to massage. You can take your massage in a private room with a bath or in a curtained-off area.

The communal baths ($25) contain hot and cold tubs, a large Japanese-style bath, a sauna, a steam room, and showers. Bang the gong for quiet if your fellow bathers are speaking too loudly. The clothing-optional baths are open for men only on Monday, Thursday, and Saturday; women bathe on Wednesday, Friday, and Sunday. Bathing suits are required on Tuesday, when the baths are coed.

Men and women can reserve private rooms daily. ✉ *1750 Geary Blvd., Japantown* ☎ *415/922–6000* 🌐 *www.kabukisprings.com.*

WHERE TO EAT

Make no mistake, San Francisco is one of America's top food cities. Some of the biggest landmarks are restaurants; and for some visitors, chefs like Daniel Patterson are just as big a draw as Alcatraz. In fact, on a Saturday, the Ferry Building—a temple to local eating—may attract more visitors than the Golden Gate Bridge: cheeses, breads, "salty pig parts," homemade delicacies, and sensory-perfect vegetables and fruits attract rabidly dedicated aficionados. You see, San Franciscans are a little loco about their edibles. If you ask them what their favorite season is, don't be surprised if they respond, "tomato season."

Some renowned restaurants are booked weeks or even months in advance. But you can get lucky at the last minute if you're flexible—and friendly. Most restaurants keep a few tables open for walk-ins and VIPs. Show up for dinner early (5:30 pm) or late (after 9 pm) and politely inquire about any last-minute vacancies or cancellations.

Use the coordinate (⊕ A1) at the end of each listing to locate a site on the corresponding map.

8

WHAT IT COSTS

	$	$$	$$$	$$$$
Restaurants	under $16	$16–$22	$23–$30	over $30

Restaurant prices are the average cost of a main course at dinner or, if dinner is not served, at lunch.

UNION SQUARE AND CHINATOWN

$$$$ MODERN AMERICAN Fodor's Choice ★

🍴 **Liholiho Yacht Club.** Big-hearted, high-spirited cooking has made Chef Ravi Kapur's lively restaurant one of the toughest reservations in town. The menu is inspired but not defined by the chef's native Hawaii. **Known for:** poke; Hawaiian-inspired food; lively buzz. [$] *Average main: $35* ✉ *871 Sutter St., Union Sq.* ☎ *415/440–5446* 🌐 *www.lycf.com* 🕒 *Closed Sun. No lunch.* ⊕ *D4.*

$$$ CHINESE

🍴 **Mister Jiu's.** Brandon Jew's ambitious, graceful restaurant offers the chef's contemporary, farm-to-table interpretation of Chinese cuisine. This is the place for hot-and-sour soup garnished with nasturtiums and pot stickers made with Swiss chard and local chicken. **Known for:** modern Chinese food; cocktails. [$] *Average main: $30* ✉ *28 Waverly Pl., Chinatown* ☎ *415/857–9688* 🌐 *www.misterjius.com* 🕒 *Closed Sun. and Mon. No lunch.* ⊕ *F3.*

HOW TO EAT LIKE A LOCAL

San Francisco may well be the most piping-red-hot dining scene in the nation now. After all, with a booming tech industry, there are mouths to feed. Freedom to do what you want. Innovation. Eccentricity. These words define the culture, the food, and the cuisine of the city by the bay. Get in on what locals know by enjoying their favorite foods.

FOOD TRUCKS

This is where experimentation begins, where the overhead is low, and risk-taking is fun. From these mobile kitchens careers are launched. A food meet-up called "Off the Grid" happens in season at Fort Mason where you can have a progressive dinner among the 25 or so trucks. Year-round the convoy roams to different locations, selling things like Korean poutine, Indian burritos, and Vietnamese burgers. Each dish seems to reflect a refusal to follow the norm.

DIM SUM

The tradition of dim sum took hold in San Francisco when Chinese immigrants from Guangdong Province arrived with Cantonese cuisine. These earlier settlers eventually established teahouses and bakeries that sold dim sum, like the steamed dumplings stuffed with shrimp (*har gow*) or pork (*shao mai*). Now carts roll from table to table in Chinatown restaurants—and other parts of the city. Try the grilled and fried bite-size savories but also the sweets like *dan tat,* an egg custard tart.

BARBECUE

Whaaa? San Francisco barbecue? And what would that be? You can bet it's meat from top purveyors nearby. The city is surrounded by grazing lands, where the animals and their minders, the ranchers, are king. Until now, meats came simply plated. Now it's messy, with smokiness, charred crusts, and gorgeous marbling. But you may never hear of a San-Fran-style barbecue because, in the words of one chef, we're "nondenominational." You'll see it all: Memphis, Texas, Carolina, and Kansas City.

ICE CREAM

How ice cream became so popular in a place that spends many of its 365 days below the 75 degree mark is a mystery. But the lines attest to the popularity of the frozen dessert that gets its own San Francisco twist. This is the vanilla-bean vanilla and Tcho chocolate crowd. Bourbon and cornflakes? Reposado tequila? Cheers to that. Diversity and local produce is blended into flavors like ube (purple yam), yuzu, and Thai latte. Vegans, we got you covered, too.

BURRITOS

This stuffed tortilla got its Bay Area start in the 1960s in the Mission District. Because the size and fillings distinguish it from other styles, it became known as the Mission burrito. Look for rice (Southern Californians are cringing), beans, salsa, and enough meat in the burrito for two meals. The aluminum foil keeps the interior neat, in theory. Popular choices are *carne asada* (beef) and *carnitas* (pork). But

then there's *lengua* (beef tongue) and *birria* (goat). This is a hands-on meal. No utensils, please.

COFFEE

Coffee roasters here are like sports teams in other cities. You pick one of the big five or six to be loyal to, and defend it tirelessly. San Francisco favorites source impeccably and blend different beans as if they were wine making. In addition, a few of the big names—Four Barrel, Sightglass, Ritual, Blue Bottle—roast their own to control what they grind and pour at their outlets across the city—and now nationally and internationally.

FARMERS' MARKETS

These are our new grocery stores. They're the places to discover the latest in fruits, vegetables, and dried beans—much of it grown within a 60-mile radius. Cheeses, cured salami, breads, and nuts are sampled. Then there are the local ready-to-eat snacks, like pizza and *huevos rancheros*. The most popular market is the one on Saturday at the Ferry Plaza.

Opposite: Several farmers' markets occupy the Ferry Building; top right: dim sum; bottom right: the food truck

8

$$ CHINESE FAMILY 🍴 **R&G Lounge.** Salt-and-pepper Dungeness crab is a delicious draw at this bright, three-level Cantonese eatery that excels in the crustacean. A menu with photographs will help you sort through other HK specialties, including Peking duck and shrimp-stuffed bean curd. **Known for:** crab; Cantonese specialties; extensive menu. [$] *Average main: $19* ✉ *631 Kearny St., Chinatown* ☎ *415/982–7877* 🌐 *www.rnglounge.com* ✣ *F3.*

SOMA

$$$$ MODERN AMERICAN Fodor's Choice ★ 🍴 **Benu.** Chef Corey Lee's three-Michelin-star fine-dining mecca is a must-stop for those who hop from city to city, collecting memorable meals. Each of the tasting menu's 15-plus courses is impossibly meticulous, a marvel of textures and flavors. **Known for:** high-end dining; tasting menu; good service. [$] *Average main: $285* ✉ *22 Hawthorne St., SoMa* ☎ *415/685–4860* 🌐 *www.benusf.com* 🕒 *Closed Sun. and Mon. No lunch* ✣ *G5.*

$$$ CONTEMPORARY Fodor's Choice ★ 🍴 **In Situ.** Benu chef Corey Lee's restaurant at SFMOMA is an exhibition of its own, with a rotating menu comprised of dishes from 80 famous chefs around the world. You might taste David Chang's sausage and rice cakes, Rene Redzepi's wood sorrel granita, or Wylie Dufresne's shrimp grits. **Known for:** global influences; originality; museum location. [$] *Average main: $30* ✉ *151 3rd St., SoMa* ☎ *415/941–6050* 🌐 *insitu.sfmoma.org* 🕒 *Closed Wed. No dinner Mon. and Tues.* ✣ *F5.*

$$$ AMERICAN Fodor's Choice ★ 🍴 **Marlowe.** Hearty American bistro fare and hip design draw crowds to this Anna Weinberg–Jennifer Puccio production. The menu boasts one of the city's best burgers, and the dining room gleams with white penny tile floors and marble countertops. **Known for:** burgers; strong drinks; festive atmosphere. [$] *Average main: $27* ✉ *500 Brannan St., SoMa* ☎ *415/777–1413* 🌐 *www.marlowesf.com* 🕒 *No lunch weekends* ✣ *G6.*

$$$ MODERN AMERICAN Fodor's Choice ★ 🍴 **Trou Normand.** Thad Vogler's second endeavor (Bar Agricole was the first) delivers a fun boozy evening in stunning surroundings. Located off the lobby of the art deco–era Pacific Telephone building, it excels at house-cured salami and charcuterie and classic brandy-based cocktails. **Known for:** house-made charcuterie; brandy-based cocktails. [$] *Average main: $26* ✉ *140 New Montgomery St., SoMa* ☎ *415/975–0876* 🌐 *www.trounormandsf.com* ✣ *G4.*

$$$ PIZZA 🍴 **Una Pizza Napoletana.** Inside this bare-bones SoMa spot you'll find one of the best Neapolitan-style pizzas outside of Italy. Chef-owner and Manhattan transplant Anthony Mangieri is an obsessive artisan, carefully making each and every pizza by hand. **Known for:** Neapolitan-style pizza; brief menu. [$] *Average main: $25* ✉ *210 11th St., SoMa* ☎ *415/861–3444* 🌐 *www.unapizza.com* 🕒 *Closed Sun.–Tues.* ✣ *D6.*

HAYES VALLEY

$$ JAPANESE

🍴 **Nojo Ramen.** For a little bonhomie before the symphony, it's hard to go wrong with this buzzy (and typically crowded) ramen spot. Noodles are the star of the menu, and deservedly so, but you'll also find izakaya-style small plates and comfort food like chicken teriyaki. **Known for:** ramen with chicken-based (paitan) broth; Japanese comfort foods; long lines. [$] *Average main: $17* ✉ *231 Franklin St., Hayes Valley* ☎ *415/896–4587* 🌐 *www.nojosf.com* 🕒 *Closed Mon. No lunch.* ✥ *C6.*

$$$$ MODERN AMERICAN Fodor's Choice ★

🍴 **Rich Table.** Sardine potato chips and porcini doughnuts are the most popular bites at co-chefs Evan and Sarah Rich's lively restaurant—and the most indicative of its creativity. The mains are also clever stunners: try one of the proteins or pastas, like the Douglas fir gnocchi. **Known for:** creative food; freshly baked bread. [$] *Average main: $34* ✉ *199 Gough St., Hayes Valley* ☎ *415/355–9085* 🌐 *www.richtablesf.com* 🕒 *No lunch* ✥ *C6.*

$$$ MEDITERRANEAN Fodor's Choice ★

🍴 **Zuni Café.** After one bite of Zuni's succulent brick-oven-roasted whole chicken with Tuscan bread salad, you'll understand why the two-floor café is a perennial star. Its long copper bar is a hub for a disparate mix of patrons who commune over oysters on the half shell and cocktails and wine. **Known for:** famous roast chicken; classic San Francisco dining. [$] *Average main: $30* ✉ *1658 Market St., Hayes Valley* ☎ *415/552–2522* 🌐 *www.zunicafe.com* 🕒 *Closed Mon.* ✥ *C6.*

FINANCIAL DISTRICT

$$$ ITALIAN

🍴 **Cotogna.** This urban trattoria is just as in demand as its fancier big sister, Quince, next door. The draw here is Chef Michael Tusk's flavorful, rustic, seasonally driven Italian cooking. **Known for:** rustic Italian; fantastic wine list. [$] *Average main: $25* ✉ *490 Pacific Ave., Financial District* ☎ *415/775–8508* 🌐 *www.cotognasf.com* ✥ *F2.*

$$$ ITALIAN

🍴 **Perbacco.** Chef Staffan Terje understands the cuisine of northern Italy. From the complimentary basket of skinny, brittle breadsticks to the pappardelle with short rib ragu, his entire menu is a delectable paean to the region. **Known for:** pasta stuffed with meat and cabbage; housemade cured meats; authentic Northern Italian cuisine. [$] *Average main: $30* ✉ *230 California St., Financial District* ☎ *415/955–0663* 🌐 *www.perbaccosf.com* 🕒 *Closed Sun. No lunch Sat.* ✥ *G3.*

$$ CHINESE FAMILY

🍴 **Yank Sing.** This bustling teahouse serves some of San Francisco's best dim sum to office workers on weekdays and boisterous families on weekends. The several dozen varieties prepared daily include both the classic and the creative. **Known for:** classic dim sum; Shanghai soup dumplings. [$] *Average main: $16* ✉ *49 Stevenson St., Financial District* ☎ *415/541–4949* 🌐 *www.yanksing.com* 🕒 *No dinner* ✥ *F4.*

NOB HIL AND RUSSIAN HILL

$$ SEAFOOD Fodor's Choice ★

🍴 **Swan Oyster Depot.** Half fish market and half diner, this small, slim, family-run seafood operation, open since 1912, has no tables, just a narrow marble counter with about 18 stools. Most people come in to buy perfectly fresh salmon, halibut, crabs, and other seafood to take home.

8

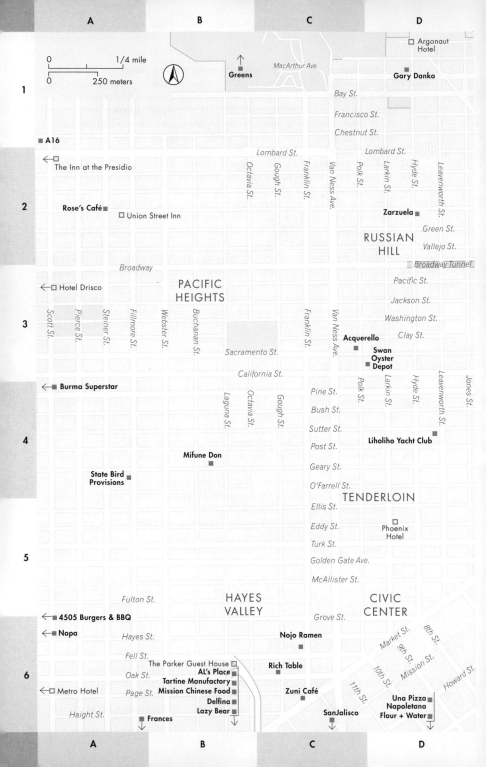

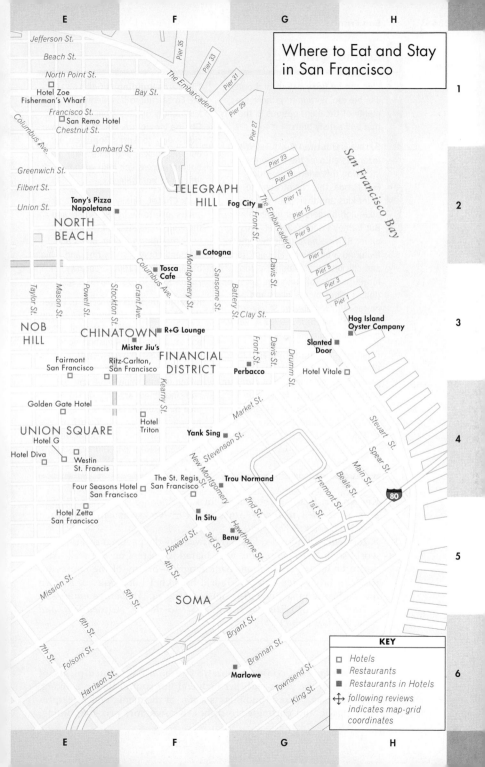

Eating with Kids

Kids can be fussy eaters, and parents can be, too. Fortunately, there are plenty of excellent options in the city that will satisfy both.

Barney's Gourmet Burgers. With locations all over the Bay Area, including this one not far from Fort Mason, this chain caters to older kids and their parents with mile-high burgers and giant salads. But Barney's doesn't forget "kids under 8," who have their own menu featuring a burger, an all-beef frank, and chicken strips. And they don't forget parents, offering a nice selection of wines by the glass and beer on tap. ⊠ *3344 Steiner St., near Union St.* ☎ *415/563–0307* ⊕ *www. barneyshamburgers.com 3:C6.*

City View Restaurant. Nearby in Chinatown, City View Restaurant serves a varied selection of dim sum, with tasty pork buns for kids and more-exotic fare for adults. ⊠ *662 Commercial St., near Kearny St.* ☎ *415/398–2838 1:E4.*

The Ferry Building *(1:G4)*on the Embarcadero has plenty of kid-friendly options, from **Mijita Cocina Mexicana,** which has its own kids' menu, to **Gott's Roadside,** for burgers, shakes, and more. (And the outdoor access can help keep the little ones entertained.)

Park Chalet. Finally, both kids and adults love to be by the ocean, and the Park Chalet, hidden behind the two-story Beach Chalet, offers pizza, mac and cheese, sticky ribs, and a big banana split. ⊠ *1000 Great Hwy., at Fulton St.* ☎ *415/386–8439 3:A3.*

Rosamunde Sausage Grill. In Lower Haight, the small Rosamunde Sausage Grill serves just that—a slew of different sausages, from Polish to duck to *Weisswurst* (Bavarian veal). You get your choice of two toppings, like grilled onions, sauerkraut, and chili, and since there are only six stools, plan on take-out. ■**TIP**➔ Head to nearby Duboce Park, with its cute playground. ⊠ *545 Haight St., between Steiner and Fillmore Sts.* ☎ *415/437–6851 3:D3.*

Known for: fresh seafood; long lines. $ *Average main: $18* ⊠ *1517 Polk St., Polk Gulch* ☎ *415/673–1101* ▭ *No credit cards* ☉ *Closed Sun. No dinner* ✛ *D3.*

$$
TAPAS

✗ **Zarzuela.** Full-blooded Spaniards swear by the paella at this tiny old-world-style bistro, complete with matador posters on the wall. Also not to be missed is the homemade sangria—or any of the impressive roster of tapas prepared by Madrid-bred chef Lucas Gasco. **Known for:** authentic tapas; not-to-be-missed sangria. $ *Average main: $21* ⊠ *2000 Hyde St., Russian Hill* ☎ *415/346–0800* ☉ *Closed Sun. and Mon. No lunch* ✛ *D2.*

VAN NESS/POLK

$$$$
ITALIAN
Fodor's Choice
★

✗ **Acquerello.** Chef-co-owner Suzette Gresham has elicited plenty of swoons over the years with her high-end but soulful Italian cooking. Her Parmesan *budino* (pudding) is a star of the menu, which features both classic and cutting-edge dishes. **Known for:** prix-fixe dining;

Parmesan budino; extensive Italian wine list. [$] *Average main: $95* ✉ *1722 Sacramento St., Polk Gulch* ☎ *415/567–5432* 🌐 *www.acquerello.com* 🕑 *Closed Sun. and Mon. No lunch* ✣ *C3.*

NORTH BEACH

$$$ PIZZA FAMILY 🍴 **Tony's Pizza Napoletana.** Locals hotly debate who makes the city's best pizza, and for many Tony Gemignani takes the prize. Repeatedly crowned the World Champion Pizza Maker at the World Pizza Cup in Naples, he's renowned here for his flavorful dough and impressive range. **Known for:** World Champion Pizza chef; multiple pizza ovens and pie styles; family dining. [$] *Average main: $27* ✉ *1570 Stockton St., North Beach* ☎ *415/835–9888* 🌐 *www.tonyspizzanapoletana.com* 🕑 *Closed Tues.* ✣ *E2.*

$$$ ITALIAN 🍴 **Tosca Cafe.** Following a much-heralded revamp, this 1919 boho classic continues to attract both celebs and local scenesters. The room is dark and clubby, and the food skews Italian, with a raft of pastas and antipasti. **Known for:** Italian-American comfort food; tasty cocktails; signature roast chicken for two. [$] *Average main: $28* ✉ *242 Columbus Ave., North Beach* ☎ *415/986–9651* 🌐 *www.toscacafesf.com* 🕑 *No lunch* ✣ *F3.*

ON THE WATERFRONT

FISHERMAN'S WHARF

$$$$ AMERICAN 🍴 **Gary Danko.** This San Francisco classic has earned a legion of fans—and a Michelin star—for its namesake chef's refined and creative cooking. The cost of a meal is pegged to the number of courses, from three to five, and the menu spans a classic yet Californian style that changes seasonally. **Known for:** prix-fixe menu; fine dining; extensive wine list. [$] *Average main: $87* ✉ *800 N. Point St., Fisherman's Wharf* ☎ *415/749–2060* 🌐 *www.garydanko.com* 🕑 *No lunch* 👔 *Jacket required* ✣ *D1.*

EMBARCADERO

$$ AMERICAN FAMILY 🍴 **Fog City.** All but hidden on a far-flung stretch of the Embarcadero, this 21st-century diner is well worth the hike. It's best known for its updated classics, like a short-rib BLT with kimchi mayo and corn bread that emerges hot from the wood-fired oven. **Known for:** updated diner food; excellent cocktails; views of Battery St. and the Embarcadero. [$] *Average main: $21* ✉ *1300 Battery St., Embarcadero* ☎ *415/982–2000* 🌐 *www.fogcitysf.com* ✣ *G2.*

$$ SEAFOOD 🍴 **Hog Island Oyster Company.** A thriving oyster farm north of San Francisco in Tomales Bay serves up its harvest at this raw bar and restaurant in the Ferry Building. Devotees come here for impeccably fresh oysters and clams on the half shell. **Known for:** fresh oysters; first-rate seafood stew; busy raw bar. [$] *Average main: $17* ✉ *Ferry Bldg., Embarcadero at Market St., Embarcadero* ☎ *415/391–7117* 🌐 *www.hogislandoysters.com* ✣ *H3.*

$$$ VIETNAMESE 🍴 **Slanted Door.** If you're looking for homey Vietnamese food served in a down-to-earth dining room at a bargain-basement price, *don't* stop here. Celebrated chef-owner Charles Phan has mastered the

8

upmarket, Western-accented Vietnamese menu. **Known for:** upscale Vietnamese food; great cocktails. $ *Average main: $30* ✉ *Ferry Bldg., Embarcadero at Market St., Embarcadero* ☎ *415/861–8032* ⊕ *www. slanteddoor.com* ✛ *H3.*

THE MARINA

$$$ ✕ **A16.** Named after a highway that runs through Southern Italy, this
ITALIAN   trattoria specializes in the food from that region, done very, very well. The menu is stocked with pizza and rustic pastas like *maccaronara* with *ragu napoletana* and house-made salted ricotta, as well as entrées like roasted chicken with sage salsa verde. **Known for:** excellent Southern Italian food; mostly Southern Italian wine list; lively bar. $ *Average main: $25* ✉ *2355 Chestnut St., Marina* ☎ *415/771–2216* ⊕ *www. a16pizza.com* ✆ *No lunch Mon. and Tues.* ✛ *A1.*

$$$ ✕ **Greens.** Owned and operated by the San Francisco Zen Center, this
VEGETARIAN   legendary vegetarian restaurant gets some of its fresh produce from the center's organic Green Gulch Farm. Despite the lack of meat, hearty dishes from chef Annie Somerville—such as green curry and wild-mushroom-leek pizza—really satisfy. **Known for:** sweeping views; hearty vegetarian food. $ *Average main: $24* ✉ *Bldg. A, Fort Mason, 2 Marina Blvd., Marina* ☎ *415/771–6222* ⊕ *www.greensrestaurant.com* ✆ *No lunch Mon.* ✛ *B1.*

COW HOLLOW

$$$ ✕ **Rose's Café.** Although it's open morning until night, this cozy café is
ITALIAN   most synonymous with brunch. Sleepy-headed locals turn up for delights
FAMILY   like the breakfast pizza of smoked ham, eggs, and fontina and the French toast with caramelized apples. **Known for:** popular Sunday brunch; breakfast pizza; top-notch ingredients. $ *Average main: $28* ✉ *2298 Union St., Cow Hollow* ☎ *415/775–2200* ⊕ *www.rosescafesf.com* ✛ *A2.*

THE CASTRO

$$$ ✕ **Frances.** Still one of the hottest tickets in town, chef Melissa Perello's
MODERN   simple, sublime restaurant is a consummate date-night destination.
AMERICAN   Perello's seasonal California-French cooking is its own enduring love affair. **Known for:** seasonal menu; neighborhood gem; tough reservation. $ *Average main: $30* ✉ *3870 17th St., Castro* ☎ *415/621–3870* ⊕ *www.frances-sf.com* ✆ *Closed Mon. No lunch* ✛ *A6.*

THE MISSION

$$ ✕ **AL's Place.** AL is Chef Aaron London, and his place is a sunny, white-
MODERN   washed corner spot that serves inventive, Michelin-starred vegetable-for-
AMERICAN   ward cooking. London's menu changes frequently, but some dishes, like lightly cured trout and grits with seasonal produce, stick around. **Known for:** seasonal cooking; inventive vegetable-heavy menu; fries with cult following. $ *Average main: $17* ✉ *1499 Valencia St., Mission* ☎ *415/416–6136* ⊕ *www.alsplacesf.com* ✆ *Closed Mon. and Tues. No lunch.* ✛ *B6.*

$$$ ITALIAN Fodor's Choice ★ 🍴 **Delfina.** To find Craig and Annie Stoll's cultishly adored Northern Italian spot, just look for the crowds. They're a constant fixture here, as are deceptively simple, exquisitely flavored dishes like the signature spaghetti with plum tomatoes. **Known for:** signature spaghetti with plum tomatoes; long waits; much-lauded panna cotta. [$] *Average main: $27* ✉ *3621 18th St., Mission District* ☎ *415/552–4055* 🌐 *www.delfinasf.com* 🕒 *No lunch* ✥ *B6.*

$$$ ITALIAN 🍴 **Flour + Water.** This hot spot is synonymous with pasta, though its blistery thin-crust Neapolitan pizzas are also top notch. The grand experience here is the seven-course pasta-tasting menu (extra for wine pairings). **Known for:** difficult to get a reservation; delicious pizzas and pastas; noisy scene. [$] *Average main: $26* ✉ *2401 Harrison St., Mission District* ☎ *415/826–7000* 🌐 *www.flourandwater.com* 🕒 *No lunch* ✥ *D6.*

$$$$ MODERN AMERICAN 🍴 **Lazy Bear.** There's no end to the buzz of chef David Barzelay's pop-up turned permanent, or the quest for a ticket to one of his modern American dinners. A reservation for the 14-plus-course prix-fixe menu that changes monthly is required. **Known for:** hot-ticket often resold; communal dining; dinner party setup. [$] *Average main: $160* ✉ *3416 19th St., Mission District* ☎ *415/874–9921* 🌐 *www.lazybearsf.com* 🕒 *Closed Sun. and Mon. No lunch.* ✥ *B6.*

$ CHINESE 🍴 **Mission Chinese Food.** While the setting is somewhat one-star, the food draws throngs for its bold, cheerfully inauthentic riffs on Chinese cuisine. The kitchen pumps out some fine and super-fiery kung pao pastrami as well as other dishes made with quality meats and ingredients, like salt cod fried rice with mackerel confit, and sour chili chicken. **Known for:** kung pao pastrami; salt cod fried rice; to-go spot due to long waits. [$] *Average main: $14* ✉ *2234 Mission St., Mission District* ☎ *415/863–2800* 🌐 *www.missionchinesefood.com* 🕒 *Closed Wed.* ✥ *B6.*

$ MEXICAN FAMILY 🍴 **SanJalisco.** This colorful old-time, sun-filled, family-run restaurant is a neighborhood favorite, and not only because it serves breakfast all day—though the hearty *chilaquiles* hit the spot. On weekends, adventurous eaters may opt for *birria,* a spicy barbecued goat stew, or *menudo,* a tongue-searing soup made from beef tripe. **Known for:** breakfast all day; beef-tripe menudo; delicious sangria. [$] *Average main: $11* ✉ *901 S. Van Ness Ave., Mission District* ☎ *415/648–8383* 🌐 *www.sanjalisco.com* ✥ *C6.*

$$$$ MODERN AMERICAN FAMILY 🍴 **Tartine Manufactory.** Little Tartine bakery has expanded big time, with this sunny, cathedral-like space in the Heath Ceramics building. This is where you come for Chad Robertson's bread and Liz Prueitt's pastries, but also for breakfast, lunch, and dinner. **Known for:** Chad Robertson's bread; Liz Prueitt's pastries; seasonal salads. [$] *Average main: $32* ✉ *595 Alabama St., Mission District* ☎ *415/757–0007* 🌐 *www.tartinemanufactory.com* 🕒 *No dinner Mon. and Tues.* ✥ *B6.*

JAPANTOWN

$ JAPANESE FAMILY 🍴 **Mifune Don.** Thin brown soba and thick white udon are the stars at this long-popular outpost of a celebrated Osaka restaurant. There's usually a line, but the house-made noodles, served both hot and cold and with a score of toppings, are worth the wait (and the line moves quickly).

Known for: house-made soba and udon; savory Japanese pancakes; long lines. $ *Average main: $12* ✉ *22 Peace Plaza, Suite 560, Japantown* ☎ *415/346–1993* ◷ *Closed Tues.* ✛ *B4.*

WESTERN ADDITION

$$
BARBECUE

✕ **4505 Burgers & BBQ.** Noted butcher Ryan Farr is behind the tender, deliciously charred brisket at this hipster-chic barbecue shack. The smoker here works overtime, churning out an array of meats that can be had by the plate and pound. **Known for:** smoked meats; delicious sides; juicy burgers. $ *Average main: $17* ✉ *705 Divisadero, at Grove St., Western Addition* ☎ *415/231–6993* ⊕ *www.4505meats. com* ✛ *A6.*

$$$
AMERICAN

✕ **Nopa.** This is the good-food granddaddy of the hot corridor of the same name (NoPa equals North of the Panhandle). The Cali-rustic fare here draws dependable crowds, especially on the weekends. **Known for:** California cooking; flatbread topped with bacon and Treviso cheese; lively crowd. $ *Average main: $24* ✉ *560 Divisadero St., Western Addition* ☎ *415/864–8643* ⊕ *www.nopasf.com* ◷ *No lunch weekdays* ✛ *A6.*

$$$
MODERN
AMERICAN
Fodor's Choice
★

✕ **State Bird Provisions.** It's more or less impossible to nab a reservation at Stuart Brioza and Nicole Krasinski's game-changing, Michelin-starred restaurant. But if you do walk in and brave the 90-plus-minute wait, you'll eventually be rewarded with inventive bites served from dim sum–style carts. **Known for:** dim sum–style dining; long waits. $ *Average main: $30* ✉ *1529 Fillmore St., Western Addition* ☎ *415/795–1272* ⊕ *www.statebirdsf.com* ◷ *No lunch* ✛ *A4.*

THE RICHMOND

$
ASIAN

✕ **Burma Superstar.** Locals make the trek to the "Avenues" for this perennially crowded spot's flavorful, well-prepared Burmese food. Its signature dish is the extraordinary tea leaf salad, a combo of spicy, salty, crunchy, and sour that is mixed table-side. **Known for:** tea leaf salad; samusa soup; long lines. $ *Average main: $15* ✉ *309 Clement St., Richmond* ☎ *415/387–2147* ⊕ *www.burmasuperstar.com* ✛ *A4.*

WHERE TO STAY

San Francisco accommodations are diverse, ranging from cozy inns and kitschy motels, to chic little inns and true grande dames, housed in century-old structures and sleek high-rises. While the tech boom has skyrocketed the prices of even some of the most dependable low-cost options, luckily, some Fodor's faves still offer fine accommodations without the jaw-dropping prices to match those steep hills. In fact, the number of reasonably priced accommodations is impressive.

Hotel reviews have been shortened. For full information, visit Fodors. com. Use the coordinate (✛ A1) at the end of each listing to locate a site on the corresponding map.

WHAT IT COSTS				
	$	$$	$$$	$$$$
Hotels	under $150	$150–$249	$250–$350	over $350

Hotel prices are the lowest cost of a standard double room in high season.

UNION SQUARE

$ B&B/INN FAMILY Fodor's Choice ★ **Golden Gate Hotel.** Budget seekers looking for accommodations around Union Square will enjoy this four-story Edwardian with bay windows, an original birdcage elevator, hallways lined with historical photographs, and rooms decorated with antiques, wicker pieces, and Laura Ashley bedding and curtains. **Pros:** friendly staff; free Wi-Fi; spotless rooms; comfortable bedding; good location if you're a walker. **Cons:** some rooms share a bath; resident cat and dog, so not good for guests with allergies; some rooms on small side. [$] *Rooms from: $145* ✉ *775 Bush St., Union Sq.* ☎ *415/392–3702, 800/835–1118* 🌐 *www.goldengatehotel.com* 🛏 *23 rooms* 🍴 *Breakfast* ⊕ *E4.*

$$ HOTEL FAMILY **Hotel Diva.** Entering this magnet for urbanites craving modern decor requires stepping over footprints, handprints, and autographs embedded in the sidewalk by visiting stars; in the rooms, designer carpets complement mid-century-modern chairs and brushed-steel headboards whose shape mimics that of ocean waves. **Pros:** punchy design; in the heart of the theater district; accommodating staff. **Cons:** few frills; tiny bathrooms (but equipped with eco-friendly bath products); many rooms are small. [$] *Rooms from: $189* ✉ *440 Geary St., Union Sq.* ☎ *415/885–0200, 800/553–1900* 🌐 *www.hoteldiva.com* 🛏 *130 rooms* 🍴 *No meals* ⊕ *E4.*

$$ HOTEL **Hotel Triton.** One of San Francisco's early concept boutique hotels, the Triton may have been eclipsed by newcomers in both style and substance, but its staff remains attentive and the hotel's location at the convergence of Chinatown, the Financial District, and Union Square keeps it worthy of consideration. **Pros:** attentive service; arty environs; good location. **Cons:** rooms and baths are on the small side; hallways feel cramped; needs a reboot. [$] *Rooms from: $219* ✉ *342 Grant Ave., Union Sq.* ☎ *415/394–0500, 877/793–9931* 🌐 *www.hoteltriton.com* 🛏 *140 rooms* 🍴 *No meals* ⊕ *F4.*

$$$$ HOTEL **Westin St. Francis.** The survivor of two major earthquakes, some headline-grabbing scandals, and even an attempted presidential assassination, this grande dame that dates to 1904 remains ever above the fray. **Pros:** prime Union Square location; great views from some rooms; special weekend rates part of year. **Cons:** rooms in original building can be small; public spaces lack the panache of days gone by. [$] *Rooms from: $356* ✉ *335 Powell St., Union Sq.* ☎ *415/397–7000, 800/917–7458* 🌐 *www.westinstfrancis.com* 🛏 *1,195 rooms* 🍴 *No meals* ⊕ *E4.*

SOMA

$$$$ HOTEL

🏨 **Four Seasons Hotel San Francisco.** Occupying floors 5 through 17 of a skyscraper, the Four Seasons delivers subdued elegance in rooms with contemporary artwork, fine linens, floor-to-ceiling windows that overlook Yerba Buena Gardens or downtown, and bathrooms with deep soaking tubs and glass-enclosed showers. **Pros:** near museums, galleries, restaurants, shopping, and clubs; terrific fitness facilities; luxurious rooms and amenities. **Cons:** pricey; rooms can feel sterile. [$] *Rooms from: $525* ✉ *757 Market St., SoMa* ☎ *415/633–3000, 800/332–3442, 800/819–5053* 🌐 *www.fourseasons.com/sanfrancisco* 🛏 *277 rooms* 🍴 *No meals* ✣ *F4.*

$$$ HOTEL Fodor's Choice ★

🏨 **Hotel Zetta San Francisco.** With a playful lobby lounge, the London-style Cavalier brasserie, and slick-yet-homey tech-friendly rooms, this trendy redo behind a stately 1913 neoclassical facade is a leader in the SoMa hotel scene. **Pros:** tech amenities and arty design; fine restaurant and lounge; noteworthy fitness center. **Cons:** lots of hubbub and traffic; no bathtubs; aesthetic mildly too frenetic for some guests. [$] *Rooms from: $289* ✉ *55 5th St., SoMa* ☎ *415/543–8555* 🌐 *hotelzetta.com* 🛏 *116 rooms* 🍴 *No meals* ✣ *E5.*

$$$$ HOTEL Fodor's Choice ★

🏨 **The St. Regis San Francisco.** Across from Yerba Buena Gardens and SFMOMA, the luxurious and modern St. Regis is favored by celebrities such as Lady Gaga and Al Gore. **Pros:** excellent views; stunning lap pool; luxe spa. **Cons:** expensive rates; small front-desk area; cramped space for passenger unloading. [$] *Rooms from: $358* ✉ *125 3rd St., SoMa* ☎ *415/284–4000* 🌐 *www.stregis.com/sanfrancisco* 🛏 *260 rooms* 🍴 *No meals* ✣ *F4.*

THE TENDERLOIN

$$ HOTEL

🏨 **Phoenix Hotel.** A magnet for the boho crowd, the Phoenix is retro and low-key, with bamboo furniture, white bedspreads, and original pieces by local artists, as well as modern amenities like iHome docking stations. **Pros:** mellow staffers set boho tone; cheeky design, hip restaurant/bar; free parking. **Cons:** somewhat seedy location; no elevators; can be loud in the evenings. [$] *Rooms from: $249* ✉ *601 Eddy St., Tenderloin* ☎ *415/776–1380, 800/248–9466* 🌐 *www.thephoenixhotel.com* 🛏 *44 rooms* 🍴 *Breakfast* ✣ *D5.*

HAYES VALLEY

$ HOTEL Fodor's Choice ★

🏨 **Metro Hotel.** These tiny rooms, with simple yet modern decor and equipped with private, if small, bathrooms, are within walking distance to the lively Haight, Hayes Valley, Panhandle, NoPa, and Castro neighborhoods. **Pros:** can't beat the price; out-of-downtown location; friendly staffers. **Cons:** small rooms and bathrooms; street noise; only difficult street parking available. [$] *Rooms from: $107* ✉ *319 Divisadero St., Hayes Valley* ☎ *415/861–5364* 🌐 *www.metrohotelsf.com* 🛏 *24 rooms* 🍴 *No meals* ✣ *A6.*

NOB HILL

$$$$ HOTEL 🏨 **Fairmont San Francisco.** Dominating the top of Nob Hill like a European palace, the Fairmont indulges guests in luxury—rooms in the main building, adorned in sapphire blues with platinum and pewter accents, have high ceilings, decadent beds, and marble bathrooms; rooms in the newer Tower, many with fine views, have a neutral color palette with bright-silver notes. **Pros:** huge bathrooms; stunning lobby; great location. **Cons:** some older rooms are small; hills can be challenging for those on foot. [$] *Rooms from: $459* ✉ *950 Mason St., Nob Hill* ☎ *415/772–5000, 800/257–7544* 🌐 *www.fairmont.com/san-francisco* 🛏 *592 rooms* 🍴 *No meals* ✥ *E3.*

$$$$ HOTEL Fodor's Choice ★ 🏨 **Ritz-Carlton, San Francisco.** A tribute to beauty and attentive, professional service, the Ritz-Carlton emphasizes luxury and elegance, which is evident in the Ionic columns that grace the neoclassical facade and the crystal chandeliers that illuminate marble floors and walls in the lobby. **Pros:** terrific service; beautiful surroundings; Parallel 37 restaurant and Lobby Lounge. **Cons:** expensive; hilly location; no pool. [$] *Rooms from: $570* ✉ *600 Stockton St., at California St., Nob Hill* ☎ *415/296–7465, 800/542–8680* 🌐 *www.ritzcarlton.com/sanfrancisco* 🛏 *336 rooms* 🍴 *No meals* ✥ *E3.*

NORTH BEACH

$ HOTEL Fodor's Choice ★ 🏨 **San Remo Hotel.** A few blocks from Fisherman's Wharf, this three-story 1906 Italianate Victorian—once home to longshoremen and Beat poets—has a narrow stairway from the street leading to the front desk and labyrinthine hallways. **Pros:** inexpensive rates; free Wi-Fi; rooftop penthouse (reserve way ahead) has private deck with Coit Tower views. **Cons:** some rooms are dark; only the penthouse suite has a private bath; parking (discounted fee) is off-site. [$] *Rooms from: $119* ✉ *2237 Mason St., North Beach* ☎ *415/776–8688, 800/352–7366* 🌐 *www.sanremohotel.com* 💳 *No credit cards* ⏲ *64 rooms* 🍴 *No meals* ✥ *E1.*

FISHERMAN'S WHARF

$$$ HOTEL FAMILY Fodor's Choice ★ 🏨 **Argonaut Hotel.** The Argonaut's spacious guest rooms have exposed-brick walls, wood-beam ceilings, and best of all, windows that open to the sea air and the sounds of the waterfront; many rooms enjoy Alcatraz and Golden Gate Bridge views. **Pros:** bay views; near Hyde Street cable car; toys for the kids. **Cons:** nautical theme isn't for everyone; cramped public areas; far from crosstown attractions. [$] *Rooms from: $269* ✉ *495 Jefferson St., at Hyde St., Fisherman's Wharf* ☎ *415/563–0800, 866/415–0704* 🌐 *www.argonauthotel.com* 🛏 *252 rooms* 🍴 *No meals* ✥ *D1.*

$$$ HOTEL 🏨 **Hotel Zoe Fisherman's Wharf.** Multimillion-dollar renovations in 2017 transformed the dowdy former Best Western Tuscan into a smart-looking boutique hotel with guest-room interiors inspired by luxury Mediterranean yachts. **Pros:** cozy feeling; steps from Fisherman's Wharf; smart-looking contemporary design. **Cons:** congested touristy area; small rooms. [$] *Rooms from: $279* ✉ *425 N. Point St., at Mason St., Fisherman's Wharf* ☎ *415/561–1100, 800/648–4626* 🌐 *www.hotelzoesf.com* 💳 *No credit cards* 🛏 *221 rooms* 🍴 *No meals* ✥ *E1.*

EMBARCADERO

$$$$ HOTEL FAMILY Fodor's Choice ★ [🏨] **Hotel Vitale.** The emphasis on luxury and upscale relaxation at this eight-story bay-front property is apparent in every thoughtful detail: little vases of lavender mounted outside each room; limestone-lined baths stocked with top-of-the-line products; the penthouse-level day spa with soaking tubs set in a rooftop bamboo forest. **Pros:** family-friendly studios; great waterfront views; penthouse spa. **Cons:** some rooms feel cramped; "urban fee" adds further expense to an already pricey property; only partial bay views from some rooms. [$] *Rooms from: $385* ✉ *8 Mission St., Embarcadero* ☎ *415/278–3700, 888/890–8688* 🌐 *www.hotelvitale.com* 🛏 *200 rooms* 🍴 *No meals* ✥ *H3.*

THE MARINA, COW HOLLOW, AND THE PRESIDIO

$$$ B&B/INN Fodor's Choice ★ [🏨] **The Inn at the Presidio.** Built in 1903 and opened as a hotel in 2012, this two-story, Georgian Revival–style structure once served as officers' quarters but now has 26 guest rooms—most of them suites—complete with gas fireplaces and modern-meets-salvage-store finds such as wrought-iron beds, historic black-and-white photos, and Pendleton blankets. **Pros:** Golden Gate Bridge views; away-from-it-all feeling yet still in the city; Presidio's hiking and biking trails, Disney museum, and other attractions. **Cons:** no on-site restaurant; no elevator; challenging to get a taxi; far from downtown attractions. [$] *Rooms from: $295* ✉ *42 Moraga Ave., Presidio* ☎ *415/800–7356* 🌐 *www.innatthepresidio.com* 🛏 *26 rooms* 🍴 *Breakfast* ✥ *A2.*

$$ B&B/INN Fodor's Choice ★ [🏨] **Union Street Inn.** Antiques, unique artwork, and such touches as candles, fresh flowers, wineglasses, and fine linens make rooms in this green-and-cream 1902 Edwardian popular with honeymooners and those looking for a romantic getaway with an English countryside ambience. **Pros:** personal service; excellent full breakfast; romantic setting. **Cons:** parking is difficult; no air-conditioning; no elevator. [$] *Rooms from: $249* ✉ *2229 Union St., Cow Hollow* ☎ *415/346–0424* 🌐 *www.unionstreetinn.com* 🛏 *6 rooms* 🍴 *Breakfast* ✥ *A2.*

THE MISSION

$$ B&B/INN Fodor's Choice ★ [🏨] **The Parker Guest House.** Two yellow 1909 Edwardian houses enchant travelers wanting an authentic San Francisco experience; dark hallways and steep staircases lead to bright earth-toned rooms with private tiled baths (most with tubs), comfortable sitting areas, and cozy linens. **Pros:** handsome affordable rooms; just steps from Dolores Park and the vibrant Castro District on a Muni line; elaborate gardens. **Cons:** stairs can be challenging for those with limited mobility. [$] *Rooms from: $179* ✉ *520 Church St., Mission District* ☎ *415/621–4139* 🌐 *parkerguesthouse.com* 🛏 *21 rooms* 🍴 *Breakfast* ✥ *B6.*

PACIFIC HEIGHTS AND JAPANTOWN

$$$$
HOTEL
Fodor'sChoice
★

Hotel Drisco. Pretend you're a denizen of one of San Francisco's wealthiest residential neighborhoods while you stay at this understated, elegant 1903 Edwardian hotel. **Pros:** full renovation of property in 2017; great service and many amenities; quiet residential retreat. **Cons:** far from downtown (but free weekday-morning chauffeur service); room-rate uptick since renovation; on a steep hill. $ *Rooms from: $499* ✉ *2901 Pacific Ave., Pacific Heights* ☎ *415/346–2880, 800/634–7277* ⊕ *www.hoteldrisco.com* ⇆ *48 rooms* ○ *Breakfast* ✦ *A3.*

NIGHTLIFE

After hours, business folk and the working class give way to costume-clad partygoers, hippies and hipsters, downtown divas, frat boys, and those who prefer something a little more clothing-optional.

Entertainment information is printed in the "Datebook" section and the more calendar-based "96 Hours" section of the *San Francisco Chronicle* (⊕ *www.sfgate.com*) . Also consult any of the free alternative weeklies, notably the *SF Weekly* (⊕ *www.sfweekly.com*), which blurbs nightclubs and music, and the *San Francisco Bay Guardian* (⊕ *www.sfbg.com*), which lists neighborhood, avant-garde, and budget events. SF Station (⊕ *www.sfstation.com*; online only) has an up-to-date calendar of entertainment goings-on.

You're better off taking public transportation or taxis on weekend nights, unless you're heading downtown (Financial District or Union Square) and are willing to park in a lot. There's only street parking in North Beach, the Mission, Castro, and the Haight, and finding a spot can be practically impossible. Muni stops running between 1 am and 5 am but has its limited Owl Service on a few lines—including the K, N, L, 90, 91, 14, 24, 38, and 22—every 30 minutes. Service cuts have put a dent in frequency; check ⊕ *www.sfmuni.com* for current details. You can sometimes hail a taxi on the street in well-trodden nightlife locations like North Beach or the Mission, but you can also call for one (*415/626–2345 Yellow Cab, 415/648–3181 Arrow*). The best option by far is booking a taxi with a smartphone-based app (*www.uber.com, www.lyft.com*). ■**TIP→ Cabs in San Francisco are more expensive than in other areas of the United States; expect to pay at least $15 to get anywhere within the city. Keep in mind that BART service across the bay stops shortly after midnight.**

8

UNION SQUARE

BARS

Harry Denton's Starlight Room. Forget low-key drinks—the only way to experience Harry Denton's is to go for a show. Cough up the cover charge and enjoy the opulent, over-the-top decor and entertainment (some of the best cover bands in the business, usually playing Top 40 hits from the '60s, '70s, and '80s). Velvet booths and romantic lighting help re-create the 1950s high life on the 21st floor of the Sir

Francis Drake Hotel, and the small dance floor is packed on Friday and Saturday nights. Jackets are preferred for men. Call ahead—the room is sometimes closed for private events on weekdays. ⊠ *Sir Francis Drake Hotel, 450 Powell St., between Post and Sutter Sts., Union Sq.* ☎ *415/395–8595* ⊕ *www.starlightroomsf.com.*

Pacific Cocktail Haven. PCH for short, this neighborhood hangout has taken over the space that once belonged to the Latin sensation Cantina. Having a convivial aura and industrial-chic decor, PCH hits all the right notes. Plus the well-chosen and unique ingredients mean there's a little something for everyone. And the glassware is as dazzling as the elixirs inside. ■**TIP→** The must-try cocktail is the Oh Snap!, a concoction of gin, sugar snap peas, citrus, and absinthe. ⊠ *580 Sutter St., at Mason St., Union Sq.* ☎ *415/398–0195* ⊕ *www.pacificcocktailsf.com* ⊘ *Closed Sun.*

SOMA

BARS

City Beer Store. Called CBS by locals, this friendly tasting room cum liquor mart has a wine-bar's sensibility. Perfect for connoisseurs and the merely beer curious, CBS stocks more than 300 different bottled beers, and more than a dozen are on tap. The indecisive can mix and match six-packs to go. ■**TIP→** Come early: The small space fills up quickly on event nights. ⊠ *1168 Folsom St., at 8th St., SoMa* ☎ *415/503–1033* ⊕ *www.citybeerstore.com.*

21st Amendment Brewery. This popular brewery is known for its range of beer types, with multiple taps going at all times. In the spring, the Hell or High Watermelon—a wheat beer—gets rave reviews. ■**TIP→** Serious beer drinkers should try the Back in Black, a black IPA-style beer this brewpub helped pioneer. The space has an upmarket warehouse feel, though exposed wooden ceiling beams, framed photos, whitewashed brick walls, and hardwood floors make it feel cozy. It's a good spot to warm up before a Giants game and an even better place to party after they win. ⊠ *563 2nd St., between Federal and Brannan Sts., SoMa* ☎ *415/369–0900* ⊕ *www.21st-amendment.com.*

GAY NIGHTLIFE

The Stud. Glam trans women, gay bears, tight-teed pretty boys, ladies and their ladies, and a handful of straight onlookers congregate here to dance to live DJ sounds and watch world-class drag performers on the small stage. The entertainment is often campy, pee-your-pants funny, and downright fantastic. Each night's music is different—from funk, soul, and hip-hop to '80s tunes and disco favorites. ■**TIP→** At Frolic, the Stud's most outrageous party (second Saturday of the month), club goers dance the night away dressed as bunnies, kittens, and even stranger creatures. ⊠ *399 9th St, at Harrison St., SoMa* ☎ *415/863–6623* ⊕ *www.studsf.com* ⊘ *Closed Mon.*

THE TENDERLOIN

BARS

Fodor's Choice ★ **Bourbon & Branch.** Bourbon & Branch reeks of Prohibition-era speakeasy cool. It's not exclusive, though: everyone is granted a password. The place has sex appeal, with tin ceilings, bordello-red silk wallpaper, intimate booths, and low lighting; loud conversations and cell phones are not allowed. The menu of expertly mixed cocktails and quality bourbon and whiskey is substantial, though the servers aren't always authorities. ■TIP→ Your reservation dictates your exit time, which is strictly enforced. There's also a speakeasy within the speakeasy called Wilson & Wilson, which is more exclusive, but just as funky. ✉ *501 Jones St., at O'Farrell St., Tenderloin* ☎ *415/346-1735* ⊕ *www.bourbonandbranch.com.*

MUSIC CLUBS

Fodor's Choice ★ **Great American Music Hall.** You can find top-drawer entertainment at this eclectic nightclub. Acts range from the best in blues, folk, and jazz to up-and-coming college-radio and American-roots artists to indie rockers such as OK Go, Mates of State, and Cowboy Junkies. The colorful marble-pillared emporium (built in 1907 as a bordello) also accommodates dancing at some shows. Pub grub is available on most nights. ✉ *859 O'Farrell St., between Polk and Larkin Sts., Tenderloin* ☎ *415/885–0750* ⊕ *www.slimspresents.com.*

HAYES VALLEY

BARS

Fodor's Choice ★ **Smuggler's Cove.** With the decor of a pirate ship and a slew of rum-based cocktails, you half expect Captain Jack Sparrow to sidle up next to you at this offbeat, Disney-esque hangout. But don't let the kitschy ambience fool you. The folks at Smuggler's Cove take rum so seriously they even make their own, which you can sample along with more than 200 other offerings, some of them vintage and very hard to find. A punch card is provided so you can try all 70 cocktails and remember where you left off without getting shipwrecked. The small space fills up quickly, so arrive early. ✉ *650 Gough St., at McAllister St., Hayes Valley* ☎ *415/869–1900* ⊕ *www.smugglerscovesf.com.*

NORTH BEACH

BARS

Fodor's Choice ★ **Vesuvio Cafe.** If you're hitting only one bar in North Beach, it should be this one. The low-ceilinged second floor of this raucous boho hangout, little altered since its 1960s heyday (when Jack Kerouac frequented the place), is a fine vantage point for watching the colorful Broadway Street and Columbus Avenue intersection. Another part of Vesuvio's appeal is its diverse clientele, from older neighborhood regulars and young couples to Bacchanalian posses. ✉ *255 Columbus Ave., at Broadway St., North Beach* ☎ *415/362–3370* ⊕ *www.vesuvio.com.*

8

CABARET

Club Fugazi. The claim to fame here is *Beach Blanket Babylon,* a wacky musical send-up of San Francisco moods and mores that has been going strong since 1974, making it the longest-running musical revue anywhere. Although the choreography is colorful, the singers brassy, and the satirical songs witty, the real stars are the comically exotic costumes and famous ceiling-high "hats"—which are worth the price of admission alone. The revue sells out as early as a month in advance, so order tickets as far ahead as possible. Those under 21 are admitted only to the Sunday matinee. ■TIP➜ If you don't shell out the extra money for reserved seating, you won't have an assigned seat—so get your cannoli to go and arrive at least 30 minutes prior to showtime to get in line. ✉ *678 Green St., at Powell St., North Beach* ☎ *415/421–4222* ⊕ *www. beachblanketbabylon.com.*

MUSIC CLUBS

Bimbo's 365 Club. The plush main room and adjacent lounge of this club, here since 1951, retain a retro vibe perfect for the "Cocktail Nation" programming that keeps the crowds entertained. For a taste of the old-school San Francisco nightclub scene, you can't beat it. Indie low-fi and pop bands such as Stephen Malkmus and the Jicks and Camera Obscura play here. ✉ *1025 Columbus Ave., at Chestnut St., North Beach* ☎ *415/474–0365* ⊕ *www.bimbos365club.com.*

EMBARCADERO

BARS

Hard Water. This waterfront restaurant and bar with stunning bay views pays homage to America's most iconic spirit—bourbon—with a wall of whiskeys and a lineup of specialty cocktails. The menu, crafted by Charles Phan of Slanted Door fame, includes spicy pork-belly cracklings, corn-bread-crusted alligator, and other fun snacks. ✉ *Pier 3, Suite 3–102, at Embarcadero, Embarcadero* ☎ *415/392–3021* ⊕ *www.hardwaterbar.com.*

THE WESTERN SHORELINE

BARS

The Riptide. A cozy cabin bar that's the perfect finale for beachgoers, Riptide is a surfer favorite, but you don't have to own a board to feel at home. You'll find classic beers, good food, and all at wallet-friendly prices. There's live music most nights, which swings somewhere between bluegrass to karaoke. Many tourists fooled by San Francisco's definition of summer end up warming their popsicle toes at the bar's fireplace. Sunday's feature a bacon Bloody Mary, great for hangovers. ✉ *3639 Taraval St, Sunset* ☎ *415/681–8433* ⊕ *www.riptidesf.com.*

THE MISSION

BARS

Fodor's Choice ★ **El Rio.** A dive bar in the best sense has a calendar chock-full of events, from free bands and films to Salsa Sunday (seasonal), all of which keep Mission kids coming back. Bands play several nights a week, and there are plenty of other events. No matter what day you attend, expect to find a diverse gay-straight crowd. When the weather's warm, the large patio out back is especially popular, and the midday dance parties are *the* place to be. ⊠ *3158 Mission St., between César Chavez and Valencia Sts., Mission District* ☎ *415/282–3325* ⊕ *www.elriosf.com.*

Zeitgeist. It's a bit divey, a bit rock and roll, but a good place to relax with a cold one or an ever-popular (and ever-strong) Bloody Mary in the large beer "garden" (there's not much greenery) on a sunny day. Grill food is available, and if you're lucky. one of the city's most famous food-cart operators, the Tamale Lady, will drop by. If you own a trucker hat, a pair of Vans, and a Pabst Blue Ribbon T-shirt, you'll fit right in. ⊠ *199 Valencia St., at Duboce Ave., Mission District* ☎ *415/255–7505* ⊕ *www.zeitgeistsf.com.*

GAY NIGHTLIFE

Martuni's. A mixed crowd enjoys cocktails in the semi-refined environment of this bar where the Castro, the Mission, and Hayes Valley intersect; variations on the martini are a specialty. In the intimate back room a pianist plays nightly, and patrons take turns boisterously singing show tunes. Martuni's often gets busy after symphony and opera performances—Davies Hall and the Opera House are both within walking distance. ■ TIP➔ The Godiva Chocolate Martini is a crowd favorite. ⊠ *4 Valencia St., at Market St., Mission District* ☎ *415/241–0205.*

POTRERO HILL

MUSIC CLUBS

Bottom of the Hill. This is a great live-music dive—in the best sense of the word—and truly the epicenter for Bay Area indie rock. The club has hosted some great acts over the years, including the Strokes and the Throwing Muses. Rap and hip-hop acts occasionally make it to the stage. ⊠ *1233 17th St., at Texas St., Potrero Hill* ☎ *415/621–4455* ⊕ *www.bottomofthehill.com.*

WESTERN ADDITION

MUSIC CLUBS

The Fillmore. This is *the* club that all the big names, from Coldplay to Clapton, want to play. San Francisco's most famous rock-music hall presents national and local acts: rock, reggae, grunge, jazz, folk, acid house, and more. Go upstairs to view the amazing collection of rock posters lining the walls. At the end of each show, free apples are set near the door, and staffers hand out collectible posters. ■ TIP➔ Avoid steep service charges by purchasing tickets at the club's box office on Sunday from 10 to 4. ⊠ *1805 Geary Blvd., at Fillmore St., Western Addition* ☎ *415/346–6000* ⊕ *www.thefillmore.com.*

8

PERFORMING ARTS

Sophisticated, offbeat, and often ahead of the curve, San Francisco's performing arts scene supports world-class opera, ballet, and theater productions, along with alternative-dance events, avant-garde plays, groundbreaking documentaries, and a slew of spoken-word and other literary happenings.

The best guide to the arts is printed in the "Datebook" section and the "96 Hours" section of the *San Francisco Chronicle* (⊕ *www.sfgate. com*). Also check out the city's free alternative weeklies, including *SF Weekly* (⊕ *www.sfweekly.com*) and the *San Francisco Bay Guardian* (⊕ *www.sfbg.com*).

Online, SF Station (⊕ *www.sfstation.com*) has a frequently updated arts and nightlife calendar. *San Francisco Arts Monthly* (⊕ *www.sfarts. org*), which is published at the end of the month, has arts features and events listings, plus a helpful "Visiting San Francisco?" section. For offbeat, emerging-artist performances, consult CounterPULSE (⊕ *www. counterpulse.org*).

TICKETS

City Box Office. This charge-by-phone service sells tickets for many performances and lectures. You can also buy tickets online, or in person on weekdays from 9:30 to 5:30. ✉ *180 Redwood St., Suite 100, off Van Ness Ave., between Golden Gate Ave. and McAllister St., Civic Center* ☎ *415/392–4400* ⊕ *www.cityboxoffice.com*.

San Francisco Performances. SFP brings an eclectic array of top-flight global music and dance talents to various venues—mostly the Yerba Buena Center for the Arts, Davies Symphony Hall, and Herbst Theatre. Artists have included Yo-Yo Ma, Edgar Meyer, the Paul Taylor Dance Company, and Midori. Tickets can be purchased in person through City Box Office, online, or by phone. ✉ *500 Sutter St., Suite 710, Financial District* ☎ *415/392–2545* ⊕ *www.sfperformances.org*.

TIX Bay Area. Half-price, same-day tickets for many local and touring shows go on sale (cash only) at the TIX booth in Union Square, which is open daily from 10 to 6. Discount purchases can also be made online. ✉ *350 Powell St., at Geary St., Union Sq.* ☎ *415/433–7827* ⊕ *www. tixbayarea.org*.

DANCE

Fodor's Choice
★

San Francisco Ballet. For ballet lovers, the nation's oldest professional company is reason alone to visit the Bay Area. SFB's performances, for the past three decades under the direction of Helgi Tomasson, have won critical raves. The primary season runs from February through May. The repertoire includes full-length ballets such as *Don Quixote* and *Sleeping Beauty*; the December presentation of *The Nutcracker* is truly spectacular. The company also performs bold new dances from star choreographers such as William Forsythe and Mark Morris, alongside modern classics by George Balanchine and Jerome Robbins. Tickets are available at the **War Memorial Opera House.** ✉ *War Memorial Opera House, 301 Van Ness Ave., at Grove St., Civic Center* ☎ *415/865–2000* ⊕ *www.sfballet.org*.

FILM

Fodor'sChoice ★ **Castro Theatre.** A large neon sign marks the exterior of this 1,400-plus-seat Art Deco movie palace whose exotic interior transports you back to 1922, when the theater first opened. High-profile festivals present films here, along with classic revivals and foreign flicks. There are a few cult-themed drag shows every month. ■ TIP➜ **Lines for the Castro's popular sing-along movie musicals often trail down the block.** ✉ *429 Castro St., near Market St., Castro* ☎ *415/621–6120* ⊕ *www.castrotheatre.com.*

MUSIC

Fodor'sChoice ★ **San Francisco Symphony.** One of America's top orchestras performs from September through May, with additional summer performances of light classical music and show tunes. The orchestra and its charismatic music director, Michael Tilson Thomas, known for his daring programming of 20th-century American works, often perform with soloists of the caliber of Andre Watts, Gil Shaham, and Renée Fleming. The symphony's adventurous projects include its collaboration with the heavy-metal band Metallica. ■ TIP➜ **Deep discounts on tickets are often available through Travelzoo, Groupon, and other vendors.** ✉ *Davies Symphony Hall, 201 Van Ness Ave., at Grove St., Civic Center* ☎ *415/864–6000* ⊕ *www.sfsymphony.org.*

SFJAZZ Center. Jazz legends Branford Marsalis and Herbie Hancock have performed at the snazzy center, as have Rosanne Cash and world-music favorite Esperanza Spaulding. The sight lines and acoustics here impress. Shows often sell out quickly. ✉ *201 Franklin St., Hayes Valley* ☎ *866/920–5299* ⊕ *www.sfjazz.org.*

MUSIC FESTIVALS

Fodor'sChoice ★ **Stern Grove Festival.** The nation's oldest continual free summer music festival hosts Sunday-afternoon performances of symphony, opera, jazz, pop music, and dance. The amphitheater is in a beautiful eucalyptus grove, perfect for picnicking before the show. World-music favorites such as Ojos de Brujas, Seu Jorge, and Shuggie Otis get the massive crowds dancing. ■ TIP➜ **Shows generally start at 2 pm, but arrive hours earlier if you want to see the performances up close—and dress for cool weather, as the fog often rolls in.** ✉ *Sigmund Stern Grove, Sloat Blvd. at 19th Ave., Sunset* ☎ *415/252–6252* ⊕ *www.sterngrove.org.*

OPERA

Fodor'sChoice ★ **San Francisco Opera.** Founded in 1923, this internationally recognized organization has occupied the War Memorial Opera House since the building's completion in 1932. From September through January and June through July, the company presents a dozen or so operas. SF opera frequently collaborates with European companies and presents unconventional, sometimes edgy projects designed to attract younger audiences. Translations are projected above the stage during most non-English productions. ✉ *War Memorial Opera House, 301 Van Ness Ave., at Grove St., Civic Center* ☎ *415/864–3330 tickets* ⊕ *www.sfopera.com* ☞ *Box office: 199 Grove St., at Van Ness Ave.; open Mon. 10–5, Tues.–Fri. 10–6.*

8

PERFORMING ARTS CENTERS

FodorśChoice **War Memorial Opera House.** With its soaring vaulted ceilings and marble
★ foyer, this elegant 3,146-seat venue, built in 1932, rivals the Old World
theaters of Europe. Part of the San Francisco War Memorial and Performing Arts Center, which also includes Davies Symphony Hall and
Herbst Theatre, this is the home of the San Francisco Opera and the
San Francisco Ballet. ⊠ *301 Van Ness Ave., at Grove St., Civic Center*
☎ *415/621–6600* ⊕ *www.sfwmpac.org.*

FodorśChoice **Yerba Buena Center for the Arts.** Across the street from the San Fran-
★ cisco Museum of Modern Art and abutting a lovely urban garden, this
performing arts complex schedules interdisciplinary art exhibitions,
touring and local dance troupes, music, film programs, and contemporary theater events. You can depend on the quality of the productions at Yerba Buena. Film buffs often come here to check out the San
Francisco Cinematheque (*www.sfcinematheque.org*), which showcases
experimental film and digital media. And dance enthusiasts can attend
concerts by a roster of city companies that perform here, including
Smuin Ballet/SF (*www.smuinballet.org*), ODC/San Francisco (*www.
odcdance.org*), the Margaret Jenkins Dance Company (*www.mjdc.org*),
and Alonzo King's Lines Ballet (*www.linesballet.org*). The Lamplighters
(*www.lamplighters.org*), an alternative opera that specializes in Gil-
bert and Sullivan, also performs here. ⊠ *3rd and Howard Sts., SoMa*
☎ *415/978–2787* ⊕ *www.ybca.org.*

THEATER

American Conservatory Theater. One of the nation's leading regional theater companies presents about eight plays a year, from classics to contemporary works, often in repertory. The season runs from early fall to
late spring. In December ACT stages a beloved version of Charles Dick-
ens's *A Christmas Carol.* ⊠ *415 Geary St., Union Sq.* ☎ *415/749–2228*
⊕ *www.act-sf.org.*

SHOPPING

With its grand department stores and funky secondhand boutiques,
San Francisco summons a full range of shopping experiences. From the
anarchist bookstore to the mouthwatering specialty-food purveyors at
the gleaming Ferry Building, the local shopping opportunities reflect the
city's various personalities. Visitors with limited time often focus their
energies on the high-density Union Square area, where several major
department stores tower over big-name boutiques. But if you're keen
to find unique local shops, consider moving beyond the square's radius.

Each neighborhood has its own distinctive finds, whether it's 1960s housewares, cheeky stationery, or vintage Levi's. If shopping in San Francisco
has a downside, it's that real bargains can be few and far between. Sure,
neighborhoods such as the Lower Haight and the Mission have thrift shops
and other inexpensive stores, but you won't find many discount outlets in
the city, where rents are sky-high and space is at a premium.

UNION SQUARE

ART GALLERIES

Fodor'sChoice **Berggruen Gallery.** Twentieth-century American and European paintings
★ are displayed throughout three airy floors. Some recent exhibitions have
included the works of Robert Kelly and Isca Greenfield-Sanders. Look
for thematic shows here, too; past exhibits have had titles such as Summer Highlights and Four Decades. ☒ *10 Hawthorne St., at Howard St.,
Union Sq.* ☎ *415/781–4629* ⊕ *www.berggruen.com.*

Fodor'sChoice **Fraenkel Gallery.** This renowned gallery represents museum-caliber pho-
★ tographers or their estates, including Nicholas Nixon, Nan Goldin,
Richard Misrach, and Garry Winogrand. Recent shows have included
work by Robert Adams, Idris Khan, and Hiroshi Sugimoto. Most
shows feature one or two artists, but the annual Several Exceptionally
Good Recently Acquired Pictures showcases the range of works the
gallery exhibits. ☒ *49 Geary St., 4th fl., between Kearny St. and Grant
Ave., Union Sq.* ☎ *415/981–2661* ⊕ *fraenkelgallery.com* ☙ *Closed
Sun. and Mon.*

CLOTHING: MEN AND WOMEN

Fodor'sChoice **Margaret O'Leary.** If you can only buy one piece of clothing in San Fran-
★ cisco, make it a hand-loomed cashmere sweater by this Irish-born local
legend. The perfect antidote to the city's wind and fog, the sweaters are
so beloved by San Franciscans that some of them never wear anything
else. Pick up an airplane wrap for your trip home, or a media cozy
to keep your tech toasty. Another store is in Pacific Heights, at 2400
Fillmore Street. ☒ *1 Claude La., at Sutter St., just west of Kearny St.,
Union Sq.* ☎ *415/391–1010* ⊕ *www.margaretoleary.com.*

Scotch & Soda. With clean, tailored lines and deep solid colors, there is
something elegant yet cutting-edge for every age here. Based on Amsterdam couture, and carrying European labels, this hive of a shop is cool
but friendly; it also has an old but new feel to it. The Bodycon Peplum
dress is a classic, as is the men's stretch wool blazer. This is a good place
to visit if you're looking for a new pair of denims, or a cool shirt for a
night out. ☒ *59 Grant Ave., between Geary and O'Farrell Sts., Union
Sq.* ☎ *415/644–8334* ⊕ *www.scotch-soda.com.*

DEPARTMENT STORES

Fodor'sChoice **Gump's.** It's a San Francisco institution, dating to the 19th century, and
★ it's a strikingly luxurious one. The airy store exudes a museumlike vibe,
with its large decorative vases, sumptuous housewares, and Tahitian-
pearl display. It's a great place to pick up gifts, such as the Golden
Gate Bridge note cards or silver-plated butter spreaders in a signature
Gump's box. ☒ *135 Post St., near Kearny St., Union Sq.* ☎ *415/982–
1616* ⊕ *www.gumps.com.*

FURNITURE, HOUSEWARES, AND GIFTS

Fodor'sChoice **Diptyque.** The original Diptyque boutique in Paris has attracted a long
★ line of celebrities. You can find the full array of scented candles and
fragrances in this chic shop that would be at home on the boulevard
St-Germain. Trademark black-and-white labels adorn the popular L'eau
toilet water, scented with geranium and sandalwood. Candles come in

8

traditional and esoteric scents, including lavender, basil, leather, and fig tree. Also available are Mariage Frères teas. ⊠ *73 Geary St., at Grant Ave., Union Sq.* ☏ *415/402–0600* ⊕ *www.diptyqueparis.com.*

CHINATOWN

TOYS AND GADGETS

Chinatown Kite Shop. The kites sold here range from basic diamond shapes to box- and animal-shaped configurations. ■ TIP→ Colorful dragon kites make great souvenirs. ⊠ *717 Grant Ave., near Sacramento St., Chinatown* ☏ *415/989–5182* ⊕ *www.chinatownkite.com.*

SOMA

BOOKS

Fodor's Choice
★

Chronicle Books. This local beacon of publishing produces inventively designed fiction, cookbooks, art books, and other titles, as well as diaries, planners, and address books—all of which you can purchase at three airy and attractive spaces. The other stores are at 680 2nd Street, near AT&T Park, and 1846 Union Street, in Cow Hollow. ⊠ *Metreon Westfield Shopping Center, 165 4th St., near Howard St., SoMa* ☏ *415/369–6271* ⊕ *www.chroniclebooks.com.*

FOOD AND DRINK

K&L Wine Merchants. More than any other wine store, this one has an ardent cult following around town. The friendly staffers promise not to sell what they don't taste themselves, and weekly events—on Thursday from 5 pm to 6:30 pm and Saturday from noon to 3 pm—open the tastings to customers. The best-seller list for varietals and regions for both the under- and over-$30 categories appeals to the wine lover in everyone. ⊠ *855 Harrison St., at 4th St., SoMa* ☏ *415/896–1734* ⊕ *www.klwines.com.*

HAYES VALLEY

FOOD AND DRINK

Arlequin Wine Merchant. If you like the wine list at Absinthe Brasserie, you can walk next door and pick up a few bottles from its highly regarded sister establishment. This small, unintimidating shop carries hard-to-find wines from small producers. Why wait to taste? Crack open a bottle on the patio out back. ⊠ *384 Hayes St., at Gough St., Hayes Valley* ☏ *415/863–1104* ⊕ *www.arlequinwinemerchant.com.*

Miette Confiserie. There is truly nothing sweeter than a cellophane bag tied with blue-and-white twine and filled with malt balls or chocolate sardines from this European-style apothecary. Grab a gingerbread cupcake or a tantalizing macaron or some shortbread. The pastel-color cake stands make even window-shopping a treat. ⊠ *449 Octavia Blvd., between Hayes and Fell Sts., Hayes Valley* ☏ *415/626–6221* ⊕ *www.miette.com.*

NORTH BEACH

FOOD AND DRINK

Fodor's Choice ★ **Molinari Delicatessen.** This store has been making its own salami, sausages, and cold cuts since 1896. Other homemade specialties include meat and cheese ravioli, tomato sauces, and fresh pastas. ■ TIP→ **Do like the locals: grab a made-to-order sandwich for lunch and eat it at one of the sidewalk tables or over at Washington Square Park.** ✉ *373 Columbus Ave., at Vallejo St., North Beach* ☎ *415/421–2337* ⊕ *www. molinarisalame.com.*

EMBARCADERO

FARMERS' MARKETS

Fodor's Choice ★ **Ferry Plaza Farmers' Market.** The partylike Saturday edition of the city's most upscale and expensive farmers' market places baked goods, gourmet cheeses, smoked fish, and fancy pots of jam alongside organic basil, specialty mushrooms, heirloom tomatoes, handcrafted jams, and juicy-ripe locally grown fruit. On Saturday about 100 vendors pack in along three sides of the building, and sandwiches and other prepared foods are for sale in addition to fruit, vegetable, and other samples free for the nibbling. Smaller markets take place on Tuesday and Thursday. (The Thursday one doesn't operate from about late December through March.) ✉ *Ferry Plaza, at Market St., Embarcadero* ☎ *415/291–3276* ⊕ *www.ferrybuildingmarketplace.com.*

THE HAIGHT

MUSIC

Fodor's Choice ★ **Amoeba Music.** With more than 2.5 million new and used CDs, DVDs, and records at bargain prices, this warehouselike offshoot of the Berkeley original carries titles you can't find on Amazon. No niche is ignored—from electronica and hip-hop to jazz and classical—and the stock changes daily. ■ TIP→ **Weekly in-store performances attract large crowds.** ✉ *1855 Haight St., between Stanyan and Shrader Sts., Haight* ☎ *415/831–1200* ⊕ *www.amoeba.com.*

THE MISSION

ART GALLERIES

Southern Exposure. An artist-run, nonprofit gallery, this is an established venue for cutting-edge art. In addition to exhibitions, lectures, performances, and film, video screenings take place. ✉ *3030 20th St., at Alabama St., Mission District* ☎ *415/863–2141* ⊕ *soex.org* ⊗ *Closed Sun. and Mon.*

FURNITURE, HOUSEWARES, AND GIFTS

Fodor's Choice ★ **Paxton Gate.** Elevating gardening to an art, this serene shop offers beautiful earthenware pots, amaryllis and narcissus bulbs, decorative garden items, and coffee-table books such as *An Inordinate Fondness for Beetles.* The collection of taxidermy and preserved bugs provides more unusual gift ideas. A couple of storefronts away is too-cute Paxton

Gate Curiosities for Kids, jam-packed with retro toys, books, and other stellar finds. ⊠ *824 Valencia St., between 19th and 20th Sts., Mission District* ☎ *415/824–1872* ⊕ *www.paxtongate.com.*

PACIFIC HEIGHTS

BEAUTY

BeneFit Cosmetics. You can find this locally based line of cosmetics and skin-care products at Macy's and Sephora, but it's much more fun to come to one of the eponymous boutiques. No-pressure salespeople dab you with whimsical makeup such as Ooh La Lift concealer and Tinted Love, a stain for lips and cheeks. ⊠ *2117 Fillmore St., between California and Sacramento Sts., Pacific Heights* ☎ *415/567–0242* ⊕ *www.benefitcosmetics.com.*

JAPANTOWN

BOOKS

Kinokuniya Bookstore. The selection of English-language books about Japanese culture—everything from medieval history to origami instructions—is one of the finest in the country. Kinokuniya is the city's biggest seller of Japanese-language books. Dozens of glossy Asian fashion magazines attract the young and trendy; the manga and anime books and magazines are wildly popular, too. ⊠ *Kinokuniya Bldg., 1581 Webster St., at Geary Blvd., Japantown* ☎ *415/567–7625* ⊕ *www.kinokuniya.com/us.*

THE BAY AREA

WELCOME TO THE BAY AREA

TOP REASONS TO GO

★ **Bite into the "Gourmet Ghetto":** Eat your way through this area of North Berkeley, starting with a slice of perfect pizza from Cheese Board Pizza (just look for the line).

★ **Find solitude at Point Reyes National Seashore:** Hike beautifully rugged—and often deserted—beaches at one of the most beautiful places on Earth, period.

★ **Sit on a dock by the bay:** Admire the beauty of the Bay Area from the rocky, picturesque shores of Sausalito or Tiburon.

★ **Go barhopping in Oakland's hippest hood:** Spend an evening swinging through the watering holes of Uptown, Oakland's artsy-hip and fast-rising corner of downtown.

★ **Walk among giants:** Walking into Muir Woods, a mere 12 miles north of the Golden Gate Bridge, is like entering a cathedral built by God.

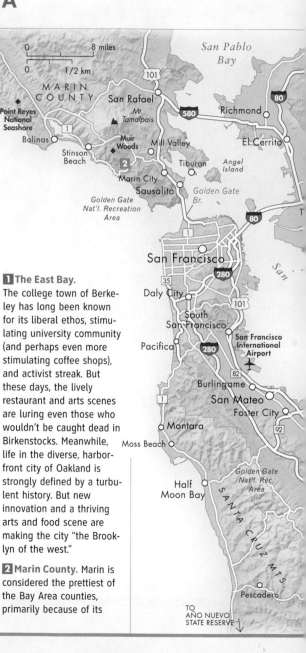

1 The East Bay.
The college town of Berkeley has long been known for its liberal ethos, stimulating university community (and perhaps even more stimulating coffee shops), and activist streak. But these days, the lively restaurant and arts scenes are luring even those who wouldn't be caught dead in Birkenstocks. Meanwhile, life in the diverse, harborfront city of Oakland is strongly defined by a turbulent history. But new innovation and a thriving arts and food scene are making the city "the Brooklyn of the west."

2 Marin County. Marin is considered the prettiest of the Bay Area counties, primarily because of its wealth of open space. Anchored by water on three sides, the county is mostly parkland, including long stretches of undeveloped coastline. The picturesque small towns here—Sausalito, Tiburon, Mill Valley, and Bolinas among them—may sometimes look rustic, but most are in a dizzyingly high tax bracket.

Berkeley

Redwood Regional Park

THE EAST BAY

Oakland

880

Oakland International Airport

San Leandro

580

Hayward

92

880

Union City

680

Belmont

Fremont

101

84

San Francisco Bay National Wildlife Refuge

Redwood City

84

880

35

Palo Alto

101

Milpitas

237

Mountain View

280

85

Santa Clara

101

280

TO BIG BASIN REDWOODS STATE PARK

85

San Jose

Francisco Bay

24

1

580

GETTING ORIENTED

East of the city, across the San Francisco Bay, lie Berkeley and Oakland, in what most Bay Area residents refer to as the East Bay. These two towns have distinct personalities, but life here feels more relaxed than in the city—though every bit as vibrant.

Cross the Golden Gate Bridge and head north to reach Marin County's rolling hills and green expanses, where residents enjoy an haute-suburban lifestyle. Farther afield, the wild land-scapes of the Muir Woods, Mt. Tamalpais, Stinson Beach, and Point Reyes National Seashore await.

9

Updated by A. K. Carroll

It's rare for a metropolis to compete with its suburbs for visitors, but the view from any of San Francisco's hilltops shows that the Bay Area's temptations extend far beyond the city limits. East of the city are the energetic urban centers of Berkeley and Oakland. Famously radical Berkeley is also comfortably sophisticated, while Oakland has an arts and restaurant scene so hip that it pulls San Franciscans across the bay. To the north is Marin County with its dramatic coastal beauty and chic, affluent villages.

PLANNING

WHEN TO GO

As with San Francisco, you can visit the rest of the Bay Area any time of year, and it's especially nice in late spring and fall. Unlike San Francisco, though, the surrounding areas are reliably sunny in summer—it gets hotter as you head inland. Even the rainy season has its charms, as otherwise golden hills turn a rich green and wildflowers become plentiful. Precipitation is usually the heaviest between November and March. Berkeley is a university town, so it's easier to navigate the streets and find parking near the university between semesters, but there's also less buzz around town.

GETTING HERE AND AROUND

BART TRAVEL

Using public transportation to reach Berkeley or Oakland is ideal. The under- and aboveground BART (Bay Area Rapid Transit) trains make stops in both towns. Trips to either take about a half hour one-way from the center of San Francisco. BART does not serve Marin County.

Contacts BART. ☎ *510/465–2278* ⊕ *www.bart.gov.*

BOAT AND FERRY TRAVEL

For sheer romance, nothing beats the ferry; there's service from San Francisco to Sausalito, Tiburon, and Larkspur in Marin County, and to Alameda and Oakland in the East Bay.

The Golden Gate Ferry crosses the bay to Larkspur and Sausalito from San Francisco's Ferry Building (✉ *Market St. and the Embarcadero*). Blue & Gold Fleet ferries depart daily for Sausalito and Tiburon from Pier 41 at Fisherman's Wharf; weekday commuter ferries leave from the Ferry Building for Tiburon. The trip to either Sausalito or Tiburon takes from 25 minutes to an hour. Purchase tickets from terminal vending machines.

The Angel Island–Tiburon Ferry sails to the island daily from April through October and on weekends the rest of the year.

The San Francisco Bay Ferry runs several times daily between San Francisco's Ferry Building or Pier 41 and Oakland's Jack London Square by way of Alameda. The trip lasts from 25 to 45 minutes, and leads to Oakland's waterfront shopping and restaurant district. Purchase tickets on board.

Boat and Ferry Lines Angel Island–Tiburon Ferry. ☎ 415/435–2131 ⊕ www.angelislandferry.com. **Blue & Gold Fleet.** ☎ 415/705–8200 ⊕ www.blueandgoldfleet.com. **Golden Gate Ferry.** ☎ 415/921–5858 ⊕ www.goldengateferry.org. **San Francisco Bay Ferry.** ☎ 707/643–3779, 800/643–3779 ⊕ sanfranciscobayferry.com.

BUS TRAVEL

Golden Gate Transit buses travel north to Sausalito, Tiburon, and elsewhere in Marin County from the Transbay Temporary Terminal (located at Howard and Main, two blocks south of Market) and other points in San Francisco. For Mt. Tamalpais State Park and West Marin (Stinson Beach, Bolinas, and Point Reyes Station), take any route to Marin City and then transfer to the West Marin Stagecoach. San Francisco Muni buses primarily serve the city, though the 76X does cross the Golden Gate and end at the Marin Headlands Visitors Center on weekends.

Though less speedy than BART, over 30 AC Transit bus lines provide service to and from the Transbay Temporary Terminal and throughout the East Bay, even after BART shuts down. The F and FS lines will get you to Berkeley, while lines C, P, B, and O take you to Oakland and Piedmont.

Bus Lines AC Transit. ☎ 510/891–4777 ⊕ www.actransit.org. **Golden Gate Transit.** ☎ 511 ⊕ www.goldengatetransit.org. **San Francisco Muni.** ☎ 311 ⊕ www.sfmta.com. **West Marin Stagecoach.** ☎ 511 ⊕ www.marintransit.org.

CAR TRAVEL

To reach the East Bay from San Francisco, take Interstate 80 East across the San Francisco–Oakland Bay Bridge. For U.C. Berkeley, merge onto Interstate 580 West and take exit 11 for University Avenue. For Oakland, merge onto Interstate 580 East. To reach downtown, take Interstate 980 West from Interstate 580 East and exit at 14th Street. Travel time varies depending on traffic, but should take about 30 minutes (or an hour if it's rush hour).

9

For all points in Marin, head north on U.S. 101 and cross the Golden Gate Bridge. Sausalito, Tiburon, the Marin Headlands, and Point Reyes National Seashore are all accessed off U.S. 101. The scenic coastal route, Highway 1, also called Shoreline Highway and Panoramic for certain stretches, can be accessed off U.S. 101 as well. Follow this road to Muir Woods, Mt. Tamalpais State Park, Muir Beach, Stinson Beach, and Bolinas. From Bolinas, you can continue north on Highway 1 to Point Reyes.

RESTAURANTS

The Bay Area is home to many popular and innovative restaurants, such as Chez Panisse in Berkeley and Commis in Oakland—for which reservations must be made well in advance. There are also countless casual but equally tasty eateries to test out; expect an emphasis on organic seasonal produce, locally raised meats, craft cocktails, and curated wine menus. Marin's dining scene trends toward the sleepy side, so be sure to check hours ahead of time. *Restaurant reviews have been shortened. For full information, visit Fodors.com.*

HOTELS

With a few exceptions, hotels in Berkeley and Oakland tend to be standard-issue, but many Marin hotels package themselves as cozy retreats. Summer in Marin is often booked well in advance, despite weather that can be downright chilly. Check for special packages during this season. *Hotel reviews have been shortened. For full information, visit Fodors.com.*

WHAT IT COSTS			
$	**$$**	**$$$**	**$$$$**
Restaurants			
under $16	$16–$22	$23–$30	over $30
Hotels			
under $150	$150–$199	$200–$250	over $250

Restaurant prices are the average cost of a main course at dinner or, if dinner is not served, at lunch. Hotel prices are the lowest cost of a standard double room in high season.

TOURS

Fodor'sChoice **Best Bay Area Tours.** Morning and afternoon tours of Muir Woods and
★ Sausalito include at least 90 minutes in the redwoods before heading on to Sausalito. On returning to the city, tours make a scenic stop in the Marin Headlands to enjoy fantastic views. Knowledgeable guides lead small tours in comfortable vans, and hotel pickup is included, though park entrance is not. Another tour option includes a visit to Muir Woods and Wine Country exploration. ☎ 877/705–8687 ⊕ *bestbayareatours.com* ✉ *From $60.*

THE EAST BAY

To many San Franciscans, the East Bay is a world away. But don't fall into that trap, because there's much to see on the other side of the Bay Bridge—industrial-chic Emeryville, the rolling hills of Orinda, and the upscale shopping suburb of Walnut Creek to name a few. Add on Berkeley, with its world-class university, and edgy Oakland, with its booming arts culture, nightlife, and restaurant scenes, and you've got plenty of reasons to venture east.

BERKELEY

2 miles northeast of Bay Bridge.

Berkeley is the birthplace of the Free Speech Movement, the radical hub of the 1960s, the home of arguably the nation's top public university, and a frequent site of protests and political movements. The city of 115,000 is also a culturally diverse breeding ground for social trends, a bastion of the counterculture, and an important center for Bay Area writers, artists, and musicians. Berkeley residents, students, and faculty spend hours nursing coffee concoctions while they read, discuss, and debate at the dozens of cafés that surround campus. It's the quintessential university town, with numerous independent bookstores, countless casual eateries, myriad meetups, and thousands of cyclists.

Oakland may have Berkeley beat when it comes to ethnic diversity and cutting-edge arts, but unless you're accustomed to sipping hemp milk lattes while planning a protest prior to yoga, you'll likely find Berkeley charmingly offbeat.

GETTING HERE AND AROUND

BART is the easiest way to get to Berkeley from San Francisco. Exit at the Downtown Berkeley station, and walk a block up Center Street to get to the western edge of campus. AC Transit buses F and FS lines stop near the university and 4th Street shopping. By car, take Interstate 80 East across the Bay Bridge, merge onto Interstate 580 West, and take the University Avenue exit through downtown Berkeley or take the Ashby Avenue exit and turn left on Telegraph Avenue. Once you arrive, explore on foot. Berkeley is very pedestrian-friendly.

ESSENTIALS

Visitor Information Koret Visitor Center. ⊠ *2227 Piedmont Ave., at California Memorial Stadium* ☎ *510/642–5215* ⊕ *visit.berkeley.edu.* **Visit Berkeley.** ⊠ *2030 Addison St., Suite 102* ☎ *510/549–7040, 800/847–4823* ⊕ *www.visitberkeley.com.*

EXPLORING

TOP ATTRACTIONS

4th Street. Several blocks centering on 4th Street north of University Avenue have evolved from light industrial uses into an upscale shopping and dining district. The compact area is busiest on bright weekend afternoons. The Stained Glass Garden, Builders Booksource, and the Apple Store are among shoppers' favorites, along with a slew of boutiques, a fascinating reptile-filled Vivarium, and several wonderful paper stores. ⊠ *4th St. between University Ave. and Cedar St.* ⊕ *www.fourthstreet.com.*

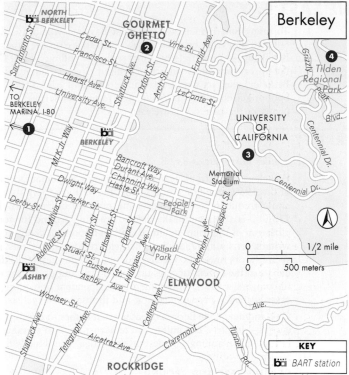

QUICK
BITES

Cheese Board Pizza. A jazz combo entertains the line that usually snakes down the block outside Cheese Board Pizza; it's that good. The cooperatively owned takeout spot and restaurant draws devoted customers with the smell of just-baked garlic on the pie of the day. **Known for:** vegetarian pizza by the slice or slab; live music performances. ⊠ *1504–1512 Shattuck Ave., at Vine St.* ☎ *510/549-3183* ⊕ *cheeseboardcollective.coop/pizza.*

Fodor'sChoice ★

Gourmet Ghetto. The success of Alice Water's Chez Panisse defined California cuisine and attracted countless other food-related enterprises to a stretch of Shattuck Avenue now known as the Gourmet Ghetto. Foodies will do well to spend a couple of hours here poking around the shops, grabbing a quick bite, or indulging in a full meal.

The line stretches down the block in front of **Cheese Board Pizza** (*1512 Shattuck*), where live jazz bands serenade diners who spill out onto the sidewalk and median. Next door is the **Cheese Board Collective** and its fabulous bakery and cheese counter. Nearby, **César** (*1515 Shattuck*) wine bar and tapas house provides afternoon quaffs and late-night drinks, while the food stands of the **Epicurious Garden** (*1509–1513 Shattuck*) sell everything from sushi to gelato. In the back of the upscale food court, a small terraced garden winds up four levels to the **Imperial Tea Court,** a zenlike teahouse rife with imports and tea ware.

Across Vine, the **Vintage Berkeley** (*2113 Vine*) wineshop offers regular tastings and a great selection of reasonably priced bottles within the walls of a historic former pump house. Coffee lovers can head to the original **Peet's Coffee & Tea** at the corner of Walnut and Vine (*2124 Vine*) or venture to No. 1600 for a cup of Philz custom-blend coffee.

South of Cedar Street is the art-filled **Guerilla Cafe** (No. 1620), a

> **A TASTING TOUR**
>
> For an unforgettable foodie experience, book a **Culinary Walking Tour** with Edible Excursions (*415/806-5970 www.edible-excursions.net*). Come hungry for knowledge and noshing. Tours ($105) take place on Thursdays at 11 and Saturdays at 10.

breakfast and lunch spot beloved for its waffles (and Blue Bottle Coffee). Also look for the **Local Butcher Shop** (No. 1600), which sells locally sourced meat and hearty made-to-order sandwiches. For high-end food at takeout prices, try the salads, sandwiches, and signature potato puffs at **Grégoire**, around the corner on Cedar Street (No. 2109) or pastrami, latkes, and other Jewish deli fare at local favorite **Saul's Restaurant and Delicatessen** (No. 1475). **Masse's Pastries** with its delicate tortes, dainty eclairs, and decadent desserts (No. 1469) is a museum of edible artwork. We could go on, but you get the idea. ✉ *Shattuck Ave. between Delaware and Rose Sts., North Berkeley* ⊕ *www.gourmetghetto.org.*

FAMILY

Fodor's Choice

★

Tilden Regional Park. Stunning bay views, a scaled-down steam train, and a botanic garden that boasts the nation's most complete collection of California plant life are the hallmarks of this 2,000-acre park in the hills just east of the U.C. Berkeley campus. The garden's visitors center offers tours, as well as information about Tilden's other attractions, including its picnic spots, Lake Anza swimming site, golf course, and hiking trails (the paved **Nimitz Way,** at Inspiration Point, is a popular hike with wonderful sunset views). ■**TIP➔** Children love Tilden's interactive Little Farm and vintage carousel. ✉ *Tilden Regional Park, 2501 Grizzly Peak Blvd., Tilden Park* ☎ *510/544-2747 Park Office* ⊕ *www. ebparks.org/parks/tilden* ▨ *Free to park and botanic garden.*

University of California. Known simply as "Cal," the founding campus of California's university system is one of the leading intellectual centers in the United States and a major site for scientific research. Chartered in 1868, the university sits on 178 oak-covered acres split by Strawberry Creek; it's bound by Bancroft Way to the south, Hearst Avenue to the north, Oxford Street to the west, and Gayley Road to the east. Campus highlights include bustling and historic **Sproul Plaza** (*Bancroft Way and Sather Rd.*), the seven floors and 61-bell carillon of **Sather Tower** (*Campanile Esplanade*), the nearly 3 million artifacts in the **Phoebe A. Hearst Museum of Anthropology** (Kroeber Hall), hands-on **Lawrence Hall of Science** (*1 Centennial Dr.*), the vibrant 34-acre **Botanical Gardens** (*200 Centennial Dr.*), and the eclectic and extensive collections housed in the **Art Museum & Pacific Film Archive** (*2155 Center*). ✉ *Berkeley* ☎ *510/642-6000* ⊕ *www.berkeley.edu.*

9

The University of California is the epicenter of Berkeley's energy and activism.

University of California Botanical Garden. Thanks to Berkeley's temperate climate, over 10,000 types of plants from all corners of the world flourish in the 34-acre University of California Botanical Garden. Free garden tours are given regularly. Benches and shady picnic tables make this a relaxing place for a snack with a breathtaking view. ⊠ *200 Centennial Dr.* ☎ *510/643–2755* ⊕ *botanicalgarden.berkeley.edu* ⊡ *$10.*

WHERE TO EAT

Dining in Berkeley may be low-key when it comes to dress, but it's top-of-class in quality, even in less-refined spaces. Late diners beware: Berkeley is an "early to bed" kind of town.

$
DINER
FAMILY

✕ **Bette's Oceanview Diner.** Checkered floors, vintage burgundy booths, and an old-time jukebox set the scene at this retro-chic diner. The wait for a seat at breakfast can be quite long; luckily Bette's To Go is always an option. **Known for:** soufflé pancakes; spicy scrambles; meatloaf and gravy. Ⓢ *Average main: $13* ⊠ *1807 4th St., near Delaware St., 4th Street* ☎ *510/644–3230* ⊕ *www.bettesdiner.com* ☽ *No dinner.*

$$$$
MODERN
AMERICAN
Fodor's Choice
★

✕ **Chez Panisse Café & Restaurant.** Alice Waters's legendary eatery is known for its locally sourced ingredients, formal prix-fixe menus, and personal service, while its upstairs café offers simpler fare in a more casual setting. Both menus change daily and legions of loyal fans insist that Chez Panisse lives up to its reputation. **Known for:** sustainably sourced meats; inventive use of seasonal ingredients. Ⓢ *Average main: $125* ⊠ *1517 Shattuck Ave., at Vine St., North Berkeley* ☎ *510/548–5525 restaurant, 510/548–5049 café* ⊕ *www.chezpanisse.com* ☽ *Closed Sun. No lunch in the restaurant.*

$$ MODERN MEXICAN Fodor's Choice ★ 🍴 **Comal.** Relaxed yet trendy, Comal's cavernous indoor dining space and intimate back patio and fire pit draw a diverse, decidedly casual crowd for creative Mexican-influenced fare and well-crafted cocktails. The menu centers on small dishes that lend themselves to sharing and are offered alongside more than 100 tequilas and mezcals. **Known for:** margaritas and mezcal; fresh fish tacos; wood-fired entrées. [$] *Average main: $16* ✉ *2020 Shattuck Ave., near University Ave., Downtown* ☎ *510/926–6300* 🌐 *www.comalberkeley.com* 🕒 *No lunch.*

$$$ MODERN ITALIAN 🍴 **Corso.** This lively spot serves up a seasonal menu of excellent Florentine cuisine and Italian wines in a sparse but snazzy space. The open kitchen dominates a room, which includes closely spaced tables and festive flickering candles. **Known for:** handcrafted pasta; housemade salumi; Northern Italian specialties; extensive wine list. [$] *Average main: $24* ✉ *1788 Shattuck Ave., at Delaware St., North Berkeley* ☎ *510/704–8004* 🌐 *www.corsoberkeley.com* 🕒 *No lunch.*

$$ MODERN AMERICAN 🍴 **Gather.** All things local, organic, seasonal, and sustainable reside harmoniously under one roof at Gather. This haven for vegans, vegetarians, and carnivores alike is a vibrant, well-lit space that boasts funky light fixtures, shiny wood furnishings, and banquettes made of recycled leather belts. **Known for:** sustainable Californian cuisine; wood-fired pizzas; crispy brussels sprouts. [$] *Average main: $22* ✉ *2200 Oxford St., at Allston Way* ☎ *510/809–0400* 🌐 *www.gatherrestaurant.com.*

$$$ JAPANESE Fodor's Choice ★ 🍴 **Ippuku.** More Tokyo street chic than standard sushi house, this *izakaya*—the Japanese equivalent of a bar with appetizers—is decked with bamboo-screen booths. Servers pour an impressive array of sakes and *shōchū* and serve up surprising fare. **Known for:** shōchū selection; charcoal-grilled yakitori skewers. [$] *Average main: $25* ✉ *2130 Center St., Downtown* ☎ *510/665–1969* 🌐 *www.ippukuberkeley.com* 🕒 *Closed Mon. No lunch.*

$ CAFÉ 🍴 **1951 Coffee.** The first java spot of its kind, 1951 Coffee Company is a nonprofit coffee shop inspired and powered by refugees. In addition to crafting high-caliber coffee drinks and dishing out local pastries and sandwiches, this colorful café also serves as an inspiring advocacy space for refugees. Just three blocks south of campus, it's a favorite meet-up spot for locals and students alike. **Known for:** Verve coffee; Starter Bakery pastries; chai latte. [$] *Average main: $7* ✉ *2410 Channing Way, at Dana St.* ☎ *510/848–6252 ext. 270* 🌐 *1951coffee.com.*

$$$ MODERN AMERICAN 🍴 **Rivoli.** Italian-inspired dishes using fresh California ingredients star on a menu that changes regularly. Inventive offerings are served in a tight modern dining room with captivating views of the lovely back garden. **Known for:** line-caught fish and sustainably sourced meats; curated wine list. [$] *Average main: $28* ✉ *1539 Solano Ave., at Neilson St.* ☎ *510/526–2542* 🌐 *www.rivolirestaurant.com* 🕒 *No lunch.*

$ AMERICAN FAMILY Fodor's Choice ★ 🍴 **Saul's.** High ceilings and red-leather booths add to the friendly, retro atmosphere of Saul's deli, a Berkeley institution that is well known for its homemade sodas and enormous sandwiches. Locals swear by the pastrami sandwiches, stuffed-cabbage rolls, and challah French toast. **Known for:** pastrami sandwich; deli hash. [$] *Average main: $15* ✉ *1475 Shattuck Ave., near Vine St., North Berkeley* ☎ *510/848–3354* 🌐 *www.saulsdeli.com* 🕒 *Closed Thanksgiving and Yom Kippur.*

Famed Berkeley restaurant Chez Panisse focuses on seasonal local ingredients.

WHERE TO STAY

For inexpensive lodging, investigate University Avenue, west of campus. The area can be noisy, congested, and somewhat dilapidated, but it does include a few decent motels and chain properties. All Berkeley lodgings, except for the swanky Claremont, are strictly mid-range.

$$
HOTEL

The Bancroft Hotel. Renovated in 2012, this eco-friendly boutique hotel—across from the U.C. campus—is quaint, charming, and completely green. **Pros:** closest hotel in Berkeley to U.C. campus; friendly staff; many rooms have good views. **Cons:** some rooms are quite small; despite renovation, the building shows its age with thin walls; no elevator. $ *Rooms from: $160* ✉ *2680 Bancroft Way* ☎ *510/549–1000, 800/549–1002 toll-free* ⊕ *bancrofthotel.com* ⇄ *22 rooms* ⦿*Breakfast.*

$$$$
HOTEL
FAMILY
Fodor'sChoice
★

Claremont Resort and Spa. Straddling the Oakland–Berkeley border, this amenities-rich Fairmont property—which celebrated its centennial in 2015—beckons like a gleaming white castle in the hills. **Pros:** amazing spa; supervised child care; solid business amenities; excellent dining and bar options; nearby hiking trails. **Cons:** parking is pricey; mandatory facilities charge. $ *Rooms from: $299* ✉ *41 Tunnel Rd., at Ashby and Domingo Aves., Claremont* ☎ *510/843–3000, 800/257–7544 reservations* ⊕ *www.fairmont.com/claremont-berkeley* ⇄ *276 rooms* ⦿*No meals.*

$$$
HOTEL
Fodor'sChoice
★

Hotel Shattuck Plaza. This historic boutique hotel sits amid Berkeley's downtown arts district, just steps from the U.C. campus and a short walk from the Gourmet Ghetto. **Pros:** central location near public transit; special date night and B&B packages; modern facilities; good views;

great restaurant; pet friendly; free pass to nearby YMCA. **Cons:** public and street parking only; limited on-site fitness center. [$] *Rooms from: $209* ✉ *2086 Allston Way, at Shattuck Ave., Downtown* ☎ *510/845–7300* 🌐 *www.hotelshattuckplaza.com* 🛏 *199 rooms* 🍴 *No meals.*

NIGHTLIFE AND PERFORMING ARTS

NIGHTLIFE

Fodor's Choice ★ **Freight & Salvage Coffeehouse.** Some of the most talented practitioners of folk, jazz, gospel, blues, world-beat, and bluegrass perform in this nonprofit coffeehouse, one of the country's finest folk music and story-telling venues. Most tickets cost less than $30. ✉ *2020 Addison St., between Shattuck Ave. and Milvia St.* ☎ *510/644–2020* 🌐 *www.thefreight.org.*

Fodor's Choice ★ **Tupper & Reed.** Housed in the former music shop of John C. Tupper and Lawrence Reed, this music-inspired cocktail haven features a symphony of carefully crafted libations, which are mixed with live music performed by local musicians. The historic 1925 building features a reservations-only balcony bar, cozy nooks, antique fixtures, a pool table, and romantic fireplaces. ✉ *2271 Shattuck Ave., at Kitteredge St., Downtown* ☎ *510/859–4472* 🌐 *www.tupperandreed.com.*

PERFORMING ARTS

Berkeley Repertory Theatre. One of the region's most highly respected and innovative repertory theaters, Berkeley Rep performs the work of classic and contemporary playwrights. Well-known pieces such as *Tartuffe* and *Macbeth* mix with world premieres and edgier fare like Green Day's *American Idiot* and Lemony Snicket's *The Composer Is Dead*. The theater's complex is in the heart of downtown Berkeley's arts district, near BART's Downtown Berkeley station. ✉ *2025 Addison St., near Shattuck Ave.* ☎ *510/647–2949* 🌐 *www.berkeleyrep.org.*

Cal Performances. Based out of U.C. Berkeley, this series runs from September through May. It features a varied bill of internationally acclaimed artists ranging from classical soloists to the latest jazz, world-music, theater, and dance ensembles. Past performers include Alvin Ailey American Dance Theatre, the National Ballet of China, Peter Sellars, and Yo-Yo Ma. ✉ *101 Zellerbach Hall, Suite 4800, Dana Str. and Bancroft Way* ☎ *510/642–9988* 🌐 *calperformances.org.*

SHOPPING

Fodor's Choice ★ **Amoeba Music.** Heaven for audiophiles and movie collectors, this legendary Berkeley favorite is *the* place to head for new and used CDs, vinyl, cassettes, VHS tapes, Blu-ray discs, and DVDs. The massive and ever-changing stock includes thousands of titles for all music tastes, as well as plenty of Amoeba merch. There are branches in San Francisco and Hollywood, but this is the original. ✉ *2455 Telegraph Ave., at Haste St.* ☎ *510/549–1125* 🌐 *www.amoeba.com.*

Kermit Lynch Wine Merchant. Credited with taking American appreciation of Old World wines to a higher level, this small shop is a great place to peruse as you educate your palate. The friendly salespeople will happily direct you to the latest French and Italian bargains. ✉ *1605 San Pablo Ave., at Cedar St.* ☎ *510/524–1524* 🌐 *www.kermitlynch.com* 🕒 *Closed Sun. and Mon.*

Moe's Books. The spirit of Moe—the creative, cantankerous, cigar-smoking late proprietor—lives on in this world-famous four-story house of new and used books. Students and professors come here to browse the large selection, which includes literary and cultural criticism, art titles, and literature in foreign languages. ⊠ *2476 Telegraph Ave., near Haste St.* ☏ *510/849–2087* ⊕ *www.moesbooks.com.*

OAKLAND

East of Bay Bridge.

In contrast to San Francisco's buzz and beauty and Berkeley's storied counterculture, Oakland's allure lies in its amazing diversity. Here you can find a Nigerian clothing store, a Gothic revival skyscraper, a Buddhist meditation center, and a lively salsa club, all within the same block.

Oakland's multifaceted nature reflects its colorful and tumultuous history. Once a cluster of Mediterranean-style homes and gardens that served as a bedroom community for San Francisco, the town had a major rail terminal and port city by the turn of the 20th century. Already a hub of manufacturing, Oakland became a center for shipbuilding and industry when the United States entered World War II. New jobs in the city's shipyards, railroads, and factories attracted thousands of laborers from across the country, including sharecroppers from the Deep South, Mexican Americans from the southwest, and some of the nation's first female welders. Neighborhoods were imbued with a proud but gritty spirit, along with heightened racial tension. In the wake of the civil rights movement, racial pride gave rise to militant groups like the Black Panther Party, but they were little match for the economic hardships and racial tensions that plagued Oakland. In many neighborhoods the reality was widespread poverty and gang violence—subjects that dominated the songs of such Oakland-bred rappers as the late Tupac Shakur. The highly publicized protests of the Occupy Oakland movement in 2011 and 2012 and the #BlackLivesMatter movement of 2014 and 2015 illustrate just how much Oakland remains a mosaic of its past.

Oakland's affluent reside in the city's hillside homes and wooded enclaves like Claremont, Piedmont and Montclair, which provide a warmer, more spacious alternative to San Francisco, while a constant flow of newcomers ensures continued diversity, vitality, and growing pains. Many neighborhoods to the west and south of the city center have yet to be touched by gentrification, but a renovated downtown and vibrant arts scene has injected new energy into the city. Even San Franciscans, often loath to cross the Bay Bridge, come to Uptown and Temescal for the nightlife, arts, and restaurants.

Everyday life here revolves around the neighborhood. In some areas, such as Piedmont and Rockridge, you'd swear you were in Berkeley or San Francisco's Noe Valley. Along Telegraph Avenue just south of 51st Street, Temescal is littered with hipsters and pulsing with creative culinary and design energy. These are perfect places for browsing, eating, or relaxing between sightseeing trips to Oakland's architectural gems, rejuvenated waterfront, and numerous green spaces.

GETTING HERE AND AROUND

Driving from San Francisco, take Interstate 80 East across the Bay Bridge, then take Interstate 580 East to the Grand Avenue exit for Lake Merritt. To reach downtown and the waterfront, take Interstate 980 West from Interstate 580 East and exit at 12th Street; exit at 18th Street for Uptown. For Temescal, take Interstate 580 East to Highway 24 and exit at 51st Street.

By BART, use the Lake Merritt Station for the Oakland Museum and southern Lake Merritt; the Oakland City Center–12th Street Station for downtown, Chinatown, and Old Oakland; and the 19th Street Station for Uptown, the Paramount Theatre, and the north side of Lake Merritt.

By bus, take the AC Transit's C and P lines to get to Piedmont in Oakland. The O bus stops at the edge of Chinatown near downtown Oakland.

Oakland's Jack London Square is an easy hop on the ferry from San Francisco. Those without cars can take advantage of the free Broadway Shuttle, which runs from the Jack London Square to 27th Street via downtown on weekdays and Friday and Saturday nights.

Be aware of how quickly neighborhoods can change. Walking is generally safe downtown and in the Piedmont and Rockridge areas, but avoid walking west and southeast of downtown, especially at night.

Shuttle Contact Broadway Shuttle. ⊕ *www.meetdowntownoak.com.*

ESSENTIALS

Visitor Information Visit Oakland. ⊠ *481 Water St., near Broadway, Jack London Square* ☎ *510/839–9000* ⊕ *www.visitoakland.org.*

EXPLORING

TOP ATTRACTIONS

FAMILY

Fodor'sChoice

★

Oakland Museum of California. This museum surveys the state's art, history, and natural wonders in three galleries of absorbing, interactive exhibits. Travel through myriad ecosystems, from the sand dunes of the Pacific to the volcanic Mt. Shasta, and discover over 2,000 species in the expansive Gallery of California Natural Sciences. Explore disparate integrated stories in the rambling Gallery of California History, which includes everything from Ohlone baskets to Gold Rush era artifacts. Of particular interest in the Gallery of California Art are photographs by Dorothea Lange and paintings by members of the Bay Area figurative school. Stop by the Blue Oak café for a snack or relax for a minute in the flower gardens, which are open to the public at no charge during hours of operation. ∎TIP➔ On Friday evenings the museum gets lively, with live music, food trucks, and half-price admission. ⊠ *1000 Oak St., at 10th St., Downtown* ☎ *510/318–8400, 888/625–6873 toll-free* ⊕ *museumca.org* ⊠ *$16, free 1st Sun. of month* ⊙ *Closed Mon. and Tues.*

Fodor'sChoice

★

Paramount Theatre. A glorious Art Deco specimen, the Paramount operates as a venue for concerts and performances of all kinds, from the Oakland Symphony to Jerry Seinfeld and Elvis Costello. The popular classic movie nights start off with a 30-minute Wurlitzer concert. ∎TIP➔ Docent-led tours, offered the first and third Saturday of the month, are fun and informative. ⊠ *2025 Broadway, at 20th St., Uptown* ☎ *510/465–6400* ⊕ *www.paramounttheatre.com* ⊠ *Tour $5.*

9

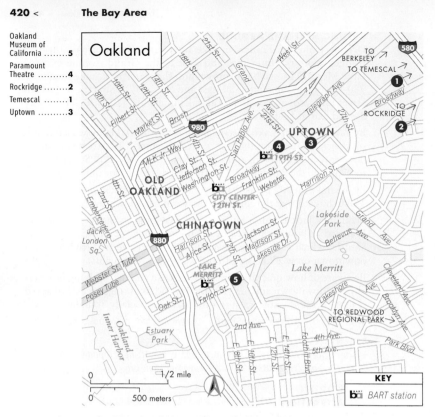

Oakland

FAMILY
Fodor's Choice
★
Rockridge. This fashionable upscale neighborhood is one of Oakland's most desirable places to live. Explore the tree-lined streets that radiate out from **College Avenue** just north and south of the Rockridge BART station for a look at California Craftsman bungalows at their finest. By day College Avenue between Broadway and Alcatraz Avenue is crowded with shoppers buying fresh flowers, used books, and clothing; by night the same folks are back for handcrafted meals, artisan wines, and locally brewed ales. With its specialty-food shops and quick bites to go, **Market Hall,** an airy European-style marketplace at Shafter Avenue, is a hub of culinary activity. ⊠ *College Ave., between Alcatraz Ave. and Broadway, Rockridge* ⊕ *www.rockridgedistrict.com.*

Fodor's Choice
★
Temescal. Centering on Telegraph Avenue between 40th and 51st Streets, Temescal (the Aztec term for "sweat house") is a low-pretension, mon-eyed-hipster hood with young families and middle-aged folks thrown into the mix. A critical mass of excellent eateries draws folks from around the Bay Area; there's veteran **Doña Tomás** (*5004 Telegraph Ave.*) and favorites **Pizzaiola** (*5008 Telegraph Ave.*) and **Aunt Mary's** (*4640 Telegraph Ave.*) as well as **Bakesale Betty** (*5098 Telegraph Ave.*), where folks line up for the fried-chicken sandwich. Old-time dive bars and smog-check stations share space with the trendy children's cloth-ing shop **Ruby's Garden** (*5026 Telegraph Ave.*) and the stalwart **East**

Bay Depot for Creative Reuse (*4695 Telegraph Ave.*), where you might find a bucket of buttons or 1,000 muffin wrappers among birdcages, furniture, lunch boxes, and ribbon.

Around the corner, **Temescal Alley** (*49th St.*), a tucked-away lane of tiny storefronts, crackles with the creative energy of local makers. Surprising finds can be had at **Crimson Horticultural Rarities** (*No. 470*) or at the home-decor shop at **Bounty and Feast** (*No. 482*). Don't miss grabbing a sweet scoop at **Curbside Creamery** (*No. 482*). ✉ *Telegraph Ave., between 40th and 51st Sts., Temescal* 🌐 *www.temescaldistrict.org.*

Fodor's Choice ★ **Uptown.** This is where nightlife and cutting-edge art happens in Oakland, along the Telegraph Avenue/Broadway corridor north of downtown. Dozens of galleries cluster around Telegraph, showing everything from photography and site-specific installations to glasswork and fiber arts. The first Friday of each month, thousands descend for **Art Murmur** (*oaklandartmurmur.org*), a late-night gallery event that has expanded into **First Friday** (*oaklandfirstfridays.org*), a veritable neighborhood festival featuring food trucks, street vendors, and live music along Telegraph Avenue.

Lively restaurants with a distinctly urban vibe make Uptown a dining destination every night of the week. Favorites include craft cocktails and eclectic Japanese-inspired fare at **Hopscotch** (*1915 San Pablo Ave.*), beautiful beverages and stylish cuisine at Art Deco **Flora** (*1900 Telegraph Ave.*), tasty tapas and modern Spanish fare at trendy **Duende** (*468 19th*), upscale Southern comfort food at elegant **Picán** (*2295 Broadway*), and innovative Oaxacan fare and mezcal magic at **Calavera** (*2337 Broadway*) just to name a few.

Toss in the bevy of bars and there's plenty within walking distance to keep you busy for an entire evening: **Cafe Van Kleef** (*1621 Telegraph Ave.*), the friendly jumble that started it all Uptown; **Bar Three Fifty-Five** (*355 19th St.*), a house of great cocktails; strikingly beautiful but low-key **Dogwood** (*1644 Telegraph Ave.*), which has tasty nibbles; **Drake's Dealership** (*2325 Broadway*), with its spacious hipster-friendly beer garden; **Lost and Found** (*2040 Telegraph Ave.*), home of draft brews and cornhole boards; and **Somar** (*1727 Telegraph Ave.*), a bar, music lounge, and gallery in one. Uptown's shopping is exploding as well, with local goods at the fore; be sure to stop by **Oaklandish** (*1444 Broadway*) for T-shirts, jeans, and everything Oaktown. The **Paramount Theatre** *(2025 Broadway)*, **Fox Theater** *(1807 Telegraph Ave.)*, and other art-deco architectural gems distinguish this neighborhood. ✉ *Oakland* ✥ *Telegraph Ave. and Broadway from 14th to 27th Sts.*

9

WHERE TO EAT

$$ MEDITERRANEAN 🍴 **À Côté.** This Mediterranean hot spot is all about seasonal small plates, cozy tables, family-style eating, and excellent wine. Heavy wooden tables, intimate dining nooks, natural light, and a heated patio make this an ideal destination for couples, families, and the after-work crowd. **Known for:** Pernod mussels; exquisite small plates; global and regional wine list. [$] *Average main: $22* ✉ *5478 College Ave., at Taft Ave., Rockridge* ☎ *510/655–6469* 🌐 *acoterestaurant.com* ⏲ *No lunch.*

$ SOUTHERN FAMILY Fodor's Choice ★

🍴 **Brown Sugar Kitchen.** Influenced by Tanya Holland's African American heritage and French culinary education, the menu at this bustling little West Oakland dining destination features local, organic ingredients and sweet and savory dishes paired with sumptuous wines. The dining room is small, but inviting with a long, sleek counter, red-leather stools, and spacious booths and tables. **Known for:** fried chicken and cornmeal waffles; bacon-cheddar-scallion biscuits; smoked chicken and shrimp gumbo. [$] *Average main: $15* ✉ *2534 Mandela Pkwy., at 26th St., West Oakland* ☎ *510/839–7685* 🌐 *www.brownsugarkitchen.com* 🕒 *Closed Mon. No dinner.*

$$$ MODERN MEXICAN

🍴 **Calavera.** This Oaxacan-inspired hot spot offers inventive and elevated plates in an industrial-chic space with lofty ceilings, warm wooden tables, exposed brick walls, and heated outdoor dining. Innovative cocktails like the salted-air margarita come from a beautiful bar with a library of over 100 agaves. **Known for:** innovative and beautiful cocktails; wide selection of tequilas and mezcal; carnitas tacos served in nixtamal heirloom corn tortillas; fresh ceviche. [$] *Average main: $25* ✉ *2337 Broadway, at 24th St., Uptown* ☎ *510/338–3273* 🌐 *calaveraoakland.com* 🕒 *Closed Mon.*

$$$$ AMERICAN

🍴 **Camino.** Russell Moore cooked at Chez Panisse for two decades before he and Allison Hopelain opened this restaurant, which focuses on simple, seasonal, straightforward dishes that are cooked in an enormous, crackling *camino* (Italian for "fireplace"). Served on redwood tables in a Craftsman-meets-refectory-style dining room, the ever-changing menu has only three entrées—each cooked over its own open fire—that feature top-notch ingredients and pair perfectly with creative craft cocktails. **Known for:** wood-fired dishes; craft cocktails. [$] *Average main: $32* ✉ *3917 Grand Ave., at Boulevard Way, Grand Lake* ☎ *510/547–5035* 🌐 *www.caminorestaurant.com* 🕒 *Closed Tues. No lunch* ☞ *No tipping.*

$$$$ AMERICAN Fodor's Choice ★

🍴 **Commis.** A slender, unassuming storefront houses the only East Bay restaurant with a Michelin star (two of them, in fact). The room is minimalist and polished: nothing distracts from the artistry of chef James Syhabout, who creates a multicourse dining experience based on the season and his distinctive vision. **Known for:** inventive multicourse tasting menu; Michelin-winning execution. [$] *Average main: $149* ✉ *3859 Piedmont Ave., at Rio Vista Ave., Piedmont* ☎ *510/653–3902* 🌐 *commisrestaurant.com* 🕒 *Closed Mon. and Tues. No lunch.*

$$ INDIAN

🍴 **Juhu Beach Club.** All the color, flavor, and fun of Mumbai's Juhu Beach is contained within the brightly colored walls of this festive funky Temescal eatery. Childhood memories, Indian street food, and family recipes have inspired Preeti Mistry's menu of spicy starters, savory sliders, inventive drinks, and edgy modern main courses. **Known for:** pav slider sandwiches; modern takes on traditional street food; refreshing drinks (both boozy and booze-free). [$] *Average main: $22* ✉ *5179 Telegraph Ave., at 51st St., Temescal* ☎ *510/652–7350* 🌐 *juhubeachclub.com.*

$$ ITALIAN FAMILY

🍴 **Pizzaiolo.** Chez Panisse alum Charlie Hallowell helms the kitchen of this rustic-chic Oakland institution. Diners of all ages perch on wooden chairs with red-leather backs and nosh on farm-to-table Italian fare from a daily changing menu. **Known for:** seasonal wood-fired pizza; delicious daily breakfast pastries; rustic California-Italian entrées. [$] *Average main: $22* ✉ *5008 Telegraph Ave., at 51st St., Temescal* ☎ *510/652–4888* 🌐 *www.pizzaiolooakland.com* 🕑 *Closed Sun. No lunch.*

$$$ MEDITERRANEAN Fodor's Choice ★ 🍴 **Shakewell.** Two *Top Chef* vets opened this stylish Lakeshore restaurant, which serves creative and memorable Mediterranean small plates in a lively setting that features an open kitchen, wood-fired oven, communal tables, and snug seating. As the name implies, well-crafted cocktails are shaken (or stirred) and poured with panache. **Known for:** wood-oven paella; Spanish and Mediterranean small plates; craft cocktails. [$] *Average main: $25* ✉ *3407 Lakeshore Ave., near Mandana Blvd.* ☎ *510/251–0329* 🌐 *www.shakewelloakland.com* 🕑 *Closed Mon. No lunch Tues.*

WHERE TO STAY

$$ HOTEL 🏨 **Best Western Plus Bayside Hotel.** Sandwiched between the serene Oakland Estuary and an eight-lane freeway, this all-suites property has handsome accommodations with balconies or patios, many overlooking the water. **Pros:** attractive, budget-conscious choice; free parking; free shuttle to and from airport, Jack London Square, and downtown; scenic water views. **Cons:** not within walking distance of anything of interest; freeway-side rooms can be loud. [$] *Rooms from: $159* ✉ *1717 Embarcadero, off I–880, at 16th St. exit* ☎ *510/356–2450* 🌐 *hotelsinooaklandca.h.bestwestern.com* 🛏 *81 rooms* 🍽 *Breakfast.*

$$ HOTEL FAMILY 🏨 **Waterfront Hotel.** This thoroughly modern, pleasantly appointed Joie de Vivre property sits among the many high-caliber restaurants of Jack London Square. **Pros:** great location; lovely views; dog-friendly; excellent hotel restaurant, Lungomare; complimentary wine-and-cheese hour during the week; free shuttle service to downtown (limited hours); easy access to the ferry. **Cons:** passing trains can be noisy on city side; parking is pricey. [$] *Rooms from: $180* ✉ *10 Washington St., Jack London Square* ☎ *510/836–3800 front desk, 888/842–5333 reservations* 🌐 *www.jdvhotels.com* 🛏 *145 rooms* 🍽 *No meals.*

NIGHTLIFE

Back when rent was still relatively cheap, artists flocked to Oakland, giving rise to a cultural scene—visual arts, indie music, spoken word, film—that's still buzzing, especially in Uptown. Trendy new spaces pop up regularly and the beer-garden renaissance is already well-established. Whether you're a self-proclaimed beer snob or just someone who enjoys a cold drink on a sunny day, there's something for everyone. Oakland's nightlife scene is less crowded and more intimate than what you'll find in San Francisco. Music is just about everywhere, though the most popular venues are downtown.

BARS

Fodor's Choice ★ **Café Van Kleef.** Long before Uptown got hot, the late Peter Van Kleef was serving stiff fresh-squeezed greyhounds, telling tales about his collection of pop culture mementos, and booking live music at Café Van Kleef, a funky café-bar that crackles with creative energy—there's still live music every weekend. This local favorite still serves some of the stiffest drinks in town. ✉ *1621 Telegraph Ave., between 16th and 17th Sts., Uptown* ☎ *510/763–7711* 🌐 *cafevankleef.com.*

The Layover Music Bar and Lounge. Bright, bold, and unabashedly bohemian, this hangout filled with recycled furniture is constantly evolving because everything is for sale, from the artwork to the pillows, rugs, and lamps. The busy bar serves up signature organic cocktails, and live entertainment includes comedy shows, storytelling, and local DJs. ⊠ *1517 Franklin St., near 15th St., Uptown* ☎ *510/834–1517* ⊕ *www.oaklandlayover.com.*

Make Westing. This sprawling industrial-chic space is always abuzz with hipsters playing bocce, the post-work crowd sipping old-fashioneds, or pretheater couples passing mason jars of Dungeness crab dip. The patio's your best bet for a conversation on a busy evening. ⊠ *1741 Telegraph Ave., at 18th St., Uptown* ☎ *510/251–1400* ⊕ *makewesting.com.*

BREWPUBS AND BEER GARDENS

Beer Revolution. Hard-core beer geeks: with hundreds of bottled beers and 50 taps, this craft beer and bottle shop is for you. Tear yourself away from the beer lists and grab a table on the patio. ⊠ *464 3rd St., at Broadway, Jack London Square* ☎ *510/452–2337* ⊕ *www.beer-revolution.com.*

FAMILY
Fodor's Choice
★

Lost & Found. The diversions on the spacious, succulent-filled patio include Ping-Pong, cornhole, and community tables full of chilled-out locals. The beer selection ranges from blue collar to Belgian and a seasonal menu focuses on internationally inspired small bites. ⊠ *2040 Telegraph Ave., at 21st St., Uptown* ☎ *510/763–2040* ⊕ *www.lostand-found510.com* ☯ *Closed Mon.*

The Trappist. Brick walls, dark wood, soft lighting, and a buzz of conversation set a warm and mellow tone inside this old Victorian space that's been renovated to resemble a traditional Belgian pub. The setting (which includes two bars and a back patio) is definitely a draw, but the real stars are the artisan beers—more than a hundred Belgian, Dutch, and North American brews. Light fare includes bar snacks and meat and cheese boards. ⊠ *460 8th St., near Broadway, Old Oakland* ☎ *510/238–8900* ⊕ *www.thetrappist.com.*

ROCK, POP, HIP-HOP, FOLK, AND BLUES CLUBS

Fox Theater. This renovated 1928 theater, Oakland's favorite performance venue, is a remarkable feat of Mediterranean Moorish architecture and has seen the likes of Willie Nelson, Counting Crows, Rebelution, and B.B. King, to name a few. The venue boasts good sight lines, a state-of-the-art sound system, brilliant acoustics, and a restaurant and bar, among other amenities. ⊠ *1807 Telegraph Ave., between 18th and 19th Sts., Uptown* ☎ *510/302–2250* ⊕ *thefoxoakland.com.*

Fodor's Choice
★

Yoshi's. Opened in 1972 as a sushi bar, Yoshi's has evolved into one of the area's best jazz and live music venues. The full Yoshi's experience includes traditional Japanese and Asian fusion cuisine in the adjacent restaurant. ⊠ *510 Embarcadero W, between Washington and Clay Sts., Jack London Square* ☎ *510/238–9200* ⊕ *www.yoshis.com* ☜ *$20–$80.*

SHOPPING

Pop-up shops and stylish, locally focused stores are scattered throughout the funky alleys of Old Oakland, Uptown, Rockridge, and Temescal, while the streets around Lake Merritt and Grand Lake offer more modest boutiques.

Maison d'Etre. Close to the Rockridge BART station, this store epitomizes the Rockridge neighborhood's funky-chic shopping scene. Look for high-end housewares and impulse buys like whimsical watches, imported fruit-tea blends, and funky slippers. ⊠ *5640 College Ave., at Keith Ave., Rockridge* ☎ *510/658–2801* ⊕ *maisondetre.com.*

Fodor's Choice **Oaklandish.** This is the place for Oaktown swag. What started in 2000 as
★ a public art project of local pride has become a celebrated brand around the bay, and a portion of the proceeds from hip Oaklandish brand T-shirts and accessories supports grassroots nonprofits committed to bettering the local community. It's good-looking stuff for a good cause. ⊠ *1444 Broadway, near 15th St., Uptown* ☎ *510/251–9500* ⊕ *oaklandish.com.*

MARIN COUNTY

Marin is, quite simply, a knockout—its abundance of protected parkland, open-space preserves, and rugged coastline are some of the most breathtaking and ecologically diverse in the world. The territory ranges from chaparral, grassland, and coastal scrub to broadleaf, redwood, and evergreen forest. It's well worth the drive over the Golden Gate Bridge to explore the stunning Marin Headlands and the sprawling beauty of Point Reyes National Seashore and its 80 miles of shoreline.

While Cyra McFadden's literary soap opera, *The Serial,* depicted Marin County as a bastion of hot-tubbing and "open" marriages, increasingly jet-set Marinites spend more time on outdoor activities, including surfing, cycling, kayaking, and hiking. Adrenaline junkies mountain bike down Mt. Tamalpais, while solitary folk wander along Point Reyes's empty beaches. Artists and musicians who arrived in the 1960s set a boho tone for mellow country towns, but much of Marin is undeniably chic, with high-tech companies making their mark in the local economy; this *is* one of the wealthiest counties in the nation.

After exploring Marin's natural beauty, consider a stop in one of its lovely villages. Most cosmopolitan is Sausalito, the town just over the Golden Gate Bridge from San Francisco. Across the inlet from Sausalito, Tiburon and Belvedere are lined with grand homes that regularly appear on fund-raising circuits, and to the north, landlocked Mill Valley is a hub of wining and dining and tony boutiques. Book Passage, a noted bookseller in the next town, Corte Madera, hosts regular readings by top-notch authors, and Larkspur, San Anselmo, and Fairfax beyond have walkable downtown areas, each a bit folksier than the next but all with good restaurants and shops and a distinct sense of place.

In general, the farther west you go, the more rural things become. Separated from the inland county by the slopes and ridges of giant Mt. Tamalpais, West Marin beckons to mavericks, artists, ocean lovers, and free spirits. Stinson Beach has tempered its isolationist attitude to accommodate out-of-towners, as have Inverness and Point Reyes Station. Bolinas, on the other hand, would prefer to keep to itself.

VISITOR INFORMATION

Contact Marin Convention & Visitors Bureau. ⊠ *1 Mitchell Blvd., Suite B, San Rafael* ☎ *415/925–2060* ⊕ *www.visitmarin.org.*

9

THE MARIN HEADLANDS

Due west of the Golden Gate Bridge's northern end.

The term *Golden Gate* has become synonymous with the world-famous bridge, but it was first given to the narrow waterway that connects the Pacific and the San Francisco Bay. To the north of the Golden Gate Strait lies the Marin Headlands, part of the Golden Gate National Recreation Area (GGNRA), which boasts some of the area's most dramatic scenery.

GETTING HERE AND AROUND

Driving from San Francisco, head north on U.S. 101. Just after you cross the Golden Gate Bridge, take exit 442 for Alexander Avenue. Keep left at the fork and follow signs for "San Francisco/U.S. 101 South", go through the tunnel under the freeway, and turn right up the hill. Muni bus 76X runs hourly from Sutter and Sansome Streets to the Marin Headlands Visitor Center on weekends and major holidays only.

EXPLORING

TOP ATTRACTIONS

FAMILY

Fodor's Choice

★

Marin Headlands. The headlands stretch from the Golden Gate Bridge to Muir Beach. Photographers perch on the southern headlands for spectacular shots of the city and bridge. Equally remarkable are the views north along the coast and out to the ocean, where the Farallon Islands are visible on clear days.

The headlands' strategic position at the mouth of San Francisco Bay made them a logical site for military installations from 1890 through the Cold War. Today you can explore the crumbling concrete batteries where naval guns once protected the area. The headlands' main attractions are centered on Fts. Barry and Cronkhite, which are separated by Rodeo Lagoon and Rodeo Beach, a dark stretch of sand that attracts sand-castle builders and dog owners.

The visitor center is a worthwhile stop for its exhibits on the area's history and ecology, and kids enjoy the "please touch" educational sites and small play area inside. You can pick up guides to historic sites and wildlife, and get information about programming and guided walks. ⊠ *Golden Gate National Recreation Area, Visitors Center, Fort Barry Chapel, Ft. Barry, Bldg. 948, Field and Bunker Rds., Sausalito* ☎ *415/331–1540* ⊕ *www.nps.gov/goga/marin-headlands.htm.*

FAMILY

Point Bonita Lighthouse. A restored beauty that still guides ships to safety with its original 1855 refractory lens, the lighthouse anchors the southern headlands. Half the fun of a visit is the steep half-mile walk from the parking area through a rock tunnel, across a suspension bridge, and down to the lighthouse. Signposts along the way detail the bravado of surfmen, as the early lifeguards were called, and the tenacity of the "wickies," the first keepers of the light. ■TIP➜ **Call about 90-minute full-moon tours.** ⊠ *End of Conzelman Rd., Ft. Barry, Bldg. 948, Sausalito* ☎ *415/331–1540* ⊕ *www.nps.gov/goga/pobo.htm* ☉ *Closed Tues.–Fri.*

SAUSALITO

2 miles north of Golden Gate Bridge.

Bougainvillea-covered hillsides and an expansive yacht harbor give Sausalito the feel of an Adriatic resort. The town sits on the northwestern edge of San Francisco Bay, where it's sheltered from the ocean by the Marin Headlands; the mostly mild weather here is perfect for strolling and outdoor dining. Nevertheless, morning fog and afternoon winds can roll over the hills without warning, funneling through the central part of Sausalito once known as Hurricane Gulch.

South of Bridgeway, which snakes between the bay and the hills, a waterside esplanade is lined with restaurants on piers that lure diners with good seafood and even better views. Stairs along the west side of Bridgeway and throughout town climb into wooded hillside neighborhoods filled with both rustic and opulent homes, while back on the northern portion of the shoreline, harbors shelter a community of over 400 houseboats. As you amble along Bridgeway past shops and galleries, you'll notice the absence of basic services. Find them and more on Caledonia Street, which runs parallel to Bridgeway and inland a couple of blocks. While ferry-side shops flaunt kitschy souvenirs, smaller side streets and narrow alleyways offer eccentric jewelry and handmade crafts.

■ TIP→ The ferry is the best way to get to Sausalito from San Francisco; you get more romance (and less traffic) and disembark in the heart of downtown.

Sausalito developed its bohemian flair in the 1950s and '60s, when creative types, including artist Jean Varda, poet Shel Silverstein, and madam Sally Stanford, established an artists' colony and a houseboat community here (this is Otis Redding's "Dock of the Bay"). Both the spirit of the artists and the neighborhood of floating homes persist. For a close-up view of the quirky community, head north on Bridgeway, turn right on Gate Six Road, park where it dead-ends, and enter through the unlocked gates.

GETTING HERE AND AROUND

From San Francisco by car or bike, follow U.S. 101 north across the Golden Gate Bridge and take exit 442 for Alexander Avenue, just past Vista Point; continue down the winding hill to the water to where the road becomes Bridgeway. Golden Gate Transit buses will drop you off in downtown Sausalito, and the ferries dock downtown as well. The center of town is flat, with plenty of sidewalks and bay views. It's a pleasure and a must to explore on foot.

ESSENTIALS

Visitor Information Sausalito Chamber of Commerce. ⊠ *1913 Bridgeway* ☎ *415/331–7262 ext. 10* ⊕ *www.sausalito.org.* **Sausalito Information Kiosk.** ⊠ *El Portal St.* ✛ *At the foot of El Portal St. at the Ferry Pier* ☎ *415/331–1093* ⊕ *www.oursausalito.com.*

Marin County

0   5 mi

0   5 km

EXPLORING

Sally Stanford Drinking Fountain. There's an unusual historic landmark on the Sausalito Ferry Pier—a drinking fountain inscribed "Have a drink on Sally" in remembrance of Sally Stanford, the former San Francisco brothel madam who became Sausalito's mayor in the 1970s. Sassy Sally would have appreciated the fountain's eccentric attachment: a knee-level basin with the inscription "Have a drink on Leland," in memory of her beloved dog. ⊠ *Sausalito Ferry Pier, Anchor St. at Humboldt St., off the southwest corner of Gabrielson Park* ⊕ *www.oursausalito.com/sausalito-ferry-1.html.*

QUICK BITES

Hamburgers Sausalito. Patrons queue up daily outside this tiny street-side shop for organic Angus beef patties that are made to order on a wheel-shaped grill. Brave the line (it moves fast) and take your food to the esplanade to enjoy fresh air and bay-side views. **Known for:** legendary burgers. ⊠ **737 Bridgeway, at Anchor St.** ☎ **415/332–9471** ⊗ **No dinner.**

Sausalito Ice House Visitors Center and Museum. The local historical society operates this dual educational exhibit and visitor center, where you can get your bearings, learn some history, and find out what's happening in town. ⊠ *780 Bridgeway, at Bay St.* ☎ *415/332–0505* ⊕ *www.sausalitohistoricalsociety.com* ⊗ *Closed Mon.*

Viña del Mar Plaza and Park. The landmark Plaza Viña del Mar, named for Sausalito's sister city in Chile, marks the center of town. Adjacent to the parking lot and ferry pier, the plaza is flanked by two 14-foot-tall elephant statues, which were created for the San Francisco Panama–Pacific International Exposition in 1915. It also features a picture-perfect fountain that's great for people-watching. ⊠ *Bridgeway and El Portal St.* ⊕ *www.oursausalito.com/parks-in-sausalito/vina-del-mar-park.html.*

WHERE TO EAT

$$
SEAFOOD
FAMILY
Fodor'sChoice
★

✕ **Fish.** If you're looking for fresh sustainably caught seafood, head to this gleaming dockside fish house a mile north of downtown. Order at the counter—cash only—and then grab a seat by the floor-to-ceiling windows or at a picnic table on the pier, overlooking the yachts and fishing boats. **Known for:** fish of the day; barbecued oysters; sustainably caught, fire-grilled entrées. $ *Average main: $20* ⊠ *350 Harbor Dr., at Gate 5 Rd., off Bridgeway* ☎ *415/331–3474* ⊕ *www.331fish.com* ▭ *No credit cards* ⊂ *Cash only.*

$$$
FRENCH

✕ **Le Garage.** Brittany-born Olivier Souvestre serves traditional French bistro fare in a relaxed, bay-side setting that feels more sidewalk café than the converted garage that it is. The restaurant seats only 35 inside and 15 outside, so make reservations or arrive early. **Known for:** PEI mussels and house-cut fries; weekend brunch. $ *Average main: $26* ⊠ *85 Liberty Ship Way, Suite 109* ☎ *415/332–5625* ⊕ *www.legaragebistrosausalito.com* ⊂ *No reservations for weekend brunch.*

$$$
ITALIAN

✕ **Poggio.** A hillside dining destination, Poggio serves modern Tuscan-style comfort food in a handsome, Old World–inspired space whose charm spills onto the sidewalks. An extensive and ever-changing menu of antipasti, pasta, hearty entrées, and pizzas emerges from the open kitchen's wood-fired oven. **Known for:** fresh local ingredients and traditional Northern Italian dishes; rotisserie chicken with property-grown organic herbs and vegetables; polpettini meatballs. $ *Average main: $30* ⊠ *777 Bridgeway, at Bay St.* ☎ *415/332–7771* ⊕ *www.poggiotrattoria.com.*

$$$
JAPANESE
Fodor'sChoice
★

✕ **Sushi Ran.** Sushi aficionados swear that this tiny, stylish restaurant—in business for more than three decades—is the Bay Area's best option for raw fish, but don't overlook the excellent Pacific Rim fusions, a melding of Japanese ingredients and French cooking techniques. Book in advance or expect a wait, which you can soften by sipping one of the bar's 45 by-the-glass sakes. **Known for:** fish imported from Tokyo's famous Tsukiji market; local miso glazed black cod. $ *Average main: $30* ⊠ *107 Caledonia St., at Pine St.* ☎ *415/332–3620* ⊕ *www.sushiran.com* ⊙ *No lunch weekends.*

WHERE TO STAY

$$
B&B/INN

☷ **Hotel Sausalito.** Handcrafted furniture and tasteful original art and reproductions give this Mission Revival-style inn the feel of a small European hotel. **Pros:** great staff; central location; solid mid-range hotel; vouchers to nearby Cafe Tutti provided. **Cons:** no room service; some rooms are small; daily public parking fee. $ *Rooms from: $175* ⊠ *16 El Portal, at Bridgeway* ☎ *415/332–0700* ⊕ *www.hotelsausalito.com* ⇱ *16 rooms* ⦿| *No meals.*

9

$$$$
B&B/INN

☷ **The Inn Above Tide.** The balconies at the Inn Above Tide literally hang over the water, and each of its rooms has a perfect 10 view that takes in wild Angel Island as well as the city lights across the bay. **Pros:** great complimentary breakfast; minutes from restaurants and attractions; central but tranquil setting. **Cons:** costly daily parking; some rooms are on the small side; five rooms have no balcony. $ *Rooms from: $380* ☒ *30 El Portal* ☎ *415/332–9535, 800/893–8433* ⊕ *www.innabovetide. com* ⌘ *31 rooms* ⏣ *Breakfast.*

TIBURON

7 miles north of Sausalito, 11 miles north of Golden Gate Bridge.

On a peninsula that was named Punta de Tiburon (Shark Point) by 18th-century Spanish explorers, this beautiful Marin County community retains the feel of a village—it's more low-key than Sausalito—despite the encroachment of commercial establishments from the downtown area. The harbor faces Angel Island across Raccoon Strait, and San Francisco is directly south across the bay—which means the views from the decks of harbor restaurants are major attractions. Since 1884, when the San Francisco and North Pacific Railroad relocated their ferry terminal facilities to the harbor town, Tiburon has centered on the waterfront. ■ TIP➜ The ferry is the most relaxing (and fastest) way to get here, and allows you to skip traffic and parking problems.

GETTING HERE AND AROUND

Blue & Gold Fleet ferries travel between San Francisco and Tiburon daily. By car, head north from San Francisco on U.S. 101 and get off at CA 131/Tiburon Boulevard/East Blithedale Avenue (Exit 447). Turn right onto Tiburon Boulevard and drive just over 4 miles to downtown. Golden Gate Transit serves downtown Tiburon from San Francisco; watch for changes during evening rush hour. Tiburon's Main Street is made for wandering, as are the footpaths that frame the water's edge.

ESSENTIALS

Visitor Information Tiburon. ☒ *Town Hall, 1505 Tiburon Blvd.* ☎ *415/435-7373* ⊕ *www.destinationtiburon.org.*

EXPLORING

FAMILY **Ark Row.** The second block of Main Street is known as Ark Row and has a tree-shaded walk lined with antiques and specialty stores. Some of the buildings are actually old 19th-century ark houseboats that floated in Belvedere Cove before being beached and transformed into stores. ■ TIP➜ If you're curious about architectural history, the Tiburon Heritage & Arts Commission has a self-guided walking-tour map, available online and at local businesses. ☒ *Ark Row, Main St., south of Juanita La.* ⊕ *tiburonheritageandarts.org.*

Old St. Hilary's Landmark and John Thomas Howell Wildflower Preserve. The architectural centerpiece of this attraction is a stark-white 1888 Carpenter Gothic church that overlooks the town and the bay from its hillside perch. Surrounding the church, which was dedicated as a historical monument in 1959, is a wildflower preserve that's spectacular in May and June, when the rare black or Tiburon jewel flower blooms. Expect a steep walk uphill to reach the preserve. The Landmarks Society will arrange guided tours by appointment. ■ **TIP→ The hiking trails behind the landmark wind up to a peak that has views of the entire Bay Area.** ✉ *201 Esperanza St., off Mar West St. or Beach Rd.* ☎ *415/435–1853* 🌐 *landmarkssociety.com/landmarks/st-hilarys/* ⏲ *Church closed Mon.–Sat. and Nov.–Mar.*

WHERE TO EAT

$$$ AMERICAN 🍴 **The Caprice.** For more than 50 years this Tiburon landmark that overlooks the bay has been the place to come to mark special occasions with local wines and European-American comfort food. The views are spectacular, and soft-yellow walls and starched white tablecloths help to make the space bright and light. **Known for:** seared sea scallops; shellfish risotto; rack of lamb; California wines. [$] *Average main: $28* ✉ *2000 Paradise Dr.* ☎ *415/435–3400* 🌐 *www.thecaprice.com* ⏲ *No lunch.*

$$$ SICILIAN 🍴 **Luna Blu.** Friendly, informative staff serve Sicilian-inspired seafood in this lively sliver of an Italian restaurant just a stone's throw from the ferry. Take a seat on the heated patio overlooking the bay, or cozy up with friends on one of the high-sided booths near the bar. **Known for:** sustainably caught seafood and local, organic ingredients; weekend English tea service. [$] *Average main: $25* ✉ *35 Main St.* ☎ *415/789–5844* 🌐 *lunablurestaurant.com* ⏲ *Closed Tues. No lunch weekdays.*

$ AMERICAN FAMILY 🍴 **New Morning Cafe.** Omelets and scrambles are served all day long at this homey triangular bay-side café with sunny outdoor seating. If you're past morning treats, choose from the many soups, salads, and sandwiches, best enjoyed at picnic tables. **Known for:** hearty American breakfast fare. [$] *Average main: $13* ✉ *1696 Tiburon Blvd., near Juanita Ln.* ☎ *415/435–4315* ⏲ *No dinner.*

$$$ AMERICAN 🍴 **Sam's Anchor Cafe.** Open since 1920, this casual dockside restaurant, rife with plastic chairs and blue-checked oilcloths, is the town's most famous eatery. Most people flock to the deck for beers, views, sunsets, and exceptionally tasty seafood. **Known for:** cioppino; Painted Hills natural beef burgers; patio beverages. [$] *Average main: $24* ✉ *27 Main St.* ☎ *415/435–4527* 🌐 *www.samscafe.com.*

WHERE TO STAY

$$$$ B&B/INN 🏨 **Waters Edge Hotel.** Checking into this stylish downtown hotel feels like tucking away into an inviting retreat by the water—the views are stunning and the lighting is perfect. **Pros:** complimentary wine and cheese for guests every evening; restaurants/sights are minutes away; free bike rentals for guests; pet-friendly; free Wi-Fi. **Cons:** downstairs rooms lack privacy and balconies; paid self-parking; fitness center is off-site. [$] *Rooms from: $279* ✉ *25 Main St., off Tiburon Blvd.* ☎ *415/789–5999, 877/789–5999* 🌐 *www.marinhotels.com* 🛏 *23 rooms* 🍽 *Breakfast.*

9

MILL VALLEY

2 miles north of Sausalito, 4 miles north of Golden Gate Bridge.

Chic and woodsy Mill Valley has a dual personality. Here, as elsewhere in the county, the foundation is a superb natural setting. Virtually surrounded by parkland, the town lies at the base of Mt. Tamalpais and contains dense redwood groves traversed by countless creeks. But this is no lumber camp. Smart restaurants and chichi boutiques line streets that have been traversed by more rock stars than one might suspect.

The rustic village flavor isn't a modern conceit, but a holdover from the town's early days as a center for the lumber industry. In 1896, the Mt. Tamalpais Scenic Railroad—dubbed "The Crookedest Railroad in the World" because of its curvy tracks—began transporting visitors from Mill Valley to the top of Mt. Tam and down to Muir Woods, and the town soon became a vacation retreat for city slickers. The trains stopped running in the 1930s, as cars became more popular, but the old railway depot still serves as the center of town: the 1929 building has been transformed into the popular Depot Bookstore & Cafe, at 87 Throckmorton Avenue.

The small downtown area has the constant bustle of a leisure community; even at noon on a Tuesday, people are out shopping for fancy cookware, eco-friendly home furnishings, and boutique clothing.

GETTING HERE AND AROUND

By car from San Francisco, head north on U.S. 101 and get off at CA 131/Tiburon Boulevard/East Blithedale Avenue (Exit 447). Turn left onto East Blithedale Avenue and continue west to Throckmorton Avenue; turn left to reach Lytton Square, then park. Golden Gate Transit buses serve Mill Valley from San Francisco. Once here, explore the town on foot.

ESSENTIALS

Visitor Information Mill Valley Chamber of Commerce and Visitor Center. ⊠ *85 Throckmorton Ave.* ☎ *415/388-9700* ⊕ *www.millvalley.org.*

EXPLORING

FAMILY **Lytton Square.** Mill Valley locals congregate on weekends to socialize in the coffeehouses and cafés near the town's central square, but it bustles most of the day. Shops, restaurants, and cultural venues line the nearby streets. ⊠ *Miller and Throckmorton Aves.*

▌OFF THE
BEATEN
PATH

Marin County Civic Center. A wonder of arches, circles, and skylights just 10 miles north of Mill Valley, the Civic Center was Frank Lloyd Wright's largest public project and has been designated a national and state historic landmark, as well as a UNESCO World Heritage Site. One-hour docent-led tours leave from the café on the second floor Wednesday mornings at 10:30. Or grab a self-guided tour map from the center's gift shop or website. ⊠ *3501 Civic Center Dr., off N. San Pedro Rd., San Rafael* ☎ *415/473-3762 Visitor Services Office* ⊕ *www.marincounty. org/depts/cu/tours* ☞ *Free admission; $10 tour fee.*

WHERE TO EAT

$$$
AMERICAN
✕**Balboa Café.** With intimate lighting, rich wood accents, and fresh-pressed white linens, this modern California café offers an upscale dining experience complete with classic cocktails, an extensive wine list, and beautiful bistro-inspired dishes that feature locally sourced ingredients. The bar is always bustling, with a daily happy hour that extends into dinner; brunch is served on the weekends. **Known for:** Balboa burger; local wines; huevos rancheros; Dungeness crab risotto; Japanese himachi crudo. ⓢ *Average main: $24* ✉ *38 Miller Ave., at Sunnyside Ave.* ☎ *415/381–7321* ⊕ *balboacafemv.com* ⊗ *No lunch Mon.*

$$$
AMERICAN
✕**Buckeye Roadhouse.** House-smoked meats and fish, grilled steaks, classic salads, and decadent desserts bring locals and visitors back again and again to this 1937 lodge-style roadhouse. Enjoy a Marin martini at the cozy mahogany bar or sip local wine beside the river-rock fireplace. **Known for:** oysters dingo; chili-lime "brick" chicken; smoked beef brisket. ⓢ *Average main: $30* ✉ *15 Shoreline Hwy., off U.S. 101* ☎ *415/331–2600* ⊕ *www.buckeyeroadhouse.com.*

$$$$
CONTEMPORARY
✕**El Paseo.** Rock & Roll Hall of Famer Sammy Hagar helped to restore this 1947 California Mission–style restaurant, which reopened in 2011 with a Spanish-influenced California cuisine menu. The secluded brick walkway, bougainvillea-framed courtyard, and candlelit dining room provide the perfect setting for a romantic night out. **Known for:** deviled eggs with crispy chorizo; Akaushi steak frites; patio-side paella; daily happy hour. ⓢ *Average main: $32* ✉ *17 Throckmorton Ave., at E. Blithedale Ave.* ☎ *415/388–0741* ⊕ *www.elpaseomillvalley. com* ⊗ *No lunch.*

$$$$
CONTEMPORARY
Fodor's Choice
★
✕**Molina.** A cozy and clean aesthetic, a convivial vibe, and impeccable cuisine have turned this snug neighborhood spot into a destination restaurant. Owner-chef (and DJ) Todd Shoberg creates a modest nightly menu of small plates, entrées, and desserts that focus on wood-fired offerings and the freshest local ingredients. **Known for:** California coastal dishes; curated wine menu. ⓢ *Average main: $32* ✉ *17 Madrona St., between Lovell and Throckmorton Aves.* ☎ *415/383–4200* ⊕ *www. molinarestaurant.com* ⊗ *No lunch.*

WHERE TO STAY

$$$$
B&B/INN
▦ **Mill Valley Inn.** The only hotel in downtown Mill Valley is comprised of a main building, the Creek House, with smart-looking European-inspired rooms, and two small cottages tucked among the trees. **Pros:** minutes from local shops and restaurants; some rooms have balconies, soaking tubs, and fireplaces; free parking; free mountain bikes. **Cons:** limited room service; dark in winter because of surrounding trees; some rooms are not accessible via elevator. ⓢ *Rooms from: $289* ✉ *165 Throckmorton Ave., near Miller Ave.* ☎ *415/389–6608, 855/334–7946* ⊕ *www.marinhotels.com* ⤐ *25 rooms* ⦿|*Breakfast.*

$$
B&B/INN
▦ **Mountain Home Inn.** Abutting 40,000 acres of state and national parks, this airy wooden inn sits on the skirt of Mt. Tamalpais, where you can follow hiking trails all the way to Stinson Beach. **Pros:** amazing terrace and views; peaceful, remote setting; in-room massage available; cooked-to-order breakfast. **Cons:** nearest town is a 12-minute

9

drive away; restaurant can get crowded on sunny weekend days; no on-site fitness option. $ Rooms from: $199 ⌧ 810 Panoramic Hwy., at Edgewood Ave. ☏ 415/381–9000 ⊕ www.mtnhomeinn.com ⟿ 10 rooms ⦿ Breakfast.

NIGHTLIFE

BREWPUS AND BEERGARDENS

Mill Valley Beerworks. A great place to rest your feet after shopping or hiking, this neighborhood taproom serves a rotating selection of local and imported drafts and bottles. A simple menu of small plates and mains includes locally sourced cheeses, brussels sprouts, and burgers. ⌧ 173 Throckmorton Ave. ☏ 415/888–8218 ⊕ millvalleybeerworks.com.

MUSIC VENUES

Sweetwater Music Hall. With the help of part-owner Bob Weir of the Grateful Dead, this renowned nightclub and café reopened in a historic Masonic Hall in 2012. Famous as well as up-and-coming bands play on most nights, and local stars such as Bonnie Raitt and Huey Lewis have been known to stop in for a pickup session. ⌧ 19 Corte Madera Ave., between Throckmorton and Lovell Aves. ☏ 415/388–3850, 877/987–6487 tickets ⊕ www.sweetwatermusichall.com.

MUIR WOODS NATIONAL MONUMENT

12 miles northwest of the Golden Gate Bridge.

Climbing hundreds of feet into the sky, *Sequoia sempervirens* are the tallest living things on Earth—some are more than 1,800 years old. One of the last remaining old-growth stands of these redwood behemoths, Muir Woods is nature's cathedral: imposing, awe-inspiring, reverence-inducing, and not to be missed.

GETTING HERE AND AROUND

If you drive to Muir Woods on a weekend or during peak season, expect to find epic traffic jams around the tiny parking areas and adjacent roads. Do yourself a favor and take a shuttle if you can. Marin Transit's Route 66 Muir Woods shuttle (*$5 round-trip* ⊕ www.marintransit.org) provides regular transport from the Sausalito ferry landing, as well as Marin City, on a seasonal schedule. Private bus tours run year-round. To drive directly from San Francisco by car, take U.S. 101 north across the Golden Gate Bridge to exit 445B for Mill Valley/Stinson Beach, then follow signs for Highway 1 north and Muir Woods.

EXPLORING

FAMILY
Fodor'sChoice
★

Muir Woods National Monument. Nothing gives perspective like walking among some of the world's last old-growth redwoods. The 550 acres of Muir Woods National Monument contain some of the most majestic redwoods in the world—some more than 250 feet tall. Though much of California's 2 million acres of redwood forest were lost to the logging industry, this stand was saved from destruction by William and Elizabeth Kent, who purchased the land in 1905, and later gifted it to the federal government. Theodore Roosevelt declared the space a national monument in 1908 and Kent named it after naturalist John Muir, whose environmental campaigns helped to establish the national park system.

DID YOU KNOW?

The gorgeous old-growth redwood trees in Muir Woods are often enveloped in fog, which provides the moisture to help them survive the dry summers.

Part of the Golden Gate National Recreation Area, Muir Woods is a pedestrian's park. The popular 2-mile main trail, which begins at the park headquarters, has been covered by a wooden boardwalk, and provides easy access to streams, ferns, azaleas, and redwood groves. Summer weekends can prove busy, so if you prefer a little serenity, consider taking a more challenging route, such as the **Dipsea Trail** which climbs west from the forest floor to soothing views of the ocean and the Golden Gate Bridge. For a complete list of trails, which vary in difficulty and distance, check with rangers.

Picnicking and camping aren't allowed, and neither are pets. Crowds can be large, especially from May through October, so try to come early in the morning or late in the afternoon. The **Muir Woods Visitor Center** has books and exhibits about redwood trees and the woods' history; the **Muir Woods Trading Company** serves hot food, organic pastries, and other tasty snacks, and the gift shop offers plenty of souvenirs.

■**TIP→** Cell service in the park is limited, so plan directions and communication ahead of time. ⊠ *1 Muir Woods Rd., off Panoramic Hwy., Mill Valley* ☎ *415/388–2595 park information, 511 Marin transit* ⊕ *www.nps.gov/muwo* ⊡ *$10; free on government holidays.*

MT. TAMALPAIS STATE PARK

13 miles northwest of Golden Gate Bridge.

The view of Mt. Tamalpais from all around the bay can be a beauty, but that's nothing compared to the views *from* the mountain, which range from jaw-dropping to spectacular and take in San Francisco, the East Bay, the coast, and beyond—on a clear day, all the way to the Farallon Islands, 25 miles away.

GETTING HERE AND AROUND

By car, take U.S. 101 north across the Golden Gate Bridge and exit 445B for Mill Valley/Stinson Beach. Continue north on Highway 1, which will turn into Panoramic Highway. By bus, take Golden Gate Transit to Marin City; in Marin City transfer to the West Marin Stagecoach, Route 61, and get off at Pantoll Ranger Station (*415/226–0855* ⊕ *www.marintransit. org/stage.html*). Once here, the only way to explore is on foot or by bike.

EXPLORING

FAMILY
Fodor's Choice
★

Mt. Tamalpais State Park. Although the summit of Mt. Tamalpais is only 2,571 feet high, the mountain rises practically from sea level, dominating the topography of Marin County. Adjacent to Muir Woods National Monument, Mt. Tamalpais State Park affords views of the entire Bay Area and the Pacific Ocean to the west. The name for the sacred mount comes from the Coast Miwok tribe and means "west hill," though some have tied it to a folktale about the "sleeping maiden" in the mountain's profile. For years the 6,300-acre park has been a favorite destination for hikers. There are more than 200 miles of trails, some rugged but many developed for easy walking through meadows, grasslands, and forests and along creeks. Mt. Tam, as it's called by locals, is also the birthplace (in the 1970s) of mountain biking, and today many spandex-clad bikers whiz down the park's winding roads.

The park's major thoroughfare, Panoramic Highway, snakes its way up from U.S. 101 to the **Pantoll Ranger Station** and then drops down to the town of Stinson Beach. Pantoll Road branches off the highway at the station, connecting up with Ridgecrest Boulevard. Along these roads are numerous parking areas, picnic spots, scenic overlooks, and trailheads. Parking is free along the roadside, but there's an $8 fee (cash or check only) at the ranger station and additional charges for walk-in campsites and group use.

The **Mountain Theater,** also known as the Cushing Memorial Amphitheatre, is a natural 4,000-seat amphitheater that was reconstructed with stone by the Civilian Conservation Corps in the 1930s. It has showcased summer "Mountain Plays" since 1913.

The **Rock Spring Trail** starts at the Mountain Theater and gently climbs for 1½ miles to the **West Point Inn,** which was once a stop on the Mt. Tam railroad route. Relax at a picnic table and stock up on water before forging ahead, via Old Railroad Grade Fire Road and the Miller Trail, to Mt. Tam's Middle Peak, which is another 1½–2 miles depending on route.

Starting from the Pantoll Ranger Station, the precipitous **Steep Ravine Trail** brings you past stands of coastal redwoods and, in the springtime, small waterfalls. Take the connecting **Dipsea Trail** to reach the town of Stinson Beach and its swath of golden sand. ■**TIP→** If you're too weary to make the 3½-mile trek back up, Marin Transit Bus 61 takes you from Stinson Beach back to the ranger station. ✉ *Pantoll Ranger Station, 3801 Panoramic Hwy., at Pantoll Rd.* ☎ *415/388–2070* ⊕ *www.parks.ca.gov.*

BEACH TOWNS

9

The winds whip wildly around Marin County's miles of coastline. The unruly waves and cool breeze make it more of an adventure than your typical day at the beach. Still, the natural beauty, rocky shores, and stunning views are nothing to balk at.

GETTING HERE AND AROUND
If you're driving, take U.S. 101 north to exit 445B (Highway 1 toward Mill Valley/Stinson Beach) and follow signs. Public transit serves Stinson Beach and Bolinas, but not Muir Beach.

MUIR BEACH

12 miles northwest of Golden Gate Bridge, 6 miles southwest of Mill Valley.

Except on the sunniest of weekends, Muir Beach is relatively quiet, but the drive here can be quite the scenic adventure.

GETTING HERE AND AROUND
A car is the best way to reach Muir Beach. From Highway 1, follow Pacific Way southwest ¼ mile.

EXPLORING

Green Gulch Farm Zen Center. Giant eucalyptus trees frame the long and winding road that leads to this tranquil Buddhist practice center. Meditation programs, tea instruction, gardening classes, and various other workshops and events take place here; there's also an extensive organic garden. Visitors are welcome to roam the property and walk through the gardens that reach down toward Muir Beach. Public Sunday programs are especially geared toward visitors. ⌧ *1601 Shoreline Hwy., at Green Gulch Rd.* ☎ *415/383–3134 welcome center* ⊕ *www.sfzc.org* ▧ *free.*

BEACHES

FAMILY **Muir Beach.** Small but scenic, this beach—a rocky patch of shoreline off Highway 1 in the northern Marin Headlands—is a good place to stretch your legs and gaze out at the Pacific. Locals often walk their dogs here; families and cuddling couples come for picnicking and sunbathing. At one end of the sand are waterfront homes (and occasional nude sunbathers) and at the other are the bluffs of the Golden Gate National Recreation Area. A land bridge connects directly from the parking lot to the beach, as well as a short trail that leads to a scenic overlook and connects to other coastal paths. **Amenities:** parking (free); toilets. **Best for:** solitude; sunsets; walking. ⌧ *100 Pacific Way, off Shoreline Hwy.* ⊕ *www.nps.gov/goga/planyourvisit/muirbeach.htm.*

WHERE TO STAY

$$$ 🛏 **Pelican Inn.** From its slate roof to its whitewashed plaster walls, this

B&B/INN   inn looks so Tudor that it's hard to believe it was built in the 1970s, but the Pelican is English to the core, with its cozy upstairs guest rooms (no elevator), draped half-tester beds, a sun-filled solarium, and bangers and grilled tomatoes for breakfast. **Pros:** five-minute walk to beach; great bar and restaurant; peaceful setting. **Cons:** 20-minute drive to nearby attractions; rooms are quite small and rustic; remote location; limited amenities. $ *Rooms from: $222* ⌧ *10 Pacific Way, off Hwy. 1* ☎ *415/383–6000* ⊕ *www.pelicaninn.com* ⏎ *7 rooms* ⏐⊙⏐ *Breakfast.*

STINSON BEACH

20 miles northwest of Golden Gate Bridge.

This laid-back hamlet is all about the beach, and folks come from all over the Bay Area to walk its sandy, often windswept shore. Ideal day trip: a morning hike at Mt. Tam followed by lunch at one of Stinson's unassuming eateries and a leisurely beach stroll.

GETTING HERE AND AROUND

If you're driving, take U.S. 101 to the Mill Valley/Stinson Beach/Highway 1 exit and follow the road west and then north. By bus, take Golden Gate Transit to Marin City and then transfer to the West Marin Stagecoach (61) for Bolinas.

BEACHES

FAMILY **Stinson Beach.** When the fog hasn't rolled in, this expansive stretch of sand is about as close as you can get in Marin to the stereotypical feel of a Southern California beach. There are several clothing-optional areas, among them a section called Red Rock Beach. ⚠ Swimming at

Stinson Beach can be dangerous; the undertow is strong and sharks sightings, though infrequent, have occurred; lifeguards are on duty May–September. On any hot summer weekend, roads to Stinson are packed and the parking lot fills, so factor this into your plans. The town itself—population 600, give or take—has a nonchalant surfer vibe, with a few good eating options and pleasant hippie-craftsy browsing. **Amenities:** food and drink; lifeguards; parking (free); showers; toilets. **Best for:** nudists; sunset; surfing; swimming; walking. ✉ *Hwy. 1, 1 Calle Del Sierra* ☎ *415/868–0942 lifeguard tower* 🌐 *www.stinsonbeachonline.com* ☞ *No pets allowed on the beach.*

WHERE TO EAT AND STAY

$$ AMERICAN FAMILY 🍴 **Parkside Cafe.** The Parkside is popular for its 1950s beachfront snack bar, but the adjoining café, coffee bar, marketplace, and bakery shouldn't be missed either. A full menu featuring fresh ingredients, local seafood, wood-fired pizzas, and just-baked breads is served. **Known for:** local seafood; clam chowder; rustic house-made breads. [$] *Average main: $21* ✉ *43 Arenal Ave., off Shoreline Hwy.* ☎ *415/868–1272* 🌐 *www.parksidecafe.com.*

$$ AMERICAN Fodor's Choice ★ 🍴 **Sand Dollar Restaurant.** Constructed from three barges that were floated over from Tiburon in the 1920s, this family-owned restaurant still attracts wayfarers from Muir Beach to Bolinas. Sip whiskey at the bar or nosh on local seafood and down a beer on the deck, preferably on warm summer weekends, when live jazz and blue grass draw a vibrant crowd. **Known for:** fresh seafood; local oysters; sunny patio for dining and drinking. [$] *Average main: $20* ✉ *3458 Shoreline Hwy.* ☎ *415/868–0434* 🌐 *www.stinsonbeachrestaurant.com.*

$$ B&B/INN FAMILY 🏨 **Sandpiper Lodging.** Recharge, rest, and enjoy the local scenery at this ultrapopular lodging that books up months, even years, in advance. **Pros:** beach chairs, towels, and toys provided; lush gardens with BBQ; minutes from the beach and town; free resident car parking. **Cons:** walls are thin; limited amenities. [$] *Rooms from: $165* ✉ *1 Marine Way, off Arenal Ave.* ☎ *415/868–1632* 🌐 *www.sandpiperstinsonbeach.com* 🛏 *11 rooms* 🍽 *No meals.*

$ B&B/INN 🏨 **Stinson Beach Motel.** Built in the 1930s, this motel is surrounded by flowering greenery, and rooms are clean, simple, and summery. **Pros:** minutes from the beach; cozy, unpretentious rooms; kitchenettes in cottages. **Cons:** smaller rooms are cramped. [$] *Rooms from: $140* ✉ *3416 Shoreline Hwy.* ☎ *415/868–1712* 🌐 *www.stinsonbeachmotel.com* 🛏 *8 rooms* 🍽 *No meals.*

9

POINT REYES NATIONAL SEASHORE

Bear Valley Visitor Center is 12 miles north of Bolinas.

With sandy beaches stretching for miles, a dramatic rocky coastline, a gem of a lighthouse, and idyllic, century-old dairy farms, Point Reyes National Seashore is one of the most varied and strikingly beautiful corners of the Bay Area.

GETTING HERE AND AROUND

From San Francisco, take U.S. 101 north, head west at Sir Francis Drake Boulevard (Exit 450B) toward San Anselmo, and follow the road just under 20 miles to Bear Valley Road. From Stinson Beach or Bolinas, drive north on Highway 1 and turn left on Bear Valley Road. If you're going by bus, take one of several Golden Gate Transit buses to Marin City; in Marin City transfer to the West Marin Stagecoach (you'll switch buses in Olema). Once at the visitor center, the best way to get around is on foot.

EXPLORING

FAMILY **Bear Valley Visitor Center.** A life-size orca model hovers over the center's engaging exhibits about the wildlife and history of the Point Reyes National Seashore. The rangers at the barnlike facility are fonts of information about beaches, whale-watching, hiking trails, and camping. Restrooms are available, as well as trailhead parking and a picnic area with barbecue grills. Winter hours may be shorter and summer weekend hours may be longer; call or check the website for details. ⊠ *Bear Valley Visitor Center, 1 Bear Valley Visitor Center Access Rd., west of Hwy. 1, off Bear Valley Rd., Point Reyes Station* ☎ *415/464–5100* ⊕ *www. nps.gov/pore/planyourvisit.*

FAMILY **Duxbury Reef.** Excellent tide pooling can be had along the 3-mile shore-
Fodor'sChoice line of Duxbury Reef; it's the most extensive tide pool area near Point
★ Reyes National Seashore, as well as one of the largest shale intertidal reefs in North America. Look for sea stars, barnacles, sea anemones, purple urchins, limpets, sea mussels, and the occasional abalone. But check a tide table (*tidesandcurrents.noaa.gov*) or the local papers if you plan to explore the reef—it's accessible only at low tide. The reef is a 30-minute drive from the Bear Valley Visitor Center. Take Highway 1 south from the center, turn right at Olema–Bolinas Road (keep an eye peeled; the road is easy to miss), left on Horseshoe Hill Road, right on Mesa Road, left on Overlook Drive, and then right on Elm Road, which dead-ends at the Agate Beach County Park parking lot. ✚ *At Duxbury Point, 1 mile west of Bolinas* ⊕ *www.ptreyes.org/ activities/tidepools.*

FAMILY **Palomarin Field Station & Point Reyes Bird Observatory.** Birders adore Point Blue Conservation Science, which maintains the Palomarin Field Station and the Point Reyes Bird Observatory (PRBO) that are located in the southernmost part of Point Reyes National Seashore. The Field Station, open daily from sunrise to sunset, has excellent interpretive exhibits, including a comparative display of real birds' talons. The surrounding woods harbor some 200 bird species. As you hike the quiet trails through forest and along ocean cliffs, you're likely to see biologists banding birds to aid in the study of their life cycles. ■ TIP➔ Visit Point Blue's website for detailed directions and to find out when banding will occur. ⊠ *999 Mesa Rd., Bolinas* ☎ *415/868–0655 field station, use ext. 395 to check conditions, 707/781–2555 head- quarters* ⊕ *www.pointblue.org.*

FAMILY
Fodor's Choice
★

Point Reyes Lighthouse & Visitor Center. In operation since December 1, 1870, this lighthouse—which was decommissioned in 1975—is one of the premier attractions of the Point Reyes National Seashore. It occupies the tip of Point Reyes, 21 miles from the Bear Valley Visitor Center, a scenic 40-minute drive over hills scattered with longtime dairy farms. The lighthouse originally cast a rotating beam lighted by four concentric wicks that burned lard oil. Keeping the wicks lighted and the 6,000-pound Fresnel lens soot-free in Point Reyes's perpetually foggy climate was a constant struggle that reputedly drove a few early attendants to alcoholism and insanity.

■TIP→ The lighthouse is one of the best spots on the coast for watching gray whales. On both legs of their annual migration, the magnificent animals pass close enough to see with the naked eye. Southern migration peaks in mid-January, and the whales head back north in March; see the slower mothers and calves in late April and early May. Humpback whales can be spotted feeding in the summer months.

On busy whale-watching weekends (from late December through mid-April), buses shuttle visitors from the Drakes Beach parking lot to the top of the stairs leading down to the lighthouse and the road is closed to private vehicles. However you've arrived, consider whether you have it in you to walk down—and up—the 308 steps to the lighthouse. The view from the bottom is worth the effort, but the whales are also visible from the cliffs above the lighthouse. Keep in mind that the parking lot is a quarter-mile trek from the visitor center and the lighthouse steps are open only during visitor center hours. ■TIP→ Winds can be chilly, and food, water, gas, and other resources are scarce, so be sure to come prepared. ⊠ *Lighthouse Visitor Center, 27000 Sir Francis Drake Blvd., western end of Sir Francis Drake Blvd., Inverness* ☎ *415/669–1534 visitor center* ⊕ *www.nps.gov/pore/planyourvisit/lighthouse.htm* ⊗ *Closed Tues.–Thurs.* ☞ *Fee for weekend shuttle.*

FAMILY
Fodor's Choice
★

Point Reyes National Seashore. One of the Bay Area's most spectacular treasures and the only national seashore on the West Coast, the 71,000-acre Point Reyes National Seashore encompasses hiking trails, secluded beaches, and rugged grasslands as well as Point Reyes itself, a triangular peninsula that juts into the Pacific. The town of **Point Reyes Station** is a one-main-drag affair with some good places to eat and gift shops that sell locally made and imported goods.

When explorer Sir Francis Drake sailed along the California coast in 1579, he allegedly missed the Golden Gate and San Francisco Bay, but he did land at what he described as a convenient harbor. In 2012 the federal government conceded a centuries-long debate and officially recognized Drake's Bay, which flanks the point on the east, as that harbor, designating the spot a National Historic Landmark and silencing competing claims in the 433-year-old controversy. Today Point Reyes's hills and dramatic cliffs attract other kinds of explorers: hikers, whale-watchers, and solitude seekers.

The infamous San Andreas Fault runs along the park's eastern edge and up the center of Tomales Bay; take the short **Earthquake Trail** from the visitor center to see the impact near the epicenter of the 1906 earthquake that devastated San Francisco. A half-mile path from the visitor center leads to **Kule Loklo,** a reconstructed Miwok village that sheds light on the daily lives of the region's first inhabitants. From here, trails also lead to the park's hike-in campgrounds (no car camping).

■**TIP**➔ **In late winter and spring, take the short walk at Chimney Rock, just before the lighthouse, to the Elephant Seal Overlook.** Even from the cliff, the male seals look enormous as they spar, growling and bloodied, for resident females.

You can experience the diversity of Point Reyes's ecosystems on the scenic **Coast Trail,** which starts at the Palomarin Trailhead, just outside Bolinas. From here, it's a 3-mile trek through eucalyptus groves and pine forests and along seaside cliffs to beautiful and tiny Bass Lake. To reach the Palomarin Trailhead, take Olema–Bolinas Road toward Bolinas, turn right on Mesa Road, follow signs to Point Blue Conservation Science, and then continue until the road dead-ends.

The 4.7-mile-long (one-way) **Tomales Point Trail** follows the spine of the park's northernmost finger of land through a Tule Elk Preserve, providing spectacular ocean views from the high bluffs. Expect to see elk, but keep your distance from the animals. To reach the moderately easy hiking trail, take Sir Francis Drake Boulevard through the town of Inverness; when you come to a fork, veer right to stay on Pierce Point Road and continue until you reach the parking lot at Pierce Point Ranch. ⊠ *Bear Valley Visitor Center, 1 Bear Valley Visitor Center Access Rd., west of Hwy. 1, off Bear Valley Rd., Point Reyes Station* ☎ *415/464–5100* ⊕ *www.nps.gov/pore.*

WHERE TO EAT

$$
PIZZA
FAMILY
✕ **Café Reyes.** Sunny patio seating, hand-tossed pizza, and organic local ingredients are the selling points of this laid-back café. The semi-industrial dining room, which is built around a brick oven, features glazed concrete floors, warm-painted walls, and ceilings high enough to accommodate full-size market umbrellas. **Known for:** wood-fired pizza; Drake's Bay fresh oysters; outdoor patio dining. $ *Average main: $16* ⊠ *11101 Hwy. 1, Point Reyes Station* ☎ *415/663–9493* ⊗ *Closed Mon. and Tues.*

$$$
SEAFOOD
FAMILY
Fodor'sChoice
★
✕ **Hog Island Oyster Co. Marshall Oyster Farm & the Boat Oyster Bar.** Take a short trek north on Highway 1 to the gritty mecca of Bay Area oysters—the Hog Island Marshall Oyster Farm. For a real culinary adventure, arrange to shuck and barbecue your own oysters on one of the outdoor grills (all tools supplied, reservations required), or for the less adventurous, the Boat Oyster Bar is an informal outdoor café that serves raw and BBQ oysters, local snacks, and tasty beverages. **Known for:** fresh, raw, and BBQ oysters. $ *Average main: $25* ⊠ *20215 Shoreline Hwy.* ☎ *415/663–9218* ⊕ *hogislandoysters.com/locations/marshall* ⊗ *Oyster Bar closed Tues.–Thurs. No dinner.*

$$
ITALIAN
Fodor'sChoice
★
✕ **Osteria Stellina.** Chef-owner Christian Caiazzo's menu of "Point Reyes Italian" cuisine puts an emphasis on showcasing hyperlocal ingredients like Marin-grown kale and Sonoma cheese. Pastas, pizzas, and a handful of entrées are served in a rustic-contemporary space with a raw bar that serves local oysters all day long. **Known for:** locally sourced

9

produce and seafood; fresh oysters; inventive pizzas; decadent desserts. [$] *Average main: $20* ✉ *11285 Hwy. 1, at 3rd St., Point Reyes Station* ☎ *415/663–9988* 🌐 *www.osteriastellina.com.*

$$$$ AMERICAN 🍴 **Sir and Star at the Olema.** With lovely garden views, creative and cryptically named dishes, and upscale-rustic decor that somehow incorporates taxidermied animals, this historic roadhouse (located within the Olema Inn) elicits both rants and raves, often from diners sharing the same table. The locally focused menu of California cuisine changes seasonally; a special prix fixe is offered by reservation on Saturday evenings. **Known for:** inventive presentation of local ingredients; avant-garde small plates. [$] *Average main: $35* ✉ *10000 Sir Francis Drake Blvd., at Hwy. 1, Olema* ☎ *415/663–1034* 🌐 *sirandstar.com* 🕒 *Closed Mon. and Tues. No lunch.*

$$ AMERICAN 🍴 **Station House Cafe.** In good weather, hikers fresh from the park fill the Station House's lovely outdoor garden as well as its homey indoor tables, banquettes, and bar stools, so prepare for a wait. The community-centric eatery is locally focused and serves a blend of modern and classic California dishes comprised of organic seasonal ingredients, sustainable hormone-free meats, and wild-caught seafood. **Known for:** signature popovers; hearty breakfast items; local fresh seafood. [$] *Average main: $22* ✉ *11180 Hwy. 1, at 2nd St., Point Reyes Station* ☎ *415/663–1515* 🌐 *www.stationhousecafe.com* 🕒 *Closed Wed.*

NAPA AND
SONOMA

WELCOME TO NAPA AND SONOMA

TOP REASONS TO GO

★ **Touring wineries:** Let's face it: this is the reason you're here, and the range of excellent sips to sample would make any oenophile (or novice drinker, for that matter) giddy.

★ **Biking:** Gentle hills and vineyard-laced farmland make Napa and Sonoma perfect for combining leisurely back-roads cycling with winery stops.

★ **Browsing the farmers' markets:** Many towns in Napa and Sonoma have seasonal farmers' markets, each rounding up an amazing variety of local produce.

★ **A meal at The French Laundry:** Chef Thomas Keller's Yountville restaurant is one of the country's best. The mastery of flavors and attention to detail are subtly remarkable.

★ **Wandering di Rosa:** Though this art and nature preserve is just off the busy Carneros Highway, it's a relatively unknown treasure. The galleries and gardens are filled with hundreds of artworks.

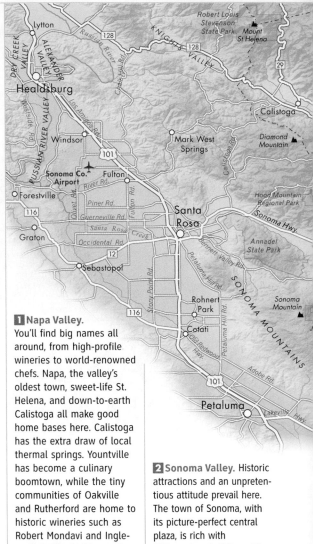

1 **Napa Valley.** You'll find big names all around, from high-profile wineries to world-renowned chefs. Napa, the valley's oldest town, sweet-life St. Helena, and down-to-earth Calistoga all make good home bases here. Calistoga has the extra draw of local thermal springs. Yountville has become a culinary boomtown, while the tiny communities of Oakville and Rutherford are home to historic wineries such as Robert Mondavi and Inglenook. Rutherford in particular is the source for outstanding Cabernet Sauvignon.

2 **Sonoma Valley.** Historic attractions and an unpretentious attitude prevail here. The town of Sonoma, with its picture-perfect central plaza, is rich with 19th-century buildings. Glen Ellen, meanwhile, has a special connection with author Jack London.

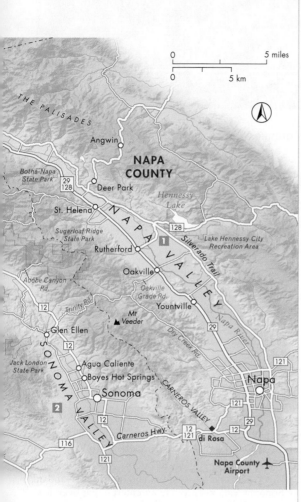

GETTING ORIENTED

The Napa and Sonoma valleys run parallel, northwest to southeast , and are separated by the Mayacamas Mountains. Southwest of Sonoma Valley are several other important viticultural areas in Sonoma county, including the Dry Creek, Alexander, and Russian River Valleys. The Carneros, which spans southern Sonoma and Napa counties, is just north of San Pablo Bay.

10

Updated by
Daniel Mangin

In California's premier wine region, the pleasures of eating and drinking are celebrated daily. It's easy to join in at famous wineries and rising newcomers off country roads, or at trendy in-town tasting rooms. Chefs transform local ingredients into feasts, and gourmet groceries sell perfect picnic fare. Yountville, Healdsburg, and St. Helena have small-town charm as well as luxurious inns, hotels, and spas, yet the natural setting is equally sublime, whether experienced from a canoe on the Russian River or the deck of a winery overlooking endless rows of vines.

The Wine Country is also rich in history. In Sonoma you can explore California's Spanish and Mexican pasts at the Sonoma Mission, and the origins of modern California wine making at Buena Vista Winery. Some wineries, among them St. Helena's Beringer and Rutherford's Inglenook, have cellars or tasting rooms dating to the late 1800s. Calistoga is a flurry of late-19th-century Steamboat Gothic architecture, though the town's oldest-looking building, the medieval-style Castello di Amorosa, is a 21st-century creation.

Tours at the Napa Valley's Beringer, Mondavi, and Inglenook—and at Buena Vista in the Sonoma Valley—provide an entertaining overview of Wine Country history. The tour at the splashy visitor center at St. Helena's Hall winery will introduce you to 21st-century wine-making technology, and over in Glen Ellen's Benziger Family Winery you can see how its vineyard managers apply biodynamic farming principles to grape growing. At numerous facilities you can play winemaker for a day at seminars in the fine art of blending wines. If that strikes you as too much effort, you can always pamper yourself at a luxury spa.

To delve further into the fine art of Wine Country living, pick up a copy of *Fodor's Napa and Sonoma.*

PLANNING

WHEN TO GO

High season extends from April through October. In summer, expect the days to be hot and dry, the roads filled with cars, and traffic heavy at the tasting rooms. Hotel rates are highest during the height of harvest, in September and October. Then and in summer book lodgings well ahead. November, except for Thanksgiving week, and December before Christmas are less busy. The weather in Napa and Sonoma is pleasant nearly year-round. Daytime temperatures average from about 55°F during winter to the 80s in summer, when readings in the 90s and higher are common. April, May, and October are milder but still warm. The rainiest months are usually from December through March.

GETTING HERE AND AROUND

AIR TRAVEL

Wine Country regulars often bypass San Francisco and Oakland and fly into Santa Rosa's Charles M. Schulz Sonoma County Airport (STS) on Alaska, Allegiant, and American, nonstop from several West Coast cities, Las Vegas, and Phoenix. Several major agencies rent cars here. ■TIP➔ Alaska allows passengers flying out of STS to check up to one case of wine for free.

BUS TRAVEL

Bus travel is an inconvenient way to explore the Wine Country, though it is possible. Take Golden Gate Transit from San Francisco to connect with Sonoma County Transit buses. VINE connects with BART commuter trains in the East Bay and the San Francisco Bay Ferry in Vallejo *(see Ferry Travel, below)*. VINE buses serve the Napa Valley and connect the towns of Napa and Sonoma.

CAR TRAVEL

Driving your own car is by far the most convenient way to get to and explore the Wine Country. In light traffic, the trip from San Francisco or Oakland to the southern portion of either Napa or Sonoma should take about an hour. Distances between Wine Country towns are fairly short, and in normal traffic you can drive from one end of the Napa or Sonoma valley to the other in less than an hour. Although this is a mostly rural area, the usual rush hours still apply, and high-season weekend traffic can often be slow.

Five major roads serve the region. U.S. 101 and Highways 12 and 121 travel through Sonoma County. Highway 29 and the parallel, more scenic, and often less crowded Silverado Trail travel north–south between Napa and Calistoga.

The easiest way to travel between the Napa Valley and Sonoma County is along Highway 12/121 to the south, or Highway 128 to the north. Travel between the middle sections of either area requires taking the slow, winding drive over the Mayacamas Mountains on the Oakville Grade, which links Oakville, in Napa, and Glen Ellen, in Sonoma.

■TIP➔ If you're wine tasting, either select a designated driver or be careful of your wine intake—the police keep an eye out for tipsy drivers.

10

From San Francisco to Napa: Cross the Golden Gate Bridge, then go north on U.S. 101. Head east on Highway 37 toward Vallejo, then north on Highway 121, aka the Carneros Highway. Turn left (north) when Highway 121 runs into Highway 29.

From San Francisco to Sonoma: Cross the Golden Gate Bridge, then go north on U.S. 101, east on Highway 37 toward Vallejo, and north on Highway 121. When you reach Highway 12, take it north to the town of Sonoma. For Sonoma County destinations north of Sonoma Valley stay on U.S. 101, which passes through Santa Rosa and Healdsburg.

From Berkeley and Oakland: Take Interstate 80 north to Highway 37 west, then on to Highway 29 north. For the Napa Valley, continue on Highway 29; to reach Sonoma County, head west on Highway 121.

FERRY TRAVEL

The San Francisco Bay Ferry sails from the Ferry Building and Pier 41 in San Francisco to Vallejo, where you can board VINE Bus 11 to the town of Napa. Buses sometimes fill in for the ferries.

RESTAURANTS

Farm-to-table Modern American cuisine is the prevalent style in the Napa Valley and Sonoma County, but this encompasses both the delicate preparations of Thomas Keller's highly praised The French Laundry and the upscale comfort food served throughout the Wine Country. The quality (and hype) often means high prices, but you can also find appealing, inexpensive eateries, especially in the towns of Napa, Calistoga, Sonoma, and Santa Rosa, and many high-end delis prepare superb picnic fare. At pricey restaurants you can save money by having lunch instead of dinner. With a few exceptions (noted in individual restaurant listings), dress is informal. *Restaurant reviews have been shortened. For full information, visit Fodors.com.*

HOTELS

The fanciest accommodations are concentrated in the Napa Valley towns of Yountville, Rutherford, St. Helena, and Calistoga; Sonoma County's poshest lodgings are in Healdsburg. The spas, amenities, and exclusivity of high-end properties attract travelers with the means and desire for luxury living. The cities of Napa and Santa Rosa are the best bets for budget hotels and inns, but even at a lower price point you'll still find a touch of Wine Country glamour. On weekends, two- or even three-night minimum stays are commonly required at smaller lodgings. Book well ahead for stays at such places during the busy summer or fall season. If your party will include travelers under age 16, inquire about policies regarding younger guests; some smaller lodgings discourage (or discreetly forbid) children. *Hotel reviews have been shortened. For full information, visit Fodors.com.*

WHAT IT COSTS			
$	**$$**	**$$$**	**$$$$**
Restaurants under $16	$16–$22	$23–$30	over $30
Hotels under $200	$200–$300	$301–$400	over $400

Restaurant prices are the average cost of a main course at dinner or, if dinner is not served, at lunch. Hotel prices are for the lowest cost of a standard double room in high season.

TASTINGS AND TOURS

Many wineries require reservations for tours, seminars, and tastings, which in most cases are made through booking websites such as Cellar-Pass and VinoVisit. A good scheduling strategy is to book appointment-only wineries in the morning, saving the ones that allow walk-ins until the afternoon. That way, if lunch or other winery visits take longer than expected you won't be stressed about having to arrive at later stops at a precise time.

Many visitors prefer to leave the scheduling and driving to seasoned professionals. Whether you want to tour wineries in a van or bus along with other passengers or spring for a private limo, there are plenty of operators who can accommodate you. Tours generally last from five to seven hours and stop at four or five wineries. Rates vary from $80 per person to $250 or more, depending on the vehicle and whether the tour includes other guests. On most tours, at least one stop includes a behind-the-scenes look at production facilities and the chance to meet winemakers or others involved in the wine-making process. Most tour operators will pick you up at your hotel or a specified meeting place. You can also book a car and driver by the hour for shorter trips. Rates for limo generally run from $50 to $85 per hour, and there's usually a two- or three-hour minimum. ■TIP→ Some tours include lunch and tasting and other fees, but not all do, so ask.

THE NAPA VALLEY

10

With more than 500 wineries and many of the biggest brands in the business, the Napa Valley is the Wine Country's star. With a population of about 79,000, Napa, the valley's largest town, lures with its cultural attractions and (relatively) reasonably priced accommodations. A few miles farther north, compact Yountville is densely packed with top-notch restaurants and hotels, and Rutherford and Oakville are renowned for their Cabernet Sauvignon–friendly soils. Beyond them, St. Helena teems with elegant boutiques and restaurants, and casual Calistoga, known for spas and hot springs, has the feel of an Old West frontier town.

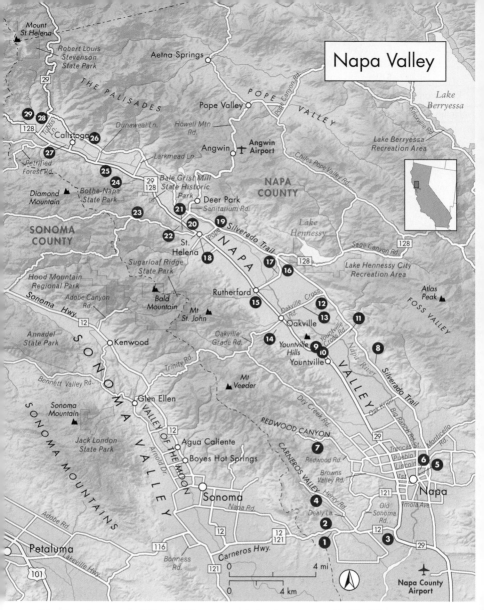

Napa Valley

Mount St Helena

Robert Louis Stevenson State Park

THE PALISADES

Aetna Springs

POPE VALLEY

Pope Valley

Lake Berryessa

Dunaweal Ln.

Howell Mtn. Rd.

Larkmead Ln.

Angwin

Angwin Airport

Lake Berryessa Recreation Area

Calistoga

Petrified Forest Rd.

Bale Grist Mill State Historic Park

Chiles Pope Valley Rd.

NAPA COUNTY

Diamond Mountain

Bothe-Napa State Park

Deer Park

Sanitarium Rd.

Lake Hennessy

SONOMA COUNTY

St. Helena

Silverado Trail

Sage Canyon Rd.

Lake Hennessy City Recreation Area

Sugarloaf Ridge State Park

Hood Mountain Regional Park

Adobe Canyon Rd.

Bald Mountain

Mt St. John

Rutherford

Oakville Cross Rd.

Atlas Peak

FOSS VALLEY

Sonoma Hwy.

Annadel State Park

Kenwood

Oakville Grade Rd.

Oakville

Yountville Cross Rd.

Napa River

Silverado Trail

Trinity Rd.

Oakville

Yountville Hills

Yountville

Mt Veeder

Glen Ellen

SONOMA MOUNTAINS

Bennett Valley Rd.

Sonoma Mountain

VALLEY OF THE MOON

REDWOOD CANYON

Dry Creek Rd.

Jack London State Park

Agua Caliente

Arnold Dr.

Boyes Hot Springs

CARNEROS VALLEY

Redwood Rd.

Browns Valley Rd.

Napa Valley Henry Rd.

Franklin St.

Pueblo Lincoln

Napa

Adobe Rd.

Sonoma

Napa Rd.

Dealy La.

Old Sonoma Rd.

Imola Ave.

Petaluma

Lakeville Hwy.

Bonness Rd.

Carneros Hwy.

0   4 mi

0   4 km

Napa County Airport

NAPA

46 miles northeast of San Francisco.

After many years as a blue-collar burg detached from the Wine Country scene, the Napa Valley's largest town (population about 80,000) has evolved into one of its shining stars. Masaharu Morimoto and other chefs of note operate restaurants here, swank hotels and inns can be found downtown and beyond, and the nightlife options include the West Coast edition of the famed Blue Note jazz club. A walkway that follows the Napa River has made downtown more pedestrian-friendly, and the Oxbow Public Market, a complex of high-end food purveyors, is popular with locals and tourists. Nearby Copia, operated by the Culinary Institute of America, hosts cooking demonstrations and other activities open to the public and has a shop and a restaurant. If you establish your base in Napa, plan on spending at least a half day strolling the downtown district.

GETTING HERE AND AROUND

Downtown Napa lies a mile east of Highway 29—take the 1st Street exit and follow the signs. Ample parking, much of it free for the first three hours and some for the entire day, is available on or near Main Street. Several VINE buses serve downtown and beyond.

EXPLORING

TOP ATTRACTIONS

Artesa Vineyards & Winery. From a distance the modern, minimalist architecture of Artesa blends harmoniously with the surrounding Carneros landscape, but up close its pools, fountains, and the large outdoor sculptures by resident artist Gordon Huether of Napa make a vivid impression. So, too, do the wines: mostly Chardonnay and Pinot Noir but also Cabernet Sauvignon, Merlot, and other limited releases like Albariño and Tempranillo. You can sample wines by themselves without a reservation or, at tastings for which a reservation is required, paired with chocolate, cheese, or tapas. ■TIP→ The tour, conducted daily, explores wine making and the winery's history. ⌧ *1345 Henry Rd., off Old Sonoma Rd. and Dealy La., Napa* ☎ *707/224–1668* ⊕ *www.artesawinery.com* ⌧ *Tastings $25–$60, tour $40 (includes tasting).*

Fodor'sChoice **di Rosa.** A formidable array of artworks from the 1960s to the present
★ by Northern California artists is displayed on this 217-acre property. The works can be found not only in galleries and in the former residence of its late founder, Rene di Rosa, but also throughout the surrounding landscape. Some works were commissioned especially for di Rosa, among them Paul Kos's meditative *Chartres Bleu,* a video installation in a chapel-like setting that replicates a stained-glass window from the cathedral in Chartres, France. ■TIP→ You can view the current temporary exhibition and a few permanent works at the Gatehouse Gallery, but to experience the breadth of the collection you'll need to book a tour. ⌧ *5200 Sonoma Hwy./Hwy. 121, Napa* ☎ *707/226–5991* ⊕ *www.dirosaart.org* ⌧ *Gatehouse Gallery $5, tours $12–$15* ☉ *Closed Mon. and Tues.*

10

Continued on page 462

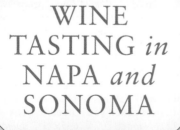

WINE
TASTING *in*
NAPA *and*
SONOMA

Whether you're a serious wine collector making your annual pilgrimage to Nothern California's Wine Country or a newbie who doesn't know the difference between a Merlot and Mourvèdre but is eager to learn, you can have a great time touring Napa and Sonoma wineries. Your gateway to the wine world is the tasting room, where staff members are happy to chat with curious guests.

VISITING WINERIES

Tasting rooms range from the grand to the humble, offering everything from a few sips of wine to in-depth tours of facilities and vineyards. Many are open for drop-in visits, usually daily from around 10 am to 5 pm. Others require guests to make reservations. First-time visitors frequently enjoy the history-oriented tours at Charles Krug and Inglenook, or ones at Mondavi and J Vineyards that highlight the process as well. The environments at some wineries reflect their founders' other interests: art and architecture at Artesa and Hall St. Helena, movie making at Francis Ford Coppola, and medieval history at the Castello di Amorosa.

Many wineries describe their pourers as "wine educators," and indeed some of them have taken online or other classes and have passed an exam to prove basic knowledge of appellations, grape varietals, vineyards, and wine-making techniques. The one constant, however, is a deep, shared pleasure in the experience of wine tasting. To prepare you for winery visits, we've covered the fundamentals: tasting rooms, fees and what to expect, and the types of tours wineries offer.

Fees. In the past few years, tasting fees have skyrocketed. Most Napa wineries charge $25 or $30 to taste a few wines, though $40, $50, or even $75 fees aren't unheard of. Sonoma wineries are often a bit cheaper, in the $15 to $35 range, and you'll still find the occasional freebie.

Some winery tours are free, in which case you're usually required to pay a separate fee if you want to taste the wine. If you've paid a fee for the tour—generally from $20 to $40—your wine tasting is usually included in that price.

10

(opposite page) Carneros vineyards in autumn, Napa Valley. (top) Pinot Gris grapes. (bottom) Bottles from Far Niente winery.

MAKING THE MOST OF YOUR TIME

■**Call ahead.** Some wineries require reservations to visit or tour. It's wise to check before visiting.

■**Come on weekdays.** Especially between June and October, try to visit on weekdays to avoid traffic-clogged roads and crowded tasting rooms. For more info on the best times of year to visit, see this chapter's Planner.

■**Get an early start.** Tasting rooms are often deserted before 11 am or so, when most visitors are still lingering over a second cup of coffee. If you come early, you'll have the staff's undivided attention. You'll usually encounter the largest crowds between 3 and 5 pm.

(top) Sipping and swirling in the DeLoach tasting room. (bottom) Learning about barrel aging at Robert Mondavi Winery.

■**Schedule strategically.** Visit appointment-only wineries in the morning and ones that allow walk-ins in the afternoon. It'll spare you the stress of being "on time" for later stops.

■**Hit the Trail.** Beringer, Mondavi, and other high-profile wineries line heavily trafficked Highway 29, but the going

is often quicker on the Silverado Trail, which runs parallel to the highway to the east. You'll find famous names here, too, among them the sparkling wine house Mumm Napa Valley, but the traffic is often lighter and sometimes the crowds as well.

Domaine Carneros.

AT THE BAR

In most tasting rooms, you'll be handed a list of the wines available that day. The wines will be listed in a suggested tasting order, starting with the lightest-bodied whites, progressing to the most intense reds, and ending with dessert wines. If you can't decide which wines to choose, tell the server what types of wines you usually like and ask for a recommendation.

The server will pour you an ounce or so of each wine you select. As you taste it, feel free to take notes or ask questions. Don't be shy—the staff are there to educate you about the wine. If you don't like a wine, or you've simply tasted enough, feel free to pour the rest into one of the dump buckets on the bar.

TOURS

Tours tend to be the most exciting (and the most crowded) in September and October, when the harvest and crush-

ing are underway. Tours typically last from 30 minutes to an hour and give you a brief overview of the winemaking process. At some of the older wineries, the tour guide might focus on the history of the property.

■ TIP➔ If you plan to take any tours, wear comfortable shoes, since you might be walking on wet floors or dirt or gravel pathways or stepping over hoses or other equipment.

MONEY-SAVING TIPS

■ Many hotels and B&Bs distribute coupons for free or discounted tastings to their guests—don't forget to ask.

■ If you and your travel partner don't mind sharing a glass, servers are happy to let you split a tasting.

■ Some wineries will refund all or part of the tasting fee if you buy a bottle. Usually one fee is waived per bottle purchased, though sometimes you must buy two or three.

■ Almost all wineries will also waive the fee if you join their wine club program. However, this typically commits you to buying a certain number of bottles on a regular basis, so be sure you really like the wines before signing up.

Preston of Dry Creek bottles only estate-grown grapes.

TOP 2-DAY ITINERARIES

First-Timer's Napa Tour

Start: Oxbow Public market, Napa. Get underway by browsing the shops selling wines, spices, locally grown produce, and other fine foods, for a taste of what the Wine Country has to offer.

Inglenook, Rutherford. The tour here is a particularly fun way to learn about the history

of Napa winemaking—and you can see the old, atmospheric, ivy-covered château.

Frog's Leap, Rutherford. Friendly, unpretentious, and knowledgeable staff makes this place great for wine newbies. (Make sure you get that reservation lined up.)

Dinner and Overnight: St. Helena. Splurge at Meadowood Napa Valley and you won't need to leave the property for

Domaine Carneros

di Rosa Preserve

121

12

Old Sonoma Rd.

Oxbow Public Market
Napa
29

NAPA COUNTY

Robert Mondavi

Far Niente

Yountville

Oakville

KEY
First-Timer's Napa Tour
Wine Buff's Tour

Silverado Trail

Stag's Leap Wine Cellars

Wine Buff's Tour

Start: Stag's Leap Wine Cellars, Yountville, Napa. Famed for its Cabernet Sauvignon and Bordeaux blends.

Silver Oak, Oakville. Schedule a tour of this celebrated winery and taste the flagship Cabernet Sauvignon.

Mumm Napa, Rutherford. Come for the bubbly—which is available in a variety of tastings—stay for the photography exhibits.

Dinner and Overnight: Yountville. Have dinner at one of the Thomas Keller restaurants. Splurge at Bardessono; save at

Maison Fleurie.

Next Day: Robert Mondavi, Oakville. Spring for the reserve room tasting so you can sip the top-of-the-line wines, especially the Cabernet Sauvignon. Head across Highway 29 to the Oakville Grocery to pick up a picnic lunch.

an extravagant dinner at its restaurant. Save at El Bonita Motel with dinner at Gott's.

Next Day: Poke around St. Helena's shops, then drive to Yountville for lunch.

di Rosa, Napa. Call ahead to book a one- or two-hour tour of the acres of gardens and galleries, which

are chock-full of thousands of works of art.

Domaine Carneros, Napa. Toast your trip with a glass of outstanding bubbly.

Sonoma Backroads

Far Niente, Oakville. You have to make a reservation and the fee for the tasting and tour is steep, but the

payoff is an especially intimate winery experience. You'll taste excellent Cabernet and Chardonnay, then end your trip on a sweet note with a dessert wine.

Start: Iron Horse Vineyards, Russian River Valley.
Soak up a view of vine-covered hills and Mount St. Helena while sipping a sparkling wine or Pinot Noir at this beautifully rustic spot.

Dutton-Goldfield Winery, Russian River Valley.
A terrific source for Pinot Noir and Chardonnay, the stars of this valley.

Dinner and Overnight: Forestville. Go all out with a stay at the Farmhouse Inn, whose award-winning restaurant is one of the best in all of Sonoma.

Next Day: Westside Road, Russian River Valley.
This scenic route, which follows the river, is crowded with worthwhile wineries like Arista and Rochioli—but it's not crowded with visitors. Pinot fans will find a lot to love. Picnic at either winery and enjoy the view.

Balletto Vineyards, Santa Rosa. End on an especially relaxed note with a walk through the vineyards and a patio tasting.

10

WINE TASTING 101

TAKE A GOOD LOOK.

Hold your glass by the stem, raise it to the light, and take a close look at the wine. Check for clarity and color. (This is easiest to do if you can hold the glass in front of a white background.) Any tinge of brown usually means that the wine is over the hill or has gone bad.

BREATHE DEEP.

1. Sniff the wine once or twice to see if you can identify any smells.

2. Swirl the wine gently in the glass. Aerating the wine this way releases more of its aromas. (It's called "volatilizing the esters," if you're trying to impress someone.)

3. Take another long sniff. You might notice that experienced wine tasters spend more time sniffing the wine than drinking it. This is because this step is where the magic happens. The number of scents you might detect is almost endless, from berries, apricots, honey, and wildflowers to leather, cedar, or even tar. Does the wine smell good to you? Do you detect any "off" flavors, like wet dog or sulfur?

AT LAST! TAKE A SIP.

1. Swirl the wine around your mouth so that it makes contact with all your taste buds and releases more of its aromas. Think about the way the wine feels in your mouth. Is it watery or rich? Is it crisp or silky? Does it have a bold flavor, or is it subtle? The weight and intensity of a wine are called its body.

2. Hold the wine in your mouth for a few seconds and see if you can identify any developing flavors. More complex wines will reveal many different flavors as you drink them.

SPIT OR SWALLOW.

The pros typically spit, since they want to preserve their palate (and sobriety!) for the wines to come, but you'll find that swallowers far outnumber the spitters in the winery tasting rooms. Whether you spit or swallow, notice the flavor that remains after the wine is gone (the finish).

Sniff

Sip

DODGE THE CROWDS

To avoid bumping elbows in the tasting rooms, look for wineries off the main drags of Highway 29 in Napa and Highway 12 in Sonoma. The back roads of the Russian River, Dry Creek, and Alexander valleys, all in Sonoma, are excellent places to explore. In Napa, try the northern end. Also look for wineries that are open by appointment only; they tend to schedule visitors carefully to avoid a big crush at any one time.

HOW WINE IS MADE

1. CRUSHING
Harvested grapes go into a stemmer-crusher, which separates stems from fruit and crushes the grapes to release "free-run" juice.

2. PRESSING
Remaining juice is gently extracted from grapes. Usually done by pressing grapes against the walls of a tank with an inflatable bladder.

3. FERMENTING
Extracted juice (and also grape skins and pulp, when making red wine) goes into stainless-steel tanks or oak barrels to ferment. During fermentation, sugars convert to alcohol.

4. AGING
Wine is stored in stainless-steel or oak casks or barrels, or sometimes in concrete vessels, to develop flavors.

5. RACKING
Wine is transferred to clean barrels; sediment is removed. Wine may be filtered and fined (clarified) to improve its clarity, color, and sometimes flavor.

6. BOTTLING
Wine is bottled either at the winery or at a special facility, then stored again for bottle-aging.

10

WHAT'S AN APPELLATION?

American Viticultural Area (AVA) or, more commonly, an appellation. What can be confusing is that some appellations encompass smaller subappellations. The Rutherford, Oakville, and Mt. Veeder AVAs, for instance, are among the Napa Valley AVA's 15 subappellations. Wineries often buy grapes from outside their AVA, so their labels might reference different appellations. A winery in the warmer Napa Valley, for instance, might source Pinot Noir grapes from the cooler Russian River Valley, where they grow better. The appellation listed on a label always refers to where a wine's grapes were grown, not to where the wine was made. By law, if a label bears the name of an appellation, 85% of the grapes must come from it.

Wine and contemporary art find a home at di Rosa.

Domaine Carneros. A visit to this majestic château is an opulent way to enjoy the Carneros District—especially in fine weather, when the vineyard views are spectacular. The château was modeled after an 18th-century French mansion owned by the Taittinger family. Carved into the hillside beneath the winery, the cellars produce sparkling wines reminiscent of those made by Taittinger, using only Los Carneros AVA grapes. The winery sells flights and glasses of its sparklers, Chardonnay, Pinot Noir, and other wines. Enjoy them all with cheese and charcuterie plates, caviar, or smoked salmon. Seating is in the Louis XV–inspired salon or on the terrace overlooking the vines. The tour covers traditional methods of making sparkling wines. Both tours and tastings are by appointment only. ⊠ *1240 Duhig Rd., at Hwy. 121, Napa* ☎ *707/257–0101, 800/716–2788* ⊕ *www.domainecarneros.com* ⊡ *Tastings $10–$250, tour $50.*

Fodor'sChoice ★ **Oxbow Public Market.** The market's two dozen stands provide an introduction to Northern California's diverse artisanal food products. Swoon over decadent charcuterie at the Fatted Calf (great sandwiches, too), slurp oysters at Hog Island, or chow down on duck or salmon tacos at C Casa. You can sample wine (and cheese) at the Oxbow Cheese & Wine Merchant, ales at Fieldwork Brewery's taproom, and barrel-aged cocktails and handcrafted vodkas at the Napa Valley Distillery. Napa Bookmine is among the few nonfood vendors here. ■**TIP**➜ **If you don't mind eating at the counter, you can select a steak at the Five Dot Ranch meat stand and pay $8 above market price ($12 with two sides) to have it grilled on the spot, a real deal for a quality slab.** ⊠ *610 and 644 1st St., at McKinstry St., Napa* ⊕ *www.oxbowpublicmarket.com.*

WORTH NOTING

Etude Wines. You're apt to see or hear hawks, egrets, Canada geese, and other wildlife on the grounds of Etude, known for its sophisticated Pinot Noirs. Although the winery and its light-filled tasting room are in Napa County, the grapes for its flagship Carneros Estate Pinot Noir come from the Sonoma portion of Los Carneros, as do those for the rarer Heirloom Carneros Pinot Noir. Chardonnay, Pinot Blanc, Pinot Noir, and other wines are poured daily at the tasting bar and in good weather on the patio. Pinot Noirs from Carneros, the Sonoma Coast, Oregon, and Santa Barbara County are compared at the Study of Pinot Noir sessions ($50), for which reservations are required. ■ TIP➜ Single-vineyard Napa Valley Cabernets are another Etude emphasis; those from Rutherford and Oakville are particularly good. ✉ *1250 Cuttings Wharf Rd., 1 mile south of Hwy. 121, Napa* ☎ *707/257–5782* ⊕ *www.etudewines.com* 🖰 *Tastings $20–$50.*

The Hess Collection. About 9 miles northwest of Napa, up a winding road ascending Mt. Veeder, this winery is a delightful discovery. The limestone structure, rustic from the outside but modern and airy within, contains Swiss owner Donald Hess's world-class art collection, including large-scale works by contemporary artists such as Andy Goldsworthy, Anselm Kiefer, and Robert Rauschenberg. Cabernet Sauvignon is a major strength, and the 19 Block Cuvée, Mount Veeder, a Cabernet blend, shows off Malbec and other estate varietals. Tastings outdoors in the garden and the courtyard take place from spring to fall, with cheese or nuts and other nibbles accompanying the wines. ■ TIP➜ Among the wine-and-food pairings offered year-round, most of which involve a guided tour of the art collection, is a fun one showcasing locally made artisanal chocolates. ✉ *4411 Redwood Rd., west off Hwy. 29 at Trancas St./Redwood Rd. exit, Napa* ☎ *707/255–1144* ⊕ *www.hesscollection.com* 🖰 *Tastings $25–$175, art gallery free.*

Napa Valley Wine Train. Several centuries-old restored Pullman railroad cars and a two-story 1952 Vista Dome car with a curved glass roof travel a leisurely, scenic route between Napa and St. Helena. All trips include a well-made lunch or dinner. Guests on the Quattro Vino tour enjoy a four-course lunch and tastings at four wineries, with stops at one or two wineries incorporated into other tours. Murder-mystery plays are among the regularly scheduled special events. ■ TIP➜ It's best to make this trip during the day, when you can enjoy the vineyard views. ✉ *1275 McKinstry St., off 1st St., Napa* ☎ *707/253–2111, 800/427–4124* ⊕ *www.winetrain.com* 🖰 *From $146.*

Stag's Leap Wine Cellars. A 1973 Stag's Leap Wine Cellars S.L.V. Cabernet Sauvignon put this winery and the Napa Valley on the enological map by placing first in the famous Judgment of Paris tasting of 1976. The grapes for that wine came from a vineyard visible from the stone-and-glass Fay Outlook & Visitor Center, which has broad views of a second fabled Cabernet vineyard (Fay) and the promontory that gives both the winery and the Stags Leap District AVA their names. The top-of-the-line Cabernets from these vineyards are poured at the $45 Estate Collection Tasting. Among the other options are a cave tour and tasting and special wine-and-food pairings. ✉ *5766 Silverado Trail, at Wappo Hill Rd., Napa* ☎ *707/261–6410* ⊕ *www.cask23.com* 🖰 *Tasting $45, tours (with tastings by appointment only) $75 and up.*

10

WHERE TO EAT

$$$ ✕**The Corner Napa.** Equal parts 21st-century gentleman's club and
MODERN brooding urban loft, this downtown restaurant seduces with a suave
AMERICAN palette of marble, leather, bronze, and polished walnut surfaces. Chef
Fodor'sChoice Dustin Falcon's cuisine is similarly elegant, with pickled pearl onions,
★ apple, sherry, and candied pecans elevating a garden beets salad, and
Sicilian pistachio, Medjool dates, spiced yogurt, and fried naan balls
playing well with each other and their dish's centerpiece, pan-seared
Spanish octopus. **Known for:** contemporary decor; international wine
list; specialty cocktails and rare spirits. $ *Average main: $28* ⊠ *660
Main St., near 5th St., Napa* ☎ *707/927–5552* ⊕ *www.cornerbarnapa.
com* ⊘ *Closed Mon. No lunch Tues.–Sat.*

$$$ ✕**Grace's Table.** A dependable, varied, three-squares-a-day menu makes
ECLECTIC this modest corner restaurant occupying a brick-and-glass storefront
many Napans' go-to choice for a simple meal. Iron-skillet corn bread
with lavender honey and butter shows up at all hours, with chilaquiles
scrambled eggs a breakfast favorite, savory fish tacos a lunchtime staple,
and cassoulet and pork osso buco risotto popular for dinner. **Known
for:** congenial staffers; good beers on tap; eclectic menu focusing on
France, Italy, and the Americas. $ *Average main: $24* ⊠ *1400 2nd St.,
at Franklin St., Napa* ☎ *707/226–6200* ⊕ *www.gracestable.net.*

$$$$ ✕**La Toque.** Chef Ken Frank's La Toque is the complete package: his
MODERN imaginative modern American cuisine, served in a formal dining space,
AMERICAN is complemented by a wine lineup that earned the restaurant a coveted
Fodor'sChoice *Wine Spectator* Grand Award. Built around seasonal local ingredients,
★ the prix-fixe menu, which changes frequently, might include potato rösti
with caviar, sole with eggplant and almond-hazelnut *picada* sauce, and
five-spice Liberty Farm duck breast with black trumpet mushrooms.
Known for: elaborate preparations; astute wine pairings. $ *Average
main: $80* ⊠ *Westin Verasa Napa, 1314 McKinstry St., off Soscol Ave.,
Napa* ☎ *707/257–5157* ⊕ *www.latoque.com* ⊘ *No lunch.*

$$$ ✕**Miminashi.** Japanese *izakaya*—gastropubs that serve appetizers
JAPANESE downed with sake or cocktails—provided the inspiration for chef Curtis
Fodor'sChoice Di Fede's buzz-worthy downtown Napa restaurant. Ramen, fried rice,
★ and yakitori anchor the menu, whose highlights include smoked-trout
potato croquettes, crispy skewered chicken skin, and the ooh-inspiring
okonomiyaki pancake with bacon and cabbage, topped by dried fer-
mented tuna flakes. **Known for:** soft-serve ice cream for dessert and
from to-go window; wines and sakes that elevate the cuisine. $ *Aver-
age main: $28* ⊠ *821 Coombs St., near 3rd St., Napa* ☎ *707/254–9464*
⊕ *miminashi.com* ⊘ *No lunch weekends.*

$$$$ ✕**Morimoto Napa.** *Iron Chef* star Masaharu Morimoto is the big name
JAPANESE behind this downtown Napa hot spot where everything is delightfully
overdone, right down to the desserts. Organic materials such as twisting
grapevines above the bar and rough-hewn wooden tables seem simulta-
neously earthy and modern, creating a fitting setting for the gorgeously
plated Japanese fare, from sashimi served with grated fresh wasabi to
elaborate concoctions that include sea-urchin carbonara made with
udon noodles. **Known for:** elaborate concoctions; gorgeous plating;
omakase menu. $ *Average main: $36* ⊠ *610 Main St., at 5th St., Napa*
☎ *707/252–1600* ⊕ *www.morimotonapa.com.*

$$$$
MODERN
AMERICAN
Fodor'sChoice
★

✗**Torc.** *Torc* means "wild boar" in an early Celtic dialect, and owner-chef Sean O'Toole, who formerly helmed kitchens at top Manhattan, San Francisco, and Yountville establishments, occasionally incorporates the restaurant's namesake beast into his eclectic offerings. O'Toole and his team enhance dishes such as roast chicken—recently prepared with Florence fennel, hedgehog mushroom, pickle lily, and bergamot—with style and precision. **Known for:** gracious service; specialty cocktails; Bengali sweet-potato pakora and deviled-egg appetizers. Ⓢ *Average main: $33* ✉ *1140 Main St., at Pearl St., Napa* ☎ *707/252–3292* ⊕ *www.torcnapa.com* ☾ *Closed Tues. No lunch weekdays.*

$$$
SPANISH
Fodor'sChoice
★

✗**ZuZu.** At festive ZuZu the focus is on tapas, paella, the signature suckling pig, and other Spanish favorites often downed with cava or sangria. Regulars revere the paella, made with Spanish *bomba* rice, and small plates that might include white anchovies with sliced egg and rémoulade on grilled bread. **Known for:** singular flavors and spicing; Latin jazz on the stereo; sister restaurant La Taberna for bar bites three doors south. Ⓢ *Average main: $29* ✉ *829 Main St., near 3rd St., Napa* ☎ *707/224–8555* ⊕ *www.zuzunapa.com* ☾ *No lunch weekends.*

WHERE TO STAY

$$$
HOTEL
Fodor'sChoice
★

▦**Andaz Napa.** Part of the Hyatt family, this boutique hotel with an urban-hip vibe has luxurious rooms with flat-screen TVs, laptop-size safes, and white-marble bathrooms stocked with high-quality bath products. **Pros:** proximity to downtown restaurants, theaters, and tasting rooms; access to modern fitness center; complimentary beverage upon arrival; complimentary snacks and nonalcoholic beverages in rooms. **Cons:** parking can be a challenge on weekends; unremarkable views from some rooms. Ⓢ *Rooms from: $359* ✉ *1450 1st St., Napa* ☎ *707/687–1234* ⊕ *andaznapa.com* ⤳ *141 rooms* �‖ *No meals.*

$$$$
RESORT
Fodor'sChoice
★

▦**Carneros Resort & Spa.** Freestanding board-and-batten cottages with rocking chairs on each porch are simultaneously rustic and chic at this luxurious property made even more so by a $6.5 million makeover. **Pros:** cottages have lots of privacy; beautiful views from hilltop pool and hot tub; heaters on private patios. **Cons:** a long drive to destinations up-valley. Ⓢ *Rooms from: $600* ✉ *4048 Sonoma Hwy./Hwy. 121, Napa* ☎ *707/299–4900, 888/400–9000* ⊕ *www.thecarnerosinn.com* ⤳ *86 rooms* ❥ *No meals.*

$$
B&B/INN
Fodor'sChoice
★

▦**Inn on Randolph.** A few calm blocks from the downtown action, the restored Inn on Randolph is a sophisticated haven celebrated for its gourmet gluten-free breakfasts and snacks. **Pros:** quiet residential neighborhood; gourmet breakfasts; sophisticated decor; romantic setting. **Cons:** a bit of a walk from downtown. Ⓢ *Rooms from: $299* ✉ *411 Randolph St., Napa* ☎ *707/257–2886* ⊕ *www.innonrandolph.com* ⤳ *10 rooms* ❥ *Breakfast.*

$$
B&B/INN

▦**Napa River Inn.** Part of a complex of restaurants, shops, a nightclub, and a spa, this waterfront inn is within easy walking distance of downtown hot spots. **Pros:** wide range of room sizes and prices; near downtown action; pet friendly. **Cons:** river views could be more scenic; some rooms get noise from nearby restaurants. Ⓢ *Rooms from: $299* ✉ *500 Main St., Napa* ☎ *707/251–8500, 877/251–8500* ⊕ *www.napariverinn.com* ⤳ *66 rooms* ❥ *Breakfast.*

10

NIGHTLIFE AND PERFORMING ARTS

Fodor's Choice
★ **Blue Note Napa.** The famed New York jazz room's West Coast club hosts national headliners such as Chris Botti, Dee Dee Bridgewater, and Coco Montoya, along with local talents such as Lavay Smith & Her Red Hot Skillet Lickers. Chef Jessica Sedlacek, formerly of The French Laundry and Bouchon in Yountville, supplies the culinary pizzazz—hearty entrées such as boneless crispy chicken and a massive pork chop, and lighter fare that includes raw oysters, chicken wings, and bacon-inflected potato fritters (an instant hit). ✉ *Napa Valley Opera House, 1030 Main St., at 1st St., Napa* ☎ *707/603–1258* ⊕ *www.bluenotenapa.com.*

Cadet Wine + Beer Bar. Cadet plays things urban-style cool with a long bar, high-top tables, an all-vinyl soundtrack, and a low-lit, generally loungelike feel. The two owners describe their outlook as "unabashedly pro-California," but their lineup of 150-plus wines and beers circles the globe. The crowd here is youngish, the vibe festive. ✉ *930 Franklin St., at end of pedestrian alley between 1st and 2nd Sts., Napa* ☎ *707/224–4400* ⊕ *www.cadetbeerandwinebar.com.*

YOUNTVILLE

9 miles north of the town of Napa.

These days Yountville is something like Disneyland for food lovers. You could stay here for a week and not exhaust all the options—several of them owned by The French Laundry's Thomas Keller—and the tiny town is full of small inns and high-end hotels that cater to those who prefer to walk (not drive) after an extravagant meal. It's also well located for excursions to many big-name Napa wineries, especially those in the Stags Leap District, from which big, bold Cabernet Sauvignons helped make the Napa Valley's wine-making reputation.

GETTING HERE AND AROUND

Downtown Yountville sits just off Highway 29. Approaching from the south take the Yountville exit—from the north take Madison—and proceed to Washington Street, home to the major shops and restaurants. Yountville Cross Road connects downtown to the Silverado Trail, along which many noted wineries do business. The free Yountville Trolley serves the town daily from 10 am to 7 pm (on-call service until 11 except on Sunday).

EXPLORING

TOP ATTRACTIONS

Fodor's Choice
★ **Cliff Lede Vineyards.** Inspired by his passion for classic rock, owner and construction magnate Cliff Lede named the blocks in his Stags Leap District vineyard after hits by the Grateful Dead and other bands. The vibe at his efficient, high-tech winery is anything but laid-back, however. Cutting-edge agricultural and enological science informs the vineyard management and wine making here. Architect Howard Backen designed the winery and its tasting room, where Lede's Sauvignon Blanc, Cabernet Sauvignons, and other wines, along with some from sister winery FEL, which produces much-lauded Anderson Valley Pinot Noirs, are poured. ■TIP➔ Walk-ins are welcome at the tasting bar, but appointments are required for the veranda outside and a nearby gallery that

often displays rock-related art. ✉ *1473 Yountville Cross Rd., off Silverado Trail, Yountville* ☎ *707/944–8642* 🌐 *cliffledevineyards.com* 🎫 *Tastings $30–$50.*

Fodor'sChoice ★ **Ma(i)sonry Napa Valley.** An art-and-design gallery that also pours the wines of about two dozen limited-production wineries, Ma(i)sonry occupies a manor house constructed in 1904 from Napa River stone. Tasting flights of wines by distinguished winemakers such as Heidi Barrett, Philippe Melka, and Thomas Rivers Brown can be sampled in fair weather in the sculpture garden, in a private nook, or at the communal redwood table, and in any weather indoors among the contemporary artworks and well-chosen *objets*—which might include 17th-century furnishings, industrial lamps, or slabs of petrified wood. ■ **TIP→ Walk-ins are welcome, space permitting, but during summer, at harvest, and on weekends and holidays it's best to book in advance.** ✉ *6711 Washington St., at Pedroni St., Yountville* ☎ *707/944–0889* 🌐 *www.maisonry.com* 🎫 *Tasting $35–$55.*

Fodor'sChoice ★ **Stewart Cellars.** Three stone structures meant to mimic Scottish ruins coaxed into modernity form this complex that includes public and private tasting spaces, a bright outdoor patio, and a café with accessible vegan- and carnivore-friendly cuisine. The attention to detail in the ensemble's design mirrors that of the wines, whose grapes come from Stagecoach, Beckstoffer Las Piedras (for the intense Nomad Cabernet), and other coveted vineyards. Although Cabernet is the focus, winemaker Blair Guthrie, with input from consulting winemaker Paul Hobbs, also makes Chardonnay, Pinot Noir, and Merlot. ■ **TIP→ On sunny days this is a good stop around lunchtime, when you can order a meal from the café and a glass of wine from the tasting room—for permit reasons this must be done separately—and enjoy them on the patio.** ✉ *6752 Washington St., near Pedroni St., Yountville* ☎ *707/963–9160* 🌐 *www.stewartcellars.com* 🎫 *Tastings $35–$85.*

WHERE TO EAT

$$$$ MODERN AMERICAN Fodor'sChoice ★ 🍴 **Ad Hoc.** At this low-key dining room with zinc-top tables and wine served in tumblers, superstar chef Thomas Keller offers a single, fixed-price menu nightly, with a small but decadent Sunday brunch. The dinner selection might include smoked beef short ribs with creamy herb rice and charred broccolini, or sesame chicken with radish kimchi and fried rice. **Known for:** casual cuisine; great price for a Thomas Keller meal; don't-miss buttermilk-fried-chicken night. [$] *Average main: $55* ✉ *6476 Washington St., at Oak Circle, Yountville* ☎ *707/944–2487* 🌐 *www.adhocrestaurant.com* ⏲ *No lunch Mon.–Sat.; no dinner Tues. and Wed.* ☞ *Call a day ahead to find out the next day's menu.*

$$$ FRENCH Fodor'sChoice ★ 🍴 **Bistro Jeanty.** Escargots, cassoulet, *daube de boeuf* (beef stewed in red wine), and other French classics are prepared with the utmost precision at this country bistro whose lamb tongue and other obscure delicacies delight daring diners. Regulars often start with the rich tomato soup in a flaky puff pastry before proceeding to sole meunière or coq au vin, completing the French sojourn with warm apple tarte tatin and other authentic desserts. **Known for:** traditional preparations; oh-so-French ambience. [$] *Average main: $27* ✉ *6510 Washington St., at Mulberry St., Yountville* ☎ *707/944–0103* 🌐 *www.bistrojeanty.com.*

$$$ FRENCH Fodor's Choice ★

🍴 **Bouchon.** The team that created The French Laundry is also behind this place, where everything—the lively and crowded zinc-topped bar, the elbow-to-elbow seating, the traditional French onion soup—could have come straight from a Parisian bistro. Roasted chicken with leeks and oyster mushrooms and steamed mussels served with crispy, addictive *frites* (french fries) are among the perfectly executed entrées. **Known for:** bistro classics; rabbit and salmon rillettes. [$] *Average main: $27* ✉ *6534 Washington St., near Humboldt St., Yountville* ☎ *707/944–8037* 🌐 *www.bouchonbistro.com.*

$$$$ AMERICAN Fodor's Choice ★

🍴 **The French Laundry.** An old stone building laced with ivy houses chef Thomas Keller's destination restaurant. Some courses on the two prix-fixe menus, one of which highlights vegetables, rely on luxe ingredients such as *calotte* (cap of the rib eye); other courses take humble elements like fava beans and elevate them to art. **Known for:** signature starter "oysters and pearls"; intricate flavors; superior wine list. [$] *Average main: $310* ✉ *6640 Washington St., at Creek St., Yountville* ☎ *707/944–2380* 🌐 *www.frenchlaundry.com* ⏲ *No lunch Mon.–Thurs.* 👔 *Jacket required* ☞ *Reservations essential weeks ahead (call or check website for precise instructions).*

$$$ AMERICAN

🍴 **Mustards Grill.** Cindy Pawlcyn's Mustards fills day and night with fans of her hearty cuisine, equal parts updated renditions of traditional American dishes—what Pawlcyn dubs "deluxe truck stop classics"—and fanciful contemporary fare. Barbecued baby back pork ribs and a lemon-lime tart piled high with brown-sugar meringue fall squarely in the first category, with sweet corn tamales with tomatillo-avocado salsa and wild mushrooms representing the latter. **Known for:** roadhouse setting; convivial mood; hoppin' bar. [$] *Average main: $27* ✉ *7399 St. Helena Hwy./Hwy. 29, 1 mile north of Yountville, Napa* ☎ *707/944–2424* 🌐 *www.mustardsgrill.com.*

$ LATIN AMERICAN Fodor's Choice ★

🍴 **Protéa Restaurant.** A meal at Yountville's The French Laundry motivated Puerto Rico–born Anita Cartagena to pursue a career as a chef, which she did for several years at nearby Ciccio and elsewhere before opening this perky storefront serving Latin-inspired multi-culti fast-food cuisine. What's in season and the chef's whims determine the order-at-the-counter fare, but Puerto Rican rice bowls (often with pork), empanadas, and sweet-and-sour ramen stir-fries make regular appearances. **Known for:** patio and rooftop seating; beer and wine lineup; eager-to-please staff. [$] *Average main: $13* ✉ *6488 Washington St., at Oak Circle, Yountville* ☎ *707/415–5035* 🌐 *www.proteayv.com.*

$$$ MODERN AMERICAN Fodor's Choice ★

🍴 **Redd.** Chef Richard Reddington's culinary influences include California, Mexico, Europe, and Asia, but his dishes, like his minimalist dining room, feel modern and unfussy. The glazed pork belly with apple puree, set amid a pool of soy caramel, is an example of the East-meets-West style, and the seafood preparations—among them petrale sole, clams, and chorizo poached in a saffron-curry broth—exhibit a similar transcontinental dexterity. **Known for:** five-course tasting menu; street-side outdoor patio; cocktails and small plates at the bar. [$] *Average main: $30* ✉ *6480 Washington St., at Oak Circle, Yountville* ☎ *707/944–2222* 🌐 *www.reddnapavalley.com.*

$$ ITALIAN 🍴 **Redd Wood.** Chef Richard Reddington's casual restaurant specializes in thin-crust wood-fired pizzas and contemporary variations on rustic Italian classics. With sausage soup laced with cabbage and turnip, pizzas such as the white anchovy with herb sauce and mozzarella, and the pork-chop entrée enlivened by persimmon, Redd Wood does for Italian comfort food what nearby Mustards Grill does for the American version: it spruces it up but retains its innate pleasures. **Known for:** industrial decor; easygoing service. [$] *Average main: $21* ✉ *North Block Hotel, 6755 Washington St., at Madison St., Yountville* ☎ *707/299–5030* 🌐 *www.redd-wood.com.*

WHERE TO STAY

$$$$ RESORT Fodor's Choice ★ 🏨 **Bardessono.** Although Bardessono bills itself as the "greenest luxury hotel in America," there's nothing spartan about its accommodations; arranged around four landscaped courtyards, the rooms have luxurious organic bedding, gas fireplaces, and huge bathrooms with walnut floors. **Pros:** large rooftop lap pool; excellent spa, with in-room treatments available. **Cons:** expensive; limited view from some rooms. [$] *Rooms from: $700* ✉ *6526 Yount St., Yountville* ☎ *707/204–6000* 🌐 *www.bardessono.com* 🛏 *62 rooms* 🍴 *No meals.*

$$ B&B/INN 🏨 **Maison Fleurie.** A stay at this comfortable inn places you within easy walking distance of Yountville's fine restaurants. **Pros:** smallest rooms a bargain; outdoor hot tub; pool (open in season); free bike rental. **Cons:** breakfast room can be crowded at peak times. [$] *Rooms from: $219* ✉ *6529 Yount St., Yountville* ☎ *707/944–2056, 800/788–0369* 🌐 *www.maisonfleurienapa.com* 🛏 *13 rooms* 🍴 *Breakfast.*

$$$ HOTEL 🏨 **Napa Valley Lodge.** Clean rooms in a convenient motel-style setting draw travelers willing to pay more than at comparable lodgings in the city of Napa to be within walking distance of Yountville's tasting rooms, restaurants, and shops. **Pros:** clean rooms; filling continental breakfast; large pool area. **Cons:** no elevator; lacks amenities of other Yountville properties. [$] *Rooms from: $350* ✉ *2230 Madison St., Yountville* ☎ *707/944–2468, 888/944–3545* 🌐 *www.napavalleylodge.com* 🛏 *55 rooms* 🍴 *Breakfast.*

$$$$ HOTEL 🏨 **North Block Hotel.** With chic Tuscan style, this 20-room hotel has dark-wood furniture and a brown-and-sage decor. **Pros:** extremely comfortable beds; attentive service; room service by Redd Wood restaurant. **Cons:** outdoor areas get some traffic noise. [$] *Rooms from: $420* ✉ *6757 Washington St., Yountville* ☎ *707/944–8080* 🌐 *northblockhotel.com* 🛏 *20 rooms* 🍴 *No meals.*

SPORTS AND THE OUTDOORS

BALLOONING

Napa Valley Aloft. Between 8 and 12 passengers soar over the Napa Valley in balloons that launch from downtown Yountville. Rates include preflight refreshments and a huge breakfast. ✉ *V Marketplace, 6525 Washington St., near Mulberry St., Yountville* ☎ *707/944–4400, 855/944–4408* 🌐 *www.nvaloft.com* 🎟 *From $220.*

BIKING

FodorsChoice   **Napa Valley Bike Tours.** With dozens of wineries within 5 miles, this shop
★   makes a fine starting point for guided and self-guided vineyard and
wine-tasting excursions. The outfit also rents bikes. ✉ *6500 Washington
St., at Mulberry St., Yountville* ☎ *707/944–2953* ⊕ *www.napavalleybik-
etours.com* 🖙 *From $124 (½-day guided tour).*

SPAS

FodorsChoice   **The Spa at Bardessono.** Many of this spa's patrons are hotel guests who
★   take their treatments in their rooms' large, customized bathrooms—all
of them equipped with concealed massage tables—but the main facility
is open to guests and nonguests alike. An in-room treatment popular
with couples starts with massages in front of the fireplace and ends
with a whirlpool bath and a split of sparkling wine. For the two-hour
Yountville Signature treatment, which can be enjoyed in-room or at
the spa, a shea-butter-enriched sugar scrub is applied, followed by a
massage with antioxidant Chardonnay grape-seed oil and a hydrating
hair-and-scalp treatment. The spa engages massage therapists skilled in
Swedish, Thai, and several other techniques. In addition to massages,
the services include facials, waxing, and other skin-care treatments, as
well as manicures and pedicures. ✉ *Bardessono Hotel, 6526 Yount St.,
at Mulberry St., Yountville* ☎ *707/204–6050* ⊕ *www.bardessono.com/
spa* 🖙 *Treatments $60–$630.*

SHOPPING

V Marketplace. This two-story redbrick market, which once housed a
winery, a livery stable, and a brandy distillery, now contains clothing
boutiques, art galleries, a chocolatier, and food, wine, and gift shops.
Celebrity chef Michael Chiarello operates a restaurant (Bottega), a tasting room for his wines, and Ottimo, with pizza, fresh mozzarella, and
other stands plus retail items. Show some love to the shops upstairs,
especially Knickers and Pearls (lingerie and loungewear), Montecristi
Panama Hats (Johnny Depp found one he liked), and Lemondrops
(kids' clothing and toys). ✉ *6525 Washington St., near Mulberry St.,
Yountville* ☎ *707/944–2451* ⊕ *www.vmarketplace.com.*

OAKVILLE

2 miles northwest of Yountville.

A large butte that runs east–west just north of Yountville blocks the
cooling fogs from the south, facilitating the myriad microclimates of
the Oakville AVA, home to several high-profile wineries.

GETTING HERE AND AROUND

Driving along Highway 29, you'll know you've reached Oakville
when you see the Oakville Grocery on the east side of the road. You
can reach Oakville from the Sonoma County town of Glen Ellen by
heading east on Trinity Road from Highway 12. The twisting route,
along the mountain range that divides Napa and Sonoma, eventually
becomes the Oakville Grade. The views on this drive are breathtaking,
though the continual curves make it unsuitable for those who suffer
from motion sickness.

EXPLORING
TOP ATTRACTIONS

B Cellars. The chefs take center stage in the open-hearth kitchen of this boutique winery's hospitality house, and with good reason: creating food-friendly wines is B Cellars's raison d'être. Visits to the Oakville facility—all steel beams, corrugated metal, and plate glass yet remarkably cozy—begin with a tour of the winery's culinary garden and caves. Most guests return to the house to sample wines paired with small bites, with some visitors remaining in the caves for exclusive tastings of Cabernet Sauvignons from several historic vineyards of Andy Beckstoffer, a prominent grower. Kirk Venge, whose fruit-forward style well suits the winery's food-oriented approach, crafts these and other wines, among them red and white blends and single-vineyard Cabernets from other noteworthy vineyards. ■TIP→ The B Cellars wine-and-food pairings, all strictly by appointment, are outstanding. ⊠ *703 Oakville Cross Rd., west of Silverado Trail, Oakville* ☎ *707/709–8787* ⊕ *www.bcellars.com* ✉ *Tastings $37–$135.*

Fodor's Choice
★
Far Niente. Guests arriving at Far Niente are welcomed by name and treated to a glimpse of one of the Napa Valley's most beautiful properties. By appointment only, small groups are escorted through the historic 1885 stone winery, including some of the 40,000 square feet of aging caves, for a lesson on the labor-intensive method of making Far Niente's flagship wines: a Cabernet Sauvignon blend and a Chardonnay. Next on the agenda is a peek at the Carriage House, which holds a gleaming collection of classic cars. The seated tasting of wines and cheeses that follows concludes on a sweet note with Dolce, a late-harvest wine made from Semillon and Sauvignon Blanc grapes. ⊠ *1350 Acacia Dr., off Oakville Grade Rd., Oakville* ☎ *707/944–2861* ⊕ *www. farniente.com* ✉ *Tasting and tour $75.*

Fodor's Choice
★
Silver Oak. The first review of this winery's Napa Valley Cabernet Sauvignon declared the debut 1972 vintage not all that good and, at $6 a bottle, overpriced. Oops. The celebrated Bordeaux-style Cabernet blend, still the only Napa Valley wine bearing its winery's label each year, evolved into a cult favorite, and Silver Oak founders Ray Duncan and Justin Meyer received worldwide recognition for their signature use of exclusively American oak to age the wines. At the Oakville tasting room, constructed out of reclaimed stone and other materials from a 19th-century Kansas flour mill, you can sip the current Napa Valley vintage, its counterpart from Silver Oak's Alexander Valley operation, and a library wine without an appointment. One is required for tours, private tastings, and food-wine pairings. ⊠ *915 Oakville Cross Rd., off Hwy. 29, Oakville* ☎ *707/942–7022* ⊕ *www.silveroak.com* ✉ *Tastings $30–$75, tour $50 (includes tasting).*

10

RUTHERFORD

2 miles northwest of Oakville.

With its singular microclimate and soil, Rutherford is an important viticultural center, with more big-name wineries than you can shake a corkscrew at. Cabernet Sauvignon is king here. The well-drained, loamy soil is ideal for those vines, and since this part of the valley gets plenty of sun, the grapes develop exceptionally intense flavors.

GETTING HERE AND AROUND

Wineries around Rutherford are dotted along Highway 29 and the parallel Silverado Trail north and south of Rutherford Road/Conn Creek Road, on which wineries can also be found.

EXPLORING

TOP ATTRACTIONS

FAMILY

Fodor's Choice

★

Frog's Leap. John Williams, owner of Frog's Leap, maintains a sense of humor about wine that translates into an entertaining yet informative experience—if you're a novice, the tour here is a fun way to begin your education. You'll taste wines that might include Zinfandel, Merlot, Chardonnay, Sauvignon Blanc, and an estate-grown Cabernet Sauvignon. The winery includes a barn built in 1884, 5 acres of organic gardens, an eco-friendly visitor center, and a frog pond topped with lily pads. Reservations are required for all visits here. ■TIP→ The tour is recommended, but you can also just sample wines either inside or on a porch overlooking the garden. ⊠ 8815 Conn Creek Rd., Rutherford ☎ 707/963–4704, 800/959–4704 ⊕ www.frogsleap.com ⌨ Tastings $20–$25; tour $25.

Inglenook. Filmmaker Francis Ford Coppola began his wine-making career in 1975, when he bought part of the historic Inglenook estate. Over the decades he reunited the original property acquired by Inglenook founder Gustave Niebaum, remodeled Niebaum's ivy-covered 1880s château, and purchased the rights to the Inglenook name. The Inglenook Experience ($50), an escorted tour of the château, vineyards, and caves, ends with a seated tasting of wines paired with artisanal cheeses. Among the topics discussed are the winery's history and the evolution of Coppola's signature wine, Rubicon, a Cabernet Sauvignon–based blend. The Heritage Tasting ($45), which also includes a Rubicon pour, is held in the opulent Pennino Salon. Reservations are required for some tastings and tours, and are recommended for all. ■TIP→ Walk-ins can sip wines by the glass or bottle at The Bistro, a wine bar with a picturesque courtyard. ⊠ 1991 St. Helena Hwy./Hwy. 29, at Hwy.128, Rutherford ☎ 707/968–1100, 800/782–4266 ⊕ www.inglenook.com ⌨ Tastings $45–$50, private experiences from $75.

Mumm Napa. In Mumm's light-filled tasting room or adjacent outdoor patio you can enjoy bubbly by the flight, but the sophisticated sparkling wines, elegant setting, and vineyard views aren't the only reasons to visit. An excellent gallery displays original Ansel Adams prints and presents temporary exhibitions by premier photographers. Winery tours cover the major steps in making sparklers. For a leisurely tasting of several vintages of the top-of-the-line DVX wines, book an Oak Terrace tasting ($50; reservations recommended Friday through Sunday). ■TIP→ Carlos Santana fans may want to taste the sparklers the musician makes in collaboration with Mumm's winemaker, Ludovic Dervin. ⊠ 8445 Silverado Trail, 1 mile south of Rutherford Cross Rd., Rutherford ☎ 707/967–7700, 800/686–6272 ⊕ www.mummnapa.com ⌨ Tastings $20–$50, tour $40 (includes tasting).

Frog's Leap's picturesque country charm extends all the way to the white picket fence.

WHERE TO EAT AND STAY

$$$$ MODERN AMERICAN Fodor's Choice ★ 🍴 **Restaurant at Auberge du Soleil.** Possibly the most romantic roost for a dinner in all the Wine Country is a terrace seat at the Auberge du Soleil resort's illustrious restaurant, and the Mediterranean-inflected cuisine more than matches the dramatic vineyard views. The prix-fixe dinner menu, which relies largely on local produce, might include veal sweetbreads and chanterelles in a caramelized shallot sauce or prime beef pavé with hearts of palm, lobster mushrooms, and bok choy. **Known for:** polished service; comprehensive wine list; over-the-top weekend brunch. [$] *Average main: $115* ✉ *Auberge du Soleil, 180 Rutherford Hill Rd., off Silverado Trail, Rutherford* ☎ *707/963–1211, 800/348–5406* 🌐 *www.aubergedusoleil.com.*

$$$ AMERICAN Fodor's Choice ★ 🍴 **Rutherford Grill.** Dark-wood walls, subdued lighting, and red leather banquettes make for a perpetually clubby mood at this trusty Rutherford hangout. Many entrées—steaks, burgers, fish, succulent rotisserie chicken, and barbecued pork ribs—emerge from an oak-fired grill operated by master technicians. **Known for:** French dip sandwich; reasonably priced wine list. [$] *Average main: $29* ✉ *1180 Rutherford Rd., at Hwy. 29, Rutherford* ☎ *707/963–1792* 🌐 *www.rutherfordgrill.com.*

$$$$ RESORT Fodor's Choice ★ 🏨 **Auberge du Soleil.** Taking a cue from the olive-tree-studded landscape, this hotel with a renowned restaurant and spa cultivates a luxurious look that blends French and California style. **Pros:** stunning views over the valley; spectacular pool and spa areas; the most expensive suites are fit for a superstar. **Cons:** stratospheric prices; least expensive rooms get some noise from the bar and restaurant. [$] *Rooms from: $875* ✉ *180 Rutherford Hill Rd., Rutherford* ☎ *707/963–1211, 800/348–5406* 🌐 *www.aubergedusoleil.com* 🛏 *50 rooms* 🍽 *Breakfast.*

ST. HELENA

2 miles northwest of Oakville.

Downtown St. Helena is a symbol of how well life can be lived in the Wine Country. Sycamore trees arch over Main Street (Highway 29), a funnel of outstanding restaurants and tempting boutiques. At the north end of town looms the hulking stone building of the Culinary Institute of America at Greystone. Weathered stone and brick buildings from the late 1800s give off that gratifying whiff of history.

The town got its start in 1854, when Henry Still built a store. Still wanted company, so he donated land lots on his town site to anyone who wanted to erect a business. Soon he was joined by a wagon shop, a shoe shop, hotels, and churches. Dr. George Crane planted a vineyard in 1858, and was the first to produce wine in commercially viable quantities. A German winemaker named Charles Krug followed suit a couple of years later, and other wineries soon followed.

GETTING HERE AND AROUND

Downtown stretches along Highway 29, called Main Street here. Many wineries lie north and south of downtown along Highway 29. More can be found off Silverado Trail, and some of the most scenic spots are on Spring Mountain, which rises southwest of town.

EXPLORING
TOP ATTRACTIONS

Charles Krug Winery. A historically sensitive renovation of its 1874 Redwood Cellar Building transformed the former production facility of the Napa Valley's oldest winery into an epic hospitality center. Charles Krug, a Prussian immigrant, established the winery in 1861 and ran it until his death in 1892. Italian immigrants Cesare Mondavi and his wife, Rosa, purchased Krug in 1943, and operated it with their sons Peter and Robert (who later opened his own winery). Krug, still run by Peter's family, specializes in small-lot Yountville and Howell Mountain Cabernet Sauvignons and makes Chardonnay, Merlot, Pinot Noir, Sauvignon Blanc, Zinfandel, and a Zinfandel port. The tour is by appointment only. ■TIP➜ To sample the small-lot Cabernets, book a Family Reserve & Limited Release Tasting ($40). ⊠ *2800 Main St./ Hwy. 29, across from the Culinary Institute of America, St. Helena* ☎ *707/967–2229* ⊕ *www.charleskrug.com* ✉ *Tastings $20–$40, tour $60 (includes tasting).*

Fodor's Choice ★ **Hall St. Helena.** The Cabernet Sauvignons produced here are works of art and the latest in organic-farming science and wine-making technology. A glass-walled tasting room allows guests to see in action some of the high-tech equipment winemaker Steve Leveque employs to craft wines that also include Merlot, Cabernet Franc, and Sauvignon Blanc. Westward from the second-floor tasting area, rows of neatly spaced Cabernet vines capture the eye, and beyond them the tree-studded Mayacamas Mountains. The main guided tour takes in the facility, the grounds, and a restored 19th-century winery, passing by artworks—inside and out—by John Baldessari, Jaume Plensa, Jesús Moroles, and other contemporary talents. ■TIP➜ Among the engaging seminars here is the

Ultimate Cabernet Experience ($125), the winery's flagship tasting of current and library releases, as well as wines still aging in barrel. ✉ *401 St. Helena Hwy./Hwy. 29, near White La., St. Helena* ☎ *707/967–2626* ⊕ *www.hallwines.com* ✑ *Tastings $40–$250, tours $40–$50.*

Fodor's Choice **Joseph Phelps Vineyards.** An appointment is required for tastings at the
★ winery started by the late Joseph Phelps, but it's well worth the effort—all the more so after an inspired renovation of the main redwood structure, a classic of 1970s Northern California architecture. Known for wines crafted with grace and precision, Phelps does produce fine whites, but the blockbusters are red, particularly the Cabernet Sauvignon and the luscious-yet-subtle Bordeaux-style blend called Insignia. In good weather, one-hour seated tastings take place on a terrace overlooking vineyards and oaks. At 90-minute tastings as thoughtfully conceived as the wines, guests explore such topics as wine-and-cheese pairing, wine blending, and the role oak barrels play in wine making. Participants in the blending seminar mix the various varietals that go into the Insignia blend. ✉ *200 Taplin Rd., off Silverado Trail, St. Helena* ☎ *707/963–2745, 800/707–5789* ⊕ *www.josephphelps.com* ✑ *Tastings and seminars $75–$200.*

Pride Mountain Vineyards. This winery 2,200 feet up Spring Mountain straddles Napa and Sonoma counties, confusing enough for visitors but even more complicated for the wine-making staff: government regulations require separate wineries and paperwork for each side of the property. It's one of several amusing Pride Mountain quirks, but winemaker Sally Johnson's "big red wines," including a Cabernet Sauvignon that earned 100-point scores from a major wine critic two years in a row, are serious business. At tastings and on tours you can learn about the farming and cellar strategies behind Pride's acclaimed Cabs (the winery also produces Syrah, a Cab-like Merlot, Viognier, and Chardonnay among others). The tour, which takes in vineyards and caves, also includes tastings of wine still in barrel. ■**TIP➔ The views here are knock-your-socks-off gorgeous.** ✉ *4026 Spring Mountain Rd., off St. Helena Rd. (extension of Spring Mountain Rd. in Sonoma County), St. Helena* ☎ *707/963–4949* ⊕ *www.pridewines.com* ✑ *Tastings $20–$75.*

10

WORTH NOTING

Beringer Vineyards. Brothers Frederick and Jacob Beringer opened the winery that still bears their name in 1876. One of California's earliest bonded wineries, it is the oldest one in the Napa Valley never to have missed a vintage—no mean feat, given Prohibition. Frederick's grand Rhine House Mansion, built in 1884, serves as the reserve tasting room. Here, surrounded by Belgian art-nouveau hand-carved oak and walnut furniture and stained-glass windows, you can sample wines that include a limited-release Chardonnay, a few big Cabernets, and a Sauterne-style dessert wine. A less expensive tasting takes place in the original stone winery. Reservations are required for some tastings and recommended for tours. ■**TIP➔ The one-hour Taste of Beringer ($50) tour of the property and sensory gardens surveys the winery's history and wine making and concludes with a seated wine-and-food pairing.** ✉ *2000 Main St./Hwy. 29, near Pratt Ave., St. Helena* ☎ *707/963–8989, 866/708–9463* ⊕ *www.beringer.com* ✑ *Tastings $25–$125, tours $30–$50.*

Culinary Institute of America at Greystone. The West Coast headquarters of the country's leading school for chefs is in the 1889 Greystone Cellars, an imposing building once the world's largest stone winery. On the ground floor you can check out the quirky Corkscrew Museum and browse the Spice Islands Marketplace shop, stocked with gleaming gadgets and many cookbooks. The Bakery Café by illy serves soups, salads, sandwiches, and baked goods. One-day and multiday cooking and beverage classes take place weekly, public cooking demonstrations on weekends. Students run the Gatehouse Restaurant, which serves lunch and dinner except during semester breaks. ✉ *2555 Main St./Hwy. 29, St. Helena* ☎ *707/967–1100* 🌐 *www.ciachef.edu/california* 🎫 *Museum free, cooking demonstrations $25, class prices vary.*

WHERE TO EAT

$$ MODERN AMERICAN Fodor's Choice ★ 🍴 **Cindy's Backstreet Kitchen.** At her up-valley outpost, Cindy Pawlcyn serves variations on the comfort food she made popular at Mustards Grill, but spices things up with dishes influenced by Mexican, Central American, and occasionally Asian cuisines. Along with staples such as meat loaf with garlic mashed potatoes and beef and duck burgers served with impeccable fries, the menu might include a rabbit tostada or curried chicken salad. **Known for:** warm pineapple upside-down cake; ethereal parfait. [$] *Average main: $22* ✉ *1327 Railroad Ave., at Hunt St., 1 block east of Main St., St. Helena* ☎ *707/963–1200* 🌐 *www.cindysbackstreetkitchen.com.*

$$ ITALIAN Fodor's Choice ★ 🍴 **Cook St. Helena.** A curved marble bar spotlit by contemporary art-glass pendants adds a touch of style to this downtown restaurant whose Northern Italian cuisine pleases with similarly understated sophistication. Mussels with house-made sausage in a spicy tomato broth, chopped salad with pancetta and pecorino, and the daily changing risotto are among the dishes regulars revere. **Known for:** top-quality ingredients; reasonably priced local and international wines; Cook Tavern two doors down for beer, wine, and cocktail-friendly small plates. [$] *Average main: $22* ✉ *1310 Main St., near Hunt Ave., St. Helena* ☎ *707/963–7088* 🌐 *www.cooksthelena.com.*

$$$ MODERN AMERICAN 🍴 **Farmstead at Long Meadow Ranch.** Housed in a high-ceilinged former barn, Farmstead revolves around an open kitchen where executive chef Stephen Barber's team prepares meals with grass-fed beef and lamb, fruits and vegetables, eggs, olive oil, wine, honey, and other ingredients from parent company Long Meadow Ranch. Entrées might include wood-grilled trout with fennel, brussels sprouts, pears, and hazelnuts, or a pork chop with broccolini, jalapeño grits, and apple chutney. **Known for:** Tuesday fried-chicken night; house-made charcuterie; seasonal cocktails. [$] *Average main: $24* ✉ *738 Main St., at Charter Oak Ave., St. Helena* ☎ *707/963–4555* 🌐 *www.longmeadowranch.com/farmstead-restaurant.*

$$$ MODERN AMERICAN Fodor's Choice ★ 🍴 **Goose & Gander.** The pairing of food and drink at G&G is as likely to involve cool cocktails as wine. Main courses such as grilled sturgeon, pork loin with sweet-potato hash, and Wagyu beef with Bordelaise sauce work well with starters that might include lamb merguez toast and mushroom soup from wild and cultivated fungi. **Known for:** intimate main dining room with fireplace; alfresco dining on patio in good weather; basement bar among Napa's best drinking spots. [$] *Average*

main: $29 ✉ 1245 Spring St., at Oak St., St. Helena ☎ 707/967–8779 🌐 www.goosegander.com.

$ AMERICAN 🍴 **Gott's Roadside.** A 1950s-style outdoor hamburger stand goes upscale at this spot whose customers brave long lines to order breakfast sandwiches, juicy burgers, root-beer floats, and garlic fries. Choices not available a half century ago include the ahi tuna burger and the chili-spice-marinated chicken breast served with Mexican slaw. **Known for:** tasty (if pricey) 21st-century diner cuisine; shaded picnic tables (arrive early or late for lunch to get one); second branch at Napa's Oxbow Public Market. [$] *Average main: $13 ✉ 933 Main St./Hwy. 29, St. Helena ☎ 707/963–3486 🌐 www.gotts.com ☞ Reservations not accepted.*

$$$$ MODERN AMERICAN 🍴 **Press.** Few taste sensations surpass the combination of a sizzling steak and a Napa Valley red, a union the chef and sommeliers at Press celebrate with a reverence bordering on obsession. Grass-fed beef cooked on the cherry-and-almond-wood-fired grill and rotisserie is the star—especially the rib eye for two—but the cooks also prepare pork chops, free-range chicken, fish, and even vegetarian dishes such as carrot and yellow-eye bean cassoulet. **Known for:** extensive wine cellar; impressive cocktails; casual-chic ambience. [$] *Average main: $48 ✉ 587 St. Helena Hwy./Hwy. 29, at White La., St. Helena ☎ 707/967–0550 🌐 www.pressstheleena.com ⏲ Closed Tues. No lunch.*

$$$$ MODERN AMERICAN Fodor's Choice ★ 🍴 **The Restaurant at Meadowood.** Chef Christopher Kostow has garnered rave reviews—and three Michelin stars for several years running—for creating a unique dining experience. Patrons choosing the Tasting Menu option ($275 per person) enjoy their meals in the dining room, its beautiful finishes aglow with warm lighting, but up to four guests can select the Counter Menu ($500 per person) for the chance to sit in the kitchen and watch Kostow's team prepare the food. **Known for:** complex cuisine; first-class service; romantic setting. [$] *Average main: $275 ✉ 900 Meadowood La., off Silverado Trail N, St. Helena ☎ 707/967–1205, 800/458–8080 🌐 www.therestaurantatmeadowood.com ⏲ Closed Sun. No lunch ☞ Jacket suggested but not required.*

$$$$ MEDITERRANEAN Fodor's Choice ★ 🍴 **Terra.** In an 1884 fieldstone building, chef Hiro Sone gives an unexpected twist to Italian and southern French cuisine, though for a few dishes, among them the signature sake-marinated black cod in a shiso broth, he draws on his Japanese background. Homey yet elegant desserts, courtesy of Sone's wife, Lissa Doumani, might include a chocolate mousseline with chocolate–peanut butter crunch and toasted marshmallow. **Known for:** prix-fixe menu; old-school romance and service; Bar Terra for cocktails, lighter fare à la carte. [$] *Average main: $85 ✉ 1345 Railroad Ave., off Hunt Ave., St. Helena ☎ 707/963–8931 🌐 www.terrarestaurant.com ⏲ Closed Tues. No lunch.*

WHERE TO STAY

$ HOTEL 🏨 **El Bonita Motel.** The tidy rooms at this roadside motel are nice enough for budget-minded travelers, and the landscaped grounds and picnic tables put this property a cut above similar accommodations. **Pros:** cheerful rooms; hot tub; microwaves and mini-refrigerators. **Cons:** road noise is a problem in some rooms. [$] *Rooms from: $196 ✉ 195 Main St./Hwy. 29, St. Helena ☎ 707/963–3216, 800/541–3284 🌐 www.elbonita.com 🛏 52 rooms 🍽 Breakfast.*

$$$ ⊡ **Harvest Inn by Charlie Palmer.** Although this inn sits just off High-
HOTEL way 29, its patrons remain mostly above the fray, strolling 8 acres
of landscaped gardens, enjoying views of the vineyards adjoining the
property, partaking in spa services, and drifting to sleep in beds adorned
with fancy linens and down pillows. **Pros:** garden setting; spacious
rooms; well-trained staff. **Cons:** some lower-price rooms lack elegance;
high weekend rates. Ⓢ *Rooms from: $354* ⊠ *1 Main St., St. Helena*
☎ *707/963–9463, 800/950–8466* ⊕ *www.harvestinn.com* ↵ *78 rooms*
†⊙*Breakfast.*

$$$$ ⊡ **Meadowood Napa Valley.** Founded in 1964 as a country club, Meado-
RESORT wood has evolved into a five-star resort, a gathering place for Napa's
Fodor's Choice wine-making community, and a celebrated dining destination. **Pros:**
★ superb restaurant; hiking trails; gracious service; all-organic spa. **Cons:**
very expensive; far from downtown St. Helena. Ⓢ *Rooms from: $650*
⊠ *900 Meadowood La., St. Helena* ☎ *707/963–3646, 800/458–8080*
⊕ *www.meadowood.com* ↵ *85 rooms* †⊙ *No meals.*

CALISTOGA

3 miles northwest of St. Helena.

With false-fronted, Old West–style shops and 19th-century inns and
hotels lining its main drag, Lincoln Avenue, Calistoga comes across as
more down-to-earth than its more polished neighbors. Don't be fooled,
though. On its outskirts lie some of the Wine Country's swankest (and
priciest) resorts and its most fanciful piece of architecture, the medieval-
style Castello di Amorosa winery.

Calistoga was developed as a spa-oriented getaway from the start. Sam
Brannan, a gold rush–era entrepreneur, planned to use the area's natural
hot springs as the centerpiece of a resort complex. His venture failed,
but old-time hotels and bathhouses—along with some glorious new
spas—still operate. You can come for an old-school mud bath, or go
completely 21st century and experience lavish treatments based on the
latest innovations in skin and body care.

GETTING HERE AND AROUND
Highway 29 heads east (turn right) at Calistoga, where in town it is
signed as Lincoln Avenue. If arriving via the Silverado Trail, head west
at Highway 29/Lincoln Avenue.

EXPLORING
TOP ATTRACTIONS
Ca' Toga Galleria d'Arte. The boundless wit, whimsy, and creativity of
the Venetian-born Carlo Marchiori, this gallery's owner-artist, finds
expression in paintings, watercolors, ceramics, sculptures, and other
artworks. Marchiori often draws on mythology and folktales for his
inspiration. A stop at this magical gallery may inspire you to tour **Villa
Ca' Toga,** the artist's fanciful Palladian home, a tromp-l'oeil tour de
force open for tours from May through October on Saturday mornings
only, by appointment. ⊠ *1206 Cedar St., near Lincoln Ave., Calistoga*
☎ *707/942–3900* ⊕ *www.catoga.com* ⊘ *Closed Tues. and Wed.*

Fodor's Choice
★
Schramsberg. On a Diamond Mountain site first planted to grapes in the early 1860s, Schramsberg produces sparkling wines using the *méthode traditionnelle* (aka *méthode champenoise*). A fascinating tour covering Schramberg's history and wine-making techniques precedes the tasting. In addition to glimpsing the winery's historic architecture you'll visit caves, some dug in the 1870s by Chinese laborers, where 2 million–plus bottles are stacked in gravity-defying configurations. Tastings include generous pours of very different bubblies. To learn more about them, consider attending the session at which the wines are paired with cheeses; not held every day, this tasting focuses on the ways wine influences our experience of food and vice versa. All visits here are by appointment. ✉ *1400 Schramsberg Rd., off Hwy. 29, Calistoga* ☎ *707/942–4558, 800/877–3623* ⊕ *www.schramsberg.com* 🍷 *Tastings and tours $65–$120.*

Fodor's Choice
★
Venge Vineyards. As the son of Nils Venge, the first winemaker to earn a 100-point score from the wine critic Robert Parker, Kirk Venge had a hard act to follow. Now a consultant to exclusive wineries himself, Kirk is an acknowledged master of balanced, fruit-forward Bordeaux-style blends. At his casual ranch-house tasting room you can sip wines that might include the estate Bone Ash Cabernet Sauvignon, an Oakville Merlot, a Syrah from the Stagecoach Vineyard in the Vaca hills, and the Silencieux Cabernet, a blend of grapes from several appellations. Tastings are by appointment only. ■**TIP**➔ With its views of the well-manicured Bone Ash Vineyard and, west across the valley, Diamond Mountain, the ranch house's porch would make for a magical perch even if Venge's wines weren't works of art in themselves. ✉ *4708 Silverado Trail, 1½ miles south of downtown, near Dunaweal La., Calistoga* ☎ *707/942–9100* ⊕ *www.vengevineyards.com* 🍷 *Tasting $25* ⊙ *Reservations recommended 3–4 wks in advance for weekend visits.*

WORTH NOTING

Castello di Amorosa. An astounding medieval structure complete with drawbridge and moat, chapel, stables, and secret passageways, the Castello commands Diamond Mountain's lower eastern slope. Some of the 107 rooms contain replicas of 13th-century frescoes (cheekily signed, "[the-artist's-name].com"), and the dungeon has an iron maiden from Nuremberg, Germany. You must pay for a tour to see most of Dario Sattui's extensive eight-level property, though with a basic tasting you'll have access to part of the complex. Bottlings of note include several Italian-style wines, including La Castellana, a robust "super Tuscan" blend of Cabernet Sauvignon, Sangiovese, and Merlot; and Il Barone, a deliberately big Cab made largely from Rutherford grapes. ■**TIP**➔ The two-hour Royal Food & Wine Pairing Tour by sommelier Mary Davidek ($85, by appointment only) is among the Wine Country's best. ✉ *4045 N. St. Helena Hwy./Hwy. 29, near Maple La., Calistoga* ☎ *707/967–6272* ⊕ *www.castellodiamorosa.com* 🍷 *Tastings $25–$35, tours $40–$85 (include tastings).*

Chateau Montelena. Set amid a bucolic northern Calistoga landscape, this winery helped establish the Napa Valley's reputation for high-quality wine making. At the pivotal Paris tasting of 1976, the Chateau Montelena 1973 Chardonnay took first place, beating out four white

10

All it needs is a fair maiden: Castello di Amorosa's re-created castle.

Burgundies from France and five other California Chardonnays, an event immortalized in the 2008 movie *Bottle Shock*. A 21st-century Napa Valley Chardonnay is always part of a Current Release Tasting ($25)—the winery also makes Sauvignon Blanc, Riesling, a fine estate Zinfandel, and Cabernet Sauvignon—or you can opt for a Limited Release Tasting ($50) focusing more on Cabernets. The walking Estate Tour takes in the grounds and covers the history of this stately property whose stone winery building was erected in 1888. Guests board a vehicle for the seasonal Vineyard Tour. Tours and some tastings require a reservation. ✉ *1429 Tubbs La., off Hwy. 29, Calistoga* ☎ *707/942–5105* ⊕ *www.montelena.com* 🍷 *Tastings $25–$75, tours $40–$78.*

Tamber Bey Vineyards. Endurance riders Barry and Jennifer Waitte share their passion for horses and wine at their glam-rustic winery north of Calistoga. Their 22-acre Sundance Ranch remains a working equestrian facility, but the site has been revamped to include a state-of-the-art winery with separate fermenting tanks for grapes from Tamber Bey's vineyards in Yountville, Oakville, and elsewhere. The winemakers produce three Chardonnays and a Sauvignon Blanc, but the stars are several subtly powerful reds, including the flagship Oakville Cabernet Sauvignon and a Yountville Merlot. A recent vintage of the top-selling wine, the Rabicano blend, contained Cabernet Sauvignon, Merlot, Petit Verdot, and Cabernet Franc. Visits to taste or tour require an appointment. ✉ *1251 Tubbs La., at Myrtledale Rd., Calistoga* ☎ *707/942–2100* ⊕ *www.tamberbey.com* 🍷 *Tastings $35–$65, tour $10 extra.*

WHERE TO EAT

$$$
MODERN
AMERICAN
Fodor'sChoice
★

✗**Evangeline.** Brandon Sharp, formerly of nearby Solbar, opened this restaurant whose gas-lamp-style lighting fixtures, charcoal-black hues, and bistro cuisine evoke old New Orleans with a California twist. Executive chef Gustavo Rios puts a jaunty spin on dishes that might include shrimp étouffée or grilled salmon with a chicory salad; the elaborate weekend brunch, with everything from buttermilk waffles to shrimp po'boys, is an up-valley favorite. **Known for:** outdoor courtyard; palate-cleansing Sazeracs and signature old-fashioneds; gumbo ya-ya and addictive fried pickles. $ *Average main: $24* ✉ *1226 Washington St., near Lincoln Ave., Calistoga* ☎ *707/341–3131* ⊕ *www.evangelinenapa.com* ☽ *No lunch weekdays.*

$$
MODERN
AMERICAN

✗**Sam's Social Club.** Tourists, locals, and spa guests—some of the latter in bathrobes after treatments—assemble at this resort restaurant for breakfast, lunch, bar snacks, or dinner. Lunch options include pizzas, sandwiches, an aged-cheddar burger, and entrées such as chicken paillard, with the burger reappearing for dinner along with grilled salmon, rib-eye steak frites, and similar fare, perhaps preceded by oysters and other cocktail-friendly starters. **Known for:** casual atmosphere; active patio scene; thin-crust lunch pizzas. $ *Average main: $22* ✉ *Indian Springs Resort and Spa, 1712 Lincoln Ave., at Wappo Ave., Calistoga* ☎ *707/942–4969* ⊕ *www.samssocialclub.com.*

$$$$
MODERN
AMERICAN
Fodor'sChoice
★

✗**Solbar.** As befits a restaurant at a spa resort, the sophisticated menu at Solbar is divided into "healthy, lighter dishes" and "hearty cuisine," with the stellar wine list's many half-bottle selections encouraging moderation, too. On the lighter side, grilled yellowfin tuna might come with charred carrots, mole amarillo, and toasted pumpkin seeds, with heartier options recently including a wood-grilled pork tenderloin with jasmine rice, chili-laced cashews, and mustard greens. **Known for:** stylish dining room; festive outdoor patio; Sunday brunch. $ *Average main: $33* ✉ *Solage Calistoga, 755 Silverado Trail, at Rosedale Rd., Calistoga* ☎ *877/684–9146* ⊕ *www.solagecalistoga.com/solbar.*

WHERE TO STAY

$$$$
RESORT
Fodor'sChoice
★

🏠**Calistoga Ranch.** Spacious cedar-shingle lodges throughout this posh wooded property have outdoor living areas, and even the restaurant, spa, and reception space have outdoor seating and fireplaces. **Pros:** many lodges have private hot tubs on the deck; lovely hiking trails on the property; guests have reciprocal facility privileges at Auberge du Soleil and Solage Calistoga. **Cons:** innovative indoor-outdoor organization works better in fine weather than in rain or cold. $ *Rooms from: $895* ✉ *580 Lommel Rd., Calistoga* ☎ *707/254–2800, 855/942–4220* ⊕ *www.calistogaranch.com* ⤳ *50 guest lodges* ⓘⓞⓘ *No meals.*

$$
B&B/INN
Fodor'sChoice
★

🏠**Embrace Calistoga.** Extravagant hospitality defines the Napa Valley's luxury properties, but Embrace Calistoga—the renamed Luxe Calistoga still run by the same attentive owners—takes the prize in the "small lodging" category. **Pros:** attentive owners; marvelous breakfasts; restaurants, tasting rooms, and shopping within walking distance. **Cons:** the hum of street traffic. $ *Rooms from: $269* ✉ *1139 Lincoln Ave., Calistoga* ☎ *707/942–9797* ⤳ *5 rooms* ⓘⓞⓘ *Breakfast.*

10

$$ RESORT
Indian Springs Resort and Spa. Stylish Indian Springs—operating as a spa since 1862—ably splits the difference between laid-back and chic in accommodations that include lodge rooms, dozens of suites, 14 duplex cottages, three stand-alone bungalows, and two houses. **Pros:** palm-studded grounds with outdoor seating areas; on-site Sam's Social Club restaurant; enormous mineral pool. **Cons:** lodge rooms are small. [$] *Rooms from: $239* ✉ *1712 Lincoln Ave., Calistoga* ☎ *707/942–4913* 🌐 *www.indianspringscalistoga.com* 🛏 *113 rooms* 🍴 *No meals.*

$$$$ RESORT
Fodor's Choice ★
Solage Calistoga. The aesthetic at this 22-acre property is Napa Valley barn meets San Francisco loft: guest rooms have high ceilings, polished concrete floors, recycled walnut furniture, and all-natural fabrics in soothingly muted colors. **Pros:** great service; complimentary bikes; separate pools for kids and adults. **Cons:** vibe may not suit everyone. [$] *Rooms from: $530* ✉ *755 Silverado Trail, Calistoga* ☎ *855/942–7442, 707/226–0800* 🌐 *www.solagecalistoga.com* 🛏 *89 rooms* 🍴 *No meals.*

SPAS

Fodor's Choice ★
Spa Solage. This eco-conscious spa has reinvented the traditional Calistoga mud and mineral-water therapies. Case in point: the hour-long "Mudslide," a three-part treatment that includes a mud body mask (in a heated lounge), a soak in a thermal bath, and a power nap in a sound-vibration chair. The mud here is a mix of clay, volcanic ash, and essential oils. Traditional spa services—combination Shiatsu-Swedish and other massages, full-body exfoliations, facials, and waxes—are available, as are fitness and yoga classes. ✉ *755 Silverado Trail, at Rosedale Rd., Calistoga* ☎ *707/226–0825, 855/790–6023* 🌐 *www.solagecalistoga.com/spa* 🎫 *Treatments $110–$510.*

SPORTS AND THE OUTDOORS

Calistoga Bikeshop. Options here include regular and fancy bikes that rent for $28 and up for two hours, and there's a self-guided Cool Wine Tour ($110) that includes tastings at three or four small wineries. ✉ *1318 Lincoln Ave., near Washington St., Calistoga* ☎ *707/942–9687* 🌐 *www.calistogabikeshop.net.*

THE SONOMA VALLEY

The birthplace of modern California wine making—Count Aragon Haraszthy opened Buena Vista Winery here in 1857—Sonoma Valley seduces with its unpretentious attitude and pastoral landscape. Tasting rooms, restaurants, and historic sites, among the latter the last mission established in California by Franciscan friars, abound near Sonoma Plaza. Beyond downtown Sonoma, the wineries and attractions are spread out along gently winding roads. Sonoma County's half of the Carneros District lies within Sonoma Valley, whose other towns of note include Glen Ellen and Kenwood. Sonoma Valley tasting rooms are often less crowded than those in Napa or northern Sonoma County, especially midweek, and the vibe here, though sophisticated, is definitely less sceney.

SONOMA

14 miles west of Napa, 45 miles northeast of San Francisco.

One of the few towns in the valley with multiple attractions not related to food and wine, Sonoma has plenty to keep you busy for a couple of hours before you head out to tour the wineries. And you needn't leave town to taste wine. There are about three dozen tasting rooms within steps of the tree-filled Sonoma plaza, some of which pour wines from more than one winery. The valley's cultural center, Sonoma was founded in 1835 when California was still part of Mexico.

GETTING HERE AND AROUND

Highway 12 (signed as Broadway near Sonoma Plaza) heads north into Sonoma from Highway 121 and south from Santa Rosa into downtown Sonoma, where (signed as West Spain Street) it travels east to the plaza. Parking is relatively easy to find on or near the plaza, and you can walk to many restaurants, shops, and tasting rooms. Signs point the way to several wineries a mile or more east of the plaza.

EXPLORING
TOP ATTRACTIONS

Gundlach Bundschu. "Gun lock bun shoe" gets you close to pronouncing this winery's name correctly, though everyone here shortens it to Gun Bun. The Bundschu family, which has owned most of this property since 1858, makes reds that include Cabernet Franc, Cabernet Sauvignon, Merlot, and a Bordeaux-style blend of each vintage's best grapes. Gewürztraminer, Chardonnay, and two rosés are also in the mix. Parts of the 1870 stone winery where standard tastings ($20) unfold are still used for wine making. For a more comprehensive experience, book a cave tour ($40), a Pinzgauer vehicle vineyard tour ($60), or a Heritage Reserve ($85) pairing of limited-release wines with small gourmet bites. Some tastings and all tours are by appointment only. ■TIP➔ On some summer days you can enjoy the outdoor Vista Courtyard's broad vineyard views while tasting wines paired with cheese and charcuterie ($30). ✉ *2000 Denmark St., at Bundschu Rd., off 8th St. E, 3 miles southeast of Sonoma Plaza, Sonoma* ☎ *707/938–5277* ⊕ *www.gunbun. com* ✇ *Tastings $20–$30, tours $40–$85 (include tastings).*

Fodor's Choice
★ **Patz & Hall.** Sophisticated single-vineyard Chardonnays and Pinot Noirs are the trademark of this respected winery whose tastings take place in a fashionable single-story residence 3 miles southeast of Sonoma Plaza. It's a Wine Country adage that great wines are made in the vineyard—the all-star fields represented here include Hyde, Durell, and Gap's Crown—but winemaker James Hall routinely surpasses peers with access to the same fruit, proof that discernment and expertise (Hall is a master at oak aging) play a role, too. You can sample wines at the bar and on some days on the vineyard-view terrace beyond it, but to learn how food friendly these wines are, consider the Salon Tasting, at which they're paired with gourmet bites crafted with equal finesse. Tastings are by appointment only. ✉ *21200 8th St. E, near Peru Rd., Sonoma* ☎ *707/265–7700* ⊕ *www.patzhall.com* ✇ *Tastings $30–$60.*

10

Ram's Gate Winery. Stunning views, ultrachic architecture, and wines made from grapes grown by acclaimed producers make a visit to Ram's Gate an event. The welcoming interior spaces—think Restoration Hardware with a dash of high-style whimsy—open up to the entire western Carneros. In fine weather you'll experience the cooling breezes that sweep through the area while sipping sophisticated wines, mostly Pinot Noirs and Chardonnays, but also Pinot Blanc, Sauvignon Blanc, Cabernet Sauvignon, and Syrah. With grapes sourced from the Sangiacomo, Hudson, and other illustrious vineyards, winemaker Jeff Gaffner focuses on creating balanced wines that express what occurred in nature that year. All visits are by appointment only. ■ TIP➜ You can sip current releases at the tasting bar ($40), take a tour-and-taste ($65), or tour and enjoy wines paired with food ($90). ⊠ *28700 Arnold Dr./Hwy. 121, Sonoma* ☎ *707/721–8700* ⊕ *www.ramsgatewinery.com* ⊠ *Tastings $40–$90; tour $65 (includes tasting)* ⊙ *Closed Tues. and Wed.*

Fodor's Choice ★ **Scribe.** Andrew and Adam Mariani, sons of California walnut growers, established Scribe in 2007 on land first planted to grapes in 1858 by Emil Dresel, a German immigrant. Dresel's claims to fame include cultivating Sonoma's first Riesling and Sylvaner, an achievement the brothers honor by growing both varietals on land he once farmed. Using natural wine-making techniques they craft bright, terroir-driven wines from those grapes, along with Chardonnay, Pinot Noir, Syrah, and Cabernet Sauvignon. In restoring their property's 1915 Mission Revival–style hacienda the brothers preserved various layers of history—original molding and light fixtures, for instance, but also fragments of floral-print wallpaper and 1950s newspapers. Now a tasting space, the hacienda served during Prohibition as a bootleggers' hideout, and its basement harbored a speakeasy: two intriguing tales among many associated with this historic site. Tastings are by appointment only. ⊠ *2100 Denmark St., off Napa Rd., Sonoma* ☎ *707/939–1858* ⊕ *scribewinery.com* ⊠ *Tasting price varies; contact winery.*

Sonoma Mission. The northernmost of the 21 missions established by Franciscan friars in California, Sonoma Mission was founded in 1823 as Mission San Francisco Solano. It serves as the centerpiece of **Sonoma State Historic Park,** which includes several other sites in Sonoma and nearby Petaluma. Some early mission structures were destroyed, but all or part of several remaining buildings date to the days of Mexican rule over California. Worth a look are the **Sonoma Barracks,** a half block west of the mission at 20 East Spain Street, which housed troops under the command of General Mariano Guadalupe Vallejo, who controlled vast tracts of land in the region. **General Vallejo's Home,** a Victorian-era structure, is a few blocks west. ⊠ *114 E. Spain St., at 1st St. E, Sonoma* ☎ *707/938–9560* ⊕ *www.parks.ca.gov/?page_id=479* ⊠ *$3, includes same-day admission to other historic sites.*

Fodor's Choice ★ **Walt Wines.** You could spend a full day sampling wines in the tasting rooms bordering or near Sonoma Plaza, but be sure not to miss Walt, which specializes in Pinot Noir from Sonoma County, Mendocino County (just to the north), California's Central Coast, and Oregon's Willamette Valley. Walk-ins are welcome to taste several wines inside a mid-1930s Tudor-inspired home or, weather permitting, at backyard

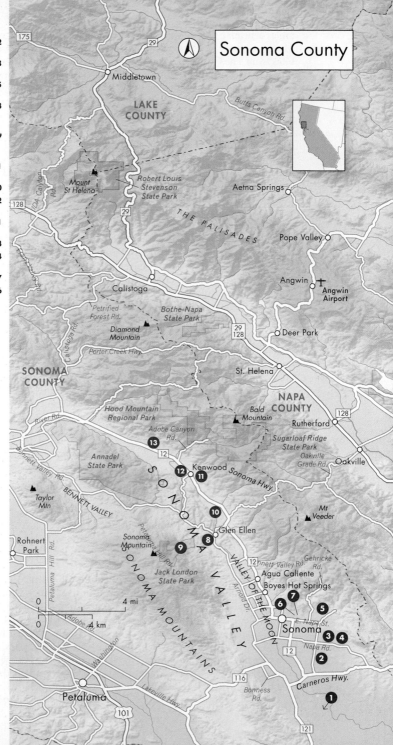

Sonoma County

tables beneath a tall, double-trunk redwood tree. To see how winemaker Megan Gunderson Paredes's wines pair with food—in this case small bites from The Girl & the Fig across the street—make a reservation for the Root 101: A Single Vineyard Exploration. At both tastings you'll learn about the origins of this sister winery to Hall St. Helena. ⊠ *380 1st St. W, at W. Spain St., Sonoma* ☎ *707/933–4440* ⊕ *www.waltwines. com* ✉ *Tastings $30–$60.*

WORTH NOTING

Buena Vista Winery. The birthplace of modern California wine making has been transformed into an entertaining homage to the accomplishments of the 19th-century wine pioneer Count Agoston Haraszthy. Tours pass through the original aging caves dug deep into the hillside by Chinese laborers, and banners, photos, and artifacts inside and out convey the history made on this site. Reserve tastings ($40) include library and current releases, plus barrel samples. The rehabilitated former press house (used for pressing grapes into wine), which dates to 1862, hosts the standard tastings. Chardonnay, Pinot Noir, several red blends, and a vibrant Petit Verdot are the strong suits here. Tours are by appointment only. ■ TIP➔ The high-tech Historic Wine Tool Museum displays implements, some decidedly low-tech, used to make wine over the years. ⊠ *18000 Old Winery Rd., off E. Napa St., Sonoma* ☎ *800/926–1266* ⊕ *www.buenavistawinery.com* ✉ *Tastings $20–$50, tours $25–$40.*

WHERE TO EAT

$$$
AMERICAN
Fodor's Choice
★

✕ **Cafe La Haye.** The dining room is compact, the open kitchen even more so, but chef Jeffrey Lloyd turns out understated, sophisticated fare emphasizing local ingredients. Chicken, beef, pasta, and fish get deluxe treatment without fuss or fanfare—the daily roasted chicken and the risotto specials are always good. **Known for:** Napa-Sonoma wine list with clever French complements; signature butterscotch pudding dessert; owner Saul Gropman on hand to greet diners. $ *Average main: $24* ⊠ *140 E. Napa St., at 1st St. E, Sonoma* ☎ *707/935–5994* ⊕ *www.cafelahaye.com* ⊘ *Closed Sun. and Mon. No lunch.*

$$$
MODERN
AMERICAN

✕ **El Dorado Kitchen.** This restaurant owes its visual appeal to its clean lines and handsome decor, but the eye inevitably drifts westward to the open kitchen, where executive chef Armando Navarro's crew crafts dishes full of subtle surprises. The menu might include ahi tuna tartare with wasabi tobiko caviar as a starter, with paella awash with seafood and dry-cured Spanish chorizo sausage among the entrées. **Known for:** subtle tastes and textures; truffle-oil fries with Parmesan; spiced crepes and other desserts. $ *Average main: $26* ⊠ *El Dorado Hotel, 405 1st St. W, at W. Spain St., Sonoma* ☎ *707/996–3030* ⊕ *www.eldoradosonoma.com/restaurant.*

$$$
FRENCH
Fodor's Choice
★

✕ **The Girl & the Fig.** At this hot spot for inventive French cooking inside the historic Sonoma Hotel bar you can always find a dish with owner Sondra Bernstein's signature figs on the menu, whether it's a fig-and-arugula salad or an aperitif blending sparkling wine with fig liqueur. Also look for duck confit, a burger with matchstick fries, and wild flounder meunière. **Known for:** wine list emphasis on Rhône varietals; artisanal cheese platters; croques monsieurs and eggs Benedict at Sunday brunch. $ *Average main: $24* ⊠ *Sonoma Hotel, 110 W. Spain St., at 1st St. W, Sonoma* ☎ *707/938–3634* ⊕ *www.thegirlandthefig.com.*

$$$ AMERICAN Fodor's Choice ★ 🍴 **Harvest Moon Cafe.** Everything at this little restaurant with an odd, zigzag layout is so perfectly executed and the vibe is so genuinely warm that a visit here is deeply satisfying. The ever-changing menu might include homey dishes such as grilled half chicken with baked polenta or pan-seared Hawaiian ono with jasmine rice and eggplant. **Known for:** friendly service; back patio with central fountain. [$] *Average main: $25* ✉ *487 1st St. W, at W. Napa St., Sonoma* ☎ *707/933–8160* 🌐 *www.harvestmooncafesonoma.com* ⏲ *Closed Tues. No lunch.*

$$$$ PORTUGUESE Fodor's Choice ★ 🍴 **LaSalette Restaurant.** Born in the Azores and raised in Sonoma, chef-owner Manuel Azevedo serves three- and five-course prix-fixe meals inspired by his native Portugal. The wood-oven-roasted fish is always worth trying, and there are usually boldly flavored lamb and pork dishes, along with soups, stews, salted cod, and other hearty fare. **Known for:** authentic Portuguese cuisine; sophisticated spicing; olive-oil cake with queijo fresco (fresh cheese) ice cream. [$] *Average main: $55* ✉ *452 1st St. E, near E. Spain St., Sonoma* ☎ *707/938–1927* 🌐 *www.lasalette-restaurant.com.*

$$$$ MODERN AMERICAN 🍴 **Oso Sonoma.** Chef David Bush, who achieved national recognition for his food pairings at St. Francis Winery, owns this barlike small-plates restaurant whose menu evolves throughout the day. Lunch might see mole braised pork-shoulder tacos or an achiote chicken sandwich, with dinner fare perhaps of steamed mussels, harissa roasted salmon, or roasted forest mushrooms with baby spinach and polenta. **Known for:** bar menu between lunch and dinner; Korean soju cocktails; decor of reclaimed materials. [$] *Average main: $32* ✉ *9 E. Napa St., at Broadway, Sonoma* ☎ *707/931–6926* 🌐 *www.ososonoma.com* ⏲ *No lunch Mon.–Wed.*

$ AMERICAN 🍴 **Sunflower Caffé.** Cheerful art and brightly painted walls set a jolly tone at this casual eatery whose assets include sidewalk seating with Sonoma Plaza views and the verdant patio out back. Omelets and waffles are the hits at breakfast, with the smoked duck breast sandwich, served on a baguette and slathered with caramelized onions, a favorite for lunch. **Known for:** combination café, gallery, and wine bar; local cheeses and hearty soups; free Wi-Fi. [$] *Average main: $13* ✉ *421 1st St. W, at W. Spain St., Sonoma* ☎ *707/996–6645* 🌐 *www.sonomasunflower.com* ⏲ *No dinner.*

10

WHERE TO STAY

$$ B&B/INN 🏨 **Inn at Sonoma.** They don't skimp on the little luxuries here: wine and hors d'oeuvres are served every evening in the lobby, and the cheerfully painted rooms are warmed by gas fireplaces. **Pros:** last-minute specials are a great deal; free soda available in the lobby. **Cons:** on a busy street rather than right on the plaza. [$] *Rooms from: $220* ✉ *630 Broadway, Sonoma* ☎ *707/939–1340, 888/568–9818* 🌐 *www.innatsonoma.com* 🛏 *27 rooms* 🍽 *Breakfast.*

$$$ HOTEL Fodor's Choice ★ 🏨 **MacArthur Place Hotel & Spa.** Guests at this 7-acre boutique property five blocks south of Sonoma Plaza bask in ritzy seclusion in plush accommodations set amid landscaped gardens. **Pros:** secluded garden setting; high-style furnishings; on-site steak house. **Cons:** a bit of a walk from the plaza; some traffic noise audible in street-side rooms. [$] *Rooms from: $399* ✉ *29 E. MacArthur St., Sonoma* ☎ *707/938–2929, 800/722–1866* 🌐 *www.macarthurplace.com* 🛏 *64 rooms* 🍽 *Breakfast.*

$ ⌂ **Sonoma Creek Inn.** The small but cheerful rooms at this motel-style inn
B&B/INN are individually decorated with painted wooden armoires, cozy quilts, and
FAMILY brightly colored contemporary artwork. **Pros:** clean, well-lighted bathrooms; lots of charm for the price; popular with bicyclists. **Cons:** office not
staffed 24 hours a day; a 10-minute drive from Sonoma Plaza. $ *Rooms
from: $145 ⊠ 239 Boyes Blvd., off Hwy. 12, Sonoma ☎ 707/939–9463,
888/712–1289 ⊕ www.sonomacreekinn.com ⇝ 16 rooms* ⦿| *No meals.*

SPAS

Willow Stream Spa at Fairmont Sonoma Mission Inn & Spa. With 40,000
square feet and 30 treatment rooms, the Wine Country's largest spa provides every amenity you could possibly want, including pools and hot tubs
fed by local thermal springs. Although the place fills with patrons in summer and on some weekends, the vibe is always soothing. The signature
bathing ritual includes an exfoliating shower, dips in two mineral-water
soaking pools, an herbal steam, and a dry-salt sauna and rain tunnel. The
regime draws to a close with cool-down showers. Other popular treatments involve alkaline baths, aloe-gel wraps, and massages in styles from
Swedish to Thai. For a touch of the exotic designed to leave your skin
luminous, try a caviar facial. The most requested room among couples
is outfitted with a two-person copper bathtub. ⊠ *100 Boyes Blvd./Hwy.
12, 2½ miles north of Sonoma Plaza, Sonoma ☎ 707/938–9000 ⊕ www.
fairmont.com/sonoma/willow-stream ⊠ Treatments $65–$528.*

SHOPPING

Sonoma Plaza is a shopping magnet, with tempting boutiques and specialty food purveyors facing the square or within a block or two.

G's General Store. The inventory of this "modern general store" runs the
gamut from cute bunny LED nightlights and Euro-suave kitchen utensils to bright-print shirts and a log-and-leather sofa fit for a ski chalet.
The owner used to buy for Smith & Hawken and Williams-Sonoma,
so expect upscale merch presented with style. ⊠ *19 W. Napa St., near
Broadway, Sonoma ☎ 707/933–8082 ⊕ www.ggeneralstore.com.*

Fodor's Choice   **Sonoma Valley Certified Farmers Market.** To discover just how bountiful the
★   Sonoma landscape is—and how talented its farmers and food artisans
are—head to Depot Park, just north of the Sonoma Plaza, on Friday
morning. This market is considered Sonoma County's best. ⊠ *Depot
Park, 1st St. W, at the Sonoma Bike Path, Sonoma ☎ 707/538–7023
⊕ www.svcfm.org.*

GLEN ELLEN

7 miles north of Sonoma.

Unlike its flashier Napa Valley counterparts, Glen Ellen eschews well-groomed sidewalks lined with upscale boutiques and restaurants, preferring instead its crooked streets, some with no sidewalks at all, shaded
with stands of old oak trees. Jack London, who represents Glen Ellen's
rugged spirit, lived in the area for many years; the town commemorates
him with place names and nostalgic establishments. Hidden among
sometimes-ramshackle buildings abutting Sonoma and Calabasas creeks
are low-key shops and galleries worth poking through, and several fine
dining establishments.

GETTING HERE AND AROUND

Glen Ellen sits just off Highway 12. From the north or south, take Arnold Drive west and follow it south less than a mile. The walkable downtown straddles a half-mile stretch of Arnold Drive.

EXPLORING

Fodor's Choice ★ **Benziger Family Winery.** One of the best-known Sonoma County wineries sits on a sprawling estate in a bowl with 360-degree sun exposure, the benefits of which are explored on tram tours that depart several times daily. Guides explain Benziger's biodynamic farming practices and provide a glimpse of the extensive cave system. The regular tram tour costs $25; another tour costing $50 concludes with a seated tasting. Known for Chardonnay, Cabernet Sauvignon, Merlot, Pinot Noir, and Sauvignon Blanc, the winery is a beautiful spot for a picnic. ■TIP➜ Reserve a seat on the tram tour through the winery's website or arrive early in the day on summer weekends and during harvest season. ⊠ *1883 London Ranch Rd., off Arnold Dr., Glen Ellen* ☎ *707/935–3000, 888/490–2739* ⊕ *www.benziger.com* ✉ *Tastings $20–$40, tours $25–$50.*

Fodor's Choice ★ **Jack London State Historic Park.** The pleasures are pastoral and intellectual at author Jack London's beloved Beauty Ranch. You could easily spend the afternoon hiking some of the 30-plus miles of trails that loop through meadows and stands of oaks, redwoods, and other trees. Manuscripts and personal artifacts depicting London's travels are on view at the House of Happy Walls Museum, which provides an overview of the writer's life and literary passions. A short hike away lie the ruins of Wolf House, which burned down just before London was to move in. Also open to visitors are a few outbuildings and the restored Cottage, a wood-framed building where he penned many of his later works. He's buried on the property. ■TIP➜ Well-known performers headline the park's Broadway Under the Stars series, a hot ticket in summer. ⊠ *2400 London Ranch Rd., off Arnold Dr., Glen Ellen* ☎ *707/938–5216* ⊕ *www.jacklondonpark.com* ✉ *Parking $10 ($5 walk-in or bike), includes admission to museum; cottage $4.*

Fodor's Choice ★ **Lasseter Family Winery.** Immaculately groomed grapevines dazzle the eye at John and Nancy Lasseter's secluded winery, and it's no accident: Phil Coturri, Sonoma Valley's premier organic and biodynamic vineyard manager, tends them. Even the landscaping, which includes an insectary to attract beneficial bugs, is meticulously maintained. Come harvesttime, winemaker Julia Lantosca oversees gentle processes that transform the fruit into wines of purity and grace: a Semillon–Sauvignon Blanc blend, two rosés, and Bordeaux and Rhône reds. As might be expected of a storyteller as accomplished as John, whose screenwriting credits include *Toy Story, Cars,* and other Pixar features, evocative labels illustrate the tale behind each wine. These stories are well told on tours that precede tastings of wines, paired with local artisanal cheeses, in an elegant room whose east-facing window frames vineyard and Mayacamas Mountains views. All visits are by appointment only. ⊠ *1 Vintage La., off Dunbar Rd., Glen Ellen* ☎ *707/933–2814* ⊕ *www.lasseterfamilywinery.com* ✉ *Tastings (some with tours) $25–$45.*

10

Hitching a ride on the Benziger Family Winery tram tour

WHERE TO EAT

$$ ITALIAN Fodor's Choice ★ 🍴 **Aventine Glen Ellen.** A Wine Country cousin to chef Adolfo Veronese's same-named San Francisco and Hollywood establishments, this Italian restaurant occupies an 1839 sawmill from California's Mexican period. Veronese's varied menu includes several pizzas (the seasonal one with black truffle honey, béchamel, and wild arugula is a savory masterpiece), an equal number of pasta dishes, a daily risotto, and several meat and fish entrées. **Known for:** chicken parmigiana the envy of local Sicilian grandmothers; outdoor patio overlooking Sonoma Creek. [$] *Average main: $20* ✉ *Jack London Village, 14301 Arnold Dr., ¾ mile south of downtown, Glen Ellen* ☎ *707/934–8911* 🌐 *www.aventinehospitality.com/glen-ellen* 🕒 *Closed Mon. and Tues.*

$$ FRENCH 🍴 **The Fig Cafe.** The compact menu at this cheerful bistro, a Glen Ellen fixture, focuses on California and French comfort food—pot roast and duck confit, for instance, as well as thin-crust pizza. Steamed mussels are served with crispy fries, which also accompany the sirloin burger, and weekend brunch brings out locals and tourists for French toast, corned-beef hash, and pizza with applewood-smoked bacon and poached eggs. **Known for:** casual ambience; no corkage fee, so good for enjoying your winery discoveries. [$] *Average main: $18* ✉ *13690 Arnold Dr., at O'Donnell La., Glen Ellen* ☎ *707/938–2130* 🌐 *www.thefigcafe.com* 🕒 *No lunch weekdays.*

$$$ ECLECTIC Fodor's Choice ★ 🍴 **Glen Ellen Star.** Chef Ari Weiswasser honed his craft at The French Laundry, Daniel, and other bastions of culinary finesse, but at his Wine Country outpost he prepares haute-rustic cuisine, much of it emerging from a wood-fired oven that burns a steady 600°F. Crisp-crusted, richly sauced Margherita and other pizzas thrive in the torrid heat,

as do tender whole fish entrées and vegetables roasted in small iron skillets. **Known for:** kitchen-view counter for watching chefs cook; enclosed patio; Weiswasser's sauces, emulsions, and spices. [$] *Average main: $28* ✉ *13648 Arnold Dr., at Warm Springs Rd., Glen Ellen* ☎ *707/343–1384* 🌐 *glenellenstar.com* 🕒 *No lunch.*

WHERE TO STAY

$$ B&B/INN Fodor's Choice ★ 🏨 **Gaige House.** Asian objets d'art and leather club chairs cozied up to the lobby fireplace are just a few of the graceful touches in this luxurious but understated bed-and-breakfast. **Pros:** beautiful lounge areas; lots of privacy; excellent service; full breakfasts, afternoon wine and appetizers. **Cons:** sound carries in the main house; the least expensive rooms are on the small side. [$] *Rooms from: $275* ✉ *13540 Arnold Dr., Glen Ellen* ☎ *707/935–0237, 800/935–0237* 🌐 *www.gaige.com* 🛏 *23 rooms* 🍴 *Breakfast.*

$$ B&B/INN Fodor's Choice ★ 🏨 **Olea Hotel.** The husband-and-wife team of Ashish and Sia Patel operate this boutique lodging that's at once sophisticated and down-home country casual. **Pros:** beautiful style; welcoming staff; chef-prepared breakfasts; complimentary wine throughout stay. **Cons:** fills up quickly on weekends; minor road noise in some rooms. [$] *Rooms from: $288* ✉ *5131 Warm Springs Rd., west off Arnold Dr., Glen Ellen* ☎ *707/996–5131* 🌐 *www.oleahotel.com* 🛏 *15 rooms* 🍴 *Breakfast.*

KENWOOD

4 miles north of Glen Ellen.

Tiny Kenwood consists of little more than a few restaurants, shops, tasting rooms, and a historic train depot, now used for private events. But hidden in this pretty landscape of meadows and woods at the north end of Sonoma Valley are several good wineries, most just off the Sonoma Highway. Varietals grown here at the foot of the Sugarloaf Mountains include Sauvignon Blanc, Chardonnay, Zinfandel, and Cabernet Sauvignon.

GETTING HERE AND AROUND

To get to Kenwood from Glen Ellen, head northeast on Arnold Drive and north on Highway 12. Sonoma Transit Bus 30 and Bus 38 serve Kenwood from Glen Ellen and Sonoma.

10

EXPLORING

TOP ATTRACTIONS

Fodor's Choice ★ **B Wise Vineyards Cellar.** The stylish roadside tasting room of this producer of small-lot reds sits on the valley floor, but B Wise's winery and vineyards occupy a prime spot high in the Moon Mountain District AVA. B Wise made its name crafting big, bold Cabernets. One comes from owner Brion Wise's mountain estate and another from the nearby Monte Rosso Vineyard, some of whose Cabernet vines are among California's oldest. These hearty mountain-fruit Cabs contrast with a suppler one from the Napa Valley's Coombsville AVA. Mark Herold, known for several cult wines, makes the Cabernets with Massimo Monticelli, who's responsible for the rest of the uniformly excellent lineup: Sonoma Coast Chardonnay; Russian River Valley, Sonoma

Coast, and Willamette Valley (Oregon) Pinot Noir; and estate Syrah, Petite Sirah, Petit Verdot, and Zinfandel. ⊠ *9077 Sonoma Hwy., at Shaw Ave., Kenwood* ☎ *707/282–9169* ⊕ *www.bwisevineyards.com* 🍷 *Tasting $20.*

Kunde Estate Winery & Vineyards. On your way into Kunde you pass a terrace flanked by fountains, virtually coaxing you to stay for a picnic with views over the vineyard. Family owned for more than a century, Kunde prides itself on producing 100% estate wines from its 1,850-acre property, which rises 1,400 feet from the valley floor. Kunde's whites include several Chardonnays and a Sauvignon Blanc, with Cabernet Sauvignon, Merlot, and a Zinfandel from 1880s vines among the reds. Two wines of note available only through the winery, both in the Destination Series, are the Red Dirt Red blend of seven varietals and the Dunfillan Cuvée, made from Cabernet and Syrah grapes. ■TIP➜ **Make a reservation for the Mountain Top Tasting, a tour by luxury van that ends with a sampling of reserve wines.** ⊠ *9825 Sonoma Hwy./Hwy. 12, Kenwood* ☎ *707/833–5501* ⊕ *www.kunde.com* 🍷 *Tastings $15–$50, Mountain Top Tasting $50, grounds and cave tour free.*

St. Francis Winery. Nestled at the foot of Mt. Hood, St. Francis has earned national acclaim for its wine-and-food pairings. With its red-tile roof and bell tower and views of the Mayacamas Mountains just to the east, the winery's California Mission–style visitor center occupies one of Sonoma County's most scenic locations. The charm of the surroundings is matched by the mostly red wines, including rich, earthy Zinfandels from the Dry Creek, Russian River, and Sonoma valleys. Chef Bryan Jones's five-course small bites-and-wine-pairings ($68)— Liberty duck breast cassoulet with one of the Zins, for example—are offered from Thursday through Monday; pairings with cheeses and charcuterie ($35) are available daily. ⊠ *100 Pythian Rd., off Hwy. 12, Kenwood* ☎ *888/675–9463, 707/833–0242* ⊕ *www.stfranciswinery. com* 🍷 *Tastings $15–$68.*

THE NORTH COAST

from the Sonoma Coast to
Redwood State Parks

Visit Fodors.com for advice, updates, and bookings

WELCOME TO THE NORTH COAST

TOP REASONS TO GO

★ **Scenic coastal drives:** There's hardly a road here that *isn't* scenic.

★ **Wild beaches:** This stretch of California is one of nature's masterpieces. Revel in the unbridled, rugged coastline, without a building in sight.

★ **Dinnertime:** When you're done hiking the beach, refuel with delectable food; you'll find everything from fish tacos to foie gras.

★ **Romance:** Here you can end almost every day with a perfect sunset.

★ **Wildlife:** Watch for migrating whales, sunbathing sea lions, and huge Roosevelt elk with majestic antlers.

1 The Sonoma Coast. As you enter Sonoma County from the south on Highway 1, you pass first through gently rolling pastureland. North of Bodega Bay dramatic shoreline scenery takes over. The road snakes up, down, and around sheer cliffs and steep inclines—some without guardrails—where cows seem to cling precariously. Stunning vistas (or cottony fog) and hairpin turns make for an exhilarating drive.

2 The Mendocino Coast. The timber industry gave birth to most of the small towns along this stretch of coastline. Although tourism now drives the economy, the region has retained much of its old-fashioned charm. The beauty of the landscape, of course, has not changed. Inland lies the Anderson Valley, whose wineries mostly grow cool-climate grapes.

3 Redwood Country. There's a different state of mind in Humboldt County. Here, instead of spas, there are old-time hotels. Instead of wineries, there are breweries. The landscape is primarily thick redwood forest; the interior mountains get snow in winter and sizzle in summer while the coast sits covered in fog. Until as late as 1924 there was no road north of Willits; the coastal towns were reachable only by sea. That legacy is apparent in the communities of today: Eureka and Arcata, both former ports, are sizeable, but otherwise towns are tiny and nestled in the woods, and people have an independent spirit that recalls the original homesteaders.

4 Redwood State Parks. For a pristine encounter with giant redwoods, make the trek to these coastal parks where even casual visitors have easy access to the trees.

Smith River
199
SISKIYOU MOUNTAINS
Point St. George
Crescent City
101
96
KLAMATH
Klamath
Redwood National
& State Parks **4**
Orick
Patrick's Point
State Park
Trinidad
96
McKinleyville
Willow Creek
3 Arcata
Arcata Bay
Eureka
299
Humboldt Bay
Fortuna
Ferndale
Hydesville
Cape
Mendocino
Rio
Dell
36
Hayfork
Point
Gorda
Humboldt
Redwoods
State Park
Garberville
Leggett
Laytonville
101
Fort Bragg
1
Willits
Mendocino
Little River
20
Albion
2 Elk
128
Ukiah
20
Lucerne
Kelseyville
Clearlake
Point Arena
Cloverdale
Lower Lake
Gualala
1
Stewarts
Point **1**
Healdsburg
Calistoga
Jenner
101
Saint Helena
Occidental
Santa Rosa
Bodega Bay
Sebastopol
29
Napa
Petaluma
Sonoma
Inverness
Novato
Vallejo
Point Reyes
1
Richmond
80
Concord
National Seashore
Bolinas
Berkeley
San Francisco
Oakland
Daly City

PACIFIC OCEAN

COAST RANGES

KLAMATH MOUNTAINS

KING MTN RANGE

ANDERSON VALLEY

Pacific Coast Hwy

0   30 mi
0   30 km

GETTING ORIENTED

It's all but impossible to explore the Northern California coast without a car. Indeed, you wouldn't want to—driving here is half the fun. The main road is Highway 1, two lanes that twist and turn (sometimes 180 degrees) up cliffs and down through valleys. Towns appear every so often, but this is mostly a land of green pasture, dense forest, and natural, undeveloped coastline. ■TIP→ Pace yourself: Most drivers stop frequently to appreciate the views, and you can't safely drive faster than 30 or 40 mph on many portions of the highway. Don't plan to drive too far in one day.

Updated by
Daniel Mangin

The spectacular coastline between Marin County and the Oregon border defies expectations. The landscape is defined by the Pacific Ocean, but instead of boardwalks and bikinis there are ragged cliffs and pounding waves— and the sunbathers are mostly sea lions. Instead of strip malls and freeways, you'll find a single-lane road that follows a fickle shoreline. Although the towns along the way vary from deluxe spa retreat to hippie hideaway, all are reliably sleepy—and that's exactly why many Californians escape here to enjoy nature unspoiled.

This stretch of Highway 1 is made up of numerous little worlds, each different from the last. From Point Reyes toward Bodega Bay, the land spreads out into green, rolling pastures and sandy beaches. The road climbs higher and higher as it heads north through Sonoma County, and in Mendocino County the coastline follows the ins and outs of lush valleys where rivers pour down from the forests and into the ocean. At Humboldt County the highway heads inland to the redwoods, and then returns to the shoreline at the tidal flats surrounding the ports of Eureka and Arcata. Heading north to the Oregon border, the coast is increasingly wild and lined with giant redwood trees.

When you travel the North Coast, turn off your phone; you won't have much of a signal anyway. Everything about life here says slow down. If you don't, you might miss a noble Roosevelt elk grazing in a roadside field or a pod of migrating whales cruising along the shore.

PLANNING

WHEN TO GO

The North Coast is a year-round destination, though when you go determines what you will see. The migration of the Pacific gray whales is a wintertime phenomenon, which lasts roughly from mid-December to early April. Wildflowers follow the winter rain, as early as January in southern areas through June and July farther north. Summer is the high season for tourists, but spring, fall, and even winter are arguably better times to visit. The pace is slower, towns are quieter, and lodging is cheaper.

The coastal climate is similar to San Francisco's, although winter nights are colder than in the city. In July and August thick fog can drop temperatures to the high 50s, but fear not. You need only drive inland a few miles to find temperatures that are often 20 degrees higher.

GETTING HERE AND AROUND

AIR TRAVEL

Arcata/Eureka Airport (ACV), 14 miles north of Eureka in McKinleyville, is served by subsidiaries of Alaska and United, and a few other small airlines. Taking City Cab to Eureka costs about $55 and takes roughly 25 minutes. Door-to-door Airporter shuttle rides cost $20 to Arcata and Trinidad, $24 to Eureka, and $50 to Ferndale for the first person, $5 for each additional person.

Airport Contacts Arcata/Eureka Airport. ⊠ *3561 Boeing Ave., McKinleyville* ☎ *707/445–9651* ⊕ *flyhumboldt.org.*

Ground Transportation Contacts City Cab. ☎ *707/442–4551* ⊕ *www.cityambulance.com/CityCab.htm.* **Door-to-Door Airporter.** ☎ *888/338–5497, 707/839–4186* ⊕ *www.doortodoorairporter.com.*

BUS TRAVEL

Greyhound buses travel along U.S. 101 from San Francisco to Garberville, Eureka, and Arcata. Humboldt Transit Authority connects Eureka, Arcata, and Trinidad.

Bus Contacts Greyhound. ☎ *800/231–2222* ⊕ *www.greyhound.com.* **Humboldt Transit Authority.** ☎ *707/443–0826* ⊕ *www.hta.org.*

CAR TRAVEL

U.S. 101 has excellent services, but long stretches separate towns along Highway 1. ■ **TIP→** If you're running low on fuel and see a gas station, stop for a refill. Twisting Highway 1 is the scenic route to Mendocino from San Francisco, but the fastest one is U.S. 101 north to Highway 128 west (from Cloverdale) to Highway 1 north. The quickest route to the far North Coast is straight up U.S. 101.

Road Conditions Caltrans. ☎ *800/427–7623* ⊕ *www.dot.ca.gov.*

RESTAURANTS

Restaurants here, a few with regional reputations but most off the culinary world's radar, entice diners with dishes fashioned from the abundant fresh seafood and locally grown vegetables and herbs. Attire is usually informal, though at pricier establishments dressy casual is the norm. Most kitchens close at 8 or 8:30 and few places serve past 9:30. Many restaurants close in January or early February. *Restaurant reviews have been shortened. For full information, visit Fodors.com.*

HOTELS

Restored Victorians, rustic lodges, country inns, and vintage motels are among the accommodations available here. Few have air-conditioning (the ocean breezes make it unnecessary), and many have no phones or TVs in the rooms. Budget accommodations are rare, but in winter you're likely to find reduced rates and nearly empty lodgings. In summer and on the weekends, though, make bed-and-breakfast reservations as far ahead as possible—rooms at the best inns often sell out months in advance. *Hotel reviews have been shortened. For full information, visit Fodors.com.*

WHAT IT COSTS				
	$	$$	$$$	$$$$
RESTAURANTS	under $16	$16–$22	$23–$30	over $30
HOTELS	under $120	$120–$175	$176–$250	over $250

Restaurant prices are the average cost of a main course at dinner or, if dinner is not served, at lunch, excluding sales tax of 7.5–8¼%. Hotel prices are the lowest cost of a standard double room in high season, excluding service charges and 8%–11% tax.

VISITOR INFORMATION

Contacts Humboldt County Convention and Visitors Bureau. ⊠ *322 1st St., Eureka* ☎ *707/443–5097, 800/346–3482* ⊕ *redwoods.info.* **Sonoma County Tourism.** ☎ *707/522–5800, 800/576–6662* ⊕ *www.sonomacounty.com.* **Visit Mendocino County.** ⊠ *345 N. Franklin St., Fort Bragg* ☎ *707/964–9010, 866/466–3636* ⊕ *www.visitmendocino.com.*

THE SONOMA COAST

State parks and beaches and small seaside towns line Sonoma County's rugged, photogenic coastline. Highway 1 curves its way more than 55 miles from Marin to Mendocino County. Along the way you can tidepool, walk the beach, and hike redwood-studded trails. From some of the higher perches you might spot a whale in winter.

BODEGA BAY

23 miles west of Santa Rosa.

From this working town's busy harbor west of Highway 1, commercial boats pursue fish and Dungeness crab. In 1962 Alfred Hitchcock shot *The Birds* in the area. The Tides Wharf complex, an important location, is no longer recognizable, but a few miles inland, in Bodega, you can find Potter Schoolhouse, now a private residence.

Surfers check out the waves near Bodega Bay on the Sonoma Coast.

GETTING HERE AND AROUND

To reach Bodega Bay, exit U.S. 101 at Santa Rosa and take Highway 12 west (called Bodega Highway west of Sebastopol) 23 miles to the coast. A scenic alternative is to take U.S. 101's East Washington Street/ Central Petaluma exit and follow signs west to Bodega Bay; just after you merge onto Highway 1, you'll pass through down-home Valley Ford. Mendocino Transit Authority (⊕ *mendocinotransit.org*) Route 95 buses serve Bodega Bay.

EXPLORING

Sonoma Coast Vineyards. This boutique winery with an oceanview tasting room makes cool-climate Chardonnays and Pinot Noirs from grapes grown close to the Pacific. The Antonio Mountain and Balistreri Family Vineyards Pinot Noirs stand out among wines that also include a mildly oaky Sauvignon Blanc, a Syrah, and a well-balanced sparkler. ⊠ *555 Hwy. 1* ☎ *707/921–2860* ⊕ *www.sonomacoastvineyards.com* ⊠ *$20.*

BEACHES

Fodor'sChoice
★

Sonoma Coast State Park. The park's gorgeous sandy coves stretch for 17 miles from Bodega Head to 4 miles north of Jenner. **Bodega Head** is a popular whale-watching perch in winter and early spring, and **Rock Point, Duncan's Landing,** and **Wright's Beach,** at about the halfway mark, have good picnic areas. Rogue waves have swept people off the rocks at Duncan's Landing Overlook, so don't stray past signs warning you away. Calmer **Shell Beach,** about 2 miles north, is known for beachcombing, tidepooling, and fishing. Walk the blufftop **Kortum Trail** or drive about 2½ miles north of Shell Beach to **Blind Beach.** Near the mouth of the Russian River just north of here at **Goat Rock Beach,** you'll find harbor seals; pupping season is from March through August. Bring binoculars and walk north from the parking lot to view the seals. During summer, lifeguards are on duty at some beaches, but strong rip currents and heavy surf keep most visitors on shore. **Amenities:** parking; toilets. **Best for:** solitude; sunset; walking. ⊠ *Park Headquarters/Salmon Creek Ranger Station, 3095 Hwy. 1, 2 miles north of Bodega Bay* ☎ *707/875–3483* ⊕ *www.parks.ca.gov* 🖼 *$8 per vehicle.*

WHERE TO EAT AND STAY

$
SEAFOOD
Fodor'sChoice
★
✕ **Spud Point Crab Company.** Crab sandwiches, clam chowder New England or Manhattan style, and house-made crab cakes with roasted red pepper sauce star on the brief menu of this shacklike operation. Place your order inside, and enjoy your meal to go or at one of the marina-view picnic tables outside. **Known for:** family-run operation; opens at 9 am; superb chowder; seafood cocktails. **$** *Average main: $9* ⊠ *1910 Westshore Rd.* ☎ *707/875–9472* ⊕ *www.spudpointcrab.com* ☉ *No dinner.*

$$$$
MODERN
AMERICAN
Fodor'sChoice
★
✕ **Terrapin Creek Cafe & Restaurant.** Intricate but not fussy cuisine based on locally farmed ingredients and the fruits de mer has made this restaurant the darling of western Sonoma County. Start with raw Marin Miyagi oysters, rich mushroom soup, or (in-season) Dungeness crab-meat ragout before moving on to halibut or other fish pan-roasted to perfection. **Known for:** intricate cuisine; a top Bay Area "foodies" choice. **$** *Average main: $31* ⊠ *1580 Eastshore Rd.* ☎ *707/875–2700* ⊕ *www.terrapincreekcafe.com* ☉ *Closed Tues. and Wed.*

$$$$
HOTEL
Fodor'sChoice
★
🛏 **Bodega Bay Lodge.** Looking out to the ocean across a wetland, the lodge's shingle-and-river-rock buildings contain Bodega Bay's finest accommodations. **Pros:** fireplaces and patios or balconies in most rooms; operated by a trusted upscale California brand; ocean views. **Cons:** pricey in-season; parking lot in foreground of some rooms' views; fairly long drive to other fine-dining restaurants. **$** *Rooms from: $350* ⊠ *103 Coast Hwy. 1* ☎ *707/875–3525, 888/875–2250* ⊕ *www.bodegabaylodge.com* ⟿ *83 rooms* 🍽 *No meals.*

$
HOTEL
🛏 **Bodega Harbor Inn.** As humble as can be, this is one of the few places on this stretch of the coast with rooms for around $100 a night. **Pros:** budget choice; rooms for larger groups; ocean views from public areas and some rooms. **Cons:** an older facility; nondescript rooms; behind a shopping center. **$** *Rooms from: $99* ⊠ *1345 Bodega Ave.* ☎ *707/875–3594* ⊕ *www.bodegaharborinn.com* ⟿ *16 rooms* 🍽 *No meals.*

SPORTS AND THE OUTDOORS
WHALE-WATCHING

Fodor'sChoice
★
Bodega Bay Sailing Adventures. Part salty dog and part jolly entertainer, Captain Rich conducts three-hour Bodega Bay tours on his 33-foot sailboat. Whales are often sighted from winter into early spring, and sea lions and harbor seals commonly appear. The sunset tour is especially fun. ⊠ *Meeting place near sport fishing center, 1418 Bay Flat Rd.* ☎ *707/318–2251* ⊕ *www.bodegabaysailing.org* 🖼 *From $95.*

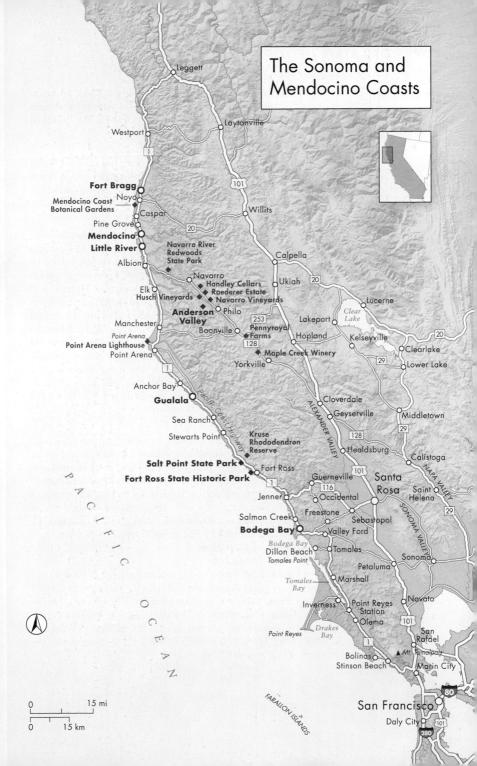

The Sonoma and
Mendocino Coasts

Leggett

Laytonville

Westport

101

Fort Bragg
Noyo
Mendocino Coast
Botanical Gardens
Caspar
Pine Grove
20
Willits
Mendocino
Little River
Navarro River
Redwoods
State Park
Albion
Calpella
Navarro
Elk
Handley Cellars
Roederer Estate
Husch Vineyards
Navarro Vineyards
Ukiah
20
Anderson
Valley
Philo
Lucerne
Manchester
Boonville
253
Pennyroyal
Farms
Lakeport
Clear
Lake
Point Arena
128
Maple Creek Winery
Hopland
Kelseyville
Clearlake
Point Arena Lighthouse
Point Arena
Yorkville
29
Lower Lake
1
Anchor Bay
Pacific Coast Highway
Cloverdale
Middletown
Gualala
Geyserville
Sea Ranch
128
Stewarts Point
Kruse
Rhododendron
Reserve
ALEXANDER VALLEY
Healdsburg
29
Calistoga
Salt Point State Park
Fort Ross
NAPA VALLEY
Fort Ross State Historic Park
101
Guerneville
Santa
Rosa
Saint
Helena
1
Jenner
116
Occidental
29
Salmon Creek
Freestone
Sebastopol
SONOMA VALLEY
Bodega Bay
Valley Ford
Bodega Bay
Tomales
Dillon Beach
Sonoma
Tomales Point
Petaluma
Tomales
Bay
Marshall
Novato
Inverness
Point Reyes
Station
101
Olema
San
Rafael
Point Reyes
Drakes
Bay
Mt. Tamalpais
Bolinas
Marin City
Stinson Beach
80
PACIFIC OCEAN
San Francisco
FARALLON ISLANDS
Daly City
280

0   15 mi

0   15 km

FORT ROSS STATE HISTORIC PARK

22 miles north of Bodega Bay.

With its reconstructed Russian Orthodox chapel, stockade, and officials' quarters, Fort Ross looks much the way it did after the Russians made it their major California coastal outpost in 1812. An excellent museum documents the fort's history.

GETTING HERE AND AROUND

From Bodega Bay, take Highway 1 north to Fort Ross. From Santa Rosa, head west on Highway 116 about 33 miles to Jenner, then north 12 miles on Highway 1. The Mendocino Transit Authority (🌐 *mendocinotransit.org*) Route 95 bus serves the area.

EXPLORING

FAMILY **Fort Ross State Historic Park.** Russian settlers established Fort Ross in 1812 on land they leased from the native Kashia people. The Russians hoped to gain a foothold in the Pacific coast's warmer regions and to produce crops and other supplies for their Alaskan fur-trading operations. In 1841, with the local marine mammal population depleted and farming having proven unproductive, the Russians sold their holdings to John Sutter, later of gold-rush fame. The land was privately ranched for decades, and became a state park in 1909. One original Russian-era structure remains, as does a cemetery. The rest of the compound has been reconstructed to look much as it did during Russian times. An excellent small museum documents the history of the fort, the Kashia people, and the ranch and state-park eras. ✉ *19005 Hwy. 1, Jenner* ☎ *707/847–3437* 🌐 *www.fortross.org* 🎫 *$8 per vehicle* ☞ *No dogs allowed past parking lot and picnic area.*

WHERE TO EAT AND STAY

$$$ MODERN AMERICAN 🍴 **Coast Kitchen.** On a sunny afternoon or at sunset, glistening ocean views from the Coast Kitchen's outdoor patio and indoor dining space elevate dishes emphasizing seafood and local produce both farmed and foraged. Starters like a baby gem lettuce and chicory salad and buttermilk brined fried quail precede entrées that include seared ahi tuna and aged rib eye. **Known for:** oceanview patio (frequent whale sightings in winter and spring); Sonoma County cheeses, wines, and produce; fresh ingredients. [$] *Average main: $25* ✉ *Timber Cove, 21780 Hwy. 1, 3 miles north of Fort Ross State Historic Park, Jenner* ☎ *707/847-3231* 🌐 *www.coastkitchensonoma.com.*

$$$$ RESORT Fodor's Choice ★ 🏨 **Timber Cove Resort.** Restored well beyond its original splendor, this resort anchored to a craggy oceanfront cliff is by far the Sonoma Coast's coolest getaway. **Pros:** dramatic sunsets; grand public spaces; destination restaurant. **Cons:** almost too cool for the laid-back Sonoma Coast; pricey oceanview rooms; occasional hospitality miscues. [$] *Rooms from: $290* ✉ *21780 Hwy. 1, Jenner* ☎ *707/847–3231* 🌐 *www.timbercoveresort.com* 🛏 *46 rooms* 🍽 *No meals.*

SALT POINT STATE PARK

6 miles north of Fort Ross.

Enjoy dramatic views, forested acres, and a rocky, rugged shoreline along Highway 1's 5-mile route through this park. With the hiking, picnicking, horseback riding, scuba diving, and fishing opportunities, you'll want to stay a while.

GETTING HERE AND AROUND

Exit U.S. 101 in Santa Rosa and travel west on Highway 116 about 33 miles to Jenner, then north 18 miles on Highway 1 to reach the park. Mendocino Transit Authority (🌐 *mendocinotransit.org*) Route 95 buses serve the area.

EXPLORING

Salt Point State Park. For 5 miles, Highway 1 winds through this park, 6,000 acres of forest, meadows, and rocky shoreline. Heading north, the first park entrance (on the right) leads to forest hiking trails and several campgrounds. The next entrance—the park's main road—winds through meadows and along the wave-splashed coastline. This is also the route to the visitor center and **Gerstle Cove,** a favorite spot for scuba divers and sunbathing seals. Next along the highway is **Stump Beach Cove,** with picnic tables, toilets, and a ¼-mile walk to the sandy beach. The park's final entrance is at **Fisk Mill Cove,** where centuries of wind and rain erosion have carved unusual honeycomb patterns in the sandstone called "tafonis." A five-minute walk uphill from the parking lot leads to a dramatic view of **Sentinel Rock,** an excellent spot for sunsets.

Just up the highway, narrow, unpaved Kruse Ranch Road leads to the **Kruse Rhododendron State Reserve,** where each May thousands of rhododendrons bloom within a quiet forest of redwoods and tan oaks. ✉ *25050 Hwy. 1* ☎ *707/847–3221, 707/865–2391* 🌐 *www.parks.ca.gov* 🎟 *$8 per vehicle.*

WHERE TO STAY

$$$$ B&B/INN 🏨 **Sea Ranch Lodge.** Wide-open oceanview vistas and minimalist design keep the focus on nature at this tranquil lodge 29 miles north of Jenner. **Pros:** all rooms are oceanfront; on-site spa; peaceful experience. **Cons:** remote location; some guests find decor dated; expensive in-season. [$] *Rooms from: $274* ✉ *60 Sea Walk Dr., Sea Ranch* ☎ *707/785–2371, 800/732–7262* 🌐 *www.searanchlodge.com* 🛏 *19 rooms* 🍴 *Breakfast.*

THE MENDOCINO COAST

The rocky coastline north of Sonoma County will take your breath away, and not only because the setting is so much more dramatic than the prototypical sandy So-Cal beach: hairpin turns and abrupt switchbacks are the order of the day from Gualala in the south past Fort Bragg in the north.

GUALALA

16 miles north of Salt Point State Park.

This former lumber port on the Gualala River has become a headquarters for exploring the coast. The busiest town on Highway 1 between Bodega Bay and Mendocino, it has all the basic services plus some galleries and gift shops.

GETTING HERE AND AROUND

To make the 71-mile trip from Santa Rosa to Gualala, head north on U.S. 101 to River Road (Exit 494) and drive west to the Pacific Ocean. At Jenner, turn north on Highway 1. From the town of Mendocino, head south on Highway 1 for 35 miles. Mendocino Transit Authority (🌐 *mendocinotransit.org*). Routes 75 and 95 buses serve the area from Santa Rosa.

EXPLORING

Gualala Arts Center. Stop here to see free exhibits of regional art. The center also runs the Dolphin Gallery behind the post office in town. ✉ *46501 Gualala Rd.* ☎ *707/884–1138* 🌐 *www.gualalaarts.org.*

Gualala Point Regional Park. This 195-acre park with picnic areas and a long, sandy beach is an excellent whale-watching spot from December through April. Birders and hikers head here year-round. Take the Bluff Top Trail for ocean vistas, the River Trail for views of the Gualala River estuary, a wildlife haven. ✉ *42401 Hwy. 1, 1 mile south of Gualala* ☎ *707/785–2377* 🌐 *www.sonoma-county.org/parks/pk_glala.htm* 🎟 *$7 per vehicle (day use).*

EN ROUTE

Point Arena Lighthouse. For an outstanding view of the ocean and, in winter, migrating whales, take the marked road off Highway 1 north of town to the 115-foot lighthouse. It's possible to stay out here, in one of four rental units ($$–$$$$), all of which have full kitchens. On weekends there's a two-night minimum. ✉ *45500 Lighthouse Rd., off Hwy. 1, Point Arena* ✥ *15 miles north of Gualala (33 miles south of Mendocino), head northwest on Lighthouse Rd.* ☎ *707/882–2809, 877/725–4448* 🌐 *www.pointarenalighthouse.com* 🎟 *Tour $7.50 ($5 if no tour).*

WHERE TO EAT AND STAY

$$$$ AMERICAN

🍴 **St. Orres.** Inside one of this lodge's two Russian-style onion-dome towers is a spectacular atrium dining room where locally farmed and foraged ingredients appear in dishes such as garlic flan with black chanterelles and rack of wild boar with apple-pear latkes. The prix-fixe menu includes soup and salad but no appetizer or dessert (available à la carte). **Known for:** elaborate weekend brunch; romantic setting; small-plates à la carte menu in bar. [$] *Average main: $50* ✉ *36601 S. Hwy. 1, 3 miles north of Gualala* ☎ *707/884–3335 restaurant* 🌐 *www.saintorres.com* 🕓 *No lunch weekdays. Occasionally closed midweek in winter.*

$$$ HOTEL Fodor's Choice ★

🏨 **Mar Vista Cottages.** Escape to nature and retro-charm at these refurbished, gadget-free 1930s cottages, four of which have two bedrooms and eight with one bedroom. **Pros:** commune-with-nature solitude; peaceful retreat; walking path to beach. **Cons:** no other businesses within walking distance; no TVs or phones in rooms; two-night minimum on weekends. [$] *Rooms from: $190* ✉ *35101 S. Hwy 1, 5 miles north of Gualala* ☎ *707/884–3522, 877/855–3522* 🌐 *www.marvista-mendocino.com* 🛏 *12 rooms* 🍴 *No meals.*

ANDERSON VALLEY

29 miles north of Point Arena.

At the town of Albion, Highway 128 leads southeast into the Anderson Valley, Mendocino's primary wine-growing region. Most of the first 13 miles wind through redwood forest along the Navarro River, then the road opens up to reveal farms and vineyards. In the towns of Philo, Boonville, and Yorkville you'll find eclectic bed-and-breakfasts, small eateries, and dozens of wineries.

Tasting rooms here are more low-key than their counterparts in Napa, but the wineries here produce world-class wines, particularly Pinot Noirs and Gewürztraminers, whose grapes thrive in the moderate coastal climate. Many wineries straddle Highway 128, mostly in Navarro and Philo with a few east of Boonville, where the Anderson Valley Brewing Company has been producing quality ales for more than three decades.

GETTING HERE AND AROUND

From the coast, pick up Highway 128 at Albion. From inland points south, take Highway 128 northwest from U.S. 101 at Cloverdale. From inland points north, exit U.S. 101 in Ukiah and take Highway 253 southwest 17 miles to Boonville. Mendocino Transit Authority (🌐 *mendocinotransit.org*) Route 75 buses serve the area.

EXPLORING

TOP ATTRACTIONS

Fodor's Choice ★ **Anderson Valley Brewing Company.** Brewery tours, tastings in the Tap Room, and 18 holes of disc golf provide a diversified experience at the home of Boont Amber Ale, double and triple Belgian style ales, and other consistent award-winning brews. Local winemakers clear their palates with the Bourbon Barrel Stout, aged in Wild Turkey barrels. ✉ *17700 Hwy. 253, Boonville* ☎ *707/895–2337* 🌐 *www.avbc.com* 🎟 *Tastings from $10.*

Goldeneye Winery. The Napa Valley's well-respected Duckhorn Wine Company makes Pinot Noirs here from local grapes, along with a Gewürztraminer, a Pinot Gris, a Chardonnay, and a blush Vin Gris of Pinot Noir. Leisurely tastings take place in either a restored farmhouse or on a patio with vineyard and redwood views. ✉ *9200 Hwy. 128, Philo* ☎ *800/208–0438, 707/895–3202* 🌐 *www.goldeneyewinery.com* 🎟 *Tastings $15–$45* 🕒 *Closed. Tues. and Wed. in Jan. and Feb.*

Lula Cellars. Seventeen miles inland from Highway 1, the fun, relaxing, and pet-friendly Lula is among the Anderson Valley wineries closest to the coast. Owner-winemaker Jeff Hansen, who started Lula in 2007 after decamping from the Napa Valley, produces Sauvignon Blanc, Gewürztraminer, Zinfandel, and a rosé of Zinfandel and Pinot Noir, but his four Pinot Noirs, each flavorful and with its own personality, are the highlights. ✉ *2800 Guntley Rd., at Hwy. 128, Philo* ☎ *707/895–3737* 🌐 *www.lulacellars.com* 🎟 *$5.*

You'll find excellent vintages and great places to taste wine in the Anderson Valley—but it's much more laid-back than Napa.

Maple Creek Winery. Chardonnay, Pinot Noir, and Zinfandel are the specialties of this winery whose artist owner, Tom Rodrigues, also makes Merlot, two dessert wines, and the intriguing Cowboy Red, a blend of Zinfandel, Merlot, and Carignane. If the art that adorns Maple Creek labels looks familiar, there's a reason: Tom's also responsible for ones at the Napa Valley's Far Niente and other top wineries. Picnickers are welcome (wines are sold by the glass). ⊠ *20799 Hwy. 128* ☎ *707/895–3001* ⊕ *www.maplecreekwine.com* ☜ *$10.*

FAMILY **Navarro River Redwoods State Park.** Described by locals as the "11-mile-long redwood tunnel to the sea," this park that straddles Highway 128 is great for walks amid second-growth redwoods and for summer swimming in the gentle Navarro River. In late winter and spring, when the river is higher, you also can fish, canoe, and kayak. ⊠ *Hwy. 128, 2 miles east of Hwy. 1, Navarro* ☎ *707/937–5804* ⊕ *www.parks.ca.gov.*

Navarro Vineyards. A visit to this family-run winery is a classic Anderson Valley experience. Make time if you can for a vineyard tour—the guides draw from years of hands-on experience to explain every aspect of production, from sustainable farming techniques to the choices made in aging and blending. Best known for Alsatian varietals such as Gewürztraminer and Riesling, Navarro also makes Chardonnay, Pinot Noir, and other wines. The tasting room sells cheese and charcuterie for picnickers. ⊠ *5601 Hwy. 128, Philo* ☎ *707/895–3686, 800/537–9463* ⊕ *www.navarrowine.com* ☜ *Tasting free.*

FAMILY **Pennyroyal Farms.** At this Boonville ranch with a contempo-barn tasting Fodor's Choice room you can sample estate Sauvignon Blanc, one of Mendocino's best ★ rosés, and velvety Pinot Noirs, along with cheeses made on the premises from goat and sheep milk. Tours of the farmstead (reservations recommended) take place daily at 10 and 2. The wines, cheeses, pastoral setting, and especially the darlin' goats win most guests' hearts. On weekends, chefs prepare panini, salads, and other meals enjoyed on the patio on sunny days. ⊠ *14930 Hwy. 128, Boonville* ☎ *707/895–2410* ⊕ *www.pennyroyalfarm. com* ✉ *Tastings $5–$15, tours $20* ⊘ *No tours Tues. and Wed.*

WORTH NOTING

Handley Cellars. International folk art collected by winemaker Milla Handley adorns the tasting room at this Anderson Valley pioneer whose lightly oaked Chardonnays and Pinot Noirs earn high praise from wine critics. The winery, which has a patio picnic area, also makes Gewürztraminer, Pinot Gris, Riesling, Zinfandel, very good sparklers, and several other wines. ⊠ *3151 Hwy. 128, Philo* ☎ *707/895–3876, 800/733–3151* ⊕ *www.handleycellars.com* ✉ *Tasting free.*

Husch Vineyards. A former pony barn houses the cozy tasting room of the Anderson Valley's oldest winery. Wines of note include Gewürztraminer, Chardonnay, Pinot Noir, and a Zinfandel from old-vine grapes. You can picnic on the deck here or at tables under grape arbors. ⊠ *4400 Hwy. 128, Philo* ☎ *800/554–8724* ⊕ *www.huschvineyards. com* ✉ *Tasting free.*

Roederer Estate. The Anderson Valley is particularly hospitable to Pinot Noir and Chardonnay grapes, the two varietals used to create Roederer's sparkling wines. The view of vineyards and rolling hills from the patio is splendid. ⊠ *4501 Hwy. 128, Philo* ☎ *707/895–2288* ⊕ *www. roedererestate.com* ✉ *Tasting $6.*

WHERE TO EAT AND STAY

$$$
MODERN
AMERICAN
Fodor'sChoice
★

✕ **Bewildered Pig.** Chef Janelle Weaver cooked for seven years at a prestigious appointment-only Napa Valley winery, perfecting skills that serve her well at her low-key yet polished roadside restaurant. On her Mendocentric menu, which might include braised English short ribs or herbed gnocchi Parisienne with smoked pork jus, Weaver credits the many local farmers and producers who supply her ingredients. **Known for:** cast-iron Dutch-oven sourdough bread; phenomenally fresh salads; vegan, gluten-free options. Ⓢ *Average main: $28* ⊠ *1810 Hwy. 128, Philo* ☎ *707/895–2088* ⊕ *www.bewilderedpig.com* ⊘ *Closed Mon. and Tues. No lunch.*

$
AMERICAN
Fodor'sChoice
★

✕ **Lauren's.** Boonville locals and frequent visitors love Lauren's for its down-home vibe and healthful comfort food—veggie and ground-beef burgers, pizzas, pot roast, chicken tostadas, meat loaf, and curry noodle bowls—many of whose ingredients are grown or produced nearby. Chocolate brownie sundaes and (seasonally) apple tarts and honey-baked pears are among the desserts worth a trip on their own. **Known for:** down-home vibe; diverse Mendocino wine selection ; trivia nights 2nd and 4th Thursday of the month. Ⓢ *Average main: $15* ⊠ *14211 Hwy. 128, Boonville* ☎ *707/895–3869* ⊕ *laurensgoodfood.com* ⊘ *Closed Mon. No dinner Sun. (except for occasional pop-ups) and Mon. No lunch Mon.–Wed.*

$
AMERICAN

✕ **Mosswood Market Café and Bakery.** Pastries for breakfast; wraps, salads, hot soup, and sandwiches for lunch; and espresso drinks all day powered by Sonoma County's Flying Goat Coffee make this sweet café in downtown Boonville a fine stop for a quick bite. Order at the counter and enjoy your meal—the oven roasted turkey and chicken mango wraps and Reuben and albacore tuna sandwiches are among the lunchtime choices—at tables inside or out front. **Known for:** empanadas; Danishes and scones; vegan options. $ *Average main: $10* ✉ *14111 Hwy. 128, Boonville* ☎ *707/895–3635.*

$$$$
AMERICAN
Fodor'sChoice
★

✕ **Table 128.** Proprietor Johnny Schmitt and his staff prepare one prix-fixe meal per night (reservations essential on summer and fall weekends), with platters of food brought to the table for sharing. Expect an expertly prepared entrée like prosciutto-wrapped halibut or slow-roasted lamb, a sophisticated side dish (radicchio with polenta, perhaps, or curried cauliflower soup), and panna cotta or a fruit tart for dessert. **Known for:** home cooking done at a high level; fresh oysters and paella on summer Sundays; tree-shaded outdoor patio. $ *Average main: $58* ✉ *Boonville Hotel, 14050 Hwy. 128, Boonville* ☎ *707/895–2210* ⊕ *www.boonvillehotel.com* ☾ *No lunch. Closed Mon.–Thurs. Nov.–Apr., closed Tues. and Wed. May–Oct.*

$$$
HOTEL

🛏 **Boonville Hotel.** From the street this looks like a standard small-town hotel with seven free-standing cottages out back in the garden, but once you cross the threshold you begin to sense the laid-back sophistication that makes the entire Anderson Valley so appealing. **Pros:** stylish but homey; beautiful gardens and grounds; on-site Table 128 restaurant for prix-fixe meals served family style. **Cons:** two-night stay required on most weekends; not great for kids; lacks big-hotel amenities. $ *Rooms from: $195* ✉ *14050 Hwy. 128, Boonville* ☎ *707/895–2210* ⊕ *www. boonvillehotel.com* ⇆ *15 rooms* ⦿| *Breakfast.*

$$$$
HOTEL
Fodor'sChoice
★

🛏 **The Philo Apple Farm.** Two founders of the renowned Napa Valley restaurant The French Laundry are among the owners of this farm with three tasteful, inviting cottages and one guest room set in an organic heirloom apple orchard. **Pros:** rustic-contemporary touches in cottages and room; working farm; relaxing back-to-nature experience. **Cons:** occasionally hot in summer; few "activities"; room service only upon request. $ *Rooms from: $300* ✉ *18501 Greenwood Rd., Philo* ☎ *707/895–2333* ⊕ *www.philoapplefarm.com* ⇆ *4 rooms* ⦿| *Breakfast.*

LITTLE RIVER

5 miles north of Anderson Valley.

The town of Little River is not much more than a post office and a convenience store; Albion, its neighbor to the south, is even smaller. Along this winding portion of Highway 1, though, you'll find numerous inns and restaurants, all of them quiet and situated to take advantage of the breathtaking ocean views.

GETTING HERE AND AROUND

From inland points south, exit U.S. 101 at Cloverdale and follow Highway 128 northwest about 56 miles to Highway 1, then head north 7 miles. From points north, exit U.S. 101 in Ukiah at Highway 253 and follow it west 17 miles to Boonville, where you'll pick up Highway 128 and drive northwest to Highway 1. Mendocino Transit Authority (⊕ *mendocinotransit.org*) Route 60 buses serve the area.

EXPLORING

Van Damme State Park. Best known for its beach, this park is a prime abalone diving spot. Upland trails lead through lush riparian habitat and the bizarre **Pygmy Forest,** where acidic soil and poor drainage have produced mature cypress and pine trees that are no taller than a person. The visitor center has displays on ocean life and the historical significance of the redwood lumber industry along the coast. ✉ *Little River Park Rd., off Hwy. 1* ☎ *707/937–5804* 🌐 *www.parks.ca.gov.*

WHERE TO EAT AND STAY

$$$ FRENCH Fodor's Choice ★ 🍴 **Ledford House.** The only thing separating this bluff-top wood-and-glass restaurant from the Pacific Ocean is a great view. Entrées evoke the flavors of southern France and include hearty bistro dishes—stews, cassoulets, and pastas—and large portions of grilled meats and freshly caught fish (though the restaurant also is vegetarian friendly). **Known for:** Mendocino-centric wine list; live jazz nightly; oceanview bar. [$] *Average main: $26* ✉ *3000 N. Hwy. 1, Albion* ☎ *707/937–0282* 🌐 *www.ledfordhouse.com* 🕒 *Closed Mon. and Tues. and late-Feb.–early-Mar. and mid-Oct.–early Nov. No lunch.*

$$$ B&B/INN 🏨 **Albion River Inn.** Contemporary New England–style cottages at this inn overlook the dramatic bridge and seascape where the Albion River empties into the Pacific. **Pros:** marvelous ocean views; great bathtubs; romantic glassed-in restaurant. **Cons:** often foggy in summer; no TV in rooms; could use uptick in style. [$] *Rooms from: $195* ✉ *3790 N. Hwy. 1, Albion* ☎ *707/937–1919, 800/479–7944* 🌐 *albionriverinn.com* 🛏 *22 rooms* 🍽 *Breakfast.*

MENDOCINO

3 miles north of Little River.

A flourishing logging town in the late-19th century, Mendocino seduces 21st-century travelers with windswept cliffs, phenomenal Pacific Ocean views, and boomtown-era New England–style architecture. Following the timber industry's mid-20th-century decline, artists and craftspeople began flocking here, and so did Hollywood: Elia Kazan chose Mendocino as the backdrop for his 1955 film adaptation of John Steinbeck's *East of Eden,* starring James Dean, and the town stood in for fictional Cabot Cove, Maine, in the long-running TV series *Murder, She Wrote.* As the arts community thrived, restaurants, cafés, and inns sprang up. Today, the small downtown area consists almost entirely of places to eat and shop.

GETTING HERE AND AROUND

From U.S. 101, exit at Cloverdale and follow Highway 128 northwest about 56 miles and Highway 1 north 10 miles. Mendocino Transit Authority (🌐 *mendocinotransit.org*) Route 60 buses serve the area.

EXPLORING

Ford House. The restored Ford House, built in 1854, serves as the visitor center for Mendocino Headlands State Park and the town. The house has a scale model of Mendocino as it looked in 1890, when it had 34 water towers and a 12-seat public outhouse. From the museum, you can head out on a 3-mile trail across the spectacular seaside cliffs that border the town. ✉ *45035 Main St., west of Lansing St.* ☎ *707/937–5397* 🌐 *mendoparks.org/mendocino-headlands-state-park-ford-house-museum* 🎫 *$2.*

WHERE TO EAT AND STAY

$$$ AMERICAN
🍴 **Cafe Beaujolais.** The yellow Victorian cottage that houses this popular restaurant is surrounded by a garden of heirloom and exotic plantings. Local ingredients find their way into appetizers such as butter-braised beets and Dungeness crab cakes and entrées like pan-roasted California sturgeon and duck two ways (crispy-skin breast and leg confit). **Known for:** breads from a wood-fired brick oven; Mendocino wines; garden of heirloom and exotic plantings. [$] *Average main: $30* ✉ *961 Ukiah St.* ☎ *707/937–5614* 🌐 *www.cafebeaujolais.com* ⏲ *No lunch Mon. and Tues.*

$$$$ B&B/INN Fodor's Choice ★
🏨 **Brewery Gulch Inn.** The feel is modern yet tasteful at this smallish inn. **Pros:** luxury in tune with nature; peaceful ocean views; complimentary wine hour and light buffet. **Cons:** must drive to town; expensive in-season; two-night minimum on weekends. [$] *Rooms from: $350* ✉ *9401 N. Hwy. 1, 1 mile south of Mendocino* ☎ *707/937–4752, 800/578–4454* 🌐 *www.brewerygulchinn.com* 🛏 *11 rooms* 🍽 *Breakfast.*

$$ B&B/INN Fodor's Choice ★
🏨 **Glendeven Inn Mendocino.** If Mendocino is the New England village of the West Coast, then Glendeven is the local country manor with sea views. **Pros:** great ocean views; elegant; romantic. **Cons:** not within walking distance of town; on the main drag; two-night minimum on weekends. [$] *Rooms from: $170* ✉ *8205 N. Hwy. 1* ☎ *707/937–0083, 800/822–4536* 🌐 *glendeven.com* 🛏 *6 rooms, 4 suites* 🍽 *Breakfast.*

$$$ B&B/INN
🏨 **MacCallum House.** Set on two flower-filled acres in the middle of town, this inn is a perfect mix of Victorian charm and modern luxury. **Pros:** excellent breakfast; central location; outstanding restaurant. **Cons:** luxury suites on a separate property are more modern; some rooms in main house lack charm; some guests find the look dated. [$] *Rooms from: $179* ✉ *45020 Albion St.* ☎ *707/937–0289, 800/609–0492* 🌐 *www.maccallumhouse.com* 🛏 *30 rooms* 🍽 *Breakfast.*

SPORTS AND THE OUTDOORS

Catch-A-Canoe and Bicycles Too. Rent kayaks and regular and outrigger canoes here year-round, as well as mountain and suspension bicycles. The outfit's tours explore Big River and its estuary. ✉ *Stanford Inn by the Sea, Comptche-Ukiah Rd., east of Hwy. 1* ☎ *707/937–0273* 🌐 *www.catchacanoe.com* 🎫 *From $65.*

FORT BRAGG

10 miles north of Mendocino.

Fort Bragg is a working-class town that many feel is the most authentic place on the coast. The city maintains a local feel since most people who work at the area hotels and restaurants also live here, as do many artists. A stroll down Franklin Street, one block east of Highway 1, takes you past bookstores, antiques shops, and boutiques.

GETTING HERE AND AROUND

From U.S. 101 at Willits follow Highway 20 west about 33 miles to Highway 1. Mendocino Transit Authority (🌐 *mendocinotransit.org*) Route 60 buses serve the town.

The North Coast is famous for its locally caught Dungeness crab; be sure to try some during your visit.

EXPLORING

Fodor's Choice
★

Mendocino Coast Botanical Gardens. Something beautiful is always abloom in these marvelous gardens. Along 3½ miles of trails, including pathways with ocean views and observation points for whale-watching, lie a profusion of flowers. The rhododendrons are at their peak from April through June; the dahlias begin their spectacular show in August and last into October. In winter the heather and camellias add more than a splash of color. The main trails are wheelchair accessible. ⊠ *18220 N. Hwy. 1, 2 miles south of Fort Bragg* ☎ *707/964–4352* ⊕ *www.gardenbythesea.org* ⊠ *$15.*

Museum in the Triangle Tattoo Parlor. At the top of a steep staircase, this several-room museum pays homage to Fort Bragg's rough-and-tumble past with memorabilia that includes early 20th-century Burmese tattooing instruments, pictures of astonishing tattoos from around the world, and a small shrine to the late sword-swallowing sideshow king Captain Don Leslie. ⊠ *356-B N. Main St.* ☎ *707/964–8814* ⊕ *www.triangletattoo.com* ⊠ *Free.*

Pacific Star Winery. When the sun's out and you're sipping wine while viewing whales or other sea creatures swimming offshore, this blufftop winery's outdoor tasting spaces feel mystical and magical. Equally beguiling on a brooding stormy day, Pacific Star has still more aces up its sleeve: engaging owners, and cheery staffers pouring a lineup of obscure varietals like Charbono and Brunello, a cousin of Sangiovese. The wines, among them a vibrant Mendocino Zin, are good, and they're reasonably priced. ■**TIP→ A downtown tasting room (401 North Main Street) opens daily each afternoon.** ⊠ *33000 N. Hwy. 1, 12 miles north of downtown* ☎ *707/964–1155* ⊕ *www.pacificstarwinery.com* ⊠ *Tasting $5* ⊗ *Closed Tues. and Wed.*

FAMILY **The Skunk Train.** A reproduction train travels the route of its 1920s predecessor, a fume-spewing gas-powered motorcar that shuttled passengers along a rail line dating from the 1880s logging days. Nicknamed the Skunk Train, the original traversed redwood forests inaccessible to automobiles. The main round-trip trek between Fort Bragg and the town of Northspur, 21 miles inland, takes a little over four hours. There are also shorter excursions to the town of Willits as well as seasonal and holiday-themed tours. ✉ *Foot of Laurel St., west of Main St.* ☎ *707/964–6371, 866/457–5865* 🌐 *www.skunktrain.com* 🎟 *From $25.*

BEACHES

Glass Beach. A gravel path on Elm Street three blocks west of Main Street leads to wild coastline with miles of blufftop trails. The sandy coves nearest the road contain dazzling sea glass (from the city dump once in this area) the surf pulverized into beautiful treasures. Some of the glass disappeared after early 2017 storms, but there's still some to see. Don't take any with you, though; it's against the law. There's no swimming at this beach either, for safety's sake. **Amenities:** parking (free); toilets. **Best for:** sunset; walking. ✉ *Elm St. and Old Haul Rd.* 🌐 *www.parks.ca.gov* 🎟 *Free.*

MacKerricher State Park. This park begins at Glass Beach, known for its sea glass, and stretches north for 9 miles, beginning with rocky headlands that taper into dunes and sandy beaches. The headland is a good place for whale-watching from December to mid-April. Fishing at Lake Cleone (a freshwater lake stocked with trout), canoeing, hiking, tidepooling, jogging, bicycling, beachcombing, camping, and harbor seal watching at Laguna Point are among the popular activities, many of which are accessible to the mobility-impaired. Be vigilant for rogue waves—don't turn your back on the sea. Dogs must be leashed. **Amenities:** parking; toilets. **Best for:** solitude; sunset; walking. ✉ *24100 MacKerricher Park Rd., off Hwy. 1, 3 miles north of town* ☎ *707/937–5804* 🌐 *www.parks.ca.gov* 🎟 *Free.*

WHERE TO EAT AND STAY

$ AMERICAN FAMILY 🍴 **Cowlick's Ice Cream.** Candy-cap mushroom (tastes like maple syrup) and black raspberry chocolate chunk are among this fun ice cream shop's top-selling flavors. Chocolate, mocha almond fudge, and ginger appear year-round, supplemented by blackberry-cheesecake, pumpkin, eggnog, and other seasonal offerings; the sorbets might include lemon, pear, or strawberry. **Known for:** handmade ice cream; chai, yellow-cake batter, and other wiggy flavors. [$] *Average main: $5* ✉ *250 N. Main St.* ☎ *707/962–9271* 🌐 *www.cowlicksicecream.com.*

$ ITALIAN 🍴 **Piaci Pub and Pizzeria.** The seats are stools and your elbows might bang a neighbor's, but nobody seems to mind at this casual spot for thin-crust pizzas (more than a dozen types), focaccia, and calzones. The food—there are several salads, too—is simple, but everything is carefully prepared and comes out tasty. **Known for:** cash-only; well-chosen beers; dog-friendly outdoor tables. [$] *Average main: $15* ✉ *120 W. Redwood Ave.* ☎ *707/961–1133* 🌐 *www.piacipizza.com* 💳 *No credit cards* 🕓 *No lunch Sun.*

$$$$ B&B/INN Fodor's Choice ★ 🏨 **Inn at Newport Ranch.** Attention to detail in both design and hospitality make for an incomparable stay at this 2,000-acre working cattle ranch with 1½ miles of private coastline. **Pros:** over-the-top design; mesmerizing Pacific views; horse riding, oceanside cocktails by a fire pit, and other diversions. **Cons:** all this design and glamour comes at a price; lengthy drive back from Mendocino and Fort Bragg restaurants at night; coast can be foggy in summer. [$] *Rooms from: $350* ✉ *31502 N. Hwy. 1* ☎ *707/962–4818* 🌐 *theinnatnewportranch.com* 🛏 *11 rooms* 🍴 *Breakfast.*

$$ B&B/INN Fodor's Choice ★ 🏨 **Weller House Inn.** It's hard to believe that this house was abandoned and slated for demolition when it was purchased in 1994 and carefully restored. **Pros:** handcrafted details; radiant heat in the wood floors; colorful and tasteful rooms. **Cons:** some guests find it too old-fashioned; pet cleaning fee; no TVs in rooms. [$] *Rooms from: $150* ✉ *524 Stewart St.* ☎ *707/964–4415* 🌐 *www.wellerhouse.com* 🛏 *9 rooms* 🍴 *Breakfast.*

SPORTS AND THE OUTDOORS

WHALE-WATCHING

All Aboard Adventures. Captain Tim of All Aboard operates whale-watching trips from late December through April. ✉ *Noyo Harbor, 32410 N. Harbor Dr.* ☎ *707/964–1881* 🌐 *www.allaboardadventures.com* 🎫 *From $40.*

REDWOOD COUNTRY

North of Mendocino in Humboldt County stand some of California's tallest and oldest redwoods. Many are easily accessible along or not too far off U.S. 101.

HUMBOLDT REDWOODS STATE PARK

86 miles northeast of Fort Bragg, 46 miles south of Eureka.

Conservationists banded together a century ago as the Save the Redwoods League and scored a key victory when a memorial grove was dedicated in 1921. That grove is now part of Humboldt Redwoods State Park, which these days has grown to nearly 53,000 acres, about a third of which are filled with untouched old-growth coast redwoods.

GETTING HERE AND AROUND

Access the park right off U.S. 101. *(See Bus Travel, at the beginning of this chapter, for Humboldt County public transportation information.)*

EXPLORING

FAMILY Fodor's Choice ★ **Avenue of the Giants.** Some of the tallest trees on Earth tower over this magnificent 32-mile stretch of two-lane blacktop, also known as Highway 254, that follows the south fork of the Eel River through Humboldt Redwoods State Park. The highway runs more or less parallel to U.S. 101 from Phillipsville in the south to the town of Pepperwood in the north. A brochure available at either end of the highway or the **visitor center,** 2 miles south of Weott, contains a self-guided tour, with short and long hikes through various redwood groves. A trail at **Founders Grove** passes by several impressive trees, among them the fallen 362-foot-long

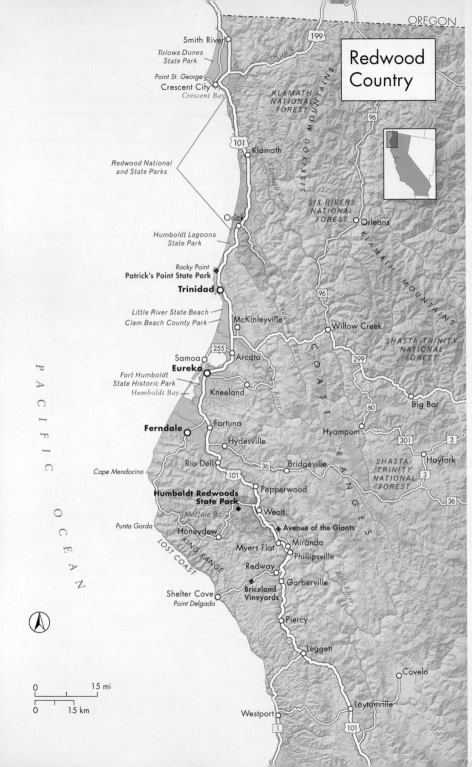

Dyerville Giant, whose root base points skyward 35 feet. The tree can be reached via a short trail that begins 4 miles north of the visitor center. About 6 miles north of the center lies **Rockefeller Forest.** The largest remaining old-growth coast redwood forest, it contains more than a third of the 100 tallest trees in the world. ⊠ *Humboldt Redwoods State Park Visitor Center, Hwy. 254, Weott* ☎ *707/946–2263* ⊕ *www.parks. ca.gov* ⊠ *Free; $8 day-use fee for Williams Grove.*

OFF THE
BEATEN
PATH

Briceland Vineyards. Lean yet flavorful Humboldt County Pinot Noirs are the specialty of this three-decades-old winery set amid the trees. In good weather the delightfully low-key tastings take place in front of the weathered original winery building. Guests sip Gewürztraminer (surprisingly dry), Viognier, or other whites before sampling Pinots and perhaps Syrah or Zinfandel. ■ TIP→ From late May through August drop-ins are welcome 1–5 on weekends, otherwise tastings are by appointment. ⊠ *5959 Briceland Rd., 10½ miles southwest of Avenue of the Giants southern entrance* ✛ *Take Briceland Rd. 5½ miles west from Redwood Dr. in Redway (from north, U.S. 101 Exit 642; from south, Exit 639B)* ☎ *707/923–2429* ⊕ *bricelandvineyards.com* ⊠ *Tastings $15.*

FERNDALE

35 miles northwest of Weott, 19 miles south of Eureka.

Ferndale, best known for its colorful Victorian architecture, much of it Stick-Eastlake, is well worth the 5-mile detour off U.S. 101. Many shops carry a self-guided tour map that highlights the most interesting historic buildings. Gift shops and ice-cream stores comprise a fair share of the businesses here, but Ferndale remains a fully functioning small town, and descendants of the Portuguese and Scandinavian dairy farmers who settled here continue to raise dairy cows in the surrounding pastures.

GETTING HERE AND AROUND

To get to Ferndale from U.S. 101, follow Highway 211 southwest 5 miles. Public transit doesn't serve the town.

EXPLORING

Ferndale Historic Cemetery. The well-worn gravestones at Ferndale's east-side cemetery provide insight into the hard, often short lives of the European immigrants who cultivated this area in the mid-18th century. At the top of the hill, sweeping (and photogenic) vistas unfold of the town, its farms, and the ocean. ⊠ *Craig St. and Berding St.* ⊠ *Free.*

Ferndale Museum. The main building of this museum exhibits Victoriana and historical photographs and has a display of an old-style barbershop and another of Wiyot Indian baskets. In the annex are a horse-drawn buggy, a re-created blacksmith's shop, and antique farming, fishing, and dairy equipment. Don't miss the historic Bosch-Omori seismograph, installed in 1933 in Ferndale; it's still checked daily for recordings of earthquake activity. ⊠ *515 Shaw Ave.* ☎ *707/786–4466* ⊕ *www.ferndale-museum.org* ⊠ *$2* ⊘ *Closed Jan., Mon. yr-round, Tues. Oct.–Dec. and Feb.–May.*

Lost Coast Scenic Drive. A loop drive counterclockwise from Ferndale yields amazing ocean views and winds through forests and small towns before heading into Humboldt Redwoods State Park and then back up U.S. 101 toward the starting point. The road has numerous curves and some rugged stretches in need of repair, but driving this 100 or so mile stretch is exhilarating. ■TIP➔ Allot four hours for this excursion. ⊠ *Ferndale* ✛ *Head southwest from Ferndale on Wildcat Ave., which soon becomes Mattole Rd. Follow Mattole west to the coast, south to Petrolia, and east to Honeydew and the park. At U.S. 101 head north back toward Ferndale.* ⊕ *redwoods.info/showrecord.asp?id=3870.*

WHERE TO STAY

$$
B&B/INN

🏨 **Gingerbread Mansion.** A dazzler that rivals San Francisco's "painted ladies," this Victorian mansion has detailed exterior spindle work, turrets, and gables. **Pros:** elegant decor; relaxing atmosphere; friendly staff. **Cons:** some may find the place gaudy; two-night minimum on weekends; lacks standard hotel amenities. $ *Rooms from: $165* ⊠ *400 Berding St.* ☎ *707/786–4000* ⊕ *www.gingerbread-mansion.com* ⤴ *11 rooms* ♸ *Breakfast.*

SHOPPING

Blacksmith Shop. With two storefronts in Ferndale, this shop celebrates the survival of traditional blacksmithing arts in the area. The hand-forged works sold here range from flatware to furniture, and especially nice are the rough-handled chef's knives—so sharp there are Band-Aids stuffed in behind the display, just in case. ⊠ *455 and 491 Main St.* ☎ *707/786–4216* ⊕ *www.ferndaleblacksmith.com.*

EUREKA

19 miles north of Ferndale.

With a population of 27,000, Eureka is the North Coast's largest city, a good place to fuel up, buy groceries, and learn a little about the region's mining, timber, and fishing pasts. The chamber of commerce visitor center has maps of self-guided driving tours of the town's nearly 100 Victorians, among them the flamboyant 1886 Queen Anne–style **Carson Mansion**, at 143 M Street. The home can only be viewed from outside, but it's worth a look and a photo or two. Art galleries and antiques stores liven up the district from C to I street between 2nd and 3rd streets, and a walking pier extends into the harbor.

GETTING HERE AND AROUND

U.S. 101 travels through Eureka. Eureka Transit (⊕ *www.eurekatransit. org*) buses serve the town.

VISITOR CENTER

Eureka Chamber of Commerce. ⊠ *2112 Broadway* ☎ *707/442–3738* ⊕ *www.eurekachamber.com.*

EXPLORING

Blue Ox Millworks. This woodshop is among a handful in the country specializing in Victorian-era architecture, but what makes it truly unique is that its craftspeople use antique tools to do the work. Visitors can watch craftsmen use printing presses, lathes, and other equipment to create gingerbread trim, fence pickets, and other signature Victorian embellishments. The shop is less interesting on Saturday, when most craftspeople take the day off. ✉ *1 X St.* ☎ *707/444–3437, 800/248–4259* 🌐 *www.blueoxmill.com* *$10* ⏲ *Closed Sat. Dec.–Mar., Sun. yr-round.*

WHERE TO EAT AND STAY

$ AMERICAN

Lost Coast Brewery and Cafe. This bustling microbrewery is the best place in town to relax with a pint of ale or porter. Soups and salads, plus burgers, tacos, and light meals are served for lunch and dinner. **Known for:** outstanding beers; happy hour weekdays 4–6; brewery tours. $ *Average main: $12* ✉ *617 4th St.* ☎ *707/445–4480* 🌐 *www.lostcoast.com.*

$$$ AMERICAN Fodor's Choice ★

Restaurant 301. The chef at the elegant restaurant inside the Carter House uses ingredients selected from the farmers' market, local cheese makers and ranchers, and the on-site gardens. The dishes (there's always a fresh seafood offering) are prepared with a delicate hand and a sensuous imagination. **Known for:** one of California's best wine lists; à la carte, prix-fixe options; bar menu (weekday happy hour's a deal). $ *Average main: $29* ✉ *301 L St.* ☎ *707/444–8062, 800/404–1390* 🌐 *carterhouse.com* ⏲ *No lunch.*

$$$ HOTEL Fodor's Choice ★

Carter House Inns. Owner Mark Carter says he trains his staff always to say yes; whether it's breakfast in bed or an in-room massage, someone here will get you what you want. **Pros:** elegant ambience; every detail in place; aim-to-please service. **Cons:** not suitable for children; expensive restaurant; two-night minimum on weekends. $ *Rooms from: $189* ✉ *301 L St.* ☎ *707/444–8062, 800/404–1390* 🌐 *www.carterhouse.com* *32 rooms* *Breakfast.*

SPORTS AND THE OUTDOORS

WHALE-WATCHING

Humboats Kayak Adventures. You can rent kayaks and book kayaking tours that from December to June include whale-watching trips. Half-day river kayaking trips pass beneath massive redwoods; the whale-watching outings get you close enough for good photos. ✉ *Woodley Island Marina, 601 Startare Dr., Dock A* ☎ *707/443–5157* 🌐 *www.humboats.com* *From $30 rentals, $55 tours.*

TRINIDAD

23 miles north of Eureka.

A mellow base for exploring the southern portion of Redwood National Park, coastal Trinidad got its name from the Spanish mariners who entered the bay on Trinity Sunday, June 9, 1775. Formerly the principal trading post for mining camps along the Klamath and Trinity rivers, these days Trinidad is a quiet and genuinely charming community with several beaches and ample sights and activities to entertain low-key visitors.

GETTING HERE AND AROUND

Trinidad sits right off U.S. 101. From Interstate 5, head west from Redding on Highway 299 and north on U.S. 101 north of Arcata. Redwood Transit System (🌐 *www.redwoodtransit.org*) provides bus service.

EXPLORING

Patrick's Point State Park. On a forested plateau almost 200 feet above the surf, the park has stunning views of the Pacific, great whale- and sea lion–watching spots, campgrounds, picnic areas, bike paths, and hiking trails through old-growth spruce forest. There are also tidal pools at Agate Beach, a re-created Yurok Indian village, and a small visitor center with exhibits. It's uncrowded and sublimely quiet here. Dogs are not allowed on trails or the beach. ✉ *U.S. 101, 5 miles north of Trinidad* ☎ *707/677–3570* 🌐 *www.parks.ca.gov* 🎟 *$8 per vehicle.*

BEACHES

FAMILY **Clam Beach County Park and Little River State Beach.** These two adjoining oceanfront areas stretch for several miles south of Trinidad. The sandy beach here is exceptionally wide. Beachcombing and savoring fabulous sunsets are favorite activities. The two parks share day-use facilities. **Amenities:** parking; toilets. **Best for:** solitude; sunset; walking. ✉ *Clam Beach Dr. & U.S. 101, 6 miles south of Trinidad* ☎ *707/445–7651* 🌐 *www.parks.ca.gov* 🎟 *Free (day use).*

WHERE TO EAT AND STAY

$$$ AMERICAN Fodor's Choice ★ 🍴 **Larrupin' Cafe.** Set in a two-story house on a quiet country road north of town, this restaurant—one of the best places to eat on the North Coast—is often thronged with people enjoying fresh seafood, Cornish game hen, mesquite-grilled ribs, and vegetarian dishes. The garden setting and candlelight stir thoughts of romance. **Known for:** garden setting; outside patio; smoked beef brisket. [$] *Average main: $29* ✉ *1658 Patrick's Point Dr.* ☎ *707/677–0230* 🌐 *www.larrupin.com* 🕒 *No lunch.*

$$$$ B&B/INN 🏨 **Trinidad Bay Bed and Breakfast Inn.** Staying at this small Cape Cod–style inn perched above Trinidad Bay is like spending the weekend at a friend's vacation house. **Pros:** great location above bay; lots of light; tall windows in Tidepool room. **Cons:** main house can feel crowded at full occupancy; expensive in summer; two-night minimum on weekends. [$] *Rooms from: $275* ✉ *560 Edwards St.* ☎ *707/677–0840* 🌐 *www.trinidadbaybnb.com* 🛏 *4 rooms* 🍽 *Breakfast.*

$$$$ B&B/INN 🏨 **Turtle Rocks Oceanfront Inn.** This comfortable inn has the best view in Trinidad, and the builders have made the most of it, adding private, glassed-in decks to each room so that guests can fully enjoy the ocean and sunning sea lions. **Pros:** great ocean views; comfortable king beds; surrounding landscape left natural and wild. **Cons:** no businesses within walking distance; interiors may be too spare for some guests; can be foggy here in summer. [$] *Rooms from: $295* ✉ *3392 Patrick's Point Dr., 4½ miles north of town* ☎ *707/677–3707* 🌐 *www.turtlerocksinn.com* 🛏 *6 rooms* 🍽 *Breakfast.*

REDWOOD NATIONAL PARK

WELCOME TO REDWOOD NATIONAL PARK

TOP REASONS TO GO

★ **Giant trees:** These mature coastal redwoods are the tallest trees in the world.

★ **Hiking to the sea:** The park's trails wind through majestic redwood groves, and many connect to the Coastal Trail, which runs along the western edge of the park.

★ **Rare wildlife:** Mighty Roosevelt elk favor the park's flat prairie and open lands; seldom-seen black bears roam the backcountry; trout and salmon leap through streams; and Pacific gray whales swim along the coast during their spring and fall migrations.

★ **Stepping back in time:** Hike mossy and mysterious Fern Canyon Trail and explore a prehistoric scene of lush vegetation and giant ferns—a memorable scene in *Jurassic Park 2* was shot here.

★ **Getting off-the-grid:** Amid the majestic redwoods you're out of cell-phone range, offering a rare opportunity to disconnect..

1 Del Norte Coast Redwoods State Park. The rugged terrain of this far northwestern corner of California combines stretches of treacherous surf, steep cliffs, and forested ridges. On a clear day it's postcard-perfect; with fog, it's mysterious and mesmerizing.

2 Jedediah Smith Redwoods State Park. Gargantuan old-growth redwoods dominate the scenery here. The Smith River cuts through canyons and splits across boulders, carrying salmon to the inland creeks where they spawn.

3 Prairie Creek Redwoods State Park. The forests here give way to spacious, grassy plains where abundant wildlife thrives. Roosevelt elk are a common sight in the meadows and down to Gold Bluffs Beach, where a short trail leads to Fern Canyon.

4 Orick Area. The highlight of the southern portion of Redwood National and State Parks is the Tall Trees Grove. It's difficult to reach and requires a special pass, but it's worth the hassle—this section has some of the tallest coast redwood trees. The current world-record holder, a 379-footer named Hyperion, was discovered outside the grove in 2006.

12

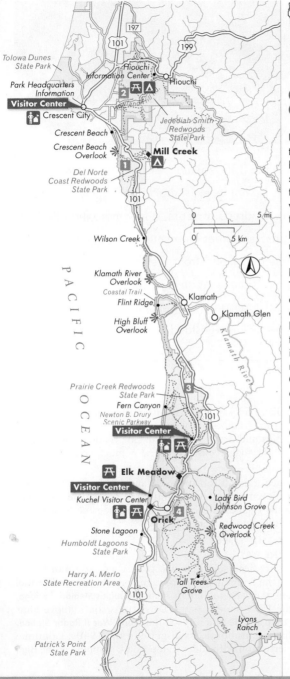

CALIFORNIA

GETTING ORIENTED

U.S. 101 weaves through the southern portion of Redwood National Park, skirts around the center, and then slips back through redwoods in the north and on to Crescent City. The entire park spans about 50 miles north to south. The Kuchel Visitor Center, Prairie Creek Redwoods State Park, Tall Trees Grove, Fern Canyon, and Lady Bird Johnson Grove are in the southern section. In the central section, where the Klamath River Overlook is the dominant feature, the narrow, mostly graveled Coastal Drive loop yields ocean vistas. To the north are Mill Creek Trail, Enderts Beach, and Crescent Beach Overlook in Del Norte Coast Redwoods State Park, as well as Jedediah Smith Redwoods State Park, Stout Grove, Little Bald Hills, and Simpson-Reed Grove.

Updated by
Daniel Mangin

Soaring more than 350 feet high, the coastal redwoods that give this park its name are miracles of efficiency—some have survived hundreds of years, a few more than two millennia. These massive trees glean nutrients from the rich alluvial flats at their feet and from the moisture and nitrogen trapped in their uneven canopy. Their huge, thick-bark trunks can hold thousands of gallons of water, reservoirs that have helped them withstand centuries of firestorms.

PLANNING

WHEN TO GO

Campers and hikers flock to the park from mid-June to early September. The crowds disappear in winter, but you'll have to contend with frequent rains and nasty potholes on side roads. Temperatures fluctuate widely: the foggy coastal lowland is much cooler than the higher-altitude interior.

The average annual rainfall is between 90 and 100 inches, most of it falling between November and April. During the dry summer, thick fog rolling in from the Pacific veils the forests, providing the redwoods a large portion of their moisture intake.

PLANNING YOUR TIME
REDWOOD IN ONE DAY

From Crescent City head south on U.S. 101. A mile south of Klamath, detour onto the 8-mile-long, narrow, and mostly unpaved **Coastal Drive** loop. Along the way, you'll pass the old **Douglas Memorial Bridge,** destroyed in the 1964 flood. Coastal Drive turns south above Flint Ridge. In less than a mile you'll reach the **World War II Radar Station,** which looks like a farmhouse, its disguise in the 1940s. Continue south to the intersection with Alder Camp Road, stopping at the **High Bluff Overlook.**

From the Coastal Drive turn left to reconnect with U.S. 101. Head south to reach **Newton B. Drury Scenic Parkway,** a 10-mile drive through an old-growth redwood forest with access to numerous trailheads. This road is open to all noncommercial vehicles. Along the way, stop at **Prairie Creek Visitor Center,** housed in a small redwood lodge. Enjoy a picnic lunch and an engaging tactile walk in a grove behind the lodge on the Revelation Trail, which was designed for vision-impaired visitors. Back on the parkway head north less than a mile and drive out on unpaved **Cal-Barrel Road,** which leads east through redwood forests. Return to the parkway, continue south about 2 miles to reconnect with U.S. 101, and turn west on mostly unpaved **Davison Road** (motorhomes/RVs and trailers are prohibited). In about 30 minutes you'll curve right to **Gold Bluffs Beach.** Continue north to the **Fern Canyon** trailhead. Return to U.S. 101, and drive south to the turnoff for the **Thomas H. Kuchel Visitor Center.** Pick up free permits—only 50 a day are granted—to visit the **Tall Trees Grove** and head north on U.S. 101 to the turnoff for **Bald Hills Road,** a steep route (motorhomes/RVs and trailers are not advised). If you visit the grove, allow at least four hours round-trip from the information center. You could also bypass the turnoff to the grove and continue south on Bald Hills Road to 3,097-foot **Schoolhouse Peak.** For a simpler jaunt, turn onto Bald Hills Road and follow it for 2 miles to the **Lady Bird Johnson Grove Nature Loop Trail.** Take the footbridge to the easy 1-mile loop, which follows an old logging road through a mature redwood forest. ■TIP➜ Motorhomes/RVs and trailers are **not** allowed on Coastal Drive, Cal-Barrel Road, and Davison Road, and are not advised on Bald Hills Road.

GETTING HERE AND AROUND

CAR TRAVEL

U.S. 101 runs north–south the entire length of the park. You can access all the main park roads via U.S. 101 and U.S. 199, which runs east–west through the park's northern portion. Many roads within the park aren't paved, and winter rains can turn them into obstacle courses; sometimes they're closed completely. Motorhomes/RVs and trailers aren't permitted on some routes. The drive from San Francisco to the park's southern end takes about five hours via U.S. 101. From Portland it takes roughly the same amount of time to reach the park's northern section by way of Interstate 5 to U.S. 199. ■TIP➜ Don't rely solely on GPS, which is not always accurate; closely consult park maps, available at the visitor information centers.

PARK ESSENTIALS

PARK FEES AND PERMITS

Admission to Redwood National Park and the related state parks is free. To visit the popular Tall Trees Grove, you must get a free permit at the Kuchel Visitor Center in Orick. The fee to camp at the state parks is $35. Free permits, available at the Kuchel, Crescent City, and (summer only) Hiouchi visitor centers, are needed to stay at all designated backcountry camps.

PARK HOURS

The park is open year-round, 24 hours a day.

Plants and Wildlife in Redwood

Coast redwoods, the world's tallest trees, grow in the moist, temperate climate of California's North Coast. The current record holder, topping out at 379 feet (or 386, depending on who's measuring), was found in the Redwood Creek watershed in 2006. These ancient giants thrive in an environment that exists in only a few hundred coastal miles along the Pacific Ocean. They commonly live 600 years—though some have been around for more than 2,000 years.

DIVERSE, COMPLEX
A healthy redwood forest is diverse and includes Douglas firs, western hemlocks, tan oaks, and madrone trees. The complex soils of the forest floor support a profusion of ferns, mosses, and fungi, along with numerous shrubs and berry bushes. In spring, California rhododendron bloom all over, providing a dazzling purple and pink contrast to the dense greenery.

OLD-GROWTH FORESTS
Redwood National and State Parks hold nearly 50% of California's old-growth redwood forests. Of the original 3,125 square miles (2 million acres) in the Redwoods Historic Range, only 4% survived logging that began in 1850. A quarter of these trees are privately owned and on managed land. The rest are on public tracts.

WILDLIFE SPECIES
In the park's backcountry, you might spot mountain lions, black bears, black-tailed deer, river otters, beavers, and minks. Roosevelt elk roam the flatlands, and the rivers and streams teem with salmon and trout. Gray whales, seals, and sea lions cavort near the coastline. More than 400 species of birds have been recorded in the parks, which are located along the Pacific Flyway.

VISITOR INFORMATION
Park Contact Information Redwood National and State Parks. ✉ *1111 2nd St., Crescent City* ☎ *707/465-7335* ⊕ *www.nps.gov/redw.*

VISITOR CENTERS
Hiouchi Information Center. This small center at Jedediah Smith Redwoods State Park has exhibits about the area flora and fauna and screens a park film. A starting point for ranger programs, the center has restrooms and a picnic area. ✉ *U.S. 199, 2 miles west of Hiouchi and 9 miles east of Crescent City* ✣ *Southeast of entrance to Jedediah Smith Campground* ☎ *707/458-3294* ⊕ *www.nps.gov/redw.*

Fodor's Choice ★ **Prairie Creek Visitor Center.** In a small redwood lodge, this center has a massive stone fireplace. The wildlife displays include a section of a tree a young elk died beside. Because of the peculiar way the redwood grew around the elk's skull, the tree appears to have antlers. The center has information about summer programs in Prairie Creek Redwoods State Park, and you'll find a gift shop, a picnic area, restrooms, and exhibits on flora and fauna. Roosevelt elk often roam the vast field adjacent to the center, and several trailheads begin nearby. Stretch your legs with an easy stroll along **Revelation Trail,** a short loop that starts behind the lodge. ✉ *Prairie Creek Rd., off U.S. 101 near southern end of Newton B. Drury Scenic Pkwy., Orick* ☎ *707/488-2039* ⊕ *www.parks.ca.gov/prairiecreek.*

Fodor'sChoice ★ **Thomas H. Kuchel Visitor Center.** The park's southern section contains the largest and best of the Redwoods visitor centers. Rangers here dispense brochures, advice, and free permits to drive up the access road to Tall Trees Grove. Whale-watchers find the center's deck an excellent observation point, and bird-watchers enjoy the nearby Freshwater Lagoon, a popular layover for migrating waterfowl. Many of the center's exhibits are hands-on and kid-friendly. ⊠ *Off U.S. 101 beside Redwood Creek Beach County Park, Orick* ☎ *707/465–7765* ⊕ *www.nps.gov/redw.*

12

EXPLORING

SCENIC DRIVES

Coastal Drive. The 8-mile, narrow, and mostly unpaved Coastal Drive takes about one hour to traverse. Weaving through stands of redwoods, the road yields close-up views of the Klamath River and expansive panoramas of the Pacific. Recurring landslides have closed sections of the original road; this loop, closed to trailers and RVs, is all that remains. Hikers access the Flint Ridge section of the Coastal Trail off the drive. ⊠ *Klamath* ✛ *1 mile south of Klamath off U.S. 101; take Klamath Beach Rd. exit and follow signs.*

Fodor'sChoice ★ **Newton B. Drury Scenic Parkway/Big Tree Wayside.** This paved 10-mile route threads through Prairie Creek Redwoods State Park and old-growth redwoods. It's open to all noncommercial vehicles. North of the Prairie Creek Visitor Center you can make the 0.8-mile walk to Big Tree Wayside and observe Roosevelt elk in the prairie. ⊠ *Orick* ✛ *Entrances off U.S. 101 about 5 miles south of Klamath and 5 miles north of Orick.*

SCENIC STOPS

Crescent Beach Overlook. The scenery here includes ocean views and, in the distance, Crescent City and its working harbor. In balmy weather this is a great place for a picnic. From the overlook you can spot migrating gray whales between November and April. ⊠ *Off Enderts Beach Rd., 4½ miles south of downtown Crescent City.*

Fodor'sChoice ★ **Fern Canyon.** Enter another world and be surrounded by 50-foot canyon walls covered with sword, deer, and five-finger ferns. Allow an hour to explore the ¼-mile-long vertical garden along a 0.7-mile loop. From the northern end of Gold Bluffs Beach it's an easy walk, although you'll have to wade across or scamper along planks that traverse a small stream several times (in addition to driving across a couple of streams on the way to the parking area). But the lush, otherworldly surroundings, which appeared in *Jurassic Park 2,* are a must-see when creeks aren't running too high. Motorhomes/RVs and all trailers are prohibited on the road to Fern Canyon. You can also hike to the canyon from Prairie Creek Visitor Center along the moderately challenging West Ridge–Friendship Ridge–James Irvine Loop, 12½ miles round-trip.

Good Reads

■ The *Redwood Official National and State Parks Handbook,* published by the Redwood Parks Association, covers the area's ecology, botany, natural and cultural history, and common wildlife.

■ Richard Preston's spellbinding *The Wild Trees: A Story of Passion and Daring* chronicles the redwood-climbing exploits of several botanists fiercely passionate about California's endangered tall trees and the ecosystem that supports them.

■ If you plan on hiking, stop at one of the visitor centers and purchase the inexpensive *Redwood National Park Trail Guide,* with details about more than 200 miles of trails.

⊠ *North of Gold Bluffs Beach, Orick ✛ 2¾ miles north of Orick, take Davison Rd. northwest off U.S. 101 and follow signs to Gold Bluffs Beach* ⊕ *www.nps.gov/redw.*

Lady Bird Johnson Grove. One of the park's most accessible spots to view big trees, the grove was dedicated by, and named for, the former first lady. A 1-mile nature loop follows an old logging road through a mature redwood forest. Allow 45 minutes to complete the trail. ⊠ *Bald Hills Rd., Orick ✛ 1 mile north of Orick off U.S. 101, then 2½ miles to trailhead* ⊕ *www.nps.gov/redw.*

Tall Trees Grove. At the Kuchel and other visitor centers you can obtain a free permit to make the steep 14-mile drive to this redwood grove that once contained the world-record holder for tallest tree. Rangers dispense only 50 permits maximum a day, first come, first served. The hike from the trailhead parking lot is 4 miles round-trip. ⊠ *Tall Trees Access Rd., off Bald Hills Rd., Orick ✛ 1 mile north of Orick, head east and south from U.S. 101 on Bald Hills Rd. for about 7 miles, then southwest on unpaved access road about 6½ miles to trailhead* ☞ *Trailers and RVs not allowed in trailhead parking lot.*

SPORTS AND THE OUTDOORS

BICYCLING

Besides the roadways, you can bike on several trails. Best bets include the 11-mile Lost Man Creek Trail, which begins 3 miles north of Orick; the 12-mile round-trip Coastal Trail (Last Chance Section), which starts at the southern end of Enderts Beach Road and becomes steep and narrow as it travels through dense slopes of foggy redwood forests; and the 19-mile, single-track Ossagon Trail Loop, on which you're likely to see elk as you cruise through redwoods before coasting oceanside toward the end.

CLOSE UP

Best Campgrounds in Redwood

Within a 30-minute drive of Redwood National and State Parks are roughly 60 public and private camping facilities. None of the four primitive areas in Redwood—DeMartin, Flint Ridge, Little Bald Hills, and Nickel Creek—is a drive-in site. You will need to get a free permit from any visitor center except Prairie Creek before camping in these campgrounds, and along Redwood Creek in the backcountry. Bring your own water because drinking water isn't available at any of these sites. These campgrounds, plus Gold Bluffs Beach, are first come, first served.

If you'd rather drive than hike in, Redwood has four developed campgrounds—Elk Prairie, Gold Bluffs Beach, Jedediah Smith, and Mill Creek—that are within the state-park boundaries. None has RV hookups, and some length restrictions apply. Fees are $35 in state park campgrounds. For details and reservations, call ☎ *800/444–7275* or check ⊕ *www.reserveamerica.com.*

Elk Prairie Campground. Roosevelt elk frequent this popular campground adjacent to a prairie and old-growth

redwoods. ⊠ *On Newton B. Drury Scenic Pkwy., 6 miles north of Orick in Prairie Creek Redwoods State Park* ☎ *800/444–7275.*

Gold Bluffs Beach Campground. You can camp in tents right on the beach at this Prairie Creek Redwoods State Park campground near Fern Canyon. ⊠ *At end of Davison Rd., 5 miles south of Prairie Creek Visitor Center off U.S. 101* ☎ *800/444–7275.*

Jedediah Smith Campground. This is one of the few places to camp—in tents or RVs—within groves of old-growth redwood forest. ⊠ *10 miles east of Crescent City on U.S. 199* ☎ *800/444–7275.*

Mill Creek Campground. Redwoods tower over large Mill Creek, in Del Norte Coast Redwoods State Park. ⊠ *East of U.S. 101, 7 miles southeast of Crescent City* ☎ *800/444–7275.*

Nickel Creek Campground. An easy hike gets you to these five primitive sites in Redwood National Park; near tide pools, they have great ocean views. ⊠ *On Coastal Trail ½ mile from end of Enderts Beach Rd.* ☎ *707/465–7335.*

12

HIKING

MODERATE

Coastal Trail. This easy-to-difficult trail runs most of the park's length; smaller sections that vary in difficulty are accessible at frequent, well-marked trailheads. The moderate-to-difficult **DeMartin section** leads past 6 miles of old-growth redwoods and through prairie. If you're up for a real workout, hike the brutally difficult but stunning **Flint Ridge section**, 4½ miles of steep grades and numerous switchbacks past redwoods and Marshall Pond. The moderate 5½-mile-long **Klamath section,** which connects the Wilson Creek Picnic Area and the Klamath River Overlook, with a short detour to Hidden Beach and its tide pools, provides coastal views and whale-watching opportunities. *Moderate.* ⊠ *Klamath ✛ Trailheads: DeMartin, U.S. 101 mile markers 12.8 (south) and 15.6 (north); Flint Ridge, Douglas Bridge parking area,* *north end of Coastal Dr. (east), and off Klamath Beach Rd. (west); Klamath, Requa Rd. at Klamath River Overlook (south), Wilson Creek Picnic Area, off U.S. 101 (north)* ⊕ *www.nps.gov/redw.*

KAYAKING

With many miles of often shallow rivers, streams, and estuarial lagoons, kayaking is a popular pastime in the park.

OUTFITTERS

Humboats Kayak Adventures. You can rent kayaks and book kayaking tours that from December to June include whale-watching trips. Half-day river kayaking trips pass beneath massive redwoods; the whale-watching outings get you close enough for good photos. ⊠ *Woodley Island Marina, 601 Startare Dr., Dock A, Eureka* ☎ *707/443–5157* ⊕ *www.humboats.com* ⌑ *From $30 rentals, $55 tours.*

Fodor's Choice **Kayak Zak's.** This outfit rents kayaks and stand-up paddleboards, good
★ for touring the beautiful estuarial and freshwater lagoons of Humboldt Lagoons State Park. You can also book a guided nature paddle. Rentals at the Stone Lagoon Visitor Center take place year-round, and on most summer weekends Kayak Zak's sets up a trailer at nearby Big Lagoon. The lagoons are stunning. Herds of Roosevelt elk sometimes traipse along the shoreline of Big Lagoon; raptors, herons, and water-fowl abound in both lagoons; and you can paddle across Stone Lagoon to a spectacular secluded Pacific-view beach. ⊠ *Stone Lagoon Visitor Center, 115336 U.S. 101, about 5½ miles south of Orick, Trinidad* ☎ *707/498–1130* ⊕ *www.kayakzak.com* ⌑ *From $30.*

WHALE-WATCHING

Good vantage points for whale-watching include Crescent Beach Over-look, the Kuchel Visitor Center in Orick, points along the Coastal Trail, and the Klamath River Overlook. From late November through January is the best time to see their southward migrations; from February through April the whales return, usually passing closer to shore.

THE INLAND EMPIRE

East of Los Angeles to Temecula

WELCOME TO THE INLAND EMPIRE

TOP REASONS TO GO

★ **Wine Country:** The idyllic, ever-expanding Temecula Valley is home to family-owned and resort-style wineries cooled by faint ocean breezes.

★ **The Mission Inn:** One of the most unusual hotels in America, Riverside's rambling, eclectic Mission Inn feels like an urban Hearst Castle.

★ **Apple country:** In the Oak Glen apple-growing region, you can attend an old-fashioned hoedown, take a wagon ride, and sample apple pies and homemade ciders.

★ **Soothing spas:** The lushly landscaped grounds, bubbling hot springs, and playful mud baths of Glen Ivy are ideal spots to unwind; Kelly's Spa at the historic Mission Inn provides a cozy Tuscan-style retreat.

★ **Alpine escapes:** Breathe in the clean mountain air or get cozy at a bed-and-breakfast at great mountain hideaways like Lake Arrowhead and Big Bear.

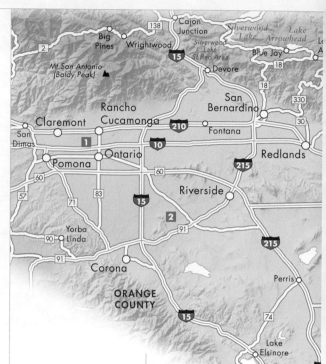

1 The Western Inland Empire. At the foot of 10,064-foot-high Mt. Baldy in the San Gabriel Mountains, the community of Claremont is known for the prestigious seven-school Claremont Colleges complex. A classic tree-shaded, lively, sophisticated college town, Claremont resembles trendy sections of Los Angeles more than the laid-back Inland Empire.

2 Riverside Area. In the late 1700s, Mexican settlers called this now-suburban region Valle de Paraíso. Citrus-growing here began in 1873, when homesteader Eliza Tibbets planted two navel-orange trees in her yard. The area's biggest draws are the majestic Mission Inn, with its fine restaurants and unique history and architecture, and Glen Ivy Hot Springs in nearby Corona.

GETTING ORIENTED

Several freeways provide access to the Inland Empire from Los Angeles and San Diego. Temecula lines up along interstates 10 and 215; and Corona, Riverside, and San Bernardino lie along Highway 91. As a Los Angeles bedroom community, the area sees nasty freeway congestion on Highway 60 and interstates 10 and 15, so try to avoid driving during rush hour, usually from 6 to 9 am and 3:30 to 7 pm.

3 San Bernardino Mountains. Lake Arrowhead and always-sunny Big Bear are the recreational centers of this area. Though the two are geographically close, they're distinct in appeal. Lake Arrowhead, with its cool mountain air, trail-threaded woods, and brilliant lake, draws a summertime crowd. Big Bear's ski and snowboarding slopes, cross-country trails, and cheerful lodges come alive in winter and provide a quiet retreat in summer. Even if you're not interested in visiting the resorts themselves, the Rim of the World Scenic Byway (Highway 18), which connects Big Bear Lake and Lake Arrowhead at an elevation up to 8,000 feet, is a magnificent drive. On a clear day, you'll feel that you can see forever.

4 The Temecula Valley. Life is quieter in the southern portion of the Inland Empire than it is to the north. In this corner of Riverside County, the town of Temecula is an oasis of the good life for locals and visitors alike.

Updated by
Daniel Mangin

Threaded with rolling vineyards, homey agricultural towns, and mountain retreats, the Inland Empire has a humble allure. Often bypassed because of its freeway maze and suburban sprawl, this historically rich region offers visitors a quiet and quirky alternative to metropolitan Los Angeles and San Diego. You can hurtle down a 7,000-foot ski slope perched above a clear blue lake, hike or snowshoe in serene forests, and taste wines wrought by Temecula's misty mornings and subtle ocean breezes.

For fresh California flavors, explore apple country in Oak Glen, and trace the roots of the state's navel orange industry in Riverside, while the San Bernardino Mountains offer Big Bear Lake, Lake Arrowhead, and plentiful recreational opportunities.

PLANNING

WHEN TO GO
The climate varies greatly, depending on what part of the Inland Empire you're visiting. Summer temperatures in the mountains and in Temecula, 20 miles from the coast, usually hover around 80°F, though it's not uncommon for Riverside to reach temperatures of 100°F or higher. From September to March this area is subject to Santa Ana winds, sometimes strong enough to overturn trucks on the freeway. In winter, temperatures in the mountains and in Temecula usually range from 30°F to 55°F, and in the Riverside area from 40°F to 60°F. Most of the ski areas open when the first natural snow falls (usually in November) and close in mid-March.

GETTING HERE AND AROUND
AIR TRAVEL
Ontario International Airport (ONT) is the local airport. Aeromexico, Alaska, American, Delta, Southwest, United, and Volaris fly here.

Airport Contacts Ontario International Airport. ⊠ *2500 E. Airport Dr., Archibald Ave. exit off I–10, Ontario* ☎ *909/937–2700* ⊕ *www.flyontario.com.*

CAR TRAVEL

Avoid Highway 91 if possible; it's almost always backed up from Corona through Orange County. Check with Caltrans for information about highway conditions, or dial 511 or log onto the IE511 website, which also has bus–train trip planners.

Contacts Caltrans. ☎ *800/427–7623* ⊕ *www.dot.ca.gov.* **IE511.** ☎ *877/694–3511* ⊕ *www.ie511.org.*

TRAIN TRAVEL

■**TIP→** Many locals get around on Metrolink, which is clean and quick, and generally a much nicer way to travel than by bus. Metrolink trains stop at several stations on the Inter-County, San Bernardino, and Riverside lines. You can buy tickets and passes at station vending machines, or by telephone. The IE511 website *(Car Travel, above)* has bus–train trip planners; dial 511 for recorded train-schedule information.

Train Contacts Metrolink. ☎ *800/371–5465* ⊕ *www.metrolinktrains.com.*

RESTAURANTS

Downtown Riverside is home to a few ambitious restaurants, along with the familiar chains. The college town of Claremont has creative contemporary and ethnic fare. Innovative cuisine has become the norm in Temecula, especially at winery restaurants, some of whose chefs specialize in farm-to-table cuisine. The options are more limited in the smaller mountain communities; typically, each town supports a single upscale restaurant, along with fast-food outlets, steak-and-potatoes family spots, and perhaps an Italian or Mexican eatery. Universally, dining out is casual. *Restaurant reviews have been shortened. For full information, visit Fodors.com.*

HOTELS

In the San Bernardino Mountains many accommodations are bed-and-breakfasts or rustic cabins, though Lake Arrowhead and Big Bear offer more luxurious resort lodging. Rates for Big Bear lodgings fluctuate widely, depending on the season. When winter snow brings droves of Angelenos to the mountains for skiing, expect to pay sky-high prices for any kind of room. Most establishments require a two-night stay on weekends. In Riverside the landmark Mission Inn is the marquee accommodation. In the Wine Country, lodgings can be found at wineries, golf resorts, and chain hotels. *Hotel reviews have been shortened. For full information, visit Fodors.com.*

WHAT IT COSTS			
$	$$	$$$	$$$$
Restaurants under $16	$16–$22	$23–$30	over $30
Hotels under $120	$120–$175	$176–$250	over $250

Restaurant prices are the average cost of a main course at dinner or, if dinner is not served, at lunch, excluding sales tax of 7¾%–9¼%. Hotel prices are the lowest cost of a standard double room in high season, excluding service charges and 7¾%–13% tax.

THE WESTERN INLAND EMPIRE

Straddling the line between Los Angeles and San Bernardino counties, the western section of the Inland Empire is home to some of California's oldest vineyards and original citrus orchards. Now a busy suburban community, it holds the closest ski slopes to metro Los Angeles. Claremont, home to a collection of high-ranking colleges, is also here.

GETTING HERE AND AROUND

To reach this area from Los Angeles, take Interstate 10, which bisects the Western Inland Empire west to east; from Pasadena, take Interstate 210, which runs parallel to the north. Take Highway 57 from Anaheim. Some areas are quite walkable, especially the Claremont Colleges, where you can stroll through parks from one school building to another.

The Foothill Transit Bus Line serves Claremont. Metrolink serves the area from Los Angeles and elsewhere.

ESSENTIALS

Bus Contacts Foothill Transit. ☎ *800/743–3463* ⊕ *www.foothilltransit.org.*

CLAREMONT

26 miles north of Anaheim, 27 miles east of Pasadena.

The seven Claremont Colleges are among the most prestigious in the nation, lending the town an ambitious and creative energy. The campuses are all laid out cheek-by-jowl; as you wander from one leafy street to the next, you won't be able to tell where one college ends and the next begins.

Claremont was originally the home of the Sunkist citrus growers cooperative movement. Today Claremont Village, home to descendants of those early farmers, is bright and lively—a beautifully restored lemon-packing house, built in 1922, now hosts numerous shops and cafés in College Heights. The business district village, with streets named for prestigious eastern colleges, is walkable and appealing with a collection of boutiques, fancy food emporiums, cafés, and lounges. The downtown district is a beautiful place to visit, with Victorian, Craftsman, and Spanish Colonial buildings.

GETTING HERE AND AROUND

If you're driving, exit Interstate 10 at Indian Hill Boulevard, and drive north to Claremont. Parking can be difficult, although there are metered spots. Overnight parking is prohibited within the village; however there is a parking structure adjacent to the College Heights Packing House that is also north of the freeway; exit Garey and drive toward the mountains. You can reach this area by public transportation, but you'll need a car to get around unless you plan to spend all your time in the Claremont Village.

ESSENTIALS

Visitor Information Claremont Chamber of Commerce. ✉ *205 Yale Ave.* ☎ *909/624–1681* ⊕ *www.claremontchamber.org.*

EXPLORING

Claremont Heritage. College walking tours, historic home tours, and nature tours are conducted throughout the year by Claremont Heritage. On the first Saturday of each month the organization gives guided walking tours ($5) of the village. Self-guided tour maps can be found on the group's website. ✉ *840 N. Indian Hill Blvd.* ☎ *909/621–0848* 🌐 *www.claremontheritage.org* 🎟 *$5.*

Pomona College Museum of Art. This small campus museum exhibits contemporary art, works by old masters, and Native American art and artifacts. Highlights include a mural by Mexican artist Jose Clemente Orozco, first-edition Goya etchings, and 15th- and 16th-century Italian panel paintings. Thursday-night Art After Hours events often include music by local bands. *Skyspace: Dividing the Light,* alumnus James Turrell's stunning light installation in Draper Courtyard, is best experienced before sunrise or sunset. ✉ *333 N. College Ave.* ✣ *Skyscape: Draper Courtyard, 6th St. and College Way* ☎ *909/621–8283* 🌐 *www.pomona.edu/museum* 🎟 *Free* ⏲ *Museum closed Mon.; Skyspace closed Tues.–Fri. Sept.–May.*

QUICK BITES

Bert & Rocky's Cream Company. The sinfully innovative concoctions at this local ice cream store include mint Oreo, blueberry-cheesecake, and the Elvis special with bananas and peanut butter. The vanilla's delightful, too. **Known for:** 200-plus ice cream flavors; homemade waffle cones; caramel-covered apples. ✉ *242 Yale Ave.* ☎ *909/625–1852* 🌐 *www.bertandrockys.com.*

Fodor's Choice ★

Rancho Santa Ana Botanic Garden. Founded in 1927 by Susanna Bixby Bryant, a wealthy landowner and conservationist, the garden is dedicated to the preservation of native California plant species. You can meander here for hours enjoying the shade of an oak tree canopy or take a guided tour of the grounds, whose 86 acres of ponds and greenery shelter California wild lilacs, big berry manzanitas, four-needled piñons, and other specimens. Countless bird species also live here. **■ TIP→** Guided tram tours are offered the third Sunday of the month (reserve by the 15th of the preceding month). ✉ *1500 N. College Ave.* ☎ *909/625–8767* 🌐 *www.rsabg.org* 🎟 *Garden $8, tram tour $10 (includes garden admission).*

WHERE TO EAT

$$ ITALIAN

🍴 **Il Mattone Trattoria Italiana.** Locals line up on weekends for a table at this busy spot where waiters zip through small rooms to deliver fresh and beautifully seasoned fare from an extensive Italian menu. Popular dishes include pappardelle with Bolognese ragout and cioppino Livornese (seafood stew). **Known for:** cheerful family-run operation; many ingredients from Inland Empire suppliers; bread pudding made with ciabatta and crème anglaise. [$] *Average main: $19* ✉ *201 N. Indian Hill Blvd.* ☎ *909/624–1516* 🌐 *www.ilmattoneusa.com.*

$$ ECLECTIC

🍴 **Packing House Wines.** At this shop, bar, and restaurant inside a former orange-packing house, you can purchase wines from around the world and enjoy them on-site. Throughout the day pair your selection with seasonal small plates and specialty cheeses and, for dinner, entrées like poke tostadas with sushi-grade ahi tuna and an organic beef burger with smoked bacon, aged cheddar, and spicy tomato aioli. **Known for:** admirable by-the-glass wine selection; reasonable corkage fee; fine stop for wine and nibbles but also for dinner. $ *Average main: $16* ✉ *540 W. 1st St.* ☎ *909/445–9463* ⊕ *www.packinghousewines. com* ◷ *Closed Mon.*

$$$$ ✕ **Tutti Mangia Italian Grill.** A favorite of college students and their visit-
ITALIAN ing parents, this storefront dining room has a warm and cozy feel and menu choices that include long-bone pork chops, osso buco, and pan-roasted salmon with blood-orange rosemary sauce. Bruschetta, fried calamari, zucchini flowers stuffed with goat cheese, and other small plates, some seasonal, always entice. **Known for:** wide selection of first and second courses and sides; martini and wine bar happy hour except Sunday; heart-healthy low-calorie menu items. $ *Average main: $40* ✉ *102 Harvard Ave.* ☎ *909/625–4669* ⊕ *www.tuttimangia.com* ◷ *No lunch weekends.*

$$$ ✕ **Walter's Restaurant.** With a menu that samples cuisines from Europe
ECLECTIC to India, Walter's is where locals dine, sip wine, and chat—outside on the sidewalk, on the lively patio, or in a cozy setting inside. The diverse possibilities include omelets, sausages and eggs, and burritos for breakfast; salads, soups, pastas, and kebabs for lunch; and everything from fried chicken to tandoori shrimp for dinner. **Known for:** Afghan battered fries with hot sauce; happy hour weekdays 4–7, weekends 8 am–closing. $ *Average main: $24* ✉ *310 N. Yale Ave.* ☎ *909/624–4914* ⊕ *www.waltersrestaurant.com.*

WHERE TO STAY

$$$ ▥ **Casa 425.** This boutique inn on a corner opposite the College Heights
B&B/INN Lemon Packing House entertainment and shopping complex is the most
Fodor's Choice attractive lodging option in Claremont Village. **Pros:** within walking
★ distance of attractions and restaurants; bicycles available; most rooms have soaking tubs. **Cons:** occasional noise. $ *Rooms from: $195* ✉ *425 W. 1st St.* ☎ *866/450–0425* ⊕ *www.foursisters.com* ⇆ *28 rooms* ⦿ *Some meals.*

$$ ▥ **DoubleTree by Hilton Hotel Claremont.** The hotel of choice for parents
HOTEL visiting children attending local colleges has spacious rooms clustered
FAMILY in three Spanish-style buildings that surround a flower-decked central courtyard. **Pros:** convenient to colleges; swimming pool; chocolate chip cookies. **Cons:** small bathrooms. $ *Rooms from: $169* ✉ *555 W. Foot-hill Blvd.* ☎ *909/626–2411* ⊕ *www.doubletreeclaremont.com* ⇆ *190 rooms* ⦿ *No meals.*

NIGHTLIFE

Being a college town, Claremont has many bars and cafés, some of which showcase bands.

Flappers Comedy Club. A typical stand-up venue that sometimes hosts celebrity comics, Flappers is a branch of a Burbank club. ✉ *532 W. 1st St., at N. Oberlin Ave.* ☎ *818/845–9721* ⊕ *www.flapperscomedy.com* ▱ *$10–$22, some shows free* ◷ *Closed Mon.–Wed.*

SPORTS AND THE OUTDOORS
SKIING
Mt. Baldy Ski Resort. The 10,064-foot mountain's real name is Mt. San Antonio, but Mt. Baldy Ski Resort—the oldest ski area in Southern California—takes its name from the treeless slopes. The Mt. Baldy base lies at 6,500 feet, and four chairlifts ascend to 8,600 feet. The resort is known for its steep triple-diamond runs; the longest of the 26 runs here is 2,100 vertical feet. The resort also operates a ski and snowboard park. Backcountry skiing is available via shuttle in the spring, and there's a school on weekends for kids ages 5 to 12. ■TIP➔ Winter or summer, you can take a scenic chairlift ride ($29) to the Top of the Notch restaurant and hiking and mountain-biking trails. ⊠ *8401 Mt. Baldy Rd., Mt. Baldy* ☎ *909/982–0800* ⊕ *www.mtbaldyskilifts.com* ☜ *$69 full-day lift ticket* ☞ *Closed weekdays May–Oct. (days and hrs may vary yr-round, so check to confirm).*

WATER PARK **Raging Waters.** This tropical-theme water park 10 miles west of Clare-
FAMILY mont is the largest water park in Southern California. It has numerous chutes and slides with such names as Neptune's Fury, Thunder Rapids, Dragon's Den, and the scary dark Tunnel of Terror. When you're ready for a break, head over to the sandy beach lagoon and relax, or go to the Snack Shack. Complimentary life jackets are provided for youngsters. Locker rentals run from $12 to $20; inner tube rental is free. For a special treat, rent a cabana (from $119 to $300) and order lunch. Check the website for online coupons. ⊠ *111 Raging Waters Dr., San Dimas Ave., off Hwy. 57, San Dimas* ☎ *909/802–2200* ⊕ *www.ragingwaters. com* ☜ *$43–$46; parking (cash only) $15* ☞ *Closed Oct.–late May and sometimes (days vary, so call ahead) late May–Sept.*

RIVERSIDE AREA

Historic Riverside lies at the heart of the Inland Empire. Major highways linking it to other regional destinations spoke out from this city to the north, south, and east.

GETTING HERE AND AROUND
The most direct route from Los Angeles to Riverside is by Highway 60 (Pomona Freeway). From San Diego take Interstate 15 northeast to the junction with Highway 60. From North Orange County, Highway 91 is the best route.

ESSENTIALS
Bus Contacts Omnitrans. ☎ *800/966–6428* ⊕ *www.omnitrans.org.* **Riverside Transit Authority.** ☎ *951/565–5000* ⊕ *www.riversidetransit.com.*

CORONA

25 miles southeast of Claremont.

Corona's Temescal Canyon is named for the dome-shaped mud saunas that the Luiseño Indians built around the area's artesian hot springs in the early 19th century. Starting in 1860, weary Butterfield Overland Stage Company passengers stopped here to relax in the soothing mineral springs. In 1890 Mr. and Mrs. W.G. Steers turned the springs into Glen Ivy Hot Springs, whose popularity has yet to fade.

GETTING HERE AND AROUND

Primarily a bedroom community, Corona lies at the intersection of Interstate 15 and Highway 91. The many roadside malls make it a convenient stop for food or gas.

EXPLORING

FAMILY **Tom's Farms.** Opened as a produce stand along Interstate 15 in 1974, Tom's Farms has grown to include a locally popular hamburger stand, a furniture showroom, and a sweets shop. You can still buy produce here, but the big draws are various weekend attractions for children: tractor driving, Tom's mining company, a petting zoo, a children's train, a pony ride, free magic shows, face painting, and an old-style carousel. Most cost a modest fee. Of interest for adults is the wine-and-cheese shop, which has more than 600 varieties of wine, including some from the nearby Temecula Valley. ⊠ *23900 Temescal Canyon Rd.* ☎ *951/277–4422* ⊕ *www.tomsfarms.com* ✏ *Free, attraction fees vary; wine tasting $5.*

SPAS

Glen Ivy Hot Springs Spa. Colorful bougainvillea and birds-of-paradise surround the secluded Glen Ivy, which offers a full range of facials, manicures, pedicures, body wraps, and massages. Some treatments are performed in underground granite chambers known collectively as the Grotto. The Under the Oaks treatment center holds eight open-air massage rooms surrounded by waterfalls and ancient oak trees. Don't bring your best bikini if you plan to dive into the red clay of Club Mud. Paying the admission fee entitles you to lounge here all day. Make reservations for treatments, which cost extra. ⊠ *25000 Glen Ivy Rd.* ☎ *888/453–6489* ⊕ *www.glenivy.com* ✏ *Admission Tues.–Thurs. $46, Fri.–Mon. $64; treatments $25–$175.*

RIVERSIDE

14 miles northeast of Corona, 34 miles northeast of Anaheim.

By 1882 Riverside was home to more than half of California's citrus groves, making it the state's wealthiest city per capita in 1895. The prosperity produced a downtown area of opulent architecture, which is well preserved today. Main Street's pedestrian strip is lined with antiques and gift stores, art galleries, salons, and the UCR/California Museum of Photography.

GETTING HERE AND AROUND

Downtown Riverside lies north of Highway 91 at the University Avenue exit. The Mission Inn is at the corner of Mission Inn Avenue and Orange Street, and key museums, shops, and restaurants are nearby. You can park around here and walk to them.

EXPLORING

Mission Inn Museum. The crown jewel of Riverside is the Mission Inn, a Spanish-Revival hotel whose elaborate turrets, clock tower, mission bells, and flying buttresses rise above downtown. Docents of the

Navel Oranges in California: Good as Gold

In 1873 a woman named Eliza Tibbets changed the course of California history when she planted two Brazilian navel-orange trees in her Riverside garden.

The trees flourished in the area's warm climate and rich soil—and before long Tibbett's garden was producing the sweetest seedless oranges anyone had ever tasted. After winning awards at several major exhibitions, Tibbets realized she could make a profit from her trees. She sold buds to the increasing droves of citrus farmers flocking to the Inland Empire, and by 1882, almost 250,000 citrus trees had been planted in Riverside alone. California's citrus industry had been born.

Today Riverside still celebrates its citrus-growing heritage. The downtown Marketplace district contains several restored packing houses, and the Riverside Metropolitan Museum is home to a permanent exhibit of historic tools and machinery once used in the industry. The University of California at Riverside still remains at the forefront of citrus research; its Citrus Variety Collection includes specimens of 1,000 different fruit trees from around the world.

13

Mission Inn Foundation, whose museum contains displays depicting the building's illustrious history, lead guided tours. Taking his cues from the Spanish missions in San Gabriel and Carmel, architect Arthur B. Benton designed the initial wing, which opened in 1903. Locals G. Stanley Wilson and Peter Weber are credited with the grand fourth section, the Rotunda Wing, completed in 1931. You can climb to the top of its five-story spiral stairway, or linger in the Courtyard of the Birds, where a tinkling fountain and shady trees invite meditation. You can also peek inside the St. Francis Chapel, where celebrities such as Bette Davis, Humphrey Bogart, and Richard and Pat Nixon tied the knot before the Mexican cedar altar. Ten U.S. presidents have patronized the Presidential Lounge, a bright, wood-panel bar. ⊠ *3696 Main St.* ☎ *951/788–9556* ⊕ *www.missioninnmuseum.org* ⊠ *Admission $2, tour $13.*

Riverside Art Museum. Hearst Castle architect Julia Morgan designed this museum that houses a significant collection of paintings by Southern California landscape artists, including William Keith, Robert Wood, and Ralph Love. Major temporary exhibitions are mounted year-round. ⊠ *3425 Mission Inn Ave., at Lime St.* ☎ *951/684–7111* ⊕ *www.riversideartmuseum.org* ⊠ *$5; free 1st Thurs. of month 6–9* ☉ *Closed Mon.*

Fodor's Choice
★
UCR/California Museum of Photography. With a collection that includes thousands of Kodak Brownie and Zeiss Ikon cameras, this museum—the centerpiece of UCR ARTSblock—surveys the history of photography *and* the devices that produced it. Exhibitions, some of contemporary images, others historically oriented, are always top-notch and often incorporate photographs from the permanent collection of works by Ansel Adams, Imogen Cunningham, and other greats. ⊠ *3824 Main St.* ☎ *951/827–4787* ⊕ *artsblock.ucr.edu/Exhibition* ⊠ *$3 (includes same-day admission to two other facilities)* ☉ *Closed Sun. and Mon.*

WHERE TO EAT AND STAY

$$$
ITALIAN
✕ **Mario's Place.** The clientele is as beautiful as the food at this intimate jazz and supper club across the street from the Mission Inn. The northern Italian cuisine is first-rate—try the pear-and-Gorgonzola wood-fired pizza, followed by the star-anise panna cotta for dessert. Jazz groups play on Friday and Saturday night in the restaurant's lounge. **Known for:** classy setting; live jazz on Friday and Saturday; first-rate northern Italian cuisine. $ *Average main: $27* ⊠ *3646 Mission Inn Ave.* ☎ *951/684–7755* ⊕ *www.mariosplace.com* ⊘ *Closed Sun.*

$
AMERICAN
✕ **Simple Simon's Bakery & Bistro.** Expect to wait in line at this popular little sandwich shop on the pedestrian-only shopping strip outside the Mission Inn. At lunchtime, salads, soups, and sandwiches on house-baked breads are served; standouts include the chicken-apple sausage sandwich and the roast lamb sandwich topped with grilled eggplant, roasted red pepper, and tomato-fennel sauce. **Known for:** specialty sandwiches for lunch; pastries, eggs dishes, and French toast for breakfast; vegetarian and vegan items. $ *Average main: $11* ⊠ *3639 Main St., near 6th St.* ☎ *951/369–6030* ⊘ *Closed Sun. No dinner.*

$$$
HOTEL
FAMILY
Fodor's Choice
★
⛩ **Mission Inn and Spa.** One of California's most historic hotels, the inn grew from a modest adobe lodge in 1876 to the grand Spanish-Revival structure it is today. **Pros:** fascinating historic site; luxurious rooms; family friendly. **Cons:** train noise can be deafening at night; old style not for everyone; expensive rates. $ *Rooms from: $219* ⊠ *3649 Mission Inn Ave.* ☎ *951/784–0300, 800/843–7755* ⊕ *www.missioninn.com* ⇨ *265 rooms* ⊙ *No meals.*

OAK GLEN

33 miles northeast of Riverside.

More than 60 varieties of apples are grown in Oak Glen. This rustic village in the foothills above Yucaipa is home to acres of farms, produce stands, country shops, and homey cafés. The town really comes alive during the fall harvest (from September through December), which is celebrated with piglet races, live entertainment, and other events. Many farms also grow berries and stone fruit, which are available in summer. Most of the apple farms lie along Oak Glen Road.

GETTING HERE AND AROUND

Oak Glen is tucked into a mountainside about halfway up the San Bernardinos. Exit Interstate 10 at Yucaipa Boulevard, heading east to the intersection with Oak Glen Road, a 5-mile loop along which you'll find most of the shops, cafés, and apple orchards.

ESSENTIALS

Visitor Information Oak Glen Apple Growers Association. ⊕ *www.oakglen.net.*

EXPLORING

Mom's Country Orchards. Oak Glen's informal information center is at Mom's, where you can head to the samples bar and learn about the nuances of apple tasting, or warm up with a hot cider heated on an antique stove. Organic produce, local honey, apple butter, and jams are also specialties here. ✉ *38695 Oak Glen Rd.* ☎ *909/797–4249* 🌐 *momsoakglen.com.*

FAMILY **Oak Tree Village.** This 14-acre children's park has miniature train rides, trout fishing, gold panning, exotic animal exhibits, shops, and a petting zoo and several eateries. Some activities don't take place year-round. ✉ *38480 Oak Glen Rd.* ☎ *909/797–4420* 🌐 *www.oaktreevillageoakglen.net* 🎟 *$5.*

BEFORE YOU GO PICKING

Be sure to call before visiting the farms, most of which are family run. Unpasteurized cider—sold at some farms—should not be consumed by children, the elderly, or those with weakened immune systems.

Rileys at Los Rios Rancho. The fantastic country store at this 100-acre apple farm sells jams, syrups, and candied apples. Drop by the bakery for a hot tri-tip sandwich before heading outside to the picnic grounds for lunch. During the fall you can pick your own apples and pumpkins, take a hayride, or enjoy live bluegrass music. On the rancho grounds, the **Oak Glen Preserve** contains 400 acres of nature trails. The diverting Hummingbird Garden of native plants is near the entrance; just beyond the garden is an outdoor display of plows and other farm machinery. ✉ *39611 Oak Glen Rd.* ☎ *909/797–1005* 🌐 *www.losriosrancho.com* 🕒 *Closed Mon. and Tues. Dec.–Sept.*

FAMILY **Riley's Farm.** Employees dress in period costumes at this interactive, kid-friendly ranch. Riley's hosts school groups from September to June, and individuals can join the groups by reservation. You can hop on a hayride, take part in a barn dance, pick your own apples, press some cider, or throw a tomahawk while enjoying living-history performances. The farm is also home to Colonial Chesterfield, a replica New England–style estate where costumed 18th-century reenactors offer lessons in cider pressing, candle dipping, colonial games, and etiquette. ✉ *12261 S. Oak Glen Rd.* ☎ *909/797–7534* 🌐 *www.rileysfarm.com* 🎟 *Free to visit ranch, fees vary for activities* 🕒 *Closed Mon. and Tues.*

WHERE TO EAT

$ AMERICAN 🍴 **Apple Annie's Restaurant and Bakery.** You won't leave hungry from this country-western diner, popular with locals for its family-style seven-course dinners. Perennial favorites include the Annie deluxe burger and the beefeater melt. **Known for:** hefty meals; 5-pound apple pies; comfortable, rustic decor. [$] *Average main: $12* ✉ *38480 Oak Glen Rd.* ☎ *909/797–2311.*

$ AMERICAN 🍴 **Law's Oak Glen Coffee Shop.** Since 1953, this old-fashioned coffee shop has been serving up hot java, hearty breakfasts and lunches, and famous apple pies. Menu stalwarts include meat loaf, country-fried steak, and Reuben sandwiches. **Known for:** apple pie; classic American diner grub; hearty breakfast. [$] *Average main: $9* ✉ *38392 Oak Glen Rd.* ☎ *909/797–1642* 🌐 *www.lawsoakglen.com* 🕒 *No dinner.*

SAN BERNARDINO MOUNTAINS

One of three transverse mountain ranges that lie in the Inland Empire, the San Bernardino range holds the tallest peak in Southern California, San Gorgonio Mountain, at 11,503 feet. It's frequently snowcapped in winter, providing the region's only challenging ski slopes. In summer the forested hillsides and lakes provide a cool retreat from the city for many locals.

LAKE ARROWHEAD

37 miles northeast of Riverside.

Lake Arrowhead Village is an alpine community with lodgings, shops, outlet stores, and eateries that descend a hill to the lake. Outside the village, access to the lake and its beaches is limited to area residents and their guests.

GETTING HERE AND AROUND

Lake Arrowhead is most easily accessed via Highway 18 off Highway 210's Exit 76. Also called the Rim of the World, Highway 18 straddles a mountainside ledge at elevation 5,000 feet, revealing fabulous views. At the Lake Arrowhead turnoff, Highway 173, you'll descend into a wooded bowl surrounding the lake. The village itself is walkable, but hilly. Highway 173 winding along the east side of the lake offers scenic blue water views through the forest.

ESSENTIALS

Visitor Information Lake Arrowhead Communities Chamber of Commerce. ✉ *28200 Hwy. 189, Suite 207* ☎ *909/337–3715* 🌐 *lakearrowhead.net.*

EXPLORING

Lake Arrowhead Queen. One of the few ways visitors can access Lake Arrowhead is on a 50-minute *Lake Arrowhead Queen* cruise, operated daily from the Lake Arrowhead Village marina. ✉ *28200 Hwy. 189, Bldg. C-100* ☎ *909/336–6992* 🌐 *lakearrowheadqueen.com* 🎟 *$17* ☞ *Purchase tickets at nearby Leroy's Boardshop.*

WHERE TO EAT AND STAY

$ CAFÉ FAMILY

🍴 **Belgian Waffle Works.** This dockside eatery steps from the *Lake Arrowhead Queen* is quaint and homey, with country decor and beautiful lake views. Dive into a mud-pie Belgian waffle with chocolate fudge sauce or try a Belgian s'more with a marshmallow-and-chocolate sauce—burgers, pulled pork sandwiches, tuna melts, chili, meat loaf, chicken dishes, and salads are among the other fare. **Known for:** 17 different waffles; Inland Empire microbrews and Belgian beers; great Lake Arrowhead views from outdoor patio. [$] *Average main: $9* ✉ *28200 Hwy. 189, Suite 150* ☎ *909/337–5222* 🌐 *belgianwaffle.com* 🕒 *No dinner from early Sept.–late May.*

$$$ RESORT FAMILY Fodor's Choice ★

🏨 **Lake Arrowhead Resort and Spa.** This lakeside lodge offers water or forest views from private patios or balconies, and there's a warm and comfy atmosphere throughout thanks to the many fireplaces. **Pros:** beautiful views from most rooms; on-site spa; delicious dining. **Cons:** some rooms have thin walls; some rooms overlook parking

lot; some rooms lack balconies. $ *Rooms from: $189* ✉ *27984 Hwy.
189* ☎ *909/336–1511* ⊕ *www.lakearrowheadresort.com* ⇄ *173 rooms*
❏|*No meals.*

SPORTS AND THE OUTDOORS
WATERSKIING
McKenzie Waterski School. Summer ski-boat rides and waterskiing and
wakeboarding lessons are available through this school in summer.
✉ *28200 Hwy. 189* ☎ *909/337–3814* ⊕ *www.mckenziewaterskischool.
com* ⇄ *From $50.*

13

BIG BEAR LAKE

24 miles east of Lake Arrowhead.

When Angelenos say they're going to the mountains, they usually mean
Big Bear, where alpine-style villages surround the 7-mile-long lake. The
south shore has ski slopes, the Big Bear Alpine Zoo, water-sports opportunities, restaurants, and lodgings that include Apples Bed & Breakfast
Inn. The more serene north shore offers easy to moderate hiking and
biking trails, splendid alpine scenery, a fascinating nature center, and
the gorgeous Windy Point Inn.

GETTING HERE AND AROUND
Driving is the best way to get to and explore the Big Bear area. But
there are alternatives. The Mountain Area Regional Transit Authority
(MARTA) provides bus service to and in San Bernardino Mountain
communities and connects with Metrolink and Omnitrans.

ESSENTIALS
Bus Contacts Mountain Transit. ☎ *909/878–5200* ⊕ *www.mountaintransit.org.*

Visitor Information Big Bear Lake Visitors Bureau. ✉ *630 Bartlett Rd., near
Big Bear Blvd.* ☎ *800/424–4232* ⊕ *www.bigbear.com.*

EXPLORING
FAMILY **Alpine Slide at Magic Mountain.** Take a ride down a twisting Olympic-
style bobsled course in winter, or beat the summer heat on a dual
waterslide at Alpine Slide, which also has an 18-hole miniature golf
course and go-karts. ■TIP➜ In winter, when snow makes high-eleva-
tion roads impassable, taking the lift here affords the best lake views.
✉ *800 Wildrose La., at Big Bear Blvd.* ☎ *909/866–4626* ⊕ *www.
alpineslidebigbear.com* ⇄ *$6 single rides, $25 5-ride pass, $30 all-
day snow-play pass.*

FAMILY **Big Bear Alpine Zoo.** This rescue and rehabilitation center specializes
in animals native to the San Bernardino Mountains. Its residents
may include black and (non-native) grizzly bears, bald eagles, coyotes, mountain lions, wolves, and bobcats. A presentation at which
guests learn about an individual animal takes place daily at noon,
with shorter sessions at 1, 2, and 3. ■TIP➜ The zoo is scheduled to
move to a nearby location in 2019. Phone or check website for details.
✉ *43285 Goldmine Dr., at Moonridge Rd.* ☎ *909/584–1299* ⊕ *www.
bigbearzoo.com* ⇄ *$12.*

At 7 miles long, Big Bear Lake is a favorite for Angelenos seeking respite from the city.

FAMILY
Fodor's Choice
★

Big Bear Discovery Center. At this nature center you can sign up for canoe and kayak tours of Big Bear Lake, a naturalist-led tour of the Baldwin Lake Ecological Reserve in the spring and summer, and winter snowshoe tours. Exhibits here explain the area's flora and fauna, and staffers provide maps and camping and hiking information. ✉ *40971 N. Shore Dr. (Hwy. 38), 2½ miles east of town center, Fawnskin* ☎ *909/382–2790* ⊕ *www.mountainsfoundation.org/big-bear-discovery-center* ⛶ *Free* ☉ *Closed Tues. and Wed.*

Big Bear Marina. The paddle wheeler *Big Bear Queen* departs from the marina for 90-minute lake tours. The marina also rents fishing boats, jet skis, kayaks, and canoes. ✉ *500 Paine Ct.* ☎ *909/866–3218* ⊕ *www.bigbearmarina.com* ⛶ *$20* ☉ *Closed early Sept.–May.*

FAMILY

Time Bandit Pirate Ship. Featured in the 1981 movie *Time Bandits*, this small-scale replica of a 17th-century English galleon cruises Big Bear Lake. The ship travels along the southern lakeshore to 6,743-foot-high Big Bear Dam; along the way you'll pass big bayfront mansions, some owned by celebrities. A sightseeing excursion with the crew dressed up like pirates, the cruise is popular with kids and adults. There's a bar, but no dining, on board. ✉ *Holloway's Marina and RV Park, 398 Edgemoor Rd.* ☎ *909/878–4040* ⊕ *www.bigbearboating.com/lake-cruise.html* ⛶ *$22* ☉ *Closed Nov.–Mar.*

WHERE TO EAT

$$$
MODERN
AMERICAN

✕ **Black Kat Fine Dining & Wine Room.** Floor-to-ceiling murals of vineyards and wine cellars decorate this 2017 newcomer whose international wine selection impresses as much as its seasonal menu. You can stop in for just wine, pair it with a cheese plate or an ahi poke or other small appetizer, or order a full entrée—perhaps delicate Dover sole or a massive rib eye. **Known for:** impressive wine selection; small plates, full meals; upscale casual vibe. $ *Average main: $25* ⊠ *560 Pine Knot Ave.* ☎ *909/878–0401* ⊕ *www.theblackkat.com.*

$ ✕**Himalayan Restaurant.** It's best to order family style at this no-frills
NEPALESE storefront restaurant so that everyone gets a taste of the many Nep-
FAMILY alese and Indian delicacies offered. Customer favorites include the
Fodor's Choice spicy *mo-mo* (pot stickers), *daal* (green lentils), lamb and shrimp
★ curry vindaloo, fish and chicken masala, and clay-oven-roasted tandoori meats and seafood. **Known for:** family-style dining; lamb and shrimp-curry vindaloo; aromatic teas and lemonades. $ *Average main: $14* ⊠ *672 Pine Knot Ave.* ☎ *909/878–3068* ⊕ *www.himalayanbigbear.com.*

$$ ✕**Peppercorn Grille.** Filling pizzas, pastas, and steak and fish dishes make
AMERICAN this clubby-looking restaurant a fine choice after a long day of skiing in winter or hiking in summer. Start with the signature New England clam chowder (bacon bits add a smoky touch) and follow it up with a salad with the zesty house Peppercorn Ranch dressing before moving on to a flat-iron steak or scallop and shrimp pasta entrée. **Known for:** heated outdoor patio; New England clam chowder; root-beer float desserts. $ *Average main: $22* ⊠ *553 Pine Knot Ave.* ☎ *909/ 866–5405* ⊕ *www. peppercorngrille.com.*

WHERE TO STAY

$$$ 🏨 **Apples Bed & Breakfast Inn.** Despite its location on a busy road to the
B&B/INN ski lifts, the inn feels remote and peaceful, thanks to the surrounding pines. **Pros:** large rooms; free snacks and movies; delicious big breakfast. **Cons:** some traffic noise; fussy decor; sometimes feels busy. $ *Rooms from: $198* ⊠ *42430 Moonridge Rd.* ☎ *909/866–0903* ⊕ *www.applesbigbear.com* ⤳ *21 rooms* |◎| *Breakfast.*

$$$ 🏨 **Gold Mountain Manor.** Each room at this restored 1928 log mansion
B&B/INN has its own theme based on a rich Hollywood history: the Clark Gable
Fodor's Choice room, for example, contains the Franklin stove that once warmed the
★ honeymoon suite Gable and actress Carole Lombard shared. **Pros:** romantic setting; gracious hosts; snowshoes and kayaks available. **Cons:** somewhat thin walls; narrow corridors; many stairs. $ *Rooms from: $179* ⊠ *1117 Anita Ave., Big Bear City* ☎ *909/585–6997* ⊕ *www.goldmountainmanor.com* ⤳ *7 rooms* |◎| *Breakfast; Some meals.*

$$$ 🏨 **Lodge at Big Bear Lake.** Resembling a giant log cabin, the four-story
HOTEL Lodge, formerly Northwoods and now run by Holiday Inn's resort division, pays homage to Big Bear's mountain roots with the lobby's antler chandelier and stone fireplace. **Pros:** pool heated in winter; ski packages available; game room for kids. **Cons:** some rooms lack balconies or patios; some noise at night ; rate increases when it snows. $ *Rooms from: $249* ⊠ *40650 Village Dr.* ☎ *909/866–3121, 800/866–3121* ⊕ *www.northwoodsresort.com* ⤳ *140 rooms, 7 suites* |◎| *No meals.*

13

SPORTS AND THE OUTDOORS

BOATS AND CHARTERS

Pine Knot Landing Marina. This full-service marina rents fishing boats, pontoon boats, and kayaks and sells bait, ice, and snacks. You can take water skiing lessons here or pick up some Jet Skis and parasailing equipment. On weekends from late April through September, the paddle wheeler *Miss Liberty* leaves from the landing for a 90-minute tour ($22) of Big Bear Lake. Refreshments are available on board. ✉ *439 Pine Knot Blvd.* ☎ *909/866–7766* ⊕ *pineknotmarina.com.*

HORSEBACK RIDING

Baldwin Lake Stables. Explore the forested mountain on horseback on a group or private guided trail ride (from an hour to half a day) arranged by this outfit that in summer has a petting zoo for kids and offers pony rides on weekends. ✉ *46475 Pioneertown Rd., Big Bear City* ☎ *909/585–6482* ⊕ *www.baldwinlakestables.com* 🖾 *From $50 per hr.*

SKIING

Big Bear Mountain Resorts. Two distinct resorts, Bear Mountain and Snow Summit, comprise Southern California's largest winter playground, one of the few that challenge skilled skiers. The complex offers 438 skiable acres, 55 runs, and 26 chairlifts, including four high-speed quads. The vibe is youthful at Bear, which has beginner slopes (training available) and the after-ski hangout The Scene. Snow Summit holds challenging runs and is open for night skiing. Although lift tickets are valid on both mountains and a shuttle connects the two mountains so you don't have to drive, on weekends and holidays, when the resort is often crowded, it's best to stay on one mountain. Bear rents skis and boards.

The resorts are open in summer for mountain biking, hiking, golfing, and some special events. The Snow Summit Scenic Sky Chair zips to the mountain's 8,200-foot peak, where the Skyline Taphouse ($), a casual outdoor barbecue restaurant, has breathtaking views of the lake and San Gorgonio Mountain. ✉ *Big Bear, 880 Summit Blvd., off Moonridge Rd.* ☎ *844/462–2327* ⊕ *www.bigbearmountainresorts. com* 🖾 *$89–$99.*

THE TEMECULA VALLEY

The southern end of the Inland Empire is devoted to the good life. Its most visited destination, Temecula, lying at the base of Mt. San Jacinto, is a popular wine region where you'll find vineyards, tasting rooms, fine dining, and cozy lodgings.

TEMECULA

43 miles south of Riverside, 60 miles north of San Diego, 90 miles southeast of Los Angeles.

Fodor's Choice ★ Temecula, with its rolling green vineyards, country inns, and first-rate restaurants, bills itself as "Southern California Wine Country." The region is home to about four dozen wineries, several of which offer spas, fine dining, or luxury lodging and shopping. Not to be missed are the small, family-run vineyards whose devotion to showcasing Temecula's unique combination of climates and soils—the terroir, as the French call it—results in some impressive wines.

The name Temecula comes from a word Luiseño Indians translate from their native tongue as "place of the sun." The city goes with "where the sun shines through the mist," which also describes ideal conditions for growing wine grapes. Intense afternoon sun and cool nighttime temperatures, complemented by ocean breezes that flow through the Rainbow and Santa Margarita gaps in the coastal range, help grapevines flourish in the area's granite soil. Once best known for Chardonnay, Temecula Valley winemakers are moving in new directions, producing Rhône varietals like Viognier and Syrah along with Cabernet Sauvignon, Malbec, and other Bordeaux reds.

Most wineries charge from $15 to $25 for a tasting that includes several wines. On its website the Temecula Valley Winegrowers Association offers suggestions for self-guided winery tours and has coupons good for tasting discounts.

GETTING HERE AND AROUND
Interstate 15 cuts right through Temecula. Many wineries can be found on the east side of the freeway along Rancho California Road; with another large grouping on the eastern portion of De Portola Road. Old Town Temecula lies west of the freeway along Front Street.

TOURS
Destination Temecula. Full-day winery tours run by Destination Temecula include stops at three wineries, lunch, and time to explore Old Town Temecula. The company picks up participants in Old Town Temecula and at San Diego and Anaheim hotels. ☎ *951/695–1232* ⊕ *www. destem.com* ✉ *From $129.*

Grapeline Wine Country Shuttle. Enthusiastic local experts lead lively tours of Temecula Valley wineries, including excursions that incorporate insider visits with vintners and catered picnic lunches. Full- and half-day tours (from $95) are offered, with private or shared transportation by luxury SUV, limousine, or coach bus. Participants are picked up at area hotels, in Old Town Temecula, and elsewhere in Southern California. ☎ *951/693–5755, 888/894–6379* ⊕ *www.gogrape.com* ✉ *From $95.*

VISITOR INFORMATION
Temecula Valley Winegrowers Association. ☎ *951/699–3626* ⊕ *www.temeculawines.org.*

Visit Temecula Valley. ✉ *28690 Mercedes St.* ☎ *951/491–6085, 888/363–2852* ⊕ *www.visittemeculavalley.com.*

EXPLORING
TOP ATTRACTIONS
Doffo Winery. This Italian-Argentine wine-making family with a 30-acre property at the Temecula Valley's northeastern edge takes a passionate and quirky approach. Winemaker Damian Doffo and his father, Marcelo, play music for their vines, whose grapes go into small-lot wines, among them a rich Syrah and the signature Malbec, from estate grapes. Tastings of these and other wines take place inside a refurbished garage.

The family's racing and vintage motorcycles, which guests can view on free self-guided walking tours, are displayed in an open-air showroom nearby. ✉ *36083 Summitville St.* ☎ *951/676–6989* ⊕ *www.doffowines. com* 🍷 *Tastings $20–$30, tour $65.*

Fodor's Choice   **Hart Family Winery.** A perennial crowd-pleaser, this winery specializes in
★   well-crafted red wines made by Jim Hart, whose father and mother, Joe and Nancy, started the winery in the 1970s. Syrah, Cabernet Franc, and Cabernet Sauvignon are among the stars, but Hart Family also works with little known varietals like Aleatico, used in a marvelous dessert wine. ✉ *41300 Ave. Biona, off Rancho California Rd.* ☎ *951/676–6300* ⊕ *www.hartfamilywinery.com* 🍷 *Tasting $12.*

Miramonte Winery. Temecula's hippest winery sits high on a hilltop. Rhône-style whites (including the Four Torch Blanc blend of Grenache Blanc) and reds like the estate Syrah and Opulent blend of Grenache, Syrah, and Mourvèdre are the strong suits, though the Tempranillo and rosé have their partisans. Taste inside at the casual bar, outside on the deck, perhaps with an artisanal cheese plate. On Friday and Saturday night from 7 to 10, the winery goes into party mode with tastings of wine and beer, live music, and dancing that spills into the vineyards. ✉ *33410 Rancho California Rd.* ☎ *951/506–5500* ⊕ *www.miramontewinery.com* 🍷 *Tastings $17–$20, tours $75 (reservations required).*

Old Town Temecula. For a bit of old-fashioned fun, head to Old Town Temecula, where turn-of-the-20th-century-style storefronts and boardwalks extend for 12 blocks. Along with dozens of restaurants and boutiques, there are antiques stores, tasting rooms, hip brewpubs, a performing arts center and jazz club, and art galleries. ✉ *Front St., between Rancho California Rd. and Hwy. 79* ☎ *888/363–2852* ⊕ *www. visittemeculavalley.com.*

FAMILY   **Pennypickle's Workshop—Temecula Children's Museum.** If you have the kids along, check out the fictional 7,500-square-foot workshop of Professor Phineas T. Pennypickle, PhD. This elaborately decorated children's museum is filled with secret passageways, machines, wacky contraptions, and time-travel inventions. ■TIP→ Take one of the two-hour tours offered daily to get the most out of your visit. ✉ *42081 Main St.* ☎ *951/308–6376* ⊕ *www.pennypickles.org* 🍷 *$5* ☾ *Closed Mon.*

Ponte Family Estates. Lush gardens and more than 300 acres of vineyards provide a rustic, elegant setting at Ponte, whose small-lot bottlings range from sparkling wines and light whites to very fine Cabernet Sauvignon and Malbec reds. Another favorite in the light-filled tasting room is the flagship Super T wine, a Cabernet Sauvignon–Sangiovese blend. To find out how the wines are made, take the Premium Tour ($85) by electric bus of the vineyards and production facility. The tour (reservation required) concludes with a wine and cheese tasting. The shaded outdoor Restaurant at Ponte serves salads, wood-fired pizzas, and seafood daily for lunch, and on Friday and Saturday for dinner. ✉ *35053 Rancho California Rd.* ☎ *951/694–8855* ⊕ *www.pontewinery. com* 🍷 *Tasting $20, tours $40–$85* ☾ *No dinner Sun.–Thurs.*

WORTH NOTING

Callaway Vineyard and Winery. One of Temecula's oldest wineries is centered on a stunning steel-and-glass cube with vineyard views all around. Callaway made its reputation with Chardonnay, but these days is also known for Roussanne, Viognier, Cabernet Sauvignon, and Syrah. The winery's Meritage Restaurant specializes in tapas, salads, and sandwiches. ✉ *32720 Rancho California Rd.* ☎ *951/676–4001* ⊕ *www.callawaywinery.com* 🍷 *Tasting $20; tour and tasting $25.*

Europa Village. Though all of this luxury wine resort's dining, lodging, winery, and other components won't be completed for a few years, a pleasant tasting room here serves wines made from French, Spanish, and Italian varietals. The selections range from Vermentino, Albariño, and other light whites to reds like Syrah and Primitivo. Winemaker dinners take place in the village, which also presents live music on some weekend nights. ✉ *33475 La Serena Way, off Rancho California Rd.* ☎ *888/383–8767* ⊕ *www.europavillage.com* 🍷 *Tasting $15.*

Leoness Cellars. Bordeaux and Rhône blends are the specialties of this 20-acre hilltop estate with magnificent views of Cabernet Sauvignon vines. If it's available, try the winemaker's pride and joy, the Mélange de Reves (Blend of Dreams), made from the traditional Rhône combo of Grenache, Syrah, and Mourvèdre. Winery tours take in the vineyards and the wine-making areas. The tours require a reservation, as do wine-and-food pairing sessions that might include fruits and cheeses or, in the case of dessert wines, chocolates. Leoness's popular French-inspired restaurant is open from Friday through Sunday. ✉ *38311 De Portola Rd.* ☎ *951/302–7601* ⊕ *www.leonesscellars.com* 🍷 *Tasting $16–$20; tours with tasting $30–$125.*

Mount Palomar Winery. One of the original Temecula Valley wineries, opened in 1969, Mount Palomar introduced Sangiovese, a varietal that has proven perfectly suited to the region's soil and climate. New owners have transformed the homey winery into a grand Mediterranean villa with acres of gardens and trees. The Sangiovese is worth a try, as are the Solera Cream Sherry (ask how it's made) and the popular Cloudbreak, an inky red blend with a Petit Verdot base. Annata Bistro/Bar, open daily for lunch and dinner, presents live entertainment on Friday night. ✉ *33820 Rancho California Rd.* ☎ *951/676–5047* ⊕ *www.mountpalomar.com* 🍷 *Tastings $16 Mon.–Thurs., $20 Fri.– Sun.*

Temecula Valley Museum. A good introduction to Temecula, this two-story museum on the edge of Old Town focuses on the valley's role in California's history, from the early days of the Luiseño Indians and the mission and cattle-ranching periods to the present era of wine making and tourism. A permanent second-floor exhibit is devoted to Erle Stanley Gardner, the prolific author of the Perry Mason mysteries and a longtime Temecula resident. ✉ *28314 Mercedes St.* ☎ *951/694–6450* ⊕ *temeculavalleymuseum.org* 🍷 *$5* ⊙ *Closed Sun. and Mon.*

Wiens Family Cellars. A winery on the rise, Wiens promotes its "Big Reds"—among them the Reserve Primitivo and a Tempranillo–Petite Sirah blend—but many visitors often wind up taking home a bottle of the perky-fruity Amour De L'Orange sparkling wine. Other wines of note include the Ruby Port and the Dulce Maria, made from Chardonnay and Muscat Canelli grapes. The ambience at Wiens is informal, but the cordial tasting-room staffers are well informed about the wines they enthusiastically pour. ✉ *35055 Via Del Ponte* ☎ *951/694–9892* 🌐 *www.wienscellars.com* 🎟 *Tasting $20.*

Wilson Creek Winery & Vineyards. One of Temecula's busiest tasting rooms sits amid inviting, parklike grounds. Wilson is known for its Almond Champagne, but the winery also produces appealing still wines. Among these the Petite Sirah, Viognier, reserve Syrah, reserve Zinfandel, and late-harvest Zinfandel all merit a taste. The on-site gluten-free Creekside Grill Restaurant serves sandwiches, salads, vegetable potpie, and seasonal entrées such as Mexican white sea bass. Dine inside or select a picnic spot, and the servers will deliver your meal to you. Nine guest rooms are available for overnight stays. ✉ *35960 Rancho California Rd.* ☎ *951/699–9463* 🌐 *www.wilsoncreekwinery.com* 🎟 *Tasting $20.*

WHERE TO EAT AND STAY

$$$ CONTEMPORARY

🍴 **Café Champagne.** With its bubbling fountain, flowering trellises, and vineyard views, the spacious patio at Thornton Winery's café is the perfect place to lunch on a sunny day. The kitchen, which faces the French-country–style dining room, turns out pan-seared New York steak, chicken with pesto risotto, sandwiches, and other hearty fare. **Known for:** bacon cheeseburger and New York steak sandwich; Sunday brunch; live music on Friday night. [$] *Average main: $24* ✉ *Thornton Winery, 32575 Rancho California Rd.* ☎ *951/699–0099* 🌐 *www.thorntonwine.com.*

$$$ MEDITERRANEAN

🍴 **Meritage Restaurant at Callaway Vineyards.** Impressively prepared cuisine and stunning Temecula Valley views from a shaded terrace make a visit to the restaurant at Callaway winery a memorable occasion. Pomegranate *pico de gallo* (salsa), radish and ginger vinaigrette, and other inventive flourishes add piquancy and pep to the mostly Mediterranean dishes, which include tapas made from slow-roasted meats and fresh seafood. **Known for:** stunning valley views; tapas from slow-roasted meats and fresh seafood; wines and craft beers. [$] *Average main: $25* ✉ *32720 Rancho California Rd., east of Butterfield Stage Rd.* ☎ *951/587–8889* 🌐 *www.callawaywinery.com* 🕒 *No dinner Mon.–Thurs.*

$$ MODERN AMERICAN

🍴 **1909.** Superb cocktails and craft-beer samplers, a something-for-everyone menu, and the always swingin' streetside patio have made this gastropub one of Old Town's jolliest hangouts. Starters like blue corn Kobe beef hot dogs, smoked chicken wings, and crab and shrimp empanadas pair well with the drinks; standout mains include the 1909 burger (love the bacon-onion jam) and braised lamb shank. **Known for:** superb cocktails; streetside patio; popular weekend brunch. [$] *Average main: $19* ✉ *28656 Front St.* ☎ *951/619–1909* 🌐 *www.1909temecula.com.*

$$ MODERN AMERICAN FAMILY

🍴 **Public House.** A low-key gastropub inside a restored 1950s home, this Old Town spot with a sunlit patio hosts live music on weekends. A roasted 16-ounce New York steak over mashed potatoes satisfies carnivores; and the mixed arugula and quinoa with roasted red beet and goat cheese is a hit with those seeking more healthful fare. **Known for:** low-key vibe; diverse menu items; Southern California craft beers. [$] *Average main: $21* ✉ *41971 Main St.* ☎ *951/676–7305* 🌐 *www.publicrestaurants.com/public-house-temecula.*

$$$ HOTEL 🏨 **Ponte Vineyard Inn.** Slow down in old Californio Rancho style at this hotel on the grounds of the Ponte Family Estate winery. **Pros:** huge rooms; excellent winery on-site; gracious service. **Cons:** many weddings; can feel remote; pets not allowed. [$] *Rooms from: $200* ✉ *35001 Rancho California Rd.* ☎ *951/587-6688* 🌐 *www.pontevineyardinn.com* 🛏 *60 rooms* 🍴 *No meals.*

$$$ RESORT 🏨 **South Coast Winery Resort and Spa.** Spacious vineyard villas, an all-suites hotel, an excellent restaurant, a spa with a saltwater pool, and a working winery—South Coast blends these elements into one luxurious, harmonious location. **Pros:** good wine-country location; quiet, private villas; beautiful grounds. **Cons:** can be very busy; many weddings; two-night minimum much of the year. [$] *Rooms from: $199* ✉ *34843 Rancho California Rd.* ☎ *951/587-9463* 🌐 *www.wineresort.com* 🛏 *132 rooms* 🍴 *No meals.*

$$$ RESORT 🏨 **Temecula Creek Inn.** Most of the rooms at this property that sprawls over 360 acres have private patios or balconies overlooking the championship golf course. **Pros:** beautiful grounds; top golf course; course views from most rooms. **Cons:** nongolfers may feel out of place; often busy; location away from Old Town and wineries. [$] *Rooms from: $209* ✉ *44501 Rainbow Canyon Rd.* ☎ *951/694-1000, 888/976-3404* 🌐 *www.temeculacreekinn.com* ⛳ *Green fees $80–$100, 27 holes, 6800 yards, par 36* 🛏 *130 rooms* 🍴 *No meals.*

NIGHTLIFE

Old Town Temecula Community Theater. An entertainment complex that holds two venues, the Old Town Theater offers a full season of performances ranging from classical ballet and symphonies to jazz. The Temecula Valley Players offer Broadway musicals through June. At the adjacent, intimate Merc theater you can hear small jazz and country groups. ✉ *42051 Main St.* ☎ *866/653-8696* 🌐 *www.temeculatheater.org.*

Pechanga Resort and Casino. Casino gambling is the main attraction here, and there are several entertainment venues. Headliners such as Paul Anka, Jill Scott, and Jerry Seinfeld have appeared at the Pechanga Theater; the intimate Comedy Club books up-and-coming talent. HBO and Fox Sports championship boxing matches draw thousands of fans. The largest Indian casino in California, Pechanga has a 517-room hotel, a golf course, a spa, and an RV park. ✉ *45000 Pechanga Pkwy.* ☎ *888/732-4264, 951/770-1819* 🌐 *www.pechanga.com.*

SPORTS AND THE OUTDOORS

GOLF

Temecula has several championship golf courses cooled by the valley's ocean breezes.

The Legends Golf Club. The tiered greens, five lakes, and many blind spots make for challenging rounds at this club's Ted Robinson–designed championship course. ✉ *41687 Temeku Dr.* ☎ *951/694-9998* 🌐 *thelegendsgc.com* 🎟 *$49–$65* ⛳ *18 holes, 6636 yards, par 72.*

Redhawk Golf Club. Considered one of the best 18-hole public golf courses in California, the Ron Fream–designed championship golf course is designed to take advantage of Temecula's tree-studded rolling hills set against craggy mountains. Watch out for wind, doglegs, skinny sand traps, and tiered greens. Rico's Cantina here offers Mexican and Southwestern items for breakfast and lunch. ⊠ *45100 Redhawk Pkwy.* ☎ *951/302–3850* ⊕ *www.redhawkgolfcourse.com* ⊠ *$44–$62* ⅃ *18 holes, 7110 yards, par 72.*

Temecula Creek Inn Golf Resort. Ted Robinson and Dick Rossen designed this Wine Country resort's three picturesque nine-hole courses. Stonehouse, the most challenging one, demands precise tee shots. ⊠ *44501 Rainbow Canyon Rd.* ☎ *951/676–2405* ⊕ *www.temeculacreekinn. com* ⊠ *$80 weekdays; $100 weekends* ⅃ *Creek: 9 holes, 3348 yards, par 36; Oaks: 9 holes, 3436 yards, par 36; Stonehouse: 9 holes, 3257 yards, par 36.*

HOT-AIR BALLOONING

California Dreamin'. Float serenely above Temecula's vineyards and country estates on an early-morning balloon adventure. The ride includes champagne, coffee, a pastry breakfast, and a souvenir photo. ⊠ *Flights depart from La Vindemia Vineyard, 33133 Vista Del Monte Rd.* ☎ *800/373–3359* ⊕ *www.californiadreamin.com* ⊠ *$148 weekdays and Sun., Sat. $178.*

FAMILY **Balloon and Wine Festival.** This festival at Lake Skinner each June consists of three days of partying, wine and food tastings, live entertainment, vendors, and early-morning balloon ascensions. Many kids' activities are scheduled. Camping is popular; there are 400 sites at the lake, including RV sites nearby. ⊠ *37701 Warren Rd.* ☎ *951/676–6713* ⊕ *www.tvbwf.com* ⊠ *$23–$33 1-day pass, $60 3-day pass; tasting extra.*

SHOPPING

Rancho Fruit Market. This cheerful little shop sells honey, "uglies" (shrivel-skinned but deliciously sweet tangerines), and other locally sourced produce. Much of it is organic, and the prices are reasonable. Sweet tooths head straight for the chocolate-dipped fruit and caramel apples. ⊠ *28670 Old Town Front St.* ☎ *951/676–5519.*

Temecula Lavender Co. Owner Jan Schneider offers an inspiring collection of the herb that fosters peace, purification, sleep, and longevity. Bath salts, hand soaps, essential oil, even dryer bags to freshen up the laundry—she's got it all. ⊠ *28561 Old Town Front St.* ☎ *951/676–1931* ⊕ *www.temeculalavenderco.com.*

Temecula Olive Oil Company. While you're shopping in Old Town, stop by the cool tasting room here for a sample of extra-virgin olive oils, flavored balsamic vinegars and sea salts, bath products, and Mission, Ascalano, and Italian olives. Guided tours of the ranch where the olives are grown are available. ⊠ *28653 Old Town Front St., Suite H* ☎ *951/693–4029* ⊕ *www.temeculaoliveoil.com.*

PALM SPRINGS

WELCOME TO PALM SPRINGS

TOP REASONS TO GO

★ **Year-round sunshine:** The Palm Springs area has 350 days of sun each year, and the weather is usually ideal for playing one of the area's more than 100 golf courses.

★ **Spa under the stars:** Many resorts and small hotels now offer after-dark spa services, including outdoor soaks and treatments you can savor while sipping wine under the clear, starry sky.

★ **Personal pampering:** The resorts here have it all, beautifully appointed rooms packed with amenities, professional staffs, sublime spas, and delicious dining options.

★ **Divine desert scenery:** You'll probably spend a lot of time taking in the gorgeous 360-degree natural panorama, a flat desert floor surrounded by 10,000-foot mountains rising into a brilliant blue sky.

★ **The Hollywood connection:** The Palm Springs area has more celebrity ties than any other resort community. So keep your eyes open for your favorite star.

1 Palm Springs. A hideaway for celebrities, artists, politicians, and sports personalities since the mid-century, Palm Springs retains the luster of its golden era. Most visitors spend their days lounging poolside at a posh resort or an artsy inn, enjoying a well-crafted meal at an upscale restaurant, or shopping for treasures at the Uptown Design District before heading back to sip martinis under the stars.

2 The Desert Resorts. East of Palm Springs on Highway 111 lie several towns, each containing strip malls, gated communities, and huge resort complexes. Palm Desert is the Coachella Valley's answer to Rodeo Drive in Beverly Hills, with walkable downtown dining options aplenty. The golfing havens of Rancho Mirage, Indian Wells, and La Quinta cater to moneyed outdoor types.

3 Along Twentynine Palms Highway. The towns of Yucca Valley, Joshua Tree, and Twentynine Palms punctuate Twentynine Palms Highway (Highway 62)—the northern highway from the desert resorts to Joshua Tree National Park—and provide visitor information, lodging, and other services to park visitors.

4 Anza-Borrego Desert. If you're looking for a break from the action, you'll find solitude and solace in this 600,000-acre desert landscape.

Pioneertown
Yucca Valley
62
Morongo Valley
COVINGTON H
LITTLE SAN BERNARDINO
Desert Hot Springs
Dillon Rd
10
INDIO H
Palm Springs Airport
111
Palm Springs
1
San Jacinto Peak
Cathedral City
Rancho Mirage
2
Palm Desert
Indian Wells
Santa Rosa & San Jacinto Mountains National Monument
74
COYOTE CANYON
Borrego Springs

GETTING ORIENTED

14

The Palm Springs resort area lies within the Colorado Desert, on the western edge of the Coachella Valley. The area holds seven cities that are strung out along Highway 111, with Palm Springs at the northwestern end of the strip and Indio at the southeastern end. North of Palm Springs, between Interstate 10 and Highway 62, is Desert Hot Springs. Northeast of Palm Springs, the towns of the Morongo Valley lie along Twentynine Palms Highway (Highway 62), which leads to Joshua Tree National Park. Head south on Highway 86 from Indio to reach Anza-Borrego Desert State Park and the Salton Sea. All of the area's attractions are easy day trips from Palm Springs.

Updated
by Cheryl
Crabtree

With the Palm Springs area's year-round sunshine, luxurious spas, chef-driven restaurants, and see-and-be-seen pool parties, it's no wonder that Hollywood A-listers and weekend warriors make the desert a getaway. Stretching south and east of the city along Highway 111, the desert resort towns—Cathedral City, Rancho Mirage, Palm Desert, Indian Wells, La Quinta, and Indio, along with Desert Hot Springs to the north—teem with resorts, golf courses, and shopping centers. Yucca Valley, Joshua Tree, and other artistic communities lie farther north and northeast. To the south, the wildflowers of Anza-Borrego Desert State Park herald the arrival of spring.

The Palm Springs area has long been a playground for the celebrity elite. In the 1920s Al Capone opened the Two Bunch Palms Hotel in Desert Hot Springs (with multiple tunnels to help him avoid the police); Marilyn Monroe was discovered poolside in the late 1940s at a downtown Palm Springs tennis club; Elvis and Priscilla Presley honeymooned here—the list goes on.

Over the years the desert arts scene has blossomed as spectacularly as the wildflowers of Anza-Borrego. Downtown Palm Springs is laden with urban-chic contemporary artwork (check out the Backstreet Arts District), but the surrounding rural areas are also artist enclaves: Yucca Valley, Joshua Tree, Pioneertown, and Twentynine Palms all have noteworthy galleries, art installations, and natural scenic views. Each April attention centers on Indio, where the Coachella Valley Music and Arts Festival, California's largest outdoor concert, culls droves of Angelenos, and music lovers from all over the world.

PLANNING

WHEN TO GO

Desert weather is best between January and April, the height of the visitor season. The fall months are nearly as lovely, but less crowded and less expensive (although autumn draws many conventions and business travelers). In summer, a popular time with European visitors, daytime temperatures may rise above 110°F (though evenings cool to the mid-70s); some attractions and restaurants close or reduce their hours during this time.

GETTING HERE AND AROUND

AIR TRAVEL

14

Palm Springs International Airport serves California's desert communities. Air Canada, Alaska, Allegiant, American, Delta, JetBlue, Sun Country, United, Virgin America, and WestJet all fly to Palm Springs, some only seasonally. Yellow Cab of the Desert serves the airport, which is about 3 miles from downtown. The fare is $3 to enter the cab and about $3.12 per mile.

Airport Information Palm Springs International Airport. ⊠ *3200 E. Tahquitz Canyon Way, Palm Springs* ☎ *760/320–3882 info line, 760/318–3800* ⊕ *www.palmspringsairport.com.*

Airport Transfers Yellow Cab of the Desert. ⊠ *75150 St. Charles Pl., Palm Desert* ☎ *760/340–8294* ⊕ *www.yellowcabofthedesert.com.*

BUS TRAVEL

Greyhound provides service to Palm Springs from many cities. SunBus, operated by the SunLine Transit Agency, serves the entire Coachella Valley, from Desert Hot Springs to Mecca.

Bus Contacts Greyhound. ☎ *800/231–2222* ⊕ *www.greyhound.com.* **SunLine Transit Agency.** ☎ *800/347–8628* ⊕ *www.sunline.org.*

CAR TRAVEL

The desert resort communities occupy a 20-mile stretch between Interstate 10 to the east, and Palm Canyon Drive (Highway 111), to the west. The region is about a two-hour drive east of the Los Angeles area and a three-hour drive northeast of San Diego. It can take twice as long to make the trip from Los Angeles to the desert on winter and spring weekends because of heavy traffic. From Los Angeles take the San Bernardino Freeway (Interstate 10) east to Highway 111. From San Diego, Interstate 15 heading north connects with the Pomona Freeway (Highway 60), leading to the San Bernardino Freeway east.

To reach Borrego Springs from Los Angeles, take Interstate 10 east past the desert resorts area to Highway 86 south to the Borrego Salton Seaway (Highway S22) west. You can reach the Borrego area from San Diego via Interstate 8 to Highway 79 through Cuyamaca State Park. This will take you to Highway 78 in Julian, which you follow east to Yaqui Pass Road (S3) into Borrego Springs.

TAXI TRAVEL

Yellow Cab of the Desert serves the entire Coachella Valley. The fare is $3 to enter a cab and about $3 per mile.

TRAIN TRAVEL

The Amtrak Sunset Limited, which runs between Florida and Los Angeles, stops in Palm Springs.

Train Contact Amtrak. ☎ *800/872-7245* ⊕ *www.amtrakcalifornia.com.*

HEALTH AND SAFETY

Never travel alone in the desert. Let someone know your trip route, destination, and estimated time and date of return. Before setting out, make sure your vehicle is in good condition. Stay on main roads, and watch out for horses and range cattle.

Drink at least a gallon of water a day (three gallons if you're hiking or otherwise exerting yourself). Dress in layered clothing and wear comfortable, sturdy shoes and a hat. Keep snacks, sunscreen, and a first-aid kit on hand. If you suddenly have a headache or feel dizzy or nauseous, you could be suffering from dehydration. Get out of the sun immediately and drink plenty of water. Dampen your clothing to lower your body temperature.

Do not enter mine tunnels or shafts. Avoid canyons during rainstorms. Never place your hands or feet where you can't see them: rattlesnakes, scorpions, and black widow spiders may be hiding there.

TOURS

Art in Public Places. Several self-guided tours cover the works in Palm Desert's 150-piece Art in Public Places collection. Each tour is walkable or drivable. Maps and information about guided tours (one Saturday each month) are available at the city's visitor center and online. ✉ *Palm Desert Visitor Center, 73510 Fred Waring Dr., Palm Desert* ☎ *760/568–1441* ⊕ *www.palm-desert.org/arts-entertainment/public-art* ✏ *Free.*

Best of the Best Tours. One of the valley's largest outfits leads tours into Andreas Canyon, along the celebrity circuit, or to view windmills up close. ☎ *760/320–1365* ⊕ *www.thebestofthebesttours.com* ✏ *From $40.*

Big Wheel Bike Tours. This outfit delivers rental mountain, three-speed, and tandem bikes to area hotels. The company also conducts full- and half-day escorted on- and off-road bike tours, and also offers hiking and jeep tours to Joshua Tree National Park and the San Andreas Fault. Guides are first-rate. ✉ *Palm Springs* ☎ *760/779–1837* ⊕ *www.bwbtours.com* ✏ *$105 per person.*

Desert Adventures. This outfit's two- to four-hour jeep, SUV, or van tours explore Joshua Tree National Park, Indian Canyon, Mecca Hills Painted Canyons, and the San Andreas Fault. The groups are small and the guides are knowledgeable. Departures are from Palm Springs and/or La Quinta; hotel pickups are available. ☎ *760/324–5337* ⊕ *www.red-jeep.com* ✏ *From $79.*

Trail Discovery Hiking Tours. For more than two decades, this outfit has been guiding hikers of all abilities through the desert canyons of the Palm Springs area. Tours include Joshua Tree National Park, Indian Canyons, San Jacinto State Park, and sections of the Pacific Crest Trail. ☎ *760/413–1575* ⊕ *www.palmspringshiking.com* ✏ *From $75.*

14

RESTAURANTS

An influx of talented chefs has expanded the dining possibilities of a formerly staid scene. The meat-and-potatoes crowd still has plenty of options, but you'll also find fresh seafood superbly prepared and contemporary Californian, Asian, Indian, and vegetarian cuisine, and Mexican food abounds. Most restaurants have early-evening happy hours, with discounted drinks and small-plate menus. Restaurants that remain open in July and August frequently discount deeply; others close in July and August or offer limited service. *Restaurant reviews have been shortened. For full information, visit Fodors.com.*

HOTELS

In general you can find the widest choice of lodgings in Palm Springs, from tiny bed-and-breakfasts and chain motels to business and resort hotels. Massive resort properties predominate in down-valley communities, such as Palm Desert and Rancho Mirage. You can stay in the desert for as little as $100, or splurge for luxury digs at more than $1,000 a night. Rates vary widely by season and expected occupancy—a $200 room midweek can jump in price to $450 on Saturday.

Hotel and resort prices are frequently 50% cheaper in summer and fall than in winter and early spring. From January through May prices soar, and lodgings book up far in advance. You should book well ahead for stays during events such as Modernism Week or the Coachella and Stagecoach music festivals.

Most resort hotels charge a daily fee of up to $40 that is not included in the room rate; be sure to ask about extra fees when you book. Many hotels are pet-friendly and offer special services, though these also come with additional fees. Small boutique hotels and bed-and-breakfasts have plenty of character and are popular with hipsters and artsy types; discounts are sometimes given for extended stays. Casino hotels often offer good deals on lodging. Take care, though, when considering budget lodgings; other than reliable chains, they may not be up to par. *Hotel reviews have been shortened. For full information, visit Fodors.com.*

WHAT IT COSTS			
	$	$$	$$$	$$$$
Restaurants	under $16	$16–$22	$23–$30	over $30
Hotels	under $120	$120–$175	$176–$250	over $250

Restaurant prices are the average cost of a main course at dinner or, if dinner is not served, at lunch. Hotel prices are the lowest cost of a standard double room in high season.

NIGHTLIFE

Desert nightlife is concentrated and abundant in Palm Springs, with plenty of bars and clubs, but the action centers on hotel bars and lively pool parties. Arts festivals occur on a regular basis, especially in winter and spring. *Palm Springs Life* magazine (⊕ *www.palmspringslife.com*), available at hotels and visitor centers, has nightlife listings, as does the *Desert Sun* newspaper (⊕ *www.mydesert.com*).

PALM SPRINGS

A tourist destination since the late 19th century, Palm Springs evolved into an ideal hideaway for early Hollywood celebrities who slipped into town to play tennis, lounge poolside, attend a party or two, and unless things got out of hand, steer clear of gossip columnists. But the area blossomed in the 1930s after actors Charlie Farrell and Ralph Bellamy bought 200 acres of land for $30 an acre and opened the Palm Springs Racquet Club, which soon listed Ginger Rogers, Humphrey Bogart, and Clark Gable among its members.

Today, Palm Springs is embracing its glory days. Owners of resorts, bed-and-breakfasts, and galleries have renovated mid-century modern buildings, luring a new crop of celebs and high-powered executives. LGBTQ travelers, twentysomethings, and families also sojourn here. Pleasantly touristy Palm Canyon Drive is packed with alfresco restaurants, many with views of the bustling sidewalk, along with indoor cafés and semi-chic shops. Farther west is the Uptown Design District, the area's shopping and dining destination. Continuing east on Palm Canyon Drive just outside downtown lie resorts and boutique hotels that host lively pool parties and house exclusive dining establishments and trendy bars.

GETTING HERE AND AROUND

Palm Springs is 90 miles southeast of Los Angeles on Interstate 10. Most visitors arrive in the Palm Springs area by car from the Los Angeles or San Diego area via this freeway, which intersects with Highway 111 north of Palm Springs. Tahquitz Canyon Way marks the division between north and south on major streets (e.g., North and South Palm Canyon Drive). Once in Palm Springs, take advantage of the free Palm Springs Buzz, an air-conditioned pet-friendly trolley that loops around town Thursday through Sunday every 15 minutes from Via Escuela to Smoketree (⊕ *buzzps.com*).

ESSENTIALS

Visitor Information Greater Palm Springs Convention and Visitors Bureau. ⊠ *Visitor Center, 70–100 Hwy. 111, at Via Florencia, Rancho Mirage* ☎ *760/770–9000, 800/967–3767* ⊕ *www.visitgreaterpalmsprings.com.* **Palm Springs Visitors Center Downtown.** ⊠ *100 S. Palm Canyon Dr.* ✛ *In Welwood Murray Memorial Library* ☎ *760/323–8296* ⊕ *www.visitpalmsprings.com.* **Palm Springs Visitors Center North.** ⊠ *2901 N. Palm Canyon Dr.* ☎ *760/778–8418, 800/347–7746* ⊕ *www.visitpalmsprings.com.*

EXPLORING

TOP ATTRACTIONS

Elvis's Honeymoon Hideaway. The hideaway of the King of rock 'n' roll and his young bride, Priscilla, during their first year of marriage, this house perches on a hilltop abutting the San Jacinto Mountains. A stunning example of local mid-century modern architecture, it is rich in Elvis lore, photos, and furnishings. Docents describe the fabulous parties that took place here, attended by celebrities and local legends. Built in 1962 by Robert Alexander, one of Palm Spring's largest developers,

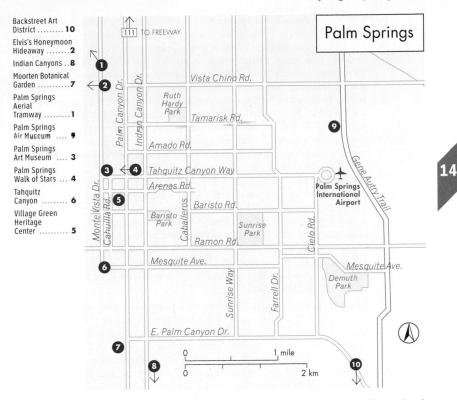

Palm Springs

14

the house consists of four perfect circles, each set on a different level. At the time, *Look* magazine described the structure as the "house of tomorrow," and indeed many of its features are standard in the homes of today. ⊠ *1350 Ladera Circle* ☏ *760/322–1192* ⊕ *www.elvishoneymoon.com* ⊡ *$30.*

FAMILY

Fodor's Choice

★

Indian Canyons. The Indian Canyons are the ancestral home of the Agua Caliente, part of the Cahuilla people. You can see remnants of their ancient life, including rock art, house pits and foundations, irrigation ditches, bedrock mortars, pictographs, and stone houses and shelters atop cliff walls. Short easy walks through the canyons reveal palm oases, waterfalls, and, in spring, wildflowers. Tree-shaded picnic areas are abundant. The attraction includes three canyons open for touring: Palm Canyon, noted for its stand of Washingtonia palms; Murray Canyon, home of Peninsula bighorn sheep and a herd of wild ponies; and Andreas Canyon, where a stand of fan palms contrasts with sharp rock formations. Ranger-led hikes to Palm and Andreas canyons are offered daily for an additional charge. The trading post at the entrance to Palm Canyon has hiking maps and refreshments, as well as Native American art, jewelry, and weaving. ⊠ *38520 S. Palm Canyon Dr., south of Acanto Dr.* ☏ *760/323–6018* ⊕ *www.indian-canyons.com* ⊡ *$9, ranger hikes $3* ⊙ *Closed Mon.–Thurs. July–Sept.*

Palm Springs Aerial Tramway. A trip on the tramway provides a 360-degree view of the desert through the picture windows of rotating cars. The 2½-mile ascent through Chino Canyon, the steepest vertical cable ride in the United States, brings you to an elevation of 8,516 feet in less than 20 minutes. On clear days, which are common, the view stretches 75 miles—from the peak of Mt. San Gorgonio in the north to the Salton Sea in the southeast. Stepping out into the snow at the summit is a winter treat. At the top, a bit below the summit of Mt. San Jacinto, are several diversions. Mountain Station has an observation deck, two restaurants, a cocktail lounge, apparel and gift shops, picnic facilities, a small wildlife exhibit, and a theater that screens movies on the history of the tramway and the adjacent Mount San Jacinto State Park and Wilderness. Take advantage of free guided and self-guided nature walks through the state park, or if there's snow on the ground, rent skis, snowshoes, or snow tubes. The tramway generally closes for maintenance in mid-September. ■TIP➔ Ride-and-dine packages are available in late afternoon. The tram is a popular attraction; to avoid a two-hour or longer wait, arrive before the first car leaves in the morning. ⊠ *1 Tramway Rd., off N. Palm Canyon Dr. (Hwy. 111)* ☎ *888/515–8726* ⊕ *www. pstramway.com* ⊠ *$25.95, ride-and-dine package $36* ⊗ *Closed 2 wks in Sept. for maintenance.*

Palm Springs Air Museum. This museum's impressive collection of World War II aircraft includes a B-17 Flying Fortress bomber, a P-51 Mustang, a Lockheed P-38, and a Grumman TBF Avenger. Among the cool exhibits are model warships, a Pearl Harbor diorama, and a Grumman Goose into which kids can crawl. Photos, artifacts, memorabilia, and uniforms are also on display, and educational programs take place on Saturday. Flight demonstrations are scheduled regularly. Biplane rides are offered on Saturday. ⊠ *745 N. Gene Autry Trail* ☎ *760/778–6262* ⊕ *palmspringsairmuseum.org* ⊠ *$16.50.*

Palm Springs Art Museum. This world-class art museum focuses on photography, modern architecture, and the traditional arts of the Americas. Galleries are bright and open. The permanent collection includes shimmering works in glass by Dale Chihuly, Ginny Ruffner, and William Morris. You'll also find handcrafted furniture by the late actor George Montgomery, mid-century modern architectural photos by Julius Shulman, enormous Native American baskets, and works by artists like Allen Houser, Arlo Namingha, and Fritz Scholder. The museum also displays significant works of 20th-century sculpture by Henry Moore, Marino Marina, Deborah Butterfield, and Mark Di Suvero. The Annenberg Theater presents plays, concerts, lectures, operas, and other cultural events. ⊠ *101 Museum Dr., off W. Tahquitz Canyon Dr.* ☎ *760/322–4800* ⊕ *www.psmuseum.org* ⊠ *$12.50, free Thurs. 4–8 during Villagefest* ⊗ *Closed Wed.*

Tahquitz Canyon. On ranger-led tours of this secluded canyon on the Agua Caliente Reservation you can view a spectacular 60-foot waterfall, rock art, ancient irrigation systems, and native wildlife and plants. Tours are conducted several times daily; participants must be able to navigate 100 steep rock steps. (You can also take a self-guided tour of the 1.8-mile trail.) At the visitor center at the canyon entrance, watch a short video, look at artifacts, and pick up a map. ⊠ *500 W. Mesquite Ave., west of S. Palm Canyon Dr.* ☎ *760/416–7044* ⊕ *www.tahquitzcanyon.com* 🖅 *$12.50* ⊘ *Closed Mon.–Thurs. July–Sept.*

WORTH NOTING

Backstreet Art District. Galleries and live-work studios just off East Canyon Drive showcase the works of a number of highly acclaimed artists. Painter and ceramicist Linda Maxson, fine artist Chris Hoffman at Fusion Art Gallery, and new and emerging artists at Rebel Art Space are among the stars here. ■TIP➔ On the first Wednesday evening of the month, the galleries are open from 5 to 8. ⊠ *2600 S. Cherokee Way* ⊕ *www.backstreetartdistrict.com* 🖅 *Free* ⊘ *Most galleries closed Mon. and Tues.*

Moorten Botanical Garden. In the 1920s, Chester "Cactus Slim" Moorten and his wife Patricia opened this showpiece for desert plants—now numbering in the thousands—that include an ocotillo, a massive elephant tree, a boojum tree, and vine cacti. Their son Clark now operates the garden. ■TIP➔ Take a stroll through the Cactarium to spot rare finds such as the welwitschia, which originated in the Namib Desert in southwestern Africa. ⊠ *1701 S. Palm Canyon Dr.* ☎ *760/327–6555* ⊕ *www.moortengarden.com* 🖅 *$5* ⊘ *Closed Wed.*

Palm Springs Walk of Stars. Along the walk, more than 300 bronze stars are embedded in the sidewalk (à la Hollywood Walk of Fame) to honor celebrities with a Palm Springs connection. Frank, Elvis, Marilyn, Dinah, Lucy, Ginger, Liz, and Liberace have all received their due. Those still around to walk the Walk and see their stars include Nancy Sinatra and Kathy Griffin. ⊠ *Palm Canyon Dr., around Tahquitz Canyon Way, and Tahquitz Canyon Way, between Palm Canyon and Indian Canyon Drs.* ☎ *760/320–3129* ⊕ *www.palmsprings.com/stars.*

Village Green Heritage Center. Three small museums at the Village Green Heritage Center illustrate early life in Palm Springs. The centerpiece, the **Agua Caliente Cultural Museum,** traces the culture and history of the Cahuilla tribe with several exhibits. The **McCallum Adobe** and the **Cornelia White House** hold the collection of the Palm Springs Historical Society. **Rudy's General Store Museum** is a re-creation of a 1930s general store. ⊠ *219–221 S. Palm Canyon Dr.* ☎ *760/323–8297* ⊕ *www.pshistoricalsociety.org* 🖅 *Agua Caliente free, McCallum $2, Rudy's $1* ⊘ *Closed Tues.*

SINATRA'S TWIN PALMS ESTATE

Among the homes Old Blue Eyes owned in the desert was a mid-century modern jewel at 1148 East Alejo Road known as Twin Palms. Designed by local architect E. Stewart Williams and completed in 1947, the house had floor-to-ceiling windows typical of the time. The pool became famous for its piano shape. Frank Sinatra lived at Twin Palms until 1957, resurfacing later in Rancho Mirage.

14

WHERE TO EAT

$$ MEDITERRANEAN

🍴 **Alicante.** This sidewalk café near the Plaza Theatre is one of the best people-watching spots in Palm Springs. Pasta, pizza, and veal scaloppine are among the hearty items on the lunch and dinner menus. **Known for:** separate tapas menu; paella; cioppino. [$] *Average main: $20* ✉ *140 S. Palm Canyon Dr., at La Plaza* ☎ *760/325–9464* 🌐 *www.alicanteps.com.*

$ AMERICAN Fodor's Choice ★

🍴 **Cheeky's.** The artisanal bacon bar and hangover-halting mimosas attract legions to this breakfast and lunch joint, but brioche French toast and other favorites also contribute to the epic wait on weekends (no reservations accepted). Huevos rancheros, a gem salad with green goddess dressing, and other farm-centric dishes entice the foodie crowd. **Known for:** homemade pastries and sausages; local organic ingredients; grass-fed burger topped with house bacon. [$] *Average main: $12* ✉ *622 N. Palm Canyon Dr., at E. Granvia Valmonte* ☎ *760/327–7595* 🌐 *www.cheekysps.com* 🕓 *Closed Tues. No dinner.*

$$$ MODERN AMERICAN

🍴 **Copley's on Palm Canyon.** Chef Manion Copley prepares innovative cuisine in a setting that's straight out of Hollywood—a hacienda once owned by Cary Grant. Dine in the clubby house or under the stars in the garden. **Known for:** romantic patio dining; fresh seafood and meats with innovative flavors; sweet and savory herb ice creams. [$] *Average main: $28* ✉ *621 N. Palm Canyon Dr., at E. Granvia Valmonte* ☎ *760/327–9555* 🌐 *www.copleyspalmsprings.com* 🕓 *No lunch. Closed July and Aug.*

$$$ AMERICAN Fodor's Choice ★

🍴 **EIGHT4NINE.** The dazzling interior design and eclectic Pacific Coast dishes made from scratch lure locals and visitors alike to this swank yet casual restaurant and lounge in the Uptown Design District. Sink into white patent leather chairs or comfy sofas in the lounge where you can gaze at historic celebrity photos, or choose a table in a grand corridor with a collection of private rooms, or in the outdoor patio with mountain views. **Known for:** nearly everything made from scratch; four-course chef's menu; all-day happy hour in lounge. [$] *Average main: $28* ✉ *849 N. Palm Canyon Dr.* ☎ *760/325–8490* 🌐 *eight4nine.com.*

$$ MODERN MEXICAN

🍴 **El Mirasol at Los Arboles.** Chef Felipe Castañeda owns two Mexican restaurants in Palm Springs—this one, part of Los Arboles Hotel, is outside on a charming patio set amid flower gardens and shaded by red umbrellas. Castañeda prepares classic combinations of tacos, tamales, and enchiladas, along with specialties such as double-cooked pork and *pollo en pipián* (chicken with a pre-Columbian sauce made of ground roasted pumpkin seeds and dry chilies). **Known for:** classic Mexican dishes; great vegetarian options; garden setting. [$] *Average main: $20* ✉ *266 Via Altamira, off N. Indian Canyon Dr.* ☎ *760/459–3136,* 🌐 *www.elmirasolrestaurants.com.*

$$$$ FRENCH

🍴 **Le Vallauris.** A longtime favorite that occupies the historic Roberson House, Le Vallauris is popular with ladies who lunch, all of whom get a hug from the maître d'. The Belgian-French-inspired menu changes daily, and each day it's handwritten on a white board. **Known for:** prix-fixe menus for lunch and dinner; lovely tree-shaded garden; romantic setting. [$] *Average main: $35* ✉ *385 W. Tahquitz Canyon Way, west of Palm Canyon Dr.* ☎ *760/325–5059* 🌐 *www.levallauris.com* 🕓 *Closed July and Aug.*

$$$$
MODERN
AMERICAN

✕ **Purple Palm.** The hottest tables in Palm Springs are those that surround the pool at the Colony Palms Hotel, where the hip and elite pay homage to Purple Gang mobster Al Wertheimer, who reportedly built the hotel in the mid-1930s. Now it's a casual, convivial place where you can dine alfresco surrounded by a tropical garden near the pool. **Known for:** craft cocktails; happy hour and weekend brunch; extensive international wine list. Ⓢ *Average main: $31* ✉ *572 N. Indian Canyon Dr., at E. Granvia Valmonte* ☎ *800/557–2187* ⊕ *www.colonypalmshotel.com.*

$$$$
MODERN
AMERICAN

✕ **Spencer's Restaurant.** The swank dining space inside the Palm Springs Tennis Club Resort occupies a historic mid-century modern structure, but the cuisine of chef Eric Wadlund, a local star with a national reputation, is the main attraction. Crab cakes, kung pao calamari, and crispy flash-fried oysters are favorite starters. **Known for:** French–Pacific Rim influences; romantic patio; elegant dining room. Ⓢ *Average main: $35* ✉ *701 W. Baristo Rd.* ☎ *760/327–3446* ⊕ *www.spencersrestaurant.com.*

14

$$
MODERN
AMERICAN

✕ **Trio.** The owners of this high-energy Uptown Design District restaurant claim that it's "where Palm Springs eats," and it certainly seems so on nights when the lines to get in run deep. The menu includes home-style staples such as Yankee pot roast, crawfish pie, and other dishes, along with veggie burgers and other vegetarian and gluten-free items. **Known for:** local artwork; inventive desserts; ample vegetarian and gluten-free options. Ⓢ *Average main: $22* ✉ *707 N. Palm Canyon Dr.* ☎ *760/864–8746* ⊕ *www.triopalmsprings.com.*

$$$
INTERNATIONAL

✕ **The Tropicale.** Tucked onto a side-street corner, the Tropicale is a mid-century-style watering hole with a contemporary vibe. The bar and main dining room hold cozy leather booths; flowers and water features brighten the outdoor area. **Known for:** globe-trotting menu; happy hour (all night on Wednesday); weekly specials. Ⓢ *Average main: $30* ✉ *330 E. Amado Rd., at N. Calle Encilia* ☎ *760/866–1952* ⊕ *www. thetropicale.com* ⊗ *No lunch.*

$
AMERICAN
FAMILY
Fodor'sChoice
★

✕ **Tyler's Burgers.** Families, singles, and couples head to Tyler's for simple lunch fare that appeals to carnivores and vegetarians alike. Expect mid-20th-century America's greatest hits: heaping burgers, stacks of fries, root beer floats, milk shakes; on weekends, be prepared to wait with the masses. **Known for:** house-made cole slaw; excellent burgers and fries; delicious shakes. Ⓢ *Average main: $9* ✉ *149 S. Indian Canyon Dr., at La Plaza* ☎ *760/325–2990* ⊕ *www.tylersburgers.com* ⊗ *Closed Sun. late May–mid-Feb. Closed mid-July–early Sept.*

$$$$
AMERICAN

✕ **Workshop Kitchen + Bar.** Chef Michael Beckman's Uptown Design District hot spot pairs high-quality California cuisine with creative cocktails in a sleek, almost utilitarian setting. The outdoor patio lures the oversize sunglasses Sunday brunch crowd, who slurp cava mimosas and artisanal cocktails; inside, the sleek concrete booths are topped with black leather cushions. **Known for:** most ingredients sourced from within a 100-mile radius; artisanal cocktails; own charcuterie and cheese shop in same complex. Ⓢ *Average main: $32* ✉ *800 N. Palm Canyon Dr., at E. Tamarisk Rd.* ☎ *760/459–3451* ⊕ *www.workshoppalmsprings.com* ⊗ *No lunch Mon.–Sat.*

WHERE TO STAY

$$$ ⛵ **Ace Hotel and Swim Club.** With the hotel's vintage feel and hippie-chic
RESORT decor, it would be no surprise to find guests gathered around cozy communal fire pits enjoying feel-good '60s music. **Pros:** Amigo Room has
late-night dining; poolside stargazing deck; weekend DJ scene at the pool.
Cons: party atmosphere not for everyone; limited amenities; casual staff
and service. $ *Rooms from: $189* ⊠ *701 E. Palm Canyon Dr.* 🕾 *760/325–
9900* ⊕ *www.acehotel.com/palmsprings* ⌁ *188 rooms* ⍾ *No meals.*

$$ ⛵ **Alcazar Palm Springs.** Amid an area known as the Movie Colony,
HOTEL Alcazar features ample, blazing-white guestrooms that wrap around a
sparkling pool; some rooms have Jacuzzis, and many have private patios
or fireplaces. **Pros:** walking distance of downtown; parking on-site;
bikes available. **Cons:** limited service; wall air-conditioners; resort fee.
$ *Rooms from: $159* ⊠ *622 N. Indian Canyon Dr.* 🕾 *760/318–9850*
⊕ *www.alcazarpalmsprings.com* ⌁ *34 rooms* ⍾ *No meals.*

$$$$ ⛵ **ARRIVE.** During the day, sip cocktails from the indoor outdoor bar
HOTEL (which doubles as the reception desk), and lounge in the pool on an
Fodor's Choice inflatable seahorse, or dance to a live DJ; at night, relax outside in the
★ hot tub and socialize around the communal fire pits (half of the rooms
also come with a private patio and fireplace), or cozy up in your king-
size bed among tasteful modern furnishings, and wake to sunny mountain views. **Pros:** private cabanas with misting systems; great restaurant,
artisanal ice-cream shop, and local coffee shop on-site; free valet. **Cons:**
only king rooms available; shower offers little privacy; party scene may
not suit everyone. $ *Rooms from: $329* ⊠ *1551 N. Palm Canyon Dr.*
🕾 *760/507–1650* ⊕ *www.arrivehotels.com* ⌁ *32 rooms* ⍾ *No meals.*

$$$$ ⛵ **Avalon Hotel Palm Springs.** A visit to the Avalon, formerly the Viceroy,
RESORT is like entering a tableau of bright white and yellow, reminiscent of a sun-
filled desert day; guest rooms for two and villas for three or more, some
with fireplaces and private patios, are spread out over four tree-shaded
acres. **Pros:** poolside cabanas; complimentary fitness classes; luxurious
on-site Estrella Spa and stylish restaurant Chi Chi. **Cons:** popular wedding site. $ *Rooms from: $400* ⊠ *415 S. Belardo Rd.* 🕾 *844/328–2566*
⊕ *www.avalonpalmsprings.com* ⌁ *79 rooms* ⍾ *No meals.*

$ ⛵ **Casa Cody.** The service is personal and gracious at this historic bed-
B&B/INN and-breakfast near the Palm Springs Art Museum; spacious studios
and one- and two-bedroom suites hold Santa Fe–style rustic furnishings. **Pros:** former hangout of Charlie Chaplin; friendly ambience; some
rooms come with fireplaces, patios, and/or kitchens. **Cons:** old buildings; limited amenities. $ *Rooms from: $99* ⊠ *175 S. Cahuilla Rd.*
🕾 *760/320–9346, 800/231–2639* ⊕ *www.casacody.com* ⌁ *29 rooms*
⍾ *Breakfast.*

$$$$ ⛵ **Colony Palms Hotel.** This hotel has been a hip place to stay since the
HOTEL 1930s, when gangster Al Wertheimer built it to front his casino, bar, and
brothel; it later became the Howard Hotel, owned by local luminaries
Robert Stewart Howard (his dad owned the fabled racehorse Seabiscuit)
and actress Andrea Leeds (the couple hosted a young Frank Sinatra,
Elizabeth Taylor, and Liberace), and today it still attracts a younger
crowd. **Pros:** rooms open to pool in the central courtyard; attentive
staff; fireplaces and whirlpool tubs in many rooms. **Cons:** high noise

level outside; not for families with young children. [$] *Rooms from: $299* ✉ *572 N. Indian Canyon Dr.* ☎ *760/969–1800, 800/577–2187* 🌐 *www.colonypalmshotel.com* 🛏 *57 rooms* 🍴 *No meals.*

$$$ B&B/INN 🏨 **East Canyon Hotel & Spa.** The vibe is social and the rooms are spacious at this classy resort whose gracious hosts serve a primarily gay clientele. **Pros:** elegant but laid-back feel; attentive service; complimentary poolside cocktails. **Cons:** some guests may find decor too masculine. [$] *Rooms from: $189* ✉ *288 E. Camino Monte Vista* ☎ *760/320–1928, 877/324–6835* 🌐 *www.eastcanyonps.com* 🛏 *15 rooms* 🍴 *Breakfast.*

TRIBAL WEALTH

The Agua Caliente Band of Cahuilla Indians owns nearly half the land in the Palm Springs area. Wanting to encourage the railroad to bring their trains through the desert, Congress granted half the land to the railroad and the other half to the Native Americans. The Cahuilla were granted all the even-numbered one-square-mile sections—but they were unable to develop the land for years due to litigation. The resulting patchwork of developed and vacant land can still be seen today, though the Cahuilla are making up for lost time by opening new hotels and casinos.

$$ HOTEL Fodor's Choice ★ 🏨 **Hotel California.** Expect homey accommodations for all budgets at this delightful hotel that's decked out in rustic Mexican furniture. **Pros:** comfortable design; friendly hosts; free limo service in the evenings. **Cons:** away from downtown. [$] *Rooms from: $175* ✉ *424 E. Palm Canyon Dr.* ☎ *760/322–8855* 🌐 *www.palmspringshotelcalifornia.com* 🛏 *14 rooms* 🍴 *No meals.*

$$ HOTEL 🏨 **The Hyatt Palm Springs.** The best-situated downtown hotel in Palm Springs, the Hyatt has spacious suites where you can watch the sun rise over the city, or set behind the mountains from your bedroom's balcony. **Pros:** underground parking; restaurant plus two outdoor bar-lounges; daily sunset hour with free wine, beer, and appetizers. **Cons:** lots of business travelers; some street noise. [$] *Rooms from: $159* ✉ *285 N. Palm Canyon Dr.* ☎ *760/322–9000* 🌐 *palmsprings.hyatt.com* 🛏 *197 suites* 🍴 *No meals.*

$$$ B&B/INN Fodor's Choice ★ 🏨 **Korakia Pensione.** The painter Gordon Coutts, best known for desert landscapes, constructed this Moroccan villa in 1924 as an artist's studio, and these days creative types gather in the main house and the adjacent Mediterranean-style villa to soak up the spirit of that era. **Pros:** design-minded decor; complimentary breakfast; yoga on weekends. **Cons:** might not appeal to those who prefer standard resorts; no TVs or phones in rooms. [$] *Rooms from: $239* ✉ *257 S. Patencio Rd.* ☎ *760/864–6411* 🌐 *www.korakia.com* 🛏 *20 rooms, 8 rental units* 🍴 *No meals.*

$$$ B&B/INN 🏨 **La Maison.** Offering all the comforts of home, this small bed-and-breakfast contains large rooms that surround the terra-cotta–tiled and very comfortable pool area, where you can spend quiet time soaking up the sun or taking a dip. **Pros:** restaurants nearby; quiet; genial hosts. **Cons:** on busy Highway 111; rooms open directly onto pool deck. [$] *Rooms from: $220* ✉ *1600 E. Palm Canyon Dr.* ☎ *760/325–1600* 🌐 *www.lamaisonpalmsprings.com* 🛏 *13 rooms* 🍴 *Breakfast.*

CLOSE UP

Palm Springs Modernism

Some of the world's most forward-looking architects designed and constructed buildings around Palm Springs between 1940 and 1970; and modernism, also popular elsewhere in California in the years after World War II, became an ideal fit for desert living, because it minimizes the separation between indoors and outdoors. See-through houses with glass exterior walls are common. Oversize flat roofs provide shade from the sun, and many buildings' sculptural forms reflect nearby landforms. The style is notable for elegant informality, clean lines, and simple landscaping.

Most obvious to visitors are three buildings that are part of the Palm Springs Aerial Tramway complex, built in the 1960s. Albert Frey, a Swiss-born architect, designed the soaring A-frame Tramway Gas Station, visually echoing the pointed peaks behind it. Frey also created the glass-walled Valley Station, from which you get your initial view of the Coachella Valley before you board the tram to the Mountain Station, designed by E. Stewart Williams.

Frey, a Palm Springs resident for more than 60 years, also designed the indoor-outdoor City Hall, Fire Station No. 1, and numerous houses. His second home, perched atop stilts on the hillside above the Palm Springs Art Museum, affords a sweeping view of the Coachella Valley through glass walls. The classy Movie Colony Hotel, one of the first buildings Frey designed in the desert, may seem like a typical 1950s motel with rooms surrounding a swimming pool now, but when it was built in 1935, it was years ahead of its time.

Donald Wexler, who honed his vision with Los Angeles architect Richard Neutra, brought new ideas about the use of materials to the desert, where he teamed up with William Cody on a number of projects, including the terminal at the Palm Springs Airport. Many of Wexler's buildings have soaring overhanging roofs, designed to provide shade from the blazing desert sun. Wexler also experimented with steel framing back in 1961, but the metal proved too expensive. Seven of his steel-frame houses can be seen in a neighborhood off Indian Canyon and Frances drives.

The Palm Springs Modern Committee sponsors Modernism Week in mid-February, when you can visit some of the most remarkable buildings in the area. Visit 🌐 *www.psmodcom.org* for an app that guides you to the most interesting buildings.

$$ B&B/INN Fodor's Choice ★ 🏨 **Orbit In Hotel.** The architectural style of this hip inn on a quiet backstreet dates back to the late 1940s and '50s—nearly flat roofs, wide overhangs, glass everywhere—and the period feel continues inside. **Pros:** saltwater pool; in-room spa services; Orbitini cocktail hour. **Cons:** best for couples; style not to everyone's taste; staff not available 24 hours. [$] *Rooms from: $169* ✉ *562 W. Arenas Rd.* ☎ *760/323–3585, 877/996–7248* 🌐 *www.orbitin.com* 🛏 *9 rooms* 🍴 *Breakfast.*

$$$$ RESORT Fodor's Choice ★ 🏨 **The Parker Palm Springs.** A cacophony of color and over-the-top contemporary art assembled by New York City–based designer Jonathan Adler mixes well with the brilliant desert garden, three pools (two outdoor), fire pits, and expansive spa of this hip hotel that attracts a stylish, worldly clientele. **Pros:** fun in the sun; celebrity clientele; on-site Palm

Springs Yacht Club Spa; design-centric. **Cons:** pricey drinks and wine; a bit of a drive from downtown; resort fee ($35). [$] *Rooms from: $325* ✉ *4200 E. Palm Canyon Dr.* ☎ *760/770–5000, 800/543–4300* 🌐 *www.theparkerpalmsprings.com* 🛏 *144 rooms* 🍴 *No meals.*

$$$$ RESORT **Riviera Resort & Spa.** A party place built in 1958 and renovated in 2008, the Riviera attracts young, well-heeled, bikini-clad guests who hang out around the pool by day, and at the Bikini Bar by night. **Pros:** personal fire pits throughout the property; hip vibe; excellent spa. **Cons:** high noise level outdoors; party atmosphere; location at north end of Palm Springs. [$] *Rooms from: $300* ✉ *1600 N. Indian Canyon Dr.* ☎ *760/327–8311* 🌐 *rivierapalmsprings.com* 🛏 *449 rooms* 🍴 *No meals.*

14

$$ HOTEL Fodor's Choice ★ **The Saguaro.** A startling, rainbow-hued oasis—the brainchild of Manhattan-based architects Peter Stamberg and Paul Aferiat—the Saguaro caters to pet-toting partygoers who appreciate its lively pool and casual- and fine-dining options. **Pros:** excellent on-site dining; daily yoga; shuttle service to downtown. **Cons:** a few miles from downtown. [$] *Rooms from: $169* ✉ *1800 E. Palm Canyon Dr.* ☎ *760/323–1711* 🌐 *thesaguaro.com* 🛏 *244 rooms* 🍴 *No meals.*

$$$$ RESORT FAMILY **Smoke Tree Ranch.** A world apart from Palm Springs' pulsating urban village, the area's most under-the-radar resort complex occupies 400 pristine desert acres surrounded by mountains and unspoiled vistas. **Pros:** priceless privacy; simple luxury; recreational activities like horseback riding and more. **Cons:** no glitz; limited entertainment options; family atmosphere not for everyone. [$] *Rooms from: $400* ✉ *1850 Smoke Tree La.* ☎ *760/327–1221, 800/787–3922* 🌐 *www.smoketreeranch.com* ⏲ *Closed Apr.–late Oct.* 🛏 *49 cottages, includes 18 suites* 🍴 *All-inclusive; Some meals.*

$$$ B&B/INN **Sparrows Lodge.** Rustic earthiness meets haute design at the adult-centered Sparrows, just off Palm Springs' main drag. **Pros:** unique design; intimate property; private patios. **Cons:** rooms feel a little dark; some guests might deem them charmless; no TVs or phones in rooms. [$] *Rooms from: $249* ✉ *1330 E. Palm Canyon Dr.* ☎ *760/327–2300* 🌐 *www.sparrowshotel.com* 🛏 *20 rooms* 🍴 *Breakfast.*

$$$$ B&B/INN Fodor's Choice ★ **Willows Historic Palm Springs Inn.** An opulent Mediterranean-style mansion built in the 1920s to host the rich and famous, this luxurious hillside bed-and-breakfast has gleaming hardwood and slate floors, stone fireplaces, frescoed ceilings, hand-painted tiles, iron balconies, antiques throughout, and a 50-foot waterfall that splashes into a pool outside the dining room. **Pros:** luxurious; sublime service; expansive breakfast. **Cons:** closed from June to September; pricey. [$] *Rooms from: $395* ✉ *412 W. Tahquitz Canyon Way* ☎ *760/320–0771, 800/966–9597* 🌐 *www.thewillowspalmsprings.com* 🛏 *8 rooms* 🍴 *Breakfast.*

NIGHTLIFE AND PERFORMING ARTS

NIGHTLIFE

BARS AND PUBS

Bootlegger Tiki. Palm Springs tiki-drink traditions, especially during the daily happy hour, draw loyal patrons to Bootlegger, which occupies the same space as Don the Beachcomber in the 1950s. ✉ *1101 N. Palm Canyon Dr.* ☎ *760/318-4154.*

Fodor's Choice
★

Draughtsman. In the Uptown Design District and part of the ARRIVE hotel, this upscale pub focuses on Palm Springs and SoCal craft beers, classic cocktails, and modern comfort food, as well as classics like chicken pot pie and short rib poutine. Hang out in the contemporary indoor space with soaring ceilings and watch sports, or chill on the patio where you can play cornhole or foosball. ⊠ *1501 N. Palm Canyon Dr.* ☎ *760/507–1644* ⊕ *draughtsmanpalmsprings.com.*

Purple Room Supper Club. In an elegant venue within the Club Trinidad Hotel, this swinging '60s-era supper club offers live entertainment six nights a week. Come for drinks, dinner, and dancing Tuesday through Thursday night (no cover charge, but reservations are recommended). On Friday and Saturday night, dine at 6 pm and watch a scheduled show at 8 pm (reserve tickets in advance). Try to time your visit to catch *The Judy Show*, actor/owner Michael Holmes's Sunday evening comical tribute to Judy Garland, Bette Davis, Katharine Hepburn, and other stars (tickets required). ⊠ *1900 E. Palm Canyon Dr.* ☎ *760/322–4422* ⊕ *www.purpleroompalmsprings.com.*

Tonga Hut. The sibling of L.A.'s oldest tiki hut (opened in 1958 in North Hollywood), Tonga Hut Palm Springs transports guests to Polynesia with an authentic tiki vibe, pupu platters, and tropical drinks. It's on the second floor of a building in the heart of the downtown strip—try to nab a table on the lanai where you can experience the action from above. The bar and dining area are also fun and lively spaces; ask about the telephone booth that leads to a secret room, available for private parties. ⊠ *254 N. Palm Canyon Dr.* ☎ *760/322–4449* ⊕ *www.tongahut.com.*

Fodor's Choice
★

Village Pub. With live entertainment, DJs, and friendly service, this popular bar caters to a young crowd. Happy hour is fantastic. On weekend days there is live music as well. ⊠ *266 S. Palm Canyon Dr., at Baristo Rd.* ☎ *760/323–3265* ⊕ *www.palmspringsvillagepub.com.*

CASINOS

Casino Morongo. A 20-minute drive west of Palm Springs, this casino has 2,600 slot machines, video games, the Vibe nightclub, plus Vegas-style shows. ⊠ *49500 Seminole Dr., off I-10, Cabazon* ☎ *800/252–4499, 951/849–3080* ⊕ *www.morongocasinoresort.com.*

Spa Resort Casino. This resort holds 1,000 slot machines, blackjack tables, a high-limit room, four restaurants, two bars, and the Cascade Lounge for entertainment. ⊠ *401 E. Amado Rd., at N. Calle Encilia* ☎ *888/999–1995* ⊕ *www.sparesortcasino.com.*

DANCE CLUBS

Zelda's Nightclub. At this Palm Springs institution, the high-energy DJs, dancing, and drinking are still going strong and the dance floor is still thumping with Latin, hip-hop, and sounds from the '60s, '70s, and '80s. Zelda's offers bottle service in the VIP Sky Box. ⊠ *611 S. Palm Canyon Dr., at E. Camino Parocela* ☎ *760/325–2375* ⊕ *www.zeldasnightclub. com* ⊗ *Closed Mon.*

GAY AND LESBIAN

The Dinah. In late March, when the world's finest female golfers hit the links for the Annual LPGA ANA Inspiration Championship in Rancho Mirage, thousands of lesbians converge on Palm Springs for a four-day party popularly known as The Dinah. ☎ *888/923–4624* ⊕ *thedinah.com.*

Hunter's Video Bar. Drawing a young gay and straight crowd, Hunter's is a club-scene mainstay. ✉ *302 E. Arenas Rd., at Calle Encilia* ☎ *760/323–0700* ⊕ *huntersnightclubs.com.*

Fodor'sChoice ★ **Toucans Tiki Lounge.** A friendly place with a tropical–rain forest setting, Toucans serves festive drinks and hosts live entertainment and theme nights. On Sunday it seems as though all of Palm Springs has turned out for drag night. ✉ *2100 N. Palm Canyon Dr., at W. Via Escuela* ☎ *760/416–7584* ⊕ *www.toucanstikilounge.com.*

White Party Palm Springs. Held during spring break, the White Party draws tens of thousands of gay men from around the world for four days of parties and events. ✉ *Palm Springs* ⊕ *jeffreysanker.com.*

THEMED ENTERTAINMENT

Fodor'sChoice ★ **Ace Hotel and Swim Club.** Events are held here nearly every night, including film screenings, full moon parties, live concerts, DJs, and dancing. Many are free, and some are family friendly. The poolside venue makes most events fun and casual. ✉ *701 E. Palm Canyon Dr., at Calle Palo Fierro* ☎ *760/325–9900* ⊕ *www.acehotel.com.*

PERFORMING ARTS

ARTS CENTERS

Annenberg Theater. Broadway shows, operas, lectures, Sunday-afternoon chamber concerts, and other events take place at the Palm Springs Art Museum's handsome theater. ✉ *101 N. Museum Dr., at W. Tahquitz Canyon Way* ☎ *760/325–4490* ⊕ *www.psmuseum.org.*

FESTIVALS

Modernism Week. Each February the desert communities celebrate the work of the architects and designers who created the Palm Springs "look" in the '40s, '50s, and '60s. Described these days as mid-century modern—you'll also see the term "desert modernism" used—these structures were created by Albert Frey, Richard Neutra, William F. Cody, John Lautner, and other notables. The 11-day event features lectures, a modernism show, films, vintage car and trailer shows, galas, and home and garden tours. A shorter preview week happens in October. ✉ *Palm Springs* ⊕ *www.modernismweek.com.*

FILM

Palm Springs International Film Festival. In mid-January this 12-day festival brings stars and nearly 200 feature films from several dozen countries, plus panel discussions, short films, and documentaries, to various venues. The weeklong "Shortfest," celebrating more than 300 short films, takes place in June. ✉ *Palm Springs* ☎ *760/322–2930, 800/898–7256* ⊕ *www.psfilmfest.org.*

14

Palm Springs is a golfer's paradise: the area is home to more than 125 courses.

SHOPPING

BOUTIQUES

Fodor's Choice
★ **Just Fabulous.** Find everything from original photography and art, coffee table books, greeting cards, designer home decor, candles, and many other eclectic items at this fun gift shop that celebrates the area's retro-modern lifestyle and desert dolce vita. ⊠ *515 N. Palm Canyon Dr.* ☎ *760/864–1300* ⊕ *bjustfabulous.com.*

Fodor's Choice
★ **Trina Turk Boutique.** Celebrity designer Trina Turk's empire takes up a city block in the Uptown Design District. Turk, famous for men's and women's outdoor wear, reached out to another celebrity, interior designer Kelly Wearstler, to create adjoining clothing and residential boutiques. Lively fabrics brighten up the many chairs and couches for sale at the residential store, which also carries bowls, paintings, and other fun pieces to spiff up your home. ⊠ *891 N. Palm Canyon Dr.* ☎ *760/416–2856* ⊕ *www.trinaturk.com.*

OUTLET MALLS

Fodor's Choice
★ **Desert Hills Premium Outlets.** About 20 miles west of Palm Springs lies one of California's largest outlet centers. The 180 brand-name discount fashion shops include Jimmy Choo, Neiman Marcus, Versace, Saint Laurent Paris, J. Crew, Armani, Gucci, and Prada. ⊠ *48400 Seminole Rd., off I–10, Cabazon* ☎ *951/849–5018* ⊕ *www.premiumoutlets.com.*

SHOPPING DISTRICTS

Fodor's Choice
★ **Uptown Design District.** A loose-knit collection of consignment and secondhand shops, galleries, and lively restaurants extends north of Palm Springs' downtown. The theme here is decidedly retro. Many businesses

sell mid-century modern furniture and decorator items, and others carry clothing and estate jewelry. One spot definitely worth a peek is **Shag, the Store,** the gallery of fine art painter Josh Agle. For antique costume jewelry check out **Dazzles.** If you dig the mid-mod aesthetic, breeze through the furnishings at **Towne Palm Springs.** ✉ *N. Palm Canyon Dr., between Amado Rd. and Vista Chino.*

SPAS

Fodor's Choice ★ **Estrella Spa at the Avalon Hotel Palm Springs.** This spa earns top honors each year for the indoor/outdoor experience it offers with a touch of Old Hollywood ambience. You can enjoy your massage in one of four outdoor treatment cabanas in a garden, experience a sugar or salt scrub, get a facial or pedicure fireside, or receive a full-body treatment with lemon crystals. Whatever the treatment, you can use the spa's private pool, take a break for lunch, and order a drink from the hotel's bar. ✉ *Avalon Hotel Palm Springs, 415 S. Belardo Rd.* ☎ *760/318–3000* ⊕ *www.avalonpalmsprings.com* ✂ *Salon. Services: facials, specialty massages, prenatal massages, outdoor treatments, wellness classes. $145, 60-min massage, $260, spa package.*

Feel Good Spa at the Ace Hotel. The Feel Good Spa within its own dedicated facility at the Ace Hotel reopened in 2017 after a head-to-toe renovation, and has five treatment rooms. The estheticians use local clay, mud, sea algae, and other natural ingredients, which you can purchase at the on-site shop. ✉ *701 E. Palm Canyon Dr.* ☎ *760/866–6188* ⊕ *www.acehotel.com/palmsprings* ✂ *Fully equipped gym. Services: wraps and scrubs, massage, facials, in-room treatments, salon, wellness classes, yoga. $110, 60-min massage.*

Palm Springs Yacht Club. It's all about fun at the Parker Palm Springs hotel's yacht club. Guests receive a complimentary cocktail while lounging in a poolside tent. Before spa treatments, you can choose music from a playlist and the staff will stream it to your room. When you're ready to crash, wander over to the outdoor café for a burger and Pimm's. Treatments might feature local clay or stones, or a Thai massage. ✉ *4200 E. Palm Canyon Dr.* ☎ *760/321–4606* ⊕ *www.theparkerpalmsprings. com/spa* ✂ *Sauna, steam room, indoor pool. Services: scrubs and wraps, massage, facials, manicures, pedicures, waxing, salon, fitness center with TechnoGym equipment, dining and cocktails. $195, 60-min massage.*

THE DESERT RESORTS

The term *desert resorts* refers to the communities along or just off Highway 111—Cathedral City, Rancho Mirage, Palm Desert, Indian Wells, Indio, and La Quinta—along with Desert Hot Springs *(see Along Twentynine Palms Highway)*, which is north of Palm Springs off Highway 62 and Interstate 10.

14

RANCHO MIRAGE

4 miles southeast of Cathedral City.

The rich and famous of Rancho Mirage live in beautiful estates and patronize elegant resorts and expensive restaurants. Although many mansions here are concealed behind the walls of gated communities and country clubs, the grandest of them all, Sunnylands, the Annenberg residence, is open to the public as a museum and public garden.

The city's golf courses host many high-profile tournaments. You'll find some of the desert's fanciest resorts in Rancho Mirage, and plenty of peace and quiet.

GETTING HERE AND AROUND

Due east of Cathedral City, Rancho Mirage stretches from Ramon Road on the north to the hills south of Highway 111. The western border is Da Vall Drive, the eastern one Monterey Avenue. Major east–west cross streets are Frank Sinatra Drive and Country Club Drive. Most shopping and dining spots are on Highway 111.

EXPLORING

The Annenberg Retreat at Sunnylands. The stunning 25,000-square-foot winter home and retreat of the late Ambassador Walter H. and Leonore Annenberg opened to the public in 2012. You can spend a whole day enjoying the 9 glorious acres of gardens (see website schedule of free guided walks, classes, and other programs), or take a guided 90-minute tour of the residence (reservations essential), a striking mid-century modern edifice designed by A. Quincy Jones. Floor-to-ceiling windows frame views of the gardens and Mount San Jacinto, and the expansive rooms hold furnishings from the 1960s and later, along with impressionist art (some original, some replicas). The history made here is as captivating as the surroundings. Eight U.S. presidents—from Dwight Eisenhower to Barack Obama—and their First Ladies have visited Sunnylands; Ronald and Nancy Reagan were frequent guests. Britain's Queen Elizabeth and Prince Philip also relaxed here, as did Princess Grace of Monaco and Japanese Prime Minister Toshiki Kaifu. Photos, art, letters, journals, and mementos provide insight into some of the history that unfolded here. ✉ *37–977 Bob Hope Dr., south of Gerald Ford Dr.* ☎ *760/202–2222* 🌐 *www.sunnylands.org* 🎫 *House tours $45, tickets available online 2 wks in advance; guided bird tour $35; open-air shuttle tour of grounds, $20; visitor center and gardens free* ⏲ *Closed Mon.–Wed. Closed July and Aug. and during retreats.*

FAMILY **Children's Discovery Museum of the Desert.** This museum features a number of hands-on exhibits, including a miniature rock-climbing area, a magnetic sculpture wall, make-it-and-take-it-apart projects, a rope maze, and an area for toddlers. Kids can paint a VW Bug, work as chefs in the museum's pizza parlor, assemble their own cars on a racetrack, and build pies out of arts and crafts supplies. ✉ *71–701 Gerald Ford Dr., at Bob Hope Dr.* ☎ *760/321–0602* 🌐 *www.cdmod.org* 🎫 *$10* ⏲ *Closed Mon. May–Dec.*

Koffi. Locals often hit this chain to get their caffeine fix, and it's a fine pit stop for pastries, pre-made sandwiches, and bagels. This outpost is the roasting facility, so the beans here are as fresh as they come. ✉ *71–380 Hwy. 111* ☎ *760/340–2444* 🌐 *www.kofficoffee.com.*

WHERE TO EAT AND STAY

$$$ MEDITERRANEAN **Catalan.** At this restaurant known for its beautifully prepared Mediterranean cuisine you can dine inside or under the stars in the atrium. The service here is attentive, and the menu roams Spain, Italy, California and beyond. **Known for:** attentive service; delicious paella with clams; happy hour with inventive cocktails. *Average main: $27* ✉ *70026 Hwy. 111* ☎ *760/770–9508* 🌐 *www.catalanrestaurant.com* ⏲ *Closed Mon.*

$ MEXICAN FAMILY **Las Casuelas Nuevas.** Hundreds of artifacts from Guadalajara, Mexico, lend festive charm to this casual restaurant, which has an expansive garden patio. Tamales and shellfish dishes are among the specialties—expect more traditional Mexican fare, rather than California-influenced creations. **Known for:** vast tequila menu; weekend live entertainment; lively happy hour. *Average main: $15* ✉ *70–050 Hwy. 111* ☎ *760/328–8844* 🌐 *www.lascasuelasnuevas.com.*

$$$ RESORT **Agua Caliente Casino, Resort, Spa.** As in Las Vegas, the Agua Caliente casino is in the lobby, but once you get into the spacious, beautifully appointed rooms of the resort, all of the cacophony at the entrance is forgotten. **Pros:** poolside cabanas outfitted with TV and Wi-Fi; package deals include access to Indian Canyons Golf Course; on-site Sunstone Spa. **Cons:** casino ambience; not appropriate for kids. *Rooms from: $250* ✉ *32–250 Bob Hope Dr.* ☎ *888/999–1995* 🌐 *www.hotwatercasino.com* *366 rooms* *No meals.*

$$$$ RESORT FAMILY 🏨 **Omni Rancho Las Palmas Resort & Spa.** The desert's most family-friendly resort, this large venue holds Splashtopia, a huge water-play zone. **Pros:** rooms come with private balconies or patios; trails for hiking and jogging; nightly entertainment. **Cons:** second-floor rooms accessed by very steep stairs; golf course surrounds rooms; resort hosts conventions. [$] *Rooms from: $299* ✉ *41-000 Bob Hope Dr.* ☎ *760/568–2727, 888/444–6664* 🌐 *www.rancholaspalmas.com* 🛏 *444 rooms* 🍴 *No meals.*

$$$$ RESORT FAMILY Fodor's Choice ★ 🏨 **The Ritz Carlton, Rancho Mirage.** On a hilltop perch overlooking the Coachella Valley, this luxury resort spoils guests with exemplary service and comforts that include a trio of pools, access to the desert's finest spa, and private outdoor sitting areas for each room. **Pros:** fire pit overlooking Coachella Valley; access to Mission Hills golf courses and tennis; spa that's a destination in itself. **Cons:** hefty rates; some airport noise; resort and parking fees ($30 each). [$] *Rooms from: $489* ✉ *68900 Frank Sinatra Dr.* ☎ *760/321–8282* 🌐 *www.ritzcarlton.com* 🛏 *244 rooms* 🍴 *No meals.*

$$$$ RESORT FAMILY 🏨 **The Westin Mission Hills Golf Resort & Spa.** A sprawling resort on 360 acres, the Westin offers a slew of activities for all ages and is surrounded by fairways and putting greens, two family-friendly pools (one lagoon-style with a 75-foot waterslide) and an adults-only pool. **Pros:** gorgeous grounds; first-class golf facilities; daily activity programs for kids and adults. **Cons:** rooms are spread out; pricey. [$] *Rooms from: $369* ✉ *71333 Dinah Shore Dr.* ☎ *760/328–5955, 800/937–8461* 🌐 *www.westinmissionhills.com* 🛏 *552 rooms* 🍴 *No meals.*

NIGHTLIFE

Agua Caliente Casino. This elegant and surprisingly quiet casino contains 1,300 slot machines, 36 table games, an 18-table poker room, a high-limit room, a no-smoking area, and six restaurants. The Show, the resort's concert theater, presents acts such as The Moody Blues, Joe Bonamassa, and Sophia Loren, as well as live sporting events. ✉ *32–250 Bob Hope Dr., at E. Ramon Rd.* ☎ *760/321–2000* 🌐 *www.hotwater-casino.com.*

SPORTS AND THE OUTDOORS

GOLF

ANA Inspiration Championship. The best female golfers in the world compete in this championship held in late March or early April. ✉ *Mission Hills Country Club* ☎ *760/834–8872* 🌐 *www.anainspiration.com.*

Fodor's Choice ★ **Westin Mission Hills Resort Golf Club.** Golfers at the Westin Mission Hills have two courses to choose from, the Pete Dye and the Gary Player Signature. They're both great, with amazing mountain views and wide fairways, but if you've only got time to play one, choose the Dye. The club is a member of the Troon Golf Institute, and has several teaching facilities, including the Westin Mission Hills Resort Golf Academy and the *Golf Digest* Golf School. ■ **TIP→ The resort's Best Available Rate program guarantees golfers (with a few conditions) the best Internet rate possible.** ✉ *71333 Dinah Shore Dr.* ☎ *760/328–3198* 🌐 *www.playmissionhills.com* 💵 *Gary Player, $74–$180; Pete Dye, $114–$172* 🏌 *Pete Dye Resort: 18 holes, 5525 yards, par 72; Gary Player Signature: 18 holes, 5327 yards, par 70.*

SHOPPING

MALL

The River at Rancho Mirage. This shopping-dining-entertainment complex holds 20 high-end shops, including the SoCal darling Diane's Beachwear, all fronting a faux river with cascading waterfalls. Also here are a 12-screen cinema, an outdoor amphitheater, and many restaurants including Fleming's Prime Steakhouse and Babe's Bar-B-Que and Brewery. ⊠ *71–800 Hwy. 111, at Bob Hope Dr.* ☎ *760/341–2711* ⊕ *www.theriveratranchomirage.com.*

SPAS

Fodor's Choice ★ **The Ritz Carlton Spa, Rancho Mirage.** Two hundred–plus suspended quartz crystals guard the entrance of the desert's premier spa. With private men's and women's areas, a co-ed outdoor soaking tub, food service, and some of the kindest spa technicians around, guests can expect pampering par excellence. The signature Spirit of the Mountains treatment, which starts with a full-body exfoliation, includes a massage, and ends with a body wrap and a scalp massage with lavender oil, is a blissful experience. The gym, equipped with state-of-the-art machines, is open 24/7. Private trainers are available to guide your workout; wellness classes are also available. ⊠ *68900 Frank Sinatra Drive* ☎ *760/202–6170* ⊕ *www.ritzcarlton.com* ⚬ *Fully equipped gym. Salon. Services: body wraps, body scrubs, facials, mineral baths, specialty massages, outdoor treatments, waxing, wellness classes. $165, 50-min massage; $330, signature package.*

The Spa at Mission Hills. The emphasis at this spa in a quiet corner of the Weston Mission Hills Resort is on comfort rather than glitz and glamour. Attentive therapists incorporate coconut milk, lemon balm, mint, thyme, red algae, hydrating honey, and other botanicals into their treatments. Yoga and other wellness classes are also available. ⊠ *71333 Dinah Shore Dr.* ☎ *760/770–2134* ⊕ *www.spaatmissionhills.com* ⚬ *Steam room. Gym with: machines, cardio, pool. Services: rubs and scrubs, massages, facials, nail services. $125, 50-min massage.*

PALM DESERT

2 miles southeast of Rancho Mirage.

Palm Desert is a thriving retail and business community with popular restaurants, private and public golf courses, and premium shopping along the main commercial drag, El Paseo. Each October, the Palm Desert Golf Cart Parade launches "the season" with a procession of 80 golf carts decked out as floats buzzing up and down El Paseo. The town's stellar sight to see is the Living Desert complex.

GETTING HERE AND AROUND

Palm Desert stretches from north of Interstate 10 to the hills south of Highway 111. West–east cross streets north to south are Frank Sinatra Drive, Country Club Drive (lined on both sides with gated golfing communities), and Fred Waring Drive. Monterey Avenue marks the western boundary, and Washington Street forms the eastern edge.

EXPLORING

Fodor's Choice ★ **El Paseo.** West of and parallel to Highway 111, this mile-long Mediterranean-style shopper's paradise is lined with fountains, courtyards, and upscale boutiques. You'll find shoe salons, jewelry stores, children's shops, two dozen restaurants, and nearly as many art galleries. The strip is a pleasant place to stroll, window-shop, people-watch, and exercise your credit cards. ■**TIP**➔ **In winter and spring a free bright-yellow shuttle ferries shoppers from store to store and back to their cars.** ⊠ *Between Monterey and Portola Aves.* ☎ *877/735–7273* ⊕ *www. elpaseo.com.*

FAMILY **Fodor's**Choice ★ **Living Desert.** Come eye-to-eye with wolves, coyotes, mountain lions, cheetahs, bighorn sheep, golden eagles, warthogs, and owls at the 1,800-acre Living Desert. Easy to challenging scenic trails traverse desert terrain populated with plants of the Mojave, Colorado, and Sonoran deserts. In recent years the park has expanded its vision to include Australia and Africa. At the 3-acre African WaTuTu village you'll find a traditional marketplace as well as camels, leopards, hyenas, and other African animals. Children can pet African domesticated animals, including goats and guinea fowl, in a "petting kraal." Gecko Gulch is a children's playground with crawl-through underground tunnels, climb-on snake sculptures, a carousel, and a Discovery Center that holds ancient Pleistocene animal bones. Elsewhere, a small enclosure contains butterflies and hummingbirds, and a cool model train travels through miniatures of historic California towns. ■**TIP**➔ **A garden center sells native desert flora, much of which is unavailable elsewhere.** ⊠ *47900 Portola Ave., south from Hwy. 111* ☎ *760/346–5694* ⊕ *www. livingdesert.org* ☞ *$20.*

Palm Springs Art Museum in Palm Desert. A satellite branch of the Palm Springs Art Museum, this gallery space tucked into a desert garden at the west entrance to El Paseo exhibits cutting-edge works by contemporary sculptors and painters. The on-site restaurant **Cuistot** (*760/340– 1000, www.cuistotrestaurant.com*) is a splendid, if pricey, place to enjoy French cuisine. ⊠ *72–567 Hwy. 111* ✛ *in El Paseo* ☎ *760/346–5600* ⊕ *www.psmuseum.org/palm-desert* ☞ *Free* ☉ *Closed Mon.*

Santa Rosa and San Jacinto Mountains National Monument. Administered by the U.S. Bureau of Land Management, this monument protects Peninsula bighorn sheep and other wildlife on 280,000 acres of desert habitat. Stop by the visitor center for an introduction to the site and information about the natural history of the desert. A landscaped garden displays native plants and frames an impressive view. The well-informed staff can recommend hiking trails that show off the beauties of the desert. ■**TIP**➔ **Free guided hikes are offered on Thursday and Saturday.** ⊠ *51–500 Hwy. 74* ☎ *760/862–9984* ⊕ *www.blm.gov* ☞ *Free.*

WHERE TO EAT AND STAY

$ AMERICAN **Fodor's**Choice ★ ✕ **Bouchee.** Devotees of this La Quinta favorite come here for farm-to-table Euro-style meals and deli items. Order the salads or gorgeous sandwiches—the salmon salad is to die for—at the counter, then retire to the French-inspired dining area, or the shaded outdoor terrace. **Known for:** premade dinner to go; gourmet wine and cheese shop;

locally sourced ingredients. $ *Average main: $10 ⊠ 72–785 Hwy. 111 ⊹ off Plaza Way near El Paseo* ☎ *442/666–3296* ⊕ *www.boucheecafeanddeli.com* ⊗ *No dinner.*

$$ ✕ **Clementine's Gourmet Marketplace**
ECLECTIC
Fodor'sChoice
★
and Cafe. A favorite of families, lunching ladies, and couples, Clementine's presents an artful mix of Mediterranean flavors. Diners at the café perch at long wooden communal tables to tuck into baked egg Ficelle, lamb burgers, and other specialties, but this space's nerve center is the take-out counter and kitchen that brims with pre-made salads, boulangerie-style meats and cheeses, and decadent French-inspired pastries and desserts. **Known for:** Mediterranean market vibe; cocktail bar and happy hour; regular evening special events. $ *Average main: $18 ⊠ 72990 El Paseo* ☎ *760/834–8814* ⊕ *www.clementineshop.com* ⊗ *No dinner.*

$$$$ ✕ **Pacifica Seafood.** Choice seafood, rooftop dining, and reduced prices
SEAFOOD
at sunset draw locals and visitors to this busy restaurant on the second floor of the Gardens of El Paseo. Seafood that shines in dishes such as butter-poached Maine lobster tail, grilled Pacific swordfish, and barbecued sugar-spiced salmon arrives daily from San Diego; the menu also includes chicken, steaks, and meal-size salads. **Known for:** inventive sauces and glazes; bar with 150 different vodkas; lower-price sunset menu. $ *Average main: $38 ⊠ 73505 El Paseo* ☎ *760/674–8666* ⊕ *www.pacificaseafoodrestaurant.com* ⊗ *No lunch June–Aug.*

$$$ 🛏 **Desert Springs J. W. Marriott Resort and Spa.** With a dramatic U-shape
RESORT
FAMILY
design, this sprawling hotel, which attract business travelers, couples, and families alike, is set on 450 landscaped acres and wraps around the desert's largest private lake. **Pros:** gondola rides on the lake to restaurants; popular lobby bar; wonderful spa. **Cons:** crowded in-season; high resort fee; long walk from lobby to rooms. $ *Rooms from: $259 ⊠ 74–855 Country Club Dr.* ☎ *760/341–2211, 888/538–9459* ⊕ *www. desertspringsresort.com* ⇆ *884 rooms* ⦶ *No meals.*

GREEN PALM DESERT

The City of Palm Desert's ambitious plan to reduce energy consumption includes incentives to install efficient pool pumps, air-conditioners, refrigeration, and lighting. The city has banned drive-through restaurants and made golf carts legal on city streets.

14

PERFORMING ARTS

McCallum Theatre. The principal cultural venue in the desert, this theater hosts productions from fall through spring. *Fiddler on the Roof* has played here; Lily Tomlin, Willie Nelson, and Michael Feinstein have performed, and Joffrey Ballet dancers have pirouetted across the stage. ⊠ *73–000 Fred Waring Dr.* ☎ *760/340–2787* ⊕ *www.mccallumtheatre.com.*

SPORTS AND THE OUTDOORS
BALLOONING

Fantasy Balloon Flights. Sunrise excursions over the southern end of the Coachella Valley lift off at 6 am and take from 60 to 90 minutes; a traditional champagne toast follows the landing. Afternoon excursions are timed to touch down at sunset. ⊠ *Palm Desert* ☎ *760/568–0997* ⊕ *www.fantasyballoonflight.com* ⇆ *$195.*

GOLF

Desert Willow Golf Resort. Praised for its environmentally smart design, this public golf resort planted water-thrifty turf grasses and doesn't use pesticides. The Mountain View course has four configurations; Firecliff is tournament quality with five configurations. A public facility, Desert Willow is one of the country's top-rated golf courses. ✉ *38–995 Desert Willow Dr., off Country Club Dr.* ☎ *760/346–0015* 🌐 *www.desertwillow.com* 🎫 *Mountain View from $65, Firecliff from $65* ⛳ *Mountain View: 18 holes, 7079 yards, par 72; Firecliff: 18 holes, 7056 yards, par 72.*

INDIAN WELLS

5 miles east of Palm Desert.

For the most part a quiet and exclusive residential enclave, Indian Wells hosts major golf and tennis tournaments throughout the year, including the BNP Paribus Open tennis tournament. Three hotels share access to championship golf and tennis facilities, and there are several noteworthy resort spas and restaurants.

GETTING HERE AND AROUND

Indian Wells lies between Palm Desert and La Quinta, with most resorts, restaurants, and shopping set back from Highway 111.

WHERE TO EAT AND STAY

$$$$ AMERICAN
🍴 **Vue Grille and Bar at the Indian Wells Golf Resort.** This not-so-private restaurant at the Indian Wells Golf Resort offers a glimpse of how the country-club set lives. The service is impeccable, and the outdoor tables provide views of mountain peaks that seem close enough to touch. **Known for:** farm-to-table cuisine; grilled steaks and seafood; flatbreads and burgers. [$] *Average main: $34* ✉ *44-500 Indian Wells La.* ☎ *760/834–3800* 🌐 *www.vuegrilleandbar.com.*

$$$$ RESORT FAMILY Fodor's Choice ★
🏨 **Hyatt Grand Regency Indian Wells Resort.** This stark-white resort adjacent to the Golf Resort at Indian Wells is one of the grandest in the desert. **Pros:** excellent business services; butler service in some rooms; very pet friendly. **Cons:** big and impersonal; spread out over 45 acres; noisy public areas. [$] *Rooms from: $350* ✉ *44–600 Indian Wells La.* ☎ *760/776–1234* 🌐 *indianwells.regency.hyatt.com* 🛏 *480 rooms, 40 villas* 🍽 *No meals.*

$$$$ RESORT
🏨 **Miramonte Resort & Spa.** A warm bit of Tuscany against a backdrop of the Santa Rosa Mountains characterizes the most intimate of the Indian Wells hotels. **Pros:** gorgeous gardens; daily wellness classes; one of the desert's best spas. **Cons:** adult-oriented; limited resort facilities on site; rooms could use some sprucing up. [$] *Rooms from: $279* ✉ *45000 Indian Wells La.* ☎ *760/341–2200* 🌐 *www.miramonteresort.com* 🛏 *215 rooms* 🍽 *Some meals.*

$$$$ RESORT FAMILY
🏨 **Renaissance Indian Wells Resort and Spa.** The centerpiece of this luxurious resort, adjacent to the Golf Resort at Indian Wells, is an eight-story atrium lobby, onto which most rooms open. **Pros:** adjacent to golf-tennis complex; kids club; bicycles available. **Cons:** higher noise level in rooms surrounding pool; somewhat impersonal ambience. [$] *Rooms from: $289* ✉ *44–400 Indian Wells La.* ☎ *760/773–4444* 🌐 *www.renaissancehotels.com* 🛏 *560 rooms* 🍽 *No meals.*

SPORTS AND THE OUTDOORS

GOLF

Fodor's Choice ★ **Golf Resort at Indian Wells.** Adjacent to the Hyatt Regency Indian Wells, this complex includes the Celebrity Course, designed by Clive Clark and twice a host to the PGA's Skins game (lots of water here), and the Players Course, designed by John Fought to incorporate views of the surrounding mountain ranges. Both courses consistently rank among the best public courses in California. **■TIP→ It's a good idea to book tee times well in advance, up to 60 days.** ✉ *44–500 Indian Wells La.* ☎ *760/346–4653* 🌐 *www.indianwellsgolfresort.com* 🎫 *Both courses $69–$219* ⛳ *Celebrity Course: 18 holes, 7050 yards, par 72; Players Course: 18 holes, 7376 yards, par 72.*

TENNIS

BNP Paribas Open. Drawing 200 of the world's top players, this tennis tournament takes place at Indian Wells Tennis Garden for two weeks in March. Various ticket plans are available, with some packages including stays at the adjoining Hyatt Regency Indian Wells or Renaissance Esmeralda resorts. ✉ *78200 Miles Ave.* ☎ *800/999–1585* 🌐 *www.bnpparibasopen.com.*

SPAS

Fodor's Choice ★ **The Well.** A luxurious 12,000-square-foot facility, The Well draws on international treatments and ingredients to indulge the senses and relax the body. Treatments such as hot stone and full-body massages, table yoga, and a couples' Pittura Festa experience, which involves painting each other with colorful therapeutic muds, are well worth the splurge. Sugar or salt exfoliating scrubs may well restore the soul in addition to the skin. ✉ *Miramonte Resort, 45–000 Indian Wells La.* ☎ *866/843–9355* 🌐 *www.miramonteresort.com* ☞ *Services: facials, nail care, solo and couple's massages, scrubs, and other body therapies. $165, 60-min massage.*

LA QUINTA

4 miles south of Indian Wells.

The desert became a Hollywood hideout in the 1920s, when La Quinta Hotel (now La Quinta Resort and Club) opened, introducing the Coachella Valley's first golf course. Old Town La Quinta is a popular attraction; the area holds dining spots, shops, and galleries.

GETTING HERE AND AROUND

Most of La Quinta lies south of Highway 111. The main drag through town is Washington Street.

WHERE TO EAT AND STAY

$$$$ AMERICAN 🍴 **Arnold Palmer's.** From the photos on the walls to the trophy-filled display cases to the putting green for diners awaiting a table, Arnie's essence infuses this restaurant. Families gather in the spacious restaurant for birthdays and Sunday dinners, and the service is always attentive. **Known for:** homemade meat loaf; top-notch wine list; entertainment most nights. [$] *Average main: $34* ✉ *78164 Ave. 52, near Desert Club Dr.* ☎ *760/771–4653* 🌐 *www.arnoldpalmersrestaurant.com.*

$$$$ BISTRO Fodor's Choice ★ 🍴 **Lavender Bistro.** This romantic bistro makes diners feel like they've been transported to southern France. The spacious outdoor atrium is decked out with flowers, fountains, and twinkling lights. **Known for:** live music on the patio and in the fireside lounge; organic ingredients; extensive locavore menu. [$] *Average main: $34* ✉ *78073 Calle Barcelona* ☎ *760/564–5353* 🌐 *www.lavender-bistro.com* ⏲ *Closed June–Sept.*

$$$$ RESORT FAMILY 🏨 **La Quinta Resort and Club.** Opened in 1926 and now a member of the Waldorf-Astoria Collection, the desert's oldest resort is a lush green oasis set on 45 acres. **Pros:** individual swimming pools in some rooms; gorgeous gardens; pet and family friendly. **Cons:** a party atmosphere sometimes prevails; spotty housekeeping/maintenance. [$] *Rooms from: $329* ✉ *49499 Eisenhower Dr.* ☎ *760/564–4111* 🌐 *www.laquintaresort.com* 🛏 *586 rooms, 210 villas* 🍽 *No meals.*

THE FIRST CELEBRITY HOTEL

Frank Capra probably started the trend when he booked a casita at the then-new, very remote La Quinta Hotel (now Resort) to write the script for the movie *It Happened One Night*. The movie went on to earn an Academy Award, and Capra continued to book that room whenever he had some writing to do. A long line of Hollywood stars followed Capra's example over the years; the current list includes Oprah Winfrey, Adam Sandler, and Christina Aguilera.

PERFORMING ARTS

La Quinta Arts Festival. More than 200 artists participate each March in a four-day juried show that's considered one of the best in the West. The event, held at La Quinta Civic Center, includes sculptures, paintings, watercolors, fiber art, and ceramics. ✉ *78495 Calle Tampico* ☎ *760/564–1244* 🌐 *www.lqaf.com* 🎟 *$20; multiday tickets $25.*

SPORTS AND THE OUTDOORS

GOLF

Fodor's Choice ★ **PGA West.** A world-class golf destination where Phil Mickelson and Jack Nicklaus play, this facility includes five resort courses and four private ones. Courses meander through indigenous desert landscapes, water features, and bunkers. The Norman, Nick Tournament, and TPC Stadium courses are "shot-makers" courses made for pros. TPC highlights include its two lakes, "San Andreas Fault" bunker, and island green called "Alcatraz." The Norman course has tight fairways and small greens. ✉ *49–499 Eisenhower Dr.* ☎ *760/564–5729 for tee times* 🌐 *www.pgawest.com* 🎟 *Mountain Course, $159–$229; Dunes, $119–$189; Greg Norman, $159–$229; TPC Stadium, $189–$269; Jack Nicklaus Tournament, $159–$229* ⛳ *Mountain Course: 18 holes, 6732 yards, par 72; Dunes: 18 holes, 6712 yards, par 72; Greg Norman: 18 holes, 7156 yards, par 72; TPC Stadium: 18 holes, 7300 yards, par 72; Jack Nicklaus Tournament: 18 holes, 7204 yards, par 72.*

SHOPPING

SPAS

Spa La Quinta. The gorgeous Spa La Quinta may be the grandest spa in the entire desert. At this huge stand-alone facility you'll find everything from massages to facials to salon services, plus a beautiful garden setting with a large fountain, flowers galore, plenty of nooks where you can hide out and enjoy the sanctuary, and a Jacuzzi with a waterfall. ✉ *49499 Eisenhower Dr.* ☎ *760/777–4800* 🌐 *www.laquintaresort.com* ☞ *Fitness center with cardio. Services: aromatherapy, body wraps and scrubs, massage, skin care, salon services, water therapies. $170, 50-min massage; $195, 30-min HydraFacial.*

INDIO

5 miles east of Indian Wells.

Indio is the home of the renowned date shake: an extremely thick and sweet milk shake made with dates. The city and surrounding countryside generate 95% of the dates grown and harvested in the United States. If you take a hot-air balloon ride, you will likely drift over the tops of date palm trees.

GETTING HERE AND AROUND

Indio is east of Indian Wells and north of La Quinta. Highway 111 runs right through Indio, and Interstate 10 skirts it to the north.

EXPLORING

FAMILY **National Date Festival and Riverside County Fair.** Indio celebrates its raison d'être each February at its date festival and county fair. The mid-month festivities include an Arabian Nights pageant, camel and ostrich races, and exhibits of local dates, plus monster truck shows, a demolition derby, a nightly musical pageant, and a rodeo. ✉ *Riverside County Fairgrounds, 82–503 Hwy. 111* ☎ *800/811–3247, 760/863–8247* 🌐 *www.datefest.org* 🎟 *$10, parking $10.*

Shields Date Garden and Café. Sample, select, and take home some of Shields's locally grown dates. Ten varieties are available, including the giant supersweet royal medjools, along with specialty date products such as date crystals, stuffed dates, confections, and local honey. At the Shields Date Garden Café you can try an iconic date shake, dig into date pancakes, or go exotic with a date tamale. Breakfast and lunch are served daily. ✉ *80–225 Hwy. 111* ☎ *760/347–0996* 🌐 *www.shieldsdategarden.com* 🕒 *No dinner.*

WHERE TO EAT

$$ SICILIAN 🍴 **Ciro's Ristorante and Pizzeria.** Serving pizza and pasta since the 1960s, this popular casual restaurant has a few unusual pies on the menu, including cashew with three cheeses. The decor is classic pizza joint, with checkered tablecloths and bentwood chairs. **Known for:** daily pasta specials; classic Italian dishes; house-made, hand-tossed pizza dough. [$] *Average main: $16* ✉ *81–963 Hwy. 111* ☎ *760/347–6503* 🌐 *www.cirosofindio.com* 🕒 *No lunch Sun.*

$$$ AMERICAN 🍴 **Jackalope Ranch.** It's worth the drive to Indio to sample flavors of the Old West, 21st-century style. Inside a rambling 21,000-foot building,

holding a clutch of indoor/outdoor dining spaces, you may be seated near an open kitchen, a bar, fountains, fireplaces, or waterworks. Jackalope can be a busy, noisy place; ask for a quiet corner if that's your pleasure. **Known for:** Western-style barbecue; casual, down-home locals hangout; lively vibe. [$] *Average main: $30* ✉ *80–400 Hwy. 111* ☎ *760/342–1999* 🌐 *www.thejackaloperanch.com.*

NIGHTLIFE AND PERFORMING ARTS

MUSIC FESTIVALS

Fodor's Choice ★ **Coachella Valley Music and Arts Festival.** Among Southern California's biggest parties, the festival draws hundreds of thousands of rock music fans to Indio each April for two weekends of live concerts. Headliners include acts such as Lady Gaga, Kendrick Lamar, Lorde, Phantogram, Jack Johnson, and Radiohead. Many attendees camp on-site, but to give your ears a rest post-concert you might want to stay at a nearby hotel. **■ TIP→ The festival sells out before the lineup is announced, so expect to pay big bucks if you haven't purchased tickets by late fall.** ✉ *Empire Polo Club, 81–800 Ave. 51* 🌐 *www.coachella.com.*

EN ROUTE **Coachella Valley Preserve.** For a glimpse of how the desert appeared before development, head northeast from Palm Springs to this preserve. It has a system of sand dunes and several palm oases that were formed because the San Andreas Fault lines here allow water flowing underground to rise to the surface. A mile-long walk along Thousand Palms Oasis reveals pools supporting the tiny endangered desert pupfish and more than 183 bird species. Families like the relatively flat trail that is mostly shaded. The preserve has a visitor center, nature and equestrian trails, restrooms, and picnic facilities. Guided hikes are offered October–March. **■ TIP→ Be aware that it's exceptionally hot in summer here.** ✉ *29200 Thousand Palms Canyon Rd., Thousand Palms* ☎ *760/343–2733* 🌐 *www.coachellavalleypreserve.org* 🎟 *Free* ⏲ *Visitor center closed June–Aug.*

ALONG TWENTYNINE PALMS HIGHWAY

Designated a California Scenic Highway, the Twentynine Palms Highway connects two of the three entrances to Joshua Tree National Park and provides gorgeous high-desert views, especially in winter and spring when you might find yourself driving beneath snowcapped peaks or through a field of wildflowers. Park entrances are located at Joshua Tree and Twentynine Palms. Yucca Valley and Twentynine Palms have lodging and dining options, and other services. Along the way, look out for the eye-catching artwork by artists associated with the avant-garde High Desert Test Sites (🌐 *www.highdeserttestsites.com).*

DESERT HOT SPRINGS

9 miles north of Palm Springs.

Desert Hot Springs's famous hot mineral waters, thought by some to have curative powers, bubble up at temperatures of 90°F to 148°F and flow into the wells of more than 40 hotel spas.

GETTING HERE AND AROUND

Desert Hot Springs lies due north of Palm Springs. Take Gene Autry Trail north to Interstate 10, where the street name changes to Palm. Continue north to Pierson Boulevard, the town's center.

EXPLORING

Cabot's Pueblo Museum. Cabot Yerxa, the man who found the spring that made Desert Hot Springs famous, built a quirky four-story, 35-room pueblo between 1939 and his death in 1965. Now a museum run by the city of Desert Hot Springs—Yerxa was the town's first mayor—the Hopi-inspired adobe structure is filled with memorabilia of his time as a homesteader; his encounters with Hollywood celebrities at the nearby Bar-H Ranch; his expedition to the Alaskan gold rush; and many other events. The home, much of it crafted out of materials Yerxa recycled from the desert, can only be seen on hour-long tours. Outside, walk the grounds to a lookout with amazing desert views. ✉ *67–616 E. Desert View Ave., at Eliseo Rd.* ☎ *760/329–7610* 🌐 *www.cabotsmuseum.org* 🎫 *$13* 🕒 *Closed Mon. Oct.–May., closed Mon. and Tues. June–Sept.* ☞ *Tours 9:30, 10:30, 11:30, 1:30, 2:30 Oct.–May, and 9:30, 10:30, 11:30 June–Sept. Tours limited to 12 people.*

WHERE TO STAY

$$$ HOTEL 🏨 **The Spring.** Designed for those who want to detox, lose weight, or chill out in the mineral pools, The Spring delivers quiet and personal service atop a Desert Hot Springs hill. **Pros:** access to mineral pools 24 hours a day; complimentary continental breakfast; spa and lodging packages available. **Cons:** rooms lack character. [$] *Rooms from: $199* ✉ *12699 Reposo Way* ☎ *760/251–6700* 🌐 *www.the-spring.com* 🛏 *12 rooms* 🍴 *Breakfast.*

SHOPPING

SPAS

Fodor's Choice ★ **Two Bunch Palms.** This iconic retreat has long been a favorite with Los Angeles yogis for its peaceful, palm-shaded grounds and hot springs pools. Big changes occurred in 2014, with new rooms added and a fresh look for the existing ones. Guests can still purchase a day pass to soak in the grotto, attend yoga classes, lounge on the grounds, and enjoy a spa treatment or two. ■ **TIP→ This is an adults-only, whispers-only destination.** ✉ *67–425 Two Bunch Palms Tr.* ☎ *760/676–5000* 🌐 *www.twobunchpalms.com* 🎫 *Day pass $25 weekdays, $40 weekends* ☞ *Services: facials, nail care, solo and couple's massages, breath work, water, and other therapies; treatments from $135, 60-min massage.*

YUCCA VALLEY

30 miles northeast of Palm Springs.

One of the high desert's fastest-growing cities, Yucca Valley is emerging as a bedroom community for people who work as far away as Ontario, 85 miles to the west. In this suburb you can shop for necessities, get your car serviced, grab coffee or purchase vintage furnishings, and chow down at fast-food outlets. Just up Pioneertown Road you'll find the most-talked-about dining establishment in the desert, Pappy and Harriet's, the famed performance venue that hosts big-name talent.

GETTING HERE AND AROUND

The drive to Yucca Valley on Highway 62/Twentynine Palms Highway passes through the Painted Hills and drops down into a valley. Take Pioneertown Road north to the Old West outpost.

EXPLORING

FAMILY **Hi-Desert Nature Museum.** Creatures that make their homes in Joshua Tree National Park are the focus here. A small live-animal display includes scorpions, snakes, lizards, and small mammals. You'll also find rocks, minerals, and fossils from the Paleozoic era, taxidermy, and Native American artifacts. There's also a children's area and art exhibits. ✉ *Yucca Valley Community Center, 57116 Twentynine Palms Hwy.* ☎ *760/369–7212* 🌐 *hidesertnaturemuseum.org* 🎟 *Free* 🕒 *Closed Sun.–Wed.*

Pioneertown. In 1946 Roy Rogers, Gene Autry, the Sons of the Pioneers (the music group for whom the town is named), and Russ Hayden built Pioneertown, an 1880s-style Wild West movie set complete with hitching posts, saloon, and an OK Corral. You can stroll past wooden and adobe storefronts and feel like you're back in the Old West. Or not: Pappy and Harriet's Pioneertown Palace, now the town's top draw, has evolved into a hip venue for indie and mainstream performers such as Dengue Fever, Neko Case, and Robert Plant. ✉ *53688 Pioneertown Rd., Pioneertown* ✥ *4 miles north of Yucca Valley* 🌐 *pappyandharriets.com.*

WHERE TO EAT AND STAY

$$$ AMERICAN FAMILY Fodor's Choice ★ 🍴 **Pappy & Harriet's Pioneertown Palace.** Smack in the middle of what looks like the set of a Western is this cozy saloon where you can have dinner, relax over a drink at the bar, and catch some great indie bands or legendary artists—Leon Russell, Sonic Youth, Paul McCartney, and Robert Plant—have all played here. Pappy & Harriet's may be in the middle of nowhere, but you'll need reservations for dinner on weekends, especially on Sunday night. **Known for:** live music several days/nights a week; Tex-Mex, Santa Maria-style barbecue; fun and lively atmosphere. [$] *Average main: $25* ✉ *53688 Pioneertown Rd., Pioneertown* ☎ *760/365–5956* 🌐 *www.pappyandharriets.com* 🕒 *Closed Tues. and Wed.*

$ HOTEL 🏨 **Best Western Joshua Tree Hotel & Suites.** This hotel has spacious, nicely appointed rooms decorated in soft desert colors. **Pros:** convenient to Joshua Tree National Park; pleasant lounge; pool and hot tub. **Cons:** on a busy highway; limited service. [$] *Rooms from: $116* ✉ *56525 Twentynine Palms Hwy.* ☎ *760/365–3555* 🌐 *www.bestwestern.com* 🛏 *95 rooms* 🍽 *Breakfast.*

$ RENTAL 🏨 **Rimrock Ranch Cabins.** The quiet beauty of the surrounding desert attracts Hollywood writers, artists, and musicians to circa-1940s housekeeping cabins, an Airstream trailer, the Hatch House duplex, and lodge rooms. **Pros:** quiet desert hideaway; fun vibe for music fans; rich music heritage on site. **Cons:** rustic cabins will not appeal to resort seekers; far from most services. [$] *Rooms from: $90* ✉ *53688 Pioneertown Rd., Pioneertown* ☎ *760/228–0130, 818/557–6383* 🌐 *www.rimrockranchpioneertown.com* 🛏 *7 rental units* 🍽 *No meals.*

JOSHUA TREE

12 miles east of Yucca Valley.

Artists and renegades have long found solace in the small upcountry desert town of Joshua Tree, home to artsy vintage shops, cafés, and B&Bs and a gateway to Joshua Tree National Park. Those who zip through town might wonder what all the hype is about, but if you slow down and spend time chatting with the folks in this funky community, you'll find much to love.

GETTING HERE AND AROUND

Highway 62 is the main route to and through Joshua Tree. Most businesses are here or along Park Boulevard as it heads toward the park.

ESSENTIALS

Visitor Information Joshua Tree Visitor Center. ✉ *6554 Park Blvd.* ☎ *760/366–1855.*

EXPLORING

Fodor's Choice ★ **Noah Purifoy Foundation.** This vast 10-acre art installation full of "assemblage art" on a sandy tract of land in the town of Joshua Tree honors the work of artist Noah Purifoy. The sculptures blend with the spare desert in an almost post-apocalyptic way. Purifoy lived most of his life in this desert until his death is 2004. He used found materials to make commentary on social issues. His art has been showcased at LACMA, J. Paul Getty Museum, MOCA, and many more. ✉ *63030 Blair Lane* ☎ *213/382–7516* 🌐 *www.noahpurifoy.com* 🎫 *Free* 🕒 *Closes at sunset.*

WHERE TO EAT AND STAY

$ AMERICAN 🍴 **Crossroads Cafe.** Mexican breakfasts, chicken-cilantro soup, and hearty sandwiches are among the draws at this Joshua Tree institution for prehike breakfasts, birthday lunches, and early dinners. Taxidermied animals and beer-can lights hint at the community's consciousness, while the tattooed waitresses and slew of veggie options make it clear the Crossroads is unlike anywhere else in San Bernardino County. **Known for:** rustic wooden interior and bar; hearty and affordable meals; vegetarian and vegan dishes. [$] *Average main: $12* ✉ *61715 Twentynine Palms Hwy.* ☎ *760/366–5414* 🌐 *crossroadscafejtree.com.*

$$$$ B&B/INN Fodor's Choice ★ 🏨 **Sacred Sands.** The dramatic exterior of this strawbale house, atop a mountain near Joshua Tree National Park's western entrance, hints at the design-forward intentions of the friendly owners, Scott and Steve. **Pros:** hot tubs infused with tea tree oil and Epsom salts; extravagant breakfasts; indoor and outdoor showers. **Cons:** expensive for the area; few nearby dining options. [$] *Rooms from: $329* ✉ *63155 Quail Springs Rd.* ☎ *760/424–6407* 🌐 *www.sacredsands.com* 🛏 *4 rooms* 🍽 *Breakfast.*

TWENTYNINE PALMS

12 miles east of Joshua Tree.

The main gateway town to Joshua Tree National Park, Twentynine Palms is also the location of the U.S. Marine Air Ground Task Force Training Center. You can find services, supplies, and lodging in town.

Check out the sculptures made of found materials at the Noah Purifoy Foundation in Joshua Tree.

GETTING HERE AND AROUND

Highway 62 is the main route to and through Twentynine Palms. Most businesses here center around Highway 62 and Utah Trail, 3 miles north of Joshua Tree's entrance.

ESSENTIALS

Visitor Information Twentynine Palms Visitor Center and Gallery. ✉ 73484 Twentynine Palms Hwy. ☎ 760/367–6197 ⊕ www.visit29.org.

EXPLORING

Oasis of Murals. Twenty-six murals painted on the sides of buildings depict the history and current lifestyle of Twentynine Palms. If you drive around town, you can't miss the murals, but you can also pick up a free map from the Twentynine Palms Visitor Center. ✉ *Twentynine Palms* ⊕ *www.action29palmsmurals.com.*

29 Palms Art Gallery. This gallery features work by local painters, sculptors, and jewelry makers inspired by the desert landscape. If you find yourself inspired as well, sign up for one of the day-long art workshops. ✉ 74055 Cottonwood Dr. ☎ 760/367–7819 ⊕ www.29palmsartgallery. com ⊘ Closed Mon.–Wed. Also closed Thurs. in summer.

WHERE TO STAY

$$
B&B/INN
🏨 **Campbell House.** To the wealthy pioneer who erected the stone mansion now occupied by this bed-and-breakfast, expense was no object, which is evident in the 50-foot-long planked maple floor in the great room, the intricate carpentry on the walls, and the huge stone fireplaces that warm the house on the rare cold night. **Pros:** elegant rooms and public spaces; spa services and massage room; great horned owls on

property. **Cons:** somewhat isolated location; three-story main building doesn't have an elevator. $ *Rooms from: $145* ⊠ *74744 Joe Davis Dr.* ☎ *760/367–3238* ⊕ *www.campbellhouse29palms.com* ➽ *2 rooms, 10 cottages* ⎢⊙⎢ *Breakfast.*

$$
B&B/INN
FAMILY
Fodor'sChoice
★

⛱ **29 Palms Inn.** The closest lodging to the entrance to Joshua Tree National Park, the funky 29 Palms Inn scatters a collection of adobe and wood-frame cottages, some dating back to the 1920s and 1930s, over 70 acres of grounds that include the ancient Oasis of Mara, a popular destination for birds and bird-watchers year-round. **Pros:** gracious hospitality; exceptional bird-watching; popular with artists. **Cons:** rustic accommodations; limited amenities. $ *Rooms from: $165* ⊠ *73950 Inn Ave.* ☎ *760/367–3505* ⊕ *www.29palmsinn.com* ➽ *20 rooms, 4 guesthouses* ⎢⊙⎢ *Breakfast.*

14

ANZA-BORREGO DESERT

Largely uninhabited, the Anza-Borrego Desert is popular with those who love solitude, silence, space, starry nights, light, and sweeping mountain vistas. This desert lies south of the Palm Springs area, stretching along the western shore of the Salton Sea down toward Interstate 8 along the Mexican border. Isolated from the rest of California by mile-high mountains to the north and west, most of this desert falls within the borders of Anza-Borrego Desert State Park, which at more than 600,000 acres is the largest state park in the contiguous United States.

For thousands of years Native Americans of the Cahuilla and Kumeyaay people inhabited this area, spending their winters on the warm desert floor and their summers in the mountains. The first Europeans—a party led by the Spanish explorer Juan Baptiste de Anza—crossed this desert in 1776. Anza, for whom the desert is named, made the trip through here twice. Roadside signs along Highways 86, 78, and S2 mark the route of the Anza expedition, which spent Christmas Eve 1776 in what is now Anza-Borrego Desert State Park. Seventy-five years later thousands of immigrants on their way to the goldfields up north crossed the desert on the Southern Immigrant Trail, remnants of which remain along Highway S2. Permanent settlers arrived early in the 20th century, and by the 1930s the first adobe resort cottage had been built.

BORREGO SPRINGS

59 miles south of Indio.

The permanent population of Borrego Springs, set squarely in the middle of Anza-Borrego Desert State Park, hovers around 2,500. From September through June, when temperatures stay in the '80s and '90s, you can engage in outdoor activities such as hiking, nature study, golfing, tennis, horseback riding, and mountain biking. If winter rains cooperate, Borrego Springs puts on some of the best wildflower displays in the low desert. In some years the desert floor is carpeted with color: yellow dandelions and sunflowers, pink primrose, purple sand verbena, and blue wild heliotrope. The bloom generally lasts from late February through April. For current information on wildflowers around Borrego Springs, call Anza-Borrego Desert State Park's wildflower hotline (*760/767–4684*).

GETTING HERE AND AROUND

You can access Anza Borrego by taking the Highway 86 exit from Interstate 10, south of Indio. Highway 86 passes through Coachella and along the western shore of the Salton Sea. Turn west on Highway S22 at Salton City and follow it to Peg Leg Road, where you turn south until you reach Palm Canyon Drive. Turn west and the road leads to the center of Borrego Springs, Christmas Circle, where most major roads come together. Well-marked roads radiating from the circle will take you to the most popular sites in the state park. If coming from the San Diego area, drive east on Interstate 8 to the Cuyamaca Mountains, exit at Highway 79, and enjoy the lovely 23-mile drive through the mountains until you reach Julian; head east on Highway 78 and follow signs to Borrego Springs.

ESSENTIALS

Visitor Information Borrego Springs Chamber of Commerce & Visitors Bureau. ⊠ *786 Palm Canyon Dr.* ☎ *760/767–5555, 800/559–5524* ⊕ *www.borregospringschamber.com.*

EXPLORING

Fodor's Choice
★

Anza-Borrego Desert State Park. One of the richest living natural-history museums in the nation, this state park is a vast, nearly uninhabited wilderness where you can step through a field of wildflowers, cool off in a palm-shaded oasis, count zillions of stars in the black night sky, and listen to coyotes howl at dusk. The landscape, largely undisturbed by humans, reveals a rich natural history. There's evidence of a vast inland sea in the piles of oyster beds near Split Mountain and of the power of natural forces such as earthquakes and flash floods. In addition, recent scientific work has confirmed that the Borrego Badlands, with more than 6,000 meters of exposed fossil-bearing sediments, is likely the richest such deposit in North America, telling the story of 7 million years of climate change, upheaval, and prehistoric animals. Evidence has been unearthed of sabre-toothed cats, flamingos, zebras, and the largest flying bird in the northern hemisphere beneath the now-parched sand. Today the desert's most treasured inhabitants are the herds of elusive and endangered native bighorn sheep, or borrego, for which the park is named. Among the strange desert plants you may observe are the gnarly elephant trees. As these are endangered, rangers don't encourage visitors to seek out the secluded grove at Fish Creek, but there are a few examples at the visitor center garden. After a wet winter you can see a short-lived but stunning display of cacti, succulents, and desert wildflowers in bloom.

The park is unusually accessible to visitors. Admission to the park is free, and few areas are off-limits. There are two developed campgrounds, but you can camp anywhere; just follow the trails and pitch a tent wherever you like. There are more than 500 miles of dirt roads, two huge wilderness areas, and 110 miles of riding and hiking trails. Many sites can be seen from paved roads, but some require driving on dirt roads, for which rangers recommend you use a four-wheel-drive vehicle. When you do leave the pavement, carry the appropriate supplies: a cell phone (which may be unreliable in some areas), a shovel and other tools, flares, blankets, and plenty of water. The canyons are susceptible to flash flooding, so inquire about weather conditions (even on sunny days) before entering. ■TIP→ Borrego resorts, restaurants, and the state park have Wi-Fi, but the service is spotty at best. If you need to talk to someone in the area, it's best to find a phone with a landline.

The sites and hikes listed below are arranged by region of the park and distance from the Visitor Center: in the valley and hills surrounding Borrego Springs, near Tamarisk Campground, along Highway S2, south of Scissors Crossing, and south of Ocotillo Wells.

Stop by the **Visitor Center** to get oriented, to pick up a park map, and to learn about weather, road, and wildlife conditions. Designed to keep cool during the desert's blazing-hot summers, the center is built underground, beneath a demonstration desert garden containing examples of most of the native flora and a little pupfish pond. Displays inside the center illustrate the natural history of the area. Picnic tables are scattered throughout, making this a good place to linger and enjoy the view.

14

A 1½-mile trail leads to **Borrego Palm Canyon,** one of the few native palm groves in North America. The canyon, about 1 mile west of the Visitor Center, holds a grove of more than 1,000 native fan palms, a stream, and a waterfall. Wildlife is abundant along this route. This moderate hike is the most popular in the park.

With a year-round stream and lush plant life, **Coyote Canyon,** approximately 4½ miles north of Borrego Springs, is one of the best places to see and photograph spring wildflowers. Portions of the canyon road follow a section of the old Anza Trail. This area is closed between June 15 and September 15 to allow native bighorn sheep undisturbed use of the water. The dirt road that gives access to the canyon may be sandy enough to require a four-wheel-drive vehicle.

The late-afternoon vista of the Borrego badlands from **Font's Point,** 13 miles east of Borrego Springs, is one of the most breathtaking views in the desert, especially when the setting sun casts a golden glow in high relief on the eroded mountain slopes. The road from the Font's Point turnoff can be rough enough to make using a four-wheel-drive vehicle advisable; inquire about road conditions at the Visitor Center before starting out. Even if you can't make it out on the paved road, you can see some of the view from the highway.

East of Tamarisk Grove campground (13 miles south of Borrego Springs), the **Narrows Earth Trail** is a short walk off the road. Along the way you can see evidence of the many geologic processes involved in forming the canyons of the desert, such as a contact zone between two earthquake faults, and sedimentary layers of metamorphic and igneous rock.

The 1.6-mile round trip **Yaqui Well Nature Trail** takes you along a path to a desert water hole where birds and wildlife are abundant. It's also a good place to look for wildflowers in spring. At the trailhead across from Tamarisk Campground you can pick up a brochure describing what can be seen along the trail.

Traversing a boulder-strewn trail is the easy, mostly flat **Pictograph/ Smuggler's Canyon Trail.** At the end is a collection of rocks covered with muted red and yellow pictographs painted within the last hundred years or so by Native Americans. Walk about ½ mile beyond the pictures to reach Smuggler's Canyon, where an overlook provides views of the Vallecito Valley. The hike, from 2 to 3 miles round-trip, begins in Blair Valley, 6 miles southeast of Highway 78, off Highway S2, at the Scissors Crossing intersection.

Just a few steps off the paved road, **Carrizo Badlands Overlook** offers a view of eroded and twisted sedimentary rock that obscures the fossils of the mastodons, saber-tooths, zebras, and camels that roamed this region a million years ago. The route to the overlook through Earthquake Valley and Blair Valley parallels the Southern Emigrant Trail. It's off Highway S2, 40 miles south of Scissors Crossing.

Geology students from all over the world visit the Fish Creek area of Anza-Borrego to explore the canyon through Split Mountain. The narrow gorge with 600-foot walls was formed by an ancient stream. Fossils in this area indicate that a sea once covered the desert floor. From Highway 78 at Ocotillo Wells, take Split Mountain Road south 9 miles. ✉ *Visitor Center, 200 Palm Canyon Dr., Hwy. S22* ☎ *760/767–4205, 760/767–4684 wildflower hotline* 🌐 *www.parks.ca.gov* 🎟 *Free; day use parking in campground areas $10* ☞ *Make a campground reservation at: reservecalifornia.com.*

FAMILY
Fodor's Choice ★

Galleta Meadows. At Galleta Meadows, camels, llamas, saber-toothed tigers, tortoises, and monumental gomphotherium (a sort of ancient elephant) appear to roam the earth again. These life-size bronze figures are of prehistoric animals whose fossils can be found in the Borrego Badlands. The collection of more than 130 sculptures created by Ricardo Breceda was commissioned by the late Dennis Avery, who installed the works of art on property he owned for the entertainment of locals and visitors. Maps are available from Borrego Springs Chamber of Commerce. ✉ *Borrego Springs Rd., from Christmas Circle to Henderson Canyon* ☎ *760/767–5555* 🎟 *Free.*

WHERE TO EAT

$$ MODERN AMERICAN

🍴 **The Arches.** On the edge of the Borrego Springs Resort, Golf Club & Spa's golf course, set beneath a canopy of grapefruit trees, The Arches is a pleasant place to eat. For breakfast you'll find burritos alongside French toast; omelets and eggs benedict; or for lunch (best enjoyed on the patio) or dinner, the options include sandwiches, salads, and entrées such as spinach and mushroom tortellini, shrimp basted in seafood oil and simmered in a green coconut curry broth, and burgers topped with smoked bacon in a brioche bun. **Known for:** light fare; nightly specials; popular happy hour. [$] *Average main: $22* ✉ *1112 Tilting T Dr.* ☎ *760/767–5700* 🌐 *www.borregospringsresort.com/dining.asp* 🕒 *Summer hrs vary; call ahead.*

$$$ AMERICAN

🍴 **Carlee's Place.** Sooner or later most visitors to Borrego Springs wind up at Carlee's Place for a drink and a bite to eat. The extra-large menu has everything: burgers, salads, seafood, sandwiches, and prime rib. **Known for:** all-American down-home setting; martinis and classic cocktails; relatively affordable fare. [$] *Average main: $25* ✉ *660 Palm Canyon Dr.* ☎ *760/767–3262.*

$ MEXICAN

🍴 **Carmelita's Mexican Grill and Cantina.** A friendly, family-run eatery tucked into a back corner of what is called "The Mall," Carmelita's draws locals and visitors all day, whether it's for a hearty breakfast, a cooked-to-order enchilada or burrito, or to tip back a brew at the bar. The menu lists typical combination plates (enchiladas, burritos, tamales, and tacos). **Known for:** dog-friendly outdoor patio; house-made masa dough; full bar with sports TVs. $ *Average main: $14* ✉ *575 Palm Canyon Dr.* ☎ *760/767–5666.*

$$$
MODERN
AMERICAN

✕ **Coyote Steakhouse.** The upscale Coyote Steakhouse at the Palms at Indian Head hotel caters to those who want a fancy dinner, particularly hunks of filet mignon or rack of lamb served at candlelit tables with white tablecloths overlooking the pool. Pet owners will appreciate the canine menu, whose treats include house-made peanut-butter dog cookies. **Known for:** romantic candlelit dining room; pork tenderloin and prime rib; classic mid-century setting. $ *Average main: $30* ✉ *2220 Hoberg Rd.* ☎ *760/767–7788* ⊕ *www.thepalmsatindianhead.com* ☉ *Coyote Steakhouse, no breakfast or lunch; Red Ocotillo, no breakfast or lunch July and Aug.*

$
MEXICAN

✕ **Los Jilberto's Taco Shop.** A casual local favorite for affordable Mexican dishes, Jilberto's serves up big burritos and meaty enchiladas. **Known for:** authentic Mexican dishes cooked to order; all-day breakfast menu; reasonable prices. $ *Average main: $9* ✉ *655 Palm Canyon Dr.* ☎ *760/767–1008* ⊕ *www.losjilbertostacoshop.com* ▬ *No credit cards.*

WHERE TO STAY

$$$
RESORT
FAMILY
Fodor's Choice
★

🏨 **La Casa Del Zorro.** The draws at this desert hideaway a short drive from Anza Borrego State Park include three guest-only pools, a hot tub, five night-lit tennis courts and two pickle ball courts, a yoga studio, a spa, a restaurant, and the lively Fox Den Bar. The 42-acre property pays tribute to its surroundings with a cactus garden, a fire pit, and two tall, welded-metal animal sculptures by local artist Ricardo Breceda. **Pros:** private pool or hot tub in many casitas; Butterfield Room serves strawberry French toast; on-site spa, bar, and restaurant. **Cons:** service can be spotty. $ *Rooms from: $189* ✉ *3845 Yaqui Pass Rd.* ☎ *760/767–0100* ⊕ *www.lacasadelzorro.com* 🛏 *48 rooms, 19 casitas* ⊗ *No meals.*

SPORTS AND THE OUTDOORS

GOLF

Borrego Springs Resort, Golf Club & Spa. The two 9-hole courses here, Mesquite and Desert Willow, are generally played as an 18-hole round by most golfers, starting with Mesquite. Both courses have natural desert landscaping and mature date palms. ✉ *1112 Tilting T Dr.* ☎ *760/767–3330* ⊕ *www.borregospringsresort.com* ⛳ *From $35* ⛳ *18 holes, 6760 yards, par 71* ☞ *Closed June–Sept. Closed Thurs. Oct.–May.*

SHOPPING

Anza-Borrego State Park Store. The Anza-Borrego Foundation, a land conservation group, runs this store that sells guidebooks, maps, clothing, desert art, and gifts for kids. Its enthusiastic staffers also assist with trip planning. Foundation guides organize hikes, naturalist talks, classes, research programs, and nature walks. ✉ *587 Palm Canyon Dr., No. 110* ☎ *760/767–0446* ⊕ *www.theabf.org* ☉ *Closed weekends June–Sept., and Thurs. Oct.–May.*

Borrego Outfitters. This contemporary general store stocks high-end outdoor gear, hiking essentials, personal care items from Burt's Bees,

14

footwear from Teva and Thymes, swimsuits, and tabletop items. You can browse through racks of clothing and piles of hats, all suited to the desert climate. ⊠ *579 Palm Canyon Dr.* ☎ *760/767–3502* ⊕ *www. borregooutfitters.com.*

SALTON SEA

30 miles southeast of Indio, 29 miles east of Borrego Springs.

The Salton Sea, one of the largest inland seas on Earth, is the product of both natural and artificial forces. The sea occupies the Salton Basin, a remnant of prehistoric Lake Cahuilla. Over the centuries the Colorado River flooded the basin and the water drained into the Gulf of California. In 1905 a flood once again filled the Salton Basin, but the exit to the gulf was blocked by sediment. The floodwaters remained in the basin, creating a saline lake 228 feet below sea level, about 35 miles long and 15 miles wide, with a surface area of nearly 380 square miles. The sea, which lies along the Pacific Flyway, supports 400 species of birds. Fishing for tilapia, boating, camping, and bird-watching are popular activities year-round.

GETTING HERE AND AROUND

Salton Sea State Recreation Area includes about 14 miles of coastline on the northeastern shore of the sea, about 30 miles south of Indio via Highway 111. The Sonny Bono Salton Sea National Wildlife Refuge fills the southernmost tip of the sea's shore. To reach it from the recreation area, continue south about 60 miles to Niland; continue south to Sinclair Road, and turn west following the road to the Refuge Headquarters.

EXPLORING

FAMILY **Salton Sea State Recreation Area.** This huge recreation area on the sea's north shore draws thousands each year to its playgrounds, hiking trails, fishing spots, and boat launches. Ranger-guided bird walks take place on Saturday; you'll see migrating and native birds including Canada geese, pelicans, and shorebirds. ⊠ *100–225 State Park Rd., North Shore* ☎ *760/393–3052* ⊕ *www.parks.ca.gov* ☒ *$7.*

Sonny Bono Salton Sea National Wildlife Refuge. The 2,200-acre wildlife refuge here, on the Pacific Flyway, is a wonderful spot for viewing migratory birds. There's an observation deck where you can watch Canada geese, and along the trails you might view eared grebes, burrowing owls, great blue herons, ospreys, and yellow-footed gulls. ⚠ **Though the scenery is beautiful, the waters here give off an unpleasant odor, and the New River, which empties into the sea, is quite toxic.** ⊠ *906 W. Sinclair Rd., Calipatria* ☎ *760/348–5278* ⊕ *www.fws.gov/refuge/ sonny_bono_salton_sea/* ☒ *Free* ☉ *Closed weekends Mar.–Oct.*

JOSHUA TREE
NATIONAL PARK

WELCOME TO
JOSHUA TREE NATIONAL PARK

TOP REASONS TO GO

★ **Rock climbing:** Joshua Tree is a world-class site with challenges for climbers of just about every skill level.

★ **Peace and quiet:** Roughly two hours from Los Angeles, this great wilderness is the ultimate escape from technology.

★ **Stargazing:** You'll be mesmerized by the Milky Way flowing across the summer sky. For spectacular natural fireworks, visit in mid-August during the Perseid meteor shower and watch shooting stars streak overhead.

★ **Wildflowers:** In spring, the hillsides explode in a patchwork of yellow, blue, pink, and white.

★ **Sunsets:** Twilight is a magical time here, especially during the winter, when the setting sun casts a golden glow on the mountains.

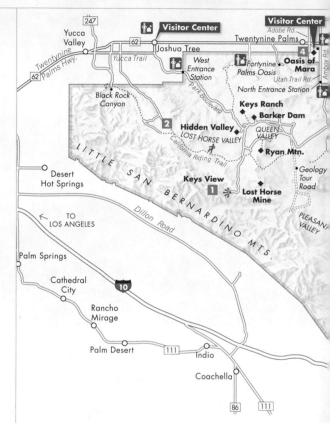

1 **Keys View.** This is the most dramatic overlook in the park—on clear days you can see Signal Mountain in Mexico.

2 **Hidden Valley.** Crawl between the big rocks and you'll understand why this boulder-strewn area was once a cattle rustlers' hideout.

3 **Cholla Cactus Garden.** Come here in the late afternoon, when the spiky stalks of the bigelow (jumping) cholla cactus are backlit against an intense blue sky.

4 **Oasis of Mara.** Walk the nature trail around this desert oasis, which the first settlers, the Serrano, dubbed "the place of little springs and much grass."

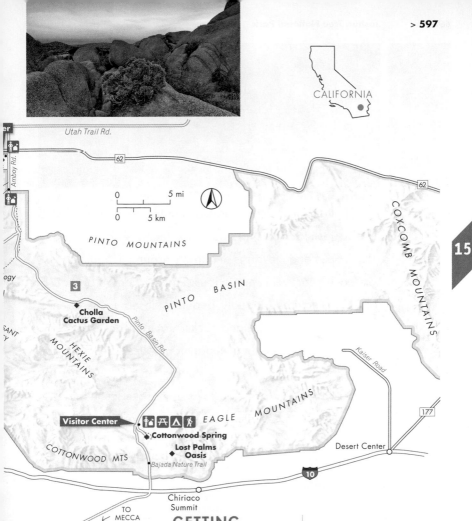

CALIFORNIA

Utah Trail Rd.

62

0 —— 5 mi
0 —— 5 km

PINTO MOUNTAINS

PINTO BASIN

Pinto Basin Rd.

Cholla Cactus Garden

3

HEXIE MOUNTAINS

Visitor Center

EAGLE MOUNTAINS

Cottonwood Spring

Lost Palms Oasis

Bajada Nature Trail

COTTONWOOD MTS

Desert Center

177

Kaiser Road

COXCOMB MOUNTAINS

62

10

Chiriaco Summit

TO ← MECCA

15

GETTING ORIENTED

Daggerlike tufts grace the branches of the namesake trees of Joshua Tree National Park in southeastern California, where the arid Mojave Desert meets the sparsely vegetated Colorado Desert (part of the Sonoran Desert, which lies across California, Arizona, and Northern Mexico).

Passenger cars are fine for paved areas, but you'll need four-wheel drive for many of the rugged backcountry roadways. At the park's most popular sites, parking is limited. Joshua Tree does not have public transportation.

Updated by
Steve Pastorino

One of the last great wildernesses in the continental United States, Joshua Tree National Park teems with fascinating landscapes and life-forms. It attracts around 1.5 million visitors each year, yet is mysteriously quiet at dawn and dusk. The park features ruggedly beautiful desert scenery, enormous boulders and jagged rocks, natural cactus gardens, and lush oases shaded by elegant fan palms. The landscape shifts abruptly from the arid stubble of the low Sonoran Desert to vast stands of the park's namesake Joshua trees in the higher, wetter Mojave Desert. Members of the yucca family of shrubs, the plants' unruly limbs are said to have reminded Mormon pioneers of the prophet Joshua's outstretched arms reaching toward heaven.

PLANNING

WHEN TO GO
October through May, when the desert is cooler, is when most visitors arrive. Daytime temperatures range from the mid-70s in December and January to mid-90s in October and May. Lows can dip to near freezing in midwinter, and you may even encounter snow at the higher elevations. Summers can be torrid, with daytime temperatures reaching 110°F.

PLANNING YOUR TIME
JOSHUA TREE IN ONE DAY
After stocking up on water, snacks, and lunch in Yucca Valley or Joshua Tree (you won't find any supplies inside the park), begin your visit at the **Joshua Tree Visitor Center**, where you can pick up maps and peruse

exhibits to get acquainted with what awaits you. Enter the park itself at the nearby **West Entrance Station** and continue driving along the highly scenic and well-maintained **Park Boulevard.** Stop first at **Hidden Valley,** where you can relax at the picnic area or hike the easy 1-mile loop trail. After a few more miles turn left onto the spur road that takes you to the trailhead for the **Barker Dam Nature Trail.** Walk the easy 1.3-mile loop to view a water tank ranchers built to quench their cattle's thirst; along the way you'll spot birds and a handful of cactus varieties. Return to Park Boulevard and head south; you'll soon leave the main road again for the drive to **Keys View.** The easy loop trail here is only 0.25 mile, but the views extend for miles in every direction—look for the San Andreas Fault, the Salton Sea, and nearby mountains. Return to Park Boulevard, where you'll find **Cap Rock,** another short loop trail winding amid rock formations and Joshua trees.

Continuing along Park Boulevard, the start of the 18-mile self-guided **Geology Tour Road** will soon appear on your right. A brochure outlining its 16 stops is available here; note that the round-trip will take about two hours, and high-clearance vehicles are recommended after stop 9. ■TIP→ Do not attempt if it has recently rained. Back on Park Boulevard, you'll soon arrive at the aptly named **Skull Rock.** This downright spooky formation is next to the parking lot; a nearby trailhead marks the beginning of a 1.7-mile nature trail. End your day with a stop at the **Oasis Visitor Center** in Twentynine Palms, where you can stroll through the historic **Oasis of Mara,** popular with area settlers.

GETTING HERE AND AROUND
AIR TRAVEL
Palm Springs International Airport is the closest major airport to Joshua Tree National Park. It's about 45 miles from the park. The drive from Los Angeles International Airport to Joshua Tree takes about two hours.

CAR TRAVEL
An isolated island of pristine wilderness—a rarity these days—Joshua Tree National Park is within a short drive of 11 million Southern California residents. Most visitors, in fact, make the two-hour drive from the Los Angeles area to enjoy a weekend of solitude in 792,726 acres of untouched desert. The urban sprawl of Palm Springs (home to the nearest airport) is 45 miles away, but gateway towns Joshua Tree, Yucca Valley, and Twentynine Palms are just north of the park. If you're staying in the Palm Springs area, you can enjoy the highlights of the park in one day, including a stop for a picnic at a scenic spot.

■TIP→ If you'd prefer not to drive, most Palm Springs area hotels can arrange a half- or full-day tour that hits the highlights of Joshua Tree National Park. But you'll need to spend two or three days camping here to truly experience the quiet beauty of the desert.

PARK ESSENTIALS
PARK FEES AND PERMITS
Park admission is $25 per car, $12 per person on foot, bicycle, motorcycle, or horse. The Joshua Tree Pass, good for one year, is $40.

15

PARK HOURS

The park is open every day, around the clock, but visitor centers are staffed from approximately 8 am to 5 pm. The park is in the Pacific time zone.

CELL-PHONE RECEPTION

Cell phones don't work in most areas of the park. There are no telephones in the interior of the park.

EDUCATIONAL OFFERINGS

LECTURES

The Desert Institute at Joshua Tree National Park. The nonprofit educational partner of the park offers a full schedule of lectures, classes, and hikes. Class topics include basket making, painting, and photography, while field trips include workshops on cultural history, natural science, and how to survive in the desert. ⊠ *74485 National Park Dr., Twentynine Palms* ☎ *760/367–5525* ⊕ *www.joshuatree.org.*

Stargazing. At Joshua Tree National Park you can tour the Milky Way on summer evenings using binoculars. Rangers also offer programs on some evenings when the moon isn't visible. Pick up a schedule at a visitor center. ⊠ *Cottonwood Campground Amphitheater and Oasis Visitor Center.*

RANGER PROGRAMS

Evening Programs. Rangers present hour-long lectures, often on Friday or Saturday evening, at Black Rock Canyon Nature Center, Cottonwood Amphitheater, Indian Cove Amphitheater, and Jumbo Rocks Campground. Topics range from natural history to local lore. The schedule is posted at the visitor centers. ⊠ *Joshua Tree National Park* ⊠ *Free.*

Fodor'sChoice
★
Keys Ranch Tour. A guide takes you through the former home of a family that homesteaded here for 60 years. In addition to the ranch, a workshop, store, and schoolhouse are still standing, and the grounds are strewn with vehicles and mining equipment. The 90-minute tour, which begins at the Keys Ranch gate, tells the history of the family that built the ranch. Tickets are $10, and reservations are required. ⊠ *Hidden Valley Picnic Area* ☎ *760/367–5522* ⊕ *www.nps.gov/jotr.*

TOURS

Big Wheel Tours. Based in Palm Desert, Big Wheel Tours offers van excursions, Jeep tours, and hiking trips through the park. Bicycle tours (road and mountain bike) are available outside the park boundary. Pickups are available at Palm Springs area hotels. ⊠ *74850 42nd Ave., Palm Desert* ☎ *760/779–1837* ⊕ *www.bwbtours.com* ⊠ *From $119.*

Trail Discovery. You can get a full day of exploring Joshua Tree with Trail Discovery, along with information on the park's plants, animals, geography, and history. Park admission, bottled water, hip packs, snacks, and fruit are included. Transportation is not provided. ☎ *760/413–1575* ⊕ *www.palmspringshiking.com* ⊠ *From $95.*

VISITOR INFORMATION

Park Contact Information Joshua Tree National Park. ⊠ *74485 National Park Dr., Twentynine Palms* ☎ *760/367–5500* ⊕ *www.nps.gov/jotr.*

VISITOR CENTERS

Cottonwood Visitor Center. The south entrance is the closest to Interstate 10, the east–west highway from Los Angeles to Phoenix. Exhibits in this small center, staffed by rangers and volunteers, illustrate the region's natural history. The center also has restrooms. ⊠ *Cottonwood Spring, Pinto Basin Rd.* ⊕ *www.nps.gov/jotr.*

Joshua Tree Visitor Center. This visitor center has interesting exhibits illustrating park geology, cultural and historic sites, and hiking and rock-climbing activities. There's also a small bookstore and café. Restrooms with flush toilets are on the premises. ⊠ *6554 Park Blvd., Joshua Tree* ☎ *760/366–1855* ⊕ *www.nps.gov/jotr.*

> ### PLANTS AND WILDLIFE IN JOSHUA TREE
>
> Joshua Tree will shatter your notions of the desert as a wasteland. Life flourishes here, as flora and fauna have adapted to heat and drought. In most areas you'll be walking among native Joshua trees, ocotillos, and yuccas. One of the best spring desert wildflower displays in Southern California blooms here. You'll see plenty of animals—reptiles such as nocturnal sidewinders, birds like golden eagles or burrowing owls, and occasionally mammals like coyotes and bobcats.

15

Oasis Visitor Center. Exhibits here illustrate how Joshua Tree was formed, reveal the differences between the park's two types of desert, and demonstrate how plants and animals eke out an existence in this arid climate. Take the ½-mile nature walk through the nearby Oasis of Mara, which is alive with cottonwood trees, palm trees, and mesquite shrubs. Facililies include picnic tables, restrooms, and a bookstore. ⊠ *74485 National Park Dr., Twentynine Palms* ☎ *760/367–5500* ⊕ *www.nps.gov/jotr.*

EXPLORING

SCENIC DRIVES

Park Boulevard. If you have time only for a short visit, driving Park Boulevard is your best choice. Traversing the most scenic portions of Joshua Tree, this well-paved road connects the north and west entrances in the park's high desert section. Along with some sweeping desert views, you'll see jumbles of splendid boulder formations, stands of Joshua trees, and Hidden Valley and Barker Dam, remnants of the area's wild and woolly past. From the Oasis Visitor Center, drive south. After about 5 miles, the road forks; turn right and head west toward Jumbo Rocks (clearly marked with a road sign). ⊠ *Joshua Tree National Park.*

Pinto Basin Road. This paved road takes you from high Mojave desert to low Colorado desert. A long, slow drive, the route runs from the main part of the park to Interstate 10; it can add as much as an hour to and from Palm Springs (round-trip), but the views and roadside exhibits make it worth the extra time. From the Oasis Visitor Center, drive south. After about 5 miles, the road forks; take a left and continue another 9 miles to the Cholla Cactus Garden, where the sun fills the cactus needles with light. Past that is the Ocotillo Patch, filled with spindly plants bearing razor-sharp thorns and, after a rain, bright green leaves and brilliant red flowers. Side trips from this route require a 4X4. ⊠ *Joshua Tree National Park.*

HISTORIC SITES

FAMILY **Hidden Valley.** This legendary cattle-rustlers' hideout is set among big boulders along a 1-mile loop trail. Kids love to scramble on and around the rocks. There are shaded picnic tables here. ⊠ *Park Blvd.* ✛ *14 miles south of west entrance.*

Fodor'sChoice **Keys Ranch.** This 150-acre ranch, which once belonged to William and ★ Frances Keys and is now on the National Historic Register, illustrates one of the area's most successful attempts at homesteading. The couple raised five children under extreme desert conditions. Most of the original buildings, including the house, school, store, and workshop, have been restored to the way they were when William died in 1969. The only way to see the ranch is on one of the 90-minute walking tours usually offered Friday–Sunday, October–May, and weekends in summer; advance reservations required. ⊠ *Joshua Tree National Park* ✛ *2 miles north of Barker Dam Rd.* ☎ *760/367–5522* ⊕ *www.nps.gov/jotr/ planyourvisit/ranchtour.htm* ⬚ *$10, available at Joshua Tree and Oasis visitor centers.*

SCENIC STOPS

Barker Dam. Built around 1900 by ranchers and miners to hold water for cattle and mining operations, the dam now collects rainwater and is a good place to spot wildlife such as the elusive bighorn sheep. ⊠ *Barker Dam Rd.* ✛ *Off Park Blvd., 10 miles south of west entrance.*

Cholla Cactus Garden. This stand of bigelow cholla (sometimes called jumping cholla, since its hooked spines seem to jump at you) is best seen and photographed in late afternoon, when the backlit spiky stalks stand out against a colorful sky. ⊠ *Pinto Basin Rd.* ✛ *20 miles north of Cottonwood Visitor Center.*

Cottonwood Spring. Home to the native Cahuilla people for centuries, this spring provided water for travelers and early prospectors. The area, which supports a large stand of fan palms, is one of the best stops for bird-watching, as migrating birds (and bighorn sheep) rely on the water as well. A number of gold mines were located here, and the area still has some remains, including an *arrastra* (a gold ore–grinding tool) and concrete pillars. ⊠ *Cottonwood Visitor Center.*

Fortynine Palms Oasis. A short drive off Highway 62, this site is a bit of a preview of what the park's interior has to offer: stands of fan palms, interesting petroglyphs, and evidence of fires built by early American Indians. Since animals frequent this area, you may spot a coyote, bobcat, or roadrunner. ⊠ *End of Canyon Rd.* ✛ *4 miles west of Twentynine Palms.*

Fodor's Choice
★ **Keys View.** At 5,185 feet, this point affords a sweeping view of the Santa Rosa Mountains and Coachella Valley, the San Andreas Fault, the peak of 11,500-foot Mt. San Gorgonio, the shimmering surface of Salton Sea, and—on a rare clear day—Signal Mountain in Mexico. Sunrise and sunset are magical times, when the light throws rocks and trees into high relief before bathing the hills in brilliant shades of red, orange, and gold. ⊠ *Keys View Rd.* ✛ *16 miles south of park's west entrance.*

Lost Palms Oasis. More than 100 fan palms comprise the largest group of the exotic plants in the park. A spring bubbles from between the rocks, but disappears into the sandy, boulder-strewn canyon. The 7.5-mile round-trip hike is not for everyone. Bring plenty of water! ⊠ *Cottonwood Visitor Center.*

Ocotillo Patch. Stop here for a roadside exhibit on the dramatic display made by the red-tipped succulent after even the shortest rain shower. ⊠ *Pinto Basin Rd.* ✛ *About 3 miles east of Cholla Cactus Gardens.*

15

SPORTS AND THE OUTDOORS

HIKING

There are more than 190 miles of hiking trails in Joshua Tree, ranging from quarter-mile nature trails to 35-mile treks. Some connect with each other, so you can design your own desert maze. Remember that drinking water is hard to come by—you won't find water in the park except at the entrances. Bring along at least a gallon per person for all but the shortest hikes, more if the weather is hot.

EASY

Cap Rock. This ½-mile wheelchair-accessible loop—named after a boulder that sits atop a huge rock formation like a cap—winds through fascinating rock formations and has signs that explain the geology of the Mojave Desert. *Easy.* ⊠ *Joshua Tree National Park* ✛ *Trailhead: at junction of Park Blvd. and Keys View Rd.*

Skull Rock Trail. The 1.7-mile loop guides hikers through boulder piles, desert washes, and a rocky alley. It's named for what is perhaps the park's most famous rock formation, which resembles the eye sockets and nasal cavity of a human skull. Access the trail from within Jumbo Rocks Campground or from a small parking area on the highway just east of the campground. *Easy.* ⊠ *Joshua Tree National Park* ✛ *Trailhead: at Jumbo Rocks Campground.*

MODERATE

Mastodon Peak Trail. Some boulder scrambling is required on this 3-mile hike that loops up to the 3,371-foot Mastodon Peak, but the journey rewards you with stunning views of the Salton Sea. The trail passes through a region where gold was mined from 1919 to 1932, so be on the lookout for open mines. The peak draws its name from a large rock formation that early miners believed looked like the head of a prehistoric behemoth. *Moderate.* ⊠ *Joshua Tree National Park* ✛ *Trailhead: at Cottonwood Spring Oasis.*

Fodor's Choice **Ryan Mountain Trail.** The payoff for hiking to the top of 5,461-foot Ryan
★ Mountain is one of the best panoramic views of Joshua Tree. From here
you can see Mt. San Jacinto, Mt. San Gorgonio, Lost Horse Valley, and
the Pinto Basin. You'll need two to three hours to complete the 3-mile
round-trip with 1,000-plus feet of elevation gain. *Moderate.* ⊠ *Joshua
Tree National Park* ✤ *Trailhead: at Ryan Mountain parking area, 16
miles southeast of park's west entrance, or Sheep Pass, 16 miles southwest of Oasis Visitor Center.*

ROCK CLIMBING

With an abundance of weathered igneous boulder outcroppings, Joshua
Tree is one of the nation's top winter-climbing destinations. There are
more than 4,500 established routes offering a full menu of climbing
experiences—from bouldering for beginners in the Wonderland of
Rocks to multiple-pitch climbs at Echo Rock and Saddle Rock. The
best-known climb in the park is Hidden Valley's Sports Challenge Rock.
A map inside the *Joshua Tree Guide* shows locations of selected wilderness and nonwilderness climbs.

TOURS AND OUTFITTERS
Joshua Tree Rock Climbing School. The school offers several programs,
from one-day introductory classes to multiday programs for experienced climbers, and provides all needed equipment. Beginning classes,
offered year-round on most weekends, are limited to six people age eight
or older. ⊠ *Joshua Tree National Park* ☎ *760/366–4745, 800/890–4745*
⊕ *www.joshuatreerockclimbing.com* ✉ *From $195.*

Vertical Adventures Rock Climbing School. About 1,000 climbers each
year learn the sport in Joshua Tree National Park through this school.
Classes, offered September–May, meet at a designated location in the
park, and all equipment is provided. ⊠ *Joshua Tree National Park*
☎ *800/514–8785* ⊕ *www.vertical-adventures.com* ✉ *From $145.*

MOJAVE DESERT

WELCOME TO MOJAVE DESERT

TOP REASONS TO GO

★ **Nostalgia:** Old neon signs, historic motels, and restored (or neglected but still striking) rail stations abound across this desert landscape. Don't miss the classic eateries along the way, including Summit Inn in Oak Hills and Emma Jean's Holland Burger Cafe in Victorville.

★ **Death Valley wonders:** Visit this distinctive landscape to tour some of the most varied desert terrain in the world.

★ **Great ghost towns:** California's gold rush brought miners to the Mojave, and the towns they left behind have their own unique charms.

★ **Cool down in Sierra country:** Head up U.S. 395 toward Bishop to visit the High Sierra, home to majestic Mt. Whitney.

★ **Explore ancient history:** The Mojave Desert is replete with rare petroglyphs, some dating back almost 16,000 years.

1 The Western Mojave. Stretching from the town of Ridgecrest to the base of the San Gabriel Mountains, the western Mojave is a varied landscape of ancient Native American petroglyphs, tufa towers, and hillsides covered in bright orange poppies.

2 The Eastern Mojave. Joshua trees and cacti dot a predominantly flat landscape that is interrupted by dramatic, rock-strewn mountains. The area is largely uninhabited, so be cautious when driving the back roads, where towns and services are scarce.

GETTING ORIENTED

Mojave Desert, once part of an ancient inland sea, is one of the largest swaths of open land in Southern California. Its boundaries include the San Gabriel and San Bernardino mountain ranges to the south; the areas of Palmdale and Ridgecrest to the west; Death Valley to the north; and Needles and Lake Havasu in Arizona to the east. The area is distinguishable by its wide-open sandy spaces, peppered with creosote bushes, Joshua trees, cacti, and abandoned homesteads. You can access the Mojave via interstates 40 and 15, highways 14 and 95, and U.S. 395.

16

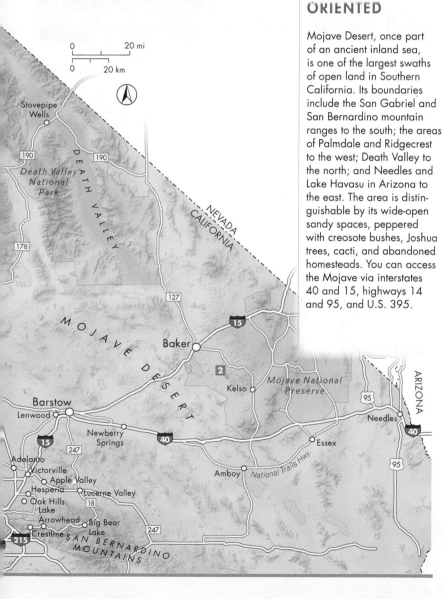

0   20 mi
0   20 km

Stovepipe Wells

190   190

Death Valley National Park

178

DEATH VALLEY

NEVADA
CALIFORNIA

127

M O J A V E   D E S E R T

15

Baker

2

Kelso

Mojave National Preserve

95

ARIZONA

Barstow
Lenwood

Newberry Springs

40

Essex

Needles

40

95

15

247

Adelanto
Victorville
Apple Valley
Hesperia
Oak Hills Lake
Arrowhead   Big Bear Lake
Crestline
215

18

Lucerne Valley

Amboy   National Trails Hwy.

247

S A N   B E R N A R D I N O
M O U N T A I N S

Updated by
Joan Patterson

Dust and desolation, tumbleweeds and rattlesnakes, barren landscapes and failed dreams—these are the bleak images that come to mind when most people hear the word *desert*. Yet the remote regions east of the Sierra Nevada possess a singular beauty, the vast open spaces populated with spiky Joshua trees, undulating sand dunes, faulted mountains, and dramatic rock formations. With a few exceptions the area is not heavily peopled, providing expanses in which visitors can both lose and find themselves.

The topography is extreme; while Death Valley drops to almost 300 feet below sea level and contains the lowest (and hottest) spot in North America, the Mojave Desert, which lies to the south, has elevations ranging from 3,000 to 5,000 feet.

PLANNING

WHEN TO GO

Spring and fall are the best seasons to tour the desert. Winters are generally mild, but summers can be cruel. If you're on a budget, be aware that room rates drop as the temperatures rise.

GETTING HERE AND AROUND

AIR TRAVEL

McCarran International Airport in Las Vegas is the nearest airport to many eastern Mojave destinations. Needles Airport and Inyokern Airport serve small, private planes.

Contacts Inyokern Airport. ⊠ *1669 Airport Rd., off Hwy. 178, 9 miles west of Ridgecrest, Inyokern* ☎ *760/377–5844* ⊕ *www.inyokernairport.com.* **McCarran International Airport.** ⊠ *5757 Wayne Newton Blvd., Las Vegas* ☎ *702/261–5211* ⊕ *www.mccarran.com.* **Needles Airport.** ⊠ *711 Airport Rd., Needles* ☎ *760/247–2371* ⊕ *cms.sbcounty.gov/airports.*

BUS TRAVEL

Greyhound provides bus service to Barstow, Victorville, and Palmdale; check with the chambers of commerce about local bus service, which is generally more useful to residents than to tourists.

Contacts Greyhound. ☎ *800/231–2222* ⊕ *www.greyhound.com.*

CAR TRAVEL

The major north–south route through the western Mojave is U.S. 395, which intersects with Interstate 15 between Cajon Pass and Victorville. Farther west, Highway 14 runs north–south between Inyokern (near Ridgecrest) and Palmdale. Two major east–west routes travel through the Mojave: to the north, Interstate 15 to Las Vegas, Nevada; to the south, Interstate 40 to Needles. At the intersection of the two interstates, in Barstow, Interstate 15 veers south toward Victorville and Los Angeles, and Interstate 40 gives way to Highway 58 west toward Bakersfield.

■ **TIP→** For the latest Mojave traffic and weather, tune in to the Highway Stations (98.1 FM near Barstow, 98.9 FM near Essex, and 99.7 FM near Baker). Traffic can be especially troublesome Friday through Sunday, when thousands of Angelenos head to Las Vegas for a bit of R&R.

16

Contacts Caltrans Current Highway Conditions. ☎ *800/427–7623* ⊕ *www.dot.ca.gov.*

TRAIN TRAVEL

Amtrak trains traveling east and west stop in Victorville, Barstow, and Needles, but the stations aren't staffed, so you'll have to purchase tickets in advance and handle your own baggage. The Barstow station is served daily by Amtrak California motor coaches that stop in Los Angeles, Bakersfield, Las Vegas, and elsewhere.

Contacts Amtrak. ☎ *800/872–7245* ⊕ *www.amtrak.com.*

HEALTH AND SAFETY

Let someone know your trip route, destination, and estimated time of return. Before setting out, make sure your vehicle is in good condition. Carry water, a jack, tools, and towrope or chain. Keep an eye on your gas gauge and try to keep the needle above half. Stay on main roads, and watch out for wildlife, horses, and cattle.

Drink at least a gallon of water a day (more if you're hiking or otherwise exerting yourself). Dress in layered clothing and wear comfortable, sturdy shoes and a hat. Keep snacks, sunscreen, and a first-aid kit on hand. If you have a headache or feel dizzy or nauseous, you could be suffering from dehydration. Get out of the sun immediately and drink plenty of water. Dampen your clothing to lower your body temperature. Do not enter abandoned mine tunnels or shafts of which there are hundreds in the Mojave Desert. The structures may be unstable, and there may be hidden dangers such as pockets of bad air. Avoid canyons during rainstorms. Floodwaters can quickly fill up dry riverbeds and cover or wash away roads. Never place your hands or feet where you can't see them: rattlesnakes, scorpions, and black widow spiders may be hiding there.

Contacts Barstow Community Hospital. ⊠ *820 E. Mountain View St., Barstow* ☎ *760/256–1761* ⊕ *www.barstowhospital.com.* **BLM Rangers.** ☎ *916/978–4400* ⊕ *www.blm.gov/ca.* **San Bernardino County Sheriff.** ☎ *760/256–4838 in Barstow, 760/733–4448 in Baker* ⊕ *cms.sbcounty.gov/sheriff.*

HOURS OF OPERATION

Early morning is the best time to visit sights and avoid crowds, but some museums and visitor centers don't open until 10. If you schedule your town arrivals for the late afternoon, you can drop by the visitor centers just before closing hours to line up an itinerary for the next day.

RESTAURANTS

Throughout the desert, dining is a fairly simple affair. There are chain establishments in Ridgecrest, Victorville, and Barstow, as well as some ethnic eateries.

HOTELS

Chain hotel properties and roadside motels are the desert's primary lodging options. The tourist season runs from late May through September. Reservations are rarely a problem, but it's still wise to make them. *Hotel reviews have been shortened. For full information, please visit Fodors.com.*

WHAT IT COSTS			
$	$$	$$$	$$$$
Restaurants	under $16	$16–$22	$23–$30	over $30
Hotels	under $120	$120–$175	$176–$250	over $250

Restaurant prices are the average cost of a main course at dinner or, if dinner is not served, at lunch, excluding sales tax of 7.75%. Hotel prices are the lowest cost of a standard double room in high season, excluding service charges and 7.25% tax.

TOURS

Sierra Club. The San Gorgonio Chapter of the Sierra Club and the chapter's Mojave Group conduct interesting field trips and desert excursions. Activities are often volunteer-run and free, but participants are sometimes required to cover parking and other expenses. ☎ *951/684–6203* ⊕ *sangorgonio2.sierraclub.org* ✉ *Some free; fee tour prices vary.*

VISITOR INFORMATION

Contacts Barstow Welcome Center. ⊠ *2796 Tanger Way, Barstow* ☎ *760/253–4782* ⊕ *www.visitcalifornia.com/destination/california-welcome-centers-desert.* **Bureau of Land Management.** ⊠ *California Desert District Office, 22835 Calle San Juan De Los Lagos, Moreno Valley* ☎ *951/697–5200* ⊕ *www.blm.gov/ca.* **Death Valley Chamber of Commerce.** ☎ *888/600–1844* ⊕ *www.deathvalleychamber.org.*

THE WESTERN MOJAVE

This vast area is especially beautiful along U.S. 395. From January through March, wildflowers are in bloom and temperatures are manageable. Year-round, snowcapped mountain peaks are irresistible sights.

LANCASTER

8 miles north of Palmdale.

Points of interest around Lancaster include a state poppy reserve that bursts to life in the spring and Edwards Air Force Base, which offers a fascinating tour of historical military aircraft. Lancaster was founded in 1876, when the Southern Pacific Railroad arrived. Before that, several Native American tribes, some of whose descendants still live in the surrounding mountains, inhabited it.

GETTING HERE AND AROUND

From the Los Angeles basin, take Highway 14, which proceeds north to Mojave and Highway 58, a link between Bakersfield and Barstow. Regional Metrolink trains serve Lancaster from the Los Angeles area. Local transit exists, but a car is the best way to experience this area.

16

ESSENTIALS

Visitor Information Destination Lancaster. ⊠ *554 W. Lancaster Blvd.* ☎ *661/948–4518* ⊕ *www.destinationlancasterca.org.*

EXPLORING
TOP ATTRACTIONS

Antelope Valley Indian Museum. This museum got its start as a private collection of American Indian antiquities gathered in the 1920s by artist and amateur naturalist Howard Arden Edwards. Today, his Swiss chalet-style home is a state museum known for one-of-a-kind artifacts from California, Southwest, and Great Basin native tribes, including ancient tools, artwork, basketry, and rugs. To get here, exit north off Highway 138 at 165th Street East and follow the signs, or take the Avenue K exit off Highway 14. ⊠ *15701 E. Ave. M* ☎ *661/946–3055* ⊕ *www.avim.parks.ca.gov* ⊠ *$3.*

Antelope Valley Poppy Reserve. The California poppy, the state flower, can be spotted throughout the state, but this quiet park holds the densest concentration. Eight miles of trails wind through 1,745 acres of hills carpeted with poppies and other wildflowers, including a paved section that allows wheelchair access. Keep in mind that poppy flowers will curl up their petals if it's too windy or cold, so plan accordingly. ■TIP➜ Blooming season is usually March through May. On a clear day at any time of year, you'll be treated to sweeping views of Antelope Valley. ⊠ *15101 Lancaster Rd., west off Hwy. 14, Ave. I Exit* ☎ *661/724–1180 wildflower hotline, 661/946–6092* ⊕ *www.parks. ca.gov/?page_id=627* ⊠ *$10 per vehicle.*

OFF THE BEATEN PATH

Exotic Feline Breeding Compound's Feline Conservation Center. About two dozen species of wild cats, from the unusual, weasel-size jaguarundi to leopards, tigers, and jaguars, inhabit this small, orderly facility. You can see the cats up close (behind barrier fences) in the parklike public zoo

and research center, and docents are available to answer questions. ✉ *Rhyolite Ave. off Mojave-Tropico Rd., Rosamond* ☎ *661/256–3793* ⊕ *www.wildcatzoo.org* ◉ *$7* ☽ *Closed Wed.*

WORTH NOTING

Air Force Flight Test Museum at Edwards Air Force Base. This museum, at what many consider to be the birthplace of supersonic flight, chronicles the rich history of flight testing. Numerous airplanes are on exhibit, from the first F-16B to the only remaining YF-22. While those with approved base entry have access to regular museum hours, a general-public tour takes place once a month. The 3½-hour tour includes indoor museum exhibits and driving tours of the aircraft. The tour requires a reservation and you have to provide basic information for a background check at least a week in advance (a month for non-U.S. residents), but be aware that slots fill up fast. On the base's website, click Tours for details. ✉ *Edwards Air Force Base Visitor Control Center , 405 S. Rosamond Blvd., Edwards* ☎ *661/277–8050, 661/277–3510* ⊕ *www. afftcmuseum.org* ◉ *Free.*

	HIKING IN THE MOJAVE DESERT

> Hiking trails are abundant throughout the desert and along the eastern base of the Sierra, meandering toward sights that you can't see from the road. Some of the best trails are unmarked; ask locals for directions. Whether you're exploring the high or low desert, wear sunscreen, protective clothing, and a hat. Watch for tarantulas, black widows, scorpions, snakes, and other creatures.

16

Antelope Valley Winery/Donato Family Vineyard. Cyndee and Frank Donato purchased the Los Angeles–based McLester Winery in 1990 and moved it to Lancaster, where the high-desert sun and nighttime chill work their magic on wine grapes such as Merlot, Zinfandel, and Sangiovese. In addition to tastings, the winery hosts a Saturday farmers' market (from May through November between 9 and noon) and sells grass-fed buffalo and other game and exotic meats such as venison, pheasant, and wild boar. ✉ *42041 20th St. W, at Ave. M* ☎ *661/722–0145, 888/282–8332* ⊕ *www.avwinery.com* ◉ *Winery free, tasting $6.50 to $15.*

OFF THE BEATEN PATH

Devil's Punchbowl Natural Area. A mile from the San Andreas Fault, the namesake of this attraction is a natural bowl-shaped depression in the earth, framed by 300-foot rock walls. At the bottom is a stream, which you can reach via a moderately strenuous 1-mile hike. You also can detour on a short nature trail; at the top an interpretive center has displays of native flora and fauna, including live animals such as snakes, lizards, and birds of prey. ✉ *28000 Devil's Punchbowl Rd., south of Hwy. 138, Pearblossom* ☎ *661/944–2743* ◉ *Free.*

St. Andrew's Abbey. Nestled in the foothills of the Antelope Valley, this peaceful enclave is both Benedictine monastery and restful retreat for those wanting to get away from the bustle of everyday life. Day visitors can walk the lush tree-lined grounds, including a large, shaded pond teeming with ducks and red-eared turtles, or browse the well-stocked gift shop for religious keepsakes. An extensive collection of ceramic tiles in the image of saints and angels by Father Maur van

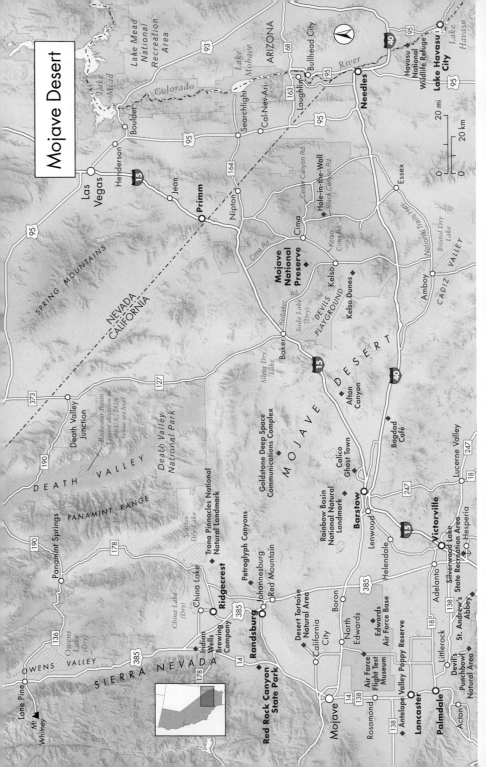

Mojave Desert

Doorslaer, a Belgian monk whose work U.S. and Canadian collectors favor, are among the items sold here to help sustain the monastery and its good works. ✉ *31001 N. Valyermo Rd., south of Hwy. 138, Valyermo* ☎ *888/454–5411, 661/944–2178 ceramics studio* ⊕ *www. saintsandangels.org* ✍ *Free.*

RED ROCK CANYON STATE PARK

48 miles north of Lancaster.

On the stretch of Highway 14 that slices through Red Rock Canyon State Park, it's easy to become caught up in the momentum of rushing to your "real" destination. But it would be a shame not to stop for this deeply beautiful canyon, with its rich, layered colors and Native American heritage.

GETTING HERE AND AROUND
The only practical way to get here is by car, taking Highway 14 north from the Palmdale-Lancaster area or south from Ridgecrest.

Red Rock Canyon State Park. A geological feast for the eyes with its layers of pink, white, red, and brown rock, this remote canyon is also a region of fascinating biological diversity—the ecosystems of the Sierra Nevada, the Mojave Desert, and the Basin Range all converge here. Native Americans known as the Kawaiisu lived here some 20,000 years ago; later, Mojave Indians roamed the land for centuries. You can still see remains of gold mining operations in the park, and movies such as *Jurassic Park* have been shot here. For a quiet nature trail a little off the beaten path try the 0.75-mile loop at Red Cliffs Natural Preserve on Highway 14, across from the entrance to the Ricardo Campground. ✉ *Visitor Center, 37749 Abbott Dr., off Hwy. 14, Cantil* ☎ *661/946–6092* ⊕ *www.parks. ca.gov* ✍ *$6 per vehicle.*

16

RIDGECREST

28 miles northeast of Red Rock Canyon State Park, 77 miles south of Lone Pine.

A military town that serves the U.S. Naval Weapons Center to its north, Ridgecrest has scores of stores, restaurants, and hotels. With about 25,000 residents, it's the last city of any significant size you'll encounter as you head northeast toward Death Valley National Park. It's a good base for visiting regional attractions such as the Trona Pinnacles and Petroglyph Canyons.

GETTING HERE AND AROUND
Arrive here by car via U.S. 395 or, from the Los Angeles area, Highway 14. The local bus service is of limited use to tourists.

ESSENTIALS
Transportation Contacts Ridgerunner Transit. ☎ *760/499–5040* ⊕ *ridgecrest-ca.gov/transit/transit.*

Visitor Information Ridgecrest Area Convention and Visitors Bureau. ✉ *643 N. China Lake Blvd., Suite C* ☎ *760/375–8202, 800/847–4830* ⊕ *www.racvb.com.*

EXPLORING

TOP ATTRACTIONS

FAMILY
Fodor's Choice ★
Petroglyph Canyons. Thousands of well-preserved images of animals and humans are scratched or pecked into dark basaltic rocks at Big Petroglyph and Little Petroglyph canyons in the Coso Mountain range, the largest concentration of ancient rock art in the Northern Hemisphere. The canyons lie within the million-acre U.S. Naval Weapons Center at China Lake. Only the drawings of Little Petroglyph can be visited, and only on a guided tour arranged in advance through the Maturango Museum. Tour participants must be U.S. citizens over 10 years of age, and fill out an online application to obtain security clearance. Detailed information about the spring and fall tours, which fill up fast, is provided on the museum's website. ✉ *100 E. Las Flores Ave.* ☎ *760/375–6900* 🌐 *www.maturango.org* 🎟 *$55* ⏲ *Closed Jan. and Feb. and July and Aug.*

Trona Pinnacles National Natural Landmark. Fantastic-looking formations of calcium carbonate, known as tufa, were formed underwater along fault lines in the bed of what is now Searles Dry Lake. Some of the more than 500 spires stand as tall as 140 feet, creating a landscape so surreal that it doubled for outer-space terrain in the film *Star Trek V.*

An easy-to-walk ½-mile trail allows you to see the tufa up close, but wear sturdy shoes—tufa cuts like coral. The best road to the area can be impassable after a rainstorm. ✉ *Pinnacle Rd.* ✥ *5 miles south of Hwy. 178, 18 miles east of Ridgecrest* ☎ *760/384–5400 Ridgecrest BLM office* 🌐 *www.recreation.gov.*

OFF THE BEATEN PATH

Indian Wells Brewing Company. After driving through the hot desert, you'll surely appreciate a cold one at Indian Wells Brewing Company, where master brewer Rick Lovett lovingly crafts his Lobotomy Bock, Amnesia I.P.A., and Lunatic Lemonade, among others. If you have the kids along, grab a six-pack of his specialty root beer, black cherry, orange, or cream soda. ✉ *2565 N. Hwy. 14, 2 miles west of U.S. 395, Inyokern* ☎ *760/377–5989* 🌐 *www.mojavered.com.*

WORTH NOTING

FAMILY
Maturango Museum. The museum contains interesting exhibits that survey the Upper Mojave Desert area's art, history, and geology, and sponsors tours of the amazing rock drawings in Petroglph Canyons. ✉ *100 E. Las Flores Ave., at Hwy. 178* ☎ *760/375–6900* 🌐 *www.maturango.org* 🎟 *$5, kids under 18 free.*

WHERE TO STAY

$$ HOTEL
🏨 **Hampton Inn & Suites Ridgecrest.** Clean and reliable, the Hampton has a well-equipped exercise room, pool, spotless Internet service, and complimentary breakfast. **Pros:** attentive, friendly service; good breakfast; big rooms. **Cons:** a rather strong chain vibe. [$] *Rooms from: $159* ✉ *104 E. Sydnor Ave.* ☎ *760/446–1968* 🛏 *93 rooms* 🍴 *Breakfast.*

$$$ HOTEL
🏨 **SpringHill Suites Ridgecrest.** The spacious rooms and contemporary feel of this all-suites Marriott brand hotel make this a welcome choice after a long drive in the desert. **Pros:** spacious rooms; good breakfast; helpful staff. **Cons:** pricey. [$] *Rooms from: $194* ✉ *113 E. Sydnor Ave.* ☎ *888/236–2427, 760/446–1630* 🌐 *www.marriott.com/hotels/travel/iyksh-springhill-suites-ridgecrest* 🛏 *93 studio suites* 🍴 *Breakfast.*

RANDSBURG

21 miles south of Ridgecrest, 26 miles east of Red Rock Canyon State Park.

Randsburg and nearby Red Mountain and Johannesburg make up the Rand Mining District, which first boomed with the discovery of gold in the Rand Mountains in 1895. Rich tungsten ore, used in World War I to make steel alloy, was discovered in 1907, and silver was found in 1919. The boom has gone bust, but the area still has some residents, a few antiques shops, and plenty of character. Butte Avenue is the main drag in Randsburg, whose tiny city jail, just off Butte, is among the original buildings still standing. An archetypal Old West cemetery perched on a hillside looms over Johannesburg.

GETTING HERE AND AROUND

Arriving by car is the best transportation option. From Red Rock Canyon, drive east on Redrock Randsburg Road. From Ridgecrest, drive south on South China Lake Road and U.S. 395.

EXPLORING

Rand Desert Museum. The colorful history of the Rand Mining District during its heyday is celebrated in this small museum, including historical mining photographs, documents, and artifacts. ⊠ *161 Butte Ave.* ☎ *760/371–0965* ⊕ *www.randdesertmuseum.com* 🗐 *Free* ⊗ *Closed weekdays.*

OFF THE BEATEN PATH

Desert Tortoise Natural Area. It may not always be easy to spot the elusive desert tortoise in this peaceful protected habitat but the approximately 40-square-mile area often blazes with wildflowers in the spring and early summer. It is also a great spot to see desert kit fox, red-tailed hawks, cactus wrens, and Mojave rattlesnakes; walking paths and a small interpretive center are part of the experience. ⊠ *8 miles northeast of California City via Randsburg Mojave Rd.* ☎ *951/683–3872* ⊕ *www. tortoise-tracks.org* 🗐 *Free.*

General Store. Built as Randsburg's Drug Store in 1896, the General Store is one of the area's few surviving ghost-town buildings with an original tin ceiling, light fixtures, and 1904-era marble-and-stained-glass soda fountain. You can still enjoy a phosphate soda from that same fountain, or a lunch of burgers, hot dogs, and chili. ⊠ *35 Butte Ave.* ☎ *760/374–2143* ⊕ *www.randsburggeneralstore.com* ⊗ *Closed Tues.–Thurs.*

White House Saloon. This still-surviving saloon served miners and cowboys when it was first established way back in 1897; nowadays tourists and bikers sidle up to the bar for a burger, ice-cold brew, and a giant dose of Old West nostalgia. ⊠ *168 Butte Ave.* ☎ *760/374–2464* ⊗ *Closed Mon.–Thurs.*

16

THE EASTERN MOJAVE

Majestic, wide-open spaces define this region, with the Mojave National Preserve being one of the state's most remote but rewarding destinations.

VICTORVILLE

87 miles south of Ridgecrest.

At the southwest corner of the Mojave is the sprawling town of Victorville, a town with a rich Route 66 heritage and a museum dedicated to the Mother Road. Victorville was named for Santa Fe Railroad pioneer Jacob Nash Victor, who drove the first locomotive through the Cajon Pass here in 1885. Once home to Native Americans, the town later became a rest stop for Mormons and missionaries. In 1941 George Air Force Base, now an airport and storage area, brought scores of military families to the area, many of which have stayed on to raise families of their own.

GETTING HERE AND AROUND

Drive here on Interstate 15 from Los Angeles or Las Vegas, or from the north via U.S. 395. Amtrak and Greyhound also serve the town. There are local buses, but touring by car is more practical.

ESSENTIALS

Transportation Information The Victor Valley Transit Authority. ☎ *760/948–3030* ⊕ *www.vvta.org.*

Visitor Information Victor Valley Chamber of Commerce. ✉ *14174 Green Tree Blvd., at St. Andrews Dr.* ☎ *760/245–6506* ⊕ *www.vvchamber.com.*

EXPLORING

TOP ATTRACTIONS

California Route 66 Museum. Visitors from around the world still think of Historic Route 66 as one of the best ways to see the real America and this 4,500-square-foot museum is chock-full of memorabilia such as maps and postcards, photographs, paintings, and nostalgic displays that bring the iconic highway's history to life. Friendly museum volunteers are more than happy to answer questions and take your picture inside the flower-painted VW Love Bus. ✉ *16825 S. D St., between 5th and 6th Sts.* ☎ *760/951–0436* ⊕ *www.califrt66museum.org* ▨ *Free.*

WORTH NOTING

FAMILY **Mojave Narrows Regional Park.** This 840-acre park is one of the few spots where the Mojave River flows aboveground and the result is open pastures, wetlands, and two lakes surrounded by cottonwoods and cattails. Amenities include camping, fishing, equestrian/walking trails, and a large playground with waterpark. ✉ *18000 Yates Rd., north on Ridgecrest Rd. off Bear Valley Rd.* ☎ *760/245–2226* ⊕ *cms.sbcounty.gov/parks* ▨ *$8 weekdays, $10 weekends and holidays* ⊙ *Closed Tues. and Wed.*

Silverwood Lake State Recreation Area. One of the desert's most popular boating and fishing areas, 1,000-acre Silverwood Lake also has campgrounds and a beach with a lifeguard. You can rent boats; fish for trout, largemouth bass, crappie, and catfish; and hike and bike the trails. In winter, bald eagles nest in the tall Jeffrey pines by the shore. ✉ *14651*

Cedar Cir., at Cleghorn Rd., off Hwy. 138, Hesperia ☎ *760/389–2303* 🌐 *www.parks.ca.gov* 🎫 *$10 per car, $10 per boat.*

WHERE TO EAT AND STAY

$ DINER 🍴 **Emma Jean's Holland Burger Cafe.** The short-order cook and his grill are literally center stage in this tiny, family-owned restaurant along Historic Route 66, which has changed little since it first opened in 1947. It's the peach cobbler, Brian burger, and fried chicken that keep locals lining up at the door, but anyone wanting a glimpse of 20th-century Americana can get their kicks here, too. **Known for:** Route 66 memorabilia; historical diner. [$] *Average main: $8* ✉ *17143 N. D St., at Water Power Housing Dr.* ☎ *760/243–9938* 💳 *No credit cards* 🕑 *Closed Sun. No dinner.*

$ AMERICAN FAMILY 🍴 **Molly Brown's Country Cafe.** There's no mystery why this place is a locals' favorite. The cozy eatery offers a mouthwatering breakfast menu that includes everything from chicken fried steak to a sizzling garden skillet brimming with fresh vegetables; pair it with a slice of homemade pumpkin bread. **Known for:** hearty breakfasts; locals' favorite; homemade breads. [$] *Average main: $10* ✉ *15775 Mojave Dr.* ☎ *760/241–4900* 🌐 *www.mollybrownscountrycafe.com.*

$$ HOTEL FAMILY 🏨 **Courtyard Marriott Victorville Hesperia.** Rooms are spacious and contemporary, and there is both an indoor pool and large outdoor patio and pool area ideal for large groups. **Pros:** convenient location off I–15; some rooms with desert views; two pools; free Wi-Fi. **Cons:** breakfast only with certain room rates; bistro menu options limited. [$] *Rooms from: $136* ✉ *9619 Mariposa Rd., Hesperia* ☎ *760/956–3876* 🌐 *www.marriott.com* 🛏 *123 rooms, 8 suites.*

$ HOTEL FAMILY 🏨 **La Quinta Inn and Suites Victorville.** This small hotel offers a touch more than your typical chain, with contemporary decor in cozy earth tones and spacious rooms. **Pros:** near shopping mall; helpful staff; hot breakfast; outdoor pool and Jacuzzi. **Cons:** some freeway noise. [$] *Rooms from: $109* ✉ *12000 Mariposa Rd., Hesperia* ☎ *760/949–9900* 🌐 *www.lq.com* 🛏 *53 rooms, 22 suites* 🍽 *Breakfast.*

BARSTOW

32 miles northeast of Victorville.

Barstow was born in 1886, when a subsidiary of the Atchison, Topeka, and Santa Fe Railway began construction of a Harvey House depot and hotel here. The depot has been restored and includes two free museums, the family-friendly Calico Ghost Town is just north of town, and there are well-known chain motels and restaurants right off Interstate 15 if you need a rest and refuel before the next stop.

GETTING HERE AND AROUND

Driving here on Interstate 15 from Los Angeles or Las Vegas is the best option, although you can reach Barstow via Amtrak or Greyhound. The local bus service is helpful for sights downtown.

ESSENTIALS

Transportation Information **Barstow Area Transit/Victor Valley Transit.** ☎ *760/948–3030* 🌐 *vvta.org.*

Many of the buildings in the popular Calico Ghost Town are authentic.

Visitor Information Barstow Area Chamber of Commerce and Visitors Bureau. ⊠ 229 E. Main St. ☎ 760/256–8617 ⊕ www.barstowchamber. com. **California Welcome Center.** ⊠ 2796 Tanger Way, Suite 100, off Lenwood Rd. ☎ 760/253–4782 ⊕ www.visitcalifornia.com/attraction/ california-welcome-center-barstow.

EXPLORING
TOP ATTRACTIONS

FAMILY **Calico Ghost Town.** This former silver-mining boom town was started in
Fodor's Choice 1881 and within a few years boasted 500 mines and 22 saloons. Its recon-
★ struction by Walter Knott of Knott's Berry Farm makes it more about G-rated family entertainment than the town's gritty past, but that doesn't seem to take away from the fun of panning for (fool's) gold, touring the original tunnels of Maggie Mine or taking a leisurely ride on the Calico Odessa Railroad. Five of the original buildings are still standing, such as the impressive Lane's General Store, and its setting among the stark beauty of the Calico Hills can make a stroll along this once-bustling Main Street downright peaceful. ■TIP→ Calico also has ghost tours and regular events such as the yearly bluegrass festival on Mother's Day weekend. ⊠ 36600 Ghost Town Rd., off I–15, Yermo ☎ 760/254–2122 ⊕ cms. sbcounty.gov/parks/Parks/CalicoGhostTown.aspx ⊠ $8.

Casa Del Desierto Harvey House. This historic train depot was built around 1911 (the original 1885 structure was destroyed by fire) and was one of the original Harvey Houses, providing dining and lodging for weary travelers along the rail lines. Waitresses at the depots were popularized in movies such as *The Harvey Girls* with Judy Garland. It now houses offices and two museums: the Western American Railroad and Route 66

Mother Road, but you can still walk along the porticos of the impressive Spanish Renaissance Classical building, or stroll into the restored lobby where you'll find the original staircase, terrazzo floor, and copper chandeliers. ⊠ *681 N. 1st Ave., near Riverside Dr.* ☎ *760/255–1890 Route 66 museum* ⊕ *www.barstowharveyhouse.com.*

FAMILY
Fodor'sChoice
★

Goldstone Deep Space Communications Complex. Friendly and enthusiastic staffers conduct guided tours of this 53-square-mile complex. Tours start at the Goldstone Museum, where exhibits detail past and present space missions and Deep Space Network history. From there, you'll drive out to see the massive concave antennas, starting with those used for early manned space flights and culminating with the 24-story-tall "listening" device. This is one of only three complexes in the world that make up the Deep Space Network, tracking and communicating with spacecraft throughout our solar system. ■**TIP➔** Appointments are required; contact the complex to reserve a slot. ⊠ *Ft. Irwin Military Base, Ft. Irwin Rd. off I–15, 35 miles north of Barstow* ☎ *760/255– 8688* ⊕ *www.gdscc.nasa.gov.*

Rainbow Basin National Natural Landmark. Many science-fiction movies set on Mars have been filmed at this landmark 8 miles north of Barstow. Huge slabs of red, orange, white, and green stone tilt at crazy angles like ships about to capsize and traces of ancient beasts such as mastodons and bear-dogs, which roamed the basin up to 16 million years ago have been discovered in its fossil beds. The dirt road around the basin is narrow and bumpy so vehicles with higher clearance are recommended and rain can quickly turn the road to mud; at times, only four-wheel-drive vehicles are permitted. ⊠ *Fossil Bed Rd., 3 miles west of Fort Irwin Rd. (head north from I–15)* ☎ *760/252–6000* ⊕ *www.recreation.gov.*

Skyline Drive-In Theatre. Check out a bit of surviving Americana at this dusty drive-in, where you can watch the latest Hollywood flicks among the Joshua trees and starry night sky. Keep in mind the old-time speakers are no more; sound is tuned in via car radio. ⊠ *31175 Old Hwy. 58* ☎ *760/256–3333* 💵 *$9 per person* ⊙ *Closed in winter.*

FAMILY
Western America Railroad Museum. You can almost hear the murmur of passengers and rhythmic, metal-on-metal clatter as you stroll past the old cabooses, railcars and engines, such as Sante Fe number 95, that are on display outside the historic Barstow station where this museum is located. The next stop is the indoor portion of the collection, including a train simulator, rail equipment, model railroad display and other memorabilia. A handful of artifacts from the depot's Harvey House days are on display, as well as period dining-car china from railways around the country. ⊠ *Casa Del Desierto, 685 N. 1st Ave., near Riverside Dr.* ☎ *760/256– 9276* ⊕ *www.barstowrailmuseum.org* ⊙ *Closed Mon.–Thurs.*

WORTH NOTING

Afton Canyon. Because of its colorful, steep walls, Afton Canyon is often called the Grand Canyon of the Mojave. It was carved over thousands of years by the rushing waters of the Mojave River, which makes one of its few aboveground appearances here. The dirt road that leads to the canyon is ungraded in spots, so it is best to explore it in an all-terrain vehicle. ⊠ *Off Afton Rd., 36 miles northeast of Barstow via I–15* ⊕ *www.recreation.gov.*

16

Bagdad Café. Tourists from all over the world flock to this Route 66 eatery where the 1987 film of the same name was shot. Built in the 1940s, the divey Bagdad Café's walls are crammed with memorabilia donated by visitors famous and otherwise. The very limited bill of fare includes the Bagdad omelet and a buffalo burger with fries, but this place is really about soaking up the Route 66-Americana vibe. ✉ *46548 National Trails Hwy., at Nopal La., Newberry Springs* ☎ *760/257–3101.*

FAMILY **Mojave River Valley Museum.** The floor-to-ceiling collection of local history, both quirky and conventional, includes Ice Age fossils such as a giant mammoth tusk dug up in 2006, Native American artifacts, 19th-century handmade quilts, and displays on early settlers. Entrance is free and there's a little gift shop with a nice collection of books about the area. ■ **TIP→ The story about Possum Trot and its population of folk-art dolls is not to be missed.** ✉ *270 E. Virginia Way, at Belinda St.* ☎ *760/256–5452* 🌐 *www.mojaverivervalleymuseum.org.*

WHERE TO EAT AND STAY

$$$ STEAKHOUSE 🍴 **Idle Spurs Steakhouse.** This spacious steak-and-seafood restaurant, with its Western-style memorabilia and cheerful white fairy lights, has been a favorite among locals for decades. The menu is very basic no-frills steakhouse fare, but the service is friendly and it's a bit of cozy, mid-century charm in the middle of the Mojave. **Known for:** locals' favorite ; family run; dated but cozy. [$] *Average main: $24* ✉ *690 Old Hwy. 58, at Camarillo Ave.* ☎ *760/256–8888* 🌐 *thespurs.us* 🕒 *Closed Mon.*

$ AMERICAN FAMILY 🍴 **Peggy Sue's 50s Diner.** Checkerboard floors and life-size versions of Elvis and Marilyn Monroe greet you at this funky '50s coffee shop and pizza parlor in the middle of the Mojave. Outside, kids can play by the duck pond before heading in to spin a tune on the jukebox or order from the soda fountain. **Known for:** movie, TV memorabilia; over-the-top '50s vibe; gift shop. [$] *Average main: $10* ✉ *35654 W. Yermo Rd., at Daggett-Yermo Rd., Yermo* ☎ *760/254–3370* 🌐 *www.peggysuesdiner.com.*

$ AMERICAN 🍴 **Slash X Ranch Cafe.** Known as a favorite stop for off-roaders, this rowdy Wild West-esque watering hole 8 miles south of main street Barstow is named for the cattle ranch that preceded it. Hearty fare such as burgers and giant breakfast burritos are served up here.There's a large outdoor patio area and if you've got the time, try to count the multitude of customer ball caps tacked to the ceiling. **Known for:** cold beer; good-time vibe. [$] *Average main: $10* ✉ *28040 Barstow Rd., at Powerline Rd.* ☎ *760/252–1197* 🌐 *slashxoffroad.com* 🕒 *Closed Mon.–Wed.*

$$ HOTEL 🏨 **Ayres Hotel Barstow.** In a sea of chain hotels this one has a few homespun touches up its sleeves, such as the free on-site dinner on Tuesday and Thursday evening. **Pros:** clean rooms, engaged management; entirely nonsmoking. **Cons:** pricey for Barstow. [$] *Rooms from: $139* ✉ *2812 Lenwood Rd.* ☎ *760/307–3121* 🌐 *www.ayreshotels.com/ayres-hotel-barstow* 🛏 *92 rooms* 🍽 *Breakfast.*

MOJAVE NATIONAL PRESERVE

Visitor center 118 miles east of Barstow, 58 miles west of Needles.

The 1.6 million acres of the Mojave National Preserve hold a surprising abundance of plant and animal life—especially considering their elevation (nearly 8,000 feet in some areas). There are traces of human history here as well, including abandoned army posts and vestiges of mining and ranching towns.

GETTING HERE AND AROUND

A car is the best way to access the preserve, which lies between interstates 15 and 40. Kelbaker Road bisects the park from north to south; northbound from I–40, Essex Road gets you to Hole-in-the-Wall on pavement but is graveled beyond there.

EXPLORING

Hole-in-the-Wall. Created millions of years ago by volcanic activity, Hole-in-the-Wall formed when gases were trapped between layers of deposited ash, rock, and lava; the gas bubbles left holes in the solidified material.

You will encounter one of California's most distinctive hiking experiences here. Proceeding clockwise from a small visitor center, you walk gently down and around a craggy hill, past cacti and fading petroglyphs to Banshee Canyon, whose pockmarked walls resemble Swiss cheese. From there you head back out of the canyon, supporting yourself with widely spaced iron rings (some of which wiggle precariously from their rock moorings) as you ascend a 50-foot incline that deposits you back near the visitor center. The one-hour adventure can be challenging but wholly entertaining. ■ TIP➜ There are no services (gas or food) nearby; be sure to fill your tank and pack some snacks before heading out here. ✉ *Mojave National Preserve* ☎ *760/252–6104* ⊕ *www.nps.gov/moja* ✑ *Free.*

Fodor's Choice
★ **Kelso Dunes.** As you enter the preserve from the south, you'll pass miles of open scrub brush, Joshua trees, and beautiful red-black cinder cones before encountering the Kelso Dunes. These golden, fine-sand slopes cover 70 square miles, reaching heights of 600 feet. You can reach them via a short walk from the main parking area, but be prepared for a serious workout. When you reach the top of a dune, kick a little bit of sand down the lee side and listen to the sand "sing." North of the dunes, in the town of Kelso, is the Mission revival–style **Kelso Depot Visitor Center.** The striking building, which dates to 1923, contains several rooms of desert- and train-themed exhibits. ✉ *For Kelso Depot Visitor Center, take Kelbaker Rd. exit from I–15 (head south 34 miles) or I–40 (head north 22 miles)* ☎ *760/252–6100, 760/252–6108* ⊕ *www.nps.gov/moja* ✑ *Free.*

NEEDLES

150 miles east of Barstow.

Along Route 66 and the Colorado River, Needles is a decent base for exploring Mojave National Preserve and other desert attractions. Founded in 1883, the town, named for the jagged mountain peaks that overlook the city, served as a stop along the Santa Fe railroad line.

GETTING HERE AND AROUND

Greyhound and Amtrak both pass through town daily, though most travelers arrive by car, either via Interstate 40 (east–west) or Highway 95 (north–south). Needles Area Transit is the local bus service.

ESSENTIALS

Bus Information Needles Area Transit. ☎ 866/669–6309 ⊕ www.cityof-needles.com.

Visitor Information Needles Chamber of Commerce. ✉ 100 G St., at Front St. ☎ 760/326–2050 ⊕ www.needleschamber.com.

EXPLORING

FAMILY
Fodor's Choice
★

Havasu National Wildlife Refuge. In 1941, after the construction of Parker Dam, President Franklin D. Roosevelt set aside Havasu National Wildlife Refuge, a 30-mile stretch of land along the Colorado River between Needles and Lake Havasu City. Best seen by boat, this beautiful waterway is punctuated with isolated coves, sandy beaches, and Topock Marsh, a favorite nesting site of herons, egrets, and other waterbirds. You can see wonderful petroglyphs on the rocky red canyon cliffs of Topock Gorge. The refuge has three points that provide boat access to Topock Marsh, though not to the lower Colorado River. ■ TIP→ Spring is by far the best time to visit, as the river is more likely to be robust and wildflowers in bloom. ✉ Off I–40, 13 miles southeast of Needles ☎ 760/326–3853 ⊕ www.fws.gov/refuge/havasu.

OFF THE
BEATEN
PATH

London Bridge. London Bridge dates back to the 1830s when it spanned the River Thames in London, England, then was taken apart in the late 1960s and reconstructed piece-by-piece in, of all places, the planned community of Lake Havasu City, AZ. Today, it is a draw for curious tourists (even Brits who remember it at the original location) and connects the city to a small island. Riverbanks on both sides have numerous restaurants, hotels, and RV parks. ✉ Lake Havasu City ☎ 928/855–4115 ⊕ www.havasuchamber.com.

WHERE TO EAT AND STAY

$
PIZZA

✕ River City Pizza. This inexpensive pizza place off Interstate 40 is a local favorite and offers a range of specialty pies, hearty appetizers, subs and pasta. Top it off with a mug of cold lager, or a glass of wine out on the small patio. **Known for:** locals' favorite; unique pizza menu. $ Average main: $12 ✉ 1901 Needles Hwy. ☎ 760/326–9191 ⊕ www.rivercitypizzaco.com.

$
HOTEL

Best Western Colorado River Inn. One of the best hotels in town, this Best Western offers a handful of larger rooms with pull-out couches, a voucher for a free breakfast at the cafe next door, and an attractive pool area that offers some precious shade. **Pros:** good rates; clean rooms; nice pool. **Cons:** town's dead at night (and not much livelier during the day); occasional train noise. $ Rooms from: $90 ✉ 2371 Needles Hwy. ☎ 760/326–4552, 800/780–7234 ⊕ www.bestwestern.com ⌁ 63 rooms ⦿ Breakfast.

$
RESORT
FAMILY

Fender's River Road Resort. On a calm section of the Colorado River, this funky little 1960s-era Route 66 motel-resort is off the beaten path in a town that's in the proverbial middle of nowhere. **Pros:** on the river; friendly staff; peaceful. **Cons:** several minutes from the freeway; rooms could use refreshing. $ Rooms from: $66 ✉ 3396 Needles Hwy. ☎ 760/326–3423 ⊕ www.fendersresort.com ⌁ 10 rooms, 31 RV sites, 10 campsites.

DEATH VALLEY
NATIONAL PARK

WELCOME TO DEATH VALLEY NATIONAL PARK

TOP REASONS TO GO

★ **Roving rocks:** Death Valley's Racetrack is home to moving boulders, an unexplained phenomenon that has scientists baffled.

★ **Lowest spot on the continent:** Stand on the lowest spot on the continent at Badwater, 282 feet below sea level.

★ **Wildflower explosion:** During the spring, this desert landscape is ablaze with greenery and colorful flowers, especially between Badwater and Ashford Mill.

★ **Ghost towns:** Death Valley is renowned for its Wild West heritage and is home to dozens of crumbling settlements including Ballarat, Cerro Gordo, Chloride City, Greenwater, Harrisburg, Keeler, Leadfield, Panamint City, Rhyolite, and Skidoo.

★ **Naturally amazing:** From canyons to sand dunes to salt flats and dry lake beds, Death Valley serves up plenty of geological treasures.

1 Central Death Valley. Furnace Creek sits in the heart of Death Valley—if you have only a short time in the park, head here. You can visit gorgeous Golden Canyon, Zabriskie Point, the Salt Creek Interpretive Trail, and Artist's Drive, among other popular points of interest.

2 Northern Death Valley. This region is uphill from Furnace Creek, which means marginally cooler temperatures. Be sure to stop by Rhyolite Ghost Town on Highway 374 before entering the park and exploring colorful Titus Canyon, and jaw-dropping Ubehebe Crater.

3 Southern Death Valley. This is a desolate area, but there are plenty of sights that help convey Death Valley's rich history. Don't miss the Dublin Gulch Caves.

4 Western Death Valley.
Panamint Springs Resort is
a nice place to grab a meal
and get your bearings
before moving on to quaint
Darwin Falls, smooth rolling
sand dunes, beehive-
shaped Wildrose Charcoal
Kilns, and historic Stovepipe
Wells Village.

CALIFORNIA

GETTING ORIENTED

Death Valley National Park
covers 5,310 square miles,
ranges from 6 to 60 miles
wide, and measures 140
miles north to south. Within
the park, the Panamint
Range parallels Death Valley
to the west, the Amargosa
Range to the east. Nearly
the entire park lies in southeastern California, with a
small eastern portion crossing over into Nevada.

17

Rhyolite
(ghost town)
Beatty
Titus
Canyon
374
95
TO
LAS VEGAS

AMARGOSA RANGE

DEATH

Historic
Stovepipe Well

Stovepipe Wells
Village

**Salt Creek
Interpretive Trail**

Devil's
Cornfield

Harmony
Borax Works
Interpretive Trail

190

Visitor Center

Furnace Creek

Amargosa
Valley

373

Emigrant
Canyon Rd. Golden Canyon
Interpretive Trail

Artist's Drive

Zabriskie Point
Twenty Mule Team Canyon

Artist's
Palette

190

Death Valley
Junction

Wildrose
Charcoal
Kilns

Devil's
Golf Course

Natural Bridge

Natural Bridge
Canyon

TO
PAHRUMP,
LAS VEGAS

Mahogany
Flat

Badwater

Dante's View

127

VALLEY

Badwater Basin
Lowest elevation in
the U.S., 282 ft.
below sea level

Panamint City
(ghost town)

3

Tint indicates
area below sea level

178

Shoshone

Dublin
Gulch
Caves

Ashford Mill
(ruins)

127

Saratoga
Spring

TO
BAKER &
I-15

Updated by
Steve Pastorino

The desert is no Disneyland. With its scorching summer heat and vast, sparsely populated tracts of land, it's not often at the top of the list when most people plan their California vacations. But the natural riches of Death Valley—the largest national park outside Alaska—are overwhelming: rolling waves of sand dunes, black cinder cones thrusting up hundreds of feet from a blistered desert floor, riotous sheets of wildflowers, bizarrely shaped Joshua trees basking in the orange glow of a sunset, tiny pupfish that enthrall youngsters, and a silence that is both dramatic and startling.

PLANNING

WHEN TO GO

Most of the park's one million annual visitors come between late fall and early spring, taking advantage of moderate temperatures and the lack of rainfall. During these cooler months you will need to book a room in advance, but don't worry: the park never feels crowded. If you visit in summer, believe everything you've ever heard about desert heat—it can be brutal, with temperatures often topping 120°F. The dry air wicks moisture from the body without causing a sweat, so drink plenty of water. Bring sunglasses, a hat, and sufficient clothing to block the sun's rays and the wind. Flash floods are fairly common; sections of roadway can be flooded or washed away, as they were after a major flood in 2015. The wettest month is February, when the park receives an average of 0.3 inch of rain.

FESTIVALS AND EVENTS
MAY
Bishop Mule Days. Entertainment at this five-day festival over the Memorial Day weekend includes top country-music stars, an arts-and-crafts fair, barbecues, country dances, the longest-running nonmotorized parade in the U.S., and more than 700 mules competing in 181 events. Admission is free. ⊠ *1141 N. Main St., Bishop* ☎ *760/872–4263* ⊕ *www.muledays.org.*

PLANNING YOUR TIME
DEATH VALLEY IN ONE DAY
If you begin the day in Furnace Creek, you can see several sights without doing much driving. Bring plenty of water with you, and some food, too. Get up early and drive the 20 miles on Badwater Road to **Badwater,** which looks out on the lowest point in the Western Hemisphere and is a dramatic place to watch the sunrise. Returning north, stop at **Natural Bridge,** a medium-size conglomerate rock formation that has been hollowed at its base to form a span across the canyon, and then at the **Devil's Golf Course,** so named because of the large pinnacles of salt present here. Detour to the right onto **Artist's Drive,** a 9-mile one-way, northbound route that passes **Artist's Palette.** The reds, yellows, oranges, and greens come from minerals in the rocks and the earth. Four miles north of Artist's Drive you will come to the **Golden Canyon Interpretive Trail,** a 2-mile round-trip that winds through a canyon with colorful rock walls. Just before Furnace Creek, take Highway 190 3 miles east to **Zabriskie Point,** overlooking dramatic, furrowed red-brown hills and the **Twenty Mule Team Canyon.** Return to Furnace Creek, where you can grab a meal and visit the museum at the Furnace Creek Visitor Center. Heading north from Furnace Creek, pull off the highway and take a look at the **Harmony Borax Works.**

GETTING HERE AND AROUND
AIR TRAVEL
The closest airport to the park with commercial service, Las Vegas McCarren International Airport, is 130 miles away, so you'll still need to drive a couple of hours to reach the park. Roughly 160 miles to the west, Burbank's Bob Hope Airport is the second-closest airport.

CAR TRAVEL
It can take more than three hours to cross from one side of the park to another, so it's important to choose an entrance point that makes sense for what you want to see. If you're driving from Los Angeles, enter through the western portion along Highway 395; if you're coming from Las Vegas, enter from the north at Beatty, Nevada, or via the central entrance at Death Valley Junction. Travelers from Orange County, San Diego, and the Inland Empire should access the park via Interstate 15 North at Baker.

Distances can be deceiving within the park: what seems close can be very far away. Much of the park can be viewed on regularly scheduled bus tours, but these often don't allow time for hikes to sites not seen from the road, such as Salt Creek, Golden Canyon, and Natural Bridge. The best option is to drive to a number of the sites, get out of the car, and walk.

17

When driving in Death Valley, reliable maps are important, as signage is often limited or, in a few places, nonexistent. Bring a phone but don't rely on cell coverage exclusively in every remote area, and pack plenty of food and water (3 gallons per person per day is recommended). Cars, especially in summer, should be prepared for the hot, dry weather too. Some of the park's most spectacular canyons are only accessible via four-wheel-drive vehicles but if this is the way you want to travel, make sure the trip is well-planned and use a backcountry map. Be aware of possible winter closures or driving restrictions because of snow. The National Park Service's website (⊕ *nps.gov/deva*) stays up-to-date on road closures during the wet (and popular) months. ⚠ One of the park's signature landmarks, Scotty's Castle, and the eight-mile road connecting it to the park border may be closed until 2019 due to damage from a 2015 flood.

Driving Information California Highway Patrol. ☎ *800/427–7623 recorded info from CalTrans, 760/872–5900 live dispatcher at Bishop Communications Center* ⊕ *www.chp.ca.gov.* **California State Department of Transportation Hotline.** ☎ *800/427–7623* ⊕ *www.dot.ca.gov.*

PARK ESSENTIALS
PARK FEES AND PERMITS
The entrance fee is $25 per vehicle and $12 for those entering on foot or bike. The payment, valid for seven consecutive days, is collected at the park's ranger stations, self-serve fee stations, and the visitor center at Furnace Creek. Annual park passes, valid only at Death Valley, are $50.

A permit is not required for groups of 14 or fewer, but if you're planning an overnight visit to the backcountry, complete a registration form at the Furnace Creek Visitor Center. Backcountry camping is allowed in areas that are at least 2 miles from maintained campgrounds and the main paved or unpaved roads and ¼ mile from water sources. Most abandoned mining areas are restricted to day use.

PARK HOURS
The park is open year-round, and can be visited day or night. Most facilities within the park remain open year-round, daily 8–6.

CELL-PHONE RECEPTION
Results vary, but in general you should be able to get fairly good cell-phone reception on the valley floor. In the surrounding mountains, however, don't count on it.

EDUCATIONAL OFFERINGS
RANGER PROGRAMS
FAMILY **Junior Ranger Program.** Children can join this program at any of the three visitor centers, where they can pick up a workbook and complete up to 15 projects (based on their age) to earn a souvenir badge. ✉ *Death Valley National Park.*

RESTAURANTS
Inside the park, if you're looking for a special evening out in Death Valley, head to the Inn at Death Valley Dining Room, where you'll be spoiled with fine wines and juicy steaks. It's also a great spot to start the day with a hearty gourmet breakfast. Most other eateries within

the park are mom-and-pop-type places with basic American fare. Outside the park, dining choices are much the same, with little cafés and homey diners serving up coffee shop–style burgers, chicken, and steaks. If you're vegetarian or vegan, BYOB (bring your own beans).

HOTELS

It's difficult to find lodging anywhere in Death Valley that doesn't have breathtaking views of the park and surrounding mountains. Most accommodations, aside from the Inn at Death Valley, are homey and rustic. Rooms fill up quickly during the fall and spring seasons, and reservations are required about three months in advance for the prime weekends.

Outside the park, head to Beatty or Amargosa Valley in Nevada for a bit of nightlife and casino action. The western side of Death Valley, along the eastern Sierra Nevada, is a gorgeous setting, though it's quite a distance from Furnace Creek. Here, you can stay in the historic Dow Villa Motel, where John Wayne spent many a night, or head farther south to the ghost towns of Randsburg or Cerro Gordo for a true Wild West experience. *Hotel reviews have been shortened. For full information, visit Fodors.com.*

WHAT IT COSTS				
	$	$$	$$$	$$$$
Restaurants	under $12	$12–$20	$21–$30	over $30
Hotels	under $100	$100–$150	$151–$200	over $200

Restaurant prices are the average cost of a main course at dinner, or if dinner is not served, at lunch. Hotel prices are the lowest cost of a standard double room in high season.

17

TOURS

Death Valley Adventure Tour (*Adventure Motorcycle [AdMo] Tours*). Motorcycle enthusiasts can sign up for a guided Death Valley Adventure Tour that starts and ends in Las Vegas. The five-day tour through Death Valley covers 800 miles. The tours, which run October through May, include hotel accommodations, gasoline, breakfasts, two dinners, snacks, a support vehicle, and a professional guide. To join, you'll need a motorcycle driver's license and experience with off-road and all-terrain riding. ⌧ *Death Valley* ☏ *760/249–1105* ⊕ *www.admotours.com* ✉ *From $3,568.*

Furnace Creek Visitor Center programs. This center has many programs, including ranger-led hikes that explore natural wonders such as Golden Canyon, nighttime stargazing parties with telescopes, and evening ranger talks. There are also occasional programs at the Borax Museum at Furnace Creek Ranch and the historic Harmony Borax Works mining site, first established in 1883. Visit the website for a complete list. ⌧ *Furnace Creek Visitor Center, Rte. 190, 30 miles northwest of Death Valley Junction, Death Valley* ☏ *760/786–2331* ⊕ *www.nps.gov/deva/ planyourvisit/tours.htm* ✉ *Free.*

Pink Jeep Tours Las Vegas. A 10-passenger luxury vehicle with oversized viewing windows will pick you up at most Strip hotels for visits to landmarks such as Dante's Peak, Furnace Creek, Devil's Golf Course, and Zabriskie Point. The tours run from about 7 am to 4 pm from September through May, are professionally narrated, and include lunch and bottled water. ✉ *3629 W. Hacienda Ave., Las Vegas* ☎ *888/900–4480* ⊕ *pinkjeeptourslasvegas.com* ✉ *From $275.*

VISITOR INFORMATION

Park Contact Information Death Valley National Park. ☎ *760/786–3200* ⊕ *www.nps.gov/deva.*

VISITOR CENTERS

⚠ The popular visitor center at Scotty's Castle is closed until at least 2019 as a result of a major flash flood in 2015 that damaged the structure and destroyed the access road.

Furnace Creek Visitor Center and Museum. The exhibits and artifacts here provide a broad overview of how Death Valley formed; you can pick up maps at the bookstore run by the Death Valley Natural History Association. This is also the place to sign up for ranger-led walks (available November through April) or check out a live presentation about the valley's cultural and natural history. The helpful center offers regular showings of a 20-minute film about the park and children can get their free Junior Ranger booklet here, packed with games and information about the park and its critters. ✉ *Hwy. 190, Death Valley* ✛ *30 miles northwest of Death Valley Junction* ☎ *760/786–3200* ⊕ *www.nps.gov/deva.*

EXPLORING

SCENIC DRIVE

Artist's Drive. This 9-mile, one-way route skirts the foothills of the Black Mountains and provides intimate views of the changing landscape. Once inside the palette, the huge expanses of the valley are replaced by the small-scale natural beauty of pigments created by volcanic deposits or sedimentary layers. It's a quiet, lonely drive, and shouldn't be rushed. Reach Artist's Palette by heading south on Badwater Road from its intersection with Route 190. ✉ *Death Valley National Park.*

HISTORIC SITES

Charcoal Kilns. Ten well-preserved stone kilns, each 25 feet high and 30 feet wide, stand as if on parade. The kilns, built by Chinese laborers for a mining company in 1877, were used to burn wood from pinyon pines to turn it into charcoal. The charcoal was then transported over the mountains into Death Valley, where it was used to extract lead and silver from the ore mined there. If you hike nearby Wildrose Peak, you will be rewarded with terrific views of the kilns. ✉ *Wildrose Canyon Rd., Death Valley* ✛ *37 miles south of Stovepipe Wells.*

CLOSE UP

Plants and Wildlife in Death Valley

There's a general misconception that Death Valley National Park consists of mile upon endless mile of flat desert sands, scattered cacti, and an occasional cow skull. Many people don't realize that across the valley floor from Badwater—the lowest point in the Western Hemisphere—Telescope Peak towers at 11,049 feet above sea level. The extreme topography of Death Valley is a lesson in geology. Two hundred million years ago seas covered the area, depositing layers of sediment and fossils. Between 3.5 million and 5 million years ago faults in the Earth's crust and volcanic activity pushed and folded the ground, causing mountain ranges to rise and the valley floor to drop. The valley was then filled periodically by lakes, which eroded the surrounding rocks into fantastic formations and deposited the salts that now cover the floor of the basin.

Most animal life in Death Valley (51 mammal, 36 reptile, 307 bird, and 3 amphibian species) is found near the limited sources of water. The bighorn sheep spend most of their time in the secluded upper reaches of the park's rugged canyons and ridges. Coyotes often can be seen lazing in the shade next to the golf course and have been known to run onto the fairways to steal a golf ball. The only native fish in the park is the pupfish, which grows to slightly longer than one inch. In winter, when the water is cold, the fish lie dormant in the bottom mud, becoming active again in spring. Because they are wary of large moving shapes, you must stand quietly over a pool at Salt Creek to see them.

Botanists say there are more than 1,000 species of plants here (21 exist nowhere else in the world), though many annual plants lie dormant as seeds for all but a few months in spring, when rains trigger a bloom. The rest congregate around the few water sources. Most of the low-elevation vegetation grows around the oases at Furnace Creek and Scotty's Castle, where oleanders, palms, and salt cedar grow. At higher elevations you will find pinyon, juniper, and bristlecone pine.

17

Harmony Borax Works. Death Valley's mule teams hauled borax from here to the railroad town of Mojave, 165 miles away. The teams plied the route until 1889, when the railroad finally arrived in Zabriskie. Constructed in 1883, one of the oldest buildings in Death Valley houses the Borax Museum, 2 miles south of the borax works at the Inn at Furnace Creek (between the restaurants and the post office). Originally a miners' bunkhouse, the building once stood in Twenty Mule Team Canyon. Now it displays mining machinery and historical exhibits. The adjacent structure is the original mule-team barn. ⊠ *Harmony Borax Works Rd., west of Hwy. 190, 2 miles north of Furnace Creek* ⊕ *www. nps.gov/deva/historyculture/harmony.htm.*

FAMILY
Fodor's Choice
★

Scotty's Castle. This Moorish-style mansion, begun in 1924 and never completed, takes its name from Walter Scott, better known as Death Valley Scotty. An ex-cowboy, prospector, and performer in Buffalo Bill's Wild West Show, Scotty always told people the castle was his, financed by gold from a secret mine. In reality, there was no mine, and the house belonged to a Chicago millionaire named Albert Johnson, whom Scott had finagled into investing in the fictitious mine. Despite the con, Johnson and Scott became great friends. The house functioned for a while as a hotel and still contains works of art, imported carpets, handmade European furniture, and a tremendous pipe organ. ⚠ **The structure and its access road were significantly damaged during a flash flood in 2015 and are closed to the public until at least 2019.** ⊠ *Scotty's Castle Rd. (Hwy. 267), Death Valley ✛ 53 miles north of Salt Creek Interpretive Trail* ☏ *760/786–2392* ⊕ *www.nps.gov/deva* 🎫 *$15.*

SCENIC STOPS

Artist's Palette. So called for the contrasting colors of its volcanic deposits and sedimentary layers, this is one of the signature sights of Death Valley. Artist's Drive, the approach to the area, is one-way heading north off Badwater Road, so if you're visiting Badwater from Furnace Creek, come here on the way back. The drive winds through foothills of sedimentary and volcanic rocks. About 4 miles into the drive, a short side road veers right to a parking lot that's a few hundred feet before the "palette," whose natural colors include shades of green, gold, and pink. ⊠ *Off Badwater Rd., Death Valley ✛ 11 miles south of Furnace Creek.*

Badwater. At 282 feet below sea level, Badwater is the lowest spot on land in North America—and also one of the hottest. Stairs and wheelchair ramps descend from the parking lot to a wooden platform that overlooks a sodium chloride pool, a small but remarkably persistent reminder that the valley floor used to contain a lake. You can continue past the platform on a broad, white path that peters out after a half mile or so. Badwater is one of the most popular and easily accessible sites within the park. From this lowest point, be sure to look across to Telescope Peak, which towers more than 2 miles above the valley floor. ⊠ *Badwater Rd., Death Valley ✛ 19 miles south of Furnace Creek.*

Fodor's Choice
★

Dante's View. This lookout is 5,450 feet above sea level in the Black Mountains. In the dry desert air you can see across most of 160-mile-long Death Valley. The view is astounding. Take a 10-minute, mildly strenuous walk from the parking lot toward a series of rocky overlooks, where with binoculars you can spot some of Death Valley's signature sites. A few interpretive signs point out the highlights below in the valley and across, in the Sierra. Getting here from Furnace Creek takes about an hour—time well invested. ⊠ *Dante's View Rd., Death Valley ✛ Off Hwy. 190, 35 miles from Badwater, 20 miles south of Twenty Mule Team Canyon.*

Devil's Golf Course. Thousands of miniature salt pinnacles carved into surreal shapes by the desert wind dot this wildly varied landscape. The salt was pushed up to the earth's surface by pressure created as underground salt- and water-bearing gravel crystallized. Get out of your vehicle and take a closer look; you'll see perfectly round holes descending into the ground. ⊠ *Badwater Rd., Death Valley ✛ 13 miles south of Furnace Creek. Turn right onto dirt road and drive 1 mile.*

Golden Canyon. Just South of Furnace Creek, these glimmering mountains are perhaps best known for their role in the original *Star Wars.* The canyon is also a fine hiking spot, with gorgeous views of the Panamint Mountains, ancient dry lake beds, and alluvial fans. ⊠ *Hwy. 178, Death Valley ⊹ From the Furnace Creek Visitor Center, drive 2 miles south on Hwy. 190, then 2 miles south on Hwy. 178 to the parking area. The lot has a kiosk with trail guides.*

Racetrack. Getting here involves a 28-mile journey over a rough dirt road, but the reward is well worth the trip. Where else in the world do rocks move on their own? This phenomenon has baffled scientists for years and is perhaps one of the last great natural mysteries. The best research on the rocks shows the movement requires a rare confluence of conditions: rain and then cold to create a layer of ice that becomes a sail for gusty winds that push the rocks along—sometimes for several hundred yards. When the mud dries, a telltale trail remains. The trek to the Racetrack can be made in a sedan, but beware—sharp rocks can slash tires; a truck or SUV with thick tires, high clearance, and a spare tire are suggested. ⊠ *Death Valley ⊹ 27 miles west of Ubehebe Crater via dirt road.*

Sand Dunes at Mesquite Flat. These dunes, made up of minute pieces of quartz and other rock, are ever-changing products of the wind-rippled hills, with curving crests and a sun-bleached hue. The dunes are the most photographed destination in the park, and you can see them at their best at sunrise and sunset. Keep your eyes open for animal tracks—you may even spot a coyote or fox. Bring plenty of water, and note where you parked your car: It's easy to become disoriented in this ocean of sand. If you lose your bearings, climb to the top of a dune and scan the horizon for the parking lot. ⊠ *Death Valley ⊹ 19 miles north of Hwy. 190, northeast of Stovepipe Wells Village.*

Stovepipe Wells Village. This tiny 1926 town, the first resort in Death Valley, takes its name from the stovepipe that an early prospector left to indicate where he found water. The area contains a motel, restaurant, convenience store, RV hookups, swimming pool, and landing strip, though first-time park visitors are better off staying in Furnace Creek, which is more central. Off Highway 190, on a 3-mile gravel road immediately southwest, are the multicolor walls of Mosaic Canyon. ⊠ *Hwy. 190, Death Valley ⊹ 2 miles from Sand Dunes, 77 miles east of Lone Pine* ☎ *760/786–2387* ⊕ *www.deathvalleyhotels.com.*

Titus Canyon. This popular one-way, 27-mile drive starts at Nevada Highway 374 (Daylight Pass Road), 2 miles from the park's boundary. Along the way you'll see Leadville Ghost Town and finally the spectacular limestone and dolomite narrows. Toward the end, a two-way section of gravel road leads you into the mouth of the canyon from Scotty's Castle Road. This drive is steep, bumpy, and narrow. High-clearance vehicles are strongly recommended. ⊠ *Death Valley National Park ⊹ Access road off Nevada Hwy. 374, 6 miles west of Beatty, NV.*

Twenty Mule Team Canyon. This canyon was named in honor of the 20-mule teams that, between 1883 and 1889, carried 10-ton loads of borax through the burning desert (though they didn't actually pass through this canyon). Along the 2.7-mile, one-way loop road off

DID YOU KNOW?

One of the best ways to experience Artist's Palette—a beautiful landscape of colorful mineral deposits—is by following Artist's Drive, a 9-mile one-way road through the area.

Highway 190, you'll find the soft rock walls reach high on both sides, making it seem like you're on an amusement-park ride. Remains of prospectors' tunnels are visible here, along with some brilliant rock formations. ⊠ *20 Mule Team Rd.* ✛ *Off Hwy. 190, 4 miles south of Furnace Creek, 20 miles west of Death Valley Junction.*

Ubehebe Crater. At 500 feet deep and ½ mile across, this crater resulted from underground steam and gas explosions about 3,000 years ago. Volcanic ash spreads out over most of the area, and the cinders lie as deep as 150 feet, near the crater's rim. Trek down to the crater's floor or walk around it on a fairly level path. Either way, you need about an hour and will be treated to fantastic views. The hike from the floor can be strenuous. ⊠ *N. Death Valley Hwy., Death Valley* ✛ *8 miles northwest of Scotty's Castle.*

Zabriskie Point. Although only about 710 feet in elevation, this is one of Death Valley National Park's most scenic spots, overlooking a striking panorama of wrinkled, multicolor hills. It's a great place to watch the sunrise, but it can be bustling any time of day. Pair it with a drive out to magnificent Dante's View. ⊠ *Hwy. 190, Death Valley* ✛ *5 miles south of Furnace Creek.*

SPORTS AND THE OUTDOORS

BICYCLING

Mountain biking is permitted on any of the back roads and roadways open to the public (bikes aren't permitted on hiking trails). Visit ⊕ *www.nps.gov/deva/planyourvisit/bikingandmtbiking.htm* for a list of suggested routes for all levels of ability. Bicycle Path, a 4-mile round-trip trek from the visitor center to Mustard Canyon, is a good place to start. Bike rentals are available at the Oasis at Death Valley, by the hour or by the day.

TOURS AND OUTFITTERS

Escape Adventures (*Escape Adventures*). Mountain bike into the heart of Death Valley on the Spirit of the Mojave Mountain Bike Adventure, a six-day trip through the national park. The 110-mile journey (on single-track trails) includes accommodations (both camping and inns). Bikes, tents, sleeping bags, helmets, and other gear may be rented for an additional price. Tours are available February–April and October only. ⊠ *Death Valley National Park* ☎ *800/596–2953, 702/838–6966* ⊕ *www.escapeadventures.com* ⊑ *From $1,190.*

BIRD-WATCHING

Approximately 350 bird species have been identified in Death Valley. The best place to see the park's birds is along the Salt Creek Interpretive Trail, where you can spot ravens, common snipes, killdeer, spotted sandpipers, and great blue herons. Along the fairways at Furnace Creek Golf Course, you can see kingfishers, peregrine falcons, hawks, Canada geese, yellow warblers, and the occasional golden eagle. Scotty's Castle, closed until at least 2019, draws wintering birds from around the globe that are attracted to its running water, shady trees, and shrubs. Other good spots to find birds are at Saratoga Springs, Mesquite Springs, Travertine Springs, and Grimshaw Lake near Tecopa.

You can download a complete park bird checklist, divided by season, at ⊕ *www.nps.gov/deva/learn/nature/upload/death-valley-bird-checklist. pdf.* Rangers at Furnace Creek Visitor Center often lead birding walks through various locations between November and March.

FOUR-WHEELING

Maps and SUV guidebooks for four-wheel-drive and other backcountry roads (including the popular Cottonwood/Marble canyons, Racetrack, Eureka Dunes, Saratoga Springs, and Warm Springs Canyon) are offered at the Furnace Creek Visitor Center. Remember: never travel alone and be sure to pack plenty of water and snacks. The park recommends checking ⊕ *www.nps.gov/deva/planyourvisit/backcountryroads. htm* for back-road conditions before setting out. Driving off established roads is strictly prohibited in the park.

ROADS

Butte Valley. This 21-mile road in the southwest part of the park climbs from 200 feet below sea level to an elevation of 4,700 feet. The geological formations along the drive reveal the development of Death Valley. ☒ *Trailhead on Warm Spring Canyon Rd., Death Valley ✛ 50 miles south of Furnace Creek Visitor Center.*

Warm Springs Canyon. If you have a four-wheel-drive vehicle and nerves of steel, this route takes you past Warm Springs talc mine and through Butte Valley, over Mengel Pass and toward **Geologists Cabin,** a charming and cheery little cabin where you can spend the night, if nobody else beats you to it. The park suggests checking their website or asking a ranger to check current conditions on all backcountry roads. The cabin, which sits under a cottonwood tree, has a fireplace, table and chairs, and a sink. Farther up the road, the cabins at Mengel's Home and Russell Camp are also open for public use. Keep the historic cabins clean and restock any items that you use. ☒ *Warm Springs Canyon Rd., off Hwy. 190/Badwater Rd., Death Valley.*

GOLF

Furnace Creek Golf Course. Golfers rave about how their drives carry at altitude, so what happens on the lowest golf course in the world (214 feet below sea level)? Its improbably green fairways are lined with date palms and tamarisk trees, and its level of difficulty is rated surprisingly high. You can rent clubs and carts, and there are golf packages available for The Oasis at Death Valley guests. In winter, reservations are essential. ☒ *Hwy. 190, Furnace Creek* ☎ *760/786–2301* ⊕ *www. oasisatdeathvalley.com* ☒ *From $35* ⅂ *18 holes, 6215 yards, par 70.*

17

HIKING

Plan to hike before or after midday in the spring, summer, or fall, unless you're in the mood for a masochistic baking. Carry plenty of water, wear protective clothing, and keep an eye out for black widows, scorpions, snakes, and other potentially dangerous creatures. Some of the best trails are unmarked; if the opportunity arises, ask for directions.

EASY

FAMILY
Fodor's Choice
★

Darwin Falls. This lovely 2-mile round-trip hike rewards you with a refreshing year-round waterfall surrounded by thick vegetation and a rocky gorge. No swimming or bathing is allowed, but it's a beautiful place for a picnic. Adventurous hikers can scramble higher toward more rewarding views of the falls. *Easy.* ⊠ *Death Valley National Park* ⊹ *Trailhead: access the 2-mile graded dirt road and parking area off Hwy. 190, 1 mile west of Panamint Springs Resort.*

Natural Bridge Canyon. A rough 2-mile access road from Badwater Road leads to a trailhead. From there, set off to see interesting geological features in addition to the bridge, which is ¼ mile away. The one-way trail continues for a few hundred meters, but scenic returns diminish quickly and eventually you're confronted with climbing boulders. *Easy.* ⊠ *Death Valley* ⊹ *Trailhead: access road off Badwater Rd., 15 miles south of Furnace Creek.*

FAMILY
Salt Creek Interpretive Trail. This trail, a ½-mile boardwalk circuit, loops through a spring-fed wash. The nearby hills are brown and gray, but the floor of the wash is alive with aquatic plants such as pickleweed and salt grass. The stream and ponds here are among the few places in the park to see the rare pupfish, the only native fish species in Death Valley. Animals such as bobcats, fox, coyotes, and snakes visit the spring, and you may also see ravens, common snipes, killdeer, and great blue herons. *Easy.* ⊠ *Death Valley* ⊹ *Trailhead: off Hwy. 190, 14 miles north of Furnace Creek.*

MODERATE

Fall Canyon. This is a 3-mile, one-way hike from the Titus canyon parking area. First, walk ½ mile north along the base of the mountains to a large wash, then go 2½ miles up the canyon to a 35-foot dry fall. You can continue by climbing around to the falls on the south side. *Moderate.* ⊠ *Death Valley National Park* ⊹ *Trailhead: access road off Scotty's Castle Rd., 33 miles northwest of Furnace Creek.*

FAMILY
Mosaic Canyon. A gradual uphill trail (4 miles round-trip) winds through the smoothly polished, marbleized limestone walls of this narrow canyon. There are dry falls to climb at the upper end. *Moderate.* ⊠ *Death Valley* ⊹ *Trailhead: access road off Hwy. 190, ½ mile west of Stovepipe Wells Village.*

DIFFICULT

Fodor's Choice
★

Telescope Peak Trail. The 14-mile round-trip (with 3,000 feet of elevation gain) begins at Mahogany Flat Campground, which is accessible by a rough dirt road. The steep and at some points treacherous trail winds through pinyon, juniper, and bristlecone pines, with excellent views of Death Valley and Panamint Valley. Ice axes and crampons may be necessary in winter—check at the Furnace Creek Visitor Center. It takes a minimum of six grueling hours to hike to the top of the 11,049-foot peak and then return. Getting to the peak is a strenuous endeavor; take plenty of water and only attempt it in fall unless you're an experienced hiker. *Difficult.* ✉ *Death Valley* ✣ *Trailhead: off Wildrose Rd., south of Charcoal Kilns.*

HORSEBACK AND CARRIAGE RIDES

TOURS AND OUTFITTERS

FAMILY **Furnace Creek Stables.** Set off on a one- or two-hour guided horseback, carriage, or haywagon ride from Furnace Creek Stables. The rides traverse trails with views of the surrounding mountains, where multicolor volcanic rock and alluvial fans form a background for date palms and other vegetation. Evening carriage rides take passengers around the golf course and The Ranch at Death Valley. The stables are open October–May only. ✉ *Hwy. 190, Furnace Creek* ☎ *760/614–1018* 🌐 *www.furnacecreekstables.net* 🎟 *From $55.*

SHOPPING

Experienced desert travelers carry a cooler stocked with food and beverages. You're best off replenishing your food stash in Ridgecrest, Barstow, or Pahrump, larger towns that have a better selection and nontourist prices.

Ranch General Store. This convenience store carries groceries, souvenirs, camping supplies, and other basics. ✉ *Hwy. 190, Furnace Creek* ☎ *760/786–2345* 🌐 *www.oasisatdeathvalley.com/activities/shopping/.*

17

WHERE TO EAT

$ AMERICAN 🍴 **19th Hole.** Next to the clubhouse of the world's lowest golf course, this open-air spot serves hamburgers, hot dogs, chicken, and sandwiches. The full-service bar has a drive-through service for golfers in carts. **Known for:** kielbasa dog; breakfast burrito; golf cart drive-through. [$] *Average main: $8* ✉ *Furnace Creek Golf Course, Hwy. 190, Furnace Creek* ☎ *760/786–2345* 🌐 *www.oasisatdeathvalley.com/dining/* ⏲ *Closed mid-May–mid-Oct. No dinner.*

$$$$ AMERICAN Fodor's Choice ★ 🍴 **Inn at Death Valley Dining Room.** Fireplaces, beamed ceilings, and spectacular views provide a visual feast to match this fine-dining restaurant's ambitious menu. Dinner entrées include fare such as salmon, free-range chicken, and filet mignon, and there's a seasonal menu of vegetarian dishes. **Known for:** views of surrounding desert; old-school charm; can be pricey. [$] *Average main: $38* ✉ *Inn at Death Valley, Hwy. 190, Furnace Creek* ☎ *760/786–3385* 🌐 *www.furnacecreekresort.com* ⏲ *Closed mid-May–mid-Oct.*

$$ AMERICAN 🍴 **Panamint Springs Resort Restaurant.** This is a great place for steak and a beer—choose from more than 150 different beers and ales—or pasta and a salad. In summer, evening meals are served outdoors on the porch, which has spectacular views of Panamint Valley. [$] *Average main: $15* ✉ *Hwy. 190, Death Valley* ✣ *31 miles west of Stovepipe Wells* ☎ *775/482–7680* 🌐 *www.panamintsprings.com/services/dining-bar.*

WHERE TO STAY

For the busy season (November–March) you should make reservations for lodgings within the park several months in advance.

$$$$ HOTEL Fodor's Choice ★ **The Inn at Death Valley.** Built in 1927, and currently undergoing an extensive renovation, this adobe-brick-and-stone lodge in one of the park's greenest oases offers Death Valley's most luxurious accommodations. **Pros:** refined; comfortable; great views. **Cons:** services reduced during low season (July and August); expensive; annoying resort fee. [$] *Rooms from: $499* ✉ *Furnace Creek Village, near intersection of Hwy. 190 and Badwater Rd., Death Valley* ☎ *760/786–2345* 🌐 *www.oasisatdeathvalley.com* 🕒 *Closed mid-May–June and Sept.–mid-Oct.* 🛏 *66 rooms* 🍴 *No meals.*

$ B&B/INN **Panamint Springs Resort.** Ten miles inside the west entrance of the park, this low-key resort overlooks the sand dunes and peculiar geological formations of the Panamint Valley. **Pros:** slow-paced; friendly; peaceful and quiet after sundown. **Cons:** far from the park's main attractions; Internet very limited; most rooms don't have TV. [$] *Rooms from: $94* ✉ *Hwy. 190, Death Valley* ✣ *28 miles west of Stovepipe Wells* ☎ *775/482–7680* 🌐 *www.panamintsprings.com* 🛏 *15 rooms, 5 cabins* 🍴 *No meals.*

$$$$ RESORT **The Ranch at Death Valley.** Originally the crew headquarters for the Pacific Coast Borax Company, the four buildings here have motel-style rooms that are good for families. **Pros:** good family atmosphere; central location. **Cons:** rooms can get hot despite air-conditioning; parking near your room can be problematic. [$] *Rooms from: $279* ✉ *Hwy. 190, Furnace Creek* ☎ *760/786–2345, 800/236-7916* 🌐 *www.oasisatdeathvalley.com* 🛏 *224 rooms* 🍴 *No meals.*

$$ HOTEL **Stovepipe Wells Village.** If you prefer quiet nights and an unfettered view of the night sky and nearby sand dunes and Mosaic Canyon, this property is for you. **Pros:** intimate, relaxed; no big-time partying; authentic desert-community ambience. **Cons:** isolated; cheapest patio rooms very small; limited Wi-Fi access. [$] *Rooms from: $140* ✉ *Hwy. 190, Stovepipe Wells* ☎ *760/786–2387* 🌐 *www.escapetodeathvalley.com* 🛏 *83 rooms* 🍴 *No meals.*

EASTERN SIERRA

WELCOME TO EASTERN SIERRA

TOP REASONS TO GO

★ **Hiking:** Whether you walk the paved loops in the national parks or head off the beaten path into the backcountry, a hike through groves and meadows or alongside streams and waterfalls will allow you to see, smell, and feel nature up close.

★ **Winter fun:** Famous for its incredible snow-pack—some of the deepest in the North American continent—the Sierra Nevada has something for every winter-sports fan.

★ **Live it up:** Mammoth Lakes is eastern California's most exciting resort area.

★ **Road trip heaven:** Legendary Highway 395 is one of California's most scenic byways, and stops in Independence, Lone Pine, Bishop, and Bodie Ghost Town give you a glimpse of Old West history.

★ **Go with the flow:** Fish, float, raft, and row in the abundant lakes, hot springs, creeks, and rivers.

1 Owens Valley. Lying in the shadow of the Eastern Sierra Nevada and Mount Whitney—the tallest peak in the contiguous USA—the stunningly scenic Owens Valley stretches along U.S. 395 from the town of Olancha, in the south, to the Mono–Inyo county line, in the north. The White Mountains border the valley on the east. This high-desert region, with tiny Old West towns and numerous hiking trails and fishing spots, offers many opportunities for off-the-beaten-track adventures in an uncrowded, pristine setting.

2 Mammoth Lakes. A jewel in the vast Eastern Sierra Nevada, the Mammoth Lakes area lies just east of the Sierra crest, on the backside of Yosemite and the Ansel Adams Wilderness. It's a place of rugged beauty, where giant sawtooth mountains drop into the vast deserts of the Great Basin. In winter, 11,053-foot-high Mammoth Mountain offers the finest skiing and snowboarding in California—sometimes as late as June or even July. Once the snows melt, Mammoth transforms itself into a warm-weather playground, with fishing, mountain biking, golfing, hiking, and horseback riding.

Nine deep-blue lakes are spread throughout the Mammoth Lakes Basin, and another 100 lakes dot the surrounding countryside.

GETTING ORIENTED

The transition between Los Angeles and the Mojave Desert and the rugged Eastern Sierra may be the most dramatic in California sightseeing; as you head into the mountains, your temptation to stop the car and gawk will increase with every foot gained in elevation. U.S. 395 is the main north–south road on the eastern side of the Sierra Nevada, at the western edge of the Great Basin, and a gateway to Death Valley National Park. It's one of California's most beautiful highways; plan to snap pictures at roadside pullouts, and be sure to check out the small towns and attractions along the way. Highway 395 is generally open year-round, which gives you easy access to winter sports, spring wildflower viewing, summer hiking, and fall leaf peeping.

18

3 East of Yosemite National Park. The area to the east of Yosemite National Park includes some ruggedly handsome, albeit desolate, terrain, most notably around Mono Lake, just east of Lee Vining. The June Lake Loop area, between Mammoth Lakes and Lee Vining, is often called the "Switzerland of California" for its series of lakes and creeks bordered by towering peaks. Northeast of Lee Vining is Bodie State Historic Park, a well-preserved ghost town that dates back to California's Gold Rush era.

Map labels: Bridgeport, Bodie Ghost Town/State Historic Park, 167, Mono Lake, NEVADA, CALIFORNIA, Lee Vining, 120, June Lake Loop, Inyo National Forest, Mammoth Lakes, Crowley Lake, 6, Mammoth Mountain (11,053 ft.), 395, WHITE MOUNTAINS, Oasis, Bishop, 168, Kaiser Peak, Owens River, SIERRA NEVADA, Big Pine, North Palisade, Kings Canyon National Park, Olancha, Independence, OWENS VALLEY, INYO MOUNTAINS, Death Valley National Park, 198, 243, Lone Pine, Mount Whitney 14,494 ft., Owens Lake (Dry), Sequoia National Park, Woodlake, Three Rivers, Visalia, 198, 190, 136, Exeter, Farmersville, Lindsay, 190, Porterville, 190, 41, 395, 0 20 mi, 0 20 km

Updated
by Cheryl
Crabtree

The Eastern Sierra's granite peaks and giant sequoias bedazzle heart and soul so completely that for many visitors the experience surpasses that at more famous urban attractions. Most of the Sierra's wonders lie within national parks, but outside them deep-blue Mono Lake and its tufa towers never cease to astound. The megaresort Mammoth Lakes, meanwhile, lures skiers and snowboarders in winter and hikers and mountain bikers in summer.

The Eastern Sierra is accessed most easily via Highway 395, which travels the length of the region from the Mojave Desert in the south to Bridgeport in the north. Main towns along the route include Lone Pine, Independence, Bishop, Mammoth Lakes, June Lake, and Lee Vining, a small town at the eastern endpoint of Tioga Road from Yosemite National Park. Pristine lakes and rolling hills outside the parks offer year-round opportunities for rest and relaxation. Or not. In winter the thrill of the slopes—and their relative isolation compared to busy Lake Tahoe—draws a hearty breed of outdoor enthusiasts. In summer a hike through groves and meadows or alongside streams and waterfalls allows you to see, smell, and feel nature up close.

PLANNING

GETTING HERE AND AROUND
AIR TRAVEL
Three main airports provide access to the Eastern Sierra: Fresno Yosemite International (FAT), on the western side, and, on the eastern side, Mammoth–Yosemite (MMH), 6 miles east of Mammoth Lakes, and Reno–Tahoe (RNO), 130 miles north of Mammoth Lakes via U.S. 395. Alaska, Allegiant, American, Delta, Frontier, JetBlue, Southwest, United, and a few other carriers serve Fresno and Reno. Alaska, United, and JetSuiteX serve Mammoth Lakes.

Airports Fresno Yosemite International Airport (*FAT*). ⊠ *5175 E. Clinton Ave., Fresno* ☎ *800/244-2359 automated information, 559/454-2052 terminal info desk* ⊕ *www.flyfresno.com.* **Mammoth Yosemite Airport.** ⊠ *1200 Airport Rd., Mammoth Lakes* ☎ *760/934-2712, 888/466-2666* ⊕ *www.visitmammoth. com/fly.* **Reno-Tahoe International Airport.** ⊠ *2001 E. Plumb La., Reno* ☎ *775/328-6400* ⊕ *www.renoairport.com.*

BUS TRAVEL

Eastern Sierra Transit Authority buses serve Mammoth Lakes, Bishop, and other eastern Sierra towns along Highway 395, from Reno in the north to Lancaster in the south. In summer YARTS (Yosemite Area Regional Transportation System) connects Yosemite National Park with Mammoth Lakes, June Lake, and Lee Vining in the Eastern Sierra, and Central Valley cities and towns in the west, including Fresno and Merced. This is a good option during summer, when parking in Yosemite Valley and elsewhere in the park can be difficult.

Bus Contacts Eastern Sierra Transit Authority. ☎ *760/872-1901 general, 760/924-3184 Mammoth Lakes* ⊕ *www.estransit.com.* **YARTS.** ☎ *877/989-2787, 209/388-9589* ⊕ *www.yarts.com.*

CAR TRAVEL

Interstate 5 and Highway 99 travel north–south along the western side of the Sierra Nevada. U.S. 395 follows a roughly parallel route on the eastern side. In summer, Tioga Pass Road in Yosemite National Park opens to car and bus travel, intersecting with U.S. 395 at Lee Vining.

From San Francisco: Head east on Interstate 80 to Sacramento, then continue on Interstate 80 to U.S. 395, east of Lake Tahoe's north shore, or take U.S. 50 to Lake Tahoe's south shore and continue on 207E to U.S. 305, then head south.

From Los Angeles: Head north on Interstate 5, exiting and continuing north onto Highway 14 and later onto U.S. 395.

■**TIP→** Gas stations are few and far between in the Sierra, so fill your tank when you can. Between October and May heavy snow may cover mountain roads. Always check road conditions before driving. Carry tire chains, and know how to install them. On Interstate 80 and U.S. 50 chain installers assist travelers (for $40), but elsewhere you're on your own.

Travel Reports Caltrans Current Highway Conditions. ☎ *800/427-7623* ⊕ *www.dot.ca.gov.*

TRAIN TRAVEL

Amtrak's daily *San Joaquin* train stops in Fresno and Merced, where you can connect to YARTS for travel to Yosemite National Park and in summer to smaller gateway towns, including Mammoth Lakes, June Lake, and Lee Vining.

Train Contact Amtrak. ☎ *800/872-7245, 215/856-7952 international* ⊕ *www.amtrak.com.*

18

RESTAURANTS

Most small towns in the Sierra Nevada have at least one restaurant. Standard American fare is the norm, but you'll also find sophisticated cuisine. With few exceptions, dress is casual. Local grocery stores and delis stock picnic fixings, good to have on hand should the opportunity for an impromptu meal under giant trees emerge. *Restaurant reviews have been shortened. For full information, visit Fodors.com.*

HOTELS

The lodgings in Mammoth Lakes and nearest Yosemite National Park generally fill up the quickest; book hotels everywhere in the Eastern Sierra well in advance in summer. *Hotel reviews have been shortened. For full information, visit Fodors.com.*

Hotel Contacts Mammoth Reservations. ☎ *800/223–3032* ⊕ *www. mammothreservations.com.*

WHAT IT COSTS			
$	$$	$$$	$$$$
Restaurants	under $16	$16–$22	$23–$30	over $30
Hotels	under $120	$120–$175	$176–$250	over $250

Restaurant prices are the average cost of a main course at dinner or, if dinner is not served, at lunch. Hotel prices are the lowest cost of a standard double room in high season.

TOURS

Mammoth All Weather Shuttle. This outfit operates summer tours from Mammoth Lakes to Yosemite; north to June Lake, Mono Lake, and Bodie Ghost Town; and around the lakes region. The company also transfers passengers from the Mammoth Yosemite Airport into town, drops off and picks up hikers at trailheads, and runs charters to Bishop, Los Angeles, Reno, and Las Vegas airports—useful when inclement weather causes flight cancellations at Mammoth's airport. ⊠ *Mammoth Lakes* ☎ *760/709–2927* ⊕ *www.mawshuttle.com* 🚌 *From $60.*

VISITOR INFORMATION

Eastern Sierra Visitor Center. Pull off the 395 at this one-stop, interagency center for visitor, wilderness, and highway information, plus views of Mount Whitney. You can also pick up wilderness permits, rent or buy bear-resistant food containers, and picnic on the grounds. It's open year-round from 9 to 5 (8 to 5 May–October). ✛ *2 miles south of Lone Pine, at junctions of U.S. Hwy. 395 and CA Hwy. 136* ☎ *760/876–6200* ⊕ *www.fs.usda.gov/recarea/inyo/recarea/?recid=20698.*

Mammoth Lakes Tourism. ⊠ *Mammoth Lakes* ☎ *760/934–2712, 888/466–2666* ⊕ *www.visitmammoth.com.*

Mono County Tourism. ⊠ *Mammoth Lakes* ☎ *800/845–7922* ⊕ *mono-county.org.*

OWENS VALLEY

Along U.S. 395 east of the Sierra Nevada.

In this undervisited region the snowcapped Sierra Nevada range abruptly and majestically rises to the west, and the high desert whistles to the east. In between are a series of roadside towns full of character, history, and outfits that cater to adventurers and other visitors. The best dining and lodging options can be found along U.S. 395 in Lone Pine and Bishop.

LONE PINE

30 miles west of Panamint Valley.

Mt. Whitney towers majestically over this tiny community, which supplied nearby gold- and silver-mining outposts in the 1860s, and for the past century the town has been touched by Hollywood glamour: several hundred movies, TV episodes, and commercials have been filmed here.

GETTING HERE AND AROUND

Arrive by car via U.S. 395 from the north or south, or Highway 190 or Highway 138 from Death Valley National Park. No train or regularly scheduled bus service is available.

ESSENTIALS

Visitor Information Lone Pine Chamber of Commerce. ⊠ *120 S. Main St., at Whitney Portal Rd.* ☎ *760/876–4444* ⊕ *www.lonepinechamber.org.*

EXPLORING

18

TOP ATTRACTIONS

Alabama Hills. Drop by the Lone Pine Visitor Center for a map of the Alabama Hills and take a drive up Whitney Portal Road (turn west at the light) to this wonderland of granite boulders. Erosion has worn the rocks smooth; some have been chiseled to leave arches and other formations. The hills have become a popular location for rock climbing. Tuttle Creek Campground sits among the rocks, with a nearby stream for fishing. The area has served as a scenic backdrop for hundreds of films; ask about the self-guided tour of the various movie locations at the visitor center. ⊠ *Whitney Portal Rd., 4½ miles west of Lone Pine.*

Mt. Whitney. Straddling the border of Sequoia National Park and Inyo National Forest–John Muir Wilderness, Mt. Whitney (14,496 feet) is the highest mountain in the contiguous United States. A favorite game for travelers passing through Lone Pine is trying to guess which peak is Mt. Whitney. Almost no one gets it right, because Mt. Whitney is hidden behind other mountains. There is no road that ascends the peak, but you can catch a glimpse of the mountain by driving curvy Whitney Portal Road west from Lone Pine into the mountains. The pavement ends at the trailhead to the top of the mountain, which is also the start of the 211-mile John Muir Trail from Mt. Whitney to Yosemite National Park. Day and overnight permits are required to ascend Mt. Whitney. The highly competitive lottery for these permits opens on February 1st. At the portal, a restaurant (known for its pancakes) and a small store cater to hikers and campers staying at Whitney Portal Campground. You can see a waterfall from the parking lot and go fishing in a small trout pond. The portal area is closed from mid-October to early May; the road closes when snow conditions require. ✉ *Whitney Portal Rd., west of Lone Pine* 🌐 *www.fs.usda.gov/attmain/inyo.*

WORTH NOTING

Museum of Western Film History. Hopalong Cassidy, Barbara Stanwyck, Roy Rogers, John Wayne—even Robert Downey Jr.—are among the stars who have starred in Westerns and other films shot in the Alabama Hills and surrounding dusty terrain. The marquee-embellished museum relates this Hollywood-in-the-desert tale via exhibits and a rollicking 20-minute documentary. ✉ *701 S. Main St., U.S. 395* ☎ *760/876–9909* 🌐 *www.museumofwesternfilmhistory.org* 🎟 *$5.*

WHERE TO EAT AND STAY

$ AMERICAN 🍴 **Alabama Hills Café & Bakery.** The extensive breakfast and lunch menus at this eatery just off the main drag include many vegetarian items. Portions are huge. **Known for:** many vegetarian and vegan options; convenient refueling stop on the 395; on-site bakery. [$] *Average main: $13* ✉ *111 W. Post St., at S. Main St.* ☎ *760/876–4675.*

$$$ AMERICAN 🍴 **Seasons Restaurant.** This inviting, country-style diner serves all kinds of traditional American fare. For a special treat, try the medallions of Cervena elk, smothered in port wine, dried cranberries, and toasted walnuts; finish with the Baileys Irish Cream cheesecake or the lemon crème brûlée for dessert. **Known for:** high-end dining in remote area; steaks and wild game; children's menu. [$] *Average main: $27* ✉ *206 S. Main St.* ☎ *760/876–8927* 🌐 *www.seasonslonepine.com* 🕓 *No lunch. Closed Mon.*

$ HOTEL 🏨 **Dow Villa Motel and Dow Hote.** Built in 1923 to cater to the film industry, the Dow Villa Motel and the historic Dow Hotel sit in the center of Lone Pine. **Pros:** clean rooms; great mountain views; in-room whirlpool tubs in motel. **Cons:** some rooms share bathrooms. [$] *Rooms from: $119* ✉ *310 S. Main St.* ☎ *760/876–5521, 800/824–9317* 🌐 *www.dowvillamotel.com* 🛏 *95 rooms* 🍽 *No meals.*

INDEPENDENCE

17 miles north of Lone Pine.

Named for a military outpost that was established near here in 1862, sleepy Independence has some wonderful historic buildings and is worth a stop for two other reasons. The Eastern California Museum provides a marvelous overview of regional history, and 6 miles south of the small downtown lies the Manzanar National Historic Site, one of 10 camps in the West where people of Japanese descent were confined during the Second World War.

GETTING HERE AND AROUND

Greyhound passes through town, but most travelers arrive by car on U.S. 395.

EXPLORING

TOP ATTRACTIONS

FAMILY **Eastern California Museum.** The highlights of this museum dedicated to Inyo County and the Eastern Sierra's history include photos and artifacts from the Manzanar War Relocation Center, Paiute and Shoshone baskets, and a yard full of equipment used by early miners and ranchers. ⌧ *155 N. Grant St., at W. Center St.* ☏ *760/878–0258* ⊕ *www. inyocounty.us/ecmsite* ▦ *Free.*

Fodor'sChoice **Manzanar National Historic Site.** A reminder of an ugly episode in U.S. his-
★ tory, the former Manzanar War Relocation Center is where more than 11,000 Japanese-Americans were confined behind barbed-wire fences between 1942 and 1945. A visit here is both deeply moving and inspiring—the former because it's hard to comprehend that the United States was capable of confining its citizens in such a way, the latter because those imprisoned here showed great pluck and perseverance in making the best of a bad situation. Most of the buildings from the 1940s are gone, but two sentry posts, the auditorium, and numerous Japanese rock gardens remain. One of eight guard towers and two barracks have been reconstructed, and a mess hall has been restored. Interactive exhibits inside the barracks include audio and video clips from people who were incarcerated in Manzanar during WWII. You can drive the one-way dirt road on a self-guided tour past various ruins to a small cemetery, where a monument stands. Signs mark where the barracks, a hospital, a school, and the fire station once stood. An outstanding 8,000-square-foot interpretive center has exhibits and documentary photographs and screens a short film. ⌧ *Independence* ✢ *West side of U.S. 395 between Independence and Lone Pine* ☏ *760/878–2194* ⊕ *www.nps.gov/manz* ▦ *Free.*

WORTH NOTING

FAMILY **Mt. Whitney Fish Hatchery.** A delightful place for a family picnic, the hatchery was one of California's first trout farms. The Tudor Revival–style structure, completed in 1917, is an architectural stunner, its walls nearly 3 feet thick with locally quarried granite. Fish production ceased in 2007 after a fire and subsequent mudslide, but dedicated volunteers staff the facility and raise trout for display purposes in a large pond out front. Bring change for the fish-food machines. ⌧ *1 Golden Trout Circle, 2 miles north of town* ☏ *760/279-1592* ⊕ *www.wildlife.ca.gov/ Fishing/Hatcheries/Mount-Whitney* ▦ *Free (donations welcomed)* ⊙ *Closed mid-Dec.–mid-Apr. Closed Tues. and Wed.*

EN
ROUTE **Ancient Bristlecone Pine Forest.** About an hour's drive from Independence or Bishop you can view some of the oldest living trees on Earth, some of which date back more than 40 centuries. The world's largest bristlecone pine can be found in Patriarch Grove, while the world's oldest known living tree is along Methusula Trail in Schulman Grove. Getting to Patriarch Grove is slow going along the narrow dirt road, especially for sedans with low clearance. ⌧ *Schulman Grove visitor center, White Mountain Rd., Bishop* ✢ *From U.S. 395, turn east onto Hwy. 168 and follow signs for 23 miles* ⊕ *www.fs.usda.gov/main/inyo/home* ▦ *$3.*

18

EN
ROUTE
Schulman Grove Visitor Center. At the Schulman Grove Visitor Center, open late May–October, you can learn about the bristlecone and take a walk to the 4,700-year-old Methuselah tree. ☎ *760/873–2500* ⊕ *www.bishopvisitor.com* ✆ *Closed Nov.–mid-May.*

BISHOP

43 miles north of Independence.

One of the biggest towns along U.S. 395, bustling Bishop has views of the Sierra Nevada and the White and Inyo mountains. First settled by the Northern Paiute Indians, the area was named in 1861 for cattle rancher Samuel Bishop, who established a camp here. Paiute and Shoshone people reside on four reservations in the area. Bishop kicks off the summer season with its Mule Days Celebration. Held over Memorial Day weekend, the five-day event includes mule races, a rodeo, an arts-and-crafts show, and country-music concerts.

GETTING HERE AND AROUND

To fully enjoy the many surrounding attractions, you should get here by car. Arrive and depart via U.S. 395 or, from Nevada, U.S. 6. Local transit provides limited service to nearby tourist sites.

ESSENTIALS

Bus Information Eastern Sierra Transit Authority. ☎ *760/872–1901* ⊕ *www.estransit.com.*

Visitor Information Bishop Chamber of Commerce. ✉ *690 N. Main St., at Park St.* ☎ *760/873–8405, 888/395–3952* ⊕ *www.bishopvisitor.com.*

EXPLORING

FAMILY **Laws Railroad Museum.** The laid-back and wholly nostalgic railroad museum celebrates the Carson and Colorado Railroad Company, which set up a narrow-gauge railroad yard here in 1883. Among the exhibits are a self-propelled car from the Death Valley Railroad, a stamp mill from an area mine, and a full village of rescued buildings, including a post office, the original 1883 train depot, and a restored 1900 ranch house. Many of the buildings are full of "modern amenities" of days gone by. ✉ *200 Silver Canyon Rd., off U.S. 6, 4.5 miles north of town* ☎ *760/873–5950* ⊕ *www.lawsmuseum.org* ✆ *$5 suggested donation.*

Mule Days Celebration. For five days around Memorial Day weekend more than 30,000 tourists and locals pack into Bishop to celebrate the humble mule. Activities include what organizers bill as the longest nonmotorized parade in the world, a rodeo, and good old-fashioned country-and-western concerts. ✉ *1141 N. Main St.* ☎ *760/872–4263* ⊕ *www.muledays.org.*

WHERE TO EAT AND STAY

$ ✕ **Erick Schat's Bakkerÿ.** A bustling stop for motorists traveling to and
BAKERY   from Mammoth Lakes, this shop is crammed with delicious pastries, cookies, rolls, and other baked goods. The biggest draw, though, is the sheepherder bread, a hand-shaped and stone hearth–baked sourdough that was introduced during the gold rush by immigrant

Basque sheepherders in 1907. **Known for:** sheepherder bread and pastries; convenient place to stock up; hefty sandwiches. [$] *Average main: $10* ✉ *763 N. Main St., near Park St.* ☎ *760/873–7156* 🌐 *www.erickschatsbakery.com.*

$$ B&B/INN 🏨 **Bishop Creekside Inn.** The nicest spot to stay in Bishop, this clean and comfortable mountain-style hotel is a good base from which to explore the town or go skiing and trout fishing nearby. **Pros:** nice pool; spacious and modern rooms. **Cons:** pets not allowed. [$] *Rooms from: $170* ✉ *725 N. Main St.* ☎ *760/872–3044, 800/273–3550* 🌐 *www.bishopcreeksideinn.com* 🛏 *89 rooms* 🍴 *Breakfast.*

SPORTS AND THE OUTDOORS

The Owens Valley is trout country; its glistening alpine lakes and streams are brimming with feisty rainbow, brown, brook, and golden trout. Good spots include Owens River, the Owens River gorge, and Pleasant Valley Reservoir. Although you can fish year-round here, some fishing is catch-and-release. Bishop is the site of fishing derbies throughout the year, including the Blake Jones Blind Bogey Trout Derby in March. Rock-climbing, mountain biking, and hiking are also popular Owens Valley outdoor activities.

FISHING

Reagan's Sporting Goods. Stop at Reagan's to pick up bait, tackle, and fishing licenses and to find out where the fish are biting. They can also recommend guides. ✉ *963 N. Main St.* ☎ *760/872–3000* 🌐 *www.reagansportinggoods.com.*

TOURS

Sierra Mountain Center. The guided experiences Sierra Mountain offers include hiking, skiing, snowshoeing, rock-climbing, and mountain-biking trips for all levels of expertise. ✉ *200 S. Main St.* ☎ *760/873–8526* 🌐 *www.sierramountaincenter.com* 🎟 *From $130.*

Sierra Mountain Guides. Join expert guides on custom and scheduled alpine adventures, from backcountry skiing and mountaineering to backpacking and mountain running. Programs range from half-day forays to treks that last several weeks. ✉ *312 N. Main St.* ☎ *760/648–1122* 🌐 *www.sierramtnguides.com* 🎟 *From $150.*

MAMMOTH LAKES

30 miles south of the eastern edge of Yosemite National Park.

International real-estate developers joined forces with Mammoth Mountain Ski Area to transform the once sleepy town of Mammoth Lakes (elevation 7,800 feet) into an upscale ski destination. Relatively sophisticated dining and lodging options can be found at the Village at Mammoth complex, and multimillion-dollar renovations to tired motels and restaurants have revived the "downtown" area of Old Mammoth Road. Also here is the hoppin' Mammoth Rock 'n' Bowl, a two-story activity, dining, and entertainment complex. Winter is high season at Mammoth; in summer, the room rates drop.

Twin Lakes, in the Mammoth Lakes region, is a great place to unwind.

GETTING HERE AND AROUND

The best way to get to Mammoth Lakes is by car. The town is about 2 miles west of U.S. 395 on Highway 203, signed as Main Street in Mammoth Lakes and Minaret Road west of town. In summer and early fall (until the first big snow) you can drive to Mammoth Lakes east through Yosemite National Park on scenic Tioga Pass Road; signed as Highway 120 outside the park, the road connects to U.S. 395 north of Mammoth. In summer YARTS provides once-a-day public-transit service between Mammoth Lakes and Yosemite Valley. The shuttle buses of Eastern Sierra Transit Authority serve Mammoth Lakes and nearby tourist sites.

ESSENTIALS

Visitor Information Mammoth Lakes Visitor Center. ⊠ *Welcome Center, 2510 Main St., near Sawmill Cutoff Rd.* ☎ *760/934–2712, 888/466–2666* ⊕ *www.visitmammoth.com.*

EXPLORING

TOP ATTRACTIONS

Fodor'sChoice ★ **Devils Postpile National Monument.** Volcanic and glacial forces sculpted this formation of smooth, vertical basalt columns. For a bird's-eye view, take the short, steep trail to the top of a 60-foot cliff. To see the monument's second scenic wonder, **Rainbow Falls**, hike 2 miles past Devils Postpile. A branch of the San Joaquin River plunges more than 100 feet over a lava ledge here. When the water hits the pool below, sunlight turns the resulting mist into a spray of color. From mid-June to early September, day-use visitors must ride the shuttle bus from the

Mammoth Mountain Ski Area to the monument. ✉ *Mammoth Lakes* ✛ *13 miles southwest of Mammoth Lakes off Minaret Rd. (Hwy. 203)* ☎ *760/934–2289, 760/872–1901 shuttle* ⊕ *www.nps.gov/depo* 💲 *$10 per vehicle (allowed when the shuttle isn't running, usually early Sept.– mid-Oct.), $7 per person shuttle.*

Fodor's Choice
★
Mammoth Lakes Basin. Mammoth's seven main lakes are popular for fishing and boating in summer, and a network of multiuse paths connects them to the North Village. First comes Twin Lakes, at the far end of which is Twin Falls, where water cascades 300 feet over a shelf of volcanic rock. Also popular are Lake Mary, the largest lake in the basin; Lake Mamie; and Lake George. ■TIP➔ Horseshoe Lake is the only lake in which you can swim. ✉ *Lake Mary Rd., off Hwy. 203, southwest of town.*

Mammoth Rock 'n' Bowl. A sprawling complex with sweeping views of the Sherwin Mountains, Mammoth Rock 'n' Bowl supplies one-stop recreation, entertainment, and dining. Downstairs are 12 bowling lanes, lounge areas, Ping-Pong and foosball tables, dartboards, and a casual bar-restaurant ($$) serving burgers, pizzas, and small plates. The upstairs floor has three golf simulators, a pro shop, and Mammoth Rock Brasserie ($$$), an upscale dining room and lounge. ■TIP➔ If the weather's nice, sit on the outdoor patio or the upstairs deck and enjoy the unobstructed vistas. ✉ *3029 Chateau Rd., off Old Mammoth Rd.* ☎ *760/934–4200* ⊕ *mammothrocknbowl.com* 💲 *Bowling: $7 per game per person evenings and weekends, $5 before 5 pm and after 10 pm; $3 shoe rental.*

FAMILY
Fodor's Choice
★
Panorama Gondola. Even if you don't ski, ride the gondola to see Mammoth Mountain, the aptly named dormant volcano that gives Mammoth Lakes its name. Gondolas serve skiers in winter and mountain bikers and sightseers in summer. The high-speed, eight-passenger gondolas whisk you from the chalet to the summit, where you can learn about the area's volcanic history in the interpretive center, have lunch in the café, and take in top-of-the-world views. Standing high above the tree line, you can look west 150 miles across the state to the Coastal Range; to the east are the highest peaks of Nevada and the Great Basin beyond. You won't find a better view of the Sierra High Country without climbing. ■TIP➔ The air is thin at the 11,053-foot summit; carry water, and don't overexert yourself. ✉ *Boarding area at Main Lodge, off Minaret Rd. (Hwy. 203), west of village center* ☎ *760/934–0745, 800/626–6684* ⊕ *www.mammothmountain.com* 💲 *$29.*

WORTH NOTING

Hot Creek Fish Hatchery. This outdoor fish hatchery has the breeding ponds for many of the fish—typically from 3 to 5 million annually— with which the state stocks Eastern Sierra lakes and rivers. In recent years budget cuts have reduced these numbers, but locals have formed foundations to keep the hatchery going. For more details, take the worthwhile self-guided tour. ■TIP➔ Kids enjoy feeding the fish here. ✉ *121 Hot Creek Hatchery Rd., off U.S. 395 (airport exit), about 10 miles southeast of Mammoth Lakes* ☎ *760/934–2664* 💲 *Free.*

18

Hot Creek Geological Site. Forged by an ancient volcanic eruption, the geological site is a landscape of boiling hot springs, fumaroles, and occasional geysers. Swimming is prohibited—the water can go from warm to boiling in a short time—but you can look down from the parking area into the canyon to view the steaming volcanic features, a very cool sight indeed. Fly-fishing for trout is popular upstream from the springs. ✉ *Hot Creek Hatchery Rd., off U.S. 395 (airport exit), about 10 miles southeast of Mammoth Lakes* ☎ *760/924–5501* 🌐 *www.fs.usda.gov/inyo* 🎟 *Free.*

Minaret Vista. The glacier-carved sawtooth spires of the Minarets, the remains of an ancient lava flow, are best viewed from the Minaret Vista. Pull off the road, park your car in the visitors' viewing area, and walk along the path, which has interpretive signs explaining the spectacular peaks, ridges, and valleys beyond. ✉ *Off Hwy. 203, 1¼ mile west of Mammoth Mountain Ski Area.*

Village at Mammoth. This huge complex of shops, restaurants, and luxury accommodations is the town's tourist center, and the venue for many special events—check the website for the weekly schedule. The complex is also the transfer hub for the free public transit system, with fixed routes throughout the Mammoth Lakes area. The free village gondola starts here and travels up the mountain to Canyon Lodge and back. ■ **TIP→ Unless you're staying in the village and have access to the on-site lots, parking can be very difficult here.** ✉ *100 Canyon Blvd.* ☎ *760/924–1575* 🌐 *villageatmammoth.com.*

WHERE TO EAT

$$ CAFÉ 🍴 **Black Velvet.** Start your day the way scores of locals do—with a stop at the slick Black Velvet espresso bar for Belgian waffles, baked treats, and coffee drinks made from small batches of beans roasted on-site. Then return in the afternoon or evening to hang out with friends in the upstairs wine bar (open 4 to 9), It's also a great place to hang out with a steamy cup of organic tea or a craft beer and log onto the free Wi-Fi. **Known for:** small-batch coffee roasting; small-lot wines by the glass; Belgian waffles. [$] *Average main: $16* ✉ *3343 Main St., Suite F* ☎ 🌐 *www.blackvelvetcoffee.com.*

$ WINE BAR 🍴 **Bleu Handcrafted Foods.** Handcrafted artisanal cheeses and meats, wine and beer tastings, bread baked on-site, and specialty meats and seafood draw patrons to Bleu, a combination market and wine bar. Bleu also cooks up savory pub fare at The Eatery at Mammoth Brewing Company. **Known for:** array of meats and cheeses; wine tasting; order-ahead box lunches. [$] *Average main: $12* ✉ *3325 Main St., Unit C* ☎ *760/914–2538* 🌐 *www.bleufoods.com.*

$ AMERICAN 🍴 **Burgers.** Don't even think about coming to this bustling restaurant unless you're hungry. Burgers is known, appropriately enough, for its burgers and sandwiches, and everything comes in mountainous portions. **Known for:** great service; hefty portions; burgers and seasoned fries. [$] *Average main: $13* ✉ *6118 Minaret Rd., across from the Village* ☎ *760/934–6622* 🌐 *www.burgersrestaurant.com* ⏲ *Closed 2 wks in May and 4–6 wks in Oct. and Nov.*

$$ AMERICAN

🍴 **Mammoth Brewing Company.** Steps from the Village gondola and main bus transfer hub, this brewery lures hungry patrons with about a dozen craft beers on tap and tasty grub cooked up by Bleu Handcrafted Foods. Tasting flights, a contemporary vibe at two spacious bar areas, and a beer garden add to the appeal. **Known for:** craft beer made on-site; upscale pub food; popular local hangout. [$] *Average main: $16* ✉ *18 Lake Mary Rd.* ✥ *At intersection of Main St. and Minaret Rd.* ☎ *760/934–7141* 🌐 *mammothbrewingco.com.*

$$$ STEAKHOUSE FAMILY

🍴 **The Mogul.** Come here for straightforward steaks—top sirloin, New York, filet mignon, and T-bone. The only catch is that the waiters cook them, and the results vary depending on their experience. **Known for:** traditional alpine atmosphere; servers custom-grill your order; all-you-can-eat salad bar. [$] *Average main: $30* ✉ *1528 Tavern Rd., off Old Mammoth Rd.* ☎ *760/934–3039* 🌐 *www.themogul.com* 🕓 *No lunch.*

$$$ AMERICAN

🍴 **Petra's Bistro & Wine Bar.** The ambience at Petra's—quiet, dark, and warm (there's a great fireplace)—complements its seductive meat and seafood entrées and smart selection of mostly California-made wines. The service is top-notch. **Known for:** romantic atmosphere; attentive service; lively downstairs bar. [$] *Average main: $29* ✉ *Alpenhof Lodge, 6080 Minaret Rd.* ☎ *760/934–3500* 🌐 *www.petrasbistro.com* 🕓 *Closed Mon. No lunch.*

$$$$ AMERICAN Fodor'sChoice ★

🍴 **Restaurant at Convict Lake.** The lake is one of the most spectacular spots in the Eastern Sierra, and the food here lives up to the view. Beef Wellington, rack of lamb, and pan-seared local trout, all beautifully prepared, are among the specialties. [$] *Average main: $34* ✉ *Convict Lake Rd. off U.S. 395, 4 miles south of Mammoth Lakes* ☎ *760/934–3803* 🌐 *www.convictlake.com* 🕓 *No lunch early Sept.–mid-June.*

$$ MODERN AMERICAN FAMILY

🍴 **Toomey's.** A passionate baseball fan, chef Matt Toomey designed this casual space near the Village Gondola to resemble a dugout, and decorated it with baseball memorabilia. After a day outdoors, relax over lobster taquitos, giant chicken wings, fish tacos, and Angus beef sliders. **Known for:** lobster taquitos and fish tacos; curbside take-out delivery to your car; homemade organic and gluten-free desserts. [$] *Average main: $20* ✉ *6085 Minaret Rd., at the Village* ☎ *760/924–4408* 🌐 *www.toomeyscatering.com.*

18

WHERE TO STAY

$$ B&B/INN

🏨 **Alpenhof Lodge.** Across from the Village at Mammoth, this mom-and-pop motel offers basic comforts and a few niceties such as the attractive pine furniture. **Pros:** convenient for skiers; reasonable rates. **Cons:** some bathrooms are small; rooms above pub can be noisy. [$] *Rooms from: $159* ✉ *6080 Minaret Rd., Box 1157* ☎ *760/934–6330, 800/828–0371* 🌐 *www.alpenhof-lodge.com* 🛏 *54 rooms, 3 cabins* 🍽 *Breakfast.*

$$$ RESORT Fodor'sChoice ★

🏨 **Double Eagle Resort and Spa.** Lofty pines tower over this very fine spa retreat on the June Lake Loop. **Pros:** pretty setting; spectacular indoor pool; 1½ miles from June Mountain Ski Area. **Cons:** expensive; remote. [$] *Rooms from: $249* ✉ *5587 Hwy. 158, Box 736, June Lake* ☎ *760/648–7004* 🌐 *www.doubleeagle.com* 🛏 *17 2-bedroom cabins, 16 rooms, 1 3-bedroom house* 🍽 *No meals.*

$$ ⌂ **Holiday Haus.** A short walk from the Village, Holiday Haus emerged
HOTEL from a property-wide renovation as a collection of contemporary moun-
tain-activity-themed rooms and suites—many with full kitchens—at
relatively affordable prices. **Pros:** free parking and Wi-Fi; good option
for groups and families; walk to the Village. **Cons:** showers, no tubs in
most rooms; no 24-hour desk; basic breakfast. $ *Rooms from: $124*
✉ *3905 Main St.* ☎ *760/934-2414* ⊕ *holidayhausmotelandhostel.com*
⌨ *23 rooms,1 cabin, 1 26-bed hostel.*

$$$ ⌂ **Juniper Springs Resort.** Tops for slope-side comfort, these condomin-
RESORT ium-style units have full kitchens and ski-in ski-out access to the moun-
tain. **Pros:** bargain during summer; direct access to the slopes; good
views. **Cons:** no nightlife within walking distance; no air-conditioning. $ *Rooms from: $199* ✉ *4000 Meridian Blvd.* ☎ *760/924-1102,
800/626-6684* ⊕ *www.mammothmountain.com* ⌨ *204 studios and
apartments* ⦿| *No meals.*

$$ ⌂ **Mammoth Mountain Inn.** If you want to be within walking distance of the
RESORT Mammoth Mountain Main Lodge, this is the place. **Pros:** great location;
big rooms; a traditional place to stay. **Cons:** can be crowded in ski season.
$ *Rooms from: $134* ✉ *1 Minaret Rd.* ☎ *760/934-2581, 800/626-6684*
⊕ *www.mammothmountain.com* ⌨ *124 rooms, 91 condos.*

$$$ ⌂ **Sierra Nevada Resort & Spa.** A full-service resort in the heart of Old Mam-
RESORT moth, the Sierra Nevada has it all: three restaurants, four bars, a dedicated
spa facility, on-site ski and snowboard rentals, a seasonal pool and Jacuzzi,
seasonal miniature golf, and room and suite options in three buildings. **Pros:**
many on-site amenities; walk to restaurants on property or downtown;
complimentary shuttle service. **Cons:** must drive or ride a bus or shuttle
to the slopes; thin walls in older rooms. $ *Rooms from: $199* ✉ *164 Old
Mammoth Rd.* ☎ *760/934-2515, 800/824-5132, 760/934-7319* ⊕ *thesier-
ranevadaresort.com* ⌨ *143 rooms, 6 townhomes* ⦿| *No meals.*

$$$ ⌂ **Tamarack Lodge Resort & Lakefront Restaurant.** On the edge of the John
RESORT Muir Wilderness Area, where cross-country ski trails lace the woods,
Fodor'sChoice this 1924 lodge looks like something out of a snow globe. **Pros:** rus-
★ tic; eco-sensitive; many nearby outdoor activities. **Cons:** pricey; shared
bathrooms for some main lodge rooms. $ *Rooms from: $239* ✉ *Lake
Mary Rd., off Hwy. 203* ☎ *760/934-2442, 800/626-6684* ⊕ *www.
tamaracklodge.com* ⌨ *46 rooms and cabins* ⦿| *No meals.*

$$$ ⌂ **The Village Lodge.** With their exposed timbers and peaked roofs, these
RESORT four-story condo buildings at the epicenter of Mammoth's dining and
nightlife scene pay homage to Alpine style. **Pros:** central location; clean;
big rooms; good restaurants nearby. **Cons:** pricey; can be noisy outside.
$ *Rooms from: $239* ✉ *1111 Forest Trail* ☎ *760/934-1982, 800/626-
6684* ⊕ *www.mammothmountain.com* ⌨ *277 units* ⦿| *No meals.*

$$$$ ⌂ **Westin Monache Resort.** On a hill just steps from the Village at Mam-
RESORT moth, the Westin provides full-service comfort and amenities close to
Fodor'sChoice restaurants, entertainment, and free public transportation. **Pros:** upscale
★ amenities; prime location; free gondola to the slopes is across the street.
Cons: long, steep stairway down to village; added resort fee. $ *Rooms
from: $359* ✉ *50 Hillside Dr.* ☎ *760/934-0400, 888/627-8154 reserva-
tions, 760/934-4686* ⊕ *www.westinmammoth.com* ⌨ *230 rooms and
suites* ⦿| *No meals.*

CLOSE UP

Camping in the Eastern Sierra

Camping in the Sierra Nevada means gazing up at awe-inspiring constellations and awakening to the sights of nearby meadows and streams and the unforgettable landscape of giant granite. Dozens of campgrounds, from remote, tents-only areas to sprawling full-service facilities close to the main attractions, operate in the Eastern Sierra. Be aware that Yosemite National Park's most accessible campgrounds can be jam-packed and claustrophobic in the summer. Luckily, there are many options to the east, including calm and beautiful sites such as Lake Mary Campground in the Mammoth Lakes

area. The following campsites are recommended. Reserve sites at www. recreation.gov.

Convict Lake Campground. A 10-minute drive south of Mammoth, this campground near the Convict Lake Resort is run by the U.S. Forest Service. ⊠ *Convict Lake Rd., 2 miles off U.S. 395* ☎ *760/924–5501* ⌁ *88 campsites.*

Lake Mary Campground. There are few sites as beautiful as this lakeside campground at 8,900 feet, open from June to September. ⊠ *Lake Mary Loop Dr., off Hwy. 203* ☎ *760/924– 5501* ▭ *No credit cards* ⌁ *48 sites (tent or RV)* ▯❍▮ *No meals.*

SPORTS AND THE OUTDOORS

BIKING

Fodor'sChoice
★

Mammoth Mountain Bike Park. The park opens when the snow melts, usually by July, and has 100-plus miles of single-track trails—from mellow to super-challenging. Chairlifts and shuttles provide trail access, and rentals are available. ⊠ *Mammoth Mountain Ski Area* ☎ *760/934–0677, 800/626-6684* ⊕ *www.mammothmountain.com* ⌁ *$55 day pass.*

FISHING

The main fishing season runs from the last Saturday in April until the end of October; there are opportunities for ice fishing in winter. Crowley Lake is the top trout-fishing spot in the area; Convict Lake, June Lake, and the lakes of the Mammoth Basin are other prime spots. One of the best trout rivers is the San Joaquin, near Devils Postpile. Hot Creek, a designated Wild Trout Stream, is renowned for fly-fishing (catch-and-release only).

Kittredge Sports. This outfit rents rods and reels and conducts guided trips. ⊠ *3218 Main St., at Forest Trail* ☎ *760/934–7566* ⊕ *kittredgesports.com.*

Sierra Drifters Guide Service. To maximize your time on the water, get tips from local anglers, or better yet, book a guided fishing trip, contact Sierra Drifters. ⊠ *Mammoth Lakes* ☎ *760/935–4250* ⊕ *www.sierradrifters.com.*

18

HIKING

Hiking in Mammoth is stellar, especially along the trails that wind through alpine scenery around the Lakes Basin. Carry lots of water; and remember, the air is thin at 8,000-plus feet.

Visit the Mammoth Lakes Trail System website (⊕ *www.mammoth-trails.org*) for descriptions of more than 300 miles of trails, maps, and a wealth of information on recreation in Mammoth Lakes and the Inyo National Forest in all seasons.

U.S. Forest Service Ranger Station. Stop at the ranger station, just east of the town of Mammoth Lakes, for an area trail map and permits for backpacking in wilderness areas. ⊠ *2510 Main St., Hwy. 203* ☎ *760/924–5501* ⊕ *www.fs.usda.gov/main/inyo.*

EASY

Convict Lake Loop. This 2.8-mile trail loops gently around deep blue Convict Lake, a popular site for anglers. Feast your eyes on stunning views of tall peaks, glistening water, and aspen and cottonwood groves while you hike. *Easy.* ⊠ *Trailhead: at Convict Lake, 9 miles south of Mammoth Lakes.*

FAMILY **Minaret Falls.** Hike along portions of both the Pacific Crest and John Muir trails on this scenic trail (3 miles round-trip) that leads to Devil's Postpile, Minaret Falls, and natural volcanic springs. This is a good family hike, especially in late summer when the water has receded a bit and kids can climb boulders and splash around. *Easy.* ⊠ *Trailhead: At Devil's Postpile National Monument.*

MODERATE

Emerald Lake and Sky Meadows. The first part of this trail travels through shady pine forest along Coldwater Creek to bright-green Emerald Lake (1.8 miles round-trip). Extend the hike by climbing up a trail along an inlet stream up to Gentian Meadow and Sky Meadows (4 miles round-trip), especially beautiful in July and August when various alpine wildflowers, fed by snowmelt, are at their peak splendor. *Moderate.* ⊠ *Trailhead: Coldwater Campground, Mammoth Lakes.*

DIFFICULT

Duck Lake. This popular and busy trail (11 miles round-trip) heads up Coldwater Canyon along Mammoth Creek, past a series of spectacular lakes and wildflower meadows over 10,797-foot Duck Pass to dramatic Duck Lake, which eventually links up with the John Muir Trail. *Difficult.* ⊠ *Trailhead: Coldwater Campground.*

HORSEBACK RIDING

Stables around Mammoth are typically open from June through September.

Mammoth Lakes Pack Outfit. This company runs day and overnight horseback and mule trips and will shuttle you to the high country. ⊠ *Lake Mary Rd., between Twin Lakes and Lake Mary* ☎ *888/475–8747,* ⊕ *www.mammothpack.com.*

McGee Creek Pack Station. These folks customize pack trips or will shuttle you to camp alone. ⊠ *2990 McGee Creek Rd., Crowley Lake* ☎ *760/935–4324 summer, 760/878–2207, 800/854–7407* ⊕ *www. mcgeecreekpackstation.com.*

SKIING

In winter, check the On the Snow website or call the Snow Report for information about Mammoth weather conditions.

FAMILY **June Mountain Ski Area.** Snowboarders especially dig June Mountain, a compact, low-key resort north of Mammoth Mountain. Three beginner-to-intermediate terrain areas—the Surprise Fun Zone, Mambo Playground, and Bucky's Adventure—are for both skiers and boarders. There's rarely a line for the lifts here: if you must ski on a weekend and want to avoid the crowds, this is the place to come, and in a storm it's better protected from wind and blowing snow than Mammoth is. (If it starts to storm, you can use your Mammoth ticket at June.) The services include a rental-and-repair shop, a ski school, and a sports shop. There's food, but the options are better at Mammoth. ■TIP➜ Kids 12 and under ski and ride free. ✉ *3819 Hwy. 158/June Lake Loop, off U.S. 395, 22 miles northwest of Mammoth, June Lake* ☎ *760/648–7733, 888/586–3686* ⊕ *www.junemountain.com* ✉ *From $99* ✆ *35 trails on 1,400 acres, rated 35% beginner, 45% intermediate, 20% advanced. Longest run 2 miles, base 7,545 feet, summit 10,190 feet. Lifts: 7.*

Fodor'sChoice **Mammoth Mountain Ski Area.** One of the West's largest and best ski areas,
★ Mammoth has more than 3,500 acres of skiable terrain and a 3,100-foot vertical drop. The views from the 11,053-foot summit are some of the most stunning in the Sierra. Below, you'll find a 6½-mile-wide swath of groomed boulevards and canyons, as well as pockets of tree-skiing and a dozen vast bowls. Snowboarders are everywhere on the slopes; there are thirteen outstanding freestyle terrain parks of varying difficulty, with jumps, rails, tabletops, and giant super pipes—this is the location of several international snowboarding competitions, and, in summer, mountain-bike meets. Mammoth's season begins in November and often lingers into July. Lessons and equipment are available, and there's a children's ski and snowboard school. Mammoth runs free shuttle-bus routes around town and to the ski area, and the Village Gondola runs from the Village complex to Canyon Lodge. However, only overnight guests are allowed to park at the Village for more than a few hours. ■TIP➜ The main lodge is dark and dated, unsuited in almost every way for the crush of ski season. **Facilities:** 150 trails; 3,500 acres; 3,100-foot vertical drop; 28 lifts. ✉ *Minaret Rd., west of Mammoth Lakes, Rte. 203, off U.S. 395* ☎ *760/934–2571, 800/626–6684, 760/934–0687 shuttle* ⊕ *www.mammothmountain. com* ✉ *From $135.*

Tamarack Cross Country Ski Center. Trails at the center, adjacent to Tamarack Lodge, meander around several lakes. Rentals are available. ✉ *Lake Mary Rd., off Hwy. 203* ☎ *760/934–5293, 760/934–2442* ⊕ *tamaracklodge.com* ✉ *$58 all-inclusive day rate.*

SKI RENTALS AND RESOURCES

Fodor'sChoice **Black Tie Ski Rentals.** Skiers and snowboarders love this rental outfit
★ whose staffers will deliver and custom-fit equipment for free. They also offer slope-side assistance. ✉ *Mammoth Lakes* ☎ *760/934–7009* ⊕ *mammothskis.com.*

18

Why Is There So Much Snow?

The Sierra Nevada receives some of the deepest snow anywhere in North America. In winter, houses literally get buried, and homeowners have to build tunnels to their front doors (though many install enclosed wooden walkways). In the high country, it's not uncommon for a single big storm to bring 10 feet of snow and for 30 feet of snow to accumulate at the height of the season. In the enormous bowls of Mammoth Mountain, you might ski past a tiny pine that looks like a miniature Christmas tree—until you remember that more than 30 feet of tree is under the snow.

To understand the weather, you have to understand the terrain. The Sierra Nevada are marked by a gentle western rise from sea level to the Sierra crest, which tops out at a whopping 14,494 feet at Sequoia National Park's Mt. Whitney, the highest point in the continental United States. On the eastern side of the crest, at the escarpment, the mountains drop sharply—as much as 5,000 feet—giving way to the Great Basin and the high-mountain deserts of Nevada and Utah.

When winter storms blow in off the Pacific, carrying vast stores of water with them, they race across the relatively flat, 100-mile-wide Central Valley. As they ascend the wall of mountains, though, the decrease in temperature and the increase in pressure on the clouds force them to release their water. Between October and April, that means snow—lots of it. Storms can get hung up on the peaks for days, dumping foot after foot of the stuff. By the time they finally cross over the range and into the Great Basin, there isn't much moisture left for the lower elevations on the eastern side. This is why, if you cross the Sierra eastward on your way to U.S. 395, you'll notice that brightly colored wildflowers and forest-green trees give way to pale-green sagebrush and brown sand as you drop out of the mountains.

The coastal cities and farmlands of the rest of the state depend heavily on the water from the Sierra snowpack. Most of the spring and summer runoff from the melting snows is caught in reservoirs in the foothills and routed to farmlands and cities throughout the state via a complex system of levees and aqueducts, which you'll no doubt see in the foothills and Central Valley, to the west of the range. But much of the water remains in the mountains, forming lakes, most notably giant Lake Tahoe to the north, Mono Lake to the east, and the thousands of little lakes along the Sierra Crest. The lakes are an essential part of the ecosystem, providing water for birds, fish, and plant life.

Footloose. When the U.S. Ski Team visits Mammoth and needs boot adjustments, everyone heads to Footloose, the best place in town—and possibly all California—for ski-boot rentals and sales, as well as custom insoles. ⊠ *3043 Main St., at Mammoth Rd.* ☎ *760/934–2400* ⊕ *www. footloosesports.com.*

Kittredge Sports. Advanced skiers should consider this outfit, which has been around since the 1960s. ✉ *3218 Main St.* ☎ *760/934–7566* ⊕ *kittredgesports.com.*

OntheSnow.com. Get the latest ski and snow reports and weather forecasts for Mammoth Mountain and other resorts, in English and several other languages. ⊕ *www.onthesnow.com/california/mammoth-mountain-ski-area/ski-resort.html.*

Snow Report. For information on winter conditions around Mammoth, call the Snow Report. ✉ *Mammoth Lakes* ☎ *760/934–7669, 888/766–9778.*

FAMILY **Woolly's Tube Park & Snow Play.** Ride a lift to the top of the hill and whoosh down in a high-speed snow tube as often as you like during a 1¼-hour session. The park has six lanes, a heated deck, and snack shop. Discounts available for a second session if you're not ready to stop riding. Little ones can hang out in the snow play area with sleds and saucers. ✉ *9000 Minaret Rd.* ☎ *800/626–6684 reservations, 760/934–7533 direct line* ⊕ *www.mammothmountain.com* 💲 *$34–$39 first session (must be 42" tall to ride), play area $15.*

SNOWMOBILING

Mammoth Snowmobile Adventures. Mammoth Snowmobile Adventures conducts guided tours along wooded trails. ✉ *Mammoth Mountain Main Lodge* ☎ *760/934–9645, 800/626–6684* ⊕ *www.mammothmountain.com* 💲 *From $109.*

EAST OF YOSEMITE NATIONAL PARK

18

Most people enter Yosemite National Park from the west, having driven out from the Bay Area or Los Angeles. The eastern entrance on Tioga Pass Road (Highway 120 off Highway 395), however, provides stunning, sweeping views of the High Sierra. Gray rocks shine in the bright sun, with scattered, small vegetation sprinkled about the mountainside. To drive from Lee Vining to Tuolumne Meadows is an unforgettable experience, but keep in mind that the road tends to be closed for at least seven months of the year.

LEE VINING

20 miles east of Tuolumne Meadows, 30 miles north of Mammoth Lakes.

Tiny Lee Vining is known primarily as the eastern gateway to Yosemite National Park (summer only) and the location of vast and desolate Mono Lake. Pick up supplies at the general store year-round, or stop here for lunch or dinner before or after a drive through the high country. In winter the town is all but deserted, except for the ice climbers who come to scale frozen waterfalls.

GETTING HERE AND AROUND

Lee Vining is on U.S. 395, north of the road's intersection with Highway 120 and on the south side of Mono Lake. In summer YARTS public transit can get you here from Yosemite Valley, but you'll need a car to explore the area.

ESSENTIALS

Visitor Information **Lee Vining Chamber of Commerce.** ☎ *760/647-6629* 🌐 *www.leevining.com.* **Mono Basin National Forest Scenic Area Visitor Center.** ✉ *Visitor Center Dr., off U.S. 395, 1 mile north of Hwy. 120* ☎ *760/647-3044* 🌐 *www.monolake.org/visit/vc.*

EXPLORING

Fodor's Choice ★ **Mono Lake.** Since the 1940s Los Angeles has diverted water from this lake, exposing striking towers of tufa, or calcium carbonate. Court victories by environmentalists have meant fewer diversions, and the lake is rising again. Although to see the lake from U.S. 395 is stunning, make time to visit South Tufa, whose parking lot is 5 miles east of U.S. 395 off Highway 120. There in summer you can join the naturalist-guided **South Tufa Walk,** which lasts about 90 minutes. The **Scenic Area Visitor Center,** off U.S. 395, is a sensational stop for its interactive exhibits and sweeping Mono Lake views (closed in winter). In town at U.S. 395 and 3rd Street, the **Mono Lake Committee Information Center & Bookstore,** open from 9 to 5 daily (extended hours in summer), has more information about this beautiful area. ✉ *Hwy. 120, east of Lee Vining* ☎ *760/647–3044 visitor center, 760/647–6595 info center* 🌐 *www.monolake.org* 🎟 *Free.*

EN ROUTE **June Lake Loop.** Heading south from Lee Vining, U.S. 395 intersects the June Lake Loop. This gorgeous 17-mile drive follows an old glacial canyon past Grant, June, Gull, and other lakes before reconnecting with U.S. 395 on its way to Mammoth Lakes. ■ **TIP→ The loop is especially colorful in fall.** ✉ *Hwy. 158 W.*

WHERE TO EAT AND STAY

$$ AMERICAN 🍴 **Tioga Gas Mart & Whoa Nelli Deli.** This might be the only gas station in the United States serving craft beers and lobster taquitos, but its appeal goes beyond novelty. Succulent fish tacos with mango salsa and barbecued ribs with a huckleberry glaze are among the many well-executed dishes. **Known for:** fish tacos; regular live music; convenient location. [$] *Average main: $16* ✉ *Hwy. 120 and U.S. 395* ☎ *760/647–1088* 🌐 *www.whoanelliedeli.com* ⏲ *Closed early Nov.–late Apr.*

$$ B&B/INN 🏨 **Lake View Lodge.** Enormous rooms and landscaping that includes several shaded sitting areas set this motel apart from its competitors in town. **Pros:** attractive; peaceful; clean; friendly staff. **Cons:** could use updating. [$] *Rooms from: $129* ✉ *51285 U.S. 395* ☎ *760/647–6543, 800/990–6614* 🌐 *www.lakeviewlodgeyosemite.com* 🛏 *76 rooms, 12 cottages.*

BODIE STATE HISTORIC PARK

31 miles northeast of Lee Vining.

Bodie State Historic Park's scenery is spectacular, with craggy, snow-capped peaks looming over vast prairies. The town of Bridgeport is the gateway to the park, and the only supply center for miles around. Bridgeport's claim to fame is that most of the 1947 film-noir classic *Out of the Past,* starring Robert Mitchum in his prime as a private eye whose past catches up with him, was filmed here. In winter, much of Bridgeport shuts down.

GETTING HERE AND AROUND

A car is the best way to reach this area. Bodie is on Highway 270 about 13 miles east of U.S. 395.

EXPLORING

Fodor's Choice **Bodie Ghost Town.** The mining village of Rattlesnake Gulch, abandoned
★   mine shafts, and the remains of a small Chinatown are among the sights at this fascinating ghost town. The town boomed from about 1878 to 1881, but by the late 1940s all its residents had departed. A state park was established here in 1962, with a mandate to preserve everything in a state of "arrested decay." Evidence of Bodie's wild past survives at an excellent museum, and you can tour an old stamp mill where ore was crushed into fine powder to extract gold and silver. Bodie lies 13 miles east of U.S. 395 off Highway 270. The last 3 miles are unpaved, and snow may close the highway from late fall through early spring. No food, drink, or lodging is available in Bodie. ⊠ *Bodie Rd., off Hwy. 270, Bodie* ☎ *760/647–6445* ⊕ *www. parks.ca.gov/bodie/* ✉ *$8.*

YOSEMITE
NATIONAL PARK

WELCOME TO YOSEMITE NATIONAL PARK

TOP REASONS TO GO

★ **Wet and wild:** An easy stroll brings you to the base of Lower Yosemite Fall, where roaring springtime waters make for misty lens caps and lasting memories.

★ **Tunnel vision:** Approaching Yosemite Valley, Wawona Road passes through a mountainside and emerges before one of the park's most heart-stopping vistas.

★ **Inhale the beauty:** Pause to smell the light, pristine air as you travel about the High Sierra's Tioga Pass and Tuolumne Meadows, where 10,000-foot granite peaks just might take your breath away.

★ **Walk away:** Leave the crowds behind—but do bring along a buddy—and take a hike somewhere along Yosemite's 800 miles of trails.

★ **Powder your nose:** Winter's hush floats into Yosemite on snowflakes. Lift your face to the sky and listen to the trees.

1 **Yosemite Valley.** At an elevation of 4,000 feet, in roughly the center of the park, beats Yosemite's heart. This is where you'll find the park's most famous sights and biggest crowds.

2 **Wawona and Mariposa Grove.** The park's southern tip holds Wawona, with its grand old hotel and pioneer history center, and the Mariposa Grove of Giant Sequoias. These are closest to the south entrance, 35 miles (a one-hour drive) south of Yosemite Village.

3 **Tuolumne Meadows.** The highlight of east-central Yosemite is this wildflower-strewn valley with hiking trails, nestled among sharp, rocky peaks. It's a 1½-hour drive northeast of Yosemite Valley along Tioga Road (closed mid-October–late May).

4 **Hetch Hetchy.** The most remote, least visited part of Yosemite accessible by automobile, this glacial valley is dominated by a reservoir and veined with wilderness trails. It's near the park's western boundary, about a half-hour drive north of the Big Oak Flat entrance.

CALIFORNIA

GETTING ORIENTED

Yosemite is so large that you can think of it as five parks. Yosemite Valley, famous for waterfalls and cliffs, and Wawona, where the giant sequoias stand, are open all year. Hetch Hetchy, home of less-used backcountry trails, is most accessible from late spring through early fall. The subalpine high country, Tuolumne Meadows, is open for summer hiking and camping; in winter it's accessible via cross-country skis or snowshoes. Yosemite Ski & Snowboard Area (formerly Badger Pass) is open in winter only. Most visitors spend their time along the park's southwestern border, between Wawona and Big Oak Flat entrance; a bit farther east in Yosemite Valley and Yosemite Ski & Snowboard Area; and along the east–west corridor of Tioga Road, which spans the park north of Yosemite Valley and bisects Tuolumne Meadows.

19

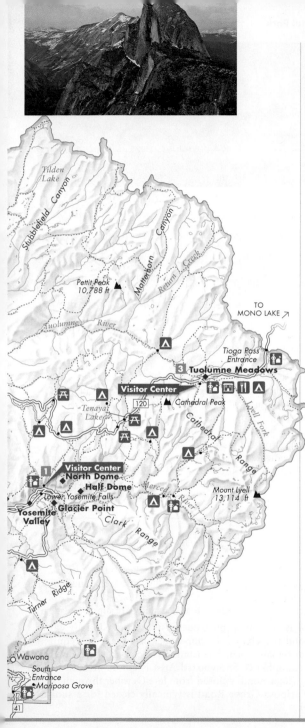

Tilden Lake

Stubblefield Canyon

Matterhorn Canyon

Return Creek

Pettit Peak
10,788 ft

Tuolumne River

TO MONO LAKE ↗

Tioga Pass Entrance

3 Tuolumne Meadows

Visitor Center

120

Cathedral Peak

Tenaya Lake

Cathedral Range

Lyell Fork

1 Visitor Center
North Dome
Half Dome

Lower Yosemite Falls

Glacier Point

Merced River

Mount Lyell
13,114 ft

Yosemite Valley

Clark Range

Turner Ridge

Wawona
South Entrance
Mariposa Grove

41

Updated
by Cheryl
Crabtree

By merely standing in Yosemite Valley and turning in a circle, you can see more natural wonders in a minute than you could in a full day pretty much anywhere else. Half Dome, Yosemite Falls, El Capitan, Bridalveil Fall, Sentinel Dome, the Merced River, white-flowering dogwood trees, maybe even bears ripping into the bark of fallen trees or sticking their snouts into beehives—it's all in Yosemite Valley.

In the mid-1800s, when tourists were arriving to the area, the valley's special geologic qualities and the giant sequoias of Mariposa Grove 30 miles to the south so impressed a group of influential Californians that they persuaded President Abraham Lincoln to grant those two areas to the state for protection on June 30, 1864. On October 1, 1890—thanks largely to lobbying efforts by naturalist John Muir and Robert Underwood Johnson, the editor of *Century Magazine*—Congress set aside an additional 1,500 square miles for Yosemite National Park; the valley and Mariposa Grove remained under state control until 1906, when they merged with the national park.

PLANNING

WHEN TO GO

During extremely busy periods—such as weekends and holidays throughout the year—you will experience delays at the entrance gates. For smaller crowds, visit midweek. Or come January through April, when the park is a bit less busy and the days usually are sunny and clear.

Summer rainfall is rare. In winter, heavy snows occasionally cause road closures, and tire chains or four-wheel drive may be required on the roads that remain open. The road to Glacier Point beyond the turnoff for Yosemite Ski & Snowboard Area is closed after the first major snowfall; Tioga Road is closed from late October through May or mid-June. Mariposa Grove Road is typically closed for a shorter period in winter.

PLANNING YOUR TIME
YOSEMITE IN ONE DAY

Begin at the **Valley Visitor Center,** where you can watch the documentary *Spirit of Yosemite* (which inexplicably shows no animals other than one deer). A minute's stroll from there is the **Indian village of the Ahwahnee,** which recalls American Indian life circa 1870. Take another 20 minutes to see the **Yosemite Museum.** Then, hop aboard the free shuttle to Yosemite Falls and hike the **Lower Yosemite Fall Trail** to the base of the falls. Then proceed via shuttle or a 20-minute walk to lunch at **Yosemite Valley Lodge.**

Next choose one of three things: leisurely exploring **Half Dome Village (formerly Curry Village)**—perhaps going for a swim or ice-skating, shopping, renting a bike, or having a beer on the deck; checking out family-friendly **Happy Isles Nature Center** and the adjacent nature trail; or hiking up the **Mist Trail** to the Vernal Fall footbridge to admire the view.

Hop back on the shuttle, then disembark at **The Majestic Yosemite Hotel (formerly The Ahwahnee).** Step into the Great Lounge, which has a magnificent fireplace and Indian artwork, and sneak a peek into the Dining Room, if you're up for a splurge. Get back on the shuttle, and head to **Yosemite Village,** where you can grab some food. Get back in your car and drive to **El Capitan picnic area** and enjoy an outdoor evening meal. At this time of day, "El Cap" should be sun-splashed. (You will have gotten several good looks at world-famous **Half Dome** throughout the day.) Any sunlight left? If so, continue driving on around to take a short hike at the base of **Bridalveil Fall.**

GETTING HERE AND AROUND
AIR TRAVEL

The closest airport to the south and west entrances is Fresno Yosemite International Airport (FAT). Mammoth Yosemite Airport (MMH) is closest to the east entrance.

19

BUS AND TRAIN TRAVEL

Amtrak's daily San Joaquin train stops in Merced and connects with YARTS buses that travel to Yosemite Valley along Highway 140 from Merced. YARTS buses also travel along Highway 41 from Fresno, and Highway 120 from Sonora, with scheduled stops at towns along the way. Once you're in Yosemite you can take advantage of the free shuttle buses, which operate on low emissions, have 21 stops, and run from 7 am to 10 pm year-round. Buses run about every 10 minutes in summer, a bit less frequently in winter. A separate (but also free) summer-only shuttle runs out to El Capitan. Also in summer, you can take the morning "hikers' bus" from Yosemite Valley to Tuolumne or pay to ride the bus up to Glacier Point. During the snow season, buses run regularly between Yosemite Valley and Yosemite Ski & Snowboard Area.

CAR TRAVEL

Roughly 200 miles from San Francisco, 300 miles from Los Angeles, and 500 miles from Las Vegas, Yosemite takes a while to reach—and its many sites and attractions merit much more time than what rangers say is the average visit: four hours.

Of the park's four entrances, Arch Rock is the closest to Yosemite Valley. The road that goes through it, Route 140 from Merced and Mariposa, is a scenic western approach that snakes alongside the boulder-packed Merced River. Route 41, through Wawona, is the way to come from Los Angeles (or Fresno, if you've flown in and rented a car). Route 120, through Crane Flat, is the most direct route from San

> **PLAN YOUR VISIT**
>
> It's wise to visit the Plan Your Visit section of the park website, ⊕ *nps.gov/yose*, for helpful tips and practical information such as water safety, bears and food storage, and how to avoid rare diseases such as plague and hantavirus.

Francisco. The only way in from the east is Tioga Road, which may be the best route in terms of scenery—though due to snow accumulation it's open for a frustratingly short amount of time each year (typically early June through mid-October).

There are few gas stations within Yosemite (Crane Flat and Wawona; none in the valley), so fuel up before you reach the park. From late fall until early spring, the weather is especially unpredictable, and driving can be treacherous. You should carry chains during this period as they are required when roads are icy and when it snows.

PARK ESSENTIALS
PARK FEES AND PERMITS

The admission fee, valid for seven days, is $30 per vehicle, $25 per motorcycle, or $15 per individual.

If you plan to camp in the backcountry or climb Half Dome, you must have a wilderness permit. Availability of permits depends upon trailhead quotas. It's best to make a reservation, especially if you will be visiting May through September. You can reserve two days to 26 weeks in advance by phone, mail, or fax (preferred method) (⊠ *Box 545, Yosemite, CA 95389* ☏ *209/372–0740* 🖷 *209/372–0739*); you'll pay $5 per person plus $5 per reservation if and when your reservations are confirmed. You can download the reservation forms from ⊕ *www.nps.gov/yose/planyourvisit/upload/wildpermitform. pdf*. Without a reservation, you may still get a free permit on a first-come, first-served basis at wilderness permit offices at Big Oak Flat, Hetch Hetchy, Tuolumne Meadows, Wawona, the Wilderness Center in Yosemite Village, and Yosemite Valley in summer. From fall to spring, visit the Valley Visitor Center.

PARK HOURS

The park is open 24/7 year-round. All entrances are open at all hours, except for Hetch Hetchy entrance, which is open roughly dawn to dusk. Yosemite is in the Pacific time zone.

CELL-PHONE RECEPTION

Cell-phone reception depends on the service provider and can be hit or miss everywhere in the park. There are public telephones at park entrance stations, visitor centers, all restaurants and lodging facilities in the park, gas stations, and in Yosemite Village.

EDUCATIONAL OFFERINGS

CLASSES AND SEMINARS

Art Classes. Professional artists conduct workshops in watercolor, etching, drawing, and other mediums. Bring your own materials or purchase the basics at the Yosemite Art Center. Children under 12 must be accompanied by an adult. The center also offers beginner art workshops and children's art and family craft programs ($5–$15 per person). ⊠ *Art Activity Center, Yosemite Village* ☎ *209/372–1442* ⊕ *www.yosemiteconservancy.org* ☞ *$15* ⊗ *No classes Sun. Closed Dec.–Feb.*

Yosemite Outdoor Adventures. Naturalists, scientists, and park rangers lead multihour to multiday educational outings on topics from woodpeckers to fire management to pastel painting. Most sessions take place spring through fall, but a few focus on winter phenomena. ⊠ *Yosemite National Park* ☎ *209/379–2317* ⊕ *www.yosemiteconservancy.org* ☞ *From $99.*

MUSEUMS

Nature Center at Happy Isles. Designed for children, this old-fashioned museum has dioramas with several stuffed animals, including a baby bear. A rotating selection of hands-on, kid-friendly exhibits teaches tykes and their parents about the park's ecosystem. Books, toys, T-shirts, and water bottles are stocked in the small gift shop. ⊠ *Yosemite National Park* ✛ *Off Southside Dr., about ¾ mile east of Half Dome Village* ☞ *Free* ⊗ *Closed Oct.–Apr.*

Yosemite Museum. This small museum consists of a permanent exhibit that focuses on the history of the area and the people who once lived here. An adjacent gallery promotes contemporary and historic Yosemite art in revolving gallery exhibits. A docent demonstrates traditional Native American basket-weaving techniques a few days a week. ⊠ *Yosemite Village* ☎ *209/372–0299* ☞ *Free.*

RANGER PROGRAMS

Junior Ranger Program. Children ages seven and up can participate in the informal, self-guided Junior Ranger program. A park activity handbook is available at the Valley Visitor Center, the Nature Center at Happy Isles, and the Wawona Visitor Center. Once kids complete the book, rangers present them with a badge and, in some cases, a certificate. ⊠ *Valley Visitor Center or the Nature Center at Happy Isles* ☎ *209/372–0299.*

Ranger-Led Programs. Rangers lead entertaining walks and give informative talks several times a day from spring to fall. The schedule is more limited in winter, but most days you can find a program somewhere in the park. In the evenings at Yosemite Valley Lodge and Half Dome Village, lectures, slide shows, and documentary films present unique perspectives on Yosemite. On summer weekends, campgrounds at Half Dome Village and Tuolumne Meadows host sing-along campfire programs. Schedules and locations are posted on bulletin boards throughout the park as well as in the indispensable *Yosemite Guide,* which is distributed to visitors as they arrive at the park. ⊠ *Yosemite National Park* ⊕ *nps.gov/yose.*

19

RESTAURANTS

Yosemite National Park has a couple of moderately priced restaurants in lovely (which almost goes without saying) settings: the Mountain Room at Yosemite Valley Lodge and Wawona Hotel's dining room. The Majestic Yosemite Hotel (formerly The Ahwahnee) provides one of the finest dining experiences in the country.

Otherwise, food service is geared toward satisfying the masses as efficiently as possible. Yosemite Valley Lodge's food court is the valley's best lower-cost, hot-food option; Half Dome Village Pavilion's offerings are overpriced and usually fairly bland, but you can get decent pizzas on the adjacent outdoor deck. In Yosemite Valley Village, the Village Grill whips up burgers and fries, Degnan's Deli has made-to-order sandwiches, and Loft Pizzeria has a chaletlike open dining area in which you can enjoy pizza, salads, and desserts.

The White Wolf Lodge and Tuolumne Meadows Lodge—both off Tioga Road and therefore guaranteed open only from early June through September—have small restaurants where meals are competently prepared. Tuolumne Meadows also has a grill, and the gift shop at Glacier Point sells premade sandwiches, snacks, and hot dogs. During the ski season you'll also find one at Yosemite Ski & Snowboard Area, off Glacier Point Road.

HOTELS

Indoor lodging options inside the park appear more expensive than initially seems warranted, but that premium pays off big-time in terms of the time you'll save—unless you are bunking within a few miles of a Yosemite entrance, you will face long commutes to the park when you stay outside its borders (though the Yosemite View Lodge, on Route 140, is within a reasonable half-hour's drive of Yosemite Valley).

Because of Yosemite National Park's immense popularity—not just with tourists from around the world but with Northern Californians who make weekend trips here—reservations are all but mandatory. Book up to one year ahead. ■TIP➔ If you're not set on a specific hotel or camp but just want to stay somewhere inside the park, call the main reservation number to check for availability and reserve (888/413–8869 or 602/278–8888 international). Park lodgings have a seven-day cancellation policy, so you may be able to snag last-minute reservations.

⚠ A trademark dispute with the former park concessioner, Delaware North, has resulted in Yosemite National Park changing the names of several historic park lodges and properties, including the iconic Ahwahnee. This guide uses the new names: Yosemite Lodge at the Falls is now Yosemite Valley Lodge; The Ahwahnee is now The Majestic Yosemite Hotel; Curry Village is now Half Dome Village; Wawona Hotel is now Big Trees Lodge; and Badger Pass Ski Area is now Yosemite Ski & Snowboard Area. For the latest information visit the Yosemite National Park website.

Hotel reviews have been shortened. For full information, visit Fodors.com.

WHAT IT COSTS				
	$	**$$**	**$$$**	**$$$$**
Restaurants	under $12	$12–$20	$21–$30	over $30
Hotels	under $100	$100–$150	$151–$200	over $200

Restaurant prices are the average cost of a main course at dinner, or if dinner is not served, at lunch. Hotel prices are the lowest cost of a standard double room in high season.

TOURS

Fodor's Choice ★ **Ansel Adams Camera Walks.** Photography enthusiasts shouldn't miss these 90-minute guided camera walks offered four mornings (Monday, Tuesday, Thursday, and Saturday) each week by professional photographers. All are free, but participation is limited to 15 people. Meeting points vary, and advance reservations are essential. ⊠ *Yosemite National Park* ☎ *209/372–4413* ⊕ *www.anseladams.com* ☞ *Free.*

Discover Yosemite. This outfit operates daily tours to Yosemite Valley, Mariposa Grove, and Glacier Point in 14- and 29-passenger vehicles. The Highway 41 route stops in Bass Lake, Oakhurst, and Fish Camp, and the Highway 140 route departs from Mariposa, Midpines, and El Portal. Rates include lunch. Sunset tours to Sentinel Dome are additional summer options. ☎ *559/642–4400, 800/585–0565* ⊕ *www.discoveryosemite.com* ☞ *From $124.*

VISITOR INFORMATION

Park Contact Information Yosemite National Park. ☎ *209/372–0200* ⊕ *www.nps.gov/yose.*

VISITOR CENTERS

Valley Visitor Center. Learn about Yosemite Valley's geology, vegetation, and human inhabitants at this visitor center, which is also staffed with helpful rangers and contains a bookstore with a wide selection of books and maps. Two films, including one by Ken Burns, alternate on the half hour in the theater behind the visitor center. ⊠ *Yosemite Village* ☎ *209/372–0200* ⊕ *www.nps.gov/yose.*

Yosemite Conservation Heritage Center. This small but striking National Historic Landmark (formerly Le Conte Memorial Lodge), with its granite walls and steeply pitched shingle roof, is Yosemite's first permanent public information center. Step inside to see the cathedral-like interior, which contains a library and environmental exhibits. To find out about evening programs, check the kiosk out front. ⊠ *Southside Dr., about ½ mile west of Half Dome Village* ⊕ *sierraclub.org/yosemite-heritage-center* ☽ *Closed Mon., Tues., and Oct.–Apr.*

19

EXPLORING

HISTORIC SITES

Indian Village of Ahwahnee. This solemn smattering of structures, accessed by a short loop trail behind the Yosemite Valley Visitor Center, is a look at what Native American life might have been like in the 1870s. One interpretive sign points out that the Miwok people referred to the 19th-century newcomers as "Yohemite" or "Yohometuk," which have been translated as meaning "some of them are killers." ⊠ *Northside Dr., Yosemite Village* 🖼 *Free.*

Pioneer Yosemite History Center. Some of Yosemite's first structures—those not occupied by Native Americans, that is—were relocated here in the 1950s and 1960s. You can spend a pleasurable and informative half hour walking about them and reading the signs, perhaps springing for a self-guided-tour pamphlet (50¢) to further enhance the history lesson. Weekends and some weekdays in the summer, costumed docents conduct free blacksmithing and "wet-plate" photography demonstrations, and for a small fee you can take a stagecoach ride. ⊠ *Rte. 41, Wawona* 🖀 *209/375–9531* 🖼 *Free* ☉ *Closed Mon., Tues., and mid-Sept.–early June.*

SCENIC STOPS

El Capitan. Rising 3,593 feet—more than 350 stories—above the valley, El Capitan is the largest exposed-granite monolith in the world. Since 1958, people have been climbing its entire face, including the famous "nose." You can spot adventurers with your binoculars by scanning the smooth and nearly vertical cliff for specks of color. ⊠ *Yosemite National Park* ✛ *Off Northside Dr., about 4 miles west of the Valley Visitor Center.*

Fodor's Choice **Glacier Point.** If you lack the time, desire, or stamina to hike more than
★ 3,200 feet up to Glacier Point from the Yosemite Valley floor, you can drive here—or take a bus from the valley—for a bird's-eye view. You are likely to encounter a lot of day-trippers on the short, paved trail that leads from the parking lot to the main overlook. Take a moment to veer off a few yards to the Geology Hut, which succinctly explains and illustrates what the valley looked like 10 million, 3 million, and 20,000 years ago. ⊠ *Yosemite National Park* ✛ *Glacier Point Rd., 16 miles northeast of Rte. 41* 🖀 *209/372–0200* ☉ *Closed late Oct.–mid-May.*

Fodor's Choice **Half Dome.** Visitors' eyes are continually drawn to this remarkable gran-
★ ite formation that tops out at more than 4,700 feet above the valley floor. Despite its name, the dome is actually about three-quarters intact. You can hike to the top of Half Dome on an 8.5-mile (one-way) trail whose last 400 feet must be ascended while holding onto a steel cable. Permits are required (and checked on the trail), and available only by lottery. Call *877/444–6777* or visit *www.recreation.gov* well in advance of your trip for details. Back down in the valley, see Half Dome reflected in the Merced River by heading to Sentinel Bridge just before sundown. The brilliant orange light on Half Dome is a stunning sight. ⊠ *Yosemite National Park* ⊕ *www.nps.gov/yose/planyourvisit/halfdome.htm.*

The Tunnel View viewpoint offers one of the most famous views of Yosemite with Bridalveil Falls, Half Dome, and the Yosemite Valley.

Hetch Hetchy Reservoir. When Congress approved the O'Shaughnessy Dam in 1913, pragmatism triumphed over aestheticism. Some 2.5 million residents of the San Francisco Bay Area continue to get their water from this 117-billion-gallon reservoir. Although spirited efforts are being made to restore the Hetch Hetchy Valley to its former, pristine glory, three-quarters of San Francisco voters in 2012 ultimately opposed a measure to even consider draining the reservoir. Eight miles long, the reservoir is Yosemite's largest body of water, and one that can be seen up close from several trails. ⊠ *Hetch Hetchy Rd., about 15 miles north of the Big Oak Flat entrance station.*

High Country. The above-tree-line, high-alpine region east of the valley— a land of alpenglow and top-of-the-world vistas—is often missed by crowds who come to gawk at the more publicized splendors. Summer wildflowers, which usually pop up mid-July through August, carpet the meadows and mountainsides with pink, purple, blue, red, yellow, and orange. On foot or on horseback are the only ways to get here. For information on trails and backcountry permits, check with the visitor center. ⊠ *Yosemite National Park.*

Mariposa Grove of Giant Sequoias. Of Yosemite's three sequoia groves— the others being Merced and Tuolumne, both near Crane Flat well to the north—Mariposa is by far the largest and easiest to walk around. Grizzly Giant, whose base measures 96 feet around, has been estimated to be one of the largest in the world. Perhaps more astoundingly, it's about 1,800 years old. Up the hill, you'll find more sequoias, a small museum, and fewer people. Summer weekends are usually crowded here.

GOOD READS

■ *The Photographer's Guide to Yosemite*, by Michael Frye, is an insider's guide to the park, with maps for shutterbugs looking to capture perfect images.

■ John Muir penned his observations of the park he long advocated for in *The Yosemite*.

■ *Yosemite and the High Sierra*, edited by Andrea G. Stillman and John Szarkowski, features beautiful reproductions of landmark photographs by Ansel Adams, accompanied by excerpts from the photographer's journals written when Adams traveled in Yosemite National Park in the early 20th century.

■ An insightful collection of essays accompanies the museum-quality artworks in *Yosemite: Art of an American Icon*, by Amy Scott.

■ Perfect for budding botanists, *Sierra Nevada Wildflowers*, by Karen Wiese, identifies more than 230 kinds of flora growing in the Sierra Nevada region.

Please note that due to major reconstruction the lower grove, which includes Grizzly Giant, Fallen Monarch, and the California Tunnel Tree, will be closed until late fall 2017. Shuttle service will resume when the grove reopens. Check the Yosemite website before visiting this area. ⊠ *Yosemite National Park ✛ Rte. 41, 2 miles north of the south entrance station* ⊕ *www.nps.gov/yose/planyourvisit/mg.htm.*

Sentinel Dome. The view from here is similar to that from Glacier Point, except you can't see the valley floor. A moderately steep 1.1-mile path climbs to the viewpoint from the parking lot. Topping out at an elevation of 8,122 feet, Sentinel is more than 900 feet higher than Glacier Point. ⊠ *Glacier Point Rd., off Rte. 41.*

Tuolumne Meadows. The largest subalpine meadow in the Sierra (at 8,600 feet) is a popular way station for backpack trips along the Pacific Crest and John Muir trails. The setting is not as dramatic as Yosemite Valley, 56 miles away, but the almost perfectly flat basin, about 2½ miles long, is intriguing, and in July it's resplendent with wildflowers. The most popular day hike is up Lembert Dome, atop which you'll have breathtaking views of the basin below. Keep in mind that Tioga Road rarely opens before June and usually closes by mid-October. ⊠ *Tioga Rd. (Rte. 120), about 8 miles west of the Tioga Pass entrance station.*

WATERFALLS

Yosemite's waterfalls are at their most spectacular in May and June. When the snow starts to melt (usually peaking in May), streaming snowmelt spills down to meet the Merced River. By summer's end, some falls, including the mighty Yosemite Falls, trickle or dry up. Their flow increases in late fall, and in winter they may be hung dramatically with ice. Even in drier months, the waterfalls can be breathtaking. If you choose to hike any of the trails to or up the falls, be sure to wear shoes with no-slip soles; the rocks can be extremely slick. Stay on trails at all times.

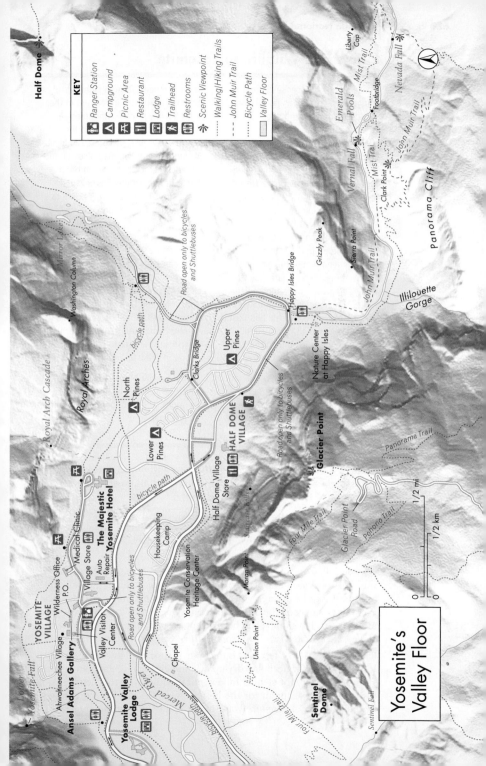

Yosemite's Valley Floor

CLOSE UP

Plants and Wildlife in Yosemite

Dense stands of incense cedar and Douglas fir—as well as ponderosa, Jeffrey, lodgepole, and sugar pines—cover much of the park, but the stellar standout, quite literally, is the *Sequoiadendron giganteum*, the giant sequoia. Sequoias grow only along the west slope of the Sierra Nevada between 4,500 and 7,000 feet in elevation. Starting from a seed the size of a rolled-oat flake, each of these ancient monuments assumes remarkable proportions in adulthood; you can see them in the Mariposa Grove of Big Trees. In late May the valley's dogwood trees bloom with white, starlike flowers. Wildflowers, such as black-eyed Susan, bull thistle, cow parsnip, lupine, and meadow goldenrod, peak in June in the valley and in July at higher elevations.

The most visible animals in the park—aside from the omnipresent western gray squirrels, which fearlessly attempt to steal your food at every campground and picnic site—are the mule deer. Though sightings of bighorn sheep are infrequent in the park itself, you can sometimes see them on the eastern side of the Sierra Crest, just off Route 120 in Lee Vining Canyon. You may also see the American black bear, which often has a brown, cinnamon, or blond coat. The Sierra Nevada is home to thousands of bears, and you should take all necessary precautions to keep yourself—and the bears—safe. Bears that acquire a taste for human food can become very aggressive and destructive and often must be destroyed by rangers, so store all your food and even scented toiletries in the bear lockers located at many campgrounds and trailheads, or use bear-resistant canisters if you'll be hiking in the backcountry.

Watch for the blue Steller's jay along trails, near public buildings, and in campgrounds, and look for golden eagles soaring over Tioga Road.

■TIP→ Visit the park during a full moon and you can stroll without a flashlight and still make out the ribbons of falling water, as well as silhouettes of the giant granite monoliths.

Bridalveil Fall. This 620-foot waterfall is often diverted dozens of feet one way or the other by the breeze. It is the first marvelous site you will see up close when you drive into Yosemite Valley. ⊠ *Yosemite Valley, access from parking area off Wawona Rd.*

Nevada Fall. Climb Mist Trail from Happy Isles for an up-close view of this 594-foot cascading beauty. If you don't want to hike (the trail's final approach is quite taxing), you can see it—albeit distantly—from Glacier Point. Stay safely on the trail, as there have been fatalities in recent years after visitors have fallen and been swept away by the water. ⊠ *Yosemite Valley, access via Mist Trail from Nature Center at Happy Isles.*

Ribbon Fall. At 1,612 feet, this is the highest single fall in North America. It's also the first waterfall to dry up in summer; the rainwater and melted snow that create the slender fall evaporate quickly at this height. Look just west of El Capitan for the best view of the fall from the base of Bridalveil Fall. ⊠ *Yosemite Valley, west of El Capitan Meadow.*

Vernal Fall. Fern-covered black rocks frame this 317-foot fall, and rainbows play in the spray at its base. You can get a distant view from Glacier Point, or hike to see it close up. You'll get wet, but the view is worth it. ⊠ *Yosemite Valley, access via Mist Trail from Nature Center at Happy Isles.*

Fodor'sChoice **Yosemite Falls.** Actually three falls, they together constitute the highest
★   combined waterfall in North America and the fifth highest in the world. The water from the top descends a total of 2,425 feet, and when the falls run hard, you can hear them thunder across the valley. If they dry up—that sometimes happens in late summer—the valley seems naked without the wavering tower of spray. If you hike the mile-long loop trail (partially paved) to the base of the Lower Fall in spring, prepare to get wet. You can get a good full-length view of the falls from the lawn of Yosemite Chapel, off Southside Drive. ⊠ *Yosemite Valley, access from Yosemite Valley Lodge or trail parking area.*

SPORTS AND THE OUTDOORS

BIKING

One enjoyable way to see Yosemite Valley is to ride a bike beneath its lofty granite monoliths. The eastern valley has 12 miles of paved, flat bicycle paths across meadows and through woods, with bike racks at convenient stopping points. For a greater challenge but at no small risk, you can ride on 196 miles of paved park roads—but bicycles are not allowed on hiking trails or in the backcountry. Kids under 18 must wear a helmet.

TOURS AND OUTFITTERS

Yosemite bike rentals. You can arrange for rentals from Yosemite Valley Lodge and Half Dome Village bike stands. Bikes with child trailers, baby-jogger strollers, and wheelchairs are also available. The cost for bikes is $12.50 per hour, or $30.50 a day. ⊠ *Yosemite Valley Lodge or Half Dome Village* ☎ *209/372–4386* ⊕ *www.travelyosemite.com.*

19

BIRD-WATCHING

More than 250 bird species have been spotted in the park, including the sage sparrow, pygmy owl, blue grouse, and mountain bluebird. Park rangers lead free bird-watching walks in Yosemite Valley a few days each week in summer; check at a visitor center or information station for times and locations. Binoculars sometimes are available for loan.

TOURS

Birding seminars. The Yosemite Conservancy organizes day- and weekend-long seminars for beginner and intermediate birders, as well as bird walks a few times a week. They can also arrange private naturalist-led walks any time of year. ⊠ *Yosemite National Park* ☎ *209/379–2321* ⊕ *www.yosemiteconservancy.org* ⊠ *From $99.*

HIKING

TOURS AND OUTFITTERS

Wilderness Center. This facility provides free wilderness permits, which are required for overnight camping (advance reservations are available for $5 per person plus $5 per reservation and are highly recommended for popular trailheads in summer and on weekends). The staff here also provides maps and advice to hikers heading into the backcountry, and rents and sells bear-resistant canisters, which are required if you don't have your own. ⊠ *Between the Ansel Adams Gallery and the post office, Yosemite Village* ☎ *209/372–0308.*

Yosemite Mountaineering School and Guide Service. From April to November, you can learn to climb, hire a guide, or join a two-hour to full-day trek with Yosemite Mountaineering School. They also rent gear and lead backpacking and overnight excursions. Reservations are recommended. In winter, cross-country ski programs are available at Yosemite Ski & Snowboard Area. ⊠ *Yosemite Mountain Shop, Half Dome Village* ☎ *209/372–8344* ⊕ *yosemitemountaineering.com.*

EASY

Fodor's Choice ★ **Yosemite Falls Trail.** Yosemite Falls is the highest waterfall in North America. The upper fall (1,430 feet), the middle cascades (675 feet), and the lower fall (320 feet) combine for a total of 2,425 feet, and when viewed from the valley appear as a single waterfall. The ¼-mile trail leads from the parking lot to the base of the falls. Upper Yosemite Fall Trail, a strenuous 7.2-mile round-trip climb rising 2,700 feet, takes you above the top of the falls. Lower trail: *Easy.* Upper trail: *Difficult.* ⊠ *Yosemite National Park* ⊹ *Trailhead: off Camp 4, north of Northside Dr.*

MODERATE

Mist Trail. Except for Lower Yosemite Fall, more visitors take this trail (or portions of it) than any other in the park. The trek up to and back from Vernal Fall is 3 miles. Add another 4 miles total by continuing up to 594-foot Nevada Fall; the trail becomes quite steep and slippery in its final stages. The elevation gain to Vernal Fall is 1,000 feet, and to Nevada Fall an additional 1,000 feet. The Merced River tumbles down both falls on its way to a tranquil flow through the valley. *Moderate.* ⊠ *Yosemite National Park* ⊹ *Trailhead: at Happy Isles.*

Fodor's Choice ★ **Panorama Trail.** Few hikes come with the visual punch that this 8½-mile trail provides. It starts from Glacier Point and descends to Yosemite Valley. The star attraction is Half Dome, visible from many intriguing angles, but you also see three waterfalls up close and walk through a manzanita grove. If you take the last bus from the valley floor to Glacier Point before starting your hike, you might run out of daylight before you finish. *Moderate.* ⊠ *Yosemite National Park* ⊹ *Trailhead: at Glacier Point.*

DIFFICULT

Fodor's Choice ★ **John Muir Trail to Half Dome.** Ardent and courageous trekkers continue on from Nevada Fall to the top of Half Dome. Some hikers attempt this entire 10- to 12-hour, 16¾-mile round-trip trek in one day; if you're planning to do this, remember that the 4,800-foot elevation gain and

the 8,842-foot altitude will cause shortness of breath. Another option is to hike to a campground in Little Yosemite Valley near the top of Nevada Fall the first day, then climb to the top of Half Dome and hike out the next day. Get your wilderness permit (required for a one-day hike to Half Dome, too) at least a month in advance. Be sure to wear hiking boots and bring gloves. The last pitch up the back of Half Dome is very steep—the only way to climb this sheer rock face is to pull yourself up using the steel cable handrails, which are in place only from late spring to early fall. Those who brave the ascent will be rewarded with an unbeatable view of Yosemite Valley below and the high country beyond. Only 300 hikers per day are allowed atop Half Dome, and they all must have permits, which are distributed by lottery, one in the spring before the season starts and another two days before the climb. Contact *www.recreation.gov* for details. *Difficult.* ⊠ *Yosemite National Park* ✛ *Trailhead: at Happy Isles* ⊕ *www.nps. gov/yose/planyourvisit/halfdome.htm.*

HORSEBACK RIDING

Reservations for guided trail rides must be made in advance at the hotel tour desks or by phone. Scenic trail rides range from two hours to a half day; four- and six-day High Sierra saddle trips are also available.

TOURS AND OUTFITTERS

Big Trees Stable. Two-hour rides at these stables start at $65, and half-day rides are $88.50. Reservations are recommended. ⊠ *Rte. 41, Wawona* ☎ *209/375–6502* ⊕ *www.travelyosemite.com/things-to-do/horseback-mule-riding/* 🎟 *From $65.*

RAFTING

Rafting is permitted only on designated areas of the Middle and South Forks of the Merced River. Check with the Valley Visitor Center for closures and other restrictions.

OUTFITTERS

Half Dome Village Recreation Center. The per-person rental fee ($31) at Half Dome Village Recreation Center covers the four- to six-person raft, two paddles, and life jackets, plus a return shuttle at the end of your trip. ⊠ *South side of Southside Dr., Half Dome Village* ☎ *209/372–4386* ⊕ *www.travelyosemite.com/things-to-do/rafting/* 🎟 *From $31.*

ROCK CLIMBING

The granite canyon walls of Yosemite Valley are world-renowned for rock climbing. El Capitan, with its 3,593-foot vertical face, is the most famous, but there are many other options here for all skill levels.

TOURS AND OUTFITTERS

Yosemite Mountaineering School & Guide Service. The one-day basic lesson at Yosemite Mountaineering School and Guide Service includes some bouldering and rappelling, and three or four 60-foot climbs. Climbers must be at least 10 years old and in reasonably good physical condition. Intermediate and advanced classes include instruction in first aid, anchor building, multipitch climbing, summer snow climbing, and big-wall climbing. There's a Nordic program in the winter. ⊠ *Yosemite Mountain Shop, Half Dome Village* ☎ *209/372–8444* ⊕ *www.travelyosemite.com* ✉ *From $148.*

WINTER SPORTS

The beauty of Yosemite under a blanket of snow has long inspired poets and artists, as well as ordinary folks. Skiing and snowshoeing activities in the park center on Yosemite Ski & Snowboard Area, California's oldest snow-sports resort, which is about 40 minutes away from the valley on Glacier Point Road. Here you can rent equipment, take a lesson, have lunch, join a guided excursion, and take the free shuttle back to the valley after a drink in the lounge.

ICE-SKATING

Half Dome Village Ice Rink. Winter visitors have skated at this outdoor rink for decades, and there's no mystery why: it's a kick to glide across the ice while soaking up views of Half Dome and Glacier Point. ⊠ *South side of Southside Dr., Half Dome Village* ☎ *209/372–8319* ⊕ *www.travelyosemite.com* ✉ *$10 per session, $4 skate rental.*

SKIING AND SNOWSHOEING

Yosemite Ski & Snowboard Area. California's first ski resort has five lifts and 10 downhill runs, as well as 90 miles of groomed cross-country trails. Free shuttle buses from Yosemite Valley operate between December and the end of March, weather permitting. Lessons, backcountry guiding, and cross-country and snowshoeing tours are also available. You can rent downhill, telemark, and cross-country skis, plus snowshoes and snowboards. **Facilities:** 10 trails; 90 acres; 800-foot vertical drop; 5 lifts. ⊠ *Yosemite National Park* ✛ *Badger Pass Rd., off Glacier Point Rd., 18 miles from Yosemite Valley* ☎ *209/372–8430* ⊕ *www.travelyosemite.com/winter/yosemite-ski-snowboard-area/* ✉ *Lift ticket: from $48.*

Yosemite Cross-Country Ski School. The highlight of Yosemite's cross-country skiing center is a 21-mile loop from Yosemite Ski & Snowboard Area to Glacier Point. You can rent cross-country skis for $25 per day at the Cross-Country Ski School, which also rents snowshoes ($24 per day) and telemarking equipment ($30). ☎ *209/372–8444* ⊕ *www.travelyosemite.com.*

Yosemite Mountaineering School. This branch of the Yosemite Mountaineering School, open at the Yosemite Ski & Snowboard Area during ski season only, conducts snowshoeing, cross-country skiing, telemarking, and skate-skiing classes starting at $35. ⊠ *Badger Pass Ski Area* ☎ *209/372–8444* ⊕ *www.yosemitepark.com.*

Yosemite Ski & Snowboard Area School. The gentle slopes of Yosemite Ski & Snowboard Area make the ski school an ideal spot for children and beginners to learn downhill skiing or snowboarding for as little as $70 for a group lesson. ☎ *209/372–8430* ⊕ *www.travelyosemite.com.*

19

SHOPPING

Ansel Adams Gallery. Framed prints of the famed nature photographer's best works are on sale here, as are affordable posters. New works by contemporary artists are available, along with American Indian jewelry and handicrafts. The gallery's elegant camera shop conducts photography workshops, from free camera walks a few mornings a week to five-day workshops. ⊠ *Northside Dr., Yosemite Village* ☎ *209/372–4413.*

Majestic Hotel Gift Shop. This shop sells more upscale items, such as American Indian crafts, photographic prints, handmade ceramics, and elegant jewelry. For less expensive gift items, browse the small book selection, which includes writings by John Muir. ⊠ *The Majestic Yosemite Hotel, Ahwahnee Rd.* ☎ *209/372–1409.*

Yosemite Mountain Shop. A comprehensive selection of camping, hiking, backpacking, and climbing equipment, along with experts who can answer all your questions, make this store a valuable resource for outdoors enthusiasts. This is the best place to ask about climbing conditions and restrictions around the park, as well as purchase almost any kind of climbing gear. ⊠ *Half Dome Village* ☎ *209/372–8396.*

NEARBY TOWNS

Marking the southern end of the Sierra's gold-bearing mother lode, **Mariposa** is the last town before you enter Yosemite on Route 140 to the west of the park. In addition to a fine mining museum, Mariposa has numerous shops, restaurants, and service stations.

Motels and restaurants dot both sides of Route 41 as it cuts through the town of **Oakhurst,** a boomtown during the Gold Rush that is now an important regional refueling station in every sense of the word, including organic foods and a full range of lodging options. Oakhurst has a population of about 3,000 and sits 15 miles south of the park.

Almost surrounded by the Sierra National Forest, **Bass Lake** is a warm-water reservoir whose waters can reach 80 degrees F in summer. Created by a dam on a tributary of the San Joaquin River, the lake is owned by Pacific Gas and Electric Company and is used to generate electricity as well as for recreation.

As you climb in elevation along Highway 41 northbound, you see nothing but trees until you get to **Fish Camp,** where there's a post office and general store, but no gasoline. (For gas, head 7 miles north to Wawona, in Yosemite, or 14 miles south to Oakhurst.)

Near the park's eastern entrance, the tiny town of **Lee Vining** is home to the eerily beautiful, salty Mono Lake, where millions of migratory birds nest. Visit **Mammoth Lakes,** about 40 miles southeast of Yosemite's Tioga Pass entrance, for excellent skiing and snowboarding in winter, with fishing, mountain biking, hiking, and horseback riding in summer. Nine deep-blue lakes form the Mammoth Lakes Basin, and another hundred dot the surrounding countryside. Devils Postpile National Monument sits at the base of Mammoth Mountain.

Visitor Information Mammoth Lakes Tourism. ⊠ *2510 Main St., Mammoth Lakes* ☎ *760/934–2712, 888/466–2666* ⊕ *www.visitmammoth.com.* **Mono Lake Information Center and Bookstore.** ☎ *760/647–6595* ⊕ *www.leevining. com.* **Tuolumne County Visitors Bureau.** ⊠ *193 S. Washington St., Sonora* ☎ *209/533–4420, 800/446–1333* ⊕ *visittuolumne.com.* **Visit Yosemite/Madera County.** ⊠ *40343 Hwy. 41, Oakhurst* ☎ *559/683–4636* ⊕ *www.yosemitethisyear. com.* **Yosemite Mariposa County Tourism Bureau.** ⊠ *5065 Hwy. 140, Suite E, Mariposa* ☎ *209/742–4567, 866/425–3366* ⊕ *www.yosemite.com.*

NEARBY ATTRACTIONS

FAMILY **California State Mining and Mineral Museum.** A California state park since 1999, the museum has displays on gold-rush history including a replica hard-rock mine shaft to walk through, a miniature stamp mill, and a 13-pound chunk of crystallized gold. ⊠ *5005 Fairground Rd., off Hwy. 49, Mariposa* ☎ *209/742–7625* ⊕ *www.parks.ca.gov* ☑ *$4.*

Fresno Flats Historical Village and Park. For a dose of colorful foothills history, make a quick stop at this engaging local museum centered around two 1870s houses. ⊠ *School Rd. and Indian Springs Rd., Oakhurst* ☎ *559/683–6570* ⊕ *www.fresnoflatsmuseum.org.*

Yosemite Gateway Gallery Row. Find out what mountain art is all about at this enclave of five galleries representing dozens of painters, sculptors, and other artists. ⊠ *40982 Hwy. 41, 1¼ mile north of Hwy. 49, Oakhurst* ☎ *559/683–5551* ⊕ *www.yosemitegatewaygalleryrow.com* ☑ *Free.*

FAMILY **Yosemite Mountain Sugar Pine Railroad.** Travel back to a time when powerful steam locomotives hauled massive log trains through the Sierra. This 4-mile, narrow-gauge railroad excursion takes you near Yosemite's south gate. There's a moonlight special ($58), with dinner and entertainment, and you can pan for gold ($10) and visit the free museum. ⊠ *56001 Hwy. 41, 8 miles south of Yosemite, Fish Camp* ☎ *559/683–7273* ⊕ *www.ymsprr.com* ☑ *$22* ⊙ *Closed Nov.–Mar. Closed some weekdays Apr. and Oct.*

19

AREA ACTIVITIES

BOATING AND RAFTING

TOURS
Zephyr Whitewater Expeditions. This outfitter conducts half-day to three-day white-water trips on the Tuolumne, Merced, and American rivers for paddlers of all experience levels. ☎ *800/431–3636 reservations, 209/532–6249* ⊕ *www.zrafting.com* ☑ *From $109.*

NIGHTLIFE

Queen's Inn Wine Bar & Beer Garden. A combination wine bar, tasting room, and small inn, this popular hangout on a bluff above the Fresno River serves about 100 wines by the glass or flight, plus microbrews and imported beers. At the tasting room, open from Wednesday through

Sunday between 11 and 5, you can sample ($5 tasting fee) Tempranillo, Pinot Gris, and other limited-production wines. ✉ *41139 Hwy. 41, Oakhurst* ☎ *559/683–4354* 🌐 *www.queensinn.com/wine-bar-beer-garden/* 🕓 *Closed Sun.–Tues.*

WHERE TO EAT

IN THE PARK

In addition to the dining options listed here, you'll find fast-food grills and cafeterias, plus temporary snack bars, hamburger stands, and pizza joints lining park roads in summer. Many dining facilities in the park are open summer only.

$$$ AMERICAN 🍴 **Big Trees Lodge Dining Room.** Watch deer graze on the meadow while you dine in the romantic, candlelit dining room of the whitewashed Big Trees Lodge (formerly the Wawona Hotel), which dates from the late 1800s. The American-style cuisine favors fresh ingredients and flavors; trout and flatiron steaks are menu staples. [$] *Average main: $28* ✉ *8308 Wawona Rd., Wawona* ☎ *209/375–1425* 🕓 *Closed most of Dec., Jan., Feb., and Mar.*

$$$$ EUROPEAN Fodor's Choice ★ 🍴 **The Majestic Yosemite Hotel Dining Room.** Formerly the Ahwahnee Hotel Dining Room, rave reviews about the dining room's appearance are fully justified—it features towering windows, a 34-foot-high ceiling with interlaced sugar-pine beams, and massive chandeliers. Although many continue to applaud the food, others have reported that they sense a dip in the quality both in the service and what is being served. [$] *Average main: $39* ✉ *The Majestic Yosemite Hotel, Ahwahnee Rd., about ¾ mile east of Yosemite Valley Visitor Center, Yosemite Village* ☎ *209/372–1489* 🌐 *www.travelyosemite.com.*

$$$ AMERICAN Fodor's Choice ★ 🍴 **Mountain Room.** Though good, the food becomes secondary when you see Yosemite Falls through this dining room's wall of windows—almost every table has a view. The chef makes a point of using locally sourced, organic ingredients whenever possible, so you can be assured of fresh vegetables to accompany the hearty main courses, such as steaks and seafood, as well as vegetarian and even vegan options. [$] *Average main: $28* ✉ *Yosemite Valley Lodge, Northside Dr., about ¾ mile west of the visitor center, Yosemite Village* ☎ *209/372–1403* 🌐 *www.travelyosemite.com* 🕓 *No lunch except Sun. brunch.*

$$ FAST FOOD 🍴 **Village Grill Deck.** If a burger joint is what you've been missing, head to this bustling eatery in Yosemite Village that serves veggie, salmon, and a few other burger varieties in addition to the usual beef patties. Order at the counter by 5 pm, then take your tray out to the deck and enjoy your meal under the trees. [$] *Average main: $12* ✉ *Yosemite Village* ✣ *100 yards east of Yosemite Valley Visitor Center* ☎ *209/372–1207* 🌐 *www.travelyosemite.com* 🕓 *Closed Oct.–May. No dinner.*

PICNIC AREAS

Considering how large the park is and how many visitors come here—some 5 million people every year, most of them just for the day—it is somewhat surprising that Yosemite has few formal picnic areas, though in many places you can find a smooth rock to sit on and enjoy breathtaking views along with your lunch. The convenience stores all sell picnic supplies, and prepackaged sandwiches and salads are widely available. Those options can come in especially handy during the middle of the day, when you might not want to spend precious daylight hours in such a spectacular setting sitting in a restaurant for a formal meal. *None of the below options has drinking water available; most have some type of toilet.*

Cathedral Beach. You may have some solitude picnicking here, as this spot usually has fewer people than picnic areas at the eastern end of the valley. *Southside Dr. underneath spirelike Cathedral Rocks.*

Church Bowl. Tucked behind The Majestic Yosemite Hotel, this picnic area nearly abuts the granite walls below the Royal Arches. If you're walking from the village with your supplies, this is the shortest trek to a picnic area. *Behind The Majestic Yosemite Hotel, Yosemite Valley.*

El Capitan. Come here for great views that look straight up the giant granite wall above. *Northside Dr., at western end of valley.*

Sentinel Beach. Usually crowded in season, this area is right alongside a running creek and the Merced River. *Southside Dr., just south of Swinging Bridge.*

Swinging Bridge. This picnic area is just before the little wooden footbridge that crosses the Merced River, which babbles pleasantly by. *Southside Dr., east of Sentinel Beach.*

OUTSIDE THE PARK

$$$$
AMERICAN

✕**Ducey's on the Lake/Ducey's Bar & Grill.** With elaborate chandeliers sculpted from deer antlers, the lodge-style restaurant at Ducey's attracts boaters, locals, and tourists with its lake views and standard lamb, beef, seafood, and pasta dishes. It's also open for breakfast: try the Bass Lake seafood omelet, huevos rancheros, or the Rice Krispies–crusted French toast. **Known for:** steaks and fresh fish; lake views. $ *Average main: $31 ⊠ Pines Resort, 54432 Rd. 432, Bass Lake* ☎ *559/642–3131* ⊕ *www.basslake.com.*

$$$$
EUROPEAN
Fodor'sChoice
★

✕**Erna's Elderberry House.** Erna Kubin-Clanin, the grande dame of Château du Sureau, created this culinary oasis, stunning for its understated elegance, gorgeous setting, and impeccable service. Earth-tone walls and wood beams accent the dining room's high ceilings, and arched windows reflect the glow of candles. **Known for:** elite waitstaff; romantic setting; seasonal prix-fixe and à la carte menus. $ *Average main: $48 ⊠ Château du Sureau, 48688 Victoria La., off Hwy. 41, Oakhurst* ☎ *559/683–6800* ⊕ *www.elderberryhouse.com* ☾ *No lunch Mon.–Sat.*

$$
AMERICAN
Fodor'sChoice
★

✕**South Gate Brewing Company.** Locals pack this family-friendly, industrial-chic restaurant to socialize and savor small-lot beers, crafted onsite, along with tasty meals. The creative pub fare runs a wide gamut, from shepherd's pie Wellington and thin-crust brick-oven pizzas to fish tacos, fish-and-chips, vegan black-bean burgers, and slow-roasted pulled-pork sandwiches. **Known for:** craft beer; homemade desserts;

19

live-music calendar. $ *Average main: $14 ⊠ 40233 Enterprise Dr., off Hwy. 49, north of Von's shopping center, Oakhurst ☎ 559/692–2739 ⊕ southgatebrewco.com.*

WHERE TO STAY

At press time, a still-ongoing trademark dispute with a former park concessioner resulted in Yosemite National Park changing the names of several historic park lodges and properties, including the iconic Ahwahnee. This guide has changed the historic names, with some references to the former. The changes include: Yosemite Lodge at the Falls is Yosemite Valley Lodge, The Ahwahnee is The Majestic Yosemite Hotel, Curry Village is Half Dome Village, Wawona Hotel is Big Trees Lodge, and Badger Pass Ski Area is Yosemite Ski & Snowboard Area.

IN THE PARK

$$
HOTEL
Big Trees Lodge. This 1879 National Historic Landmark at Yosemite's southern end (formerly Wawona Hotel) is a Victorian-era mountain resort, with whitewashed buildings, wraparound verandas, and pleasant, no-frills rooms decorated with period pieces. **Pros:** lovely building; peaceful atmosphere. **Cons:** few modern amenities, such as phones and TVs; an hour's drive from Yosemite Valley; shared bathrooms in half the rooms. $ *Rooms from: $148 ⊠ 8308 Wawona Rd., Wawona ☎ 888/413–8869 ⊕ www.travelyosemite.com ۩ Closed Dec.–Mar., except mid-Dec.–Jan. 2 ☜ 104 rooms, 50 with bath ❍ Breakfast.*

$$
HOTEL
Half Dome Village. Opened in 1899 as a place for budget-conscious travelers, Half Dome Village (formerly Curry Village) has plain accommodations: standard motel rooms, simple cabins with either private or shared baths, and tent cabins with shared baths. **Pros:** close to many activities; family-friendly atmosphere. **Cons:** not that economical after a recent price surge; can be crowded; sometimes a bit noisy. $ *Rooms from: $133 ⊠ South side of Southside Dr. ☎ 888/413– 8869, 602/278–8888 international ⊕ www.travelyosemite.com ☜ 583 rooms and cabins ❍ No meals.*

$$$$
HOTEL
Fodor's Choice
★
The Majestic Yosemite Hotel. Formerly the Ahwahnee, this National Historic Landmark is constructed of sugar-pine logs and features Native American design motifs; public spaces are enlivened with art deco flourishes, Persian rugs, and elaborate iron- and woodwork. **Pros:** best lodge in Yosemite; helpful concierge. **Cons:** expensive rates; some reports that service has slipped in recent years. $ *Rooms from: $458 ⊠ Ahwahnee Rd., about ¾ mile east of Yosemite Valley Visitor Center, Yosemite Village ☎ 801/559–4884 ⊕ www.travelyosemite.com ☜ 125 rooms and suites ❍ No meals.*

$$
HOTEL
White Wolf Lodge. Set in a subalpine meadow, the rustic accommodations at White Wolf Lodge make it an excellent base camp for hiking the backcountry. **Pros:** quiet location; near some of Yosemite's most beautiful, less crowded hikes; good restaurant. **Cons:** far from the valley. $ *Rooms from: $138 ⊠ Yosemite National Park ✛ Off Tioga Rd. (Rte. 120), 25 miles west of Tuolumne Meadows and 15 miles east of Crane*

Flat ☎ *801/559–4884* ⏲ *Closed mid-Sept.–mid-June* 🛏 *24 tent cabins, 4 cabins* 🍴 *No meals.*

$$$$ HOTEL 🏨 **Yosemite Valley Lodge.** This 1915 lodge near Yosemite Falls (formerly Yosemite Lodge at the Falls) is a collection of numerous two-story, glass-and-wood structures tucked beneath the trees. **Pros:** centrally located; dependably clean rooms; lots of tours leave from out front. **Cons:** can feel impersonal; prices recently skyrocketed. [$] *Rooms from: $247* ✉ *9006 Yosemite Valley Lodge Dr., Yosemite Village* ☎ *888/413–8869* 🌐 *www.travelyosemite.com/* 🛏 *245 rooms* 🍴 *No meals.*

LODGING TIP

Reserve your room or cabin in Yosemite as far in advance as possible. You can make a reservation up to a year before your arrival (within minutes after the reservation office makes a date available, The Majestic Yosemite Hotel, Yosemite Valley Lodge, and Big Trees Lodge often sell out their weekends, holiday periods, and all days between May and September).

OUTSIDE THE PARK

$$$ HOTEL FAMILY 🏨 **Best Western Plus Yosemite Gateway Inn.** Perched on 11 hillside acres, Oakhurst's best motel has carefully tended landscaping and rooms with stylish contemporary furnishings and hand-painted murals of Yosemite. **Pros:** close to park's southern entrance; on-site restaurant; indoor and outdoor swimming pools; frequent deer and wildlife sightings. **Cons:** some rooms on the small side; Internet connection can be slow. [$] *Rooms from: $160* ✉ *40530 Hwy. 41, Oakhurst* ☎ *559/683–2378* 🌐 *www.yosemitegatewayinn.com* 🛏 *149 rooms* 🍴 *No meals.*

$$$$ RESORT Fodor's Choice ★ 🏨 **Château du Sureau.** The inn here is straight out of a children's book: every room is impeccably styled with European antiques, sumptuous fabrics, fresh-cut flowers, and oversize soaking tubs. **Pros:** luxurious; great views; sumptuous spa facility. **Cons:** expensive; cost might not seem worth it to guests not spa-oriented. [$] *Rooms from: $420* ✉ *48688 Victoria La., Oakhurst* ☎ *559/683–6860* 🌐 *www.chateausureau.com* 🛏 *10 rooms, 1 villa* 🍴 *Breakfast.*

$$$$ RESORT FAMILY 🏨 **Evergreen Lodge at Yosemite.** Amid the trees near Yosemite National Park's Hetch Hetchy entrance, this sprawling property is perfect for families. **Pros:** near the underrated Hetch Hetchy Valley; family atmosphere; clean cabins. **Cons:** not cheap; about an hour's drive to Yosemite Valley. [$] *Rooms from: $275* ✉ *33160 Evergreen Rd., 33 miles north of El Portal, 30 miles east of town of Groveland, Groveland* ☎ *209/379–2606* 🌐 *www.evergreenlodge.com* 🛏 *88 cabins.*

$$$ B&B/INN 🏨 **Homestead Cottages.** Set on 160 acres of rolling hills that once held a Miwok village, these cottages (the largest sleeps six) have gas fireplaces, fully equipped kitchens, and queen-size beds. **Pros:** remote location; quiet setting; friendly owners. **Cons:** might be too quiet for some. [$] *Rooms from: $189* ✉ *41110 Rd. 600, 2½ miles off Hwy. 49, Ahwahnee* ☎ *559/683–0495* 🌐 *www.homesteadcottages.com* 🛏 *6 cottages* 🍴 *Breakfast.*

19

Best Campgrounds in Yosemite

If you are going to concentrate solely on valley sites and activities, you should endeavor to stay in one of the "Pines" campgrounds, which are clustered near Half Dome Village and within an easy stroll from that busy complex's many facilities. For a more primitive and quiet experience, and to be near many backcountry hikes, try one of the Tioga Road campgrounds.

National Park Service Reservations Office. Reservations are required at many of Yosemite's campgrounds. You can book a site up to five months in advance, starting on the 15th of the month. Unless otherwise noted, book your site through the central National Park Service Reservations Office. If you don't have reservations when you arrive, many sites, especially those outside Yosemite Valley, are available on a first-come, first-served basis. ☎ 877/444–6777 reservations, 518/885–3639 international, 888/448–1474 customer service ⊕ www.recreation.gov.

Bridalveil Creek. This campground sits among lodgepole pines at 7,200 feet, above the valley on Glacier Point Road. From here, you can easily drive to Glacier Point's magnificent valley views. ✉ From Rte. 41 in Wawona, go north to Glacier Point Rd. and turn right; entrance to campground is 25 miles ahead on right side.

Camp 4. Formerly known as Sunnyside Walk-In, and extremely popular with rock climbers, who don't mind that a total of six are assigned to each campsite; no matter how many are in your group, this is the only valley campground available on a first-come, first-served basis. ✉ Base of Yosemite Falls Trail, just west of Yosemite Valley Lodge on Northside Dr., Yosemite Village.

Housekeeping Camp. Composed of three concrete walls and covered with two layers of canvas, each unit has an open-ended fourth side that can be closed off with a heavy white canvas curtain. You can rent "bedpacks," consisting of blankets, sheets, and other comforts. ✉ Southside Dr., ½ mile west of Half Dome Village.

Porcupine Flat. Sixteen miles west of Tuolumne Meadows, this campground sits at 8,100 feet. If you want to be in the high country, this is a good bet. ✉ Rte. 120, 16 miles west of Tuolumne Meadows.

Tuolumne Meadows. In a wooded area at 8,600 feet, just south of its namesake meadow, this is one of the most spectacular and sought-after campgrounds in Yosemite. ✉ Rte. 120, 46 miles east of Big Oak Flat entrance station.

Upper Pines. This is one of the valley's largest campgrounds and the closest one to the trailheads. Expect large crowds in the summer—and little privacy. ✉ At east end of valley, near Half Dome Village.

Wawona. Near the Mariposa Grove, just downstream from a popular fishing spot, this year-round campground has larger, less densely packed sites than campgrounds in the valley. ✉ Rte. 41, 1 mile north of Wawona.

White Wolf. Set in the beautiful high country at 8,000 feet, this is a prime spot for hikers from early July to mid-September. ✉ Tioga Rd., 15 miles east of Big Oak Flat entrance.

CAMPING IN BEAR COUNTRY

The national parks' campgrounds and some campgrounds outside the parks provide food-storage boxes that can keep bears from pilfering your edibles (portable canisters for backpackers can be rented in most park stores). It's imperative that you move all food, coolers, and items with a scent (including toiletries, toothpaste, chewing gum, and air fresheners) from your car (including the trunk) to the storage box at your campsite; day-trippers should lock food in bear boxes provided at parking lots. If you don't, a bear may break into your car by literally peeling off the door or ripping open the trunk, or ransack your tent. The familiar tactic of hanging your food from high tree limbs is not an effective deterrent, as bears easily can scale trees. In the southern Sierra, bear canisters are the only effective and proven method for preventing bears from getting human food.

$$$$
B&B/INN

☷ **Narrow Gauge Inn.** The well-tended rooms at this family-owned property have balconies with views of the surrounding woods and mountains. **Pros:** close to Yosemite's south entrance; nicely appointed rooms; wonderful balconies. **Cons:** rooms can be a bit dark; dining options are limited, especially for vegetarians. $ *Rooms from: $209* ⊠ *48571 Hwy. 41, Fish Camp* ☏ *559/683–7720, 888/644–9050* ⊕ *www.narrowgauge-inn.com* ⤵ *26 rooms* ◎ *Breakfast.*

$$$$
RESORT
FAMILY
Fodor's Choice
★

☷ **Rush Creek Lodge.** This sleek, nature-inspired complex occupies 20 acres on a wooded hillside and includes a pool and hot tubs, a restaurant and tavern with indoor/outdoor seating, a guided recreation program, an amphitheater, and a general store. **Pros:** close to Yosemite's Big Oak Flat entrance; YARTS bus stops here and connects with Yosemite Valley and Sonora. **Cons:** no TVs; pricey in high season; remote setting. $ *Rooms from: $350* ⊠ *34001 Hwy. 120, Groveland* ✛ *25 miles east of Groveland, 23 miles north of Yosemite Valley* ☏ *209/379–2373* ⊕ *www.rushcreeklodge.com* ⤵ *143 rooms and suites* ◎ *No meals.*

$$$$
HOTEL

☷ **Sierra Sky Ranch.** Off Highway 41 just 10 miles south of the Yosemite National Park, this 19th-century cattle ranch near a hidden grove of giant sequoia trees provides a restful, rustic retreat. **Pros:** peaceful setting; historic property; full hot breakfast. **Cons:** some rooms on the small side; not in town. $ *Rooms from: $229* ⊠ *50552 Rd. 632, Oakhurst* ☏ *559/683–8040* ⊕ *www.sierraskyranch.com* ⤵ *26 rooms* ◎ *Breakfast.*

$$$
RESORT

☷ **Tamarack Lodge Resort.** Tucked away on the edge of the John Muir Wilderness Area, where cross-country ski trails loop through the woods, this 1924 lodge looks like something out of a snow globe. **Pros:** rustic but not run-down; tons of nearby outdoor activities. **Cons:** thin walls; some shared bathrooms. $ *Rooms from: $169* ⊠ *Lake Mary Rd., off Rte. 203, Mammoth Lakes* ☏ *760/934–2442, 800/237–6879* ⊕ *www.tamaracklodge.com* ⤵ *45 rooms and cabins* ◎ *No meals.*

19

$$$$ RESORT FAMILY Fodor's Choice ★ **Tenaya Lodge.** One of the region's largest hotels, Tenaya Lodge is ideal for people who enjoy wilderness treks by day but prefer creature comforts at night. **Pros:** rustic setting with modern comforts; exceptional spa and exercise facility; close to Yosemite; activities for all ages. **Cons:** so big it can seem impersonal; pricey during summer. [$] *Rooms from: $379* ✉ *1122 Hwy. 41, Fish Camp* ☎ *559/683–6555, 888/514–2167* 🌐 *www.tenayalodge.com* 🛏 *302 rooms* 🍴 *No meals.*

$$$$ B&B/INN **Yosemite Lodging at Big Creek Inn.** A romantic bed-and-breakfast in a woodsy setting south of the park, the inn offers perks that place it ahead of the competition. **Pros:** friendly, knowledgeable innkeeper; hearty home-cooked breakfast; intimate setting. **Cons:** with only three rooms it books up quickly; no pets allowed. [$] *Rooms from: $269* ✉ *1221 Hwy. 41, Fish Camp* ☎ *559/641–2828* 🌐 *www.yosemiteinn.com* 🛏 *3 rooms* 🍴 *Breakfast.*

SEQUOIA AND KINGS CANYON NATIONAL PARKS

WELCOME TO SEQUOIA AND KINGS CANYON NATIONAL PARKS

TOP REASONS TO GO

★ **Gentle giants:** You'll feel small—in a good way—walking among some of the world's largest living things in Sequoia's Giant Forest and Kings Canyon's Grant Grove.

★ **Because it's there:** You can't even glimpse it from the main part of Sequoia, but the sight of majestic Mount Whitney is worth the trip to the eastern face of the High Sierra.

★ **Underground exploration:** Far older even than the giant sequoias, the gleaming limestone formations in Crystal Cave will draw you along dark, marble passages.

★ **A grander-than-Grand Canyon:** Drive the twisting Kings Canyon Scenic Byway down into the jagged, granite Kings River Canyon, deeper in parts than the Grand Canyon.

★ **Regal solitude:** To spend a day or two hiking in a subalpine world of your own, pick one of the many trailheads at Mineral King.

1 **Giant Forest–Lodgepole Village.** One of the most heavily visited areas of Sequoia contains major sights such as Giant Forest, General Sherman Tree, Crystal Cave, and Moro Rock.

2 **Grant Grove Village–Redwood Canyon.** The "thumb" of Kings Canyon National Park is its busiest section, where Grant Grove, General Grant Tree, Panoramic Point, and Big Stump are the main attractions.

3 **Cedar Grove.** The drive through the high-country portion of Kings Canyon National Park to Cedar Grove Village, on the canyon floor, reveals magnificent granite formations of varied hues. Rock meets river in breathtaking fashion at Zumwalt Meadow.

4 **Mineral King.** In the southeast section of Sequoia, the highest road-accessible part of the park is a good place to hike, camp, and soak up the unspoiled grandeur of the Sierra Nevada.

5 **Mount Whitney.** The highest peak in the Lower 48 stands on the eastern edge of Sequoia; to get there from Giant Forest you must either backpack eight days through the mountains or drive nearly 400 miles around the park to its other side.

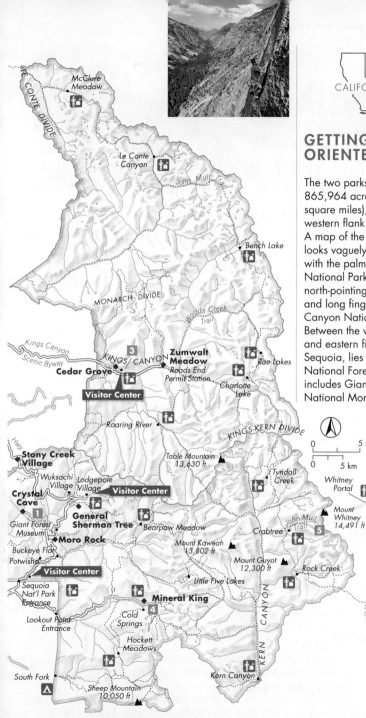

CALIFORNIA

GETTING ORIENTED

The two parks comprise 865,964 acres (1,353 square miles), mostly on the western flank of the Sierra. A map of the adjacent parks looks vaguely like a mitten, with the palm of Sequoia National Park south of the north-pointing, skinny thumb and long fingers of Kings Canyon National Park. Between the western thumb and eastern fingers, north of Sequoia, lies part of Sequoia National Forest, which includes Giant Sequoia National Monument.

McClure Meadow

LE CONTE DIVIDE

Le Conte Canyon

John Muir Trail

Bench Lake

MONARCH DIVIDE

Woods Creek Trail

Kings Canyon Scenic Byway

KINGS / CANYON

Zumwalt Meadow
Roads End
Permit Station

Rae Lakes

Cedar Grove

Charlotte Lake

Visitor Center

Roaring River

KINGS–KERN DIVIDE

Stony Creek Village

Table Mountain 13,630 ft

Tyndall Creek

Whitney Portal

0   5 mi
0   5 km

Wuksachi Village

Lodgepole Village

Visitor Center

Mount Whitney 14,491 ft

Crystal Cave

General Sherman Tree

Bearpaw Meadow

Giant Forest Museum

John Muir Trail

Crabtree

20

Moro Rock

Mount Kaweah 13,802 ft

Buckeye Flat

Potwisha

Mount Guyot 12,300 ft

Rock Creek

Little Five Lakes

Visitor Center

Sequoia Nat'l Park Entrance

Mineral King

Lookout Point Entrance

Cold Springs

Hockett Meadows

KERN CANYON

South Fork

Sheep Mountain 10,050 ft

Kern Canyon

Updated
by Cheryl
Crabtree

Although *Sequoiadendron giganteum* is the formal name for the redwoods that grow here, everyone outside the classroom calls them sequoias, big trees, or Sierra redwoods. Their monstrously thick trunks and branches, remarkably shallow root systems, and neck-craning heights are almost impossible to believe, as is the fact they can live for more than 2,500 years. Many of these towering marvels are in the Giant Forest stretch of Generals Highway, which connects Sequoia and Kings Canyon national parks.

Next to or a few miles off the 46-mile Generals Highway are most of Sequoia National Park's main attractions and Grant Grove Village, the orientation hub for Kings Canyon National Park. The two parks share a boundary that runs from the Central Valley in the west, where the Sierra Nevada foothills begin, to the range's dramatic eastern ridges. Kings Canyon has two portions: the smaller is shaped like a bent finger and encompasses Grant Grove Village and Redwood Mountain Grove (two of the parks' largest concentration of sequoias), and the larger is home to stunning Kings River Canyon, whose vast, unspoiled peaks and valleys are a backpacker's dream. Sequoia is in one piece and includes Mount Whitney, the highest point in the lower 48 states (although it is impossible to see from the western part of the park and is a chore to ascend from either side).

PLANNING

WHEN TO GO

The best times to visit are late spring and early fall, when temperatures are moderate and crowds thin. Summertime can draw hordes of tourists to see the giant sequoias, and the few, narrow roads mean congestion at peak holiday times. If you must visit in summer, go during the week. By contrast, in wintertime you may feel as though you have the parks all to yourself. But because of heavy snows, sections of the main park roads can be closed without warning, and low-hanging clouds can move in and obscure mountains and valleys for days. From early October to late April, check road and weather conditions before venturing out. ■TIP→ Even in summer, you can escape hordes of people just walking ¼ to ½ mile off the beaten path on a less-used trail.

PLANNING YOUR TIME

SEQUOIA NATIONAL PARK IN ONE DAY

After spending the night in Visalia or Three Rivers—and provided your vehicle's length does not exceed 22 feet—shove off early on Route 198 to the **Sequoia National Park entrance.** Pull over at the **Hospital Rock** picnic area to gaze up at the imposing granite formation of Moro Rock, which you later will climb. Heed signs that advise "10 mph" around tight turns as you climb 3,500 feet on **Generals Highway** to the **Giant Forest Museum.** Spend a half hour here, then examine trees firsthand by circling the lovely **Round Meadow** on the **Big Trees Trail,** to which you must walk from the museum or from its parking lot across the road.

Get back in your car and continue a few miles north on Generals Highway to see the jaw-dropping **General Sherman Tree.** Then set off on the **Congress Trail** so that you can be further awed by the Senate and House big-tree clusters. Buy lunch at the **Lodgepole** complex, 2 miles to the north, and eat at the nearby **Pinewood** picnic area. Now you're ready for the day's big exercise, the mounting of **Moro Rock.**

You can drive there or, if it is summer, park at the museum lot and take the free shuttle. Count on spending at least an hour for the 350-step ascent and descent, with a pause on top to appreciate the 360-degree view. Get back in the car, or on the shuttle, and proceed past the **Tunnel Log** to **Crescent Meadow.** Spend a relaxing hour or two strolling on the trails that pass by, among other things, **Tharp's Log.** By now you've probably renewed your appetite; head to **Sequoia Barbequeat Wuksachi Lodge** (summer evenings only) or the restaurant at **Wuksachi Lodge.**

KINGS CANYON NATIONAL PARK IN ONE DAY

Enter the park via the **Kings Canyon Scenic Byway** (Route 180), having spent the night in Fresno or Visalia. Better yet, wake up already in **Grant Grove Village,** perhaps in the **John Muir Lodge.** Stock up for a picnic with takeout food from the **Grant Grove Restaurant,** or purchase prepackaged food from the nearby market. Drive east a mile to see the **General Grant Tree** and compact **Grant Grove's** other sequoias. If it's no later than midmorning, walk up the short trail at **Panoramic Point,** for a great view of Hume Lake and the High Sierra. Either way, return to Route 180 and continue east. Stop at Junction View to take in several noteworthy peaks that tower over Kings Canyon. From here, visit **Boyden Cavern** or continue to **Cedar Grove Village,** pausing along the way for a gander at **Grizzly Falls.** Eat at a table by the **South Fork of the Kings River,** or on the deck off the Cedar Grove Snack Bar. Now you are ready for the day's highlight, strolling **Zumwalt Meadow,** which lies a few miles past the village.

20

After you have enjoyed that short trail and the views it offers of **Grand Sentinel** and **North Dome,** you might as well go the extra mile to **Roads End,** where backpackers embark for the High Sierra wilderness. Make the return trip—with a quick stop at **Roaring River Falls**—past Grant Grove and briefly onto southbound **Generals Highway.** Pull over at the **Redwood Mountain Overlook** and use binoculars to look down upon the world's largest sequoia grove, then drive another couple of miles to the **Kings Canyon Overlook,** where you can survey some of what you have done today. If you've made reservations and have time, have a late dinner at **Wuksachi Lodge.**

GETTING HERE AND AROUND

AIR TRAVEL

The closest airport to Sequoia and Kings Canyon national parks is Fresno Yosemite International Airport (FAT).

Airport Contacts Fresno Yosemite International Airport (FAT). ⊠ 5175 E. Clinton Way, Fresno ☎ 800/244-2359 automated info, 559/454-2052 terminal info desk ⊕ www.flyfresno.com.

CAR TRAVEL

Sequoia is 36 miles east of Visalia on Route 198; Grant Grove Village in Kings Canyon is 56 miles east of Fresno on Route 180. There is no automobile entrance on the eastern side of the Sierra. Routes 180 and 198 are connected by Generals Highway, a paved two-lane road that sometimes sees delays at peak times due to ongoing improvements. The road is extremely narrow and steep from Route 198 to Giant Forest, so keep an eye on your engine temperature gauge, as the incline and congestion can cause vehicles to overheat; to avoid overheated brakes, use low gears on downgrades.

If you are traveling in an RV or with a trailer, study the restrictions on these vehicles. Do not travel beyond Potwisha Campground on Route 198 with an RV longer than 22 feet; take straighter, easier Route 180 instead. Maximum vehicle length on Generals Highway is 40 feet, or 50 feet combined length for vehicles with trailers.

Generals Highway between Lodgepole and Grant Grove is sometimes closed by snow. The Mineral King Road from Route 198 into southern Sequoia National Park is closed 2 miles below Atwell Mill either on November 1 or after the first heavy snow. The Buckeye Flat–Middle Fork Trailhead road is closed from mid-October to mid-April when the Buckeye Flat Campground closes. The lower Crystal Cave Road is closed when the cave closes (typically in November). Its upper 2 miles, as well as the Panoramic Point and Moro Rock–Crescent Meadow roads, close with the first heavy snow. Because of the danger of rockfall, the portion of Kings Canyon Scenic Byway east of Grant Grove closes in winter. For current road and weather conditions, call ☎ 559/565-3341.

■**TIP→** Snowstorms are common from late October through April. Unless you have a four-wheel-drive vehicle with snow tires, you should carry chains and know how to install them.

PARK ESSENTIALS
PARK FEES AND PERMITS
The admission fee is $30 per vehicle, $25 per motorcycle, and $15 per person for those who enter by bus, on foot, bicycle, horse, or any other mode of transportation; it is valid for seven days in both parks. U.S. residents over the age of 62 pay $10 for a lifetime pass, and permanently disabled U.S. residents are admitted free.

If you plan to camp in the backcountry, you need a permit, which costs $15 for hikers or $30 for stock users (e.g., horseback riders). One permit covers the group. Availability of permits depends upon trailhead quotas. Reservations are accepted by mail or email for a $15 processing fee, beginning March 1, and must be made at least 14 days in advance (☎ 559/565–3766). Without a reservation, you may still get a permit on a first-come, first-served basis starting at 1 pm the day before you plan to hike. For more information on backcountry camping or travel with pack animals (horses, mules, burros, or llamas), contact the Wilderness Permit Office (☎ 530/565–3766).

PARK HOURS
The parks are open 24/7 year-round. They are in the Pacific time zone.

EDUCATIONAL OFFERINGS
Educational programs at the parks include museum-style exhibits, ranger- and naturalist-led talks and walks, film and other programs, and sightseeing tours, most of them conducted by either the park service or the nonprofit Sequoia Natural History Association. Exhibits at the visitor centers and the Giant Forest Museum focus on different aspects of the park: its history, wildlife, geology, climate, and vegetation—most notably the giant sequoias. Weekly notices about programs are posted at the visitor centers and elsewhere.

Grant Grove Visitor Center at Kings Canyon National Park has maps of self-guided park tours. Ranger-led walks and programs take place throughout the year in Grant Grove. Cedar Grove and Forest Service campgrounds have activities from Memorial Day to Labor Day. Check bulletin boards or visitor centers for schedules.

20

EXHIBITS
Giant Forest Museum. Well-imagined and interactive displays at this worthwhile stop provide the basics about sequoias, of which there are 2,161 with diameters exceeding 10 feet in the approximately 2,000-acre Giant Forest. ⊠ *Sequoia National Park ✛ Generals Hwy., 4 miles south of Lodgepole Visitor Center* ☎ 559/565–4480 *☛ Free ☞ Shuttle: Giant Forest or Moro Rock–Crescent Meadow.*

PROGRAMS AND SEMINARS
Evening Programs. The Sequoia Parks Conservancy presents films, hikes, and evening lectures during the summer and winter. From May through October the popular Wonders of the Night Sky programs celebrate the often stunning views of the heavens experienced at both parks. ⊠ *Sequoia National Park* ☎ 559/565–4251 ⊕ *www.exploresequoiakingscanyon.com.*

Free Nature Programs. Almost any summer day, ½-hour to 1½-hour ranger talks and walks explore subjects such as the life of the sequoia, the geology of the park, and the habits of bears. Giant Forest, Lodgepole Visitor Center, and Wuksachi Village are frequent starting points. Look for less frequent tours in the winter from Grant Grove. Check bulletin boards throughout the park for the week's offerings. ⊕ *www. exploresequoiakingscanyon.com.*

Seminars. Expert naturalists lead seminars on a range of topics, including birds, wildflowers, geology, botany, photography, park history, backpacking, and pathfinding. Reservations are required. Information about times and prices is available at the visitor centers or through the Sequoia Parks Conservancy. ⊠ *Sequoia National Park* ☎ *559/565–4251* ⊕ *www. exploresequoiakingscanyon.com.*

TOURS

Fodor's Choice
★ **Sequoia Field Institute.** The Sequoia Parks Conservancy's highly regarded educational division conducts single-day and multiday "EdVenture" tours that include backpacking hikes, natural-history walks, cross-country skiing, kayaking excursions, and motorcoach tours. ⊠ *47050 Generals Hwy., Unit 10, Three Rivers* ☎ *559/565–4251* ⊕ *www.exploresequoia-kingscanyon.com* ☎ *From $275 for a ½-day guided tour.*

Sequoia Sightseeing Tours. This locally owned operator's friendly, knowledgeable guides conduct daily interpretive sightseeing tours in Sequoia and Kings Canyon. Reservations are essential. The company also offers private tours. ⊠ *Three Rivers* ☎ *559/561–4189* ⊕ *www.sequoiatours. com* ☎ *From $69 tour of Sequoia; from $139 tour of Kings Canyon.*

RESTAURANTS

In Sequoia and Kings Canyon national parks, you can treat yourself (and the family) to a high-quality meal in a wonderful setting in the Peaks restaurant at Wuksachi Lodge, but otherwise you should keep your expectations modest. A good strategy is to embrace outdoor eating. You can grab bread, spreads, drinks, and fresh produce at one of several small grocery stores, or get take-out food from the Grant Grove Restaurant, the Cedar Grove snack bar, or one of the two small Lodgepole eateries. The summertime Sequoia Barbeque at Wuksachi Lodgeue is a hybrid experience between dining in and picnicking out. Between the parks and just off Generals Highway, the Montecito Sequoia Lodge has a year-round buffet. *Restaurant reviews have been shortened. For full information, visit Fodors.com.*

HOTELS

Hotel accommodations in Sequoia and Kings Canyon are limited, and—although they are clean and comfortable—tend to lack much in-room character. Keep in mind, however, that the extra money you spend on lodging here is offset by the time you'll save by being inside the parks. You won't be faced with a 60- to 90-minute commute from the less-expensive motels in Three Rivers (by far the most charming option), Visalia, and Fresno. Reserve as far in advance as you can, especially for summertime stays. *Hotel reviews have been shortened. For full information, visit Fodors.com.*

WHAT IT COSTS				
	$	**$$**	**$$$**	**$$$$**
Restaurants	under $12	$12–$20	$21–$30	over $30
Hotels	under $100	$100–$150	$151–$200	over $200

Restaurant prices in the reviews are the average cost of a main course at dinner, or if dinner is not served, at lunch. Hotel prices are the lowest cost of a standard double room in high season, excluding taxes and service charges.

VISITOR INFORMATION
National Park Service Sequoia and Kings Canyon National Parks. ⊠ *47050 Generals Hwy. (Rte. 198), Three Rivers* 🖀 *559/565–3341* ⊕ *nps.gov/seki.*

SEQUOIA VISITOR CENTERS
Foothills Visitor Center. Exhibits here focus on the foothills and resource issues facing the parks. You can pick up books, maps, and a list of ranger-led walks, and get wilderness permits. ⊠ *47050 Generals Hwy., Rte. 198, 1 mile north of Ash Mountain entrance, Sequoia National Park* 🖀 *559/565–3341.*

Lodgepole Visitor Center. Along with exhibits on the area's history, geology, and wildlife, the center screens an outstanding 22-minute film about bears. You can buy books, maps, and tickets to cave tours and the Wolverton barbecue here. ⊠ *Sequoia National Park* ✛ *Generals Hwy. (Rte. 198), 21 miles north of Ash Mountain entrance* 🖀 *559/565–3341* ⊘ *Closed Oct.–Apr.* ☞ *Shuttle: Giant Forest or Wuksachi-Lodgepole-Dorst.*

KINGS CANYON VISITOR CENTERS
Cedar Grove Visitor Center. Off the main road and behind the Sentinel Campground, this small ranger station has books and maps, plus information about hikes and other activities. ⊠ *Kings Canyon National Park* ✛ *Kings Canyon Scenic Byway, 30 miles east of Rte. 180/198 junction* 🖀 *559/565–3341* ⊘ *Closed mid-Sept.–mid-May.*

Kings Canyon Park Visitor Center. The center's 15-minute film and various exhibits provide an overview of the park's canyon, sequoias, and human history. Books, maps, and weather advice are dispensed here, as are (if available) free wilderness permits. ⊠ *Kings Canyon National Park* ✛ *Grant Grove Village, Generals Hwy. (Rte. 198), 3 miles northeast of Rte. 180, Big Stump entrance* 🖀 *559/565–3341.*

20

SEQUOIA NATIONAL PARK

EXPLORING

SCENIC DRIVES
Fodor's Choice ★ **Generals Highway.** One of California's most scenic drives, this 46-mile road is the main asphalt artery between Sequoia and Kings Canyon national parks. Some portions are also signed as Route 180, others as Route 198. Named after the landmark Grant and Sherman trees that leave so many visitors awestruck, Generals Highway runs from Sequoia's

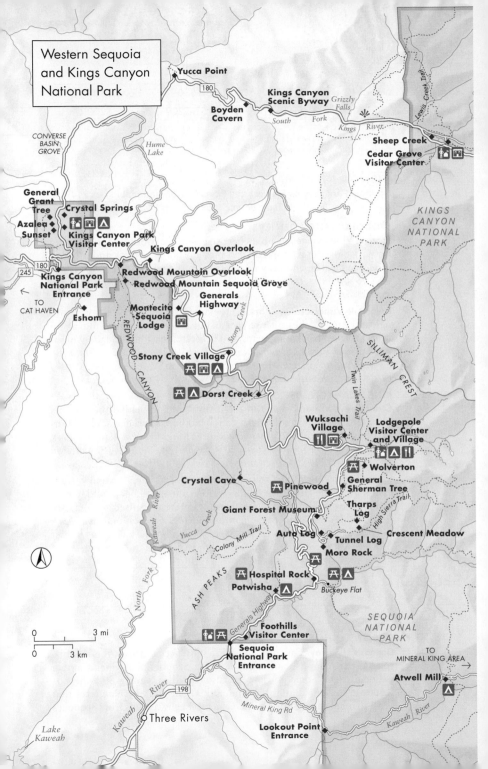

Western Sequoia and Kings Canyon National Park

Yucca Point

Kings Canyon Scenic Byway

Boyden Cavern

Grizzly Falls

South Fork

Kings River

Lewis Creek Trail

Sheep Creek

Cedar Grove Visitor Center

CONVERSE BASIN GROVE

Hume Lake

KINGS CANYON NATIONAL PARK

General Grant Tree

Crystal Springs

Azalea

Sunset

Kings Canyon Park Visitor Center

Kings Canyon National Park Entrance

Kings Canyon Overlook

TO CAT HAVEN

Redwood Mountain Overlook

Redwood Mountain Sequoia Grove

Eshom

Montecito Sequoia Lodge

Generals Highway

Stony Creek

REDWOOD CANYON

Stony Creek Village

SILLIMAN CREST

Dorst Creek

Twin Lakes Trail

Wuksachi Village

Lodgepole Visitor Center and Village

Wolverton

Crystal Cave

Pinewood

General Sherman Tree

Kaweah River

Giant Forest Museum

Tharps Log

High Sierra Trail

Crescent Meadow

Yucca Creek

Colony Mill Trail

Auto Log

Tunnel Log

Moro Rock

ASH PEAKS

Hospital Rock

North Fork

Potwisha

Buckeye Flat

SEQUOIA NATIONAL PARK

Generals Highway

Foothills Visitor Center

TO MINERAL KING AREA

Sequoia National Park Entrance

Atwell Mill

Three Rivers

Lake Kaweah

Kaweah River

Mineral King Rd

Kaweah River

Lookout Point Entrance

0   3 mi

0   3 km

Foothills Visitor Center north to Kings Canyon's Grant Grove Village. Along the way, it passes the turnoff to Crystal Cave, the Giant Forest Museum, Lodgepole Village, and other popular attractions. The lower portion, from Hospital Rock to the Giant Forest, is especially steep and winding. If your vehicle is 22 feet or longer, avoid that stretch by entering the parks via Route 180 (from Fresno) rather than Route 198 (from Visalia or Three Rivers). Take your time on this road—there's a lot to see, and wildlife can scamper across at any time. ⊠ *Sequoia National Park.*

SCENIC STOPS

Sequoia National Park is all about the trees, and to understand the scale of these giants you must walk among them. If you do nothing else, get out of the car for a short stroll through one of the groves. But there is much more to the park than the trees. Try to access one of the vista points that provide a panoramic view over the forested mountains. Generals Highway (on Routes 198 and 180) will be your route to most of the park's sights. A few short spur roads lead from the highway to some sights, and Mineral King Road branches off Route 198 to enter the park at Lookout Point, winding east from there to the park's southernmost section.

Auto Log. Before its wood showed signs of severe rot, cars drove right on top of this giant fallen sequoia. Now it's a great place to pose for pictures or shoot a video. ⊠ *Sequoia National Park ✛ Moro Rock–Crescent Meadow Rd., 1 mile south of Giant Forest.*

Crescent Meadow. A sea of ferns signals your arrival at what John Muir called the "gem of the Sierra." Walk around for an hour or two and you might decide that the Scotland-born naturalist was exaggerating a wee bit, but the verdant meadow is quite pleasant and you just might see a bear. Wildflowers bloom here throughout the summer. ⊠ *Sequoia National Park ✛ End of Moro Rock–Crescent Meadow Rd., 2.6 miles east off Generals Hwy. ☞ Shuttle: Moro Rock–Crescent Meadow.*

Fodor's Choice ★ **Crystal Cave.** One of more than 200 caves in Sequoia and Kings Canyon, Crystal Cave is composed largely of marble, the result of limestone being hardened under heat and pressure. It contains several eye-popping formations. There used to be more, but some were damaged or obliterated by early-20th-century dynamite blasting. You can only see the cave on a tour. The Daily Tour ($16), a great overview, takes about 50 minutes. To immerse yourself in the cave experience—at times you'll be crawling on your belly—book the exhilarating Wild Cave Tour ($135). Purchase Daily Tour tickets at either the Foothills or Lodgepole visitor center; they're not sold at the cave itself. ⊠ *Crystal Cave Rd., off Generals Hwy.* ☎ *877/444–6777* ⊕ *www.explorecrystalcave.com* 💲 *$16* 🕙 *Closed Oct.–late May.*

Fodor's Choice ★ **General Sherman Tree.** The 274.9-foot-tall General Sherman is one of the world's tallest and oldest sequoias, and it ranks No. 1 in volume, adding the equivalent of a 60-foot-tall tree every year to its approximately 52,500 cubic feet of mass. The tree doesn't grow taller, though—it's dead at the top. A short, wheelchair-accessible trail leads to the tree from Generals Highway, but the main trail (½ mile) winds down from a parking lot off Wolverton Road. The walk

20

back up the main trail is steep, but benches along the way provide rest for the short of breath. ⊠ *Sequoia National Park ✛ Main trail Wolverton Rd. off Generals Hwy. (Rte. 198)* ⌁ *Shuttle: Giant Forest or Wolverton–Sherman Tree.*

Mineral King Area. A subalpine valley of fir, pine, and sequoia trees, Mineral King sits at 7,500 feet at the end of a steep, winding road. This is the highest point to which you can drive in the park. It is open only from Memorial Day through late October. ⊠ *Sequoia National Park ✛ Mineral King Rd., 25 miles east of Generals Hwy. (Rte. 198)* ☉ *Closed late Oct.–May.*

Fodor's Choice
★

Moro Rock. Sequoia National Park's best nontree attraction offers panoramic views to those fit and determined enough to mount its 350 or so steps. In a case where the journey rivals the destination, Moro's stone stairway is so impressive in its twisty inventiveness that it's on the National Register of Historic Places. The rock's 6,725-foot summit overlooks the Middle Fork Canyon, sculpted by the Kaweah River and approaching the depth of Arizona's Grand Canyon, although smoggy, hazy air often compromises the view. ⊠ *Sequoia National Park ✛ Moro Rock–Crescent Meadow Rd., 2 miles east off Generals Hwy. (Rte. 198) to parking area* ⌁ *Shuttle: Moro Rock–Crescent Meadow.*

Tunnel Log. This 275-foot tree fell in 1937, and soon a 17-foot-wide, 8-foot-high hole was cut through it for vehicular passage (not to mention the irresistible photograph) that continues today. Large vehicles take the nearby bypass. ⊠ *Sequoia National Park ✛ Moro Rock–Crescent Meadow Rd., 2 miles east of Generals Hwy. (Rte. 198)* ⌁ *Shuttle: Moro Rock–Crescent Meadow.*

SPORTS AND THE OUTDOORS

The best way to see Sequoia is to take a hike. Unless you do so, you'll miss out on the up-close grandeur of mist wafting between deeply scored, red-orange tree trunks bigger than you've ever seen. If it's winter, put on some snowshoes or cross-country skis and plunge into the snow-swaddled woodland. There are not too many other outdoor options: no off-road driving is allowed in the parks, and no special provisions have been made for bicycles. Boating, rafting, and snowmobiling are also prohibited.

BIRD-WATCHING

More than 200 species of birds inhabit Sequoia and Kings Canyon national parks. Not seen in most parts of the United States, the white-headed woodpecker and the pileated woodpecker are common in most mid-elevation areas here. There are also many hawks and owls, including the renowned spotted owl. Species are diverse in both parks due to the changes in elevation, and range from warblers, kingbirds, thrushes, and sparrows in the foothills to goshawk, blue grouse, red-breasted nuthatch, and brown creeper at the highest elevations. The Sequoia Parks Conservancy (☎ 559/565–4251 ⊕ *www.sequoiaparksconservancy.org*) has information about bird-watching in the southern Sierra.

CROSS-COUNTRY SKIING

For a one-of-a-kind experience, cut through the groves of mammoth sequoias in Giant Forest. Some of the Crescent Meadow trails are suitable for skiing as well; none of the trails is groomed. You can park at Giant Forest. Note that roads can be precarious in bad weather. Some advanced trails begin at Wolverton.

Alta Market and Ski Shop. Rent cross-country skis and snowshoes here. Depending on snowfall amounts, instruction may also be available. Reservations are recommended. Marked trails cut through Giant Forest, about 5 miles south of Wuksachi Lodge. ⊠ *Sequoia National Park ✛ At Lodgepole, off Generals Hwy. (Rte. 198)* ☎ *559/565–3301* ☞ *Shuttle: Wuksachi-Lodgepole-Dorst.*

FISHING

There's limited trout fishing in the creeks and rivers from late April to mid-November. The Kaweah River is a popular spot; check at visitor centers for open and closed waters. Some of the park's secluded backcountry lakes have good fishing. A California fishing license, required for persons 16 and older, costs about $15 for one day, $24 for two days, and $47 for 10 days (discounts are available for state residents and others). For park regulations, closures, and restrictions, call the parks at ☎ *559/565–3341* or stop at a visitor center. Licenses and fishing tackle are usually available at Hume Lake.

California Department of Fish and Game. The department supplies fishing licenses and provides a full listing of regulations. ☎ *916/928–5805* ⊕ *www.wildlife.ca.gov.*

HIKING

The best way to see the park is to hike it. The grandeur and majesty of the Sierra is best seen up close. Carry a hiking map and plenty of water. Visitor center gift shops sell maps and trail books and pamphlets. Check with rangers for current trail conditions, and be aware of rapidly changing weather. As a rule of thumb, plan on covering about a mile per hour.

EASY

Fodor's Choice ★ **Big Trees Trail.** This hike is a must, as it does not take long and the setting is spectacular: beautiful Round Meadow surrounded by many mature sequoias, with well-thought-out interpretive signs along the path that explain the ecology on display. The 0.7-mile Big Trees Trail is wheelchair accessible. Parking at the trailhead lot off Generals Highway is for cars with handicap placards only. The round-trip loop from the Giant Forest Museum is about a mile long. *Easy.* ⊠ *Sequoia National Park ✛ Trailhead: off Generals Hwy. (Rte. 198), near the Giant Forest Museum* ☞ *Shuttle: Giant Forest.*

Fodor's Choice ★ **Congress Trail.** This 2-mile trail, arguably the best hike in the parks in terms of natural beauty, is a paved loop that begins near General Sherman Tree. You'll get close-up views of more big trees here than on any other Sequoia hike. Watch for the clusters known as the House and Senate. The President Tree, also on the trail, supplanted the General Grant Tree in 2012 as the world's second largest in volume (behind the General Sherman). An offshoot of the Congress Trail leads to Crescent

20

Meadow, where in summer you can catch a free shuttle back to the Sherman parking lot. *Easy.* ⊠ *Sequoia National Park* ✛ *Trailhead: off Generals Hwy. (Rte. 198), 2 miles north of Giant Forest* ☞ *Shuttle: Giant Forest.*

Crescent Meadow Trails. A 1-mile trail loops around lush Crescent Meadow to Tharp's Log, a cabin built from a fire-hollowed sequoia. From there you can embark on a 60-mile trek to Mount Whitney, if you're prepared and have the time. Brilliant wildflowers bloom in midsummer. *Easy.* ⊠ *Sequoia National Park* ✛ *Trailhead: the end of Moro Rock–Crescent Meadow Rd., 2.6 miles east off Generals Hwy. (Rte. 198)* ☞ *Shuttle: Moro Rock–Crescent Meadow.*

MODERATE

Tokopah Falls Trail. This trail with a 500-foot elevation gain follows the Marble Fork of the Kaweah River for 1.75 miles one-way and dead-ends below the impressive granite cliffs and cascading waterfall of Tokopah Canyon. The trail passes through a mixed-conifer forest. It takes 2½ to 4 hours to make the round-trip journey. *Moderate.* ⊠ *Sequoia National Park* ✛ *Trailhead: off Generals Hwy. (Rte. 198), ¼ mile north of Lodgepole Campground* ☞ *Shuttle: Lodgepole-Wuksachi-Dorst.*

DIFFICULT

Mineral King Trails. Many trails to the high country begin at Mineral King. Two popular day hikes are Eagle Lake (6.8 miles round-trip) and Timber Gap (4.4 miles round-trip). At the Mineral King Ranger Station (*559/565–3768*) you can pick up maps and check about conditions from late May to late September. *Difficult.* ⊠ *Sequoia National Park* ✛ *Trailheads: at end of Mineral King Rd., 25 miles east of Generals Hwy. (Rte. 198).*

HORSEBACK RIDING

Trips take you through forests and flowering meadows and up mountain slopes.

TOURS AND OUTFITTERS

Grant Grove Stables. Grant Grove Stables isn't too far from parts of Sequoia National Park, and is perfect for short rides from June to September. Reservations are recommended. ☎ *559/335–9292 summer, 559/799–7247 off-season* ⊕ *www.visitsequoia.com/grant-grove-stables. aspx* ⊠ *From $40.*

KINGS CANYON NATIONAL PARK

EXPLORING

SCENIC DRIVES

Fodor's Choice   **Kings Canyon Scenic Byway.** The 30-mile stretch of Route 180 between
★   Grant Grove Village and Zumwalt Meadow delivers eye-popping scenery—granite cliffs, a roaring river, waterfalls, and Kings River Canyon itself—much of which you can experience at vista points or on easy walks. The canyon comes into view about 10 miles east of the village at **Junction View.** Five miles beyond, at **Yucca Point,** the canyon is thousands of feet deeper than the more famous Grand Canyon. **Canyon**

DID YOU KNOW?

Sequoias once grew throughout the Northern Hemisphere, until they were almost wiped out by glaciers. Some of the fossils in Arizona's Petrified Forest National Park are extinct sequoia species.

View, a special spot 1 mile east of the Cedar Grove Village turnoff, showcases evidence of the area's glacial history. Here, perhaps more than anywhere else, you'll understand why John Muir compared Kings Canyon vistas with those in Yosemite. Driving the byway takes about an hour each way without stops. ⊠ *Kings Canyon National Park ✛ Rte. 180 north and east of Grant Grove village.*

HISTORIC SITES

Fallen Monarch. This toppled sequoia's hollow base was used in the second half of the 19th century as a home for settlers, a saloon, and even to stable U.S. Cavalry horses. As you walk through it (assuming entry is permitted, which is not always possible), notice how little the wood has decayed, and imagine yourself tucked safely inside, sheltered from a storm or protected from the searing heat. ⊠ *Kings Canyon National Park ✛ Grant Grove Trail, 1 mile north of Kings Canyon Park Visitor Center.*

SCENIC STOPS

Kings Canyon National Park consists of two sections that adjoin the northern boundary of Sequoia National Park. The western portion, covered with sequoia and pine forest, contains the park's most visited sights, such as Grant Grove. The vast eastern portion is remote high country, slashed across half its southern breadth by the deep, rugged Kings River Canyon. Separating the two is Sequoia National Forest, which encompasses Giant Sequoia National Monument. The Kings Canyon Scenic Byway (Route 180) links the major sights within and between the park's two sections.

General Grant Tree. President Coolidge proclaimed this to be the "nation's Christmas tree," and 30 years later President Eisenhower designated it as a living shrine to all Americans who have died in wars. Bigger at its base than the General Sherman Tree, it tapers more quickly. It's estimated to be the world's third-largest sequoia by volume. A spur trail winds behind the tree, where scars from a long-ago fire remain visible. ⊠ *Kings Canyon National Park ✛ Trailhead: 1 mile north of Grant Grove Visitor Center.*

Redwood Mountain Sequoia Grove. One of the world's largest sequoia groves, Redwood contains within its 2,078 acres nearly 2,200 sequoias whose diameters exceed 10 feet. You can view the grove from afar at an overlook or hike 6 to 10 miles down into the richest regions, which include two of the world's 25 heaviest trees. ⊠ *Kings Canyon National Park ✛ Drive 6 miles south of Grant Grove on Generals Hwy. (Rte. 198), then turn right at Quail Flat; follow it 2 miles to the Redwood Canyon trailhead.*

SPORTS AND THE OUTDOORS

The siren song of beauty, challenge, and relative solitude (by national parks standards) draws hard-core outdoors enthusiasts to the Kings River Canyon and the backcountry of the park's eastern section. Backpacking, rock-climbing, and extreme-kayaking opportunities abound, but the park also has day hikes for all ability levels. Winter brings sledding, skiing, and snowshoeing fun. No off-road driving or bicycling is allowed in the park, and snowmobiling is also prohibited.

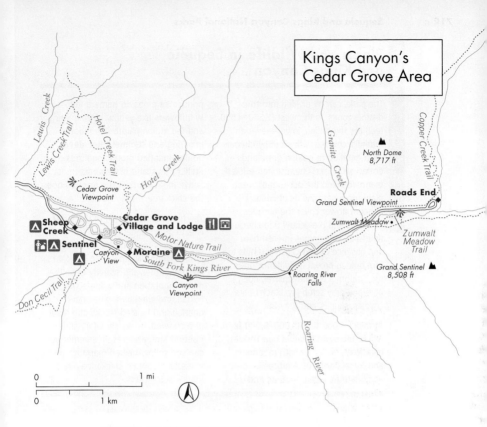

Kings Canyon's
Cedar Grove Area

Lewis Creek
Lewis Creek Trail
Hotel Creek Trail
Cedar Grove Viewpoint
Hotel Creek
Sheep Creek
Sentinel
Canyon View
Cedar Grove Village and Lodge
Moraine
Motor Nature Trail
Canyon Viewpoint
South Fork Kings River
Don Cecil Trail
Granite Creek
North Dome 8,717 ft
Copper Creek Trail
Roads End
Grand Sentinel Viewpoint
Zumwalt Meadow
Zumwalt Meadow Trail
Grand Sentinel 8,508 ft
Roaring River Falls
Roaring River

0   1 mi
0   1 km

CROSS-COUNTRY SKIING

Roads to Grant Grove are accessible even during heavy snowfall, making the trails here a good choice over Sequoia's Giant Forest when harsh weather hits.

HIKING

You can enjoy many of Kings Canyon's sights from your car, but the giant gorge of the Kings River Canyon and the sweeping vistas of some of the highest mountains in the United States are best seen on foot. Carry a hiking map—available at any visitor center—and plenty of water. Check with rangers for current trail conditions, and be aware of rapidly changing weather. Except for one trail to Mount Whitney, permits are not required for day hikes.

Roads End Permit Station. You can obtain wilderness permits, maps, and information about the backcountry at this station, where bear canisters, a must for campers, can be rented or purchased. When the station is closed (typically October–mid-May, complete a self-service permit form. ⊠ *Kings Canyon National Park ✛ Eastern end of Kings Canyon Scenic Byway, 6 miles east of Cedar Grove Visitor Center.*

20

CLOSE UP

Plants and Wildlife in Sequoia and Kings Canyon

The parks can be divided into three distinct zones. In the west (1,500–4,500 feet) are the rolling, lower-elevation foothills, covered with shrubby chaparral vegetation or golden grasslands dotted with oaks. Chamise, red-barked manzanita, and the occasional yucca plant grow here. Fields of white popcorn flower cover the hillsides in spring, and the yellow fiddleneck flourishes. In summer, intense heat and absence of rain cause the hills to turn golden brown. Wildlife includes the California ground squirrel, noisy blue-and-gray scrub jay, black bears, coyotes, skunks, and gray fox.

At middle elevation (5,000–9,000 feet), where the giant sequoia belt resides, rock formations mix with meadows and huge stands of evergreens—red and white fir, incense cedar, and

ponderosa pines, to name a few. Wildflowers like yellow blazing star and red Indian paintbrush bloom in spring and summer. Mule deer, golden-mantled ground squirrels, Steller's jays, and black bears (most active in fall) inhabit the area, as does the chickaree.

The high alpine section of the parks is extremely rugged, with a string of rocky peaks reaching above 13,000 feet to Mount Whitney's 14,494 feet. Fierce weather and scarcity of soil make vegetation and wildlife sparse. Foxtail and whitebark pines have gnarled and twisted trunks, the result of high wind, heavy snowfall, and freezing temperatures. In summer you can see yellow-bellied marmots, pikas, weasels, mountain chickadees, and Clark's nutcrackers.

EASY

Big Stump Trail. From 1883 until 1890, logging was done here, complete with a mill. The 1-mile loop trail, whose unmarked beginning is a few yards west of the Big Stump entrance, passes by many enormous stumps. *Easy.* ⊠ *Kings Canyon National Park* ⊕ *Trailhead: near Big Stump Entrance, Generals Hwy. (Rte. 180).*

Fodor's Choice
★
Grant Grove Trail. Grant Grove is only 128 acres, but it's a big deal. More than 120 sequoias here have a base diameter that exceeds 10 feet, and the **General Grant Tree** is the world's third-largest sequoia by volume. Nearby, the Confederacy is represented by the **Robert E. Lee Tree,** recognized as the world's 11th-largest sequoia. Also along the easy-to-walk trail are the **Fallen Monarch** and the **Gamlin Cabin,** built by 19th-century pioneers. *Easy.* ⊠ *Kings Canyon National Park* ⊕ *Trailhead: off Generals Hwy. (Rte. 180), 1 mile north of Kings Canyon Park Visitor Center.*

Roaring River Falls Walk. Take a shady five-minute walk to this forceful waterfall that rushes through a narrow granite chute. The trail is paved and mostly accessible. *Easy.* ⊠ *Kings Canyon National Park* ⊕ *Trailhead: 3 miles east of Cedar Grove Village turnoff from Kings Canyon Scenic Byway.*

Fodor'sChoice **Zumwalt Meadow Trail.** Rangers say this is the best (and most popular)
★ day hike in the Cedar Grove area. Just 1.5 miles long, it offers three
visual treats: the South Fork of the Kings River, the lush meadow,
and the high granite walls above, including those of Grand Sentinel
and North Dome. *Easy.* ⊠ *Kings Canyon National Park ✚ Trailhead:
4½ miles east of Cedar Grove Village turnoff from Kings Canyon
Scenic Byway.*

MODERATE
Big Baldy. This hike climbs 600 feet and 2 miles up to the 8,209-foot
summit of Big Baldy. Your reward is the view of Redwood Canyon.
Round-trip the hike is 4 miles. *Moderate.* ⊠ *Kings Canyon National
Park ✚ Trailhead: 8 miles south of Grant Grove on Generals Hwy.
(Rte. 198).*

Redwood Canyon Trails. Two main trails lead into Redwood Canyon
Grove, the world's largest sequoia grove. The 6.5-mile **Hart Tree and
Fallen Goliath Loop** passes by a 19th-century logging site, pristine
Hart Meadow, and the hollowed-out Tunnel Tree before accessing a
side trail to the grove's largest sequoia, the 277.9-foot-tall Hart Tree.
The 6.4-mile **Sugar Bowl Loop** provides views of Redwood Mountain
and Big Baldy before winding down into its namesake, a thick grove
of mature and young sequoias. *Moderate.* ⊠ *Kings Canyon National
Park ✚ Trailhead: off Quail Flat. Drive 5 miles south of Grant Grove
on Generals Hwy. (Rte. 198), turn right at Quail Flat and proceed
1½ miles to trailhead.*

DIFFICULT
Hotel Creek Trail. For gorgeous canyon views, take this trail from Cedar
Grove up a series of switchbacks until it splits. Follow the route left
through chaparral to the forested ridge and rocky outcrop known as
Cedar Grove Overlook, where you can see the Kings River Canyon
stretching below. This strenuous 5-mile round-trip hike gains 1,200 feet
and takes three to four hours to complete. *Difficult.* ⊠ *Kings Canyon
National Park ✚ Trailhead: at Cedar Grove Pack Station, 1 mile east
of Cedar Grove Village.*

HORSEBACK RIDING
One-day destinations by horseback out of Cedar Grove include Mist
Falls and Upper Bubb's Creek. In the backcountry, many equestrians
head for Volcanic Lakes or Granite Basin, ascending trails that reach
elevations of 10,000 feet. Costs per person range from $35 for a one-
hour guided ride to around $250 per day for fully guided trips for which
the packers do all the cooking and camp chores.

TOURS AND OUTFITTERS
Cedar Grove Pack Station. Take a day ride or plan a multiday adventure
along the Kings River Canyon with Cedar Grove Pack Station. Popular
routes include the Rae Lakes Loop and Monarch Divide. Closed early
September–late May. ⊠ *Kings Canyon National Park ✚ Kings Canyon
Scenic Byway, 1 mile east of Cedar Grove Village* ☎ *559/565–3464*
⊕ *www.nps.gov/seki/planyourvisit/horseride.htm* ☏ *From $40 per hr
or $100 per day.*

20

CLOSE UP

Mount Whitney

At 14,494 feet, Mount Whitney is the highest point in the contiguous United States and the crown jewel of Sequoia National Park's wild eastern side. The peak looms high above the tiny, high-mountain desert community of Lone Pine, where numerous Hollywood Westerns have been filmed. The high mountain ranges, arid landscape, and scrubby brush of the eastern Sierra are beautiful in their vastness and austerity.

Despite the mountain's scale, you can't see it from the more traveled west side of the park because it is hidden behind the Great Western Divide. The only way to access Mount Whitney from the main part of the park is to circumnavigate the Sierra Nevada via a 10-hour, nearly 400-mile drive outside the park. No road ascends the peak; the best vantage point from which to catch a glimpse of the mountain is at the end of Whitney Portal Road. The 13 miles of winding road leads from U.S. 395 at Lone Pine to the trailhead for the hiking route to the top of the mountain. Whitney Portal Road is closed in winter.

Mt. Whitney Trail. The most popular route to the summit, the Mt. Whitney Trail can be conquered by very fit and experienced hikers. If there's snow on the mountain, this is a challenge for expert mountaineers only. All overnighters must have a permit, as must day hikers on the trail beyond Lone Pine Lake, about 2½ miles from the trailhead. From May through October, permits are distributed via a lottery run each February by Recreation.gov. The Eastern Sierra Interagency Visitor Center (*760/876–6222*), on Route 136 at U.S. 395 about a mile south of Lone Pine, is a good resource for information about permits and hiking. ⊠ *Kings Canyon National Park* ☎ *760/873–2483 trail reservations* ⊕ *www.fs.usda.gov/inyo.*

Grant Grove Stables. A one- or two-hour trip through Grant Grove leaving from the stables provides a taste of horseback riding in Kings Canyon. Closed October–early June. ⊠ *Kings Canyon National Park* ✛ *Rte. 180, ½ mile north of Grant Grove Visitor Center* ☎ *559/335– 9292 mid-June–Sept.* ⊕ *www.nps.gov/seki/planyourvisit/horseride.htm* ☞ *From $45.*

SLEDDING AND SNOWSHOEING

In winter, Kings Canyon has a few great places to play in the snow. Sleds, inner tubes, and platters are allowed at both the Azalea Campground area on Grant Tree Road, ¼ mile north of Grant Grove Visitor Center, and at the Big Stump picnic area, 2 miles north of the lower Route 180 entrance to the park.

Snowshoeing is good around Grant Grove, where you can take occasional naturalist-guided snowshoe walks from mid-December through mid-March as conditions permit. Grant Grove Market rents sleds and snowshoes.

NEARBY TOWNS

Numerous towns and cities tout themselves as "gateways" to the parks, with some more deserving of the title than others. One that certainly merits the name is frisky **Three Rivers,** a Sierra foothills hamlet (population 2,200) along the Kaweah River. Close to Sequoia's Ash Mountain and Lookout Point entrances, Three Rivers is a good spot to find a room when park lodgings are full. Either because Three Rivers residents appreciate their idyllic setting or because they know that tourists are their bread and butter, you'll find them almost uniformly pleasant and eager to share tips about the best spots for "Sierra surfing" the Kaweah's smooth, moss-covered rocks or where to find the best cell-phone reception (it's off to the cemetery for Verizon customers).

Visalia, a Central Valley city of about 128,000 people, lies 58 miles southwest of Sequoia's Wuksachi Village and 56 miles southwest of the Kings Canyon Park Visitor Center. Its vibrant downtown contains several good restaurants. If you're into Victorian and other old houses, drop by the visitor center and pick up a free map of them. A clear day's view of the Sierra from Main Street is spectacular, and even Sunday night can find the streets bustling with pedestrians. Visalia provides easy access to grand Sequoia National Park and the serene Kaweah Oaks Preserve.

Closest to Kings Canyon's Big Stump entrance, **Fresno,** the main gateway to the southern Sierra region, is about 55 miles west of Kings Canyon and about 85 miles northwest of Wuksachi Village. This Central Valley city of nearly a half-million people is sprawling and unglamorous, but it has all the cultural and other amenities you'd expect of a major crossroads.

GETTING HERE AND AROUND

Sequoia Shuttle. In summer the Sequoia Shuttle connects Three Rivers to Visalia and Sequoia National Park. ☎ *877/287–4453* ⊕ *www.sequoiashuttle.com* ⌨ *$15 round-trip.*

Visitor Information Fresno/Clovis Convention & Visitors Bureau. ✉ *1550 E. Shaw Ave., Suite 101, Fresno* ☎ *559/981–5500, 800/788–0836* ⊕ *www. playfresno.org.* **Sequoia Foothills Chamber of Commerce.** ✉ *42268 Sierra Dr., Three Rivers* ☎ *559/561–3300* ⊕ *www.threerivers.com.* **Visalia Convention & Visitors Bureau.** ✉ *Kiosk, 303 E. Acequia Ave., at S. Bridge St., Visalia* ☎ *559/334–0141, 800/524–0303* ⊕ *www.visitvisalia.org.*

20

NEARBY ATTRACTIONS

OFF THE
BEATEN
PATH

Exeter Murals. More than two dozen murals in the Central Valley city of Exeter's cute-as-a-button downtown make it worth a quick detour if you're traveling on Route 198. Several of the murals, which depict the area's agricultural and social history, are quite good. All adorn buildings within a few blocks of the intersection of Pine and E streets. If you're hungry, the **Wildflower Cafe,** at 121 South E Street, serves inventive salads and sandwiches. Shortly after entering Exeter head west on Pine Street (it's just before the water tower) to reach downtown. ✉ *Exeter* ✛ *Rte. 65, 2 miles south of Rte. 198, about 11 miles east of Visalia* ⊕ *cityofexeter.com/about-8187/gallery/murals.*

OFF THE
BEATEN
PATH

Colonel Allensworth State Historic Park. It's worth the slight detour off Highway 99 to learn about and pay homage to the dream of Allen Allensworth and other black pioneers who in 1908 founded Allensworth, the only California town settled, governed, and financed by African Americans. At its height, the town prospered as a key railroad transfer point, but after cars and trucks reduced railroad traffic and water was diverted for Central Valley agriculture, the town declined and was eventually deserted. Today the restored and rebuilt schoolhouse, library, and other structures commemorate Allensworth's heyday, as do festivities that take place each October. ✉ *4129 Palmer Ave., off Hwy. 43; from Hwy. 99 at Delano, take Garces Hwy. west to Hwy. 43 north; from Earlimart, take County Rd. J22 west to Hwy. 43 south, Allensworth* 🕾 *661/849–3433* ⊕ *www.parks.ca.gov* 🖃 *$6 per car.*

FAMILY
Fodor's Choice
★

Forestiere Underground Gardens. Sicilian immigrant Baldassare Forestiere spent four decades (1906–46) carving out an odd, subterranean realm of rooms, tunnels, grottoes, alcoves, and arched passageways that once extended for more than 10 acres between Highway 99 and busy, mall-pocked Shaw Avenue. Though not an engineer, Forestiere called on his memories of the ancient Roman structures he saw as a youth and on techniques he learned digging subways in New York and Boston. Only a fraction of his prodigious output is on view, but you can tour his underground living quarters, including bedrooms (one with a fireplace), the kitchen, living room, and bath, as well as a fishpond and auto tunnel. Skylights allow exotic full-grown fruit trees to flourish more than 20 feet belowground. ✉ *5021 W. Shaw Ave., 2 blocks east of Hwy. 99, Fresno* 🕾 *559/271–0734* ⊕ *www.undergroundgardens.com* 🖃 *$17* ⊘ *Closed Dec.–Feb.*

Kaweah Oaks Preserve. Trails at this 344-acre wildlife sanctuary off the main road to Sequoia National Park lead past majestic valley oak, sycamore, cottonwood, and willow trees. Among the 134 bird species you might spot are hawks, hummingbirds, and great blue herons. Bobcats, lizards, coyotes, and cottontails also live here. The Sycamore Trail has digital signage with QR codes you can scan with your smartphone to access plant and animal information. ✉ *Follow Hwy. 198 for 7 miles east of Visalia, turn north on Rd. 182, and proceed ½ mile to gate on left side, Visalia* 🕾 *559/738–0211* ⊕ *www.sequoiariverlands.org* 🖃 *Free.*

Project Survival's Cat Haven. Take the rare opportunity to glimpse a Siberian lynx, a clouded leopard, a Bengal tiger, and other endangered wild cats at this conservation facility that shelters more than 30 big cats. A guided hour-long tour along a quarter mile of walkway leads to fenced habitat areas shaded by trees and overlooking the Central Valley. ✉ *38257 E. Kings Canyon Rd. (Rte. 180), 15 miles west of Kings Canyon National Park, Dunlap* 🕾 *559/338–3216* ⊕ *www.cathaven.com* 🖃 *$15.*

Sequoia National Forest and Giant Sequoia National Monument. Delicate spring wildflowers, cool summer campgrounds, and varied winter-sports opportunities—not to mention more than half of the world's giant sequoia groves—draw outdoorsy types year-round to this sprawling district surrounding the national parks. Together, the forest and monument cover nearly 1,700 square miles, south from the Kings River and east from the foothills along the San Joaquin Valley. The monument's groves are both north and south of Sequoia National Park. One of the most popular is the **Converse Basin Grove,** home of the Boole Tree, the forest's largest sequoia. The grove is accessible by car on an unpaved road.

The Hume Lake Forest Service District Office, at 35860 Kings Canyon Scenic Byway (Route 180), has information about the groves, along with details about recreational activities. In springtime, diversions include hiking among the wildflowers that brighten the foothills. The floral display rises with the heat as the mountain elevations warm up in summer, when hikers, campers, and picnickers become more plentiful. The abundant trout supply attracts anglers to area waters, including 87-acre **Hume Lake,** which is also ideal for swimming and nonmotorized boating. By fall the turning leaves provide the visual delights, particularly in the Western Divide, Indian Basin, and the Kern Plateau. Winter activities include downhill and cross-country skiing, snowshoeing, and snowmobiling. ⊠ *Sequoia National Park* ✣ *Northern Entrances: Generals Hwy. (Rte. 198), 7 miles southeast of Grant Grove; Hume Lake Rd. between Generals Hwy. (Rte. 198) and Kings Canyon Scenic Byway (Rte. 180); Kings Canyon Scenic Byway (Rte. 180) between Grant Grove and Cedar Grove. Southern Entrances: Rte. 190 east of Springville; Rte. 178 east of Bakersfield* ☏ *559/784–1500 forest and monument, 559/338–2251 Hume Lake* ⊕ *www.fs.usda.gov/sequoia.*

AREA ACTIVITIES

SPORTS AND THE OUTDOORS

BOATING AND RAFTING

Hume Lake. This reservoir, built by loggers in the early 1900s, is now the site of several church-affiliated camps, a gas station, and a public campground. Outside Kings Canyon's borders, Hume Lake offers intimate views of the mountains. Summer lodge room rentals start at $150. ⊠ *Hume Lake Rd., off Kings Canyon Hwy., 8 miles northeast of Grant Grove, 64144 Hume Lake Rd., Hume* ☏ *559/305-7770* ⊕ *www.humelake.org.*

Kaweah White Water Adventures. Kaweah's trips include a two-hour excursion (good for families) through Class III rapids, a longer paddle through Class IV rapids, and an extended trip (typically Class IV and V rapids). ⊠ *40443 Sierra Dr., Three Rivers* ☏ *559/740–8251* ⊕ *www. kaweah-whitewater.com* ▣ *$50–$120 per person.*

Kings River Expeditions. This outfit arranges one- and two-day whitewater rafting trips on the Kings River. ⊠ *1840 W. Shaw Ave., Clovis* ☏ *559/233–4881, 800/846–3674* ⊕ *www.kingsriver.com* ▣ *From $145.*

HORSEBACK RIDING

Wood 'n' Horse Training Stables. For hourly horseback rides or riding lessons, contact this outfit. ⊠ *42846 N. Fork Dr., Three Rivers* ☏ *559/561–4268* ⊕ *www.wdnhorse.com.*

20

WHERE TO EAT

IN THE PARKS

SEQUOIA

$ CAFÉ 🍴 **Lodgepole Market, Deli, and Snack Bar.** The choices here run the gamut from simple to very simple, with the three counters only a few strides apart in a central eating complex. For hot food, including burgers, hot dogs, and pizzas, venture into the snack bar. [$] *Average main: $10* ✉ *Next to Lodgepole Visitor Center, Sequoia National Park* ☎ *559/565–3301.*

$$$ MODERN AMERICAN 🍴 **The Peaks.** Huge windows run the length of the Wuksachi Lodge's high-ceilinged dining room, and a large fireplace on the far wall warms both body and soul. The diverse dinner menu—by far the best at both parks—reflects a commitment to locally sourced and sustainable products. [$] *Average main: $28* ✉ *Wuksachi Lodge, 64740 Wuksachi Way, Wuksachi Village* ☎ *559/565–4070* 🌐 *www.visitsequoia.com/the-peaks-restaurant.aspx.*

$$$ BARBECUE 🍴 **Sequoia Barbeque at Wuksachi Lodge.** Weather permitting, diners congregate nightly for traditional Old West barbecue. After the meal, listen to a naturalist talk, join in an interactive living history presentation, and clear your throat for a campfire sing-along. [$] *Average main: $25* ✉ *Sequoia National Park* ✣ *Wolverton Rd., 1½ mile northeast off Generals Hwy. (Rte. 198)* ☎ *559/565–4070* ⏲ *No lunch. Closed early Sept.–mid-June.*

KINGS CANYON

$$ AMERICAN 🍴 **Cedar Grove Snack Bar.** The menu here is surprisingly extensive, with dinner entrées such as pasta, pork chops, trout, and steak. For breakfast, try the biscuits and gravy, French toast, pancakes, or cold cereal. [$] *Average main: $15* ✉ *Cedar Grove Village, Kings Canyon National Park* ☎ *559/565–0100* ⏲ *Closed Oct.–May.*

OUTSIDE THE PARKS

$ CAFÉ 🍴 **Antoinette's Coffee and Goodies.** For smoothies, well-crafted espresso drinks, breakfast bowls, and pumpkin chocolate-chip muffins and other homemade baked goods, stop for a spell at this convivial coffee shop. Antoinette's is known as the town's hub for vegan and gluten-free items. **Known for:** plentiful vegan and gluten-free items; Wi-Fi on site. [$] *Average main: $7* ✉ *41727 Sierra Dr., Three Rivers* ☎ *559/561–2253* 🌐 *www.antoinettescoffeeandgoodies.com* ⏲ *Closed Tues. No dinner.*

$$ AMERICAN 🍴 **Buckaroo Diner.** Set on a bluff overlooking the Kaweah River, the boho-chic Buckaroo serves fresh, house-made dishes made with seasonal organic ingredients. A local couple started the restaurant in 2014, first operating out of a food truck and later expanding into a building that housed the original 'ol Buckaroo restaurant for decades. **Known for:** lemon ricotta pancakes for brunch; fried organic chicken; daily specials. [$] *Average main: $14* ✉ *41695 Sierra Dr., Three Rivers* ☎ *559/465–5088* 🌐 *theolbuckaroo.com* ⏲ *No lunch weekdays. Closed Tues.–Weds.*

$$
MODERN
AMERICAN
✕ **Café 225.** High ceilings and contemporary decor contribute to the relaxed and sophisticated atmosphere at this popular downtown restaurant. Chef-owner Karl Merten can often be spotted at area markets seeking out locally grown ingredients for his seasonally changing dishes. **Known for:** wood-fired rotisserie menu items; fresh local ingredients; sophisticated vibe. $ *Average main: $19* ✉ *225 W. Main St., Visalia* ☎ *559/733–2967* ⊕ *www.cafe225.com* ☾ *Closed Sun.*

$$$
AMERICAN
✕ **Gateway Restaurant and Lodge.** The view's the draw at this roadhouse that overlooks the Kaweah River as it plunges out of the high country. The Gateway serves everything from osso buco and steaks to shrimp in Thai chili sauce. **Known for:** scenic riverside setting; fine dining in otherwise casual town; popular bar. $ *Average main: $29* ✉ *45978 Sierra Dr., Three Rivers* ☎ *559/561–4133* ⊕ *www.gateway-sequoia.com.*

$
AMERICAN
✕ **The Lunch Box.** A casual downtown café and bakery, the Lunch Box serves healthful meals at reasonable prices. Choose from nearly 50 types of hot and cold sandwiches and wraps, more than 20 different salads, and soups such as chicken noodle and Tuscan tomato. **Known for:** fresh, healthful local ingredients; quick service; many menu option and combinations. $ *Average main: $10* ✉ *112 N. Court St., at Main St., Visalia* ☎ *559/635–8624* ⊕ *lunchboxcateringcompany.com* ☾ *Closed Sun.*

$$$
MODERN
AMERICAN
✕ **School House Restaurant & Tavern.** A Wine Country–style establishment that sources ingredients from the on-site gardens and surrounding farms and orchards, this popular restaurant occupies a redbrick 1921 schoolhouse in the town of Sanger. Chef Ryan Jackson, who grew up on local fruit farms, returned home after stints cooking at prestigious Napa Valley restaurants to create seasonal menus from the bounty of familiar backyards. **Known for:** fresh ingredients from neighboring farms and orchards; historic country setting; convenient stop between Kings Canyon and Fresno. $ *Average main: $27* ✉ *1018 S. Frankwood Ave., at Hwy. 180 (King's Canyon Rd.), 20 miles east of Fresno, Sanger* ☎ *559/787–3271* ⊕ *schoolhousesanger.com* ☾ *Closed Mon. and Tues.*

$
AMERICAN
✕ **Sierra Subs and Salads.** This well-run sandwich joint satisfies carnivores and vegetarians alike with crispy-fresh ingredients prepared with panache. Depending on your preference, the centerpiece of the Bull's Eye sandwich, for instance, will be roast beef or a portobello mushroom, but whichever you choose, the accompanying flavors—of ciabatta bread, horseradish-and-garlic mayonnaise, roasted red peppers, Havarti cheese, and spinach—will delight your palate. **Known for:** many vegetarian, vegan, and gluten-free options; weekly specials. $ *Average main: $8* ✉ *41717 Sierra Dr., Three Rivers* ☎ *559/561–4810* ⊕ *www.sierrasubsandsalads.com* ☾ *Closed Mon. No dinner.*

$$$$
EUROPEAN
Fodor's Choice
★
✕ **The Vintage Press.** Built in 1966, this is the best restaurant in the Central Valley. The California–Continental cuisine includes dishes such as crispy veal sweetbreads with a port-wine sauce and filet mignon with a cognac-mustard sauce. **Known for:** wine list with more than 900 selections; chocolate Grand Marnier cake and other homemade desserts and ice creams. $ *Average main: $32* ✉ *216 N. Willis St., Visalia* ☎ *559/733–3033* ⊕ *www.thevintagepress.com.*

20

Best Campgrounds in Sequoia and Kings Canyon

Campgrounds in Sequoia and Kings Canyon occupy wonderful settings, with lots of shade and nearby hiking trails. Some campgrounds are open year-round, others only seasonally. Except for Bearpaw (around $350 a night including meals), fees at the campgrounds range from $12 to $35, depending on location and size. There are no RV hookups at any of the campgrounds; expect a table and a fire ring with a grill at standard sites. Only Bearpaw, Lodgepole, Dorst Creek, Potwisha, and Buckeye Flat accept reservations, and for all of these you'll need to book well ahead. The rest are first come, first served. Campgrounds around Lodgepole and Grant Grove get busy in summer with vacationing families. Keep in mind that this is black-bear country and carefully follow posted instructions about storing food. Bear-proof metal containers are provided at many campgrounds.

IN SEQUOIA

Atwell Mill Campground. At 6,650 feet, this peaceful, tent-only campground is just south of the Western Divide. ⊠ *Mineral King Rd., 20 miles east of Rte. 198* ☎ *559/565–3341.*

Bearpaw High Sierra Camp. Classy camping is the order of the day at this tent hotel and restaurant. Make reservations starting on January 2. ⊠ *High Sierra Trail, 11.5 miles from Lodgepole Village* ☎ *888/252–5757* ⊕ *www.visitsequoia.com.*

Dorst Creek Campground. Wildlife sightings are common at this large campground at elevation 6,700 feet. ⊠ *Generals Hwy., 8 miles north of*

Lodgepole Visitor Center ☎ *559/565–3341 or 877/444–6777.*

Lodgepole Campground. The largest Lodgepole-area campground is also the noisiest, though things quiet down at night. ⊠ *Off Generals Hwy. beyond Lodgepole Village* ☎ *559/565–3341 or 877/444–6777.*

Potwisha Campground. On the Marble Fork of the Kaweah River, this midsize campground, open year-round, at elevation 2,100 feet gets no snow in winter and can be hot in summer. ⊠ *Generals Hwy., 4 miles north of Foothills Visitor Center* ☎ *559/565–3341 or 877/444–6777.*

IN KINGS CANYON

Azalea Campground. Of the three campgrounds in the Grant Grove area, Azalea is the only one open year-round. It sits at 6,500 feet amid giant sequoias. ⊠ *Kings Canyon Scenic Byway, ¼ mile north of Grant Grove Village* ☎ *559/565–3341.*

Sentinel Campground. At 4,600 feet and within walking distance of Cedar Grove Village, Sentinel fills up fast in summer. ⊠ *Kings Canyon Scenic Byway, ¼ mile west of Cedar Grove Village* ☎ *559/565–3341.*

Sheep Creek Campground. Of the overflow campgrounds, this is one of the prettiest. ⊠ *Off Kings Canyon Scenic Byway, 1 mile west of Cedar Grove Village* ☎ *No phone.*

Sunset Campground. Many of the easiest trails through Grant Grove are adjacent to this large camp, near the giant sequoias at 6,500 feet. ⊠ *Off Generals Hwy., near Grant Grove Visitor Center* ☎ *No phone.*

WHERE TO STAY

IN THE PARKS

SEQUOIA

$$
RESORT

Silver City Mountain Resort. High on Mineral King Road, this privately owned resort has rustic cabins and Swiss-style chalets, all with at least a stove, refrigerator, and sink. **Pros:** rustic setting; friendly staff; "off the grid" ambience. **Cons:** electricity (by generator) available only between noon and 10 pm. $ *Rooms from: $120* ✉ *Sequoia National Park* ✛ *Mineral King Rd., 21 miles southeast of Rte. 198* ☎ *559/561–3223* ⊕ *www.silvercityresort.com* ⊘ *Closed Nov.–late May* ⇥ *11 units, 6 with shared bath* ⊖ *No meals.*

$$$$
HOTEL
Fodor's Choice
★

Wuksachi Lodge. The striking cedar-and-stone main building is a fine example of how a structure can blend effectively with lovely mountain scenery. **Pros:** best place to stay in the parks; lots of wildlife. **Cons:** rooms can be small; main lodge is a few-minutes' walk from guest rooms; slow Wi-Fi. $ *Rooms from: $229* ✉ *64740 Wuksachi Way, Wuksachi Village* ☎ *559/565–4070, 888/252–5757* ⊕ *www.visitsequoia.com/lodging.aspx* ⇥ *102 rooms* ⊖ *No meals.*

KINGS CANYON

$$
HOTEL

Cedar Grove Lodge. Backpackers like to stay here on the eve of long treks into the High Sierra wilderness, so bedtimes tend to be early. **Pros:** a definite step up from camping in terms of comfort. **Cons:** impersonal; not everybody agrees it's clean enough. $ *Rooms from: $141* ✉ *Kings Canyon Scenic Byway, Kings Canyon National Park* ☎ *866/807–3598* ⊕ *www.visitsequoia.com/Cedar-Grove-Lodge.aspx* ⊘ *Closed mid-Oct.–mid-May* ⇥ *21 rooms* ⊖ *No meals.*

$
HOTEL

Grant Grove Cabins. Some of the wood-panel cabins here have heaters, electric lights, and private baths, but most have woodstoves, battery lamps, and shared baths. **Pros:** warm, woodsy feel; clean. **Cons:** can be difficult to walk up to if you're not in decent physical shape; costly for what you get. $ *Rooms from: $94* ✉ *Kings Canyon Scenic Byway in Grant Grove Village, Kings Canyon National Park* ☎ *866/807–3598* ⊕ *www.visitsequoia.com/Grant-Grove-Cabins.aspx* ⇥ *33 cabins, 9 with bath; 17 tent cabins* ⊖ *No meals.*

$$$
HOTEL

John Muir Lodge. In a wooded area in the hills above Grant Grove Village, this modern, timber-sided lodge has rooms and suites with queen- or king-size beds and private baths. **Pros:** open year-round; common room stays warm; quiet. **Cons:** check-in is down in the village. $ *Rooms from: $200* ✉ *Kings Canyon Scenic Byway, ¼ mile north of Grant Grove Village, 86728 Highway 180, Kings Canyon National Park* ☎ *866/807–3598* ⊕ *www.visitsequoia.com/john-muir-lodge.aspx* ⇥ *36 rooms* ⊖ *No meals.*

20

OUTSIDE THE PARKS

The only lodging immediately outside the parks is in Three Rivers. Options include inns, chain and mom-and-pop motels, and riverside cabins. Numerous chain properties operate in Visalia or Fresno (your favorite is likely represented in one or both cities), about an hour from the south and north entrances, respectively.

$$$ HOTEL FAMILY
Montecito-Sequoia Lodge. Outdoor activities are what this year-round family resort is all about, including many that are geared toward teenagers and small children. **Pros:** friendly staff; great for kids; lots of fresh air and planned activities. **Cons:** can be noisy with all the activity; some complaints about cleanliness; not within national park. [$] *Rooms from: $179* ✉ *63410 Generals Hwy., 11 miles south of Grant Grove, Sequoia National Forest* ☎ *559/565–3388, 800/227–9900* 🌐 *www.montecitosequoia.com* 🕓 *Closed 1st 2 wks of Dec.* 🛏 *37 rooms, 13 cabins* 🍴 *All meals.*

$$ B&B/INN Fodor's Choice ★
Rio Sierra Riverhouse. Guests at Rio Sierra come for the river views, the sandy beach, and the proximity to Sequoia National Park (6 miles away), but invariably end up raving equally about the warm, laid-back hospitality of proprietress Mars Roberts. **Pros:** seductive beach; winning hostess; river views from all rooms; contemporary ambience. **Cons:** books up quickly in summer; some road noise audible in rooms. [$] *Rooms from: $185* ✉ *41997 Sierra Dr., Hwy. 198, Three Rivers* ☎ *559/561–4720* 🌐 *www.rio-sierra.com* 🛏 *5 rooms* 🍴 *No meals* ☞ *2-night min stay on summer weekends.*

$ B&B/INN
The Spalding House. This restored Colonial Revival inn is decked out with antiques, oriental rugs, handcrafted woodwork, and glass doors. **Pros:** warm feel; old-time atmosphere; great place for a twilight stroll. **Cons:** no TVs in rooms. [$] *Rooms from: $95* ✉ *631 N. Encina St., Visalia* ☎ *559/739–7877* 🌐 *www.thespaldinghouse.com* 🛏 *3 suites* 🍴 *Breakfast.*

SACRAMENTO AND THE GOLD COUNTRY

WELCOME TO SACRAMENTO AND THE GOLD COUNTRY

TOP REASONS TO GO

★ **Gold Rush:** Marshall Gold Discovery State Park is where it all started—it's a must-see—but there are historic and modern gems all along California Highway 49 from Nevada City to Mariposa.

★ **State Capital:** Easygoing Sacramento offers sights like the Capitol and historic Old Sacramento.

★ **Bon Appétit:** Sacramento has emerged as a foodie destination in the past decade, but its celebrations of food, drink, and culture date back to the gold-rush parade of immigrants.

★ **Wine Tasting:** With bucolic scenery and friendly tasting rooms, the Gold Country's Shenandoah Valley has become an acclaimed wine-making region, specializing in Zinfandel.

★ **Rivers, Sequoias, and Caverns:** Natural beauty here is rich (stream beds are still lined with gold), high (sequoias in Calaveras Big Trees State Park), and deep (Moaning Cavern's main chamber is big enough to hold the Statue of Liberty).

1 Sacramento and Nearby. The gateway to the Gold Country, the seat of state government, and an agricultural hub, Sacramento plays many important contemporary roles. About 2.5 million people live in the metropolitan area, which offers up more sunshine and lower prices than coastal California.

2 The Gold Country—South. South of its junction with U.S. 50, Highway 49 traces in asphalt the famed Mother Lode. The peppy former gold-rush towns strung along the road have for the most part been restored, many with money from a modern-day boom in vineyards and wineries.

3 The Gold Country—North. Highway 49 north of Placerville links the towns of Coloma, Auburn, Grass Valley, and Nevada City. Most are gentrified versions of once-rowdy mining camps, vestiges of which remain in roadside museums, old mining structures, and restored homes now serving as inns.

21

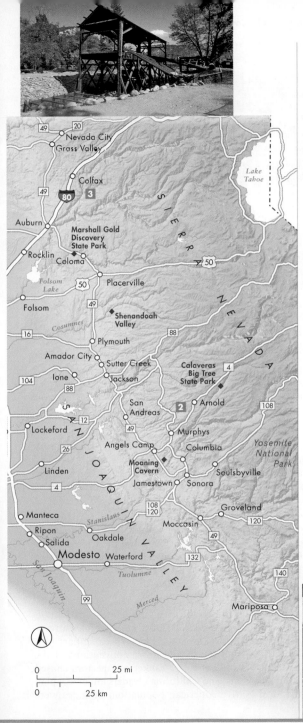

GETTING ORIENTED

The Gold Country is a largely rural destination popular with those seeking a reasonably priced escape from Southern California and the Bay Area. Sacramento and Davis are in an enormous valley just west of the Sierra Nevada range. Foothill communities Nevada City, Auburn, Placerville, and Sutter Creek were products of the gold rush, and remain popular stopovers with travelers en route to Lake Tahoe.

Updated by
Steve Pastorino

The Gold Country is one of California's less expensive and more sublime destinations, a region of the Sierra Nevada foothills that's filled with natural and cultural pleasures. Visitors come for the boomtowns and ghost towns; to explore art galleries and shop for antiques; to savor "farm-to-fork" restaurants and delicious wine at tasting rooms; and to rest at friendly, atmospheric inns. Spring brings wildflowers, and in fall the hills are colored by bright red berries and changing leaves. Because it offers plenty of outdoor diversions, the Gold Country is a great place to take kids.

Old Sacramento's museums provide a good introduction to the region's considerable history, but the Gold Country's heart lies along Highway 49, which winds the approximately 300-mile north–south length of the historic mining area. The highway—often a twisting, hilly, two-lane road—begs for a convertible with the top down.

A new era dawned for California when James Marshall turned up a gold nugget in the tailrace of a sawmill he was constructing along the American River. On January 24, 1848, Mexico and the United States were still wrestling for ownership of what would become the Golden State. Marshall's discovery helped compel the United States to tighten its grip on the region, and prospectors from all over the world soon came to seek their fortunes in the Mother Lode.

As gold fever seized the nation, California's population of 15,000 swelled to 265,000 within three years. The mostly young, male adventurers who arrived in search of gold—the '49ers—became part of a culture that discarded many of the button-down conventions of the eastern states. It was also a violent time. Yankee prospectors chased Mexican miners off their claims, and California's leaders initiated a plan to exterminate the local Native American population. Bounties were paid and private militias were hired to wipe out the Native Americans or sell them into slavery. California was to be dominated by the Anglo.

The gold-rush boom lasted scarcely 20 years, but it changed California forever, producing 546 mining towns, of which fewer than 250 remain. The hills of the Gold Country were alive, not only with prospecting and mining but also with business, the arts, gambling, and a fair share of crime. Opera houses went up alongside brothels, and the California State Capitol, in Sacramento, was built partly with the gold dug out of the hills.

The mild climate and rich soil in and around Sacramento Valley are responsible for the region's current riches: fresh and bountiful food and high-quality wines. Gold Country restaurants and wineries continue to earn national acclaim, and they're without the high prices of the Bay Area and Sonoma and Napa wine regions. There's a growing local craft-beer scene, too.

PLANNING

WHEN TO GO

The Gold Country is most pleasant in spring, when the wildflowers are in bloom, and in fall. Summers can be hot in the valley (temperatures of 100°F are fairly common), so head for the hills. Sacramento winters tend to be cool, with occasionally foggy or rainy days. Throughout the year Gold Country towns stage community and ethnic celebrations. In December many towns are decked out for Christmas.

GETTING HERE AND AROUND

AIR TRAVEL

Sacramento International Airport (SMF) is served by Aeromexico, Alaska, American, Delta, Hawaiian, JetBlue, Southwest, United, and Volaris. A taxi from the airport to Downtown Sacramento costs about $40, but services like Lyft and Uber often cost much less. The Super Shuttle fare starts at $13. Public buses *(Bus and Light-Rail Travel)* are also an option.

Contacts Sacramento International Airport. ✉ *6900 Airport Blvd., 12 miles northwest of downtown off I–5, Sacramento* ☎ *916/929–5411* ⊕ *www.sacramento.aero/smf.* **Super Shuttle.** ☎ *800/258–3826* ⊕ *www.supershuttle.com.*

BUS AND LIGHT-RAIL TRAVEL

Greyhound serves Sacramento from San Francisco and Los Angeles. Sacramento Regional Transit serves the capital area with buses and light-rail vehicles. Yolobus public buses Nos. 42A and 42B connect SMF airport and Downtown Sacramento, West Sacramento, Davis, and Woodland.

Contacts Greyhound. ✉ *420 Richards Blvd.* ☎ *916/444-6858* ⊕ *www.greyhound.com.* **Sacramento Regional Transit.** ☎ *916/321–2877* ⊕ *www.sacrt.com.* **Yolobus.** ☎ *530/666–2877, 916/371–2877* ⊕ *www.yolobus.com.*

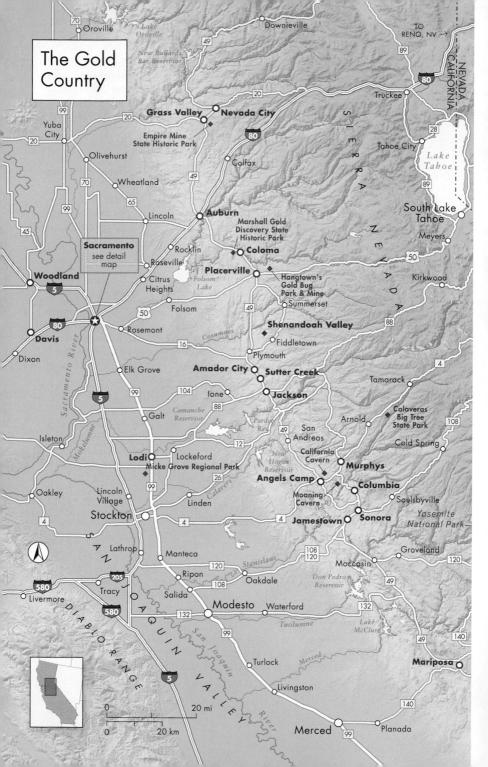

CAR TRAVEL

Interstate 5 (north–south) and Interstate 80 (east–west) are the two main routes into and out of Sacramento. From Sacramento, three highways fan out toward the east, all intersecting with historic Highway 49: Interstate 80 heads northeast 34 miles to Auburn; U.S. 50 goes east 40 miles to Placerville; and Highway 16 angles southeast 45 miles to Plymouth. Highway 49, also called the Golden Chain highway, is one of America's great drives. It's an excellent two-lane road that winds and climbs through the foothills and valleys, linking the principal Gold Country towns. Traveling by car is the only practical way to explore the Gold Country.

TRAIN TRAVEL

One of the most authentic ways to relive the Old West is traveling via train. On the Amtrak *California Zephyr,* you can ride the same route traveled by prospectors in the late 1800s. Docents from the Sacramento Railroad Museum ride the route from Sacramento to Reno daily, and are available to answer questions. The route into the Sierra Nevadas is memorable, especially if you book a sleeper car. Amtrak trains serve Sacramento and Davis from San Jose, Oakland, and Emeryville (Amtrak buses transport passengers from San Francisco's Ferry Building to Emeryville). Amtrak also runs trains and connecting motor coaches from the Central Valley.

Contacts Amtrak. ⊠ *401 I St.* ☎ *800/872–7245* ⊕ *www.amtrak.com.*

RESTAURANTS

American, Italian, Chinese, and Mexican are common Gold Country fare, but chefs also prepare ambitious European, French, and contemporary regional cuisine that mixes California ingredients with cosmopolitan preparations. Grass Valley's meat- and vegetable-stuffed *pasties,* introduced by 19th-century gold miners from Cornwall, are one of the region's more unusual treats.

HOTELS

Sacramento has plenty of full-service hotels, budget motels, and small inns. Larger towns along Highway 49—among them Auburn, Grass Valley, and Jackson—have chain motels and inns. Many Gold Country bed-and-breakfasts occupy former mansions, miners' cabins, and other historic buildings. *Hotel reviews have been shortened. For full information, visit Fodors.com.*

Contacts Amador Council of Tourism. ⊠ *460 Sutter Hill Road, Suite D, Sutter Creek* ☎ *209/267–9249, 877/868–7262* ⊕ *www.touramador.com.* **California Association of Bed & Breakfast Inns.** ☎ *800/373–9251* ⊕ *www.cabbi.com/region/gold-country.*

VISITOR INFORMATION

Contacts Amador County Chamber of Commerce & Visitors Bureau. ⊠ *115 Main St., Jackson* ☎ *209/223–0350* ⊕ *amadorchamber.com.* **El Dorado County Visitors Authority.** ⊠ *542 Main St., Placerville* ☎ *530/621–5885, 800/457–6279* ⊕ *visit-eldorado.com.* **Grass Valley/Nevada County Chamber of Commerce.** ⊠ *128 E. Main St., Grass Valley* ☎ *530/273–4667* ⊕ *www.grassvalleychamber.com.* **Tuolumne County Visitors Bureau.** ⊠ *542 W. Stockton Rd., Sonora* ☎ *209/533–4420, 800/446–1333* ⊕ *www.yosemitegoldcountry.com.* **Yosemite/Mariposa County Tourism Bureau.** ⊠ *5158 Hwy. 140, Mariposa* ☎ *209/742–4567* ⊕ *www.yosemiteexperience.com.*

WHAT IT COSTS			
	$	$$	$$$	$$$$
Restaurants	under $16	$16–$22	$23–$30	over $30
Hotels	under $120	$120–$175	$176–$250	over $250

Restaurant prices are the average cost of a main course at dinner or, if dinner is not served, at lunch, excluding sales tax. Hotel prices are the lowest cost of a standard double room in high season, excluding taxes.

SACRAMENTO AND NEARBY

California's capital is an ethnically diverse city, with sizable Mexican, Hmong, and Ukrainian populations, among many others.

SACRAMENTO

87 miles northeast of San Francisco; 384 miles north of Los Angeles.

All around the Golden State's seat of government you'll experience echoes of the gold-rush days, most notably in Old Sacramento, whose wooden sidewalks and horse-drawn carriages on cobblestone streets lend the waterfront district a 19th-century feel. The California State Railroad Museum and other venues hold artifacts of state and national significance, and historic buildings house shops and restaurants. River cruises and train rides are fun family diversions for an hour or two.

Due east of Old Sacramento is Downtown, where landmarks include the Capitol building and the surrounding Capitol Park. Golden 1 Center, the new sports and concert venue, and the convention center are also here. The area is a little uneven economically, but revitalization is taking full effect.

Farther east, starting at about 15th Street, lies the city's most interesting neighborhood, Midtown, a mix of genteel Victorian edifices, ultramodern lofts, and innovative restaurants and cozy wine bars. The neighborhood springs to life on the second Saturday evening of the month, when art galleries hold open houses and the sidewalks are packed. A few intersections are jumping most evenings when the weather's good; they include the corner of 20th and L Streets in what's known as Lavender Heights, the center of the city's gay and lesbian community.

GETTING HERE AND AROUND

Most people drive to Sacramento and get around by car. Yellow Cab, Lyft, and Uber are reliable cab options.

BUS TRAVEL   Sacramento Regional Transit buses and light-rail vehicles serve the area. The No. 30 DASH shuttle bus links Old Sacramento, Midtown, and Sutter's Fort.

CAR TRAVEL   Assuming that traffic is not a factor (though it often is), Sacramento is a 90-minute drive from San Francisco and a seven-hour drive from Los Angeles. Parking garages serve Old Sacramento and other tourist spots; on-street parking in Downtown can be difficult to find.

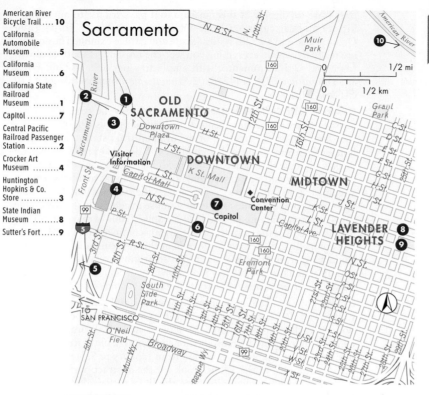

21

ESSENTIALS

Transportation Contacts Sacramento Regional Transit. ☎ 916/321–2877
⊕ www.sacrt.com. **Yellow Cab Co. of Sacramento.** ☎ 916/444–2222
⊕ www.yellowcabsacramento.com.

Visitor Information Old Sacramento Visitor Information Center. ✉ 1002
2nd St. ☎ 916/442–7644 ⊕ www.oldsacramento.com. **Sacramento Convention
and Visitors Bureau.** ✉ 1608 I St., Downtown ☎ 916/808–7777
⊕ www.visitsacramento.com.

EXPLORING
TOP ATTRACTIONS

American River Bicycle Trail. The Jedediah Smith Memorial Trail, as it's
formally called, runs for 32 miles from Old Sacramento to Beals Point
in Folsom. Walk or ride a bit of it and you'll see why local cyclists and
pedestrians adore its scenic lanes, if not always each other: confronta-
tions do occur between humorless speeders and meandering gawkers.
Enjoy great views of the American River and the bluffs overlooking it.
■ **TIP→** Bring lunch or a snack. Pretty parks and picnic areas dot the
trail. ✉ Old Sacramento ⊕ www.americanriverbiketrail.com.

California Automobile Museum. More than 150 automobiles—from
Model Ts, Hudsons, and Studebakers to modern-day electric-powered

ones—are on display at this museum that pays tribute to automotive history and car culture. Check out a replica of Henry Ford's 1896 Quadracycle and a 1920s roadside café and garage exhibit. The docents are ready to explain everything you see. The museum is south of downtown and Old Sacramento, with ample free parking. ⊠ *2200 Front St., Downtown* ☎ *916/442–6802* ⊕ *www.calautomuseum.org* ⊠ *$10* ⊙ *Closed Tues.*

FAMILY **California State Railroad Museum.** Near what was the terminus of the transcontinental and Sacramento Valley railroads, this 100,000-square-foot museum is a re-creation of the original train station and roundhouse. There are 19 steam locomotives and dozens of railroad cars on display along with a variety of other exhibits. You can walk through a post-office car and peer into cubbyholes and canvas mailbags, enter a sleeping car that simulates the swaying on the roadbed and the flashing lights of a passing town at night, or glimpse inside the first-class dining car. The room containing the gold "Last Spike," one of two cast in 1869 to commemorate the completion of the transcontinental railroad, is quietly compelling. Kids have lots of fun at this museum and can become Junior Engineers. ■ **TIP→** You can visit an original roundhouse, not just a replica, at Railtown 1897 in Jamestown, near Sonora. ⊠ *125 I St., at 2nd St., Old Sacramento* ☎ *916/323–9280* ⊕ *www.csrmf.org* ⊠ *$12.*

Fodor's Choice **Capitol.** Built in 1869 and entirely renovated (and seismologically retrofitted) in 1982, the Capitol's 128-foot gilded dome encapsulates ★ both a working museum and the active seat of California's government. Wander freely by reproductions of century-old state offices and into legislative chambers (in session from January to September) decorated in the style of the 1890s. Look for the abstract portrait of Gov. Edmund "Jerry" Brown, alongside the likes of Ronald Reagan and Arnold Schwarzenegger. Guides conduct tours of the building and the 40-acre Capitol Park, which contains a rose garden, a fragrant display of camellias (Sacramento's city flower), and California Veterans Memorials. ■ **TIP→** Wander the Capitol's botanical grounds to glimpse the diverse collection of trees, shrubs, and flowers, including some 1,200 trees from around the world. The original deodar cedars on the west side date back to 1872. ⊠ *Capitol Mall and 10th St., Downtown* ☎ *916/324–0333* ⊕ *capitolmuseum.ca.gov* ⊠ *Free.*

Fodor's Choice **Crocker Art Museum.** Established in 1885 with a collection first assembled by California Supreme Court judge E.B. Crocker and his wife, Marga-★ ret, the Crocker contains a fine collection of Californian, American, and Asian art. A highlight is the magnificent *Great Canyon of the Sierra, Yosemite* (1871) by Thomas Hill. The museum has exceptional holdings of master drawings as well as an impressive collection of international ceramics and works from Europe, Asia, and Africa. A huge contemporary wing was added in 2010 and regularly hosts outstanding traveling exhibitions. Recent exhibitions have included works by Toulouse-Lautrec, Ansel Adams, Diego Rivera, and William S. Rice. ⊠ *216 O St., at 3rd St., Downtown* ☎ *916/808–7000* ⊕ *www.crockerartmuseum.org* ⊠ *$10* ⊙ *Closed Mon.*

WORTH NOTING

FAMILY **California Museum.** California's authentic artifacts—from the State Constitution to surfing magazines—are on display at this unique celebration of the Golden State. Witness life behind the barbed wire of a WWII–era Japanese internment camp, visit a Chinese herb shop maintained by a holographic proprietor, or find familiar names inducted into the annually expanded California Hall of Fame. Steinbeck, Disney, and Earhart are among many you'll know just by their surname. ✉ *1020 O St., at 11th St., Downtown* ☎ *916/653–7524* 🌐 *www.californiamuseum.org* 🎫 *$9* 🕒 *Closed Mon.*

FAMILY **Central Pacific Railroad Passenger Station.** At this reconstructed 1876 depot there's rolling stock to admire, a typical waiting room, and a small restaurant. Part of the year a train departs from the freight depot, south of the passenger station, making a 45-minute out-and-back trip that starts along the banks of the Sacramento River. ✉ *930 Front St., at J St., Old Sacramento* ☎ *916/445–5995* 🌐 *www.csrmf.org* 🎫 *Train rides $12; first class $20* 🕒 *Closed Oct.–Mar.; call for hrs.*

Huntington, Hopkins & Co. Store. Picks, shovels, gold pans, and other paraphernalia used by gold-rush miners are on display at this re-creation of a 19th-century hardware store. Though it's named for two of the Big Four railroad barons, their store was far more elaborate. ✉ *113 I St., at Front St., Old Sacramento* ☎ *916/323–7234* 🌐 *www.californiarailroad.museum* 🎫 *Free.*

State Indian Museum. Adjacent to Sutter's Fort, this small but engaging museum explores the lives and history of California's native peoples. Among the interesting displays is one about Ishi, the last Yahi Indian to emerge from the mountains, in 1911. Arts-and-crafts exhibits, a demonstration village, knowledgeable rangers, and an evocative video offer a fascinating portrait of the history and lifestyle of the state's earliest inhabitants. ✉ *2618 K St., at 26th St., Midtown* ☎ *916/324–0971* 🌐 *www.parks.ca.gov* 🎫 *$5.*

FAMILY **Sutter's Fort.** German-born Swiss immigrant John Augustus Sutter founded Sacramento's earliest Euro-American settlement in 1839. Eight years later, assistance from Sutter's Fort helped save some members of the Donner Party. A self-guided tour includes a blacksmith's shop, bakery, prison, living quarters, and livestock areas. Costumed docents sometimes reenact fort life, demonstrating crafts, food preparation, and firearms maintenance. ✉ *2701 L St., at 27th St., Midtown* ☎ *916/445–4422* 🌐 *www.suttersfort.org* 🎫 *$5 most days, $7 on interpretive program days.*

WHERE TO EAT

$$$ NORTHERN ITALIAN Fodor's Choice ★

🍴 **Biba.** Since 1986, nationally recognized chef and owner Biba Caggiano has prepared northern Italian cuisine in her inviting restaurant near Sutter's Fort. The Capitol crowd flocks here for menus that change quarterly, with staples such as a 10-layer lasagne with Bolognese sauce, braised lamb shanks, and house-made gnocchi. **Known for:** celebrity chef; 10-layer lasagne; elegant but comfortable dining room. [$] *Average main: $28* ✉ *2801 Capitol Ave., at 28th St., Midtown* ☎ *916/455–2422* 🌐 *www.biba-restaurant.com* 🕒 *Closed Sun. No lunch Mon. or Sat.*

$$$$ MODERN AMERICAN 🍴 **Ella.** With fresh white calla lilies on the tables, ivory linen curtains, and distressed-wood shutters installed across the ceiling, this swank restaurant and bar near the Capitol building is artfully designed and thoroughly modern. Ella's decor matches the stellar California–French farm-to-table cuisine served within. **Known for:** fresh, seasonal local ingredients; classy dining room, cocktail selection, and wine list. [$] *Average main: $38* ✉ *1131 K St., Downtown* ☎ *916/443–3772* 🌐 *www.elladiningroomandbar.com* 🕓 *No lunch Sat. Closed Sun.*

$$$$ AMERICAN Fodor's Choice ★ 🍴 **The Firehouse.** The city's first brick firehouse has been restored with elegant dining spaces that showcase Chef Jay Veregge's award-winning contemporary menu. Creative dishes range from foie gras and carpaccio to locally sourced specialty beef cuts. **Known for:** steaks and seafood; sophisticated menu and setting; celeb clientele. [$] *Average main: $41* ✉ *1112 2nd St., at L St., Old Sacramento* ☎ *916/442–4772* 🌐 *www.firehouseoldsac.com* 🕓 *No lunch weekends.*

$$ MODERN AMERICAN 🍴 **Hook & Ladder Manufacturing Company.** Youthful and interesting, with found-art decorative elements and exposed vents, this historic former fire station is a favorite stop for creative cocktails, craft beers, and delicious farm-to-fork fare. Delectable salads and soups are enhanced by the area's year-round farmers' markets. **Known for:** carefully sourced ingredients; small bites; happy hour. [$] *Average main: $22* ✉ *1630 S. St., Midtown* ☎ *916/442–4885* 🌐 *www.hookandladder916.com.*

$$$ JAPANESE FUSION 🍴 **Kru.** Owner and inventive sushi chef Billy Ngo has earned a reputation for serving some of the freshest and most interesting sushi in Sacramento at this hip and stylish mod-Japanese restaurant. Try the sunshine roll, with spicy tuna, walu (escolar), and shrimp tempura and the surprising bite of green apples, lemon, and sweet chili. **Known for:** nearly two dozen styles of rolls; creative sushi; impressive sake, wine, and whisky offerings. [$] *Average main: $25* ✉ *3135 Folsom St., Midtown* ☎ *916/551–1559* 🌐 *www.krurestaurant.com* 🕓 *No lunch weekends.*

$$$ AMERICAN Fodor's Choice ★ 🍴 **Magpie Cafe.** This hip Midtown eatery with a casual vibe takes its food quite seriously: nearly all the produce is sourced locally, and menus are printed each day, reflecting availability from local farms. The array of small-batch farmstead cheeses, all from California, is mouthwatering (especially the Point Reyes Blue, drizzled with honey). **Known for:** California cheeses; new menus daily; homemade ice-cream sandwiches. [$] *Average main: $25* ✉ *1601 16th St., Midtown* ☎ *916/452–7594* 🌐 *www.magpiecafe.com* 🕓 *No dinner Sun.*

$$$ EUROPEAN Fodor's Choice ★ 🍴 **The Waterboy.** Rural French cooking with locally sourced, seasonal, high-quality (often organic) ingredients is the hallmark of this upscale Midtown restaurant that's as appealing for a casual meal with friends as it is for a drawn-out romantic dinner for two. The artisanal-cheese and antipasto plates are appealing starters for sharing, but you can't go wrong with marinated olives or oysters (in season). **Known for:** exceptional French cooking; quality local ingredients; welcoming chef. [$] *Average main: $28* ✉ *2000 Capitol Ave., at 20th St., Midtown* ☎ *916/498–9891* 🌐 *www.waterboyrestaurant.com* 🕓 *No lunch weekends.*

WHERE TO STAY

$$$ B&B/INN **Amber House Bed & Breakfast Inn.** Veer from the beaten path of traditional lodging at Amber House Inn's two historic homes—a 1905 Craftsman-style home and an 1895 Dutch colonial–revival home—just 1 mile from the Capitol. **Pros:** Midtown location; attentive service. **Cons:** freeway access isn't easy; not exactly kid-friendly. [$] *Rooms from: $199* ✉ *1315 22nd St., Midtown* ☎ *916/444–8085,* 🌐 *www.amberhouse.com* 🛏 *10 rooms* 🍴 *Breakfast.*

$$$ HOTEL Fodor's Choice ★ **The Citizen Hotel.** This boutique hotel built within the historic 1926 Cal Western Life building is dapper and refined, with marble stairs, striped wallpaper, and plush velvet chairs, lending the place a Roaring '20s charm. **Pros:** hip, sophisticated decor; smooth and solicitous service; terrific restaurant and bar. **Cons:** rooms near elevator can be noisy; rates vary widely depending on conventions, legislature, season. [$] *Rooms from: $208* ✉ *926 J St., Downtown* ☎ *916/447–2700* 🌐 *www.thecitizenhotel.com* 🛏 *198 rooms* 🍴 *No meals.*

$$ HOTEL **Delta King.** Wake up to the sound of geese taking flight along the river when you book a stay in one of Sacramento's most unusual and historic relics, a carefully restored riverboat hotel, permanently moored on Old Sacramento's waterfront. **Pros:** unique lodgings; steps from historic Old Town shopping and dining. **Cons:** slanted floors can feel a bit jarring; rooms are cramped. [$] *Rooms from: $156* ✉ *1000 Front St., Old Sacramento* ✥ *At the end of K St.* ☎ *916/444–5464, 800/825–5464* 🌐 *www.deltaking.com* 🛏 *44 rooms* 🍴 *Breakfast.*

$$$ HOTEL **Embassy Suites by Hilton Sacramento Riverfront.** Immediately adjacent to Sacramento's iconic Tower Bridge, this property has huge common areas, updated large rooms, locally commissioned public art, and a well-deserved reputation for exceptional customer service. **Pros:** best river view in town; proximity to Old Town and downtown. **Cons:** the atrium feels sterile. [$] *Rooms from: $219* ✉ *100 Capitol Mall, Downtown* ☎ *916/326–5000* 🌐 *embassysuites3.hilton.com* 🛏 *242 suites* 🍴 *Breakfast.*

$$$ HOTEL **Hyatt Regency Sacramento.** With a marble-and-glass lobby and luxurious rooms, this hotel across from the Capitol and adjacent to the convention center is one of Sacramento's finest. **Pros:** Capitol Park is across the street; some rooms have small balconies; excellent service. **Cons:** nearby streets can feel a little dodgy at night; somewhat impersonal. [$] *Rooms from: $239* ✉ *1209 L St., Downtown* ☎ *916/443–1234, 800/633–7313* 🌐 *sacramento.regency.hyatt.com* 🛏 *505 rooms* 🍴 *No meals.*

NIGHTLIFE AND PERFORMING ARTS

NIGHTLIFE

Blue Cue. A billiard lounge with a bright blue door, the Blue Cue is upstairs from the popular Mexican restaurant Centro. Wednesday night's trivia contest is a spirited event. ✉ *1004 28th St., at J St., Midtown* ☎ *916/441–6810* 🌐 *www.bluecue.com.*

Dive Bar. Live "mermaids" and "mermen" swim in a massive tank above the bar at this lively downtown nightspot known for its extensive list of craft cocktails and local beers. ✉ *1016 K St., Downtown* ☎ *916/737–5999* 🌐 *divebarsacramento.com.*

Fox and Goose. This casual pub with live music serves fish-and-chips, Cornish pasties, and other traditional items—plus vegetarian and vegan fare—on weekdays until 9:30. Music and revelry go until 2 am on weekends. ⊠ *1001 R St., at 10th St., Downtown* ☎ *916/443–8825* ⊕ *www. foxandgoose.com.*

Harlow's. This sceney restaurant draws a youngish crowd to its art-deco bar-nightclub, inviting patio, and Sacramento's most diverse live-music lineup after 9 pm. ⊠ *2708 J St., at 27th St., Midtown* ☎ *916/441–4693* ⊕ *www.harlows.com.*

Streets Pub and Grub. A favorite among Anglophiles, Streets is open until 2 am nightly. Darts and TV soccer, anyone? ⊠ *1804 J St., at 18th St., Midtown* ☎ *916/498–1388* ⊕ *www.streetspubandgrub.com.*

PERFORMING ARTS

California Musical Theatre. This group presents Broadway shows at the Sacramento Community Center Theater and the summer Music Circus musicals (think *Oklahoma, Annie*) at the theater-in-the-round Wells Fargo Pavilion. ⊠ *1419 H St., at 14th St., Downtown* ☎ *916/557–1999* ⊕ *www.calmt.com.*

Crest Theatre. It's worth peeking inside the Crest even if you don't catch a show there, just to see the swirling and flamboyant art-deco design in the foyer, or to dine at the new Empress Tavern restaurant within. It's a beloved venue for classic and art-house films, along with concerts and other cultural events. ⊠ *1013 K St., at 10th St., Downtown* ☎ *916/476–3356* ⊕ *www.crestsacramento.com.*

SHOPPING

Greater Sacramento is filled with familiar shops. To try something new but maybe find something old, wander through Midtown, especially J, K, and L Streets between 16th and 26th Streets.

Westfield Galleria at Roseville. From Sears to Nordstrom to Tiffany & Co., this shopping complex is a sprawling, heavily trafficked collection of chain stores and restaurants. It's always jumping. ⊠ *1151 Galleria Blvd., north of Sacramento off I–80 Exit 105A, Roseville* ⊕ *www.westfield.com/galleriaatroseville.*

WOODLAND

20 miles northwest of Sacramento.

In its heyday, Woodland was among California's wealthiest cities. Established by gold seekers and entrepreneurs, it later became an agricultural gold mine. The legacy of the old land barons lives on in the restored Victorian and Craftsman architecture downtown; the best examples are south of Main Street on College, Elm, 1st, and 2nd Streets. The town's top attraction is the splendid California Agriculture Museum.

GETTING HERE AND AROUND

Yolobus (⊕ *www.yolobus.com*) serves downtown Woodland from Sacramento, but it's far more practical to drive here via Interstate 5.

ESSENTIALS

Visitor Information Woodland Chamber of Commerce. ✉ 307 1st St., at Dead Cat Alley ☎ 530/662-7327 ⊕ www.woodlandchamber.org.

EXPLORING

FAMILY | **California Agriculture Museum.** This gigantic space provides a marvelous overview of the entire history of motorized agricultural vehicles through dozens and dozens of threshers, harvesters, combines, tractors, and more. A separate wing surveys the evolution of the truck, with an emphasis on ones used for farm work. ✉ 1962 Hays La., off County Rd. 102 ☎ 530/666-9700 ⊕ www.CaliforniaAgMuseum.org ✉ $10 ⊗ Closed Mon. and Tues.

Woodland Opera House. On the U.S. National Register of Historic Places, this 1896 structure hosted minstrel shows, John Philip Sousa's marching band, and early vaudeville acts before closing for six decades. Now restored, it hosts plays, musicals, and concerts year-round. If the box office is open, ask for a backstage tour or a peek at the auditorium. ✉ 340 2nd St. ☎ 530/666-9617 ⊕ www.woodlandoperahouse.org.

WHERE TO EAT

$$
AMERICAN | ✗ **Kitchen428 and Mojo's Lounge.** Originally built in 1891 to house luxury apartments, the Jackson building roared back to life in 2012 as Woodland's best restaurant, showcasing locally sourced California cuisine from filet mignon to cioppino. A friendly, stylish, and "green" place, Mojo's rewards like-minded customers; ride a bike here, and you'll receive 10% off your bill. **Known for:** local and sustainable menu; historic building; weekend brunch. $ Average main: $21 ✉ 428 1st St., off Main St. ☎ 530/661-0428 ⊕ www.mojoskitchen428.com.

DAVIS

10 miles west of Sacramento.

Davis began as a rich agricultural area and remains one, but it doesn't feel like a cow town. It's home to the University of California at Davis, whose 35,000-plus students hang at downtown cafés, galleries, and bookstores (most of the action takes place between 1st and 4th and C and G Streets), lending the city a decidedly college-town feel.

GETTING HERE AND AROUND

Most people arrive here by car via Interstate 80. In a pinch, you can get here via Yolobus (⊕ www.yolobus.com) from Sacramento. Downtown is walkable. Touring by bicycle is also a popular option—Davis is very flat.

ESSENTIALS

Visitor Information Davis Chamber of Commerce. ✉ 640 3rd St. ☎ 530/756-5160 ⊕ www.?schamber.com.

EXPLORING

University of California, Davis. A top research university, UC Davis educates many of the Wine Country's vintners and grape growers, in addition to farmers, veterinarians, and brewmasters, too. Campus tours depart from Buehler Alumni and Visitors Center. On a tour or not, worthy stops include the **Arboretum** (⊕ arboretum.ucdavis.edu), the **Manetti Shrem Museum of Art** (⊕ manettishremmuseum.ucdavis.edu), and the **Mondavi Center for the Performing Arts** (⊕ *mondaviarts.org*), a striking modern glass structure that presents top-tier artists. ⊠ *Visitor Center, 550 Alumni La.* ☎ *530/752–8111 for tour information* ⊕ *visit.ucdavis.edu.*

LODI

41 miles north of Modesto, 34 miles south of Sacramento.

With about 100,000 acres of mostly rich alluvial soils planted to more than six-dozen grape varietals—more types than in any other California viticultural area—Lodi is a major a wine-making grape hub, particularly for Zinfandel. Eighty or so wineries do business in Lodi and neighboring Acampo, Lockeford, and Woodbridge. Founded on agriculture, Lodi was once the watermelon capital of the country. Today it's surrounded by fields of asparagus, pumpkins, beans, safflowers, sunflowers, kiwis, melons, squashes, peaches, and cherries. Lodi itself retains an old rural charm. You can stroll downtown or visit a wildlife refuge, all the while benefiting from a Sacramento River delta breeze that keeps this microclimate cooler in summer than anyplace else in the area.

GETTING HERE AND AROUND

Most of Lodi lies to the west of Highway 99, several miles east of Interstate 5. Buses and Amtrak trains stop here frequently. Although the GrapeLine bus (☎ *209/333–6806*) can get you around town and to many of the wineries, you are better off with your own vehicle.

ESSENTIALS

Visitor Information Lodi Conference & Visitors Bureau. ⊠ *25 N. School St.* ☎ *209/365–1195, 800/798–1810* ⊕ *www.visitlodi.com.*

EXPLORING

TOP ATTRACTIONS

Lodi Wine & Visitor Center. A fine place to sample Lodi wines, the center has a tasting bar and viticultural exhibits. You can also buy wine and pick up a free winery map. The knowledgeable pourers can suggest wineries to explore. ⊠ *2545 W. Turner Rd., at Woodhaven La.* ☎ *209/365–0621* ⊕ *www.lodiwine.com* ⊠ *Tasting $7.*

Lucas Winery. David Lucas was one of the first local producers to start making serious wine, and today his Zinfandels are among Lodi's most sought-after vintages. In addition to fruity Zins, Lucas makes a light Chardonnay with subtle oaky flavors. The 90-minute tour and tasting will get you up to speed on the Lodi wine appellation. ⊠ *18196 N. Davis Rd., at W. Turner Rd.* ☎ *209/368–2006* ⊕ *www.lucaswinery.com* ⊠ *Tastings $10–$55, tour (includes tasting) $55* ⊗ *Closed Mon. and Tues.*

Fodor's Choice ★ **M2 Wines.** With its translucent polycarbonate panels, concrete floor, and metal framing, this winery's high-ceilinged tasting room strikes an iconoclastic, industrial-sleek pose along an otherwise relentlessly rural lane north of Lodi. The Soucie Vineyard old-vine Zinfandel and the Trio Red Wine blend are the flagships. ⊠ *2900 E. Peltier Rd., Acampo* ✦ *Near Lower Sacramento Rd.* ☎ *209/339–1071* ⊕ *www.m2wines.com* ⊠ *Tasting $10* ⊗ *Closed Tues. and Wed.*

Fodor's Choice ★ **Michael David Winery.** Fifth-generation farmers turned winery owners Michael and David Phillips operate their tasting room at the rustic roadside **Phillips Farms Fruit Stand,** where they also sell their family's gorgeous produce. Michael David is well known for Zinfandels, among them 7 Deadly Zins. **■ TIP→ Breakfast or lunch at the café here is a treat.** ✉ *4580 W. Hwy. 12, at N. Ray Rd.* ☎ *209/368–7384* 🌐 *www.michaeldavidwinery.com* 🎟 *Tastings $5–$10* 🕒 *No reserve tasting Mon.–Thurs.*

WORTH NOTING

Berghold Estate Winery. The tasting room at Berghold recalls an earlier wine era with its vintage Victorian interior, including restored, salvaged mantlepieces, leaded glass, and a 26-foot-long bar. The wines—among them Viognier, Cabernet Sauvignon, Merlot, Syrah, and Zinfandel—pay homage to French winemaking styles. ✉ *17343 N. Cherry Rd., off E. Victor Rd./Hwy. 12* ☎ *209/333–9291* 🌐 *bergholdvineyards.com* 🎟 *Tasting $10* 🕒 *Closed Mon.–Wed.*

FAMILY **Micke Grove Regional Park.** This 258-acre, oak-shaded park has a Japanese tea garden, picnic tables, children's play areas, an agricultural museum, a zoo, a golf course, and a water-play feature. **Fun Town at Micke Grove,** a family-oriented amusement park, is geared toward younger children. ✉ *11793 N. Micke Grove Rd., off Hwy. 99 Armstrong Rd. exit, 5 miles south of downtown* ☎ *209/953–8800 park info, 209/369–7330 Fun Town, 209/331–2010 zoo* 🎟 *Parking $5 weekdays, $6 weekends and holidays; pets $1 (leash required); Fun Town ride prices vary; zoo $5.*

Van Ruiten Family Vineyards. For an affordable experience of what Lodi's hardworking old Zinfandel vines can produce, sample the Van Ruiten Old Vine Zin and the Reserve Sideways Lot 69 Old Vine Zin. Other wines of note include the Chardonnays and the Cabernet-Shiraz blend. ✉ *340 W. Hwy. 12* ☎ *209/334–5722* 🌐 *www.vrwinery.com* 🎟 *Tastings $10–$15.*

WHERE TO EAT

$$ AMERICAN 🍴 **The Dancing Fox Winery and Bakery.** This is a good downtown stop for coffee and fresh pastries, a granola parfait, or more filling breakfast selections. The Dancing Fox also serves lunch and dinner and has a tasting room for its eponymous wines. **Known for:** fresh organic breads and pizzas; many dishes baked in Spanish wood-fired oven; historic downtown setting. [$] *Average main: $19* ✉ *203 S. School St.* ☎ *203/366–2634* 🌐 *www.dancingfoxwinery.com* 🕒 *Closed Mon. No dinner Sun.*

$$$ ITALIAN 🍴 **Pietro's Trattoria.** Lodi's go-to spot for Italian–American classics wins fans for its quality ingredients, Tuscan-courtyard ambience, and plant-filled outdoor patio (reservations essential on weekends). Expect straightforward, well-executed renditions of chicken and veal piccata, filling lasagna and fettucine Alfredo (with chicken or prawns), pizzas, and the like, all delivered with informal good cheer by the cadre of servers. **Known for:** wine list focused on local vintages; Italian-American classics; authentic Tuscan atmosphere. [$] *Average main: $25* ✉ *317 E. Kettleman La.* ☎ *209/368–0613* 🌐 *www.pietroslodi.com* 🕒 *Closed Sun. No lunch Mon.*

$$$$ MODERN AMERICAN Fodor's Choice ★ 🍴 **Towne House Restaurant.** Lodi power breakfasts and lunches and special-occasion dinners often take place in the distinguished rooms of this former residence behind, and part of, the Wine and Roses hotel. Painted in rich, textured hues offset by wide white molding, the rooms exude a subtle sophistication matched by the cuisine of executive chef John Hitchcock. Jazz musicians perform nightly in the lounge, noteworthy for its specialty cocktails and selection of local wines by the glass. **Known for:** 70-plus local wines by the glass; nightly live music; fresh seasonal local ingredients. [$] *Average main: $40* ✉ *2505 W. Turner Rd., at Woodhaven La.* ☎ *209/371–6160* 🌐 *winerose.com/towne-house-restaurant.*

WHERE TO STAY

$$ B&B/INN 🏨 **The Inn at Locke House.** Built between 1862 and 1882, the inn occupies a pioneer doctor's family home that rates a listing on the National Register of Historic Places. **Pros:** friendly; quiet; lovely. **Cons:** remote; can be hard to find. [$] *Rooms from: $149* ✉ *19960 Elliott Rd., Lockeford* ☎ *209/727–5715* 🌐 *www.theinnatlockehouse.com* 🛏 *5 rooms* 🍽 *Breakfast.*

$$$$ HOTEL 🏨 **Wine & Roses Hotel and Restaurant.** Set on 7 acres amid a tapestry of informal gardens, this hotel has cultivated a sense of refinement typically associated with Napa or Carmel. **Pros:** luxurious; relaxing; quiet. **Cons:** expensive; some guests mention that walls are thin. [$] *Rooms from: $259* ✉ *2505 W. Turner Rd.* ☎ *209/334–6988* 🌐 *www.winerose.com* 🛏 *66 rooms* 🍽 *No meals.*

SPORTS AND THE OUTDOORS

Lodi Lake Park. Shaded by grand old elms and oaks, the lake's banks are much cooler in summer than other spots in town. You can swim, watch birds, picnic, and rent a kayak, canoe, or pedal boat here. ✉ *1101 W. Turner Rd., at Mills Ave.* ☎ *209/333–6742* 🌐 *www.lodi.gov/prcs/lodi-lake.html* 🎟 *$5 vehicle entrance fee, $3 public swimming.*

THE GOLD COUNTRY—SOUTH

This hilly region has an old-timey vibe. It's rich with antiques shops, quaint coffee shops, and delightfully appointed Victorian B&Bs.

PLACERVILLE

44 miles east of Sacramento.

It's hard to imagine now, but in 1849 about 4,000 miners staked out every gully and hillside in Placerville, turning the town into a rip-roaring camp of log cabins, tents, and clapboard houses. The area was then known as Hangtown, a graphic allusion to the nature of frontier justice. It took on the name Placerville in 1854 and became an important supply center for the miners. (*Placer* is defined roughly as valuable minerals found in riverbeds or lakes.) Mark Hopkins, Philip Armour, and John Studebaker were among the industrialists who got their starts here. Today Placerville ranks among the hippest towns in the region, its Main Street abuzz with indie shops, coffeehouses, and wine bars, many of them inside rehabbed historic buildings.

GETTING HERE AND AROUND

You'll need a car to get to and around Placerville; it's a 45-minute drive from Sacramento via U.S. 50.

EXPLORING

FAMILY **Apple Hill.** During the fall harvest season (September through December), the members of the Apple Hill Growers Association open their orchards and vineyards for apple and berry picking, picnicking, and wine and cider tasting. Start your tour at High Hill Ranch, where there are fishing ponds for kids (they'll clean and pack the fish for you). Nibble on apple doughnuts or buy jewelry from local crafters. Stop at Larsen Apple Barn, a legacy farm. Family-favored Kid's Inc. serves apple pies and empanadas, and you can sample Cabernet and Bordeaux-style blends at Grace Patriot Wines and fresh-pressed juices at Barsotti. Stop at Wofford Acres Vineyard just to see a dramatic view of the American River canyon below. ■ **TIP→** Traffic on weekends is often backed up, so take the Camino exit or go during the week to avoid the crowds (although kid-centric events are on weekends). ✉ *About 5 miles east of Hwy. 49; take Camino exit from U.S. 50* ☎ *530/644–7692* 🌐 *www.applehill.com.*

FAMILY **Hangtown's Gold Bug Park & Mine.** Take a self-guided tour of this fully lighted mine shaft within a park owned by the City of Placerville. The worthwhile audio tour (included) makes clear what you're seeing. ■ **TIP→ A shaded stream runs through the park, and there are picnic facilities.** ✉ *2635 Goldbug La., off Bedford Ave., 1 mile off U.S. 50* ☎ *530/642–5207* 🌐 *www.goldbugpark.org* 🎟 *Park free; mine tour $7.*

WHERE TO EAT AND STAY

$ VEGETARIAN 🍴 **The Cozmic Cafe.** Crowds come for healthful wraps, burritos, sandwiches, salads, and the like, including vegan and vegetarian options. Portions are big, prices are low, and the ambience is distinctly communal and small town. **Known for:** healthy eats; live music. [$] *Average main: $9* ✉ *594 Main St.* ☎ *530/642–8481* 🌐 *www.ourcoz.com* 🕒 *Closed Mon.*

$$$$ B&B/INN FAMILY Fodor's Choice ★ 🏨 **Eden Vale Inn.** Handcrafted by the owners, this lavish but rustic B&B occupies a converted turn-of-the-20th-century hay barn, the centerpiece of which is a 27-foot slate fireplace that rises to a sloping roof of timber beams. **Pros:** rooms are exceptionally plush; the patio and grounds are stunning; plenty of places outside for kids to run. **Cons:** expensive for the area, plus two-night minimum on weekends; book summer weekends well in advance. [$] *Rooms from: $318* ✉ *1780 Springvale Rd.* ☎ *530/621–0901* 🌐 *www.edenvaleinn.com* 🛏 *7 rooms* 🍽 *Breakfast.*

$$ B&B/INN 🏨 **Seasons Bed & Breakfast.** One of Placerville's oldest buildings, a gold stamp mill that dates to 1859, has been transformed into a lovely and relaxing oasis with a main house, cottages, and gardens filled with paintings and sculptures. **Pros:** quiet setting; short walk to downtown; attentive hosts. **Cons:** better for romantics than business travelers. [$] *Rooms from: $135* ✉ *2934 Bedford Ave.* ☎ *530/626–4420* 🌐 *www.theseasons.net* 🛏 *3 rooms, 1 cottage* 🍽 *Breakfast.*

SHENANDOAH VALLEY

20 miles south of Placerville.

The most concentrated Gold Country wine-touring area lies in the hills of the Shenandoah Valley, east of Plymouth. Robust Zinfandel is the primary grape grown here, but vineyards here produce plenty of other varietals, from Rhône blends to Italian Barberas and Sangioveses. Most wineries are open for tastings at least on weekend afternoons, and some of the top ones are open daily; several have shaded picnic areas. **■ TIP→ This region is gaining steam as a less-congested alternative to the Napa Valley.**

GETTING HERE AND AROUND

Reach the Shenandoah Valley by turning east on Fiddletown Road in Plymouth, between Placerville and Sutter Creek, and then north on Plymouth-Shenandoah Road. You will need a car to explore the valley and its vineyards.

EXPLORING

Shenandoah Vineyards. A plummy Barbera and an almost chocolaty Zinfandel top this winery's repertoire, but for a contrast you can also try a startlingly crisp Sauvignon Blanc. The Tempranillo is also good. An adjacent gallery sells contemporary art, pottery, photographs, and souvenirs. **■ TIP→ Shenandoah is affiliated with the nearby Sobon Estate Winery, which has an engaging on-site museum about the area.** ✉ *12300 Steiner Rd., Plymouth* ☎ *209/245–4455* 🌐 *www.sobonwine.com* 🎟 *Tasting $5.*

Terre Rouge and Easton Wines. The winery of Bill Easton and Jane O'Riordan has two labels with two different wine-making styles: Terre Rouge focuses on Rhône-style wines, while Easton covers old-vine Zinfandel and Barbera. The winery has had good results with inky, soft Syrahs and Enigma, a Rhône-style white blend of Marsanne, Viognier, and Roussane. **■ TIP→ You can picnic on the shaded patio here and there's a pétanque court nearby.** ✉ *10801 Dickson Rd., Plymouth* ☎ *209/245–4277* 🌐 *www.terrerougewines.com* 🎟 *Tasting $5* 🕒 *Closed Tues. and Wed.*

Vino Noceto. Noceto draws raves for its Sangiovese wines which range from light and fruity to rich and heavy. Look for the Little Red Barn, where you'll find welcoming owners Suzy and Jim Gullett offering tastings and tours seven days a week. They also produce small lots of wines from other varietals. ✉ *11011 Shenandoah Rd., at Dickson Rd., Plymouth* ☎ *209/245–6556* 🌐 *www.noceto.com* 🎟 *Tasting free.*

WHERE TO EAT

$$$$ MODERN AMERICAN Fodor's Choice ★

🍴 **Taste.** A serendipitous find on the dusty streets of tiny Plymouth, Taste serves eclectic modern dishes made from fresh local fare. Phyllo-wrapped mushroom "cigars" are a small-plate staple, and quail, rack of lamb, and duck confit are examples of chef Mark Berkner's sustainably sourced, creative dishes. **Known for:** fine dining in tiny Plymouth; knowledgeable sommeliers. [$] *Average main: $33* ✉ *9402 Main St., Plymouth* ☎ *209/245–3463* 🌐 *www.restauranttaste.com* 🕒 *Closed Wed. No lunch weekdays.*

AMADOR CITY

6 miles south of Plymouth.

The history of tiny Amador City (population 200) mirrors the boom-bust-boom cycle of many Gold Country towns. With an output of $42 million in gold, its Keystone Mine was one of the most productive in the Mother Lode. After all the gold was extracted, the miners cleared out, and the area suffered. Amador City now derives its wealth from tourists, who come to browse through its antiques and specialty shops.

GETTING HERE AND AROUND

Park where you can along Old Highway 49 (a bypass diverts Highway 49 traffic around Sutter Creek and Amador City), and walk around.

WHERE TO STAY

$$ **Imperial Hotel.** Located on the bend in this one-block town, the whim-
B&B/INN sically decorated mock-Victorian rooms at this 1879 hotel give a modern twist to the excesses of the Gold Rush. **Pros:** unique history-evoking stay; good restaurant and bar. **Cons:** the hotel and bar are the town nightlife. $ *Rooms from: $130* ✉ *14202 Old Hwy. 49* ☎ *209/267–9172* ⊕ *www.imperialamador.com* ↝ *9 rooms* ⦿*Breakfast.*

SUTTER CREEK

2 miles south of Amador City.

Sutter Creek is a charming conglomeration of balconied buildings, Victorian homes, and neo–New England structures. The stores on Main Street (formerly part of Highway 49, which was rerouted) are worth visiting for works by the many local artists and craftspeople.

GETTING HERE AND AROUND

Arrive here by car on Highway 49. There's no public transit, but downtown is walkable. The visitor center organizes walking tours.

ESSENTIALS

Information Sutter Creek Visitor Center. ✉ *71A Main St.* ☎ *209/267–1344* ⊕ *www.suttercreek.org.*

EXPLORING

Monteverde Store Museum. This store, opened 1896, is a relic from the past: its final owner walked out more than four decades ago and never returned. These days you can peruse what he left behind, including typical wares from a century ago, an elaborate antique scale, and a chair-encircled potbellied stove. ✉ *3 Randolph St.* ☎ *209/267–0493.*

WHERE TO STAY

$$ **Days Inn Sutter Creek.** Relative to the cost of boutique inns and bed-
HOTEL and-breakfast hotels in the region, the Days Inn offers a clean, updated
FAMILY place to stay in Gold Country at a reasonable price. **Pros:** easy, especially with families, pets and/or oversized vehicles; clean. **Cons:** you can walk to historic downtown, but sidewalks aren't great. $ *Rooms from: $155* ✉ *271 Hanford St.* ☎ *209/267–9177* ⊕ *www.wyndhamhotels.com/days-inn/sutter-creek-california/days-inn-sutter-creek/overview* ↝ *52 rooms* ⦿*Breakfast.*

$$
B&B/INN

⚐ **Eureka Street Inn.** The lead- and stained-glass windows and the origi-
nal redwood paneling, wainscoting, and beams—and, oh yes, those
gas-log fireplaces in most rooms—lend the Eureka Street Inn a cozy
feel. **Pros:** quiet location; lovely porch; engaging owners. **Cons:** two-
night stay required at times. Ⓢ *Rooms from: $155* ✉ *55 Eureka St.*
☎ *209/267–5500, 800/399–2389* ⊕ *www.eurekastreetinn.com* ⬟ 4
rooms ⊚ *Breakfast.*

$$$
B&B/INN

⚐ **The Foxes Inn of Sutter Creek.** The rooms in this 1857 yellow-clapboard
house are handsome, with high ceilings, antique beds, and armoires;
five have gas fireplaces. **Pros:** lovely inside and out; friendly owners.
Cons: two-night minimum stay at times. Ⓢ *Rooms from: $199* ✉ *77
Main St.* ☎ *209/267–5882, 800/987–3344* ⊕ *www.foxesinn.com* ⬟ 7
rooms ⊚ *Breakfast.*

$$$
B&B/INN

⚐ **Grey Gables Inn.** Charming if you like lace and frills, this inn—with
rooms named after British poets—brings the English countryside to
Gold Country. **Pros:** English-manor feel; tasteful interiors and grounds;
complimentary bottle of wine in rooms. **Cons:** adjacent to busy main
drag into town; two-night stay required at times. Ⓢ *Rooms from: $220*
✉ *161 Hanford St.* ☎ *209/267–1039, 800/473–9422* ⊕ *www.greyga-
bles.com* ⬟ 10 *rooms* ⊚ *Breakfast.*

JACKSON

8 miles south of Sutter Creek.

Jackson wasn't the Gold Country's rowdiest town, but the party lasted
longer here than most anywhere else: "girls' dormitories" (aka brothels)
and nickel slot machines flourished until the mid-1950s. Jackson also
had the world's deepest and richest gold mines, the Kennedy and the
Argonaut, which together produced $70 million in gold. Most of the
miners who worked the lode were of Serbian or Italian origin, and they
gave the town a European character that persists to this day. Jackson
has pioneer cemeteries whose headstones tell the stories of local Serbian
and Italian families. The city's official website (⊕ *ci.jackson.ca.us*; *click
on "Visitor Center"*) has great cemetery and walking-tour maps; there
are some interesting shops downtown.

GETTING HERE AND AROUND

Arrive by car on Highway 49. You can walk to downtown sights but
otherwise will need a car.

EXPLORING

Kennedy Gold Mine. On weekends, docents offer guided surface tours of
one of the most prolific mines of the gold-rush era. Exhibits inside the
remaining buildings illustrate how the mine used "skips" to lower min-
ers and materials into the mile-long shaft, and to carry ore and tailings
to the surface. Plan for 90 minutes to enjoy the guided tour. ✉ *Kennedy
Mine Rd., at Argonaut La.* ✛ *½ mile east of Hwy. 49* ☎ *209/223–9542*
⊕ *www.kennedygoldmine.com* ▱ *Free; guided tours $10.*

Preston Castle. History buffs and ghost hunters regularly make the trip
to this fantastically creepy building that was built to house troubled
youth in 1894. Having fallen into a state of disrepair, the building is

DID YOU KNOW?

You can still pan for gold, but any shiny stuff will usually be worthless iron pyrite. Here a young prospector tries his hand at Marshall Gold Discovery State Park.

California's Gold Rush

When James W. Marshall burst into John Sutter's Mill on January 24, 1848, carrying flecks of gold in his hat, the millwright unleashed the glittering California gold rush with these immortal words: "Boys, I believe I've found a gold mine!" Before it was over, drowsy San Francisco had become the boomtown of the Golden West, Columbia's mines alone yielded $87,000,000, and California's Mother Lode—a vein of gold-bearing quartz that stretched 150 miles across the Sierra Nevada foothills—had been nearly tapped dry. Even though the gold rush soon became the gold bust, today you can still strike it rich by visiting the historic sites where it all happened. Journey down the Gold Country Highway—a serpentine, nearly 300-milelong two-lane route appropriately numbered 49—to find pure vacation treasure: fascinating Mother Lode towns, rip-roaring mining camps, and historic strike sites. In fact, in Placerville—as the former Hangtown, this spot saw so much new money and crime that outlaws were hanged in pairs—you can still pan the streams.

BOOM TO BUST

From imagination springs adventure, and perhaps no event in the 19th century provoked more wild adventures than the California gold rush of 1848 to 1855. **January 24, 1848:** James W. Marshall spies specks of bright rock in the streambed at his sawmill's site. **May, 1848:** California's coastal communities empty out as prospectors flock to the hills to join the "forty-eighters." **August 19, 1848:** *The New York Herald* is the first East Coast newspaper to report a gold rush in California. **October 13, 1849:** California's state constitution is approved in Monterey. The state's new motto becomes "Eureka!" **1855:** The California gold rush effectively ends, as digging for the precious mineral becomes increasingly difficult, and large corporations monopolize mining operations.

HOW TO PAN FOR GOLD

Grab any non-Teflon-coated pan with sloping sides and head up to "them thar hills." Find a stream—preferably one containing black sand—you can stoop beside, and then scoop out sediment to fill your pan. Add water, then gently shake the pan sideways, back and forth. This allows any gold to settle at the bottom. Pick out and toss away any larger rocks. Keep adding water, keep shaking the pan, and slowly pour the loosened waste gravel over the rim of the pan, making sure not to upend the pan while doing so. If you're left with gold, yell "Eureka!" then put it in a glass container. Your findings may not make you rich, but will entitle you to bragging rights. If you'd rather go with a guide, plenty of attractions and museums in the Gold Country will let you try your hand at prospecting.

slowly undergoing a full renovation. Tours are available by appointment and on certain Tuesdays and Saturdays (it's best to call ahead to confirm schedule). Ask about evening and overnight tours when tales of paranormal activity are truly spooky. The dramatic Romanesque Revival structure has appeared on TV's *Ghost Hunters*, and during tours of this 156-room building you'll learn all sorts of spine-tingling tales, including one about a student murdering a housekeeper and then rolling her up in a carpet. ✉ *909 Palm Dr., 12 miles west of Jackson via Hwys. 88 and 104, Ione* ☎ *209/256–3623* 🌐 *www.prestoncastle.com* 🎟 *$15* ⏲ *Closed Sept.-Mar.*

WHERE TO EAT AND STAY

$ AMERICAN FAMILY ✕ **Mel and Faye's Diner.** Since 1956, the Gillman family has been serving up its famous "Moo Burger" with two patties and special sauce—so big it still makes cow sounds, presumably. Breakfast is available all day at this homey diner. **Known for:** Moo burgers; milk shakes. [$] *Average main: $12* ✉ *31 Highway 88* ☎ *209/223–0853* 🌐 *www.melandfayes.homestead.com.*

$ HOTEL **Hotel Leger.** Dramatically remodeled in 2013 as part of a makeover television show ("Hotel Impossible"), this convivial old saloon and hotel was a rowdy miners' haunt during the gold rush. **Pros:** rich in history; friendly and accommodating proprietors. **Cons:** some might not appreciate the creaky wood floors; rooms above the saloon can be noisy. [$] *Rooms from: $115* ✉ *8304 Main St., Mokelumme Hill* ☎ *209/286–1401* 🌐 *www.hotelleger.com* *13 rooms* 🍴 *No meals.*

ANGELS CAMP

20 miles south of Jackson.

Angels Camp is famous chiefly for its May jumping-frog contest, based on Mark Twain's short story "The Celebrated Jumping Frog of Calaveras County." The writer reputedly heard the story of the jumping frog from Ross Coon, proprietor of Angels Hotel, which has been in operation since 1856. It's a favorite destination these days among outdoor adventurers, who love exploring the subterranean caverns and fishing for salmon, trout, and bass in the area's crystal clear rivers and lakes.

GETTING HERE AND AROUND

Angels Camp is at the intersection of Highway 49 and Highway 4. You'll need a car to get here and around.

EXPLORING

FAMILY Fodor's Choice ★ **Angels Camp Museum.** Learn about Mark Twain's "The Celebrated Jumping Frog of Calaveras County" and check out mining equipment and relics from the gold-rush era. The grounds include a carriage house, little red schoolhouse, and mercantile store. ✉ *753 S. Main St.* ☎ *209/736–2963* 🌐 *www.angelscampmuseumfoundation.org* 🎟 *$5.*

FAMILY **California Cavern.** A ½-mile subterranean trail winds through large chambers and past underground streams and lakes. There aren't many steps to climb, but it's a strenuous walk with some narrow passageways and steep spots. The caverns, at a constant 55°F, contain crystalline formations not found elsewhere, and the 80-minute guided tour explains local history and geology. ✉ *9565 Cave City Rd., 9 miles east of San Andreas on Mountain Ranch Rd., then about 3 miles on Cave City Rd., Mountain Ranch* ☎ *209/736–2708* 🌐 *www.caverntours.com* 🎟 *$17.50.*

FAMILY Fodor's Choice ★ **Moaning Cavern.** For a different sort of underground jewel, wander into an ancient limestone cave, where stalactites and stalagmites, not gold and silver, await you. Take the 235-step spiral staircase built in 1922 into this vast cavern, or more intrepid explorers can rappel into the chamber—ropes and instruction are provided. Outside there are three zip lines, starting at $45 per person, and a climbing tower. ✉ *5350 Moaning Cave Rd., off Parrotts Ferry Rd., about 2 miles south of Vallecito, Vallecito* ☎ *209/736–2708* ⊕ *www.caverntours. com* ✇ *$17.50.*

MURPHYS

10 miles northeast of Angels Camp.

Murphys is the Gold Country's most compact, orderly town, with enough shops and restaurants to keep families busy for at least a half day, and more than 20 tasting rooms within walking distance. A well-preserved town of white-picket fences, Victorian houses, and interesting shops, it exhibits an upscale vibe. Horatio Alger and Ulysses S. Grant came through here, staying at what's now called the Murphys Historic Hotel & Lodge when they, along with many other 19th-century tourists, came to investigate the giant sequoia groves in nearby Calaveras Big Trees State Park.

GETTING HERE AND AROUND

Murphys is 10 miles northeast of Highway 49 on Highway 4. You'll need to drive here. Parking can be difficult on summer weekends.

EXPLORING

FAMILY

Fodor'sChoice

★

Calaveras Big Tree State Park. The park protects hundreds of the largest and rarest living things on the planet—magnificent giant sequoia redwood trees. Some are 3,000 years old, 90 feet around at the base, and 250 feet tall. There are campgrounds, cabin rentals, and picnic areas; swimming, wading, fishing, and sunbathing on the Stanislaus River are popular in summer. Enjoy the "three senses" trail, designated for the blind, with interpretive signs in braille that guide visitors to touch the bark and encourage children to slow down and enjoy the forest in a more sensory way. ✉ *Off Hwy. 4, 15 miles northeast of Murphys, 4 miles northeast of Arnold, Angels Camp* ☎ *209/795–2334* ⊕ *www. parks.ca.gov* ✇ *$10 per vehicle.*

Ironstone Vineyards. Tours here take in spectacular gardens and underground tunnels cooled by a waterfall, and include the automated performance of a restored silent-movie-era pipe organ. On display near the tasting room is a 44-pound specimen of crystalline gold. The winery, known for Merlot, Cabernet Sauvignon, and Cabernet Franc, hosts concerts and other events. Its deli has picnic items. ■ TIP→ Ironstone is worth a visit even if you don't drink wine. ✉ *1894 6 Mile Rd.* ⊹ *From Jones St. in town, head south on Scott St.* ☎ *209/728–1251* ⊕ *www. ironstonevineyards.com* ✇ *Tasting $5.*

WHERE TO EAT AND STAY

$$

AMERICAN

✕ **Grounds.** From risotto to rib eye, this bustling bistro and coffee shop has something for all palates. Lighter grilled vegetables, chicken, sandwiches, salads, and homemade soups always shine here. **Known for:** potato pancakes at breakfast; carefully curated wine list. Ⓢ *Average main: $22* ✉ *402 Main St.* ☎ *209/728–8663* ⊕ *www.groundsrestaurant. com* ☉ *No dinner Mon. and Tues.*

$$ HOTEL **Murphys Historic Hotel & Lodge.** This 1855 stone hotel, whose register claims to have seen the signatures of Mark Twain, John Wayne, Susan B. Anthony, and Ulysses S. Grant is a 19th-century throwback in the heart of Murphys. **Pros:** historic ambience; great bar; rumors suggest it's haunted, if you're into that. **Cons:** original building lacks modern amenities; newer building has motel feel; restaurant can be noisy. [$] *Rooms from: $140* ✉ *457 Main St.* ☎ *209/728–3444, 800/532–7684* 🌐 *www.murphyshotel.com* 🛏 *29 rooms* 🍴 *No meals.*

COLUMBIA

14 miles south of Angels Camp.

Columbia is the gateway for Columbia State Historic Park, one of the Gold Country's most visited sites. The historic Fallon House Theater is a great place for families to participate in living history activities like candle dipping and soap making on weekends. There are several inviting spots for a picnic in the area.

GETTING HERE AND AROUND

The only way to get here is by car, via either Highway 4 (the northern route) or Highway 49 (the southern) from Angels Camp.

EXPLORING

FAMILY Fodor's Choice ★ **Columbia State Historic Park.** Columbia is both a functioning community and a historically preserved gold-rush town. Usually you can ride a stagecoach, pan for gold, and watch a blacksmith working at an anvil. Street musicians perform in summer. Restored or reconstructed buildings include a Wells Fargo Express office, a Masonic temple, an old-fashioned candy store, saloons, a firehouse, churches, a school, and a newspaper office. At times, all are staffed to simulate a working 1850s town. The park also includes the must-stop **Historic Fallon House Theater,** where Broadway-quality shows are performed Wednesday through Sunday—Mark Twain once performed in this gorgeous Victorian structure. The town's two 19th-century historic lodgings, the Fallon Hotel ($) and City Hotel ($–$$) perch you in the past; to reserve a hotel or cottage go to *www.reserveamerica.com.* ✉ *11255 Jackson St.* ☎ *209/588–9128* 🌐 *www.parks.ca.gov/columbia* 🎟 *Free.*

SONORA

4 miles south of Columbia.

Miners from Mexico founded Sonora and made it the biggest town in the Mother Lode. Following a period of racial and ethnic strife, the Mexican settlers moved on, and Yankees built the commercial city visible today. Sonora's historic downtown section sits atop the Big Bonanza Mine, one of the richest in the state. Another mine, on the site of nearby Sonora High School, yielded 990 pounds of gold in a single week in 1879. Reminders of the gold rush are everywhere in Sonora, in prim Victorian houses, typical Sierra-stone storefronts, and awning-shaded sidewalks. Reality intrudes beyond the town's historic heart, with strip malls, shopping centers, and modern motels.

GETTING HERE AND AROUND

Arrive in Sonora by car via Highway 49 (if coming from Columbia, drive south on Parrots Ferry Road). Parking can be difficult on the busy main drag, Washington Street (Highway 49).

EXPLORING

Tuolumne County Museum and History Centers. The small museum occupies a historic gold-rush-era building that served as a jail until 1960. Vintage firearms and paraphernalia, gold specimens, and Me-Wuk baskets are among the many artifacts on display. ✉ *158 W. Bradford St.* ☎ *209/532–1317* 🌐 *www.tchistory.org* 🎟 *Free* 🕒 *Closed Sun.*

WHERE TO EAT AND STAY

$ AMERICAN 🍴 **Diamondback Grill and Wine Bar.** The bright decor and refined atmosphere suggest more ambitious fare, but burgers are what this place is about. Locals crowd the tables, especially after 6 pm, for the ground-meat patties, beer-battered onion rings, veggie burgers, and fine wines. **Known for:** half-pound burgers and garlic fries; wine bar and wine club. [$] *Average main: $12* ✉ *93 S. Washington St.* ☎ *209/532–6661* 🌐 *www.thediamondbackgrill.com.*

$$ B&B/INN 🏨 **Barretta Gardens Bed and Breakfast Inn.** Perfect for a romantic getaway or peaceful escape, this inn's elegant Victorian rooms and three antiques-filled parlors are furnished with period pieces. **Pros:** lovely grounds; delicious breakfasts; great location. **Cons:** only seven rooms. [$] *Rooms from: $159* ✉ *700 S. Barretta St.* ☎ *209/532–6039, 800/206–3333* 🌐 *www.barrettagardens.com* 🛏 *7 rooms* 🍽 *Breakfast.*

JAMESTOWN

4 miles south of Sonora.

Compact Jamestown supplies a touristy view of gold-rush-era life. Shops in brightly colored buildings along Main Street sell antiques and gift items. You can try your hand at panning for gold here or explore a bit of railroad history.

GETTING HERE AND AROUND

Jamestown lies at the intersection of north–south Highway 49 and east–west Highway 108. You'll need a car to tour here.

EXPLORING

FAMILY **Gold Prospecting Adventures.** You'll get a real feel (sort of) for the life of a prospector on the three-hour gold-panning excursions led by this outfit's congenial tour guides. You might even strike gold at the Jimtown Mine. Reservations recommended—call ahead to confirm hours and fees. ✉ *18170 Main St.* ☎ *209/984–4653, 800/596–0009* 🌐 *www.goldprospecting.com.*

FAMILY Fodor's Choice ★ **Railtown 1897.** A must for rail enthusiasts and families with kids, this is one of the most intact early roundhouses (maintenance facilities) in North America. You can hop aboard a steam train for a 40-minute journey—bring along the family dog if you'd like. The docents entertain guests with tales about the history of locomotion. Listen to the original rotor and pulleys in the engine house and take in the smell of axle grease. Walk through a genteel passenger car with dusty-green velvet seats and ornate metalwork, where Grace Kelly and Gary Cooper filmed a scene in the epic Western *High Noon*. You can also climb onto a historic train to see where the fireman once shoveled coal into the tender. ✉ *18115 5th Ave.* ☎ *209/984–3953* 🌐 *www.railtown1897.org* 🎟 *Roundhouse tour $5; train ride $15.*

WHERE TO STAY

$ RESORT 🏨 **Black Oak Casino Resort.** About 12 miles east of Jamestown off Highway 108, this flashy, contemporary property appeals heavily to casino gamers, but it's also just a nice place to stay with well-outfitted rooms (comfy bedding, down pillows, and alarm clocks with MP3 players) and a central Gold Country location. **Pros:** clean and spacious rooms; plenty of diversions on hand for both kids and adults. **Cons:** must go through smoky casino to reach bowling alley and restaurants; there's nothing quaint or historic about this place. [$] *Rooms from: $99* ✉ *19400 Tuolumne Rd. N, Tuolumne* ☎ *209/928–9300* 🌐 *www.blackoakcasino.com* 🛏 *148 rooms* 🍴 *No meals.*

$$ B&B/INN 🏨 **McCaffrey House Bed and Breakfast Inn.** Surrounded by trees on the edge of the Stanislaus National Forest, McCaffrey's appeal lies in its remoteness. **Pros:** rooms outfitted with stoves and Amish quilts; wonderful nearby hiking; romantically remote. **Cons:** too remote for some. [$] *Rooms from: $169* ✉ *23251 Hwy. 108, Twain Harte* ☎ *209/586–0757, 888/586–0757* 🌐 *www.mccaffreyhouse.com* 🛏 *9 rooms* 🍴 *Breakfast.*

$$ B&B/INN 🏨 **National Hotel.** In business since 1859, the National has survived the gold rush, gambling, prostitution, at least two fires, a ghost named Flo, and Prohibition, and stands today a well-maintained property with all the authentic character and charm its storied past suggests. **Pros:** feels straight out of a Western movie; authentic character; great brunches. **Cons:** not much happens in town after dark. [$] *Rooms from: $140* ✉ *18183 Main St.* ☎ *209/984–3446,* 🌐 *www.national-hotel.com* 🛏 *9 rooms* 🍴 *Breakfast.*

MARIPOSA

50 miles south of Jamestown.

Mariposa marks the southern end of the Mother Lode. Much of the land in this area was part of a 44,000-acre land grant Colonel John C. Fremont acquired from Mexico before gold was discovered and California became a state. Many people stop here on the way to Yosemite National Park, about an hour's drive east on Highway 140.

GETTING HERE AND AROUND

If driving, take Highway 49 or Highway 140. YARTS (🌐 *www.yarts.com*), the regional transit system, can get you to Mariposa from the Central Valley town of Merced (where you can also transfer from Amtrak) or from Yosemite Valley. Otherwise, you'll need a car to get here and around.

EXPLORING

FAMILY **California State Mining and Mineral Museum.** A California state park since 1999, the museum has displays on gold-rush history including a replica hard-rock mine shaft to walk through, a miniature stamp mill, and a

13-pound chunk of crystallized gold. ✉ *5005 Fairground Rd., off Hwy. 49* ☎ *209/742–7625* 🌐 *www.parks.ca.gov* 🎟 *$4.*

Mariposa Museum and History Center. You'll leave this small museum feeling like you just found your own gold nugget. Detailed exhibits, both indoors and out, tell the history of Mariposa County. Visit a replica of a typical miner's cabin; see a working stamp mill; tour the blacksmith shop. Artifacts, photographs, and maps, along with the knowledgeable staff, will capture your imagination and transport you back to 1849. ✉ *5119 Jessie St.* ☎ *209/966–2924* 🌐 *www.mariposamuseum.com* 🎟 *$5.*

WHERE TO EAT

$$ AMERICAN 🍴 **Savoury's.** Seafood, pasta, and portobello mushrooms are some of the savory treats that draw high praise from locals at the kind of refined and competent spot that you'd expect in an urban environment, not in mellow Mariposa. Vegetarians and vegans will find lots of options. **Known for:** well-prepared American food from seafood to steak; high-quality food and service. [$] *Average main: $20* ✉ *5034 Hwy. 140* ☎ *209/966–7677* 🕓 *Closed Wed. No lunch.*

THE GOLD COUNTRY—NORTH

Gold has had a significant presence along this northern stretch of Highway 49, whose highlights include the bucolic Empire State Historic Park and Coloma, where the discovery of a few nuggets triggered the gold rush.

COLOMA

On Highway 49 between Placerville (8 miles) and Auburn (18 miles).

The California gold rush started in Coloma. "My eye was caught with the glimpse of something shining in the bottom of the ditch," James Marshall recalled. Marshall himself never found any more "color," as gold came to be called.

GETTING HERE AND AROUND

A car is the only practical way to get to Coloma, via Highway 49. Once parked, you can walk to all the worthwhile sights.

EXPLORING

FAMILY Fodor's Choice ★ **Marshall Gold Discovery State Historic Park.** Most of Coloma lies within the historic park along the banks of the south fork of the American River. Though crowded with tourists in summer, Coloma hardly resembles the mob scene it was in 1849, when 2,000 prospectors staked out claims along the streambed. The town's population grew to 4,000, supporting seven hotels, three banks, and many stores and businesses. But when reserves of the precious metal dwindled, prospectors left as quickly as they had come. A working reproduction of an 1840s mill lies near the spot where James Marshall first saw gold. Trails lead to the mill, remnants of buildings and mining equipment, and to a statue of Marshall with sublime views. ■ **TIP→ For $7 per person, rangers give gold-panning lessons on the hour, year-round.** ✉ *310 Back St., off Hwy. 49* ☎ *530/622–3470* 🌐 *www.parks.ca.gov* 🎟 *$8 per vehicle.*

AUBURN

18 miles northwest of Coloma; 34 miles northeast of Sacramento.

Located halfway between San Francisco and Reno on Interstate 80, Auburn is enjoying a renaissance buoyed by its central location to many gold-rush sites, outdoor recreation opportunities, and thriving farms and vineyards. The self-proclaimed "endurance capital of the world" is abuzz almost every summer weekend with running, cycling, rafting or kayaking, and equestrian events. Downtown Auburn has its own gold-rush charm with narrow climbing streets, cobblestone lanes, wooden sidewalks, and many original buildings. **■TIP→ Fresh produce, flowers, baked goods, and gifts are for sale at the farmers' market, held on Saturday morning year-round.**

GETTING HERE AND AROUND

Amtrak serves Auburn, though most visitors arrive by car on Highway 49 or Interstate 80. Once downtown, you can tour on foot.

EXPLORING

Bernhard Museum Complex. Party like it's 1889 at this space whose main structure opened in 1851 as the Traveler's Rest Hotel and for 100 years was the residence of the Bernhard family. The congenial docents, dressed in Victorian garb, describe the family's history and 19th-century life in Auburn. ✉ *291 Auburn–Folsom Rd.* ☎ *530/889–6500* 🌐 *www.placer.ca.gov* 🎟 *Free.*

FAMILY **Gold Rush Museum.** You'll get a feel for life in the mines at this museum whose highlights include a re-created mine tunnel and an indoor gold-panning stream. ✉ *601 Lincoln Way* ☎ *530/889–6506* 🎟 *Free.*

Placer County Courthouse. Visible from the highway and an easy detour on your drive to or from Lake Tahoe, Auburn's standout structure is the Placer County Courthouse. The classic gold-dome building houses the Placer County Museum, which documents the area's history—Native American, railroad, agricultural, and mining—from the early 1700s to 1900. Look for the Thomas Kinkade original painting and the wall safe housing gold nuggets valued at more than $300,000 today. ✉ *101 Maple St.* ☎ *530/889–6500* 🎟 *Free.*

WHERE TO EAT AND STAY

$ AMERICAN FAMILY 🍴 **Auburn Alehouse.** This craft brewer serves up the best beer in Gold Country along with decent gastropub fare in this historic American Block building, the centerpiece of Auburn's old town since 1856. Gold Country Pilsner, Old Town Brown, and Hop Donkey Red Ale are all Great American Beer Festival award winners, and you can see them being brewed through glass walls behind the dining area. **Known for:** historic building; award-winning pilsner. [$] *Average main: $12* ✉ *289 Washington St.* ☎ *530/885–2537* 🌐 *www.auburnalehouse.com.*

$ AMERICAN FAMILY 🍴 **Awful Annie's.** One of Auburn's favorite old-time breakfast and lunch spots retains all its old charm in its new home at the north end of town. The breakfast menu is mouthwatering, from "awful" waffles to chili omelets, Bloody Marys, burgers, and sandwiches. **Known for:** best breakfast in the foothills; Grandma's bread pudding. [$] *Average main: $10* ✉ *13460 Lincoln Way* ☎ *530/888–9857* 🌐 *www.awfulannies.com* 🕓 *No dinner.*

Almost 6 million ounces of gold were extracted from the Empire Mine.

$$$ MODERN AMERICAN **Fodor's Choice** ★

🍴 **Carpe Vino.** What started as a boutique wine retailer has become a must-visit experience for foodies who appreciate chef Eric Alexander's hearty and imaginative French-inspired dishes and this gem's charming setting, tucked into an old downtown saloon and mine with a handsome old bar. The sophisticated fare is presented in a nonchalant, almost effortless way, as if ingredients rolled right from the farm basket onto your plate. **Known for:** 500 wines, one rock-star chef; impeccable service; 21-plus only. [$] *Average main: $28* ✉ *1568 Lincoln Way* ☎ *530/823–0320* 🌐 *www.carpevinoauburn.com* 🕓 *Closed Sun. and Mon.*

$$ HOTEL FAMILY

🏨 **Holiday Inn Auburn Hotel.** Above the freeway across from Old Town, this hotel has a welcoming lobby and chain-standard but updated and nice rooms. **Pros:** Auburn's nicest hotel; great base for Gold Country exploring; on-site restaurant. **Cons:** can't walk to Old Town restaurants and shops. [$] *Rooms from: $165* ✉ *120 Grass Valley Hwy.* ☎ *530/887–8787, 800/814–8787* 🌐 *www.auburnhi.com* 🛏 *96 rooms* 🍽 *No meals.*

GRASS VALLEY

24 miles north of Auburn.

More than half of California's total gold production was extracted from mines around Grass Valley, including the Empire Mine, which, along with the North Star Mining Museum, is among the Gold Country's most fascinating attractions.

GETTING HERE AND AROUND

You'll need a car to get here. Take Highway 20 east from Interstate 5 or west from Interstate 80. Highway 49 is the north–south route into town. Gold Country Stage vehicles (☎ *530/477–0103* Weekdays 7–6) serve some attractions. Expect to wait, though.

EXPLORING

FAMILY Fodor's Choice ★ **Empire Mine State Historic Park.** Starting with the "secret map" that mine management hid from miners, you can relive the days of gold, grit, and glory, when this mine was one of the biggest and most prosperous hard-rock gold mines in North America. Empire Mine yielded an estimated 5.8 million ounces of gold from 367 miles of underground passages. You can walk into a mine shaft and peer into dark, deep recesses, and almost imagine what it felt like to work this vast operation. Dressed-up docents portraying colorful characters who shaped Northern California's history share stories about the period. The grounds have the exquisite Bourn Cottage (call for tour times), picnic tables, and gentle trails—perfect for a family outing. ✉ *10791 E. Empire St.* ☎ *530/273–8522* 🌐 *www.empiremine.org* 🎟 *$7.*

Holbrooke Hotel. This landmark hotel ($$) is a Main Street icon. Built in 1851, it hosted entertainer Lola Montez and writer Mark Twain as well as Ulysses S. Grant and other U.S. presidents. The hotel is best appreciated as a sight rather than a lodging option (it begs a renovation) but the restaurant-saloon ($$) is worth a visit as one of the oldest operating west of the Mississippi. ✉ *212 W. Main St.* ☎ *530/273–1353, 800/933–7077* 🌐 *www.holbrooke.com.*

FAMILY **North Star Mining Museum.** Housed in a former powerhouse, the museum displays the 32-foot-high Pelton Water Wheel, said to be the largest ever built. It was used to power mining operations and was a forerunner of the modern turbines that generate hydroelectricity. Hands-on displays are geared to children. You can picnic nearby. ✉ *10933 Allison Ranch Rd.* ☎ *530/264–7569* 🌐 *www.nevadacountyhistory.org* 🎟 *Donation requested.*

WHERE TO EAT

$ MEXICAN 🍴 **Maria's Mexican Restaurant.** The bright adobe walls and the colorful Talavera tile are as welcoming as the fragrance of owner Maria Ramos's fresh-cooked dishes with Mexican chilies, avocado, and garlic. Go for the beef *Chicana,* which includes peppers, tomatoes, and onions; the shredded and sautéed beef has a completely different flavor and texture than beef fajitas. **Known for:** house salsas and sauces; authentic Mexican food; 70 tequilas at the round cantina bar. [$] *Average main: $15* ✉ *226 E. Main St.* ☎ *530/274–2040* 🌐 *www.mariasgrassvalley.com.*

NEVADA CITY

4 miles north of Grass Valley.

Nevada City, once known as the Queen City of the Northern Mines, is the most appealing of the northern Mother Lode towns. The iron-shutter brick buildings that line the narrow downtown streets contain antiques shops, galleries, boutiques, B&Bs, restaurants, and a winery.

Horse-drawn-carriage tours add to the romance, as do gas street lamps. At one point in the 1850s, Nevada City had a population of nearly 10,000—enough to support much cultural activity. Today, about 3,000 people live here.

GETTING HERE AND AROUND

You'll need a car to get here. Take Highway 20 east from Interstate 5 or west from Interstate 80. Highway 49 is the north–south route into town. Gold Country Stage vehicles (☎ *530/477–0103* 🕒 *Weekdays 7–6*) serve some attractions.

ESSENTIALS

Visitor Information Nevada City Chamber of Commerce. ✉ *132 Main St.* ☎ *530/265–2692* 🌐 *www.nevadacitychamber.com.*

EXPLORING

Nevada City Winery. For an unassuming winery located in a garage, Nevada City Winery has earned a loyal following for its wine club, the tasting-room ambience, the service team's friendliness, and the quality of its reds—especially Syrah and Zinfandel. ✉ *Miners Foundry Garage, 321 Spring St., at Bridge St.* ☎ *530/265–9463, 800/203–9463* 🌐 *www.ncwinery.com* 🎫 *Tasting and tour free.*

WHERE TO EAT AND STAY

$$$ EUROPEAN 🍴 **Friar Tuck's.** Popular Friar Tuck's specializes in creative, interactive fondues and has an extensive menu of seafood, steaks, and pasta dishes, too. The sparkling interior has a late-19th-century ambience—it's one of Nevada City's best indoor spaces. **Known for:** cheese fondue; rebuilt in 14 months after burning to the ground in 2002; live music nightly. [$] *Average main: $27* ✉ *111 N. Pine St.* ☎ *530/265–9093* 🌐 *friartucks.com* 🕒 *No lunch.*

$ AMERICAN 🍴 **South Pine Cafe.** Locals flock here for lobster Benedict, chorizo breakfast tacos, and other dishes that are anything but your ordinary eggs and pancake fare. Imaginative burritos and burgers highlight the lunch menu, and there are plenty of vegan, gluten-free, and organic options, too. **Known for:** creative cooking; homemade muffins all day; vegan and gluten-free options. [$] *Average main: $13* ✉ *110 S. Pine St.* ☎ *530/265–0260* 🌐 *www.southpinecafe.com* 🕒 *No dinner.*

$ HOTEL FAMILY 🏨 **Outside Inn.** It looks like a typical one-story motel, but Outside Inn offers a variety of unique accommodations inspired by nature or activities in nature (there's a climbing wall in the rock-climbing suite), in an ideal location to enjoy Northern California's four seasons. **Pros:** character and comfort; a fun reinvention of a motel; convenient to trails and hikes. **Cons:** rooms are on the smaller side; a half mile from town. [$] *Rooms from: $109* ✉ *575 E. Broad St.* ☎ *530/265–2233* 🌐 *www.outsideinn.com* 🛏 *15 rooms* 🍽 *No meals.*

LAKE TAHOE

with Reno, Nevada

WELCOME TO LAKE TAHOE

TOP REASONS TO GO

★ **The lake:** Blue, deep, and alpine pure, Lake Tahoe is far and away the main reason to visit this High Sierra paradise.

★ **Skiing:** Daring black-diamond runs or baby-bunny bumps—whether you're an expert, a beginner, or somewhere in between, the numerous Tahoe-area ski parks abound with slopes to suit your skills.

★ **The great outdoors:** A ring of national forests and recreation areas linked by miles of trails makes Tahoe excellent for nature lovers.

★ **Dinner with a view:** You can picnic lakeside at state parks or dine in restaurants perched along the shore.

★ **A date with lady luck:** Whether you want to roll dice, play the slots, or hope the blackjack dealer goes bust before you do, you'll find round-the-clock gambling at the casinos on the Nevada side of the lake and in Reno.

1 California Side. With the exception of Stateline, Nevada—which, aside from its casino-hotel towers, seems almost indistinguishable from South Lake Tahoe, California—the California side is more developed than the Nevada side. Here you can find both commercial enterprises—restaurants, motels, lodges, ski resorts, residential subdivisions—and public-access facilities, such as historic sites, parks, campgrounds, marinas, and beaches.

2 Nevada Side. You don't need a highway sign to know when you've crossed from California into Nevada: the flashing lights and elaborate marquees of casinos announce legal gambling in garish hues. But you'll find more here than tables and slot machines. Reno, the Biggest Little City in the World, has a vibrant arts scene and a serene downtown Riverwalk. And when you really need to get away from the chip-toting crowds, you can hike through pristine wilderness at Lake Tahoe–Nevada State Park, or hit the slopes near Incline Village.

GETTING ORIENTED

In the northern section of the Sierra Nevada mountain range, the Lake Tahoe area covers portions of four national forests, several state parks, and rugged wilderness areas with names like Desolation and Granite Chief. Lake Tahoe, the star attraction, straddles California and Nevada and is one of the world's largest, clearest, and deepest alpine lakes. The region's proximity to the Bay Area and Sacramento to the west and Reno to the east draws thrill seekers during ski season and again in summer when water sports, camping, and hiking are the dominant activities.

22

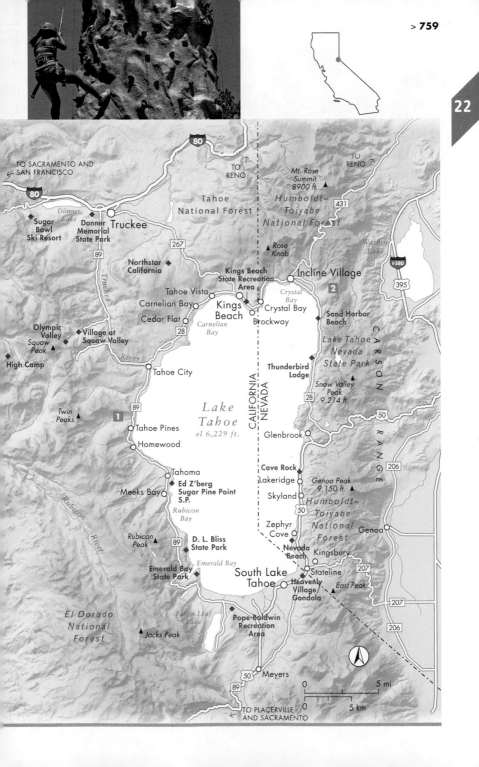

TO SACRAMENTO AND
← SAN FRANCISCO

TO
RENO

TO
RENO

Mt. Rose
Summit
8900 ft.

80

Tahoe
National Forest

Humboldt–
Toiyabe
National Forest

Washoe
Lake

I-580

Donner
Lake

Sugar
Bowl
Ski Resort

Donner
Memorial
State Park

Truckee

267

431

Rose
Knob

89

Northstar
California

Kings Beach
State Recreation
Area

Incline Village

2

395

Tahoe Vista

Crystal
Bay

Carnelian Bay

Kings
Beach

Crystal Bay

Sand Harbor
Beach

Cedar Flat

28

Brockway

Olympic
Valley
Squaw
Peak

Village at
Squaw Valley

Carnelian
Bay

Lake Tahoe
Nevada
State Park

C
A
R
S
O
N

Truckee River

High Camp

Tahoe City

Thunderbird
Lodge

Snow Valley
Peak
9,214 ft.

28

R
A
N
G
E

50

Twin
Peaks

89

1

Lake
Tahoe
el 6,229 ft.

CALIFORNIA
NEVADA

Glenbrook

Tahoe Pines

Homewood

Cave Rock

Lakeridge

Genoa Peak
9,150 ft.

206

Tahoma

Meeks Bay

Ed Z'berg
Sugar Pine Point
S.P.

Skyland

Rubicon
Bay

Humboldt–
Toiyabe
National
Forest

50

Rubicon River

Rubicon
Peak

89

D. L. Bliss
State Park

Zephyr
Cove

Genoa

Emerald Bay

Nevada
Beach

Kingsbury

Emerald Bay
State Park

South Lake
Tahoe

Stateline

207

El Dorado
National
Forest

Fallen Leaf
Lake

Heavenly
Village/
Gondola

East Peak

207

Jacks Peak

Pope-Baldwin
Recreation
Area

206

50

Meyers

0   5 mi

89

0   5 km

TO PLACERVILLE
AND SACRAMENTO

Updated by
Daniel Mangin

Whether you swim, fish, sail, or simply rest on its shores, you'll be wowed by the overwhelming beauty of Lake Tahoe, the largest alpine lake in North America. Famous for its cobalt-blue water and surrounding snowcapped peaks, Lake Tahoe straddles the state line between California and Nevada. The border gives this popular Sierra Nevada resort region a split personality. About half its visitors are intent on low-key sightseeing, hiking, camping, and boating. The rest head directly to the Nevada side, where bargain dining, big-name entertainment, and the lure of a jackpot draw them into the glittering casinos.

To explore the lake area and get a feel for its many differing communities, drive the 72-mile road that follows the shore through wooded flatlands and past beaches, climbing to vistas on the rugged southwest side of the lake and passing through busy commercial developments and casinos on its northeastern and southeastern edges. Another option is to actually go out *on* the 22-mile-long, 12-mile-wide lake on a sightseeing cruise or kayaking trip.

The lake, the communities around it, the state parks, national forests, and protected tracts of wilderness are the region's main draws, but other nearby destinations are gaining in popularity. Truckee, with an Old West feel and innovative restaurants, entices visitors looking for a relaxed pace and easy access to Tahoe's north shore and Olympic Valley ski parks. And today Reno, once known only for its casinos, attracts tourists with its buzzing arts scene, downtown riverfront, and campus events at the University of Nevada.

PLANNING

WHEN TO GO

A sapphire-blue lake shimmering deep in the center of an ice-white wonderland—that's Tahoe in winter. But those blankets of snow mean lots of storms that often close roads and force chain requirements on the interstate. In summer the roads are open, but the lake and lodgings are clogged with visitors seeking respite from valley heat. If you don't ski, the best times to visit are early fall—September and October—and late spring. The crowds thin, prices dip, and you can count on Tahoe being beautiful.

Most Lake Tahoe accommodations, restaurants, and even a handful of parks are open year-round, but many visitor centers, mansions, state parks, and beaches are closed from October through May. During those months, winter-sports enthusiasts swamp Tahoe's downhill resorts and cross-country centers, North America's largest concentration of skiing facilities. In summer it's cooler here than in the scorched Sierra Nevada foothills, the clean mountain air is bracingly crisp, and the surface temperature of Lake Tahoe is an invigorating 65°F to 70°F (compared with 40°F to 50°F in winter). This is also the time, however, when it may seem as if every tourist at the lake—100,000 on peak weekends—is in a car on the main road circling the shoreline (especially on Highway 89, just south of Tahoe City; on Highway 28, east of Tahoe City; and on U.S. 50 in South Lake Tahoe). Christmas week and July 4th are the busiest times, and prices go through the roof; plan accordingly.

GETTING HERE AND AROUND
AIR TRAVEL

The nearest airport to Lake Tahoe is Reno–Tahoe International Airport (RNO), in Reno, 50 miles northeast of the closest point on the lake. Airlines serving RNO include Alaska, Allegiant, American, Delta, Jet-Blue, Southwest, United, and Volaris. Except for Allegiant, these airlines plus Aeromexico and Hawaiian serve Sacramento International Airport (SMF), 112 miles from South Lake Tahoe. North Lake Tahoe Express runs buses ($49 each way) between RNO and towns on the lake's western and northern shores, plus Incline Village, Truckee, Squaw Valley, and Northstar. South Tahoe Airporter runs buses ($29.75 one-way, $53 round-trip) between Reno–Tahoe Airport and resort hotels in the South Lake Tahoe area.

Airport Contacts Reno Tahoe International Airport. ⊠ 2001 E. Plumb La., off U.S. 395/I–580, at Reno-Tahoe International Airport Exit, Reno ☎ 775/328–6400 ⊕ www.renoairport.com. **Sacramento International Airport.** ⊠ 6900 Airport Blvd., 12 miles northwest of downtown off I–5, Sacramento ☎ 916/929–5411 ⊕ www.sacramento.aero/smf.

Transfer Contacts North Lake Tahoe Express. ☎ 866/216–5222 ⊕ www.northlaketahoeexpress.com. **South Tahoe Airporter.** ☎ 775/325–8944, 866/898–2463 ⊕ southtahoeairporter.com.

BUS TRAVEL

Greyhound stops in San Francisco, Sacramento, Truckee, and Reno. BlueGO ($2 per ride) provides year-round local service in South Lake Tahoe. On the north shore, Tahoe Area Regional Transit (TART; $1.75) operates buses between Tahoma and Incline Village and runs shuttles to Truckee. RTC RIDE buses ($2) serve the Reno area. All local rides require exact change.

In winter, BlueGO provides free ski shuttle service from South Lake Tahoe hotels and resorts to various Heavenly Mountain ski lodge locations. Most of the major ski resorts offer shuttle service to nearby lodging.

Bus Contacts Greyhound. ☎ *800/231–2222* ⊕ *www.greyhound.com.* **BlueGO.** ☎ *530/541–7149* ⊕ *www.tahoetransportation.org/transit/south-shore-services.* **RTC RIDE.** ☎ *775/348–7433* ⊕ *www.rtcwashoe.com.* **Tahoe Area Regional Transit (TART).** ☎ *530/550–1212, 800/736–6365* ⊕ *www.placer.ca.gov/ departments/works/transit/tart.*

CAR TRAVEL

Lake Tahoe is 198 miles northeast of San Francisco, a drive of less than four hours in good weather and light traffic—if possible avoid heavy weekend traffic, particularly leaving the San Francisco area for Tahoe on Friday afternoon and returning on Sunday afternoon. The major route is Interstate 80, which cuts through the Sierra Nevada about 14 miles north of the lake. From there Highway 89 and Highway 267 reach the west and north shores, respectively.

U.S. 50 is the more direct route to the south shore, a two-hour drive from Sacramento. From Reno you can get to the north shore by heading south on U.S. 395/Interstate 580 for 10 miles, then west on Highway 431 for 25 miles. For the south shore, head south on U.S. 395/Interstate 580 through Carson City, and then turn west on U.S. 50 (56 miles total).

The scenic 72-mile highway around the lake is marked Highway 89 on the southwest and west shores, Highway 28 on the north and northeast shores, and U.S. 50 on the east and southeast. Sections of Highway 89 sometimes close during snowy periods, usually at Emerald Bay because of avalanche danger, which makes it impossible to complete the circular drive around the lake. Interstate 80, U.S. 50, and U.S. 395/Interstate 580 are all-weather highways, but there may be delays while snow is cleared during major storms.

Interstate 80 is a four-lane freeway; much of U.S. 50 is only two lanes with no center divider. Carry tire chains from October through May, or rent a four-wheel-drive vehicle. Most rental agencies do not allow tire chains to be used on their vehicles; ask when you book.

Contacts California Highway Patrol. ☎ *530/577–1001 South Lake Tahoe* ⊕ *www.chp.ca.gov.* **Caltrans Current Highway Conditions.** ☎ *800/427–7623* ⊕ *www.dot.ca.gov.* **Nevada Department of Transportation Road Information.** ☎ *877/687–6237* ⊕ *nvroads.com.* **Nevada Highway Patrol.** ☎ *775/687–5300* ⊕ *nhp.nv.gov.*

TRAIN TRAVEL

Amtrak's cross-country rail service makes stops in Truckee and Reno. Amtrak also operates several buses daily between Reno and Sacramento to connect with coastal train routes.

Train Contact Amtrak. ☎ *800/872-7245* ⊕ *www.amtrak.com.*

22

RESTAURANTS

On weekends and in high season, expect a long wait at the more popular restaurants. And expect to pay resort prices almost everywhere. During the "shoulder seasons" (from April to May and September to November), some places may close temporarily or limit their hours, so call ahead. Also, check local papers for deals and discounts during this time, especially two-for-one coupons. Many casinos use their restaurants to attract gamblers. Marquees often tout "$8.99 prime rib dinners" or "$4.99 breakfast specials." Some of these meals are downright lousy and they are usually available only in the coffee shops and buffets, but at those prices, it's hard to complain. The finer restaurants in casinos deliver pricier food, as well as reasonable service and a bit of atmosphere. Unless otherwise noted, even the most expensive area restaurants welcome customers in casual clothes. *Restaurant reviews have been shortened. For full information, visit Fodors.com.*

HOTELS

Quiet inns on the water, suburban-style strip motels, casino hotels, slope-side ski lodges, and house and condo rentals throughout the area constitute the lodging choices at Tahoe. The crowds come in summer and during ski season; reserve as far in advance as possible, especially for holiday periods when prices skyrocket. Spring and fall give you a little more leeway and lower—sometimes significantly lower, especially at casino hotels—rates. Check hotel websites for the best deals.

Head to South Lake Tahoe for the most activities and the widest range of lodging options. Heavenly Village in the heart of town has an ice rink, cinema, shops, fine-dining restaurants, and simple cafés, plus a gondola that will whisk you up to the ski park. Walk two blocks south from downtown, and you can hit the casinos.

Tahoe City, on the west shore, has a small-town atmosphere and is accessible to several nearby ski resorts. A few miles northwest of the lake, Squaw Valley USA has its own self-contained upscale village, an aerial tram to the slopes, and numerous outdoor activities once the snow melts.

Looking for a taste of Old Tahoe? The north shore with its woodsy backdrop is your best bet, with Carnelian Bay and Tahoe Vista on the California side. And across the Nevada border are casino resorts where Hollywood's glamour-stars once romped. *Hotel reviews have been shortened. For full information, visit Fodors.com.*

WHAT IT COSTS				
	$	$$	$$$	$$$$
Restaurants	under $16	$16–$22	$23–$30	over $30
Hotels	under $120	$120–$175	$176–$250	over $250

Restaurant prices are the average cost of a main course at dinner or, if dinner is not served, at lunch. Hotel prices are the lowest cost of a standard double room in high season.

OUTDOORS AND BACKCOUNTRY TIPS

If you're planning to spend any time outdoors around Lake Tahoe, whether hiking, climbing, skiing, or camping, be aware that weather conditions can change quickly in the Sierra. To avoid hypothermia, always bring a pocket-size, fold-up rain poncho (available in all sporting-goods stores) to keep you dry. Wear long pants and a hat. Carry plenty of water. Because you'll likely be walking on granite, wear sturdy, closed-toe hiking boots, with soles that grip rock. If you're going into the backcountry, bring a signaling device (such as a mirror), emergency whistle, compass, map, energy bars, and water purifier. When heading out alone, tell someone where you're going and when you expect to return.

If you plan to ski, be aware of resort elevations. In the event of a winter storm, determine the snow level before you choose the resort you'll ski. Often the level can be as high as 7,000 feet, which means rain at some resorts' base areas but snow at others.

BackCountry, in Truckee, operates an excellent website with current information about how and where to (and where not to) ski, mountain bike, and hike in the backcountry around Tahoe. The store also stocks everything from crampons to transceivers. For storm information, check the National Weather Service's website; for ski conditions, visit ⊕ onthesnow.com. For reservations at campgrounds in California state parks, contact Reserve California. If you plan to camp in the backcountry of the national forests, you'll need to purchase a wilderness permit, which you can pick up at the forest service office or at a ranger station at any forest entrance. If you plan to ski the backcountry, check the U.S. Forest Service's recorded information for conditions.

Contacts and Information BackCountry. ✉ 11400 Donner Pass Rd., at Meadow Way, Truckee ☎ 530/582-0909 Truckee ⊕ www.thebackcountry.net. **National Weather Service.** ⊕ www.wrh.noaa.gov/rev. **OntheSnow.com.** ⊕ www.onthesnow.com/california/skireport.html. **Reserve California.** ⊕ www. reservecalifornia.com. **U.S. Forest Service.** ✉ Office, 35 College Dr., South Lake Tahoe ☎ 530/543-2600 general backcountry information, 530/587-3558 backcountry information recording after office hours ⊕ www.fs.usda.gov/ltbmu.

SKIING AND SNOWBOARDING

The mountains around Lake Tahoe are bombarded by blizzards throughout most winters and sometimes in fall and spring; 10- to 12-foot bases are common. Indeed, the Sierras often have the deepest snowpack on the continent, but because of the relatively mild temperatures over the Pacific, falling snow can be very heavy and wet—it's nicknamed "Sierra Cement" for a reason. The upside is that you can sometimes ski and board as late as May (snowboarding is permitted at all Tahoe ski areas). The major resorts get extremely crowded on weekends. If you're going to ski on a Saturday, arrive early and quit early. Avoid moving with the masses: eat at 11 am or 1:30 pm, not noon. Also consider visiting the ski areas with few high-speed lifts or limited lodging and real estate at their bases: Alpine Meadows, Sugar Bowl, Homewood, Mt. Rose, Sierra-at-Tahoe, Diamond Peak, and Kirkwood. And to find out the true ski conditions, talk to waiters and bartenders—most of them are ski bums.

The Lake Tahoe area is also a great destination for Nordic skiers. Cross-country skiing at the resorts can be costly, but you get the benefits of machine grooming and trail preparation. If it's bargain Nordic you're after, take advantage of thousands of acres of public forest and parkland trails.

TOURS

Lake Tahoe Balloons. Take a hot-air balloon flight over the lake from mid-May through mid-October with this company that launches and lands its balloons on a boat. The four-hour excursion begins shortly after sunrise and ends with a traditional champagne toast. ⊠ *Tahoe Keys Marina, at end of Venice Dr. East, South Lake Tahoe* ☎ *530/544–1221, 800/872–9294* ⊕ *www.laketahoeballoons.com* ✉ *From $295* ☞ *From $299.*

MS Dixie II. The 520-passenger *MS Dixie II*, a stern-wheeler, sails year-round from Zephyr Cove to Emerald Bay on sightseeing and dinner cruises. ⊠ *Zephyr Cove Marina, 760 U.S. Hwy. 50, near Church St., Zephyr Cove* ☎ *775/589–4906, 800/238–2463* ⊕ *www.zephyrcove. com/cruises* ✉ *From $51* ☞ *$59.*

North Lake Tahoe Ale Trail. The concept of these great self-guided tours is simple: bike or walk one of North Lake Tahoe's dozens of fantastic trails, then reward yourself with a craft brew (or two) at an ale house near the end of the trail you choose. A dedicated website has an interactive map, descriptions, and short videos pairing trails and drinking spots. There are also suggestions for paddleboarders and kayakers. ⊕ *www.gotahoenorth.com/things/north-lake-tahoe-ale-trail.*

Sierra Cloud. From May to September, the *Sierra Cloud*, a 41-passenger catamaran, departs from the Hyatt Regency beach at Incline Village and cruises the north and east shore areas. ⊠ *Hyatt Regency Lake Tahoe, 111 Country Club Dr., Incline Village* ☎ *775/831–4386* ⊕ *www.awsincline.com* ✉ *From $65* ☞ *$80.*

Tahoe Gal. Docked in Tahoe City this old-style 120-passenger paddlewheeler departs daily from June through September and on some days in May on brunch, lunch, happy hour, and sunset tours of Emerald Bay and Lake Tahoe's north and west shores. Specialty excursions include ones with live music or other entertainment. ⚠ **Closed October–April and some days in May.** ⊠ *Departures from Lighthouse Center, 952 N. Lake Blvd., Tahoe City* ☎ *800/218–2464* ⊕ *www.tahoegal. com* ✉ *From $28.*

Tahoe Boat Cruises. From mid-May to mid-October, this company offers barbecue lunch, happy-hour, sunset, and champagne cruises (from $50) aboard the *Safari Rose*, an 80-foot-long wooden motor yacht. Shuttle-bus pick-up service is available. ⊠ *Departures from Ski Run Marina, 900 Ski Run Blvd., South Lake Tahoe* ☎ *888/867–6394* ⊕ *www. tahoecruises.com* ⊠ *From $34.*

Fodor's Choice **Thunderbird Lodge Cruise & Tour.** From mid-May to mid-October, the cap-★ tain of the *Tahoe*, a classic wooden boat, takes passengers on an east shore cruise whose highlights are a walking tour and picnic lunch at the Thunderbird Lodge, a historic mansion. ⊠ *Departures from Zephyr Cove Pier, 760 U.S. 50, Zephyr Cove* ☎ *775/230–8907* ⊕ *www.cruise-tahoe.com/public-cruises* ⊠ *$139.*

VISITOR INFORMATION

Contacts Go Tahoe North. ☎ *530/581–6900, 888/434–1262* ⊕ *www.gotahoenorth.com.* **Visit Lake Tahoe South.** ☎ *775/588–5900, 800/288–2463* ⊕ *tahoesouth.com.*

THE CALIFORNIA SIDE

The most hotels, restaurants, ski resorts, and state parks are on the California side of the lake, but you'll also encounter the most conges-tion and developed areas.

SOUTH LAKE TAHOE

60 miles south of Reno, 198 miles northeast of San Francisco.

The city of South Lake Tahoe's raison d'être is tourism: the casinos of adjacent Stateline, Nevada; the ski slopes at Heavenly Mountain; the beaches, docks, bike trails, and campgrounds all around the south shore; and the backcountry of Eldorado National Forest and Desolation Wilderness. Less appealing are the strip malls, old-school motels, and low-rise prefab buildings lining U.S. 50, the city's main drag. Although in recent years a few jazzed-up motels and new boutique hotels have joined a few longtime high-quality inns, many places provide little more than basic accommodation. The small city's saving grace is its conve-nient location, bevy of services, and gorgeous lake views.

GETTING HERE AND AROUND

The main route into and through South Lake Tahoe is U.S. 50; signs say "Lake Tahoe Boulevard" in town. Arrive by car or, if coming from Reno airport, take the South Tahoe Express bus. BlueGO operates daily bus service in the south shore area year-round, plus a ski shuttle from the large hotels to Heavenly Mountain Resort in the winter.

ESSENTIALS

Visitor Information Visit Lake Tahoe South. ⊠ *Visitor Center, 169 U.S. Hwy. 50, at Kingsbury Grade, Stateline* ☎ *775/588–5900, 800/288–2463* ⊕ *tahoe-south.com* ⊠ *Visitor Center, 3066 Lake Tahoe Blvd., at San Francisco Ave.* ☎ *530/541–5255* ⊕ *tahoesouth.com.*

EXPLORING

FAMILY
Fodor'sChoice
★

Heavenly Gondola. Whether you ski or not, you'll appreciate the impressive view of Lake Tahoe from the Heavenly Gondola. Its eight-passenger cars travel from Heavenly Village 2.4 miles up the mountain in 15 minutes. When the weather's fine, you can take one of three hikes around the mountaintop and then have lunch at Tamarack Lodge. ⊠ *4080 Lake Tahoe Blvd.* ☎ *775/586–7000, 800/432–8365* ⊕ *www. skiheavenly.com* ☒ *$52.*

Heavenly Village. This lively complex at the base of the Heavenly Gondola has good shopping, an arcade for kids, a cinema, a brewpub, a skating rink in winter, miniature golf in summer, and the Loft for magic shows and other live entertainment. Base Camp Pizza Co., Azul Latin Kitchen, and Kalani's for seafood stand out among the several restaurants. ⊠ *1001 Heavenly Village Way, at U.S. 50* ⊕ *www.theshopsatheavenly.com.*

WHERE TO EAT

$$
MEDITERRANEAN

✕ **Artemis Lakefront Cafe.** A festive marina restaurant with a heated outdoor patio, Artemis reveals its Greek influences in breakfast dishes like baklava French toast and gyros and egg pita wraps. All day, though, the menus encompass more familiar options (eggs Benedict in the morning, burgers and grilled mahi mahi later on). **Known for:** heated outdoor patio; many Greek-influenced menu items; festive atmosphere. $ *Average main: $19* ⊠ *900 Ski Run Blvd.* ☎ *530/542–3332* ⊕ *www. artemislakefrontcafe.com.*

$$
ECLECTIC

✕ **Blue Angel Café.** A favorite of locals, who fill the dozen or so wooden tables, this cozy spot with Wi-Fi serves basic sandwiches and salads along with internationally inspired dishes like chipotle shrimp tacos and Thai curry. On cold days warm up with wine or an espresso in front of the stone fireplace. **Known for:** varied menu; locals' hangout; easy-going staff. $ *Average main: $17* ⊠ *1132 Ski Run Blvd., at Larch Ave.* ☎ *530/544–6544* ⊕ *www.blueangelcafe.com.*

$$$$
ECLECTIC
Fodor'sChoice
★

✕ **Evan's American Gourmet Cafe.** Its excellent service, world-class cuisine, and superb wine list make this intimate restaurant the top choice for high-end dining in South Lake. Inside a converted cabin, Evan's serves creative American cuisine that includes catch-of-the-day seafood offerings and meat dishes such as rack of lamb marinated with rosemary and garlic and served with raspberry demi-glace. **Known for:** intimate atmosphere; world-class cuisine; superb wine list. $ *Average main: $33* ⊠ *536 Emerald Bay Rd., Hwy. 89, at 15th St.* ☎ *530/542–1990* ⊕ *evanstahoe.com* ⊙ *No lunch.*

$$$$
ASIAN

✕ **Kalani's at Lake Tahoe.** Fresh-off-the-plane seafood gets delivered from the Honolulu fish market to Heavenly Village's sleekest (and priciest) restaurant. The white-tablecloth dining room is decked out with carved bamboo, a burnt-orange color palette, and a modern-glass sculpture, all of which complement contemporary Pacific Rim specialties such as melt-from-the-bone baby-back pork ribs with sesame-garlic soy sauce. **Known for:** fresh Hawaiian seafood; inventive and traditional sushi combinations; upscale setting. $ *Average main: $36* ⊠ *1001 Heavenly Village Way, #26, at U.S. 50* ☎ *530/544–6100* ⊕ *www.kalanis.com.*

$ ✕ **My Thai Cuisine.** Fantastic flavors and gracious owners have earned this
THAI   humble roadside restaurant the loyalty of Tahoe residents and regular
visitors. The aromatic dishes include crab pad Thai, basil lamb, sizzling
shrimp, and numerous curries. **Known for:** many vegetarian options;
lunch specials a steal; lively atmosphere. $ *Average main: $14* ✉ *2108
Lake Tahoe Blvd., ¼-mile north of "Y" intersection of U.S. 50 and
Hwy. 89* ☎ *530/544-3232* ⊕ *www.thairestaurantsouthlaketahoe.com.*

$$$ ✕ **Nepheles Restaurant.** The mood is low-key but the California cuisine
AMERICAN   is outstanding at this small white-tablecloth restaurant inside an old
cabin. Start with escargots or herb crab cakes with Thai chili aioli
before moving on to one of several creative salads—perhaps the fruit
and Gorgonzola on a mesclun mix—and an entrée like elk medallions,
shrimp pasta, or grilled portobello stuffed with ratatouille. **Known
for:** chef with a deft touch; house-baked breads; full bar, good wine
list. $ *Average main: $25* ✉ *1169 Ski Run Blvd.* ☎ *530/544-8130*
⊕ *www.nepheles.com.*

$$ ✕ **Scusa! Italian Ristorante** This longtime favorite turns out big plates of
ITALIAN   veal scallopine, chicken piccata, and garlicky linguine with clams—
straightforward Italian-American food (and lots of it), served in an intimate dining room warmed by a crackling fire on many nights. There's
an outdoor patio that's open in warm weather. **Known for:** intimate
dining room; outdoor patio; classic Italian-American food. $ *Average
main: $22* ✉ *2543 Lake Tahoe Blvd., at Sierra Blvd.* ☎ *530/542-0100*
⊕ *www.scusalaketahoe.com* ◷ *No lunch.*

$ ✕ **Sprouts Natural Foods Cafe.** If it's in between normal mealtimes and
AMERICAN   you're hungry for something healthful, head to this order-at-the-counter
Fodor'sChoice   café for salads, overstuffed wraps, hot sandwiches, homemade vegan
★   soups, all-day breakfasts, and the best smoothies in town. Dine at
wooden tables in the cheery contemporary indoor space or out front
on the patio, or just order food to go. **Known for:** fresh, healthy cuisine; vegan and vegetarian friendly; congenial staff. $ *Average main:
$9* ✉ *3123 Harrison Ave., U.S. 50 at Alameda Ave.* ☎ *530/541-6969*
⊕ *www.sproutscafetahoe.com* ▭ *No credit cards.*

WHERE TO STAY

$$ 🏨 **Base Camp South Lake Tahoe.** This spunky three-floor boutique hotel
HOTEL   near the Heavenly Gondola, Stateline casinos, and several good res-
Fodor'sChoice   taurants provides solid value in a hip yet family-friendly setting. **Pros:**
★   convenient location; great for groups; cool public spaces include rooftop
hot tub with mountain views. **Cons:** communal dinners won't appeal
to all travelers; near a busy area; not on the lake. $ *Rooms from: $169*
✉ *4143 Cedar Ave., off U.S. 50* ☎ *530/208-0180* ⊕ *www.basecampta-
hoesouth.com* ⤳ *74 rooms* ⊙| *Breakfast.*

$$$ 🏨 **Black Bear Lodge.** The rooms and cabins at this well-appointed inn fea-
B&B/INN   ture 19th-century American antiques, fine art, and fireplaces; cabins also
Fodor'sChoice   have kitchenettes. **Pros:** near Heavenly skiing; within walking distance
★   of good restaurants; good for groups. **Cons:** no room service; lacks big-
hotel amenities; social types may find setting too sedate. $ *Rooms from:
$199* ✉ *1202 Ski Run Blvd.* ☎ *530/544-4451* ⊕ *www.tahoeblackbear.
com* ⤳ *9 rooms* ⊙| *Breakfast.*

$$$ HOTEL **Hotel Azure.** Across the road from a beach, the former Inn by the Lake began 2017 totally revamped (to the tune of $3.5 million), as a high-end motel meets boutique hotel. **Pros:** clean, spacious rooms; good work spaces and tech amenities; short drive to Heavenly Mountain. **Cons:** on busy Lake Tahoe Boulevard; no bell or room service; some sound bleed-through from room to room. [$] *Rooms from: $180* ✉ *3300 Lake Tahoe Blvd.* ☎ *530/542–0330, 800/877–1466* 🌐 *www.hotelazuretahoe.com* 🛏 *99 rooms* 🍴 *No meals.*

$$$ RESORT **Marriott's Grand Residence and Timber Lodge.** You can't beat the location of these two gigantic, modern condominium complexes right at the base of Heavenly Gondola, smack in the center of town. **Pros:** central location; great for families; near excellent restaurants. **Cons:** can be jam-packed on weekends; no room service; lacks serenity. [$] *Rooms from: $200* ✉ *1001 Heavenly Village Way* ☎ *530/542–8400 Marriott's Grand Residence, 800/845–5279, 530/542–6600 Marriott's Timber Lodge* 🌐 *www.marriott.com* 🛏 *431 rooms* 🍴 *No meals.*

$$ RESORT **Sorensen's Resort.** Escape civilization by staying in a log cabin at this woodsy 165-acre resort within the Eldorado National Forest, 20 minutes south of town. **Pros:** gorgeous, rustic setting; on-site restaurant; outdoor activities. **Cons:** nearest nightlife is 20 miles away; lacks amenities of larger properties; basic furnishings. [$] *Rooms from: $135* ✉ *14255 Hwy. 88, Hope Valley* ☎ *530/694–2203, 800/423–9949* 🌐 *www.sorensensresort.com* 🛏 *36 rooms* 🍴 *No meals.*

NIGHTLIFE

Most of the area's nightlife is concentrated in the casinos over the border in Stateline. To avoid slot machines and blinking lights, try the California-side nightspots in and near Heavenly Village.

BARS

The Loft. Crowd-pleasing magic shows and other entertainment, DIY s'mores, and a casual-industrial setting keep patrons happy at this Heavenly Village bar and lounge where kids aren't out of place. The mood is upbeat, the specialty cocktails are potent, and if you're in the mood for dinner the kitchen turns out Italian fare more tasty than one might expect at such a venue. ✉ *1001 Heavenly Village Way* ☎ *530/523–8024* 🌐 *www.thelofttahoe.com.*

Mc P's Taphouse & Grill. You can hear live bands—rock, jazz, blues, alternative—on most nights at Mc P's while you sample a few of the 40 beers on draft. Lunch and dinner (pub grub) are served daily. ✉ *4125 Lake Tahoe Blvd., Ste A, near Friday Ave.* ☎ *530/542–4435.*

SPORTS AND THE OUTDOORS

FISHING

Tahoe Sport Fishing. One of the area's largest and oldest fishing-charter services offers morning and afternoon trips. Outings include all necessary gear and bait, and the crew cleans and packages your catch. ✉ *900 Ski Run Blvd., off U.S. 50* ☎ *530/541–5448, 800/696–7797 in CA* 🌐 *www.tahoesportfishing.com* 🎟 *From $110.*

HIKING

Desolation Wilderness. Trails within the 63,960-acre wilderness lead to gorgeous backcountry lakes and mountain peaks. It's called Desolation Wilderness for a reason, so bring a topographic map and compass, and carry water and food. You need a permit for overnight camping (*877/444–6777*). In summer you can access this area by boarding a boat taxi ($14 one-way) at **Echo Chalet** (*9900 Echo Lakes Rd., off U.S. 50, 530/659–7207, www.echochalet.com*) and crossing Echo Lake. The Pacific Crest Trail also traverses Desolation Wilderness. ⊠ *El Dorado National Forest Information Center* ☎ *530/644–2349* ⊕ *www.fs.usda.gov/eldorado.*

ICE-SKATING

FAMILY **Heavenly Village Outdoor Ice Rink.** If you're here in winter, practice your jumps and turns at this rink between the gondola and the cinema. ⊠ *1001 Heavenly Village Way* ☎ *530/542–4230* ⊕ *www.theshopsatheavenly.com* 💲 *$22, includes skate rental.*

South Lake Tahoe Ice Arena. For year-round fun, head to this NHL regulation–size indoor rink where you can rent equipment and sign up for lessons. *Hrs vary; call or check website for public skate times.* ⊠ *1176 Rufus Allen Blvd.* ☎ *530/544–7465* ⊕ *tahoearena.com* 💲 *$15; includes skate rental.*

KAYAKING

Kayak Tahoe. Sign up for lessons and excursions (to the south shore, Emerald Bay, and Sand Harbor), offered from May through September. You can also rent a kayak and paddle solo on the lake. ⊠ *Timber Cove Marina, 3411 Lake Tahoe Blvd., at Balbijou Rd.* ☎ *530/544–2011* ⊕ *www.kayaktahoe.com* 💲 *From $40.*

MOUNTAIN BIKING

Tahoe Sports Ltd. You can rent road and mountain bikes and get tips on where to ride from the friendly staff at this full-service sports store. ⊠ *Tahoe Crescent V Shopping Center, 4000 Lake Tahoe Blvd., Suite 7* ☎ *530/542–4000* ⊕ *www.tahoesportsltd.com.*

SKIING

If you don't want to pay the high cost of rental equipment at the resorts, you'll find reasonable prices and expert advice at Tahoe Sports Ltd. (*Mountain Biking, above*).

Fodor'sChoice **Heavenly Mountain Resort.** Straddling two states, vast Heavenly Mountain Resort—composed of nine peaks, two valleys, and four base-lodge areas, along with the largest snowmaking system in the western United States—pairs terrain for every skier with exhilarating Tahoe Basin views. Beginners can choose wide, well-groomed trails, accessed from the California Lodge or the gondola from downtown South Lake Tahoe; kids have short and gentle runs in the Enchanted Forest area all to themselves. The Sky Express high-speed quad chair whisks intermediate and advanced skiers to the summit for wide cruisers or steep tree-skiing. Mott and Killebrew canyons draw experts to the Nevada side for steep chutes and thick-timber slopes. For snowboarders and tricksters, there are five different terrain parks.

22

The ski school is big and offers everything from learn-to-ski packages to canyon-adventure tours. Call about ski and boarding camps. Skiing lessons are available for children ages four and up; there's day care for infants older than six weeks. Summertime thrill seekers participate in Epic Discovery—fun for the whole family that includes a mountain coaster, zip lines, a climbing wall, ropes courses, hiking opportunities, and a learning center. **Facilities:** 97 trails; 4,800 acres; 3,427-foot vertical drop; 30 lifts ⊠ *Ski Run Blvd., off U.S. 50* ☎ *775/586–7000, 800/432–8365* ⊕ *www.skiheavenly.com* ✉ *Lift ticket $137.*

Hope Valley Outdoors. Operating from a yurt at Pickett's Junction, Hope Valley provides lessons and equipment rentals to prepare you for cross-country skiing and snowshoeing. The outfit has more than 60 miles of trails through Humboldt–Toiyabe National Forest, about 10 of which are groomed. ⊠ *Hwy. 88, at Hwy. 89, Hope Valley* ☎ *530/721–2015* ⊕ *www.hopevalleycrosscountry.com.*

Kirkwood Ski Resort. Thirty-six miles south of Lake Tahoe, Kirkwood is the hard-core skiers' and boarders' favorite south-shore mountain, known for its craggy gulp-and-go chutes, sweeping cornices, steep-aspect glade skiing, and high base elevation. But there's also fantastic terrain for newbies and intermediates down wide-open bowls, through wooded gullies, and along rolling tree-lined trails. Families often head to the Timber Creek area, a good spot to learn to ski or snowboard. Tricksters can show off in two terrain parks on jumps, wall rides, rails, and a half-pipe, all visible from the base area. The mountain normally gets hammered with more than 600 inches of snow annually, and often has the most in all of North America. If you're into out-of-bounds skiing, check out Expedition Kirkwood, a backcountry-skills program that teaches basic safety awareness. Kirkwood is also the only Tahoe resort to offer Cat-skiing. If you're into cross-country, the resort has 80 km (50 miles) of superb groomed-track skiing, with skating lanes, instruction, and rentals. Nonskiers can snowshoe, snow-skate, and go dogsledding or snow-tubing. The children's ski school has programs for ages 3 to 12. **Facilities:** 87 trails; 2,300 acres; 1,100-foot vertical drop; 15 lifts. ⊠ *1501 Kirkwood Meadows Dr., off Hwy. 88, 14 miles west of Hwy. 89, Kirkwood, Kirkwood* ☎ *800/967–7500 information, 209/258–7248 cross-country, 209/258–7293 lodging information, 209/258–7332 snow phone* ⊕ *www.kirkwood.com* ✉ *Lift ticket $107.*

Sierra-at-Tahoe. Wind-protected and meticulously groomed slopes, excellent tree-skiing, and gated backcountry skiing are among the draws at this low-key but worthy resort. Extremely popular with snowboarders, Sierra has several terrain parks, including Halfpipe, with 18-foot walls and a dedicated chairlift. For beginners, Sierra-at-Tahoe has more than 100 acres of learning terrain, and there's a snow-tubing hill. **Facilities:** 46 trails; 2,000 acres; 2,250-foot vertical drop; 14 lifts. ⊠ *1111 Sierra-at-Tahoe Rd., 12 miles from South Lake Tahoe off U.S. 50, past Echo Summit, Twin Bridges* ☎ *530/659–7453 information, 530/659–7475 snow phone* ⊕ *www.sierraattahoe.com* ✉ *Lift ticket $101.*

POPE-BALDWIN RECREATION AREA

5 miles west of South Lake Tahoe.

To the west of downtown South Lake Tahoe, U.S. 50 and Highway 89 come together, forming an intersection nicknamed "the Y." If you head northwest on Highway 89, also called Emerald Bay Road, and follow the lakefront, commercial development gives way to national forests and state parks. One of these is Pope-Baldwin Recreation Area.

GETTING HERE AND AROUND

The entrance to the Pope-Baldwin Recreation Area is on the east side of Emerald Bay Road. The area is closed to vehicles in winter, but you can cross-country ski here.

EXPLORING

Tallac Historic Site. At this site you can stroll or picnic lakeside year-round, and then in late spring and summer you can also explore three historic estates. The **Pope House** is the magnificently restored 1894 mansion of George S. Pope, who made his money in shipping and lumber and played host to the business and cultural elite of 1920s America. The **Baldwin Museum** is in the estate that once belonged to entrepreneur "Lucky" Baldwin; today it houses a collection of family memorabilia and Washoe Indian artifacts. The **Valhalla** (*valhallatahoe.com*), with a spectacular floor-to-ceiling stone fireplace, belonged to Walter Heller. Its Grand Hall and a lakeside boathouse, refurbished as a theater, host summertime concerts, plays, and cultural activities. Docents conduct tours of the Pope House in summer; call for tour times. ⊠ *Hwy. 89* ☎ *530/541–5227 late May–mid-Sept., 530/543–2600 year-round* ⊕ *tahoeheritage.org* 🎫 *Free, summer guided site walk $5, Pope House tour $10* ⊗ *House and museum closed late Sept.–late May.*

FAMILY **Taylor Creek Visitor Center.** At this center operated by the U.S. Forest Service you can visit the site of a Washoe Indian settlement; walk self-guided trails through meadow, marsh, and forest; and inspect the Stream Profile Chamber, an underground display with windows right into Taylor Creek. In fall you may see spawning kokanee salmon digging their nests. In summer Forest Service naturalists organize discovery walks and evening programs. ⊠ *Hwy. 89, 3 miles north of junction with U.S. 50* ☎ *530/543–2674 late May–Oct., 530/543–2600 year-round* ⊕ *www.fs.usda.gov/recarea/ltbmu/recarea/?recid=11785* 🎫 *Free.*

EMERALD BAY STATE PARK

4 miles west of Pope-Baldwin Recreation Area.

You can hike, bike, swim, camp, scuba dive, kayak, or tour a lookalike Viking castle at this state park. Or you can simply enjoy the most popular tourist stop on Lake Tahoe's circular drive: the high cliff overlooking Emerald Bay, famed for its jewel-like shape and color.

GETTING HERE AND AROUND

The entrance to Emerald Bay State Park is on the east side of a narrow, twisting section of Highway 89. Caution is the key word for both drivers and pedestrians. The park is closed to vehicles in winter.

Fjord-like Emerald Bay is possibly the most scenic part of Lake Tahoe.

EXPLORING

Fodor's Choice
★

Emerald Bay. A massive glacier millions of years ago carved this 3-mile-long and 1-mile-wide fjordlike inlet. Famed for its jewel-like shape and colors, the bay surrounds Fannette, Tahoe's only island. Highway 89 curves high above the lake through Emerald Bay State Park; from the Emerald Bay lookout, the centerpiece of the park, you can survey the whole scene. This is one of the don't-miss views of Lake Tahoe. The light is best in mid- to late morning, when the bay's colors really pop. ⊠ *Hwy. 89, 20 miles south of Tahoe City* ☎ *530/525–7232* ⊕ *www. parks.ca.gov* ⊠ *$10 parking fee.*

Vikingsholm. This 38-room estate was completed in 1929 and built as a precise copy of a 1,200-year-old Viking castle, using materials native to the area. Its original owner, Lora Knight, furnished it with Scandinavian antiques and hired artisans to build period reproductions. The sod roof sprouts wildflowers each spring. There are picnic tables nearby and a gray-sand beach for strolling. A steep 1-mile-long trail from the Emerald Bay lookout leads down to Vikingsholm, and the hike back up is hard (especially if you're not yet acclimated to the elevation), although there are benches and stone culverts to rest on. At the 150-foot peak of Fannette Island are the ruins of a stone structure known as the Tea House, built in 1928 so that Knight's guests could have a place to enjoy afternoon refreshments after a motorboat ride. The island is off-limits from February through mid-June to protect nesting Canada geese. The rest of the year it's open for day use. ⊠ *Hwy. 89* ☎ *530/525–7232* ⊕ *www.vikingsholm.com* ⊠ *Day-use parking fee $10; mansion tour $10* ☉ *Closed late Sept.–late May.*

SPORTS AND THE OUTDOORS

HIKING

Eagle Falls. To reach these falls, leave your car in the parking lot of the Eagle Falls picnic area (near Vikingsholm; arrive early for a good spot), and walk up the short but fairly steep canyon nearby. You'll have a brilliant panorama of Emerald Bay from this spot near the boundary of Desolation Wilderness. For a strenuous full-day hike, continue 5 miles, past Eagle Lake, to Upper and Middle Velma Lakes. Pick up trail maps at Taylor Creek Visitor Center in summer, or year-round at the main U.S. Forest Service Office in South Lake Tahoe, at 35 College Drive. ⊠ *Hwy. 89, South Lake Tahoe.*

D.L. BLISS STATE PARK

3 miles north of Emerald Bay State Park, 17 miles south of Tahoe City.

This park shares six miles of shoreline with adjacent Emerald Bay State Park, and has two white-sand beaches. Hike the Rubicon Trail for stunning views of the lake.

GETTING HERE AND AROUND

The entrance to D.L. Bliss State Park is on the east side of Highway 89 just north of Emerald Bay. No vehicles are allowed in when the park is closed for the season.

EXPLORING

D.L. Bliss State Park. This park takes its name from Duane LeRoy Bliss, a 19th-century lumber magnate. At one time Bliss owned nearly 75% of Tahoe's lakefront, along with local steamboats, railroads, and banks. The park shares 6 miles of shoreline with Emerald Bay State Park; combined the two parks cover 1,830 acres, 744 of which the Bliss family donated to the state. At the north end of Bliss is Rubicon Point, which overlooks one of the lake's deepest spots. Short trails lead to an old lighthouse and Balancing Rock, which weighs 250,000 pounds and balances on a fist of granite. The 4.5-mile Rubicon Trail—one of Tahoe's premier hikes—leads to Vikingsholm and provides stunning lake views. Two white-sand beaches front some of Tahoe's warmest water. ⊠ *Hwy. 89* ☎ *530/525–3345, 800/777–0369* ⊕ *www.parks.ca.gov* ⌑ *$10 per vehicle, day use.*

ED Z'BERG SUGAR PINE POINT STATE PARK

8 miles north of D. L. Bliss State Park, 10 miles south of Tahoe City.

Visitors love to hike, swim, and fish here in the summer, but this park is also popular in winter, when a small campground remains open. Eleven miles of cross-country ski and snowshoe trails allow beginners and experienced enthusiasts alike to whoosh through pine forests and glide past the lake.

GETTING HERE AND AROUND

The entrance to Sugar Pine Point is on the east side of Highway 89, about a mile south of Tahoma. A bike trail links Tahoe City to the park.

22

EXPLORING

Hellman-Ehrman Mansion. The main attraction at Sugar Pine Point State Park is Ehrman Mansion, a 1903 stone-and-shingle summer home furnished in period style. In its day it was the height of modernity, with electric lights and complete indoor plumbing. Also in the park are a trapper's log cabin from the mid-19th century, a nature preserve with wildlife exhibits, a lighthouse, the start of the 10-mile biking trail to Tahoe City, and an extensive system of hiking and cross-country skiing trails. If you're feeling less ambitious, you can relax on the sun-dappled lawn behind the mansion and gaze out at the lake. ✉ *Hwy. 89* ☎ *530/525–7982 mansion in season, 530/525–7232 year-round* 🌐 *www.parks.ca.gov* 🎟 *$10 per vehicle, day use; mansion tour $10.*

Ed Z'Berg Sugar Pine Point State Park. Named for a state lawmaker who sponsored key conservation legislation, Lake Tahoe's largest state park has 2,000 acres of dense forests and nearly 2 miles of shore frontage. A popular spot during snow season, Sugar Pine provides 11 miles of cross-country trails and winter camping on a first-come, first-served basis. Rangers lead full-moon snowshoe tours from January to March. ✉ *Hwy. 89, 1 mile south of Tahoma* ☎ *530/525–7982, 530/525–7232 year-round* 🌐 *www.parks.ca.gov* 🎟 *$10 per vehicle, day use.*

TAHOMA

1 mile north of Ed Z'berg Sugar Pine Point State Park, 23 miles south of Truckee.

With its rustic waterfront vacation cottages, Tahoma exemplifies life on the lake in its quiet early days before bright-lights casinos and huge crowds proliferated. In 1960 Tahoma was host of the Olympic Nordic-skiing competitions. Today there's little to do here except stroll by the lake and listen to the wind in the trees, making it a favorite home base for mellow families and nature buffs.

GETTING HERE AND AROUND

Approach Tahoma by car on Highway 89, called West Lake Boulevard in this section. From the northern and western communities, take a TART bus to Tahoma. A bike trail links Tahoe City to Tahoma.

WHERE TO STAY

$$$ B&B/INN 🏨 **Tahoma Meadows B&B Cottages.** With sixteen individually decorated little red cottages sitting beneath towering pine trees, it's hard to beat this serene property for atmosphere and woodsy charm. **Pros:** lovely setting; good choice for families; close to Homewood ski resort. **Cons:** far from the casinos; may be too serene for some guests; old-style decor. [$] *Rooms from: $199* ✉ *6821 W. Lake Blvd.* ☎ *530/525–1553, 866/525–1553* 🌐 *www.tahomameadows.com* 🛏 *16 rooms* 🍴 *Breakfast.*

SPORTS AND THE OUTDOORS

SKIING

Homewood Mountain Resort. Schuss down these slopes for fantastic views—the mountain rises across the road from the Tahoe shoreline. This small, usually uncrowded resort is the favorite area of locals on a snowy day, because you can find lots of untracked powder. It's also the most protected and least windy Tahoe ski area during a storm; when every other resort's lifts are on wind hold, you can almost always count on Homewood's to be open. There's only one high-speed chairlift, but there are rarely any lines, and the ticket prices are some of the cheapest around—kids 5 to 12 ski for $24, and those four and under are free. The resort may look small as you drive by, but most of it isn't visible from the road. **Facilities:** 64 trails; 2,010 acres; 1,625-foot vertical drop; 8 lifts. ✉ *5145 W. Lake Blvd., Hwy. 89, 6 miles south of Tahoe City, Homewood* ☎ *530/525–2992 information, 530/525–2900 snow phone* 🌐 *www.skihomewood.com* 🎫 *Lift ticket $59.*

TAHOE CITY

9 miles north of Tahoma, 14 miles south of Truckee.

Tahoe City is the only lakeside town with a charming downtown area good for strolling and window-shopping. Stores and restaurants are all within walking distance of the Outlet Gates, where water is spilled into the Truckee River to control the surface level of the lake.

GETTING HERE AND AROUND

Tahoe City is at the junction of Highway 28, also called North Lake Boulevard, and Highway 89 where it turns northwest toward Squaw Valley and Truckee. TART buses serve the area.

ESSENTIALS

Visitor Information Go Tahoe North. ☎ *530/581–6900, 888/434–1262* 🌐 *www.gotahoenorth.com.*

EXPLORING

Gatekeeper's Museum. This museum preserves a little-known part of the region's history. Between 1910 and 1968 the gatekeeper who lived on this site was responsible for monitoring the level of the lake, using a winch system (still used today and visible just outside the museum) to keep the water at the correct level. Also here, the fantastic Marion Steinbach Indian Basket Museum displays intricate baskets from 85 tribes. ✉ *130 W. Lake Blvd.* ☎ *530/583–1762* 🌐 *www.northtahoemuseums.org* 🎫 *$5* 🕒 *Closed Mon.–Wed. early-Sept.–late May.*

WHERE TO EAT

$ ECLECTIC

🍴 **Cafe Zenon.** Straightforward Vietnamese pho noodle soup is served all day at chef Suzanne Nguyen's restaurant at Tahoe City's public golf course, but she also prepares everything from poutine and kimchi hot dogs to pork and green beans. The Vietnamese French Dip, a local favorite, substitutes pho broth for the traditional beef. **Known for:** classic Vietnamese dishes; mushroom skillet with a fried egg for weekend breakfast; golf course setting (skating rink in winter). [$] *Average main: $11* ✉ *251 N. Lake Blvd.* ☎ *530/583–1517* 🌐 *www.cafezenon.com* 🕒 *Closed Mon.–Tues. No breakfast weekdays.*

$$$$ AMERICAN Fodor's Choice ★

🍴 **Christy Hill.** Huge windows reveal stellar lake views at this Euro–Cal restaurant serving seafood, beef, and vegetarian entrées, along with small plate offerings. The extensive wine list and exceptionally good desserts earn accolades, as do the gracious service and casual vibe.

Known for: Euro–Cal menu; romantic choice; dinner on the deck. $ *Average main: $31* ✉ *115 Grove St., at N. Lake Blvd.* ☎ *530/583–8551* ⊕ *www.christyhill.com* ◷ *No lunch.*

$ | AMERICAN

✗ **Fire Sign Café.** There's often a wait for breakfast and lunch at this great little diner 2 miles south of Tahoe City, but it's worth it. The pastries are made from scratch, the salmon is smoked in-house, the salsa is hand cut, and there's real maple syrup for the many types of pancakes and waffles. **Known for:** pastries from scratch; many pancakes and waffles; fruit cobbler. $ *Average main: $11* ✉ *1785 W. Lake Blvd., at Fountain Ave.* ☎ *530/583–0871* ⊕ *www.firesigncafe.com* ◷ *No dinner.*

$$$$ | ECLECTIC

✗ **Wolfdale's.** Consistent, inspired cuisine makes Wolfdale's one of the top restaurants on the lake, albeit among the most expensive as well. The imaginative entrées, many involving seafood, merge Asian and European cooking, and everything from teriyaki glaze to smoked fish is made in-house. **Known for:** imaginative entrées; lake view; elegantly simple dining room. $ *Average main: $33* ✉ *640 N. Lake Blvd., near Grove St.* ☎ *530/583–5700* ⊕ *www.wolfdales.com* ◷ *Closed Tues. No lunch.*

WHERE TO STAY

$$ | B&B/INN | FAMILY | Fodor'sChoice | ★

🛏 **Basecamp Tahoe City.** A downtown motel for the 21st century, Basecamp charms its guests with a combination of industrial, retro, and rustic styles. **Pros:** lively public spaces; stylish rooms; passionate staff. **Cons:** some road noise; lacks amenities of large properties; 8-minute walk to local beach. $ *Rooms from: $149* ✉ *955 N. Lake Blvd.* ☎ *530/580–8430* ⊕ *www.basecamptahoecity.com* ⤴ *24 rooms* ⦿ *Breakfast.*

$$ | B&B/INN

🛏 **Cottage Inn.** Avoid the crowds by staying in one of these charming circa-1938 log cottages under the towering pines on the lake's west shore. **Pros:** romantic, woodsy setting; each room has a fireplace; full breakfast. **Cons:** no kids under 12; weak Wi-Fi; old-school decor. $ *Rooms from: $150* ✉ *1690 W. Lake Blvd.* ☎ *530/581–4073, 800/581–4073* ⊕ *www.thecottageinn.com* ⤴ *22 rooms* ⦿ *Breakfast.*

$$ | RESORT

🛏 **Granlibakken Tahoe.** A condo community with its own snow-play area in winter, this secluded 74-acre resort's name means "a hillside sheltered by fir trees" in Norwegian. **Pros:** fitness and wellness orientation; secluded location; pool and spa treatments. **Cons:** some guests find the location too secluded; more for families than romantic interludes; conference activities and weddings. $ *Rooms from: $160* ✉ *725 Granlibakken Rd.* ☎ *530/583–4242 front desk, 800/543–3221 reservations* ⊕ *granlibakken.com* ⤴ *165 rooms* ⦿ *Breakfast.*

$$$ | HOTEL | Fodor'sChoice | ★

🛏 **Sunnyside Steakhouse and Lodge.** The views are superb and the hospitality gracious at this lakeside lodge three miles south of Tahoe City. **Pros:** complimentary Continental breakfast and afternoon tea; most rooms have balconies overlooking the lake; lively bar and restaurant. **Cons:** can be pricey for families; can be noisy in summer; pricey entrées at steak house. $ *Rooms from: $200* ✉ *1850 W. Lake Blvd., Box 5969* ☎ *530/583–7200, 800/822–2754* ⊕ *www.sunnysideresort.com* ⤴ *23 rooms* ⦿ *Breakfast.*

22

SPORTS AND THE OUTDOORS

RAFTING

FAMILY **Truckee River Rafting.** In summer you can take a self-guided raft trip down a gentle 5-mile stretch of the Truckee River. This outfitter will shuttle you back to Tahoe City at the end of your two- to three-hour trip. On a warm day, this makes a great family outing. ⊠ *175 River Rd., near W. Lake Blvd.* ☎ *530/583–1111* ⊕ *www.truckeeriverrafting. com* ⌦ *From $35.*

SKIING

Fodor's Choice **Alpine Meadows Ski Area.** With an average 450 inches of snow annually,
★ Alpine has some of Tahoe's most reliable conditions. It's usually one of the first areas to open in November and one of the last to close in May or June. Alpine isn't the place for show-offs; instead, you'll find down-to-earth alpine fetishists. The two peaks here are well suited to intermediate skiers, with a number of runs for experts only. Snowboarders and hot-dog skiers will find a terrain park with a super-pipe, rails, and tabletops, as well as a boarder-cross course. Alpine is a great place to learn to ski and has a ski school that coaches those with physical and mental disabilities. On Saturday, because of the limited parking, there's more acreage per person than at other resorts. Lift tickets are good at neighboring Squaw Valley; a free shuttle runs all day between the two ski parks. **Facilities:** 100 trails; 2,400 acres, 1,802-foot vertical drop; 13 lifts. ⊠ *2600 Alpine Meadows Rd., off Hwy. 89, 6 miles northwest of Tahoe City and 13 miles south of Truckee* ☎ *530/583–4232, 800/403–0206* ⊕ *www.squawalpine.com* ⌦ *Lift ticket $114.*

Tahoe Dave's Skis and Boards. You can rent skis, boards, and snowshoes at this shop, which has the area's best selection of downhill rental equipment. ⊠ *590 N. Lake Blvd.* ☎ *530/583–6415* ⊕ *www.tahoedaves.com.*

OLYMPIC VALLEY

7 miles north of Tahoe City to Squaw Valley Road; 8½ miles south of Truckee.

Olympic Valley got its name in 1960, when Squaw Valley USA, the ski resort here, hosted the Winter Olympics. Snow sports remain the primary activity, but once summer comes, you can hike into the adjacent Granite Chief Wilderness, explore wildflower-studded alpine meadows, or lie by a swimming pool in one of the Sierra's prettiest valleys.

GETTING HERE AND AROUND

Squaw Valley Road, the only way into Olympic Valley, branches west off Highway 89 about 8 miles south of Truckee. TART connects the Squaw Valley ski area with the communities along the north and west shores, and Truckee, with year-round public transportation. Squaw Valley Ski Resort provides a free shuttle to many stops in those same areas.

EXPLORING

High Camp. You can ride the Squaw Valley Aerial Tram to this activity hub, which at 8,200 feet commands superb views of Lake Tahoe and the surrounding mountains. In summer, go for a hike, sit by the pool, or have a cocktail and watch the sunset. In winter you can ski,

Squaw Valley USA has runs for skiers of all ability levels, from beginner to expert trails.

ice-skate, snow-tube, or go for a full-moon snowshoe hike. There's also a restaurant, a lounge, and a small Olympic museum. Pick up trail maps at the tram building. ⊠ *Aerial Tram Bldg., Squaw Valley* ☎ *800/403–0206* ⊕ *www.squawalpine.com/events-things-do/aerial-tram-rides* ⊠ *Aerial Tram, $44.*

FAMILY **Village at Squaw Valley.** The centerpiece of Olympic Valley is a pedestrian mall at the base of several four-story ersatz Bavarian stone-and-timber buildings, where you'll find restaurants, high-end condo rentals, boutiques, and cafés. ⊠ *1750 Village East Rd.* ☎ *530/584–1000, 800/403–0206 information, 800/731–8021 condo reservations* ⊕ *www.squawalpine.com/explore/about/squaw-valley-village-map.*

WHERE TO EAT

$ ✕ **Fireside Pizza Company.** Adults might opt for the signature pear and
PIZZA Gorgonzola pizza at this modern Italian restaurant, but most kids
FAMILY clamor for the house favorite: an Italian-sausage-and-pepperoni combo with a bubbly blend of four cheeses. Salads and pasta dishes round out the menu at this family-friendly spot. **Known for:** inventive pizzas; good, inexpensive dining option in a pricey area; family friendly. $ *Average main: $15* ⊠ *The Village at Squaw Valley, 1985 Squaw Valley Rd., #25* ☎ *530/584–6150* ⊕ *www.firesidepizza.com.*

$$$ ✕ **Graham's of Squaw Valley.** Sit by a floor-to-ceiling river-rock hearth
ECLECTIC under a knotty-pine peaked ceiling in this well-run restaurant's intimate dining room. The southern European–inspired menu changes often, but expect hearty entrées such as grilled beef tenderloin with wild mushroom sauce, along with lighter-fare small plates like quail with fig demi-glace or tasty crab salad. **Known for:** hearty entrées, small plates;

highly regarded wine list; fireside bar for appetizers. [$] *Average main: $30* ✉ *Christy Inn Lodge, 1650 Squaw Valley Rd.* ☎ *530/581–0454* ⏲ *Closed Mon. and Tues. No lunch.*

$$$$ AMERICAN Fodor's Choice ★ 🍴 **PlumpJack Cafe.** The menu at this chic restaurant for serious foodies changes seasonally, but look for rib-eye steak in a green peppercorn demi glace, seared diver scallops with toasted Israeli cous cous, and inventive vegetarian dishes. Rather than complicated, heavy sauces, the chef uses simple reductions to complement a dish. **Known for:** chic setting; clean, dynamic flavors; varied, reasonably priced wines. [$] *Average main: $39* ✉ *1920 Squaw Valley Rd.* ☎ *530/583–1578* 🌐 *www.plumpjackcafe.com* ⏲ *No lunch (except at bar).*

WHERE TO STAY

$$$ HOTEL Fodor's Choice ★ 🏨 **PlumpJack Squaw Valley Inn.** Stylish and luxurious, this two-story, cedar-sided inn has a snappy, sophisticated look and laid-back sensibility, perfect for the Bay Area cognoscenti who flock here on weekends. **Pros:** small and intimate; loaded with amenities; personable and attentive service. **Cons:** not the best choice for families with small children; not all rooms have tubs; laid-back sensibility may not work for some guests. [$] *Rooms from: $225* ✉ *1920 Squaw Valley Rd.* ☎ *530/583–1576, 800/323–7666* 🌐 *www.plumpjacksquawvalleyinn.com* 🛏 *56 rooms* 🍽 *Breakfast.*

$$$$ RESORT 🏨 **Resort at Squaw Creek.** This multi-facility Squaw Valley resort offers a plethora of year-round activities. **Pros:** every conceivable amenity; private chairlift to Squaw Valley USA for ski-in, ski-out; attractive furnishings. **Cons:** so large it can feel impersonal; high in-season rates; a lot of hubbub during ski season. [$] *Rooms from: $279* ✉ *400 Squaw Creek Rd.* ☎ *530/583–6300, 800/327–3353* 🌐 *www.squawcreek.com* 🛏 *405 rooms* 🍽 *No meals.*

$$$ HOTEL 🏨 **The Village at Squaw Valley USA.** Right at the base of the slopes, at the center point of Olympic Valley, the Village's condominiums (from studio to three bedrooms) come complete with gas fireplaces, daily maid service, and heated slate-tile bathroom and kitchen floors. **Pros:** family-friendly; near Village restaurants and shops; at base of slopes. **Cons:** claustrophobia-inducing crowds on weekends; nicely appointed but not high style. [$] *Rooms from: $199* ✉ *1750 Village East Rd.* ☎ *530/584–1000, 888/259–1428* 🌐 *www.squawalpine.com/lodging* 🛏 *198 rooms* 🍽 *No meals.*

SPORTS AND THE OUTDOORS

GOLF

Resort at Squaw Creek Golf Course. For beautiful views of Squaw Valley's surrounding peaks, play this narrow, challenging championship course designed by Robert Trent Jones, Jr. The design emphasizes accuracy over distance, especially on the front nine. All fees include a golf cart plus valet parking; rates drop after noon and again after 3 pm. ✉ *400 Squaw Creek Rd.* ☎ *530/583–6300, 530/581–6637 pro shop* 🌐 *www.destinationhotels.com/squawcreek/recreation* 🎟 *$89 weekdays; $99 weekends* ⛳ *18 holes, 6,931 yards, par 71.*

ICE-SKATING

FAMILY **Olympic Ice Pavilion.** Ice-skate here from late November to early March. A ride up the mountain in the Aerial Tram costs $44, plus $14 for skate rental and one hour of skate time. In summer the pavilion converts into a roller-skating rink. Year-round, you get fabulous views of the lake and the Sierra Nevada. ✉ *1960 Squaw Valley Rd., High Camp, Squaw Valley* ☎ *800/403–0206* ⊕ *www.squawalpine.com/ events-things-do/ice-skating.*

22

SKIING

Fodor'sChoice **Squaw Valley USA.** Known for some of the toughest skiing in the Tahoe ★ area, this park was the centerpiece of the 1960 Winter Olympics. Today it's the definitive North Tahoe ski resort and among the top-three megaresorts in California (the other two are Heavenly and Mammoth). Although Squaw has changed significantly since the Olympics, the skiing is still world-class and extends across vast bowls stretched between six peaks. Experts often head directly to the untamed terrain of the infamous KT-22 face, which has bumps, cliffs, and gulp-and-go chutes, or to the nearly vertical Palisades, where many famous extreme-skiing films have been shot. Fret not, beginners and intermediates: you have plenty of wide-open, groomed trails at High Camp (which sits at the *top* of the mountain) and around the more challenging Snow King Peak. Snowboarders and show-off skiers can tear up the five fantastic terrain parks, which include a giant super-pipe. Ski passes are good at neighboring Alpine Meadows; free shuttles run all day between the two ski parks. **Facilities:** 170 trails; 3,600 acres; 2,850-foot vertical drop; 29 lifts. ✉ *1960 Squaw Valley Rd., off Hwy. 89, 7 miles northwest of Tahoe City* ☎ *800/731–8021 lodging reservations, 530/452–4355 snow phone, 800/403–0206 information* ⊕ *www.squawalpine.com* ⌨ *Lift ticket $124.*

Tahoe Dave's Skis and Boards. If you don't want to pay resort prices, you can rent and tune downhill skis and snowboards at this shop. ✉ *3039 Hwy. 89, at Squaw Valley Rd.* ☎ *530/583–5665* ⊕ *www. tahoedaves.com.*

TRUCKEE

13 miles northwest of Kings Beach, 14 miles north of Tahoe City.

Formerly a decrepit railroad town in the mountains, Truckee is now the trendy first stop for many Tahoe visitors. The town was officially established around 1863, and by 1868 it had gone from a stagecoach station to a major stopover for trains bound for the Pacific via the new transcontinental railroad. Every day, freight trains and Amtrak's *California Zephyr* still idle briefly at the depot in the middle of town. The visitor center inside the depot has a walking-tour map of historic Truckee.

Across from the station, where Old West facades line the main drag, you'll find galleries, gift shops, boutiques, a wine-tasting room, old-fashioned diners, and several good restaurants.

GETTING HERE AND AROUND

Truckee is off Interstate 80 between highways 89 and 267. Greyhound and Amtrak stop here, and TART buses serve the area.

ESSENTIALS

Visitor Information Truckee Donner Chamber of Commerce and the California Welcome Center. ✉ *Amtrak depot, 10065 Donner Pass Rd., near Spring St.* ☎ *530/587–8808 chamber of commerce, 866/443–2027 welcome center* 🌐 *www.truckee.com.*

EXPLORING

Donner Memorial State Park and Emigrant Trail Museum. The park and museum commemorate the 89 members of the Donner Party, westward-bound pioneers who became trapped in the Sierra in the winter of 1846–47 in snow 22 feet deep. Barely more than half survived, some by resorting to cannibalism. The absorbing Emigrant Trail Museum in the visitor center contains exhibits about the Donner Party, regional Native Americans, and railroad and transportation development in the area. In the park, you can picnic, hike, camp, and go boating, fishing, and waterskiing in summer; winter brings cross-country skiing and snowshoeing on groomed trails. ✉ *12593 Donner Pass Rd., off I–80, 2 miles west of Truckee* ☎ *530/582–7892 museum* 🌐 *www.parks.ca.gov* 🎫 *$10 parking, day use ($5 in winter).*

WHERE TO EAT

$$$ ECLECTIC Fodor's Choice ★

🍴 **Cottonwood Restaurant & Bar.** Perched above town on the site of North America's first chairlift, this local institution has a bar decked out with old wooden skis, sleds, skates, and photos of Truckee's early days. The ambitious menu includes grilled steak, baby-back short ribs with honey-chipotle barbecue sauce, and butternut-squash raviolis with sage brown butter—plus fresh-baked breads and desserts. **Known for:** local institution; ambitious menu; hilltop views. [$] *Average main: $26* ✉ *10142 Rue Hilltop Rd., off Brockway Rd., ¼ mile south of downtown* ☎ *530/587–5711* 🌐 *www.cottonwoodrestaurant.com* 🕒 *No lunch.*

$$ AMERICAN

🍴 **FiftyFifty Brewing Company.** In this Truckee brewpub the warm red tones and comfy booths, plus a pint of the Donner Party porter (or a shot of bourbon), will take the nip out of a cold day on the slopes. The menu includes salads, burgers, inventive pizzas, barbecued ribs, pan-seared salmon, and the house specialty, a pulled-pork sandwich. **Known for:** inventive pizzas; pulled-pork sandwich; après-ski action. [$] *Average main: $20* ✉ *11197 Brockway Rd., near Martis Valley Rd.* ☎ *530/587–2337* 🌐 *www.fiftyfiftybrewing.com.*

$ AMERICAN Fodor's Choice ★

🍴 **Marty's Cafe.** You'd never know from this café's laid-back decor that the namesake owner-chef's resume includes stints at fancy restaurants from Beverly Hills to Kennebunkport. Marty's hearty breakfasts (like the house-made granola or the fried egg sandwich with bacon and Gruyère on toasted French bread) and lunches—burgers, hoagies, "char dogs," sloppy joes, and a winning chicken and avocado BLT—are served from opening until closing. **Known for:** hearty breakfasts and lunches served all day; daily specials and seasonal salads; ebullient hospitality. [$] *Average main: $14* ✉ *10115 Donner Pass Rd.* ☎ *530/550–8208* 🌐 *martyscafetruckee.com* 🕒 *No dinner.*

$$$ ECLECTIC 🍴 **Moody's Bistro, Bar & Beats.** Head here for contemporary-Cal cuisine in a sexy dining room with pumpkin-color walls, burgundy velvet banquettes, and art-deco fixtures. The earthy, sure-handed cooking features organically grown ingredients: look for ahi poke, snazzy pizzas bubbling-hot from a brick oven, braised lamb shanks, pan-roasted wild game, fresh seafood, and organic beef. **Known for:** lighter fare for lunch; summer alfresco dining; live music in bar some nights. [$] *Average main: $25* ✉ *10007 Bridge St., at Donner Pass Rd.* ☎ *530/587–8688* 🌐 *www.moodysbistro.com.*

$$$ ITALIAN 🍴 **Pianeta Ristorante.** A town favorite for a decade-plus, Pianeta serves high-style Italian cuisine in a warmly lit bilevel redbrick space on Truckee's historic main drag. Start with a beef carpaccio antipasto plate or perhaps house-made spicy-fennel and mild sausages, following up with a pasta course of ravioli Bolognese (both pasta and sauce made in-house), an entrée of ragout with spicy sausage and Mexican prawns—or both. **Known for:** house-made sausages, pastas, and sauces; warmly lit redbrick space; well-conceived wine list. [$] *Average main: $25* ✉ *10096 Donner Pass Rd.* ☎ *530/587–4694* 🌐 *www.pianetarestauranttruckee.com* 🕒 *No lunch.*

$ AMERICAN 🍴 **Squeeze In.** Meet the locals at Truckee's top choice for breakfast, thanks to the dozens of omelets and several variations on eggs Benedict along with banana-walnut pancakes and French toast oozing with cream cheese. At lunch savor homemade soups and sandwiches. **Known for:** omelets and eggs Benedict; homemade soups. [$] *Average main: $13* ✉ *10060 Donner Pass Rd., near Bridge St.* ☎ *530/587–9814* 🌐 *www.squeezein.com* 🕒 *No dinner.*

$$$ AMERICAN 🍴 **Truckee Tavern & Grill.** The wood-fired grill in this downtown restaurant turns out steaks, chicken, and chops along with buffalo tri-tip and other house specialties. Non-carnivores enjoy pasta (linguine with ricotta and vegetables) and fish (salmon with green-lentil ragout) entrées. **Known for:** wood-fired meats; pasta and fish entrées; small-batch gin and whiskey. [$] *Average main: $26* ✉ *10118 Donner Pass Rd., near Spring St.* ☎ *530/587–3766* 🌐 *www.truckeetavern.com* 🕒 *No lunch.*

WHERE TO STAY

$$ HOTEL 🏨 **Cedar House Sport Hotel.** The clean, spare lines of the Cedar House's wooden exterior evoke a modern European feel, while energy-saving heating, cooling, and lighting systems emphasize the owners' commitment to sustainability. **Pros:** environmentally friendly; hip yet comfortable; heated-tile bathroom floors. **Cons:** some bathrooms on the small side; not all bathrooms have tubs; about a mile from historic downtown Truckee. [$] *Rooms from: $170* ✉ *10918 Brockway Rd.* ☎ *530/582–5655, 866/582–5655* 🌐 *www.cedarhousesporthotel.com* 🛏 *40 rooms* 🍽 *Breakfast.*

$$$ RESORT 🏨 **Northstar California Resort.** The area's most complete destination resort entices families with its sports activities and concentration of restaurants, shops, and accommodations. **Pros:** array of lodging types; on-site shuttle; several dining options in Northstar Village. **Cons:** family accommodations are very pricey; lacks intimacy; some units not as attractive as others. [$] *Rooms from: $249* ✉ *100 Northstar Dr., off Hwy. 267, 6 miles southeast of Truckee* ☎ *530/562–1010, 800/466–6784* 🌐 *www.northstarcalifornia.com* 🛏 *250 rooms* 🍽 *No meals.*

$$$$
RESORT
Fodor's Choice
★

⛄ **Ritz-Carlton Highlands Court, Lake Tahoe.** Nestled mid-mountain on the Northstar ski resort, the plush accommodations of the four-story Ritz-Carlton have floor-to-ceiling windows for maximum views, along with fireplaces, cozy robes, and down comforters. **Pros:** superb service; gorgeous setting; ski-in, ski out convenience. **Cons:** prices as breathtaking as the views; resort fee and mandatory valet parking add to cost of stay; must go off-site for golf and tennis. Ⓢ *Rooms from: $362* ✉ *13031 Ritz-Carlton Highlands Court* ☏ *530/562–3000, 800/241–3333* ⊕ *www.ritzcarlton.com/laketahoe* ➬ *169 rooms* ◯❙ *No meals.*

$$
B&B/INN

⛄ **River Street Inn.** On the banks of the Truckee River, this 1885 wood-and-stone inn has uncluttered, comfortable rooms that are simply decorated, with attractive, country-style wooden furniture and extras like flat-screen TVs. **Pros:** tidy rooms; good value; in historic downtown Truckee. **Cons:** parking is a half-block from inn; decor is simple; noise from on-site restaurant and bar and nearby trains. Ⓢ *Rooms from: $145* ✉ *10009 E. River St.* ☏ *530/550–9290, 530/550–9222 restaurant* ⊕ *www.riverstreetinntruckee.com* ➬ *7 rooms* ◯❙ *Breakfast.*

SPORTS AND THE OUTDOORS

GOLF

Coyote Moon Golf Course. With towering pine trees lining the fairways and no houses to spoil the view, this course is as beautiful as it is challenging. Fees include a shared cart; the greens fee drops at 1 pm and dips again at 3. ✉ *10685 Northwoods Blvd., off Donner Pass Rd.* ☏ *530/587–0886* ⊕ *www.coyotemoongolf.com* ⛳ *$175* ⛳ *18 holes, 7177 yards, par 72* ☉ *Closed late fall–late spring.*

Northstar California Golf. Robert Muir Graves designed this course that combines hilly terrain and open meadows. The front nine holes here are open-links style, while the challenging back nine move through tight, tree-lined fairways. Fees starting at $55 for nine holes include a shared cart, and twilight rates begin at 2 pm. ✉ *168 Basque Dr., off Northstar Dr., west off Hwy. 267* ☏ *530/562–3290 pro-shop* ⊕ *www.northstarcalifornia.com/info/summer/golf.asp* ⛳ *$55 for 9 holes, $85 for 18 holes* ⛳ *18 holes, 6781 yards, par 72.*

Old Greenwood. Beautiful mountain and forest views add to the pleasure of a round played at north Lake Tahoe's only Jack Nicklaus Signature Golf Course. The regular fees are high, but there's a $75 twilight rate beginning at 4 pm. ✉ *12915 Fairway Dr., off Overland Trail Rd., off I–80, Exit 190* ☏ *530/550–7010* ⊕ *www.golfintahoe.com/old-greenwood/course* ⛳ *$150–$200* ⛳ *18 holes, 7518 yards, par 72.*

MOUNTAIN BIKING

Cyclepaths Mountain Bike Adventures. This combination full-service bike shop and bike-adventure outfitter offers instruction in mountain biking, guided tours, tips for self-guided bike touring, bike repairs, and books and maps on the area. ✉ *Pioneer Center, 10825 Pioneer Trail, Suite 105* ☏ *530/582–1890* ⊕ *www.cyclepaths.net.*

Northstar California Bike Park. In summer Northstar's ski slopes transform into a magnificent lift-served bike park with 100 miles of challenging terrain, including the aptly named Livewire trail. Guided tours, multiday retreats, and downhill, cross-country, and endurance races are available for riders of all abilities. ⊠ *Northstar Dr., off Hwy. 267* ☏ *530/562–1010* ⊕ *www.northstarcalifornia.com/bike-and-hike/mtn-biking-rentals.aspx* ⛷ *Lift $59.*

SKIING

Boreal Mountain Resort. These slopes have 380 skiable acres and 500 vertical feet of terrain visible from the freeway. Lift-served snow-tubing and night skiing go until 9. ⊠ *19749 Boreal Ridge Rd., at I–80, Boreal/Castle Peak exit, Soda Springs* ☏ *530/426–3666* ⊕ *www.rideboreal.com.*

Donner Ski Ranch. This ski park has 505 acres and 750 vertical feet. A popular area with kids in this small, family-friendly park is the Tubing Hill. Riders whisk down the slope in a huge inflated inner tube and then go back to the top on a moving carpet. ⊠ *19320 Donner Pass Rd., Norden* ☏ *530/426–3635* ⊕ *www.donnerskiranch.com.*

Fodor's Choice ★ **Northstar California.** Meticulous grooming and long cruisers make this resort a paradise for intermediate skiers and a fine choice for families. Although the majority of the trails are intermediate in difficulty, advanced skiers and riders have access to Lookout Mountain's more than two dozen expert trails and 347 acres of gated terrain and steeps. The diversity of terrain in proximity makes it easier for families and groups with varying skills to hang out with each other. As for terrain parks, the ones here are considered among North America's best, with features that include a 420-foot-long super-pipe, a half-pipe, rails and boxes, and lots of kickers. The Cross Country, Snowshoe and Telemark Center, located mid-mountain, is the starting point for a network of 35 km (22 miles) of groomed trails, including double-set tracks and skating lanes. The trails are also fat-bike friendly, so nonskiers can enjoy the park, too. The school has programs for skiers ages three and up, and on-site care is available for tots two and older. **Facilities:** 97 trails; 3,170 acres; 2,280-foot vertical drop; 20 lifts. ⊠ *5001 Northstar Dr.* ☏ *530/562–1010 information, 800/466–6784 lodging, 530/562–1330 snow phone* ⊕ *www.northstarcalifornia.com* ⛷ *Lift ticket $126.*

Royal Gorge. If you love to cross-country, don't miss Royal Gorge, which serves up 200 km (124 miles) of track for all abilities, eight trail systems on a whopping 6,000 acres, a ski school, and nine warming huts. Because the complex, affiliated with Sugar Bowl, sits right on the Sierra Crest, the views are drop-dead gorgeous. ⊠ *9411 Pahatsi Dr., off I–80, Soda Springs/Norden exit, Soda Springs* ☏ *530/426–3871, 800/500–3871* ⊕ *www.royalgorge.com.*

Sugar Bowl Ski Resort. Opened in 1939 by Walt Disney, this is the oldest—and one of the best—resorts at Tahoe. Atop Donner Summit, it receives an incredible 500 inches of snowfall annually. Four peaks are connected by 1,650 acres of skiable terrain, with everything from gentle groomed corduroy to wide-open bowls to vertical rocky chutes and outstanding tree skiing. Snowboarders can hit two terrain parks with numerous boxes, rails, and jumps. Because it's more compact than some of the area's megaresorts, there's a gentility here that distinguishes Sugar Bowl from its competitors, making this a great place for families and

22

a low-pressure, low-key place to learn to ski. It's not huge, but there's some very challenging terrain (experts: head to the Palisades). There's limited lodging at the base area. Facilities: 102 trails; 1,650 acres; 1,500-foot vertical drop; 12 lifts. ⊠ *629 Sugar Bowl Rd., off Donner Pass Rd., 3 miles east of I–80 Soda Springs/Norden exit, 10 miles west of Truckee, Norden* ☎ *530/426–9000 information and lodging reservations, 530/426–1111 snow phone, 866/843–2695 lodging referral* ⊕ *www.sugarbowl.com* ⊡ *Lift ticket $115.*

Tahoe Dave's. You can save money by renting skis and boards at this shop, which has the area's best selection and also repairs and tunes equipment. ⊠ *10200 Donner Pass Rd., near Spring St.* ☎ *530/582–0900* ⊕ *www.tahoedaves.com.*

Tahoe Donner. Just north of Truckee, this park covers 120 acres and 600 vertical feet; the cross-country center includes 51 trails on 100 km (62 miles) of groomed tracks on 4,800 acres, with night skiing on Wednesday in January and February. ⊠ *11603 Snowpeak Way* ☎ *530/587–9444* ⊕ *www.tahoedonner.com.*

CARNELIAN BAY TO KINGS BEACH

5–10 miles northeast of Tahoe City.

The small lakeside commercial districts of Carnelian Bay and Tahoe Vista service the thousand or so locals who live in the area year-round and the thousands more who have summer residences or launch their boats here. Kings Beach, the last town heading east on Highway 28 before the Nevada border, is full of basic motels and rental condos, restaurants, and shops.

GETTING HERE AND AROUND

To reach Kings Beach and Carnelian Bay from the California side, take Highway 89 north to Highway 28 north and then east. From the Nevada side, follow Highway 28 north and then west. TART provides public transportation in this area.

BEACHES

FAMILY   **Kings Beach State Recreation Area.** The north shore's 28-acre Kings Beach State Recreation Area, one of the largest such areas on the lake, is open year-round. The 700-foot-long sandy beach gets crowded in summer with people swimming, sunbathing, Jet Skiing, riding in paddleboats, spiking volleyballs, and tossing Frisbees. If you're going to spend the day, come early to snag a table in the picnic area; there's also a good playground. **Amenities:** food and drink; parking (fee); toilets; water sports. **Best For:** sunrise; sunset; swimming; windsurfing. ⊠ *8318 N. Lake Blvd., Hwy. 28, Kings Beach* ☎ *530/546–7248* ⊕ *www.parks. ca.gov* ⊡ *$10 parking fee.*

WHERE TO EAT AND STAY

$$$$ ✕ **Gar Woods Grill and Pier.** The view's the thing at this lakeside stalwart,
ECLECTIC   where you can watch the sun shimmer on the water through the dining room's plateglass windows or from the heated outdoor deck. Grilled steak and fish are menu mainstays, but be sure to try specialties like crab chilis rellenos and pomegranate braised pork ribs. **Known for:** lake

views; grilled steak and fish; better bet price wise for lunch or weekend breakfast. $ *Average main: $35* ✉ *5000 N. Lake Blvd., Hwy. 28, Carnelian Bay* ☎ *530/546–3366* 🌐 *www.garwoods.com.*

$$$ ECLECTIC 🍴 **Soule Domain.** Rough-hewn wood beams, a vaulted wood ceiling, and, in winter, a roaring fireplace lend high romance to this cozy 1927 pine-log cabin next to the Tahoe Biltmore casino. Chef-owner Charlie Soule's specialties include curried almond chicken, fresh sea scallops poached in champagne with a kiwi and mango cream sauce, and a vegan sauté judiciously flavored with ginger, jalapeños, sesame seeds, and teriyaki sauce. **Known for:** cozy, romantic setting; skilfully prepared cuisine; suave service. $ *Average main: $27* ✉ *9983 Cove St., ½ block up Stateline Rd. off Hwy. 28, Kings Beach* ✣ *Restaurant is just west of Tahoe Biltmore casino at California-Nevada border.* ☎ *530/546–7529* 🌐 *www.souledomain.com* 🕒 *No lunch.*

$$$ AMERICAN 🍴 **Spindleshanks American Bistro and Wine Bar.** A local favorite on the Old Brockway Golf Course, Spindleshanks serves mostly classic American cooking—ribs, steaks, and seafood updated with adventurous sauces—as well as house-made ravioli. Savor a drink from the full bar or choose a wine from the extensive list while you enjoy views of Lake Tahoe or the historic greens where Bing Crosby hosted his first golf tournament in 1934. **Known for:** classic American cooking; Lake Tahoe views; outdoor patio. $ *Average main: $24* ✉ *400 Brassie Ave., at Hwy. 267 & N. Lake Tahoe Blvd., Kings Beach* ☎ *530/546–2191* 🌐 *www.spindleshankstahoe.com.*

$ HOTEL FAMILY 🏨 **Ferrari's Crown Resort.** Great for families with kids, the family-owned and-operated Ferrari's has straightforward motel rooms in a resort setting. **Pros:** family-friendly; lakeside location; a few rooms value-priced. **Cons:** older facility; unappealing exterior; thin walls. $ *Rooms from: $115* ✉ *8200 N. Lake Blvd., Kings Beach* ☎ *530/546–3388, 800/645–2260* 🌐 *www.tahoecrown.com* 🛏 *72 rooms* 🍽 *Breakfast.*

$$$$ B&B/INN 🏨 **Mourelatos Lakeshore Resort.** At first glance this family-run waterfront property looks like a slightly above-average two-story motel, but with a private beach, two hot tubs, ceaselessly alluring lake and mountain vistas, and summertime barbecuing, kayaking, and other extras it legitimately lays claim to the title of resort. **Pros:** private beach; some rooms have full kitchens; summertime barbecuing and kayaking. **Cons:** decor a tad dated; books up quickly for summer; some rooms lack sufficient heat in winter. $ *Rooms from: $290* ✉ *6834 N. Lake Blvd., Tahoe Vista* ☎ *530/546–9500* 🌐 *www.mlrtahoe.com* 🛏 *32 rooms* 🍽 *Breakfast.*

$ HOTEL FAMILY 🏨 **Rustic Cottages.** These charming clapboard cottages sit clustered beneath tall pine trees across the road from Lake Tahoe and a little beach. **Pros:** woodsy Old Tahoe feel; expanded Continental breakfast; good value. **Cons:** older facility; some rooms are very small; lacks big-hotel amenities. $ *Rooms from: $109* ✉ *7449 N. Lake Blvd., Tahoe Vista* ☎ *530/546–3523, 888/778–7842* 🌐 *www.rusticcottages.com* 🛏 *20 rooms* 🍽 *Breakfast.*

THE NEVADA SIDE

The difference on the Nevada side of the lake from Crystal Bay south to Stateline, is, of course, gambling. Crystal Bay contains a few casinos whose glory has long faded, and Incline Village has a casino (at the Hyatt Lake Tahoe), but Stateline has the main gaming action. Top scenic stops along the shore include Sand Harbor, Zephyr Cove, and Nevada Beach.

INCLINE VILLAGE

3 miles east of Crystal Bay.

Incline Village dates to the early 1960s, when an Oklahoma developer bought 10,000 acres north of Lake Tahoe. His idea was to sketch out a plan for a town without a central commercial district, hoping to prevent congestion and to preserve the area's natural beauty. One-acre lakeshore lots originally fetched $12,000 to $15,000; today you couldn't buy the same land for less than several million.

GETTING HERE AND AROUND

From the California side, reach Incline Village via Highway 89 or 267 to Highway 28. From South Lake Tahoe, take U.S. 50 north to Highway 28 north. TART serves the communities along Lake Tahoe's north and west shores from Incline Village to Tahoma.

ESSENTIALS

Visitor Information Lake Tahoe Incline Village/Crystal Bay Visitors Bureau. ⊠ *969 Tahoe Blvd.* ☎ *775/832–1606, 800/468–2463* ⊕ *www.gotahoenorth.com.*

EXPLORING

Lakeshore Drive. Take this beautiful drive to see some of the most expensive real estate in Nevada. The route is discreetly marked: to find it, start at the Hyatt hotel and drive westward along the lake. ⊠ *Incline Village.*

Fodor'sChoice   **Thunderbird Lodge.** George Whittell, a San Francisco socialite who once
★   owned 40,000 acres of property along the lake, began building this lodge in 1936, completing it in 1941. You can tour the mansion and the grounds by reservation only, and though it's pricey to do so, you'll be rewarded with a rare glimpse of a time when only the very wealthy had homes at Tahoe. The lodge is accessible via a bus from the Incline Village Visitors Bureau, a catamaran from the Hyatt in Incline Village ($120), or a 1950 wooden cruiser from Tahoe Keys Marina in South Lake Tahoe, which includes Continental breakfast and lunch ($139). ⊠ *5000 Hwy. 28* ☎ *775/832–8752 lodge info, 800/468–2463 reservations, bus tour, 775/588–1881, 888/867–6394 Tahoe Keys boat, 775/831–4386 Hyatt Incline catamaran* ⊕ *www.thunderbirdtahoe.org/ tours* 🎫 *$39 bus tour, $120 and $139 for boat tours.*

BEACHES

Lake Tahoe–Nevada State Park and Sand Harbor Beach. Protecting much of the lake's eastern shore from development, this park comprises several sections that stretch from Incline Village to Zephyr Cove. Beaches and trails provide access to a wilder side of the lake, whether you're into cross-country skiing, hiking, or just relaxing at a picnic. With a gently sloping beach for lounging, crystal-clear water for swimming and snorkeling, and a picnic area shaded by cedars and pines, **Sand Harbor Beach** is so popular that it sometimes fills to capacity by 11 am on summer weekends. Boaters have two launch ramps. A handicap-accessible nature trail has interpretive signs and beautiful lake views. Pets are not allowed. **Amenities**: food and drink; parking ($12 mid-Apr.–mid-Oct., $7 rest of the year); toilets; water sports. **Best For**: snorkeling; sunset; swimming; walking. ✉ *Sand Harbor Beach, Hwy. 28, 3 miles south of Incline Village* ☎ *775/831–0494* 🌐 *parks.nv.gov/parks/sand-harbor*.

WHERE TO EAT AND STAY

$$$ ECLECTIC

🍴 **Fredrick's Fusion Bistro.** Copper-top tables lend a chic look to the dining room at this intimate bistro. The menu consists of a mélange of European and Asian dishes—braised short ribs, roasted duck with caramel-pecan glaze, fresh sushi rolls—most of them prepared with organic produce and free-range meats. **Known for:** chic and intimate; organic, free-range meat in most dishes; fireside tables. [$] *Average main: $24* ✉ *907 Tahoe Blvd., at Village Blvd.* ☎ *775/832–3007* 🌐 *fredricksbistro.com* ⏲ *Closed Sun. and Mon. No lunch.*

$$$$ FRENCH

🍴 **Le Bistro.** Incline Village's hidden gem changed owners in late 2016 but is still going strong, serving French-country cuisine in a relaxed, romantic dining room. The five-course prix-fixe menu ($65) may include dishes like pâté de campagne, escargots, herb-crusted roast lamb, and fresh fish, paired with award-winning wines if you choose. **Known for:** romantic dining room; five-course prix-fixe meal with wine pairings; gracious, attentive service. [$] *Average main: $65* ✉ *120 Country Club Dr., #29, off Lakeshore Blvd.* ☎ *775/831–0800* ⏲ *Closed Sun. and Mon. No lunch.*

$ AMERICAN Fodor's Choice ★

🍴 **Mountain High Sandwich Company.** An all-natural deli serving breakfast and lunch, Mountain High may well be the only place in Tahoe to find coconut chia seed pudding and similar delicacies. More familiar fare—biscuits and sausage gravy for breakfast, house-smoked tri-tip sandwiches for lunch—is also on the menu, with many selections gluten-free and vegan or vegetarian friendly. **Known for:** casual atmosphere; inventive soups; sustainable practices. [$] *Average main: $9* ✉ *120 Country Club Dr., Suite 28* ☎ *775/298–2636* 🌐 *www.mountainhighsandwichco.com.*

$ SOUTHERN

🍴 **T's Mesquite Rotisserie.** There's nothing fancy about T's (it looks like a small snack bar), but the mesquite-grilled chicken and tri-tip steaks are delicious and inexpensive—a rare combination in pricey Incline Village. It's mainly a take-out spot; seating is limited. **Known for:** chicken and tri-tip steaks; delicious and inexpensive; meals for take-out. [$] *Average main: $9* ✉ *901 Tahoe Blvd., at Village Blvd.* ☎ *775/831–2832* 💳 *No credit cards.*

$$$$ RESORT

🏨 **Hyatt Regency Lake Tahoe.** A full-service destination resort on 26 acres of prime lakefront property, the Hyatt has a range of luxurious accommodations, from tower-hotel rooms to lakeside cottages. **Pros:** incredible views; low-key casino; luxurious accommodations. **Cons:** pricey (especially for families); feels corporate; smallish beach. [$] *Rooms from: $379* ✉ *111 Country Club Dr.* ☎ *775/832–1234, 888/899–5019* 🌐 *www.laketahoe.hyatt.com* 🛏 *422 rooms* 🍽 *No meals.*

Get to Sand Harbor Beach in Lake Tahoe–Nevada State Park early; the park sometimes fills to capacity before lunchtime in summer.

SPORTS AND THE OUTDOORS
GOLF

Incline Championship. Robert Trent Jones Sr. designed this challenging course of tightly cut, tree-lined fairways laced with water hazards that demand accuracy as well as distance skills. Greens fee includes a cart, except for the 4:30 pm Super Twilight rate of $3 per hole (cart $25). ⊠ *955 Fairway Blvd., at Northwood Blvd., north off Hwy. 28* ☎ *866/925–4653 reservations, 775/832–1146 pro shop* ⊕ *www.your-tahoeplace.com/golf-incline* ⊴ *$170 weekdays, $190 weekends* ⅄ *18 holes, 7106 yards, par 72.*

Incline Mountain. Robert Trent Jones, Jr. designed this executive (shorter) course that requires accuracy more than distance skills. The greens fee includes a cart. ⊠ *690 Wilson Way, at Golfer's Pass, south off Hwy. 431* ☎ *866/925–4653 reservations, 775/832–1150 pro shop* ⊕ *www.yourta-hoeplace.com/golf-incline* ⊴ *$65–$70* ⅄ *18 holes, 3527 yards, par 58.*

MOUNTAIN BIKING

Flume Trail Bikes. You can rent bikes and get helpful tips from this company, which also operates a bike shuttle to popular trailheads. ⊠ *1115 Tunnel Creek Rd., at Ponderosa Ranch Rd., off Hwy. 28* ☎ *775/298–2501* ⊕ *www.flumetrailtahoe.com* ⊴ *From $39.*

SKIING

Diamond Peak. A fun family mood prevails at Diamond Peak, which has affordable rates and many special programs. Snowmaking covers 75% of the mountain, and runs are groomed nightly. The ride up the 1-mile Crystal Express rewards you with fantastic views. Diamond Peak is less crowded than Tahoe's larger ski parks and provides free shuttles to nearby lodgings. A great place for beginners and interme-diates, it's appropriately priced for families. Though there are some steep-aspect black-diamond runs, advanced skiers may find the acre-age too limited. For snowboarders there's a small terrain park. **Facili-ties:** 30 trails; 655 acres; 1,840-foot vertical drop; 7 lifts. ⊠ *1210 Ski Way, off Country Club Dr.* ☎ *775/832–1177* ⊕ *www.diamondpeak. com* ⊠ *Lift ticket $79.*

Mt. Rose Ski Tahoe. At this park, ski some of Tahoe's highest slopes and take in bird's-eye views of Reno, the lake, and Carson Valley. Though more compact than the bigger Tahoe resorts, Mt. Rose has the area's highest base elevation and consequently the driest snow. The mountain has a wide variety of terrain. The most challenging is the Chutes, 200 acres of gulp-and-go advanced-to-expert vertical. Intermediates can choose steep groomers or mellow, wide-open boulevards. Beginners have their own corner of the mountain, with gentle, wide slopes. Boarders and tricksters have three terrain parks to choose from, on opposite sides of the mountain, allowing them to follow the sun as it tracks across the resort. The mountain gets hit hard in storms; check conditions before heading up during inclement weather or on a windy day. **Facilities:** 61 trails; 1,200 acres; 1,800-foot vertical drop; 8 lifts. ⊠ *22222 Mt. Rose Hwy., Hwy. 431, 11 miles north of Incline Village, Reno* ☎ *775/849–0704, 800/754–7673* ⊕ *www.skirose.com* ⊠ *Lift ticket $109.*

Tahoe Meadows Snowplay Area. This is the most popular area near the north shore for noncommercial cross-country skiing, sledding, tubing, snowshoeing, and snowmobiling. ⊠ *Off Hwy. 431, between Incline Village and Mt. Rose.*

ZEPHYR COVE

22 miles south of Incline Village.

The largest settlement between Incline Village and the Stateline area is Zephyr Cove, a tiny resort. It has a beach, marina, campground, picnic area, coffee shop in a log lodge, rustic cabins, and nearby riding stables.

GETTING HERE AND AROUND

From the north shore communities, reach Zephyr Cove by following Highway 28 along the eastern side of the lake. From South Lake Tahoe, take U.S. 50 north and then west. Public transportation isn't available in Zephyr Cove.

EXPLORING

Cave Rock. Near Zephyr Cove, this 75 feet of solid stone at the southern end of Lake Tahoe–Nevada State Park is the throat of an extinct vol-cano. The impressive outcropping towers over a parking lot, a lakefront picnic ground, and a boat launch. The views are some of the best on the lake; this is a good spot to stop and take a picture. However, this area is a sacred burial site for the Washoe Indians, and climbing up to the cave, or through it, is prohibited. ⊠ *U.S. 50, 4 miles north of Zephyr Cove* ☎ *775/831–0494* ⊕ *www.parks.nv.gov/parks/lake-tahoe-nevada-state-park-2* ⊠ *$10 mid-Apr.–mid-Oct.; $7 rest of yr.*

WHERE TO EAT AND STAY

$$$ ITALIAN 🍴 **Capisce?** The signature mushroom and tomato sauce is so thick it's called "gravy" at this handsome roadside restaurant whose menu emphasizes old favorites from the Italian-American side of the family that runs it. The mildly spicy concoction adds zest to cioppino—seafood stew, here served on risottolike white-wine rice—and to house-made raviolis that many diners order half slathered with it and the other half with a velvety butter and Parmesan cheese sauce. **Known for:** handsome high-ceilinged dining room; old family recipes; full bar patronized by many locals. [$] *Average main: $26* ✉ *178 U.S. 50* ☎ *775/ 580–7500* 🌐 *www.capiscelaketahoe.com* 🕒 *Closed Mon. No lunch.*

$$$ RENTAL FAMILY 🏨 **Zephyr Cove Resort.** Beneath towering pines at the lake's edge stand 28 cozy, modern vacation cabins with peaked knotty-pine ceilings. **Pros:** family-friendly; cozy cabins; old-school ambience. **Cons:** lodge rooms are basic; can be noisy in summer; not all cabins have fireplaces. [$] *Rooms from: $200* ✉ *760 U.S. 50, 4 miles north of Stateline* ☎ *775/589–4906, 800/238–2463* 🌐 *www.zephyrcove.com* 🛏 *32 rooms* 🍽 *No meals.*

STATELINE

5 miles south of Zephyr Cove.

Stateline is the archetypal Nevada border town. Its four high-rise casinos are as vertical and contained as the commercial district of South Lake Tahoe, on the California side, is horizontal and sprawling. And Stateline is as relentlessly indoors-oriented as the rest of the lake is focused on the outdoors. This small strip is where you'll find the most concentrated action at Lake Tahoe: restaurants (including typical casino buffets), showrooms with semi-famous headliners and razzle-dazzle revues, tower-hotel rooms and suites, and 24-hour casinos.

GETTING HERE AND AROUND

From South Lake Tahoe take U.S. 50 north across the Nevada border to reach Stateline and its casinos. If coming from Reno's airport, take U.S. 395/Interstate 580 south to Carson City, and then head west on U.S. 50 to the lake and head south. Or take the South Tahoe Express bus. BlueGO operates daily bus service.

BEACHES

Nevada Beach. Although less than a mile long, this is the widest beach on the lake and especially good for swimming (many Tahoe beaches are rocky). You can boat and fish here, and there are picnic tables, barbecue grills, and a campground beneath the pines. This is the best place to watch the July 4th or Labor Day fireworks, but most of the summer the subdued atmosphere attracts families and those seeking a less-touristy spot. **Amenities:** parking ($8 fee), water sports, toilets. **Best For:** sunrise, swimming, walking. ✉ *Elk Point Rd., off U.S. 50, 3 miles north of Stateline* ☎ *530/543–2600, 877/444–6777 camping reservations* 🌐 *www.fs.usda.gov/detail/ltbmu/recreation/?cid=stelprdb5134175* ☞ *Dogs permitted on leash in picnic areas but not on beach.*

22

WHERE TO EAT AND STAY

$$
AMERICAN
Fodor'sChoice
★

╳ **Brooks Bar & Deck.** Stateline's best spot for lunch or a casual dinner serves up clever takes on comfort cuisine—tacos, burgers, daily changing grilled-cheese panini, and a crispy-chicken sandwich with Sriracha aioli. Although this is the Edgewood Tahoe resort's golf-course restaurant, you needn't have finished 18 holes to enjoy the food and lake, forest, and golf course views from the high-ceilinged restaurant or stone-floored outdoor deck. **Known for:** casual comfort food; outdoor deck; eclectic clientele. $ *Average main: $19* ✉ *Edgewood Tahoe, 100 Lake Pkwy.* ☎ *775/588–6183* ⊕ *www.edgewoodtahoe.com.*

$
HOTEL

🖥 **Harrah's Tahoe Hotel/Casino.** The hotel's major selling point is that every room has two full bathrooms, a boon if you're traveling with family. **Pros:** central location; great midweek values; two full bathrooms in every room. **Cons:** can get noisy; uneven housekeeping; lacks intimacy. $ *Rooms from: $109* ✉ *15 U.S. 50, at Stateline Ave.* ☎ *775/588–6611, 800/427–7247* ⊕ *www.caesars.com/harrahs-tahoe* ⤴ *512 rooms* ⦿ *No meals.*

$
HOTEL

🖥 **Harveys Resort Hotel/Casino.** This resort began as a cabin in 1944, and now it's Tahoe's largest casino-hotel; premium rooms have custom furnishings, oversize marble baths, minibars, and good lake views. **Pros:** hip entertainment; just a few blocks north of the Heavenly Gondola; good lake views. **Cons:** can get loud at night; high summer rates; large property. $ *Rooms from: $119* ✉ *18 U.S. 50, at Stateline Ave.* ☎ *775/588–2411, 800/648–3361* ⊕ *www.caesars.com/harveys-tahoe* ⤴ *742 rooms* ⦿ *No meals.*

$
HOTEL

🖥 **Lakeside Inn and Casino.** The smallest of the Stateline casinos, the property has good promotional room rates and simple, attractive accommodations in two-story motel-style buildings separate from the casino. **Pros:** daily dining specials; casino separate from accommodations; no resort or parking fee. **Cons:** some rooms are on the small side; some rooms are dark; motel-style buildings. $ *Rooms from: $109* ✉ *168 U.S. 50, at Kingsbury Grade* ☎ *775/588–7777, 800/624–7980* ⊕ *lakesideinn.com* ⤴ *124 rooms* ⦿ *No meals.*

$$$$
RESORT
Fodor'sChoice
★

🖥 **The Lodge at Edgewood Tahoe.** The lodge, which debuted in mid-2017 on a prime lakefront parcel, makes a bold impression with its stone and walnut Great Hall, whose four-story wall of windows frames views across Lake Tahoe to grand Mt. Tallac. **Pros:** prime lakefront location; haute-rustic design; all rooms have balconies and fireplaces. **Cons:** high rates in-season; some rooms have no lake views; long walk to pool and hot tub from some rooms. $ *Rooms from: $300* ✉ *100 Lake Pkwy.* ☎ *775/588–2787, 888/881–8659* ⊕ *www.edgewoodtahoe.com/lodge* ⤴ *154 rooms.*

NIGHTLIFE

Each of the major casinos has its own showroom, featuring everything from comedy to magic acts to sexy floor shows to Broadway musicals.

LIVE MUSIC

Harveys Outdoor Summer Concert Series. Harveys Lake Tahoe books outdoor concerts on weekends in summer with headliners such as The Who, Paul Simon, and Lenny Kravitz. ✉ *18 U.S. 50* ☎ *775/588–2411* ⊕ *www.caesars.com/harveys-tahoe/shows.html.*

South Shore Room. Classic acts like Robin Trower and the Yardbirds play Harrah's big showroom, along with comedians like Louie Anderson and the psychedelic Pink Floyd Laser Spectacular show. ✉ *Harrah's Lake Tahoe, 15 U.S. 50* ☎ *775/586–6244 tickets, 775/588–6611* ⊕ *www.caesars.com/harrahs-tahoe/shows.html.*

SPORTS AND THE OUTDOORS

GOLF

Edgewood Tahoe. Golfers of all skill levels enjoy this scenic lakeside course that has four sets of tees, offering a variety of course lengths. The greens fee includes an optional cart. ✉ *100 Lake Pkwy., at U.S. 50* ☎ *775/588–3566, 866/761–4653* ⊕ *www.edgewood-tahoe.com* ✉ *$140–$260 (varies throughout season)* 🏌 *18 holes, 7529 yards, par 72.*

RENO

32 miles east of Truckee, 38 miles northeast of Incline Village.

Established in 1859 as a trading station at a bridge over the Truckee River, Reno grew along with the silver mines of nearby Virginia City and the transcontinental railroad that chugged through town. Train officials named it in 1868, but gambling—legalized in 1931—put Reno on the map. This is still a gambling town, with most of the casinos crowded into five square blocks downtown, but a thriving university scene and outdoor activities also attract tourists.

Parts of downtown are sketchy, but things are changing. Reno now touts family-friendly activities like kayaking on the Truckee, museums, and a downtown climbing wall. With over 300 days of sunshine annually, temperatures year-round in this high-mountain-desert climate are warmer than at Tahoe, though rarely as hot as in Sacramento and the Central Valley, making strolling around town a pleasure.

GETTING HERE AND AROUND

Interstate 80 bisects Reno east–west, U.S. 395 north–south (south of town the road is signed U.S. 395/Interstate 580). Greyhound and Amtrak stop here, and several airlines fly into Reno-Tahoe International Airport. RTC Ride provides bus service.

ESSENTIALS

Bus Contact RTC Ride. ✉ *Transit Center, E. 4th and Lake Sts.* ☎ *775/348–7433* ⊕ *www.rtcwashoe.com.*

Visitor Information Reno Tahoe USA Visitor Center. ✉ *11 N. Sierra St.* ☎ *775/827–7650, 800/367–7366* ⊕ *www.visitrenotahoe.com.*

EXPLORING

TOP ATTRACTIONS

FAMILY
Fodor'sChoice
★

National Automobile Museum. Antique and classic automobiles, including an Elvis Presley Cadillac, a Mercury coupe driven by James Dean in the movie *Rebel Without a Cause,* and the experimental and still futuristic-looking 1938 Phantom Corsair, are all on display at this museum. ✉ *10 S. Lake St., at Mill St.* ☎ *775/333–9300* ⊕ *www.automuseum.org* ✉ *$12.*

22

Riverwalk District. The makeover of Reno's waterfront has transformed this formerly dilapidated area into the toast of the town. The Riverwalk itself is a half-mile promenade on the north side of the Truckee River, which flows around lovely Wingfield Park, where outdoor festivals and other events take place. On the third Saturday of each month, local merchants host a **Wine Walk** between 2 and 5. For $20 you receive a wine glass and can sample fine wines at participating shops, bars, restaurants, and galleries. In July, look for stellar outdoor art, opera, dance, and kids' performances as part of the monthlong **Artown festival** (*renoisartown.com*), presented mostly in Wingfield Park. Also at Wingfield is the **Truckee River Whitewater Park.** With activities for all skill levels, it's become a major attraction for water-sports enthusiasts. ✉ *Riverwalk, north side of Truckee River between Lake and Ralston Sts.* ⊕ *www.renoriver.org.*

WORTH NOTING

Nevada Museum of Art. A dramatic four-level structure designed by Will Bruder houses this splendid museum's collection, which focuses on themes such as the Sierra Nevada/Great Basin and altered-landscape photography. The building's exterior torqued walls are sided with a black zinc-based material that has been fabricated to resemble textures found in the Black Rock Desert. Inside the building, a staircase installed within the central atrium is lit by skylights and suspended by a single beam attached to the atrium ceiling. ✉ *160 W. Liberty St., and Hill St.* ☎ *775/329–3333* ⊕ *www.nevadaart.org* 🎟 *$10* ⊗ *Closed Mon. and Tues.*

WHERE TO EAT

$$$
FRENCH
Fodor'sChoice
★

✗ **Beaujolais Bistro.** Across from the Truckee River, this Reno favorite serves earthy, country-style French food with zero pretension. Expect classics like escargots, steak frites with red wine sauce, cassoulet, and crisp sweetbreads with madeira, along with fish and vegetarian selections. **Known for:** country-style French; intimate atmosphere. $ *Average main: $29* ✉ *753 Riverside Dr., near Winter St.* ☎ *775/323–2227* ⊕ *www.beaujolaisbistro.com* ⊗ *No lunch. Closed Mon.*

$$$
AMERICAN
Fodor'sChoice
★

✗ **4th St. Bistro.** For deliciously simple, smart cooking, head to this charming little bistro on the edge of town. The chef-owner uses organic produce and meats in her soulful preparation of dishes like grilled cobia wrapped in Serrano ham or Moroccan spiced organic chicken breast with braised rainbow chard and couscous. **Known for:** soulful preparation; organic produce and meats; fireplace in winter, deck dining in summer. $ *Average main: $30* ✉ *3065 W. 4th St.* ☎ *775/323–3200* ⊕ *www.4thstbistro.com* ⊗ *Closed Sun. and Mon. No lunch.*

WHERE TO STAY

$
HOTEL

🏨 **Eldorado Hotel Casino.** In the middle of glittering downtown, this resort's huge tower has rooms overlooking either the mountains or the lights of the city. **Pros:** fun; good food; amusingly kitschy decor. **Cons:** noisy. $ *Rooms from: $60* ✉ *345 N. Virginia St.* ☎ *775/786–5700, 800/879–8879* ⊕ *www.eldoradoreno.com* 🛏 *679 rooms, 137 suites* ⊗ *No meals.*

$ HOTEL **Harrah's Reno.** Of the big-name casino hotels in downtown Reno, double-towered Harrah's remains a reliable choice with its large guest rooms, decorated in browns and pale gold tones, overlooking downtown and the entire mountain-ringed valley. **Pros:** good location; great online midweek rates; large guest rooms. **Cons:** large property; impersonal service; some housekeeping lapses. [$] *Rooms from: $70* ✉ *219 N. Center St., at E. 2nd St.* ☎ *775/786–3232, 800/427–7247* 🌐 *www.harrahsreno.com* 🛏 *928 rooms* 🍴 *No meals.*

$ HOTEL **Peppermill Reno.** A few miles removed from downtown's flashy main drag, this property set a high standard for luxury in Reno, especially in the Tuscan Tower, whose 600 baroque suites have plush king-size beds, marble bathrooms, and European soaking tubs. **Pros:** luxurious rooms; casino decor; good coffee shop. **Cons:** deluge of neon may be off-putting to some; enormous size; mostly expensive dining. [$] *Rooms from: $109* ✉ *2707 S. Virginia St., at Peppermill La.* ☎ *775/826–2121, 866/821–9996* 🌐 *www.peppermillreno.com* 🛏 *1,623 rooms* 🍴 *No meals.*

NIGHTLIFE

CASINOS

Eldorado. Action packed, with lots of slots and popular bar-top video poker, this casino also has good coffee-shop and food-court fare. Don't miss the Fountain of Fortune with its massive Florentine-inspired sculptures. ✉ *345 N. Virginia St., at W. 4th St.* ☎ *775/786–5700, 800/879–8879* 🌐 *www.eldoradoreno.com.*

Peppermill. A few miles from downtown, this casino is known for its excellent restaurants and neon-bright gambling areas. The Fireside cocktail lounge is a blast. ✉ *2707 S. Virginia St., at Peppermill La.* ☎ *775/826–2121, 866/821–9996* 🌐 *www.peppermillreno.com.*

Silver Legacy. A 120-foot-tall mining rig and video poker games draw gamblers to this razzle-dazzle casino. ✉ *407 N. Virginia St., at W. 4th St.* ☎ *775/325–7411, 800/215–7721* 🌐 *www.silverlegacyreno.com.*

THE FAR NORTH

with Lake Shasta, Mt. Shasta, and
Lassen Volcanic National Park

WELCOME TO THE FAR NORTH

TOP REASONS TO GO

★ **Mother Nature's wonders:** California's Far North has more rivers, streams, lakes, forests, and mountains than you'll ever have time to explore.

★ **Rock and roll:** With two volcanoes to entice you—Lassen and Shasta—you can learn firsthand what happens when a mountain blows its top.

★ **Fantastic fishing:** Whether you like casting from a riverbank or letting your line bob beside a boat, you'll find fabulous fishing in all the northern counties.

★ **Cool hops:** On a hot day there's nothing quite as inviting as a visit to Chico's world-famous Sierra Nevada Brewery. Take the tour, and then savor a chilled glass on tap at the adjacent brewpub.

★ **Shasta:** Wonderful in all its forms: lake, dam, river, mountain, forest, and town.

1 From Chico to Mt. Shasta. The Far North is bisected, south to north, by Interstate 5, which passes through several historic towns and state parks, as well as miles of mountainous terrain. Halfway to the Oregon border is Lake Shasta, a favorite recreation destination, and farther north stands the spectacular snowy peak of Mt. Shasta.

2 The Backcountry. East of Interstate 5, the Far North's main corridor, dozens of scenic two-lane roads crisscross the wilderness, leading to dramatic mountain peaks and fascinating natural wonders. Small towns settled in the second half of the 19th century seem frozen in time, except that they are well equipped with tourist amenities.

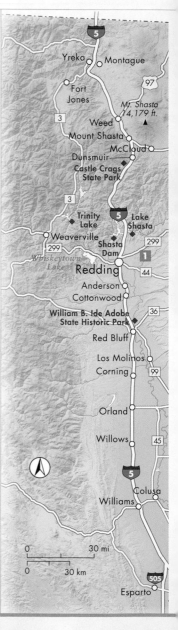

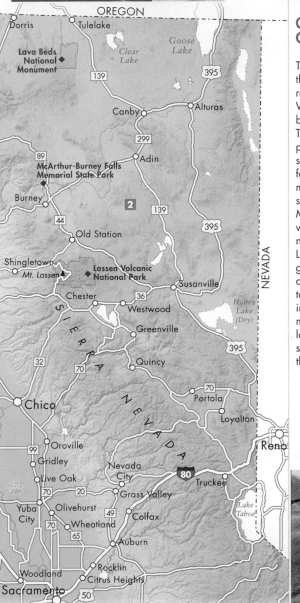

GETTING ORIENTED

23

The Far North is a vast area that stretches from the upper reaches of the Sacramento Valley north to the Oregon border and east to Nevada. The region includes all or part of eight counties with sparsely populated rural farming and mountain communities, as well as thriving small cities in the valley. Much of the landscape was shaped by two volcanoes—Mt. Shasta and Mt. Lassen—that draw amateur geologists, weekend hikers, and avid mountain climbers to their rugged terrain. An intricate network of high-mountain watersheds feeds lakes large and small, plus streams and rivers that course through several forests.

Updated by
Daniel Mangin

The Far North's soaring mountain peaks, trail-filled national forests, alpine lakes, and wild rivers teeming with trout make it the perfect destination for outdoor enthusiasts, including hikers, cyclists, kayakers, and bird-watchers. You won't find many hot nightspots or cultural enclaves in this region, but you will find crowd-free national and state parks, crystal-clear mountain streams, superlative hiking and fishing, plus small towns worth exploring. And the spectacular landscapes of Lassen Volcanic National Park and Mt. Shasta are sure to impress.

The wondrous landscape of California's northeastern corner is the product of volcanic activity. At the southern end of the Cascade Range, Lassen Volcanic National Park is the best place to witness the Far North's fascinating geology. Beyond the sulfur vents and bubbling mud pots, the park owes much of its beauty to 10,457-foot Mt. Lassen and 50 wilderness lakes.

The most enduring image of the region, though, is Mt. Shasta, whose 14,179-foot snowcapped peak beckons outdoor adventurers of all kinds. There are many versions of Shasta to enjoy—the mountain, the lake, the river, the town, the dam, and the forest—all named after the Native Americans known as the Shatasla, or Sastise, who once inhabited the region.

PLANNING

WHEN TO GO

Heat scorches the valley in summer. Temperatures above 110°F are common, but the mountains provide cool respite. Fall throughout the Far North is beautiful, rivaled only by spring, when wildflowers bloom and mountain creeks fed by the snowmelt splash through the forests. Winter is usually temperate in the valley, but cold and snowy in high country. Some tourist attractions are closed in winter.

GETTING HERE AND AROUND

AIR TRAVEL

For the cheapest fares, fly into Sacramento and then rent a car—you'll need one anyway—and drive north. Redding, which is served by PenAir and United, has a small airport. There's no shuttle service, but you can take a taxi for about $32 to downtown Redding.

Air Contacts Redding Municipal Airport. ⊠ *6751 Woodrum Circle, off Airport Rd., Redding* ☎ *530/224-4320* ⊕ *www.cityofredding.org/departments/airports.*

Ground Transportation Anytime Taxi. ☎ *530/828-7962 for Chico transfers.* **Road Runner Taxi.** ☎ *530/241-7433 for Redding transfers* ⊕ *www.roadrunnertaxicab.com.*

BUS TRAVEL

Greyhound buses stop in Chico, Red Bluff, Redding, and Weed. TRAX buses serve Corning and Red Bluff. STAGE buses serve Dunsmuir and Mt. Shasta. Various other transit authorities provide local public transit *(see individual town listings for details).*

Bus Contacts Greyhound. ☎ *800/231-2222* ⊕ *www.greyhound.com.* **STAGE.** ☎ *530/842-8295* ⊕ *www.co.siskiyou.ca.us/content/transportation-division-stage.* **TRAX.** ☎ *530/385-2877* ⊕ *www.taketrax.com.*

CAR TRAVEL

Interstate 5 runs up the center of California through Red Bluff and Redding. Chico is east of Interstate 5 on Highway 32. Lassen Volcanic National Park can be reached by Highway 36 from Red Bluff or (except in winter) Highway 44 from Redding. Highway 299 connects Weaverville and Redding. Check weather reports and carry detailed maps, warm clothing, and tire chains whenever you head into mountainous terrain in winter.

Road Conditions Caltrans. ☎ *800/427-7623* ⊕ *www.dot.ca.gov.*

TRAIN TRAVEL

Amtrak serves Chico, Redding, and Dunsmuir.

Train Contact Amtrak. ☎ *800/872-7245* ⊕ *www.amtrak.com.*

RESTAURANTS

Redding, the urban center of the Far North, and college-town Chico have the greatest selection of restaurants. Cafés and simple eateries are the rule in the smaller towns. Dress is always informal. *Restaurant reviews have been shortened. For full information, visit Fodors.com.*

HOTELS

Chain hotels and motels predominate in this region, with the occasional small rustic or Victorian inn. Wilderness resorts close in fall and reopen after the snow season ends in May. For summer holiday weekends in towns such as Mt. Shasta, Dunsmuir, and Chester, and at camping sites within state or national parks, make lodging reservations well in advance. *Hotel reviews have been shortened. For full information, visit Fodors.com.*

B&B Info California Association of Boutique & Breakfast Inns. ☎ *800/373-9251* ⊕ *www.cabbi.com/region/Mount-Shasta.*

WHAT IT COSTS				
	$	$$	$$$	$$$$
Restaurants	under $16	$16–$22	$23–$30	over $30
Hotels	under $120	$120–$175	$176–$250	over $250

Restaurant prices are the average cost of a main course at dinner or, if dinner is not served, at lunch. Hotel prices are the lowest cost of a standard double room in high season.

VISITOR INFORMATION

Contacts **Shasta Cascade Wonderland Association.** ⊠ *Shasta Outlets, 1699 Hwy. 273, off I-5, Exit 667, Anderson* ☎ *530/365-7500, 800/474-2782* ⊕ *www. shastacascade.com.* **Trinity County Chamber of Commerce.** ⊠ *509 Main St., Weaverville* ☎ *530/623-6101* ⊕ *www.trinitycounty.com.* **Visit Siskiyou.** ☎ *530/926-3696 Mt. Shasta Chamber of Commerce* ⊕ *visitsiskiyou.org.*

FROM CHICO TO MT. SHASTA

From blooming almond orchards in the fertile Sacramento River valley to forested mountains and the dominating peak of a dormant volcano, this section of the Far North entices tourists in all seasons.

CHICO

86 miles north of Sacramento.

The Sacramento Valley town of Chico (Spanish for "small") offers a welcome break from the monotony of Interstate 5. The Chico campus of California State University, the scores of local artisans, and the area's agriculture (primarily almond orchards) all influence the culture here. Chico's claim to fame, however, is the Sierra Nevada Brewery, which keeps beer drinkers across the country happy with its distinctive brews.

GETTING HERE AND AROUND

Highway 99, off Interstate 5 from the north or south, and Highway 32 east off the interstate, intersect Chico. Amtrak and Greyhound stop here, and Butte Regional Transit's B-Line buses serve the area. Chico's downtown neighborhoods are great for walking.

ESSENTIALS

Bus Contact **B-Line.** ☎ *530/342-0221* ⊕ *www.blinetransit.com.*

Visitor Information **Chico Chamber of Commerce.** ⊠ *441 Main St., Suite 150, near E. 5th St.* ☎ *530/891-5556, 800/852-8570* ⊕ *www.chicochamber.com.*

TOURS

Sacramento River Eco Tours. Wildlife biologist Henry Lomeli guides boat tours down the Sacramento River to explore its diverse fish, fowl, and plant life. ⊠ *Chico* ☎ *530/864-8594* ⊕ *www.sacramentoriverecotours. com* ✉ *From $85.*

EXPLORING

Bidwell Mansion State Historic Park. Built between 1865 and 1868 by General John Bidwell, the founder of Chico, this mansion was designed by Henry W. Cleaveland, a San Francisco architect. Bidwell and his wife welcomed many distinguished guests to their pink Italianate home, including President Rutherford B. Hayes, naturalist John Muir, suffragist Susan B. Anthony, and General William T. Sherman. A one-hour tour takes you through most of the mansion's 26 rooms. ✉ *525 The Esplanade, at Memorial Way* ☎ *530/895–6144* 🌐 *www.parks.ca.gov/parkindex* 🎟 *$6* 🕒 *Closed Tues.–Fri.*

Bidwell Park. The sprawling 3,670-acre Bidwell Park is a community green space straddling Big Chico Creek, where scenes from *Gone With the Wind* and the 1938 version of *Robin Hood* (starring Errol Flynn) were filmed. The region's recreational hub, it includes a golf course, swimming areas, and biking, hiking, horseback riding, and in-line skating trails. Chico Creek Nature Center serves as the official information site for Bidwell Park. ✉ *1968 E. 8th St., off Hwy. 99* ☎ *530/891–4671* 🌐 *www.bidwellpark.org* 🎟 *Park free, nature center $4* 🕒 *Nature center closed Sun.–Tues.*

Fodor's Choice ★ **Sierra Nevada Brewing Company.** This pioneer of the microbrewery movement still has a hands-on approach to beer making. Tour the brew house and see how the beer is produced—from the sorting of hops through fermentation and bottling, and concluding with a complimentary tasting. You can also enjoy lunch or dinner in the taproom. **■ TIP→ Tours fill up fast; call or sign up online before you visit.** ✉ *1075 E. 20th St., at Sierra Nevada St.* ☎ *530/345–2739 taproom, 530/899–4776 tours* 🌐 *www.sierranevada.com* 🎟 *Free.*

WHERE TO EAT AND STAY

$$$ STEAKHOUSE Fodor's Choice ★ 🍴 **5th Street Steakhouse.** Hand-cut steak is the star in this refurbished early 1900s building, the place to come when you're craving red meat, a huge baked potato, or some fresh seafood. Exposed redbrick walls warm the dining rooms, and a long mahogany bar catches the overflow crowds that jam the place on weekends. **Known for:** weekday happy hour 4:30–6; weekend crowds; prime cuts of beef with white tablecloth service. [$] *Average main: $30* ✉ *345 W. 5th St., at Normal Ave.* ☎ *530/891–6328* 🌐 *www.5thstreetsteakhouse.com* 🕒 *No lunch Sat.–Thurs.*

$ AMERICAN 🍴 **Madison Bear Garden.** This downtown favorite inside a historic structure lies two blocks south of the Chico State campus. It's a great spot for checking out the college scene while enjoying a burger and a brew. **Known for:** beer selection; curly fries; lengthy weekday happy hours. [$] *Average main: $8* ✉ *316 W. 2nd St., at Salem St.* ☎ *530/891–1639* 🌐 *www.madisonbeargarden.com.*

$$ HOTEL 🏨 **Hotel Diamond.** Crystal chandeliers and gleaming century-old wood floors and banisters welcome guests into the foyer of this restored 1904 gem near Chico State University. **Pros:** great downtown location; refined rooms, some with bay windows and fireplaces; one of the town's best restaurants. **Cons:** street scene can be noisy on weekends; some rooms are small; some rooms lack tubs. [$] *Rooms from: $132* ✉ *220 W. 4th St., near Broadway* ☎ *530/893–3100, 866/993–3100* 🌐 *www.hoteldiamondchico.com* 🛏 *43 rooms* 🍽 *Breakfast.*

CORNING

29 miles northwest of Chico, 50 miles south of Redding.

Signs along Highway 99 and Interstate 5 beckon travelers to Corning, whose favorable soil and plentiful sunshine have made the town a center of olive cultivation and olive oil manufacturing. At several tasting rooms you can sample olives, olive oil, and other products.

GETTING HERE AND AROUND

Corning lies just off Interstate 5 at Exit 631. From Chico take Highway 99 for 17½ miles and follow signs west to Corning. TRAX provides weekday bus service from Red Bluff.

EXPLORING

Fodor's Choice
★

Lucero Olive Oil. As a brand Lucero dates back to the mid-2000s, but the family that started the company began farming olives in the Corning area in 1947. Lucero's Extra Virgin olive oils have won countless awards in California and abroad. In the tasting room adjacent to the mill you can taste oils like Ascalona and Koroneiki and ones infused with lemon, chili, and other flavors, sometimes paired with excellent balsamic vinegars. ⊠ *2120 Loleta Ave., off Hwy. 99 W, 1 mile south of Solano St.* ☎ *530/824–2190* ⊕ *www.lucerooliveoil.com* ☜ *Free.*

FAMILY

Olive Pit. Three generations of the Craig family run this combination café, store, and tasting room where you can learn all about California olive production and sample olive products, craft beers and small-lot wines, and other artisanal foods. Sandwich selections at the café include muffulettas (of course) and olive burgers. Wash your choice down with a balsamic shake in flavors that include peach, coconut, strawberry, and French prune. ■TIP→ The Olive Pit opens at 7 am and closes at 8 pm. ⊠ *2156 Solano St., off I–5, Exit 631 (Corning Rd.)* ☎ *530/824–4667, 800/654–8374* ⊕ *www.olivepit.com* ☜ *Tastings free for olive oil, $5 for beer and wine.*

RED BLUFF

41 miles north of Chico.

Red Bluff is a gateway to Lassen Volcanic National Park. Established in the mid-19th century as a shipping center on the Sacramento River, and named for the color of its soil, the town, filled with dozens of restored Victorians, makes a good base for outdoor adventures in the area. The Tehama Country Visitor Center has information about wine tasting and other activities.

GETTING HERE AND AROUND

Access Red Bluff via exits off Interstate 5, or by driving north on Highway 99. Highway 36 travels east–west through town; east of the freeway it's called Antelope Boulevard, west of it Oak Street. Greyhound buses stop in Red Bluff and provide connecting service to Amtrak. TRAX (Tehama Rural Area Express) provides bus service on weekdays.

ESSENTIALS

Visitor Information Tehama Country Visitor Center. ⊠ *250 Antelope Blvd., ¼-mile east of I–5* ☎ *530/529–0133* ⊕ *www.visittehamacountry.com.*

EXPLORING

Fodor's Choice ★ **Gaumer's Jewelry.** The Gaumer family has been making and selling jewelry in Red Bluff since the 1960s, and has been collecting rocks, gems, and minerals for even longer. When the jewelry shop is open, you can tour its fascinating museum, whose displays include crystals, gemstone carvings, fossils, and fluorescent minerals. ✉ *78 Belle Mill Rd.* ✥ *From I–5, Exit 649, head west on Hwy. 36 (Antelope Blvd.); make a right on Center Ave. and immediately make another right onto Belle Mill* ☎ *530/527–6166* 🌐 *www.gaumers.com* 🎫 *Free* ⏲ *Closed weekends.*

> **RED BLUFF ROUND-UP**
>
> Check out old-time rodeo at its best during the Red Bluff Round-Up. Held the third weekend of April, this annual event attracts some of the best cowboys in the country. For more information, visit 🌐 *redbluffroundup.com.*

Tuscan Ridge Estate Winery. Depending on the day, this crowd-pleasing winery with a vineyard-view tasting room serves pizzas or antipasti to accompany some of the nearly two dozen reds and whites made here. Most of the grapes for them come from the Sierra foothills; the Zinfandel and Syrah in particular are worth seeking out. ■ **TIP→ The winery opens in the late afternoon on Thursday and Friday.** ✉ *19260 Ridge Rd.* ☎ *530/527–7393* 🌐 *www.tuscanridgeestate.com* 🎫 *Tasting $10* ⏲ *Closed Mon.–Wed.*

WHERE TO EAT AND STAY

$$ STEAKHOUSE 🍴 **Green Barn Steakhouse.** You're likely to find cowboys sporting Stetsons and spurs feasting on beef medallions, baby back ribs, and prime rib at "the Barn," Red Bluff's premier steak house. For lighter fare, try the fish or pasta entrées, but whatever you choose don't miss the bread pudding with rum sauce for dessert. **Known for:** top-quality beef; old-style Western steakhouse decor; bread pudding with rum sauce. [$] *Average main: $22* ✉ *5 Chestnut Ave., at Antelope Blvd.* ☎ *530/527–3161* 🌐 *www.greenbarnsteakhouse.com* ⏲ *Closed Sun.; no lunch Sat.*

$ HOTEL 🏨 **Hampton Inn & Suites Red Bluff.** In a town filled with budget chain properties, this three-story hotel with clean, spacious rooms and a high-ceilinged lobby qualifies as the grande dame. **Pros:** clean, spacious rooms; Wi-Fi works well; pool and business and fitness centers. **Cons:** pricey for the area; on the north end of town away from most attractions; lacks personality. [$] *Rooms from: $119* ✉ *520 Adobe Rd.* ☎ *530/529–4178* 🌐 *www.hamptoninn3.hilton.com* 🛏 *97 rooms* 🍽 *Breakfast.*

REDDING

32 miles north of Red Bluff on I–5.

As the largest city in the Far North and a gateway to Lassen Volcanic National Park's northern entrance, Redding is an ideal headquarters for exploring the surrounding countryside.

GETTING HERE AND AROUND

Interstate 5 is the major north–south route into Redding. Highway 299 bisects the city east–west, and Highway 44 connects Redding and Lassen Park's north entrance. Amtrak and Greyhound stop here.

ESSENTIALS

Bus Information **Redding Area Bus Authority.** ☎ *530/241–2877* 🌐 *www.rabaride.com.*

Visitor Information **Redding Convention and Visitors Bureau.** ✉ *Visitor center, 844 Sundial Bridge Dr.* ☎ *530/225–4100, 800/874–7562* 🌐 *www.visitredding.com.*

EXPLORING

Moseley Family Cellars. Although its street name conjures up pastoral images, this winery whose grapes come from Napa, Sonoma, Lodi, and some local vineyards is actually in an industrial park. It's still worth a visit, not only for its wines—two Chardonnays and a Grenache, Syrah, Mourvèdre red blend are among the stars—but also the hospitality of co-owner Mimi Moseley (husband Marty makes the wines), who's happy to help you plan other area winery stops. ✉ *4712 Mountain Lakes Blvd., Suite 300* ☎ *530/229–9463* 🌐 *www.moseleyfamilycellars.com* 🎟 *Tasting $10* ⏲ *Closed Mon.–Wed. (except by appointment).*

Shasta State Historic Park. Six miles west of downtown lies the former town of Shasta City, which thrived in the mid- to late 1800s. The park's 19 acres of half-ruined brick buildings and overgrown graveyards, accessed via trails, are a reminder of the glory days of the California gold rush. The former county courthouse building, jail, and gallows have been restored to their 1860s appearance. The Litsch General Store, in operation from 1850 to 1950, is now a museum, with displays of many items once sold here. ✉ *15312 Hwy. 299* ☎ *530/243–8194* 🌐 *www.parks.ca.gov/?page_id=456* 🎟 *Free to park, $3 Courthouse Museum* ⏲ *Courthouse Museum closed Mon.–Wed.*

FAMILY Fodor's Choice ★ **Turtle Bay Exploration Park.** This park has walking trails, an aquarium, an arboretum and botanical gardens, and many interactive exhibits for kids. The main draw is the stunning **Sundial Bridge,** a metal and translucent glass pedestrian walkway, suspended by cables from a single tower, spanning a broad bend in the Sacramento River. On sunny days the tower lives up to the bridge's name, casting a shadow on the ground below to mark time. Access to the bridge and arboretum is free, but there's a fee for the museum and gardens. ✉ *844 Sundial Bridge Dr.* ☎ *530/243–8850, 800/887–8532* 🌐 *www.turtlebay.org* 🎟 *Museum $16* ⏲ *Museum closed Mon. and Tues. early Sept.–mid-Mar.*

WHERE TO EAT AND STAY

$$$$ AMERICAN 🍴 **Clearie's Restaurant and Lounge.** The granddaughter of "Doc" Clearie, who ran a popular Redding restaurant long ago, returned the family name to fine-dining prominence with this white-tablecloth lounge and restaurant. Many guests begin with the signature blackberry lavender lemon drop "martini," bubbling like a cauldron courtesy of dry ice, and perhaps a baked Brie appetizer before, depending on the season, a main course like short-rib beef Stroganoff or pan-seared ahi tuna. **Known for:** white-tablecloth ambience; well-executed cuisine; decent wine list. [$] *Average main: $32* ✉ *1325 Eureka Way* ☎ *530/241–4535* 🌐 *www.cleariesrestaurant.com* ⏲ *Closed Sun.*

$ AMERICAN 🍴 **From the Hearth Artisan Bakery & Café.** A homegrown variation on the Panera theme, this extremely popular operation (as in expect a wait at peak dining hours) serves pastries, eggs and other hot dishes, and good coffee drinks, juices, and smoothies for breakfast, adding a diverse selection of wraps, panini, sandwiches, burgers, rice bowls, and soups the rest of the day. Some sandwiches are made with a bread that FTH bills as "Redding's original sourdough." There are two other locations in Redding (one downtown) and another in Red Bluff. **Known for:** baked goods; breakfast until noon on weekends; diverse selection. [$] *Average main: $11* ✉ *2650 Churn Creek Rd.* ☎ *530/646–4315* 🌐 *www.fthcafe.com.*

$$$ STEAKHOUSE 🍴 **Jack's Grill.** The original Jack opened his grill (and an upstairs brothel) in 1938—tamer these days but often jam-packed and noisy, this place is famous for its 16-ounce steaks and deep-fried shrimp and chicken dishes. What Jack's lacks in culinary finesse it more than makes up for in atmosphere. **Known for:** 1930s atmosphere; great martinis; thick slabs of beef. [$] *Average main: $24* ✉ *1743 California St., near Sacramento St.* ☎ *530/241–9705* 🌐 *www.jacksgrillredding.com* ⏲ *Closed Sun. No lunch.*

$$ AMERICAN 🍴 **Moonstone Bistro.** About a mile and a half southwest of downtown this light-filled restaurant in a strip mall prides itself on its use of seasonal organic produce, free-range meats, sustainable line-caught fish, and cage-free eggs. All day you can dine on fish tacos, a large mixed-greens salad, or burgers (standard, veggie, or teriyaki mushroom Swiss), with fish, chicken, and pasta dishes available at lunch, and heavier pork and beef dishes added for dinner. **Known for:** organic produce; all-day bistro menu; Sunday brunch. [$] *Average main: $21* ✉ *3425 Placer St., near Buenaventura Blvd.* ☎ *530/241–3663* 🌐 *www.moonstonebistro.com* ⏲ *Closed Mon. No dinner Sun.*

$$$ MODERN AMERICAN 🍴 **View 202.** The view at this glass-walled hilltop restaurant is of the Sacramento River below the wide outdoor patio and well beyond the waterway to snowcapped mountains. The New American menu emphasizes grilled meats and fish from noted California purveyors but also includes bouillabaisse and house-made ravioli. **Known for:** Sacramento River and mountain views; specialty cocktails; wine list among the North State's best. [$] *Average main: $30* ✉ *202 Hemsted Dr., off E. Cypress Ave.* ☎ *530/226–8439* 🌐 *www.view202redding.com.*

$ B&B/INN Fodor's Choice ★ 🏨 **Bridgehouse Bed & Breakfast.** In a residential area a block from the Sacramento River and a half-mile from downtown Redding, this inn contains six rooms in two side-by-side homes. **Pros:** easy hospitality; proximity to downtown and Turtle Bay; freshly baked scones at full breakfast. **Cons:** lacks pool, fitness center, and other standard hotel amenities; the two least expensive rooms are small; books up well ahead in summer. [$] *Rooms from: $119* ✉ *1455 Riverside Dr.* ☎ *530/247–7177* 🌐 *www.bridgehousebb.com* 🛏 *6 rooms* 🍽 *Breakfast.*

$$ HOTEL FAMILY 🏨 **Fairfield Inn & Suites Redding.** The three-story Fairfield's clean rooms, amiable service, 24-hour business center, mountain views from some rooms, and bright, chipper public areas make it the best choice among Redding's many chain properties. **Pros:** clean rooms; amiable service; many amenities. **Cons:** prices often higher than competitors; corporate

feel; some rooms are small. $ *Rooms from: $146* ⊠ *164 Caterpillar Rd.* ☎ *530/243–3200* ⊕ *www.marriott.com/hotels/travel/rddre* ➦ *75 rooms* ⎟◎⎟ *Breakfast.*

NIGHTLIFE

Final Draft Brewing Company. This spacious brick-walled brewpub opened in 2017 to high acclaim for its accessible ales and above-average pub grub. Try the beer-battered fish and chips with swirly fries instead of regular ones. While they're cooking, order a sampler flight to decide which of the brews to wash them down with. ⊠ *1600 California St., at Placer St.* ☎ *530/338–1198* ⊕ *www.finaldraftbrewingcompany.com.*

Wildcard Brewing Tied House. At the mellow outpost of this brewery founded in 2012 you can sample an adventurous lineup that includes a pilsner, a red ale, several IPAs, and an almost chewy oatmeal porter. The flagship North State IPA's citrus notes are amped up to good effect in the Ruby Red Grapefruit, worth checking out if on tap when you visit. ⊠ *1321 Butte St., at Pine St.* ☎ *530/255–8582* ⊕ *www.wildcardbrewingco.com.*

Woody's Brewing Company. A fun downtown hangout with a partylike vibe, Woody's has built a loyal following for its pierogi, special-recipe tater tots, and range of beers from a pilsner and fruited wheat ales to a double Belgian white IPA and the Shasta Street stout. The reasonably priced sampler flights provide a good introduction. ⊠ *1257 Oregon St., at Shasta St.* ☎ *530/768–1034* ⊕ *www.woodysbrewing.biz.*

WEAVERVILLE

46 miles west of Redding on Hwy. 299.

Chinese miners erected the 1874 Joss House that anchors Weaverville's impressive downtown historic district. The town, population about 3,600, is also a popular headquarters for family vacations and hiking, fishing, and gold-panning excursions.

GETTING HERE AND AROUND

Highway 299, east from the Pacific Coast or west from Redding, becomes Main Street in central Weaverville. Highway 36 from Red Bluff to Highway 3 heading north leads to Weaverville. Trinity Transit provides bus service.

ESSENTIALS

Visitor Information Trinity County Visitors Bureau. ⊠ *509 Main St.* ☎ *530/623–6101* ⊕ *www.visittrinity.com.*

EXPLORING

Trinity County Hal Goodyear Historical Park. For a vivid sense of Weaverville's past, visit this park, especially its **Jake Jackson Memorial Museum.** A blacksmith shop and a stamp mill (where ore is crushed) from the 1890s are still in use during certain community events. Also here are the Trinity County Courthouse's original jail cells. ⊠ *780 Main St., at Bartlett La.* ☎ *530/623–5211* ⊕ *www.trinitymuseum.org* ⊙ *Museum closed various days Jan.–Apr. and Oct.–Dec.*

Fodor's Choice ★ **Weaverville Joss House State Historic Park.** Weaverville's main attraction is the Joss House, a Taoist temple built in 1874 and called Won Lim Miao ("the temple of the forest beneath the clouds") by Chinese miners. The oldest continuously used Chinese temple in California, it attracts worshippers from around the world. With its golden altar, antique weaponry, and carved wooden canopies, the Joss House is a piece of California history that can best be appreciated on a guided 30-minute tour. ✉ *630 Main St., at Oregon St.* ☎ *530/623–5284* 🌐 *www.parks.ca.gov/?page_id=457* 🎟 *Museum free; guided tour $4* 🕒 *Closed Mon.–Wed.*

WHERE TO EAT AND STAY

$$ AMERICAN 🍴 **La Grange Café.** In 2016 new owners revived this locals'-fave restaurant and bar inside two 1854 brick buildings that rank among Weaverville's oldest structures. For lunch are salads, a few pastas, burgers, and sandwiches that include a nicely executed Monte Cristo, with most of the same repeating for dinner, supplemented by nightly specials, Angus steaks (topped with bourbon or herb butter), roasted half chicken, a pork chop, and spicy-good jambalaya. **Known for:** Angus steaks; spicy jambalaya; salads and pastas. [$] *Average main: $20* ✉ *520 Main St.* ☎ *530/623–5325* 🕒 *Closed Sun. and Mon.*

$ AMERICAN 🍴 **Mamma Llama Eatery & Cafe.** Tap into the spirit of 21st-century Weaverville at this mellow café that serves breakfast (all day) and lunch and in winter specializes in hot soups to warm body and soul. Expect all the usual suspects at breakfast along with Country Cheesy Potatoes (topped with green chili) and sausage between two biscuits topped with homemade sausage gravy; a spicy club wrap and several vegetarian sandwiches are among the lunch offerings. **Known for:** mellow vibe; good soups; espresso drinks. [$] *Average main: $9* ✉ *490 Main St.* ☎ *530/623–6363* 🌐 *www.mammallama.com.*

$$ HOTEL 🏨 **Weaverville Hotel.** Originally built during the gold rush, this beautifully restored hotel is filled with antiques and period furniture. **Pros:** gracious on-site owners; in heart of town's historic district; beautifully restored. **Cons:** no breakfast on-site; children under 12 not permitted; only one room has a TV. [$] *Rooms from: $140* ✉ *481 Main St., near Court St.* ☎ *530/623–2222, 800/750–8853* 🌐 *www.weavervillehotel.com* 🛏 *7 rooms* 🍽 *No meals.*

$ B&B/INN Fodor's Choice ★ 🏨 **Whitmore Inn.** Amid Weaverville's historic district and shaded by black locust trees, this Victorian inn near shops and restaurants has five rooms, some with a shared bath. **Pros:** Victorian style with modern touches; convenient historic district location; innkeeper generous with sightseeing tips. **Cons:** some rooms share a bath; Victorian style in most rooms not for everyone; young children not permitted. [$] *Rooms from: $100* ✉ *761 Main St.* ☎ *530/623–2509* 🌐 *www.whitmoreinn.com* 🛏 *5 rooms* 🍽 *Breakfast.*

SPORTS AND THE OUTDOORS

Weaverville Ranger Station. Check here for maps, free wilderness and campfire permits, and information about local fishing and the 600 miles of hiking trails in the 500,000-acre Trinity Alps Wilderness. ✉ *360 Main St.* ☎ *530/623–2121.*

LAKE SHASTA AREA

12 miles north of Redding.

When you think of the Lake Shasta Area, picture water, wilderness, dazzling stalagmites—and a fabulous man-made project, Shasta Dam, in the midst of it all.

GETTING HERE AND AROUND

Interstate 5 north of Redding is the main link to the Lake Shasta area. Get to the dam by passing through the tiny city of Shasta Lake. There is no local bus service.

EXPLORING

Lake Shasta. Numerous types of fish inhabit the lake, including rainbow trout, salmon, bass, brown trout, and catfish. The lake region also has California's largest nesting population of bald eagles. You can rent fishing boats, ski boats, sailboats, canoes, paddleboats, Jet Skis, and windsurfing boards at marinas and resorts along the 370-mile shoreline. ⊠ *Shasta Lake* ⊕ *www.shastacascade.com.*

Fodor's Choice
★ **Lake Shasta Caverns National Natural Landmark.** Stalagmites, stalactites, flowstone deposits, and crystals entice visitors to the Lake Shasta Caverns. To see this impressive spectacle, you must take the two-hour tour, which includes a catamaran ride across the McCloud arm of Lake Shasta and a bus ride up North Grey Rocks Mountain to the cavern entrance. The temperature in the caverns is 58°F year-round, making them a cool retreat on a hot summer day. The most awe-inspiring of the limestone rock formations is the glistening Cathedral Room, which appears to be gilded. ⊠ *20359 Shasta Caverns Rd., Exit 695 off I–5, 17 miles north of Redding, Lakehead* ☎ *530/238–2341, 800/795–2283* ⊕ *www.lakeshastacaverns.com* ⊠ *$26.*

Shasta Dam. This is the second-largest concrete dam in the United States (only Grand Coulee in Washington is bigger). The visitor center has computerized photographic tours of the dam construction, video presentations, fact sheets, and historical displays. Hour-long guided tours inside the dam and its powerhouse leave from the center. ⊠ *16349 Shasta Dam Blvd., off Lake Blvd., Shasta Lake* ☎ *530/275–4463* ⊕ *www.usbr.gov/mp/ncao/shasta* ⊠ *Free.*

SPORTS AND THE OUTDOORS

FISHING

The Fishen Hole. A couple of miles from the lake, this bait-and-tackle shop sells fishing licenses and provides information about conditions. ⊠ *3844 Shasta Dam Blvd., at Red Ave., Shasta Lake* ☎ *530/275–4123.*

HOUSEBOATING

Houseboats come in all sizes except small. As a rule, rentals are outfitted with cooking utensils, dishes, and most of the equipment you'll need—you supply the food and linens. When you rent a houseboat, you receive a short course in how to maneuver your launch before you set out. You can fish, swim, sunbathe on the flat roof, or sit on the deck and watch the world go by. Expect to spend at least $400 a day (two- or three-night minimum) for a craft that sleeps six. Bridge Bay Resort and Shasta Marina at Packers Bay are two reliable outfits.

Bridge Bay Resort. This resort offers modest lakeside lodging, a restaurant, boat and Jet Ski rentals, and a full-service marina. Houseboats for rent sleep from 8 to 13 people. ✉ *10300 Bridge Bay Rd., off I–5, Exit 690, Redding* ☎ *800/752–9669, 530/275–3021* 🌐 *www.bridgebayhouseboats.com* 🎟 *From $550 per night in summer, 2-night minimum.*

FAMILY Fodor'sChoice ★ **Shasta Marina at Packers Bay.** Packed with amenities, well-maintained, and clean, this highly regarded operator's deluxe houseboats sleep from 14 to 16 people. Some even have a hot tub onboard. ✉ *16814 Packers Bay Rd., west from I–5, Exit 693, Lakehead* ☎ *800/959–3359* 🌐 *shastalake.net* 🎟 *From $1200 per night in summer, 3-night minimum.*

DUNSMUIR

10 miles south of Mt. Shasta.

Surrounded by towering forests and boasting world-class fly-fishing in the Upper Sacramento River, tiny Dunsmuir was named for a 19th-century Scottish coal baron who offered to build a fountain if the town was renamed in his honor. You can spend the night in restored cabooses at the fun Railroad Park Resort.

GETTING HERE AND AROUND

Reach Dunsmuir via exits off Interstate 5 at the north and south ends of town. Amtrak stops here; Greyhound stops in Weed, 20 miles north. On weekdays, STAGE buses serve Dunsmuir.

ESSENTIALS

Visitor Information Dunsmuir Chamber of Commerce. ✉ *5915 Dunsmuir Ave., Suite 100* ☎ *530/235–2177* 🌐 *dunsmuir.com.*

EXPLORING

Fodor'sChoice ★ **Castle Crags State Park.** Named for its 6,000-foot glacier-polished crags, which were formed by volcanic activity centuries ago, this park offers fishing on the upper Sacramento River, hiking in the backcountry, and a view of Mt. Shasta. The crags draw climbers and hikers from around the world. The 4,350-acre park has 28 miles of hiking trails, including a 2¾-mile access trail to **Castle Crags Wilderness,** part of the **Shasta-Trinity National Forest.** There are excellent trails at lower altitudes, too, including the 1-mile Indian Creek Nature Loop Trail (near the entrance), whose theme is the local water cycle. ✉ *6 miles south of Dunsmuir, Castella/Castle Crags exit off I–5, 20022 Castle Creek Rd., Castella* ☎ *530/235–2684* 🌐 *www.parks.ca.gov/parkindex* 🎟 *$8 per vehicle, day use.*

WHERE TO EAT AND STAY

$$$ MEDITERRANEAN 🍴 **Café Maddalena.** The chef here gained experience working in top San Francisco restaurants before moving north to prepare adventurous Mediterranean fare with a French influence. Selections change seasonally but always feature a vegetarian dish, along with fish, beef, and chicken entrées. **Known for:** Euro-centric wine list; daily prix-fixe menu; outdoor dining under grape arbor. [$] *Average main: $26* ✉ *5801 Sacramento Ave.* ☎ *530/235–2725* 🌐 *www.cafemaddalena.com* 🕒 *Closed Mon.–Wed. and Jan.–mid-Feb. No lunch.*

$$
AMERICAN

✕ **Yaks on the 5.** Renowned for bacon-jalapeño and many other grass-fed burgers, Yaks has gotten so much social-media lovin' the crowds can be huge in-season, but this festive joint wins most diners' hearts with its house-made ingredients (even buns), dozens of beers, and upbeat decor and staffers. You'll pay more than expected but will likely leave feeling you got your money's worth. **Known for:** garlic, duck-chili, barbecue, and other burgers; many beers on tap; upbeat decor and staffer. $ *Average main: $17* ✉ *4917 Dunsmuir Ave.* ☎ *530/678–3517* ⊕ *www.yaks.com.*

> **FINE FISHING**
>
> The upper Sacramento River near Dunsmuir is consistently rated one of the best fishing spots in the country. Check with the chamber of commerce for local fishing guides.

$$
HOTEL
FAMILY

🚃 **Railroad Park Resort.** The antique cabooses here were collected over more than three decades and have been converted into 23 cozy motel rooms in honor of Dunsmuir's railroad legacy (there are also four cabins). **Pros:** gorgeous setting; unique accommodations; kitschy fun. **Cons:** cabooses can feel cramped; must drive to Dunsmuir restaurants; some guests find location too remote. $ *Rooms from: $135* ✉ *100 Railroad Park Rd.* ☎ *530/235–4440* ⊕ *www.rrpark.com* ⤴ *27 rooms* ❍ *No meals.*

MT. SHASTA

34 miles north of Lake Shasta.

While a snow-covered dormant volcano is the area's dazzling draw, the town of Mt. Shasta charms visitors with its small shops, friendly residents, and beautiful scenery in all seasons.

GETTING HERE AND AROUND

Three exits off Interstate 5 lead to the town of Mt. Shasta. When snow hasn't closed the route, you can take Highway 89 from the Lassen Park area toward Burney then northeast to Mt. Shasta. The ski park is off Highway 89. Greyhound stops at Weed, 10 miles north; Amtrak stops at Dunsmuir, 10 miles south. STAGE provides bus service.

ESSENTIALS

Visitor Information Mt. Shasta Chamber of Commerce and Visitors Bureau. ✉ *300 Pine St., at W. Lake St.* ☎ *530/926–4865, 800/926–4865* ⊕ *www.mtshastachamber.com.*

EXPLORING

Fodor's Choice
★

Mt. Shasta. The crown jewel of the 2.5-million-acre Shasta-Trinity National Forest, Mt. Shasta, a 14,179-foot-high dormant volcano, is a mecca for day hikers. It's especially enticing in spring, when fragrant Shasta lilies and other flowers adorn the rocky slopes. A paved road, the Everitt Memorial Highway, reaches only as far as the timberline; the final 6,000 feet are a tough climb of rubble, ice, and snow (the summit is perpetually ice-packed). Hiking enthusiasts include this trek with those to the peaks of Kilimanjaro and Mount Fuji in lists of iconic must-do mountain hikes. ■**TIP→** Always check weather predictions; sudden storms have trapped climbers with snow and freezing temperatures. ✉ *Mt. Shasta* ⊕ *www.mtshastachamber.com.*

WHERE TO EAT AND STAY

$$$ ECLECTIC 🍴 **Lilys.** This restaurant in a white-clapboard home, framed by a picket fence and arched trellis, offers an eclectic menu, starting with bourbon-glazed French toast for breakfast. Lunch and dinner selections vary seasonally but often include roasted beet salad, herb-stuffed fresh trout, a walnut garbanzo veggie burger, and marinated pork chops with cannellini beans. **Known for:** eclectic menu; flavorful vegetarian options; weekend brunch. [$] *Average main: $25* ✉ *1013 S. Mt. Shasta Blvd., at Holly St.* ☎ *530/926–3372* 🌐 *www.lilysrestaurant.com.*

$ MEXICAN 🍴 **Poncho & Lefkowitz.** The cuisine is Mexican and American at this small stand popular with locals and visitors for its burritos, quesadillas, fish tacos, tamales, sausages, and hot dogs. Order at the window and enjoy your meal at outdoor picnic tables with Mt. Shasta views. **Known for:** fish tacos; house-made strawberry lemonade; outdoor picnic tables with Mt. Shasta views. [$] *Average main: $8* ✉ *401 S. Mt. Shasta Blvd.* ☎ *530/926–1505* 🕒 *Closed Sun. and Mon.*

$ CAFÉ 🍴 **Seven Suns Coffee and Cafe.** A favorite gathering spot for locals, this small coffee shop serves specialty wraps for breakfast and lunch, plus soups and salad. Pastries, made daily, include muffins, cookies, and scones (great blackberry ones in season). **Known for:** pastries made daily; outside patio; blackberry scones in season. [$] *Average main: $9* ✉ *1011 S. Mt. Shasta Blvd., at Holly St.* ☎ *530/926–9701* 🌐 *www.mtshastacoffee.com* 🕒 *No dinner.*

$$$ HOTEL 🏨 **Best Western Tree House Motor Inn.** The clean, standard rooms at this motel less than a mile from downtown Mt. Shasta are decorated with natural-wood furnishings. **Pros:** close to ski park; indoor pool; lobby's roaring fireplace is a big plus on winter days. **Cons:** not all lodging buildings have elevators; pricier than other chain properties (though it delivers more); no free breakfast, though discount voucher provided. [$] *Rooms from: $179* ✉ *111 Morgan Way* ☎ *530/926–3101, 800/545–7164* 🌐 *www.bestwesterncalifornia.com/hotels/best-western-plus-tree-house* 🛏 *98 rooms* 🍽 *Breakfast.*

$ HOTEL 🏨 **Mount Shasta Inn & Suites.** Although its rooms are sparsely decorated with unremarkable furnishings, this two-story motel conveniently located on Mt. Shasta's main drag wins points for cleanliness and competitive rates. **Pros:** clean, spacious rooms; competitive rates; convenient location. **Cons:** no style; few amenities; front desk not staffed 24/7. [$] *Rooms from: $80* ✉ *710 S. Mt. Shasta Blvd.* ☎ *530/918–9292* 🌐 *www.mtshastainn.com* 🛏 *30 rooms* 🍽 *No meals.*

$$$ RENTAL 🏨 **Mount Shasta Resort.** Private chalets are nestled among tall pine trees along the shore of Lake Siskiyou, all with gas-log fireplaces and full kitchens. **Pros:** incredible views; romantic woodsy setting; some pet-friendly rooms for extra fee. **Cons:** kids may get bored; must drive to Mt. Shasta restaurants; some hospitality lapses. [$] *Rooms from: $179* ✉ *1000 Siskiyou Lake Blvd.* ☎ *530/926–3030, 800/958–3363* 🌐 *www.mountshastaresort.com* 🛏 *65 rooms* 🍽 *No meals.*

SPORTS AND THE OUTDOORS

HIKING

Mt. Shasta Forest Service Ranger Station. Check in here for current trail conditions and avalanche reports. ⊠ *204 W. Alma St., at Pine St.* ☎ *530/926–4511, 530/926–9613 avalanche conditions.*

MOUNTAIN CLIMBING

Fifth Season Mountaineering Shop. This shop rents bicycles and skiing and climbing equipment, and operates a recorded 24-hour climber-skier report. ⊠ *300 N. Mt. Shasta Blvd.* ☎ *530/926–3606, 530/926–5555 ski phone* ⊕ *www.thefifthseason.com.*

Shasta Mountain Guides. These guides lead hiking, climbing, and skiing tours to Mt. Shasta's summit. ⊠ *Mt. Shasta* ☎ *530/926–3117* ⊕ *shastaguides.com.*

SKIING

FAMILY **Mt. Shasta Board & Ski Park.** Three-quarters of the trails at this ski park on Mt. Shasta's southeast flank are for beginning or intermediate skiers. A package for beginners, available through the ski school, includes a lift ticket, ski rental, and a lesson. There's night skiing for those who want to see the moon rise as they schuss. The base lodge has a simple café, a ski shop, and a ski-snowboard rental shop. Facilities: 32 trails; 425 skiable acres; 1,435-foot vertical drop; 5 lifts. ⊠ *Hwy. 89 exit east from I–5, south of Mt. Shasta* ☎ *530/926–8610, 800/754–7427,* ⊕ *www. skipark.com* ⊠ *Lift ticket $64.*

THE BACKCOUNTRY

The Far North's primitive, rugged backcountry is arguably full of more natural wonders than any other region in California.

MCARTHUR–BURNEY FALLS MEMORIAL STATE PARK

52 miles southeast of Mt. Shasta, 41 miles north of Lassen Volcanic National Park.

One of the most spectacular sights in the Far North is Burney Falls, where countless ribbonlike streams pour from moss-covered crevices. You have to travel forested back roads to reach this gem, but the park's beauty is well worth the trek.

GETTING HERE AND AROUND

To get to the falls, head east off Interstate 5 on Highway 89 at Mt. Shasta. From Redding, head east on Highway 299 to Highway 89; follow signs 6 miles to the park.

EXPLORING

FAMILY **McArthur–Burney Falls Memorial State Park.** Just inside this park's southern
Fodor's Choice boundary, Burney Creek wells up from the ground and divides into
★ two falls that cascade over a 129-foot cliff into a pool below. Countless ribbonlike streams pour from hidden moss-covered crevices; resident bald eagles are frequently seen soaring overhead. You can walk a self-guided nature trail that descends to the foot of the falls, which Theodore Roosevelt—according to legend—called "the eighth wonder

DID YOU KNOW?

President Theodore Roosevelt supposedly called McArthur–Burney Falls "the eighth wonder of the world."

of the world." On warm days, swim at Lake Britton; lounge on the beach; rent motorboats, paddleboats, and canoes; or relax at one of the campsites or picnic areas. ✉ *24898 Hwy. 89, 6 miles north of Hwy. 299, Burney* ☎ *530/335–2777* ⊕ *www.parks.ca.gov/?page_id=455* ✒ *$8 per vehicle, day use.*

OFF THE BEATEN PATH

Lava Beds National Monument. Thousands of years of volcanic activity created this rugged landscape, which is distinguished by cinder cones, lava flows, spatter cones, pit craters, and more than 400 underground lava tube caves. During the Modoc War (1872–73), Modoc Indians under the leadership of their chief "Captain Jack" Kientopoos took refuge in a natural lava fortress now known as Captain Jack's Stronghold. They managed to hold off U.S. Army forces, which outnumbered them 20 to 1, for five months. When exploring this area, be sure to wear hard-soled boots and a bump hat. Bring a flashlight with you, although some are available for borrowing at the Indian Well Visitor Center, at the park's southern end. This is where summer activities such as guided walks, cave tours, and campfire programs depart from. ■TIP➔ **About 78 miles from McArthur-Burney Memorial State Park (85 miles from Mt. Shasta City), Lava Beds is extremely remote; see website for detailed driving instructions.** ✉ *1 Indian Well, Tulelake* ✛ *From McArthur-Burney state park, take Hwy. 89 south to Hwy. 299 east to Bieber-Lookout Rd. and Hwy. 139 north to Forest Service Rte. 97 west and follow signs; from Mt. Shasta City, take Hwy. 89 to Forest Service Rtes. 97 and 10* ☎ *530/667–2282* ⊕ *www.nps.gov/labe* ✒ *$15 per vehicle; $10 on foot, bicycle, or motorcycle.*

LASSEN VOLCANIC NATIONAL PARK

45 miles east of Redding, 48 miles east of Red Bluff.

Fissures and fumaroles burble and belch as reminders of Lassen Peak's dramatic eruption a century ago. Four different types of volcanoes form part of this park's fascinating geothermal landscape.

GETTING HERE AND AROUND

Whether coming from the west or the east, reach the park's southern entrance via Highway 36E, and turn onto Highway 89 for a short drive to the park. The northwest entrance is reached via Highway 44 from Redding and Susanville. No buses serve the area.

EXPLORING

Fodor's Choice ★

Volcanic Legacy Scenic Byway. This 185-mile scenic drive begins in Chester and loops through the forests, volcanic peaks, hydrothermal springs, and lava fields of Lassen National Forest and Lassen Volcanic National Park, providing an all-day excursion into dramatic wilderness. From Chester, take Highway 36 west to Highway 89 north, which within the park is called Lassen Volcanic National Park Highway, or Lassen Park Highway. Upon exiting the park at the north, follow Highway 44 east and then south to Highway 36, on which you can head back west to Chester. Parts of this route are inaccessible in winter and spring. ✉ *Lassen Volcanic National Park* ☎ *800/427–7623 CA Highway info service, 530/595–4480 Lassen Park visitor center.*

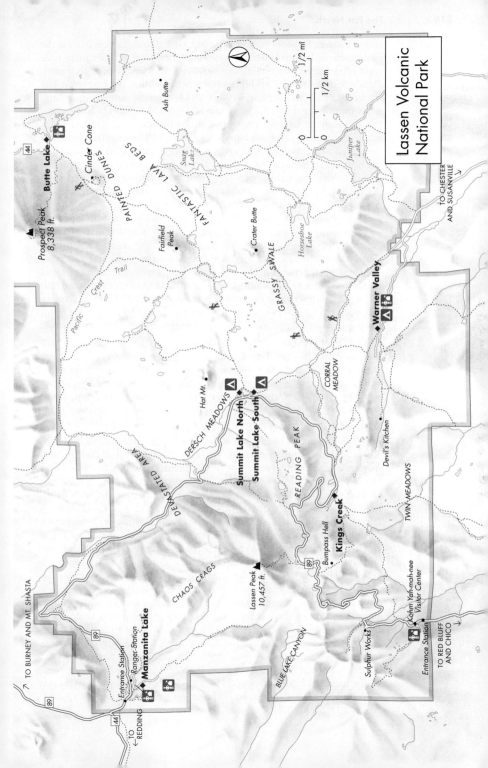

Lassen Volcanic National Park

Fodor's Choice ★ **Lassen Volcanic National Park.** A dormant plug dome, Lassen Peak is the main focus of Lassen Volcanic National Park, but this 165-square-mile tract of dense forests and alpine meadows also abounds with memorable opportunities for hiking, camping, and wildlife photography. The famed peak began erupting in May 1914, sending pumice, rock, and snow thundering down the mountain and gas and hot ash billowing into the atmosphere. Lassen's most spectacular outburst occurred in 1915, when it blew a cloud of ash almost 6 miles high. The resulting mudflow destroyed vegetation for miles; the evidence is still visible today, especially in the Devastated Area. The volcano finally came to rest in 1921. Today fumaroles, mud pots, lakes, and bubbling hot springs create a fascinating but dangerous landscape that can be viewed throughout the park, especially via a hiked descent into Bumpass Hell. Because of its significance as a volcanic landscape, Lassen became a national park in 1916. Several volcanoes—the largest of which is now Lassen Peak—have been active in the area for roughly 600,000 years. Lassen Park Road (the continuation of Highway 89 within the park) and 150 miles of hiking trails provide access to many of these wonders. ⚠ **Heed signs warning visitors to stay on the trails and railed boardwalks to avoid falling into boiling water or through thin-crusted areas.** ✉ *Mineral* 🌐 *www.nps.gov/lavo* 🎫 *$20 per car, $15 per motorcycle, $10 per person if not in motor vehicle* 🕒 *Main (Kohm Yah-mah-nee) visitor center closed Mon. and Tues. Nov.–Mar.*

FAMILY **Sulphur Works Thermal Area.** Proof of Lassen Peak's volatility becomes evident shortly after you enter the park at the southwest entrance. Sidewalks skirt boiling springs and sulfur-emitting steam vents. This area is usually the last site to close because of snow. ✉ *Lassen Park Hwy., 1 mile from southwest entrance ranger station, Lassen Volcanic National Park.*

WHERE TO EAT AND STAY

$$$ AMERICAN 🍴 **Highlands Ranch Restaurant and Bar.** Dining at the Highlands Ranch Resort's contemporary roadhouse restaurant is in a stained-wood, high-ceilinged room indoors, or out on the deck, which has views of a broad serene meadow and the hillside beyond. Among the few sophisticated eating options within Lassen Volcanic National Park's orbit, the restaurant serves regional American dishes like blackened ahi with carrot-cucumber slaw and balsamic-marinated duck with blackberries and wild mushrooms. **Known for:** striking views inside and out; small plates and burgers in the bar; inventive sauces and preparations. [$] *Average main: $20* ✉ *Highlands Ranch Resort, 41515 Hwy. 36 E* ☎ *530/595–3388* 🌐 *highlandsranchresort.com/artisans-view-restaurant* 🕒 *Hrs vary seasonally; check website or call.*

$$$$ B&B/INN Fodor's Choice ★ 🏨 **Drakesbad Guest Ranch.** With propane furnaces and kerosene lamps, everything about this century-old property in the park's remote but beautiful southeastern corner harks back to a simpler time. **Pros:** back-to-nature experience; great for family adventures; only full-service lodging inside the park. **Cons:** accessible only via a partially paved road leading out of Chester; rustic, with few in-room frills; not open year-round. [$] *Rooms from: $354* ✉ *1 Warner Valley Rd., Chester* ☎ *866/999–0914* 🌐 *www.drakesbad.com* 🕒 *Closed mid-Oct.–early June* 🛏 *19 rooms* 🍽 *All meals.*

$$$ B&B/INN Fodor's Choice ★ **Highlands Ranch Resort.** On a gorgeous 175-acre alpine meadow 10 miles from Lassen National Park's southwest entrance, this cluster of smartly designed upscale bungalows is peaceful and luxurious. **Pros:** stunning views; most luxurious accommodations near the park; friendly and helpful staff. **Cons:** pricey for the area (but you get a lot for what you pay); party types may find location too remote; books up months ahead for summer stays. [$] *Rooms from: $239* ✉ *41515 Hwy. 36 E* ☎ *530/595–3388* 🌐 *www.highlandsranchresort.com* 🕓 *Closed some Mon. and Tues. from fall to spring depending on weather; check website or call* 🛏 *7 cottages* 🍴 *Breakfast.*

SPORTS AND THE OUTDOORS

HIKING

Fodor's Choice ★ **Bumpass Hell Trail.** Boiling springs, steam vents, and mud pots are the highlights of this 3-mile round-trip hike. Expect the loop to take about two hours. During the first mile there's a gradual climb of 500 feet before a steep 300-foot descent to the basin. You'll encounter rocky patches, so wear hiking boots. Stay on trails and boardwalks near the thermal areas, as what appears to be firm ground may be only a thin crust over scalding mud. *Moderate.* ✉ *Lassen Volcanic National Park* ✣ *Trailhead: at end of paved parking area off Lassen Park Hwy., 6 miles from southwest entrance ranger station.*

Fodor's Choice ★ **Lassen Peak Hike.** This trail winds 2½ miles to the mountaintop. It's a tough climb—2,000 feet uphill on a steady, steep grade—but the reward is a spectacular view. At the peak you can see into the rim and view the entire park (and much of California's far north). Bring sunscreen, water, snacks, a first-aid kit, and, because it can be windy and cold at the summit, a jacket. ✉ *Lassen Volcanic National Park* ✣ *Trailhead: at parking area off Lassen Park Hwy., 7 miles north of southwest entrance ranger station* ☎ *530/595–4480.*

CHESTER

71 miles east of Red Bluff.

The population of this small town on Lake Almanor swells from 2,500 to nearly 5,000 in summer as tourists come to visit. Chester serves as a gateway to Lassen Volcanic National Park.

GETTING HERE AND AROUND

Chester is on Highway 36E, the main route from Red Bluff. When snow doesn't close Highway 89 in Lassen Park, visitors can take Highway 44 from Redding to Highway 89 through the park and to Highway 36E and onto Chester and Lake Almanor. Plumas County Transit provides local bus service.

ESSENTIALS

Bus Information **Plumas County Transit.** ☎ *530/283–2538* 🌐 *www.plumastransit.com.*

Visitor Information **Lake Almanor Area Chamber of Commerce and Visitors Bureau.** ✉ *328 #6 Main St., near Reynolds Rd.* ☎ *530/258–2426* 🌐 *www.lakealmanorarea.com.*

EXPLORING

Lake Almanor. This lake's 52 miles of forested shoreline are popular with campers, swimmers, waterskiers, and anglers. At an elevation of 4,500 feet, the lake warms to above 70°F for about eight weeks in summer. ⊠ *Off Hwys. 89 and 36* ☎ *530/258–2426* ⊕ *www.lakealmanorarea.com.*

WHERE TO EAT AND STAY

$
AMERICAN
Fodor'sChoice
★

✕**Cravings Cafe Espresso Bar & Bakery.** This breakfast and lunch place with vegetarian-friendly options not only satisfies diners' cravings, but with dishes like homemade slow-cooked corned-beef hash topped with two eggs and accompanied by a slice of sourdough bread it also creates them. You can get breakfast and excellent pastries all day, with soups, salads, sandwiches, and burgers on the menu for lunch. **Known for:** breakfast all day; corn-beef hash; excellent pastries. Ⓢ *Average main: $10* ⊠ *278 Main St.* ☎ *530/258–2229* ☉ *Closed Tues. and Wed.*

$$
HOTEL

⛭ **Best Western Rose Quartz Inn.** Down the road from Lake Almanor and close to Lassen Volcanic National Park, this small-town chain property is basically a motel, but the helpful staff (especially with touring plans) and amenities like good Wi-Fi and spacious breakfast area make it a good choice for a short stay. **Pros:** within easy walking distance of town's restaurants; convenient to Lassen Volcanic National Park; good Wi-Fi and other amenities. **Cons:** a little pricey; cookie-cutter decor; noise audible between rooms. Ⓢ *Rooms from: $149* ⊠ *306 Main St.* ☎ *530/258–2002* ⊕ *www.bestwestern.com* ⇆ *50 rooms* ❧○❧ *Breakfast.*

$$
B&B/INN
Fodor'sChoice
★

⛭ **Bidwell House.** Some guest rooms at this 1901 ranch house have wood-burning stoves, claw-foot tubs, and antique furnishings; a separate cottage with a kitchen sleeps six. **Pros:** unique decor in each room; beautiful wooded setting; near Lake Almanor. **Cons:** not ideal for kids; may be too remote for some guests; lacks some big-hotel amenities. Ⓢ *Rooms from: $125* ⊠ *1 Main St.* ☎ *530/258–3338* ⊕ *www.bidwellhouse.com* ⇆ *14 rooms* ❧○❧ *Breakfast.*

TRAVEL SMART CALIFORNIA

GETTING HERE AND AROUND

▋ AIR TRAVEL

Flying time to California is about 6½ hours from New York and 4¾ hours from Chicago. Travel from London to either Los Angeles or San Francisco is 11 hours and from Sydney approximately 15. Flying between San Francisco and Los Angeles takes about 90 minutes.

FROM LOS ANGELES TO:	BY AIR	BY CAR
San Diego	55 mins	2 hrs
Death Valley	No flights	5 hrs
San Francisco	1 hr 30 mins	5 hrs 40 mins
Monterey	1 hr 10 mins	5 hrs
Santa Barbara	50 mins	1 hr 40 mins
Big Sur	No flights	5 hrs 40 mins
Sacramento	1 hr 30 mins	5 hrs 30 mins

FROM SAN FRANCISCO TO:	BY AIR	BY CAR
San Jose	No flights	1 hr
Monterey	45 mins	2 hrs
Los Angeles	1 hr 30 mins	5 hrs 40 mins
Portland, OR	1 hr 50 mins	10 hrs
Mendocino	No flights	3 hrs
Yosemite NP/ Fresno	1 hr	4 hrs
Lake Tahoe/ Reno	1 hr	3 hrs 30 mins

AIRPORTS

Northern California Sacramento International Airport. ☎ 916/929–5411 ⊕ www.sacramento.aero/smf. **San Francisco International Airport.** ☎ 650/821–8211, 800/435–9736 ⊕ www.flysfo.com. **San Jose International Airport.** ☎ 408/392–3600 ⊕ www.flysanjose.com.

Southern California Hollywood Burbank Airport (*Bob Hope Airport*). ☎ 818/840–8840 ⊕ www.hollywoodburbankairport.com. **John Wayne Airport.** ☎ 949/252–5200 ⊕ www.ocair.com. **Long Beach Airport.** ☎ 562/570–2600 ⊕ www.lgb.org. **Ontario International Airport.** ☎ 909/937–2700 ⊕ www.flyontario.com. **Los Angeles International Airport.** ☎ 310/641–5700 ⊕ www.lawa.org/welcome-lax.aspx. **San Diego International Airport.** ☎ 619/400–2404 ⊕ www.san.org.

▋ BUS TRAVEL

Greyhound is the major bus carrier in California. Regional bus service is available in metropolitan areas.

Bus Information Greyhound. ☎ 800/231–2222 ⊕ www.greyhound.com.

▋ CAR TRAVEL

Two main north–south routes run through California: Interstate 5 through the middle of the state, and U.S. 101, a parallel route closer to the coast. Slower but more scenic is Highway 1, which winds along much of the coast.

From north to south, the state's main east–west routes are Interstate 80, Interstate 15, Interstate 10, and Interstate 8. Much of California is mountainous, and you may encounter winding roads and steep mountain grades.

GASOLINE

Gas stations are plentiful throughout the state. Many stay open late, except in rural areas, where Sunday hours are limited and where you may drive long stretches without a chance to refuel.

ROAD CONDITIONS

Rainy weather can make driving along the coast or in the mountains treacherous. Some smaller routes over mountain ranges and in the deserts are prone to flash flooding. When the weather is particularly

FROM LOS ANGELES TO:	ROUTE	DISTANCE
San Diego	I-5 or I-405	127 miles
Las Vegas	I-10 to I-15	270 miles
Death Valley	I-10 to I-15 to Hwy. 127 to Hwy. 190	290 miles
San Francisco	I-5 to I-580 to I-80	382 miles
Monterey	U.S. 101 to Salinas, Hwy. 68 to Hwy. 1	320 miles
Santa Barbara	U.S. 101	95 miles
Big Sur	U.S. 101 to Hwy. 1	349 miles
Sacramento	I-5	391 miles

FROM SAN FRANCISCO TO:	ROUTE	DISTANCE
San Jose	U.S. 101	50 miles
Monterey	U.S. 101 to Hwy. 156 to Hwy. 1	120 miles
Los Angeles	U.S. 101 to Hwy. 156 to I-5	382 miles
Portland, OR	I-80 to I-505 to I-5	635 miles
Mendocino	Hwy. 1	174 miles
Yosemite NP	I-80 to I-580 to I-205 to Hwy. 120 east	184 miles
Lake Tahoe/ Reno	I-80	220 miles

bad, Highway 1 may be closed due to mud and rock slides.

Many smaller roads over the Sierra Nevada are closed in winter, and if it's snowing, tire chains may be required on routes that are open. ■TIP→ It's less expensive to purchase chains before you get to the mountains. Chains or cables generally cost $30–$75, depending on tire size; cables are easier to attach than chains, but chains are more durable. Most rental-car companies prohibit chain installation on their vehicles. If you choose to disregard this rule, your insurance likely will not cover any chains-related damage.

In Northern California uniformed chain installers on Interstate 80 and U.S. 50 will apply chains for about $30 and take them off for half that. Chain installers are independent businesspeople, not highway employees. They are not allowed to sell or rent chains. On smaller roads, you're on your own.

Always carry extra clothing, blankets, water, and food when driving to the mountains in the winter, and keep your gas tank full to prevent the fuel line from freezing.

Road Conditions Caltrans Current Highway Conditions. ☎ 800/427-7623 ⊕ www.dot. ca.gov.

Weather Conditions National Weather Service. ☎ 707/443-6484 northernmost California, 831/656-1710 San Francisco Bay area and central California, 775/673-8100 Reno, Lake Tahoe, and northern Sierra, 805/988-6615 Los Angeles area, 858/675-8700 San Diego area, 916/979-3041 Sacramento area ⊕ www.weather.gov.

ROADSIDE EMERGENCIES

Dial 911 to report accidents and to reach the police, the California Highway Patrol (CHP), or the fire department. On some rural highways and on most interstates, look for emergency phones on the side of the road.

In Los Angeles, the Metro Freeway Service Patrol provides assistance to stranded motorists under nonemergency conditions. Dial 511 from a cell phone and choose the "motorist aid" option to reach them 24 hours a day.

RULES OF THE ROAD

All passengers must wear a seat belt at all times. A child must be secured in a federally approved child passenger restraint system and ride in the back seat until at least eight years of age or until the child is at least 4 feet 9 inches tall. Children who are eight but don't meet the height requirement must ride in a booster seat or a car seat. It is illegal to leave a child six years of age or younger unattended in a motor vehicle. Unless indicated, right turns are allowed at red lights after you've come to a full stop. Left turns between two one-way streets are allowed at red lights after you've come to a full stop. Drivers with a blood-alcohol level higher than 0.08 who are stopped by police are subject to arrest.

The speed limit on some interstate highways is 70 mph; unlimited-access roads are usually 55 mph. In cities, freeway speed limits are between 55 mph and 65 mph. Many city routes have commuter lanes during rush hour.

You must turn on your headlights whenever weather conditions require the use of windshield wipers. Texting on a wireless device is illegal for all drivers. If using a mobile phone while driving it must be hands-free and mounted (i.e., it's not legal having it loose on the seat or your lap). For more driving rules, refer to the Department of Motor Vehicles driver's handbook at ⊕ *www.dmv.ca.gov.*

CAR RENTAL

When you reserve a car, ask about cancellation penalties, taxes, drop-off charges (if you're planning to pick up the car in one city and leave it in another), and surcharges (for being under or over a certain age, for additional drivers, or for driving across state or country borders or beyond a specific distance from your point of rental). All these things can add substantially to your costs. Request car seats and extras such as GPS when you book.

Rates are sometimes—but not always—better if you book in advance or reserve through a rental agency's website. There are other reasons to book ahead, though: for popular destinations, during busy times of the year, or to ensure that you get certain types of cars (vans, SUVs, exotic sports cars).

■TIP➜ Make sure that a confirmed reservation guarantees you a car. Agencies

sometimes overbook, particularly for busy weekends and holiday periods.

A car is essential in most parts of California. In compact San Francisco it's better to use public transportation, taxis, or ride-sharing services to avoid parking headaches. In sprawling cities such as Los Angeles and San Diego, you'll have to take the freeways to get just about anywhere.

Rates statewide for the least expensive vehicle begin as low as $30 a day, usually on weekends, and less than $200 a week. This does not include additional fees or the tax on car rentals (8%–10%). Be sure to shop around—you can get a decent deal by shopping the major car-rental companies' websites. A few companies rent specialty cars such as convertibles or sport-utility vehicles.

In California you must have a valid driver's license and be 21 to rent a car; rates may be higher if you're under 25. Some agencies will not rent to those under 25; check when you book. Non-U.S. residents must have a license, valid for the entire rental period, with text in the Roman alphabet that clearly identifies it as a driver's license. In addition, most companies also require an international license; check in advance.

Specialty Car Agencies Beverly Hills Rent a Car. ☏ *310/923–7833* ⊕ *www.bhrentacar.com.* **Enterprise Exotic Car Rentals.** ☏ *866/458–9227* ⊕ *exoticcars.enterprise.com.* **MCar** (*Midway Car Rental*). ☏ *866/717–6802* ⊕ *www.midwaycarrental.com.*

▌ TRAIN TRAVEL

Amtrak provides rail service within California. On some trips—to Yosemite National Park, for example—passengers board motor coaches part of the way. The rail service's scenic *Coast Starlight* trip begins in Los Angeles and hugs the Pacific Coast to San Luis Obispo before it turns inland for the rest of its journey to Portland and Seattle.

Information Amtrak. ☏ *800/872–7245* ⊕ *www.amtrak.com.*

ESSENTIALS

▌ ACCOMMODATIONS

The lodgings we review are the top choices in each price category. *For an expanded review of each property, please see www.fodors.com.* We don't specify whether the facilities cost extra; when pricing accommodations, ask what's included and what costs extra. *For price information, see the planner in each chapter.*

Be sure you understand the hotel's cancellation policy. Some places allow you to cancel without any kind of penalty—even if you prepaid to secure a discounted rate—if you cancel at least 24 hours in advance. Others require you to cancel a week in advance or penalize you the cost of one night. Small inns and B&Bs are most likely to require you to cancel far in advance. Most hotels allow children under a certain age to stay in their parents' room at no extra charge, but others charge for them as extra adults; find out the cutoff age for discounts.

BED-AND-BREAKFASTS

California has more than 1,000 bed-and-breakfasts. You'll find everything from simple homestays to lavish luxury lodgings, many in historic hotels and homes. The California Association of Boutique and Breakfast Inns has about 300 member properties that you can locate and book through its website.

Reservation Services California Association of Boutique and Breakfast Inns. ☎ *800/373–9251* ⊕ *www.cabbi.com.*

▌ COMMUNICATIONS

INTERNET

Internet access is widely available in urban areas, but it can be difficult to get online in rural communities. Most hotels offer some kind of connection—usually broadband or Wi-Fi. Many hotels charge a daily fee ($10–$15) for Internet access. Cafés with free Wi-Fi are common throughout California.

▌ EATING OUT

California has led the pack in bringing natural and organic foods to the forefront of American dining. Though rooted in European cuisine, California cooking sometimes has strong Asian and Latin influences. Wherever you go, you're likely to find that dishes are made with fresh produce and other local ingredients.

The restaurants we list are the cream of the crop in each price category. *For price information, see the planner in each chapter.*

CUTTING COSTS

The better grocery and specialty-food stores have grab-and-go sections, with prepared foods on a par with restaurant cooking, perfect for picnicking (remember, it infrequently rains between May and October). At resort areas in the off-season you can often find two-for-one dinner specials at upper-end restaurants; check coupon apps or local papers or with visitor bureaus.

RESERVATIONS AND DRESS

Regardless of where you are, it's a good idea to make a reservation if you can. For popular restaurants, book as far ahead as you can (often 30 days), and reconfirm as soon as you arrive in California. (Large parties should always call ahead to check the reservations policy.)

Online reservation services make it easy to book a table. OpenTable covers many California cities.

Contacts OpenTable. ⊕ *www.opentable.com.*

▌ HEALTH

Smoking is illegal in all California bars and restaurants, including on outdoor dining patios in some cities. If you have an existing medical condition that may require emergency treatment, be aware that many rural and mountain communities have only daytime clinics, not hospitals with 24-hour emergency rooms.

Outdoor sports are a huge draw in California's moderate climate, but caution, especially in unfamiliar areas, is key. Drownings occur each year because beach lovers don't heed warnings about high surfs with their deadly rogue waves. Do not fly within 24 hours of scuba diving.

If you're spending time in the national parks or forests, be sure to follow posted instructions that outline how to avoid encounters with bears (e.g., store your food in bear lockers) and how to prevent exposure to hantavirus, carried in deer mouse droppings in remote areas.

HOURS OF OPERATION

Banks in California are typically open weekdays from 9 to 6; most are open on Saturday but close on Sunday and most holidays. Smaller shops usually operate from 10 or 11 to 6, with larger stores remaining open until 8 or later. Hours vary for museums, historical sites, and state parks, and many are closed one or more days a week, or for extended periods during off-season months.

MONEY

Los Angeles, San Diego, and San Francisco are expensive cities to visit, and rates at coastal and desert resorts are also high. A day's admission to a major theme park is more than $100 per person, though you may be able to get discounts by purchasing tickets in advance online. Hotel rates average $150 to $250 a night (though you can find cheaper places), and dinners at even moderately priced restaurants often cost $20 to $40 per person. Costs in the Gold Country, the Far North, and the Death Valley/Mojave Desert region are considerably less—many fine Gold Country bed-and-breakfasts charge around $125 a night, and some motels in the Far North and the Mojave charge less than $100.

CREDIT CARDS
It's a good idea to inform your credit-card company before you travel. Otherwise, unusual activity might prompt the company to put a hold on your card. Record all your credit-card numbers—as well as the phone numbers to call if your cards are lost or stolen—so you're prepared should something go wrong.

SAFETY

California is a safe place to visit, as long as you take the usual precautions. In large cities ask the concierge or desk clerk to point out areas on your map that you should avoid. Lock valuables in a hotel safe when you're not using them. Keep an eye on your handbag when you're out in public. Security is high (but mostly invisible) at theme parks and resorts.

When hiking, stay on trails—rangers say that the majority of hikers needing to be rescued have gone off trail—and heed signs at trailheads about dangerous situations such as cliffs with loose rocks and how to react if you encounter predatory animals that live in the area. Bring plenty of water, hike with a companion if possible, and learn to identify and avoid contact with poison oak, a ubiquitous plant in California that causes a severe rash.

TAXES

Sales tax in the state of California is 7.25%, but local taxes vary and may be as much as an additional 2.5%. Sales tax applies to all purchases except for food bought in a grocery store; food consumed in a restaurant is taxed, but take-out food is not. Hotel taxes vary widely by region, from about 8% to 16.5%.

TIME

California is in the Pacific time zone. Pacific daylight time (PDT) is in effect from mid-March through early November; the rest of the year the clock is set to Pacific standard time (PST).

▮ TIPPING

TIPPING GUIDELINES FOR CALIFORNIA	
Bartender	$1–$3 per drink, or 15%–20% per round
Bellhop	$2–$3 per bag, depending on the level of the hotel
Hotel Concierge	$5–$10 for advice and reservations, more for difficult tasks
Hotel Doorman	$2–$3 for hailing a cab
Valet Parking Attendant	$3–$5 when you get your car
Hotel Maid	$3–$5 per day; more in high-end hotels
Waiter	18%–22% (20%–25% is standard in upscale restaurants); nothing additional if a service charge is added to the bill
Skycap at Airport	$1–$2 per bag
Hotel Room-Service Waiter	15%–20% per delivery, even if a service charge was added since that fee goes to the hotel, not the waiter
Taxi Driver	15%–20%, but round up the fare to the next dollar amount
Tour Guide	15% of the cost of the tour, more depending on quality

▮ TOURS

Guided tours are a good option when you don't want to do it all yourself. You travel along with a group (sometimes large, sometimes small), stay in prebooked hotels, eat with your fellow travelers (the cost of meals is sometimes included in the price of your tour, sometimes not), and follow a schedule.

But not all guided tours are an if-it's-Tuesday-this-must-be-Yosemite experience. A knowledgeable guide can take you places that you might never discover on your own, and you may be pushed to see more than you would have otherwise.

Tours aren't for everyone, but they can be just the thing for trips to places where making travel arrangements is difficult or time-consuming.

Whenever you book a guided tour, find out what's included and what isn't. A "land-only" tour includes all your travel (by bus, in most cases) in the destination, but not necessarily your flights to and from or even within it. Also, in most cases prices in tour brochures don't include fees and taxes. And remember that you'll be expected to tip your guide (in cash) at the end of the tour.

GENERAL TOURS

Trafalgar. A dependable tour operator whose guides know California well, Trafalgar conducts nearly a dozen excursions around the state. One takes in San Francisco, Monterey, Big Sur, Yosemite, and Lake Tahoe, and another surveys the Northern California Wine Country. ☎ 866/513-1995 ⊕ www.trafalgar.com/usa 🖾 From $1695.

SPECIAL-INTEREST TOURS
BIKING

Biking is a popular way to see the California countryside, and commercial tours are available throughout the state. Most three- to five-day trips are all-inclusive—you'll stay in delightful country inns, dine at good regional restaurants, and follow experienced guides. When booking, ask about level of difficulty, as nearly every trip will involve some hill work. Tours fill up early, so book well in advance. ▮TIP→ Most airlines accommodate bikes as luggage, provided they're dismantled and boxed.

The Northern California Wine Country, with its flat valley roads, is one of the most popular destinations.

Napa and Sonoma Valley Bike Tours. Single-day bike tours through beautiful Napa and Sonoma Wine Country offer a casual pace and frequent winery stops. ⊠ 6500 Washington St., Yountville ☎ 707/251-8687 Napa tours, 707/996-2453 Sonoma tours ⊕ www.napavalleybiketours.com 🖾 From $108.

MULTISPORT TOURS

Backroads. Based in Northern California, Backroads arranges guided tours that may include biking, hiking, or gentler walking, camping, or all of these. Tours might take in the state's national parks, beaches, and forests, or wine-growing regions, with overnight stays in accommodations that range from campgrounds to deluxe small inns. ☎ *800/462–2848, 510/527–1555* ⊕ *www.backroads.com* ✉ *From $1998.*

▌ VISITOR INFORMATION

The California Travel and Tourism Commission's website takes you to each region of California, with digital visitor guides in multiple languages, driving tours, maps, welcome center locations, information on local tours, links to bed-and-breakfasts, and a complete booking center. It also links you—via the Destinations menu—to the websites of city and regional tourism offices and attractions. *For the numbers and websites of regional and city visitor bureaus and chambers of commerce, see the Planning section in each chapter.*

Contacts California Travel and Tourism Commission. ☎ *800/462–2543* ⊕ *www. visitcalifornia.com.*

INDEX

PHOTO CREDITS

16: The Mojave Desert: 605, Robert Holmes. 606, amygdala imagery/Shutterstock. 607, Robert Holmes. 608, San Bernardino County Regional Parks. 612, Merryl Edelstein, Fodors.com member. 620, Maksershov | Dreamstime.com. **Chapter 17: Death Valley National Park:** 625, Bryan Brazil/ Shutterstock. 627, Igor Karon/Shutterstock. 628, Paul D. Lemke/iStockphoto. 638–639, James Feliciano/iStockphoto. **Chapter 18: Eastern Sierra:** 643, Clicktrick | Dreamstime.com. 645 (top), David T Gomez/iStockphoto. 646 christinea78, Fodors.com member. 654, moonjazz/Flickr. 665, Douglas Atmore/iStockphoto. **Chapter 19: Yosemite National Park:** 667, Sarah P. Corley, Fodors.com member. 668, Greg Epperson/age fotostock. 669, Andy Z./Shutterstock. 670, Doug Lemke/Shutterstock. 677, Jane Rix / Shutterstock. 683, Nathan Jaskowiak/Shutterstock. **Chapter 20: Sequoia and Kings Canyon National Parks:** 695, Robert Holmes. 697, Greg Epperson/age fotostock. 698, Robert Holmes. 709, urosr/Shutterstock. **Chapter 21: Sacramento and the Gold Country:** 723 and 725 (top and bottom), Robert Holmes. 726, Andy Z./Shutterstock. 745, Ambient Images Inc./Alamy. 754, RickC/Flickr. **Chapter 22: Lake Tahoe:** 757, Tom Zikas/North Lake Tahoe. 758, Rafael Ramirez Lee/iStockphoto. 759, Janet Fullwood. 760, Jay Spooner/iStockphoto. 773, Mblach/Dreamstime.com. 779, Hank de Vre/Squaw Valley Alpine Meadows. 790, Christopher Russell/iStockphoto. **Chapter 23: The Far North:** 797, NPS. 799 (top), Andy Z./Shutterstock. 799 (bottom), NPS. 800, ThreadedThoughts/ Flickr. 815, kathycsus/Flickr. **About Our Writers:** All photos are courtesy of the writers except for the following: Michele Bigley, courtesy of Tony Belko; John Blodgett, courtesy of Tom Darnall; Cheryl Crabtree, courtesy of Bryn Berg; Denise Leto, courtesy of Kevin Finney; Daniel Mangin, courtesy of J. Rodby; Kathy McDonald, courtesy of Jeff Kirschbaum; Christine Vovakes, courtesy of Michael Vovakes; Bobbi Zane, courtesy of Leena Hanonnen.

NOTES

NOTES

NOTES

ABOUT OUR WRITERS

Native Californian **Cheryl Crabtree** has worked as a freelance writer since 1987 and regularly travels up, down, and around California for work and fun. She has contributed to *Fodor's California* since 2003 and also contributes to the *Fodor's National Parks of the West* guide. Cheryl is editor of *Montecito Magazine* and co-authors *The California Directory of Fine Wineries* book series, Central Coast and Napa, Sonoma, Mendocino editions. Her articles have appeared in many regional and national magazines. Cheryl updated the Central Coast, Monterey Bay Area, Palm Springs, Eastern Sierra, Yosemite National Park, and Sequoia & Kings Canyon National Park chapters this edition.

Daniel Mangin returned to California, where he's maintained a home for three decades, after two stints at the Fodor's editorial offices in New York City, the second one as the editorial director of Fodors.com and the Compass American Guides. With several-dozen wineries less than a half-hour's drive from home, he often finds himself transported as if by magic to a tasting room bar, communing with a sophisticated Cabernet or savoring the finish of a smooth Pinot Noir. For this edition, Daniel, the writer of *Fodor's Napa & Sonoma*, updated the Napa and Sonoma, North Coast, Redwood National Park, Far North, Inland Empire, Lake Tahoe, and Travel Smart chapters.

Steve Pastorino has visited nearly a dozen national parks on behalf of Fodor's and has favorite spots in all of them. In the summer, the long-time sports marketer and his family of five are often found at baseball diamonds. He updated the Joshua Tree National Park, Death Valley National Park, and Sacramento and the Gold Country chapters.

Joan Patterson is a freelance writer and editor based in southern Nevada who contributed to the Mojave Desert chapter for this edition and has worked on chapters in both *Fodor's Las Vegas* and *Fodor's Complete Guide to National Parks of the West*. She has worked in small-town newspaper production as a reporter, photographer, and news editor, and has been a features writer covering Las Vegas for the *Las Vegas Review-Journal* as both staff member and freelancer.

A veteran traveler, **Claire Deeks van der Lee** feels lucky to call San Diego home. Claire loves road-tripping around her adopted state of California, so it was a perfect fit for her to work on the Experience and California's Best Road Trips chapters of this book. Claire has traveled to more than 40 countries, and has contributed to *Everywhere* magazine and several Fodor's guides.

Updating our Los Angeles chapter was a team of writers from Fodor's Los Angeles: Michele Bigley, Alene Dawson, Paul Feinstein, Kathy A. McDonald, Ashley Tibbits, and Clarissa Wei.

Updating our San Diego chapter was a team of writers from Fodor's San Diego: Marlise Kast-Myers, Kai Oliver-Kurtain, Archana Ram, Juliana Shallcross, Jeff Terich, and Claire Deeks van der Lee.

Updating our San Francisco chapter was a team of writers from Fodor's San Francisco: Amanda Kuehn Carroll, Denise M. Leto, Daniel Mangin, Andrea Powell, Rebecca Flint Marx, and Jerry James Stone.